NEW BONES

Contemporary Black Writers in America

Kevin Everod Quashie
Smith College

R. Joyce Lausch
Arizona State University

Keith D. Miller
Arizona State University

Prentice
Hall

Upper Saddle River, New Jersey 07458

Library of Congress Cataloging-in-Publication Data
New bones : contemporary Black writers in America / Kevin Quashie, Joyce Lausch,
Keith Miller.
    p. cm.
  Includes index.
  ISBN 0-13-014127-5
    1. American literature—Afro-American authors.   2. American literature—20th century.
  3. Afro-Americans—Literary collections.   I. Quashie, Kevin.   II. Lausch, Joyce.
  III. Miller, Keith D.

PS508.N3 N47 2000
810.8'0896073'09045—dc21

                                                                                00-022516

Editor in Chief: Leah Jewell
Senior Acquisitions Editor: Carrie Brandon
Editorial Assistant: Sandy Hrasdzira
Managing Editor: Mary Rottino
Production Liaison: Fran Russello
Editorial/Production Supervision: Marianne Hutchinson (Pine Tree Composition)
Prepress and Manufacturing Buyer: Mary Ann Gloriande
Marketing Manager: Rachel Falk
Cover Designer: Robert Farrar-Wagner

For permission to use copyrighted material, grateful acknowledgment is made to the
copyright holders on pages 1115–1122, which are hereby made part of this copyright page.

This book was set in 10/12 Berkeley-Medium by Pine Tree Composition, Inc.,
and was printed and bound by Courier Companies, Inc.
The cover was printed by Phoenix Color Corp.

© 2001 by Prentice-Hall, Inc.
A Division of Pearson Education
Upper Saddle River, New Jersey 07458

Printed in the United States of America

10   9   8   7   6   5   4   3   2   1

ISBN 0-13-014127-5

Prentice-Hall International (UK) Limited, *London*
Prentice-Hall of Australia Pty. Limited, *Sydney*
Prentice-Hall Canada Inc., *Toronto*
Prentice-Hall Hispanoamericana, S.A., *Mexico*
Prentice-Hall of India Private Limited, *New Delhi*
Prentice-Hall of Japan, Inc., *Tokyo*
Pearson Education Asia Pte. Ltd., *Singapore*
Editora Prentice-Hall do Brasil, Ltda., *Rio de Janeiro*

CONTENTS

Ruth Forman   313

Leon Forrest   326

Ernest Gaines   329

Nikki Giovanni   352

Jewelle Gomez   366

Hattie Gossett   376

PREFACE

This book *New Bones* is an amazing collection. Of course, we can say this because of the extensive work that has been put into completing the project. But there are other reasons for holding this anthology in high esteem, including that it is the first and most extensive collection of its kind. There are other well-regarded texts that collect contemporary writings by African Americans, but those works often organize around a theme, genre, or subject matter. *New Bones* pulls together, in one well-compiled resource, writings by Black writers since 1970, the time period that many readers are most familiar with and intrigued by. What makes *New Bones* an even more exciting collection is the way that it brings together well-known writers and newer voices, creating a lovely gathering of Black voices. These are, quite literally, new bones.

In organizing the anthology we have selected works that best represent authors, but also works that introduce and expand ideas of what contemporary African-American literature is. We have chosen a broad spectrum of writing: fiction, poetry, autobiography, nonfiction essays, speeches, plays; covering a wide range of topics, including relationships, gender, history, social problems, migration, education, mythology, color, identity, language, amongst others. We have also carefully avoided, in most cases, using excerpts of works, especially with fiction, and instead used representative short fiction when possible so that the reader can appreciate the entire piece. In the cases where excerpts are used, we have offered a generous selection for context.

There are three prominent features of the anthology that bear some comment; the first is the introductory essay that precedes each writer. This essay serves to introduce the reader to the writer using biographical and career information as well as providing a brief overview of the themes and aesthetics of the included selections. These introductory essays also offer ways of reading the work, sometimes give insight on common ways that a writer or a work has been received, and often make reference to other writers in the anthology whose work evokes similar themes or ideas. In this way, the introductory essays serve to clarify the incredible web that is contemporary African-American literature.

Another important feature of *New Bones* is the inclusion of "Focused Study" sections. These focused studies aim to give a reader a more extensive introduction to a particular writer, and in this respect, those sections are significantly longer than others. Each focused study provides a longer introductory essay, a wider selection from the author's work, and at least one secondary essay relevant to the author (for example, an interview, or a critical essay). The eight such sections included are divided across genres and subject matter, and also highlight newer as well as established writers.

A final noteworthy feature is the very comprehensive introductory essay that proceeds this preface. This essay, written in very readable prose, provides a very effective introduction to contemporary African-American literature, offering insight into the historical and political factors that preceded this body of writers. The essay further explores the development of contemporary aesthetics in various genres. What is most effective about this essay is the way that it offers general and thematic frameworks with specific examples, such that readers of other works included in the anthology can readily consider texts in light of the body of information in the introduction. The anthology also includes key artwork by Black visual artists in the last thirty years, and ends with a list of writers not included in the anthology, but who are also part of this larger body of contemporary African-American writers and thinkers.

We hope that you will find this collection useful, inspiring, and engaging.

Kevin Everod Quashie
R. Joyce Lausch
Keith D. Miller

INTRODUCTION

The sharp increase in both quality and quantity of literary production from the 1970s through 1990s signals a contemporary renaissance of African American literature, one that rivals the scope and duration of the Harlem Renaissance. The number of award-winning Black authors has grown dramatically, with more in the 1980s and 1990s than in the rest of the century. Consider, for example, Derek Walcott's 1992 Nobel Prize, Toni Morrison's 1993 Nobel Prize, August Wilson's 1987 and 1990 Pulitzer Prizes, Yusef Komunyakaa's 1993 Pulitzer Prize, Maya Angelou's reading of a poem at President Clinton's 1993 inauguration, and Rita Dove's 1987 Pulitzer Prize and unprecedented two-term appointment as poet laureate. All of these achievements testify to the importance of African American literature in broader American life. Since 1990, it has not been uncommon for three or four African American authors to appear simultaneously on the *New York Times* best-seller list. With a diverse and growing audience, including a committed African American audience, Black authors are enjoying richly deserved visibility and, sometimes, fame.

In addition, scholars in the last fifteen years have placed Black literature at the center of English and Women's Studies curricula. And many universities have established African American studies programs that highlight literature.

The ascendance of African American literature after roughly 1970 is related to the vigorous, grassroots racial protest of the previous sixteen years. That protest arguably began in 1954, when JoAnn Robinson and her organization, the Women's Political Council, raised strong objections to legalized racial segregation on the buses of Montgomery, Alabama. The following year, Rosa Parks was arrested for refusing to yield her seat on a Montgomery bus to a white man. Immediately, Robinson and the Women's Policital Council distributed thousands of leaflets calling for African Americans to boycott city buses. Emerging as the leader of the Montgomery Bus Boycott, Martin Luther King, Jr., defined the protest as a Biblical struggle against American Pharaohs and part of dark-skinned peoples' worldwide rebellion against white supremacy and colonialism. When his home was bombed, King delivered an impromptu Sermon on the Porch, explaining that the boycott would only rely on the weapon of Christian love and nonviolence. In 1955 the Supreme Court vindicated the nonviolent boycotters by outlawing segregation on the buses of Montgomery.

In 1960 four African American college freshman sat down at a segregated lunch counter in Greensboro, North Carolina, and refused to leave. With no advanced planning, similar sit-ins quickly spread to more than fifty cities. Inspired by Ella Baker, youthful protesters then met to form the Student Nonviolent Coordinating Committee (SNCC), which was organized by Robert Moses, Ruby Doris Robinson, and many others. In 1961 the Congress of Racial Equality, founded by James Farmer in 1942, conducted nonviolent Freedom Rides through Alabama and Mississippi. White racists greeted Freedom Riders with severe beatings and set one bus on fire with the Freedom Riders aboard. Farmer and other Freedom Riders, not their attackers, were jailed.

Much to the chagrin of President John Kennedy, a huge, nonviolent grass-roots struggle engulfed much of the South and the nation. The most important focal points were Mississippi, where Fannie Lou Hamer, a former sharecropper, inspired many with her courage and her songleading; and Alabama, where King directed his key crusades. Following Kennedy's assassination, President Lyndon Johnson secured passage of the 1964 Civil Rights Act, the most important racial law since Reconstruction. In 1965, following protests by SNCC and King in Selma, Alabama, Johnson proposed and Congress approved the Voting Rights Acts, which guaranteed that, for the first time, African Americans could vote anywhere in the United States.

During the early 1960s, Malcolm X attracted many listeners in the urban North as he eloquently railed at White oppression, instilled racial pride, and advocated racial separation. Black writers were also involved in the process, as evidenced for example by James Baldwin: In the 1950s and 1960s, Baldwin wrote trenchant novels and nonfiction that powerfully articulated enormous anger at racial inequities; he also marched with civil rights demonstrators. Especially in Mississippi and Alabama, nonviolent civil rights activists were routinely beaten and occasionally tortured or murdered. Their racist attackers were seldom arrested and rarely convicted. The Federal Bureau of Investigation (FBI) wiretapped and harassed King and other nonviolent protesters while usually ignoring those who beat, imprisoned, tortured, and murdered them.

As activist Anne Moody explains in her classic autobiography, *Coming of Age in Mississippi* (1968), idealistic civil rights agitators grew disillusioned with every level of American government. Sounding like Malcolm X, Stokely Carmichael and other leaders in SNCC rejected the goals of racial integration and nonviolence in favor of "Black Power" and economic development. Disillusionment deepened when Malcolm X was assassinated in 1965 and when President Johnson escalated the Vietnam War, into which a disproportionately large number of African American soldiers were drafted. Some of the early objections to the war came from civil rights agitators. King denounced it in 1967. Between 1964 and 1968, rioting and burning became fairly common in large American cities, most notably Los Angeles, Detroit, and Newark. Massive disturbances were widespread following King's assassination in 1968. He had called earlier riots "the cry of the unheard."

In this context, between roughly 1965 and 1976, authors banded to form the Black Arts Movement, which sought to redefine and transform social conditions through literature. Specifically, writers furthered the freedom struggle, promoted "Black Power" and "Black Consciousness," and proclaimed the beauty of Black people. They urged self-definition, cultural unity, and community-based revolutionary politics.

Led by such figures as Amiri Baraka (LeRoi Jones), Askia Toure, and Larry Neal, the Black Arts Movement began in New York City as poets delivered angry, vernacular chants throughout Harlem. Black Arts also flourished in Los Angeles, San Francisco, Chicago, Detroit, and New Orleans. Ed Bullins, Ron Milner, and other playwrights attracted eager audiences. Authors initiated numerous journals, including *Black Dialogue,* and publishing outlets, most notably Dudley Randall's Broadside Press (in Detroit) and Haki Madhubuti's Third World Press (in Chicago). Randall published hundreds of poets, including such older luminaries as Sterling Brown and Gwendolyn Brooks and such promising writers as Nikki Giovanni, Etheridge Knight, and Sonia Sanchez. Many of these works experimented with form, often incorporating rhythms and phrases from streetcorners. A few Black Arts books, such as Baraka and Neal's anthology *Black Fire,* received broad national distribution. But large New York publishers generally avoided Black Arts writers.

During the 1960s, some feminist activists questioned the assertive, largely male public leadership of the Civil Rights Movement, whose watershed March on Washington featured a day of speechifying (including King's famous "I Have a Dream" address), but no orations by women.

Beginning in 1970, certainly the single most important characteristic of contemporary African American literary tradition is the explosion of writing by women. In 1970 Toni Cade Bambara edited *The Black Woman,* a landmark anthology that documented Black women writers' dissatisfaction with sexism, racism, and the narrow range of experience expressed in White and Black literature. They also announced their new and growing dedication to female self-determination and self-expression.

During the 1970s, Audre Lorde, Paule Marshall, Alice Walker, June Jordan, and others proposed that "Blackness" was not as unifying or as simple a concept as many in the Black Arts Movement presumed. Even during the 1960s, such writers as Adrienne Kennedy questioned the homogeneity of "Blackness" and the tendency of Black Arts to essentialize Black experience. Jordan, among others, objected to the traditional, secondary status of woman in defining "Blackness." Walker and other southern artists contested the assumption that "Blackness" was an urban phenomenon, an assumption that seemed popular among Black Arts participants, who generally lived in large cities. Lorde's poetry raised the visibility of gays and lesbians within the continuum of "Blackness." Concentrating on life in the Caribbean Basin, Marshall and others reminded readers that African Americans could not contain or define the entire experience of the African Diaspora.

The lives of Black women, long ignored or relegated to stereotype, became the focal point for most Black women writers. Their work in all genres often blended militancy, personal exploration, and self-affirmation. Alice Walker, Toni Morrison, and many others critiqued the valorization of Black manhood and the subordination of women—themes that emerged, for example, in the extremely popular, posthumously published *Autobiography of Malcolm X* (1965). Walker, Morrison, and others analyzed the intertwining complexities of sex, race, and class as an argument for the whole, healthy future of Black families and communities. Investigating gender relationships and stereotypes, they extended thematic arenas to include sexuality and spirituality, mother/daughter relationships, and women's friendships.

Poetry: Black Arts Movement and Beyond

The most prominent genre of the Black Arts Movement was poetry that was publicly performed, poetry that was heard as much as it was read. Defiantly anti-elitist, many Black Arts poets drew from the vernacular tradition of sermons, popular music, and Black speech (including signifying) to inspire audiences toward revolutionary action. The verse was free and conversational and—especially in the case of Quincy Troupe and Sonia Sanchez—deeply influenced by jazz and the blues. In some cases, poets appropriated specific American forms; Amiri Baraka, for example, initially adopted the avant-garde style of the Beat movement. Combining the rousing strategies of storyteller and preacher and the themes of radical politics and Black pride, Black Arts Poets established a rich tradition for contemporary writers to mine.

Many Black Arts poets published their best-known poetry between 1965 and 1970, as evidenced by the following catalog: Amiri Baraka, *Black Magic Poetry* (1969); Nikki Giovanni, *Black Talk/Black Judgment* (1968) and *Re: Creation* (1970); Mari Evans, *I Am a Black Woman* (1970); Haki Madhubuti, *Think Black* (1967), *Black Pride* (1968), and *Don't Cry, Scream* (1969); Etheridge Knight, *Poems from Prison* (1968); Sonia Sanchez, *Homecoming* (1969); Jayne Cortez, *Pisstained Stairs and the Monkey Man's Wares* (1969); Carolyn Rodgers, *Paper Soul* (1968) and *Songs of a Black Bird* (1969). The influence of Black Arts philosophy, valuing the unique history and culture of Black art and community, could not but help to be an important influence on literary production in the early 1970s and beyond.

A resurgence in the popularity of performance poetry, the spoken word, is a current, nationwide practice among people of many ethnicities. This phenomenon reflects the lasting impact of Beat and Black Arts oral poetry. Numerous contemporary Black poets—notable Ruth Forman, Quincy Troupe, and Wanda Coleman—continue to hone the art of performed poetry. In addition, the extremely important, centuries-old tradition of African American oratory continued to thrive in the presentations of such notables as Angela Davis, Shirley Chisholm, Barbara Jordan, Jesse Jackson, and Cornel West.

During the 1960s, some African nations moved from colonization to independence—or, as King and Malcolm X explained, from oppression to freedom. In an effort to negate the effects of White ideology, people began to investigate and celebrate African culture, which inspired a sense of common origin and helped create a "new" African American identity. Civil rights activists, including Fannie Lou Hamer, traveled to Africa; Stokely Carmichael moved there. Many Black poets—including Nikki Giovanni, Sonia Sanchez, and Amiri Baraka—also journeyed there, often returning with new styles of dress and song and vocabulary to integrate into their work. Maya Angelou and Audre Lorde also ventured to Africa for inspiration. The exploration of African mythologies and images is still common in contemporary African American poetry, as the interest in the African Diaspora thrives.

Poets expanded the territory of Black poetry in other ways as well. Throughout the 1960s and 1970s, Derek Walcott explored themes related to the West Indies. In *Poems from Prison* (1968), Etheridge Knight spotlighted the life of the underclass and, especially, the not uncommon experience of prison. In 1997, Toi Derricotte explored biracial identity—an examination that younger poet Ruth Ellen Kocher continues in *Desdemona's Fire* (1999).

Like other genres, poetry experienced a woman-driven shift in the 1970s, when Lorde published *Cables to Rage* (1970), *From a Land Where Other People Live* (1973), *New York Head Shop and Museum* (1974), *Between Our Selves* (1976), and *Coal* (1976). Lorde's prestige and audience grew with each new collection. She filled her verse with images of strong, self-affirming women, and especially in *The Black Unicorn* (1978), she integrated African mythology, establishing ties between Africa and African America and imagining wider realms of self-definition and self-assertion for Black women. Lucille Clifton wrote her second and third collections of poetry, *Good News about the Earth* (1972) and *An Ordinary Woman* (1974), which forecast her prolific production of seven more collections and a memoir during the 1980s and 1990s. With the publication of second and third collections—*New Days: Poems of Exile and Return* (1974) and *Things That I Do in the Dark* (1977)—June Jordan stepped forward as a dominant poetic force whose output would be profuse. Clifton and Jordan focused on the strength and resilience of mothers in Black communities and the dynamics of gender relationships. Clifton's concision contributed to the impact of her statements about genealogy, Christian heritage, and women's friendships, while Jordan expanded the range of poetic subjects and themes. Women poets of 1990s—including Ruth Forman, Jewelle Gomez, and Toi Derricotte—benefitted enormously from the formidable legacy of Lorde, Clifton, and Jordan.

Many poets continue to rely on the still lively sounds and rhythms of blues and jazz. Sherley Anne Williams, Quincy Troupe, and Michael S. Harper integrate musicality into the style and content of their poetry. Writing about solitary Black women and about relationships between Black men and women, Williams relies on the blues tradition with its emphasis on remembering pain and brutality and with its call to transcend pain in secular ways. She proclaims the sorrows of humanity with rhythmic delivery, call-and-response reminiscent of Black folk preaching, and a single voice—mournful, but resilient. Harper and Troupe draw more centrally on the primarily urban tradition of jazz. As it celebrates the human capacity to endure and thrive under pressure and to improvise coping strategies, jazz resonates in Harper's *Images of Kin* (1977), which negotiates African American with "American" identity and history. Jazz also vibrates in Troupe's *Weather Reports* (1991), as he integrates urban sights and sounds with Southern sensibilities and pace. With the publication of *Magic City* (1992) and *Neon Vernacular* (1993), Yusef Komunyakaa also engages in thoughtful poetic musicality.

Drama: A Continuing Social Force

During the 1960s, drama (along with poetry) deployed language as a weapon of social change and revolution. Lorraine Hansberry's famous play, *A Raisin in the Sun* (1959), anatomized gender and generational tensions within a family seeking racial equality. Amiri Baraka's *Dutchman* (1964), *The Baptism* (1967), *The Toilet* (1967), and *Four Black Revolutionary Poems* (1969) sought to break the illusion of the stage, to make drama represent living experience. *Dutchman,* which won the 1964 Obie award, addresses the oppressive powers that create and reify divisive stereotypes of race and gender, particularly those involving Black men and White women.

If Baraka is the best-known playwright of the Black Arts Movement, Adrienne Kennedy is the dramatist whose subsequent productivity is most notable. Publishing seven plays in the late 1960s, Kennedy continued to write, producing *A Movie Star Has to Star in Black and White* (1976), *Orestes and Electra* (1980), and *The Alexander Plays* (1992), a collection of four new dramas. Kennedy fills her plays with surrealistic images, dream-like interactions between characters (some of whom are played by more than one actor), masks, and nontraditional music.

Drama continues in many ways to follow the conversational style and content of Black Arts. Racism continues to be crucial to subject matter, though issues of class, gender, and sexuality have also become central. While the "lesson" or call to action is not as dominant in drama as it once was, contemporary drama still addresses structural social problems. Drama has also become increasingly fertile ground for experimentation with voice and form. Because Ntozake Shange's renowned *for colored girls who consider suicide/when the rainbow is enough* (1975) is replete with multiple perspectives, voices, settings, and dance, Shange calls her work a choreopoem. Anna Deveare Smith's exploration of contemporary racial conflict and violence in Los Angeles (*Twilight,* 1992 [1993]) and Brooklyn (*Fires in the Mirror* [1992]) are one-woman portrayals of many viewpoints surrounding the Rodney King incident and the Crown Heights class between the Hassidic Jewish and African American communities. Smith's multifaceted approach and play with narrative voice may help subsequent writers capitalize on sociological field research and what it says about race in the United States.

The most celebrated American playwright of the 1980s and early 1990s is August Wilson. Wilson often depicts African Americans in the urban North during earlier decades of the twentieth century. These characters, who typically range from the lumpen-proletariat to the lower middle class, struggle against severe restrictions that racism imposes on their lives, which combine wit, pluck, courage, pathos, and tradegy. In *Fences,* which premiered on Broadway in 1987, Wilson created his saddest and most memorable character in the charming Troy Maxson, a garbageman and former baseball player in the Negro Leagues, who is degraded by racism and his own inability to emotionally support his son and wife. With Wilson's phenomenal presence, but also with the talent and works of Smith, Shange, and others, the dramatic tradition in African American literature remains strong.

Fiction: Renewal of Narrative

Nineteen seventy proved at least as important as any year in the entire history of African American letters. In 1970, Toni Morrison, Alice Walker, and June Jordan each published their first novels: *The Bluest Eye, The Third Life of Grange Copeland,* and *His Own Where,* respectively. Morrison concentrated on the effects of internalized racism on the disintegration of a Black family in a small midwestern town. Walker focused on impoverished Black men in the South who brutalized women after being brutalized themselves by Whites. And Jordan rounded out the variation with her examination of experience in New York City. Not only did Toni Cade Bambara publish her germinal anthology, *The Black Woman,* in 1970, she also issued *Tales for Black Folks,* which demonstrated that African American stories and traditions needed to be preserved and communicated within the Black community.

Narrative fiction revived the treasure of orality and storytelling that had been practiced primarily in the mode of poetry during the Black Arts Movement. Relying on vernacular language, James Alan McPherson's stories in *Hue and Cry* (1969) depict survival under White power or loss suffered under it. John Williams's fast-paced novels, including his well-known *The Man Who Cried I Am* (1967), critiqued the continuation of racial inequities. Albert Murray's *Train Whistle Guitar* (1974) is informed by jazz and the blues. In *Mumbo Jumbo* (1972) and other novels, postmodernist Ishmael Reed—an advocate of "Neohoodooism"—harnesses wild fantasy and collage to mock diverse foibles and absurdities, including racism.

It is not that Black fiction was dormant during the 1960s, but more that poetry and drama became central to the political imperatives of the time period. Near the end of the 1960s, the publication of the texts listed above, and some that follow, led to the current contemporary interest in Black fiction, an interest that rivals the period in the 1940s and 1950s when James Baldwin, Richard

Wright, Ralph Ellison, Ann Petry, and Gwendolyn Brooks all wrote fiction of some repute. Because of an incredible contemporary community of writers, the subjects of fiction have now diverged greatly.

Setting narratives in his childhood neighborhood, John Edgar Wideman published six novels after 1970 as well as two short story collections, including *All Stories Are True* (1993). The geography and meaning of "home" resonate richly in the novels that comprise his *Homewood Trilogy* (1985). He sometimes employed variations of modernist stream of consciousness, leading readers through time without disruption and smoothly switching point of view. Wideman's overall concern is to affirm the history and survival of Black families who suffer under terrible conditions. As Wideman chooses his great-great-great-grandmother Sybela Owens as the foundation for his *Homewood Trilogy,* he demonstrates respect for tradition and ancestry.

Other novelists also reconsider the past, including slavery. Ernest Gaines's *Autobiography of Miss Jane Pittman* (1971) and Charles Johnson's *Oxherding Tale* (1982) and *Middle Passage* (1989) treat the experience of bondage. Gaines adapts the form of slave autobiography; Johnson contemplates the epistemologies of slaves and slave owners. Gayl Jones' *Corregidora* (1975), Toni Morrison's *Song of Solomon* (1977) and *Beloved* (1987), Gloria Naylor's *Mama Day* (1988), and Sherley Anne Williams' first novel, *Dessa Rose* (1986), also revisit the history and legacy of slavery, especially with respect to women's experiences. The central purpose of revising history and culture is to add to the complexity of what is already known. Thus, *Dessa Rose* focuses on slaves traveling West toward freedom. Sweet Home of Morrison's *Beloved* is not a large Southern plantation, but a small Kentucky farm. Naylor's *Mama Day* centers on the slave heritage of an island. Each of these authors asserts that slavery is a complex part of American history that needs to be reexamined continually, never forgotten, and never simplified to one story deemed "authentic." Much of this writing seeks in nonlinear ways to reconstruct the past for the purpose of understanding the present, a project in which male writers such as Ishmael Reed in *Flight to Canada* (1976) and David Bradley in *The Chaneysville Incident* (1981) are also involved. Showing appreciation for African writers, some contemporary novelists incorporate elements of African cosmology and mythology, especially the emphasis on the significance of ancestors.

While many writers revisit slavery, others build on the philosophies and heritage of dominant cultures. Intertextuality thus extends beyond precedent in the African American tradition to adoption of form and thought from other traditions. With *The Color Purple* (1982), Alice Walker engages the English tradition of the epistolary novel. Eastern philosophy is a dominant theme in James Alan McPherson's *Crabcakes* (1998) and Charles Johnson's *Middle Passage*. Naylor's *Mama Day* resonates with Shakespeare's *The Tempest;* her *Linden Hills* (1985) revises Dante's *Inferno*. Walter Mosley's *Devil in a Blue Dress* (1990), which has also been produced as a film, experiments with the form of the detective novel. Terri McMillan's *Waiting to Exhale* (1992) and *How Stella Got Her Groove Back* (1996), both produced as mainstream movies and both lingering for weeks on the *New York Times* bestseller list, popularized her as a romance writer. Octavia Butler's numerous novels, including *Wild Seed* (1980), apply devices of science fiction to illuminate slavery and oppression, while Samuel Delany's Return to Neveryon Series uses science fiction to explore sexuality. All these intertexts complicate common forms with African American themes.

Revision of "American" history and increasing acknowledgment of multiple and global heritage has created greater recognition of writers who examine the African Diaspora and immigration. The contributions of Caribbean-based writers are especially marked. Paule Marshall's *Brown Girl, Brownstones* (1959), *Praisesong for the Widow* (1983), and *Daughters* (1991) examine relationships between African Americans and Caribbeans. Michelle Cliff's *Abeng* (1984) and *No Telephone to Heaven* (1987) elide Jamaican history, myth, colonization, and constructs of race. Jamaica Kincaid's novels *Annie John* (1985), *Lucy* (1990), and *Autobiography of My Mother* (1996) and her short story collection *At the Bottom of the River* (1996) plumb the intricacies of mother-daughter relationships and colonized identities. Edwidge Danticat's *Krik? Krak!* (1995) is rich in the tradition of Haitian storytelling. The variation of Black lives and identities put forth by Caribbean-based writers notably expands the entire literature of the western hemisphere.

Fiction for children has also blossomed. Creating positive communities and encouraging positive Black identity requires educating Black children to resist discrimination and affirm history, heritage, and self. Since the Black Arts Movement insisted on a revolutionary vision of African American culture and communities, production of children's literature has proliferated. Well-known authors have written many books for children. Lucille Clifton has published more than a dozen children's books, many featuring a young African American boy, Everett Anderson, learning about his culture. June Jordan's first novel, *His Own Where* (1970), was intended for adolescents. Her *Fannie Lou Hamer* (1972) reminds a young audience of Hamer's huge importance. Sherley Anne Williams' recent *Working Cotton* (1992) is based on the poetry in *Peacock Poems* (1975), which documents a day in the life of a young girl in the field.

Autobiography: Subjectivity Spoken

While autobiographies were popular and prevalent during the 1960s (for example those of Malcolm X, King, and Anne Moody), the genre experiences an explosion in the 1970s similar to that in fiction, especially in terms of a greater number of women's voices. In 1970—the same year that Alice Walker, Toni Morrison, and June Jordan issued their first novels—Maya Angelou's *I Know Why The Caged Bird Sings* dazzled readers and became enormously famous. *Caged Bird* and Angelou's many sequels spurred the popularity of autobiography.

With the publication of *Zami* (1983), which she calls biomythography, Audre Lorde offers the first written account by a Black lesbian dealing with isolation from her Black family and culture, her outsider status in queer culture, and homophobia during the 1950s and 1960s in the United States. Lorde also imagines for herself a healing and redeeming space within the Grenadian mythology and poetic language her mother passed down to her. In her poetic memoir, *Generations* (1987), Lucille Clifton begins with the story of her great-grandmother (who was a slave), documents the life of her father (whose death and funeral work as the immediate setting), and closes with the future of her children and the perpetuation of her family's heritage. Her memoir is a communal autobiography seen through her eyes. Formally, the narrative is loose, weaving her father's stories into her own reflections and including photos of family members to people the prose poem narratives with images.

June Jordan, Nikki Giovanni, and bell hooks practice somewhat similar autobiographical strategies in their genre-conflating collections of political essays. Each weaves personal narrative into political prose, realizing that to separate the two spheres is not only arbitrary but counterproductive. Like Clifton, bell hooks in *Bone Black* (1996) and *Wounds of Passion* (1997) captures central experiences in short narrative pieces and interchanges third-person and first-person voice (especially in *Wounds*). hooks celebrates the surge in autobiographical narratives and notes the need for more experimentation and greater appreciation for honesty and creative strategies: "Constantly faced with the paucity of nonbiased information about our lives as black women and men, it is both reassuring and affirming that we are witnessing a resurgence of interest in autobiographical narratives by African Americans. . . . Experimental memoirs have become the cultural sites for more imaginative accountings of an individual's life" (*Wounds*, pp. xviii–xix). This comment is also true of the narrative memoirs by male writers. In *Brothers and Keepers* (1984) John Edgar Wideman applies strategies of modernist fiction as he considers his brother's life and prison sentence, using the narrative space imaginatively. Wideman's interest in autobiographical writing is furthered in *Fatheralong*, published in 1994. Works by writers like Nathan McCall (*Makes Me Wanna Holler*, 1994) and Mark Muthabane (*Kaffir Boy in America*, 1989) also expand the Black tradition of autobiography.

Critical and Literary Essays: Intellectual Presence

A growing tradition of African American cultural, political, and literary criticism has produced some of the most important public intellectuals in the United States. In the 1970s Alice Walker discovered the forgotten work of Zora Neale Hurston and defined it as a linchpin of American fiction. Walker's *In Search of Our Mothers' Gardens* (1983) differentiates between African American and mainstream feminism and emphasizes the importance of recognizing all forms of creativity, from quilting to gardening. Henry Louis Gates, Jr., argues in *Figures in Black: Words, Signs, and the Racial Self* (1987) and *The Signifying Monkey* (1988) that race is a construct of language and that African American texts rely on rhetorical strategies, not the direct outpouring of lived experience. Houston Baker's *Long Black Song* (1990) and *Black Studies, Rap, and the Academy* (1995) propose that texts be studied within the tradition of African American music.

Barbara Smith and her colleagues' *All The Women Are White, All the Blacks Are Men, But Some of Us Are Brave* (1982) highlights the intersections of race, gender, and sexuality and recommends such an analysis as a heuristic for reading. Both in her essays and in *Her Own Where,* June Jordan consistently supports the power and value of Black English. Audre Lorde's *Sister Outsider* (1984) challenges and broadens scholars' treatment of sexuality in African American letters. Articulating powerful social criticism, bell hooks and Cornel West dialogue in *BREAKING BREAD* (1991). In several essays in *YEARNING* (1990), hooks advocates a body of work to critique media depictions of African Americans. Varied in subject and approach, these and other philosophical texts revise the ways scholars and the public view African American culture and literature.

Broad Themes in Contemporary Black Writing

The themes that are central to Black literature post-1970 are interconnected with and reflective of developments in the genres. One principal idea is exploration of selfhood, a theme that has its roots in the experiences of forced migration and enslavement, and the unrelenting oppressive economic, social, and psychosocial conditions that African Americans endure in the U.S. landscape. This theme manifests most clearly in the autobiographical tradition. The particular approach that these writers take to self and selfhood includes a greater exploration of difference among people who are linked by racial identity; including investigations of mixed-race identity and sexuality. As the population of African America grows, the notions of community and class necessarily undergo critique and expansion. Some examples include Maya Angelou's *I Know Why the Caged Bird Sings,* which focuses on the development of identity for a young African American girl; or Bebe Moore Campbell's *Sweet Summer* (1989), which investigates the relationship between a young girl growing up in urban Philadelphia with her mother but spending sweet summer months with her father in rural North Carolina. Both writers focus on coming of age for Black girls, which was something of a literary novelty, and Campbell offers a rare commentary on Black women and their fathers. Further examples include Toi Derricotte's poetic commentary on biracial identity; Essex Hemphill's attention to the lives of Black men and their participation in Black American national and cultural politics; or Terry McMillan's romance-flavored look at Black middle class lives—all of which suggest the expansive nature of selfhood in contemporary literature.

The concept and construction of memory, which is a part of the contemporary interrogation of selfhood, is an especially fruitful theme for work in this anthology because of the relationship between memory and history, truth and time. Memory is crucial because of the inaccurate histories that have been recorded about the lives of African Americans, and the contested nature of what is called "the Black experience." Sometimes, all there is to refute an error of history is the memory of a person who dares to tell his or her truth. And still, the act of remembering is dynamic and fluid, always changing how the event or experience happened, giving new contours to the edges of the remembered thing. Memory then becomes political and necessary, but also ambivalent and imprecise. Cornelius Eady's loving meditation on the loss of his father, or Rita Dove's competing and complementary stories in *Thomas and Beulah* reveal both the struggle and the joy of memory.

A common example of how memory is engaged in the literature is in the use of slave narrative. In tune with some tendencies of post modernism, some contemporary Black writers play with time, merging past, present, and future, or using ghosts or other manifestations of ancestors to disrupt the common psychic barriers between states of time. David Bradley's *The Chaneysville Incident,* along with works by Reed, Naylor, Morrison, and Williams, reflect the increased contemporary interest in slave narrative as aesthetic. Memory as a literary and psychic construct also facilitates the interest in the African Diaspora—the literal and emotional community of people of African descent, living wherever they do in the world, whose lives are linked by forced dispersion from their homeland. The interest in Diaspora is not exclusively particular to contemporary writers. Still, the various revolutionary movements throughout the Diaspora in the decade or so that precede 1970, especially those in the Caribbean, the United States, and various West African countries, seem to have further facilitated literacy exploration of Diaspora, especially as Diasporic experiences inform processes of selfhood and self-regard.

Another prominent theme in the work of Black writers since 1970 is a passionate interest in writing and language. Writing has for many decades been of interest to African Americans, especially because the ability to write (as it represented a level of literacy) was almost a necessary requirement for freedom prior to the Emancipation Proclamation. The slaves who were able to write and read were the ones who most often had access to information necessary to break free, or who were able to engage in labor that might allow them to save money and, in a few instances, purchase their freedom. If nothing else, writing was important to selfhood and memory, important to the ability of a person to write his or her own experience of the world. The potency of slave narratives attest to this. As much, then, as Black people have yearned for writing, they have also exhibited wariness about the ways that writing and language have been used against them, for example legal documents that sanctioned enslavement, or literacy tests designed to forestall voting rights, or scientific documents that allegedly confirmed the inferiority of Black people. Morrison's character Schoolteacher in *Beloved* represents the intersection of these concerns.

Added to this historical ambivalence toward writing and language are the influences of the Black Arts Movement, which used word play to encode a Black vernacular; and of contemporary post modern and sociolinguistic critical thought, which suggests that language is, at best, unstable. The literature represented in this anthology often exhibits a high degree of word play, of using words in particular ways to speak two or more meanings, what is called signifying. Some writers use various vernaculars, or intentionally misuse words, to further contest the authority of language, but also to expand the language for their purposes. A cadre of poets—Sonia Sanchez, Angela Jackson, Jayne Cortez, Clarence Major, Quincy Troupe, and Michael Harper—have created work with strong examples of this tendency. This interest in language influences both the content and the form of the work. For example, Cortez, Troupe, and Harper are expressedly interested in writing in a jazz style, in a form that mirrors the repetition and revision that is jazz music aesthetic. This formalistic innovation reinforces the orality and performance quality that so characterized the poetry of Black Arts. Additionally, writers like Sapphire are beginning to introduce elements of hip hop into the literary tradition; this inclusion of hip hop is part of the "New Black Aesthetic" that novelist Trey Ellis argues in his essay of the same name. This special attention to form and content has been supported by the increased presence of Black studies in academic institutions. In fact, two of the more celebrated scholarly texts of Black literary criticism are Houston Baker's *Blues, Ideology and Afro-American Literature* (1984) and Henry Louis Gates Jr.'s *The Signifying Monkey,* both of which are centrally about Black literary language use.

In works since 1970, many writers and thinkers, especially various Black women, explore psychic, spiritual, and social healing and restoration. The scope of political activism often includes issues of community and nation, attempting to separate those issues from private experiences. This attempted division ignores, in Angela Davis's phrase, "the highly social character of interior lives." Such authors as Davis, Audre Lorde, Alice Walker, and bell hooks assert that both interior spaces and public issues are territory for political destruction and political restoration. In his essay included here, writer and activist Joseph Beam acknowledges these contributions of Black women and draws a direct line between their psychic and spiritual interests and his own themes. A similar connection can be seen in works by Cornelius Eady and Randall Kenan.

This attention to the psychic and spiritual capacities of self results in an interest in the power of the spirit and in the struggle toward wholeness. The aesthetic representation of wholeness does not lead to easy or simplistic resolutions, but instead allows writers to address complex issues, such as urban deterioration, or globalization of economies. Alice Walker's novel *Possessing the Secret of Joy,* where she weaves a complicated narrative about female genital mutilation is an example of the uneasy but unrelenting aesthetic investigation of peace and social justice. Ntozake Shange's *for colored girls* is another outstanding example of the use of interiority as a political site. What these writers suggest is that triumph is not always public and grand, but sometimes is quiet and sweet, personal and complicated. These texts struggle with and against nihilism, and gesture towards the possibility of transformation.

There are, of course, many other characteristics that could be said to represent, in some way, Black literature since 1970. What we offer here is not a definitive outline, but highlights of some key themes that are prominent in the works surveyed here.

What this anthology reflects is the stunning production of writing by African Americans in the past thirty years. Taken together, contemporary African American writers aim to convincingly re-envision and reframe the entire history of White and Black American race, gender, and class relations and the entire history of American literature. In many ways, they succeed, in what is a phenomenal literary and cultural achievement.

R. Joyce Lausch with Kevin Everod Quashie and Keith D. Miller

ACKNOWLEDGMENTS

We would like to acknowledge the enormous help of our editor, Carrie Brandon, at many stages of this project. Cordelia Candelaria, Myriam Chancy, Eugenia De-Lamotte, Montye Fuse, Deborah Garfield, Neal Lester, Demetria Martinez, and Jewell Parker Rhodes provided many useful suggestions and much encouragement. So did Lenore Brady, Vanessa Holford Diana, Caroline Irungu, Paul Jorgensen, Nicole Lanson, Ja'Milla C.K. Lomas, Claudia Barbosa Nogueira, Michael Pfister, and Sanderia Smith—all of whom were kind enough to write headnotes for us as well. We also acknowledge William Andrews for his astute suggestions at the very beginning of the project. Doris Miller and Andrew Jin Miller supplied inspiration.

Ai (1947–)

The poet Ai was born Florence Anthony in Albany, Texas on October 21, 1947. Of mixed ethnic heritage, which she once described as "1/2 Japanese, 1/8 Choctaw, 1/4 Black and 1/16 Irish," she took the name "Ai," which means "love" in Japanese, and has an expressed interest in exploring multiethnic identity. She completed a B.A. degree at the University of Arizona and an M.F.A. from the University of California at Irvine in 1971. Her first collection of poetry, Cruelty, *appeared in 1973 and had an immediate impact, garnering the praise of many and the criticism of others. Since then, Ai has completed five other volumes of poetry:* Killing Floor *in 1979 (which was named the Lamont Poetry Selection by the Academy of American Poets),* Sin *in 1986,* Fate *in 1991,* Greed *in 1993, and most recently,* Vice *in 1999, which is a collection of new and selected poems.*

Two qualities of Ai's poetry are readily evident and have been cited by most who read and study her poetry—its graphic and sometimes unflinching representation of violence and its use of dramatic or poetic monologue. It is true that Ai's work, and the content that her work deals with, is graphic and intense, but the representations are not gratuitous. Her work aims to show human frailty and strength, to capture both the mess and wonder that our world is. Through her use of monologue, she investigates and interrogates power relationships in social situations—a woman's relationship to and with a man; a man's relationship to his brother; a government official's relationship to the people he serves, and to himself. Her monologues are amazingly successful because they reach deep to the core of the particular persona and unearth fears, insights, and intents. She is a consummate artist in her ability to represent the timbre and contour of so many different and unlikely voices.

In "Twenty-Year Marriage," the female speaker's voice is resistant and plaintive, giving character to the relationship she shares with her partner. Ai uses well-placed, familiar images—the pickup, the fake leather thigh, the old newspapers—to represent the aged quality of this relationship, which informs the passion. The voice here is alive, you can almost hear it whisper "Come on, baby, lay me down on my back." This is what Ai does so well—captures the orality of the language by using exactly the simple and sometimes shocking words that people in the situations she is describing might use. She does not clean it up; she renders it straight and naked, not needing to make it more or less pretty than it is.

And she moves from voice to voice with ease: The male voice in "Abortion" has a different tone, a kind of resignation. Ai's characters, if one wants to call them such, always deliver a punch with their grittiness; their lives are poignant, and the lessons of the life are present and sometimes well articulated. Hence the male voice in this poem says "the poor have no children, just small people," which is an amazing commentary on poverty and systems of economic oppression. Similarly, the female voice in "Young Farm Woman Alone" muses on gender in a way that reveals an awareness of and familiarity with violence, but also a wisdom about negotiating violence.

Since her collection Sin in 1986, Ai has used her ability to create voices in a different way—she creates monologic voices that speak through and as public figures. One critic has said that the shift in Ai's work is from the "personal myth to public myth," which is partially true because Ai does start to write characters that include John F. Kennedy, Robert Oppenheimer, Joseph McCarthy, and the Atlanta child murderer. It is important, however, to realize that all of Ai's voices, even the less-recognizable and less-public ones, are still commentaries on public and political situations, as is evident in the last three selections. In "Interview with a Policeman," Ai captures the language of frustration, revealing an officer caught between his responsibility for a system's failures and his own human limitations. The poem asks the question about racism and justice and presents one character's struggle with these issues. Again, the language here is precise, capturing the frustration accurately: "You say you want this story/ in my own words,/ but you won't tell it my way."

These voices are sharp and clear, and they resonate not because they shock, but because they and the language they speak in are so familiar. They are on our televisions, in the newspapers, and just around the corner in a house down the street. These voices, as one critic once noted of Ai's poetry, cannot be ignored, and hence push us to contemplate a better place. Ai's courage in her representation and exploration of everyday violence is reminiscent of writers like Gayl Jones, and her everyday language resonates with poets like Sonia Sanchez and Carolyn Rodgers.

Kevin Everod Quashie

Twenty-Year Marriage

You keep me waiting in a truck
with its one good wheel stuck in the ditch,
while you piss against the south side of a tree.
Hurry. I've got nothing on under my skirt tonight.
That still excites you, but this pickup has no windows
and the seat, one fake leather thigh,
pressed close to mine is cold.
I'm the same size, shape, make as twenty years ago,
but get inside me, start the engine;
you'll have the strength, the will to move.
I'll pull, you push, we'll tear each other in half.
Come on, baby, lay me down on my back.
Pretend you don't owe me a thing
and maybe we'll roll out of here,
leaving the past stacked up behind us;
old newspapers nobody's ever got to read again.

Abortion

Coming home, I find you still in bed,
but when I pull back the blanket,
I see your stomach is flat as an iron.
You've done it, as you warned me you would
and left the fetus wrapped in wax paper
for me to look at. My son.
Woman, loving you no matter what you do,
what can I say, except that I've heard
the poor have no children, just small people
and there is room only for one man in this house.

Young Farm Woman Alone

What could I do with a man?—
pull him on like these oxhide boots,
the color of plums, dipped in blue ink
and stomp hell out of my loneliness,
this hoe that with each use grows sharper.

Interview with a Policeman

You say you want this story
in my own words,
but you won't tell it my way.
Reporters never do.
If everybody's racist,
that means you too.
I grab your finger
as you jab it at my chest.
So what, the minicam caught that?
You want to know all about it, right?—
the liquor store, the black kid
who pulled his gun
at the wrong time.

You saw the dollars he fell on and bloodied.
Remember how cold it was that night,
but I was sweating.
I'd worked hard, I was through
for twenty-four hours,
and I wanted some brew.
When I heard a shout,
I turned and saw the clerk
with his hands in the air,
saw the kid drop his gun
as I yelled and ran from the back.
I only fired when he bent down,
picked up his gun, and again dropped it.
I saw he was terrified,
saw his shoulder and head jerk to the side
as the next bullet hit.
When I dove down, he got his gun once more
and fired wildly.
Liquor poured onto the counter, the floor
onto which he fell back finally,
still firing now toward the door,
when his arm flung itself behind him.
As I crawled toward him,
I could hear dance music
over the sound of liquor spilling and spilling,
and when I balanced on my hands
and stared at him, a cough or spasm
sent a stream of blood out of his mouth
that hit me in the face.

Later, I felt as if I'd left part of myself
stranded on that other side,
where anyplace you turn is down,
is out for money, for drugs,
or just for something new like shoes
or sunglasses,
where your own rage
destroys everything in its wake,
including you.
Especially you.
Go on, set your pad and pencil down,
turn off the camera, the tape.
The ape in the gilded cage
looks too familiar, doesn't he,

and underneath it all,
like me, you just want to forget him.

Tonight, though, for a while you'll lie awake.
You'll hear the sound of gunshots
in someone else's neighborhood,
then, comforted, turn over in your bed
and close your eyes,
but the boy like a shark redeemed at last
yet unrepentant
will reenter your life
by the unlocked door of sleep
to take everything but his fury back.

Maya Angelou (1928–)

Maya Angelou is perhaps one of the first contemporary Black women artists of national prominence, due largely to her possession of talents in many areas—she is a fiction writer, poet, and essayist; a dancer, singer, and songwriter; an actress, film director, and producer. In the thirty years since her autobiography I Know Why the Caged Bird Sings became a publishing phenomenon, Angelou has remained active in writing and other forms of cultural production; her life experiences span many decades, and she has lived in the company of a wide range of comrades, including Malcolm X, Alvin Ailey, James Baldwin, Toni Morrison, Nick Ashford and Valerie Simpson, and Oprah Winfrey. Angelou is, to cite the title of her poem, "a phenomenal woman."

Born Marguerite Annie Johnson on April 4, 1928, in St. Louis, a young Maya moved between her place of birth and Stamps, Arkansas, living alternately with her mother and father. These two locations serve as the backdrop for her first of five autobiographical narratives, I Know Why the Caged Bird Sings, which was published in 1970 and nominated for a National Book Award. With Caged Bird, Angelou confirmed herself as a major voice of Black America, a capacity she had already attained from her documentary work with PBS and her social and political alliances. Now, she was also recognized as an exquisite teller of stories. Angelou has written four other autobiographical volumes: Gather Together in My Name (1974), Singin' and Swingin' and Gettin' Merry Like Christmas (1976), Heart of a Woman (1981), and All God's Children Need Traveling Shoes (1984). Between the publication of these works, she has also written volumes of poetry and essays (including Just Give Me A Cool Drink of Water Before I Die in 1971, which was nominated for a Pulitzer Prize; and the well-regarded And Still I Rise in 1978 and I Shall Not Be Moved in 1990) and worked in film and music. In 1993, President Clinton selected Angelou to speak at his Inauguration, for which she penned the moving epic "On the Pulse of the Morning."

Over the course of Angelou's career, she has continued to explore the incredible potency of human beings and their ability to not only survive, but to also thrive. Angelou uses storytelling, usually of her own life, to precisely articulate situations and conditions of living, and in doing so, allows the reader to not only see the triumph and humanness of struggle, but to also interrogate her or his own living as informative and triumphant. This use of autobiography is evident in the excerpt here from Caged Bird, which tells of a community listening to a Joe Louis fight on radio. For many Black Americans at the time, Joe Louis represented hope and strength, and his fights were always significant and breathtaking communal events. His humble beginnings and tremendous success in a racially charged country, and in a sport that best characterizes one-on-one confrontation, had a profound impact on Black pride collectively and individually. In Angelou's account here, she opens the chapter in dramatic fashion—in the middle of things—further heightening the tension the reader brings to the moment. She uses short paragraphs to enhance this tight rhythm and gives descriptions that strongly capture the environment in a short space of time. As with most autobiography, Angelou uses what might be called hyperbole or exaggeration for effect—for example, when she says "My race groaned" as Louis seems to be losing the fight, or when she writes "We didn't breathe. We didn't hope. We waited." These statements help not only to add to the import of the moment, but also nicely mirror Angelou's youthful narrator, whose narrative voice is filled with all the wonder that is in the voices of children her age. This short excerpt from Angelou's first book is a good example of how she uses autobiography, which later impacts writers like Bebe Moore Campbell and Marita Golden.

Much like acute description and sweet storytelling are central to Angelou's prose, use of rhythm and rhyme are key to her poetry. She uses rhythms that pull from blues, jazz, swing, and gospel traditions to create literal lyrics—sometimes short and punchy, and other times long and epic.

The one poem included here is perhaps Angelou's most recognizable: "Phenomenal Woman" (which was featured in the motion picture Poetic Justice). "Phenomenal Woman" is an anthemic poem, a strong declarative statement of self and love. It is almost defiant, and certainly celebratory; it speaks to, with, and against U.S. historical records that characterize Black women (and Black people in general) in negative ways. And yet, as is true to Angelou's use of autobiography, this poem, which can be called epic, is also deeply personal and intimate.

Angelou's collection of short prose essays Wouldn't Take Nothing for My Journey Now continues her tradition of meditative and prayerful writing, particularly focused on the condition of being female and Black. In "New Directions," she again uses her personal history (and in this case, that of her mother) to affirm the will and grace of human beings. She pays careful attention in even this short piece to color and texture, and her language is clean and pointed. In "Get-Ups," she uses a more general storytelling style to focus on the interaction between a mother and her son; and in "Style" she uses an easy prose quality, one more essay-like, to comment on a theme that in fact is reflected in both "New Directions" and "Get-Ups." Angelou's short prose exhibits both the lyrical quality of her poetry and the descriptive colorfulness of her autobiographical narratives, speaking from the "I" persona to gain clarity that is ultimately useful to a larger group than "I."

Maya Angelou's use of autobiography to present the personal as collective and political is evident throughout her work. Her rhythmic, lyrical narratives of hope and triumph celebrate humanity and have informed writing traditions of many writers who proceed her.

Kevin Everod Quashie

Joe Louis Fight

The last inch of space was filled, yet people continued to wedge themselves along the walls of the Store. Uncle Willie had turned the radio up to its last notch so that youngsters on the porch wouldn't miss a word. Women sat on kitchen chairs, dining-room chairs, stools and upturned wooden boxes. Small children and babies perched on every lap available and men leaned on the shelves or on each other.

The apprehensive mood was shot through with shafts of gaiety, as a black sky is streaked with lightning.

"I ain't worried 'bout this fight. Joe's gonna whip that cracker like it's open season."

"He gone whip him till that white boy call him Momma."

At last the talking was finished and the string-along songs about razor blades were over and the fight began.

"A quick jab to the head." In the Store the crowd grunted, "A left to the head and a right and another left." One of the listeners cackled like a hen and was quieted.

"They're in a clench, Louis is trying to fight his way out."

Some bitter comedian on the porch said, "That white man don't mind hugging that niggah now, I betcha."

"The referee is moving in to break them up, but Louis finally pushed the contender away and it's an uppercut to the chin. The contender is hanging on, now he's backing away. Louis catches him with a short left to the jaw."

A tide of murmuring assent poured out the doors and into the yard.

"Another left and another left. Louis is saving that mighty right . . ." The mutter in the Store had grown into a baby roar and it was pierced by the clang of a bell and the announcer's "That's the bell for round three, ladies and gentlemen."

As I pushed my way into the Store I wondered if the announcer gave any thought to the fact that he was addressing as "ladies and gentlemen" all the Negroes around the world who sat sweating and praying, glued to their "master's voice."

There were only a few calls for R. C. Colas, Dr. Peppers, and Hire's root beer. The real festivities would begin after the fight. Then even the old Christian ladies who taught their children and tried themselves to practice turning the other cheek would buy soft drinks, and if the Brown Bomber's victory was a particularly bloody one they would order peanut patties and Baby Ruths also.

Bailey and I lay the coins on top of the cash register. Uncle Willie didn't allow us to ring up sales during a fight. It was too noisy and might shake up the atmosphere. When the gong rang for the next round we pushed through the near-sacred quiet to the herd of children outside.

"He's got Louis against the ropes and now it's a left to the body and a right to the ribs. Another right to the body, it looks like it was low . . . Yes, ladies and gentlemen, the referee is signaling but the contender keeps raining the blows on Louis. It's another to the body, and it looks like Louis is going down."

My race groaned. It was our people falling. It was another lynching, yet another Black man hanging on a tree. One more woman ambushed and raped. A Black boy whipped and maimed. It was hounds on the trail of a man running through slimy swamps. It was a white woman slapping her maid for being forgetful.

The men in the Store stood away from the walls and at attention. Women greedily clutched the babes on their laps while on the porch the shufflings and smiles, flirtings and pinching of a few minutes before were gone. This might be the end of the world. If Joe lost we were back in slavery and beyond help. It would all be true, the accusations that we were lower types of human beings. Only a little higher than the apes. True that we were stupid and ugly and lazy and dirty and, unlucky and worst of all, that God Himself hated us and ordained us to be hewers of wood and drawers of water, forever and ever, world without end.

We didn't breathe. We didn't hope. We waited.

"He's off the ropes, ladies and gentlemen. He's moving towards the center of the ring." There was no time to be relieved. The worst might still happen.

"And now it looks like Joe is mad. He's caught Carnera with a left hook to the head and a right to the head. It's a left jab to the body and another left to the head. There's a left cross and a right to the head. The contender's right eye is bleeding and he can't seem to keep his block up. Louis is penetrating every block. The referee is moving in, but Louis sends a left to the body and it's the uppercut to the chin and the contender is dropping. He's on the canvas, ladies and gentlemen."

Babies slid to the floor as women stood up and men leaned toward the radio.

"Here's the referee. He's counting. One, two, three, four five, six, seven . . . Is the contender trying to get up again?"

All the men in the store shouted, "NO."

"—eight, nine, ten." There were a few sounds from the audience, but they seemed to be holding themselves in against tremendous pressure.

"The fight is all over, ladies and gentlemen. Let's get the microphone over to the referee . . . Here he is. He's got the Brown Bomber's hand, he's holding it up . . . Here he is . . ."

Then the voice, husky and familiar, came to wash over us—"The winnah, and still heavyweight champeen of the world . . . Joe Louis."

Champion of the world. A Black boy. Some Black mother's son. He was the strongest man in the world. People drank Coca-Colas like ambrosia and ate candy bars like Christmas. Some of the men went behind the Store and poured white lightning in their soft-drink bottles, and a few of the bigger boys followed them. Those who were not chased away came back blowing their breath in front of themselves like proud smokers.

It would take an hour or more before the people would leave the Store and head for home. Those who lived too far had made arrangements to stay in town. It wouldn't do for a Black man and his family to be caught on a lonely country road on a night when Joe Louis had proved that we were the strongest people in the world.

Phenomenal Woman

Pretty women wonder where my secret lies.
I'm not cute or built to suit a fashion model's size
But when I start to tell them,

They think I'm telling lies.
I say,
It's in the reach of my arms,
The span of my hips,
The stride of my step,
The curl of my lips.
I'm a woman
Phenomenally.
Phenomenal woman,
That's me.

I walk into a room
Just as cool as you please,
And to a man,
The fellows stand or
Fall down on their knees.
Then they swarm around me,
A hive of honey bees.
I say,
It's the fire in my eyes,
And the flash of my teeth,
The swing in my waist,
And the joy in my feet.
I'm a woman
Phenomenally.
Phenomenal woman,
That's me.

Men themselves have wondered
What they see in me.
They try so much
But they can't touch
My inner mystery.
When I try to show them,
They say they still can't see.
I say,
It's in the arch of my back,
The sun of my smile,
The ride of my breasts,
The grace of my style.
I'm a woman
Phenomenally.

Phenomenal woman,
That's me.

Now you understand
Just why my head's not bowed.
I don't shout or jump about
Or have to talk real loud.
When you see me passing,
It ought to make you proud.
I say,
It's in the click of my heels,
The bend of my hair,
the palm of my hand,
The need for my care.
'Cause I'm a woman
Phenomenally.
Phenomenal woman,
That's me.

New Directions

In 1903 the late Mrs. Annie Johnson of Arkansas found herself with two toddling sons, very little money, a slight ability to read and add simple numbers. To this picture add a disastrous marriage and the burdensome fact that Mrs. Johnson was a Negro.

When she told her husband, Mr. William Johnson, of her dissatisfaction with their marriage, he conceded that he too found it to be less than he expected, and had been secretly hoping to leave and study religion. He added that he thought God was calling him not only to preach but to do so in Enid, Oklahoma. He did not tell her that he knew a minister in Enid with whom he could study and who had a friendly, unmarried daughter. They parted amicably, Annie keeping the one-room house and William taking most of the cash to carry himself to Oklahoma.

Annie, over six feet tall, big-boned, decided that she would not go to work as a domestic and leave her "precious babes" to anyone else's care. There was no possibility of being hired at the town's cotton gin or lumber mill, but maybe there was a way to make the two factories work for her. In her words, "I looked up the road I was going and back the way I come, and since I wasn't satisfied, I decided to step off the road and cut me a new path." She told herself that she wasn't a fancy cook but that she could "mix groceries well enough to scare hungry away and from starving a man."

She made her plans meticulously and in secret. One early evening to see if she was ready, she placed stones in two five-gallon pails and carried them three miles to the cotton gin. She rested a little, and then, discarding some rocks, she walked in the darkness to the saw mill five miles farther along the dirt road. On her way back to her little house and her babies, she dumped the remaining rocks along the path.

That same night she worked into the early hours boiling chicken and frying ham. She made dough and filled the rolled-out pastry with meat. At last she went to sleep.

The next morning she left her house carrying the meat pies, lard, an iron brazier, and coals for a fire. Just before lunch she appeared in an empty lot behind the cotton gin. As the dinner noon bell rang, she dropped the savors into boiling fat and the aroma rose and floated over to the workers who spilled out of the gin, covered with white lint, looking like specters.

Most workers had brought their lunches of pinto beans and biscuits or crackers, onions and cans of sardines, but they were tempted by the hot meat pies which Annie ladled out of the fat. She wrapped them in newspapers, which soaked up the grease, and offered them for sale at a nickel each. Although business was slow, those first days Annie was determined. She balanced her appearances between the two hours of activity.

So, on Monday if she offered hot fresh pies at the cotton gin and sold the remaining cooled-down pies at the lumber mill for three cents, then on Tuesday she went first to the lumber mill presenting fresh, just-cooked pies as the lumbermen covered in sawdust emerged from the mill.

For the next few years, on balmy spring days, blistering summer noons, and cold, wet, and wintry middays, Annie never disappointed her customers, who could count on seeing the tall, brown-skin woman bent over her brazier, carefully turning the meat pies. When she felt certain that the workers had become dependent on her, she built a stall between the two hives of industry and let the men run to her for their lunchtime provisions.

She had indeed stepped from the road which seemed to have been chosen for her and cut herself a brand-new path. In years that stall became a store where customers could buy cheese, meal, syrup, cookies, candy, writing tablets, pickles, canned goods, fresh fruit, soft drinks, coal, oil, and leather soles for worn-out shoes.

Each of us has the right and the responsibility to assess the roads which lie ahead, and those over which we have traveled, and if the future road looms ominous or unpromising, and the roads back uninviting, then we need to gather our resolve and, carrying only the necessary baggage, step off that road into another direction. If the new choice is also unpalatable, without embarrassment, we must be ready to change that as well.

Style

Content is of great importance, but we must not underrate the value of style. That is, attention must be paid to not only what is said but how it is said; to what we wear, as well as how we wear it. In fact, we should be aware of all we do and of how we do all that we do.

Manners and a respect for style can be developed if one is eager and has an accomplished teacher. On the other hand, any observant person can acquire the same results without a teacher simply by carefully watching the steady march of the human parade.

Never try to take the manners of another as your own, for the theft will be immediately evident and the thief will appear as ridiculous as a robin with peacock feathers hastily stuck on. Style is as unique and nontransferable and perfectly personal as a fingerprint. It is wise to take the time to develop one's own way of being, increasing those things one does well and eliminating the elements in one's character which can hinder and diminish the good personality.

Any person who has charm and some confidence can move in and through societies ranging from the most privileged to the most needy. Style allows the person to appear neither inferior in one location nor superior in the other. Good manners and tolerance, which are the highest manifestation of style, can often transform disaster into good fortune. Many people utter insults or disparaging remarks without thinking, but a wise or stylish person takes the time to consider the positive as well as the negative possibilities in each situation. The judicious response to a gibe can disarm the rude person, removing the power to injure.

This is not another admonition to turn the other cheek, although I do think that that can be an effective ploy on certain occasions. Rather, this is an encouragement to meet adverse situations with the intent and style to control them. Falling into an entanglement with brutes will usually result in nothing more conclusive than a stimulated nervous system and an upset digestive tract.

Getups

I was a twenty-one-year-old single parent with my son in kindergarten. Two jobs allowed me an apartment, food, and child care payment. Little money was left over for clothes, but I kept us nicely dressed in discoveries bought at the Salvation Army and other secondhand shops. Loving colors, I bought for myself beautiful reds and oranges, and greens and pinks, and teals and turquoise. I chose azure dresses and blouses and sweaters. And quite often I wore them in mixtures which brought surprise, to say the least, to the eyes of people who could not avoid noticing me. In fact, I concocted what southern black women used to call "getups."

Because I was very keen that my son not feel that he was neglected or different, I went frequently to his school. Sometimes between my jobs I would just go and stand outside the fenced play area. And he would, I am happy to say, always come and acknowledge me in the colorful regalia. I always wore beads. Lots of beads. The cheaper they were, the more I got, and sometimes I wore head wraps.

When my son was six and I twenty-two, he told me quite solemnly that he had to talk to me. We both sat down at the kitchen table, and he asked with an old man's eyes and a young boy's voice, "Mother, do you have any sweaters that match?" I was puzzled at first. I said, "No," and then I understood he was talking about the pullover and cardigan sets which were popular with white women. And I said, "No, I don't," maybe a little huffily. And he said, "Oh, I wish you did. So that you could wear them to school when you come to see me."

I was tickled, but I am glad I didn't laugh because he continued, "Mother, could you please only come to school when they call you?" Then I realized that my attire, which delighted my heart and certainly activated my creativity, was an embarrassment to him.

When people are young, they desperately need to conform, and no one can embarrass a young person in public so much as an adult to whom he or she is related. Any outré action or wearing of "getups" can make a young person burn with self-consciousness.

I learned to be a little more discreet to avoid causing him displeasure. As he grew older and more confident, I gradually returned to what friends thought of as my eccentric way of dressing. I was happier when I chose and created my own fashion.

I have lived in this body all my life and know it much better than any fashion designer. I think I know what looks good on me, and I certainly know what feels good in me.

I appreciate the creativity which is employed in the design of fabric and the design of clothes, and when something does fit my body and personality, I rush to it, buy it quickly, and wear it frequently. But I must not lie to myself for fashion's sake. I am only willing to purchase the item which becomes me and to wear that which enhances my image of myself to myself.

If I am comfortable inside my skin, I have the ability to make other people comfortable inside their skins although their feelings are not my primary reason for making my fashion choice. If I feel good inside my skin and clothes, I am thus free to allow my body its sway, its natural grace, its natural gesture. Then I am so comfortable that whatever I wear looks good on me even to the external fashion arbiters.

Dress is important to mention because many people are imprisoned by powerful dictates on what is right and proper to wear. Those decisions made by others and sometimes at their convenience are not truly meant to make life better or finer or more graceful or more gracious. Many times they stem from greed, insensitivity, and the need for control.

I have been in company, not long to be sure, but in company where a purveyor of taste will look at a woman or man who enters a room and will say with a sneer, "That was last year's jacket." As hastily as possible, I leave that company, but not before I record the snide attitude which has nothing to do with the beauty or effectiveness of the garment, but rather gives the speaker a moment's sense of superiority at, of course, someone else's expense.

Seek the fashion which truly fits and befits you. You will always be in fashion if you are true to yourself, and only if you are true to yourself. You might, of course, rightly wear that style which is emblazoned on the pages of the fashion magazines of the day, or you might not.

The statement "Clothes make the man" should be looked at, reexamined, and in fact reevaluated. Clothes can make the man or woman look silly and foppish and foolish. Try rather to be so much yourself that the clothes you choose increase your naturalness and grace.

Tina McElroy Ansa (1949–)

Born in Macon, Georgia, Tina McElroy Ansa was educated at Spelman College in Atlanta. As a freelance journalist, she wrote for the Atlanta Constitution *and the* Charlotte Observer. *She also taught writing at Brunswick College, Emory University, and Spelman College.*

Her first two novels, Baby of the Family *(1989) and* Ugly Ways *(1993), emphasize family dynamics and problems in mother-daughter relationships. Her long, erotic novel,* The Hand I Fan With *(1996), presents Lena, a wealthy and exceedingly generous African American woman who helps everyone in her small town. In an exquisitely beautiful house filled with treasures from Africa, Lena only lacks one thing—a man—until she conjures a very physical male ghost who satisfies her every desire. A confident, smart, productive, and self-accepting woman, Lena seems to pose Ansa's answer to images of exploited Black women in works by Harriet Jacobs, Zora Neale Hurston, and Alice Walker, among others.*

The first selection here, "Willie Bea and Jaybird" treats a male-female sexual relationship and bears some comparison with several other stories in this anthology.

Keith D. Miller

Willie Bea and Jaybird

When Willie Bea first saw Jaybird in The Place, she couldn't help herself. She wanted him so bad she sucked in her bottom lip, cracked with the cold, then she ran her tongue so slowly over her top lip that she could taste the red Maybelline lipstick she had put on hours before. He looked like something that would be good to eat, like peach cobbler or a hot piece of buttered cornbread.

She had just entered the bar clutching her black purse under her arm and smiling to try to make herself look attractive among the 6 o'clock crowd of drinkers and dancers and socializers, every one of them glad to be done with work for the day. He was there at the end of the bar in his golden Schlitz uniform sharing a quart of Miller High Life beer with a buddy. Willie Bea noticed right away how he leaned his long frame clear across the bar, bent at the waist, his elbows resting easily on the Formica counter. There didn't seem to be a tense bone in his lean efficient body.

"He look like he could go anywhere in the world," Willie Bea thought as she followed her big-butt friend Patricia as she weaved her way to a nearby table already jammed with four of her friends, two men and two women. "If somebody put him in a white jacket and a flower in his buttonhole, he could pass for an actor in a Technicolor movie."

As the juke box stated up again, playing a driving Sam and Dave number, he looked around the bar, picked up his glass of beer and headed toward her table with his chin held high over the other patrons. When he smoothly pulled up a chair to her table and straddled it backwards, Willie Bea crossed her stick legs and pinched her friend Pat's thigh under the table to give her some Sen-Sen for her breath.

"Hey, Little Mama, you got time for a tired working man?"

She had to remember to wipe the uncomfortable moisture from the corners of her mouth with her fingertips before she could respond to him.

She still felt that way, four years after they had started going together, when she looked at him.

Nothing gave her more pleasure than to be asked her marital status with Jaybird around.

"Willie Bea, girl, where you been keeping yourself?" some big-mouthed woman would shout at her over the din of the jukebox at The Place. "I ain't seen you in a month of Sundays. You still living with your aunt, ain't you?" This last expectantly with pity.

Willie Bea would roll her shoulders and dip her ears from side to side a couple of times in feigned modesty.

"Naw, girl, I *been* moved out of my aunt's," Willie Bea would answer. "I'm married now. I live with my . . . *husband*."

The old horse's big mouth would fall open, then close, then open as if she were having trouble chewing this information.

"Husband? Married??!!"

"Uh-huh. That's my *husband* over there by the juke box. Naw, not him. My Jay is the tall light-skinned one, the one with the head full of curly hair."

Willie Bea never even bothered to look at her inquisitor when she pointed out Jay. She could hear the effect the weight of the revelation had had on the woman. And Willie Bea only glanced smugly at the old cow as she raced around the bar nearly knocking over a chair to ask her friends and companions why no one told her that skinny little shiny-faced Willie Bea had a man.

"I thought she was sitting there mighty sassy looking."

Even Willie Bea would have admitted it: Most days, she did feel sassy, and it was Jaybird who made her so. He burst into the bathroom while she was in the bathtub and pretended to take pictures of her with an imaginary camera. He teased her about flirting with Mr. Maurice who owned the store on the corner near their boardinghouse when the merchant sliced her baloney especially thin, the way she liked it.

Now, she really thought she was cute, with her little square monkey face and eager-to-please grin, a cheap jet black Prince Valiant wig set on the top of her head like a wool cap with her short hair plaited underneath and a pair of black eyeglasses so thick that her eyes looked as if they were in fish bowls.

Jaybird had done that to her. He even called her "fine," an appellation that actually brought tears to her eyes made huge and outlandish by the Coke-bottle-thick glasses.

"Fine." It was the one thing in life Willie Bea longed to be. She had no shape to speak of. She was just five feet tall and weighed about 90 pounds. But she did her best to throw that thing even though she had very little to throw.

"If I had me a big old butt like you, Pat," she would say to her friend, "ya'll couldn't stand me."

The pitiful little knot of an ass that she had was her sorrow, especially after noticing from Jaybird's gaze that he appreciated a full ass. His favorite seemed to be the big heart-shaped ones that started real low and hung and swayed like a bustle when the woman walked. Many mornings, Jay lay in bed watching Bea move around the room getting dressed and thought, "Her behind ain't no bigger than my fist." But he didn't dare say anything, even as a joke. He knew it would break her heart.

But since she knew she didn't have a big ass, she did what she had done since she was a child when someone told her what she was lacking: She pretended she did and acted as if her ass was the prize one in town. The one men in jukejoints talked about.

Wherever she went—to the market, to work cleaning houses, to The Place, downtown to shop—she dressed as if she had that ass to show off.

She wore tight little straight skirts that she made herself on her landlady's sewing machine. Skirts of cotton or wool or taffeta no wider than 12 inches across. Not that wide, really, because she wanted the skirt to "cup," if possible, under the pones of her behind and to wrinkle across her crotch in front. Using less than a yard of material and a Simplicity quickie pattern she had bought years before and worked away to tatters, she took no more than an hour to produce one of her miniature skirts.

On Sundays, when the house was empty of other boarders or quiet from their sleep, Willie Bea used her landlady's sewing machine that she kept in the parlor. The steady growl of the old foot-pedal-run Singer disturbed no one. In fact, on those Sundays she and Jaybird went out and she did no sewing, the other tenants of the large white wooden house felt an unidentified longing and found themselves on the verge of complaining about the silence.

Willie Bea looked on the ancient sewing machine, kept in mint condition by the genial landlady who always wore plaid housedresses and her thin crimpy red hair in six skinny braids, as a blessing. She didn't mind that the machine was a foot-propelled model rather than an electric one. It never occurred to her to expect anything as extravagant as that. For her, the old machine was a step up from the tedious hand-sewing that she had learned and relied on as a child. With the waist bands neatly attached and the short zippers eased into place by machine, her skirts had a finished look that would have taken her all night to accomplish by hand.

Many times, she felt herself rocking gently to the rhythm she set with her bare feet on the cold iron treadle to ease a crick in her stiff back before she realized that she had been at the job non-stop all afternoon. Just using the machine made her happy, made her think of men watching her at the bus stops in her new tight skirt and later, maybe, these same men letting some sly comment drop in front of Jaybird about her shore looking good.

She imagined Jaybird jumping in the men's faces, half-angry, half-proud, to let them know that was his *wife* they were talking about. Just thinking of Jaybird saying, "my wife" made her almost as happy as her being able to say "my husband."

She loved to go over in her head how it had come to pass, their marriage. They had been living together in one room of the boardinghouse at the top of Pleasant Hill for nearly three years, with him seeming to take for granted that they would be together for eternity and with her hardly daring to believe that he really wanted her, afraid to ask him why he picked her to love.

As with most of his decisions, movements, he surprised her.

One evening in August, he walked into their room and said, "Let's get married." As if the idea had just come to him, his and original. She responded in kind.

"Married? Married, Jay?" she said, pretending to roll the idea around in her head a while. Then, "Okay, if you want."

It was her heart's desire, the play-pretty of her dreams, being this man's wife.

She bought stiff white lace from Newberry's department store to make a loose cropped sleeveless overblouse and a yard of white polished cotton and sewed a tight straight skirt for the ceremony at the courthouse.

When they returned to their room for the honeymoon, Willie Bea thought as she watched him take off his wedding suit that no other man could be so handsome, so charming, so full of self-assured cockiness . . . and still love her.

He was tall and slender in that way that made her know that he would be lean all his life, never going sway-backed and to fat around his middle like a pregnant woman. He was lithe and strong from lifting cases and kegs of Schlitz beer all day long, graceful from leaping on and off the running board of the moving delivery truck as it made its rounds of bars and stores.

Once when he had not seen her, Willie Bea had spied him hanging fearlessly off the back of the beer truck like a prince, face directly into the wind, his eyes blinking back the wind tears, a vacant look on his face. His head full of curly hair quivering in the wind. The setting sunlight gleamed off the chrome and steel of the truck, giving a golden-orange color to the aura that Willie Bea felt surrounded him all the time.

Overcome by the sight, Willie Bea had had to turn away into an empty doorway to silently weep over the beauty of her Jaybird.

Jaybird even made love the way she knew this man would—sweet and demanding. When her friend Pat complained about her own man's harsh unfeeling fucking, Willie Bea joined in and talked about men like dogs. But first, in her own mind, she placed Jaybird outside the dog pack.

"Girl, just thank your lucky stars that you ain't hooked up with a man like Henry," Pat told her. "Although God knows they all alike. You may as well put 'em all in a crocker sack and pick one out. They all the same. One just as good as the other. Just take your pick."

"Uh-huh, girl, you know you telling the truth," Willie Bea would answer.

"Why, that old dog of mine will just wake any time of the night and go to grabbing me and sticking his hand up my nightdress. He don't say nothing, just grunt. He just goes and do his business. I could be anything, a sack of flour, that chair you sitting on."

"What you be doing?" Willie Bea asked in her soft sing-song voice even though she already knew because Pat always complained about the same thing. But she asked because she and Pat had grown up together, she had been Pat's friend longer than anyone outside of her family. And Willie Bea knew what a friend was for.

"Shoot, sometimes I just lay there like I *am* a sack of flour. I thought that would make him see I wasn't getting nothing out of his humping. Then, I saw it didn't make no difference to him whether I was having a good time or not. So, now, sometimes I push him off me just before he come. That makes him real mad. Or I tell him I got my period.

"Some nights, we just lay there jostling each other like little children jostling over a ball. I won't turn over or open up my legs and he won't stop tugging on me."

"Girl, both of ya'll crazy. That way, don't neither of you get a piece. That's too hard," Willie Bea said sincerely.

"Shoot, girl, some nights we tussle all night." Pat gave a hot dry laugh. "Henry thinks too much of hisself to fight me for it, really hit me up side my head or yell and scream 'cause with those little paper sheer walls, everybody next door would know our business. So while we fighting, it's real quiet except for some grunts and the bed squeaking."

Then, she laughed again.

"I guess that's all you'd be hearing anyway."

Willie Bea tried to laugh in acknowledgement. Once Pat told her, "Shoot, girl, I've gotten to liking the scuffling we do in bed better than I ever liked the screwing."

That made Willie Bea feel cold all over.

"It's like it make it more important," Pat continued. "Something worth fighting for. Some nights when he just reach for me like that, it's like he calling me out my name. And I turn over ready to fight.

"I would get somebody else, but they all the same, you may as well pick one from the sack as another. But look at you, Bea. You just agreeing to be nice. You don't believe that, do you?'

"I didn't say nothing," Willie Bea would rush to say. "I believe what you say about you and Henry. I believe you."

"That ain't what I mean and you know it. I'm talking about mens period."

"I know what you saying about men."

"Yeah, but you don't think they all alike, do you?" Pat asked.

Willie Bea would start dipping her head from side to side and grinning her sheepish closed-mouth grin.

"Go on and admit it, girl," Pat would prod.

After a moment, Willie Bea would admit it. "I don't know why he love me so good."

Then, Pat would sigh and urge her friend to tell her how sweet Jay was to her . . . in bed, at the table, after work. Especially in bed.

Willie Bea balked at first, each time the subject came up. But she always gave in, too. She was just dying to talk about Jaybird.

Most women she knew held the same beliefs that Pat did about men. They sure as hell didn't want to hear about her and the bliss her man brought her. She had found they may want to hear about you "can't do with him and can't do without him" or how bad he treat you and you still can't let him go. All of that. But don't be coming around them with those thick window pane eyes of hers all bright and enlarged with stories of happiness and fulfillment. Those stories cut her other girlfriends and their lives to the quick.

But her friend Pat, big-butt Pat, urged Bea to share her stories with her. Sometimes, these reminiscences made Pat smile and glow as if she were there in Willie Bea's place. But sometimes, they left her morose.

Willie Bea, noticing this at first, began leaving out details that she thought made Pat's love pale in comparison. But Pat, alert to nuances in the tales, caught on an insisted that Willie Bea never leave stuff out again if she was going to tell it.

And Willie Bea, eager to tell it all, felt as if she were pleasing her friend as much as herself. So, she continued telling stories of love and dipping her ear down toward her shoulder in a gay little shy gesture.

"When Jaybird and me doing it, he has this little gruff-like voice he uses when he talks to me."

"Talk to you? What ya'll be doing, screwing or talking?" Pat would interrupt, but not seriously.

"He says things like, 'Is that all? That ain't all. I want it all. Uh-huh.' "

At first, Willie Bea was embarrassed disclosing these secrets of her and Jaybird's passionate and tender lovemaking. But Pat seemed so enthralled by her stories that Willie Bea finally stopped fighting it and gave herself over to the joy of recounting how Jaybird loved her.

Pat never told Willie Bea that many of the women at The Place talked under their breaths when Jaybird and Willie Bea came in together.

"He may sleep in the same bed with her, but I heard he put an ironing board between 'em first," some said.

"He can't really want that little old black gal. He just like her worshipping the ground he walk on," another would add.

Pat knew Willie Bea would have tried to kill whoever said such things. But even Pat found it hard to believe sometimes that her little friend had attracted Jaybird.

Mornings, Pat watched Willie Bea step off the city bus they both took to their jobs, her too-pale dimestore stockings shining in the early light, her narrow shoulders rotating like bicycle pedals in the direction opposite the one she sent her snake hips inside her straight skirt and thought how changed her friend was by the love of Jaybird. Now, that walk is something new, Pat thought as the bus pulled away from the curb.

Willie Bea, who lived two blocks above Pat, got on the bus first, then alit first when she got near the white woman's house she cleaned five days a week. Pat stayed on until the bus reached downtown near the box factory where she worked. They rode to and from work together nearly every day.

So, one evening when Pat wasn't on the bus when she got on returning home, Willie Bea began to worry about her. All that one of Pat's co-workers on the bus said when Willie Bea asked was, "She left work early."

"I wonder if she's sick," Willie Bea thought.

She was still thinking about her friend when the bus began making its climb up Pleasant Hill. "I better stop and see 'bout her," Willie Bea thought.

She was still standing with her hand near the signal wire when the bus slowed to a stop in front of the cinder block duplex where Pat lived, and Willie Bea saw the gold of a Schiltz beer uniform slip back inside the dusty screen door of her friend's house.

The bus driver paused a good while with the bus door open waiting for Willie Bea to leave. Then, he finally hollered toward the back of the bus, "You getting off or not?"

Willie Bea turned around to the driver's back and tried to smile as she took her regular seat again. When she reached her boardinghouse, she was anxious to see Jaybird and ask him who the new man was working on the beer truck. But he wasn't home.

She sat up alone on the bed in the boardinghouse room long after it grew dark.

Willie Bea didn't know how long she had been asleep when she heard the rusty door knob turn and felt a sliver of light from the hall fall across her face. Jaybird almost never stayed out late without her or telling her beforehand.

"You okay, Jay?" she asked sleepily.

He only grunted and rubbed her back softly. "Go back to sleep, Bea," he said. "I'm coming to bed now."

Willie Bea lay waiting for Jaybird to say something more, to say where he had been, to say he saw her friend Pat that day. But he said nothing.

And when he did finally slip into bed, it felt as if an ironing board was between them.

Toni Cade Bambara (1939–1995)

Toni Cade was born in New York City on March 25, 1939, and was raised, along with a brother, by a single mother. Both protective and liberal, Toni Cade's mother insisted that her children learn Black history at home and school, an insistence that certainly influenced Bambara's own dedication to communal history and tradition. Bambara's mother also instilled in her children a sense of identity beyond gender roles, encouraging both son and daughter toward self-determination and creativity.

Her mother was the first of many influential women role models in Bambara's early life. She learned much from the women in her neighborhood whose lives demonstrated possibility and potential as much as they also evidenced the imposition of circumstance and oppression. Bambara felt "mothered" on many levels and she translated the security and variety of the women around her into the rich women characters that bring her fiction to life.

Toni Cade Bambara valued education from a young age, expending effort on her studies despite the many moves from neighborhood to neighborhood in New York City, to New Jersey, and to the South. She pursued a double major in theatre arts and English at Queens College and, in l959, started graduate work in African fiction at the City College of New York. It was during her time at City College and while working her way through school that she began to publish her fiction in various journals, though she considered her writing more of a hobby than a career.

As an academic, Bambara returned to CCNY to teach from 1965–1969, and, in 1970, began teaching at Livingston College. After five years at Livingston, Bambara was the writer in residence at Spelman College and taught at Duke University and Rutgers University.

In the last years of her life, however, Bambara focused on film and video, adapting several of her stories to film and creating a film version of the attack on the alternative Black commune MOVE in Philadelphia. Bambara remained vitally politically active and lived in Philadelphia until her death in 1995.

The publication of The Black Woman (1970), an anthology that gathered the voices of many African American women writers, signaled Bambara's own growing consciousness of her literary talents and their intersection with her political ideal. The Black Woman centered Black women's voices and experiences in a way that no other work yet had, showing the range of Black women's thinking about the Civil Rights Movement, the feminist movement, and community and personal relationships in the forms of poetry, fiction, essay, conversations, and letters. Including the voices of well-known writers Nikki Giovanni, Audre Lorde, Alice Walker, and Paule Marshall, the anthology stood as a response from Black women to being written about. The voices in The Black Woman self-

defined. Publication of the anthology solidified Bambara's reputation as a writer as well as her role as a social activist and a woman dedicated to the intersections of racism and feminism.

In the wake of The Black Woman's *success, Toni Cade exercised a form of self-definition herself, becoming Toni Cade Bambara when she found the name Bambara on a sketchbook in her great-grandmother's trunk. With a new name symbolic of her commitment to her own heritage and the history and tradition of her community, Bambara was ready to pursue her goals as writer, revolutionary, and mother, for 1970 brought not only the scholarly success, but the birth of her daughter, Karma.*

A second anthology that Bambara edited and to which she contributed, Tales and Stories for Black Folk, *was published in 1971. This anthology invited Black youth into their literary tradition through the words of established writers like Alice Walker and Langston Hughes, the works of Bambara's students at Livingston College, and Bambara's own Black fairy tales, most of them revisions of European fairy tales rich with Black English and veneration of the values of Black communities. The stories in* Tales for Black Folks *were stories Bambara wished she had enjoyed when she was a child. Her decision to include young writers alongside established writers was her way of leveling destructive hierarchies.*

Perhaps most well known as a writer of short fiction, Bambara published two widely read and highly acclaimed collections in the 1970s, the first, Gorilla, My Love *in 1972 and the second,* The Sea Birds Are Still Alive, *five years later in 1977. Many of the stories in* Gorilla, My Love *feature a spirited African American girl, not at all a victim as young Black girls were in much of the fiction of the time. Hazel, a young girl who goes to P.S. 186, is the focus of the title story of the collection. On a pecan-picking trip with her Grandaddy Vale, her brother, Baby Jason, and her uncle, Jefferson Winston Vale a.k.a. Hunca Bubba, Hazel confronts her Hunca Bubba about the woman he's in love with. Through her honest depiction of the situation through Hazel's eyes, Bambara validates Hazel's jealous pain resulting from her Hunca Bubba's "betrayal" of his promise to marry her when she grew up. Stories within the frame of the trip story fill the reader in on Hazel's general exasperation with the childhood condition of "grownups messin over kids just cause they little." Also central to Hazel's self-perception are the names she recognizes as her own—Scout, Badbird, Miss Muffin—and the way she understands their function in her life, including use of Hazel, her "real name," as absolutely necessary for serious interactions like telling your uncle he's a "lyin dawg." The language and magic of the story and collection as a whole is the music of urban Black English and the strategy of jazz improvisation as a method of storytelling. These themes are also evidenced in "My Man Bovanne."*

The Sea Birds Are Still Alive *shares the plot improvisation and Black neighborhoods of* Gorilla, My Love, *but the settings and themes of the collection evidence a broadening of political thinking and activism, a broadening due in part to Bambara's travel and work with women's groups in Cuba and Vietnam after the publication of* Gorilla, My Love. *The title story, which features Vietnamese boat people, perhaps best demonstrates this broader focus. While the stories in* The Sea Birds Are Still Alive *highlight Bambara's commitment to social activism, her attention to the individual is still also central. In "The Organizer's Wife," Bambara maintains the intimacy of narrative perspective of "Gorilla, My Love." Despite the third person narration, Virginia's exhaustion and desperation as the wife of a community organizer in jail for his ideals, as mother, and as woman in the spotlight of the community, comes through clearly. Virginia's final decision to keep the faith and maintain her commitment to the people and her husband is the victory of the story. Bambara's success is capturing Virginia's struggle of spirit and psyche in language.*

Bambara's first novel, The Salt Eaters *(1980), focuses on a character similar to Virginia of "The Organizer's Wife." At the center of the novel is the healing of an African American woman, Velma Henry, who has lost herself in pursuit of the struggle for the survival of her community. A veteran activist, Velma is exhausted by the futility of trying to save a community center when her community will not unite with her and when funding is never stable. Her suicide attempt prompts the community to respond with methods of healing that range from traditional folk methods to modern medicine. The plot weaves across time and combines thoughts, dreams, and multiple perspectives to create a work of profound fullness.*

Her second novel, originally titled If Blessings Come, *was written during the twelve years before her death and was published in October 1999 as* Those Bones Are Not My Child, *edited and with an introduction by Toni Morrison. In the novel, Bambara revisits the race relations, but more importantly the terror, of the Atlanta child murders of 1979–1981. During this time span, forty African American children lost their lives. The protagonist of this novel is Marzala Rawls Spencer, a divorced mother of three, holding down three jobs and going to night school. When her 12-year-old son Sundiata disappears, Zala is pulled into the inexpressible fear of the summer of 1980 in the city of Atlanta.*

In all of her fiction and editorial work, Bambara worked to capture in language and hope the volatile times of transition of the 1960s and 1970s and to promote a future of healthier relationships and identities, especially for Black women. In a 1983 interview with Claudia Tate published in Black Women Writers at Work *(1983), Bambara says of her role as a Black Woman writer. "As black and woman in a society systematically orchestrated to oppress each and both, we have a very particular vantage point and, therefore, have a special contribution to make to the collective intelligence, to the literature of this historical moment. . . . I am about the empowerment and development of our sisters and of our community. That sense of caring and celebration is certainly reflected in the body of my work. . . ." The readers of Bambara's legacy will certainly concur.*

R. Joyce Lausch

My Man Bovanne

Blind people got a hummin jones if you notice. Which is understandable completely once you been around one and notice what no eyes will force you into to see people, and you get past the first time, which seems to come out of nowhere, and it's like you in church again with fat-chest ladies and old gents gruntin a hum low in the throat to whatever the preacher by saying. Shakey Bee bottom lip all swole up with Sweet Peach and me explainin how come the sweet-potato bread was a dollar-quarter this time stead of dollar regular and he say uh hunh he understand, then he break into this *thizzin* kind of hum which is quiet, but fiercesome just the same, if you ain't ready for it. Which I wasn't. But I got used to it and the onliest time I had to say somethin bout it was when he was playin checkers on the stoop one time and he commenst to hummin quite churchy seem to me. So I says, "Look here Shakey Bee, I can't beat you and Jesus too." He stop.

So that's how come I asked My Man Bovanne to dance. He ain't my man mind you, just a nice ole gent from the block that we all know cause he fixes things and the kids like him. Or used to fore Black Power got hold their minds and mess em around till they can't be civil to ole folks. So we at this benefit for my niece's cousin who's runnin for somethin with this Black party somethin or other behind her. And I press up close to dance with Bovanne who blind and I'm hummin and he hummin, chest to chest like talkin. Not jammin my beasts into the man. Wasn't bout tits. Was bout vibrations. And he dug it and asked me what color dress I had on and how my hair was fixed and how I was doin without a man, not nosy but nice-like, and who was at this affair and was the canapés dainty-stingy or healthy enough to get hold of proper. Comfy and cheery is what I'm tryin to get across. Touch talkin like the heel of the hand on the tambourine or on a drum.

But right away Joe Lee come up on us and frown for dancin so close to the man. My own son who knows what kind of warm I am about; and don't grown men call me long distance and in the middle of the night for a little Mama comfort? But he frown. Which ain't right since Bovanne can't see and defend himself. Just a nice old man who fixes toasters and busted irons and bicycles and things and changes the lock on my door when my men friends get messy. Nice man. Which is not why they invited him. Grass roots you see. Me and Sister Taylor and the woman who does heads at Mamies and the man from the barber shop, we all there on account of we grass roots. And I ain't never been souther than Brooklyn Battery and no more country than the window box on my fire escape. And just yesterday my kids tellin me to take them countrified rags off my head and be cool. And now can't get Black enough to suit em. So everybody passin sayin My Man Bovanne. Big deal, keep steppin and don't even stop a minute to get the man a drink or one of them cute sandwiches or tell him what's goin on. And him standin there with a smile ready case someone do speak he want to be ready. So that's how come I pull him on the dance floor and we dance squeezin past the tables and chairs and all them coats and people standin round up in each other face talkin bout this and that but got no use for this blind man who mostly fixed skates and skooters for all these folks when they was just kids. So I'm pressed up close and we touch talkin with the hum. And here come my daughter cuttin her eye at me like she do when she tell me about my "apolitical" self like I got hoof and mouf disease and there ain't no hope at all. And I don't pay her no mind and just look up in Bovanne shadow face and tell him his stomach like a drum and he laugh. Laugh real loud. And here come my youngest, Task, with a tap on my elbow like he the third grade monitor and I'm cuttin up on the line to assembly.

"I was just talkin on the drums," I explained when they hauled me into the kitchen. I figured drums was my best defense. They can get ready for drums what with all this heritage business. And Bovanne stomach just like that drum

Task give me when he come back from Africa. You just touch it and it hum thizzm, thizzm. So I stuck to the drum story. "Just drummin that's all."

"Mama, what are you talkin about?"

"She had too much to drink," say Elo to Task cause she don't hardly say nuthin to me direct no more since that ugly argument about my wigs.

"Look here Mama," say Task, the gentle one. "We just tryin to pull your coat. You were makin a spectacle of yourself out there dancing like that."

"Dancin like what?"

Task run a hand over his left ear like his father for the world and his father before that.

"Like a bitch in heat," say Elo.

"Well uhh, I was goin to say like one of them sex-starved ladies gettin on in years and not too discriminating. Know what I mean?"

I don't answer cause I'll cry. Terrible thing when your own children talk to you like that. Pullin me out the party and hustlin me into some stranger's kitchen in the back of a bar just like the damn police. And ain't like I'm old old. I can still wear me some sleeveless dresses without the meat hangin off my arm. And I keep up with some thangs through my kids. Who ain't kids no more. To hear them tell it. So I don't say nuthin.

"Dancin with that tom," say Elo to Joe Lee, who leanin on the folks' freezer. "His feet can smell a cracker a mile away and go into their shuffle number post haste. And them eyes. He could be a little considerate and put on some shades. Who wants to look into them blown-out fuses that—"

"Is this what they call the generation gap?" I say.

"Generation gap," spits Elo, like I suggested castor oil and fricassee possum in the milk-shakes or somethin. "That's a white concept for a white phenomenon. There's no generation gap among Black people. We are a col—"

"Yeh, well never mind," says Joe Lee. "The point is Mama . . . well, it's pride. You embarrass yourself and us too dancin like that."

"I wasn't shame." Then nobody say nuthin. Them standin there in they pretty clothes with drinks in they hands and gangin up on me, and me in the third-degree chair and nary a olive to my name. Felt just like the police got hold to me.

"First of all," Task say, holdin up his hand and tickin off the offenses, "the dress. Now that dress is too short, Mama, and too low-cut for a woman your age. And Tamu's going to make a speech tonight to kick off the campaign and will be introducin you and expecting you to organize the council of elders—"

"Me? Didn nobody ask me nuthin. You mean Nisi? She change her name?"

"Well, Norton was supposed to tell you about it. Nisi wants to introduce you and then encourage the older folks to form a Council of the Elders to act as an advisory—"

"And you going to be standing there with your boobs out and that wig on your head and that hem up to your ass. And people'll say, 'Ain't that the horny bitch that was grindin with the blind dude?'"

"Elo, be cool a minute," say Task, gettin to the next finger. "And then there's the drinkin. Mama, you know you can't drink cause next thing you know you be laughin loud and carryin on," and he grab another finger for the loudness. "And then there's the dancin. You been tattooed on the man for four records straight and slow draggin even on the fast numbers. How you think that look for a woman your age?"

"What's my age?"

"What?"

"I'm axin you all a simple question. You keep talkin bout what's proper for a woman my age. How old am I anyhow?" And Joe Lee slams his eyes shut and squinches up his face to figure. And Task run a hand over his ear and stare into his glass like the ice cubes goin calculate for him. And Elo just starin at the top of my head like she goin rip the wig off any minute now.

"Is your hair braided up under that thing? If so, why don't you take it off? You always did do a neat cornroll."

"Uh huh," cause I'm thinkin how she couldn't undo her hair fast enough talking bout cornroll so countrified. None of which was the subject. "How old, I say?"

"Sixtee-one or—"

"You a damn lie Joe Lee Peoples."

"And that's another thing," say Task on the fingers.

"You know what you all can kiss," I say, gettin up and brushin the wrinkles out my lap.

"Oh, Mama," Elo say, puttin a hand on my shoulder like she hasn't done since she left home and the hand landin light and not sure it supposed to be there. Which hurt me to my heart. Cause this was the child in our happiness fore Mr. Peoples die. And I carried that child strapped to my chest till she was nearly two. We was close is what I'm tryin to tell you. Cause it was more me in the child than the others. And even after Task it was the girlchild I covered in the night and wept over for no reason at all less it was she was a chub-chub like me and not very pretty, but a warm child. And how did things get to this, that she can't put a sure hand on me and say Mama we love you and care about you and you entitled to enjoy yourself cause you a good woman?

"And then there's Reverend Trent," say Task, glancin from left to right like they hatchin a plot and just now lettin me in on it. "You were suppose to be talking with him tonight, Mama, about giving us his basement for campaign headquarters and—"

"Didn nobody tell me nuthin. If grass roots mean you kept in the dark I can't use it. I really can't. And Reven Trent a fool anyway the way he tore into the window man up there on Edgecomb cause he wouldn't take in three of them foster children and the woman not even comfy in the ground yet and the man's mind messed up and—"

"Look here," say Task. "What we need is a family conference so we can get all this stuff cleared up and laid out on the table. In the meantime I think we better get back into the other room and tend to business. And in the meantime, Mama, see if you can't get to Reverend Trent and—"

"You want me to belly rub with the Reven, that it?"

"Oh damn," Elo say and go through the swingin door.

"We'll talk about all this at dinner. How's tomorrow night, Joe Lee?" While Joe Lee being self-important I'm wonderin who's doin the cookin and how come no body ax me if I'm free and do I get a corsage and things like that. Then Joe nod that it's O.K. and he go through the swingin door and just a little hubbub come through from the other room. Then Task smile his smile, lookin just like his daddy and he leave. And it just me in this stranger's kitchen, which was a mess I wouldn't never let my kitchen look like. Poison you just to look at the pots. Then the door swing the other way and it's My Man Bovanne standin there sayin Miss Hazel but lookin at the deep fry and then at the steam table, and most surprised when I come up on him from the other direction and take him on out of there. Pass the folks pushin up towards the stage where Nisi and some other people settin and ready to talk, and folks gettin to the last of the sandwiches and the booze fore they settle down in one spot and listen serious. And I'm thinkin bout tellin Bovanne what a lovely long dress Nisi got on and the earrings and her hair piled up in a cone and the people bout to hear how we all gettin screwed and gotta form our own party and everybody there listenin and lookin. But instead I just haul the man on out of there, and Joe Lee and his wife look at me like I'm terrible, but they ain't said boo to the man yet. Cause he blind and old and don't nobody there need him since they grown up and don't need they skates fixed no more.

"Where we goin, Miss Hazel?" Him knowin all the time.

"First we gonna buy you some dark sunglasses. Then you comin with me to the supermarket so I can pick up tomorrow's dinner, which is goin to be a grand thing proper and you invited. Then we goin to my house."

"That be fine. I surely would like to rest my feet." Bein cute, but you got to let men play out they little show, blind or not. So he chat on bout how tired he is and how he appreciate me takin him in hand this way. And I'm thinkin I'll have him change the lock on my door first thing. Then I'll give the man a nice warm bath with jasmine leaves in the water and a little Epsom salt on the sponge to do his back. And then a good rubdown with rose water and olive oil. Then a cup of lemon tea with a taste in it. And a little talcum, some of that fancy stuff Nisi mother sent over last Christmas. And then a massage, a good face massage round the forehead which is the worryin part. Cause you gots to take care of the older folks. And let them know they still needed to run the mimeo machine and keep the spark plugs clean and fix the mailboxes for folks who might help us get the breakfast program goin, and the school for the little kids and the campaign and all. Cause old folks is the nation. That what Nisi was sayin and I mean to do my part.

"I imagine you are a very pretty woman, Miss Hazel."

"I surely am," I say just like the hussy my daughter always say I was.

Gorilla, My Love

That was the year Hunca Bubba changed his name. Not a change up, but a change back, since Jefferson Winston Vale was the name in the first place. Which was news to me cause he'd been my Hunca Bubba my whole lifetime, since I couldn't manage Uncle to save my life. So far as I was concerned it was a change completely to somethin soundin very geographical weatherlike to me, like somethin you'd find in a almanac. Or somethin you'd run across when you sittin in the navigator seat with a wet thumb on the map crinkly in your lap, watchin the roads and signs so when Granddaddy Vale say "Which way, Scout," you got sense enough to say take the next exit or take a left or whatever it is. Not that Scout's my name. Just the name Granddaddy call whoever sittin in the navigator seat. Which is usually me cause I don't feature sittin in the back with the pecans. Now, you figure pecans all right to be sittin with. If you thinks so, that's your business. But they dusty sometime and make you cough. And they got a way of slidin around and dippin down sudden, like maybe a rat in the buckets. So if you scary like me, you sleep with the lights on and blame it on Baby Jason and, so as not to waste good electric, you study the maps. And that's how come I'm in the navigator seat most times and get to be called Scout.

So Hunca Bubba in the back with the pecans and Baby Jason, and he in love. And we got to hear all this stuff about this woman he in love with and all. Which really ain't enough to keep the mind alive, though Baby Jason got no better sense than to give his undivided attention and keep grabbin at the photograph which is just a picture of some skinny woman in a countrified dress with her hand shot up to her face like she shame fore cameras. But there's a movie house in the background which I ax about. Cause I am a movie freak from way back, even though it do get me in trouble sometime.

Like when me a Big Brood and Baby Jason was on our own last Easter and couldn't go to the Dorset cause we'd seen all the Three Stooges they was. And the RKO Hamilton was closed readying up for the Easter Pageant that night. And the West End, the Regun and the Sunset was too far, less we had grownups with us which we didn't. So we walk up Amsterdam Avenue to the Washington and *Gorilla, My Love* playin, they say, which suit me just fine, though the "my love" part kinda drag Big Brood some. As for Baby Jason, shoot, like Granddaddy say, he'd follow me into the fiery furnace if I say come on. So we go in and get three bags of Havmore potato chips which not only are the best potato chips but the best bags for blowin up and bustin real loud so the matron come trottin down the aisle with her chunky self, flashin that flashlight dead in your eye so you can give her some lip, and if she answer back and you already finish seein the show anyway, why then you just turn the place out. Which I love to do, no lie. With Baby Jason kickin at the seat in front, egging me on, and Big Brood mumblin bout what fiercesome things we goin do. Which means me. Like when the big boys come up on us talkin bout Lemme a nickel. It's me that hide the money. Or when the bad boys in the park take Big Brood's Spaudeen way from him. It's me that jump on they back and fight awhile. And it's me that turns out the show if the matron get too salty.

So the movie come on and right away it's this churchy music and clearly not about no gorilla. Bout Jesus. And I am ready to kill, not cause I got anything gainst Jesus. Just that when you fixed to watch a gorilla picture you don't wanna get messed around with Sunday School stuff. So I am mad. Besides, we see this raggedy old brown film *King of Kings* every year and enough's enough. Grownups figure they can treat you just anyhow. Which burns me up. There I am, my feet up and my Havmore potato chips really salty and crispy and two jawbreakers in my lap and the money safe in my shoe from the big boys, and here comes this Jesus stuff. So we all go wild. Yellin, booin, stompin and carryin on. Really to wake the man in the booth up there who musta went to sleep and put on the wrong reels. But no, cause he holler down to shut up and then he turn the sound up so we really gotta holler like crazy to even hear ourselves good. And the matron ropes off the children section and flashes her light all over the place and we yell some more and some kids slip under the rope and run up and down the aisle just to show it take more than some dusty ole velvet rope to tie us down. And I'm flingin the kid in front of me's popcorn. And Baby Jason kickin seats. And it's really somethin. Then here come the big and bad matron, the one they let out in case of emergency. And she totin that flashlight like she gonna use it on somebody. This here the colored matron Brandy and her friends call Thunderbuns. She do not play. She do not smile. So we shut up and watch the simple ass picture.

Which is not so simple as it is stupid. Cause I realize that just about anybody in my family is better than this god they always talkin about. My daddy wouldn't stand for nobody treatin any of us that way. My mama specially. And I can just see it now, Big Brood up there on the cross talkin bout Forgive them Daddy cause they don't know what they doin. And my Mama say Get on down from there you big fool, whatcha think this is, playtime? And my Daddy yellin to Granddaddy to get him a ladder cause Big Brood actin the fool, his mother side of the family showin up. And my mama and her sister Daisy jumpin on them Romans beatin them with they pocketbooks. And Hunca Bubba tellin them folks on they knees they better get out the way and go get some help or they goin to get trampled on. And Granddaddy Vale sayin Leave the boy alone, if that's what he wants to do with his life we ain't got nothin to say about it. Then Aunt Daisy givin him a taste of that pocketbook, fussin bout what a damn fool old man Granddaddy is. Then everybody jumpin in his chest like the time Uncle Clayton went in the army and come back with only one leg and Granddaddy say somethin stupid about that's life. And by this time Big Brood off the cross and in the park playin handball or skully or somethin. And the family in the kitchen throwin dishes at each other, screamin bout if you hadn't done this I wouldn't had to do that. And me in the parlor trying to do my arithmetic yellin Shut it off.

Which is what I was yellin all by myself which make me a sittin target for Thunderbuns. But when I yell We want our money back, that gets everybody in chorus. And the movie windin up with this heavenly cloud music and the smart-ass up there in his hole in the wall turns up the sound again to drown us out. Then there comes Bugs Bunny which we already seen so we know we been had. No gorilla my nuthin. And Big Brood say Awwww sheeet, we goin to see the manager and get our money back. And I know from this we business. So I brush the potato chips out of my hair which is where Baby Jason like to put em, and I march myself up the aisle to deal with the manager who is a crook in the first place for lyin out there sayin *Gorilla, My Love* playin. And I never did like the man cause he oily and pasty at the same time like the bad guy in the serial, the one that got a hideout behind a push-button bookcase and play "Moonlight Sonata" with gloves on. I knock on the door and I am furious. And I am alone, too. Cause Big Brood suddenly got to go so bad even though my mama told us bout goin in them nasty bathrooms. And I hear him sigh like he disgusted when he get to the door and see only a little kid there. And now I'm really furious cause I get so tired grownups messin over kids just cause they little and can't take em to court. What is it, he say to me like I lost my mittens or wet on myself or am somebody's retarded child. When in reality I am the smartest kid P.S. 186 ever had in its whole lifetime and you can ax anybody. Even them teachers that don't like me cause I won't sing them Southern songs or back off when they tell me my questions are out of order. And cause my Mama come up there in a minute when them teachers start playin the dozens behind colored folks. She stalk in with her hat pulled down bad and that Persian lamb coat draped back over one hip on account of she got her fist planted there so she can talk that talk which gets us all hypnotized, and teacher be comin undone cause she know this could be her job and her behind cause Mama got pull with the Board and bad by her own self anyhow.

So I kick the door open wider and just walk right by him and sit down and tell the man about himself and that I want my money back and that goes for Baby Jason and Big Brood too. And he still trying to shuffle me out the door even though I'm sittin which shows him for the fool he is. Just like them teachers do fore they realize Mama like a stone on that spot and ain't backin up. So he ain't gettin up off the money. So I was forced to leave, takin the matches from under his ashtray, and set a fire under the candy stand, which closed the raggedy ole Washington down for a week. My Daddy had the suspect it was me cause Big Brood got a big mouth. But I explained right quick what the whole thing was about and I figured it was even-steven. Cause if you say Gorilla, My Love, you suppose to mean it. Just like when you say you goin to give me a party on my birthday, you gotta mean it. And if you say me and Baby Jason can go South pecan haulin with Granddaddy Vale, you better not be comin up with no stuff about the weather look uncertain or did you mop the bathroom or any other trickified business. I mean even gangsters in the movies say My word is my bond. So don't nobody get away with nothin far as I'm concerned. So Daddy put his belt back on. Cause that's the way I was raised. Like my Mama say in one of them situations when I won't back down, Okay Badbird, you right. Your point is well-taken. Not that Badbird my name, just what she say when she tired arguin and know I'm right. And Aunt Jo, who is the hardest head in the family and worse even than Aunt Daisy, she say, You absolutely right Miss Muffin, which also ain't my real name but the name she gave me one time when I got some medicine shot in my behind and wouldn't get up off her pillows for nothin. And even Grand-daddy Vale—who got no memory to speak of, so sometime you can just plain lie to him, if you want to be like that—he say, Well if that's what I said, then that's it. But this name business was different they said. It wasn't like Hunca Bubba had gone back on his word or anything. Just that he was thinkin bout gettin married and was usin his real name now. Which ain't the way I saw it at all.

So there I am in the navigator seat. And I turn to him and just plain ole ax him. I mean I come right on out with it. No sense goin all around that barn the old folks talk about. And like my mama say, Hazel—which is my real name and what she remembers to call me when she bein serious—when you got somethin on your mind, speak up and let the chips fall where they may. And if anybody don't like it, tell em to come see you mama. And Daddy look up from the paper and say, You hear your mama good, Hazel. And tell em to come see me first. Like that. That's how I was raised.

So I turn clear round in the navigator seat and say, "Look here, Hunca Bubba or Jefferson Windsong Vale or whatever your name is, you gonna marry this girl?"

"Sure am," he say, all grins.

And I say, "Member that time you was baby-sittin me when we lived at four-o-nine and there was this big snow and Mama and Daddy got held up in the country so you had to stay for two days?"

And he say, "Sure do."

"Well. You remember how you told me I was the cutest thing that ever walked the earth?"

"Oh, you were real cute when you were little," he say, which is suppose to be funny. I am not laughin.

"Well. You remember what you said?"

And Grandaddy Vale squintin over the wheel and axin Which way, Scout. But Scout is busy and don't care if we all get lost for days.

"Watcha mean, Peaches?"

"My name is Hazel. And what I mean is you said you were going to marry *me* when I grew up. You were going to wait. That's what I mean, my dear Uncle Jef-ferson," And he don't say nuthin. Just look at me real strange like he never saw me before in life. Like he lost in some weird town in the middle of night and lookin for directions and there's no one to ask. Like it was me that messed up the maps and turned the road posts round. "Well, you said it, didn't you? And Baby Jason lookin back and forth like we playin ping-pong. Only I ain't playin. I'm hurtin and I can hear that I am screamin. And Grandaddy Vale mumblin how we never gonna get to where we goin if I don't turn around and take my navigator job serious.

"Well, for cryin out loud, Hazel, you just a little girl. And I was just teasin."

"'And I was just teasin,'" I say back just how he said it so he can hear what a terrible thing it is. Then I don't say nuthin. And he don't say nuthin. And Baby Jason don't say nuthin nohow. Then Granddaddy Vale speak up. "Look here, Precious, it was Hunca Bubba what told you them things. This here, Jefferson Winston Vale." And Hunca Bubba say, "That's right. That was somebody else. I'm a new somebody."

"You a lyin dawg," I say, when I meant to say treacherous dog, but just couldn't get hold of the word. It slipped away from me. And I'm crying and crumplin down in the seat and just don't care. And Granddaddy say to hush and steps on the gas. And I'm losin my bearins and don't even know where to look on the map cause I can't see for cryin. And Baby Jason cryin too. Cause he is my blood brother and understands that we must stick together or be forever lost, what with grownups playin change-up and turnin you round every which way so bad. And don't even say they sorry.

The Organizer's Wife

The men from the co-op school were squatting in her garden. Jake, who taught the day students and hassled the town school board, was swiping at the bushy greens with his cap, dislodging slugs, raising dust. The tall gent who ran the graphics workshop was pulling a penknife open with his teeth, scraping rust from the rake she hadn't touched in weeks. Old Man Boone was up and down. Couldn't squat too long on account of the ankle broken in last spring's demonstration when the tobacco weights showed funny. Jack-in-the-box up, Boone snatched at a branch or two and stuffed his pipe—crumblings of dry leaf, bits of twig. Down, he eased string from the seams of his overalls, up again, thrumbling up tobacco from the depths of his pockets.

She couldn't hear them. They were silent. The whole morning stock-still, nothing stirring. The baby quiet too, drowsing his head back in the crook of her arm as she stepped out into the sun already up and blistering. The men began to unbend, shifting weight to one leg then the other, watching her move about the jumbled yard. But no one spoke.

She bathed the baby with the little dew that had gathered on what few leaves were left on the branches crackling, shredding into the empty rain barrels. The baby gurgled, pinching her arms. Virginia had no energy for a smile or a wince. All energy summoned up at rising was focused tightly on her two errands of the day. She took her time going back in, seeing the men shift around in the heaps of tomatoes, in the snarl of the strawberry runners. Stamped her shoe against each step, carrying the baby back in. Still no one spoke, though clearly, farmers all their lives, they surely had some one thing to say about the disarray of her garden.

The young one, whose voice she well knew from the sound truck, had his mouth open and his arm outstretched as though to speak on the good sense of turning every inch of ground to food, or maybe to rant against the crime of letting it just go. He bent and fingered the brown of the poke salad that bordered the dry cabbages, his mouth closing again. Jake rose suddenly and cleared his throat, but turned away to light Old Man Boone's pipe, lending a shoulder for the old one to hunch against, cupping the bowl and holding the match, taking a long lingering time, his back to her. She sucked her teeth and went in.

When she came out again, banding the baby's carry straps around her waist, she moved quickly, stepping into the radishes, crushing unidentifiable shoots underfoot. Jake stepped back out of the way and caught his cuffs in the rake. Jake was the first in a long line to lose his land to unpaid taxes. The bogus receipts were pinned prominently as always to his jacket pocket. Signed by someone the county said did not exist, but who'd managed nonetheless to buy up Jake's farm at auction and turn it over swiftly to the granite company. She looked from the huge safety pin to the hot, brown eyes that quickly dropped. The other men rose up around her, none taller than she, though all taller than the corn bent now, grit-laden with neglect. Out of the corner of her eye, she saw a white worm work its way into the once-silky tufts turned straw, then disappear.

"Mornin," she said, stretching out her hand.

The men mumbled quickly, clearing their throats again. Boone offering a hand in greeting, then realizing she was extending not her hand but the small, round tobacco tin in it. Graham's red tobacco tin with the boy in shiny green astride an iron horse. It was Graham's habit, when offering a smoke, to spin some tale or other about the boy on the indestructible horse, a tale the smoker would finish. The point always the same—the courage of the youth, the hope of the future. Boone drew his hand back quickly as though the red tin was aflame. She curled her hand closed and went out the gate, slowly, deliberately, fixing her tall, heavy image indelibly on their eyes.

"Good-for-nuthin."

The thought that's what they heard drift back over her shoulder. Them? The tin? The young one thought he saw her pitch it into the clump of tomatoes hanging on by the gate. But no one posed the question.

"Why didn't you say somethin?" Jake demanded of his star pupil, the orator, whose poems and tales and speeches delivered from the sound truck had done more to pull the districts together, the women all said, than all the leaflets the kids cluttered the fields with, than all the posters from the co-op's graphic workshop masking the road signs, than all the meetings which not all the folk could get to.

"Why didn't you speak?" Jake shoved the young one, and for a minute they were all stumbling, dancing nimbly to avoid destroying food that could still be salvaged.

"Watch it, watch it now," Old Boone saying, checking his foot brace and grabbing the young one up, a fistful of sleeve.

"You shoulda said somethin," the tall gent spat.

"Why me?" The young one whined—not in the voice he'd cultivated for the sound truck. "I don't know her no better than yawl do."

"One of the women shoulda come," said the tall gent.

The men looked at each other, then stared down the road. It was clear that no one knew any more how to talk to the bristling girl-woman, if ever any had.

It wasn't a shift in breeze that made the women look up, faces stuck out as if to catch the rain. 'Cause there was no breeze and there'd been no rain. And look like, one of them said, there'd be no bus either. The strained necks had more to do with sound than weather. Someone coming. A quick check said all who worked in town were already gathered at the bus stop. Someone coming could only mean trouble—fire broke out somewhere, riot in town, one of the children hurt, market closed down, or maybe another farm posted. The women standing over their vegetable baskets huddled together for conference, then broke apart to jut their bodies out over the road for a look-see. The women seated atop the bags of rags or uniforms, clustered to question each other, then scattered, some standing tiptoe, others merely leaning up from the rocks to question the market women. And in that brief second, as bodies pulled upward, the rocks blotted up more sun to sear them, sting them, sicken them with. These stones, stacked generations ago to keep the rain from washing the road away, banked higher and broader by the young folk now to keep the baking earth from breaking apart.

Virginia nodded to the women, her earrings tinkling against her neck. The "Mornins" and "How do's" came scraggly across the distance. The bus-stop plot was like an island separated from the mainland road by shimmering sheets of heat, by arid moats and gullies that had once been the drainage system, dried-out craters now misshapen, as though pitted and gouged by war.

One clear voice rising above the scattered sopranos, calling her by name, slowed Virginia down. Frankie Lee Taylor, the lead alto in the choir, was standing on the rocks waving, out of her choir robes and barely recognizable but for that red-and-yellow jumper, the obligatory ugly dress just right for the kitchens in town. "Everything all right?" the woman asked for everyone there. And not waiting for a word once Virginia's face could be read by all, she continued: "Bus comin at all, ever?"

Virginia shrugged and picked up her pace. If the six-thirty bus was this late coming, she thought, she could make the first call and be back on the road in time for the next bus to town. She wouldn't have to borrow the church station wagon after all. She didn't want to have to ask for nothing. When she saw Graham that afternoon she wanted the thing stitched up, trimmed, neat, finished.

Wanted to be able to say she asked for "nuthin from nobody and didn't nobody offer up nuthin." It'd be over with. They'd set bail and she'd pay it with the money withheld from the seed and the fertilizer, the wages not paid to the two students who used to help in the garden, the money saved 'cause she was too cranky to eat, to care. Pay the bail and unhook them both from this place. Let some other damn fool break his health on this place, the troubles.

She'd been leaving since the first day coming, the day her sister came home to cough herself to death and leave her there with nobody to look out for her 'cept some hinkty cousins in town and Miz Mama Mae, who shook her head sadly whenever the girl spoke of this place and these troubles and these people and one day soon leaving for some other place. She'd be going now for sure. Virginia was smiling now and covering a whole lotta ground.

Someone was coming up behind her, churning up the loose layers of clay, the red-and-yellow jumper a mere blur in the haze of red dust. Everyone these dry, hot days looked like they'd been bashed with a giant powder puff of henna. Virginia examined her own hands, pottery-red like the hands of her cousins seen through the beauty-parlor windows in town, hands sunk deep in the pots, working up the mud packs for the white women lounging in the chairs. She looked at her arms, her clothes, and slowed down. Not even well into the morning and already her skimpy bath ruined. The lime-boiled blouse no longer white but pink.

"Here, Gin," the woman was saying. "He a good man, your man. He share our hardships, we bear his troubles, our troubles." She was stuffing money in between the carry straps, patting the chubby legs as the baby lolled in his cloth carriage. "You tell Graham we don't forget that he came back. Lots of the others didn't, forgot. You know, Gin, that you and me and the rest of the women . . ." She was going to say more but didn't. Was turning with her mouth still open, already trotting up the road, puffs of red swirling about her feet and legs, dusting a line in that red-and-yellow jumper the way Miz Mama Mae might do making hems in the shop.

Virginia hoisted the baby higher on her back and rewound the straps, clutching the money tight, flat in her fist. She thought about Miz Mama Mae, pins in her mouth, fussing at her. "What's them hanky-type hems you doin, Gin?" she'd say, leaning over her apprentice. "When ya sew for the white folks you roll them kinda stingy hems. And you use this here oldish thread to insure a quick inheritance. But when you sew for us folks, them things got to last season in and season out and many a go-round exchange. Make some hefty hems, girl, hefty."

And Virginia had come to measure her imprisonment by how many times that same red-and-yellow jumper met her on the road, faded and fading some more, but the fairly bright hem getting wider and wider, the telltale rim recording the seasons past, the owners grown. While she herself kept busting out of her clothes, straining against the good thread, outdistancing the hefty hems. Growing so fast from babe to child to girl to someone, folks were always introducing and reintroducing themselves to her. It seemed at times that the walls wouldn't contain her, the roof wouldn't stop her. Busting out of childhood, busting out her clothes, but never busting out the place.

And now the choir woman had given her the money like that and spoken, trying to attach her all over again, root her, ground her in the place. Just when there was a chance to get free. Virginia clamped her jaws tight and tried to go blank. Tried to blot out all feelings and things—the farms, the co-op sheds, the lone gas pump, a shoe left in the road, the posters promising victory over the troubles. She never wanted these pictures called up on some future hot, dry day in some other place. She squinted, closed her eyes even, 'less the pictures cling to her eyes, store in the brain, to roll out later and crush her future with the weight of this place and its troubles.

Years before when there'd been rain and ways to hold it, she'd trotted along this road not seeing too much, trotting and daydreaming, delivering parcels to and from Miz Mama Mae's shop. She could remember that one time, ducking and dodging the clods of earth chucked up by the horse's hooves. Clods spinning wet and heavy against her skirts, her legs, as she followed behind, seeing nothing outside her own pictures but that horse and rider. Trying to keep up, keep hold of the parcel slipping all out of shape in the drizzle, trying to piece together the things she would say to him when he finally turned round and saw her. She had lived the scene often enough in bed to know she'd have to speak, say something to make him hoist her up behind him in the saddle, to make him gallop her off to the new place. She so busy dreaming, she let the curve of the road swerve her off toward the edge. Mouthing the things to say and even talking out loud with her hands and almost losing the slippery bundle, not paying good enough attention. And a ball of earth shot up and hit her square in the chest and sent her stumbling over the edge into the gully. The choir organist's robe asprawl in the current that flushed the garbage down from the hill where the townies lived, to the bottom where the folks lived, to the pit where the co-op brigade made compost heaps for independence, laughing.

Graham had pulled her up and out by the wrist, pulled her against him and looked right at her. Not at the cabbage leaves or chicory on her arms, a mango sucked hairy to its pit clinging to her clothes. But looked at her. And no screen door between them now. No glass or curtain, or shrub peeked through.

"You followin me." He grinned. And she felt herself swimming through the gap in his teeth.

And now she would have to tell him. 'Cause she had lost three times to the coin flipped on yesterday morning. Had lost to the icepick pitched in the afternoon in the dare-I-don't-I boxes her toe had sketched in the yard. Had lost at supper to the shadow slanting across the tablecloth that reached her wrist before Miz Mama Mae finished off the corn relish. Had lost that dawn to the lazy lizard, suddenly quickened in his journey on the ceiling when the sun came up. Lost against doing what she'd struggled against doing in order to win one more day of girlhood before she jumped into her womanstride and stalked out on the world. I want to come to you. I want to come to you and be with you. I want to be your woman, she did not say after all.

"I want to come to the co-op school," she said. "I want to learn to read better and type and figure and keep accounts so I can get out of . . ."—this place, she didn't say—"my situation."

He kept holding her and she kept wanting and not wanting to ease out of his grip and rescue the choir robe before it washed away.

"I had five years schooling 'fore I came here," she said, talking way too loud. "Been two years off and on at the church school . . . before you came."

"You do most of Miz Mama Mae's cipherin I hear? Heard you reading the newspapers to folks in the tobacco shed. You read well."

She tried to pull away then, thinking he was calling her a liar or poking fun some way. "Cipherin" wasn't how he talked. But he didn't let go. She expected to see her skin twisted and puckered when she looked at where he was holding her. But his grip was soft. Still she could not step back.

"You been watchin me," he said with the grin again. And looking into his face, she realized he wasn't at all like she'd thought. Was older, heavier, taller, smoother somehow. But then looking close up was not like sneaking a look from the toolshed as he'd come loping across the fields with his pigeon-toed self and in them soft leather boots she kept waiting to see fall apart from rough wear till she finally decided he must own pairs and pairs of all the same kind. Yes, she'd watched him on his rounds, in and out of the houses, the drying sheds, down at the docks, after fellowship in the square. Talking, laughing, teaching, always moving. Had watched him from the trees, through windows as he banged tables, arguing about deeds, urging, coaxing, pleading, hollering, apologizing, laughing again. In the early mornings, before Miz Mama Mae called the girls to sew, she had watched him chinning on the bar he'd slammed between the portals of the co-op school door. Huffing, puffing, cheeks like chipmunks. The dark circle of his gut sucking in purple, panting out blue. Yes, she watched him. But she said none of this or of the other either. Not then.

"I want to come to night school" was how she put it. "I don't know yet what kinda work I can do for the co-op. But I can learn."

"That's the most I ever heard you talk," he was saying, laughing so hard, he loosened his grip. "In the whole three years I've been back, that's the most—" He was laughing again. And he was talking way too loud himself.

She hadn't felt the least bit foolish standing there in the drizzle, in the garbage, tall up and full out of her clothes nearly, and Graham laughing at her. Not the least bit foolish 'cause he was talking too loud and laughing too hard. And she was going to go to his school. And whether he knew it or not, he was going to take her away from this place.

Wasn't but a piece of room the school, with a shed tacked on in back for storage and sudden meetings. The furniture was bandaged but brightly painted. The chemistry equipment was old but worked well enough. The best thing was the posters. About the co-op, about Malcolm and Harriet and Fannie Lou, about

Guinea-Bissau and Vietnam. And the posters done by the children, the pictures cut from magazines, the maps—all slapped up as though to hold the place together, to give an identity to the building so squat upon the land. The identity of the place for her was smells. The smell of mortar vibrating from the walls that were only wood. The smell of loam that curled up from the sink, mostly rusted metal. The green-and-brown smell rising up over heads sunk deep into palms as folks leaned over their papers, bearing down on stumps of pencil or hunks of charcoal, determined to get now and to be what they'd been taught was privilege impossible, what they now knew was their right, their destiny.

"Season after season," Graham was dictating that first night, leaning up against the maps with the ruler, "we have pulled gardens out of stones, creating something from nothing—creators."

Swear beading on a nose to her left, a temple to her right. Now and then a face she knew from fellowship looking up as Graham intoned the statements, tapping the ruler against the table to signal punctuation traps. And she working hard, harder than some, though she never ever did learn to speak her speak as most folks finally did. But grateful just to be there, and up in front, unlike the past when, condemned by her size, she'd been always exiled in the rear with the goldfish tanks or the rabbits that always died, giving her a suspect reputation.

"The first step toward getting the irrigation plant," he continued, crashing the ruler down, "is to organize."

"Amen," said one lady by the window, never looking up from her paper, certain she would finally train herself and be selected secretary of the church board. "That way us folks can keep track of them folks" was how she'd said it when she rose to speak her speak one summer night.

"What can defeat greed, technological superiority, and legal lawlessness," Graham had finished up, "is discipline, consciousness, and unity."

Always three sentences that folks would take home for discussion, for transformation into well-ordered paragraphs that wound up, some of them, in the co-op newsletter of on the posters or in the church's bulletin. Many became primers for the children.

Graham had been wearing the denim suit with the leather buckles the first night in class. Same fancy suit she'd caught sight of through the screen door when he'd come calling on Miz Mama Mae to buy the horse. A denim suit not country-cut at all—in fact, so *not* she was sure he would be leaving. Dudes in well-cut denim'd been coming and leaving since the days she wore but one yard of cloth. It was his would-be-moving-on clothes that had pulled her to him. But then the pull had become too strong to push against once his staying-on became clear.

She often fixed him supper in a metal cake tin once used for buttons. And Miz Mama Mae joked with the pin cushion, saying the girl weren't fooling nobody but herself sneaking around silly out there in the pantry with the button box. Telling the bobbins it was time certain folk grew up to match they size. And into the night, treadling away on the machine, the woman addressed the dress form, saying a strong, serious-type schoolteacher man had strong, serious work to do. Cutting out the paper patterns, the woman told the scissors that visiting a man in his rooms at night could mean disaster or jubilee one. And Virginia understood she would not be stopped by the woman. But some felt she was taking up too much of his time, their time. He was no longer where they could find him for homework checks or questions about the law. And Jake and Old Man Boone sullen, nervous that the midnight strategy meetings were too few now and far between. The women of the nearby district would knock and enter with trapped firefly lanterns, would shove these on the table between the couple, and make their point as Graham nodded and Virginia giggled or was silent, one.

His quilt, Graham explained, leaving the earrings on the table for her to find, was made from patches from his daddy's overalls, and scraps from Boone's wedding cutaway, white remnants from his mother's shroud, some blue from a sister's graduation, and khaki, too, snatched from the uniform he'd been proud of killing in in Korea a hundred lives ago. The day students had stitched a liberation flag in one corner. The night students had restuffed it and made a new border. She and Miz Mama Mae had stitched it and aired it. And Virginia had brought it back to him, wrapped in it. She had rolled herself all in it, to hide from him in her new earrings, childish. But he never teased that she was too big for games, and she liked that. He found her in it, his tongue finding the earrings first. Careful, girl, she'd warned herself. This could be a trap, she murmured under him.

"Be my woman," he whispered into her throat.

You don't have time for me, she didn't say, lifting his tikis and medallions up over his head. And there'd never be enough time here with so many people, so much land to work, so much to do, and the wells not even dug, she thought, draping the chains around his bedpost.

"Be my woman, Gin," he said again. And she buried her fingers in his hair and he buried his hair inside her clothes and she pulled the quilt close and closed him in, crying.

She was leaking. The earrings tinkling against her neck. The medallions clinking against the bedpost in her mind. Gray splotches stiffened in her new pink blouse, rubbing her nipples raw. But other than a dribble that oozed momentarily down her back, there was no sign of the baby aroused and hungry. If the baby slept on, she'd keep on. She wanted to reach Revun Michaels before the white men came. Came this time brazenly with the surveyors and the diggers, greedy for the granite under the earth. Wanted to catch Revun Michaels before he showed them his teeth and wouldn't hear her, couldn't, too much smiling. Wanted to hear him say it—the land's been sold. The largest passel of land in the district, the church holdings where the co-op school stood, where two storage sheds of the co-op stood, where the graphics workshop stood, where four families had lived for generations working the land. The church had sold the land. He'd say it, she'd hear it, and it'd be over with. She and Graham could go.

She was turning the bend now, forgetting to not look, and the mural the co-op had painted in eye-stinging colors stopped her. FACE UP TO WHAT'S KILLING YOU, it demanded. Below the statement a huge triangle that from a distance was just a triangle, but on approaching, as one muttered 'how deadly can a triangle be?' turned into bodies on bodies. At the top, fat, fanged beasts in smart clothes, like the ones beneath it laughing, drinking, eating, bombing, raping, shooting, lounging on the backs of, feeding off the backs of, the folks at the base, crushed almost flat but struggling to get up and getting up, topple the structure. She passed it quickly. All she wanted to think about was getting to Revun Michaels quick to hear it. Sold the land. Then she'd be free to string together the bits and scraps of things for so long bobbing about in her head. Things that had to be pieced together well, with strong thread so she'd have a whole thing to shove through the mesh at Graham that afternoon.

And would have to shove hard or he'd want to stay, convinced that folks would battle for his release, would battle for themselves, the children, the future, would keep on no matter how powerful the thief, no matter how little the rain, how exhausted the soil, 'cause this was home. Not a plot of earth for digging in or weeping over or crawling into, but home. Near the Ethiopic where the ancestral bones spoke their speak on certain nights if folks stamped hard enough, sang long enough, shouted. Home. Where "America" was sung but meant something altogether else than it had at the old school. Home in the future. The future here now developing. Home liberated soon. And the earth would recover. The rain would come. The ancient wisdoms would be revived. The energy released. Home a human place once more. The bones spoke it. The spirit spoke, too, through flesh when the women gathered at the altar, the ancient orishas still vibrant beneath the ghostly patinas some thought right to pray to, but connected in spite of themselves to the spirits under the plaster.

WE CANNOT LOSE, the wall outside the church said. She paused at the bulletin board, the call-for-meeting flyers limp in the heat. She bent to spit but couldn't raise it. She saw Revun Michaels in the schoolhouse window watching her. He'd say it. Sold the land.

Virginia wondered what the men in her ruined garden were telling themselves now about land as power and land and man tied to the future, not the past. And what would they tell the women when the bulldozers came to claim the earth, to maim it, rape it, plunder it all with that bone-deep hatred for all things natural? And what would the women tell the children dangling in the tires waiting for Jake to ring the bell? Shouting from the clubhouses built in the trees? The slashed trees oozing out money into the white man's pails, squeezing hard to prolong a tree life, forestalling the brutal cut down to stump. Then stump wasting, no more money to give, blown up out of the earth, the iron claw digging deep and merciless to rip out the taproots, leaving for the children their legacy, an open grave, gouged out by a gene-deep hatred for all things natural, for all things natural that couldn't turn a quick penny quick enough to dollar. She spit.

Revun Michaels, small and balding, was visible in the schoolhouse window. His expression carried clear out the window to her, watching her coming fast, kicking himself for getting caught in there and only one door, now that the shed was nailed on fast in back.

"Did you sell the land as well?" she heard herself saying, rushing in the doorway much too fast. "You might have waited like folks asked you. You didn't have to. Enough granite under this schoolhouse alone"—she stamped, frightening him—"to carry both the districts for years and years, if we developed it ourselves." She heard the "we ourselves" explode against her teeth and she fell back.

"Wasn't me," he stammered. "The church board saw fit to—"

"Fit!" She was advancing now, propelled by something she had no time to understand. "Wasn't nuthin fitten about it." She had snatched the ruler from its hook. The first slam hard against the chair he swerved around, fleeing. The next cracked hard against his teeth. His legs buckled under and he slid down, his face frozen in disbelief. But nothing like the disbelief that swept through her the moment "we ourselves" pushed past clenched teeth and nailed her to the place, a woman unknown. She saw the scene detached, poster figures animated: a hefty woman pursuing a scrambling man in and out among the tables and chairs in frantic games before Jake rang the bell for lessons to commence.

"And what did the white folks pay you to turn Graham in and clear the way? Disturber of the peace. What peace? Racist trying to incite a riot. Ain't that how they said it? Outside agitator, as you said. And his roots put down here long before you ever came. When you were just a twinkle in Darwin's eye." Virginia heard herself laughing. It was a good, throaty laugh and big. The man was turning round now on the floor, staring at her in amazement.

"Thirty pieces of silver, maybe? That's what you preach, tradition. Thirty pieces 'bout as traditional as—"

"Just hold on. It wasn't me that—The board of trustees advised me that this property could not be used for—"

The ruler came down on the stiff of his arm and broke. Michaels dropped between two rickety chairs that came apart on top of him. The baby cried, the woman shushed, as much to quiet the woman that was her. Calm now, she watched the man try to get up, groping the chairs the folks had put together from cast-offs for the school. Her shoe caught him at the side of his head and he went under.

The station wagon was pulling up as she was coming out, flinging the piece of ruler into the bushes. She realized then that the men had come in it, that the station wagon had been sitting all morning in her garden. That they had come to take her to see Graham. She bit her lip. She never gave folk a chance, just like Miz Mama Mae always fussed. Never gave them or herself a chance to speak the speak.

"We'll take you to him," Jake was saying, holding the door open and easing the baby off her back.

The young one shoved over. "Mother Lee who's secretarying for the board has held up the papers for the sale. We came to tell you that." He waited till she smiled to laugh. "We're the delegation that's going to confront the board this evening. Us and Frankie Lee Taylor and—"

"Don't talk the woman to death," said Boone, turning in his seat and noting her daze. He was going to say more, but the motor drowned him out. Virginia hugged the baby close and unbuttoned her blouse.

"That's one sorry piece of man," drawled Boone as they pulled out. All heads swung to the right to see the short, fat, balding preacher darting in and out among the gravestones for the sanctuary of the church. To the phone, Virginia figured. And would they jail her too, she and the baby?

Then everyone was silent before the naked breast and the sucking. Silence was what she needed. And time, to draw together tight what she'd say to Graham. How blood had spurted from Revun Michaels's ear, for one thing. Graham might not want to hear it, but there was no one else to tell it to, to explain how it was when all she thought she wanted was to hear it said flat out—land's been sold, school's no more. Not that a school's a building, she argued with herself, watching the baby, playing with the image of herself speaking her speak finally in the classroom, then realizing that she already had. By tomorrow the women would have burrowed beneath the tale of some swinging door or however Revun Michaels would choose to tell it. But would the women be able to probe and sift and explain it to her? Who could explain her to her?

And how to explain to Graham so many things. About this new growth she was experiencing, was thinking on at night wrapped in his quilt. Not like the dread growing up out of her clothes as though she'd never stop 'fore she be freak, 'cause she had stopped. And not like the new growth that was the baby, for she'd expected that, had been prepared. More like the toenail smashed the day the work brigade had stacked the stones to keep the road from splitting apart. The way the new nail pushed up against the old turning blue, against the gauze and the tape, stubborn to establish itself. A chick pecking through the shell, hard-headed and hasty and wobbly. She might talk of it this time. She was convinced she could get hold of it this time.

She recalled that last visiting time trying to speak on what was happening to her coming through the shell. But had trouble stringing her feelings about so many things together, words to drape around him, to smother all those other things, things she had said, hurled unstrung, flung out with tantrum heat at a time when she thought there would always be time enough to coolly take them back, be woman warm in some elsewhere place and make those hurtful words forgettable. But then they had come for him in the afternoon, came and got him, took him from the schoolhouse in handcuffs. And when she had visited him in the jail, leaning into the mesh, trying to push past the barrier, she could tell the way the guards hovered around her and baby that clearly they thought she could do, would do, what they had obviously tried over and over to do, till Graham was ashy and slow, his grin lax. That she could break him open so they could break him down. She almost had, not knowing it, leaking from the breast as she always did not keeping track of the time. Stuttering, whining, babbling, hanging on to the mesh with one hand, the other stuffed in her mouth, her fingers ensnarled in the skein of words coming out all tangled, knotted.

"I don't mind this so much," he'd cut in. "Time to think."

And when she pulled her fingers from her mouth, the thread broke and all her words came bouncing out in a hopeless scatter of tears and wails until something—her impatience with her own childishness, or maybe it was the obvious pleasure of the guards—made her grab herself up. She grabbed herself up abrupt, feeling in that moment what it was she wanted to say about her nights wrapped up in the quilt smelling him in it, hugging herself, grabbing herself up and trying to get to that place that was beginning to seem more of a when than a where. And the when seemed to be inside her if she could only connect.

"I kinda like the quiet," he had said. "Been a while since I've had so much time to think." And then he grinned and was ugly. Was that supposed to make her hate him? To hate and let go? That had occurred to her on the bus home. But roaming around the house, tripping on the edges of the quilt, she had rejected it. That was not the meaning of his words or that smile that had torn his face. She'd slumped in the rocking chair feeding the baby, examining her toenail for such a time.

"They never intended to dig the wells, that's clear," Old Man Boone was saying. "That was just to get into the district, get into our business, check out our strength. I was a fool," he muttered, banging his pipe against his leg remembering his hopefulness, his hospitality even. "A fool."

"Well, gaddamn, Boone," the tall gent sputtered. "Can't you read? That's what our flyers been saying all along. Don't you read the stuff we put out? Gaddamnit, Boone."

"If you don't read the flyers, you leastways knows history," the young one was saying. "When we ever invited the beast to dinner he didn't come in and swipe the napkins and start taking notes on the tablecloth 'bout how to take over the whole house?"

"Now that's the truth," Jake said, laughing. His laughter pulled Virginia forward, and she touched his arm, moved. That he could laugh. His farm stolen and he could laugh. But that was one the three most moving things about Jake, she was thinking. The way he laughed. The way he sweated. The way he made his body comfy for the children to lean against.

"Yeh, they sat right down to table and stole the chicken," said Jake.

"And took the table. And the deed." The tall gent smacked Jake on his cap.

"Yeh," Old Man Boone muttered, thinking of Graham.

"We ain't nowhere's licked yet though, huhn?"

The men looked quickly at Virginia, Jake turning clear around, so that Boone leaned over to catch the steering wheel.

"Watch it, watch it now, young feller."

"There's still Mama Mae's farm," Virginia continued, patting the baby. "Enough granite under there even if the church do—"

"But they ain't," said the young one. "Listen, we got it all figured out. We're going to bypass the robbers and deal directly with the tenant councils in the cities, and we're—"

"Don't talk the woman to death," soothed Boone. "You just tell Graham his landlady up there in the North won't have to eat dog food no more. No more in life. New day coming."

"And you tell him . . ."—Jake was turning around again—"just tell him to take his care."

By the time the bolt had lifted and she was standing by the chair, the baby fed and alert now in her arms, she had done with all the threads and bits and shards of the morning. She knew exactly what to tell him, coming through the steel door now, reaching for the baby he had not held yet, could not hold now, screened off from his father. All she wished to tell him was the bail'd been paid, her strength was back, and she sure as hell was going to keep up the garden. How else to feed the people?

Joseph Beam (1954-1988)

Joseph Fairchild Beam was central to the rise of publications by gay Black men in the 1980s. He edited one of the most important collections of writings by gay Black men, In the Life in 1986, giving space to many writers who before had either been unpublished or locally known. Beam also worked with Essex Hemphill in various east coast writing communities, and the two were collaborating on a follow-up collection, Brother to Brother when Beam died in 1988 from AIDS-related complications. In his honor, Hemphill completed the anthology.

A board member of the National Coalition of Black Lesbians and Gays, Beam was first and foremost an activist. His life as an essayist and poet reflected his commitment to activism, his unrelenting desire to make space for Black lesbians and gays to live freer of oppression and domination. In his writing, especially the essay excerpted here, Beam draws on common notions of Black community to contest the invisibility of lesbians and gays, but also to reveal how present they are in those communities. He uses anecdotes that paint scenes of communal and urban life, scenes that are familiar and recognizable (for example, the coffee shop, the outside apartment steps, the ride on the bus) and uncover the gay character in the scene. These anecdotes are sometimes filled with tension and unease, and sometimes even the threat of violence, but Beam (nor his characters) does not back down, for he is again challenging the reader to acknowledge the gay presence that for so long has been forced to be silent and invisible, even to her/his own detriment.

This use of anecdote is a version of the Black memoir, the telling of a narrative of one's life, to express commentary about social and political conditions. Beam engages this style especially in his use of "I," but is also careful to supplement his experience of the world with references to other well-known Black artists. Another rhetorical strategy that he uses here is repetition for emphasis—for example, "I remember," which as a phrase serves to tell the memory as well as also inspire and trigger it. Although Beam does not directly speak to the audience in this piece, his essay takes on a direct tone because of its use of repetition, but also because of its anecdotes; both add to the sense of intimacy of his piece.

"Brother to Brother" is an essay modeled after a style of cultural criticism that writers like Audre Lorde, Alice Walker, bell hooks, and Cornel West have made popular: the merging of popular references—so-called pop culture—with academic and scholarly examples; but also the use of a hybrid text, one that is not entirely any one form, or about one particular subject, but which moves through a variety of examples, some of them varying and disparate, toward the achievement of a single point and commentary. And in the tradition of this kind of nonfiction prose, Beam, like the Black women's traditions that he celebrates in this essay, explores the spiritual and the psychic. That is, his writing is almost like a meditation or a prayer, as much as it is also a political tract.

Beam's central point here, but also in his other work (and in the work that he helped to bring to publication) is that Black men must work to love each other—to develop those

61

ties of kinship and affinity that systems of race and gender oppression have thwarted and to become, in the truest sense, brothers to each other. The idea of brotherhood is one that Beam refigures in this essay to include his own growing relationship with his father and his sexual and nonsexual relationships with other Black men. Beam's work is an excellent example of the intentional mixing of genres of writing, as well as rhetorical strategies, which has become a contemporary revision of the Black prose essay. "Brother to Brother" is a political prayer, a statement that is at once meditation and activism.

Kevin Everod Quashie

Brother to Brother: Words from the Heart

. . . what is most important to me must be spoken, made verbal and shared, even at the risk of having it bruised or misunderstood.[1]

> I know the anger that lies inside me like I know the beat of my heart and the taste of my spit. It is easier to be angry than to hurt. Anger is what I do best. It is easier to be furious than to be yearning. Easier to crucify myself in you than to take on the threatening universe of whiteness by admitting that we are worth wanting each other.[2]

I, too, know anger. My body contains as much anger as water. It is the material from which I have built my house; blood red bricks that cry in the rain. It is what pulls my tie and gold chains taut around my neck; fills my penny loafers and my Nikes; molds my Calvins and gray flannels to my torso. It is the face and posture I show the world. It is the way, sometimes the only way, I am granted an audience. It is sometimes the way I show affection. I am angry because of the treatment I am afforded as a Black man. That fiery anger is stoked additionally with the fuels of contempt and despisal shown me be my community because I am gay. *I cannot go home as who I am.*

When I speak of home, I mean not only the familial constellation from which I grew, but the entire Black community: the Black press, the Black church, Black academicians, the Black literati, and the Black left. Where is my reflection? I am most often rendered invisible, perceived as a threat to the family, or am tolerated if I am silent and inconspicuous. I cannot go home as who I am and that hurts me deeply.

Almost every morning I have coffee at the same donut shop. Almost every morning I encounter the same Black man who used to acknowledge me from across the counter. I can only surmise that it is my earrings and earcuffs that have tipped him off that I am gay. He no longer speaks, instead looks disdainfully through me as if I were glass. But glass reflects, so I am not even that. He sees no part of himself in me—not my Blackness nor my maleness. "There's nothing in me that is not in everyone else, and nothing in everyone else that is not in me."[3]

Should our glances meet, he is quick to use his *Wall Street Journal* as a shield while I wince and admire the brown of my coffee in my cup.

I do not expect his approval—only his acknowledgment. The struggles of Black people are too perilous and too pervasive for us to dismiss one another, in such cursory fashion, because of perceived differences. Gil Scott-Heron called it "dealing in externals," that is, giving great importance to visual information and ignoring real aspects of commonality. Aren't all hearts and fists and minds needed in this struggle or will this faggot be tossed into the fire? In this very critical time everyone from the corner to the corporation is desperately needed.

> . . . [Brother] the war goes on
> respecting no white flags
> taking no prisoners
> giving no time out for women and children
> to leave the area
> whether we return their fire
> or not
> whether we're busy attaching each other
> or not.

If you could put your newspaper aside for a moment, I think you, too, would re- member that it has not always been this way between us. I remember. I remem- ber the times before different meant separate, before different meant outsider. I remember Sunday school and backyard barbeques and picnics in the Park and the Avenue and parties in dimly lit basements and skateboards fashioned from two-by-fours and b-ball and . . . I remember. I also recall secretly playing jacks and jumping rope on the back porch, and the dreams I had when I spent the night at your house.

But that was before different meant anything at all, certainly anything sub- stantial. That was prior to considerations such as too light/too dark; or good/bad hair; before college/army/jail; before working/middle class; before gay/straight. But I am no longer content on the back porch; I want to play with my jacks on the front porch. There is no reason for me to hide. Our differences should pro- mote dialogue rather than erect new obstacles in our paths.

On another day: I am walking down Spruce/Castro/Christopher Street on my way to work. A half block away, walking towards me, is another Black gay man. We have seen each other in clubs. Side by side, and at the precise moment that our eyes should meet, he studies the intricate detail of a building. I check my white sneakers for scuff marks. What is it that we see in each other that makes us avert our eyes so quickly? Does he see the same thing in me that the brother in the donut shop sees? Do we turn away from each other in order not to see our collective anger and sadness?

It is my pain I see reflected in your eyes. Our angers ricochet between us like the bullets we fire in battles which are not our own nor with each other.

The same angry face, donned for safety in the white world, is the same expression I bring to you. I am cool and unemotive, distant from what I need most. "It is easier to be furious than to be yearning. Easier to crucify myself in you . . ." And perhaps easiest to ingest that anger until it threatens to consume me, or apply a salve of substitutes to the wound.

But real anger accepts few substitutes and sneers at sublimation. The anger-hurt I feel cannot be washed down with a Coke (old or new) or a Colt 45; cannot be danced away; cannot be mollified by a white lover, nor lost in the mirror reflections of a Black lover; cannot evaporate like sweat after a Nautilus workout; nor drift away in a cloud of reefer smoke. I cannot leave it in Atlantic City, or Rio, or even Berlin when I vacation. I cannot hope it will be gobbled up by the alligators on my clothing; nor can I lose it in therapeutic catharsis. I cannot offer it to Jesus/Allah/Jah. So, I must mold and direct that fiery cool mass of angry energy—use it before it uses me! *Anger unvented becomes pain, pain unspoken becomes rage, rage released becomes violence.*

Use it to create a Black gay community in which I can build my home surrounded by institutions that reflect and sustain me. Concurrent with that vision is the necessity to repave the road home, widening it, so I can return with all I have created to the home which is my birthright.

Silence is what I hear after the handshake and the slap of five; after the salutations: what's happenin'/what's up/how you feel; after our terms of endearment: homeboy, cuzz, "girlfriend," blood, running buddy, and Miss Thing. I can hear the silence. When talking with a "girlfriend," I am more likely to muse about my latest piece or so-and-so's party at Club She-She than about the anger and hurt I felt that morning when a jeweler refused me entrance to his store because I am Black and male, and we are all perceived as thieves. I will swallow that hurt and should I speak of it, will vocalize only the anger, saying: I have bust out his fuckin' windows! Some of the anger will be exorcised, but the hurt, which has not been given voice, prevails and accumulates.

Silence is a way to grin and bear it. A way not to acknowledge how much my life is discounted each day—100% OFF ALL BLACK MEN TODAY—EVERY DAY! I strive to appear strong and silent. I learn to ingest hatred at a geometric rate and to count (silently) to 10 . . . 10 thousand . . . 10 million. But as I have learned to mute my cries of anguish, so have I learned to squelch my exclamations of joy. What remains is the rap.

My father is a warm brown man of seventy, who was born in Barbados. He is kind and gentle, and has worked hard for me so that I am able to write these words. We are not friends: he is my father, I am his son. We are silent when alone together. I do not ask him about his island childhood or his twelve years as a janitor or about the restaurant he once owned where he met my mother. He does not ask me about being gay or why I wish to write about it. Yet we are connected: his past is my present, our present a foundation for the future. I have never said to him that his thick calloused hands have led me this far and given me options he never dreamed of.

How difficult it is to speak of my appreciation, saying: Dad, I love you. *I am here because of you, much deeper than sperm meeting egg, much deeper than sighs in the night, I am here because of you.* Our love for each other, though great, may never be spoken. It is the often unspoken love that Black men give to other Black men in a world where we are forced to cup our hands over our mouths or suffer under the lash of imprisonment, unemployment, or even death. But these words, which fail, are precisely the words that are life-giving and continuing. They must be given voice. What legacy is to be found in our silence?

Because of the silence among us, each one of us, as Black boys and men maturing, must all begin the struggle to survive anew. With the incomplete knowledge of what had gone before, our struggles to endure and maintain, at best, save us only as individuals. Collectively we falter and stumble, covering up our experiences in limp aphorisms: Times are hard! Watch out for the Man! This is the depth of the sage advice we offer each other—at arm's length. We must begin to speak of our love and concern for each other as vigorously as we argue party politics or the particular merits of an athletic team. . . .

We have few traditions like those of Black women. No kitchen tables around which to assemble. No intimate spaces in which to explore our feelings of love and friendship. No books like *The Color Purple*. We gather in public places: barber shops, bars, lodges, fraternities, and street corners, places where bravado rather than intimacy are the rule. We assemble to *do* something rather than *be* with each other. We can talk about the Man, but not about how we must constantly vie with one another for the scant crumbs thrown our way. We can talk about dick and ass and pussy, but not of the fierce competition for too few jobs and scholarships. We can talk about sporting events in amazing detail, but not about how we are pitted, one against the other, as permanent adversaries. . . .

Black men loving Black men is the revolutionary act of the eighties, not only because sixties' revolutionaries like Bobby Seale, Huey Newton, and Eldridge Cleaver dare speak our name; but because as Black men we were never meant to be together—not as father and son, brother and brother—and certainly not as lovers.

Black men loving Black men is an autonomous agenda for the eighties, which is not rooted in any particular sexual, political, or class affiliation, but in our mutual survival. The ways in which we manifest that love are as myriad as the issues we must address. Unemployment, substance abuse, self-hatred, and the lack of positive images are but some of the barriers of our loving.

Black men loving Black men is a call to action, an acknowledgment of responsibility. We take care of our own kind when the night grows cold and silent. These days the nights are cold-blooded and the silence echoes with complicity.

NOTES

1. Lorde, Audre. *The Cancer Journals.* Argyle, NY: Spinster's Ink, 1980.
2. Lorde, Audre. *Sister Outsider.* Ithaca, NY: Crossing Press, 1984.
3. Baldwin, James. *Village Voice*, Vol. 29, No. 26, p. 14.

Becky Birtha (1948–)

Becky Birtha was born October 11, 1948, in Hampton, Virginia. Her great-grandmother and namesake, Rebecca Birtha, was a slave. Yet, Birtha also claims the heritage of Irish, Cherokee, and Catawba roots, a heritage that manifests itself in the multicultural slant of her fiction and poetry. Birtha's mother, Jessie Moore Birtha, was a child librarian in Hampton and introduced Birtha early to African American literature.

Birtha spent most of her childhood and youth in Philadelphia. Attending the public Philadelphia School for Girls, she took her first creative writing class before starting college at Case Western Reserve. Dropping out of school, Birtha moved to Berkeley, California, for a year, experiencing the most intense times of the Berkeley protests and People's Park. She stayed only a year before moving to Buffalo where she re-enrolled in school at the State University of New York and lived for five years. Attending both Buffalo State and SUNY Buffalo, Birtha graduated from SUNY Buffalo with a self-designed major in children's studies.

Becky Birtha is both a writer of short fiction and a poet. Her first short fiction collection, For Nights Like This One *(1983), is an insightful look at the politics of lesbian and interracial relationships. The women in the stories are both vulnerable and strong as they face their circumstances and make difficult choices about survival in a heterosexist and racist world. In her second collection of short fiction,* Lover's Choice *(1987), Birtha creates complex characters, individuals who arrive at crossroad moments that require them to make critical life-changing decisions. Again, many of the characters are involved in interracial relationships, and Birtha courageously depicts White women through Black women's eyes, writing freely from a Black lesbian perspective. In "Ice Castle" and "Her Ex-Lover," the stories that focus most directly on interracial lesbian relationships, the Black woman characters gain deeper perspective and greater psychological health in recognizing and understanding the quandaries of being involved with White women. While lesbian relationships are Birtha's primary focus, she also writes of other strong women like Leona May Moses of "Route 23; 10th and Bigler to Bethlehem Pike" who takes her children in blankets for a ride on an all-night city bus to avoid their ice-cold apartment.*

The first story of Lover's Choice, *"Johnnieruth," features a young Black woman struggling to understand herself. On one of many bike rides away from the expectations of family and community, Johnnieruth encounters a lesbian couple in a park. Seeing them embrace, she recognizes that the affection they share is inviting and familiar, that the sense of isolation she feels may indicate an aspect of herself that does not need to be negative. As Johnnieruth rides her bicycle home after the encounter, she is more sure of herself, more free, and less alone. Like "Johnnieruth," all of the stories in* Lover's Choice *highlight the resilience and strength of Black women coming to know themselves and standing firm in what they know.*

The endings of Birtha's stories are often unconventional as she foregrounds the complexity of lesbian relationships and issues, keeping the reader and her characters from falling into the clichés that too often lessen the impact and reality of themes like coming out, monogamy, and breaking up. Birtha's characters are developed emotionally and psychologically, and this complexity leads them to respond to conventional situations in complicated and unexpected ways.

Responding primarily to the end of a relationship, a familiar situation, the speaker's voice in The Forbidden Poems *(1991)*, Birtha's first collection of poetry, is driven by directness, biting humor, and emotion. As the Black woman speaker reflects on her White lover and the beauty and pain of the relationship, many of the poems are also about the loss of other loved ones. Other poems comment on the support of community and sisterhood. All elements of self—woman, Black woman, and lesbian—are essential elements of voice in the poems, as the speaker writes of putting herself back together again. The publication of the collection, finally, is a celebration of Birtha's adoption of her daughter, Tasha Alfrieda Birtha.

While Becky Birtha dedicates her writing to the women before her, including her mother and grandmother, who longed to be creative writers, most of the energy in her writing stems from her commitment to lesbian communities and the voices of women-loving women of the past three decades. Coming out as a lesbian in 1976, Birtha sees her primary audience as women like herself, women who must continually struggle to embrace self, and who need to see women like themselves in real and affirming words.

R. Joyce Lausch

Johnnieruth

Summertime. Nighttime. Talk about steam heat. This whole city get like the bathroom when somebody in there taking a shower with the door shut. Nights like that, can't nobody sleep. Everybody be outside, sitting on they steps or else dragging half they furniture out on the sidewalk—kitchen chairs, card tables— even bringing TVs outside.

Womenfolks, mostly. All the grown women around my way look just the same. They all big—stout. They got big bosoms and big hips and fat legs, and they always wearing runover house-shoes, and them shapeless, flowered numbers with the buttons down the front. Cept on Sunday. Sunday morning they all turn into glamour girls, in them big hats and long gloves, with they skinny high heels and they skinny selves in them tight girdles—wouldn't nobody ever know what they look like the rest of the time.

When I was a little kid I didn't wanna grow up, cause I never wanted to look like them ladies. I heard Miz Jenkins down the street one time say she don't mind being fat cause that way her husband don't get so jealous. She say it's more than one way to keep a man. Me, I don't have me no intentions of keeping no man. I never understood why they was in so much demand anyway, when it seem like all a woman can depend on em for is making sure she keep on having babies.

We got enough children in my neighborhood. In the summertime, even the little kids allowed to stay up till eleven or twelve o'clock at night—playing in the street and hollering and carrying on—don't never seem to get tired. Don't nobody care, long as they don't fight.

Me—I don't hang around no front steps no more. Hot nights like that, I get out my ten speed and I be gone.

That's what I like to do more than anything else in the whole world. Feel that wind in my face keeping me cool as a air conditioner, shooting along like a snowball. My bike light as a kite. I can really get up some speed.

All the guys around my way got ten speed bikes. Some of the girls got em too, but they don't ride em at night. They pedal around during the day, but at nighttime they just hang around out front, watching babies and running they mouth. I didn't get my Peugeot to be no conversation piece.

My mama don't like me to ride at night. I tried to point out to her that she ain't never said nothing to my brothers, and Vincent a year younger than me. (And Langston two years older, in case "old" is the problem.) She say, "That's different, Johnnieruth. You're a girl." Now I wanna know how is anybody gonna know that. I'm skinny as a knifeblade turned sideways, and all I ever wear is blue jeans and a Wrangler jacket. But if I bring that up, she liable to get started in on how come I can't be more of a young lady, and fourteen is old enough to start taking more pride in my appearance, and she gonna be ashamed to admit I'm her daughter.

I just tell her that my bike be moving so fast can't nobody hardly see me, and couldn't catch me if they did. Mama complain to her friends how I'm wild and she can't do nothing with me. She know I'm gonna do what I want no matter what she say. But she know I ain't getting in no trouble, neither.

Like some of the boys I know stole they bikes, but I didn't do nothing like that. I'd been saving my money ever since I can remember, every time I could get a nickel or a dime outta anybody.

When I was a little kid, it was hard to get money. Seem like the only time they ever give you any was on Sunday morning, and then you had to put it in the offering. I used to hate to do that. In fact, I used to hate everything about Sunday morning. I had to wear all them ruffly dresses—that shiny slippery stuff in the wintertime that got to make a noise every time you move your ass a inch on them hard old benches. And that scratchy starchy stuff in the summertime with all them scratchy crinolines. Had to carry a pocketbook and wear them shiny shoes. And the church we went to was all the way over on Summit Avenue, so the whole damn neighborhood could get a good look. At least all the other kids'd be dressed the same way. They boys think they slick cause they get to wear pants, but they still got to wear a white shirt and a tie; and them dumb hats they wear can't hide them baldheaded haircuts, cause they got to take the hats off in church.

There was one Sunday when I musta been around eight. I remember it was before my sister Corletta was born, cause right around then was when I put my foot down about that whole sanctimonious routine. Anyway, I was dragging my feet along Twenty-fifth Street in back of Mama and Vincent and them, when I spied this lady. I only seen her that one time, but I still remember just how she look. She don't look like nobody I ever seen before. I *know* she don't live around here. She real skinny. But she ain't no real young woman, neither. She could be old as my mama. She ain't nobody's mama—I'm sure. And she ain't wearing Sunday clothes. She got on blue jeans and a man's blue working shirt, with the tail hanging out. She got patches on her blue jeans, and she still got her chin stuck out like she some kinda African royalty. She ain't carrying no shiny pocketbook. It don't look like she care if she got any money or not, or who know it, if she don't. She ain't wearing no house-shoes, or stockings or high heels neither.

Mama always speak to everybody, but when she pass by this lady she make like she ain't even seen her. But I get me a real good look, and the lady stare right back at me. She got a funny look on her face, almost like she think she know me from some place. After she pass on by, I had to turn around to get another look, even though Mama say that ain't polite. And you know what? She was turning around, too, looking back at me. And she give me a great big smile.

I didn't know too much in them days, but that's when I first got to thinking about how it's got to be different ways to be, from the way people be around my way. It's got to be places where it don't matter to anybody if you all dressed up on Sunday morning or you ain't. That's how come I started saving money. So, when I got enough, I could go away to some place like that.

Afterwhile I begun to see there wasn't no point in waiting around for hand-outs, and I started thinking of ways to earn my own money. I used to be running errands all the time—mailing letters for old Grandma Whittaker and picking up cigarettes and newspapers up the corner for everybody. After I got bigger, I started washing cars in the summer, and shoveling people sidewalk in the wintertime. Now I got me a newspaper route. Ain't never been no girl around here with no paper route, but I guess everybody got it figured out by now that I ain't gonna be like nobody else.

The reason I got me my Peugeot was so I could start to explore. I figured I better start looking around right now, so when I'm grown, I'll know exactly where I wanna go. So I ride around every chance I get.

Last summer, I used to ride with the boys a lot. Sometimes eight or ten of us'd just go cruising around the streets together. All of a sudden my mamma decide she don't want me to do that no more. She say I'm too old to be spending so much time with boys. (That's what they tell you half the time, and the other half the time they worried cause you ain't interested in spending more time with boys. Don't make much sense.) She want me to have some girl friends, but I never seem to fit in with none of the things the girls do. I used to think I fit in more with the boys.

But I seen how Mama might be right, for once. I didn't like the way the boys was starting to talk about girls sometimes. Talking about what some girl be like from the neck on down, and talking all up underneath somebody clothes and all. Even though I wasn't really friends with none of the girls, I still didn't like it. So now I mostly just ride around by myself. And Mama don't like that neither—you just can't please her.

This boy that live around the corner on North Street, Kenny Henderson, started asking me one time if I don't ever be lonely, cause he always see me by myself. He say don't I ever think I'd like to have me somebody special to go places with and stuff. Like I'd pick him if I did! Made me wanna laugh in his face. I do be lonely, a lotta times, but I don't tell nobody. And I ain't met nobody yet that I'd really rather be with than be by myself. But I will someday. When I find that special place where everybody different, I'm gonna find somebody there I can be friends with. And it ain't gonna be no dumb boy.

I found me one place already, that I like to go to a whole lot. It ain't even really that far away—by bike—but it's on the other side of the Avenue. So I don't tell Mama and them I go there, cause they like to think I'm right around the neighborhood someplace. But this neighborhood too dull for me. All the houses look just the same—no porches, no yards, no trees—not even no parks around here. Every block look so much like every other block it hurt your eyes to look at, afterwhile. So I ride across Summit Avenue and go down that big steep hill there, and then make a sharp right at the bottom and cross the bridge over the train tracks. Then I head on out the boulevard—that's the nicest part, with all them big trees making a tunnel over the top, and lightning bugs shining in the bushes. At the end of the boulevard you get to this place call the Plaza.

It's something like a little park—the sidewalks is all bricks and they got flowers planted all over the place. The same kind my mama grow in that painted-up tire she got out front masquerading like a garden decoration—only seem like they smell sweeter here. It's a big high fountain right in the middle, and all the streetlights is the real old-fashion kind. That Plaza is about the prettiest place I ever been.

Sometimes something going on there. Like a orchestra playing music or some man or lady singing. One time they had a show with some girls doing some kinda foreign dances. They look like they were around my age. They all had on these fancy costumes, with different color ribbons all down they back. I wouldn't wear nothing like that, but it looked real pretty when they was dancing.

I got me a special bench in one corner where I like to sit, cause I can see just about everything, but wouldn't nobody know I was there. I like to sit still and think, and I like to watch people. A lotta people be coming there at night—to look at the shows and stuff, or just to hang out and cool off. All different kinda people.

This one night when I was sitting over in that corner where I always be at, there was this lady standing right near my bench. She mostly had her back turned to me and she didn't know I was there, but I could see her real good. She had on this shiny purple shirt and about a million silver bracelets. I kinda liked the way she look. Sorta exotic, like she maybe come from California or one of the islands. I mean she had class—standing there posing with her arms folded. She walk away a little bit. Then turn around and walk back again. Like she waiting for somebody.

Then I spotted this dude coming over. I spied him all the way cross the Plaza. Looking real fine. Got on a three piece suit. One of them little caps sitting on a angle. Look like leather. He coming straight over to this lady I'm watching and then she seen him too and she start to smile, but she don't move till he get right up next to her. And then I'm gonna look away, cause I can't stand to watch nobody hugging and kissing on each other, but all of a sudden I see it ain't no dude at all. It's another lady.

Now I can't stop looking. They smiling at each other like they ain't seen one another in ten years. Then the one in the purple shirt look around real quick—but she don't look just behind her—and sorta pull the other one right back into the corner where I'm sitting at, and then they put they arms around each other and kiss—for a whole long time. Now I really know I oughtta turn away, but I can't. And I know they gonna see me when they finally open they eyes. And they do.

They both kinda gasp and back up, like I'm the monster that just rose up outta the deep. And then I guess they can see I'm only a girl, and they look at one another—and start to laugh! Then they just turn around and start to walk away like it wasn't nothing at all. But right before they gone, they both look around again, and see I still ain't got my eye muscles and jaw muscles working right again yet. And the one lady wink at me. And the other one say "Catch you later."

I can't stop staring at they backs, all the way across the Plaza. And then, all of a sudden, I feel like I got to be doing something, got to be moving.

I wheel on outta the Plaza and I'm just concentrating on getting up my speed. Cause I can't figure out what to think. Them two women kissing and then, when they get caught, just laughing about it. And here I'm laughing too, for no reason at all. I'm sailing down the boulevard laughing like a lunatic, and then I'm singing at the top of my lungs. And climbing that big old hill up to Summit Avenue is just as easy as being on a escalator.

David Bradley (1950–)

David Bradley was born on September 7, 1950, in Bedford, Pennsylvania. He graduated summa cum laude, with a BA from the University of Pennsylvania in 1972. Two years later, Bradley earned his master's degree from King's College in London. His distinguished career includes being an associate professor of English at Temple University and being a guest lecturer at several other universities. Bradley earned early success with writing two novels, South Street *and* The Chaneysville Incident, *before the age of thirty-five. The* Chaneysville Incident *is the winner of the 1982 PEN/Faulkner Award and also won an American Academy and Institute of Arts and Letters grant for literature. The widespread praise for Bradley's novels resulted from his unique style of writing historical fiction, which he places in a contemporary context.*

Bradley spent his childhood and young adult life in a predominantly White town in rural Pennsylvania, which had an effect on his attitude toward the power of African Americans in the United States. Even as the Black Power Movement was gaining strength as Bradley entered the University of Pennsylvania in the late 1960s, he remained critical of the impact such a movement could have in a American society so committed to racist practice. This question about the pliability of racism informed his first novel, South Street, *which chronicles the lives of ordinary Black people in a Philadelphia ghetto. Bradley once stated, "The people of South Street were totally without power. Their lives were terrible— they just lived with the situation and made the best of it."*

Although Bradley completed South Street *as an undergraduate, his next project,* The Chaneysville Incident, *took nearly a decade to complete. Once again, with this book, Bradley revisits his roots of rural Pennsylvania. As a young man, his mother told him a story of thirteen slaves in Bedford County who were faced with the choice of death or enslavement; they chose death. Bradley was enamored with this story and ultimately chose it as the basis for the novel. The* Chaneysville Incident *is a complex novel, and the historical content is only a catalyst for Bradley's other objectives. By using historical and factual evidence, Bradley paves the way for his keen observations and descriptions about American life and how these observations may relate to the socioeconomic class structure of the United States. John, the main character and the narrative voice, is a history professor who is reluctantly planning a trip back to rural Pennsylvania to visit a dying friend. This point of view and narrative is important to the story's larger focus on regional racism and class struggle in the United States. Bradley always seems to be writing about conflict, whether it is a broad social conflict of racism, or the interpersonal conflict one has with one's partner.*

This spectrum of conflict is found within the relationship of John and his lover Judith. Racial conflict occurs during the conversations between John, a black man, and Judith, a

white woman, because they have different views about American society. As the story unfolds, Judith is constantly trying to discover John's new motivations for finding historical
facts surrounding the death of thirteen slaves from rural Pennsylvania. John's need for
discovery stems from his subjectivity as both a Black man and as a historian, and in fact,
his motivation transcends the search for historical facts, and becomes a process of self and
spiritual discovery. The interpersonal conflict stems from and relates to the larger national
conflict. John undergoes a transformation from being a historian to being a storyteller due
to the personal nature of the story he is trying to uncover. In a sense, as John makes the
transformation into a storyteller, he also becomes a time traveler in his own mind. His
journey through time, to reencounter his ancestors' experiences, has left him uncertain
about his future with Judith and his future as an academic. At the end of the novel, John
must take a leap of faith, which provides conflict, pain, and confusion for him. In the last
sentence of The Chaneysville Incident, Bradley writes about John and symbolically indicates his personal journey through time, "I reached out and held tightly to the table feeling
it solid beneath my fingers, knowing it was not moving, but feeling the room swirl around
me just the same." John realizes he must hold on to what he knows in order to ease the
intense pain and confusion caused by the struggle to discover the truth about his ancestors, a swirling, complicated spiritual passage that he is only just about to undertake.

Paul Jorgensen

197903121800 (Monday)

The storm was in its final phase. The south wind had gone, had taken with it the
moisture and the clouds. Now the sky was clear and black, the air crisp and dry
and cold as steel. Now the west wind blew. I knew it was the west wind—I could
hear it singing.

That was what I had called it when I was a child; that was what it had
sounded like to me. And that was what I had believed it was, even though nobody else thought it sounded like singing, not even Old Jack. He had claimed it
was the souls of the Indians who lived and died in the mountains, long before
the white man came, panting as they ran in pursuit of deer and bear and cata-
mount in their hunting grounds beyond the grave. But he had never argued with
my interpretation. Because it was not the kind of thing you could argue about.
He heard panting, I heard singing; we both heard something, and believed what
we wanted to believe.

Eventually there had come a time when I had not needed legends to explain
it. I had been in my last year of high school then, studying physics, and I read in
my textbook how the passage of a gas over an irregular surface sets up vibrations, the frequency of which varies in direct proportion to something, and in in-
verse proportion to something else, and I had realized that the sound I called the
singing of the wind was not singing at all, or panting, either; that it was just a

sound, like a car honking; that if you knew the shape of the land and the velocity and temperature and direction of the wind, you could sit there with your slide rule and come up with a pretty good idea of what the pitch would be. It was something that you didn't have to believe in; it was something you could know. And so I had copied down the equations in my notebook and I had waited anxiously for the first of the winter storms, and when the snow had fallen and the sky was clearing, I had gone to the far side to sit with Old Jack and drink toddies and listen to the sound the wind made and to glory in the power of *knowing* what it was. I had told him what I had learned and he had looked at me blankly, and shaken his head and said he didn't give a damn about what the book said; it was the souls of Indians. And I had realized for the first time that even though I loved him, he was an ignorant old man, no better than the savages who thought that thunder was the sound of some god's anger, and for the first time, I had argued with him about it. But then it had started, and I had left off arguing to listen. And what I had heard had filled me with cold fear. For I had not heard a sound like a car honking; I had not heard vibrations of a frequency that varied directly or inversely with anything at all; I had heard singing. I had set there, clutching my toddy, trying to perceive that sound as I had known I should, trying not to hear voices in it, trying not to hear words. But I had heard them anyway.

In the days that followed I had spent every spare minute studying the physics of sound, studying harder than I had when I had needed to pass an exam. But it made no difference. For when the west wind blew, I heard it singing. And so I had done what I had to do; I had gone away from the mountains, down to the flat land, where there were no irregularities of surface. And I had promised myself I would never hear it again, that I would never go up into the mountains again. I had kept that promise, until now. Only now I knew where the lie had been: I had stopped hearing, but I had not stopped listening.

It was cold in the cabin; I could not recall its ever being as cold there—or anywhere—before. It was the wind that made it cold, not only stabbing through every crack in the walls but slicing over the top of the chimney, creating a fearsome draft, making the fire burn strongly but without heat, making it give off nothing but a hard, cold, fierce, unholy light.

I saw Judith leave the stove—not Judith, really, just the shadow of her, moving against the glow of the stove. She set a steaming cup on the table before me. I did not need to taste it, or even smell it, to know what it was: coffee. I did not want coffee. I wanted a toddy. I needed one. But I could not expect Judith to understand that. There was a lot that I needed that she would never understand. For she was a woman and she was white, and though I loved her there were points of reference that we did not share. And never would.

We had come back easily, more easily than I would have thought possible. We had to struggle down from the hillside and out to the main road, but when we got there we found that it had been plowed and cindered, and within half a mile of walking we were offered a ride in a battered red GMC pickup by an aging farmer with a ruddy, weather-beaten face. He said little to us, only asking if we wanted a ride and how far we were going, and sharing his opinion on the timing of the inevitable shift in the wind. He dropped us at the base of the mountain, and we had made our way up. The sun was high then, and shining on that slope, and the air was cold but still; we made the climb in half an hour, and brought the car down in just a little more, slowed only by an occasional deep drift and the fact that we were going in reverse.

I bought gas in Rainsburg, and we made good time from there. I stayed in the valley, coming north through Charlesville and Beegletown, swinging west at the Narrows, tooling slowly through the Town. I expected to have to climb the Hill on foot since it was rarely—if ever—plowed, but when we got there I saw the Town's road-grader coming down; Randall Scott was an honest politician— he stayed scared.

The cabin was cold, but not as cold as I had feared it would be; there were still coals glowing in the grate. I built a tinder fire on top of them to force a draft. In half an hour the heat was coming up well, and the frost no longer blossomed before our faces. By then I had made tea, and we drank it loaded with sugar, and I heated stew and fried venison steaks, and we wolfed them down. Then I loaded the stove with wood to burn while we slept. By the time I finished, Judith was al-ready lying down, huddled under the blankets. But she wasn't sleeping—her breathing was too regular for that. I mixed myself a toddy and stood by the stove. When I had drunk it all I went to lie beside her; she moved quickly to make room. Then we lay there, listening to the fire roaring in the chimney.

"John?" she said after a while.

"What?"

"Are you going to tell me *anything?*"

"I'm not sure I can," I said.

She didn't say anything.

"Tell me what you want to know," I said.

"I want to know who the hell is buried down there," she said.

"Oh. That. Slaves are buried down there. Runaway slaves. A subject of a local legend; not much of one. No heroes doing great deeds. Nobody much has even bothered to write it down, except for one local historian, and we know about local historians. . . ."

"*John.*"

"A group of slaves came north on the Underground Railroad. They got across the Line all right, into what they probably thought was free territory. Only there wasn't any such thing. And so they were about to be captured and taken back. But they decided they'd rather die. Some kind soul in the South County did it for them. Anyway, that's the legend."

"And you think those are the people buried down there?"

"Yes," I said.

"And you think it has something to do with your . . . with Moses Wash-ington."

"Sure," I said. "You know, it's really amazing when you think about it. I mean, mathematically it's perfectly possible, but for a man to take a mathematical possibility and turn it into reality . . . it's amazing. I don't know whether you'd call it obsession or dedication, but it surely is amazing."

"John," she said. "Will you please slow down and talk to me? *What* is amazing?"

"Moses Washington's search. He started it when he was sixteen years old. He dedicated his life to it. That's easy to say, but you can't understand it until you sit down and figure out how he must have found those graves. He wouldn't have known they were there, or even what he was looking for. And so he would have had to look everywhere for something. And he would have known, before he was twenty years old, that he was going to have to do it that way and he would have had to accept, at twenty, the possibility that he was going to end up looking at every square yard of this County, on foot. And he would have had to accept the fact, at twenty, that he wasn't going to be finished until he was . . . I don't know. The odds would make it at least forty-five. And so he would have had to set up a plan, a pattern, that he was going to follow for a quarter of a century, longer than he'd been alive. It was perfectly possible; there's about a thousand square miles of County, and he could have eliminated some of it—plowed fields, rivers, towns, so forth—but even if there were a thousand square miles, he could have searched a square mile a week, which isn't much. But it would take twenty-five years. And it took longer. It took him thirty-five years, even though he naturally prowled the County most of the time. So by then he must have actually searched most of the County. Maybe all of it; maybe he missed them the first time, not knowing what he was looking for—"

"Missed the graves," she said.

"Yes."

"But how did he know that that was what he was looking for? When he found it, I mean. And how was it—"

"He knew because there were only twelve runaway slaves. That's what the legend says. Well, it says a dozen, which could be taken as an approximation, but could be dead accurate. And he knew the legend; it was one of his favorites."

"But there are thirteen graves," she said.

"That's how he knew he'd found him."

"Found who? You mean . . . C.K.?"

"Yes," I said. "C.K."

She didn't say anything.

"Thirty-five years," I said.

"Why thirty-five?" she said. "He died in 1958, right?"

"He found them in 1942," I said. "He would have found them in the fall or early winter, because the ground would have had to be clear. Or maybe he found them in the spring or summer and took the time deciding what to do."

"What did he do?"

"He joined the army," I said.

She didn't say anything.

"You know," I said, "it's funny. You spend years fiddling around with facts, trying to put them in the right places, trying to explain them with each other, and maybe you come pretty close, and everything fits except maybe one or two things, and that's usually because you've made a mistake right from the very beginning, overlooked something so obvious that when it finally dawns on you you just want to cry. I spent the better part of fifteen years wondering what happened to him in the army that made him change. I guess it seemed reasonable to assume that was where it had happened; everybody knows war changes men—that's why they keep having them. But the war didn't change Moses Washington. He would have had to change before he would go to war. Otherwise it doesn't make any sense. Moses Washington, fifty-two years old, volunteers, hell, *bribes* his way into a white man's army, a segregated army, to fight a white man's war; he would have had to change in order to do that, or have had a pretty strong reason."

"So you think he found the graves before that, and that's what changed him?"

"No," I said. "I don't think he changed at all. I think he went to war for the same reason he married my mother when he came out, for the same reason he did everything else: to get himself ready to find C.K. Washington."

"But he'd *found* him."

"No," I said. "He'd found his grave."

She didn't say anything.

"I know," I said. "It sounds like the same thing. That's what I thought too; that's the way historians think. I assumed that if Moses Washington went looking for his grandfather he'd really be looking for signs of his grandfather: records, old campsites, markers, graves, maybe even a skeleton. And he was. So I assumed that he was acting just like a historian, and when he found whatever it was, he'd set up a marker or something, and that would be it. But I forgot that Moses Washington wasn't a historian, any more than he was a moonshiner or a real estate speculator. If he was anything, he was a hunter. And he did what any good hunter does when he's going off to trail dangerous game: he left trail markers, so that if somebody wanted to they could follow him, and he more or less made sure somebody would want to. . . ."

"You're talking about you, aren't you?" she said.

"Yes," I said.

"All right," she said. "So he was a hunter, and he left a trail for you to follow. But what was the point of it if he'd already found the grave?"

"He wasn't looking for a grave," I said. "He was looking for a man. That's what he was looking for all along: a man. He knew when he came here that C.K. Washington was dead; if he wasn't he would have been a hundred years old. So he was looking for his grave or a skeleton or whatever the same way a hunter looks for a hoofprint, or bedding grounds, or signs of feeding or droppings—it was a spoor. And when he found it he did what any good woodsman would do: he put himself into the mind of the game and headed off after it."

"Wait a minute. You're saying that because C.K. Washington died there Moses Washington committed suicide there?"

"No," I said. "Not suicide. I was wrong about that. We were all wrong. Everybody thought it was an accident. The Judge thought it was murder. I thought I had discovered it was suicide. But what it really was was a . . . a hunting trip. That's where he said he was going. That's what he told his wife, and that's what he told Old Jack: he was going hunting. And that's what he did."

"That sounds . . . crazy," she said. "You're talking about a man chasing after ghosts."

"No," I said. "Ghost isn't the right word. Ghost is a word that was invented by people who didn't believe, like the names the Spaniards gave the Aztec gods. Ancestors is a better term, or—"

"I don't care what you call it. It's insane."

"Maybe," I said. "I guess maybe that's what insanity is, somebody believing in something that doesn't have any kind of reality for you. Napoleon's dead; anybody who thinks he's Napoleon is crazy. There are no ghosts; anybody who chases ghosts is crazy. The thing is, if you accept his premises, everything he did was perfectly logical. He wanted to understand dying, to look before he leaped, so he went to war. He was a hero, because he wanted to take chances, get closer to dying. He loved a woman because C.K. had loved a woman, maybe two, and Moses Washington needed to understand that. He had a son because C.K. Washington had had a son. . . ."

"Moses Washington had *two* sons," she said, "and it's still crazy."

"Only if you're a Christian. Only if you believe in heaven and hell, and all those things. Moses Washington didn't; the old ladies always said he was a heathen, and he was—he spent all that time in the church and talking to preachers and reading the Bible because he wanted to be sure the Christians were wrong. You don't throw your whole life away if you're not sure that the dead really are there, waiting for you."

"That's not crazy," she said. "That's the Goddamned Twilight Zone."

I didn't say anything.

She raised up and looked at me; I could feel her eyes on me. "You don't think so, do you?" she said.

I didn't say anything.

"No," she said. "You don't. You not only think he did that, you think it was a perfectly sane and sensible thing to do, don't you?"

I didn't say anything.

"Don't you?"

I didn't say anything.

She lay back down. "Dear God," she said.

We lay there for a while, listening to the fire, to the first low hummings as the west wind began its song.

"Anyway," she said, "it's over now. You know what happened to Moses Washington, and all that—"

"I don't know anything," I said. "I don't know what happened to C.K., and that means I don't really know anything. I just know what Moses Washington knew when he got this far."

"Oh, great," she said. "So what does that mean? You're going to put on your little Dan'l Boone costume and take your little rifle down there and blow your brains out so you can go hunting with the old men, and sit around the campfire drinking whiskey and telling lies—"

"I'm going to sleep," I said.

We lay there for a while, not talking, not touching. The song grew louder. I tried not to listen.

"I'm sorry," she said.

"Yeah," I said.

"I'm *sorry.*"

"It's all right," I said.

"Then hold me?" she said. "Please?"

I twisted around to face her, put my arms around her, felt her breath on my face, feeling the chill in it.

"Don't go away," she said. "Please."

"I won't," I said.

But I had gone away. When her breathing became slow and even, punctuated by the little catches and hesitations that, in her, meant deepest sleep, I slipped away from her, and went to sit at the table, staring into the darkness, listening to songs the wind sang as it fluted through the hills. I don't know how long I sat there; a long time. Long enough for the fire to burn low, its substance leeched away by the wailing wind. Long enough for the chill to come and set me shivering. I closed my eyes then, trying to escape the cold, knowing, as I did it, that it would not do any good. And then I heard her moving, getting up and going to the stove. I had opened my eyes and had seen her shadow moving, coming to me, bringing me coffee.

"I don't want it," I said.

"Drink it," she said.

"I don't want coffee. . . ." I caught the aroma then: strong, sweet, heady. A toddy. She had made me a toddy. I took the cup and sipped at it, once, twice. Then I drank it down, almost in a gulp, feeling the warmth spread through me. I closed my eyes. She came and took the cup from me and filled it again and brought it back, held it out to me. "Why?" I said.

"Faith," she said.

I didn't say anything.

"I know," she said. "You don't think I understand. You're right; I don't understand. But I can believe in you; I do believe in you. If you want to take that gun and blow your head off, I won't try to stop you; I don't know that I can help you, but I won't try to stop you. And I'll try to understand. And if you say you need something that I can't give you, something you need a toddy to get, then I'll make a toddy for you."

I wished the lamp were going so that I could see her face, but I could not, so I just reached out and took the cup from her hands and drank. She came and stood beside me, her hand on my shoulder, waiting while I finished. When I set the cup down she went to the stove and began to mix another. "You still hate him, don't you?"

I didn't say anything.

"That's what it is, you know," she said. "You hate him. You've hated him all along. You keep saying you made mistakes, or you didn't understand. That's true, I guess; I wouldn't really know. But I do know why you made all those mistakes. You were too busy hating him to really see him. It took you how long to figure out he killed himself? But you should have known. All the facts were there—"

"They covered them up," I said.

"'I study history because I want to know where the lies are.' That's what you told me. So now I'm supposed to believe you swallowed the biggest lie of all."

"How was I supposed to know?"

"'Why not study atrocities? History itself is atrocious.' You told me that too."

I didn't say anything.

"You know," she said, "you have to wonder. Here you are, hot-stuff historian, superscholar, able to leap to conclusions in a single bound, and half the people who know you think you're brilliant and the other half think you're crazy, but everybody agrees there's something special about you, even if they don't understand what the hell it is. You can make a bonfire by rubbing two dry facts together, so long as you're talking about the Punic Wars and Saint Francis of Assisi, or the Lost Chord and Jesus Christ. But let you come within twenty miles of where you live and it all goes out the window. Because you don't really want to know, John. You want to win. You want to beat Moses Washington and whatever—"

"No," I said. "Not now. Not anymore. Now I just want to know the truth."

"Then what's stopping you?"

"Facts," I said. "Don't you understand? There aren't any facts. All that about the runaway slaves and Moses Washington, that's extrapolation. It's not facts. I've used the facts."

"So get more facts."

"There *aren't* any more facts."

"Then forget the facts," she said.

"You were right to start with," I said. "You don't understand."

She brought the cup to me then, and I took it from her and drank it down, almost angrily. Drank it too fast. Because I realized suddenly that I had had too many toddies, that I was drunk. I set the cup down and closed my eyes, fighting off a wave of dizziness. I reached out and held tightly to the table feeling it solid beneath my fingers, knowing it was not moving, but feeling the room swirl around me just the same.

Gwendolyn Brooks (1917–)

Gwendolyn Brooks has enjoyed one of the most sustained, prolific, and distinguished careers among all American poets.

Born in Topeka, Kansas, Brooks soon moved with her parents to Chicago, where she
has sent most of her life. In 1933, after reading her early verse, Langston Hughes offered
encouragement. During the 1930s she published many poems in the Chicago Defender, a
leading African American newspaper. Her first book of poetry, A Street in Bronzeville, appeared in 1945. She quickly garnered two Guggenheim Fellowships. Another volume of
poetry, Annie Allen (1949), won the Pulitzer Prize.

During the 1960s she taught at Columbia College in Chicago, Elmhurst College, and
City College of New York. In the same decade, she drew energy from the Black Arts Movement, meeting Larry Neal, Amiri Baraka, and Haki Madhubuti. She and Madhubuti became close friends and co-workers.

Brooks's novel Maud Martha (1953) is a notable longer work. Her autobiographical
Report from Part One (1971) is both experimental and informative.

Her poems from the 1960s range from a tribute to Malcolm X to reflections on urban
riots. Most of her poetry, however, tracks the everyday lives of African Americans, especially those residing in cities. Her poems—many of which are collected in Blacks (1991)—
are paradoxically formal and casual, traditional and streetwise, metrical and vernacular.

"Two Dedications" contrasts public works of art: an officially sanctioned, enigmatic
statue by Picasso; and a vibrant African American mural on a slum wall. "when you have
forgotten Sunday: the love story" is a tender poem about a lost relationship.

Keith D. Miller

Two Dedications

I

THE CHICAGO PICASSO

August 15, 1967

"Mayor Daley tugged a white ribbon, loosing the blue percale wrap.
A hearty cheer went up as the covering slipped off the big steel
sculpture that looks at once like a bird and a woman."

—CHICAGO SUN-TIMES

(Seiji Ozawa leads the Symphony.
The Mayor smiles.
And 50,000 See.)

Does man love Art? Man visits Art, but squirms.
Art hurts. Art urges voyages—
and it is easier to stay at home,
the nice beer ready.
      In commonrooms
we belch, or sniff, or scratch.
Are raw.

But we must cook ourselves and style ourselves for Art, who
is a requiring courtesan.
We squirm.
We do not hug the Mona Lisa.
We
may touch or tolerate
an astounding fountain, or a horse-and-rider.
At most, another Lion.

Observe the tall cold of a Flower
which is as innocent and as guilty,
as meaningful and as meaningless as any
other flower in the western field.

II

THE WALL

August 27, 1967
      For Edward Christmas

"The side wall of a typical slum building on the corner of 43rd
and Langley became a mural communicating black dignity. . . ."
            —EBONY

A drumdrumdrum.
Humbly we come.
South of success and east of gloss and glass are
sandals;
flowercloth;
grave hoops of wood or gold, pendant
from black ears, brown ears, reddish-brown
and ivory ears;

black boy-men.
Black

boy-men on roofs fist out "Black Power!" Val,
a little black stampede
in African
images of brass and flowerswirl,
fists out "Black Power!"—tightens pretty eyes,
leans back on mothercountry and is tract,
is treatise through her perfect and tight teeth.

Women in wool hair chant their poetry.
Phil Cohran gives us messages and music
made of developed bone and polished and honed cult.
It is the Hour of tribe and of vibration,
the day-long Hour. It is the Hour
of ringing, rouse, of ferment-festival.

On Forty-third and Langley
black furnaces resent ancient
legislatures
of ploy and scruple and practical gelatin.
They keep the fever in,
fondle the fever.

All
worship the Wall.

I mount the rattling wood. Walter
says, "She is good." Says, "She
our Sister is." In front of me
hundreds of faces, red-brown, brown, black, ivory,
yield me hot trust, their yea and their Announcement
that they are ready to rile the high-flung ground.
Behind me, Paint
Heroes.
No child has defiled
the Heroes of this Wall this serious Appointment
this still Wing
this Scald this Flute this heavy Light this Hinge.

An emphasis is paroled.
The old decapitations are revised,
the dispossessions beakless.

And we sing.

when you have forgotten Sunday: the love story

—And when you have forgotten the bright bedclothes on a
  Wednesday and a Saturday,
And most especially when you have forgotten Sunday—
When you have forgotten Sunday halves in bed,
Or me sitting on the front-room radiator in the limping afternoon
Looking off down the long street
To nowhere,
Hugged by my plain old wrapper of no-expectation
And nothing-I-have-to-do and I'm-happy-why?
And if-Monday-never-had-to-come—
When you have forgotten that, I say,
And how you swore, if somebody beeped the bell,
And how my heart played hopscotch if the telephone rang;
And how we finally went in to Sunday dinner,
That is to say, went across the front room floor to the ink-spotted
    table in the southwest corner
To Sunday dinner, which was always chicken and noodles
Or chicken and rice
And salad and rye bread and tea
And chocolate chip cookies—
I say, when you have forgotten that,
When you have forgotten my little presentiment
That the war would be over before they got to you;
And how we finally undressed and whipped out the light and flowed
    into bed,
And lay loose-limbed for a moment in the week-end
Bright bedclothes,
Then gently folded into each other—
When you have, I say, forgotten all that,
Then you may tell,
Then I may believe
You have forgotten me well.

Octavia Butler (1947–)

Born in Pasadena, California, Octavia Butler is an acclaimed and prolific science fiction author and winner of a MacArthur Fellowship. Her early science fiction novels include Survivor *(1978),* Wild Seed *(1980), and* Clay's Ark *(1984), followed by the trilogy* Dawn *(1987),* Adulthood Rites *(1988), and* Imago *(1989).*

Butler's work incorporates standard motifs of science fiction—telepathy, alien invasions, various forms of mutation, and dystopia. But, unlike well-known White science fiction writers, Butler is deeply influenced by African American slave narratives. Her most important theme is bondage, mental and physical. In a pair of novels, Patternmaster *(1976) and* Mind of My Mind *(1977), for example, telepathy affects large numbers of people and always involves issues of power. In another novel,* Kindred *(1979), she uses time travel to project a character onto a slave plantation. A later novel,* Parable of the Sower *(1993), explores the bondage, if you will, that occurs in drug addiction.*

Like George Orwell and others, Butler creates dystopias in part to criticize contemporary culture, in her case to critique, among other things, social stratifications and power arrangements rooted in distinctions of race and gender.

Each of the very different stories included here won a prize coveted by science fiction writers—the Hugo Award. "Bloodchild" enfolds the reader, as well as its characters, in a web of trust, dependence, control, and horror. "Speech Sounds" affirms fundamental human bonds during a numbing, futuristic disaster.

Keith D. Miller

Bloodchild

My last night of childhood began with a visit home. T'Gatoi's sister had given us two sterile eggs. T'Gatoi gave one to my mother, brother, and sisters. She insisted that I eat the other one alone. It didn't matter. There was still enough to leave everyone feeling good. Almost everyone. My mother wouldn't take any. She sat, watching everyone drifting and dreaming without her. Most of the time she watched me.

I lay against T'Gatoi's long, velvet underside, sipping from my egg now and then, wondering why my mother denied herself such a harmless pleasure. Less of her hair would be gray if she indulged now and then. The eggs prolonged life, prolonged vigor. My father, who had never refused one in his life, had lived more than twice as long as he should have. And toward the end of his life, when he should have been slowing down, he had married my mother and fathered four children.

But my mother seemed content to age before she had to. I saw her turn away as several of T'Gatoi's limbs secured me closer. T'Gatoi liked our body heat and took advantage of it whenever she could. When I was little and at home more, my mother used to try to tell me how to behave with T'Gatoi—how to be respectful and always obedient because T'Gatoi was the Tlic government official in charge of the Preserve, and thus the most important of her kind to deal directly with Terrans. It was an honor, my mother said, that such a person had chosen to come into the family. My mother was at her most formal and severe when she was lying.

I had no idea why she was lying, or even what she was lying about. It *was* an honor to have T'Gatoi in the family, but it was hardly a novelty. T'Gatoi and my mother had been friends all my mother's life, and T'Gatoi was not interested in being honored in the house she considered her second home. She simply came in, climbed onto one of her special couches, and called me over to keep her warm. It was impossible to be formal with her while lying against her and hearing her complain as usual that I was too skinny.

"You're better," she said this time, probing me with six or seven of her limbs. "You're gaining weight finally. Thinness is dangerous." The probing changed subtly, became a series of caresses.

"He's still too thin," my mother said sharply.

T'Gatoi lifted her head and perhaps a meter of her body off the couch as though she were sitting up. She looked at my mother, and my mother, her face lined and old looking, turned away.

"Lien, I would like you to have what's left of Gan's egg."

"The eggs are for the children," my mother said.

"They are for the family. Please take it."

Unwillingly obedient, my mother took it from me and put it to her mouth. There were only a few drops left in the now-shrunken, elastic shell, but she squeezed them out, swallowed them, and after a few moments some of the lines of tension began to smooth from her face.

"It's good," she whispered. "Sometimes I forget how good it is."

"You should take more," T'Gatoi said. "Why are you in such a hurry to be old?"

My mother said nothing.

"I like being able to come here," T'Gatoi said. "This place is a refuge because of you, yet you won't take care of yourself."

T'Gatoi was hounded on the outside. Her people wanted more of us made available. Only she and her political faction stood between us and the hordes who did not understand why there was a Preserve—why any Terran could not be courted, paid, drafted, in some way made available to them. Or they did understand, but in their desperation, they did not care. She parceled us out to the desperate and sold us to the rich and powerful for their political support. Thus, we were necessities, status symbols, and an independent people. She oversaw the joining of families, putting an end to the final remnants of the earlier system of breaking up Terran families to suit impatient Tlic. I had lived outside with her. I had seen the desperate eagerness in the way some people looked at me. It was a little frightening to know that only she stood between us and that desperation that could so easily swallow us. My mother would look at her sometimes and say to me, "Take care of her." And I would remember that she too had been outside, had seen.

Now T'Gatoi used four of her limbs to push me away from her onto the floor. "Go on, Gan," she said. "Sit down there with your sisters and enjoy not being sober. You had most of the egg. Lien, come warm me."

My mother hesitated for no reason that I could see. One of my earliest memories is of my mother stretched alongside T'Gatoi, talking about things I could not understand, picking me up from the floor and laughing as she sat me on one of T'Gatoi's segments. She ate her share of eggs then. I wondered when she had stopped, and why.

She lay down now against T'Gatoi, and the whole left row of T'Gatoi's limbs closed around her, holding her loosely, but securely. I had always found it comfortable to lie that way, but except for my older sister, no one else in the family liked it. They said it made them feel caged.

T'Gatoi meant to cage my mother. Once she had, she moved her tail slightly, then spoke. "Not enough egg, Lien. You should have taken it when it was passed to you. You need it badly now."

T'Gatoi's tail moved once more, its whip motion so swift I wouldn't have seen it if I hadn't been watching for it. Her sting drew only a single drop of blood from my mother's bare leg.

My mother cried out—probably in surprise. Being stung doesn't hurt. Then she sighed and I could see her body relax. She moved languidly into a more comfortable position within the cage of T'Gatoi's limbs. "Why did you do that?" she asked, sounding half asleep.

"I could not watch you sitting and suffering any longer."

My mother managed to move her shoulders in a small shrug. "Tomorrow," she said.

"Yes. Tomorrow you will resume your suffering—if you must. But just now, just for now, lie here and warm me and let me ease your way a little."

"He's still mine, you know," my mother said suddenly.

"Nothing can buy him from me." Sober, she would not have permitted herself to refer to such things.

"Nothing," T'Gatoi agreed, humoring her.

"Did you think I would sell him for eggs? For long life? My son?"

"Not for anything," T'Gatoi said, stroking my mother's shoulders, toying with her long, graying hair.

I would like to have touched my mother, shared that moment with her. She would take my hand if I touched her now. Freed by the egg and the sting, she would smile and perhaps say things long held in. But tomorrow, she would remember all this as a humiliation. I did not want to be part of a remembered humiliation. Best just be still and know she loved me under all the duty and pride and pain.

"Xuan Hoa, take off her shoes," T'Gatoi said. "In a little while I'll sting her again and she can sleep."

My older sister obeyed, swaying drunkenly as she stood up. When she had finished, she sat down beside me and took my hand. We had always been a unit, she and I.

My mother put the back of her head against T'Gatoi's underside and tried from that impossible angle to look up into the broad, round face. "You're going to string me again?"

"Yes, Lien."

"I'll sleep until tomorrow noon."

"Good. You need it. When did you sleep last?'

My mother made a wordless sound of annoyance. "I should have stepped on you when you were small enough," she muttered.

It was an old joke between them. They had grown up together, sort of, though T'Gatoi had not, in my mother's life-time, been small enough for any Terran to step on. She was nearly three times my mother's present age, yet would still be young when my mother died of age. But T'Gatoi and my mother had met as T'Gatoi was coming into a period of rapid development—a kind of Tlic adolescence. My mother was only a child, but for a while they developed at the same rate and had no better friends than each other.

T'Gatoi had even introduced my mother to the man who became my father. My parents, pleased with each other in spite of their different ages, married as T'Gatoi was going into her family's business—politics. She and my mother saw each other less. But sometime before my older sister was born, my mother promised T'Gatoi one of her children. She would have to give one of us to someone, and she preferred T'Gatoi to some stranger.

Years passed. T'Gatoi traveled and increased her influence. The Preserve was hers by the time she came back to my mother to collect what she probably saw as her just reward for her hard work. My older sister took an instant liking to her and wanted to be chosen, but my mother was just coming to term with me and T'Gatoi liked the idea of choosing an infant and watching and taking part in all the phases of development. I'm told I was first caged within T'Gatoi's many limbs only three minutes after my birth. A few days later, I was given my first taste of egg. I tell Terrans that when they ask whether I was ever afraid of her. And I tell it to Tlic when T'Gatoi suggests a young Terran child for them and they, anxious and ignorant, demand an adolescent. Even my brother who had somehow grown up to fear and distrust the Tlic could probably have gone smoothly into one of their families if he had been adopted early enough. Sometimes, I think for his sake he should have been. I looked at him, stretched out on the floor across the room, his eyes open, but glazed as he dreamed his egg dream. No matter what he felt toward the Tlic, he always demanded his share of egg.

"Lien, can you stand up?" T'Gatoi asked suddenly.

"Stand?" my mother said. "I thought I was going to sleep."

"Later. Something sounds wrong outside." The cage was abruptly gone.

"What?"

"Up, Lien!"

My mother recognized her tone and got up just in time to avoid being dumped on the floor. T'Gatoi whipped her three meters of body off her couch, toward the door, and out at full speed. She had bones—ribs, a long spine, a skull, four sets of limb bones per segment. But when she moved that way, twisting, hurling herself into controlled falls, landing running, she seemed not only boneless, but aquatic—something swimming through the air as though it were water. I loved watching her move.

I left my sister and started to follow her out the door, though I wasn't very steady on my own feet. It would have been better to sit and dream, better yet to find a girl and share a waking dream with her. Back when the Tlic saw us as not much more than convenient, big, warm-blooded animals, they would pen several of us together, male and female, and feed us only eggs. That way they could be sure of getting another generation of us no matter how we tried to hold out. We were lucky that didn't go on long. A few generations of it and we would have *been* little more than convenient, big animals.

"Hold the door open, Gan," T'Gatoi said. "And tell the family to stay back."

"What is it?" I asked.

"N'Tlic."

I shrank back against the door. "Here? Alone?"

"He was trying to reach a call box, I suppose." She carried the man past me, unconscious, folded like a coat over some of her limbs. He looked young—my brother's age perhaps—and he was thinner than he should have been. What T'Gatoi would have called dangerously thin.

"Gan, go to the call box," she said. She put the man on the floor and began stripping off his clothing.

I did not move.

After a moment, she looked up at me, her sudden stillness a sign of deep impatience.

"Send Qui," I told her. "I'll stay here. Maybe I can help."

She let her limbs begin to move again, lifting the man and pulling his shirt over his head. "You don't want to see this," she said. "It will be hard. I can't help this man the way his Tlic could."

"I know. But send Qui. He won't want to be of any help here. I'm at least willing to try."

She looked at my brother—older, bigger, stronger, certainly more able to help her here. He was sitting up now, braced against the wall, staring at the man on the floor with undisguised fear and revulsion. Even she could see that he would be useless.

"Qui, go!" she said.

He didn't argue. He stood up, swayed briefly, then steadied, frightened sober.

"This man's name is Bram Lomas," she told him, reading from the man's armband. I fingered my own armband in sympathy. "He needs T'Khotgif Teh. Do you hear?"

"Bram Lomas, T'Khotgif Teh," my brother said. "I'm going." He edged around Lomas and ran out the door.

Lomas began to regain consciousness. He only moaned at first and clutched spasmodically at a pair of T'Gatoi's limbs. My younger sister, finally awake from her egg dream, came close to look at him, until my mother pulled her back.

T'Gatoi removed the man's shoes, then his pants, all the while leaving him two of her limbs to grip. Except for the final few, all her limbs were equally dexterous. "I want no argument from you this time, Gan," she said.

I straightened. "What shall I do?"

"Go out and slaughter an animal that is at least half your size."

"Slaughter? But I've never—"

She knocked me across the room. Her tail was an efficient weapon whether she exposed the sting or not.

I got up, feeling stupid for having ignored her warning, and went into the kitchen. Maybe I could kill something with a knife or an ax. My mother raised a few Terran animals for the table and several thousand local ones for their fur. T'Gatoi would probably prefer something local. An achti, perhaps. Some of those were the right size, though they had about three times as many teeth as I did and a real love of using them. My mother, Hoa, and Qui could kill them with knives. I had never killed one at all, had never slaughtered any animal. I had spent most of my time with T'Gatoi while my brother and sisters were learning the family business. T'Gatoi had been right. I should have been the one to go to the call box. At least I could do that.

I went to the corner cabinet where my mother kept her large house and garden tools. At the back of the cabinet there was a pipe that carried off waste water from the kitchen—except that it didn't anymore. My father had rerouted the waste water below before I was born. Now the pipe could be turned so that one half slid around the other and a rifle could be stored inside. This wasn't our only gun, but it was our most easily accessible one. I would have to use it to shoot one of the biggest of the achti. Then T'Gatoi would probably confiscate it. Firearms were illegal in the Preserve. There had been incidents right after the Preserve was established—Terrans shooting Tlic, shooting N'Tlic. This was before the joining of families began, before everyone had a personal stake in keeping the peace. No one had shot a Tlic in my lifetime or my mother's, but the law still stood—for our protection, we were told. There were stories of whole Terran families wiped out in reprisal back during the assassinations.

I went out to the cages and shot the biggest achti I could find. It was a handsome breeding male, and my mother would not be pleased to see me bring it in. But it was the right size, and I was in a hurry.

I put the achti's long, warm body over my shoulder—glad that some of the weight I'd gained was muscle—and took it to the kitchen. There, I put the gun back in its hiding place. If T'Gatoi noticed the achti's wounds and demanded the gun, I would give it to her. Otherwise, let it stay where my father wanted it.

I turned to take the achti to her, then hesitated. For several seconds, I stood in front of the closed door wondering why I was suddenly afraid. I knew what was going to happen. I hadn't seen it before but T'Gatoi had shown me diagrams and drawings. She had made sure I knew the truth as soon as I was old enough to understand it.

Yet I did not want to go into that room. I wasted a little time choosing a knife from the carved, wooden box in which my mother kept them. T'Gatoi might want one, I told myself, for the tough, heavily furred hide of the achti.

"Gan!" T'Gatoi called, her voice harsh with urgency.

I swallowed. I had not imagined a single moving of the feet could be so difficult. I realized I was trembling and that shamed me. Shame impelled me through the door.

I put the achti down near T'Gatoi and saw that Lomas was unconscious again. She, Lomas, and I were alone in the room—my mother and sisters probably sent out so they would not have to watch. I envied them.

But my mother came back into the room as T'Gatoi seized the achti. Ignoring the knife I offered her, she extended claws from several of her limbs and slit the achti from throat to anus. She looked at me, her yellow eyes intent. "Hold this man's shoulders, Gan."

I stared at Lomas in panic, realizing that I did not want to touch him, let alone hold him. This would not be like shooting an animal. Not as quick, not as merciful, and, I hoped, not as final, but there was nothing I wanted less than to be part of it.

My mother came forward. "Gan, you hold his right side," she said. "I'll hold his left." And if he came to, he would throw her off without realizing he had done it. She was a tiny woman. She often wondered aloud how she had produced, as she said, such "huge" children.

"Never mind," I told her, taking the man's shoulders. "I'll do it." She hovered nearby.

"Don't worry," I said. "I won't shame you. You don't have to stay and watch."

She looked at me uncertainly, then touched my face in a rare caress. Finally, she went back to her bedroom.

T'Gatoi lowered her head in relief. "Thank you, Gan," she said with courtesy more Terran than Tlic. "That one . . . she is always finding new ways for me to make her suffer."

Lomas began to groan and make choked sounds. I had hoped he would stay unconscious. T'Gatoi put her face near his so that he focused on her.

"I've stung you as much as I dare for now," she told him. "When this is over, I'll sting you to sleep and you won't hurt anymore."

"Please," the man begged. "Wait . . ."

"There's no more time, Bram. I'll sting you as soon as it's over. When T'Khotgif arrives she'll give you eggs to help you heal. It will be over soon."

"T'Khotgif!" the man shouted, straining against my hands.

"Soon, Bram." T'Gatoi glanced at me, then placed a claw against his abdomen slightly to the right of the middle, just below the left rib. There was movement on the right side—tiny, seemingly random pulsations moving his brown flesh, creating a concavity here, a convexity there, over and over until I could see the rhythm of it and knew where the next pulse would be.

Lomas's entire body stiffened under T'Gatoi's claw, though she merely rested it against him as she wound the rear section of her body around his legs. He might break my grip, but he would not break hers. He wept helplessly as she used his pants to tie his hands, then pushed his hands above his head so that I could kneel on the cloth between them and pin them in place. She rolled up his shirt and gave it to him to bite down on.

And she opened him.

His body convulsed with the first cut. He almost tore himself away from me. The sound he made . . . I had never heard such sounds come from anything human. T'Gatoi seemed to pay no attention as she lengthened and deepened the cut, now and then pausing to lick away blood. His blood vessels contracted, reacting to the chemistry of her saliva, and the bleeding showed.

I felt as though I were helping her torture him, helping her consume him. I knew I would vomit soon, didn't know why I hadn't already. I couldn't possibly last until she was finished.

She found the first grub. It was fat and deep red with his blood—both inside and out. It had already eaten its own egg case but apparently had not yet begun to eat its host. At this stage, it would eat any flesh except its mother's. Let alone, it would have gone on excreting the poisons that had both sickened and alerted Lomas. Eventually it would have begun to eat. By the time it ate its way out of Lomas's flesh, Lomas would be dead or dying—and unable to take revenge on the thing that was killing him. There was always a grace period between the time the host sickened and the time the grubs began to eat him.

T'Gatoi picked up the writhing grub carefully and looked at it, somehow ignoring the terrible groans of the man.

Abruptly, the man lost consciousness.

"Good," T'Gatoi looked down at him. "I wish you Terrans could do that at will." She felt nothing. And the thing she held . . .

It was limbless and boneless at this stage, perhaps fifteen centimeters long and two thick, blind and slimy with blood. It was like a large worm. T'Gatoi put it into the belly of the achti, and it began at once to burrow. It would stay there and eat as long as there was anything to eat.

Probing through Lomas's flesh, she found two more, one of them smaller and more vigorous. "A male!" she said happily. He would be dead before I would. He would be through his metamorphosis and screwing everything that would hold still before his sisters even had limbs. He was the only one to make a serious effort to bite T'Gatoi as she placed him in the achti.

Paler worms oozed to visibility in Lomas's flesh. I closed my eyes. It was worse than finding something dead, rotting, and filled with tiny animal grubs. And it was far worse than any drawing or diagram.

"Ah, there are more," T'Gatoi said, plucking out two long, thick grubs. You may have to kill another animal, Gan. Everything lives inside you Terrans."

I had been told all my life that this was a good and necessary thing Tlic and Terran did together—a kind of birth. I had believed it until now. I knew birth was painful and bloody, no matter what. But this was something else, something worse. And I wasn't ready to see it. Maybe I never would be. Yet I couldn't not see it. Closing my eyes didn't help.

T'Gatoi found a grub still eating its egg case. The remains of the case were still wired into a blood vessel by their own little tube or hook or whatever. That was the way the grubs were anchored and the way they fed. They took only blood until they were ready to emerge. Then they ate their stretched, elastic egg cases. Then they ate their hosts.

T'Gatoi bit away the egg case, licked away the blood. Did she like the taste? Did childhood habits die hard—or not die at all?

The whole procedure was wrong, alien. I wouldn't have thought anything about her could seem alien to me.

"One more, I think," she said. "Perhaps two. A good family. In a host animal these days, we would be happy to find one or two alive." She glanced at me. "Go outside, Gan, and empty your stomach. Go now while the man is unconscious."

I staggered out, barely made it. Beneath the tree just beyond the front door, I vomited until there was nothing left to bring up. Finally, I stood shaking, tears streaming down my face. I did not know why I was crying, but I could not stop. I went further from the house to avoid being seen. Every time I closed my eyes I saw red worms crawling over redder human flesh.

There was a car coming toward the house. Since Terrans were forbidden motorized vehicles except for certain farm equipment, I knew this must be Lomas's Tlic with Qui and perhaps a Terran doctor. I wiped my face on my shirt, struggled for control.

"Gan," Qui called as the car stopped. "What happened?" He crawled out of the low, round, Tlic-convenient car door. Another Terran crawled out the other side and went into the house without speaking to me. The doctor. With his help and a few eggs, Lomas might make it.

"T'Khotgif Teh?" I said.

The Tlic driver surged out of her car, reared up half her length before me. She was paler and smaller than T'Gatoi—probably born from the body of an animal. Tlic from Terran bodies were always larger as well as more numerous.

"Six young," I told her. "Maybe seven, all alive. At least one male."

"Lomas?" she said harshly. I liked her for the question and the concern in her voice when she asked it. The last coherent thing he had said was her name.

"He's alive," I said.

She surged away to the house without another word.

"She's been sick," my brother said, watching her go. "When I called, I could hear people telling her she wasn't well enough to go out even for this."

I said nothing. I had extended courtesy to the Tlic. Now I didn't want to talk to anyone. I hoped he would go in—out of curiosity if nothing else.

"Finally found out more than you wanted to know, eh?"

I looked at him.

"Don't give me one of *her* looks," he said. "You're not her. You're just her property."

One of her looks. Had I picked up even an ability to imitate her expressions?

"What'd you do, puke?" He sniffed the air. "So now you know what you're in for."

I walked away from him. He and I had been close when we were kids. He would let me follow him around when I was home, and sometimes T'Gatoi would let me bring him along when she took me into the city. But something had happened when he reached adolescence. I never knew what. He began keeping out of T'Gatoi's way. Then he began running away—until he realized there was no "away." Not in the Preserve. Certainly not outside. After that he concentrated on getting his share of every egg that came into the house and on looking out for me in a way that made me all but hate him—a way that clearly said, as long as I was all right, he was safe from the Tlic.

"How was it, really?" he demanded, following me.

"I killed an achti. The young ate it."

"You didn't run out of the house and puke because they ate an achti."

"I had . . . never seen a person cut open before." That was true, and enough for him to know. I couldn't talk about the other. Not with him.

"Oh," he said. He glanced at me as though he wanted to say more, but he kept quiet.

We walked, not really headed anywhere. Toward the back, toward the cages, toward the fields.

"Did he say anything?" Qui asked. "Lomas, I mean."

Who else would he mean? "He said 'T'Khotgif.'"

Qui shuddered. "If she had done that to me, she'd be the last person I'd call for."

"You'd call for her. Her sting would ease your pain without killing the grubs in you."

"You think I'd care if they died?"

No. Of course he wouldn't. Would I?

"Shit!" He drew a deep breath. "I've seen what they do. You think this thing with Lomas was bad? It was nothing."

I didn't argue. He didn't know what he was talking about.

"I saw them eat a man," he said.

I turned to face him. "You're lying!"

"*I saw them eat a man.*" He paused. "It was when I was little. I had been to the Hartmund house and I was on my way home. Halfway here, I saw a man and a Tlic and the man was N'Tlic. The ground was hilly. I was able to hide from them and watch. The Tlic wouldn't open the man because she had nothing to feed the grubs. The man couldn't go any further and there were no houses around. He was in so much pain, he told her to kill him. He begged her to kill him. Finally, she did. She cut his throat. One swipe of one claw. I saw the grubs eat their way out, then burrow in again, still eating."

His words made me see Lomas's flesh again, parasitized, crawling. "Why didn't you tell me that?" I whispered.

He looked startled as though he'd forgotten I was listening. "I don't know."

"You started to run away not long after that, didn't you?"

"Yeah. Stupid. Running inside the Preserve. Running in a cage."

I shook my head, said what I should have said to him long ago. "She wouldn't take you, Qui. You don't have to worry."

"She would . . . if anything happened to you."

"No. She'd take Xuan Hoa. Hoa . . . wants it." She wouldn't if she had stayed to watch Lomas.

"They don't take women," he said with contempt.

"They do sometimes." I glanced at him. "Actually, they prefer women. You should be around them when they talk among themselves. They say women have more body fat to protect the grubs. But they usually take men to leave the women free to bear their own young."

"To provide the next generation of host animals," he said, switching from contempt to bitterness.

"It's more than that!" I countered. Was it?

"If it were going to happen to me, I'd want to believe it was more, too."

"It *is* more!" I felt like a kid. Stupid argument.

"Did you think so while T'Gatoi was picking worms out of that guy's guts?"

"It's not supposed to happen that way."

"Sure it is. You weren't supposed to see it, that's all. And his Tlic was supposed to do it. She could sting him unconscious and the operation wouldn't have been as painful. But she'd still open him, pick out the grubs, and if she missed even one, it would poison him and eat him from the inside out."

There was actually a time when my mother told me to show respect for Qui because he was my older brother. I walked away, hating him. In his way, he was gloating. He was safe and I wasn't. I could have hit him, but I didn't think I would be able to stand it when he refused to hit back, when he looked at me with contempt and pity.

He wouldn't let me get away. Longer legged, he swung ahead of me and made me feel as though I were following him.

"I'm sorry," he said.

I strode on, sick and furious.

"Look, it probably won't be that bad with you. T'Gatoi likes you. She'll be careful."

I turned back toward the house, almost running from him.

"Has she done it to you yet?" he asked, keeping up easily. "I mean, you're about the right age for implantation. Has she—"

I hit him. I didn't know I was going to do it, but I think I meant to kill him. If he hadn't been bigger and stronger, I think I would have.

He tried to hold me off, but in the end, had to defend himself. He only hit me a couple of times. That was plenty. I don't remember going down, but when I came to, he was gone. It was worth the pain to be rid of him.

I got up and walked slowly toward the house. The back was dark. No one was in the kitchen. My mother and sisters were sleeping in their bedrooms—or pretending to.

Once I was in the kitchen, I could hear voices—Tlic and Terran from the next room. I couldn't make out what they were saying—didn't want to make it out.

I sat down at my mother's table, waiting for quiet. The table was smooth and worn, heavy and well crafted. My father had made it for her just before he died. I remembered hanging around underfoot when he built it. He didn't mind. Now I sat leaning on it, missing him. I could have talked to him. He had done it three times in his long life. Three clutches of eggs, three times being opened up and sewed up. How had he done it? How did anyone do it?

I got up, took the rifle from its hiding place, and sat down again with it. It needed cleaning, oiling.

All I did was load it.

"Gan?"

She made a lot of little clicking sounds when she walked on bare floor, each limb clicking in succession as it touched down. Waves of little clicks.

She came to the table, raised the front half of her body above it, and surged onto it. Sometimes she moved so smoothly she seemed to flow like water itself. She coiled herself into a small hill in the middle of the table and looked at me.

"That was bad," she said softly. "You should not have seen it. It need not be that way."

"I know."

"T'Khotgif—Ch'Khotgif now—she will die of her disease. She will not live to raise her children. But her sister will provide for them, and for Bram Lomas." Sterile sister. One fertile female in every lot. One to keep the family going. That sister owed Lomas more than she could ever repay.

"He'll live then?"

"Yes."

"I wonder if he would do it again."

"No one would ask him to do that again."

I looked into the yellow eyes, wondering how much I saw and understood there, and how much I only imagined. "No one ever asks us," I said. "You never asked me."

She moved her head slightly. "What's the matter with your face?"

"Nothing. Nothing important." Human eyes probably wouldn't have noticed the swelling in the darkness. The only light was from one of the moons, shining through a window across the room.

"Did you use the rifle to shoot the achti?"

"Yes."

"And do you mean to use it to shoot me?"

I stared at her, outlined in the moonlight—coiled, graceful body. "What does Terran blood taste like to you?"

She said nothing.

"What are you?" I whispered. "What are we to you?"

She lay still, rested her head on her topmost coil. "You know me as no other does," she said softly. "You must decide."

"That's what happened to my face," I told her.

"What?"

"Qui goaded me into deciding to do something. It didn't turn out very well." I moved the gun slightly, brought the barrel up diagonally under my own chin. "At least it was a decision I made."

"As this will be."

"Ask me, Gatoi."

"For my children's lives?"

She would say something like that. She knew how to manipulate people, Terran and Tlic. But not this time.

"I don't want to be a host animal," I said. "Not even yours."

It took her a long time to answer. "We use almost no host animals these days," she said. "You know that."

"You use us."

"We do. We wait long years for you and teach you and join our families to yours." She moved restlessly. "You know you aren't animals to us."

I stared at her, saying nothing.

"The animals we once used began killing most of our eggs after implantation long before your ancestors arrived," she said softly. "You know these things, Gan. Because your people arrived, we are relearning what it means to be a healthy, thriving people. And your ancestors, fleeing from their home-world, from their own kind who would have killed or enslaved them—they survived because of us. We saw them as people and gave them the Preserve when they still tried to kill us as worms."

At the word "worms," I jumped. I couldn't help it, and she couldn't help noticing it.

"I see," she said quietly. "Would you really rather die than bear my young, Gan?"

I didn't answer.

"Shall I go to Xuan Hoa?"

"Yes!" Hoa wanted it. Let her have it. She hadn't had to watch Lomas. She'd be proud. . . . Not terrified.

T'Gatoi flowed off the table onto the floor, startling me almost too much.

"I'll sleep in Hoa's room tonight," she said. "And sometime tonight or in the morning, I'll tell her."

This was going too fast. My sister Hoa had had almost as much to do with raising me as my mother. I was still close to her—not like Qui. She could want T'Gatoi and still love me.

"Wait! Gatoi!"

She looked back, then raised nearly half her length off the floor and turned to face me. "These are adult things, Gan. This is my life, my family!"

"But she's . . . my sister."

"I have done what you demanded. I have asked you!"

"But—"

"It will be easier for Hoa. She has always expected to carry other lives inside her."

Human lives. Human young who should someday drink at her breasts, not at her veins.

I shook my head. "Don't do it to her, Gatoi." I was not Qui. It seemed I could become him, though, with no effort at all. I could make Xuan Hoa my shield. Would it be easier to know that red worms were growing in her flesh instead of mine?

"Don't do it to Hoa," I repeated.

She stared at me, utterly still.

I looked away, then back at her. "Do it to me."

I lowered the gun from my throat and she leaned forward to take it.

"No," I told her.

"It's the law," she said.

"Leave it for the family. One of them might use it to save my life someday."

She grasped the rifle barrel, but I wouldn't let go. I was pulled into a standing position over her.

"Leave it here!" I repeated. "If we're not your animals, if these are adult things, accept the risk. There is risk, Gatoi, in dealing with a partner."

It was clearly hard for her to let go of the rifle. A shudder went through her and she made a hissing sound of distress. It occurred to me that she was afraid. She was old enough to have seen what guns could do to people. Now her young and this gun would be together in the same house. She did not know about the other guns. In this dispute, they did not matter.

"I will implant the first egg tonight," she said as I put the gun away. "Do you hear, Gan?"

Why else had I been given a whole egg to eat while the rest of the family was left to share one? Why else had my mother kept looking at me as though I were going away from her, going where she could not follow? Did T'Gatoi imagine I hadn't known?

"I hear."

"Now!" I let her push me out of the kitchen, then walked ahead of her toward my bedroom. The sudden urgency in her voice sounded real. "You would have done it to Hoa tonight!" I accused.

"I must do it to someone tonight."

I stopped in spite of her urgency and stood in her way. "Don't you care who?"

She flowed around me and into my bedroom. I found her waiting on the couch we shared. There was nothing in Hoa's room that she could have used. She would have done it to Hoa on the floor. The thought of her doing it to Hoa at all disturbed me in a different way now, and I was suddenly angry.

Yet I undressed and lay down beside her. I knew what to do, what to expect. I had been told all my life. I felt the familiar sting, narcotic, mildly pleasant. Then the blind probing of her ovipositor. The puncture was painless, easy. So easy going in. She undulated slowly against me, her muscles forcing the egg from her body into mine. I held on to a pair of her limbs until I remembered Lomas holding her that way. Then I let go, moved inadvertently, and hurt her. She gave a low cry of pain and I expected to be caged at once within her limbs. When I wasn't, I held on to her again, feeling oddly ashamed.

"I'm sorry," I whispered.

She rubbed my shoulders with four of her limbs.

"Do you care?" I asked. "Do you care that it's me?"

She did not answer for some time. Finally, "You were the one making the choices tonight, Gan. I made mine long ago."

"Would you have gone to Hoa?"

"Yes. How could I put my children into the care of one who hates them?"

"It wasn't . . . hate."

"I know what it was."

"I was afraid."

Silence.

"I still am." I could admit it to her here, now.

"But you came to me . . . to save Hoa."

"Yes." I leaned my forehead against her. She was cool velvet, deceptively soft. "And to keep you for myself," I said. It was so. I didn't understand it, but it was so.

She made a soft hum of contentment. "I couldn't believe I had made such a mistake with you," she said. "I chose you. I believed you had grown to choose me."

"I had, but . . ."

"Lomas."

"Yes."

"I had never known a Terran to see a birth and take it well. Qui has seen one, hasn't he?"

"Yes."

"Terrans should be protected from seeing."

I didn't like the sound of that—and I doubted that it was possible. "Not protected," I said. "Shown. Shown when we're young kids, and shown more than once. Gatoi, no Terran ever sees a birth that goes right. All we see is N'Tlic—pain and terror and maybe death."

She looked down at me. "It is a private thing. It has always been a private thing."

Her tone kept me from insisting—that and the knowledge that if she changed her mind, I might be the first public example. But I had planted the thought in her mind. Chances were it would grow, and eventually she would experiment.

"You won't see it again," she said. "I don't want you thinking any more about shooting me."

The small amount of fluid that came into me with her egg relaxed me as completely as a sterile egg would have, so that I could remember the rifle in my hands and my feelings of fear and revulsion, anger and despair. I could remember the feelings without reviving them. I could talk about them.

"I wouldn't have shot you," I said. "Not you." She had been taken from my father's flesh when he was my age.

"You could have," she insisted.

"Not you." She stood between us and her own people, protecting, interweaving.

"Would you have destroyed yourself?"

I moved carefully, uncomfortable. "I could have done that. I nearly did. That's Qui's 'away.' I wonder if he knows."

"What?"

I did not answer.

"You will live now."

"Yes." *Take care of her,* my mother used to say. Yes.

"I'm healthy and young," she said. "I won't leave you as Lomas was left—alone, N'Tlic. I'll take care of you."

Speech Sounds

There was trouble aboard the Washington Boulevard bus. Rye had expected trouble sooner or later in her journey. She had put off going until loneliness and hopelessness drove her out. She believed she might have one group of relatives left alive—a brother and his two children twenty miles away in Pasadena. That was a day's journey one-way, if she were lucky. The unexpected arrival of the bus as she left her Virginia Road home had seemed to be a piece of luck—until the trouble began.

Two young men were involved in a disagreement of some kind, or, more likely, a misunderstanding. They stood in the aisle, grunting and gesturing at each other, each in his own uncertain T stance as the bus lurched over the potholes. The driver seemed to be putting some effort into keeping them off balance. Still, their gestures stopped just short of contact—mock punches, hand games of intimidation to replace lost curses.

People watched the pair, then looked at one another and made small anxious sounds. Two children whimpered.

Rye sat a few feet behind the disputants and across from the back door. She watched the two carefully, knowing the fight would begin when someone's nerve broke or someone's hand slipped or someone came to the end of his limited ability to communicate. These things could happen anytime.

One of them happened as the bus hit an especially large pothole and one man, tall, thin, and sneering, was thrown into his shorter opponent.

Instantly, the shorter man drove his left fist into the disintegrating sneer. He hammered his larger opponent as though he neither had nor needed any weapon other than his left fist. He hit quickly enough, hard enough to batter his opponent down before the taller man could regain his balance or hit back even once.

People screamed or squawked in fear. Those nearby scrambled to get out of the way. Three more young men roared in excitement and gestured wildly. Then, somehow, a second dispute broke out between two of these three—probably because one inadvertently touched or hit the other.

As the second fight scattered frightened passengers, a woman shook the driver's shoulder and grunted as she gestured toward the fighting.

The driver grunted back through bared teeth. Frightened, the woman drew away.

Rye, knowing the methods of bus drivers, braced herself and held on to the crossbar of the seat in front of her. When the driver hit the brakes, she was ready and the combatants were not. They fell over seats and onto screaming passengers, creating even more confusion. At least one more fight started.

The instant the bus came to a full stop, Rye was on her feet, pushing the back door. At the second push, it opened and she jumped out, holding her pack in one arm. Several other passengers followed, but some stayed on the bus. Buses were so rare and irregular now, people rode when they could, no matter what. There might not be another bus today—or tomorrow. People started walking, and if they saw a bus they flagged it down. People making intercity trips like Rye's from Los Angeles to Pasadena made plans to camp out, or risked seeking shelter with locals who might rob or murder them.

The bus did not move, but Rye moved away from it. She intended to wait until the trouble was over and get on again, but if there was shooting, she wanted the protection of a tree. Thus, she was near the curb when a battered blue Ford on the other side of the street made a U-turn and pulled up in front of the bus. Cars were rare these days—as rare as a severe shortage of fuel and of relatively unimpaired mechanics could make them. Cars that still ran were as likely to be used as weapons as they were to serve as transportation. Thus, when the driver of the Ford beckoned to Rye, she moved away warily. The driver got out—a big man, young, neatly bearded with dark, thick hair. He wore a long overcoat and a look of wariness that matched Rye's. She stood several feet from him, waiting to see what he would do. He looked at the bus, now rocking with the combat inside, then at the small cluster of passengers who had gotten off. Finally he looked at Rye again.

She returned his gaze, very much aware of the old forty-five automatic her jacket concealed. She watched his hands.

He pointed with his left hand toward the bus. The dark-tinted windows prevented him from seeing what was happening inside.

His use of the left hand interested Rye more than his obvious question. Left-handed people tended to be less impaired, more reasonable and comprehending, less driven by frustration, confusion, and anger.

She imitated his gesture, pointing toward the bus with her own left hand, then punching the air with both fists.

The man took off his coat revealing a Los Angeles Police Department uniform complete with baton and service revolver.

Rye took another step back from him. There was no more LAPD, no more *any* large organization, governmental or private. There were neighborhood patrols and armed individuals. That was all.

The man took something from his coat pocket, then threw the coat into the car. Then he gestured Rye back, back toward the rear of the bus. He had something made of plastic in his hand. Rye did not understand what he wanted until he went to the rear door of the bus and beckoned her to stand there. She obeyed mainly out of curiosity. Cop or not, maybe he could do something to stop the stupid fighting.

He walked around the front of the bus, to the street side where the driver's window was open. There, she thought she saw him throw something into the bus. She was still trying to peer through the tinted glass when people began stumbling out the rear door, choking and weeping. Gas.

Rye caught an old woman who would have fallen, lifted two little children down when they were in danger of being knocked down and trampled. She could see the bearded man helping people at the front door. She caught a thin old man shoved out by one of the combatants. Staggered by the old man's weight, she was barely able to get out of the way as the last of the young men pushed his way out. This one, bleeding from nose and mouth, stumbled into another, and they grappled blindly, still sobbing from the gas.

The bearded man helped the bus driver out through the front door, though the driver did not seem to appreciate his help. For a moment, Rye thought there would be another fight. The bearded man stepped back and watched the driver gesture threateningly, watched him shout in wordless anger.

The bearded man stood still, made no sound, refused to respond to clearly obscene gestures. The least impaired people tended to do this—stand back unless they were physically threatened and let those with less control scream and jump around. It was as though they felt it beneath them to be as touchy as the less comprehending. This was an attitude of superiority, and that was the way people like the bus driver perceived it. Such "superiority" was frequently punished by beatings, even by death. Rye had had close calls of her own. As a result, she never went unarmed. And in this world where the only likely common language was body language, being armed was often enough. She had rarely had to draw her gun or even display it.

The bearded man's revolver was on constant display. Apparently that was enough for the bus driver. The driver spat in disgust, glared at the bearded man for a moment longer, then strode back to his gas-filled bus. He stared at it for a moment, clearly wanting to get in, but the gas was still too strong. Of the windows, only his tiny driver's window actually opened. The front door was open, but the rear door would not stay open unless someone held it. Of course, the air conditioning had failed long ago. The bus would take some time to clear. It was the driver's property, his livelihood. He had pasted old magazine pictures of items he would accept as fare on its sides. Then he would use what he collected to feed his family or to trade. If his bus did not run, he did not eat. On the other hand, if the inside of his bus was torn apart by senseless fighting, he would not eat very well either. He was apparently unable to perceive this. All he could see was that it would be some time before he could use his bus again. He shook his fist at the bearded man and shouted. There seemed to be words in his shout, but Rye could not understand them. She did not know whether this was his fault or hers. She had heard so little coherent human speech for the past three years, she was no longer certain how well she recognized it, no longer certain of the degree of her own impairment.

The bearded man sighed. He glanced toward his car, then beckoned to Rye. He was ready to leave, but he wanted something from her first. No. No, he wanted her to leave with him. Risk getting into his car when, in spite of his uniform, law and order were nothing—not even words any longer.

She shook her head in a universally understood negative, but the man continued to beckon.

She waved him away. He was doing what the less impaired rarely did—drawing potentially negative attention to another of his kind. People from the bus had begun to look at her.

One of the men who had been fighting tapped another on the arm, then pointed from the bearded man to Rye, and finally held up the first two fingers of his right hand as though giving two-thirds of a Boy Scout salute. The gesture was very quick, its meaning obvious even at a distance. She had been grouped with the bearded man. Now what?

The man who had made the gesture started toward her.

She had no idea what he intended, but she stood her ground. The man was half a foot taller than she was and perhaps ten years younger. She did not imagine she could outrun him. Nor did she expect anyone to help her if she needed help. The people around her were all strangers.

She gestured once—a clear indication to the man to stop. She did not intend to repeat the gesture. Fortunately, the man obeyed. He gestured obscenely and several other men laughed. Loss of verbal language had spawned a whole new set of obscene gestures. The man, with stark simplicity, had accused her of sex with the bearded man and had suggested she accommodate the other men present— beginning with him.

Rye watched him wearily. People might very well stand by and watch if he tried to rape her. They would also stand and watch her shoot him. Would he push things that far?

He did not. After a series of obscene gestures that brought him no closer to her, he turned contemptuously and walked away.

And the bearded man still waited. He had removed his service revolver, hol- ster and all. He beckoned again, both hands empty. No doubt his gun was in the car and within easy reach, but his taking it off impressed her. Maybe he was all right. Maybe he was just alone. She had been alone herself for three years. The illness had stripped her, killing her children one by one, killing her husband, her sister, her parents. . . .

The illness, if it was an illness, had cut even the living off from one another. As it swept over the country, people hardly had time to lay blame on the Soviets (though they were falling silent along with the rest of the world), on a new virus, a new pollutant, radiation, divine retribution. . . . The illness was stroke-swift in the way it cut people down and strokelike in some of its effects. But it was highly specific. Language was always lost or severely impaired. It was never regained. Often there was also paralysis, intellectual impairment, death.

Rye walked toward the bearded man, ignoring the whistling and applauding of two of the young men and their thumbs-up signs to the bearded man. If he had smiled at them or acknowledged them in any way, she would almost cer- tainly have changed her mind. If she had let herself think of the possible deadly consequences of getting into a stranger's car, she would have changed her mind. Instead, she thought of the man who lived across the street from her. He rarely washed since his bout with the illness. And he had gotten into the habit of uri- nating wherever he happened to be. He had two women already—one tending each of his large gardens. They put up with him in exchange for his protection. He had made it clear that he wanted Rye to become his third woman.

She got into the car and the bearded man shut the door. She watched as he walked around to the driver's door—watched for his sake because his gun was on the seat beside her. And the bus driver and a pair of young men had come a few steps closer. They did nothing, though, until the bearded man was in the car. Then one of them threw a rock. Others followed his example, and as the car drove away, several rocks bounced off harmlessly.

When the bus was some distance behind them, Rye wiped sweat from her forehead and longed to relax. The bus would have taken her more than halfway to Pasadena. She would have had only ten miles to walk. She wondered how far she would have to walk now—and wondered if walking a long distance would be her only problem.

At Figuroa and Washington where the bus normally made a left turn, the bearded man stopped, looked at her, and indicated that she should choose a direction. When she directed him left and he actually turned left, she began to relax. If he was willing to go where she directed, perhaps he was safe.

As they passed blocks of burned, abandoned buildings, empty lots, and wrecked or stripped cars, he slipped a gold chain over his head and handed it to her. The pendant attached to it was a smooth, glassy, black rock. Obsidian. His name might be Rock or Peter or Black, but she decided to think of him as Obsidian. Even her sometimes useless memory would retain a name like Obsidian.

She handed him her own name symbol—a pin in the shape of a large golden stalk of wheat. She had bought it long before the illness and the silence began. Now she wore it, thinking it was as close as she was likely to come to Rye. People like Obsidian who had not known her before probably thought of her as Wheat. Not that it mattered. She would never hear her name spoken again.

Obsidian handed her pin back to her. He caught her hand as she reached for it and rubbed his thumb over her calluses.

He stopped at First Street and asked which way again. Then, after turning right as she had indicated, he parked near the Music Center. There, he took a folded paper from the dashboard and unfolded it. Rye recognized it as a street map, though the writing on it meant nothing to her. He flattened the map, took her hand again, and put her index finger on one spot. He touched her, touched himself, pointed toward the floor. In effect, "We are here." She knew he wanted to know where she was going. She wanted to tell him, but she shook her head sadly. She had lost reading and writing. That was her most serious impairment and her most painful. She had taught history at UCLA. She had done freelance writing. Now she could not even read her own manuscripts. She had a houseful of books that she could neither read nor bring herself to use as fuel. And she had a memory that would not bring back to her much of what she had read before.

She stared at the map, trying to calculate. She had been born in Pasadena, had lived for fifteen years in Los Angeles. Now she was near L.A. Civic Center. She knew the relative positions of the two cities, knew streets, directions, even knew to stay away from freeways, which might be blocked by wrecked cars and destroyed overpasses. She ought to know how to point out Pasadena even though she could not recognize the word.

Hesitantly, she placed her hand over a pale orange patch in the upper right corner of the map. That should be right. Pasadena.

Obsidian lifted her hand and looked under it, then folded the map and put it back on the dashboard. He could read, she realized belatedly. He could probably write, too. Abruptly, she hated him—deep, bitter hatred. What did literacy mean to him—a grown man who played cops and robbers? But he was literate and she was not. She never would be. She felt sick to her stomach with hatred, frustration, and jealousy. And only a few inches from her hand was a loaded gun.

She held herself still, staring at him, almost seeing his blood. But her rage crested and ebbed and she did nothing.

Obsidian reached for her hand with hesitant familiarity. She looked at him. Her face had already revealed too much. No person still living in what was left of human society could fail to recognize that expression, that jealousy.

She closed her eyes wearily, drew a deep breath. She had experienced longing for the past, hatred of the present, growing hopelessness, purposelessness, but she had never experienced such a powerful urge to kill another person. She had left her home, finally, because she had come near to killing herself. She had found no reason to stay alive. Perhaps that was why she had gotten into Obsidian's car. She had never before done such a thing.

He touched her mouth and made chatter motions with thumb and fingers. Could she speak?

She nodded and watched his milder envy come and go. Now both had admitted what it was not safe to admit, and there had been no violence. He tapped his mouth and forehead and shook his head. He did not speak or comprehend spoken language. The illness had played with them, taking away, she suspected, what each valued most.

She plucked at his sleeve, wondering why he had decided on his own to keep the LAPD alive with what he had left. He was sane enough otherwise. Why wasn't he at home raising corn, rabbits, and children? But she did not know how to ask. Then he put his hand on her thigh and she had another question to deal with.

She shook her head. Disease, pregnancy, helpless, solitary agony . . . no.

He massaged her thigh gently and smiled in obvious disbelief.

No one had touched her for three years. She had not wanted anyone to touch her. What kind of world was this to chance bringing a child into even if the father were willing to stay and help raise it? It was too bad, though. Obsidian could not know how attractive he was to her—young, probably younger than she was, clean, asking for what he wanted rather than demanding it. But none of that mattered. What were a few moments of pleasure measured against a lifetime of consequences?

He pulled her closer to him and for a moment she let herself enjoy the closeness. He smelled good—male and good. She pulled away reluctantly.

He sighed, reached toward the glove compartment. She stiffened, not knowing what to expect, but all he took out was a small box. The writing on it meant nothing to her. She did not understand until he broke the seal, opened the box, and took out a condom. He looked at her, and she first looked away in surprise. Then she giggled. She could not remember when she had last giggled.

He grinned, gestured toward the backseat, and she laughed aloud. Even in her teens, she had disliked backseats of cars. But she looked around at the empty streets and ruined buildings, then she got out and into the backseat. He let her put the condom on him, then seemed surprised at her eagerness.

Sometime later, they sat together, covered by his coat, unwilling to become clothed near strangers again just yet. He made rock-the-baby gestures and looked questioningly at her.

She swallowed, shook her head. She did not know how to tell him her children were dead.

He took her hand and drew a cross in it with his index finger, then made his baby-rocking gesture again.

She nodded, held up three fingers, then turned away, trying to shut out a sudden flood of memories. She had told herself that the children growing up now were to be pitied. They would run through the downtown canyons with no real memory of what the buildings had been or even how they had come to be. Today's children gathered books as well as wood to be burned as fuel. They ran through the streets chasing one another and hooting like chimpanzees. They had no future. They were now all they would ever be.

He put his hand on her shoulder, and she turned suddenly, fumbling for his small box, then urging him to make love to her again. He could give her forgetfulness and pleasure. Until now, nothing had been able to do that. Until now, every day had brought her closer to the time when she would do what she had left home to avoid doing: putting her gun in her mouth and pulling the trigger.

She asked Obsidian if he would come home with her, stay with her.

He looked surprised and pleased once he understood. But he did not answer at once. Finally, he shook his head as she had feared he might. He was probably having too much fun playing cops and robbers and picking up women.

She dressed in silent disappointment, unable to feel any anger toward him. Perhaps he already had a wife and a home. That was likely. The illness had been harder on men than on women—had killed more men, had left male survivors more severely impaired. Men like Obsidian were rare. Women either settled for less or stayed alone. If they found an Obsidian, they did what they could to keep him. Rye suspected he had someone younger, prettier keeping him.

He touched her while she was strapping her gun on and asked with a complicated series of gestures whether it was loaded.

She nodded grimly.

He patted her arm.

She asked once more if he would come home with her, this time using a different series of gestures. He had seemed hesitant. Perhaps he could be courted.

He got out and into the front seat without responding.

She took her place in front again, watching him. Now he plucked at his uniform and looked at her. She thought she was being asked something but did not know what it was.

He took off his badge, tapped it with one finger, then tapped his chest. Of course.

She took the badge from his hand and pinned her wheat stalk to it. If playing cops and robbers was his only insanity, let him play. She would take him, uniform and all. It occurred to her that she might eventually lose him to someone he would meet as he had met her. But she would have him for a while.

He took the street map down again, tapped it, pointed vaguely northeast toward Pasadena, then looked at her.

She shrugged, tapped his shoulder, then her own, and held up her index and second fingers tight together, just to be sure.

He grasped the two fingers and nodded. He was with her.

She took the map from him and threw it onto the dashboard. She pointed back southwest—back toward home. Now she did not have to go to Pasadena. Now she could go on having a brother there and two nephews—three right-handed males. Now she did not have to find out for certain whether she was as alone as she feared. Now she was not alone.

Obsidian took Hill Street south, then Washington west, and she leaned back, wondering what it would be like to have someone again. With what she had scavenged, what she had preserved, and what she grew, there was easily enough food for them. There was certainly room enough in a four-bedroom house. He could move his possessions in. Best of all, the animal across the street would pull back and possibly not force her to kill him.

Obsidian had drawn her closer to him, and she had put her head on his shoulder when suddenly he braked hard, almost throwing her off the seat. Out of the corner of her eye, she saw that someone had run across the street in front of the car. One car on the street and someone had to run in front of it.

Straightening up, Rye saw that the runner was a woman, fleeing from an old frame house to a boarded-up storefront. She ran silently, but the man who followed her a moment later shouted what sounded like garbled words as he ran. He had something in his hand. Not a gun. A knife, perhaps.

The woman tried a door, found it locked, looked around desperately, finally snatched up a fragment of glass broken from the storefront window. With this she turned to face her pursuer. Rye thought she would be more likely to cut her own hand than to hurt anyone else with the glass.

Obsidian jumped from the car, shouting. It was the first time Rye had heard his voice—deep and hoarse from disuse. He made the same sound over and over the way some speechless people did, "Da, da, da!"

Rye got out of the car as Obsidian ran toward the couple. He had drawn his gun. Fearful, she drew her own and released the safety. She looked around to see who else might be attracted to the scene. She saw the man glance at Obsidian, then suddenly lunge at the woman. The woman jabbed his face with her glass, but he caught her arm and managed to stab her twice before Obsidian shot him.

The man doubled, then toppled, clutching his abdomen. Obsidian shouted, then gestured Rye over to help the woman.

Rye moved to the woman's side, remembering that she had little more than bandages and antiseptic in her pack. But the woman was beyond help. She had been stabbed with a long, slender boning knife.

She touched Obsidian to let him know the woman was dead. He had bent to check the wounded man who lay still and also seemed dead. But as Obsidian looked around to see what Rye wanted, the man opened his eyes. Face contorted, he seized Obsidian's just-holstered revolver and fired. The bullet caught Obsidian in the temple and he collapsed.

It happened just that simply, just that fast. An instant later, Rye shot the wounded man as he was turning the gun on her.

And Rye was alone—with three corpses.

She knelt beside Obsidian, dry-eyed, frowning, trying to understand why everything had suddenly changed. Obsidian was gone. He had died and left her—like everyone else.

Two very small children came out of the house from which the man and woman had run—a boy and girl perhaps three years old. Holding hands, they crossed the street toward Rye. They stared at her, then edged past her and went to the dead woman. The girl shook the woman's arm as though trying to wake her.

This was too much. Rye got up, feeling sick to her stomach with grief and anger. If the children began to cry, she thought she would vomit.

They were on their own, those two kids. They were old enough to scavenge. She did not need any more grief. She did not need a stranger's children who would grow up to be hairless chimps.

She went back to the car. She could drive home, at least. She remembered how to drive.

The thought that Obsidian should be buried occurred to her before she reached the car, and she did vomit.

She had found and lost the man so quickly. It was as though she had been snatched from comfort and security and given a sudden, inexplicable beating. Her head would not clear. She could not think.

Somehow, she made herself go back to him, look at him. She found herself on her knees beside him with no memory of having knelt. She stroked his face, his beard. One of the children made a noise and she looked at them, at the woman who was probably their mother. The children looked back at her, obviously frightened. Perhaps it was their fear that reached her finally.

She had been about to drive away and leave them. She had almost done it, almost left two toddlers to die. Surely there had been enough dying. She would have to take the children home with her. She would not be able to live with any other decision. She looked around for a place to bury three bodies. Or two. She wondered if the murderer were the children's father. Before the silence, the police had always said some of the most dangerous calls they went out on were domestic disturbance calls. Obsidian should have known that—not that the knowledge would have kept him in the car. It would not have held her back either. She could not have watched the woman murdered and done nothing.

She dragged Obsidian toward the car. She had nothing to dig with her, and no one to guard for her while she dug. Better to take the bodies with her and bury them next to her husband and her children. Obsidian would come home with her after all.

When she had gotten him onto the floor in the back, she returned for the woman. The little girl, thin, dirty, solemn, stood up and unknowingly gave Rye a gift. As Rye began to drag the woman by her arms, the little girl screamed, "No!"

Rye dropped the woman and stared at the girl.

"No!" the girl repeated. She came to stand beside the woman. "Go away!" she told Rye.

"Don't talk," the little boy said to her. There was no blurring or confusing of sounds. Both children had spoken and Rye had understood. The boy looked at the dead murderer and moved further from him. He took the girl's hand. "Be quiet," he whispered.

Fluent speech! Had the woman died because she could talk and had taught her children to talk? Had she been killed by a husband's festering anger or by a stranger's jealous rage? And the children . . . they must have been born after the silence. Had the disease run its course, then? Or were these children simply immune? Certainly they had had time to fall sick and silent. Rye's mind leaped ahead. What if children of three or fewer years were safe and able to learn language? What if all they needed were teachers? Teachers and protectors.

Rye glanced at the dead murderer. To her shame, she thought she could understand some of the passions that must have driven him, whomever he was. Anger, frustration, hopelessness, insane jealousy . . . how many more of him were there—people willing to destroy what they could not have?

Obsidian had been the protector, had chosen that role for who knew what reason. Perhaps putting on an obsolete uniform and patrolling the empty streets had been what he did instead of putting a gun into his mouth. And now that there was something worth protecting, he was gone.

She had been a teacher. A good one. She had been a protector, too, though only of herself. She had kept herself alive when she had no reason to live. If the illness let these children alone, she could keep them alive.

Somehow she lifted the dead woman into her arms and placed her on the backseat of the car. The children began to cry, but she knelt on the broken pavement and whispered to them, fearful of frightening them with the harshness of her long unused voice.

"It's all right," she told them. "You're going with us, too. Come on." She lifted them both, one in each arm. They were so light. Had they been getting enough to eat?

The boy covered her mouth with his hand, but she moved her face away. "It's all right for me to talk," she told him. "As long as no one's around, it's all right." She put the boy down on the front seat of the car and he moved over without being told to, to make room for the girl. When they were both in the car, Rye leaned against the window, looking at them, seeing that they were less afraid now, that they watched her with at least as much curiosity as fear.

"I'm Valerie Rye," she said, savoring the words. "It's all right for you to talk to me."

Bebe Moore Campbell (1950–)

Bebe Moore Campbell is one of the most versatile writers around today, having published works in three distinct genres—fiction, memoir, and sociological journalism. Though the styles of these three overlap, Campbell's skill is not to be taken for granted. Born in Philadelphia, Pennsylvania, she attended the University of Pittsburgh. After graduating, she worked as a public school teacher for six years, but it was writing that was to bring her great success. Campbell worked as a freelance writer, contributing over the years to pe-riodicals such as Ebony, Ms., New York Times Book Review, New York Times Magazine, Publisher's Weekly, *and* The Washington Post. *She was also a commentator for National Public Radio and has appeared on many television talk shows.*

In 1980, Campbell received a National Endowment for the Arts grant, and shortly after, her first book, Successful Women, Angry Men: Backlash in the Two-Career Mar-riage *was published by Random House. In this work, Campbell used the example of her own life, but also those of many other couples, as well as extensive research, to produce a text that reflects some of her bent as a journalist, but also exhibits her research and critical abilities. Interestingly, it is this critical skill that illuminates her second text, a memoir ti-tled* Sweet Summer: Growing Up With and Without My Dad, *published in 1989. Since this work, Campbell has published three successful novels:* Your Blues Ain't Like Mine *(1992),* Brothers and Sisters *(1994), and* Singing in the Comeback Choir *(1998).*

Campbell's Sweet Summer *is not a complete autobiography, for it does not aim to tell the entire narrative of her life. Instead, it focuses in on her life as a child of divorce, which resulted in her living during the school year with her mother in Philadelphia, and spend-ing her summers in North Carolina with her father. Because she hones in on a particular experience of her life, and even more so—she focuses on her relationship with her father—Campbell is able to write with clarity and expansion, with wit and deft. She was widely praised for her writing, but also for her choice to explore her relationship with her father; still today,* Sweet Summer *is regarded as her finest writing.*

Because of her skill in various forms of writing, Campbell writes a memoir that incor-porates gifts from other genres. For example, her memoir includes many novelistic sym-bols or constructs, such as the tension between North (Philadelphia) and South (North Carolina). Though these settings are accurate representations of the life she lived, it is also true that Campbell utilizes literary and historical aesthetics in how she remembers and memorializes these landscapes. Similarly, her interest in sociological issues, and particu-larly the relationships between men and women, further enhances her exploration of the group of women who are her Philadelphia community and the mostly male group that she interacts with in North Carolina.

It is in her use of these various elements from other genres that Campbell's gift as a storyteller becomes evident. She is a wonderful storyteller, with a keen sense of time and moment, opening with the reflective and potent statement "When my father died, old men went out of my life." The reader at this point is poised to hear her story, for she has situated herself as a reflective thinker, and an almost prophetic one at that. She handles this reflection well, writing in an easy style, using words such as "I suppose," switching to the more intimate "Daddy," and writing in fragments to achieve a rhythm that seems casual and easy, loving, but not careless.

Another of Campbell's fine achievement in this piece is how she incorporates events that are from different times: She writes about her father's death, his funeral, her dream of his interaction with her daughter, her memory of his response to being ill—all of which are different situations that she links via the idea of her father's impressiveness, of the great big heart he had, and how he moved her so. But Campbell's reflection is savvy and critical, not romantic even as it might be wistful: She remembers the pieces of him that bothered her, the concerns she had about his life, and her growing relationship with his aging body.

What most characterizes Campbell's memoir is her use of description—how she is able to capture images and personalities and actions in a phrase or series of phrases. The reader can hear her father's laugh, can see his friends, and because of Campbell's care in her writing, we can feel exactly why this man was so much a part of her sweet summer. We understand her pronounced opening statement, and her bold closing to the first chapter: that "as always, [her] life is framed by his absence."

Kevin Everod Quashie

Chapter 1

When My father died, old men went out of my life.

From the vantage point of my girlhood, he and his peers had always been old to me, even when they were not. In his last years, the reality of his graying head began to hit home. I no longer boogied the weekends away in smoke-clogged rooms that gyrated all night with Motown sounds, where I'd take a breather from the dancing by leaning up against the wall, sipping a sloe gin fizz and spewing out fire-laced rhetoric of "death to the pigs." I was a mature young wife, a mother even, three rungs from thirty, a home owner, a meal planner, who marched for an end to apartheid in front of the South African embassy only often enough to feel guilty. I made vague plans to care for him in his dotage. Care for him on a teacher's salary, in the middle of a marriage that was scratching against the blackboard with its fingernails, in a two-bedroom brick fixer-upper my husband, daughter and I had outgrown the moment we moved in. That was the plan.

When he died in 1977, I suppose, a theoretical weight was lifted, since Daddy was a paraplegic because of a car accident he'd had when I was ten months old. No doubt his senior-citizen years would have been expensive and exhausting for me. And then too, I had other potential dependents. I mused about the future, fantasized about my role as a nurturer of old people, feeling vaguely smug and settled, maybe a little bourgeois. . . .

When I thought about my father I realized that he had a strong will too, and maybe more reasons not to want to live to be older than Nana. You could see that will in the way he jutted out his chin, the quick way he moved and drove. He liked speed because it was powerful, as strong as he always wanted to be. I knew George Moore's mental powers would never be used to precipitate his leaving this earth any sooner than absolutely necessary. Right after the accident the doctors told him he wouldn't live out the year because of the damage that had been done to his kidneys. He made the decision right then. Put away the razor blade he'd been clutching and pressing to his throat when he saw his toes would never move again. Made a decision right then and there. Started drinking gallons of water a day. Doing his exercises. Praying. How he forced the sadness from his eyes I do not know. Only one time did I witness him mourning the life he might have had. It was a terrible moment, but a healing one. That split second taught me that the best part of my father, the jewel stuck deep inside his core, was determination. George Moore was about living life until it was gone, wrested from him, snatched out of his clenched fist. He would play out the hand that had been dealt. My potbellied daddy wouldn't roll off resolutely to some senior citizen's palace to sip tea and play canasta, and he sure as hell didn't know any old guy he'd want for a roommate. Unmarried men living together, unless they were in the Army or Navy or something, seemed weird to him. No, he'd see his old age, his infirmities as something quite naturally to be shared with his only child. He wouldn't want to be a burden; he'd pay his way, share his little Social Security check so he would have a legitimate gripe when there weren't any pork chops in the house. And he'd be very useful; all the Moore men, my father and my seven uncles, have always had a tendency toward workaholism. They get up early and get busy; that's in their blood. Daddy would fix all the broken radios, clocks and televisions in the house. He'd do the plumbing and put in new electrical outlets. And of course, Daddy would tend the garden, since he could make anything grow. And much as he loved children, I'd have had a super built-in baby-sitter. If there was no work, no ball game on television and he couldn't get a decent conversation going, he'd just leave, go for a ride or something. He had a car with hand controls for the accelerator and brakes. Icy streets wouldn't keep Daddy inside a house where there was nothing to do, nobody to chew the fat and trade stories with. And he wouldn't be rushing off to attend some important, purposeful meeting called by the NAACP, the Neighborhood Association, the Coalition of 100 Black Men, or even Omega Psi Phi fraternity, of which he was a very nonactive member. He'd left behind those kinds of gatherings in his other life, the one I knew nothing about, the one he titled "Before I got hurt." No, Daddy would go riding just to hang out. And not alone, either. At least that's what I thought on that day in Washington as the fragrant, moist air mixed in my hair, rendering my kitchen absolutely impassable to my wandering fingers.

I remembered the sweet North Carolina summers of my childhood, my father's snappy "C'mon, kiddo. Let's go for a ride," when life was boring sitting in Grandma Mary's house or the yard. There was a ritual my father had to endure before he and I could zoom away down the one-car-wide dirt lane that led to the larger tar road. He'd roll his wheelchair right up between his open car door and the driver's seat and hoist himself from his chair to the car seat with one powerful thrust of his body. Then he'd clutch his leg, which would invariably start twitching with involuntary muscle spasms. When the shaking stopped, he'd lean out of his car seat, snatch his chair closed, press his body into the steering wheel, pulling the back of his seat up so that he could lift his chair into the backseat of the car. This done, he'd take out a white handkerchief, wipe his drenched forehead and look over at me and grin. Then I'd hop into the seat next to his and we'd take off. In those days I was his partner, his roadie, his little minimama homegirl. In the summer he hardly went anywhere without me. And I believed, as I engaged in my humid, sun-porch reverie, my probing fingers struggling inside the tangle of my kitchen, that I would be all those things again, that when my father got old he would need me.

The thought of our living together for the first time since I was a child delighted me, since it was in such stark contrast to the female-centered home I'd grown up in after my parents separated and my mother and I moved from North Carolina to Nana's house in Philadelphia. Realistically, though, living with my father would present special challenges. There were, of course, the implications of his paralysis, and his lack of mobility was complicated by his size. There were over two hundred pounds of him sitting in that chair. He was the black man's Chief Ironside. Well, maybe Raymond Burr had a couple of pounds on him. He tried to play it off when I teased him about his gut. Daddy would pat his belly, grin and say, "The chippies' playground, baby girl." Still, Daddy would be no fun to heave up and down stairs or in and out of a bathtub, although periodically, when he set his mind on losing weight, my father dieted quite successfully and could knock off thirty or forty pounds. When he was on a diet, I don't care how many pork chops you floated under George Moore's nose, the boy wasn't eating. That kind of doggedness enabled him in his later years finally to cut loose the Winstons he had inhaled with passion when he was younger. When he set his mind on something, that was it. Nobody had more determination than Daddy. So maybe the weight wouldn't have been a problem. What would have irritated me, though, was his innate ability to run the helpless bit into the ground at times, at least with me. Maybe only with me.

The summer before he died I drove from D.C. to the outskirts of Richmond for a visit and stayed with him at the home where he boarded with an elderly widow named Mrs. Murphy. He had only recently begun working for the federal government in personnel. He was, in affirmative-action terms, a twofer: black and disabled. Finally he was beginning to make decent money. He was sick the day I came to see him, something that rarely happened to him. Aside from his useless legs, he was robust. He rarely even got so much as a cold, although, of course, from time to time he had to go into the McGuire VA Hospital for a stay to have his damaged kidneys checked out. The day I went to visit him he had the flu and was coughing like crazy, drinking water like a fiend, snorting, trying to let out his Big Daddy Jumbo Pasquotank Country farts on the sly and rattling on and on about the stock market, his latest in a long line of plans to become wealthy. To his dying day he never saw his becoming rich as something out of the realm of ordinary possibilities. His was the American dream: to work hard and have it pay off big. "Yeah, baby. Your ole daddy's gonna make us some money." He tossed off the titles of stocks and prices per share, totally losing me amid the names and numbers. Sensing my disinterest, he said disgustedly, "You ought to listen to this, girl. I'm telling you, we can make us some money." When my only response was to shrug my shoulders, Daddy shook his head. His mood turned bossy. "Bebe, go get Daddy some more cough syrup." "Bebe, go get Daddy a big ole glass of ice water." "Bebe, go empty this urine duct for your ole sick Daddy." Which was pushing it, because I hated rinsing out his urine ducts. And he knew it. But I did it that day, holding way out ahead of me the rubber duct that contained the acrid-smelling waste he could no longer control. I turned my head in the small, cramped bathroom that held his toothbrush at one end of the sink and Mrs. Murphy's teeth in a cup at the other, as I emptied the urine into the toilet, and again as I rinsed the containers out in the special buckets Mrs. Murphy kept right next to the small commode.

When I returned to his bedroom, Daddy was laid up in the bed like some imperial royal highness, flashing me a slightly wan but still very dazzling smile as I handed him his duct; I turned my head as he fiddled under the covers, attaching the thing to himself. The room needed ten shots of Air-Fresh. He cleared his throat when he finished. Then he grinned at me.

My daddy had a killer of a smile and I think he knew it. I know he knew it. His teeth were so white, so perfectly straight they were startling. Big, white, even teeth. Chiclets. And his grin was just a little crooked, and that's what made him such a charming smiler. On that particular day, I wasn't falling for his charm. "Don't ask me to do one more thing, old man," I said, as sourly as I could.

"BebebebebebeMoore," Daddy sang out, throwing his big, heavy arm around my shoulder when I stopped fussing. I was sitting on the side of his bed, one leg under me, the other leg swinging, my big toe just brushing the floor as I looked at a magazine, my hips against his very still legs. The air had returned to normal and I thought to myself, George Linwood Peter Moore, please do not funk up this room with another one of those jumbo farts. I looked up and he was smiling that killer smile. "Don't bother me, old man," I said.

What can I say? Daddy would have run my ass raggedy, but he was so charming I wouldn't have minded. To have my father at the dinner table every night, to watch television with him in the early evening, to discuss books and politics, what Ted Koppel said, to go shopping with him and take rides in his car, I would have emptied his urine ducts to have all that.

But this is what I really wanted to see: Daddy and Maia being crazy about each other. He saw his granddaughter only once before he died. She was an infant at the time and I remember he took her out of my arms because I wasn't burping her right. He showed me how to do it, which didn't surprise me because whenever my father took me to visit people there were usually little kids or babies around. The children would jump up in his lap or climb on the back of his chair. He was used to burping babies. "Where'd you get this little red thing from anyway?" he teased, propping Maia up on his lap and smiling at her, lifting her up and down and shaking her gently. "Hey there, baby girl. Hey, little bit. What her got to say to ole Grandad, huh?"

They would have loved each other. I can see Maia sitting in Granddad's lap for hours, falling asleep in his arms, waking up and giggling as he rolled his wheelchair back and forth to amuse her. I can see her standing on the bracers on the back of his chair, placing her tiny arms around his neck. And when she was older, what a pair they would have made: a little brown-skinned girl and the heavyset man in the chair, she pushing him into the park near the water when they went for rides there. Daddy would go to her school plays and to open house and watch Maia as she pirouetted across the stage or recited a Paul Laurence Dunbar poem in church, his applause the loudest in the audience, his smile the brightest.

And my uncles, my father's seven brothers, would come to visit when Daddy came to live with us. John. Elijah. Eddie. Cleat. Joe. Sammy. Norman. On Sundays my husband and I would have to put the two leaves in the dining room table to accommodate two or three of my uncles and maybe their families. And my father's men friends would visit also. It wasn't such a long ride from North Carolina or Richmond to D.C. I imagine Tank Jackson, who was also paralyzed, but from World War II, driving his block-long Lincoln to our door and the two men rolling their chairs into the backyard to have beer and pretzels and me baking something whenever my uncles or Tank came to visit, a potato pie or a coconut cake, and making lemonade too, even in the winter. It would be easy enough to tear out one of the rose bushes and have a ramp put in that would lead right to the door. When Daddy pulled himself up the ramp, as he got older, I'd stand behind him and say, "Can you make it all right, old man?"

The day before my father died I was a bridesmaid in my best friend's wedding and was staying with friends in Pittsburgh. My hostess awakened me around three or four o'clock Sunday morning and told me my uncle was on the phone. Uncle Norman's signature has always been brevity, an innate ability to get to the point with a minimum of fanfare or bullshit. When I picked up the phone he said, "Bebe, this is Norman. Your father died in a car accident this morning." Just like that. Then, "Did you hear me? Honey, did you hear Uncle Norman?"

A car accident, I thought, the phone still in my hand, Uncle Norman still talking, another car accident. That wasn't supposed to happen, is what ran through my mind. How did that happen twice in one life? Twice in two lives? Somehow, with the room spinning and my head aching, I listened to the rest of his instructions. I was to return home the next day and Uncle Cleat would take me to Richmond to identify the car and sign papers at the police station. We'd get Daddy's things at Mrs. Murphy's. Uncle Johnny, the eldest of Grandma Mary's eleven children, was having my father's body transported to North Carolina, where he would be buried in the family plot behind Grandma Mary's house. "He was coming to see you, Bebe," Uncle Norman said. "He didn't know you were out of town. You know your daddy, he just hopped in the car and got on the road. He was bringing a camera to take pictures of the baby."

When Uncle Norman said that, I remembered the pictures I'd promised to send Daddy weeks before and felt the first flicker of pain course through my body. Something swept through me, hot as lightning. All at once I was shaking and crying. God. He shouldn't have died like that, all alone out on a highway, slumped over the wheel like some fragile thing who couldn't take a good hard knock. God.

It was cool and dim in the funeral parlor, and filled with a strange odor I'd never smelled before. There were three rooms full of caskets—bronze, dark wood, light wood, pastels. A dizzying array. The funeral director was a friend of the family. Mr. Walson had an uncanny affinity for professional solemnity. He referred to Daddy as "the body." Did I wish to see the body? Was I satisfied with the appearance of the body? Did I care for knotty pine or cherry wood? He said this, his dark face devoid of all emotion, his expansive belly heaving threateningly against the dangerously thin belt around his waist. The same odd smell that filled the room clung to Mr. Walson. What was that smell? I leaned against Uncle Johnny and felt his hand on my shoulder. Upon learning that my grief was buttressed by a healthy insurance policy, Mr. Walson urged me to choose the cherry wood. I looked at Uncle Johnny questioningly; he has always known how to take charge. Maybe it comes from being the oldest. If he tells you to do something, you do it. "We'll take the cherry," he told the funeral director, who assured me he would take care of everything. But he could not, of course, take care of me. My grief was private and not covered. . . .

In the months that followed, the fat insurance checks my father left me transformed my life-style, but at that moment I could feel his death reshaping my life, or at least the life I thought I was entitled to. There are gifts that only a father can give a daughter: his daily presence, his daily molding, his thick arm across thin girlish shoulder, his solemn declaration that she is beautiful and worthy. That her skin is radiant, the flare of her nostrils pretty. *Yeah, and Daddy's baby sure does have some big, flat feet, but that's all right. That's all right now. Come here, girl, and let Daddy see those tight, pretty curls, them kitchen curls.* I was all prepared to receive daily ration of such gifts, albeit belatedly, but it was not to be. I would never serve beer and pretzels in the yard to Daddy and Tank. I would never have his company as I cleaned the dishes. He wouldn't see Maia's plays or her recitals. That was the way the cards had been dealt. I would go to my uncles, they wouldn't come to me. And the time for even those visits would later be eroded by obligations and miles. After April 1977 the old men in my life just plain thinned out.

For one thing, I got divorced and later remarried and moved far away to Los Angeles. After Grandma died, Uncle Johnny and Aunt Rena moved to Georgia near Aunt Rena's people. "You come see us," he told me before he left. "Don't forget; I'm your pop now." My Uncle Eddie finally sold his grocery store and moved from Philly to North Carolina, so I couldn't conveniently drop in at his market and chew the fat with him when I came to town to see Mom and Nana. Uncle Elijah died and I couldn't even go to his funeral, because my money was real funny that month. I sent flowers and called his wife, but what could I say? I should have been there.

My Marine uncle became a preacher. Uncle Sammy doesn't whoop and holler; his message is just plain good-sense gospel. He can even get scientific on you. When I hear his message I am thinking the whole time.

Uncle Norman and I still talk, but mostly on the telephone. My youngest uncle would call me up in hell, just to find out how I was getting treated. He is busy with his family and business. We don't see each other often.

The last time I saw Tank was a few weeks after the funeral, when he picked me up at the Greyhound bus station in Richmond and took me to get my father's car. Tank's skin is like a country night—no moon, no stars. You don't know what black is until you look in his face. Daddy always told me he wasn't much of a talker, and he's not, but he was just so nice and polite, sitting up in that big Lincoln, being my chauffeur. "Just tell me where you want to go," he said when I got into the car. We drove all over Richmond. Tank took me to where my father worked, to Mrs. Murphy's, everywhere.

Around two o'clock we pulled into McDonald's and he bought hamburgers, french fries and sodas for our lunch; the car was filled with the aroma of greasy food. We were both famished and we ate without talking at first. All you could hear was our lips smacking against our Big Macs. Al Green was singing, "Love will make a waaay . . ." on the radio. Tank looked at me and said, "Ole Be Be," as though astonished that little girls grow up and become women. He said my name the way older southerners are wont to, two distinct syllables. I love the sound. But it was weird, because as soon as he said my name like that, I caught sight of his wheelchair in the rearview mirror and at the same time thought about Maia, whom I'd left in D.C. with a girlfriend. I was still nursing her and I immediately felt pins and needles in my breasts, and when I looked at my blouse there were two huge wet milk rings. Tank looked, he looked away, then he looked again. Then he said, as if thinking aloud, "That's right. Moore's a grandaddy."

Tank's chair was very shiny in the mirror. His words hung between us real softly for a minute before I started up, which I'd sworn I wasn't going to do. I put my head on his shoulder and I just cried and cried and cried. Tears wouldn't stop. "George was right crazy about you, Be Be. Talked about you all the time. All the time," Tank said shyly. He offered up these words as the gift they were. I just nodded.

There have never been enough idle moments really to straighten out those tight, tight curls at the nape of my neck. Untangling a kitchen calls for a protracted, concentrated effort. You have to be serious. It is not a job for weak fingers on a summer's afternoon. Still, daydreaming fingers, even those caught up in tangles, reveal much.

It has proved to be true, what I felt looking into my father's satin-lined casket: my loss was more than his death, much more. Those men who used to entice me with their storytelling, yank my plaits, throw me quarters and tell me what a pretty girl I was are mostly beyond my reach now. But that's all right. When they were with me they were very much with me. My father took to his grave the short-sleeved, beer-swilling men of summer, big bellies, raucous laughter, pipe smoke and the aroma of cigars. My daddy is really gone and his vacant place is my cold, hard border. As always, my life is framed by his absence.

Maxine Clair (1939–)

Maxine Clair grew up in Kansas City, Kansas, in the 1950s. One of nine children, she developed early a strong sense of family, neighborhood, and connectedness to an African American community while living within a dominantly White Midwestern city. In many ways, Clair's childhood was idyllic, full of friends, playing in the neighborhood, going to church on Sunday—all the standards of middle America. The world of her childhood plays a large role in her short fiction.

Clair attended the University of Kansas as a medical technology major with an emphasis in microbiology. Committed to a career in the medical field, Clair worked toward success, reaching the position of Chief Technologist at Children's Hospital National Medical Center in Washington, DC.

Several years into her career, she decided that literature was her true passion. A single mother of four children, Clair quit her job and began to write poetry, living on her savings and the dream. She reviewed personal journals for poem ideas and sent poems to Random House, to be rejected with the advice that she read more. Shortly after receiving this advice, Clair applied and was accepted to the Jenny McKeen Moor workshop for nonstudents at George Washington University. She was encouraged by the organizer of the workshop, herself a Guggenheim fellow, to pursue a Master of Fine Arts degree in creative writing. Working a full-time job as a medical technologist to make ends meet for herself and her family, Clair began work toward a degree at American University.

Her collection of poetry, Coping with Gravity *(1988), and a chapbook,* October Brown, *a story revised in her first novel,* Rattlebone *(1994), are the products of her dedication to writing against the odds.*

Clair is deeply influenced by and integrates the tradition of music, especially in its place as part of her childhood community. Her mother's love for music from classical to religious to creating her own jazz compositions empowered Clair toward her own creativity. In an interview with Barbara Youree published in Potpourri Magazine, *Clair says of her language: "What I am always after, both in poetry and prose, is to get the message across with some sound, with some beauty of the words themselves. I want to fit the words together that express the rhythm and cadences that are there in life. I always want to hold on to the language. The language for me is about music." The power of language when combined with the rhythm of music communicates insight in both her poetry and prose. Highly influenced by the oral tradition, especially the Black Arts poets of the 1960s, the natural, musical rhythms of conversation fill the pages of* Rattlebone.

Clair has received remarkable critical attention for her novel Rattlebone, *which won the Friends of American Literature Fiction Award and the American Library Association's Black Caucus Award for Fiction. While Irene, the central character in the novel is African*

American, as are most of the people she interacts with, race is not the focal point of the stories, though racism does evidence itself in a few of the stories as an outside force penetrating Irene's world. Irene herself is the focal point, her growing up and her growing realizations of self, the workings of interpersonal relationships, and the range of her experience.

"Cherry Bomb" is the story of the summer before Irene's sixth grade year. Irene is between childhood and adolescence, just beginning to discover danger and sexuality. Still harboring the treasure box of childhood in which she keeps a cherry bomb and her diary and still believing in the threat of the "Hairy Man" the adults in the neighborhood use as threat against bad behavior, Irene experiences her first awkward and violating sexual encounter with Nick, a boy she likes but wishes were better behaved. The story closes with a surprising twist and Irene's stark recognition of her own mortality, a different kind of loss of innocence.

Clair is currently an associate professor of English at George Washington University in Washington, D.C. She is also a recent winner of a Guggenheim fellowship and is working on a second novel.

R. Joyce Lausch

Cherry Bomb

It was two summers before I would put my thin-penny bus token in the slot and ride the Fifth Street trolley all the way to the end of the line to junior high. Life was measured in summers then, and the expression "I am in this world, but not of it" appealed to me. I wasn't sure what it meant, but it had just the right ring for a lofty statement I should adopt. That Midwest summer broke records for straight over-one-hundred-degree days in July, and Mr. Calhoun still came around with that-old-thing of an ice truck. Our mother still bought a help-him-out block of ice to leave in the backyard for us to lick or sit on. It was the summer that the Bible's plague of locusts came. Evening sighed its own relief in a locust hum that swelled from the cattails next to the cemetery, from the bridal wreath shrubs and the pickle grass that my younger cousin, Bea, combed and braided on our side of the alley.

I kept a cherry bomb and a locked diary in the closet under the back steps where Bea, restrained by my suggestion that the Hairy Man hid there, wouldn't try to find them. It was an established, Daddy-said-so fact that at night the Hairy Man went anywhere he wanted to go but in the daytime he stayed inside the yellow house on Sherman Avenue near our school. During the school year if we were so late that the patrols boys had gone inside, we would see him in his fenced-in yard, wooly-headed and bearded, hollering things we dared not repeat until a nurse kind of woman in a bandanna came out and took him back inside the house with the windows painted light blue, which my mother said was a peaceful color for somebody shell-shocked.

If you parted the heavy coats between the raggedy mouton that once belonged to my father's mother, who, my father said, was his Heart when she died, and the putrid-colored jacket my father wore when he got shipped out to the dot in the Pacific Ocean where, he said, the women wore one piece of cloth and looked as fine as wine in the summertime, you would find yourself right in the middle of our cave-dark closet. Then, if you closed your eyes, held your hands up over your head, placed one foot in front of the other, walked until the tips of your fingers touched the smooth cool of slanted plaster all the way down to where you had to slue your feet and walk squat-legged, fell to you knees and felt around on the floor—then you would hit the strong-smelling cigar box. My box of private things.

From time to time my cousins Bea and Eddy stayed with us, and on the Fourth of July the year before, Eddy had lit a cherry bomb in a Libby's corn can and tried to lob it over the house into the alley. Before it reached the top of the porch it went off, and a piece of tin shot God-is-whipping-you straight for Eddy's eye. By the time school started that year, Eddy had a keloid like a piece of twine down the side of his face and a black patch he had to wear until he got his glass eye that stared in a fixed angle at the sky. Nick, Eddy's friend, began calling Eddy "Black-Eyed Pea."

After Eddy's accident, he gave me a cherry bomb. His last. I kept it in my cigar box as a sort of memento of good times. Even if I had wanted to explode it, my mother had threatened to do worse to us if we so much as looked at fireworks again. Except for Christmas presents, it was the first thing anybody ever gave me.

But my diary was my most private thing, except for the other kind of private thing, which Eddy's friend Nick was always telling me he was going to put his hand up my dress and feel someday when I stopped being babyish about it. I told that to my diary right along with telling the other Nick-smells-like-Dixie-Peach things I wrote every afternoon, sitting in my room with the bed that Bea and I shared pulled up against the door. I always wrote until it was time for my father to come home and take off his crusty brogans that sent little rocks of dried cement flying.

One evening after supper, I sat on the curb with Bea and Wanda calling out cars the way my father sometimes did with us from the glider on our front porch. The engine sounds, the sleekness of shapes, the intricacies of chrome in the grill-work were on his list of what he would get when his ship came in. Buick Dynaflow! Fifty-three Ford! Bea kept rock-chalk score on the curb until Nick rode up on his dump-parts bike. Situated precariously on the handlebars, he pedaled backwards, one of his easy postures. He rode his bike in every possible pose, including his favorite invention, the J.C., which had him sailing along, standing upright on the seat with his arms out in mock crucifixion.

"You wanna ride?"

Of course I wanted to, but Nick was stingy when it came to his bike, and I knew he was teasing.

"It's gettin dark, but I'll ride you up to the highway and back if you want to," he said. He sounded like he meant it.

Okay, but no fooling around," I said, and at once I was on the seat behind him, close up to his Dixie Peach hair. Pumping up and over two long hills, we rode a mile in the twilight. Later with our knees drawn up, we sat to rest on the soft bluff overlooking the yellow-stippled asphalt road, calling out cars. Beyond the highway toward the river, I could see the horizon's last flames. The faint smell of bacon rode sweetly on the breeze from the packing house upshore.

"Star light, star bright, the first star I see tonight, I wish I may, I wish I might . . ."

At first Nick wouldn't look up. "I don't see no star," he said.

I pointed. "See right up there, it's the North Star."

"How you know?"

"My mother showed it to me."

Then he looked. "Bet that ain't it."

"Bet it is. When it gets all the way dark, it'll be on the handle of the Little Dipper."

"If it's on the handle by the time the nine o'clock whistle blows, you get to ride my bike tomorrow all day. If it ain't, I get a kiss."

"Uh-uh, Nick," I said. "Let's just bet a hot pickle."

"Okay, Mamma's-Baby, okay, Miss Can't-Get-No-Brassiere, Miss Bow-Legs," and he rubbed my leg.

"Quit!" I said, and brushed his hand away. He did it again and I knocked his hand away again.

"Bet nobody ever touched your pussy."

"Ain't nobody ever going to, either."

"See if I don't," and he pushed me backwards, stuck his salty tongue in my mouth. His groping fingers up the leg of my shorts scratched when he pulled at my underpants. Then, like an arrow, fast and straight, his finger shot pain inside me. I punched him hard and he—"Ow, girl!"—stopped. I jumped up—"I'm telling"—and ran. He grabbed my ankle. His "Don't tell," then his "You better not" filled the air around me. But my own steely "I ain't scared" walked me all the way home. Halfway there I heard the pad of bike tires behind me on the brick street, and Nick sailed by, standing on the seat, his arms out in a J.C.

"Girl, I sent Eddy out looking for you, where you been?" my mother asked.

"I was up by Janice's house," I told her.

That night the tinge of pink in my underpants said that I should put epsom salts in the bathtub and hope that nothing bad had happened down there. When my mother asked me what I was doing with epsom salts, I told her, "Chiggers."

But I spelled it all out to my diary in I-am-in-this-world language. Nick: his shiny black-walnut skin, the soft fragrance of Dixie Peach in his hair, the cutoff overalls he wore with only one shoulder strap fastened so that I had to hold on to his bare shoulders even though they were sweaty. And in but-not-of-this-world language I told my diary the wish I had for him to get some kind of home training, go to church, act right, and not want to feel in my panties, and the soft kiss I wanted him to learn. I also told my diary how Eddy was pretending to be able to see with his glass eye, but how I heard him crying at night because he wanted to go with Wanda Coles and she made a fool out of him by having him watch her hand move back and forth in front of his face.

The next morning, when I gave my father his lunch box and his ice-water thermos and held the screen door for him, I saw Nick leaning and looking to be noticed in the Y of his apricot tree across the alley that was the boundary between our backyards. It was washday, a good opportunity for me to ignore him.

"Four loads before the sun gets hot," my mother said, and we rolled the washer off the back porch and into the middle of the kitchen, with two rinse tubs set side by side on my father's workbench. I stripped the beds still full of Bea and Eddy and the tobacco smell of my father and soft scent of my mother's Pond's cream. Underneath the mattress in their bedroom I always saw the same envelope of old war bonds, the small book of old ration stamps. And this time I found a magazine, *True Romance,* and inside it a card with roses on the front and a my-love-grows message, unsigned. At first I thought it must be from my father to my mother or vice versa. But as I ran to the kitchen with my discovery, I suddenly thought of my *private* cigar box, and slowly I went back up the stairs to sort out the knot of bedclothes on the floor.

Nick waited until the last sheet was stretched and pinned and the long pole was jacked up to raise the clothesline higher before he said a word.

"Found a new pedal for my bike," he yelled. I went inside the screen door but turned to see him sliding down from his perch.

"You can ride all day," he said through the screen. "Aw, hi, Miss Wilson."

"What you doing running around this early?" my mother asked him. "I know your mamma left something for you to get done 'fore she gets home," she said. "I bet you haven't even washed your face yet."

I already did everything," Nick lied. The naps on his head were still separate.

"Then you can get your friend Eddy out the bed, and y'all can go to the store for me. We need some more starch."

It tickled Nick that he had gained entrance to the goings-on of our house, and he raced up the stairs calling out, "Hey, Eddy, let's go!" I was hanging up line number two when they jostled down the unpaved alleyway, picking up rooks and throwing them at birds. "Come on, girl," my mother called. "We got a mess of overalls in here."

On washdays, when my mother said "Catch as catch can," we revelled in the break of routine, eating whatever we could find raw in a bowl for breakfast—and whatever we could get between two slices of bread for lunch. That noon, in my mother's got-to-get-this-done expression, I tried to find the secret that must have brought her the card of roses. Suppose Nick gave me such a card. But I could not picture my mother looking at the man holding the woman on the front of *True*

Romance. I made mustard-and-onion-sandwiches for me and Bea and wandered among the clotheslines, waiting for Nick to ride by so I could ignore him some more.

When the sun was at its highest point, Eddy and Nick came into the kitchen for a cool drink of water. Nick grinned at me through Eddy's entire speech to my mother about how hot it was, how the Missouri River had backed up enough from recent rains to fill the hole that wasn't even stagnant this summer, how the still water was so clear you could see the tadpoles, and how my father had said even *he* used to swim over there.

As Eddy went on, Nick said I could go swimming with them if I wanted to. I couldn't swim, and I knew that he knew it, which made his asking sweet.

"I saw the Dipper last night," he said. "You can ride my bike tomorrow since y'all have to wash today."

"I don't want to ride your bike," I said. "You don't know how to act. Besides, my father is building me one for myself, and it's going to be a girl's bike."

"You can't *make* a girl's bike," Nick said. "They don't throw away those kind of frames at the dump."

"Okay," my mother said to them. "Y'all can go. But Nick, you watch out for Eddy. He can't see as good as you can, so don't be cuttin the fool in the water. Y'all be back here 'fore supper, you hear?"

Nick winked at me. Rolling my eyes had become my best response. Undaunted, he pushed Eddy toward the screen door, and by the time it slammed, they were on Nick's bike, headed for the Missouri River hole.

My best friend, Cece, lived with her grandmother over the summer, too far away from our house. And so I hung around with Wanda most of the time, though I usually told her none of my secrets. Really, the only thing I had against Wanda was her long, straight hair in bangs and two braids that she made even longer with colored plastic clothespins clamped onto the ends.

"Can you come out?" she asked through the screen.

"Sprinkle the shirts and ball them up, and you can go," my mother said. I filled the ironing basket with sprinkled clothes and left with Wanda. Out under our crabapple tree we sat rubbing chunks of ice over our legs and arms in the still afternoon.

"I came to tell you something," Wanda said.

"What?"

"Guess," she said.

"I don't know."

"It has something to do with this," she said, and reached into the elastic band of her shorts. She struggled with the size of the thing until it cleared her pocket and held it up. "See."

It was a small, thick diary, a tan color, with letters that read FIVE YEAR DIARY in gold on the cover, and when she felt around in her pocket, a small key—all just like mine. Then deftly she unlocked the lock.

"Read this," she said. I took the book from her and confirmed that each page held a lined section for each day of five years. It was enough to see that Wanda, who wasn't even my friend, had managed to secure for herself the same precious thing I had done Miss Gray's chores for. Because Miss Gray next door was grossly overweight and couldn't get her arms up, I had oiled and braided her thick, sticky hair. I had swept her house, rugs and all. Since she couldn't get around very well, I had run to the store to get her messy tobacco, and got the boneless ham too that she said she ought to cut back on—all in order to collect two dollars' worth of dimes in a sock for the journal that would record the most vital facts about five years of my life.

That was enough without Wanda insisting that I read it.

"I can't read your writing," I said.

She took the book from my hands. "It says, 'Today I became a woman. I didn't get the cramps like everyone said I would. Now I can wear heels and red-fox stockings, and know that I have put away all the childish things I used to do. I am truly happy.' You know what that means?" she asked me.

"Yeah, that's nice," was all I could muster.

"I think every girl should have a diary, because it happens to every girl and it's a day you should always remember. You ought to get one."

"Yeah," I said.

By the time my father got home, I had done my two-faced best to convince Wanda that she would look like Lena Horne if she just wore kit curlers to bed. All the while I delighted in the way her bangs fell like a stringy rag mop in her eyes that day.

By suppertime I was sick of Wanda and happy to go looking for Eddy and Nick at the river. My mother insisted Wanda should keep me company, and so off we went, hopscotching our way on the bricks until we came to the new concrete sidewalk with cracks to avoid in the name of good luck. Down the soft slope above the highway we scooted, and when the whiz of cars broke, we flew across the highway and ran down the muddy hollow to the plain of wild onion, garlic, asparagus, and no telling what kinds of snakes to the place where the stand of short trees leaned, and the noisy rush of cars gave way to the noisy rush of river to come.

There on the ground just through the trees, Eddy lay on his back with his arms careless at his sides. Something wavelike through me made the hairs stand up on my arms, and I took off running to him. I stood above him just long enough to see his blind eye staring before he jumped awake, opening his other eye. In that instant I realized that not since the cherry-bomb accident had I seen Eddy asleep, and therefore did not know that he slept with the eye open.

"What are you doing laying here like this? Where's Nick?"

"I got too tired and Nick didn't want to come out yet," Eddy said, and he got up, pulled on his undershirt, and picked up Nick's bike at his side.

Wanda and I went to the bank of the cloudy green pool and called for Nick to come out. We called again and again. "Nick! Nick! We're going to leave you here and take your bike!"

"Nick!" Eddy called from across the water. "Nick!" Eddy called again and it went through the hairs on my arms. Wanda and I couldn't hold back our "Nick! Come on!" We looked into the pool but saw nothing through the muddy green.

We ran around the pool to Eddy's side.

"You don't think he went on over to the river, do you?"

"Not without telling me," Eddy said.

"Then where it he? Where was he when you came out?"

"He was right there." Eddy pointed. "Right out there in the middle. He can swim better than anybody. Let's just wait, hear?"

"Uh-uh," Wanda said. "We ought to get somebody. Suppose something happened to him.

I hated Wanda more than anybody and anything. "Let's just wait," I echoed Eddy.

"I'm going," Wanda said. As she ran, she yelled, "I'm going to get y'all's daddy. My mamma's going to be mad. I ain't got no business by the river."

"Nick's gonna get it. Nick's gonna get it," Eddy kept repeating as we stood looking toward the river, hoping to see Nick's white-toothed, nappy-headed self come bopping through the short trees, looking for his bike to go off on while we walked home, probably meeting my father on the way, probably telling him never mind, and most likely rolling our eyes at Wanda, who always acts like she know so much.

Nick's gonna get it. When I get my girl's bike I'm not letting him touch it unless he swears he will not show off like it's some piece of junk he doesn't have to treat right. Unless he says we can ride together up to the highway and he says he's sorry for not acting right. I am in this world, but not of it. I am in this world.

Eddy and I waited, watched the pool turn deeper green, and the sun slant light like fire through the trees.

First came my father, the sweat on his face and head shining, his arms wagging out at his sides as he sloshed through the tall grass toward us. Then Mamma behind him in her flower-print wash dress, calling us like she couldn't see we were standing right there. Then, really bad, Nick's mother with her gray and crimson elevator operator's uniform still on from work, running in high-heel shoes, calling Nick. Then Bea with Wanda and Mrs. Coles holding Puddin's hand, walking fast, then standing still outside the realm of confusion. Then the questions and Nick's mother shaking Eddy and my mother snatching her away from us and my father jumping in with his overalls on and Nick's mother crying and my mother saying, "Hush, now, it's gonna be all right," and Eddy closing his good eye tight and me saying the Lord's Prayer for us all. Then my father spitting out water and hollering and going down again and up again and hollering, "Get them kids away from here, get 'em away!" and Wanda and her mother running toward the highway, and my mother making us go stand over by the trees and Nick's mother pulling away from Mamma like she was going to jump into the water herself.

When my father laid Nick's body on the grass, I could see that Nick's hands were curled like they could never be straightened. Mamma walked his mother over to him and they held those curled-up hands until the ambulance people came and covered up his face. Nick's mother and Mamma went with them. Wanda's mother took me and Eddy and my father and Bea home in their Dynaflow.

That night Mamma held her waist and cried a lot. Eddy put his bed up to his door so that nobody could go in. My father said that I could stay up as long as I wanted and he sat out on the porch with his cigarettes. I could hear the glider creak every now and then, and I knew he was dozing and waking in the dark. Bea was so quiet in our room, she was almost not there. I sat awake in our bed for what seemed like the longest time, as if I had been sentenced to wait for something that could never come. I didn't feel at all like I would cry. Blank was what I felt, blank and swollen tight.

Groping my way, I parted the coats between the mouton and my father's rough wool, stretched my arms, and walked my hands down the ceiling to the box. Although I could not yet bring myself to throw away a month of my recorded life, my diary would not be useful, I had nothing to write. I found the cherry bomb. In the kitchen, I took the box of matches from the shelf over the stove and crept out the screen door. The glider creaked, but I stole out of the yard across the alley, through Nick's yard, out to the sidewalk and on.

From the soft bluff, I could hear the rush of the river above the hum of locusts. A fingernail sliver of moon laid out the highway gray and bent. The Little Dipper tilted. I struck a match and lit the green stem. When it sizzled, I threw it high and far, exploding the whole summer.

Michelle Cliff (1946–)

Born in Kingston, Jamaica, Michelle Cliff spent part of her childhood in New York City and part in Jamaica. She did her undergraduate and graduate studies in London. Her first important essay, "Notes on Speechlessness" (1977) appeared in Conditions II, *a lesbian journal. Subsequent works include* Abeng *(1984),* No Telephone to Heaven *(1987),* Bodies of Water *(1990), and* Free Enterprise *(1993).*

Both poet and novelist, Cliff sometimes sets narratives in the tropical West Indies and directly or indirectly treats issues of White domination. Her characters often grapple with tangled cultural forces and identities—White colonialist and Caribbean.

Somewhat reminiscent of Jean Toomer's Cane *(1923), a classic text of the Harlem Renaissance, Cliff's most recent collection of short stories,* The Store of a Million Items *(1998), might be characterized as shimmering, elusive, indirect, and highly literary. The selection below is taken from that volume.*

Keith D. Miller

transactions

I

A blond, blue-eyed child, about three years old—no one will know her exact age, ever—is sitting in the clay of a country road, as if she and the clay are one, as if she is the first human, but she is not.

She is dressed in a boy's shirt, sewn from osnaburg check, which serves her as a dress. Her face is scabbed. The West Indian sun, even at her young age, has made rivulets underneath her eyes where waters run.

She is always hungry.

She works the clay into a vessel which will hold nothing.

Lizards fly between the tree ferns that stand at the roadside.

A man is driving an American Ford, which is black and eating up the sun. He wears a Panama hat with a red band around it. He carries a different brightly colored band for each day of the week. He is pale and the band interrupts his pale-ness. His head is balding and he takes care to conceal his naked crown. In his business, appearance is important.

He is practicing his Chinese as he negotiates the mountain road, almost washed away by the rains of the night before. His abacus rattles on the seat be-side him. With each swerve and bump, and there are many, the beads of the aba-cus quiver and slide.

He is alone.

"You should see some of these shopkeepers, my dear," he tells his wife, "they make this thing sing."

His car is American and he has an American occupation. He is a traveling sales-man. He travels into the interior of the island, his car packed with American goods.

Many of the shopkeepers are Chinese, but like him, like everyone it seems, are in love with American things. He brings American things into the interior, into the clearing cut from ruinate. Novelties and necessities. Witch hazel. Super-man. Band-Aids. Zane Grey. Chili con carne. Cap guns. Coke syrup. Fruit cock-tail. Camels.

Marmalade and Marmite, Bovril and Senior Service, the weekly *Mirror* make room on the shopkeepers' shelves.

The salesman has always wanted a child. His wife says she never has. "Too many pickney in the world already," she says, then kisses her teeth. His wife is brown-skinned. He is not. He is pale, with pale eyes.

The little girl sitting in the road could be his, but the environment of his wife's vagina is acid. And then there is her brownness. Well.

And then he sees her. Sitting filthy and scabbed in the dirt road as he comes around a corner counting to a hundred in Chinese. She is crying.

Has he startled her?

He stops the car.

He and his wife have been married for twenty years. They no longer sleep next to each other. They sleep American-style as his wife calls it. She has noticed that married couples in the movies sleep apart. In "Hollywood" beds. She pre-vails on Mr. Dickens (a handyman she is considering bringing into the house in broad daylight) to construct "Hollywood" beds from mahogany.

The salesman gets out of the car and walks over to the little girl.

He asks after her people.

She points into the bush.

He lifts her up. He uses his linen hanky to wipe off her face. He blots her eye-corners, under her nose. He touches her under her chin.

"Lord, what a solemn lickle ting."

He hears her tummy grumble.

At the edge of the road there is a narrow path down a steep hillside.

The fronds of a coconut tree cast shadows across the scabs on her face. He notices they are rusty. They will need attention.

He thinks he has a plan.

At the end of the narrow path is a clearing with some mauger dogs, packed red-dirt yard, and a wattle house set on cement blocks.

The doorway, there is no door, yawns into the darkness.

He walks around the back, still holding the child, the dogs sniffing at him, licking at the little girl's bare feet.

A woman, blond and blue-eyed, is squatting under a tree. He is afraid to approach any closer, afraid she is engaged in some intimate activity, but soon enough she gets up, wipes her hand on her dress, and walks toward him.

Yes, this is her little girl, the woman says in a strangely accented voice. And the salesman realizes he's stumbled on the descendants of a shipload of Germans, sent here as convicts or cheap labor, he can't recall which. There are to this day pockets of them in the deep bush.

He balances the little girl in one arm—she weighs next to nothing—removes his hat, inclines his balding head toward the blonder woman. She lowers her blue eyes. One eye has a cloud, the start of a cataract from too much sun.

He knows what he wants.

The woman has other children, sure, too many, she says. He offers twenty American dollars, just like that, counting out the single notes, and promises the little girl will have the best of everything, always, and that he loves children and has always wanted one of his own but he and his wife have never been so blessed.

The woman says something he does not understand. She points to a small structure at the side of the house. Under a peaked roof is a statue of the Virgin Mary, a dish of water at her feet. On her head is a coronet of *lignum vitae*. She is rude but painted brightly, like the Virgins at the roadside in Bavaria, carved along routes of trade and plague. Her shawl is colored indigo.

"Liebfrau," the woman repeats.

He nods.

The Virgin's shawl is flecked with yellow, against indigo, like the Milky Way against the black of space.

The salesman is not Catholic but never mind. He promises the little girl will attend the Convent of the Immaculate Conception at Constant Spring, the very best girls' school on the island. He goes on about their uniforms. Very handsome indeed. Royal blue neckties and white dresses. Panama hats with royal blue hatbands. He points to the band around his own hat by way of explanation.

The royal blue will make his daughter's eyes bright.

This woman could not be more of a wonder to him. She is a stranger in this landscape, this century, she of an indentured status, a petty theft.

He wonders at her loneliness. No company but the Virgin Mother.

The woman extends her hand for the money, puts it in the side pocket of her dress. She strokes the head of her daughter, still in the salesman's arms.

"She can talk?"

"Jah, no mus'?"

A squall comes from inside the darkness of the house, and the woman turns, her dress becoming damp.

"Well, goodbye then," the salesman says.

She turns back. She opens her dress and presses a nipple, dripping, into the mouth of her little girl. "Bye, bye," she says. And she is gone.

He does not know what to think.

The little girl makes no fuss, not even a whimper, as he carries her away, and he is suddenly afraid he has purchased damaged goods. What if she's foolish? It will be difficult enough to convince his brown-skinned wife to bring a white-skinned child into the house. If she is fool-fool God help him.

Back at the car he tucks her into the front seat, takes his penknife and opens a small tin of fruit cocktail.

He points to the picture on the label, the glamorous maraschino cherry. "Wait till you taste this, darlin'. It come all the way from America." Does she have the least sense of what America is?

He wipes away the milk at the corners of her mouth.

He takes a spoon from the glove compartment.

"You can feed yourself?"

She says nothing, so he begins to spoon the fruit cocktail into her. Immediately she brightens and opens her mouth wide, tilting her head back like a little bird.

In no time she's finished the tin.

"Mustn't eat too fast, sweetheart. Don't want to get carsick."

"Nein, nein," she says with a voice that's almost a growl.

She closes her eyes against the sun flooding the car.

"Never mind," he says, "we'll be off soon." He wraps the spoon and empty fruit cocktail tin into a sheet of the *Daily Gleaner,* putting the package on the floor of the back seat.

Next time he will pour some condensed milk into the tinned fruit, making it even sweeter.

There's a big American woman who runs a restaurant outside Milk River. She caters to the tourists who come to take the famously radioactive waters. And to look at the crocodiles. She also lets rooms. She will let him a room for the night. In return he will give her the American news she craves. She says she once worked in the movies. He doesn't know if he believes her.

He puts the car in gear and drives away from the clearing.

His heart is full. Is this how women feel? he wonders, as he glances at the little girl, now fast asleep.

What has he done? She is his treasure, his newfound thing, and he never even asked her name. What will you call this child? the priest will ask. Now she is yours. He must have her baptized. Catholic or Anglican, he will decide.

He will have to bathe her. He will ask the American woman to help him. He will take a bathroom at the mineral spring and dip her into the famous waters, into the "healing stream," like the old song says.

He will baptize her himself. The activity of the spring, of world renown, will mend her skin. The scabs on her face are crusted over and there are more on her arms and legs. She might well have scurvy, even in the midst of a citrus grove.

But the waters are famous.

As he drives he alternates between making plans and imagining his homecoming and his wife's greeting. You must have taken leave of your senses, busha. She calls him busha when she's angry and wants him to stand back. No, busha. Is who tell you we have room fi pickney? He will say he had no choice. Was he to leave this little girl in the middle of a country road covered with dirt and sores and hungry? Tell me, busha, tell me jus' one ting: Is how many pickney you see this way on your travels, eh? Is why you don't bring one home sooner? Tell me that.

Everybody wants a child that favors them, that's all.

She will kiss her teeth.

If she will let him have his adoption, he will say, she can have the other side of the house for her and Mr. Dickens. It will be simple. Once he plays that card there will be no going back. They will split the house down the middle. That will be that.

Like is drawn to like. Fine to fine. Coarse to coarse.

There are great advantages to being a traveling salesman in this place. He learns the island by heart. Highland and floodplain, sinkhole and plateau. Anywhere a shopkeeper might toss up, fix some shelves inside a zinc-roofed shed, open shop.

He respects the relentlessness of shopkeepers. They will nest anywhere. You can be in the deepest bush and come upon a tin sign advertising Nescafé, and find a group of people gathered as if the shed were a town hall, which it well might be.

Everything is commerce, he cannot live without it.

On the road sometimes he is taken by what is around him. He is distracted by gorges, ravines possessed of an uncanny green. Anything could dwell there. If he looks closer, he will enter the island's memory, the petroglyphs of a disappeared people. The birdmen left by the Arawak.

Once he took a picnic lunch of cassava cake and fried fish and ginger beer into the burial cave at White Marl and left a piece of cassava at the feet of one of the skeletons.

He gazes at the remains of things. Stone fences, fallen, moss-covered, which might mark a boundary in Somerset. Ruined windmills. A circular ditch where a coffle marked time on a treadmill. As steady as an orbit.

A salesman is free, he tells himself. He makes his own hours, comes and goes as he pleases. People look forward to his arrival, and not just for the goods he carries. He is part troubador. If he's been to the movies in town he will recount the plot for a crowd, describe the beauty of the stars, the screen washed in color.

These people temper his loneliness.

But now, now.

Now he thinks he'll never be lonely again.

II

The Bath is located on the west bank of Milk River, just south of where the Rio Brontë, much tamer than its name, branches off.

The waters of the Bath rise through the karst, the heart of stone. The ultimate source of the Bath is an underground saline spring, which might suggest a relationship with the sea. The relationship with the sea is suggested everywhere; the limestone that composes more of the land than any other substance is nothing but the skeletons of marine creatures.

"From the sea we come, to the sea we shall return." His nursemaid used to chant this as he lay in his pram on King's Parade.

The water of the Bath is a steady temperature of ninety-one degrees Fahrenheit (thirty-three degrees Centigrade). The energy of the water is radiant, fifty-five times more active than Baden-Baden, fifty times more active than Vichy.

Such is the activity that bathers are advised not to remain immersed for more than fifteen minutes a day.

In the main building the bather may read testimonials to the healing faculties of the waters. These date to 1794, when the first bathrooms were opened.

> Lord Salisbury was cured of lowness of spirit
> Hamlet, his slave, escaped depraved apprehensions
> MAY 1797, ANNO DOMINI

> Mrs. Horne was cured of the hysteria and loss of spleen
> DECEMBER 1802, ANNO DOMINI

> The Governor's Lady regained her appetites
> OCTOBER 1817, ANNO DOMINI

> Septimus Hart, Esq., banished his dread
> JULY 1835, ANNO DOMINI

> The Hon. Catherine Dillon was cured of a mystery
> FEBRUARY 1900, ANNO DOMINI

The waters bore magical properties. Indeed, some thought the power of the Lord was in them.

The salesman's car glides into the gravel parking lot of the Little Hut, the American woman's restaurant. She named it after a movie she made with Ava Gardner and Stewart Granger. A movie she made sounds grandiose; she picked up after Miss Gardner, stood in for her during long shots.

She hears the car way back in the kitchen of the restaurant, where she's supervising Hamlet VII in the preparation of dinner. Tonight, pepper pot soup to start, followed by curried turtle, rice and peas, a Bombay mango cut in half and filled with vanilla ice cream.

The American woman, her head crowned with a thick black braid, comes out of the doorway onto the verandah that runs around the Little Hut and walks toward the salesman's car.

"Well, well, what have we got here?" She points to the passenger seat in front. "What are you? A kidnapper or something?"

She's wearing a khaki shirt with red and black epaulets, the tails knotted at her midsection, and khaki shorts. The kitchen steam has made her clothes limp, and sweat stains bloom on her back and under her arms. Her feet are bare. She wears a silver bangle around one ankle.

"Gone native" is one of her favorite ways of describing herself, whether it means bare feet, a remnant of chain, or swimming in Milk River alongside the crocodiles.

Still she depends on the salesman to bring her news of home.

"I've got your magazines, your *Jets,*" the salesman says, ignoring her somewhat bumptious remark.

It was late afternoon by now. A quick negotiation about a room for the night and then he will take his little sleepy-head, who has not stirred, to be bathed. He has great faith in the waters from all he has heard.

He asks the American woman about a room.

"There's only one available right now," she tells him. "I've been overrun."

The room is located behind the restaurant, next to the room where Hamlet VII sleeps.

The salesman, she remembers his name is Harold (he was called "Prince Hal" at school he told her), hers is Rosalind, is not crazy about sleeping in what he considers servants' quarters and tells her so.

"My daughter," he begins.

Rosalind interrupts him. "You may as well take it."

He's silent.

"It's clean and spacious," she tells him, "lots of room for you, and for her." She nods in the direction of the little girl. She can't help but be curious, aware from his earlier visits that he said he had no children, that his wife had turned her back on him, or so he said, that he equated being a traveler for an import firm with being a pirate on the Spanish Main, right down to the ribbon on his hat and his galleon of a car.

"Footloose and fancy-free" was how he described himself to her, but Rosalind didn't buy it.

He seemed like a remnant to her. So many of them did. There was something behind the thickness of green, in the crevices of bone; she wore a sign of it on her ankle.

"Very well, then. I'll take it."

"You won't be sorry."

"I need to take her to the Bath presently. Will you come?"

"Me? Why?"

"I need a woman to help me with her."

"I thought you said she was your daughter."

"I did."

"What's wrong with her?"

"Her skin is broken."

"Well, they have attendants at the Bath to help you."

"Okay, then."

Rosalind had in mind a stack of *Jets,* a pitcher of iced tea, and a break into the real world, Chicago, New York, Los Angeles, before the deluge of bathers, thirsty for something besides radioactive waters, descended on her.

"It will be fine. Just don't let her stay in too long."

"I won't."

"How much do I owe you for the magazines!"

"Not to worry."

"Well, then, the room is gratis."

That was fair. He felt a bit better.

At the Bath a white-costumed woman showed him and the little girl into a bathroom of their own. She unveiled the child and made no comment at the sores running over her tummy and back. As she dipped the child into the waters an unholy noise bounded across the room, beating against the tile, skating the surface of the waters, testing the room's closeness. "Nein! Nein!" the little girl screamed over and over again. The salesman had to cover his ears.

The waters did not bubble or churn; there was nothing to be afraid of. The salesman finally found his tongue. "What is the matter, sweetheart? You never feel water touch your skin before this?"

But the child said nothing in response, only took some gasps of breath, and suddenly he felt like a thief, not the savior he preferred.

"Nein! Nein!" she started up again, and the woman in white put her hand over his treasure's mouth, clamping it tight and holding her down in the temperate waters rising up from the karst.

She held her down the requisite fifteen minutes and then lifted her out, shaking her slightly, drying her, and only two bright tears were left, one on each cheek, and he knew if he got close enough, he would be reflected in them.

The woman swaddled the child in a white towel, saying, "No need to return this." She glanced back, in wonder he was sure, then turned the knob and was gone.

If the waters were as magic as promised, maybe he would not have to return. He lifted the little girl up in his arms and felt a sharp sensation as she sank her baby teeth into his cheek, drawing blood.

*   *   *

The salesman had tied the stack of *Jets* tightly, and Rosalind had to work the knife under the string, taking care not to damage the cover of the magazine on top. The string gave way and the stack slid apart. The faces of Jackie Wilson, Sugar Ray Robinson, and Dorothy Dandridge glanced up at her. A banner across one cover read EMMETT TILL, THE STORY INSIDE. She arranged herself on a wicker chaise on the verandah and began her return to the world she'd left behind.

She took the photographs—there were photographs—released by his mother—he was an only child—his mother was a widow—he stuttered—badly—these were some details—she took the photographs into her—into herself—and she would never let them go.

She would burn the magazine out back with the kitchen trash—drop it in a steel drum and watch the images curl and melt against turtle shell—she'd give the other magazines to Hamlet as she always did—he had a scrapbook of movie stars and prize fighters and jazz musicians.

The mother had insisted on the pictures, so said *Jet*. This is my son. Swollen by the beating—by the waters of the River Pearl—misshapen—unrecognizable—monstrous.

Hamlet hears her soft cries out in the kitchen, over the steam of turtle meat.

"Missis is all right?"

She made no answer to his question, only waved him off with one hand, the other covering the black and white likeness of the corpse. She did not want Hamlet to see where she came from.

America's waterways.

She left the verandah and went out back.

Blood trickled from the salesman's cheek.

"Is vampire you vampire, sweetheart?"

"What are you telling me?"

They were sitting on the verandah after dinner, the tourists having strolled to Milk River, guided by Hamlet, to watch the crocodiles in the moonlight.

"Are they man-eaters? Are they dangerous?" one tourist woman inquired.

"They are more afraid of you than you could possibly be of them," Hamlet told her.

The little sharp-toothed treasure was swaddled in the towel from the Bath and curled up on a chaise next to Rosalind. Tomorrow the salesman would have to buy her decent clothes.

If he decided to keep her.

But he must keep her.

"I gave a woman twenty American dollars for her."

"What is she?"

What indeed, this blond and blue-eyed thing, filled with vanilla ice cream, bathing in the moonlight that swept the verandah.

Not a hot moon tonight. Not at all.

He rubbed his cheek where the blood had dried.

"Her people came from overseas, long time ago."

They sat in the quiet, except for the backnoise of the tropics. As if unaware of any strangers around them.

Silence.

His wife would never stand for it.

He might keep his treasure here. He would pay her room and board, collect her on his travels. A lot of men had outside children. He would keep in touch with his.

Why was he such a damn coward?

Rosalind would never agree to such a scheme, that he knew.

But no harm in asking.

It would have to wait. He'd sleep on it.

But when he woke, all he woke to was a sharp pain in his cheek. He touched the place where the pain seemed keenest and felt a round hardness that did not soften to his touch but sent sharp sensations clear into his eyes.

When he raised his eyelids, the room was a blur. He waited for his vision to clear but nothing came. The red hatband was out of sight.

He felt the place in the bed where his treasure had slept.

There was a damp circle on the sheet. She was gone.

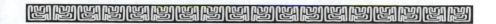

Lucille Clifton (1936–)

Lucille Clifton has bestowed on her readers the gift of two decades of poetry, autobiography, essays, and children's stories. Known for simple language and form, Clifton says of her own poetry, "I am interested in trying to render big ideas in a simple way." Perhaps the simplicity of her style is fueled by a desire for a wide and "ordinary" audience. Spanning a wide variety of topics and emotions to engage the variety in her audience, Clifton fills her poetry with precise images and memorable places and characters. her appeal is continual political protest as she imbues all of her poetry with dedication to the culture and history of Black communities. Combining Christian symbolism and commitment to Black women, Clifton depicts strong women characters and is a spokesperson for African American women and men in the struggle to maintain faith, family, and community.

Lucille Clifton was born Thelma Lucille Sayles on June 27, 1936, in Depew, New York. She learned to appreciate very early in life the power of words from her mother, Thelma, who wrote poems, and from her father, Samuel, who loved to tell stories about his ancestors.

Clifton attended Howard University from 1953–1955 where she majored in drama and wrote fiction and poetry. She next attended Fredonia State Teachers College in 1955, but didn't finish her degree because she had decided on her true and lifelong goal—she wanted to be a professional writer.

Clifton's writing took second place for many years, however, as she started her working life as a claims clerk for the New York State Division of Employment in 1958 and married Fred Clifton, a professor at the University of Buffalo, that same year. She dedicated the next eleven years of her life primarily to raising their six children, though she continued to write poetry.

Clifton's life began to center on her poetry in the late 1960s when Ishmael Reed sent some of her poems on to Langston Hughes who published them in his anthology, Poetry of the Negro, 1746–1970 *(1970). This acceptance gave her the confidence she needed. She sent some poems to Robert Hayden, another well-known poet, who presented them to YW-YMCA Poetry Center in New York City. In 1969, Clifton was awarded their Discovery Award and began work as a literature assistant for the Central Atlantic Regional Educational Laboratory at the U.S. Office of Education in Washington D.C. Her appointment to poet in residence at Coppin State College in Baltimore from 1971–1974 after the well-received 1969 publication of her first collection of poems,* Good Times, *solidified her original professional goal. She became a visiting writer at Columbia University School of Arts in 1974 and, in 1985, after her husband's 1984 death, Clifton became professor of creative writing at University of California at Santa Cruz.*

Clifton's first collection of poetry, Good Times *(1969), offers portraits of inner city life. With the simple and musical language that would become her trademark, Clifton conveys the resilience and dignity of Black families, her most common theme. After* Good Times *was published, Clifton was awarded a grant from the National Endowment for the Arts. A second NEA grant followed in 1972.*

Good News about the Earth *(1972), a second poetry collection, highlights love within the community and community heroes, ordinary people, whom Clifton links to Biblical figures. This second collection also includes her work with the blues idiom, the best example of which is "the lost baby poem," which expresses the sorrow and pain of a mother looking back, looking forward, and mourning a baby never born. Also more central to this collection than* Good Times *is the place of women in the liberation movements of the 1960s and 1970s.*

A continued focus on the strength and power of black women pervades following collections. In Ordinary Woman *(1974), Clifton traces the descendants of Caroline Donald, her great-great-grandmother. The theme of the collection is the spiritual sisterhood between extraordinary women—from the witches in the poem "In Salem" to Harriet Tubman and Sojourner Truth and "ordinary" women like Caroline Donald, Clifton herself, or the friends of the poem, "Sisters." The great truth of the collection is that "ordinary" women do not exist, that the inexplicable ways of knowing presented in the poems "New Bones" and "Roots" and the experience of mothering presented in "She Understands Me" and "i was born in a hotel" make every Black woman extraordinary.*

Two Headed Woman *(1980) centers on sisterhood and womanhood. In "homage to my hips," Clifton celebrates a full-figured woman's body, the liberation of woman, while in "to the unborn and waiting children" she admits the contradiction that suffering is as constant as celebration. Clifton also returns to religious thematic of* Good News about the Earth *in a series of poems concentrating on Mary. In these poems, Clifton uses dialect to link Black folk understanding of miracles to Mary's perception of her position. In two of the final poems of the collection, "testament" and "perhaps," Clifton compares her understanding of herself as a poet to Mary's understanding of her miracle, extending the connection between women who gain knowledge and perceive worlds through inexplicable means.*

Written after the deaths of her parents, Generations *(1976) is a memoir that documents, through the narrative of prose poems and photos, Clifton's ancestry and heritage beginning with great-great-grandmother Caroline Donald who was born in West Africa in 1822 and captured by slave traders. Lucille, Clifton's namesake and her great-grandmother, was the first legally hanged woman in Virginia. She was hanged for killing the White father of her only son. As Clifton weaves the stories of five generations, Mammy Ca'line is the link to African heritage, passing down a legacy of resistance and social responsibility.*

The legacy of Lucille Clifton herself shows no sign of ebbing. Good Woman: Poems and Memoir *(1987) brings together four volumes of poetry and the memoir.* Next: New Poems *(1987) focuses on Clifton's personal experiences and her sense of her own mortality after the death of her husband and parents. "she won't ever forgive me" is a direct expression of Clifton's fear of death and hope in living.* Next *also shows a greater global consciousness with poems like "winnie's song," "this belief," and "the woman in the camp." In* Quilting: poems 1987–90 *(1991), Clifton joins Alice Walker, Toni Morrison, and Gloria Naylor in claiming the art of quilting as creative legacy. The majority of the sections are titled after quilt patterns and, within each section, Clifton pieces together experiences to show her unique vision. Her most recent collections,* Book of Light *(1993) and* The Terrible Stories *(1996), focus on ordinary Black folk, place, story, and spirit, locating in true Clifton-fashion the sublime in the everyday and grounding the surreal in concrete images.*

In addition to poetry and memoir, Clifton has written nineteen children's books, primarily focusing on relationships of young African Americans to family and friends. The young boy, Everett Anderson, is a character in six of those books. Clifton works to clarify cultural lineage, focusing on Africans in America within a diasporic context.

Clifton's awards include a Pulitzer Prize committee citation in 1970 and nomination in 1980. She was honored as poet laureate of Maryland in 1979 and received a Juniper Prize for poetry in 1980. She also holds honorary doctorates from Goucher College and University of Maryland, both awarded in 1980.

In an interview with Naomi Thiers, Clifton discusses her perceptions of her own poetry and poetry in general. She explains her writing process and the sources that have most inspired her. The interview provides an inside look at Clifton's philosophy and practice.

In her essay, "In Her Own Images: Lucille Clifton and the Bible," Akasha (Gloria) Hull traces the Biblical tradition in Clifton's poetry, highlighting Clifton's ability to transform the images and language of patriarchal text into powerful assertions of Black feminist thought and experience. For its attention to one of Clifton's poetry's most essential characteristics, the essay adds to the richness of embracing the magic Clifton communicates.

R. Joyce Lausch

In Salem

TO JEANETTE

Weird sister
the Black witches know that
the terror is not in the moon
choreographing the dance of wereladies
and the terror is not in the broom
swinging around to the hum of cat music
nor the wild clock face grinning from the wall,
the terror is in the plain pink
at the window
and the hedges moral as fire
and the plain face of the white woman watching us
as she beats her ordinary bread.

Sisters

FOR ELAINE PHILIP ON HER BIRTHDAY

me and you be sisters.
we be the same.
me and you
coming from the same place.
me and you
be greasing our legs

touching up our edges.
me and you
be scared of rats
be stepping on roaches.
me and you
come running high down purdy street one time
and mama laugh and shake her head at
me and you.
me and you
got babies
got thirty-five
got black
let our hair go back
be loving ourselves
be loving ourselves
be sisters.
only where you sing
i poet.

New Bones

we will wear
new bones again.
we will leave
these rainy days,
break out through
another mouth
into sun and honey time.
worlds buzz over us like bees,
we be splendid in new bones.
other people think they know
how long life is
how strong life is.
we know.

Roots

call it our craziness even,
call it anything.
it is the life thing in us

that will not let us die.
even in death's hand
we fold the fingers up
and call them greens and
grow on them,
we hum them and make music.
call it our wildness then,
we are lost from the field
of flowers, we become
a field of flowers.
call it our craziness
our wildness
call it our roots,
it is the light in us
it is the light of us
it is the light, call it
whatever you have to,
call it anything.

She Understands Me

it is all blood and breaking,
blood and breaking. the thing
drops out of its box squalling
into the light. they are both squalling,
animal and cage. her bars lie wet, open
and empty and she has made herself again
out of flesh out of dictionaries,
she is always emptying and it is all
the same wound the same blood the same breaking.

if mama
could see
she would see
lucy sprawling
limbs of lucy
decorating the
backs of chairs
lucy hair
holding the mirrors up
that reflect odd
aspects of lucy.

if mama
could hear
she would hear
lucysong rolled in the
corners like lint
exotic webs of lucysighs
long lucy spiders explaining
to obscure gods.

if mama
could talk
she would talk
good girl
good girl
good girl
clean up your room.

i was born in a hotel,
a maskmaker.
my bones were knit by
a perilous knife.
my skin turned round
at midnight and
i entered the earth in
a woman jar.
i learned the world all
wormside up
and this is my yes
my strong fingers;
i was born in a bed of
good lessons
and it had made me
wise.

Breaklight

light keeps on breaking.
i keep knowing
the language of other nations.
i keep hearing
tree talk

water words
and i keep knowing what they mean.
and light just keeps on breaking.
last night
the fears of my mother came
knocking and when i
opened the door
they tried to explain themselves
and i understood
everything they said.

the thirty eighth year
of my life,
plain as bread
round as a cake
an ordinary woman.

an ordinary woman.

i had expected to be
smaller than this,
more beautiful,
wiser in Afrikan ways,
more confident,
i had expected
more than this.

i will be forty soon.
my mother once was forty.

my mother died at forty four,
a woman of sad countenance
leaving behind a girl
awkward as a stork.
my mother was thick,
her hair was a jungle and
she was very wise
and beautiful
and sad.

i have dreamed dreams
for you mama
more than once.
i have wrapped me
in your skin

and made you live again
more than once.
i have taken the bones you hardened
and built daughters
and they blossom and promise fruit
like Afrikan trees.
i am a woman now.
an ordinary woman.

in the thirty eighth
year of my life,
surrounded by life,
a perfect picture of
blackness blessed,
i had not expected this
loneliness.

if it is western,
if it is the final
Europe in my mind,
if in the middle of my life
i am turning the final turn
into the shining dark
let me come to it whole
and holy
not afraid
not lonely
out of my mother's life
into my own.
into my own.

i had expected more than this.
i had not expected to be
an ordinary woman.

the lost baby poem

the time i dropped your almost body down
down to meet the waters under the city
and run one with the sewage to the sea

what did i know about waters rushing back
what did i know about drowning
or being drowned

you would have been born into winter
in the year of the disconnected gas
and no car   we would have made the thin
walk over genesee hill into the canada wind
to watch you slip like ice into strangers' hands
you would have fallen naked as snow into winter
if you were here i could tell you these
and some other things

if i am ever less than a mountain
for your definite brothers and sisters
let the rivers pour over my head
let the sea take me for a spiller
of seas   let black men call me stranger
always   for your never named sake

the bodies broken on
the trail of tears
and the bodies melted
in middle passage
are married to rock and
ocean by now
and the mountains crumbling on
white men
the waters pulling white men down
sing for red dust and black clay
good news about the earth

adam and eve

the names
of the things
bloom in my mouth

my body opens
into brothers

homage to my hips

these hips are big hips
they need space to
move around in.
they don't fit into little
petty places. these hips
are free hips.
they don't like to be held back.
these hips have never been enslaved,
they go where they want to go
they do what they want to do.
these hips are mighty hips.
these hips are magic hips.
i have known them
to put a spell on a man and
spin him like a top!

mary

this kiss
as soft as cotton

over my breasts
all shiny bright

something is in this night
oh Lord have mercy on me

i feel a garden
in my mouth

between my legs
i see a tree

to the unborn and waiting children

i went into my mother as
some souls go into a church,
for the rest only. but there,

even there, from the belly of a
poor woman who could not save herself
i was pushed without my permission
into a tangle of birthdays.
listen, eavesdroppers; there is no such thing
as a bed without affliction;
the bodies all may open wide but
you enter at your own risk.

holy night

joseph, i afraid of stars,
their brilliant seeing.
so many eyes. such light.
joseph, i cannot still these limbs,
i hands keep moving toward i breasts,
so many stars. so bright.
joseph, is wind burning from east
joseph, i shine, oh joseph,   oh
illuminated night.

island mary

after the all been done and i
one old creature carried on
another creature's back, i wonder
could i have fought these thing?
surrounded by no son of mine save
old men calling mother like in the tale
the astrologer tell, i wonder
could i have walk away when voices
singing in my sleep? i one old woman.
always i seem to worrying now for
another young girl asleep
in the plain evening.
what song around her ear?
what star still choosing?

testament

in the beginning
was the word.

the year of our lord,
amen. i
lucille clifton
hereby testify
that in that room
there was a light
and in that light
there was a voice
and in that voice
there was a sigh
and in that sigh
there was a world.
a world a sigh a voice a light and
i
alone
in a room.

perhaps

i am going blind.
my eyes exploding,
seeing more than is there
until they burst into nothing

or going deaf, these sounds
the feathered hum of silence

or going away from my self, the cool
fingers of lace on my skin
the fingers of madness

or perhaps
in the palace of time
our lives are a circular stair
and i am turning

caroline and son

I celebrate myself, and sing myself,
And what I assume you shall assume,
For every atom belonging to me as good belongs to you.
—*Song of Myself*
WALT WHITMAN

1

She said
    I saw your notice in the Bedford newspaper and I thought isn't this interesting, so I figured I would call you and tell you that I am a Sale and I have compiled and privately printed a history of the Sale/Sayle family of Bedford County Virginia and I would be glad to send it to you. But why are you interested in the Sayles?

Her voice is sweet and white over the wires. What shall I say to this white lady? What does it matter now that Daddy is dead and I am a Clifton?

Have you ever heard of a man named John F. Sale? I ask.
Why yes, he was a great-uncle of mine, I believe. She is happy and excited.
Well, my maiden name was Sayles, I say.
What was your father's name? she asks. She is jumping through the wires.
Samuel, I say.
She is puzzled. I don't remember that name, she says.

Who remembers the names of the slaves? Only the children of slaves. The names are Caroline and Lucy and Samuel, I say. Slaves names.
    Ooooh, she cries. Oh that's just awful. And there is silence.
    Then she tells me that the slave cabins are still there at the Sale home where she lives, and the graves of the slaves are there, unmarked. The graves of my family. She remembers the name Caroline, she says, her parents were delivered by the midwife, Mammy Caroline. The midwife Mammy Caroline.
    Is the Nichols house still there? I ask.
    Still with the family in it, she says. I hear the trouble in her voice.
    And I rush to reassure her. Why? Is it in my blood to reassure this thin-voiced white lady? I am a Clifton now, I say. I only wanted to find out about these things. I am only curious, I say. It's a long time after, and I just wanted to know.
    I can help you, she sighs. I can help you.
    But I never hear her voice again.

Yet she sends the history she had compiled and in it are her family's names. And our family names are thick in her family like an omen. I see that she is the last of her line. Old and not married, left with a house and a name. I look at my husband and our six children and I feel the Dahomey women gathering in my bones.

"They called her Ca'line," Daddy would tell us. "What her African name was, I never heard her say. I asked her one time to tell me and she just shook her head. But it'll be forgot, I hollered at her, it'll be forgot. She just smiled at me and said 'Don't you worry, mister, don't you worry.'"

2

She said
    he finished his eggs and his bacon and his coffee and said Jo get me one of them True Greens and I got him his cigarette and went upstairs to get a ashtray and when I got back he was laying on the floor and blood was all on his mouth like when Mama used to have her fits and I hollered Daddy Daddy Daddy and Bobby come running down the stairs to see what was the matter and when he saw he called the rescue squad but when they got here they said he was dead. I didn't believe it.

    Punkin calling from Buffalo, talking soft and slow like she did when she was high. Lue, Lue, Daddy is dead.

    I didn't believe her. I hung up the phone and went back to reading the paper and waited for Fred and Sammy to come back home. I didn't believe Mr. Sayles Lord was dead. I didn't believe Old Brother Sayles was dead. I didn't believe the Rock was dead. I didn't believe you were dead Daddy. You said you stayed on here because we had feet of clay. I didn't believe you could die Daddy. I didn't believe you would. I didn't want you to die Daddy. You always said you would haunt us if you did.

    We drove North, seeing everything and laughing the whole way. Miss Mattie came and got the kids and I stopped by Sears and bought a black hat and Fed and Sammy got a map and we headed North, Fred driving.

    Mammy Ca'line walked North from New Orleans to Virginia in 1830. She was eight years old.

3

    "Mammy Ca'line raised me," Daddy would say. "After my Grandma Lucy died, she took care of Genie and then took care of me. She was my great-grandmother, Lucy's Mama, you know, but everybody called her Mammy like they did in them days. Oh she was tall and skinny and walked straight as a soldier, Lue. Straight like somebody marching wherever she went. And she talked with a Oxford accent! I ain't kidding. Don't let nobody tell you them old people was dumb. She talked like she was from London England and when we kids would be running and hooping and hollering all around she would come to the door and look straight at me and shake her finger and say 'Stop that Bedlam, mister, stop that Bedlam, I say.' With a Oxford accent, Lue! She was a dark old skinny lady and she raised my Daddy and then raised me, least till I was eight years old when she died. When I was eight years old. I remember everything she ever told me, cause you know when you that age you old enough to remember things. I remember everything she told me, Lue, even though she died when I was eight years old. And then I knowed about what she remembered cause that's how old she was when she got here. Eight years old."

4

Driving out of Baltimore you turn around narrow one-way streets and long-named alleys and stop in lines of school-teachers on Monday mornings. Every car had a woman driver except ours.

Where are the men, I laughed. On the corners, Sammy laughed back. Everything was funny. Everything was funny. We curved and crawled around past Ward's, past the last hamburger before the highway and broke out of the city like out of chains. Fred gunned the motor and laughed and we left Baltimore behind us. An old Black lady watched us making noise outside her country door. I could hear her head shaking. This is Maryland farm country, we be nice niggers here. I laughed at her frown. Fred nodded his head toward the front of the car. Be careful, he said, Pennsylvania is out there. We all laughed. Everything was funny.

"Walking from New Orleans to Virginia," Daddy would say, "you go through Mississippi, Alabama, Georgia, South Carolina and North Carolina. And that's the walk Mammy Ca'line took when she was eight years old. She was born among the Dahomey people in 1822, Lue. Among the Dahomey people, and she used to always say 'Get what you want, you from Dahomey women.' And she used to tell us about how they had a whole army of nothing but women back there and how they was the best soldiers in the world. And she was from among the Dahomey people and one day her and her Mama and her sister and her brother was captured and throwed on a boat and on a boat till they landed in New Orleans. And I would ask her how did you get captured, Mammy, and she would say that she was a child and I would ask her when did it happen, Mammy, and she would say 'In 1830 I walked from New Orleans to Virginia and I was eight years old.' And I would ask her what was it like on the boat and she would just shake her head. And it seems like so long ago, you know, because when I was asking her this it must have been 1908 or '9. I was just a little boy. I was a little boy and my Mama was working in the tobacco plant and my Mammy Ca'line took care of me and I took care of my brothers and my sister. My Daddy Genie was dead. He died young. He was my real Grandmother Lucy's boy and of course she was dead too. Her name was Lucille just like my sister and just like you. You named for Dahomey women, Lue."

5

Pennsylvania seemed greener than Maryland did. It smelled like spring and even when we laughed at the Welcome to Pennsylvania sign we sniffed deeply the green spring smell. My brother said the only thing wrong with Pennsylvania was that it was full of Pennsylvanians and Fred grinned and then glanced into the rear-view mirror. Sammy and I looked behind us. There was a Pennsylvanian driving behind us, driving too close to our station wagon. A whiteboy driver in a cowboy hat driving a cowboy car and bent down low and stiff over the steering wheel. Sammy and I pointed at him and laughed loud and fell down all in the seat and the poor Pennsylvania whiteboy sat straight up and gunned around us three crazy spooks driving North and sped the hell in front of us and across the mountains scared and driving like hell. Like away from hell. Fred started to speed and we strained trying to catch up with him and laugh at him some more but we looked across every mountain and he was gone. We kept on, saying we were looking for our cowboy and followed the day across the Pennsylvania green until we left spring there in the high ground and the land turned slowly grey and hard and cracking and we were nearing New York State. The promised land.

6

"When Mammy Ca'line and them got to Virginia," my Daddy would say, "the coffle was split up and she was sold to a man named Bob Donald. Her brother was sold to somebody in a close-by town and he was trained to be a blacksmith and her sister was sold to a plantation next to Bob Donald's and Mammy Ca'line got to see her sometime. Of course she never saw her Mama again cause she was sold away. Mammy Ca'line was eight years old. And I used to ask her, Mammy, don't you wish you could have seen your Mama sometime? And she would just shake her head. She never would say nothing to me about her Mama but sometime when I was a boy I would sit with her and Aunt Margaret Brown, who was her sister, while they rocked on the porch and I would hear them talking about do you remember different things. And they would say about Do you remember Nat Turner's forays when we just got here and Do you remember John Brown and the war between the states? And Mammy Ca'line would smile like at Aunt Margaret Brown and say 'I'm glad you survived it, sister, and I wonder what become of our Mama?' And they would just rock and rock."

Smoke was hanging over Buffalo like judgment. We rode silently through shortcuts we knew, and came at last into my father's street. It was night. There were no children playing. In the middle of the block the door to my father's house stood open and lighted as it had when my mother had died. Fred parked the car and we unstuck ourselves from the seats, tired and limp from laughing. My husband and my brother took my hands and we walked slowly toward the light, toward the family we had tried to escape.

We are orphans, my brother whispered. Very softly.

samuel

1

The morning of my father's funeral was grey and wet. Everything cried. Jo and Punkin and I stood waiting to be driven to the church in our stiff new black hats and veils. Sammy stood unsteady in the things that Fred had rushed out in the early morning rain and bought him. We were silent, a quiet place in the middle of girlfriends and cousins and my Aunt Lucille who had come from New Jersey in the night. She was standing as she always stood, stiff and military in the rain, surrounded by people who didn't like her. Daddy had loved his sister dearly and we resented his affection. She don't never call him, we would whisper, he always go to call her and she always want him to send for her. She don't even think about him and he crazy bout her.

She and I were in the first car and she turned to me when it came and took my arm. Lucille and Lucille. She was an old woman, an old soldier. I took her hand as we stepped into the car. I too was straight and quiet. Mammy Ca'line's great-granddaughter and great-great-granddaughter. Dahomey women. We rode to the church in silence.

2

"The generations of Caroline Donald, born free among the Dahomey people in 1822 and died free in Bedford Virginia in 1910," my Daddy would say, "and Sam Louis Sale, born a slave in America in 1777 and died a slave in the same place in around 1860
are Dabney and Gabriel and Sam and Helen and John and
Lucille,
called Lucy
who had a son named Gene by a man named Harvey Nichols
and then
she killed him,
and this boy Gene with a withered arm had three sons and a
daughter
named Willie and Harvey and Samuel and Lucille
and Samuel who is me
named his boy Sam and
his daughter Lucille.
We fooled em, Lue, slavery was terrible but we fooled them
old people. We come out of it better than they did."

3

My father was laid in the ground between his wives. The stones seemed strange to me. Edna Sayles. Thelma Sayles. I had never thought of Jo's mother as a Sayles before and the name seemed too big in my mouth. Punkin's mother waited, cooking at the house, and I thought of her and wondered where she would lie. My father was lowered into the ground between his wives and my face was wet before I realized it. I wanted to tell him something, my insides screamed. I remember everything. I believe. Everything shook and my Aunt Lucille was shaking my arm and crying. Crying without shame quietly and straight as a soldier. Mammy Mammy she was whispering in her tears, Mammy it's 1969, and we're still here. I held her hand tightly. Lucille and Lucille.

My father bumped against the earth. Like a rock.

last page of "thelma" section

And I could tell you about things we been through, some awful ones, some wonderful, but I know that the things that make us are more than that, our lives are more than the days in them, our lives are our line and we go on. I type that and I swear I can see Ca'line standing in the green of Virginia, in the green of Afrika, and I swear she makes no sound but she nods her head and smiles.

The generations of Caroline Donald born in Afrika in 1823 and
Sam Louis Sale born in America in 1777 are
Lucille
who had a son named
Genie
who had a son named
Samuel
who married
Thelma Moore and the blood became Magic and their daughter
is
Thelma Lucille
who married Fred Clifton and the blood became whole and
their children are
Sidney
Fredrica
Gillian
Alexia   four daughters and
Channing
Graham   two sons,
and the line goes on.
"Don't you worry, mister, don't you worry."

winnie song

a dark wind is blowing
the townships into town.
they have burned your house
winnie mandela
but your house has been on fire
a hundred years.
they have locked your husband
in a cage
and it has made him free.
Mandela. Mandala. Mandala
is the universe. the universe
is burning. a dark wind is blowing
the homelands into home.

this belief
in the magic of whiteness,
that it is the smooth
pebble in your hand,
that it is the godmother's
best gift,
that it explains,
allows,
assures,
entitles,
that it can sprout singular blossoms
like jack's bean
and singular verandas from which
to watch them rise,
it is a spell
winding round on itself,
grimms' awful fable,
and it turns into capetown and johannesburg
as surely as the beanstalk leads
to the giant's actual country
where jack lies broken at the
meadow's edge
and the land is in ruins,
no magic, no anything.

the woman in the camp

cbs news
lebanon
1983

they murdered
27 of my family
counting the babies
in the wombs.
some of the men
spilled seed on the ground.
how much is a thousand
thousand?

i had a child.
i taught her to love.
i should have taught her
to fear.
i have learned about blood
and bullets,
where is the love
in my education?

a woman in this camp
has 1 breast and 2 babies.
a woman in this camp
has breasts like mine.
a woman in this camp
watched the stealing
of her husband.
a woman in this camp
has eyes like mine.

alive
i never thought of other women.
if i am ever alive again
i will hold out my female hands.

the death of thelma sayles

2/13/59
age 44

i leave no tracks so my live loves
can't follow. at the river
most turn back, their souls shivering,
but my little girl stands alone on the bank
and watches. i pull my heart out of my pocket
and throw it. i smile as she catches all
she'll ever catch and heads for home
and her children. mothering
has made it strong, i whisper in her ear
along the leaves.

leukemia as white rabbit

running always running murmuring
she will be furious   she will be
furious, following a great
cabbage of a watch that tells only
terminal time, down deep into a
rabbit hole of diagnosticians shouting
off with her hair   off with her skin and
i am   i am   i am furious.

she won't ever forgive me,
the willful woman,
for not becoming a pine box
of wrinkled dust according to plan.
i can hear her repeating my dates:
1962 to 1982 or 3. mother
forgive me, mother believe
i am trying to make old bones.

Interview with Naomi Thiers

You have said that if the officers of the LA Police Department had been readers of poetry, they couldn't have beaten Rodney King.

I am certain. They couldn't have done it so easily because poetry allows you to see beyond yourself, to try to reach toward the sameness in the other.

In a way fiction doesn't?

It may be that poetry goes more directly to the inside. The brain and intellect start you thinking too much. Poetry seeks different ways of seeing and understanding, something beyond the self and larger than the sum of its parts. And that allows us to understand that humans also are larger than the sum of all their parts.

Poetry seems to have always been part of your life. In Generations *it sounded as if you knew you wanted to be a poet from the time you were a teenager.*

When I was a little girl, writing poems just came to me because I read a lot and loved the magical sound and music of language. It never occurred to me to say I wanted to be a poet. What seemed possible was being a nurse, being a teacher, or marrying a preacher. I wasn't going to do any of that! What was true about me was that I could breathe and I "made" poems. But I never thought of having a career as a poet.

What was your poetry like when you started writing?

Traditional. I loved Edna St. Vincent Millay's sonnets, and I started writing sonnets and trying to use the language as best I could. By the time I was first published I had been writing with major intent for more than twenty years. Not the intent of publishing, which is what it often is today, but attempting to serve the poem well.

You hadn't thought of trying to publish your work?

You must remember that I was born in 1936 near Buffalo, New York. The only poets I ever saw or heard of were the portraits that hung on the walls of my elementary school—old dead white men from New England with beards. Of course, it didn't seem to be a possibility for me. It's important to remember that writing and publishing poems are two different things.

Who encouraged you as a writer?

No one. I was not *discouraged.* My parents encouraged me in that they always said I could do anything I wanted to. I didn't know any other writers when I first started. I never took creative writing classes or workshops. I think it's important to say that these days.

What in your home environment went into your becoming a writer?

We were verbal people, and my parents were great readers, although neither one finished elementary school. My father could read but not write. I always say my literary antecedent was Reverend Merriweather from the Macedonia Baptist Church because of his oratory.

I hear the rhythms of the Bible in a lot of your poems.

Do you? I'll have to look for that now. I used to hear my father (who is a great Bible person) and my grandmother read the Bible. I reveled in the roll of the language, especially the King James version. The Bible must be there somewhere, because poetry comes out of all that we are, and part of what I am is someone who attended church regularly as a child. My father was Southern Baptist, and my mother was Sanctified, which is a holy roller—type religion. The church influenced me, perhaps not as much in subject matter as in energy. It's a mistake to think that we are products of what we are taught. We are products of all that we learn and some of what we are taught. I, as a child surrounded on Sunday by the vibrations of a Baptist church, must have absorbed something.

How does your spirituality relate to your writing now?

People say all the time that I'm a religious poet, although I'm not a particularly religious person. I do think I'm spiritual. I remember the day I first said to my father, "I don't think I want to go to church today." He was shocked—he didn't know how to deal with it. I'm fond of sacred places but don't like to worship in them; I always say I want to live in one. I used to visit churches, and I go to Seder; a good friend who was a priest used to take me to cathedrals. I've been to lots of different kinds of rituals, but I don't hang with any particular one.

   I married a philosopher. Toward the end of his life, if you asked my husband what he did, he would say he was a mystic. And I think he was. He did yogic practices and was interested in Eastern belief systems and traveled to India, to Tibet, to Africa.

Your sequence of poems called "The Light That Came to Lucille Clifton" seems to reflect a mystical experience.

It does. The poems reflect a kind of otherness that has been with me most of my life. I decided to write them after I heard another poet say, "It's funny I don't know much about Lucille's inner life."

So it wasn't a one-time experience but something you have experienced frequently?

Yes. The poems are pretty literal, actually.

Do you hear a voice?

Yes, I do hear voices. It's the kind of thing that's hard to explain if a person hasn't had it. An awareness of otherness has always been in my life. I accept that as I accept the rest of who I am. It doesn't get in my way.

Do you feel it's the voice of God?

No, it's just an awareness of more than the physical. Many people have that and don't quite know what to call it. They talk about hunches, intuitions; well, I have them a lot and have learned to heed them and incorporate them into my living.

And you sometimes experience your intuition as a light or a vision?

I use *light* a lot in my writing. *Lucille* means "light," and it takes on various meanings: *The Book of Light* is about clearness, seeing things whole, seeing what's there and more.

Many of your poems retell Bible character's stories in their own words.

Well, I'll speak for anybody! I wanted to find the humanity in their stories. Someone said to me once that I find the myth in the human and the human in the myth. In the new book I speak for Leda, for Atlas, for Naomi in the Bible. I always say I speak in the voices of the living *and* the dead. To feel yourself into another is what poetry can do for us, and I think I'm not bad at it. That doesn't make the stories less sacred or divine; it makes them more so to me. It is much more wonderful and miraculous to know that a poor peasant girl did something than to know that an angel did it. And I like to tell the stories: I like the Seder idea of keeping our stories known. If we know stories, we can understand more about what being human is.

In your poems and in **Generations** *you've told the story of your own family, going back to when your great-great-grandmother was brought from Africa as a slave.*

My father told those stories to me over and over. That made them seem important. He told them to whoever was present, but I listened. We must preserve the past for the future's sake. If we see our lives as an ongoing story, it's important to include all the ingredients and not have it in little compartments. I like to think of it not as "that was then, this is now" but that they all connect. For some reason I've always found the stories between the stories more interesting, wondered the hows and the whys to things. What has gone into making us who we are? Is it good or not? What is destroying us? What will keep us warm?

You seem to have a special fascination with the story of Mary.

I do like Mary, don't I? I'm fond of her.

But you seem ambivalent about whether her story is blessed or horrible.

I wonder what she thinks! I should think for her it was a mixed blessing. I think her mother, Anna, would fight this. I would, if my daughter said "Mom, I hear voices telling me I'm about to get pregnant and my kid's going to hang on a tree." I would probably say, "We will not hear this; we won't listen to that again; we will not watch the stars." I'll bet Anna wanted for her child what I want for mine: happiness, peace, some kind of family life as she defines it.

You also seem to have a fascination with the Hindu goddess Kali.

People tell me: "Lucille, you're always happy. You've always been happy. You've never had a bad time. You're always smiling." Well, how would they know? I smile a lot, and I have a sense of humor. Things happen to be very funny. But Kali had—we all have—many sides. She was both destroyer and creator, and it's always been interesting to me that she was black. And it is possible for me, too, for people, to be both creator and destroyer. I tell my students all the time that "both/and" is an African-American tradition, not "either-or."

How did you start writing children's books?

I've been publishing them as long as I've been publishing poetry. A children's book and *Good Times* were both published in 1969. I was friends with Maxine Kumin—who wrote children's books with Anne Sexton—and we worked together on a project of the Department of Education years ago. Maxine suggested that, because I have so many kids, I might try a children's book, and I found that I could. I must have been waiting to do it for a long time, although I'd never expressed that desire, because *Some of the Days of Everett Anderson* took about half an hour to write down!

You've written a series of Everett Anderson books. How did you create his character?

I wanted to write a book about a child from the projects to show that being materially poor doesn't mean being poor in spirit. Even in those days there was a tendency for girls to defer to boys in the black community. My mother didn't finish school so her brothers could go, for instance. Later, somebody pointed out that I'd written about boys all the time—I'd never noticed—so I started writing about girls, too.

Bantam has reissued seven of my children's books, including *The Black ABCs*, which has a verse for every letter, starting with "A is for Africa, land of the sun, the king of continents, the mighty one." I then talk about Africa having so many different languages, some of the world's largest rivers, and so on. I like that book because of my *X*; in those days *X* in the alphabet was always a xylophone. My *X* is for Malcolm. I was pleased to have thought of that in 1970!

I heard you say at a conference several years ago that having six children was the best thing that ever happened to your writing.

It kept me human and kept my priorities absolutely together. People are more important than things, and I know it. Kids don't let you be elitist or take yourself too seriously. They teach you all kinds of things: patience, turns of phrase, that you can handle more than you think you can, that things are never lost. To care for something besides yourself, to take yourself out of the center of your doing. I learned that there were a lot of things I didn't have to do. I learned how to keep things in my head. So, when I sit down to write, I'm not just starting: A lot has already happened.

How did you write when your children were small?

My earlier poems are shorter than my later ones, if you notice. But I can write and do other things at the same time. Everybody who has kids knows that. Somebody asked me once, "What are the optimum circumstances under which you write?" When you're in the kitchen and four of the kids have measles. One learns that one's process is what it has to be.

These kinds of questions are wonderings from the academy. It's as if poetry started there. But poetry didn't start at a desk or at a computer. The first poem came from somebody walking out of a cave somewhere and looking up and seeing the stars and saying wow! My poems are wow! Poetry is not completely an intellectual activity. Nor is it wise to think that what we wish to be is intellectuals. I am not one. Poems come out of human lives, human activities.

Is it ever hard for you being part of the academy?

I've entered the academy, but I don't put on all the academy's clothes. Mostly because I can't get very many of them on! Sometimes my feelings are hurt when I think what I do is underrated by some people, especially because they know I didn't graduate from a four-year college. But I'm good at ignoring what I feel like ignoring, and I'm grounded in myself. One of the blessings of being born an African-American woman is that I learned a long time ago not to buy other people's definitions of who I am and what I'm supposed to be like.

I've never felt that I had to limit myself in any way to be part of the academy. It is there to serve students, and I'm interested in that. I don't do a whole lot of other foolishness.

Do you have any thoughts about how poetry is taught to children?

It is taught badly in school because it's taught by people who were taught badly. People fear it. Teachers have asked me about when children are ready to learn poems, but children love the music of language. I don't presume to know what a particular child is able to understand. Some things we enjoy whether we understand them or not—like *Jabberwocky*. One of the first things I remember reading was *The Citadel* by A.J. Cronin. I was about five. I didn't know what a citadel was, but I loved the word. I got something out of it. Poetry needs to be taught, even on college campuses, because it is something that can be loved. When you hear people talk about literature, they often do not talk about that reason for it. But often we are taught that this is what a civilized person needs to know.

We have so many stereotypes about what is possible for certain kinds of people to know. So that if some folks are poor they can't know Leninism; they would not enjoy Bach. I had a student once who turned in poetry by Emily Dickinson because she thought I would only know Nikki Giovanni. The idea that I wouldn't know the world of American poetry!

Many of your poems deal with the danger of nature being destroyed.

If you're interested in life, you have to be interested in all of it, and, if you're concerned about life and its well-being, you have to be concerned even with life that does not look like oneself.

In the poem "Being Property Myself Once" and many others you make a connection between destruction of earth and oppression of people, especially minorities.

One has to see it as connected. When I think about property, how can I not associate it with coming from a line of people who were considered property? My problem—or my gift—is to have a long memory.

"The Killing of the Trees" connects destroying trees with the destruction of Native Americans.

I wrote that poem when I first moved to St. Mary's County [Md.]. I lived in a new development and had just come from California, where cutting down trees for no reason is just not done. But men were cutting down trees as if it were something wonderful; there seemed to be no feeling for preserving the landscape. And the tree did for a moment flash in my eyes as if it were a warrior chief.

Native American culture comes up in a lot of your poems.

I've always been interested in our misuse of Native American names. "They Are Afraid of Her" was the name of Crazy Horse's daughter. One man's name really translates into English as "Young Man Who Is So Fierce Even His Horses Are Fierce," yet he was called Young Man Afraid of His Horses. Isn't that awful? It's terrible to do that. Crazy Horse's native name translates as "Young Man Whose Horses Dance under Him as If They Were Enchanted." To trivialize history, including the stories and practices of other cultures, is a great mistake.

Your recent poems deal with social and political events, like Nelson Mandela being released from prison. What do you think about William Carlos William's words that it's hard to get the news from poetry but men die every day for lack of what is found there?

One of the strengths of poets is to notice what happens and to tell about it. A man in the audience at one of my readings said, "This is very interesting, but I can't really get into it because I'm a historian." And I said, "Me too." What the poet does, ideally, is talk about the history of the inside of people so that history is more than just the appearance of things.

Do you think that few modern poets write about events outside their own lives?

Poets have to write out of the music that they hear. With minority poets what sounds political is really their lives. When I talk about the black experience in America, I am not talking politics; I'm talking my life. (Gwendolyn Brooks once said that every time I walk out of my house it's a political decision.)

I was at a concert at St. Mary's once, and a wonderful pianist was playing Bach. I love Bach, and, when this man plays, Bach just rises up to the ceiling. Looking around, I started crying. A colleague asked me what was wrong, and I said, "I just wish there were more black people here." He said, "Lucille, do you have to get political?" and I said: "Wait a minute, *you* have the luxury of saying this is political. I'm talking about my life, and I have the right to that."

Do you want to say anything about Audre Lorde's death?

That was a great loss. Every brave spirit that's no longer walking around in a body diminishes the energy. That's some courage gone from the world, some strength, some truth telling, some female power. She's an underrated poet, I think.

You've seen the effects of racism and suffering, as well as richness, in the black community all your life. What are your sources of hope, and what keeps you going?

I wish I knew. I've been asked that before. Some people have been annoyed with me because I'm not bitter. See, I never expected life to be absolutely wonderful. Why would I have? But I do believe in possibility. And I, of course, have to believe that things and people can change. If I didn't believe that, why would I be writing at all?

What sounds like religious faith may just be faith in life, in the human spirit and in human possibilities. Why I have that, I have no idea. Maybe because I have survived, so I know survival is possible. Maybe it's the poet in me. Where she came from, I don't know.

(1994)

In Her Own Images:
Lucille Clifton and the Bible

AKASHA (GLORIA) HULL

The Bible has functioned as a sourcebook for Lucille Clifton throughout her il-
lustrious, twenty-five-year poetic career. In three cycles of poems written between 1972 and 1991, she directly treats many of its major characters and events.
On one level, her use of this biblical material is—in every sense of the word—
faithful; yet, in fundamental and crucial ways, she is startlingly heterodox. Perhaps the simplest way to describe her transformative mode is to say that she (1)
Africanizes, (2) feminizes, (3) sexualizes, and (4) mysticizes the original text.
Thus she rewrites it in her own image as a black and cosmically spiritual woman.
The poetic genre through which she mediates her vision is the personal, free
verse lyric but here, too, she negotiates a mutually illuminating relationship between the traditional and the new, the ordinary and the extraordinary. Invariably
lowercased, brief, and deceptively simple in form, style, and diction, her poems
ultimately authorize themselves as complexly crafted pieces redolent with both
mystical-spiritual and sociopolitical consciousness.

As important context, it should be mentioned that Lucille Clifton is one of
an impressive number of contemporary African American women writers whose
spiritual consciousness is providing both content and modality for their work.
They are writing about supranatural experiences and phenomena, and also utilizing what Toni Morrison has called "ways of knowing beyond the five senses" to
access their material. Morrison herself has spiced her novels with flying Africans,
ghosts, supernatural birth, rootworking, and so forth. She has also spoken in
propria persona about her connection through her grandmother and father to
the world of dreams and spirits (Strouse 1981). Alice Walker has said that the
characters of *The Color Purple* (1982) visited her to have her transmit their story
(A. Walker 1983); and in a later book, *The Temple of My Familiar* (1989), she
deals undramatically with such matters as karmic union, reincarnation, and the
physical materialization of energy.

Adopting science fiction, Octavia Butler deploys shape-shifters and an array
of telepathic powers, as in *Mind of My Mind* (1977) and *Wild Seed* (1980)), two of
her earlier works. Another poet, Dolores Kendrick, prefaces her 1989 volume
with these words:

The initial draft of this essay was written with the support of a 1991 postdoctoral fellowship
from the American Association of University Women. I wish to acknowledge this funding and express my sincere appreciation.

All of the unreferenced quotations of Clifton are taken from an interview I conducted with her
in May 1991. I am deeply indebted to her for this cooperation.

167

I thank these women
for coming, and I thank
the good God who sent them.

The Women of Plums

Toni Cade Bambara's novel *The Salt Eaters* (1980) is a brilliant compendium of ancient, black, and New Age spiritual wisdoms. Paule Marshall's heroine in *Praisesong for the Widow* (1983) undergoes a psychic rebirth that catapults her into ancestral visions and Yoruba gods. This list could be extended to further enforce the point that spirituality is a vital current for black women writers—just as it increasingly is for United States society and the whole of pre-twenty-first-century civilization. This special dimension of their work seems to account significantly for their current popularity, for the way unprecedented masses of readers are attracted to their writings.

Fitting generally into this movement, Lucille Clifton is yet unique in her unclouded self-revelation and the meshing of personal autobiography with her art. Spiritually endowed, she practices her gifts in both her life and her poetry. Clifton hears voices, automatically writes, reads palms, senses realities, and speaks normally unknowable truths. She and her family—which she has described as "spiritual and even perhaps mystical" (Clifton 1983)[1]—learned over time to "incorporate the nonvisible" into their everyday cosmology. How she does so makes her spirituality a force that could be described with the following adjectives: black, natural, rooted, unpretentious, practical, quietly powerful, good-natured, good-humored, ethically and politically edged, humanly respectful, lovingly shared, transformative.

Clifton's way of functioning in this area breaks down the boundaries between this world and the "other" world. Likewise, her spirituality-driven poetry transgresses categories of form, genre, and artistic convention. One very striking example of this is her poem "the light that came to lucille clifton" (from *two-headed woman*, 1980). Immediately, the use of her own, real name is arresting. In earlier poems, she had incorporated fanciful references to "lucy girl," but she had never instated herself with this degree of fullness, formality, and solemnity. Thus, with a dramatic move that upsets modesty and convention, the reader is invited to see the person behind the persona, the lady behind the mask.

Poetically working Clifton's actual experience, "the light that came" recounts a pivotal time when "a shift of knowing" makes possible the breakthrough to higher levels of awareness and personal power.

it was the summer
she understood that she had not understood
and was not mistress even

---

[1]Lucille Clifton's more recent volume *The Book of Light* (1993) adds a fourth set of texts to this category. The final section of the book is a sequence titled "brothers," "a conversation in eight poems between an aged Lucifer and God, though only Lucifer is heard" (69).

of her own off eye. then
the man escaped throwing away his tie and
the children grew legs and started walking and
she could see the peril of an
unexamined life.

(CLIFTON 1987A:209)

Among this series of concrete details is Clifton's allusion to her half-blind eye, whose functions she cannot control. This image inversely resonates with her finally being able to see that she needs to scrutinize her own autonomous be-ing more closely. However, she closes her eyes, "afraid to look for her / authenticity."

but the light insists on itself in the world;
a voice from the nondead past started talking,
she closed her ears and it spelled out in her hand
"you might as well answer the door, my child,
the truth is furiously knocking."

(209)

Thus the poem ends, with reference to an automatic writing experience and active resignation/acceptance.

In addition to incorporating her full name, this poem presents the oddness of Clifton referring to herself in the third person within a work that otherwise fits into the "I" frame of confessional or autobiographical verse. This disassociative effect is heightened by the way she linguistically distances obviously intimate elements: "the man" is her husband, "the children" her own six maturing ones (whose just-growing legs strike an almost surreal chord). These features tip the ambiance of the poem toward madness—which is reflected in its initially de-ranged lines. Yet this craziness is effectively contravened by a simultaneous, convincing lucidity.

For an epiphanic poem, "the light that came to lucille clifton" is strangely low-key; as a rendition of mystical experience, it is singularly nonelevated. Seemingly, Clifton is conveying through her form and style what she believes: that the extraordinary is really quite ordinary, nothing to get overly excited about, and available to us all. Cumulatively, this is a highly original poem. It is followed by a remarkable final sequence through which Clifton testifies to having seen the light and heard the voices of another world. Despite being called mad, she holds onto the truth of her experience and authoritatively declares in the last lyric:

in populated air
our ancestors continue.
i have seen them.
i have heard
their shimmering voices
singing.

(221)

From this point on, spiritual-mystical themes and materials become an even more prominent feature of her work.

Situated against this background of expressed—and expressive—spirituality, Lucille Clifton's handling of the Bible effects a perhaps contradictory-seeming union of Christian subject matter and her own brand of spirituality, which is certainly not traditionally religious but rather mystical in the broadest sense of the word. Having defined herself as "someone who is aware of mystery," Clifton illuminates on multiple levels the even more marvelous mysteries that lie behind received Mystery.

Moreover, her treatment of the Bible places her among contemporary women poets who, like herself, are engaged in what the critic Alicia Ostriker terms "revisionist mythmaking"—the poets' appropriation "for altered ends" of "a figure or story previously accepted and defined by a culture," including historic and quasi-historical figures, folktales, legends, and Scripture (1986: 212–13). Ostriker notes that these poets no longer hide behind the characters to make their socially seditious points but openly "deviate from or explicitly challenge the meanings attributed to mythic figures and tales." She sums up the revisionist mythmaking of this poetry thus:

> These poems generically assume the high literary status that myth confers and that women writers have often been denied because they write "personally" or "confessionally." But in them the old stories are changed, changed utterly, by female knowledge of female experience, so that they can no longer stand as foundations of collective male fantasy or as the pillars sustaining phallocentric "high" culture. Instead, they are corrections; they are representations of what women find divine and demonic in themselves; they are retrieved images of what women have collectively and historically suffered; in some cases they are instructions for survival. (Ostriker 1986:215)

Ostriker's emphasis on the legitimacy gained through employing respected cultural myths and the ultimate feminization of this material is a particularly helpful context for understanding Clifton's work.

Another necessary context is Clifton's own African American religious background. Her mother belonged to the Sanctified church, and her father was Baptist. She grew up in the Baptist church of her father, no doubt absorbing the Bible along with its interpretations and embellishments in Sunday school and sermons. Though she does not believe it "as a literal book," she herself has read the text from cover to cover. Clifton says that she finds it interesting but really does not know why she uses it so extensively in her writing: "It just interests me. The figures there interest me." One might also surmise that the Bible has possibly influenced her literary style. Both it and her poems possess a terse but affluent concreteness, an elliptical fullness.

As an African American woman, Clifton effortlessly balances a respectful—and even, one could say, affectionate—use of the Bible with her other nonorthodox attitudes, ideas, and beliefs. As is true for many of her counterparts (especially of her generation), she feels no need to rail against God and Christianity. It would be highly unusual to find someone like her expressing angry, negative sentiments about this religious code. It is too African American, too much who we are—our culture, blood, survival; the faith of our fathers and grandmothers. Not surprisingly, while Clifton relentlessly lowercases absolutely everything else, she always capitalizes "God" and his pronouns. Furthermore, as a truly spiritual person, Clifton would know that (1) fundamentally, all spiritual systems are essentially the same, and (2) they all (can) work for whoever sincerely believes and faithfully practices them.

Clifton's equipoise of contrasting doctrines can also be framed as an agile juxtaposition of folk and religious beliefs. Dianne Johnson uses this dyad in her helpful discussion of Clifton's books for children. She notes that even though, after 1947, (mostly) white writers of black children's books tended to eliminate superstition, while continuing to portray black people as religious, Clifton "sees no reason to avoid the 'superstitious' merely because it may evoke images of the 'primitive' or to deny the overlay of the superstitious with the religious." Her perpetuation of these "superstitious" images can, in fact, be "viewed as an acceptance of a world view rather than as a resignation to stereotypes" (Johnson 1990: 86–87). This notion of seeing what Clifton does as considered ontology is absolutely correct. As both her life and her work demonstrate, she accepts phenomena usually dubbed superstition as valid reality and does so from a deep rootedness in her cultural identity as an African American woman.

Johnson illustrates Clifton's syncretism of the folk and the religious with a discussion of her children's book *The Lucky Stone* (1979). This stone—originating as a talisman that helped save the life of a slave girl Mandy and subsequently handed down to generations of her successors—is now, after Emancipation, in the possession of Mandy's daughter, Vashti. One Sunday when the weather is "strange and threatnin," Vashti attends a special and very spirited church service. The last to ascend the platform to testify, Vashti does so with her mother's stone worn in a pouch around her neck. The pouch string breaks, "hurling the stone to the ground"—and just as she jumps down to retrieve it, a mighty bolt of lightning strikes the platform, destroying it with fire. In the story, Vashti's descendant, Tee, who is being told this tale by her great grandmother, whispers, "That stone was sure lucky for her." The "Grandmama" replies with a smile, "That's cause it's a lucky stone" (Johnson 1990:88). Johnson comments on the meaning of this passage:

> [T]here is little or no differentiation between the "religious" and the "superstitious" as commonly understood in everyday English. Recognizing this, the passage is both remarkable and unremarkable for the same reason—for the Black worshippers on this stormy afternoon, Vashti's shiny black stone is a savior just as God himself is a deliverer. Belief in God's power is at the base of the events taking place. Yet the power of the stone is an inextricable element too. Both are part of the acknowledged order of things. In this version of the event, in fact, it is the stone that is finally hailed as the protector. (88)

Born of African cosmology and of experiences in America that often made no "sense," this ability to live well and happily with apparent contradiction is a notable feature to African American culture. It is certainly relevant for Clifton's overall spirituality and for her handling of the Bible and Christianity in her work.

These biblical poems occur in three primary places: (1) the "some jesus" sixteen-piece final section of *good news about the earth* (1972), (2) the eight-poem sequence about Mary in *two-headed woman* (1980),and (3) the "Tree of Life" section in *quilting* (1991), which consists of ten poems revolving around Lucifer, the fallen angel. One of the most immediately striking features of all these selections is Clifton's ability to see the ordinary in the extraordinary, to bring heaven "down" to earth and make "men" of gods (the hierarchical metaphors are inappropriate.) This is a critical ingredient of her uniqueness and success. The intermingling of ordinary and extraordinary—whether she begins with one side or the other—is a characteristic feature of her consciousness and is reflected in her style. She reports that a friend of hers expresses the same idea by saying that she, Clifton, tries to find "the human in the mythology and the mythology in the human."

A single work from *Next* (1987), "my dream about God," illustrates Clifton's manipulation of these two dimensions. The beginning stanzas of the poem read:

> He is wearing my grandfather's hat.
> He is taller than my last uncle.
> when He sits to listen
> He leans forward tilting the chair
>
> where His chin cups in my father's hand.
> it is swollen and hard from creation.
> His fingers drum on His knee
> dads stern tattoo.
>
> (CLIFTON 1987B:41)

Here, God becomes anthropomorphic, family, familiar, complete with the appurtenances and mannerisms of the poet's male relatives, down to his work-hardened hands. This poem is reminiscent of Gwendolyn Brooks's "the preacher: ruminates behind the sermon" from her first collection, *A Street in Bronzeville* (1945). Brooks's work begins with the arresting lines: "I think it must be lonely to be God. / Nobody loves a master." It goes on to picture a Jehovah who strides importantly through his halls, but who has no one to take his arm, tweak his ear, or buy him a coke or beer. Perhaps, the poet wonders, "He tires of looking down. . . . Perhaps sometimes He tires of being great / In solitude. Without a hand to hold" (Brooks 1963:8). Not so with Clifton's God. He is a companionable father who, in the poem, "leans forward" and "strains to hear" his good daughter's wishes. Clifton has taken this basic conceit one step further, from the problem of Divine isolation to a solution which releases Him from His misery. Everyone is happier.

Her anthropomorphic strategies in this poem appear on a larger, amplified scale in the "some jesus" sequence. These are brief (as usual), first-person monologues, which read like soliloquies rather than like traditional dramatic monologues that assume a listener and an active context. The biblical characters—who obviously do interest Clifton—are projected as ordinary folk. They are demythologized, debunked, leveled through homely imagery and contextualizations. Cain "plants tears" in the desert every morning that his brother Abel, whom he has slain, does not rise up (1972). And Job comes to the rags of his suffering "like a good baby / to breakfast." Perhaps the most heterodox (for some readers) of Clifton's stratagems is that she further "levels" these biblical figures by making them racially black. This is apparent throughout in their language, for they speak an African American folk dialect of "be's," third-person subject–verb "disagreements," and colorful metaphor.

In addition, as if this were not enough to make her point, Clifton either clearly Africanizes history and historical context or slyly suggests their Afrocentric possibilities. Moses becomes "an old man / leaving slavery," which is literally and biblically true and also redolent of black United States history. Solomon blesses blackness in all its forms, from "the black skin of the woman" (the dark lover in his Song of Solomon or Songs) to the "black / night turning around her." On Palm Sunday, the people lay turnips for Christ's mule to walk on and wave beets and collard greens in the air (an especially humorous visualization). John the Baptist, the forerunner of Jesus Christ, announces:

> somebody coming in blackness
> like a star
> and the world be a great bush
> on his head
> . . . .
> i'm just only a baptist preacher
> somebody bigger than me coming
> in blackness like a star

> (98)

The "great bush" calls to mind God inaugurating Moses' mission by speaking to him from the burning bush, while it simultaneously—and almost as a pun—becomes a head of natural black hair, also called a "bush." After a reference like this and locutions such as "he be calling the people brother," it is almost impossible not to make John a *black* "baptist preacher."

Another arresting poem in this category is "jonah":

> what i remember
> is green
> in the trees
> and the leaves
> and the smell of mango

> and yams
> and if i had a drum
> i would send to the brothers
> —Be care full of the ocean—
>
> (97)

Speaking from the belly of the whale that swallowed him, Jonah waxes nostalgic about the sights, smells, and tastes of his tropical home. The crowning touch, however, is his yearning for one of the famed talking drums with which to warn his kin about the dangers of the ocean, a trope that spells enslavement and the Middle Passage—in addition to its accurate Bible reference.

Even in their biblical guises, many of the figures about which Clifton writes exhibit ordinary human traits—and this is probably what attracted her to them in the first place. (Limning these traits is certainly one way that Baptist preachers make their sermons interesting and effective for their congregations.) Jonah himself, for instance, runs away from responsibility, sleeps during a crisis, gets angry, inflexibly holds a grudge, and sulks (see his story in the Book of Jonah). Clifton picks up on human cues like these and refracts them in her own image. The result is sometimes surprising, sometimes humorous, and always impressive. Her working in this way fits into the anthropomorphizing tendencies of African American folktales, where characters from the Bible and even God himself are similarly "raced" and humanized. Another, earlier woman writer, Zora Neale Hurston, displays this approach in her highly original folklore collection, *Mules and Men* (1935). Finally, it must be said that transforming biblical figures into plain black folks is a move that simultaneously levels and elevates. It brings the Bible's inhabitants down to earth, while it imparts to black people some of the status of universal heroes and heroines.

Clifton treads even further into heterodox territory when she adds sexual overtones to the human characteristics that these biblical personages exhibit. Often this is ambiguously referenced and ripples as a delicate undercurrent, but for almost any perceptive reader, it is there. Attend to her poem "mary":

> this kiss
> as soft as cotton
>
> over my breasts
> all shiny bright
>
> something is in this night
> oh Lord have mercy on me
>
> i feel a garden
> in my mouth
>
> between my legs
> i see a tree
>
> (1972:99)

This poem recounts Mary, the virgin betrothed to Joseph, being "gotten with child" by the Holy Spirit. However, it adds flesh and body to traditional projections of this event, corporealizing and even eroticizing what is usually treated as a strictly nonphysical and ethereal phenomenon. In the incoherence of their grammatical structure and the vague wonder of their words, the first two "couplets" indicate a mating experience. After this, a series of short, definite sentences follow, even though fear and awe are still present—especially in the plea to God for mercy. The final two "couplets" show Mary as a visionary who sees through this present happening to its ultimate result.

The garden in her mouth is Gethsemane, the place where Christ prayed shortly before the Last Supper, and the tree is certainly representative of his subsequent Crucifixion. The sexual language—"between my legs"—and the phallic symbolism of the tree placed there circle back to the kiss and the breasts at the beginning of the poem. Given the Africanization that marks most of the poems in this series, one gives weight to the cotton in her initial simile (the picking of which assured black people's continued status as slaves to a Southern economy) and thinks about trees as the site of black men's hanging (like Christ on the cross, a comparison sometimes made for dramatic effect).

"mary" is an exellent example of how much dense matter Clifton can encapsulate in a very brief poem through their unerringly chosen diction and images. Christ's life is here, from his inception to his death, and Mary herself—as well as the supernatural event that sanctified her—have been given indelible body *and* race. Clifton's tour de force becomes all the more amazing when we compare it with the scant bit that the Bible tells. During the annunciation, Mary asks Gabriel, the angel who breaks the news, "How shall this be, seeing I know not a man?" He answers: "The Holy Ghost shall come upon thee, and the power of the Highest shall overshadow thee" (Luke 1:34–35). That is all. Clifton's poetic imagination supplies the rest. Finally, because Mary's is simultaneously a visionary and an erotic experience, the poem unites mysticism and sexuality, a combination that through the ages has been linked intuitively by thinkers both visionary and erotic.

This poem is Clifton's most overt and sustained treatment of sex and sexuality among the group. It is followed by "joseph," set at a later time when Christ is a "boy." Almost as baffled as Mary, Joseph notes that "something about this boy / has spelled my tongue." Even when his fingers "tremble" in love on Mary, his "mouth cries only / Jesus Jesus Jesus" (1972:100). Perhaps Clifton is thinking— almost as a sly joke—of the tendency of many people to call Jesus Christ's name during the rigorous pleasure of making love and thus is facilitating our identification with the poem in this personal way. Repetition and agitated rhythm are the techniques by which she also suggests sexuality in a third poem, "holy night," from the Marian cycle in *two-headed woman*. Mary is again the speaker. She concludes her troubled words to her husband with, "joseph, i shine, oh joseph, oh / illuminated night" (1980:189).

It is safe to say that Clifton "fleshes out" these biblical figures, making them more interesting and independent, and imparting to them a subjectivity greater than the object/ive status they tend to have in received religious discourse. She probes their minds, their psychologies, their personalities. As she does when she herself is the subject of a poem, she invites us to see the person behind the persona, the human behind the myth. In addition to her treatment of them on this level, Clifton further shows these characters as human beings who are being "worked," handled, used by a magic and mystery they can scarce understand. Seeing them thus enhances the mystery, but it also evokes our empathetic sympathy for the characters. All of this contributes to the success of Clifton's poems that specifically focus on Mary.

In "some jesus," Eve appeared in the first poem with Adam, and included there was the one poem that has been discussed about Mary. The remainder of the figures were male. This markedly contrasts with the religious sequence in *two-headed woman,* where all eight poems are devoted to Mary. Biblical tradition remains a kind of background, but these works are even less literally tied to the Bible. Twice in Luke, we are told that Mary "ponders" things "in her heart." Beyond this, there is silence about her thoughts. This is the kind of intriguing lacuna that Clifton's imagination fills, the kind of gaps that summon speculation and creation. In the Bible, Mary questions and then favorably responds to Gabriel. During an ensuing conversation with her cousin Elizabeth, John the Baptist's mother, about the miraculous births coming to both of them, Mary "magnifies" the Lord in ten rapturous verses (which, given the terse economy of the Bible, almost amounts to chattering). Otherwise, she is objectified in brief mentions or altogether absent from the text. Clifton constructs a very different picture.

First, she makes Mary important enough to have been the subject of an astrologer's predictions at her birth, a move paralleling all of the signs and prophecies that surround the imminence of the holy male figures. In "one-liners" as cryptic as predictions are wont to be, the astrologer accurately foresees her future. "Old men will follow" her, calling "mother mother," her "womb will blossom then die," "at a certain place" she will see something that will "break her eye" (1980:196). In phrases like these, her entire sad career as the mother of Jesus is foretold.

The second poem in the cycle continues to make her more worthy than incidental by addressing her parentage and early years: "anna speaks of the childhood of mary her daughter." Interestingly, the apocryphal gospels portray Anna's own birth of Mary as a miraculous occurrence. The Lord had "shut up" her womb, but she nevertheless gave birth to Mary after "her husband had fasted and prayed for 40 days and 40 nights in the wilderness" (Wigoder et al. 1986:662). Perhaps the scribes who established the canonical form of the Bible left out this account since such a proliferation of holy births adjacent to Jesus' might have vitiated the forces of his own. In Clifton's poem, Anna narrates her recurring dream, also prescient, about Mary being "washed in light" and looking up on a hill with her "face all long tears." Her response is:

> and shall i give her up
> to dreaming then? i fight this thing.
> all day we scrubbing   scrubbing.
>
> (197)

Her question is that of a loving, protective mother, but she has no choice of power in the matter. Her woman's work—even in its repetitive, fierce insistence—does not stay the divine plan.

Mary herself dreams of being hailed by "winged women," whom she joins. And, after her Son's birth, she reminisces in a song about her days as a "maiden" in her mother's house. While the cosmic events in which she played a leading role were evolving, she was "watching" her mother, "smiling an ordinary smile." Mary, Anna, and the astrologer all speak a form of Caribbean dialect. He says "she womb will blossom," a grammatical usage that is still current in Jamaica among other places. Ignoring standard rules of agreement, omitting auxiliary verbs, and employing the nominal for the objective possessive, Mary says "women was saying," "i afraid," and "i hands keep moving." In this way, Clifton implies a comparison between the early Christians and present-day Rastafarians. As she glosses them, they were/are both "small, somewhat despised" sects with "who knows what promise."

The Caribbean dialect is thickest in the last poem in Mary's voice, appropriately entitled "island mary":

> after the all been done and i
> one old creature carried on
> another creature's back, i wonder
> could i have fought these thing?
> surrounded by no son of mine save
> old men calling mother like in the tale
> the astrologer tell, i wonder
> could i have walk away when voices
> singing in my sleep? i one old woman.
> always i seem to worrying now for
> another young girl asleep
> in the plain evening.
> what song around her ear?
> what star still choosing?
>
> (202)

Aged, looking back, Mary summarizes her life as a "creature" of fate, wondering—in an echo of her mother—if she could have "fought." What concerns her now is the possibility that some other young girl will have to undergo a similar existence. Her worry sounds like an ultimate commentary on the action, a final choric glossing of all that has gone before.

This Marian cycle concludes with a poem that projects her into perpetuity, where she is prayed to and prayed for as the "holy woman split by sanctified seed," the "sister woman shook by the / awe full affection of the saints." Apparently, neither Mary herself or the women (presumably) who pray for her forever see her lot as an enviable one. In *Just a Sister Away: A Womanist Vision of Women's Relationships in the Bible,* black Christian feminist Renita J. Weems gives a similar, though dualistic, judgment of Mary's fate: "To be chosen by God is a humbling experience. To be used by God is an awesome experience. To be blessed by God is a joyous experience . . . most of the time" (1988:113; her ellipsis). And she calls Mary and her older cousin Elizabeth two women "trying to grapple with the hand of God in their lives, sharing with each other the blessedness and the burdensomeness of being blessed" (122).

The similarly skeptical, if not totally critical, attitude toward being singled out for divine attention that Clifton suggests in these poems about Mary is extended even further in three later works about Leda, who was "taken" by Zeus in the form of a swan (Clifton 1993:59–61). She is a woman from a different milieu than Mary's but their stories are comparable. These Leda poems lend a harsher glare to the sentiments prefigured in the earlier Marian pieces. At the outset, in images that suggest Mary's situation, Leda declares that "sometimes / it all goes badly":

> the inn is strewn with feathers,
> the old husband suspicious
> and the fur between her thighs
> is the only shining thing.
>
> (60)

Continuing to speak bitterness in the second poem, she denounces the "pyrotechnics" of these "stars spinning into phalluses / of light" and tells them that if they "want what a man wants," the next time they should "come as a man / or don't come." Whatever Clifton may have been thinking when she devised these initial images, they bitingly mimic contemporary rock supercelebrities bursting onto a stage of fireworks for a one-show-only performance. Leda's ultimate judgment is that "there is nothing luminous" about her experience:

> they took my children.
> i lived alone in the backside
> of the village.
> my mother moved to anther town.
> my father would follow me,
> when i came to the well,
> his thick lips slavering.

and at night my dreams were full
of the cursing of me fucking god
fucking me.

(59)

A ruined woman, regarded as a freak sexual object by even her own father, Leda is both the cursed and the cursing one. Using diction that never shows up elsewhere in Clifton's work, these last two lines are particularly scathing.

Clifton is aware that she has written many poems about Mary, and she says it is not "lost on her" that she currently teaches at St. Mary's College in St. Mary's City, Maryland—another coincidence that she thinks is "most interesting." Clifton reports that once, when she was listening to a speaker at the college lecture about Mary and the chosen women, she found herself thinking, "I bet some of these chosen women were quite annoyed." She admits that this "must be something that I think, and I don't know why." Whether she knows why or not, many of her women readers—be they feminists or not—will be able to comprehend her sentiment.

In sum, Clifton's work on Mary fills in the Bible's silences and invents a whole, new womanly mythology for her. Mary herself is centered and given an individuated, female primacy that in some ways reflects yet ultimately transcends her traditional status as Jesus Christ's mother. Implicit in Clifton's revision is a critique of patriarchal privilege, whether it emanates from heaven with God the Father or from his earthly sons who inscribe the story in *their* image. That she is able to accomplish her ends attests to her spiritual ability to shed her limiting ego and compassionately to project herself into other beings and consciousness. So doing, she rewrites the old myths into startling new scripts.

Certainly, Clifton's original treatment of her Christian material—from her dialect and Africanization to her bold characterization of Mary—exemplifies the strategy of "defamiliarization" that Ostriker finds in contemporary women poets. Defamiliarization draws "attention to the discrepancies between traditional concepts and the conscious mental and emotional activity of female re-vision," accentuating its argument "to make clear that there *is* an argument, that an act of theft is occurring." Colloquialism, for instance, "not only modernizes what is ancient, making us see the contemporary relevance of the past. It also reduces the verbal glow that we are trained to associate with mythic material. . . . With women poets we look at or into, but not up at, sacred things; we unlearn submission (Ostriker 1986:236).

Lucille Clifton began brooding on the figure of Lucifer with her sixth book of poetry, *quilting* (1991). Having already completed the initial manuscript, she wrote poems about the fallen angel which she "liked very much" and added them under the internal title of "Tree of Life" (continuing her pattern of naming each section with a traditional quilt design). She explains: "I think I was struck with the idea of Lucifer being the Light-Bringer, and Lucille meaning 'light.'"

Originally, she was supposed to have been named Georgia after her two grand-mothers. But when her father saw her "so pretty," he wished to name her after her mother, Thelma, who asked him to provide a second name. This became Lu-cille—after his sister and his grandmother Lucy, the "first Black woman legally hanged in the state of Virginia" (Clifton 1987a:240). Something about the Lucifer-Lucille-Light conjunction came together and she began to write these poems: "Who knows where these things come from? I swear I don't."

Clifton admits, further, that she "has a thing" with light because "there is a light. It's so hard to talk about." However, when pressed to explain, she offers the following brief story. Once she asked her supernatural source, "What is God?" and was told that "God is Love is Light is God." She continues: "I don't say God particularly because it's too externally defined, so I talk about the universe, but for me the universe is sort of like Light, big L. And I believe that there is a Light, whatever that means—and it is like that, it is like the making clear what has not been clear, being able to see what has not been seen. I just feel and instinctive trust in that. Now *why* I have no idea. That's something else again."

Her poetry reveals a preoccupation with the concept and depiction of light/Light long before she began her work on Lucifer. It first appears in *an ordinary woman* (1974) in a poem titled "roots." There, light is synonymous with the survival "craziness," "wildness," "whatever" which is "the life thing" in African American people that "will not let us die" (1974:12). A few poems later, she re-counts the genealogy of her own name, declaring proudly at the end: "mine already is / an afrikan name." Her next book, *two-headed woman* (1980), contains the already-mentioned magnificent sequence of poems that describe her encoun-ters with the light of her ancestral spirits. Writing about Clifton in *The Southern Review*, Hank Lazer believes that these poems establish her "lineage as one based on light": "We know that that light is a history, a narrative refiguring of an other-wise often ahistorical image of inward illumination. The strength of Clifton's mysticism is that it is grounded in history and in a familial mother tongue" (Lazer 1989:765). Proceeding from historical family to spirit ancestry, Clifton achieves the "inward illumination" of mystics, a transcendent sense of the "God-Spirit-Universe" complex that she images as light/Light—which is not at odds with its genesis in her concrete circumstances. Her use of the term—and her consciousness—is large enough to encompass all of these resonances.

The real conundrum, though, is how—after being told that "God is Light"—Clifton maintains her designation of Light as "personification" for "Transcendent Being," but still attaches it to Lucifer, who is God's opposite, or, at the least, is certainly not God. She responds to this puzzlement by asking, "If God is God—is there a 'not God'?"—which means that if God is everything, "He" is also Lucifer, who can then be seen as (part of) God, and hence as Light. Clearly, the ground has shifted to the philosophical-mystical-occult understanding that the separa-tive sense of God transcendent and distinct which underlies habitual, linear thinking must give way to the knowledge of God as also immanent in the whole of his creation.

Clifton grounds her depiction of Lucifer in Christian interpretation and in other—for example, Gnostic—traditions. The actual biblical basis for the mass of material about him is slight. The most extended reference occurs when the Old Testament prophet Isaiah decries the ruler of Babylon as "Lucifer": "How art thou fallen from heaven, O Lucifer, son of the morning! *how* art thou cut down to the ground, which didst weaken the nations! For thou hast said in thine heart, I will ascend into heaven, I will exalt my throne above the stars of God: . . . I will ascend above the heights of the clouds; I will be like the Most High. Yet thou shalt be brought down to hell, to the sides of the pit" (Isaiah 14:12–15). In the New Testament book of Luke, Jesus says to his faithful, "I beheld Satan as lightning fall from heaven" (Luke 10:18). These references—together with two others in Revelation and Ezekiel—lay the foundation for the "doctrine that the Devil was a great archangel who rebelled against God from pride" (Cavendish 1983:1662).

Lucifer's name, meaning "light-bearer" or "light-bringer," was the Latin name of the Morning Star (the planet Venus). In *The Woman's Encyclopedia of Myths and Secrets,* Barbara Walker finds that seventh-century Canaanite pagan scriptures included a dirge for the fallen Morning Star (which she quotes) whose words are so similar to those in Isaiah that she concludes: "Centuries later, a Jewish scribe copied this Canaanite scripture into the Bible and pretended it was written by Isaiah" (B. Walker 1983:551). She notes, too, that the "pit" was "the same as Helel, or Asherah, the god's own Mother-bride; and his descent as a lightning-serpent into her Pit represented fertilization of the abyss by masculine fire from heaven": "In short, the Light-bringer challenged the supreme solar god by seeking the favors of the Mother. This divine rivalry explains the so-called sin of Lucifer, *hubris,* which church fathers translated 'pride'—but its real meaning was 'sexual passion.'" Tellingly, during the Christian era, Lucifer "continued to be linked with both lust and lightning" (552).

Sexual passion is certainly the splendid and agitated center of Clifton's "tree of life" poems (Clifton 1991). Beginning her virtuoso changes on light, she writes a story of creation based on sex/sexuality—not simply as the forbidden something which Eve and Adam discovered when they opened their eyes with apple-knowledge, but as the motive power for events even before God spoke the world into being with his fiat, "Let there be light." An angelic narrator reporting from heaven remembers that at Lucifer's birth, when he "broke" as a flash of light "from the littlest finger / of God," the seraphim (the highest order of angels) knew that the "shimmer" and "flush" of him was "too much for / one small heaven." When he eventually falls from the kingdom, leaving it "all shadow" and the cherubim singing kaddish, "light breaks / where no light was before" as God, "the solitary brother," rises and points a wooden stick toward the garden (of Eden). Thus, Lucifer's fall and the creation of the world are synonymous. The angelic voice—speaking from a "less radiant / less sure" heaven—calls Lucifer "beautiful" and asks in trepidation, "oh lucifer / what have you done" (1991:40). Clearly, something frightfully awesome has occurred.

Whatever it is has to be inquired about in whispers (in the poem, "whispered to lucifer"), like gossip, secrets, and sex (which often travel together):

> oh son of the morning
> was it the woman
> enticed you to leave us
>
> was it to touch her
> featherless arm
> was it to curl your belly
>
> around her
> that you fell laughing
> your grace all ashard
>
>   (73)

This image of a laughing, licentious Lucifer falling, splintered and askew with abandon, is magnificent. Subsequent poems reveal that yes, indeed, it is the love of sex, or sexual love—with all of its origins and generations—which has motivated (perhaps unconsciously) the mighty upheaval in heaven. Lucifer comes to understand that his has been a divine mission, despite any and all appearances to the contrary. "Thy servant lord," he—courtly—calls himself, "bearer of lightning / and of lust." In an image that is triply copulation, fertilization, and birth (and that suggests the Gnostic premysteries), he describes his descent as a "thrust between the / legs of the earth / into this garden" (82).

Moreover, he links God with all of his doings, implicating Him in this other, sexual work of creation and simultaneously giving it sanction: "phallus and father / doing holy work." The oppositions between God's mission and Satan's, between the holy and the profane, are thus totally obliterated. Lucifer concludes his soliloquy of understanding with a rhapsodic smacking of the lips:

> oh sweet delight
> oh eden
>
> if the angels
> hear of this
>
> there will be no peace
> in heaven
>
>   (75)

His own "rebellion" has been justified. What he fell for is "sweet" enough to entice to earth another heaven full of angels (were they also to be "enlightened").

With Lucifer in the garden, it is, in Eve's words, "wild country": "brothers and sisters coupling / claw and wing / groping one another." Adam, whom she calls a "slow," "clay two-foot" (making him sound like a mentally dense, prehistoric male animal), needs her help to join the action. While she plots to "whisper into his mouth / our names" as he sleeps, he himself is struggling to "roar" erotic desire, sensing his own desperate "hunger to tunnel back / inside" her, to "reconnect the rib and clay / and to be whole again." Eve already has the words, knows the language. Satan has slid into her dreams and infected her with a hunger for her "own lush self" which has given her the necessary knowledge. Autoerotic images inspire her, becoming the basis of her quest for further pleasure. Her dreams are of

> apple
> apple snug as my breast
> in the palm of my hand
> apple sleek apple sweet
> and bright in my mouth
>   (74)

In Clifton's story, Eve leads the human fall from grace, just as she does in the Biblical tale. However, here, her revised role is a splendid one (just like Lucifer's). "Clay and morning star"—that is, Adam and Satan—follow her "bright back" out of the garden.

One poem in particular seems to support a reading of this series as Clifton's general exploration of the meaning and consequences of sexual knowledge or passion. Having given sexuality a cosmic and titanic setting, then brought it down to primeval earth, she further universalizes it in a piece that has no fixed voice or temporal situation (again, as she often does, permitting us a place of entry into the events and conversation, a way to try to connect ourselves and our lives to what she has placed before us). Titled "the garden of delight," it metaphorizes the various meanings of sex for different types of people:

> for some
> it is stone
> bare smooth
> as a buttock
> rounding
> into the crevasse
> of the world
>
> for some
> it is extravagant
> water   mouths wide
> washing together
> forever   for some
> it is fire
> for some air

and for some
certain only of the syllables
it is the element they
search their lives for

eden

for them
it is a test

(76)

Using the four basic alchemical and astrological elements, she posits four possibilities, from the grounded and fleshy earth to fire and air. Her fifth possibility is
a worldless empyrean, a sibilant search that tries the seeker for all of his or her
life. The nature of the test is left unspecified. It could be celibacy, or promiscuity,
or finding the right use(s) of eros, or whatever. The challenge for Eve, and
Adam, was initially restraint—and viewed from this angle, they surely failed.
However, looked at again in light of Clifton's perspective, their test could just as
well have been the courage to embrace: and at this they succeeded, with the aid
of Lucifer, whose mission, we must remember, was—"despite" its results—pre-
ordained ("thy servant lord . . . doing holy work").

Ultimately, Clifton seems to be saying that sexuality is life, or the way of and
to life—or that wrestling with it determines what life is about. Literally, sexual
connection is the means by which life is propagated and continues. Perhaps it
was or is this fundamental connection between the two which explains the
"Freudian slip" that resulted in the "tree of life" quilt pattern from which Clifton
titled this sequence of poems. Traditionally, there are two patterns with this
name, one that is made up solely of trees and another that has a serpent coiled
around the tree. Clifton reports that this latter "seemed right" to her. What is interesting here is that the biblical tree of knowledge has somehow been confused
with the tree of life. In Genesis chapter 2, God commands Adam not to eat "of
the tree of the knowledge of good and evil'" and it is this tree, in the middle of
the garden of Eden, from which Eve is led to pluck the fruit by the serpent.

This tree is not the tree of life, for after the Lord has discovered their actions,
He reasons: "Behold, the man is become as one of us, to know good and evil: and
now, lest he put forth his hand, and take also of the tree of life, and eat, and live
for ever," he and his partner must be driven from the garden (Genesis 3:22–24).
The question is, why have these two trees—with their attendant meanings and
symbolism—been conflated? Perhaps it is because of the instinctive linkage of
sexuality, life, and immortality through one's "generations" made by human
minds, including quiltmakers and Clifton, who certainly must know about the
two distinct trees in the garden. Additionally, there is the parallel understanding
which links knowledge and life, the belief being that without consciousness of
"good and evil" (that is, struggle and morality), there can be no life. These are

the real stakes that Clifton's human-centered poems highlight—not the old tale of obedience and transgression.

With little apparent effort, Lucille Clifton succeeds at transforming the Bible from a patriarchal to an Afrocentric, feminist, sexual, and broadly mystical text. The poetry that effects this metamorphosis is itself a kind of magic, deceptively simple but capable of producing shivers in any reader who is drawn to marvelous manifestations of the spiritual. Her favored form is the subjective, free-verse lyric, which she employs with the deliberate and open personalization that is characteristic of many contemporary women poets. She also removes the "high," "poetic" elitism from this quintessential genre, making it widely accessible, flexible, and oral. However, no matter how seemingly simple or even colloquial any poem of hers may be, it always authorizes itself as fine poetry, deftly bearing a craft that does not ever permit it to be mistaken for prosaic utterance.

Although Clifton encodes herself as female and, more than that, feminist through the content of her work (valorizing goddesses, heroines, and woman power; glorifying menstruation, menopause, motherhood, and the womb; probing the sexual abuse of young girls; ect.), she does not appear to think of her style in gendered terms except in one poem. "when i stand around among poets" contrasts the poets' "long white heads," the "great bulge" in their pants, and their "certainties" about their authorial identities and work, with the speaker's own embarrassed confession:

> i don't know how to do
> what i do in the way
> that i do it, it happens
> despite me and i pretend
>
> to deserve it,
>
> but i don't know how to do it,
> only sometimes when
> something is singing
> i listen and so far
>
> i hear

(CLIFTON 1991:79)

Her situation is not generalized to other women poets, but the poem does set up a dichotomy between abstract masculine rationality and feminine intuitiveness that appears in other of her works, notably the title selection of this *quilting* volume. However, the major difference expressed has to do with the modality of creative production. "When I stand around" suggests a connection between Clifton's spirituality and her poetics that is made explicit by some of her remarks.

Early in her career, she learned to respond when "something that was not alive, someone in spirit, wished to catch [her] attention." The electrical tingle in her arm would always result in her writing "something of value, even if it was just a little thing." Clifton theorizes the creative process in this way: "You get something and then you try to help it become what IT seems to want to be, not what you want it to be. . . . If you get a feel (and feeling seems to me to be first) for what this is trying to be, then you try to help it to do that. Not what you want it to be. Not what you think it ought to be. Not what you want your friends to think you think it ought to be. But what it seems to want to be." For her, it is a process that has more to do with feeling than external analysis: "That's why, if you can take simple words and feel them as well as know them and imbue them with real power, that works." Even poets "don't exactly know" where poems come from, but Clifton agreed that what she termed "living art" probably emanates from the realm of spirit. And, perhaps, poetry transmits from that realm better, "gets closer than prose because it has so little room to be full of crap. I think just the terseness [and urgency] of the language helps poetry, although there are many other ways."

Clearly, the openness to extraordinary vision that characterizes Clifton's life in general and the content of her poetry also helps determine her attitude toward genre and her style, making her reliant on intuitively perceived and not prescribed form. Clifton will not call herself a mystic or a mystical poet. Yet she defines language in a way that echoes the mystic's attempt to capture the noumenal world: "Language is translation of that which is beyond language. Language is a trying to express that which probably is not really expressible." Here, the epigraph that she uses for one of her poems in *The Book of Light* where Lucifer talks to God is apropos. It is a line from Carolyn Forché: "the silence of God is God." In all of her poetry about what Hurston synthesized as "God, Man, and the Devil" in one of her *Mules and Men* subtitles, Clifton confronts the classic paradox of the spiritual poet—having to render the ineffable in language, to distill what is beyond language into words. That she brings it down to earth helps, but the challenge remains.

In practice, Clifton's powerfully evocative, spare, and profoundly simple poems approximate the fleeting clarity and intensity of transcendent moments when "God-Love-Light" is apprehended. This same spiritual acuity directed toward the material realm accounts for the abundant, incisive truths about social and political realities that interpenetrate her biblical and spiritual matter, further developing the dialectic of multiple worlds that lies at the heart of her work. Without extravagance, we might say of Clifton creating what she writes about Eve:

> as she walked past
> . . . .
> into the unborn world
> chaos fell away
> before her like a cloud
> and everywhere seemed light
>
> seemed glorious
> seemed very eden.
> (CLIFTON 1991:49)

Wanda Coleman (1946–)

Born in Watts, Wanda Coleman continues to live in and write about Los Angeles. Beginning in 1977, she has published eight books of poetry and fiction, including Mad Dog Black Lady (1979), A War of Eyes and Other Stories (1988), and African Sleeping Sickness: Stories and Poems (1990). In 1984 she won a Guggenheim Fellowship for poetry.

Coleman focuses on the failures and triumphs of urban African American women struggling against anonymity, poverty, racism, sexism, and violence. Like many blues lyrics, Coleman's writing is consistently direct and stark. She spotlights issues of power and subordination. Her works typically concentrate on sexual relationships between African American male and female characters, relationships often characterized by men's severe mistreatment of women. Violence often erupts in her stories. Many of her female characters face the dilemma of wanting to express their passionate heterosexuality but contending with abusive and sometimes violent males. In the Coleman stories and poems below, solutions for female characters often prove elusive.

While most American writers prefer to ignore urban, dispossessed African American women, Wanda Coleman portrays their lives directly and sympathetically.

Keith D. Miller

Women of My Color

i follow the curve of his penis
and go down

there is a peculiar light in which women
of my color are regarded by men

being on the bottom where pressures
are greatest is least desirable
would be better to be dead i
sometimes think

there is a peculiar light in which women
of my race are regarded by black men

as saints
as mothers
as sisters
as whores

but mostly as the enemy

it's not our fault   we are victims
who have chosen to struggle and stay alive

there is a peculiar light in which women
of my race are regarded by white men
                                    as exotic
                                    as enemy

but mostly as whores

it's enough to make me cry
but i don't

following the curve of his penis
i go down

will i ever see
the sun?

Today I Am a Homicide in the North of the City

on this bus to oblivion i bleed in the seat
numb silent rider
bent to poverty/my blackness covers me like the
american flag over the coffin of some hero killed in action
unlike him i have remained unrecognized, unrewarded
eyes cloaked in the shroud of hopelessness
search advancing avenues for a noisy haven
billboards press against my face
reminders of what i can't afford to buy
laughing fantasies speed past in molded steel luxury
i get off at a dark corner
and in my too tight slacks
move into the slow graceful mood of shadow

i know my killer is out there

A Lyric

white-eyes wave across aisle
my name in underground code of poets, muttered

our suffering makes us comrades
flag of truce and a telephone number

ex-suicides, we gather, discuss new technology
not much to get fat off here

they say massachusetts, santa barbara, boulder creek
nix frisco—a silicone fag hag drag

a revolution in green candles and nam yoho renge kyo
rhythm taken captive

(she screams into my ear go back to school—fool
a barren womb indulges self-centeredness)

down the street the black and white flashes caution
this new breed of cannibal digests bone

the angels are revolting in heaven:
a drama done in clap, limp pricks and midnight calls to
        mama

The Library

walking his halls—a wonder
explore shelves behind eyes—dusty tales of s. holmes
winter afternoons curled up inside his mouth
a history scrawled in knotted brows

country winters his skin
his hands, leaves falling southern autumn
the endless canyon's cool blues of his smile

1950 lives. 1850 remembered. 1450 dreamed.

(the maidens in his fairytale are black instead of the knights)

poems gather, age, grow dry and brittle
crack beneath worn bitten nails

alone between the pages of his friends
reads love never found

The Seamstress

Mama comes home tired from the sweatshop. She is so tired her body stoops—the weight of slaving on the double-needled power-sewing machine from 7:30 in the morning till 4:20 in the afternoon. So tired she can barely push open the door. So tired we are silenced by the impact of it on her face.

Mama comes home to the imperfect dinner almost ruined by the eleven-year-old anxious to please. To the petulant ten-year-old eager to play outside. To the five-year-old banging on his red fire engine. To the three-year-old crying for lack of attention.

Mama comes home to us so tired she must lay down awhile before she does anything.

So tired, baby, I could cry.

She goes into her room and collapses into the bed. I watch from the hallway. She cries for a few minutes—a soft, plaintive whine. I go and set the table and serve the meal. I fix her a plate and take it to her on a tray. She is too tired to come to the table. *So tired, baby, I could die.*

We eat and my older brother and I do the dishes. Papa has not come home. He calls. I take the phone to her. Her side of the conversation is full of pain, anxiousness and despair. So tired she sounds.

But it's the beginning of the school term. And we need clothes for school. We need. And I watch her rise.

"You know, it was hard today. The white man boss don't want to pay me what I make. I work fast. Faster than the other girls. They get jealous of me. They try and slow me down. My floor lady is an evil witch. She won't give me the good bundles. And she lets some girls take work home to make extra money. But not me.

"I don't care. I'm so fast I do it all right there. And those Mexican girls—they make me so angry. They all the time afraid. Won't speak up for their rights. Take anything they'll give 'em. Even work for less money, which weakens all our purses. We say, 'Hey—don't be afraid.' I don't understand them Mexican girls."

She fills my ears with her days when she comes home from work. I am the one she talks to. There is no one there to listen but me. Sometimes Papa is gone three or four days without word. And my brothers—little boys too impatient for such stuff as what a woman's day is made of. And her few friends—she talks to them by phone now and then. She's too proud to tell them how hard it is for us. And since the hard times, few friends come by.

She goes into the bathroom, washes her face in cold water and dries her eyes. She goes into the front room and sits at the coffee table and slowly, carefully counts out the tickets which will determine her day's wage. I help her make the tally by reading off the numbers aloud. Her eyes are too tired to see them even with glasses. She marks them down on a sheet of paper and adds them up. Satisfied, she gathers them up and binds them with a rubber band.

I bring her fresh water from the kitchen. She drinks it in long, slow swallows, then gets up slowly and goes over to her single-needle power machine, sits and picks up the pieces that will become my new dress. Within the hour I will try it on. She will pin up the hem and then sit in front of the television and stitch it in. And tomorrow the girls at school will again envy the one who always has new clothes.

But now I watch her back curve to the machine. She threads it with quick, dark cedar hands. She switches on the lights and the motor rumbles to life and then roars. *Zip zip zip*—the dress takes shape.

And this tired. I wonder as I watch her. What must it be like? And what makes her battle it so hard and never give in?

Without Visible Means

You need, Baby. You need a lot. You too needy. I can't deal with it.

Baby, you've got everything any one man could want in a woman—looks, personality and sexual overdrive.

But you're poor.

Your poor is too big. I can't fill it. What you crave is beyond me. I can't satisfy it. I mean, ambition is one thing. But you want one hundred per cent and I've only got forty.

Cold part is I know what you need. And I'd like to be able to give it to you. But what I'd like to do and what I can do are two different thangs. As much of a provider as I'd like to be, what little I can squeeze out of the white rock will *nevah* do the j-o-b. Consequently every little thing is a crisis. Every little thing is a melodrama. It's too much.

If this were my world I'd give it to you on a platinum platter—never mind the silver. But this *iszant* my world. It's theirs. They mean to see that you and me don't amount to diddlysquat in it. And diddlysquat plus diddlysquat is nothing more.

Understand me?

The Parrr-taayyy was going on long before we showed on the set. It's nobody's fault—least nobody I can *see*. It's hardly more than I can do to wipe my own ass.

Understand me?

What's a niggah to do? Dream?

If you're dreaming you're sleeping, and both of my eyes are wide open. I'm woke. And I'm sorry to say I can't see no future for you and me. None-at-all.

It's not like that. They don't come sweeter than you. One look and you bring my nature to a rise. I mean, I'm hot for you. Since that first time we hooked up—you know—that was a righteous thrill. I say, you thrilled me! The way we do the slow dance? I couldn't get enough then, can't get enough now—of you. But there's more to a happy ending than sex, Baby. Sweet as it is it don't keep Goldie Locks in wolf pelts.

Baabee, don't be like that! You know I love you. I know you love me. But we can't use love as collateral. This *iszant* real estate. You can't build on it.

No, I'm no materialist. Let's not start calling folk out of their name. I'm not hung up on material things—so don't *mistake* me. Please see me for the man I am. I could lay up here and lay around and run you into the ground. But I'm not like that. Credit where credit is due. I'm being realistic. I'm seeing our situation—*what it is*. The things you want I can't give you no matter what. I don't have the power. And knowing that hurts, Baby. It hurts real bad. So that's why I'm leaving. That's why I've got to go. I've got no say-so. And I'm doing this for you. Why? Because—because, after a while, you yourself will ask me to leave. You yourself will put me out because I will not be living up to what you expect of me and I will not be giving you what you need.

So that's why this has to stop now.

It's best this way. For both of us. I'm saving us both a lot of pain and ugliness.

Don't cry, Baby. Wipe those weepy eyes. Come on—courage, now. Put your hands on your hips and let your backbone slip. Smile, Baby. Smile through those tears. Give a taste of those salty lips. Give a little kiss. It'll ease the pain.

There. See there?

And please, please do me one favor. Do one big thing for me. Will you? Sure you will. Just don't ever change. Be sure and stay as sweet as you are.

This is not like "goodby forever." I'll be in the neighborhood from time-to-time. And I'll drop by to check up on you, to see how you've been getting along in this world.

Remember. You'll always be in my Top Forty, Baby. Always.

There, now. Don't that make you feel better?

Jayne Cortez (1936–)

Jayne Cortez was born in Fort Huachuca, Arizona, and, early in her adulthood, lived in Southern California. In her career, Cortez has had an interest in the performance qualities of poetry, often integrating music into her poems; she is a performance poet and artist, much like Amiri Baraka and Sonia Sanchez, and is a forerunner to Sapphire's work in American Dreams. In 1964, Cortez founded the Watts Repertory Company, and in 1972, formed her own publishing company, Bola Press. Her first volume of poetry appeared in 1969, titled Pissstained Stairs and the Monkey Man's Wares. Next came Festivals and Funerals in 1971, and Scarifications in 1973. Before releasing her next collection of poetry, Cortez recorded and released a collection of her work, which gave full life to the language and rhythms of her work; the recording titled Celebrations and Solitudes was released in 1975. Since then, Cortez has produced other recordings, and also released Mouth on Paper (1977), Firespitter (1982), and Somewhere in Advance of Nowhere (1996). She has received an American Book Award, a National Endowment for the Humanities grant, and a Guggenheim award.

Cortez's poetry is intended especially to be read aloud, to capture the significance and rhythms of her use of repetitions and her language. She uses hard-sounding words, and words that are unmistakably direct and clear, to capture the power of the situation she is describing. The subtlety of her work is not in its language, but in its composition, which incorporates jazz and blues rhythms, and might even be considered an early version of hip hop vocal style. It is the beautiful musicality of her work that takes a bit of pressure off of the intensity of her poetry, which speaks to every day violations and violences in the world—for example, women under national oppression, or people in poverty.

In "I Am New York City," she claims the space of New York for herself, writing of the city as if it were part of her body, all of its passion and destruction and abundance. This strategy of defining the political and public as personal is an act of resistance, an act of subterfuge—a way to undercut both the privilege and pride New York represents, while simultaneously ripping the veil off of its ugly parts. Similarly, in "So Many Feathers," she presents the competing tensions of the myth of Josephine Baker, the African American performer who established a renowned career as a dancer and singer in France. Cortez does not become Baker, but instead speaks from the second person, revealing that the position of the poem's narrator is also a tension, part of what makes Baker's life a myth. Cortez repeats phrases, like "double-jointed" or "i remember," as a way to recreate the intensity of

Baker's life as revered exotic icon, powerful and glamorous, but also "froze[n]." The poem offers no easy answers, but instead gives an intense love-song for Josephine. Cortez also takes on another historical incident in "Shut Off the System," writing about and against the MOVE Bombing in Philadelphia in 1985. Her comment is more succinct than in "So Many Feathers" or "I Am New York City" but no less lethal. In fact, in these shorter lines, the orality rings more clearly; one can hear some voice, over a megaphone, saying "sue the city/ the county/ the state of bourgeois fear." Cortez's use of more condensed style here builds on the power of her other poems, hitting loud and clear with packed, compound phrases.

Her poem "Rape" is one of her most electric performance pieces. The poem chronicles the condition of two women, Inez and Joanne, who were raped, and is a manifesto for women's right to self-defense. In fact, Cortez cleverly refashions the language of the nation—of national security, defense, and war—and personalizes them, which is reminiscent of her making New York into a body. Rape and its ever-present threat for all women renders women's bodies as literal "combat zone[s]," and if this violence is a war against a body, then the body has a right to defend itself. Cortez inverts and subverts the logic of a society, which, too often, ignores violence done to women. But the piece is not only a statement of justification, but also a warning: that the threat of violence will only bring more violence. This stance is evidenced in the powerful last line, and its use of the inclusive pronoun "we," a literal redrawing of battle lines.

Cortez's interest and skill in poetic form is revealed in "Flame," where the poem's design not only mirrors its title, but also all of the words are centered, which speaks to the flaming fire that is so much a part of her work speaking out against violence. "Flame" is interestingly a meditative poem, most evidenced by its closing focus on the flame that is inside one's self. It is important to read this poem's self-reliant and introspective quality alongside "There It Is," which also embraces a tone that is softer (though no less resistant). From the title, which is simple and definitive and plain, Cortez begins "My friend/ they don't care/ if you're an individualist." This is another kind of battle line—a recognition of the system of violences that in fact makes no distinction for the individual and an alignment (by the speaker) with the subject of the poem, the person who is a "friend." The tone here is not resigned even in the face of the seeming inevitability of it all, but instead, the tone is caring and direct, loving and firm, but loving. The key use of repetition of the opening gesture of camaraderie helps to cushion the harsh.

This quality, what I call meditative because it speaks directly of love and comes from a quieter place, is partner to the more potent and spitting voices of Cortez's other poems. The two are not at odds, but in fact complement each other. What it does reveal is that Cortez is aware of the limitations of poetry and interested ultimately in the human life that is laid to waste by the power systems she critiques. In "Poetry," she raises exactly this point, beginning in mid-argument with "In fact/ poetry/ will not/ strike/ lightning/ through/ any/ convoy of chickens." After all its usefulness to critique and disrupt, poetry is still poetry, and a life destroyed is a life destroyed, which affirms the need for the poet (and the poetry lover) to be a daily activist.

Jayne Cortez's poetry moves like song, from blues and jazz rhythm, to the soul of the 1960s, and especially, like the vibe and power that is part of contemporary hip hop music.

Kevin Everod Quashie

I Am New York City

i am new york city
here is my brain of hot sauce
my tobacco teeth my
    mattress of bedbug tongue
legs apart   hand on chin
    war on the roof   insults
pointed fingers   pushcarts
my contraceptives all

look at my pelvis blushing

i am new york city of blood
police and fried pies
i rub my docks red with grenadine
and jelly madness in a flow of tokay
my huge skull of pigeons
my seance of peeping toms
my plaited ovaries excuse me
this is my grime my thigh of
steelspoons and toothpicks
    i imitate no one

i am new york city
of the brown spit and soft tomatoes
give me my confetti of flesh
    my marquee of false nipples
my sideshow of open beaks
    in my nose of soot
in my ox bled eyes
in my ear of saturday night specials

i eat ha ha hee hee and ho ho

i am new york city
never change never sleep never melt
my shoes are incognito
cadavers grow from my goatee
look i sparkle with shit with wishbones
my nickname is glue-me

take my face of stink bombs
my star spangled banner of hot dogs

take my beer can junta
my reptilian ass of footprints
and approach me through life
approach me through death
approach me through my widow's peak
through my slit ends my
asthmatic laugh   approach me
through my wash rag
half ankle   half elbow
massage me with your camphor tears
salute the patina and concrete
of my rat tail wig
face up   face down   piss
into the bite of our handshake

i am new york city
my skillet-head friend
my fat-bellied comrade
citizens
break wind with me

So Many Feathers

You danced a magnetic dance
in your rhinestones and satin banana G-strings
it was you who cut the river
with your pink diamond tongue
did the limbo on your back
straight from the history of southern flames
onto the stage where your body
covered in metallic flint
under black and green feathers strutted
with wings of a vulture paradise on your head
strutted among the birds
until you became terror woman of all feathers
of such terrible beauty
of such fire
such flames
all feathers Josephine
This Josephine

exploding red marble eyes in new york
this Josephine
breaking color bars in miami
this Josephine
mother of orphans
legion of honor
rosette of resistance
this Josephine before
splitting the solidarity of her beautiful feathers

Feather-woman of terror
such feathers so beautiful
Josephine
with your frosted mouth half-open
why split your flamingos
with the death white boers in durban south africa
Woman with magnificent face of Ife mask
why all the teeth for the death white boers in durban
Josephine you had every eyelash in the forest
every feather flying
why give your beaded snake-hips
to the death white boers in durban
Josephine didn't you know about the torture
chambers
made of black flesh and feathers
made by the death white boers in durban
Josephine terror-woman of terrible beauty of such
feathers
I want to understand why dance
the dance of the honorary white
for the death white boers in durban

After all Josephine
I saw you in your turquoise headdress
with royal blue sequins pasted on your lips
your fantastic legs studded with emeralds
as you kicked   as you bumped   as you leaped in the
air
then froze
your body breaking lightning in fish net
and Josephine   Josephine
what a night in harlem
what electricity
such trembling

such goose pimples
so many feathers
Josephine
dancer of the magnetic dancers
of the orange flint pelvis of the ruby navel
of the purple throat
of the feet pointing both ways
of feathers now gone
Josephine   Josephine
I remember you rosette of resistance
southern flames
Josephine of the birdheads, ostrich plumes
bananas and sparkling G-strings
Josephine of the double-jointed knees
double-jointed shoulders   double-jointed thighs
double-jointed breasts   double-jointed fingers
double-jointed toes   double-jointed eyeballs
double-jointed hip doubling
into a double squat like a double star into a giant
double snake
with the double heartbeats of a young girl
doubling into woman-hood
and grinding into an emulsified double spirit
Josephine terror-woman of feathers   i remember
Josephine of such conflicts   i remember
Josephine of such floating   i remember
Josephine of such heights   i remember
Josephine
of so many transformations   i remember
Josephine
of such beauty   i remember
Josephine of such fire   i remember
Josephine of such sheen   i remember
Josephine
so many feathers   i remember
Josephine   Josephine

Rape

What was Inez supposed to do for
the man who declared war on her body
the man who carved a combat zone between her

breasts
Was she supposed to lick crabs from his hairy ass
kiss every pimple on his butt
blow hot breath on his big toe
draw back the corners of her vagina and
hee haw like a California burro

This being war time for Inez
she stood facing the knife
the insults and
her own smell drying on the penis of
the man who raped her

She stood with a rifle in her hand
doing what a defense department will do in times of
war
And when the man started grunting and panting and
wobbling forward like
a giant log
She pumped lead into his three hundred pounds of
shaking flesh
Sent it flying to the Virgin of Guadalupe
then celebrated day of the dead rapist punk
and just what the fuck else was she supposed to do?

And what was Joanne supposed to do for
the man who declared war on her life
Was she supposed to tongue his encrusted
toilet stool lips
suck the numbers off of his tin badge
choke on his clap trap balls
squeeze on his nub of rotten maggots and
sing god bless america thank you for fucking my life
away

This being wartime for Joanne
she did what a defense department will do in times of
war
and when the piss drinking   shit sniffing guard said
I'm gonna make you wish you were dead black bitch
come here
Joanne came down with an ice pick in
the swat freak motherfucker's chest
yes in the fat neck of that racist policeman
Joanne did the dance of the ice picks and once again

from coast to coast
house to house
we celebrated day of the dead rapist punk
and just what the fuck else were we supposed to do

Flame

And it's familiar
this fact of flame
of indulging images
the salty dust devil winds
spitting into silver helmets
through shit splattered wings
the beginnings and endings
in which i salute the sun
because i know it has to come today
because a dream is like a nail
because this room peels back the hole in my cup
and so i tell you whoever you are
plastic pen, paper, dictionary
i tell you
the policemen sing
the sanitation men whistle
the distended body of military parades
fly flags in wounds of dead words
and the sad look of tribal warfare
points every second between sockets
into the same flame of the zero hour
and i know it has to come from me

There It Is

My friend
they don't care
if you're an individualist
a leftist   a rightist
a shithead or a snake

They will try to exploit you
absorb you   confine you
disconnect you   isolate you
or kill you

And you will disappear into your own rage
into your own insanity
into your own poverty
into a word a phrase a slogan a cartoon
and then ashes

The ruling class will tell you that
there is no ruling class
as they organize their liberal supporters into
white supremist lynch mobs
organize their children into
ku klux klan gangs
organize their police into
killer cops
organize their propaganda into
a device to ossify us with angel dust
pre-occupy us with western symbols in
african hair styles
innoculate us with hate
institutionalize us with ignorance
hypnotize us with a monotonous sound designed
to make us evade reality and stomp our lives away
And we are programmed to self destruct
to fragment
to get buried under covert intelligence operations of
unintelligent committees impulsed toward death
And there it is

The enemies polishing their penises between
oil wells at the pentagon
the bulldozers leaping into demolition dances
the old folks dying of starvation
the informers wearing out shoes looking for crumbs
the lifeblood of the earth almost dead in
the greedy mouth of imperialism
And my friend
they don't care
if you're an individualist
a leftist   a rightist
a shithead or a snake

They will spray you with
a virus of legionnaire's disease
fill your nostrils with

the swine flu of their arrogance
stuff your body into a tampon of
toxic shock syndrome
try to pump all the resources of the world
into their own veins
and fly off into the wild blue yonder to
pollute another planet

And if we don't fight
if we don't resist
if we don't organize and unify and
get the power to control our own lives
Then we will wear
the exaggerated look of captivity
the stylized look of submission
the bizarre look of suicide
the dehumanized look of fear
and the decomposed look of repression
forever and ever and ever
And there it is

Shut Off the System

They're pulling
human pieces of flesh
from nervous rectum
of a Black Philly Flame of Hope
sue the city
the county
the state of bourgeois fear
don't give us
the classical story
of classical excuses
from
Mister Classical
drop-the-bomb-on-the-house-Goode
no good
cancel the classes
slash the certificates
seal up roof top to the planet

Poetry

In fact
poetry
will not
strike
lightning
through
any
convoy of chickens

Today poems are like flags
flying on liquor store roof
poems are like baboons
waiting to be fed by tourists

& does it matter
how many metaphors
reach out to you
when the sun
goes down like
a stuffed bird in
tropical forest
of your solitude

In fact
poetry
will not
sing jazz
through
constricted mouth
of an anteater
no matter how many
symbols survive
to see the moon
dying in saw dust
of your toenail

Edwidge Danticat (1969–)

The first African Haitian female author to write in English and be published by a major publishing house, Edwidge Danticat captured the attention of the national media in 1995 when Krik? Krak!, *a collection of short stories garnered a National Book Award nomination (the title is the traditional opening call-and-response at a Haitian storytelling session). One year later, Granta selected her as one of the 20 Best Young American Novelists. Born in Port-au-Prince during one of Haiti's most violent periods, Danticat and her younger brother remained behind and were given over to the care of her aunt and uncle who lived in Bel Air, a poor area of Port-au-Prince; she later moved to New York City at age twelve to join her parents who had emigrated to the United States for work. When Danticat finally rejoined her parents in Brooklyn, she had to struggle not only to remake her family ties but also to learn English and cope with comments from her public school classmates who mocked her as a "boat person." "My primary feeling the whole first year was one of loss," she recalls. "Loss of my childhood, and of the people I'd left behind—and also of being lost." A difficult transition, Danticat recalls that she took refuge from the isolation she felt by writing about her native land. Danticat's affinity for storytelling and her talent for writing took precedence over her parents' desire for her to pursue a career in medicine.*

Danticat's writing has its roots in her homeland. As a child in Bel Air, she received an enduring lesson in the power of storytelling from her aunt's grandmother. "She told stories when the people would gather—folk tales with her own spin on them, and stories about the family" says Danticat. "It was call-and-response—if the audience seemed bored, the story would speed up, and if they were participating, a song would go in. The whole interaction was exciting to me." In Brooklyn, she was penning articles for a high school newspaper, New Youth Connections, *within a year of her arrival. An article she wrote in high school about her arrival in America and her reunion with her mother became the germ of her first novel,* Breath, Eyes and Memory. *After graduating from Barnard College in 1990, Danticat worked as a secretary and applied to both MBA schools and MFA programs while pursuing writing after-hours. She accepted a scholarship to Brown University's MFA program. Danticat believes that it is important for people to read things that somehow mirror their own experience. That is why she regards Barbadian-American writer Paule Marshall, whose* Brown Girl, Brownstone *tells the story of a young girl's immigrant experience, as a major influence in her own writing life.*

Breath, Eyes and Memory (1994) recounts the story of a young Haitian woman torn between her love for her mother and her sense of betrayal, particularly over a past she cannot understand. The novel, The Farming of Bones *(1998), exposes the 1937 Haitian genocide at the border of the neighboring Dominican Republic, an episode that still haunts the Haitian community. (Haitians have been emigrating to the bordering Domini-*

can Republic for work since the nineteenth century). In 1937, the anti-Haitian propaganda campaign flared into violence, resulting in the death of thousands of Haitians. (An earlier story about a survivor of the massacre, "Nineteen Thirty Seven," is included in Krik? Krak!) Danticat writes as memory and marker for both the larger audiences as well as for her family and community. She says, "It's a part of our history, as Haitians, but it's also a part of the history of the world. Writing … is an act of remembrance."

As part of a 1997 three-year grant from the Lila Acheson Wallace Foundation, Danticat also works with the National Coalition for Haitian Rights. "I often think I'm in a communal endeavor. People are investing in what I'm doing. Writers often feel as though they're writing alone, but I feel a sense of solidarity. I have a lot of collaborators! This is a part of history that's not in the history books; it's not something we talk about. But it's about survivors, and we're children of survivors."

The stories in Danticat's Krik? Krak! examine not only the painful social legacy that Danticat left behind in her homeland of Haiti, but also the delicate, sometimes agonizingly twisted ties that bind one to one's heritage. The Haiti that emerges from Danticat's stories is the one in which she grew up, a country under the rule of dictators Francois Papa Doc Duvalier and his son Jean-Claude, known as Baby Doc. The Duvaliers governed Haiti by dint of oppression and cruelty. Their brutal secret police, the Tonton Macoutes, committed many atrocities against the Haitian people. The Duvalier regime was not overthrown until 1986, but the political situation suffered upheaval until well into the 1990s. The nine stories braid together the personal, political, spiritual, and historical threads.

From the opening lines of the first-person narration of "Night Women," the reader is immersed in a spatial and temporal split, "stuck between day and night in the golden amber bronze." It is a split determined by the politics of race, class, and gender and articulated in an angle of vision that combines the stark reality of a single woman's material impoverishment/poverty with the spiritual abundance/hopefulness of ancestors and angels. This layering of history unearths a world of opposites where bodies at rest and bodies at work are forced to exist in the between, the dream places between the dances of angels and the realities of politics. Crowded with transformations that soothe and ruffle abound—boy into ghost, boy into father, mosquito into firefly, mother into prostitute. These shifting perceptions are born on generational links between mother and son, father and son, maternal ancestors ("ghost women riding the crest of waves") that define liberation possibilities that exist within the spirit and imagination.

Lenore L. Brady

Night Women

I cringe from the heat of the night on my face. I feel as bare as open flesh. Tonight I am much older than the twenty-five years that I have lived. The night is the time I dread most in my life. Yet if I am to live, I must depend on it.

Shadows shrink and spread over the lace curtain as my son slips into bed. I watch as he stretches from a little boy into the broom-size of a man, his height mounting the innocent fabric that splits our one-room house into two spaces, two mats, two worlds.

For a brief second, I almost mistake him for the ghost of his father, an old lover who disappeared with the night's shadows a long time ago. My son's bed stays nestled against the corner, far from the peeking jalousies. I watch as he digs furrows in the pillow with his head. He shifts his small body carefully so as not to crease his Sunday clothes. He wraps my long blood-red scarf around his neck, the one I wear myself during the day to tempt my suitors. I let him have it at night, so that he always has something of mine when my face is out of sight.

I watch his shadow resting still on the curtain. My eyes are drawn to him, like the stars peeking through the small holes in the roof that none of my suitors will fix for me, because they like to watch a scrap of the sky while lying on their naked backs on my mat.

A firefly buzzes around the room, finding him and not me. Perhaps it is a mosquito that has learned the gift of lighting itself. He always slaps the mosqui-toes dead on his face without even waking. In the morning, he will have tiny blood spots on his forehead, as though he had spent the whole night kissing a woman with wide-open flesh wounds on her face.

In his sleep he squirms and groans as though he's already discovered that there is pleasure in touching himself. We have never talked about love. What would he need to know? Love is one of those lessons that you grow to learn, the way one learns that one shoe is made to fit a certain foot, lest it cause discomfort.

There are two kinds of women: day women and night women. I am stuck be-tween the day and night in a golden amber bronze. My eyes are the color of dirt, almost copper if I am standing in the sun. I want to wear my matted tresses in braids as soon as I learn to do my whole head without numbing my arms.

Most nights, I hear a slight whisper. My body freezes as I wonder how long it would take for him to cross the curtain and find me.

He says, "Mommy."

I say, *"Darling."*

Somehow in the night, he always calls me in whispers. I hear the buzz of his transistor radio. It is shaped like a can of cola. One of my suitors gave it to him to plug into his ears so he can stay asleep while Mommy *works*.

There is a place in Ville Rose where ghost women ride the crests of waves while brushing the stars out of their hair. There they woo strollers and leave the stars on the path for them. There are nights that I believe that those ghost women are with me. As much as I know that there are women who sit up through the night and undo patches of cloth that they have spent the whole day weaving. These women, they destroy their toil so that they will always have more to do. And as long as there's work, they will not have to lie next to the lifeless soul of a man whose scent still lingers in another woman's bed.

The way my son reacts to my lips stroking his cheeks decides for me if he's asleep. He is like a butterfly fluttering on a rock that stands out naked in the middle of a stream. Sometimes I see in the folds of the eyes a longing for something that's bigger than myself. We are like faraway lovers, lying to one another, under different moons.

When my smallest finger caresses the narrow cleft beneath his nose, sometimes his tongue slips out of his mouth and he licks my fingernail. He moans and turns away, perhaps thinking that this too is a part of the dream.

I whisper my mountain stories in his ear, stories of the ghost women and the stars in their hair. I tell him of the deadly snakes lying at one end of a rainbow and the hat full of gold lying at the other end. I tell him that if I cross a stream of glass-clear hibiscus, I can make myself a goddess. I blow on his long eyelashes to see if he's truly asleep. My fingers coil themselves into visions of birds on his nose. I want him to forget that we live in a place where nothing lasts.

I know that sometimes he wonders why I take such painstaking care. Why do I draw half-moons on my sweaty forehead and spread crimson powders on the rise of my cheeks. We put on his ruffled Sunday suit and I tell him that we are expecting a sweet angel and where angels tread the hosts must be as beautiful as floating hibiscus.

In his sleep, his fingers tug his shirt ruffles loose. He licks his lips from the last piece of sugar candy stolen from my purse.

No more, no more, or your teeth will turn black. I have forgotten to make him brush the mint leaves against his teeth. He does not know that one day a woman like his mother may judge him by the whiteness of his teeth.

It doesn't take long before he is snoring softly. I listen for the shy laughter of his most pleasant dreams. Dreams of angels skipping over his head and occasionally resting their pink heels on his nose.

I hear him humming a song. One of the madrigals they still teach children on very hot afternoons in public schools. *Kompè Jako, domé vou?* Brother Jacques, are you asleep?

The hibiscus rustle in the night outside. I sing along to help him sink deeper into his sleep. I apply another layer of the Egyptian rouge to my cheeks. There are some sparkles in the powder, which make it easier for my visitor to find me in the dark.

Emmanuel will come tonight. He is a doctor who likes big buttocks on women, but my small ones will do. He comes on Tuesdays and Saturdays. He arrives bearing flowers as though he's come to court me. Tonight he brings me bougainvillea. It is always a surprise.

"How is your wife?" I ask.

"Not as beautiful as you."

On Mondays and Thursdays, it is an accordion player named Alexandre. He likes to make the sound of the accordion with his mouth in my ear. The rest of the night, he spends with his breadfruit head rocking on my belly button.

Should my son wake up, I have prepared my fabrication. One day, he will grow too old to be told that a wandering man is a mirage and that naked flesh is a dream. I will tell him his father has come, that an angel brought him back from Heaven for a while.

The stars slowly slip away from the hole in the roof as the doctor sinks deeper and deeper beneath my body. He throbs and pants. I cover his mouth to keep him from screaming. I see his wife's face in the beads of sweat marching down his chin. He leaves with his body soaking from the dew of our flesh. He calls me an avalanche, a waterfall, when he is satisfied.

After he leaves at dawn, I sit outside and smoke a dry tobacco leaf. I watch the piece-worker women march one another to the open market half a day's walk from where they live. I thank the stars that at least I have the days to myself.

When I walk back into the house, I hear the rise and fall of my son's breath. Quickly, I lean my face against his lips to feel the calming heat from his mouth.

"Mommy, have I missed the angels again?" he whispers softly while reaching for my neck.

I slip into the bed next to him and rock him back to sleep.

"Darling, the angels have themselves a lifetime to come to us."

Angela Davis (1944–)

Born in Birmingham, Alabama, Angela Davis attended high school in New York. During the 1960s, she protested racism and espoused Marxism. A self-proclaimed revolutionary, she was at one time listed among the FBI's most wanted criminals. But at her trial she was found innocent of government charges.

Davis became a professor and now teaches at the University of California at Santa Cruz.

As a writer, Davis is best known for her 1974 autobiography and for her many essays in which she analyzes and attacks racism, sexism, rape, class privilege, the prison system, and the exploitation of the poor. Probably no radical from the 1960s has remained as articulate and as visible in the 1990s as Angela Davis.

Below is a chapter from Davis's autobiography in which she recounts her experience in jail. In the second essay below, she analyzes and champions female blues singers, especially Gertrude "Ma" Rainey and Bessie Smith.

Keith D. Miller

Excerpts from *Angela Davis: An Autobiography*

The entire jail was shrouded in darkness when I finally reached the cell in 4b. It was no more than four and a half feet wide. The only furnishings were an iron cot bolted to the floor and a seatless toilet at the foot of the bed. Some minutes after they had locked me in, the officer in charge of that unit—another young black woman—came to the iron door. She whispered through the grating that she was shoving a piece of candy under the door. She sounded sincere enough, but I couldn't take any chances. I didn't want to be paranoid, but it was better to be too distrustful than not cautious enough. I was familiar with jailhouse "suicides" in California. For all I knew, there might be poison in the candy.

The first night in jail, I had no desire to sleep. I thought about George and his brothers in San Quentin. I thought about Jonathan. I thought about my mother and father and hoped that they would make it through this ordeal. And then I thought about the demonstration outside, about all the people who had dropped everything to fight for my freedom.

I had just been captured; a trial awaited me in California on the charges of murder, kidnapping, and conspiracy. A conviction on any one of these charges could mean death in the gas chamber. One would have thought that this was an enormous defeat. Yet, at that moment, I was feeling better than I had felt in a long time. The struggle would be difficult, but there was already a hint of victory. In the heavy silence of the jail, I discovered that if I concentrated hard enough, I could hear echoes of slogans being chanted on the other side of the walls. "Free Angela Davis." "Free All Political Prisoners."

The key rattling in the cell-gate lock startled me. A guard was opening the gate for a plump young black woman wearing a faded blue prisoner's uniform and holding a big tray in her hands.

Smiling, she said in a very soft voice, "Here's your breakfast. Do you want some coffee?"

Her gentle manner was comforting and made me feel like I was among human beings again. I sat up on the cot, thanked her and told her that I would very much like a cup of coffee.

Looking around, I realized that there was no place to put the food—the bed and the toilet were the only furnishings in the tiny cell. But the sister, obviously having gone through this many times before, had already stooped down to a squatting position and was placing the food on the floor: a small box of corn-flakes, a paper cup filled with watery milk, two pieces of plain white bread and a paper cup into which she began to pour the coffee.

"Is there any black coffee?" I asked her, partly because I didn't drink coffee with milk and partly because I wanted an excuse to exchange a few more words with her.

"When they give it to us, it's already like this," she answered, "but I'll see what I can do about getting you some black coffee tomorrow."

The guard told me I had to get ready for my court appearance. Then she slammed the gate on the young woman's exit. While she was unlocking the next cell, the sister whispered through the bars. "Don't worry about a thing. We're all on your side." And she disappeared down the corridor.

I looked down at my breakfast, and saw that a roach had already discovered it. I left it all spread out on the bare floor untouched. After I had gone through the elaborate steps involved in getting dressed for court, a matron led me down-stairs. A crowd of white men was milling around the receiving room. Seeing me, they swept toward me like vultures and clamped handcuffs around my wrists, which still ached from the previous day. Outside, shiny tin cars crowded into the cobblestone courtyard. It was still dark when the caravan reached the federal courthouse. A glimpse of the morning paper's bold-lettered headlines, peeping out from under some man's arm, stunned me: ANGELA DAVIS CAPTURED IN NEW YORK. It suddenly struck me that the huge crowd of press people summoned by the FBI the evening before had probably written similar headline stories throughout the country. Knowing that my name was now familiar to millions of people, I felt overwhelmed. Yet I knew that all this publicity was not really aimed at me as an individual. Using me as an example, they wanted to discredit the black liberation movement, the Left in general and obviously also the Communist Party. I was only the occasion for their manipulations.

The holding cell where I spent the next several hours was cleaner than the jail cell I had just left and looked like a giant, unfinished bathroom. It had sparkling white tile walls and a light-colored linoleum floor. A seatless toilet stood in one of the corners. Long metal benches lined the three walls.

One of the federal bureaucrats came into the cell.

"I have nothing to say," I told him, "until I see my lawyer."

"Your father's lawyer is waiting outside," he said.

My father's lawyer? Perhaps it was a friend posing as my "father's lawyer" in order to get permission to see me.

In a large hall filled with rows of desks, John Abt was waiting to see me. Although I had never met him before I knew about the trials in which he had successfully defended members of our Party. With a great feeling of relief, I sat down to talk with him.

"I waited for hours last night at the jail, but they refused to let me in," John said. "I had to get your father to call them before they would let me see you this morning."

He went on to explain that I was about to be arraigned on the federal charge—interstate flight to avoid prosecution. Before he had gotten very far in his discussion of the legal proceedings before us, a group of people pressed through a door at the other end of the room. Without my glasses, which the FBI had not bothered to return, the people's faces were blurred. Noticing a young black woman involved in a heated exchange with the marshals, I squinted in order to see her more clearly.

"That's Margaret!" I shouted.

Margaret Burnham was a very old friend of mine. During my youngest years, her family and mine had lived in the same housing project in Birmingham. When the Burnhams moved to New York, we visited them every summer for four years, then we alternated the visits—sometimes they would come to Birmingham and sometimes we would go to New York. Our families had been so close that I had always considered Margaret, her sisters Claudia and Linda, and her brother Charles more family than friends. I had not seen her for several years. She had been in Mississippi, gotten married and given birth to a child. I knew that she had recently graduated from law school and I assumed she was now practicing in New York.

"Margaret," I called, as loudly as I could, "come on over." Apparently this was enough to settle the argument she was having with the marshal, for he did nothing to prevent her from walking over to the desk where John and I were. It felt so good to embrace her. "Margaret," I said to her, "I'm so glad you came. You don't know how glad I am to see you." As we started talking about personal things, I almost forgot that there was business to be taken care of.

"Can you work on the case?" I asked her finally, desperately hoping she would say yes.

"You know I will, Angela," she answered, "if that's what you think I should do."

It was as if half the battle had already been won.

John Abt went on to explain the legal situation.

Back in August, Marin County had charged me with murder, kidnapping, and conspiracy to commit murder and rescue prisoners. On the basis of an FBI agent's affidavit declaring that I had been seen by "reliable sources" in Birmingham, a federal judge had issued a warrant charging me with "interstate flight to avoid prosecution." It was possible, John said, that I might be "removed" to California, which meant that without further litigation I would simply be transferred from the New York Federal District to the California Federal District. But more than likely, he surmised, I would be "turned over" to the State of New York for extradition to California, and we would be able to challenge California in the New York courts.

As we were winding up this conference, David[1] walked into the room, encircled by guards. I hadn't seen him since our arrest. He looked as if he hadn't slept either.

In a cool, crisp tone, he called out to me, "Remember now, no matter what, we're going to beat this thing."

"No talking between the prisoners," a voice announced. It could have come from any one of the marshals standing around.

"OK, David," I said, ignoring the command. "You be sure to keep strong yourself."

I had never seen a courtroom so small. With its marred walls of blond wood, it had the worn-out elegance of an old mansion. There was just enough room for the bench and a single row of chairs lining the back wall. The smallness of the courtroom exaggerated the height of the judge's bench. The judge himself was little, like his courtroom. He was wearing old-fashioned plastic-rimmed glasses, and his white hair was spread sparsely over his head. I thought about Soledad guard O. G. Miller perched in his gun tower, aiming his carbine at the three brothers he killed in the yard in January.[2]

There were no spectators. The only non-official people were reporters—and there were not very many of them. As I entered, a sister sitting in the seat closest to the door held up a copy of the hardcover edition of George's *Soledad Brother*. This was the first time I had seen the book, which I had read in manuscript.

The arraignment on the federal charges was short and to the point. All the prosecutor was required to do was to prove, for the record, that I was the Angela Davis named in the warrant. The bail figure was a farce. Who could even contemplate raising $250,000 to get me out of jail?

It was still early—late morning or early afternoon—when I returned to the holding cell. The last time I had been in the cell, my thoughts had been monopolized by the problem of finding a lawyer. Now that I had two fine lawyers whom I trusted and loved, I could no longer ward off thoughts of my imprisonment. I was alone with the shiny tile walls and the gray steel bars. Walls and bars, nothing more. I wished I had a book or, if not something to read, at least a pencil and a sheet of paper.

I fought the tendency to individualize my predicament. Pacing from one end of this cell to the other, from a bench along one wall to a bench along the other, I kept telling myself that I didn't have the right to get upset about a few hours of being alone in a holding cell. What about the brother—Charles Jordon was his name—who had spent, not hours, but days and weeks in a pitch-dark strip-cell in Soledad Prison, hardly large enough for him to stretch out on the cold cement, reeking of urine and human excrement because the only available toilet was a hole in the floor which could hardly be seen in the dark.

I thought about the scene George had described in the manuscript of his book—the brother who had painted a night sky on the ceiling of his cell, because it had been years since he had seen the moon and stars. (When it was discovered, the guards painted over it in gray.) And there was Ericka Huggins at Niantic State Farm for Women in Connecticut. Ericka, Bobby, the Soledad Brothers, the Soledad 7, the Tombs Rebels and all the countless others whose identifies were hidden behind so much concrete and steel, so many locks and chains. How could I indulge even the faintest inclination toward self-pity? Yet I paced faster across the holding cell. I walked with the determination of someone who has someplace very important to go. At the same time, I was trying not to let the jailers see my agitation.

When someone finally opened the gate, it was late in the evening. Margaret and John were waiting to accompany me to a court appearance in the same courtroom we had appeared in that morning. Aside from us, there were no "civilians" in the courtroom, not even the reporters from the morning session. I wondered what kind of secret appearance this was going to be.

The elderly judge announced that he was rescinding the bail and releasing me on my own recognizance. I was sure I had misheard his words. But already, the Feds were approaching me to unlock the handcuffs. The judge said something else, which I hardly heard, and then suddenly several New York policemen moved in to replace the federal handcuffs with their own manacles.

With the New York handcuffs binding my wrists, there was a trip to a musty police precinct office, where I was officially booked as a prisoner of the State of New York. Forms, fingerprints, mug shots—the same routine. The New York police seemed to be as confused as their surroundings. Amid all the papers haphazardly strewn on desks and counters, they were running around like novices. Their incompetence calmed me. It must have been around ten in the evening when one of them announced that there would be yet another court appearance. (Did Margaret and John know about this third court session?)

The courtroom in the New York County Courthouse was larger than any I had ever seen. Its high ceilings and interminable rows of benches made it look like a church from another era. Most courtrooms are windowless, but this one seemed especially isolated from the outside world. It was so dimly lit, with hardly anyone but policemen sitting randomly on the benches, that I had the impression that what was about to happen was supposed to be hidden from the people outside. Neither Margaret nor John was there. When they told me that I had to be arraigned before a New York judge, I said that I wasn't budging from my seat until they contacted my lawyers. I was prepared to wait the whole night.

When John finally arrived, he said that the police had directed him to the wrong courtroom. He had been running all over New York trying to find me. After hours of waiting, the court appearance lasted all of two minutes.

Back at the jail, I was so physically and emotionally exhausted that I only wanted to sleep. Even the hard cell cot in the "mental" ward felt comfortable. But as soon as I closed my eyes, I was jolted out of my exhaustion by piercing screams in a language which sounded Slavic. They came from a cell at the other end of the corridor. Footsteps approached the cell in the darkness. Voices tried to calm the woman in English but could not assuage her terror. I listened to her all night—until they took her away in the morning. [. . .]

While I was in solitary, I finally began to receive regular evening visits from several friends. An officer would stand just close enough to hear my side of the conversation. (I assumed that they summarized it in the log book.) I was not a stranger to visiting arrangements in jails, for I had visited friends and comrades in prison on many occasions. But this visiting room was by far the worst I had seen. It is not unusual to have to speak to a visitor through a glass pane, but the panes in the House of Detention were less than a square foot in size, and the rust-colored dirt that covered them made it impossible to get a clear look at the person who had come to see you. The prisoners had to stand up during these twenty-minute visits and shout into telephones which inevitably seemed to stop functioning just when the most important part of the conversation had gotten under way.

One evening while I was still in solitary, I received a visit from Kendra Alexander, who had been subpoenaed to New York along with her husband Franklin to testify before the Grand Jury in the case against David Poindexter.[3] She informed me that the demonstration protesting my solitary confinement was about to begin. They knew more or less where my room was located—I had carefully detailed the areas of Greenwich Avenue I could see from my window. The demonstrators were to gather on the corner of Greenwich and West Tenth.

I ran back upstairs. The officer guarding me was one of the friendlier ones, and turned her head and closed her ears while I spread the news. On five or six floors, the women who lived in the corridors with windows looking out on Greenwich Avenue would be able to see and hear the demonstration.

It was an enthusiastic crowd. Their shouts "Free Angela! Free all our sisters!" rang through the night. Looking down from my cell window, I became altogether engrossed in the speeches, sometimes losing the sensation of captivity, feeling my-self down there on the street with them. My mind flashed back to past demonstra-tions—"Free the Soledad Brothers," "Free Bobby and Ericka," "Free Huey," "End the war in Vietnam," "Stop police killings in our community now . . ."

Jose Stevens, a communist leader from Harlem, had wound up his speech. Franklin was addressing his words, full of passion, to all the prisoners locked up in the Women's House of Detention. Then my sister, Fania, took the megaphone. The sound of her voice shocked me back into the reality of my situation, for I momentarily had forgotten that this demonstration was centered around me. I had been so absorbed in the rally that I had actually felt as if I were down there in the streets with them. Reflecting upon the impenetrability of this fortress, on all the things that keep me separated from my comrades barely a few hundred yards away, and reflecting on my solitary confinement—this prison within a prison that kept me separated from my sisters in captivity—I felt the weight of imprisonment perhaps more at that moment than at any time before.

My frustration was immense. But before my thoughts led me further in the direction of self-pity, I brought them to a halt, reminding myself that this was precisely what solitary confinement was supposed to evoke. In such a state the keepers could control their victim. I would not let them conquer me. I trans-formed my frustration into raging energy for the fight.

Against the background of the chants ringing up from the demonstration below, I took myself to task for having indulged in self-pity. What about George, John and Fleeta, and my co-defendant, Ruchell Magee, who had endured far worse than I could ever expect to grapple with? What about Charles Jordan and his bout with that medieval strip-cell in Soledad Prison? What about those who had given their lives—Jonathan, McClain, and Christmas?

The experience of the demonstration had worked up so much tension in me that I felt none of the debilitating effects of the fast. I did an extra heavy set of exercises to sufficiently lower my energy level so I could lie in bed in relative calm. There was no question of getting a full night's sleep. On this evening, I had to be especially vigilant. All was quiet in the jail, but I was convinced that the demonstration had aroused the jailers, and I had to hold myself in readiness in case they decided to strike sometime during the night. On the tenth day of my hunger strike, at a time when I had persuaded myself that I could continue indefinitely without eating, the Federal Court handed down a ruling enjoin-ing the jail administration from holding me any longer in isolation and under maximum security conditions. They had decided—under pressure, of course—that this unwarranted punishment was meted out to me because of my political beliefs and affiliation. The court was all but saying that Commissioner of Cor-rections George McGrath and Jessie Behagan, the superintendent of the Women's House of D., were so fearful of letting the women in the jail discover what communism was that they preferred to violate my most basic constitu-tional rights.

This ruling came as a surprise. I hadn't expected it to be so swift and to the point. It was an important victory, for we had firmly established that those in the Department of Corrections in New York would not have a clear course before them when they attempted to persecute the next political prisoner delivered into their hands. At the same time, however, I did not put it past the jail administration to concoct another situation which might not be solitary confinement, but which would give me an equally bad time. This thought subdued my delight at the news of the injunction.

Next destination: seventh floor, C corridor. When I arrived, there was a big shake-up going on. Women were being moved out, others were coming in. For a moment the thought struck me that they were preparing a special corridor for informers, jailer's confidantes—and me. But as it turned out, the lawsuit had forced the administration to get on its toes—so-called "first offenders" were supposed to be jailed separately from those who had already spent time in the House of Detention. Apparently the necessary shifts were being made.

There was little time to learn my way about before all the cell gates were locked, but some of my neighbors gave me a guided tour of my 8' × 5' cell. Because mine was the corner cell—the one which could be easily spied on from the officer's desk in the main hallway—it was also the smallest one on the corridor; the double bunk made it appear even smaller. The fixtures—the bed, the tiny sink, the toilet—were all arranged in a straight line, leaving no more than a width of two feet of floor at any point in the cell.

The sisters helped me improvise a curtain in front of the toilet and sink so they could not be seen from the corridor. They showed me how to use newspaper wrapped in scrap cloth to make a seat cover so the toilet could be turned into a chair to be used at the iron table that folded down from the wall in front of it. I laughed out loud at the thought of doing all my writing while sitting on the toilet stool.

Lock-in time was approaching; a sister remembered that she had forgotten to warn me about one of the dangers of night-life in the House of D. "'Mickey' will be trying to get into your cell tonight," she said, and I would have to take precautionary steps to "keep him out."

"Mickey?" Was there some maniac the jailers let loose at night to pester the women?

The sister laughingly told me she was referring to the mice which scampered about in the darkness of the corridors looking for cell doors not securely stuffed with newspapers.

It became a nightly ritual: placing meticulously folded newspapers in the little space between the gate and the floor and halfway up the gate along the wall. Despite the preventive measures we took, Mickey could always chew through the barricade in at least one cell, and we were often awakened by the shouts of a woman calling the officer to get the mouse out. One night Mickey joined me in the top bunk. When I felt him crawling around my neck, I brushed him away thinking that it was roaches. When I finally realized what it was, I called for the broom—our only weapon against him. Apparently mousetraps were too expensive, and they were not going to exterminate.

There was one good thing about Mickey. His presence reassured us that there were no rats in the vicinity. The two never share the same turf.

In a sense our daily struggles with Mickey—with all the various makeshift means devised to get the better of him—were symbolic of a larger struggle with the system. Indulging in a flight of fancy, I would sometimes imagine that all the preparations that were made at night to ward off those creatures were the barricades being erected against that larger enemy. That hundreds of women, all over the jail, politically conscious, politically committed, were acting in revolutionary unison.

That first evening, shortly after the sister had helped me stuff the gate with newspapers, an officer called out, "Lock-in time, girls. Into your cells." As the women slid their heavy iron gates closed, loud metallic crashing noises thundered from all four corridors of the seventh floor. I could hear the same sounds at a distance echoing from throughout the jail. (In 4b, I had never been able to figure out what all this commotion was about. The first time I heard it, I thought a rebellion had been unleashed.)

The officer came around to count each prisoner, and at 9 p.m. all lights in the corridor and cells were turned off by a master switch. In the darkness, a goodnight ritual was acted out. One sister shouted goodnight to another, calling her by name. The latter, catching the identity of the voice, would shout goodnight, also calling the first sister by name. Early on, someone from my corridor called out warmly, "Good night, Angela!" But having learned hardly anyone's name, much less to recognize their voices, I was an outsider to this ritual and could only respond with a lonesome, unsupported (though no less vigorous) "goodnight." My call sparked off goodnight shouts to me, which came not only from my own corridor but from the others as well. I am sure that there had never been such a prolonged "saying of goodnights." The officers did not interrupt, though silence should have prevailed long before.

Notes

1 Editor's note: David Poindexter traveled with Davis during the two months she was underground. He was acquitted of federal charges of harboring a fugitive.

2 Editor's note: O. G. Miller was the Soledad prison guard who killed three black prisoners (W. L. Nolen, Cleveland Edwards, and Alvin Miller) on January 13, 1970. When the grand jury ruled his action was "justifiable homicide," the prisoners' riot resulted in the killing of a guard who was on duty at the time. The Soledad Brothers were charged with the murder of this guard.

3 Editor's note: Angela Davis first met Kendra and Franklin Alexander through her work with the Black Student Alliance. Franklin Alexander and Davis were active together in the organization, Black Panther Political Party, and it was as a result of Davis's growing political relationship with the Alexanders that she decided to join their organization, the Che-Lumumba Club of the Communist Party, USA. Kendra Alexander died in 1993, Franklin in 1994.

I Used To Be Your Sweet Mama: Ideology, Sexuality, and Domesticity

You had your chance and proved unfaithful
So now I'm gonna be real mean and hateful
I used to be your sweet mama, sweet papa
But now I'm just as sour as can be.
            "I USED TO BE YOUR SWEET MAMA"[1]

Like most forms of popular music, African-American blues lyrics talk about love. However, what is distinctive about the blues, particular in relation to other American popular music forms of the 1920s and 1930s, is its intellectual independence and representational freedom. One of the most obvious ways in which blues lyrics deviated from that era's established popular music culture was their provocative and pervasive sexual—including homosexual—imagery.[2]

By contrast, the popular song formulas of the period demanded saccharine and idealized non-sexual depictions of heterosexual love relationships.[3] Those aspects of lived love relationships that were not compatible with the dominant, etherealized ideology of love—such as extramarital relationships, domestic violence, and the ephemerality of many sexual partnerships—were largely banished from the established popular musical culture. These themes pervade the blues. What is even more striking is the fact that initially the professional performers of this music—the most widely heard individual purveyors of the blues—were women. Bessie Smith earned the title "Empress of the Blues" not least through the sale of three-quarters of a million copies of her first record.[4]

The historical context within which the blues developed a tradition of openly addressing both female and male sexuality reveals an ideological framework that was specifically African American.[5] Emerging during the decades following the abolition of slavery, the blues gave musical expression to the new social and sexual realities encountered by African Americans as free women and men. The former slaves' economic status had not undergone a radical transformation—they were no less impoverished than they had been during slavery.[6] It was the status of their personal relationships that was revolutionized. For the first time in the history of the African presence in North America, masses of black women and men were in a position to make autonomous decisions regarding the sexual partnerships into which they entered.[7] Sexuality thus was one of the most tangible domains in which emancipation was acted upon, and through which its meanings were expressed. Sovereignty in sexual matters marked an important divide between life during slavery and life after emancipation.

This essay is excerpted from the first chapter of Angela Y. Davis, *Blues Legacies and Black Feminism: Gertrude "Ma" Rainey, Bessie Smith, and Billie Holiday* (New York: Pantheon, 1998), copyright © 1998 by Angela Y. Davis. Reprinted by permission of Pantheon Books, a division of Random House, Inc.

Themes of individual sexual love rarely appear in the music forms produced during slavery. Whatever the reasons for this—and it may have been due to the slave system's economic management of procreation, which did not tolerate, and often severely punished, the public exhibition of self-initiated sexual relationships—I am interested here in the disparity between the individualistic, "private" nature of sexuality and the collective forms and nature of the music that was produced and performed during slavery. Sexuality after emancipation could not be adequately expressed or addressed through the musical forms existing under slavery. The spirituals and the work songs confirm that the individual concerns of black people given musical expression during slavery centered on a collective desire for an end to the system declaring them unconditional slaves to their white masters. This does not mean there was an absence of sexual meanings in the music produced by African-American slaves.[8] It means that slave music—both religious and secular—was quintessentially collective music. It was collectively performed and it gave expression to the community's yearning for freedom.[9]

The blues, on the other hand, the predominant post-slavery African-American musical form, articulated a new valuation of individual emotional needs and desires. The birth of the blues was aesthetic evidence of new psycho-social realities within the black population. This music was presented by individuals singing alone, accompanying themselves on such instruments as the banjo or guitar. The blues therefore marked the advent of a popular culture of performance, with the borders of performer and audience becoming increasingly differentiated.[10] Through the emergence of the professional blues singer—a predominantly female figure accompanied by small and large instrumental ensembles—as part of the rise of the black entertainment industry, this individualized mode of presenting popular music crystallized into a performance culture that has had an enduring influence on Africa-American music.

The spirituals, as they survived and were transformed during the post-slavery era, were both intensely religious and the aesthetic bearers of the slaves' collective aspirations for worldly freedom.[11] Under changed historical circumstances in which former slaves had closer contact with the religious practices and ideologies of the dominant culture, sacred music began to be increasingly enclosed within institutionalized religious spaces. Slave religious practices were inseparable from other aspects of everyday life—work, family, sabotage, escape. Post-slavery religion gradually lost some of this fluidity and came to be dependent on the church. As sacred music evolved from spirituals to gospel, it increasingly concentrated on the hereafter. Historian Lawrence Levine characterizes the nature of this development succinctly. "The overriding thrust of the gospel songs," he writes,

was otherworldly. Emphasis was almost wholly upon God with whom Man's relationship was one of total dependence. . . . Jesus rather than the Hebrew children dominated the gospel songs. And it was not the warrior Jesus of the spirituals but a benevolent spirit who promised His children rest and peace and justice in the hereafter.[12]

The blues rose to become the most prominent secular genre in early twenti-eth-century black American music. As it came to displace sacred music in the everyday lives of black people, it both reflected and helped to construct a new black consciousness. This consciousness interpreted God as the opposite of the Devil, religion as the not secular, and the secular as largely sexual. With the blues came the designations "God's music" and the "Devil's music." The former was performed in church—although it could also accompany work[13]—while the latter was performed in jook joints, circuses, and traveling shows.[14]

Despite the new salience of this binary opposition in the everyday life of black people, it is important to underscore the close relationship between the old music and the new. The new music had old roots, and the old music reflected a new ideological grounding of black religion. Both were deeply rooted in the same history and culture.

God and the Devil had co-habited the same universe during slavery, not as polar opposites, but rather as complex characters who had different powers and who both entered into relationships with human beings. They also sometimes engaged with each other on fairly equal terms. As Henry Louis Gates and others have argued, the Devil was often associated with the trickster god Legba or Eleg-gua in Yoruba religions.[15] Some of the folk tales Zora Neale Hurston presents in *Mules and Men* portray the devil not as evil incarnate, but as a character with whom it was possible to identify in humorous situations.[16]

In describing the religious household in which she was reared, veteran blueswoman Ida Goodson emphasizes that the blues were banned from her child-hood home. Nevertheless, she and her playmates often played and sang the blues when her parents were away. On those occasions when the parents showed up un-expectedly, they easily made the transition to gospel music without missing a beat:

> My mother and father were religious persons. And they liked music, but they like church music. They didn't like jazz like we do. And of course we could not even play jazz in our home while they were there. But just the moment they would turn their back, go to their society or church somewhere or another, we'd get our neighbor-hood children to come in there and we'd get to playing the blues and having a good time. But still we'd have one girl on the door watching to see when Mr. Goodson's coming back home or Mrs. Goodson. Because I knew if they came and caught us what we would get. . . . Whenever we'd see my father or my mother coming back home, the girl be saying, "There come Mr. Goodson 'nem." And they'd be so close up on us, we'd change the blues, singing "Jesus keep me near the cross." After that my mother and father would join us and we'd all get to singing church songs.[17]

As if reconciling the two positions—that of herself as a young musician and that of her religious parents—Goodson later explains that "The Devil got his work and God got his work."

During slavery, the sacred universe was virtually all-embracing. Spirituals helped to construct community among the slaves and infused this imagined community with hope for a better life. They retold Old Testament narratives about the Hebrew people's struggle against Pharaoh's oppression, and thereby established a community narrative of African people enslaved in North America that simultaneously transcended the slave system and encouraged its abolition. Under the conditions of US slavery, the sacred—and especially sacred music—was an important means of preserving African cultural memory. Karl Marx's comments on religion as the "opium of the people"[18] notwithstanding, the spirituals attest to the fact that religious consciousness can itself play a transformative role. As Sojourner Truth and other abolitionists demonstrated—as well as insurrectionary leaders Nat Turner and Denmark Vesey, and the Underground Railroad conductor Harriet Tubman— religion was far more than Marx's "illusory sun." Spirituals were embedded in and gave expression to a powerful yearning for freedom.[19] Religion was indeed, in Marx's words, the "soul" of "soulless conditions."[20]

The spirituals articulated the hopes of black slaves in religious terms. In the vast disappointment that accompanied emancipation—when economic and political liberation must have seemed more unattainable than ever—blues created a discourse[21] that represented freedom in more immediate and accessible terms. The material conditions for the freedom about which the slaves had sung in their spirituals seemed no closer after slavery than they had seemed before, but there were nevertheless distinct differences between the slaves' personal status under slavery and during the post-Civil War period. In three major respects, emancipation had radically transformed their personal lives: (1) there was no longer a proscription on free individual travel; (2) education was now a realizable goal for individual men and women; (3) sexuality could be explored freely by individuals who now could enter into autonomously chosen personal relationships. The new blues consciousness was shaped by and gave expression to at least two of these three transformations: travel and sexuality. In both male and female blues, travel and sexuality are ubiquitous themes, handled both separately and together. But what finally is most striking is the way the blues registered sexuality as a tangible expression of freedom; it was this dimension that most profoundly marked and defined the secularity of the blues.

James Cone offers the following definition of the blues, agreeing with C. Eric Lincoln's succinct characterization of them as "secular spirituals." Cone writes,

> They are secular in the same sense that they confine their attention solely to the immediate and affirm the bodily expression of black soul, including its sexual manifestations. They are spirituals because they are impelled by the same search for the truth of black experience.[22]

It is not necessary to accede to Cone's essentialist invocation of a single metaphysical "truth" of black experience to gain from it a key insight into why the blues were condemned as the Devil's music. It was because they drew upon and incorporated sacred consciousness and thereby posed a serious threat to religious attitudes.

Levine emphasizes the blurring of the sacred and the secular both in gospel music and in the blues. It may not have been the secularity of the blues that produced such castigation by the church, he argues, but rather, precisely their sacred nature. He writes,

> The blues was threatening not primarily because it was secular; other forms of secular music were objected to less strenuously and often not at all. Blues was threatening because its spokesmen and its ritual too frequently provided the expressive communal channels of relief that had been largely the province of religion in the past.[23]

Although both Cone and Levine make references to Mamie Smith, Ma Rainey, Bessie Smith, and other women who composed and performed blues songs, they, like most scholars, tend to view women as marginal to the production of the blues. Note that in the passage quoted above, Levine refers quite explicitly to the "spokesmen" of the blues. With the simple substitution of "spokeswomen," the argument he suggests would become more compelling and more deeply revealing of the new religious consciousness about which he writes.

Blues practices, as Levine asserts, did tend to appropriate previously religious channels of expression and this appropriation was associated with women's voices. Women summoned sacred responses to their messages about sexuality.[24] During this period, religious consciousness came increasingly under the control of institutionalized churches, and male dominance over the religious process came to be taken for granted. At the same time that male ministers were becoming a professional caste, women blues singers were performing as professional artists and attracting large audiences in revival-like gatherings. Gertrude "Ma" Rainey and Bessie Smith were the most widely known of these women. They preached about sexual love, and in doing so they articulated a collective experience of freedom, and gave voice to the most powerful evidence there was for many black people that slavery no longer existed.

The expression of socially unfulfilled dreams in the language and imagery of individual sexual love is, of course, not peculiar to the African-American experience. As part of the capitalist schism between the public and the private realms within European-derived American popular culture, however, themes of romantic love had quite different ideological implications from themes of sexuality within post-slavery African-American cultural expression. In the context of the consolidation of industrial capitalism, the sphere of personal love and domestic life in mainstream American culture came to be increasingly idealized as the arena in which happiness was to be sought.[25] This held a special significance for women, since love and domesticity were supposed to constitute the outermost limits of their lives. Full membership in the public community was the exclusive domain of men. Therefore, European-American popular songs have to be interpreted within this context and as contributing to patriarchal hegemony.

The blues did not entirely escape the influences that shaped the role of romantic love in the popular songs of the dominant culture. Nevertheless, the incorporation of personal relationships into the blues has its own historical meanings and social and political resonances. Love was not represented as an idealized realm to which unfulfilled dreams of happiness were relegated. The historical African-American vision of individual sexual love linked it inextricably with possibilities of social freedom in the economic and political realms. Unfreedom during slavery involved, among other things, a prohibition of freely chosen, enduring family relationships. Because slaves were legally defined as commodities, women of childbearing age were valued in accordance with their breeding potential and were often forced to copulate with men—viewed as "bucks"—chosen by their owners for the sole purpose of producing valuable progeny.[26] Moreover, direct sexual exploitation of African women by their white masters was a constant feature of slavery.[27] What tenuous permanence in familial relationships the slaves did manage to construct was always subject to the whim of their masters and the potential profits to be reaped from sale. The suffering caused by forced ruptures of slave families has been abundantly documented.[28]

Given this context, it is understandable that the personal and sexual dimensions of freedom acquired an expansive importance, especially since the economic and political ingredients of freedom were largely denied to black people in the aftermath of slavery. The focus on sexual love in blues music was thus quite different in meaning from the prevailing idealization of romantic love mainstream popular culture. For recently emancipated slaves, freely chosen sexual love became a mediator between historical disappointment and the new social realities of an evolving African-American community. Ralph Ellison alludes to this dimension of the blues, I think, when he notes that "their mysteriousness . . . their ability to imply far more than they state outright and their capacity to make the details of sex convey meanings which touch on the metaphysical."[29]

Sexuality was central in both men's and women's blues. During the earliest phases of their history, blues were essentially a male phenomenon. The archetypal blues singer was a solitary wandering man accompanied by his banjo or guitar, and, in the words of blues scholar Giles Oakley, his principal theme "is the sexual relationship. Almost all other themes, leaving town, train rides, work trouble, general dissatisfaction sooner or later reverts to the central concern."[30] In women's blues, which became a crucial element of the rising black entertainment industry, there was an even more pronounced emphasis on love and sexuality.

The representations of love and sexuality in women's blues often blatantly contradicted mainstream ideological assumptions regarding women and being in love. They also challenged the notion that women's "place" was in the domestic sphere. Such notions were based on the social realities of middle-class white women's lives, but were incongruously applied to all women, regardless of race or class.[31] This led to inevitable contradictions between prevailing social expectations and black women's social realities. Women of that era were expected to seek fulfillment within the confines of marriage, with their husbands functioning as provider and their children as evidence of their worth as human beings. The sparsity of allusions to marriage and domesticity in women's blues therefore becomes highly significant.

In Bessie Smith's rendition of "Sam Jones Blues"—which contains one of the few commentaries on the subject of marriage to be found in her body of work—the subject is acknowledged only in relation to its dissolution. Her performance of this song satirically accentuates the contrast between the dominant cultural construction of marriage and the stance of economic independence black women were compelled to assume for their sheer survival. Referring to a wandering husband, Bessie Smith sings,

> . . . I'm free and livin' all alone
> Say, hand me the key that unlocks my front door
> Because that bell don't read "Sam Jones" no more
> No, you ain't talkin' to Mrs Jones, you speaking to Miss Wilson now.[32]

Although the written lyrics reveal a conversation between "proper" English and black working-class English, only by listening to the song do we experience the full impact of Smith's manipulation of language in her recording. References to marriage as perceived by the dominant white culture are couched in irony. She mocks the notion of eternal matrimony—"I used to be your lofty mate"—singing genteel words with a teasing intonation to evoke white cultural conceptions. On the other hand, when she indicates the perspective of the black woman, Miss Wilson—who "used to be Mrs Jones"—she sings in a comfortable, bluesy black English. This song is remarkable for the way Smith translates into musical contrast and contention the clash between two cultures' perceptions of marriage—and particularly women's place within the institution. It is easy to imagine the testifying responses Smith no doubt evoked in her female audiences, responses that affirmed working-class black women's sense of themselves as relatively emancipated if not from marriage itself then at least from some of its most confining ideological constraints.

The protagonists in women's blues are seldom wives and almost never mothers. One explanation for the absence of direct allusions to marriage may be the different words mainstream and African-American cultures use to designate "male spouse." African-American working-class argot refers to both husbands and male lovers (and even in some cases female lovers) as "my man" or "my daddy." But these different linguistic practices cannot be considered in isolation from the social realities they represent, for they point to divergent perspectives regarding the institution of marriage.

During Bessie Smith's era most black heterosexual couples—married or not—had children. However, blues women rarely sang about mothers, fathers, and children. In the subject index to her book *Black Pearls*, black studies scholar Daphne Duval Harrison lists the following themes: advice to other women; alcohol; betrayal or abandonment; broken or failed love affairs; death; departure; dilemma of staying with man or returning to family; disease and afflictions; erotica; hell; homosexuality; infidelity; injustice; jail and serving time; loss of lover;

love; men; mistreatment; murder; other woman; poverty; promiscuity; sadness; sex; suicide; supernatural; trains; traveling; unfaithfulness; vengeance; weariness, depression and disillusionment; weight loss.[33] It is revealing that she does not include children, domestic life, husband, and marriage.

The absence of the mother figure in the blues does not imply a rejection of motherhood as such, but rather suggests that blues women found the cult of motherhood irrelevant to the realities of their lives.[34] The female figures evoked in women's blues are independent women free of the domestic orthodoxy of the prevailing representations of womanhood through which female subjects of the era were constructed. . . .

*   *   *   *   *

The woman in Ma Rainey's "Lawd Send Me a Man Blues" harbors no illusions about the relationship she desires with a man. She is lonely and is wondering "who gonna pay my board bill now." Appealing for any man she can get, she pleads, singing with a bluesy zeal,

> Send me a zulu, a voodoo, any old man
> I'm not particular, boys, I'll take what I can.[35]

Bessie Smith's "Baby Doll" conveys a similar message:

> I want to be somebody's baby doll
> So I can get my loving all the time
> I want to be somebody's baby doll
> To ease my mind.[36]

These blues women had no qualms about announcing female desire. Their songs express women's intention to "get their loving." Such affirmations of sexual autonomy and open expressions of female sexual desire give historical voice to possibilities of equality not articulated elsewhere. Women's blues and the cultural politics lived out in the careers of the blues queens put these new possibilities on the historical agenda. . . .

By focusing on the issue of misogynist violence, the first activist moments of the contemporary women's movement exposed the centrality of the ideological separation of the public and private spheres to the structure of male domination. In the early 1970s women began to speak publicly about their experiences of rape, battery, and about the violation of their reproductive rights. Obscured by a shroud of silence, these assaults against women traditionally had been regarded as a fact of private life to be shielded at all costs from scrutiny in the public sphere. That this cover-up would no longer be tolerated was the explosive meaning behind feminists' defiant notion that "the personal is political."[37]

The performances of the classic blues women—especially Bessie Smith— were one of the few cultural spaces in which a tradition of public discourse on male violence had been previously established. One explanation for the fact that the blues women of the 1920s—and the texts they present—fail to respect the taboo on speaking publicly about domestic violence is that the blues as a genre never acknowledges the discursive and ideological boundaries separating the private sphere from the public. Historically, there has been no body of literature on battering because white, well-to-do women who were in a position to write about their experiences in abusive relationships have only recently been convinced that such privately executed violence is a suitable subject for public discourse.

There is, however, a body of preserved oral culture—or "orature," to use a term employed by some scholars[38]—about domestic abuse in the songs of blues women like Gertrude Rainey and Bessie Smith. Violence against women was always an appropriate topic of women's blues. The contemporary urge to break the silence surrounding misogynist violence, and the organized political movement challenging violence against women has an aesthetic precursor in the work of the classic blues singers.

Women's blues have been accused of promoting acquiescent and therefore anti-feminist responses to misogynist abuse. It is true that some of the songs recorded by Rainey and Smith seem to exemplify acceptance of male violence—and sometimes even masochistic delight in being the target of lovers' beatings. Such claims do not take into account the extent to which blues meaning is manipulated and transformed—sometimes even into its opposite—in blues performance. Blues make abundant use of humor, satire, and irony, revealing their historic roots in slave music, wherein indirect methods of expression were the only means by which the oppression of slavery could be denounced. In this sense, the blues genre is a direct descendant of work songs, which often relied on indirection and irony to highlight the inhumanity of slave owners so that their targets were sure to misunderstand the intended meaning.[39]

Bessie Smith sings a number of songs whose lyrics may be interpreted as condoning emotional and physical abuse as attendant hazards for women involved in sexual partnerships. But close attention to her musical presentation of these songs persuades the listener that they contain implicit critiques of male abuse. In "Yes Indeed He Do," Bessie Smith's sarcastic presentation of the lyrics transforms their observations on an unfaithful, abusive and exploitative lover into a scathing critique of male violence:

> Is he true as stars above me? What kind of fool is you?
> He don't stay from home all night more than six times a week
> No, I known that I'm his Sheba and I know that he's my sheik
> And when I ask him where he's been he grabs a rocking chair
> Then he knocks me down and says it's just a love lick dear.[40]

Edward Brooks, in *The Bessie Smith Companion*, makes the following comment about this song:

Bessie delivers the song with growling gusto, as if it were really a panegyric to en exemplary lover; she relates his wrongs with the approval of virtues and it comes as a jolt when the exultation in her voice is compared with her actual words.[41]

Brooks's analysis assumes that Smith was unselfconscious in her performance of this song. He therefore misses its intentional ambiguity and complexity. Smith was an accomplished performer, actor and comedian and was therefore well acquainted with the uses of humor and irony. It is much more plausible to characterize her decision to sing "Yes Indeed He Do" with mock praise and elation as a conscious effort to highlight, in the most effective way possible, the inhumanity and misogyny of male batterers. . . .

The female characters memorialized in women's blues songs, even in their most despairing moods, do not fit the mold of the typical victim of abuse. The independent women of blues lore are women who do not think twice about wielding weapons against men who they feel have mistreated them. They frequently brandish their razors and guns, and dare men to cross the lines they draw. While acknowledging the physical mistreatment they have received at the hands of their male lovers, they do not perceive or define themselves as powerless in face of such violence. Indeed, they fight back passionately. In many songs Ma Rainey and Bessie Smith pay tribute to fearless women who attempt to avenge themselves when their lovers have been unfaithful. In "Black Mountain Blues," Bessie Smith sings:

> He met a city gal and he throwed me down
> I'm bound for Black Mountain, me and my razor and my gun
> Lord I'm bound for Black Mountain, me and my razor and my gun
> I'm gonna shoot him if he stands still and cut him if he run.[42]

In Smith's "Sinful Blues," a woman's rage also turns into violence:

> Gonna get me a gun long as my right arm
> Shoot that man because he done me wrong.
> Lord, now I've got them sinful blues.[43]

In Ma Rainey's "See See Rider Blues," the protagonist, who has discovered that her man has another woman friend, announces her intention to buy herself a pistol and to "kill my man and catch the Cannonball."[44] Her concluding resolution is: "If he don't have me, he won't have no gal at all." In Rainey's "Rough and Tumble Blues," the woman attacks not the man, but the women who have attempted to seduce him:

> I got rough and killed three women 'fore the police got the news
> 'Cause mama's on the warpath with these rough and tumble blues.[45]

The lives of many of the blues women of the twenties resembled those of the fearless women memorialized in their songs. We know that at times Bessie Smith was a victim of male violence and also that she would not hesitate to hurl violent threats—which she sometimes carried out—at the men who betrayed her. Nor was she afraid to confront the most feared embodiments of white racist terror. One evening in July of 1927, robed and hooded Ku Klux Klansmen attempted to disrupt her tent performance by pulling up the tent stakes and collapsing the entire structure. When Smith was informed of the trouble, she immediately left the tent and, according to her biographer:

> . . . ran toward the intruders, stopped within ten feet of them, placed one hand on her hip, and shook a clenched fist at the Klansmen. "What the fuck you think you're doin'," she shouted above the sound of the band. "I'll get the whole damn tent out here if I have to. You just pick up them sheets and run!"
>
> The Klansmen, apparently too surprised to move, just stood there and gawked. Bessie hurled obscenities at them until they finally turned and disappeared quietly into the darkness . . .
>
> Then she went back into the tent as if she had just settled a routine matter.[46]

Blues women were expected to deviate from the norms defining orthodox female behavior, which is why they were revered by both men and women in black working-class communities. Ida Cox's "Wild Women Don't Have the Blues" became the most famous portrait of the nonconforming, independent woman, and her "wild woman" has become virtually synonymous with the blues queen herself:

> Wild women don't worry, wild women don't have the blues
> You never get nothing by being an angel child
> You'd better change your ways and get real wild.[47]

"Prove It On Me Blues," composed by Gertrude Rainey, portrays just such a "wild woman" who affirms her independence from the orthodox norms of womanhood by boldly flaunting her lesbianism. Rainey's sexual involvement with women was no secret among her colleagues and her audiences. The advertisement for the release of "Prove It On Me Blues" showed the blues woman sporting a man's hat, jacket and tie and, while a policeman looked on, obviously attempting to seduce two women on a street corner. The song's lyrics include the following:

> Went our last night with a crowd of my friends
> They must've been women 'cause I don't like no men . . .
>
> Wear my clothes just like a fan
> Talk to the gals just like any old man.[48]

Sandra Lieb has described this song as a "powerful statement of lesbian defiance and self-worth."[49] "Prove It On Me Blues" is a cultural precursor to the lesbian cultural movement of the 1970s, which, it is interesting to note, began to crystallize around the performance and recording of lesbian-affirming songs. (In fact, in 1977, Teresa Trull recorded a cover of Ma Rainey's song for an album entitled *Lesbian Concentrate*.[50])

Hazel Carby has insightfully observed that "Prove It On Me Blues"

> vacillates between the subversive hidden activity of women loving women [and] a public declaration of lesbianism. The words express a contempt for a society that rejected lesbians. . . . But at the same time the song is a reclamation of lesbianism as long as the woman publicly names her sexual preference for herself. . . .

Carby argues that this song "engag[es] directly in defining issues of sexual preference as a contradictory struggle of social relations."[51]

"Prove It On Me Blues" suggests how the iconoclastic blueswomen of the twenties were pioneers for later historical developments. The response to this song also suggests that homophobia within the black community did not prevent blues women from challenging stereotypical conceptions of women's lives. They did not allow themselves to be enshrined by the silence imposed by mainstream society.

The blues songs recorded by Gertrude Rainey and Bessie Smith offer us a privileged glimpse of the prevailing perceptions of love and sexuality in post-slavery black communities in the United States. Both women were role models for untold thousands of their sisters to whom they delivered messages that defined the male dominance encouraged by mainstream culture. The blues women openly challenged the gender politics implicit in traditional cultural representations of marriage and heterosexual love relationships. Refusing, in the blues tradition of raw realism, to romanticize romantic relationships, they instead exposed the stereotypes and explored the contradictions of those relationships. By so doing, they redefined women's "place." They forged and memorialized images of tough, resilient and independent women who were afraid neither of their own vulnerability nor of defending their right to be respected as autonomous human beings.

NOTES

1 Bessie Smith, "I Used To Be Your Sweet Mama," Columbia 14292-D, Feb. 9, 1928. Reissued on *Empty Bed Blues*, Columbia CG 30450, 1972.

2 According to Hazel Carby, "[w]hat has been called the 'Classic Blues,' the women's blues of the twenties and early thirties, is a discourse that articulates a cultural and political struggle over sexual relations: a struggle that is directed against the objectification of female sexuality within a patriarchal order but which also tries to reclaim women's bodies as the sexual and sensuous objects of song." "It Just Be's Dat Way Sometime: The Sexual Politics of Women's Blues," *Radical America*, 20, no. 4 (June–July 1986), 12.

3 See Henry Pleasants, *The Great American Popular Singers* (New York: Simon & Schuster, 1974). According to Lawrence Levine, "the physical side of love which, aside from some tepid hand holding and lip pecking, was largely missing from popular music, was strongly felt in the blues." *Black Culture and Black Consciousness: Afro-American Thought from Slavery to Freedom* (New York: Oxford University Press, 1975), 279.

4 Bessie Smith's first recording, a cover of Alberta Hunter's "Down Hearted Blues," sold 780,000 copies in less than six months. Chris Albertson, *Bessie* (New York: Stein & Day, 1972), 46.

5   The central place of the blues in the elaboration of a post-slavery black cultural consciousness has been examined widely in works like LeRoi Jones's pioneering *Blues People* and Lawrence Levine's engaging study *Black Culture and Black Consciousness*. While both suggest important approaches to the understanding of racial dimensions of African-American culture, scant attention is accorded gender consciousness. Daphne Duval Harrison's trailblazing study *Black Pearls: Blues Queens of the 1920s* (New Brunswick: Rutgers University Press, 1988) reveals, in fact, how rich women's blues can be as a terrain for explorations of the place gender occupies in black cultural consciousness.

6   See W. E. B. Du Bois, *Black Reconstruction in America* (New York: Harcourt, Brace, 1935).

7   See Herbert Gutman, *The Black Family in Slavery and Freedom, 1750–1925* (New York: Pantheon, 1976), ch. 9.

8   Lawrence Levine cites a rowing song heard by Frances Kemble in the late 1830s and characterized by her as nonsensical, but interpreted by Chadwick Hansen as containing hidden sexual meanings.

Jenny shake her toe at me,
   Jenny gone away;
Jenny shake her toe at me,
   Jenny gone away.
Hurrah! Miss Susy, oh!
   Jenny gone away;
Hurrah! Miss Susy, oh!
   Jenny gone away.

Levine, *Black Culture and Black Consciousness*, p. 11. (Frances Anne Kemble, *Journal of a Residence on a Georgian Plantation in 1838–1839* [1863; reprint, New York: Knopf, 1961], 163–4.) "Chadwick Hansen [in "Jenny's Toe: Negro Shaking Dances in America," *American Quarterly*, 19 (1967), 554–63] has shown that in all probability what Miss Kemble heard was not the English word 'toe' but an African-derived word referring to the buttocks." The Jenny of whom the slaves were singing with such obvious pleasure was shaking something more interesting and provocative than her foot.

9   According to James Cone, "The spiritual . . . is the spirit of the people struggling to be free . . . [it] is the people's response to the societal contradictions. It is the people facing trouble and affirming, 'I ain't tired yet.' But the spiritual is more than dealing with trouble. It is a joyful experience, a vibrant affirmation of life and its possibilities in an appropriate esthetic form. The spiritual is the community in rhythm, swinging to the movement of life." *The Spirituals and the Blues: An Interpretation* (New York: Seabury, 1972), 32–3.

10 Popular musical culture in the African-American tradition continues to actively involve the audience in the performance of the music. The distinction, therefore, is not between the relatively active and relatively passive stances of the audience. Rather it is between a mode of musical presentation in which everyone involved is considered a "performer"—or perhaps in which no one, the song leader included, is considered a "performer"—and one in which the producer of the music plays a privileged role in calling forth the responses of the audience.

11 See James Cone's discussion of the liberation content of the spirituals. John Lovell, Jr (*Black Song: The Forge and the Flame*, New York: Macmillan, 1972) also emphasizes the relationship between the slave community's yearning for liberation and the music it produced in the religious tradition of Christianity.

12 Levine, *Black Culture and Black Consciousness*, 175.

13 Religious themes are to be found in some of the prison work songs recorded by folklorists such as Alan Lomax during the thirties, forties, and fifties.

14 See Giles Oakley, *The Devil's Music: A History of the Blues* (New York and London: Harcourt Brace Jovanovich, 1976), 97–9.

15 See Henry Louis Gates, Jr, *The Signifying Monkey: A Theory of African-American Literary Criticism* (New York: Oxford University Press, 1988), ch. 1.

16 See Zora Neale Hurston, *Mules and Men* (Bloomington: Indiana University Press, 1978), stories on Jack and the Devil, 164, and about "unh hunh" as a word the Devil made up, 169.

17 *Wild Women Don't Have the Blues*, dir. Christine Dall, Calliope Film Resources, 1989, videocassette.

18 When applied to the religious contours and content of slave-initiated cultural community, the infamous observation by the young Karl Marx that religion is the "opium of the people" eluci-

dates the utopian potential of slave religion; but, in this context, Marx's observation simultaneously goes too far and not far enough.

> *Religious* suffering is at the same time an *expression* of real suffering and a protest against real suffering. Religion is the sigh of the oppressed creature, the sentiment of a heartless world, and the soul of soulless conditions. It is the *opium* of the people. . . . Religion is only the illusory sun around which man revolves so long as he does not revolve around himself.

Karl Marx, "The Critique of Hegel's Philosophy of Right," in Karl Marx, *Early Writings*, ed. T. B. Bottomore (New York: McGraw-Hill, 1963), 43–4.

Marx goes too far in the sense that he assumes a necessarily and exclusively ideological relationship between religious consciousness and material conditions, i.e., that religion is fundamentally false consciousness and that the "self" or community it articulates is necessarily an illusion. Such an all-embracing conception of religion cannot account for its extra-religious dimensions. On the other hand, he does not go far enough when he dismisses the revolutionary potential of religious consciousness.

19 See Lovell, *Black Song*, chs 17 and 18.
20 Marx, "Critique of Hegel's Philosophy," 44.
21 See Houston A. Baker, Jr, *Blues, Ideology, and Afro-American Literature* (Chicago: University of Chicago Press, 1984).
22 Cone, *The Spirituals and the Blues*, 112. C. Eric Lincoln originated the term "secular spirituals."
23 Levine, *Black Culture and Black Consciousness*, 237.
24 Julio Finn argues that "the jook joint is to the blues what the church is to the spiritual, and the bluesman on stage is in his pulpit. Contrary to the 'holy' atmosphere which reigns in the church, the jook joint is characterized by its rowdiness—the noise and smoke and drinking are necessities without which its character would be fatally altered, for that would alter the music, which is in no small way shaped by it." Julio Finn, *The Bluesman* (London: Quartet, 1986), 202. Unfortunately, Finn confines his discussion to blues men and does not consider the role of women.
25 See Joan Landes, "The Public and the Private Sphere: A Feminist Reconsideration," in Johanna Meehan (ed.), *Feminists Read Habermas* (London: Routledge, 1995). According to Aida Hurtado in "Relating to Privilege: Seduction and Rejection in the Subordination of White Women and Women of Color" (*Signs: A Journal of Women and Culture in Society*, 14, no. 4 [Summer 1989]), "the public/private distinction is relevant only for the white middle and upper classes since historically the American state has intervened constantly in the private lives and domestic arrangements of the working class. Women of Color have not had the benefit of the economic conditions that underlie the public/private distinction. Instead the political consciousness of women of Color stems from an awareness that the public is *personally* political."
26 Du Bois points out that in many border states, slave-breeding became a main industry: "The deliberate breeding of a strong, big field-hand stock could be carried out by selecting proper males, and giving them the run of the likelist females. This is many Border States became a regular policy and fed the slave trade." *Black Reconstruction in America*, 44.
27 Gutman, *The Black Family*, 80, 388.
28 Slave narratives by Frederick Douglass, Solomon Northrup, and Harriet Jacobs contain poignant descriptions of family separations. See also Gutman, *The Black Family*, ch. 8.
29 Ralph Ellison, *Shadow and Act* (New York: Vintage, 1972), 245.
30 Oakley, *The Devil's Music*, 59.
31 Angela Y. Davis, *Women, Race, and Class* (New York: Random House, 1981).
32 Bessie Smith, "Sam Jones Blues," Columbia 13005-D, Sept. 24, 1923. Reissued on *Any Woman's Blues*, Columbia G 30126, 1972.
33 Harrison, *Black Pearls*, 287.
34 See Mary P. Ryan's discussion of the cult of motherhood in *Womanhood in America: From Colonial Times to the Present* (New York: Franklin Watts, 1975).
35 Gertrude "Ma" Rainey, "Lawd, Send Me a Man Blues," Paramount 12227, May 1924. Reissued on *Queen of the Blues*, Biograph BLP-12032, n.d.
36 Bessie Smith, "Baby Doll," Columbia 14147-D, May 4, 1926. Reissued on *Nobody's Blues but Mine*, Columbia CG 31093, 1972.
37 See Sara Evans's study, *Personal Politics: The Roots of Women's Liberation in the Civil Rights Movement and the New Left* (New York: Knopf, 1979).
38 See Michere Githae Mugo, *Orature and Human Rights* (Rome: Institute of South African Development Studies, NUL, Lesotho, 1991).

39 See Oakley's discussion of work and song, *The Devil's Music*, 36–46.
40 Bessie Smith, "Yes, Indeed He Do."
41 Edward Brooks, *The Bessie Smith Companion* (New York: Da Capo, 1982), 143.
42 Bessie Smith, "Black Mountain Blues," Columbia 14554-D, June 22, 1930. Reissued on *The World's Greatest Blues Singer,* Columbia CG 33, 1972.
43 Bessie Smith, "Sinful Blues," Columbia 114052-D, Dec. 11, 1924. Reissued on *The Empress,* Columbia CG 30818, 1972.
44 Gertrude "Ma" Rainey, "See See Rider Blues," Paramount 12252, Dec. 1925. Reissued on *Ma Rainey,* Milestone M-47021, 1974.
45 Gertrude "Ma" Rainey, "Rough and Tumble Blues," Paramount 12303, 1928. Reissued on *The Immortal Ma Rainey,* Milestone MLP 2001, 1966.
46 Albertson, *Bessie,* 132–3.
47 Ida Cox, "Wild Women Don't Have the Blues," Paramount 12228, 1924. Reissued on *Wild Women Don't Have the Blues,* Riverdale RLP 9374, n.d.
48 Gertrude "Ma" Rainey, "Prove It On Me Blues," Paramount 12668, June 1928. Reissued on *Ma Rainey,* Milestone M-47021, 1974.
49 Sandra Lieb, 125.
50 *Lesbian Concentrate: A Lesbianthology of Songs and Poems.* Ouvia Records MU 29729, 1977.
51 Carby, "It Just Be's Dat Way Sometime," 18.

Toi Derricotte (1941–)

Born and raised in Detroit, Michigan, Toi Derricotte took a long road toward becoming a poet of positive repute, whose works unabashedly explore difficult issues of race and gender, family and community. Derricotte attended Wayne State University, earning a B.A. in special education, and worked for years as a teacher in Detroit and New Jersey school systems. She published her first work of poetry, The Empress of the Death House (1978), which began her journey to a distinguished writing career. Since then, she has published three other books of poetry: Natural Birth (1983), Captivity (1989), and Tender (1997). In 1997, she also published The Black Notebooks: An Interior Journey, a prose collection of journal writing chronicling her process as a writer and her engagement with issues of color, race, class, and gender.

Derricotte completed a master's degree in English and Creative Writing from NYU in 1984 and has received many awards for her work, including two National Endowment for the Arts fellowships, as well as the Distinguished Pioneering of the Arts Award from the United Black Artists, the Lucille Medwick Memorial Award from the Poetry Society of America, and the Folger Shakespeare Library Poetry Book Award. As a celebrated poet, she has been an invited or visiting writer at many schools and now is a professor of English at the University of Pittsburgh.

Derricotte's passion and style has been compared to works by Audre Lorde, Pat Parker, and Cornelius Eady. Of her own writing, she has once said that she writes "confessionally," as a mode self-examination. But Derricotte's self-explorations on the page are sweet meditations and reflections that cause the reader to examine contradictions in societal constructions of race. Derricotte is particularly interested in how color and race continue to haunt a people, marking the limits of expression and the boundaries of alliance. In "Workshop on Racism," Derricotte explores the difficulty a mother faces in comforting a child who is being marginalized because of her race. The mother realizes that the issue is not just this taunting at this young age, but an issue of protection and self-regard. Here, Derricotte exploits the anecdotal form to present a narrative without an answer; the poem ends with the lovely line "Already at five the children understand, / 'black' is not a color, it is a / blazing skin." She points attention to the volatility of race, how it blazes and burns; but she also is hinting at its magic, its transformative qualities. This "blazing skin," which is both a thing to be feared and admired, is sweet and sad, like the quality she captures in the title poem from Tender.

This is what Derricotte does so well: One, she uses the anecdote to tell a particular incident, but also to reveal the larger relevance that exists in the story's particularity. Often, in this case, the anecdote ends without a definitive conclusion, leaving a world of possibility to be had in the reader's interpretation, in the particular knowledge systems the reader *brings to the poem. For example, the poem "Passing" raises questions about the highly controversial experience—where a light-skinned African American who may or may not be biracial can be mistaken for being white. Derricotte both defuses the controversy and at the same time points direct attention to the pertinent issues by asking the question "Why presume / 'passing' is based on what I leave out / and not what she fills in?" The poem ends without a conclusion, without being told what to think about passing; instead, the poem has become an occasion to think about passing, to begin one's own confession.*

The other thing Derricotte does so well is take what is intimate to her, and what is often very personal and emotional and potentially painful, and present it in clean and exquisite language. She does not get trapped using obscure references, or complicated and inaccessible ideas or form; instead, like Langston Hughes, but also like Lorde and Eady, she writes stories that are so simple they are song-like. Her language, such as that in "Tender," is evocative and precise, but not cumbersome. Furthermore, the simplicity does not offer flatness; in fact, in "Tender," Derricotte plays with the idea of meat and tender, evoking many images through her brief lines. Similarly, in "Touching/Not Touching: My Mother," the desire to put hands beneath the night dress is palpable, and the relationship between the two women represents many kinds of relationships between women who touch, and don't.

It is Derricotte's expansiveness that is her greatest triumph—the way that her own self-investigations do not close in on the reader and offer her view, but that they quietly expand out, generating possibilities for thinking through the poetic moment.

Kevin Everod Quashie

Touching / Not Touching: My Mother

i.

That first night in the hotel bedroom,
when the lights go out,
she is already sleeping (that woman who has always
claimed sleeplessness), inside her quiet breathing
like a long red gown. How can she
sleep? My heart beats as if I am alone,
for the first time, with a lover or a beast.
Will I hate her drooping mouth,
her old woman rattle? Once I nearly
suffocated on her breast. Now I can almost
touch the other side of my life.

ii.

Undressing
in the dark,
looking,

not looking,
we parade before each other,
old proud peacocks, in our stretch marks
with hanging butts. We are equals. No
more do I need to wear her high heels to step
inside the body of a woman.
Her beauty and strangeness no longer seduce
me out of myself. I show my good side, my
long back, strong mean legs, my thinness that
came from learning to hold back
from taking what's not mine. No more
a thief for love. She takes off her
bra, facing me, and I see those gorgeous
globes, soft, creamy,
high; my mouth waters.
how will I resist
crawling in beside her, putting
my hand for warmth under
her thin night dress?

Tender

The tenderest meat
comes from the houses
where you hear the least

squealing. The secret
is to give a little
wine before killing.

For Black Women Who Are Afraid

A black woman comes up to me at break in the writing
workshop and reads me her poem, but she says she
can't read it out loud because
there's a woman in a car on her way
to work and her hair is blowing in the breeze

and, since her hair is blowing, the woman must be
white, and she shouldn't write about a white woman
whose hair is blowing, because
maybe the black poets will think she wants to be
that woman and be mad at her and say she hates herself,
and maybe they won't let her explain
that she grew up in a white neighborhood
and it's not her fault, it's just what she sees.
But she has to be so careful. I tell her to write
the poem about being afraid to write,
and we stand for a long time like that,
respecting each other's silence.

Passing

A professor invites me to his "Black Lit" class; they're
reading Larson's *Passing.* One of the black
students says, "Sometimes light-skinned blacks
think they can fool other blacks,
but *I* can always tell," looking
right through me.
After I tell them I am black,
I ask the class, "Was I passing
when I was just sitting here,
before I told you?" A white woman
shakes her head desperately, as if
I had deliberately deceived her.
She keeps examining my face,
then turning away
as if she hopes I'll disappear. Why presume
"passing" is based on what I leave out
and not what she fills in?
In one scene in the book, in a restaurant,
she's "passing,"
though no one checked her at the door—
"Hey, you black?"
My father, who looked white,
told me this story: every year
when he'd go to get his driver's license,
the man at the window filling

out the form would ask,
"White or black?" pencil poised, without looking up.
My father wouldn't pass, but he might
use silence to trap a devil.
When he didn't speak, the man
would look up at my father's face.
"What did he write?"
my father quizzed me.

Workshop on Racism

Her mother is crying
because Briana came home from school screaming in agony.
Two girls in her class are named Briana
and the children distinguish them
by calling her "The Black Briana," taunting her.
She screams at her mother, "I don't want to be
'The Black Briana!'"
Her mother weeps, helplessly. "What can I do?
I give her dolls, read her
black history. How can I protect her?"
Already at five the children understand,
"black" is not a color, it is a
blazing skin.

Melvin Dixon (1950–1992)

Melvin Dixon is perhaps most well known as a writer who spoke and wrote about his homosexuality very openly, for which he was both criticized and celebrated. As an active spokesperson for gay communities and issues, Dixon integrates the complexities of gay identity and lifestyle into his work while communicating what it means to be a Black man, gay or straight. Above all, his characters strive to love themselves and to be accepted by others.

Dixon was born May 29, 1950 in Stamford, Connecticut. He graduated from Wesleyan University in 1971 with a degree in American Studies. In 1975, he earned a Ph.D. from Brown University, also in American Studies. While studying at Brown, Dixon was fortunate enough to enjoy the opportunity of working with poet Michael Harper. From 1980 until the time of his death in 1992, Dixon taught at Queens College in New York City. He died at home on October 26, 1992 of an AIDS-related illness.

As a writer, Melvin Dixon embraced both scholarship and creativity. He wrote poems, stories, novels, essays, critical studies, and translations from French with equal energy. Fueled by an incredible desire to understand his literary heritage, Dixon traveled to the Caribbean, Africa, and Europe, researching James Baldwin in Paris, Haitian poet and novelist Jacques Roumain, and West African writer Léopold Senghor, the former president of Senegal. While in Senegal and studying Senghor, Dixon studied the Négritude movement, a political and philosophical movement grounded in the French language tradition of Senghor and much like the English Pan-Africanism movement in its drive toward unification of people of African descent around a common sense of cultural origin. Dixon's dedication to comparative Black literature, a global perspective, is best evidenced through his translation work, which includes Drumbeats, Masks, and Metaphor: Contemporary Afro-American Theatre *by Genevieve Fabre (1983) and the huge undertaking of Léopold Senghor's* Collected Poetry *(1990).*

Melvin Dixon published his own first volume of poetry, Change of Territory *in 1983. The free-verse poems of* Change of Territory *document Dixon's experiences in Paris in the 1970s and express his interest in genealogy and ancestry, especially his own family's Southern heritage. His displacement in Paris affords Dixon a different perspective on self and journey, a perspective that informs the cycle of departure and return within the work.*

Dixon followed a first collection of poetry with a critical study of Black literature, Ride Out the Wilderness, *in 1987. Summarizing the aim of this work, Dixon states in the introduction: "I examine the ways in which Afro-American writers, often considered homeless, alienated from mainstream culture, and segregated in negative environments, have used language to create alternative landscapes where black culture and identity can flourish apart from any marginal, prescribed 'place.'" The underground, mountains, and the wilderness are the tropes Dixon focuses on to explain the ways in which African American writers construct "place" and home through language.*

Two novels, Trouble the Water *(1989) and* Vanishing Rooms *(1991), emphasize Dixon's dedication to the "wilderness" of sexuality and relationships.* Trouble the Water *focuses on Jordan Henry, a married college professor who must deal with the memories of a childhood friend for whom feelings extended beyond mere friendship. In* Vanishing Rooms, *Jesse, a gay man, Lonny, a homophobic adolescent, and Ruella, a heterosexual woman, all struggle to love themselves.* Vanishing Rooms *centers in love of dance, gay male fantasies, violent homophobia, and friendship. While Dixon foregrounds the psychological and social consequences of gay identity and relationships, the novel is equally about people relating to each other, trying to survive and love.*

Dixon wrote Vanishing Rooms *from the perspectives of each of the central characters. Jesse, Ruella, and Lonny communicate their thoughts and emotions in first person voice in separate chapters, the perspective shifting throughout the novel. Jesse's perspective initiates the novel, bringing the reader into the conflict and love of his relationship with Metro, a white man, city-rough and simultaneously fragile. As Jesse loses himself in the music, movement, and collaboration with Ruella during a dance rehearsal, his mind dwells on Metro. Unprepared for the police who meet him at his door to tell him of Metro's violent passing, Jesse depends on Ruella and their friendship just initiated for the strength he needs to deal with the tragedy. Ruella herself must resolve the attraction she feels toward Jesse, learn to accept both him and respect her own needs and emotions. The first chapter of Jesse's perspective is full of the power that propels the rest of the novel, imbuing it with the most intense of emotions and human interactions.*

A posthumously published collection of poetry, Love's Instruments *(1995), crowns the achievement of Dixon's short life. The poetry of* Love's Instruments *and the speech that concludes the collection, "I'll Be Somewhere Listening for My Name," serve as memorials to those who have lost their lives in the struggle against the disease, a plea for memory and action.*

Melvin Dixon will be remembered for the fact of his creative achievement, but also for the spirit that is inseparable from his words.

R. Joyce Lausch

Jesse

Metro wasn't his real name, but I called him that. It was fall of 1975. He led me by the arm out of the dark, rotting warehouse and to the pier fronting West Street. The sharp, fresh air cut through the smell of mildew stuffing my nose. The shock of the bright October sun made me blink so hard I missed a step and stumbled against him. He reached to block my fall, lifting my fingers to his nose. I squeezed his shoulders, held tight for a moment. We wobbled like two dancing drunks, vying for balance. His hands were shaking with a chill. The salt flavor of his skin left my mouth and my lips dried. I could stand and breathe again.

The lot around the pier and the warehouse looked like a deserted playground. Behind me I heard footsteps and creaking floorboards where we had been. We walked on ahead where the Hudson River lapped at soggy wooden piles. The water gurgled and sloshed with delight and the loose, stiff wood swayed in the dim flow. One post cracked free, bobbed in the sucking current, and floated away limp. I brushed off my jeans, more dusty now than blue. Wood splinters fell out of the seams. I looked at Metro to see if he noticed. His eyes were red and puffy. Maybe mine were too. His jeans were torn at the knees and just as dusty. Maybe his knees were scraped, I couldn't tell. He kept shivering, but I felt warm in the wide blade of sunlight. I squinted to see him clearer. My face wrinkled to a pout.

"Are you mad?" he asked me, brushing tangled brown hair from his face. His hand pulled out splinters. "Are you mad because I made you come here?"

"You didn't make me come," I said. "I came because I wanted to."

Metro touched my denim jacket and let go. He shook his head. "Then why are you looking like that?" he asked, his eyes holding mine.

"Like what?"

"Like you're relieved or something."

"What's gotten into you?" I said. He stepped back from me. I didn't mean to sound so annoyed. His skin had never looked so white.

"Nothing."

"I don't want to meet here again, Metro. Promise me we don't have to meet here."

"Why should I promise? You call me Metro, don't you?"

"I'm scared, that's all." I wanted to touch him again, hold him close this time.

"You didn't say that a few hours ago."

"I know. I'm sorry I didn't."

I held out my hand, reached for him, changed my mind, and searched my pockets instead. I found my watch. It was three forty-five. Damn, I was late for dance class. Today was the day for improvisations, a good chance to make an impression before auditions next month. I couldn't miss a class. Metro started to say something, but I headed away from the warehouse to catch a crosstown cab. He followed after me, his keys jangling from a leather loop on his belt. "Wait," he said.

I couldn't wait. One cab zoomed by on radio call. Another stopped.

"Wait," said Metro.

"I'm late already, man, what is it?"

"Never mind. I just thought you were angry, that's all."

"I'm not angry." I got in the cab and lowered the window.

Metro had a wild look in his eyes. His chin held hard and straight. His thin lips opened and closed, but he said nothing more. He was taller than I but his shoulders slumped, and he looked weak. He didn't raise his shoulders.

"I'm glad I came, Metro."

"You didn't like it, did you?"

I smiled. And he smiled, hesitantly at first. I knew why I was there.

He stepped back from the cab. I said, "See you later, baby. I love you," and the cab lurched forward. The driver stared at me through the rearview mirror.

I'd be gone only a few hours. Metro would be home when I got back. Yet I missed him. My stomach fluttered. Maybe it was that empty, searching look in his eyes, or his suddenly pale skin against my oily brown hands. I missed him and searched the rear window. Metro was standing in the middle of West 12th Street, oblivious to the traffic veering around him. He scared me. I wanted the cab to turn around and pick him up, but it was too late. Why was I in such a rush? But I'm always rushing, rushing to dance class, rushing home, rushing to the mailbox, rushing just to be a quick step ahead of myself.

In no time I reached the studio. At my locker, I changed into yesterday's tights, which had aired out but should have been cleaned. Splinters fell out of my clothes, from the armpits of my shirt and the seat of my pants. I must have smelled of wood and low tide. Other dancers were warming up with stretches on the floor. I wasn't too late after all. Maybe I could sweat off the stink of the warehouse, dance with my feet on firm ground, not on creaking floorboards or with anonymous shadows lurking behind crumbling walls. Maybe the aftertaste of sweat, splinters, and Metro's tangled brown hair would go away. The other dancers wouldn't suspect a thing, I hoped, prayed. No one would know where I had been.

I stretched onto the floor for a few warm-ups, then stood with my stomach held in tight. My thighs eased open in demi-plié. Next, grand plié. I breathed deeply, calmly, and pulled myself up. On relevé I felt as tall as Metro, my hands as broad as his.

Anna Louise, the dance captain, called us into formation for single-file walks with our knees turned out, chests high. Next we lined up two by two. I found myself opposite another man, and we had to hold hands while doing triplet steps across the floor. For the next round I was with a girl I hadn't seen before in class, and another black dancer at that. She was shorter than I by a good foot, dark-complexioned with broad hips and close-cropped, boyish hair. But her legs were long, and she was some match for me in the quick, crisp steps we had to execute:

> *One-two-three*   *One-two-three*
> *Up-two-three*   *Down-two-three*

Before I had a chance to say hello we were across the floor again with a leap-two-three, leap-two-three. Waltz step, then turns. Between breaths I asked her name. "Ruella," she said heavily. "Ruella McPhee."

I reached for her hand and caught her wrist. "I'm Jesse Durand."

And we were back across the floor. Turns, leaps, waltz steps, and more stretches from head to toe.

Improvisation came next. "Just listen to this song for now, then let the music move you," said Anna Louise, her hands circling in the air. She held her hips and added, "At first I thought this song was so simple, but then the words and music started to make such terrible sense that I was taken with it completely. Now you try." She gave each pair of dancers a number.

We were number three.

The song played a second time. It was then that I recognized Nina Simone's voice crooning from the single phonograph speaker as if it needed more room, was aching for it. Her voice bounced upon the empty walls of the studio. The words were those of Waring Cuney, I later found out, from a poem that still plays in my mind:

> She does not know
> Her beauty
> She thinks her brown body
> Has no glory.
>
> If she could dance
> Naked
> Under palm trees
> And see her image in the river
> She would know.

I looked at Ruella and smiled. My knees were already moving with what I wanted to say. Ruella was tapping her feet. The song spoke to her too.

> But there are no palm trees
> On the street
> And dish water gives back no images.

I thought of our house back in Hartford and my mother Jessica, who named me. She made me and my older brother Charlie wash dishes on alternate nights. We'd still fight over whose turn it was. My father made us shovel snow, take out the garbage in the cold, wash the car, scrub the kitchen floor, rake leaves into a pile, but we'd jump in it and have to rake them up again. I didn't mind the kitchen work, but I hated the outside chores. "Work builds character," my father always said. But he stopped preaching that line when he noticed my preference for baking cakes and polishing silverware.

As the song ended plaintively, Simone's voice lifted high in arabesque, her throaty tones like a bridge to cross.

When our turn came, Ruella and I held each other at arm's length and circled slowly, measuring our steps and each other. Our heads leaned in and out from the center between us. Our bodies came close. We were drawn into the music and the pain in Simone's voice. Our bodies were swaying, singing. I broke the circle of our arms, held Ruella in slight elevation, then eased her down. I spun away and halted in demi-plié. She leaped in small quick steps, then faced me. I lifted her straight up, felt myself lifting, too. I brought her down slowly, carefully, my hands broad about her waist. We stood side by side and bent legs, arms, and thighs into a heap upon the floor. Her head eased into my arms; our faces touched, hair caressed. We were almost one head. We broke free and ran from each other like frightened children. I curled into a ball and shot up in arabesque. Ruella leaped high, then stood stock still. Our hands reached out, held on, turned with open palms to the other dancers watching us. Our waists swayed, curled, stretched like whispers. Our bodies had voices of their own, and they hushed into quiet. We sank into a pile, rose up close together. Our tights made our thighs one black pillar, and our Afros became one huge head. We inched into separate positions, our hands and eyes holding onto one another. The song ended with our standing back to back like a Janus mask, facing both sides of the room at once; one looking up and ahead, the other up and behind. Quickly, on the beat, we changed sides for the last wailing chord, then held firm as two sides of one body, one voice, both of us dancing from whatever we made visible on the floor.

The class erupted into applause. Anna Louise came forward with her hands tapping out a beat in the air. "You'll have to develop that into a polished piece," she said, "and present it to us again. What do you say, class?"

The applause grew louder, filling us. I smiled at Ruella who was grinning with such beautiful teeth. She smiled at me distantly, then left the floor. When class finished for the day, I waited at the dressing room until Ruella changed into street clothes. We walked together to the subway.

"I felt something in that dance," I said.

"Me, too."

"Funny, isn't it?"

She looked at me without a word. Then she said, "I'm not sure I know what you mean."

"Dance," I said.

"Yeah," said Ruella. "I've never been that close to a guy without feeling he wants something. You know what I mean?"

"Yes." Suddenly conscious of how I looked, I brushed off my jeans, pulled my stomach in.

"How do *you* know?"

"I just know."

Ruella looked at me hard, her eyes scratching at something. Sunlight glistened in her short hair. My scalp itched with splinters I couldn't wait to scratch out. "It was strange, but beautiful," she said. "Real beautiful."

I started giggling for no reason at all.

"Look," she said. "Forget what I said just then. I don't know you, really. You're charming."

"No, I'm not. Who wants to be charming, anyway?"

"Well, graceful, then. You move gracefully."

"Thanks," I said.

"Are you auditioning for the company, too?"

"I hope so," I said.

Below us a subway train screeched to a halt. Ruella looked worried. Her mouth grew tight. "Don't make me miss my train, now."

"I won't."

"I want to be home before it gets too dark."

"Let's get together again. To work on that dance," I said.

"I don't know, really. It was great, but I'm not sure I can get that high again. That's why I don't like improvs, not really. It's like, well, meeting someone, and after the rush of excitement, it's gone."

"What about the beginning of a friendship?" I asked, watching her.

She smiled, then tried to hide it.

"We can work on the dance, at least."

"Just the dance, Jesse?" Her eyes still searching. "I've got to get going."

"See you again? In class, I mean."

"Sure."

"How far are you going?"

"To the West Side. Eighty-fourth Street." Ruella bounded down the stairs. Then she was gone.

I wanted to dance again and to keep on dancing. The song and the improvisation came back to my mind, moving my feet as I walked home up 8th Street. My stomach was still contracted and made my steps light. I sang the song over to myself, trying to imitate Simone's raspy voice, but nothing but my own flat drawl came through. I thought of Ruella, then remembered Metro waiting for me at home. I changed more than the pronouns.

> He does not know his beauty
> He thinks his pale body
> Has no glory
> If he keeps dancing naked
> On the pier . . .

No, that's not it:

> There are no palm trees
> On the pier . . .

I must have laughed out loud because people started moving away from me on the sidewalk. Some went into the street. I kept singing and smiling. I'd tell Metro about the dance, about Ruella. In that brief moment she seemed to be a place to come to, a pier without splinters, a cozy room, not a warehouse.

I thought of Metro's thighs warm against mine, how close our faces held in making love, how wiry were his hands. But how lasting were those images? I walked faster. Suddenly, my toes were burning.

I reached the apartment, but he wasn't there. I waited for him through the early evening. I scrambled some eggs for dinner and read *GQ* twice. I waited for him through the night. I waited and waited. The more I waited the stronger was my desire for him. I wanted his hands on me. My legs still ached from dance, and when they relaxed I tried to sleep.

I wanted his hands on me. I didn't mind the cracked, chewed skin, the broken fingernails with flecks of dirt along the ridge. I wanted those hands on me, the blunt knuckles, the wrinkled skin, the bony joints, the tiny hair sprouts curling out. I wanted his hands on me. And wherever those hands led, I'd follow. I'd ride the tracks of his feet and the rough guardrails of those hands. Five fingers and five more. I wanted the electricity of his touch, his hands on me. How many times did I tell him, "Just touch me. Dance your fingers on my chest, my thighs. Press my flesh. Take off my clothes real slow." But when he touched me, my excitement dwindled into fear. His hands fluttered, suddenly unsure of themselves, of where they would land and do their marvelous work. I bent low and let his fingers drum on my belly. Then calmly they stroked where my secret skin was softest. He lifted away his hands and hid them. His lips found the tender places left aching by his touch. And when my hands kneaded him in turn—everywhere—nothing afterwards felt the same.

Then morning. An alarm shooting through me like the song. A knock on the door. Police.

They asked if Metro lived there with me and I said yes. They looked as if they expected me to be white or have something to hide. They told me to come with them downtown.

Metro lay in the city morgue. He had been stabbed eight times.

I couldn't look at him long. I couldn't breathe. I couldn't see. I grabbed for something to hold on to. The room whirled red, then black. The next thing I knew I was being lifted from the floor. When I could hold steady, they wanted to know his real name. My mouth was too dry to speak. Finally, in a voice hardly my own, I said, "Jon-Michael Barthé." His name didn't sound right at all. They probably thought I was lying.

Later they wanted my name. I said, "Jesse."

"Jesse what?"

"Jesse Durand."

"Ain't that a woman's name?" asked an officer behind a desk.

"Sometimes," I said.

They made me sign some papers. Then they let me go back home.

Once inside the apartment, I double-locked the door. I went to the window and spent hours looking up and down the street. Night came and swallowed up everything alive. Nothing moved, not even the subway below. I was alone. The rooms stirred empty. The emptiness gave off a chill. My eyes wouldn't cry and wouldn't close. I wanted to scream, but I had no air. I held myself in. I couldn't stop trembling.

God, what had happened? Just yesterday we were standing together at the pier, marveling at the polluted Hudson. Then I had to get to class, dance class. I thought I was late. There was a girl I had danced with. Then the hours and hours I waited for Metro to come home. Suddenly voices filled the outer hallway. Rushing footsteps. Laughter. Banging on doors somewhere. My hands shook again and my stomach tied itself in knots. Where could I hide? But the voices went past my door and up to the last floor of the building. I was sweating. I had to talk to someone. Anyone. I called my parents long-distance but there was no answer. I called again and the line was busy. But what could I tell them? College buddy, roommate, lover dead? Not a chance. Then I fumbled through the telephone directory, found her name, number, and I dialed.

"Ruella, this is Jesse. From dance class, remember? We met yesterday. We danced. Remember?"

"Yes, yes, Jesse. But how did you get my number?" I tried to say something but couldn't. "Jesse? You still there?"

"Listen, something terrible has happened. Metro, my friend. He's been stabbed. He's dead." I couldn't say anything more and she didn't say any more. My breath caught in the phone. "I can't stay here tonight," I said. "Not alone."

"You come right over, honey," she said. "I've got plenty of room."

I took only what I'd need for the night. Once there, I looked at her and she looked at me for a long time before I turned away and searched her windows. She didn't ask any questions. I wanted to talk, to tell her everything. She said there was no rush. I wanted to say that boys named after their mothers are different, that it wasn't for the money that they stabbed Metro; he had all his money on him when his body was found. It was for something else. When I tried to talk my lips started moving faster than the sounds, and I just cried, cried, cried.

Before the morgue's cold darkness had sucked me in, I had seen the gashes like tracks all over Metro's belly and chest. His open eyes were questions I couldn't answer. I couldn't say a word. The officer pulled the sheet all the way back and turned the body over where his ass had been slashed raw. I knew why he had been killed. I tried to scream but had no wind. I needed air. That's when I must have hit the floor. I could still see those gashes. They opened everywhere, grooves of flesh and blood, lips slobbering with kisses.

Ruella put her arms around me. My stomach heaved. I bolted for the toilet and vomited until there was nothing left of the bathroom or me. I woke up in her bed. From then on I called her Rooms.

After that first night she said I could stay longer if I needed to. I told her that guys like me are different.

"Then why did you call me?" she asked.

"Because you were there."

"But why *me*, Jesse?"

"We danced, that's all."

The second night Rooms touched me by accident. I didn't move. The chilly, October night filled the bed space between us. Then her hand crept to mine and held it, caressing and easing out the chill. Slowly, I relaxed but couldn't help remembering the men who had first made me warm. Metro's name came up raw on my tongue. It needed air, more air. "Metro," I said aloud. I kept still.

"Jesse? You all right?"

Rooms drew closer to me. We held each other tight against the dark.

"Jesse? You all right?" Her voice, hovering in the chill.

Something was pricking my scalp. I pulled out one splinter after another, but they were over all of me now, and I scratched and pulled everywhere. Not wood from the warehouse floor or the rickety pier, these were glinting steel blades with my name on them. Faces I'd seen before inched from corners of the room, closing the gap between here and there, now and then. Mouths opened and sneered. Teeth got sharp. Tongues wagged and breath steamed up around me until I sank into the sheets. Now a boy's voice. Then many voices. *"Jesseeeee."* A steel blade getting close. Closer. *"Jesse!"*

"I won't hurt you," said Rooms.

Outside the bedroom window, police sirens hollered up and down the streets. Where the hell were they *then?*

I imagined how Metro came up from the IRT exit and entered our block from the corner of West 12th and Bank Street. He passed the shut newsstand. It was almost morning. Metallic edges of light cut back the night. Metro walked with the same aching sound I knew from my own scuffling feet. I could almost hear the brush of denim between his thighs, see the arch of his pelvis as he swayed arms and hips as if he owned the whole street. His eyes tried to focus on the walk; his head leaned carelessly to the side. As he neared our building he was not alone. Other shapes crawled into the street, filled it. Cigarette smoke trailed out from an alley, and the figures of boys appeared out of nowhere, riding spray-paint fumes, crackling marijuana seeds, and waves of stinking beer.

Four, five, maybe six teenagers. Maybe they were the ones. The same ones I had seen before on my way home from rehearsals. Even then their smell of a quick, cheap high had been toxic. One time they spotted me and yelled, first one, then another until I was trapped.

"Hey, nigger."

"Yeah, you."

"Naw, man, he ain't no nigger. He a faggot."

"Then he a black nigger faggot."

They laughed. I walked faster, almost running, and reached my block in a cold sweat from pretending not to hear them. But I did hear them, and the sweat and trembling in my knees would not go away, not even when I reached the door and locked myself in.

Metro didn't believe it was that bad. But what did he know? A white boy from Louisiana, New England prep schools and college. "Don't worry, baby," he said when I told him what had happened. He held my head and hands until I calmed down. "It'll be all right." And we made love slowly, deliberately, believing we were doing something right. Still, I should have known better than to take so much for granted, even in Greenwich Village where we lived. And I should have known better than to leave him alone by the pier in the condition he was in, just for a dance improvisation. He had a cold, wild look in his eyes. How could I tell how many pills he'd taken? He could have fought back. But then why hadn't I fought back when those Italian kids started yelling, "He a black nigger faggot, yeah, he a faggot, a nigger, too," and shouting and laughing so close they made acid out of every bit of safety I thought we had? Now their hate had eaten up everything.

I could still hear them, making each prove himself a man—"I ain't no faggot. Not me, man"—and drawing blood. And when Metro left the black underground of trains and screeching wheels, when he reached for air in the thick ash of night, they spotted him like found money through the stinking grates of smoke and beer. I imagined how they followed his unsteady walk, his wavering vision, his fatigue. Curses like baseball bats swung out of their mouths. The first ones were on target: "There go a faggot."

"Hey man, you a faggot?"

Metro kept walking. Like I did. *Please keep walking. Please, Metro.*

"I say that man call you a faggot. You a faggot?"

Metro said nothing. Did he even hear them? They came closer. The streets were empty. No witnesses, no help. And I was back home waiting for his knock that never came.

"Yeah, you a faggot all right. Ain't he?"

"Yeah, he a faggot."

And Metro walked faster, skipped into a run, but they caught him. Knives slipped out of their pants. Hands reached for him, caught him in a tunnel of angry metal. They told him to put his wallet back. "This ain't no fucking robbery, man." They knocked him down. Metro sprawled about wet and hurt, couldn't pull himself up.

"Who stuck him?"

"Get up, faggot. We ain't through that easy."

"Look, he's bleeding."

"Who went ahead and stuck him before we all could stick it in? Who?"

They jostled him to his feet, feeling his ass.

"When can the rest of us stick it in? We all wanna fuck him, don't we fellahs?"

"Yeah. When can we fuck him?"

And Metro was wet from the discharged knives. He stopped treading the ground. He swayed back like wood in water, his eyes stiff on the open zippers. The leader of them grinning, his mouth a crater spilling beer, said, *"Now."*

"Why did you call me?" Rooms asked.

I said nothing.

"You think I'm gay, too?"

"No," I said.

"You really loved him," said Rooms.

"Yes."

"That makes all the difference." She held me with her eyes. They cut into me. "There's something else, isn't there? Something you haven't told me."

I tasted blood in my mouth. My head felt hot.

"I can wait," she said.

I went to her window and looked out. A subway rumbled underground, then it was quiet. The lump high in my throat, about to spread all through me since yesterday, eased down for a moment. I went back to my apartment to get the rest of my things.

Rita Dove (1952–)

In 1993, Rita Dove became the first African American and the youngest individual to be appointed Poet Laureate/Consultant in Poetry of the Library of Congress, a position that she held until 1995. But prestigious awards are numerous for Dove. Ms. Dove's honors include Fulbright, Guggenheim, and Mellon fellowships, sixteen honorary doctorates, the NAACP Great American Artist Award, Glamour magazine's "Woman of the Year" Award, the New York Public Library's "Literary Lion" citation, the Golden Plate Award from the American Academy of Achievement, as well as residencies at Tuskegee Institute, the National Humanities Center, and the Rockefeller Foundation's Villa Serbelloni in Bellagio, Italy. In 1996 she received both the Heinz Award in the Arts and Humanities and the Charles Frankel Prize/National Medal in the Humanities, and in 1997 she was honored with the Sara Lee Frontrunner Award and the Barnes & Noble Writers for Writers Award.

Dove has published six poetry collections, among them Thomas and Beulah, which was awarded the Pulitzer Prize in 1987. Her first work, The Yellow House on the Corner, a collection of poems dealing with coming of age, was published in 1980 and set the tone for her word artistry, presenting poems defined by their precise imagery, lyric intensity, and masterful craft. Resisting the bounds of artistic genre, Dove also authored the novel Through the Ivory Gate and the drama The Darker Face of the Earth, which premiered at the Oregon Shakespeare Festival in 1996 and was subsequently produced at the Kennedy Center in Washington, DC, and other theaters. Her song cycle, Seven for Luck, with music by John Williams, was first performed with the Boston Symphony Orchestra at Tanglewood in 1998.

Born in Akron, Ohio in 1952 into a highly educated family, Dove was encouraged in her passion for books and became a voracious reader of everything from Langston Hughes to Shakespeare to science fiction. She went on to graduate summa cum laude from Miami University of Ohio in 1973, and then to study German at the University of Tübingen where she became a Fulbright Scholar. She also received her Masters of Fine Arts degree at the University of Iowa.

In her work Dove draws upon personal perception and emotion while integrating an awareness of history and social issues. These qualities are best evidenced in the novelistic Thomas and Beulah (1986), which commemorates the lives of her grandparents and offers a chronicle of the collective experience of African Americans during the twentieth century. She comments, "'Dusting' appeared, really out of nowhere. I didn't realize that this was Thomas' wife saying 'I want to talk. And you can't do his side without doing my side.' … So Thomas and Beulah became actually two sides of the same story." This twin, twining plait of personal and political consciousness wraps itself around the poems in the collection, gathering together stories of love, courtship, and domesticity with narratives of race, gender, and class.

With her *1989 collection of poems,* Grace Notes, *Dove allows everyday experience to infiltrate her poetry from her career in academics, first at Arizona State University (whose faculty she joined in 1981 as the only Black professor in the seventy-member English department) and at the University of Virginia (where she moved in 1989 and where she became Commonwealth Professor of English in 1993). The collection features an emphasis on musical imagery as well as a profusion of verbal notes. Grace becomes beauty, blessedness, and mercy, a trinity uniting the seemingly incomplete, ephemeral pieces. This emphasis on partial, incomplete communication testifies to Dove's commitment to exchange and expression.*

Mother Love, *published in 1995, is a cycle of extraordinary sonnets re-visioning the Demeter and Persephone myths, placing them in a contemporary global setting. Deliberate confusion of voices and shifting of personae bleed mother into daughter, daughter into woman, mother and daughter as individuals "struggling to sing in their chains." As she draws on classical Greco-Roman mythologies and the traditional poetic form of the sonnet, Dove re-covers the skeletal form of the sonnet with the musculature of historically violated race and gender issues—"a world gone awry." As she states in the Preface, "I like how the sonnet comforts even while its prim borders (but what a pretty fence!) are stultifying; one is constantly bumping up against Order."*

A latter day griot, Dove preserves and reinterprets a sense of a past culture, combining classical myth, Black history, and contemporary culture to explore and retell the individual story of woman's loss and recovery and its communal significance within a mythic framework. "Mother Love," the poem from which the collection takes its title, may be its best example of Dove's skill in complicating form and content as she takes on the personal and political implications of history, gender roles, and race. It is a cultural critique of the diasporic shattering of family and the role of Black women slaves in America. Dove turns the Petrarchan sonnet upside down, sestet first, octave after the white space—rebalancing the form, perhaps suggesting a stability provided by Black women; a strength and stability in the face of fragmentation and bondage. Women in African American communities have in the past and continue still to support and nurture the home and community, even in the perceived absence/invisibility of the Black male as husband/father.

Her latest work, On the Bus with Rosa Parks *(1999), presents an exploration of human endeavors, frail and strong, shot through with a jazzy elegance that recalls in lyric a past "Back when earth was new" and "everything was still to come." From the opening sequence to the last, these poems explore the intersection of individual fates with the grand arc of history.*

Lenore L. Brady

Mother Love

Who can forget the attitude of mothering?
        Toss me a baby and without bothering
to blink I'll catch her, sling him on a hip.
        Any woman knows the remedy for grief
is being needed: duty bugles and we'll
        climb out of exhaustion every time,

bare the nipple or tuck in the sheet,
        heat milk and hum at bedside until
they can dress themselves and rise, primed
        for Love or Glory—those one-way mirrors
girls peer into as their fledgling heroes slip
        through, storming the smoky battlefield.

So when this kind woman approached at the urging
        of her bouquet of daughters,
(one for each of the world's corners,
        one for each of the winds to scatter!)
and offered up her only male child for nursing
        (a smattering of flesh, noisy and ordinary),
I put aside the lavish trousseau of the mourner
        for the daintier comfort of pity:
I decided to save him. Each night
        I laid him on the smoldering embers,
sealing his juices in slowly so he might
        be cured to perfection. Oh, I know it
looked damning: at the hearth a muttering crone
        bent over a baby sizzling on a spit
as neat as a Virginia ham. Poor human—
        to scream like that, to make me remember.

Courtship

1.

Fine evening may I have
the pleasure . . .
up and down the block
waiting—for what? A
magnolia breeze, someone
to trot out the stars?

But she won't set a foot
in his turtledove Nash,
it wasn't proper.
Her pleated skirt fans
softly, a circlet of arrows.

King of the Crawfish
in his yellow scarf,
mandolin belly pressed tight
to his hounds-tooth vest—
his wrist flicks for the pleats
all in a row, sighing . . .

2.

. . . so he wraps the yellow silk
still warm from his throat
around her shoulders. (He made
good money; he could buy another.)
A gnat flies
in his eye and she thinks
he's crying.

Then the parlor festooned
like a ship and Thomas
twirling his hat in his hands
wondering how did I get here.
China pugs guarding a fringed settee
where a father, half-Cherokee,
smokes and frowns.
I'll give her a good life—
what was he doing,
selling all for a song?
His heart fluttering shut
then slowly opening.

Courtship, Diligence

A yellow scarf runs through his fingers
as if it were melting.
Thomas dabbing his brow.

And now his mandolin in a hurry
though the night, as they say,
is young,
though she is *getting on.*

Hush, the strings tinkle. *Pretty gal.*

Cigar-box music!
She'd much prefer a pianola
and scent in a sky-colored flask.

Not that scarf, bright as butter.
Not his hands, cool as dimes.

Dusting

Every day a wilderness—no
shade in sight. Beulah
patient among knicknacks,
the solarium a rage
of light, a grainstorm
as her gray cloth brings
dark wood to life.

Under her hand scrolls
and crests gleam
darker still. What
was his name, that
silly boy at the fair with
the rifle booth? And his kiss and
the clear bowl with one bright
fish, rippling
wound!

Not Michael—
something finer. Each dust
stroke a deep breath and
the canary in bloom.
Wavery memory: home
from a dance, the front door
blown open and the parlor
in snow, she rushed
the bowl to the stove, watched
as the locket of ice
dissolved and he
swam free.

That was years before
Father gave her up
with her name, years before
her name grew to mean
Promise, then
Desert-in-Peace.
Long before the shadow and
sun's accomplice, the tree.

Maurice.

Testimonial

Back when the earth was new
and heaven just a whisper,
back when the names of things
hadn't had time to stick;

back when the smallest breezes
melted summer into autumn,
when all the poplars quivered
sweetly in rank and file . . .

the world called, and I answered.
Each glance ignited to a gaze.
I caught my breath and called that life,
swooned between spoonfuls of lemon sorbet.

I was pirouette and flourish,
I was filigree and flame.
How could I count my blessings
when I didn't know their names?

Back when everything was still to come,
luck leaked out everywhere.
I gave my promise to the world,
and the world followed me here.

Cornelius Eady (1954–)

Born in Rochester, New York, Cornelius Eady has had much success as a poet, writing his first collection, Kartunes, in 1980. His second collection, Victims of the Latest Dance Craze (1985), won the prestigious Lamont Poetry Award from the Academy of American Poets. His later works include BOOM BOOM BOOM (1988), The Gathering of My Name (1991), You Don't Miss Your Water (1995), and Autobiography of a Jukebox (1996). Eady was nominated for a Pulitzer Prize for his work in Gathering and has been awarded various honors including fellowships from the National Endowment for the Arts and the Guggenheim, Rockefeller, and Reader's Digest Foundations. He is Associate Professor of English and Director of the Poetry Center at the State University of New York at Stony Brook.

Eady possesses an unmistakable poetic talent, one that captures images and moments with precision and clarity. His work literally sets the image to music, like a blues musician, and leaves the reader breathless and wanting more. In "Grace," he avoids the attempt to define the concept with language and instead presents scenes that are themselves manifestations of grace: "Perhaps it's these kids, / Negotiating games in the street, . . . After a week of rain, / The sun is out, a neighbor / Waxes her black sedan." Eady's narrator poses a keen eye, noticing the sunlight's "shimmer on the hood" and calling it "A simple trick / of the light." It is this description, in its bareness, that allows the reader to see the same light trick that the narrator sees. Not only does Eady give examples of grace in his poem, of things easy and magical in their composition, but his poem is also graceful—rhythmic and smooth, repeating the word "perhaps" as a hesitation, a breathing delay before unveiling another scene. The ease of the poem is that it seems uninterrupted: There is no gap between what the narrator sees, what the author writes, and what the reader takes in.

The twenty-one prose poems in one of his more recent works, You Don't Miss Your Water, are a meditation on and to his dying, and then dead, father. Many critics agree that it is in this collection that Eady's poetic gifts shine, because of the sustained emotion and expression that the love meditation requires. Many think these are his finest poems. What Eady achieves here in these five poems is various portraitures of his father's dying, but also of the impact this experience has on him, his mother, his sister, and his relationship to his work. Eady's touch on these poems—the way his poetic fingers move with surgeon-like deft—is so skilled it appears effortless. In "I Know (I'm Losing You)," he uses suspension to reveal the loss that is unspoken. For example, the naming of the loss in the title is in parentheses, which is a key move because the loss is both muted and highlighted, and does little to interrupt the affirmation of "I know." Similarly, Eady uses italicized lines to emphasize the two levels in the poem—one, the literal memory of his father's fading physical body, and two, the memory of the absence of touch between father and son. It is a beautiful moment, for the memory is fading and faded, as is the body. There are, in this poem, at least two narratives to follow, both leading to the weight of loss.

This notion of the weight of loss follows Eady through his meditation. When "A Rag, A Bone, And A Hank of Hair" begins with "I'm sitting alone with my father at the funeral parlor," it becomes clear that Eady's father is alive in his passing. The weight of a loss. In the title poem, "You Don't Miss Your Water," Eady rememorializes, a year later, his father's death, telling what his mother and his sister carry from that loss, but also his own. His memory is not romantic, just pained, and honest. "I miss his difficult waters," Eady writes, and closes with a loving return to a loving gesture that his father had made often when he was alive, but that Eady did not often return. These poems are a fine achievement because they capture Eady's skill for clean and lyric poetic line with the emotional vulnerability that exists in living. In his ability to write these poems that are so much like songs, Eady is in a tradition with Langston Hughes, but also Ethelbert Miller and Toi Derricotte.

Kevin Everod Quashie

I Know (I'm Losing You)

Have you ever touched your father's back? No,
my fingers tell me, as they try to pull up a similar
memory.

There are none. This is a place we have never
traveled to, as I try to lift his weary body onto the
bedpan.

I recall a photo of him standing in front of our
house. He is large, healthy, a stocky body in a dark
blue suit.

And now his bowels panic, feed his mind phony
information, and as I try to position him, my hands
shift, and the news shocks me more than the sight
of his balls.

O, bag of bones, this is all I'll know of his body,
the sharp ridge of spine, the bedsores, the ribs rising
up in place like new islands.

I feel him strain as he pushes, for nothing, feel his
fingers grip my shoulders. *He is slipping to dust,* my
hands inform me, *you'd better remember this.*

One Kind Favor

My father is close to death, and in his final hours, he
begins his journey by asking anyone within earshot
of his bed for a few things.

He asks to be allowed to go back home to Florida.

He asks to be able to cast off his dreary hospital
gown, to be reunited to the shape of his own clothes.

He wants someone to fetch him his shoes, now
useless for weeks, the impossible act of slipping
them on, the slight miracle of bending and tying.

In his wishes, my mother arrives and sits at his
bedside, or he changes it, and he walks back into his
house, into the living room, his old chair.

He is so close to dreaming now, and his body lifts
with the desire to fix things.

A Rag, A Bone, and A Hank of Hair

I'm sitting alone with my father at the funeral parlor.
Viewing hours have just begun, but it's midday work
week, and for a few hours it'll be just me and him, the
first time I've laid eyes on him since the phone call
woke me up.

I'm doing what a son is supposed to do, or so I've
been told, but it's hard work, sitting with what used
to love and trouble you.

Of course, his body is a bright lie in its casket,
everything that has brought him here carefully
hidden or rearranged.

Is there something I want to tell him? Anything I
can forgive?

I can only sit and wait and listen to the gospel
music as it buzzes though the speakers. *Jesus, Jesus,
Jesus.* All his time, all his struggles that I still call life.

All his trials.

You Don't Miss Your Water

At home, my mother wakes up and spends some of
her day talking back to my father's empty chair.

In Florida, my sister experiences the occasional
dream in which my father returns; they chat.

He's been dead and gone for a little over a year.
How it would please me to hear his unrecorded voice
again, now alive only in the minds of those who
remember him.

If I could, if as in the old spiritual, I could actually
get a direct phone link to the other side, I could call
him up, tell him about this small prize of a week I've
had teaching poetry at a ski resort a few miles from
Lake Tahoe, imagination jackpot, brief paradise of
letters.

How could I make him believe that I have gotten
all of this, this modern apartment, this pond in front
of my window, all from the writing of a few good
lines of verse, my father, who distrusted anything he
couldn't get his hands on?

Most likely, he would listen, then ask me, as he
always did, just for safety's sake, if my wife still had
her good-paying job.

And I can't tell you why, but this afternoon,
I wouldn't become hot and stuffy from his concern,
think "old fool," and gripe back *of course I'm still
teaching college. It's summer, you know?*

This afternoon, I miss his difficult waters. And
when he'd ask, as he always would, *how're they
treating you?* I'd love to answer back, *Fine, Daddy.
They're paying me to write about your life.*

Grace

Perhaps
It's the deep, endless
Whirr of the expressway
In the background I need to
Keep, the shadows

At this time in the afternoon,
Their fingers and blouses
Across the lawns and steps.
Perhaps it's these kids,
Negotiating games in the street,

The sight of a blue car
Parked in front of a
Blue house.
     After a week of rain,

The sun is out, a neighbor
Waxes her black sedan.
From my window I watch
The neighborhood compress
And shimmer on the hood,
A simple trick
     of the light.

Trey Ellis (1962–)

Trey Ellis was born in Washington, DC, and attended Phillips Academy, Andover, and Stanford University. After years as a journalist for Newsweek, Playboy, The Village Voice, The Washington Post Book World, Interview, Premiere, *and* The Los Angeles Times, *Ellis started writing fiction. In a short time, he was widely considered one of the best new Black writers around; his novels* Platitudes *(1988) and* Home Repairs *(1993), and most recently,* Right Here, Right Now *(1999), have all been highly reviewed and praised. Ellis is a contemporary Black artist of serious distinction not only because of his novels, but also due to his work with popular culture, especially his screenwriting. He wrote the screenplay for "The Inkwell" (Touchstone, 1992), which starred a young Laurence Tate, and for "The Tuskegee Airmen" (HBO), which was nominated for an Emmy. He has also worked on "Boomerang," "Love Fields," and "Eve's Bayou."*

"The New Black Aesthetic," published in 1989, is a prose piece that gained Ellis wide recognition and ignited much commentary by Black writers and scholars. In the essay, Ellis attempts to articulate the characteristics of a new cadre of Black artists, whom he dubs the New Black Aesthetic (NBA). Ellis's construct of an artistic movement borrows its name from the Black Arts and Aesthetic Movements of the 1960s and early 1970s, and in fact Ellis draws a close connection between that community and the one he is speaking of here: The NBA artists benefit from the social, political, and artistic strides that earlier artists made. NBA artists also benefit from the successes, however marginal, of integration, including greater access to education and to housing. The New Black Aesthetic, then, is a body of artists who are similar in age (at this point, in their thirties), and who have a different relationship to communities of Black and White people than artists might have had before: They are beholden to neither community and are interested mostly in the expression of their art and in living their lives.

Ellis does well articulating the literary and cultural phenomena that characterized the time period from the mid-1980s to the early 1990s. For one, Black presence in entertainment and popular culture was particularly high, and although it has always been true that Black people have been prevalent in entertainment, Ellis makes the keen observation that more and more Black artists and producers were directing and controlling aspects of cultural production. In effect, a Black presence was undeniable and perhaps less restricted than times before, which has an effect on the kind of art being produced.

The cumulative effect of these phenomena is that the NBA artists are what he calls "cultural mulattos"–people who grew up in White worlds (neighborhoods, for example) but who lived and experienced Black worlds and cultures. The relationship these artists have to racism is, as Ellis claims, different: They do not deny its presence, but also do not overestimate its impact. This sense of disregard for the impact of racism, which is in some ways healthy and necessary, is a direct result of the gains that the generation before have secured, even as their efforts and their steadfast critique of racism is the source of parody in some aspects of the work being produced by NBA artists.

Ellis makes an effective argument here, one that aims to outline the characteristics of a new generation of Black artists. These educated and savvy NBA artists are definitively different, he thinks, from the writers before them; their preoccupations are different as well as their products. Interestingly, Ellis's arguments here are also an expression of his own artistic agenda, an attempt to put his own work and its themes into a larger cultural context. It is important not to ignore this aspect of his essay. Yet this is not a criticism of Ellis's work or his prose here, for he is operating within a long tradition in African American literature that engages memoir in political discourse.

In many ways, Ellis's essay is accurate in its portrayal of the concerns of contemporary Black artists and how those concerns are in contradistinction to the artists who preceded them. Of course, this essay is already somewhat outdated, having been written eleven years ago. For example, the 1990s saw a greater emphasis on diasporic sensibilities—on the psychic and literal connections between the United States, countries in West Africa, and the Caribbean—than Ellis's NBA exhibits. Also, the role of hip hop as an aesthetic itself seems to play a greater role in late 1990s Black literature, as well as a struggle with and against a sense of nihilism—a recognition of the violence of the modern world, somewhat in contradistinction to the widespread positivity (which manifests in production) Ellis describes here. Still, Ellis's essay, like his fiction, is important because it boldly and nicely categorizes a character of the art of Black America in these contemporary times. His articulation of a New Black Aesthetic not only helped to crystallize (and critique) prior conversations about contemporary Black writing, but it also has inflected all such conversations that proceed from it.

Kevin Everod Quashie

The New Black Aesthetic

While the tale of how we suffer, and how we are
delighted, and how we may triumph is never new, it
always must be heard. There isn't any other tale to tell,
it's the only light we've got in all this darkness. . . .
And this tale, according to that face, that body, those
strong hands on those strings, has another aspect in
every country, and a new depth in every generation.
—JAMES BALDWIN, THE PRICE OF THE TICKET

They have recently reopened a wing of huge Junior's Restaurant in Fort Greene, Brooklyn, just so Spike Lee can talk in peace. Though some may say he looks like a black Woody Allen, he's got the mouth of a filmmaking Cassius Clay. "People aren't going to see your shit just because you're black. People didn't go see *Native Son*. I didn't think they should see *The Color Purple* and any black person who saw *Soul Man* should have been shot." I admit I was curious, so I rented *Soul Man* just last week. He shrugs. "Black people are the greatest artists on this earth, probably because we're the first people on the earth. White people know that . . . [but] I still can't catch a cab. Ask any black man. Bill Cosby couldn't catch a cab if he wanted to. They ain't stopping for him."

A few days later, on the other coast, another interview, a little different. While Mr. Lee looks meek but talks strong, I am scared of entering this old Los Angelino theater where a black rock group that tosses dead fish onto its audience and once rear-projected a porno film of an oceanically fat black woman having sex with two white men during the song "Cholly" ("I love ya Cholly with your big fat body/Oh oh golly Cholly you're just chubbly wubbly wobbly") is grinding out material for their third album (*Truth & Soul*, Columbia). Today's the 22nd birthday of Fishbone's oldest member and its namesake, drummer "Fish" Fisher, so the band isn't getting a lot of work done. Guitarist "Special K" Kendall Jones swings a half-full bottle of tequila toward me and everybody stops to watch me drink. Am I just imagining Fish's drum roll? Oh how I'd love to be able to chug the booze, smear my mouth with the back of my hand and belch, thus making these mean-looking black punks cheer and let fly guitar chord bursts like rounds from Zapata's *pistoles*. But I'm not about to throw up my magazine expense-account lunch, black male bonding ritual or no. However, they don't mind. The band members just smile and introduce themselves as they warmly shake my hand. Cocky, black West Coast Ska/punk/funkers meet buppie East Coast novelist. I guess Spike Lee is culturally somewhere in between.

Yet we all share a lot more than just skin color. Lee, Fishbone, and I, along with the battalions of other young black artists I run into more and more frequently, all grew up feeling misunderstood by both the black worlds and the white. Alienated (junior) intellectuals, we are the more and more young blacks getting back into jazz and the blues; the only ones you see at punk concerts; the ones in the bookstore wearing little, round glasses and short, neat dreads; some of the only blacks who admit liking both Jim and Toni Morrison. Eddie Murphy, Prince, and the Marsalis brothers are just the initial shock troops because now, in New York's East Village, in Brooklyn's Fort Greene, in Los Angeles, and in Harlem, all of us under thirty only ones are coming together like so many twins separated at birth—thrilled, soothed, and strengthened in being finally reunited.

> Out of this ferment will emerge something new. It reminds me of early bebop. Maybe this will spill into politics.
>
> —NOVELIST ISHMAEL REED

I now know that I'm not the only black person who sees the black aesthetic as much more than just Africa and jazz. Finally finding a large body of the like-minded armors me with the nearly undampenable enthusiasm of the born again.

And my friends and I—a minority's minority mushrooming with the current black bourgeoisie boom—have inherited an open-ended New Black Aesthetic from a few Seventies pioneers that shamelessly borrows and reassembles across both race and class lines. This muscley combination of zeal, *Glasnost,* and talent is daily commanding ever-larger chunks of the American art worlds.

Fishbone has just finished practicing and is ready to talk. Brought together by court-ordered busing out to a mostly white San Fernando Valley junior high school, the six members are the New Black Aesthetic personified. They are a mongrel mix of classes and types, and their political music sounds out this hybrid. Brothers Norwood Fisher and Fish used to bum free lunches from the Black Panthers' headquarters in East Los Angeles; Chris Dowd's father is both a Deep Purple fan and an engineer; "Special K" chose the band over Stanford. Cocky and crazy, they are now very hip among the black and white avant-gardes, yet they yearn for broader, especially black popular support. However, they refuse to pander to an audience just to top the charts. Says Fish, "If it happens, it happens, [but] we're not changing our course." Like the rest of the NBA artists, however, Fishbone's course has frequently changed, crossed, and flouted existing genres according to their own eclectic inspirations. When the band first started playing they covered art-rock songs by Rush and Pink Floyd. Later they moved on to heavy metal and punk before discovering George Clinton's spaced-out soul bands Parliament/Funkadelic and then ska, a British wedding of rock and reggae. "We're like bag people," says "Special K," "Whatever we do we take with us."

> We explored in the past but were not allowed to
> survive. I'm sure there were other kooky ethnic artists
> that were coming from the left but were discouraged.
> —AUGUST DARNELL, "KID CREOLE," 37,
> OF KID CREOLE AND THE COCONUTS

I grew up in the predominantly white, middle and working-class suburbs around Ann Arbor, Michigan, and New Haven, Connecticut, while my mother and father worked their way through the University of Michigan and Yale. At public elementary school in Hamden, Connecticut, my sister and I were the only blacks not bused in from New Haven. It wasn't unusual to be called "oreo" and "nigger" on the same day. After going to private junior high and high school in New Haven, I transferred to Phillips Academy, Andover, in the eleventh grade. At Stanford I majored in creative writing. I won't pretend to be other than a bourgie black boy, now 26 years old, who hadn't lived around a lot of other black people except my own family until I moved into Ujamaa, Stanford's black dorm, my freshman year. When a white friend I've known since the fifth grade heard I was writing this article and asked, "What do you know about black culture?," I realized I was a cultural mulatto. He didn't know I was reading *Soul on Ice, The Autobiography of Malcolm X* and listening to Richard Pryor's *That Nigger's Crazy* after school. I didn't share them with him, one of my best friends.

Just as a genetic mulatto is a black person of mixed parents who can often get along fine with his white grandparents, a cultural mulatto, educated by a multi-racial mix of cultures, can also navigate easily in the white world. And it is by and large this rapidly growing group of cultural mulattoes that fuels the NBA. We no longer need to deny or suppress any part of our complicated and some-times contradictory cultural baggage to please either white people or black. The culturally mulatto *Cosby* girls are equally as black as a black teenage welfare mother. Neither side of the tracks should forget that. Edmund Perry, bouncing from Harlem to Exeter and on his way to Stanford, might have been shot by that white police officer because the old world, both black and white, was too narrow to embrace a black prep from Harlem.

> I was so confused about my identity. I attributed a lot
> of negative things to black dance. It represented a too
> conventional, too restrictive point of view. . . . [Now]
> my work will have a black face because we are black. I
> now have an anger and a location in history that is
> bigger than me. I'm not just a loose cannon.
> —CHOREOGRAPHER BILL T. JONES, 36

Today's cultural mulattoes echo those "tragic mulattoes" critic Sterling Brown wrote about in the Thirties only when they too forget they are wholly black. Most self-deluding cultural mulattoes desperately fantasize themselves the children of William F. Buckley. However, a minority affect instead a "superblackness" and try to dream themselves back to the ghetto. Either way they are letting other people de-fine their identity. Today, there are enough young blacks torn between the two worlds to finally go out and create our own. The New Black Aesthetic says you just have to *be* natural, you don't necessarily have to *wear* one.

Lisa and Kellie Jones, 26 and 29, are Amiri Baraka (LeRoi Jones) and Hettie Cohen's daughters. Their parents were divorced when the children were young and they were raised primarily by their Jewish mother. "I was always searching for the black," says Lisa, "overcompensating as a kid." Besides working on Spike Lee's *She's Gotta Have It* and *School Daze* (she also co-authored *Uplift the Race, The Making of School Daze* with Mr. Lee), the Yale graduate founded Rodeo Cal-donia, a black women's performance-art group. After Amherst, Kellie worked at the Studio Museum of Harlem. She is now the Visual Arts Director of the Jamaica (Queens) Arts Center. Never before have individual, educated blacks and the ability to assimilate so painlessly, yet both Jones sisters didn't. Says Lisa, "I had a lot of options, but I chose [blackness]."

> Rae Dawn Chong says she's Cherokee, Chinese,
> White. . . . Look in a mirror Rae . . . you're BLACK! Go
> try and marry a fucking Kennedy and see how black
> you really are.
> —COMEDIAN CHRIS ROCK, 20

Besides the Jones sisters, many other members of the NBA are the children of Civil Rights workers or black nationalists, and we have inherited from our parents what *Village Voice* critic Greg Tate, 30, calls a "postliberated aesthetic." Though even they themselves might not have arrived at the promised land completely freed from a slave mentality, they thoroughly shielded us from its vestiges. All those Ezra Jack Keats black children's books, *Roots* parties, *For Colored Girls . . .* theater excursions, and the nationalist Christmastide holiday of Kwanzaa worked. Says Spike Lee, "My grandmother would color in the birthday cards black, the dolls brown. We knew that black people are a great race."

Yet ironically, a telltale sign of the work of the NBA is our parodying of the black nationalist movement: Eddie Murphy, 27, and his old *Saturday Night Live* character, prison poet Tyrone Green, with his hilariously awful angry black poem, "Cill [sic] My Landlord," ("See his dog/Do he bite?"); playwright George Wolfe, 34, and his parodies of both *A Raisin in the Sun* and *For Colored Girls . . .* in his hit play *The Colored Museum* ("Enter Walter-Lee-Beau-Willie-Jones. . . . His brow is heavy from 300 years of oppression."); filmmaker Reginald Hudlin, 27, and his sacrilegious *Reggie's World of Soul* with its fake commercial for a back scratcher, spatula, and toilet bowl brush all with black clenched fists on their handle ends; and Lisa Jones's character Clean Mama King who is available for both sit-ins and film walk-ons. There is now such a strong and vast body of great black work that the corny or mediocre doesn't need to be coddled. NBA artists aren't afraid to flout publicly the official, positivist black party line.

However, the works and protests of the nationalists "made us possible," says Lisa. "Though we make fun of them, if it weren't for [deceased, brilliant critic] Larry Neal and my father, we wouldn't have the freedom now to be so nonchalant." Like any new movement of artists and like most people in their mid-twenties, part of the process of stamping our own adult identities includes rebelling against our parents, cautioning ourselves against their pitfalls.

Yet our spiritual and often biological older brothers and sister, those who were artistically coming of age just as the bloom of Mr. Baraka's Black Arts Movement was beginning to fade, are our constant icons. Though during the mid-seventies they were a minority of the black-arts community, branded either counter-revolutionary, too artsy or just not good propagandists, nevertheless avant-garde artists like novelists Ishmael Reed, Clarence Major, Toni Morrison, and John Edgar Wideman; George Clinton with his spaced-out funk band Parliament/Funkadelic; conceptual artist David Hammons who has hung empty Thunderbird bottles and spades from trees; Richard Pryor with his molten parodies of black life on his early albums and short-lived television show, all helped forge our current aesthetic. Stripping themselves of both white envy and self-hate they produced supersophisticated black art that either expanded or exploded the old definitions of blackness, showing us as the intricate, uncategorizeable folks we had always known ourselves to be. These artists—what the University of Massachusetts's Pancho Savery calls the "Third Plane"—saved my generation from a decade of not-so-funky chickens and disco ducks. If it weren't for them, the

NBA—like the current young white aesthetic of kitsch Americana—would be fueled just by the junk of the Seventies: mood rings, crock pots, *Bicentennial Minutes,* "Keep On Truckin'" T-shirts, and *Josie and the Pussycats.*

But today's new black cutting edge has two advantages over the Third Plane. Though as an aesthetic the NBA might not be any newer than Ms. Morrison's *Song of Solomon* (1978), yet as a movement we finally have the numbers to leverage this point of view. For the first time in our history we are producing a critical mass of college graduates who are children of college graduates themselves. Like most artistic booms, the NBA is a post-bourgeois movement driven by a second generation of middle class. Having scraped their way to relative wealth and, too often, crass materialism, our parents have freed (or compelled) us to bite those hands that fed us and sent us to college. We now feel secure enough to attend art school instead of medical school.

Another great advantage we have over the artists of the Seventies is that today's popular culture is guided by blacks almost across the board. Between Eddie Murphy and Bill Cosby (soon to be the first entertainment billionaire), Spike Lee and Robert Townsend, playwright August Wilson and poet Rita Dove (1987's Pulitzer Prize winners), novelist Toni Morrison (1988's Pulitzer winner), Wynton and Branford Marsalis, Prince, and the explosion of rap artists, the world is not only now accustomed to black faces in the arts, but also hungers for us.

I feel the new, unflinching way NBA artists are looking at black culture is largely responsible for their popularity. No longer are too many black characters either completely cool and fearless (*Sweet Sweetback's Badaaaaas Song*) or completely loving and selfless (*Sounder*). Says Spike Lee, "The number one problem with the old reactionary school was they cared too much about what white people think." And it is precisely because Mr. Lee isn't afraid of what anyone else thinks that he dares to show his world warts and all in both his first film *She's Gotta Have It* and in this year's controversial musical *School Daze* that opened up, among other things, the previously taboo subject of intra-racial, skin-color prejudice; and gave us a black version of Jimmy the Greekesque theorizing in the form of the musical dance craze in praise of the extra-large curves of the Afro-American behind ("Da Butt") and another praising natural black hair ("Straight and Nappy"). Again with the hair, Mr. Hudlin has invented an improbable ethnic group, the Rasta-Hassidim, in his parody of a black TV news magazine; Mr. Wolfe's *Colored Museum* includes a sketch in which a pair of wigs—one Afro, one straightened—discuss the politics and love life of their owner; and in Mr. Townsend's *Hollywood Shuffle* his character defeats the villain Jheri Curl by withholding his curl activator until the man's greasy ringlets dry back up to their natural naps.

Though Third Plane playwright August Wilson, 43, wrote agitprop in the Sixties because "that was necessary, a more polemical theater," in his Pulitzer and Tony award-winning play *Fences* he didn't whitewash the bitter stubbornness of one 1950s black father just because some white people might mistake one man's flaws for across-the-board black male cruelty. And in Mr. Wilson's latest play, *Joe Turner's Come and Gone,* his characters are the polar extreme of propagandistic puppets, instead reaching lyric complexities. Terry McMillan's acclaimed first novel, *Mama,* doesn't sidestep the periodic cruelty of the protagonist's mother just because many non-blacks already believe the black family doomed. Following the lead of the Third Plane, NBA artists are now defining blacks in black contexts—so we are no longer preoccupied with the subjects of interracial dating or integration. And these artists aren't flinching before they lift the hood on our collective psyches now that they have liberated themselves from both white envy and self-hate.

Unfortunately, however, still too many blacks belie their fears of inferiority by always demanding propagandistic positivism. Mr. Lee returned to Moorehouse College a hero, but soon afterwards he and his film crew were kicked off campus while filming *School Daze.* Moorehouse president Hugh Gloster thought veteran actor Joe Seneca, who played the president of Lee's Mission College, somehow looked like Uncle Tom.

So we now find ourselves the dominant culture's "flavor of the month" as has happened before, during Reconstruction, the Twenties' Harlem Renaissance and the Sixties' Black Arts Movement, but this time, armed with savvy and hungry new institutions, like the Black Filmmaker Foundation, the Black Rock Coalition, and DefJam records, we are not only determined but also now equipped to extend this month in the sun into a lifetime.

> What blacks were doing in the 60s is coming to some
> fruition. . . . We have the framework and the
> orientation to take things further.
>
> —AUGUST WILSON

Warrington Hudlin, 35, is president of the New York-based Black Filmmaker Foundation. I met him and his brother Reginald three years ago while researching an article on black independent filmmakers, and since then they have become two of my best friends. They are about to produce and direct their first feature film for New Line Cinema. And like fellow BFF member and playwright George Wolfe (whose adaptation of Duke Ellington's jazz opera, *Queenie Pie,* will hit Broadway this Spring at the same time Gregory Hines begins rehearsing Wolfe's new musical, *Jelly Roll Morton*), the Hudlin brothers are some of the most traditionally middle class of the NBA. Artful black yuppies ("buppies"), they don't dress like either hiphop B-boys or punkish hepcats. And they aren't ashamed that many of their friends are lawyers and bankers. In fact, the BFF's relationship with those black professionals is probably what has made the ten-year-old black independent film programming, distribution, and exhibition service last so long. It is one of the first black-arts organizations that couples the creativity of the new black artists themselves with the insider's knowledge of high finance from the current flood of young black investment bankers and lawyers.

Reginald is the directorial half of this producer/director brotherhood. He is one of the youngest major-studio filmmakers in the country and his films realistically, relentlessly, and hilariously portray contemporary black working-class life. Like his friend Spike Lee, the Harvard graduate has little tolerance for the *Sounder*-esque "glory stories" of the Seventies where black "films were more obsessed with being good PR for the race than with being culturally authentic. It's as if blacks have to be spoon fed." Some of Reginald's comedy sketches, on the other hand, would be very hard to swallow if they weren't so funny. In his parody of a black TV news magazine, *Reggie's World of Soul,* he claims that "Mello Yello" soft drink is also an effective skin lightener and swears that Lionel Ritchie used to be the misshapen yellow animal "Drooper" on the Seventies' children show *The Banana Splits*.

> I don't want nobody to give me nothing, Open up the
> door (HUH!) I'll get it myself.
> —James Brown, "I Don't Want Nobody To Give Me Nothing"

The revisionism we bring to our understanding of the Civil Rights and black Nationalist movements has little to do with that of black conservatives such as Thomas Sowell of Stanford's ultra-right-wing Hoover Institute or Stanley Crouch of the *New Republic*. Nationalist pride continues to be one of the strongest forces in the black community and the New Black Aesthetic stems straight from that tradition. It is not an apolitical, art-for-art's-sake fantasy. We realize that despite this current buppie artist boom, most black Americans have seldom had it worse. But what most all the New Black Artists have in common is a commitment to what Columbia University philosopher Arthur Danto calls "Disturbatory Art"—art that shakes you up. The moral imperative of being black in America enrapts us with a militant juju that wards off cynical minimalism. In the NBA you won't find many spartan tales of suburban ennui or technicolor portraits of Fred and Barney.

Neither are the new black artists shocked by the persistence of racism as were those of the Harlem Renaissance, nor are we preoccupied with it as were those of the Black Arts Movement. For us, racism is a hard and little-changing constant that neither surprises nor enrages. Robert Townsend, 31, puts it this way, "You can sit around and complain about the white man until you're blue in the face. . . . I wasn't listening when everybody told me about the obstacles. I was too stupid to be discouraged." So he took the dominant culture's credit cards and clobbered it with a film. Terry McMillan "thinks life's a bitch no matter what color you are. You can't blame the world." We're not saying racism doesn't exist; we're just saying it's not an excuse.

> I had to fight to overcome in the institution and
> transform it; make a white institution serve a black
> person.
> —Anthony Davis, 37, composer of X,
> the opera on the life of Malcolm X

I'm at Andre Harrell's twenty-seventh birthday party. He used to work for Russel Simmons's Rush Productions which represents most all of today's rap artists (b-boys, Run D.M.C., L.L. Cool J, The Beastie Boys, Whodini, Public Enemy) but now runs his own hiphop music management company and record label, the Brooklyn-based Uptown productions. Gary Harris, a big, friendly guy who also used to work for Rush but is now an independent promoter and who knows me only from the times Andre kindly sneaks me into Nell's nightclub with his crew, was surprised to learn I studied creative writing in California. "I thought you went to M.I.T. or some [obscenity]."

So maybe members of the NBA sometimes still type people. And more often than not, at least inside the movement, their guess is going to be right. But cliquish elitism and snap judgments on the content of one's character based on the cut of one's clothes could wilt the NBA even before it has fully bloomed. Insiders too often dwell on the differences between the NBA's buppies, b-boys, and bohemians. Fortunately, however, there is a lot of cross-pollination. The Hudlin Brothers direct hiphop videos, East Village painter Fab 5. Freddie (Fred Brathwaite) is an ex-rapper, graffitiist, and now host of *Yo. MTV raps!,* and Laurie Anderson-style avant-opera singer Alva Rogers acted in *School Daze.*

Nevertheless, for hiphop b-boys, style is often as important as one's music and brand names can be more important than one's rap. Suzuki Samurai Jeeps, Moet champagne, complete Gucci or Louis Vuitton leather outfits, Kangol hats, "[heavy] duty gold" rope necklaces, four-finger rings, and crotch-first machismo are all, for the moment, rap *de rigueur.* Most all young, black intellectuals, on the other hand, wear little, round glasses, Ghanaian, kinte-cloth scarves, and increasingly, tiny, neat dreadlocks. (Unfortunately, my hair is still too short for dreads. Still, I am proud of my also-stylish "Fade" or "jar-head" cut, only one-curl-high on the sides of my head—so short you can see the scalp.) "It's going to be a real challenge for people in our little group to make sure that our movement isn't a little elitist, avant-garde thing," says Lisa Jones. However, at least for now, that is exactly what it is.

> You spend a buck in the 80s—what you get is a preacher
> Forgivin' this torture of the system that brought 'cha
> I'm on a mission and you got that right
> Addin' fuel to the fire—punch to the fight.
> —Public Enemy, "Rightstarter (Message for the Black man)"
> Yo! Bum Rush This Show DefJam/Columbia

Rap is the most innovative sound since rock & roll, making new music out of everything from sitcom sound bites to heavy-metal speed-guitar solos to record scratching. Tonight, at Andre's house party, 21-year-old balladeer Al B. Sure croons along with his album, *Al B. Sure in Effect Mode,* (Uptown/Warner Bros.). I swear at least fifteen girls and women at the party hold their knees to keep upright. A posse of rappers from New Rochelle have been invited to entertain live and nervously go through a sound check. Jam Master Jay of Run D.M.C. and Russell Simmons, 31, millionaire co-founder of DefJam records and Rush president, are both in the house. Mr. Simmons describes himself as a shrewd entrepreneur who "sells to pop America what they thought was exclusively black." And like the rest of the NBA, he is creating his own definitions of blackness no matter how loudly either white or black people might complain. Says Simmons, "Even dashiki-wearing blacks who were really important in the black movement just look at us as part of a ghetto mentality. Art shouldn't be categorized."

One categorical mistake many make is thinking that rap is only created by the hardcore children of the slums; that the black middle class is all too busy buying Polo shirts and branding their arms with fraternity emblems to care about black street culture and politics. In fact, most of the big-name rappers are middle-class black kids. Mr. Simmon's father is a former professor of black history at Pace College and his mother a school teacher. His brother is Run of Run D.M.C.; L.L. Cool J grew up around the corner. Public Enemy, Bill Stephney, 27, vice-president of DefJam records, and *Village Voice* rap critic Harry Allen, 27, all met in an Afro-American studies course at Adelphi University on Long Island where they grew up. In fact, Public Enemy's chief, Chuck D., 28, is from Roosevelt, Long Island, sharing the suburban hometown with Eddie Murphy. Nevertheless, his group slugs out the hardest, most militant rap around. Mr. Stephney, who also co-produced the Public Enemy albums *Yo! Bum Rush This Show* and *It Takes a Nation of Millions to Hold Us Back,* describes their music as "politically conscious but not preachy." They make you realize that you don't have to be black and poor to be black and angry.

> I just feel in a lot of ways black people are so much
> looser and cooler . . . just as a culture.
> —PEE-WEE HERMAN, *INTERVIEW*, JULY 1987

Two and a half years ago while I was still an "only one" having yet to discover the NBA, I had just hitchhiked my way across central Africa (something only a second-generation middle-class person would ever volunteer to do) proud of the fact I had only $80 dollars to my name and was now working my way north through Niger. The Peace Corps was kind enough to put me up for a few nights in a hostel in the country's capital of Niamey. A volunteer, Craig Wilson, then 25, was my roommate. When I met him he was wiping his little, round glasses (Peace Corps standard issue) between stanzas of the Ishmael Reed poem "I AM A COWBOY IN THE BOAT OF RA." Of course we became friends and three months later we met again back here in New York where he, now a music composer, dragged me to see a guitarist he knew at CBGBs, a hardcore club in the Bowery.

Vernon Reid, then 26, shook the sweat from his short dreads arcing out from his forehead before grinding his third encore solo into a psychotically distorted explosion. A black lead-guitarist playing funked-out heavy metal. "Well I'll be damned," I remember thinking. Backstage after the concert, he shook everyone's hand before handing out copies of a manifesto for the then newly formed Black Rock Coalition of which he is a founder: "For white artists, working under the rubric 'rock' has long meant the freedom to pimp any style of black music— funk, reggae, soul, jazz, gospel ad infinitum. . . . We too claim that same right. . . . The members of the BRC are neither novelty acts, nor carbon copies of the white bands who work America's Apartheid Oriented Rock circuit. . . . We are individuals and will accept no less than full respect for our right to be conceptually independent." I was blown away.

Since then Vernon, his band Living Colour, and the rest of the Black Rock Coalition have been written up in *Spin, Rolling Stone, Billboard, Interview,* the *Voice* (where Vernon is also a political essayist), and in the *Times.* He has played with downtown experimental music king John Zorn at Brooklyn Academy of Music's "Next Wave" festival as well as on Public Enemy's rap album *Yo! Bum Rush This Show.* Mick Jagger—who borrowed everything he knows from black bluesmen—repaid the debt, a bit, when he paid for and produced three Living Colour demos last summer. Reid's album, *Vivid* (Epic records) came out last Spring, and artist Robert Longo did the first video.

"I don't mind being in a bag as long as it's one I can define and control," he tells me last summer in the Hiro Cafe's sculpture garden, one of the many artsy-fartsy babaganush and gazpacho joints with sculpture gardens in the East Village. Next to him sit Kellie Jones and painter Fred Brathwaite, both 28. I'm the only one who orders alcohol and red meat.

"When you look into your own shit and dig in," continues Vernon, "then you'll find the universal. You won't find the universal by deciding to go after the universal." Then we all talk about how *She's Gotta Have It* crossed over so well precisely because it was so true to the black. And how Lionel Ritchie's "Dancing on the Ceiling" and Whitney Houston's "I Wanna Dance with Somebody" are so lifeless precisely because they have applied Porcelana fade cream to their once extremely soulful throats. The two now-pop singers have transformed themselves into cultural-mulatto, assimilationist nightmares; neutered mutations instead of thriving hybrids. Trying to please both worlds instead of themselves, they end up truly pleasing neither.

> I had somebody say once my black was way too black,
> And someone answer she's not black enough for me.
> —JOAN ARMATRADING, *HOW CRUEL,* TITLE TRACK, A&M RECORDS

What I'm noticing most nowadays about the New Black Aesthetic movement is its magnetism. Since anything (good) goes, almost every month a talented new black artist blows into town with a wild new cultural combination. The new Italian critics call it *"neobarocco."* Stanford philosopher Sylvia Wynter calls it "the Democratization of Perspective." I call it the most exciting period I have ever known. "We don't have to go into the white intellectual community in search of

kindred souls," says Lisa Jones. "We all considered ourselves freaky, out, rebelling against some sort of middle-class values. I can find that all in black people now." A few years ago it seemed that no young blacks were playing jazz
anymore and that the legacy would default upon sympathetic white negroes.
Now, besides Wynton and Branford Marsalis, we have bluesman Robert Cray,
guitarist Jean-Paul Bourelly, 27, pianist composers Geri Allen and saxophonist
Steve Coleman. They are all energetically taking up right where Ornette and
Thelonius and 'trane left off. We even have a black folk singer in 24-year-old,
boarding-school and Tufts University trained Tracy Chapman. So whether at the
Jamaica Arts Center where Kellie Jones works, at the Knitting Factory in the East
Village, or at the Black Filmmaker Foundation's free monthly screenings in the
HBO building in midtown Manhattan, you can experience everything from the
large-format photography of Lorna Simpson to the postmodern, post-Ailey
choreography of Fred Holland. Somehow these dry, neoconservative Eighties,
these horse latitudes for mainstream culture, are proving one of the most fertile
periods black culture has ever known. Says Fred Brathwaite, "That other culture
is definitely spent," while black people have yet to see the best days of our race.
Until a few years ago I was constantly bemoaning the fact that I wasn't in my
prime during the Black Arts Movement or the Beatnik era; I wasn't around to
slouch between Picasso and Hemingway on a couch in Gertrude Stein's salon.
But I agree with playwright George Wolfe: "*This* is an incredible time." It has
been over a year now that I don't envy any other age. I feel good.

Mari Evans (1923–)

Mari Evans is a woman of many roles—poet, playwright, storyteller, screen writer, television producer, college professor, and editor. In every role, she explores the Black community and the realities of Black women, especially. Her literary achievements include children's books, drama, poetry collections, and an anthology of critical essays on Black women writers. Evans was also producer, director, writer for the television show, "The Black Experience," broadcast from Indianapolis from 1968 to 1973.

With work spanning three decades, Mari Evans started her literary career in the midst of the Black Arts Movement, a time when artists and writers were advancing Black nationalism and a Black aesthetic. I Am A Black Woman (1970), her most well-known collection of poetry, focuses specifically on the Black community and is more overtly political than her first book, Where Is All the Music (1968). A central marker of the poetry in I Am A Black Woman is the brevity and specificity of her form, which enhances the power of image and theme in each line. In "Into Blackness Softly," for example, through the simple and lyrical image of a door closing and a number of quiet steps, Evans communicates the theme of the title. The typographical strategies of spacing words, running words together, and using lower and uppercase letters establish the rhythm and tone of the poem and are trademarks of her style. Writing about loss and the strength of Black women in the title poem, "I Am A Black Woman," Evans collapses the experiences of Black women across time, linking enslavement and Black impoverishment to global oppression, and linking resistance in the United States to African liberation and to the fight against the imperialistic oppression of people of color globally. In this poem, as in "Vive Noir," Evans reveres the resilience and faith of Black people, heroes and human, as she documents the circumstances of survival.

In Night Star (1981) and A Dark and Splendid Mass (1992), Evans's work continues to celebrate the strength, endurance, and grace of the African American community. In "Music as Heartbeat and Blood," she honors the tradition of song. In the three parts of the "Amtrak Suite," the train is cold, continuously moving, prompting a reader to see more clearly what is being passed, ignored, unchanged, unappreciated. Writing as observer and participant, Evans appeals to the African American community, asks them to see more closely, love and act more consciously. So powerful is her message that her poetry has been adopted into communal expression—album covers, television, music, and dance.

Born in Toledo, Ohio, on July 16, 1923, Evans lost her mother when she was seven and was raised primarily by her father who instilled in her a consciousness of her African heritage and who encouraged her to write. She attended the University of Toledo and is a longtime resident of Indianapolis. She was awarded an honorary doctorate in Humane Letters from Marion College in 1975 and has taught African American literature and creative writing at Indiana University, Purdue University, Northwestern University, and the

State University of New York at Albany, as well as serving as a visiting professor at Washington University and Cornell University.

R. Joyce Lausch

I Am A Black Woman

I am a black woman
the music of my song
some sweet arpeggio of tears
is written in a minor key
and I
can be heard humming in the night
Can be heard
                    humming
in the night

I saw my mate leap screaming to the sea
and I/with these hands/cupped the lifebreath
from my issue in the canebrake
I lost Nat's swinging body in a rain of tears
and heard my son scream all the way from Anzio
for Peace he never knew. . . . I
learned Da Nang and Pork Chop Hill
in anguish
Now my nostrils know the gas
and these trigger tire/d fingers
seek the softness in my warrior's beard

I
am a black woman
tall as a cypress
strong
beyond all definition still
defying place
and time
and circumstance
    assailed
        impervious
            indestructible
Look
    on me and be
renewed

into blackness softly

the hesitant door chain
back forth back
forth
  the
stealthy
  soft
   final
    ssshuuu t
jubilantly
  stepping down
   stepping down
    step
ping lightly across the lower
  hall
the shocking airfingers
  the
   receiving

    blackness
  sigh

Vive Noir!

i
am going to rise
en masse
from Inner City

    sick
   of newyork ghettos
   chicago tenements
  l a's slums
weary
  of exhausted lands
  sagging privies
  saying yessuh yessah
  yesSIR
  in an assortment
  of geographical dialects i
have seen my last
broken down plantation

even from a
distance
        i
will load all my goods
in '50 Chevy pickups '53
Fords fly United and '66
caddys i
     have packed in
     the old man and the old lady and
   wiped the children's noses
         I'm tired
           of hand me downs
             shut me ups
               pin me ins
                 keep me outs
                    messing me over have
               just had it
           baby
         from
      you . . .
i'm
gonna spread out
over America
        intrude
my proud blackness
all
     over the place
         i have wrested wheat fields
         from the forests

         turned rivers
         from their courses

         leveled mountains
         at a word
         festooned the land with
         bridges
               gemlike
            on filaments of steel
                moved
      glistening towersofBabel in place
         like blocks
    sweated a whole
    civilization

now
          i'm
gonna breathe fire
through flaming nostrils BURN
          a place for

          me

in the skyscrapers and the
schoolrooms on the green
lawns and the white
beaches
                    i'm
gonna wear the robes and
sit on the benches
make the rules and make
the arrests say
who can and who
can't
               baby you don't stand
               a
               chance
  i'm
      gonna put black angels
      in all the books and a black
      Christchild in Mary's arms i'm
      gonna make black bunnies black
      fairies black santas black
      nursery rhymes and
                         black
          ice cream
                         i'm
gonna make it a
     crime
          to be anything BUT black
          pass the coppertone

gonna make white
a twentyfourhour
lifetime
J.O.B.
               an' when all the coppertone's gone . . . ?

Music as Heartbeat and Blood

There have been men
intimate with arpeggio
with the citrus sting of cymbal
with the whirr and wisk of brush
who were themselves soft sensuous nightsongs
haunting and haunted
                    formidable
the pulse intense and complex
daysongs reworked
                    hour on disciplined hour
Men whose eyes were early evening fires
    dangerously banked
                        lashed with longing
Men who sang persuasive lovesongs soft on
alto saxophone on flute and Fender
fingers copper, lean, coercive

            Men whose other instruments were those
of tenderness of feathered touch
                    natural phrasing
etudes throbbing through quiescent
sunlit afternoons   pregnant classics
                    creative voicing, pristine
                    bass overripe throated
The stroll arrogant and dominant
thirty two measures then one note
extended breathing
                    circular
                        a linear bursting
        A virtuoso performance

Amtrak Suite I

(A DARK AND SPLENDID MASS)

Crevasse and mountainside a
dark and splendid mass, cloaked
        and threatening; a forest armed
            veterans at attention
dense, close ordered, impenetrable

The valley sister to the ravening gorge
a fading light, the lengthening shadows. There atop
the distant rise a silvered saucer
imaged in the eyes of does
                    Albino does
      a motion in the mind
The dusk drifts down
      The evening news, silt
whispered in cadence
      from another planet

Amtrak Suite II

(PASSING A PENITENTIARY, IN FULL FLIGHT)

The train in flying gear rocks past a flat red prison complex
Urged beyond its passions, its performances, to flee
the elongated fingers straining at escaping windows

Forced to race in futile contest it will neither place nor win; with
stark and fleshless dreams in swift and shifting pursuit; with
chill imaginings and opaque eyeballs prying through the clouded
thermal panes—See the train in flight, it speeds the bedrock
past untidy undergrowth and past the ragged stands of pine

Red brick walls cannot contain the narrow, barren lives, they
have no baggage and are faster than the whine of
late November wind. They lie in wait within the cages
nails unsheathed and hunger honed; a mass
undisciplined and eager, passage subsidized, their
destination of no real import for 'there' is anywhere but here
The instinct, the insatiate goal, the pure intent:
To ride-a that train each time
each time   each time   each time
      each   time

Amtrak Suite III

(FADING ORANGE SUNLIGHT ON DESERTED RUINS)

It speeds her on to where no one is waiting
Where no hand will sweep the curtain to one side nor
lift the shade a bit to peer beneath nor
crack the door to tilt the head out and inquire

of the street. The train is in control
      of Time and Situation
She is scrunched, an emptiness, a
Woman in a corner watching trees rush backwards
Caught in some relentless forward movement
Her reluctance no concern at all

It speeds her on, this train
that gives so little and imposes much
      It speeds her on
    to where no hand will sweep the curtain
    to one side nor
    lift the shade
    nor tilt the head out to
    inquire
    of the street if

    she is near
  or
      anywhere

Percival Everett (1956–)

Percival Everett was born in December 1956 in Fort Gordon, Georgia. He earned an under-graduate degree at the University of Miami in 1977 and a graduate degree from Brown University in 1982. In between those degrees, Everett also attended the University of Oregon. In his life, Everett has worked as a jazz musician, ranch worker, high school teacher, and university professor. In the latter capacity, he has worked at the University of Kentucky, the University of Notre Dame, and most recently, the University of California, Riverside.

Everett has somewhat quietly built a writing career of some reputation. I say quietly, because he is hardly a publicist for his own work or personality and has maintained his focus on capturing in writing the complexities of life in a modern world. Nonetheless, the strength of his work is not unrecognized by the literary world: He has received a D.H. Lawrence fellowship from the University of New Mexico after the publication of his first work, Suder (1983), and has been a writer-in-residence at numerous institutions. Since his first work, he has written Walk Me to the Distance *(1985),* Cutting Lisa *(1986),* The Weather and Women Treat Me Fair *(1987),* For Her Dark Skin *(1989),* Zulus *(1990),* The One That Got Away *(1992),* God's Country *(1994),* Big Picture *and* Watershed *(both 1996),* Frenzy *(1997), and* Glyph *(1999). His is a prolific career, for which there has been much critical praise.*

It is the madness and challenge of the modern world that most frequently shows up as a theme in Everett's work. In "Randall Randall," Everett writes a well-crafted and fast-paced story that is in one sense a conflict between Randall and the other people in his community. The way Randall perceives the world seems contradictory to how others perceive it. The "oddness" of the story begins with the title and the name of the character—a double name that seems on one hand like a joke, and on the other hand seems elegant, as if it commands respect. At the opening of the story, Randall is writing a letter to a neighbor about her habit of parking her car in front of the trash container, which is not only a fire hazard, but which makes it difficult for his wife, Claudia, to access that area. Randall's letter is serious and argumentative, engaging logic and a tone of legality. His wife Claudia, whose interest Randall seems to have in writing the letter, does not share his enthusiasm in relation to the letter. This initial conflict—where one is not sure whether Randall is making too much of Claudia's casual complaint about the car and the risk it poses, or if in fact Randall has a serious and necessary gripe—is the model for all the other conflicts that lead to the story's tragic end.

What Everett achieves so well in this story is the pacing—how a trip to the drugstore (where Randall is allowed to exhibit a paternal and admiring connection with Lisa, the clerk, and a foreshadowing adversarial one with Willy, the pharmacist) leads to a car theft, a police chase, the injury (death?) of a police officer, a bank misunderstanding, and eventually some physical injury (shooting? stabbing?) to Randall and perhaps his own death. Everett effectively creates situations that are not necessarily linked to each other, but that could in a moment of confusion be linked to each other, and as such, have dire consequences. In doing so, Everett uses ambiguity to sustain the idea that it is perception of the world that matters (for example, Randall and Willy's perception that the neighborhood is dangerous, and that they must protect themselves, yet ironically it is the two of them who are involved in the only dangerous activity in the story); in one's perception of the world lies the reality, the only reality.

The heart of Randall's struggle is his not wanting to be nothing, for him not to matter, which is what happens at three key scenes in the story. The first is the seeming dismissal of his letter by Holly, whose car is defiantly in the same spot after his rather long and pointed letter. Secondly, there is the interchange in McDonald's with the poor man, who Randall fears could be him; in that scene, the poor homeless man becomes Randall's shadow, his other self. Finally, there is the scene where the young person says that he is looking at nothing, as he stares at Randall. It is the reality (which is Everett's clever use of language) that allows Willy to not see Randall, but instead an ambiguous threat of the modern world.

Everett's narrative craft is reminiscent of Toni Cade Bambara's, and is a contemporary of Michelle Cliff, Randall Kenan, and Clarence Major, even as Everett's work takes a decided look at modernity.

Kevin Everod Quashie

Randall Randall

RANDALL HALPERN RANDALL

189 Wayland Avenue   Apt. 51   Providence, Rhode Island

8:10 A.M., Sunday, November 23, 1980

Miss Holly Diehl
Apt. 41
189 Wayland Avenue
Providence, RI

Dear Holly:

I am distressed that it has come to this. I had hoped that there would be no reason for me to compose this letter, but it seems the matter at hand will not straighten itself out, considering this morning's condition in the driveway rear of this building.

Please permit me to state MY SIDE of the matter in question!!!

My dear wife, a good woman who knits constantly and who makes baby booties for people she doesn't even know, has enjoyed over 20 years of extremely peaceful and harmonious relations with the tenants in this building, and I certainly have tried my best to preserve such a condition in spite of some recent goings-on such as door slamming by tenants on the fourth and sixth floors, etc.

We have attempted to quietly and without disturbing anyone else on any floor take care of the rubbish and/or garbage from our apartment . . . to the large green dumpster, as detailed in our lease and yours . . . daily (not just weekends as you seem to have deduced, per Claudia!). However, I usually do it . . . and a major reason is that Claudia suffered a fracture to her knee cap (patella) some time back when she fell on some ice outside the convenience store and had to wear a brace for weeks. And of course I have thrombophlebitis, as did our former president Mr. Nixon, two years ago, throughout my left leg and must watch myself when descending the 87 *steps down to the first floor and out the rear door of this building!!!*

I contacted Mr. Harry Bottoms following your "to whom it may concern" note (which I still have in my possession) and asked him WHO was probably the nicest and most quiet and agreeable tenant in the building—aside from him and Lucy. He said without pause that it is YOU!!! That is WHY I could not understand HOW any such fine person would block the rear door to prevent passage to the big green dumpster. . . . Aside from the probability that the fire department could NEVER get in, in case of a fire in the building!!! I remember vividly when those yellow lines were painted, and I NEVER saw any car in that area right up close blocking the door until your car was there!!!

You KNOW that once I stopped into your fine apartment and was received most cordially and enjoyed speaking with you about your plants and collection of small dinner bells, etc. I could NOT somehow believe that it was YOUR car (never thought it was for one minute) that was blocking us from the dumpster.

I was planning to seek you out for a discussion of the matter, but the condition, and it was a condition and not a situation as my wife insists, was so serious this morning that I had to state MY side of the case to Mr. Pluckett!!! I HOPE that this will be the end of it—and that my poor wife won't have to cart our waste out and around, so publicly, around three (3) sides of the building to reach the dumpster!!! Mr. Bottoms was just up here again—Claudia spoke with him at length only to discover that you and others have accused me of over-reacting. Please do not speak about me further and I shall do the same for you.

Sincerely,
R.H.R.

P.S.—I don't care what you or anyone else thinks, I am NOT a "trouble-maker" and want a peaceful home just as you no doubt do. I DO try to be alert, however, because there have been several burglaries in the 27 years Claudia has been here and the 16 years that I have been here. And of course the Osco drugstore was broken into again last week.

Randall folded the letter and sealed it in an envelope. He waved it in the air in front of his wife's face as if to say, "This should take care of it."

"It's not such a big deal, Randall," Claudia said.

"What if I were breaking the rule," Randall asked. "What if it was me? You think it would just be let go? No, it wouldn't." He sat down at the kitchen table and scratched at a chip in the formica. "No, it wouldn't and I'll tell you why. It's because she's a young woman and Pluckett's a dirty old man."

Claudia slapped a skillet onto a burner of the gas stove. She laughed.

"Shut up."

"I bet old Pluckett is down there right now having a little party with Miss Diehl." She melted butter in the pan while she opened the refrigerator.

"I only want one egg this morning." Randall said.

"Bacon or sausage?"

"Sausage."

"We're out of sausage," Claudia said.

"Then why did you ask me?"

She put the bacon on the counter next to the carton of eggs. "I wanted to give you a choice."

"But I didn't have a choice."

"You chose, didn't you? You just made the wrong choice." She cracked an egg into the hot skillet. It sizzled.

"Well, I don't want bacon," Randall said.

"Then I won't make you any."

He looked at her in her lavender robe and cream-colored slippers. She was dressed in street clothes, but still she wore that robe over them and those slippers. He hated the way the heels of her feet looked, hard and calloused, white, porous.

"Do you want toast?"

"Is there any bread?"

"Yes."

"Then, yes, I want toast."

Claudia flipped one of the eggs. "I broke your yolk," she told him. She lit a cigarette and put the lighter back down on the sill above the sink.

"I want to put plastic runners down over the carpet in the front room," Claudia said.

"Plastic runners."

"To protect the carpet from wear."

Randall laughed. "Wear? Oh, yeah, from all the visitors we get."

Claudia fell silent as she slid the eggs onto the plates. She pulled the bread from the toaster and put breakfast in front of Randall. She sat with him at the table.

Randall buttered his toast. "This neighborhood is going to hell."

Claudia tore her toast and dipped a corner of it into the yolk of her egg.

"Gangs and drugs," Randall said. "Punks." He watched Claudia eat for a while. "What's wrong with you?"

"Nothing's wrong with me."

"Something's wrong," he said.

"I'll tell you what's wrong. I don't have anybody to talk to. That's what's wrong."

"Here we go again," Randall sighed. "I'm talking to you right now."

Claudia continued to eat.

Randall put his fork down. "Listen, I'm going out to get my medicine. Is there any money in the house?"

Claudia looked up at him. "In my purse."

"What?"

"There's some money in my purse," she repeated.

Randall went into the front room and grabbed Claudia's pocketbook from the buffet. He brought it back to the doorway of the kitchen and found the money in it. "Do you need anything while I'm out?"

"No."

"I'm not going out again, so tell me now if you need anything."

"I don't need anything."

"Okay, but I asked. You can't tell me I didn't ask."

Randall walked out, pulling the door closed behind him. He went down one flight of stairs and stood at number 41. He slipped the note under the door of Holly Diehl's apartment. At that moment the door opened and there was Holly Diehl, a small woman with short blonde hair and she was looking at Randall.

"Just delivering a note to you," Randall said.

Holly Diehl bent and picked it up, looked at the envelope.

Randall realized that he had not put her name on it.

"How do you know it's for me?" she asked.

"It's for you," he said and he turned away and started walking toward the stairs.

"Is this from you?" Holly Diehl asked.

But Randall was gone. He walked down the stairs and out onto Wayland Avenue. The cold wind blew open his jacket and he pulled it closed, zipped it as he walked. He looked in through the window of the Oriental rug store where none of the salesmen spoke English, at least pretended not to speak English. Randall had gone in when the shop first opened, but when he figured out how much they were trying to tell him a rug sold for he got mad. He turned his gaze away when one of the mustached salesmen waved to him.

A blast of heat pushed through Randall when he entered the Osco drugstore and made him too hot. He unzipped his jacket and let out a breath.

"Morning, Mr. Randall," the young clerk, Susie, said. She was setting up a display of blank video tapes.

"Hi, Susie," Randall said. He liked her, liked to look at the way her make-up curved up at the corners of her eyes. He had always thought that Claudia would look good like that, but had never said anything, knew she would take it the wrong way. Claudia could try something, he thought, more make-up or wear her hair differently. She didn't even try. All she ever did was complain about her knee. Susie always smiled at him, so he knew he was still an attractive man.

At the back of the store, the druggist, a fat man named Willy, was in his booth. Randall hated looking up at the man. He didn't like Willy, was sure that the man was cheating him somehow, maybe putting less medicine in each capsule.

"How's the pressure?" Willy asked.

"Under control," Randall said. "How's yours?"

"Oh, I don't have a problem. I watch my diet and walk to work."

Randall nodded as Willy turned away to collect his medicine. "Sure you do, you fat bastard," he said under his breath.

"Excuse me?" Willy said.

"Nothing."

"Oh, I thought you said something." Willy reached through the window and handed down the vial of pills in a small white bag. "There you go."

"Thanks."

"You ought to get some exercise," Willy said. "Gotta stay in shape just to run from the thugs in this neighborhood nowadays."

"You can't outrun them bastards," Randall chuckled.

"Don't need to. Not now."

Randall nodded and walked away down the aisle of foot care items. He remembered once when he had athlete's foot and how good that spray had felt. It was funny he had thought then, and thought now, that his feet didn't usually feel good, bad, or otherwise. It was something when that spray had felt good. He met Susie at the check-out.

"Is that it?" Susie asked.

"That's it." Randall looked at her eyes. "I like your eyes," he said. "The way you paint them." He had never mentioned them to her before. "How's school?"

"Stopped going."

"Oh. Are you still going out with that guy? That cook guy." Randall remembered his white clothes from when he would pick up Susie from the drugstore.

"No. He thought he was hot stuff because he was going to Johnson and Wales."

"Oh."

"I'm trying to get a job as a cosmetician," Susie said.

"You'll be good at it. You always look really pretty." He paused, watching her nails on the register keys. "I hope you don't mind me saying that."

"No, I don't. Thank you, Mr. Randall. That will be twelve-forty-seven."

He handed her a ten and a five. "This stuff just keeps going up."

"Everything does," Susie said. She counted his change out to him. "Want your receipt?"

"I guess."

"Bye now."

Randall waved and walked away, the blast of heat at the doorway bothering him once more as he exited.

Randall paused at the entrance to his building, looked up its side to his window. He decided to walk around back and check on the situation with the driveway and dumpster. He rounded the corner and saw the car before he was there. He couldn't believe it. After all his complaining and his last letter, here was Holly Diehl's car, big as life, in the very same spot, blocking the dumpster. He saw exhaust coming out of the tailpipe and realized that the car was running. Holly Diehl must have just run inside for something. He walked to the driver's side and peered through the window at the purse on the seat. Dumb girl, Randall thought.

Mr. McRae came out of the back door with a bag of garbage and had to squeeze by the blue Honda.

"Can you believe this?" Randall said.

McRae looked at the car. "Pretty tight."

"I've begged her not to park here. It's a fire zone, you know."

McRae nodded and tossed his bag into the container. "I guess, it's not a good idea, all right." He was back at the door now. "Nice car, though." He was gone.

Randall looked at the car, then at the closed door. He thought about taking Holly Diehl's purse, to teach her a lesson, then it occurred to him that he should just take her car. He could get into her car and park it around the block. She'd get the point then.

There was no one on the street at that moment and Randall opened the car door. His heart was racing. He looked around again, then fell in behind the wheel, keeping his eye on the door of the building. He stepped on the clutch, put the car into reverse and released the brake. He backed out slowly, still watching for Holly Diehl. He drove forward away from Wayland Avenue and toward the stop sign at the corner, but he didn't stop, he rolled through it, turning right and noticing behind him a Providence city police car. The cop turned on his blue light.

Randall was sitting in Holly Diehl's car, her open pocketbook beside him. He had taken the car without her permission. He had stolen it. His foot pressed more firmly on the accelerator. The policeman honked his horn. Randall looked at him in the mirror, saw the cop see him looking. He floored it. The car lurched forward and Randall sped away toward the university. The cop turned with him and switched on his siren. Randall felt a pressure in his chest. He careened through a series of alleys and side streets and lost the police car when it slid into a white Plymouth. He saw the cop talking on his radio as he rolled out of sight.

Randall was terrified. He was a criminal on the run. Holly Diehl had no doubt called the police by now to report her car stolen. It occurred to Randall that the policeman could have gotten hurt in his crash. What if that had happened? He would be to blame. He saw the man on the radio, but what if he was calling for an ambulance? What if he had sustained internal injuries or had a bad heart? He could be dying. Randall Halpern Randall could be a murderer. He looked at the little white bag on the seat beside him. He needed one of the pills now. He tried to breathe calmly and deeply, tried to slow his body down. What he needed to do was stop the car and get out, run, hide and sneak back to his apartment. No one knew that he was the car thief. McRae had seen him by the car though. He needed to get to a phone and call Claudia, tell her to tell anyone who asked for him that he was in the bathroom or something like that. He began to slow to a stop when another siren blast pushed his foot to the floor. The tires of the blue Honda squealed as he narrowly missed hitting a woman with a sheep dog. A light snow began to fall. The cop was right behind him, talking on his radio as he drove. Randall found himself on busy Thayer Street, college students everywhere, cars everywhere, people pointing.

There were two police cars behind him now, lights flashing, sirens blowing. Randall imagined he heard his name over a loud speaker. He made a sharp right and headed down the bus-only tunnel toward downtown. The police were caught off guard by this maneuver and slammed into each other at the mouth of the tunnel.

To Randall's surprise there were no police at the bottom of the tunnel. He screeched to a halt and got out of the car, ran along Main Street for a half block, then up through someone's yard, through a couple of yards and up the hill until he was on the campus. In fact, he was suddenly back on Thayer Street, just a block from the accident involving the two police cars. People were standing around, watching, telling each other what they had seen. But no one was looking at Randall even though he was panting and his clothes were grass and dirt stained from his scurry up the hill. He walked away from the commotion, looking up at the snow, which was falling harder now. The white flakes made him think of his white bag and he remembered that he had left his medicine sitting on the seat of Holly Diehl's car.

He found a phone booth on a corner in front of a gas station. He closed the door, fumbled through the change in his pocket, dropped in a quarter and called Claudia.

"Where are you?" Claudia asked.

"Shut up and listen," he barked.

"Don't you tell me to shut up," she said. "Where are you?"

"Has anyone asked for me?"

"Randall? What's going on?"

"Has anyone asked for me?" he repeated.

"No, no one has asked for you. Why?" He could hear her sitting down on the recliner. "Where are you?"

"If anyone calls or comes by just tell them I'm in the bathroom."

"Why?"

"Just do it!"

"Don't yell at me," Claudia said.

"I'm sorry. Do it, please?" Randall hung up the phone, knowing that she wouldn't do it. An ambulance rolled by him, light flashing. The cop was hurt. He knew it. He couldn't count on Claudia. He was suddenly very cold. The snow was beginning to stick to the grass and bushes.

Randall pushed through the wind to the gas station office. He pieced together forty cents and dropped the coins into the vending machine. He collected his bag of cheese curls from the tray and pulled it open, began to eat as he watched the weather. The man behind the desk, a big greasy man, was staring at Randall. Randall left, shoving the remains of his snack into the pocket of his jacket.

Randall counted his money. He had nearly seven dollars, not enough for anything, certainly not enough for a life on the lam. If only the cop hadn't died in that collision. He was sure the matter could be straightened out if not for that. The cold air was beginning to make his lungs ache when he entered a branch of his bank that he had never visited. There was no line and he went directly to a teller, a youngish woman with big glasses and a gold crown that showed in the back of her mouth when she said,

"May I help you?"

"I'd like to withdraw some money," Randall said. He felt his pocket and realized he didn't have his checkbook. "But I'm afraid I don't have my checkbook."

"What's your account number then?" the woman said.

"I don't know."

She looked at him over the rim of her glasses.

"My name is Randall, Randall Randall," he said.

"Randall Randall," she repeated. "Would you mind waiting here for a second."

"I just want my money," Randall said.

"I'll be right back." The woman fell away from her stool and walked briskly across the floor to another woman and together they regarded Randall.

Randall looked around. The bank was empty of customers. The guard was by the door looking at him. He looked up and saw the video camera looking at him. Randall began to whistle. He turned, continuing to whistle as he moved toward the door.

"Sir," the young teller called to him, but Randall was gone. He ran down the street and around the corner, stopping finally, hands on knees, panting.

Randall went back to Thayer Street and boarded a bus. There were a couple of kids in the back and a blind man up front next to the driver. They rolled toward the tunnel, and Randall saw the faces of the policemen. Their cars were connected to purple tow trucks with Buzz painted on the doors. The bus passed by and went through the tunnel. Randall looked at his watch and thought about that armed forces ad that said soldiers did more before eight than most people did all day. It was nine-thirty.

Randall wandered into a McDonalds to get warm. He bought a cup of coffee and sat in the middle of the restaurant, away from the windows. His mind was racing but could find nowhere to go. He wouldn't be able to sit here forever. Too long, and the workers would get suspicious. Besides the little, yellow, plastic chairs hurt his butt.

A man in a tattered coat had been sitting in a booth when Randall arrived. He wasn't eating or drinking, just sitting. A kid in a McDonalds hat came and asked him to leave.

"It's cold out there," the man said.

"I'm sorry, sir, but you're going to have to leave."

"It's cold out there."

The kid looked back into the kitchen and caught the eye of another man. He said something to someone Randall couldn't see and came out to the scene.

"He won't go," the kid said.

"Sir, we're trying to run a business here," the new man said. He was tall, lanky and not too old himself. He wore a brass tag that said MANAGER.

"And I'm trying to stay the fuck alive."

"Listen," the manager was getting tough. "You gotta get out of here right now."

"Or what?" The man in the tattered clothes looked the manager up and down. "Or what? You candy-ass, made-up little prick-faced, boy scout."

The manager got mad. "Listen, asshole, the police are coming, already been called."

"The police are coming," the man repeated. "Is that because you can't *handle* the situation?" The man pulled himself up and out of the booth.

The manager and the kid fell back a step.

"Boo," the man said.

The manager got mad and started for the man in tattered clothes, but the kid stopped him.

"You'd better stop him," the man said, headed for the door. "Don't make me have to hurt the sorry-ass."

The manager stopped pushing and said. "Get out of here, you boozed-up, pathetic, homeless motherfucker."

The man in the tattered clothes stopped, held the door open, and looked back at the manager. His eyes were steady. "I ain't pathetic."

Randall watched the man walk past the window and out to the street. He got up himself and threw away his empty cup. He had to use the toilet, but he wanted to be gone when the police arrived.

Randall Randall was scared. He couldn't go home and he had no one to whom he could turn. He thought about the people who liked him. Susie liked him. He liked her. Maybe she would help him. He wondered what she could do, being just a cashier at the Osco. She could go to his apartment and get the checkbook. He would call Claudia and tell her that Susie was coming by for it, but then Claudia would see Susie and get jealous, jealous of her youth, jealous of her make-up, and then she would get mad and not give it to her. For that matter, why couldn't Claudia just bring the checkbook to him herself or even go to the bank and bring him the cash. Because she wouldn't, that was why. She had always insinuated that he was only interested in her money and this would just prove it. And what would he say when she asked him when he was coming home? It was her fault that he was in this mess. He had no problem with the dumpster, he was just worried about her knee, all her complaining.

Randall went back to his neighborhood and from a couple of blocks away he could see that things weren't quite right. There were a couple of cops standing on the sidewalk across the street from his building.

He found another pay phone, this one in the back of an arcade. This phone had a dial and it felt funny on his finger, had to work to remember his number. It was difficult for him to hear over the bells and buzzers of the nearest pinball machine, but he knew that Claudia sounded funny when she answered.

"Oh, hello, Randall," Claudia said. "Where are you, dear? You're late. I've been so worried."

Randall hung up. He looked over to find the leather-jacketed, late teens pinballer staring at him. "What are you looking at?" Randall asked.

"Nothing," the kid said, staring right at him. "I'm looking at nothing."

Randall got mad for a second, then became afraid. He left the arcade and decided the public library was a good place to hide and keep warm.

The very tall woman with the tower of books in her arms disappeared down the stairs, leaving Randall alone on the floor, he believed. He sat on a step stool in the middle of an aisle, a book full of pictures of India on his lap. He'd never wanted to go to India, and these pictures of sand and elephants and cobra snakes and people with spotted foreheads weren't causing him to want to go there now, but still he wished he were there.

He looked through many, many books about Asia, suffering through the occasional visitor to his section of the stacks. Out the window he could see the sky starting to darken, the snow still falling. The library would close soon and he figured it was best to get out without being asked, so he left.

It was nearly five and the Osco would be closing. He wanted to catch Susie as she was leaving work and ask her to help, though he wasn't sure what he would be asking her to do. Perhaps she would allow him to sleep at her place. It was much colder now and the snow was piling up.

Randall was glad it was dark, feeling he could now move about more freely. His jacket was not nearly warm enough. If he had a credit card he could just take off, go to the bus station or the airport, but he didn't have one. A life on the lam didn't sound so bad, city to city, new people.

Susie was bundled up in her long, down parka, coming out of the front door of the drugstore. The coat was a dark pink and seemed to match her eye makeup. Randall was standing at the corner of the building, at the entrance to the alley, in the shadows.

"Susie," he whispered to her, startling her. "Susie, it's me, Randall Randall."

She looked at him, clutching her bag. "Mr. Randall?" Susie did not come closer. "The police came in today asking questions about you."

"I need your help, Susie."

Susie looked up and down the street, took a step away. "Listen, I've got to go."

"I didn't do anything, Susie."

The young woman walked away, looking over her shoulder at Randall. The snow swirled around her.

Randall went back into the alley and fell to sitting on the ground, leaning against the brick wall, between a green dumpster, like the one behind his building, and some empty cardboard cartons. He heard the back door of the Osco come open and he pushed and pulled himself to his feet, his legs stiff. He saw Willy, the druggist locking up.

"Willy," Randall said.

"Who's there?"

"It's me."

Willy put the package he was holding into his other hand and reached into his pocket.

Randall moved closer. The flash hurt his eyes. He felt a dull push at his middle and he was confused. He was sitting on the ground, looking down at his lap. His ears were ringing. He moved his eyes back up to see Willy. The fat man showed fear. Randall saw something drop from the fat man's hand. Randall rocked in the cold air, then lay back, looked up at the snow.

Carolyn Ferrell *

Carolyn Ferrell's first collection of short fiction, Don't Erase Me (1997), was awarded the Los Angeles Times Art Seidenbaum Award for First Fiction in 1998. Primarily inspired by Ferrell's own inner city experience as director of a South Bronx family literacy program, the characters of Don't Erase Me struggle to survive in single-parent families, with AIDS, in an environment of gang pressure and high teenage pregnancy rates. The protagonist of the title story, Layla Jackson, is a young single mother infected with HIV by her stepfather. "Tiger Frame Glasses" features a young girl who, rather than be defeated by the cruelty of her peers, creates affirming and intricate fantasies. The lives of these urban survivors and others are not simplified, but rendered realistically in all their complexity.

Lorrie, the main character, in "Proper Library," for example, is a gay teen who needs as much love and acceptance as he has to give. He loves his mother and he loves children because they accept him, thrive on his attention, and recognize what he values in himself. Lorrie struggles in school and struggles to make good decisions about what is really best for him—the love of his friend Rakeem, or going to school, relying on the love of the children he babysits and his recognition that words are a powerful tool that can help him get beyond the constant derision from his classmates. He lives in his mind and his heart, no one around him but the children, really seeing the Lorrie he believes in.

The stories of Don't Erase Me are each as powerful and moving as Lorrie's. The dignity Ferrell allows Lorrie is characteristic of the depth with which she develops each of her characters. The language of Lorrie's innermost understandings of himself and the world around him is a combination of urban realism and poetry, exemplifying Ferrell's poetic skill and rhythm. Ferrell captures the words and thoughts of her characters in the natural patterns of their speech to render the spirit and life of their individual and intersecting lives. While the lives she portrays are bleak, they are simultaneously hopeful as each character creates meaning and love despite his or her circumstances. The people in her stories are not victims, but survivors, individuals who meet the realities of their lives head on with grace, anger, and insight. Psychology, sociology, and the poetry of language work together to create a strong and memorable collection of short fiction.

A graduate of the City University of New York, Carolyn Ferrell is a writer who is certain to produce more insightful fiction.

R. Joyce Lausch

*Birth year not available.

Proper Library

Boys, men, girls, children, mothers, babies. You got to feed them. You always got to keep them fed. Winter summer. They always have to feel satisfied. Winter summer. But then you stop and ask, Where is the food going to come from? Because it's never-ending, never-stopping. Where? Because your life is spent on feeding them and you never stop thinking about where the food is going to come from.

Formula, pancakes, syrup, milk, roast turkey with cornbread stuffing, Popsicles, love, candy, tongue kisses, hugs, kisses behind backs, hands on faces, warmth, tenderness, Boston cream pie, fucking in the butt. You got to feed them, and it's always going to be you. Winter summer.

My ma says to me, Let's practice the words this afternoon when you get home, baby. I nod to her. I don't have to use any words with her to let her know I will do what she wants. When family people come over and they see me and Ma in the kitchen like that with the words, they say she has the same face as the maid in the movies. She does have big brown hands like careful shovels, and she loves to touch and pat and warm you up with them. And when she walks, she shuffles. But if anyone is like the maid in the movies, it is Aunt Estine. She likes to give mouth, specially when I got the kids on my hands. She's sassy. She's got what people call a bad attitude. She makes sure you hear her heels clicking all the time, specially when you are lying in bed before dawn and thinking things in order, how you got to keep moving, all day long. Click, click. Ain't nobody up yet? Click. Lazy ass Negroes you better not be specting me to cook y'all breakfast when you do get up! Click, click. I'm hungry. Click. I don't care what time it is, I'm hungry y'all and I'm tired and depressed and I need someone to talk to. Well the hell with all y'all. That's my last word. Click, click, click.

My ma pats her hands on my schoolbag, which is red like a girl's, but that's all right. She pats it like it was my head. The books I have in it are: Biology, Woodworking for You, Math 1, The History of Civilization.

I'm supposed to be in Math 4, but the people keep holding me back. I know it's no real fault of mine. I been teaching the kids Math 4 from a book I took out of the Lending Mobile in the schoolyard. The kids can do most of Math 4. They like the way I teach it to them, with real live explanations, not the kind where you are supposed to have everything already in your head and it's just waiting to come out. And the kids don't ask to see if I get every one right. They trust me. They trust my smart. They just like the feel of the numbers and seeing them on a piece of paper: division of decimals, division of fractions. It's these numbers that keep them moving and that will keep them moving when I am gone. At school I just keep failing the City-Wide Tests every May and the people don't ask any questions: they just hold me back. Cousin Cee Cee said, If you wasn't so stupid you would realize the fact of them holding you back till you is normal.

The kids are almost as sad as Ma when I get ready to go to school in the morning. They cry and whine and carry on and ask me if they can sit on my lap just one more time before I go, but Ma is determined. She checks the outside of my books to make sure nothing is spilled over them or that none of the kids have torn out any pages. Things got to be in place. There has to be order if you gonna keep on moving, and Ma knows that deep down. This morning I promise to braid Lasheema's hair right quick before I go, and as I'm braiding, she's steady smiling her four-year-old grin at Shawn, who is a boy and therefore has short hair, almost a clean shave, and who can't be braided and who weeps with every strand I grease, spread, and plait.

Ma warns me, Don't let them boys bother you now, Lorrie. Don't let 'em.

I tell her, Ma, I have not let you down in a long time. I know what I got to do for you.

She smiles but I know it is a fake smile, and she says, Lorrie, you are my only son, the only real man I got. I don't want them boys to get you from me.

I tell her because it's the only thing I can tell her, You cooking up something special tonight?

Ma smiles and goes back to fixing pancake mix from her chair in the kitchen. The kids are on their way to forgetting about me 'cause they love pancakes more than anything and that is the only way I'll get out of here today. Sheniqua already has the bottle of Sugar Shack syrup and Tonya is holding her plate above her nappy lint head.

Tommy, Lula Jean's navy husband, meets me at the front door as I open it. Normally he cheers me up by testing me on Math 4 and telling me what a hidden genius I am, a still river running deep, he called it one time. He likes to tell me jokes and read stories from the Bible out loud. And he normally kisses my sister Lula Jean right where I and everybody else can see them, like in the kitchen or in the bedroom on the bed, surrounded by at least nine kids and me, all flaming brown heads and eyes. He always says, This is what love should be. And he searches into Lula Jean's face for whole minutes.

I'm leaving for Jane Addams High School and I meet Tommy and he has a lady tucked under his arm and it ain't Lula Jean. Her hair is wet and smells like mouthwash and I hate him in a flash. I never hate anybody, but now I hate him. I know that when I close the door behind me, a wave of mouths will knock Tommy and this new lady down, but it won't drown them. My sister Anita walks into the room and notices and carries them off into the bathroom, quick and silent. But before that she kisses me on my cheek and pats her hand, a small one of Ma's, on my chest. She whispers, You are my best man, remember that. She slips a letter knife in my jacket pocket. She says, If that boy puts his thing on you, cut it off. I love you, baby. She pushes me out the door.

Layla Jackson who lives in the downtown projects and who might have AIDS comes running up to me as I walk out our building's door to the bus stop. She is out of breath. I look at her and could imagine a boy watching her chest heave up and down like that and suddenly getting romantic feelings, it being so big and all, split like two kickballs bouncing. I turn my eyes to hers, which are crying. Layla Jackson's eyes are red. She has her baby Tee Tee in her arms, but it's cold out here and she doesn't have a blanket on him or nothing. I say to her, Layla, honey, you gonna freeze that baby to death.

And I take my jacket off and put it over him, the tiny miracle.

Layla Jackson says, Thanks Lorrie man I got a favor to ask you please don't tell me no please man.

Layla always makes her words into a worry sandwich.

She says, Man, I need me a new baby sitter 'cause I been took Tee Tee over to my mother's but now she don't want him with the others and now I can't do nothing till I get me a sitter.

I tell her, Layla, I'm going back to school now. I can't watch Tee Tee in the morning but if you leave him with me in the cafeteria after fifth period I'll take him on home with me.

She says, That means I got to take this brat to Introduction to Humanities with me. Shit, man. He's gonna cry and I won't pass the test on Spanish Discover-ers. Shit, man.

Then Layla Jackson thinks a minute and says, Okay, Lorrie, I'll give Tee to you at lunch in the cafeteria, bet. And I'll be 'round your place 'round six for him or maybe seven, thanks, man.

Then she bends down and kisses Tee Tee on his forehead and he glows with what I know is drinking up an oasis when you are in the desert for so long. And she turns and walks to the downtown subway, waving at me. At the corner she comes running back because she still has my jacket and Tee Tee is waving the letter knife around like a flag. She says that her cousin Rakeem was looking for me and to let me know he would be waiting for me 'round his way. *Yes.* I say to her, See you, Layla, honey.

Before I used to not go to Jane Addams when I was supposed to. I got in the habit of looking for Rakeem, Layla's cousin, underneath the Bruckner Expressway, where the Spanish women sometimes go to buy oranges and watermelons and apples cheap. He was what you would call a magnet, only I didn't know that then. I didn't understand the different flavors of the pie. I saw him one day and I had a feeling like I wanted him to sit on my lap and cradle me. That's when I had to leave school. Rakeem, he didn't stop me. His voice was just as loud as the trucks heading toward Manhattan on the Bruckner above us: This is where your real world begins, man. The women didn't watch us. We stared each other in the eyes. Rakeem taught me how to be afraid of school and of people watching us. He said, Don't go back, and I didn't. A part of me was saying that his ear was more delicious than Math 4. I didn't go to Jane Addams for six months.

On the BX 17 bus I see Tammy Ferguson and her two little ones and Joe Smalls and that white girl Laura. She is the only white girl in these Bronx projects that I know of. I feel sorry for her. She has blue eyes and red hair, and one time when the B-Crew-Girls were going to beat her butt in front of the building, she broke down crying and told them that her real parents were black from the South. She told them she was really a Negro and they all laughed and that story worked the opposite than we all thought. Laura became their friend, like the B-Crew-Girls' mascot. And now she's still their friend. People may laugh when she ain't around but she's got her back covered. She's loyal and is trying to wear her thin flippy hair in cornrows, which in the old days woulda made the B-Crew, both boys and girls, simply fall out. When Laura's around, the B-Crew-Girls love to laugh. She looks in my direction when I get on the bus and says, Faggot.

She says it loud enough for all the grown-up passengers to hear. They don't look at me, they keep their eyes on whatever their eyes are on, but I know their ears are on me. Tammy Ferguson always swears she would never help a white girl, but now she can't pass up this opportunity, so she says, You tight-ass homo, go suck some faggot dick. Tammy's kids are taking turns making handprints on the bus window.

I keep moving. It's the way I learned: keep moving. I go and sit next to Joe Smalls in the back of the bus and he shows me the Math 3 homework he got his baby's mother Tareen to do for him. He claims she is smarter now than when she was in school at Jane Addams in the spring. He laughs.

The bus keeps moving. I keep moving even though I am sitting still. I feel all of the ears on us, on me and Joe and the story of Tareen staying up till 4 A.M. on the multiplication of fractions and then remembering that she had promised Joe some ass earlier but seeing that he was sound asleep snoring anyway, she worked on ahead and got to the percent problems by the time the alarm went off. Ha ha, Joe laughs, I got my girl in deep check. Ha ha.

All ears are on us, but mainly on me. Tammy Ferguson is busy slapping the babies to keep quiet and sit still, but I can feel Laura's eyes like they are a silent machine gun. Faggot faggot suck dick faggot. Now repeat that one hundred times in one minute and that's how I am feeling.

Keep moving. The bus keeps rolling and you always have to keep moving. Like water like air like outer space. I always pick something for my mind. Like today I am remembering the kids and how they will be waiting for me after fifth period and I remember the feel of Lasheema's soft dark hair.

Soft like the dark hair that covers me, not an afro but silky hair, covering me all over. Because I am so cold. Because I am so alone. A mat of thick delicious hair that blankets me in warmth. And therefore safety. And peace. And solitude. And ecstasy. Lasheema and me are ecstatic when we look at ourselves in the mirror. She's only four and I am fourteen. We hold each other, smiling.

Keep moving. Then I am already around the corner from school while the bus pulls away with Laura still on it because she has fallen asleep in her seat and nobody has bothered to touch her.

On the corner of Prospect Avenue and Westchester where the bus lets me out, I see Rakeem waiting for me. I am not supposed to really know he's there for me and he is not supposed to show it. He is opening a Pixie Stick candy and then he fixes his droopy pants so that they are hanging off the edge of his butt. I can see Christian Dior undies. When I come nearer he throws the Pixie Stick on the ground next to the other garbage and gives me his hand just like any B-Crew-Boy would do when he saw his other crew member. Only we are not B-Crew members, we get run over by the B-Crew.

He says, Yo, man, did you find Layla?

I nod and listen to what he is really saying.

Rakeem says, Do you know that I got into Math 3? Did you hear that shit? Ain't that some good shit?

He smiles and hits me on the back and he lets his hand stay there.

I say, See what I told you before, Rakeem? You really got it in you to move on. You doing all right, man.

He grunts and looks at his sneakers. Last year the B-Crew-Boys tried to steal them from him but Rakeem screamed at them that he had AIDS from his cousin and they ran away rubbing their hands on the sides of the buildings on the Grand Concourse.

Rakeem says, Man, I don't have nothing in me except my brain that tells me: Nigger, first thing get your ass up in school. Make them know you can do it.

I say, Rakeem, you are smart, man! I wish I had your smart. I would be going places if I did.

He says, And then, Lorrie, I got to get people to like me and to stop seeing me. I just want them to think they like me. So I got to hide *me* for a while. Then you watch, Lorrie, man: *much* people will be on my side!

I say to him, Rakeem, you got Layla and baby Tee Tee and all the teachers on your side. And you got smart. You have it made.

He answers me after he fixes his droopy pants again so that they are hanging exactly off the middle of his ass: Man, they are wack! You know what I would like to do right now, Lorrie? You know what I would like? Shit, I ain't seen you since you went back to school and since I went back. Hell, you know what I would like? But it ain't happening 'cause you think I'ma look at my cousin Layla and her bastard and love them and that will be enough. But it will never be enough.

I think about sitting on his lap. I did it before but then I let months go by because it was under the Bruckner Expressway and I believed it could only last a few minutes. It was not like the kind of love when I had the kids because I believed they would last forever.

He walks backwards away, and when he gets to the corner he starts running. No one else is on the street. He shouts, Rocky's Pizza! I'ma be behind there, man. We got the school fooled. This is the master plan. I'ma be there, Lorrie! *Be there.*

I want to tell Rakeem that I have missed him and that I will not be there but he is gone. The kids are enough. The words are important. They are all enough.

The front of Jane Addams is gray-green with windows with gates over all of them. I am on the outside.

The bell rings first period and I am smiling at Mr. D'Angelo and feeling like this won't be a complete waste of a day. The sun has hit the windows of Jane Addams and there is even heat around our books. Mr. D'Angelo notices me but looks away. Brandy Bailey, who doesn't miss a thing, announces so that only us three will hear, Sometimes when a man's been married long he needs to experience a new kind of loving, ain't that what you think, Lorrie?

For that she gets thrown out of the classroom and an extra day of in-school suspension. All ears are now on me and Mr. D'Angelo. I am beyond feeling but I know he isn't. And that makes me happy in a way, like today ain't going to be a complete waste of a day.

He wipes his forehead with an imported handkerchief. He starts out saying, Class, what do we remember about the piston, the stem, and the insects? He gets into his questions and his perspiration stops and in two minutes he is free of me.

And I'm thinking: Why couldn't anything ever happen, why does every day start out one way hopeful but then point to the fact that ain't nothing ever going to happen? The people here at school call me ugly, for one. I know I got bug eyes and I know I am not someone who lovely things ever happen to, but I ask you: Doesn't the heart count? Love is a pie and I am lucky enough to have almost every flavor in mine. Mr. D'Angelo turns away from my desk and announces a surprise quiz and everybody groans and it is a sea of general unhappiness but no one is more than me, knowing that nothing will ever happen the way I'd like it to, not this flavor of the pie. And I am thinking, Mr. D'Angelo, do you know that I would give anything to be like you, what with all your smarts and words and you know how to make the people here laugh and they love you. And I would give anything if you would ask me to sit on your lap and ask me to bite into your ear so that it tingles like the bell that rips me in and out of your class. I would give anything. Love is a pie. Didn't you know that? Mr. D'Angelo, I am in silent love in a loud body.

So don't turn away. *Sweat.*

Mrs. Cabrini pulls me aside and whispers, My dear Lorrie, when are you ever going to pass this City-Wide? You certainly have the brains. And I know that your intelligence will take you far, will open new worlds for you. Put your mind to your dreams, my dear boy, and you will achieve them. You are your own universe, you are your own shooting star.

People 'round my way know me as Lorrie and the name stays. Cousin Cee Cee says the name fits and she smacks her gum in my face whenever she mentions that. She also adds that if anyone ever wants to kick my ass, she'll just stand around and watch because a male with my name and who likes it just deserves to be watched when whipped.

Ma named me for someone else. My real name is Lawrence Lincoln Jefferson Adams. It's the name on my school records. It's the name Ma says I got to put on my application to college when the time comes. She knows I been failing these City-Wide Tests and that's why she wants to practice words with me every day. She laughs when I get them wrong but she's afraid I won't learn them on my own, so she asks me to practice them with her and I do. Not every day, but a whole lot: look them up and pronounce them. Last Tuesday: *Independence. Chagrin. Symbolism. Nomenclature. Filament.* On Wednesday, only: *Apocrypha.* Ma says they have to be proper words with proper meanings from a dictionary. You got to say them right. This is important if you want to reach your destiny, Ma says.

Like for instance the word *Library.* All my life I been saying that "Liberry." And even though I knew it was a place to read and do your studying, I still couldn't call it right. Do you see what I mean? I'm about doing things, you see, *finally* doing things right.

Cousin Cee Cee always says, What you learning all that shit for? Don't you know it takes more than looking up words to get into a college, even a damn community college? Practicing words like that! Is you a complete asshole?

And her two kids, Byron and Elizabeth, come into the kitchen and ask me to teach them the words too, but Cee Cee says it will hurt their eyes to be doing all that reading and besides they are only eight and nine. When she is not around I give them words with up to ten letters, then they go back to TV with the other kids.

When we have a good word sitting, me and Ma, she smoothes my face with her hands and calls me Lawrence, My Fine Boy. She says, You are on your way to good things. You just got to do things the proper way.

We kiss each other. Her hands are like the maid in the movies. I know I am taken care of.

Zenzile Jones passes me a note in History of Civilization. It's the part where Ptolemy lets everyone know the world is round. Before I open it, I look at her four desks away and I remember the night when I went out for baby diapers and cereal and found her crying in front of a fire hydrant. I let her cry on my shoulder. I told her that her father was a sick man for sucking on her like that.

The note says, Please give me a chance.

Estine Smith, my mother's sister who wants me and the kids to call her by both names, can't get out of her past. Sometimes I try on her clothes when I'm with the kids and we're playing dress-up. My favorite dress is her blue organza without the back. I seen Estine Smith wear this during the daytime and I fell in love with it. I also admired her for wearing a dress with the back out in the day, but it was only a ten-second admiration. Because then she opens her mouth and she is forever in her past. Her favorite time to make us all go back to is when they lynched her husband, David Saul Smith, from a tree in 1986 and called the TV station to come and get a look. She can't let us go one day without reminding us in words. I never want to be like her, ever. Everybody cries when they are in her words because they feel sorry for her, and Estine Smith is not someone but a walking hainted house.

Third period. I start dreaming about the kids while the others are standing in line to use the power saw. I love to dream about the kids. They are the only others who think I am beautiful besides Ma and Anita. They are my favorite flavor of the pie, even if I got others in my mind.

Most of the time there are nine but when my other aunt, Samantha, comes over I got three more. Samantha cries in the kitchen and shows Ma her blue marks and it seems like her crying will go on forever. Me, I want to take the kids' minds away. We go into Ma's room where there is the TV and we sing songs like "Old Gray Mare" and "Bingo Was His Name O" or new ones like "Why You Treat Me So Bad?" and "I Try to Let Go." Or else I teach them Math 4. Or else I turn on the TV so they can watch Bugs or He-Man and so I can get their ironing done.

Me, I love me some kids. I need me some kids.

Joe Smalls talks to me in what I know is a friendly way. The others in Woodworking for You don't know that. They are like the rest of the people who see me and hear the action and latch on.

Joe Smalls says, Lorrie, man, that bitch Tareen got half the percentage problems wrong. Shit. Be glad you don't have to deal with no dumb-ass Tareen bitch. She nearly got my ass a F in Math 3.

I get a sad look on my face, understanding, but it's a fake look because I'm feeling the rest of the ears on us, latching, readying. I pause to heaven. I am thinking I wish Ma had taught me how to pray. But she doesn't believe in God.

Junior Sims says, Why you talking that shit, Joe, man? Lorrie don't ever worry about bitches!

Perry Samson says, No, Lorrie never ever thinks about pussy as a matter of fact. Never ever.

Franklin says, Hey, Lorrie, man, tell me what you think about, then? What can be better than figuring out how you going to get that hole, man? Tell me what?

Mr. Samuels, the teacher, turns off the power saw just when it gets to Barney Moore's turn. He has heard the laughter from underneath the saw's screeching. Everybody gets quiet. His face is like a piece of lumber. Mr. Samuels is never soft. He doesn't fail me even though I don't do any cutting or measuring or shellacking. He wants me the hell out of there.

And after the saw is turned off, Mr. Samuels, for the first time in the world, starts laughing. The absolute first time. And everybody joins in because they are afraid of this and I laugh too because I'm hoping all the ears will go off me.

Mr. Samuels is laughing Haw Haw like he's from the country. Haw Haw. Haw Haw. His face is red. Everyone cools down and is just smiling now.

Then he says, Class, don't mess with the only *girl* we got in here!

Now it's laughter again.

Daniel Fibbs says, Yeah, Mr. Samuels is *on!*

Franklin laughs, No fags allowed, you better take your sissy ass out of here 'less you want me to cut it into four pieces.

Joe Smalls is quiet and looking out the window.

Junior Sims laughs, Come back when you start fucking bitches!

Keep moving, keep moving.

I pick up my red bag and wade toward the door. My instinct is the only thing that's working, and it is leading me back to Biology. But first out the room. Inside me there is really nothing except for Ma's voice: *Don't let them boys.* But inside there is nothing else. My bones and my brain and my heart would just crumble if it wasn't for that swirling wind of nothing in me that keeps me moving and moving.

Perry laughs, I didn't know Mr. Samuels was from the South.

With his eyelashes, Rakeem swept the edges of my face. He let me know they were beautiful to him. His face went in a circle around mine and dipped in my eyes and dipped in my mouth. He traveled me to a quiet place where his hands were the oars and I drifted off to sleep. The thin bars of the shopping cart where I was sitting in made grooves in my back, but it was like they were rows of tender fingers inviting me to stay. The roar of the trucks was a lullaby.

Layla Jackson comes running up to me but it's only fourth period because she wants to try and talk some sense into Tyrone. She hands me little Tee Tee. Tyrone makes like he wants to come over and touch the baby but instead he flattens his back against the wall to listen to Layla. I watch as she oozes him. In a minute they are tongue kissing. Because they are the only two people who will kiss each other. Everyone says that they gave themselves AIDS and now have to kiss each other because there ain't no one else. People walk past them and don't even notice that he has his hand up her shirt, squeezing the kickball.

Tee Tee likes to be in my arms. I like for him to be there.

The ladies were always buying all kinds of fruits and vegetables for their families underneath the Bruckner Expressway. They all talked Spanish and made the sign of the cross and asked God for forgiveness and gossiped.

Rakeem hickeyed my neck. We were underneath the concrete bridge supports and I had my hands on the handle of a broken shopping cart, where I was sitting. Don't go back, Rakeem was telling me, don't go back. And he whispered in my ear. And I thought of all the words I had been practicing, and how I was planning to pass that City-Wide. Don't go back, he sang, and he sat me on his lap and he moved me around there. They don't need *you,* he said, and *you* don't need *them.*

But I do, I told him.

This feeling can last forever, he said.

No, it can't, I said, but I wound up leaving school for six months anyway. That shopping cart was my school.

I am thinking: It will never be more. I hold Tee Tee carefully because he is asleep on my shoulder and I go to catch the BX 17 back to my building.

Estine Smith stays in her past and that is where things are like nails. I want to tell her to always wear her blue organza without the back. If you can escape, why don't you all the time? You could dance and fling your arms and maybe even feel love from some direction. You would not perish. *You* could be free.

When I am around and she puts us in her past in her words, she tells me that if I hada twitched my ass down there like I do here, they woulda hung me up just by my black balls.

The last day Rakeem and I were together, I told him I wanted to go back, to school, to everyone. The words—I tried to explain about the words to Rakeem. I could welcome him into my world if he wanted me to. Hey, wasn't there enough room for him and me and the words?

Hell no, he shouted, and all the Spanish women turned around and stared at us. He shouted, You are an ugly-ass bastard who will always be hated big-time and I don't care what you do: this is where your world begins and this is where your world will end. Fuck you. You are a pussy, man. Get the hell out of my face.

Ma is waiting for me at the front door, wringing her hands. She says it's good that I am home because there is trouble with Tommy again and I need to watch him and the kids while she goes out to bring Lula Jean home from the movies, which is where she goes when she plans on leaving Tommy. They got four kids here and if Lula Jean leaves, I might have to drop out of school again because she doesn't want to be tied to anything that has Tommy's stamp on it.

I set Tee Tee down next to Tommy on the sofa bed where I usually sleep. Tommy wakes up and says, Hey, man, who you bringing to visit me?

I go into the kitchen to fix him some tea and get the kids' lunch ready. Sheniqua is playing the doctor and trying to fix up Shawn, who always has to have an operation when she is the doctor. They come into the kitchen to hug my legs and then they go back in the living room.

Tommy sips his tea and says, Who was that chick this morning, Lorrie, man?

I say I don't know. I begin to fold his clothes.

Tommy says, Man, you don't know these bitches out here nowadays. You want to show them love, a good time, and a real deep part of yourself and all they do is not appreciate it and try to make your life miserable.

He says, Well, at least I got Lula. Now that's some woman.

And he is asleep. Sheniqua and her brother Willis come in and ask me if I will teach them Math 4 tonight. Aunt Estine rolls into the bedroom and asks me why do I feel the need to take care of this bum, and then she hits her head on the doorframe. She is clicking her heels. She asks, Why do we women feel we always need to teach them? They ain't going to learn the right way. They ain't going to learn shit. That's why we always so alone. Click, click.

The words I will learn before Ma comes home are: *Soliloquy, Disenfranchise, Cate-chism.* I know she will be proud. This morning before I left she told me she would make me a turkey dinner with all the trimmings if I learned four new words tonight. I take out my dictionary but then the kids come in and want me to give them a bath and baby Tee Tee has a fever and is throwing up all over the place. I look at the words and suddenly I know I will know them without studying.

And I realize this in the bathroom and then again a few minutes later when Layla Jackson comes in cursing because she got a 60 on the Humanities quiz. She holds Tee but she doesn't touch him. She thinks Tyrone may be going to some group where he is meeting other sick girls and she doesn't want to be alone. She curses and cries, curses and cries. She asks me why things have to be so fucked. Her braids are coming undone and I tell her that I will tighten them up for her. That makes Layla Jackson stop crying. She says, And to top it off, Rakeem is a shit. He promised me he wouldn't say nothing but now that he's back in school he is broadcasting my shit all over the place. And that makes nobody like me. And that makes nobody want to touch me.

I put my arm around Layla. Soon her crying stops and she is thinking about something else.

But me, I know these new words and the old words without looking at them, without the dictionary, without Ma's hands on my head. Lasheema and Tata come in and want their hair to be like Layla's and they bring in the Vaseline and sit around my feet like shoes. Tommy wakes up still in sleep and shouts, Lula, get your ass on in here. Then he falls back to sleep.

Because I know I will always be able to say the words on my own. I can do the words on my own and that is what matters. I have this flavor of the pie and I will always have it. Here in this kitchen I was always safe, learning the words till my eyes hurt. The words are in my heart.

Ma comes in and shoves Lula Jean into a kitchen chair. She says, Kids, make room for your cousin, go in the other room and tell Tommy to get his lame ass out here. Layla, you can get your ass out of here and don't bring it back no more with this child sick out his mind, do your 'ho'ing somewhere out on the street where you belong. Tommy, since when I need to tell you how to treat your wife? You are a stupid heel. Learn how to be a man.

Everybody leaves and Ma changes.

She says, I ain't forgot that special dinner for you, baby. I'm glad you're safe and sound here with me. Let's practice later.

I tell her, Okay, Ma, but I got to go meet Rakeem first.

She looks at me in shock and then out the corner of my eye I can tell she wants me to say no, I'll stay, I won't go to him. Because she knows.

But I'm getting my coat on and Ma has got what will be tears on her face because she can't say no and she can't ask any questions. Keep moving.

And I am thinking of Rocky's Pizza and how I will be when I get there and how I will be when I get home. Because I am coming back home. And I am going to school tomorrow. I know the words, and I can tell them to Rakeem and I can share what I know. Now he may be ready. I want him to say to me in his mind: Please give me a chance. And I know that behind Rocky's Pizza is the only place where I don't have to keep moving. Where there is not just air in me that keeps me from crumbling, but blood and meat and strong bones and feelings. I will be me for a few minutes behind Rocky's Pizza and I don't care if it's just a few minutes. I pat my hair down in the mirror next to the kitchen door. I take Anita's letter knife out my jacket pocket and leave it on the table next to where Tommy is standing telling his wife that she never knew what love was till she met him and why does she have to be like that, talking about leaving him and shit? You keep going that way and you won't ever know how to keep a man, bitch.

Nikky Finney (1957-)

Nikky Finney was born in Conway, South Carolina, on the coast where rice fields were more prominent than cotton ones. This geographic landscape is highly relevant to Finney's poetry, especially her most recent collection, Rice (1995). After attaining a degree from Talladega College, Finney began teaching and writing in California, eventually moving back to the South, where she currently is an Associate Professor of Creative Writing at the University of Kentucky. She published one other collection, On Wings Made of Gauze (1985), and also wrote the script for the PBS documentary "For Posterity's Sake: The Story of Morgan and Marvin Smith" in 1995, which chronicles the African American twins from Lexington who became noted photographers in New York in the 1930s and 1940s. She is a founding member of the Affrilachian Poets, a collective of Appalachian writers of African descent.

What Finney achieves well in her poems is the use of the image. But more than simply evoking and engaging the image, she uses it to tell a narrative, which means that she also expands the image. Her collection Rice begins with the notion of rice and all that rice as product and production means: earth, food, basic element, miniature, the U.S. South, plantations, water-flooded fields, whiteness, seasons, reeds. In the collection, Finney brings to bear these ideas (and many more), making her collection a meditation on rice, but also rice itself—a thing of sustenance. Her poetry here is in the aesthetic tradition of Black women and men writers who explore issues of psychic and spiritual healing, which involves a visitation and reclamation of the past.

In the short piece "The Blackened Alphabet," Finney uses cooking as a construct for her expression of a Black poetic manifesto. She uses the culturally appropriate cooking method of "blackening" to suggest not only the heat and urgency of the Black poets' work, but also how locally committed and influenced the work is.

One of her longer poems, "Irons at Her Feet," works centrally with the idea of tips—of things on the edge, on the margin, almost on the outside. Her diction teases apart the notion of the edge to include things on the surface, and to suggest the depth of the surface, of where warmth and love might lie: "hot irons traveled / into waiting flannel wraps / and were shuttled / up under covers / and inbetween quilts." Finney's poem is an interior poem, digging deep into her own soul and memory, but also exploring the depths of the warmth in her grandmother's bedroom. Part of this strategy is the careful use of prepositions, which are useful parts of speech only as they are used intentionally to indicate a precise place (position) of one subject in relation to another. The poem ends with a revision of the central poetic images—heat, edges, surfaces, and exchange.

"My Centipeding Self" uses similar emphasis on image as the poetic trajectory. Here, Finney writes of a narrative psyche that is not singular, but communal. In fact, the narrative voice experiences itself as 35 women, who are linked together as a centipede. Finney plays with the number 35, as both the narrator's age ("I am 35") and also the reality of being connected to the experiences that other women have. This poem exhibits the fear and anxiety that some women feel that other women in another part of life might not feel; and still, there is the commonality—that as women, their lives are in peril and their movements are also actions of resistance and self-regard. It is an interesting construction, especially when the narrator screams in response to potential danger, and writes "but one of these women that I am / juts up her hand / for me to shut up / she knows more than me / she is at the end / I am only the head." These lines are commentary on the relationships women in different stations of life necessarily have with women in other stations, an expression of sisterhood. The lines are also expressive of the multiplicity of self that contemporary Black women talk about in their work—the various communities that they exist in and respond to.

Finally, in "Making Foots," Finney uses the colloquial expression to comment on the violence of slavery and the evidence of Black people's attempt to escape slavery. The poem presents the slave master's practice of breaking a slave's foot, a condition that is the poetic conceit that Finney explores and that she connects to foot pains that are still felt today.

Finney's poems here emphasize history and memory and often trace experience from Black woman to Black woman. This exploration of how one woman's experience passes through and to another, with both voices becoming a backbone of Black women's experiences, is a lovely articulation of a Black feminist tradition that is important for men to also hear and engage.

Kevin Everod Quashie

The Blackened Alphabet

While others sleep
My black skillet sizzles
Alphabets dance and I hit the return key
On my tired But ever jumping eyes
I want more I hold out for some   more
While others just now turn over
shut down alarms
I am on I am on
I am pencilfrying
sweet Black alphabets
In an allnight oil

Irons At Her Feet

from the coals
of her bedroom fired place
onto the tip
of my grandmother's

december winter stick
for fifteen years
hot irons traveled
into waiting flannel wraps
and were shuttled
up under covers
and inbetween quilts
where three babies lay shivering
in country quarter
night time air
hot irons
wrapped and pushed
up close
to frosting toes
irons instead of lip kisses
is what she remembers
irons instead of carmel colored fingers
that should have swaddled shoulders
like it swaddled hoes
and quiltin' needles
and spongy cow tits

everytime
i am back home
i tip into her room
tip again into her saucering cheeks
and in her half sleep
my mother reads her winters
aloud to me

My Centipeding Self

for now
without cane
I move
like an ocean of turbulent women trails
all leading South
I look behind me
as I go
and there they are

all of them
the All of me
still crossing the street
holding up more traffic
than any one young woman could
if I stop to hurry them
they will snarl the roads even more
so I keep going
stay my eyes ahead
I am 35 thundering
rainy eyed women today
I stand still for lights
but they don't
they cross whenever
however they wish
why do I wait then
is this hesitation kin to arthritis?
I don't want to know
my feet get wet in the hydrant water
that gushes me along
it is all the way up to my thighs
I dig my toes down deeper
in this 35 foot of wet sand
that the world is slowly becoming
and the line of them
the line of myselves
is still crossing
I yell at them
to hurry
to get across
so that the traffic can go again
so that the people can get on
get back to its too busy self
but I am not yet all across
there is nothing I can do
with any of them anymore
so nothing moves

The light changes again and again
I turn and twist
and they all stretch in the middle
but never separate
like something fingery and human
has touched the earthworm's belly

I am 35
I want to cross over
but someone in the volkswagon
impatiently-desperately
starts to go and
all the other traffic follows her lead
I scream
but one of these women that I am
juts up her hand
for me to shut up
she knows more than me
she is at the end
I am only the head
the traffic moves again
right on through
a steady stream of black translucent
Me's
and the spawning river
of my whole self
never stops
and I recycle this worry
and stop looking back
and marvel at all the places
where the cars have hit
and I have never run

Making Foots

Many a foot
was chopped
off an African highgrass runner
and made into
a cotton picking
plowing peg
was burned away into
two festering runaway sores
was beaten around
into a southern gentleman's original
club foot design

They went for our feet first
for what we needed most
to get 'way

My papa's feet
are bad
bad
once under roof
his shoes are always
the first to go
a special size is needed
to fit around
ankle bones broken at birth

Sore feet
standing on freedom lines
weary feet
stomping up a southern dust bowl march
simple feets
wanting just the chance
just one
to Black Gulliver jump
a Kress lunch counter
or two
and do a Zulu   Watusi   Zootsuited
step
instead of a fallen archless
wait wait wait
for the time to come

Him wanted to put his feet up
and sip himself some

Papa, how you say you'll take that coffee?
Oh Baby, just make it black and bitter like me.

My papa's feet are bad
they beat our feet around with billy clubs
and by our raggedy feet
had hoped to drag us all away

Country corners
and city curbs is where
they hold my

keepsakes
some of my brothers
who brush their I-talian skins off
on the backs
of steam pressed
pantslegs

Shoes first
they'll tell you
shoes above all else
they'll show you

If your black foot
ever wakes you up
in the night
wanting to talk about something
aching there
under the cover
out loud
for no apparent
reason

There is reason

Ruth Forman*

Ruth Forman's We Are the Young Magicians *(1993), her first collection of poetry, is the seventh collection published in the Barnard New Women Poets Series. In* We Are the Young Magicians, *Forman insists on African American idiom, the language of urban black youth, to claim identity and culture. The setting of many of her poems is South Philadelphia with its homes that "have no backyard / frontyard neither" but "black magic n brownstone steps" that feed the child's need for community and security. Forman celebrates the people, the food, the places that fill life with meaning. In terms of audience—black youth, especially young black women—and play with rhythm and language, Forman established the unique style that she would build upon in her second collection of poetry,* Renaissance *(1997).*

In both volumes of poetry, Forman embraces the tradition of poetry before her, including the word work of June Jordan, Lucille Clifton, and Audre Lorde. She honors the tradition of their poetry and the women's traditions she has known in her own life by bringing the everyday, the "ordinary," the essence of women's relationships to the page. From the braiding of hair and kitchen table conversation to the endurance of catcalls and the joy of wearing lipstick, her poems are peopled with vibrant women and a rainbow of emotions. "You So Woman," for example, stands as a hyperbolic celebration and affirmation of a Black woman's beauty: "so girl / you jus keep on / makin the sunset procrastinate n / givin the rainbows a complex..." The poem is a compliment and pick-me-up for a friend, but it is also proud encouragement for all women to embrace themselves, value themselves.

Especially prominent in her poems is her mother, a woman whose life and influence she reveres in "Momma." The death of her mother before the publication of Renaissance *makes her presence even more central to the poems of that collection, as Forman grieves and gathers herself. "Before I Leave My Doorstep to Mama's Grave," for example, is a lullaby of self-healing, a rhythmic prayer.*

In both We are the Young Magicians *and* Renaissance, *Forman varies form, communicating her messages and images in forms ranging from short haiku-like stanzas to long, persona-driven street monologues. The short poem "Strength" expresses vulnerability and need for connection through the image of fern frond, green and living and sure. The long and singing poem "Tracie Double Dutch on the Tongue" recreates the rhythm of jump rope rhyme while communicating the intersection of past and present, ancestry and innovation.*

Across form and subject, Ruth Forman's lyrics are simple and inspiring. She communicates her understanding of the layering and creativity of love and passion in the poem "Venus's Quilt;" the "you" addressed is a lover, the metaphor a quilt made of lover-cloth and lover-willingness. In the very title of the poem, "Poetry Should Ride the Bus," Forman

---

*Birth year not available.

proclaims her understanding of the function of poetry, which she reinforces throughout the poem's strategy of personification: "Poetry should hopscotch in a polka dot dress / wheel cartwheels / n hold your hand..." This poem bespeaks Forman's philosophy on the need for poetry to be accessible, to be meaningful for the community it addresses, recalling Black Arts philosophy.

Ruth Forman writes for the future of young Black girls. She writes to teach self-love and affirmation. She writes to celebrate the music and magic of growing up Black and woman.

R. Joyce Lausch

Young Cornrows Callin Out the Moon

we don have no backyard
frontyard neither
we got black magic n brownstone steps
when the sun go down

we don have no backyard
no sof grass rainbow kites mushrooms butterflies
we got South Philly summer
when the sun go down

cool after lemonade n black eye peas
full after ham hocks n hot pepper greens
corn bread coolin on the stove
n more to watch than tv

we got double dutch n freeze tag n kickball
so many place to hide n seek n
look who here Punchinella Punchinella
look who here Punchinella inna zoo

we got the ice cream man

we got the corner store
red cream pop
red nails Rick James the Bump the Rock
n we know all the cheers

we got pretty lips
we got callous feet healthy thighs n ashy knees
we got fiiine brothas we r fiiine sistas
n
we got attitude

we hold mamma knees when she snap the naps out
we got gramma tell her not to pull so hard
we got sooo cleeen cornrows when she finish
n corn bread cool on the stove

So you know
we don really want no backyard
frontyard neither
cuz we got to call out the moon
wit black magic n brownstone steps

Poetry Should Ride the Bus

poetry should hopscotch in a polka dot dress
wheel cartwheels
n hold your hand
when you walk past the yellow crackhouse

poetry should wear bright red lipstick
n practice kisses in the mirror
for all the fine young men with fades
shootin craps around the corner

poetry should dress in fine plum linen suits
n not be so educated that it don't stop in
every now n then to sit on the porch
and talk about the comins and goins of the world

poetry should ride the bus
in a fat woman's Safeway bag
between the greens n chicken wings
to be served with Tuesday's dinner

poetry should drop by a sweet potato pie
ask about the grandchildren
n sit through a whole photo album
on a orange plastic covered La-Z-Boy with no place to go

poetry should sing red revolution love songs
that massage your scalp
and bring hope to your blood
when you think you're too old to fight

yeah
poetry should whisper electric blue magic
all the years of your life
never forgettin to look you in the soul
every once in a while
n smile

You So Woman

FOR ANYA

lady
when ya purple heels hit concrete
afros swing
cool jazz hot baby
strollin by cry amen

so holy
preachas stutta
thighs so righteous
pews jump up n catch the spirit n
hymns speak in tongues

so sweet
bees leave the daffodils behind
for honey you make table sugar taste sour n
Mrs. Butterworth sho can't find a damn thing to say
when you aroun

lookin so good
cockroaches ask you to step on em
sos they can see heaven
befo
and after they die n

you love ya people so much
if you was on pilgrimage
the Sahara Desert would run to the Atlantic
jus to make sure you don't get thirsty n
camels would kiss you for choosin they back

but Africa don't got you
we do n glad too

so girl
you jus keep on
makin the sunset procrastinate n
givin the rainbows a complex
you a silk earthquake
you a velvet hurricane
n girl you so woman
i be damn
if you don't put a full moon to shame.

Momma

You taste like thick cream and almonds in your prayers
for God to watch over your children
I think of you every time I drink coffee
angels sashaying in the steam
bring memories full as the moon and slow grace
I send my love spinning
into your palms together
the palace of angels and where I find shelter.

Green Boots n Lil Honeys

n i'm waitin for the light to turn green/
n i see these two fat kentucky fried oozie-lookin brothas/
peepin me like i'm the lil cutie/wantin to jump in
their long Sanford n Son lookin hooptie/
now i'm not one to judge or nothin/
but these two look like the kind who might/
give me a free flight into the wall/
jus cuz i'm not actin right/if you know what i mean
n they smilin at me/n i'm waitin for the light to turn green
n tryin to look like i'm real into the sidewalk/
cuz that's where it's at/n i can feel these brothas
jus waitin for me to hop into the back seat/

where the springs poppin out/all the time
i'm thinkin/why these folks lookin
like i want to get with them so bad

n all the time i'm thinkin of the videos
you know/where the brotha's in the beat up car/
drivin real slow/he got money/
but he don't put it into his car/
cuz Oakland Police stop him twice as many times a night
if he had somethin like a BMW/cuz they know
if he got a dope car he a dope dealer/
anyway/it's kinda makin sense now/
cuz it's kinda in style for lil honeys
to be all over somebody big who look like
somethin white people call the police on
cuz they just look wrong/
n honeys be all over them in like twos n threes
sometimes/in the videos/i know you seen them/
so what i'm sayin is it's kinda in style to be kissin
n huggin n rubbin on somebody
who knock you out in a minute/
but still give you money to get ya nails done/
it's hip you know/in style n shit/
n i'm not one who don't like style
cuz i'm lookin kinda fly
in my knee green boots and black raiders jacket/
but you know style ain't what you see on tv

n all the time these brothas think imma get with them/
cuz they the B-boys/n they been getting some play/
n they been thinkin they can get some more
from this here honey on the corner/well
i'm jus not that much in style

n the light turns green n they cruise by real slow/
makin sure i get a good look
at em/but you know the sidewalk is what's happenin/
i told you that already/
i pretend i don't see em but i shoulda screamed on em/
SEE YOU IN THE VIDEOS/that i turn on when i'm tired
of lookin at that damn news/you know/
where war is kinda in style/
green boots n gas masks/you know/
how in high school the recruiter rolls by/
talkin bout how you can earn money/

get a education/see the world/n people hop in cuz
these folks tryin to get where they goin/wherever that is/
n they seen on tv that it's kinda in style to hop on over
to somethin that will fuck you up in a minute/
n they didn't really know it would be like that/
tryin to find a way out from where they're at/
n somebody drive by offerin all this kinda shit/
n they think it's kinda cool cuz you know/
on tv it's kinda cool to be a soldier/kinda in style/
n the big dealers just sittin up there/
thinkin you be their lil honey
or somethin/n i wonder why
they think i be down for somethin like that/why
we be down for somethin like that/
n i think it's cuz it's in style or somethin
like biker shorts n gold teeth n Ray Bans
to cover a black eye/
everybody seem like they down for alla that
cuz nobody say nothin different/
n i don't neither/i jus keep on waitin on the green light

Strength

She look like ferns
unwithered after the storm
straight green reaching for God
I want to feel the leaves whisper my cheek and tell me
how it feel to rock
how roots grow with merciless rain

I want to touch her smooth leaves
kiss them wet and feel living

Come between My Knees Child

you with the moon eyes
bring the comb and oil
let me rub it in

Head down

We know this common place this silence
you waiting
for something my fingers to tell you

today they weave a story

we not alone in this place
this is the hour of mothers always the hour of mothers
always with us in this quiet place together
listen
she say be unafraid

Head straight

let your roots lead my fingers
let the mothers dance in that space
no lines tell where you end and we begin

Child you our power

so if the singing break forth
from the oil in my fingers
be unafraid
unannounced uninvited
it is Mama
it is you through the silk in your throat

it is time to leave sorrow together

Pass the ribbons child
you with the moon eyes from crying
pass me all the colors
we go someplace not arrived
in the hour of voices unfolding a new peace

Venus's Quilt

You need to be loved
I would do it
be the one to open you like pomegranate
take your fruit between my teeth and tongue
and shine every seed

rub you between my palms until the heat come
and the numbness go away
reach into your hair
weed memories that don't belong
and lay out a welcome mat
for all sunshine

there is water in your eyes I want to travel
there is babies to be born yet and shoes to be sewn

if i could I would quilt you into my life
so you could lay just left of my mother
east of my father north of my sister
into my friend

I am Venus without a lover
fingers with soft nails and need to touch
I might ask you to swim in my memory
I might ask you to make your own
we could sit and watch them like slides

how many women should I be
for you to feel loved
how many men
for you to feel safe
how many daughters
for you to feel pride
and sons to be forever

I will be them all
barrettes and butterflies, tube sox and elbows
first drink of water last toothpaste
I will be your uncle's hand
I will be your aunt's kitchen
I will be your sunset in the morning

I am Venus
cluster of grapes in your mouth and wine coming

we are whispers in the length of the dark
we are cuffs in the folds of the universe
I can button you safe
I can hold you forever
so long as you give me your cloth

Tracie Double Dutch on the Tongue

FOR TRACIE MORRIS

Tracie Tracie sista girl what you got/what you got
me no words no place n so tired
Tracie Tracie sista girl what you got
n why ma feet gotta itch when you come round
sista girl what you got/double dutch on ya tongue
why my feet gotta itch wich ya rhythm rhythm what
rhythm rhythm what you sayin/we could fly
what you say/you know triple jump off the tongue
what yo name rhythm
well show me wich ya smooth smooth rope/I'll turn

Hand me that rope n us'll turn
one two sista, come on through sista
one two sista, come on through sista

Jump/what you/jump what you/jump what you know
on the concrete/negrita chiquita beat
cuz cornrows don't mean nothin without the grease
gotta have the grease/Dixie Peach/Always
sweet when ya finish
dang
look at ya jagged sunset step/this side of the sea
dookie gold jazz riff waves
lick the street and call feet of heavy hip quick lip sistas
inta vision sharp/rhythm hard n
somehow I know when it gonna kiss the beat
or turn it inside out to teach gravity
how to scat
make me feel like shit ain't nothin this good since Lakeside Stank
i see ya in ya dance
you leadin from the ancestors/cuz they need somethin new
well lead from the ancestors cuz they need something new

call back to the old
cuz rhythm is a place
rhythm is a place you got to step into/to not get lost

I'm steppin in too/to not get lost
one two sista, comin through sista
one two sista, comin through sista

Jump/what we/jump what we/jump what we know
on the concrete
rhythm is a place we step into to not get lost
rhythm is a place we step into to not get lost
rhythm is a place of the ancestors/in our skin n
rhythm is a place of the ancestors/in our hair
high n far out
I said/you got me juiced like a mango/waitin for the right tongue to
sail along/that's what you do just sail along
into the jagged sunset
the sweet/baby/the sweet place/sweet space/I'm in
black feet n ancestors deep in the soles the souls on our tongues
nobody can negotiate/the beat
our feet we free ankles n higher
than rainbows/they swingin
n me turnin/n us turnin/us turnin heads/always turnin
the present inside out
flyin freestyle/lead on sister
lead me on to a fantastic voyage

James Brown/Betty Carter
pack your bags get on up n jam y'all
come on n ride on the funk y'all
hopin for something to pick me up again
me hopin for something to pick me up again
me I was hopin for someone to pick me up again/I was no words n so tired
til you come along all sweet n mangoes n no nonsense

in the rainbows/elliptical propellers
freestylin/ma feet/dancin
I/I can/jump in this
double double dutch/double double no single ones
double double dutch tongues
where air is new n sidewalk cracks n feet fly old ways/no single ones
feet fly old ways/no single ones
feet fly old ways
in new forms
you teach me the place/the place with no words n alright
me slappin down this/slappin slappin down this
rhythm
present inside out/outside in/to the ancestors
the ancestors/jus holdin me

The ancestors/jus holdin me
one two sista, passin through sista
one two sista, passin through sista

Tracie Tracie what you got/double dutch on ya tongue?
Make me got up again n ready/make me got up again n ready
make me got up again
make me got
up

Before I Leave My Doorstep to Mama's Grave

    i need to give seven gifts to seven strangers

    tuck their good wishes in my new Timberlands
    the space between my sock and ankle

    i need to walk steady in love
    face above the water
    an oak tree standing in the middle of the sea

    mama i'm not ready to see you yet
    in my room
    let alone among the headstones
    of you
    Carrie
    and a baby boy i never knew

    before i leave my doorstep i need to know peace
    so i can bring you some
    like earrings
    i want to paint the sky in my joy to see you
    sherbet colors or
    sandpaintings that i used to do on the dining room table

    been pushing myself to do each next thing
    after you left
    go back to school
    move to a new house
    i can't yet push through another door
    my arms hurt from the bruises
    my smile strained

let me build my home upon my heart
let me weave my heart into my home

a place to make a nest
when all the straw i know
has turned to grass
beneath my feet a headstone and some roses

let me build my fortress
strong head ready to give seven gifts to seven strangers
open enough to let life in that fickle butterfly
ready to love you like a child
ready to hum you like an old woman
on the porch waiting for God to come down
dressed in all the spirituals she ever knew

let me weave my days in letters to you
write them upon the air in my best school cursive
codes for only you to see
they will say
i miss you, what are you doing, who is combing your hair
i love you
who holds your hand besides your sister
they will say
what are you doing?
i eat cantaloupe on my new balcony
looking down on my neighbor's white pickup
in the morning sun

let me write to you in goosebumps
and a tired neck
let me rock myself steady

i will come like nomads in pilgrimage
i will come in sandbroken feet
i will come in love
and soon
but most importantly in peace.

Leon Forrest (1937–1997)

Leon Forrest grew up on the South Side of Chicago and studied at the University of Chicago. He became a journalist and, in 1969, served as Associate Editor of Muhammed Speaks, *a newspaper issued by the Nation of Islam. Later he became a professor at Northwestern University, where he taught for many years.*

At Random House, Toni Morrison edited Forrest's first novel, There Is a Tree More Ancient Than Eden *(1973). Forrest is perhaps best known for his epic novel* Divine Days *(1992)—an extraordinary achievement praised by Morrison and Arnold Rampersad, among others. Henry Louis Gates, Jr., compares* Divine Days *to Leo Tolstoy's classic* War and Peace. *Forrest's great kaleidoscope of a novel portrays the life and mind of Joubert Antoine Jones, an Army veteran and prospective playwright who works in an urban bar and liquor store.*

As you can judge from the following excerpt from There Is a Tree, *Forrest experiments with modernist, stream-of-consciousness techniques as he treats African American themes. While his writing can be dense, multilayered, elliptical, and allusive, it is always highly engaging.*

Keith D. Miller

Excerpt from *There Is a Tree More Ancient Than Eden*

Louis Armstrong; 1900–1971. Became famous by the ominous combination of the wayward aesthetics of greedy white promoters and their whim-ridden audiences, who devoured *after* his handkerchief clown-entertainer growling singer side, while purposefully declining to deal with the cornet-trumpet art of the most influential innovator in the idiom of twentieth-century U.S. music. Often pulled away from his magical flight vision of a joyous stomping celebrating soul in flight, which he weaved through his horn, by ill health and the garbled taste of white America, Armstrong was planning to return to his revolutionary horn, even as he lay upon his deathbed. Press-music-money magnates always kept out of the news the very substantial contributions Armstrong made to the freedom movement, as they enjoyed dividing Dipper from the young and his own people on the shaky grounds that he was a "Tom" when in the end it was from the people themselves that Armstrong's towering and revolutionary power issued.

Frederick Douglass; 1817–1895. The North Star, whose shadow perhaps the great President was worthy to walk in; but only his shadow. . . .

Harriet Tubman; 1821–1913. Breedlove's antecedent. . . .

Abraham Lincoln; 1809–1865. The Father upon whose shaky, shawled shoulders the engulfing, awesome burden of the Original Sin fell, whose vacillation and compromise were really a reflection of the psychic split of the Republic and was only equaled by his bald-eagle steadfastness and undying faith that by pursuing the role of healer and savior of the nation's higher dream of itself, he could avoid the hysterical histrionics of body-soul slave-marketing merchandizing-foundation upon which the dung-tarred Soul of the Nation hung/rocked like a sweeping pendulum—yet compromise itself, had vaulted him into the seat of father over a house divided. . . .

And the gloomy-melancholy President touched a dimension of this when he indicated that perhaps this terrible war was the price we must pay for the wealth mounted up by the bondsman, but never mentioned the wealth mounted up by the North, hollowed within the bowels of Manifest Destiny/birth of a nation. . . . Who, in stovepipe hat, shawl and beard, resembled some runaway mulatto castoff—*Our American Cousin?*—who had found freedom, only to find rampant entrapment and behind that, the odd man/marginal man's love for the Union, more than for the white side and severely more than for the colored side, who had been adjudged not only three-fifths human (which meant two parts animal) but according to Judge Taney, even four years before the attempted secession, the property of the master, which is not to excuse his condescending silence but rather to suggest the Republic's ruinous mountain tobogganing into a valley attitude, in the inferno of time, space and setting, in which the Redeemer found himself trying to be greater than a politician, which was not the reason he had been chosen or even elected. . . .

Whose totality seems so awesome, even now that no historian can hold him or indeed that epoch in his mortal hands without dropping down dead with the Union itself (yet the Union endured somehow or other): thereby taking on a most prodigiously pusillanimous view of his gothic personality as if to avoid the painful duty of facing the man's totality—plucking slivers out of his sculpture—as another escape from facing the whole range of the notorious Union's riddles—thereby only reducing their own humanity and scaling down the harpoons of their own arguments into toothpicks. . . .

Found Himself the President over a land of ancestral gang-banging prisoner "runaway slaves" which did not stop with flesh-peddling, incarcerating the soul in chains, nor did it stop with human flesh, but galloped into the human genius, became hallowed in flags and colors and in the Word, gutted the deed and made of the precious filament of the flight for freedom a savage turning upon the workers' earth and made them exact imitations of the wanton barons and overlords from which they had fled. . . .

Presided over a house divided without malice, which came to apotheosize and magnify his ominous Soul, his symbolism, his Christ-myth marginality—but long after it had assassinated his body, even as it threatened to rip up the vestiges of its Soul, after electing him out of his rail-splitting rustic boyishness and frontiermanship that he would allow them to dream that they were honoring the Republic's humble runaway origins, log cabin to Capitol, who himself had by initiative, humor, happenstance, compromise, savvy, eloquence, barnyard-ness, and hard work made it, had muddled through, but who had to be assassinated as part of the will of the Republic to no longer be shepherded—or even exist in its present form—when the politician-elect suddenly attempted to be Father and mend and heal, but not dictatorially lead, which might have saved his life, but not the Union, and whose assassination was the manifestation of the collective chaos of the Republic and he dared stand in the path of a Nation's doom tobogganing descending, not realizing it could no longer live with itself. . . .

Assassinated, not only because all fathers must be killed but particularly by those who live out of the blood and profit off of that blood which is the Soul of the Nation. . . . LINCOLN—who in effect said, If this cup will pass Lord, not as I will it but as you—who had a map and a plan for getting rid of the slave question via recolonization and deportation, which was not only a foreshadowing of Garvey (and later Neo-Garveyism) but an expansion of the cherished; brilliant; slave-holding Jefferson (the old separator) who in his autobiography in 1821 (the year Harriet Tubman was born) stated in perfect Monticello-ese: "Nothing is more certainly written in the book of fate, than that these people are to be free; nor is it less certain that the two races, equally free, cannot live in the same government. Nature, habit, opinion have drawn indelible lines of distinction between them. It is still in our power to direct the process of emancipation and deportation, peaceably, and in slow degree; as that the evil will wear off insensibly." Out of the rows upon rows upon rows of unidentified graves; out of the gospel orchards of sweat chain plantations moaning down the shaking leaves of green corn and kingdoms of cotton, down the sense of possibility that was *this* dropouts' lot, even as they raced towards his assassination down down down and back back back through the rail-splitting trains which carried him home, and the long war and their short dream. . . . Back down the seven black coaches of the funeral train from Washington to Baltimore to Philadelphia to New York, Albany, Syracuse, Cleveland, Chicago, Springfield and the guilt upon the people's gawking faces upon the deed, upon their hands and blood-spot of his blood apparently hiding the spot of the Original Sin, bathing and washing their hands in the blood of slaves and then clothing their high sheriff spirit in sackcloth and the runic garb of a slave . . . but blood at the root and blood at the leaf. . . . And then they commenced to divide his parts and his effects, his memories, his sides, his geometery filling him with the durability of the old gray goose and "This is my Body this is my Blood" and the train lifting him above the decomposition streaking him homewards, as it vaulted over the harpooning horizon and back back back Lord and down down down. . . .

Ernest Gaines (1933–)

Ernest Gaines was born in Louisiana and raised on the River Lake Plantation, where, as a child, he cut sugarcane in the fields. He moved to California as a teenager and developed the desire to write. He visited libraries, trying to find himself through reading the literature of authors like William Faulkner, who write about rural Southern life.

Gaines received many awards and honors, including grants and fellowships from the National Endowment for the Arts, the Guggenheim Foundation, the American Academy and Institute of Arts and Letters, and the MacArthur Foundation. He is Writer in Residence at the University of Southwestern Louisiana and has received honorary doctorates from many universities.

Gaines wrote six novels. One of them, The Autobiography of Miss Jane Pittman *(1971), became a bestseller.* A Gathering of Old Men *(1983) was also well received, as was* A Lesson Before Dying *(1993), which won the National Book Critics Circle Award and was selected for the Oprah Winfrey Book Club.*

Gaines has a gift for finding the voice of common folks living in Louisiana. The main character in The Autobiography *is a proud, 110-year old woman who endures from slavery to the 1960s. His dominant theme in* A Gathering *and* A Lesson *is the search for male identity and the need for males to become men. In both novels Gaines seems to equate not being a man to being the lowest form of animal, the hog. Standing up for what is right and healing the mental and physical pain of being a powerless Black male in the South— those are some of the ingredients needed to become a man.*

The multi-narrator structure of A Gathering *recalls a similar form in Faulkner's* As I Lay Dying.

Taken from Bloodline *(1968), Gaines's only collection of short stories, "The Sky Is Gray" deals with the struggle of James, an eight-year-old boy, as he becomes aware of prejudice and poverty. Told from the boy's point of view, the story allows the reader to see the gargantuan task his mother faces when she takes him to the dentist.*

Sanderia Smith

The Sky Is Gray

1

Go'n be coming in a few minutes. Coming round that bend down there full speed.

And I'm go'n get out my handkerchief and wave it down, and we go'n get on it and go.

I keep on looking for it, but Mama don't look that way no more. She's looking down the road where we just come from. It's a long old road, and far 's you can see you don't see nothing but gravel. You got dry weeds on both sides, and you got trees on both sides, and fences on both sides, too. And you got cows in the pastures and they standing close together. And when we was coming out here to catch the bus I seen the smoke coming out of the cows's noses.

I look at my mama and I know what she's thinking. I been with Mama so much, just me and her, I know what she's thinking all the time. Right now it's home—Auntie and them. She's thinking if they got enough wood—if she left enough there to keep them warm till we get back. She's thinking if it go'n rain and if any of them go'n have to go out in the rain. She's thinking 'bout the hog—if he go'n get out, and if Ty and Val be able to get him back in. She always worry like that when she leaves the house. She don't worry too much if she leave me there with the smaller ones, 'cause she know I'm go'n look after them and look after Auntie and everything else. I'm the oldest and she say I'm the man.

I look at my mama and I love my mama. She's wearing that black coat and that black hat and she's looking sad. I love my mama and I want put my arm round her and tell her. But I'm not supposed to do that. She say that's weakness and that's crybaby stuff, and she don't want no crybaby round her. She don't want you to be scared, either. 'Cause Ty's scared of ghosts and she's always whipping him. I'm scared of the dark, too, but I make 'tend I ain't. I make 'tend I ain't 'cause I'm the oldest, and I got to set a good sample for the rest. I can't ever be scared and I can't ever cry. And that's why I never said nothing 'bout my teeth. It's been hurting me and hurting me close to a month now, but I never said it. I didn't say it 'cause I didn't want act like a crybaby, and 'cause I know we didn't have enough money to go have it pulled. But, Lord, it been hurting me. And look like it wouldn't start till at night when you was trying to get yourself little sleep. Then soon 's you shut your eyes— ummm-ummm, Lord, look like it go right down to your heartstring.

"Hurting, hanh?" Ty'd say.

I'd shake my head, but I wouldn't open my mouth for nothing. You open your mouth and let that wind in, and it almost kill you.

I'd just lay there and listen to them snore. Ty there, right 'side me, and Auntie and Val over by the fireplace. Val younger than me and Ty, and he sleeps with Auntie. Mama sleeps round the other side with Louis and Walker.

I'd just lay there and listen to them, and listen to that wind out there, and listen to that fire in the fireplace. Sometimes it'd stop long enough to let me get little rest. Sometimes it just hurt, hurt, hurt. Lord, have mercy.

2

Auntie knowed it was hurting me. I didn't tell nobody but Ty, 'cause we buddies and he ain't go'n tell nobody. But some kind of way Auntie found out. When she asked me, I told her no, nothing was wrong. But she knowed it all the time. She told me to mash up a piece of aspirin and wrap it in some cotton and jugg it down in that hole. I did it, but it didn't do no good. It stopped for a little while, and started right back again. Auntie wanted to tell Mama, but I told her, "Uh-uh." 'Cause I knowed we didn't have any money, and it just was go'n make her mad again. So Auntie told Monsieur Bayonne, and Monsieur Bayonne came over to the house and told me to kneel down 'side him on the fireplace. He put his finger in his mouth and made the Sign of the Cross on my jaw. The tip of Monsieur Bayonne's finger is some hard, 'cause he's always playing on that guitar. If we sit outside at night we can always hear Monsieur Bayonne playing on his guitar. Sometimes we leave him out there playing on the guitar.

Monsieur Bayonne made the Sign of the Cross over and over on my jaw, but that didn't do no good. Even when he prayed and told me to pray some, too, that tooth still hurt me.

"How you feeling?" he say.

"Same," I say.

He kept on praying and making the Sign of the Cross and I kept on praying, too.

"Still hurting?" he say.

"Yes, sir."

Monsieur Bayonne mashed harder and harder on my jaw. He mashed so hard he almost pushed me over on Ty. But then he stopped.

"What kind of prayers you praying, boy?" he say.

"Baptist," I say.

"Well, I'll be—no wonder that tooth still killing him. I'm going one way and he pulling the other. Boy, don't you know any Catholic prayers?"

"I know 'Hail Mary,'" I say.

"Then you better start saying it."

"Yes, sir."

He started mashing on my jaw again, and I could hear him praying at the same time. And, sure enough, after while it stopped hurting me.

Me and Ty went outside where Monsieur Bayonne's two hounds was and we started playing with them. "Let's go hunting," Ty say. "All right," I say; and we went on back in the pasture. Soon the hounds got on a trail, and me and Ty followed them all 'cross the pasture and then back in the woods, too. And then they cornered this little old rabbit and killed him, and me and Ty made them get back, and we picked up the rabbit and started on back home. But my tooth had started hurting me again. It was hurting me plenty now, but I wouldn't tell Monsieur Bayonne. That night I didn't sleep a bit, and first thing in the morning Auntie told me to go back and let Monsieur Bayonne pray over me some more. Monsieur Bayonne was in his kitchen making coffee when I got there. Soon 's he seen me he knowed what was wrong.

"All right, kneel down there 'side that stove," he say. "And this time make sure you pray Catholic. I don't know nothing 'bout that Baptist, and I don't want know nothing 'bout him."

3

Last night Mama say, "Tomorrow we going to town."

"It ain't hurting me no more," I say. "I can eat anything on it."

"Tomorrow we going to town," she say.

And after she finished eating, she got up and went to bed. She always go to bed early now. 'Fore Daddy went in the Army, she used to stay up late. All of us sitting out on the gallery or round the fire. But now, look like soon 's she finish eating she go to bed.

This morning when I woke up, her and Auntie was standing 'fore the fireplace. She say: "Enough to get there and get back. Dollar and a half to have it pulled. Twenty-five for me to go, twenty-five for him. Twenty-five for me to come back, twenty-five for him. Fifty cents left. Guess I get little piece of salt meat with that."

"Sure can use it," Auntie say. "White beans and no salt meat ain't white beans."

"I do the best I can," Mama say.

They was quiet after that, and I made 'tend I was still asleep.

"James, hit the floor," Auntie say.

I still made 'tend I was asleep. I didn't want them to know I was listening.

"All right," Auntie say, shaking me by the shoulder. "Come on. Today's the day."

I pushed the cover down to get out, and Ty grabbed it and pulled it back.

"You, too, Ty," Auntie say.

"I ain't getting no teef pulled," Ty say.

"Don't mean it ain't time to get up," Auntie say. "Hit it, Ty."

Ty got up grumbling.

"James, you hurry up and get in your clothes and eat your food," Auntie say. "What time y'all coming back?" she say to Mama.

"That 'leven o'clock bus," Mama say. "Got to get back in that field this evening."

"Get a move on you, James," Auntie say.

I went in the kitchen and washed my face, then I ate my breakfast. I was having bread and syrup. The bread was warm and hard and tasted good. And I tried to make it last a long time.

Ty came back there grumbling and mad at me.

"Got to get up," he say. "I ain't having no teefes pulled. What I got to be getting up for?"

Ty poured some syrup in his pan and got a piece of bread. He didn't wash his hands, neither his face, and I could see that white stuff in his eyes.

"You the one getting your teef pulled," he say. "What I got to get up for. I bet if I was getting a teef pulled, you wouldn't be getting up. Shucks; syrup again. I'm getting tired of this old syrup. Syrup, syrup, syrup. I'm go'n take with the sugar diabetes. I want me some bacon sometime."

"Go out in the field and work and you can have your bacon," Auntie say. She stood in the middle door looking at Ty. "You better be glad you got syrup. Some people ain't got that—hard 's time is."

"Shucks," Ty say. "How can I be strong."

"I don't know too much 'bout your strength," Auntie say; "but I know where you go'n be hot at, you keep that grumbling up. James, get a move on you; your mama waiting."

I ate my last piece of bread and went in the front room. Mama was standing 'fore the fireplace warming her hands. I put on my coat and my cap, and we left the house.

4

I look down there again, but it still ain't coming. I almost say, "It ain't coming yet," but I keep my mouth shut. 'Cause that's something else she don't like. She don't like for you to say something just for nothing. She can see it ain't coming, I can see it ain't coming, so why say it ain't coming. I don't say it, I turn and look at the river that's back of us. It's so cold the smoke's just raising up from the water. I see a bunch of pool-doos not too far out—just on the other side the lilies. I'm wondering if you can eat pool-doos. I ain't too sure, 'cause I ain't never ate none. But I done ate owls and blackbirds, and I done ate redbirds, too. I didn't want kill the redbirds, but she made me kill them. They had two of them back there. One my trap, one in Ty's trap. Me and Ty was go'n play with them and let them go, but she made me kill them 'cause we needed the food.

"I can't," I say. "I can't."

"Here," she say. "Take it."

"I can't," I say. "I can't. I can't kill him, Mama, please."

"Here," she say. "Take this fork, James."

"Please, Mama, I can't kill him," I say.

I could tell she was go'n hit me. I jerked back, but I didn't jerk back soon enough.

"Take it," she say.

I took it and reached in for him, but he kept on hopping to the back.

"I can't, Mama," I say. The water just kept on running down my face. "I can't," I say.

"Get him out of there," she say.

I reached in for him and he kept on hopping to the back. Then I reached in farther, and he pecked me on the hand.

"I can't, Mama," I say.

She slapped me again.

I reached in again, but he kept on hopping out my way. Then he hopped to one side and I reached there. The fork got him on the leg and I heard his leg pop. I pulled my hand out 'cause I had hurt him.

"Give it here," she say, and jerked the fork out my hand.

She reached in and got the little bird right in the neck. I heard the fork go in his neck, and I heard it go in the ground. She brought him out and helt him right in front of me.

"That's one," she say. She shook him off and gived me the fork. "Get the other one."

"I can't, Mama," I say "I'll do anything, but don't make me do that."

She went to the corner of the fence and broke the biggest switch over there she could find. I knelt 'side the trap, crying.

"Get him out of there," she say.

"I can't, Mama."

She started hitting me 'cross the back. I went down on the ground, crying.

"Get him," she say.

"Octavia?" Auntie say.

'Cause she had come out of the house and she was standing by the tree looking at us.

"Get him out of there," Mama say.

"Octavia," Auntie say, "explain to him. Explain to him. Just don't beat him. Explain to him."

But she hit me and hit me and hit me.

I'm still young—I ain't no more than eight; but I know now; I know why I had to do it. (They was so little, though. They was so little. I 'member how I picked the feathers off them and cleaned them and helt them over the fire. Then we all ate them. Ain't had but a little bitty piece each, but we all had a little bitty piece, and everybody just looked at me 'cause they was so proud.) Suppose she had to go away? That's why I had to do it. Suppose she had to go away like Daddy went away? Then who was go'n look after us? They had to be somebody left to carry on. I didn't know it then, but I know it now. Auntie and Monsieur Bayonne talked to me and made me see.

5

Time I see it I get out my handkerchief and start waving. It's still 'way down there, but I keep waving anyhow. Then it come up and stop and me and Mama get on. Mama tell me go sit in the back while she pay. I do like she say, and the people look at me. When I pass the little sign that say "White" and "Colored," I start looking for a seat. I just see one of them back there, but I don't take it, 'cause I want my mama to sit down herself. She comes in the back and sit down, and I lean on the seat. They got seats in the front, but I know I can't sit there, 'cause I have to sit back of the sign. Anyhow, I don't want sit there if my mama go'n sit back here.

They got a lady sitting 'side my mama and she looks at me and smiles little bit. I smile back, but I don't open my mouth, 'cause the wind'll get in and make that tooth ache. The lady take out a pack of gum and reach me a slice, but I shake my head. The lady just can't understand why a little boy'll turn down gum, and she reach me a slice again. This time I point to my jaw. The lady understands and smiles little bit, and I smile little bit, but I don't open my mouth, though.

They got a girl sitting 'cross from me. She got on a red overcoat and her hair's plaited in one big plait. First, I make 'tend I don't see her over there, but then I start looking at her little bit. She make 'tend she don't see me, either, but I catch her looking that way. She got a cold, and every now and then she h'ist that little handkerchief to her nose. She ought to blow it, but she don't. Must think she's too much a lady or something.

Every time she h'ist that little handkerchief, the lady 'side her say something in her ear. She shakes her head and lays her hands in her lap again. Then I catch her kind of looking where I'm at. I smile at her little bit. But think she'll smile back? Uh-uh. She just turn up her little old nose and turn her head. Well, I show her both of us can turn us head. I turn mine too and look out at the river.

The river is gray. The sky is gray. They have pool-doos on the water. The water is wavy, and the pool-doos go up and down. The bus go round a turn, and you got plenty trees hiding the river. Then the bus go round another turn, and I can see the river again.

I look toward the front where all the white people sitting. Then I look at that little old gal again. I don't look right at her, 'cause I don't want all them people to know I love her. I just look at her little bit, like I'm looking out that window over there. But she knows I'm looking that way, and she kind of look at me, too. The lady sitting 'side her catch her this time, and she leans over and says something in her ear.

"I don't love him nothing," that little old gal says out loud.

Everybody back there hear her mouth, and all of them look at us and laugh.

"I don't love you, either," I say. "So you don't have to turn up your nose, Miss."

"You the one looking," she say.

"I wasn't looking at you," I say. "I was looking out that window, there."

"Out that window, my foot," she say. "I seen you. Everytime I turned round you was looking at me."

"You must of been looking yourself if you seen me all them times," I say.

"Shucks," she say, "I got me all kind of boyfriends."

"I got girlfriends, too," I say.

"Well, I just don't want you getting your hopes up," she say.

I don't say no more to that little old gal 'cause I don't want have to bust her in the mouth. I lean on the seat where Mama sitting, and I don't even look that way no more. When we get to Bayonne, she jugg her little old tongue out at me. I make 'tend I'm go'n hit her, and she duck down 'side her mama. And all the people laugh at us again.

6

Me and Mama get off and start walking in town. Bayonne is a little bitty town. Baton Rouge is a hundred times bigger than Bayonne. I went to Baton

Rouge once—me, Ty, Mama, and Daddy. But that was 'way back yonder, 'fore Daddy went in the Army. I wonder when we go'n see him again. I wonder when. Look like he ain't ever coming back home. . . . Even the pavement all cracked in Bayonne. Got grass shooting right out the sidewalk. Got weeds in the ditch, too; just like they got at home.

It's some cold in Bayonne. Look like it's colder than it is home. The wind blows in my face, and I feel that stuff running down my nose. I sniff. Mama says use that handkerchief. I blow my nose and put it back.

We pass a school and I see them white children playing in the yard. Big old red school, and them children just running and playing. Then we pass a café, and I see a bunch of people in there eating. I wish I was in there 'cause I'm cold. Mama tells me keep my eyes in front where they belong.

We pass stores that's got dummies, and we pass another café, and then we pass a shoe shop, and that bald-head man in there fixing on a shoe. I look at him and I butt into that white lady, and Mama jerks me in front and tells me stay there.

We come up to the courthouse, and I see the flag waving there. This flag ain't like the one we got at school. This one here ain't got but a handful of stars. One at school got a big pile of stars—one for every state. We pass it and we turn and there it is—the dentist office. Me and Mama go in, and they got people sitting everywhere you look. They even got a little boy in there younger than me.

Me and Mama sit on that bench, and a white lady come in there and ask me what my name is. Mama tells her and the white lady goes on back. Then I hear somebody hollering in there. Soon 's that little boy hear him hollering, he starts hollering, too. His mama pats him and pats him, trying to make him hush up, but he ain't thinking 'bout his mama.

The man that was hollering in there comes out holding his jaw. He is a big old man and he's wearing overalls and a jumper.

"Got it, hanh?" another man asks him.

The man shakes his head—don't want open his mouth.

"Man, I thought they was killing you in there," the other man says. "Hollering like a pig under a gate."

The man don't say nothing. He just heads for the door, and the other man follows him.

"John Lee," the white lady says. "John Lee Williams."

The little boy juggs his head down in his mama's lap and holler more now. His mama tells him go with the nurse, but he ain't thinking 'bout his mama. His mama tells him again, but he don't even hear her. His mama picks him up and takes him in there, and even when the white lady shuts the door I can still hear little old John Lee.

"I often wonder why the Lord let a child like that suffer," a lady says to my mama. The lady's sitting right in front of us on another bench. She's got on a white dress and a black sweater. She must be a nurse or something herself, I reckon.

"Not us to question," a man says.

"Sometimes I don't know if we shouldn't," the lady says.

"I know definitely we shouldn't," the man says. The man looks like a preacher. He's big and fat and he's got on a black suit. He's got a gold chain, too.

"Why?" the lady says.

"Why anything?" the preacher says.

"Yes," the lady says. "Why anything?"

"Not us to question," the preacher says.

The lady looks at the preacher a little while and looks at Mama again.

"And look like it's the poor who suffers the most," she says. "I don't understand it."

"Best not to even try," the preacher says. "He works in mysterious ways—wonders to perform."

Right then little John Lee bust out hollering, and everybody turn they head to listen.

"He's not a good dentist," the lady says. "Dr. Robillard is much better. But more expensive. That's why most of the colored people come here. The white people go to Dr. Robillard. Y'all from Bayonne?"

"Down the river," my mama says. And that's all she go'n say, 'cause she don't talk much. But the lady keeps on looking at her, and so she says, "Near Morgan."

"I see," the lady says.

7

"That's the trouble with the black people in this country today," somebody else says. This one here's sitting on the same side me and Mama's sitting, and he is kind of sitting in front of that preacher. He looks like a teacher or somebody that goes to college. He's got on a suit, and he's got a book that he's been reading. "We don't question is exactly our problem," he says. "We should question and question and question—question everything."

The preacher just looks at him a long time. He done put a toothpick or something in his mouth, and he just keeps on turning it and turning it. You can see he don't like that boy with that book.

"Maybe you can explain what you mean," he says.

"I said what I meant," the boy says. "Question everything. Every stripe, every star, every word spoken. Everything."

"It 'pears to me that this young lady and I was talking 'bout God, young man," the preacher says.

"Question Him, too," the boy says.

"Wait," the preacher says. "Wait now."

"You heard me right," the boy says. "His existence as well as everything else. Everything."

The preacher just looks across the room at the boy. You can see he's getting madder and madder. But mad or no mad, the boy ain't thinking 'bout him. He looks at that preacher just 's hard 's the preacher looks at him.

"Is this what they coming to?" the preacher says. "Is this what we educating them for?"

"You're not educating me," the boy says. "I wash dishes at night so that I can go to school in the day. So even the words you spoke need questioning."

The preacher just looks at him and shakes his head.

"When I come in this room and seen you there with you book, I said to myself, 'There's an intelligent man.' How wrong a person can be."

"Show me one reason to believe in the existence of a God," the boys says.

"My heart tells me," the preacher says.

"'My heart tells me,'" the boys says. "'My heart tells me.' Sure, 'My heart tells me.' And as long as you listen to what your heart tells you, you will have only what the white man gives you and nothing more. Me, I don't listen to my heart. The purpose of the heart if to pump blood throughout the body, and nothing else."

"Who's your paw, boy?" the preacher says.

"Why?"

"Who is he?"

"He's dead."

"And your mom?"

"She's in Charity Hospital with pneumonia. Half killed herself, working for nothing."

"And 'cause he's dead and she's sick, you mad at the world?"

"I'm not mad at the world. I'm questioning the world. I'm questioning it with cold logic, sir. What do words like Freedom, Liberty, God, White, Colored mean? I want to know. That's why *you* are sending us to school, to read and to ask questions. And because we ask these questions, you call us mad. No sir, it is not us who are mad."

"You keep saying 'us'?"

"'Us.' Yes—us. I'm not alone."

The preacher just shakes his head. Then he looks at everybody in the room—everybody. Some of the people look down at the floor, keep from looking at him. I kind of look 'way myself, but soon 's I know he done turn his head, I look that way again.

"I'm sorry for you," he says to the boy.

"Why?" the boy says. "Why not be sorry for yourself? Why are you so much better off than I am? Why aren't you sorry for these other people in here? Why not be sorry for the lady who had to drag her child into the dentist office? Why not be sorry for the lady sitting on that bench over there? Be sorry for them. Not for me. Some way or the other I'm going to make it."

"No, I'm sorry for you," the preacher says.

"Of course, of course," the boy says, nodding his head. "You're sorry for me because I rock that pillar you're leaning on."

"You can't ever rock the pillar I'm leaning on, young man. It's stronger than anything man can ever do."

"You believe in God because a man told you to believe in God," the boy says. "A white man told you to believe in God. And why? To keep you ignorant so he can keep his feet on your neck."

"So now we the ignorant?" the preacher says.

"Yes," the boy says. "Yes." And he opens his book again.

The preacher just looks at him sitting there. The boy done forgot all about him. Everybody else make 'tend they done forgot the squabble, too.

Then I see that preacher getting up real slow. Preacher's a great big old man and he got to brace himself to get up. He comes over where the boy is sitting. He just stands there a little while looking down at him, but the boy don't raise his head.

"Get up, boy," preacher says.

The boy looks up at him, then he shuts his book real slow and stands up. Preacher just hauls back and hit him in the face. The boy falls back 'gainst the wall, but he straightens himself up and looks right back at that preacher.

"You forgot the other cheek," he says.

The preacher hauls back and hit him again on the other side. But this time the boy braces himself and don't fall.

"That hasn't changed a thing," he says.

The preacher just looks at the boy. The preacher's breathing real hard like he just run up a big hill. The boy sits down and opens his book again.

"I feel sorry for you," the preacher says. "I never felt so sorry for a man before."

The boy makes 'tend he don't even hear that preacher. He keeps on reading his book. The preacher goes back and gets his hat off the chair.

"Excuse me," he says to us. "I'll come back some other time. Y'all, please excuse me."

And he looks at the boy and goes out the room. The boy h'ist his hand up to his mouth one time to wipe 'way some blood. All the rest of the time he keeps on reading. And nobody else in there say a word.

8

Little John Lee and his mama come out the dentist office, and the nurse calls somebody else in. Then little bit later they come out, and the nurse calls another name. But fast 's she calls somebody in there, somebody else comes in the place where we sitting, and the room stays full.

The people coming in now, all of them wearing big coats. One of them says something 'bout sleeting, another one says he hope not. Another one says he think it ain't nothing but rain. 'Cause, he says, rain can get awful cold this time of year.

All round the room they talking. Some of them talking to people right by them, some of them talking to people clear 'cross the room, some of them talking to anybody'll listen. It's a little bitty room, no bigger than us kitchen, and I can see everybody in there. The little old room's full of smoke, 'cause you got two old men smoking pipes over by that side door. I think I feel my tooth thumping me some, and I hold my breath and wait. I wait and wait, but it don't thump me no more. Thank God for that.

I feel like going to sleep, and I lean back 'gainst the wall. But I'm scared to go to sleep. Scared 'cause the nurse might call my name and I won't hear her. And Mama might go to sleep, too, and she'll be mad if neither one of us heard the nurse.

I look up at Mama. I love my mama. I love my mama. And when cotton come I'm go'n get her a new coat. And I ain't go'n get a black one, either. I think I'm go'n get her a red one.

"They got some books over there," I say. "Want read one of them?"

Mama looks at the book, but she don't answer me.

"You got yourself a little man there," the lady says.

Mama don't say nothing to the lady, but she must've smiled, 'cause I seen the lady smiling back. The lady looks at me a little while, like she's feeling sorry for me.

"You sure got that preacher out here in a hurry," she says to that boy.

The boy looks up at her and looks in his book again. When I grow up I want be just like him. I want clothes like that and I want keep a book with me, too.

"You really don't believe in God?" the lady says.

"No," he says.

"But why?" the lady says.

"Because the wind is pink," he says.

"What?" the lady says.

The boy don't answer her no more. He just reads in his book.

"Talking 'bout the wind is pink," that old lady says. She's sitting on the same bench with the boy and she's trying to look in his face. The boy makes 'tend the old lady ain't even there. He just keeps on reading. "Wind is pink," she says again. "Eh, Lord, what children go'n be saying next?"

The lady 'cross from us bust out laughing.

"That's a good one," she says. "The wind is pink. Yes sir, that's a good one."

"Don't you believe the wind is pink?" the boys says. He keeps his head down in the book.

"Course I believe it, honey," the lady says. "Course I do," She looks at us and winks her eye. "And what color is grass, honey?"

"Grass? Grass is black."

She bust out laughing again. The boy looks at her.

"Don't you believe grass is black?" he says.

The lady quits her laughing and looks at him. Everybody else looking at him, too. The place quiet, quiet.

"Grass is green, honey," the lady says. "It was green yesterday, it's green today, and it's go'n be green tomorrow."

"How do you know it's green?"

"I know because I know."

"You don't know it's green," the boy says. "You believe it's green because someone told you it was green. If someone had told you it was black you'd believe it was black."

"It's green," the lady says. "I know green when I see green."

"Prove it's green," the boy says.

"Sure, now," the lady says. "Don't tell me it's coming to that."

"It's coming to just that," the boy says. "Words mean nothing. One means no more than the other."

"That's what it all coming to?" that old lady says. That old lady got on a turban and she got on two sweaters. She got a green sweater under a black sweater. I can see the green sweater 'cause some of the buttons on the other sweater's missing.

"Yes ma'am," the boy says. "Words mean nothing. Action is the only thing. Doing. That's the only thing."

"Other words, you want the Lord to come down here and show Hisself to you?" she says.

"Exactly, ma'am," he says.

"You don't mean that, I'm sure?" she says.

"I do, ma'am," he says.

"Done, Jesus," the old lady says, shaking her head.

"I didn't go 'long with that preacher at first," the other lady says; "but now—I don't know. When a person say the grass is black, he's either a lunatic or something's wrong."

"Prove to me that it's green," the boy says.

"It's green because the people say it's green."

"Those same people say we're citizens of these United States," the boy says.

"I think I'm a citizen," the lady says.

"Citizens have certain rights," the boy says. "Name me one right that you have. One right, granted by the Constitution, that you can exercise in Bayonne."

The lady don't answer him. She just looks at him like she don't know what he's talking 'bout. I know I don't.

"Things changing," she says.

"Things are changing because some black men have begun to think with their brains and not their hearts," the boy says.

"You trying to say these people don't believe in God?"

"I'm sure some of them do. Maybe most of them do. But they don't believe that God is going to touch these white people's hearts and change things tomorrow. Things change through action. By no other way."

Everybody sit quiet and look at the boy. Nobody says a thing. Then the lady 'cross the room from me and Mama just shakes her head.

"Let's hope that not all your generation feel the same way you do," she says.

"Think what you please, it doesn't matter," the boy says. "But it will be men who listen to their heads and not their hearts who will see that your children have a better chance than you had."

"Let's hope they ain't all like you, though," the old lady says. "Done forgot the heart absolutely."

"Yes ma'am, I hope they aren't all like me," the boy says. "Unfortunately, I was born too late to believe in your God. Let's hope that the ones who come after will have your faith—if not in your God, then in something else, something definitely that they can lean on. I haven't anything. For me, the wind is pink, the grass is black."

9

The nurse comes in the room where we all sitting and waiting and says the doctor won't take no more patients till one o'clock this evening. My mama jumps up off the bench and goes up to the white lady.

"Nurse, I have to go back in the field this evening," she says.

"The doctor is treating his last patient now," the nurse says. "One o'clock this evening."

"Can I at least speak to the doctor?" my mama asks.

"I'm his nurse," the lady says.

"My little boy's sick," my mama says. "Right now his tooth almost killing him."

The nurse looks at me. She's trying to make up her mind if to let me come in. I look at her real pitiful. The tooth ain't hurting me at all, but Mama say it is, so I make 'tend for her sake.

"This evening," the nurse says, and goes on back in the office.

"Don't feel 'jected, honey," the lady says to Mama. "I been round them a long time—they take you when they want to. If you was white, that's something else; but we the wrong color."

Mama don't say nothing to the lady, and me and her go outside and stand 'gainst the wall. It's cold out there. I can feel that wind going through my coat. Some of the other people come out of the room and go up the street. Me and Mama stand there a little while and we start walking. I don't know where we going. When we come to the other street we just stand there.

"You don't have to make water, do you?" Mama says.

"No, ma'am," I say.

We go on up the street. Walking real slow. I can tell Mama don't know where she's going. When we come to a store we stand there and look at the dummies. I look at a little boy wearing a brown overcoat. He's got on brown shoes, too. I look at my old shoes and look at his'n again. You wait till summer, I say.

Me and Mama walk away. We come up to another store and we stop and look at them dummies, too. Then we go on again. We pass a café where the white people in there eating. Mama tells me keep my eyes in front where they belong, but I can't help from seeing them people eat. My stomach starts to growling 'cause I'm hungry. When I see people eating, I get hungry; when I see a coat, I get cold.

A man whistles at my mama when we go by a filling station. She makes 'tend she don't even see him. I look back and I feel like hitting him in the mouth. If I were bigger, I say; if I was bigger, you'd see.

We keep on going. I'm getting colder and colder, but I don't say nothing. I feel that stuff running down my nose and I sniff.

"That rag," Mama says.

I get it out and wipe my nose. I'm getting cold all over now—my face, my hands, my feet, everything. We pass another little café, but this'n for white people, too, and we can't go in there, either. So we just walk. I'm so cold now I'm 'bout ready to say it. If I knowed where we was going I wouldn't be so cold, but I don't know where I going. We go, we go, we go. We walk clean out of Bayonne. Then we cross street and we come back. Same thing I seen when I got off the bus this morning. Same old trees, same old walk, same old weeds, same old cracked pave—same old everything.

I sniff again.

"That rag," Mama says.

I wipe my nose real fast and jugg that handkerchief back in my pocket 'fore my hand gets too cold. I raise my head and I can see David's hardware store. When we come up to it, we go in. I don't know why, but I'm glad.

It's warm in there. It's so warm in there you don't ever want to leave. I look for the heater, and I see it over by them barrels. Three white men standing round the heater talking in Creole. One of them comes over to see what mama want.

"Got any axe handles?" she says.

Me, Mama and the white man start to the back, but Mama stops me when we come up to the heater. She and the white man go on. I hold my hands over the heater and look at them. They go all the way to the back, and I see the white man pointing to the axe handles 'gainst the wall. Mama takes one of them and shakes it like she's trying to figure how much it weighs. Then she rubs her hand over it from one end to the other end. She turns it over and looks at the other side, then she shakes it again, and shakes her head and puts it back. She gets another one and she does it just like she did the first one, then she shakes her head. Then she gets a brown one and do it that, too. But she don't like this one, either. Then she gets another one, but 'fore she shakes it or anything, she looks at me. Look like she's trying to say something to me, but I don't know what it is. All I know is I done got warm now and I'm feeling right smart better. Mama shakes this axe handle just like she did the others, and shakes her head and says something to the white man. The white man just looks at his pile of axe handles, and when Mama pass him to come to the front, the white man just scratch his head and follows her. She tells me come on and we go on out and start walking again.

We walk and walk, and no time at all I'm cold again. Look like I'm colder now 'cause I can still remember how good it was back there. My stomach growls and I suck it in to keep Mama from hearing it. She's walking right 'side me, and it growls so loud you can hear it a mile. But Mama don't say a word.

10

When we come up to the courthouse, I look at the clock. It's got quarter to twelve. Mean we got another hour and a quarter to be out here in the cold. We go and stand 'side a building. Something hits my cap and I look up at the sky. Sleet's falling.

I look at Mama standing there. I want stand close 'side her, but she don't like that. She say that's crybaby stuff. She say you got to stand for yourself, by yourself.

"Let's go back to that office," she says.

We cross the street. When we get to the dentist office I try to open the door, but I can't. I twist and twist, but I can't. Mama pushes me to the side and she twist the knob, but she can't open the door, either. She turns 'way from the door. I look at her, but I don't move and I don't say nothing. I done seen her like this before and I'm scared of her.

"You hungry?" she says. She says it like she's mad at me, like I'm the cause of everything.

"No, ma'am," I say.

"You want eat and walk back, or you rather don't eat and ride?"

"I ain't hungry," I say.

I ain't just hungry, but I'm cold, too. I'm so hungry and cold I want to cry. And look like I'm getting colder and colder. My feet done got numb. I try to work my toes, but I don't even feel them. Look like I'm go'n die. Look like I'm go'n stand right here and freeze to death. I think 'bout home. I think 'bout Val and Auntie and Ty and Louis and Walker. It's 'bout twelve o'clock and I know they eating dinner now. I can hear Ty making jokes. He done forgot 'bout getting up early this morning and right now he's probably making jokes. Always trying to make somebody laugh. I wish I was right there listening to him. Give anything in the world if I was home round the fire.

"Come on," Mama says.

We start walking again. My feet so numb I can't hardly feel them. We turn the corner and go on back up the street. The clock on the courthouse starts hitting for twelve.

The sleet's coming down plenty now. They hit the pave and bounce like rice. Oh, Lord; oh, Lord, I pray. Don't let me die, don't let me die, don't let me die, Lord.

11

Now I know where we going. We going back of town where the colored people eat. I don't care if I don't eat. I been hungry before. I can stand it. But I can't stand the cold.

I can see we go'n have a long walk. It's 'bout a mile down there. But I don't mind. I know when I get there I'm go'n warm myself. I think I can hold out. My hands numb in my pockets and my feet numb, too, but if I keep moving I can hold out. Just don't stop no more, that's all.

The sky's gray. The sleet keeps on falling. Falling like rain now—plenty, plenty. You can hear it hitting the pave. You can see it bouncing. Sometimes it bounces two times 'fore it settles.

We keep on going. We don't say nothing. We just keep on going, keep on going.

I wonder what Mama's thinking. I hope she ain't mad at me. When summer come I'm go'n pick plenty cotton and get her a coat. I'm go'n get her a red one.

I hope they'd make it summer all the time. I'd be glad if it was summer all the time—but it ain't. We got to have winter, too. Lord, I hate the winter. I guess everybody hate the winter.

I don't sniff this time. I get out my handkerchief and wipe my nose. My hands's so cold I can hardly hold the handkerchief.

I think we getting close, but we ain't there yet. I wonder where everybody is. Can't see a soul but us. Look like we the only two people moving round today. Must be too cold for the rest of the people to move round in.

I can hear my teeth. I hope they don't knock together too hard and make that bad one hurt. Lord, that's all I need, for that bad one to start off.

I hear a church bell somewhere. But today ain't Sunday. They must be ringing for a funeral or something.

I wonder what they doing at home. They must be eating. Monsieur Bayonne might be there with his guitar. One day Ty played with Monsieur Bayonne's guitar and broke one of the strings. Monsieur Bayonne was some mad with Ty. He say Ty wasn't go'n ever 'mount to nothing. Ty can go just like Monsieur Bayonne when he ain't there. Ty can make everybody laugh when he starts to mocking Monsieur Bayonne.

I used to like to be with Mama and Daddy. We used to be happy. But they took him in the Army. Now, nobody happy no more. . . . I be glad when Daddy comes home.

Monsieur Bayonne say it wasn't fair for them to take Daddy and give Mama nothing and give us nothing. Auntie say, "Shhh, Etienne. Don't let them hear you talk like that." Monsieur Bayonne say, "It's God truth. What they giving his children? They have to walk three and a half miles to school hot or cold. That's anything to give for a paw? She's got to work in the field rain or shine just to make ends meet. That's anything to give for a husband?" Auntie say, "Shhh, Etienne, shhh." "Yes, you right," Monsieur Bayonne say. "Best don't say it in front of them now. But one day they go'n find out. One day." "Yes, I suppose so," Auntie say. "Then what, Rose Mary?" Monsieur Bayonne say. "I don't know Etienne," Auntie say. "All we can do is us job, and leave everything else in His hand. . . ."

We getting closer, now. We getting closer. I can even see the railroad tracks.

We cross the tracks, and now I see the café. Just to get in there, I say. Just to get in there. Already I'm starting to feel little better.

12

We go in, Ahh, it's good, I look for the heater; there 'gainst the wall. One of them little brown ones. I just stand there and hold my hands over it. I can't open my hands too wide 'cause they almost froze.

Mama's standing right 'side me. She done unbuttoned her coat. Smoke rises out of the coat, and the coat smells like a wet dog.

I move to the side so Mama can have more room. She opens out her hands and rubs them together. I rub mine together, too, 'cause this keep them from hurting. If you let them warm too fast, they hurt you sure. But if you let them warm just little bit at a time, and you keep rubbing them, they be all right every time.

They got just two more people in the café. A lady back of the counter, and a man on this side the counter. They been watching us ever since we come in.

Mama gets out the handkerchief and count up the money. Both of us know how much money she's got there. Three dollars. No, she ain't got three dollars, 'cause she had to pay us way up here. She ain't got but two dollars and a half left. Dollar and a half to get my tooth pulled, and fifty cents for us to go back on, and fifty cents worth of salt meat.

She stirs the money round with her finger. Most of the money is change 'cause I can hear it rubbing together. She stirs it and stirs it. Then she looks at the door. It's still sleeting. I can hear it hitting 'gainst the wall like rice.

"I ain't hungry, Mama," I say.

"Got to pay them something for they heat," she says.

She takes a quarter out the handkerchief and ties the handkerchief up again. She looks over her shoulder at the people, but she still don't move. I hope she don't spend the money. I don't want her spending it on me. I'm hungry, I'm almost starving I'm so hungry, but I don't want her spending the money on me.

She flips the quarter over like she's thinking. She's must be thinking 'bout us walking back home. Lord, I sure don't want walk home. If I thought it'd do any good to say something, I'd say it. But Mama makes up her own mind 'bout things.

She turns 'way from the heater right fast, like she better hurry up and spend the quarter 'fore she change her mind. I watch her go toward the counter. The man and the lady look at her, too. She tells the lady something and the lady walks away. The man keeps on looking at her. Her back's turned to the man, and she don't even know he's standing there.

The lady puts some cakes and a glass of milk on the counter. Then she pours up a cup of coffee and sets it 'side the other stuff. Mama pays her for the things and comes on back where I'm standing. She tells me sit down at the table 'gainst the wall.

The milk and the cakes's for me; the coffee's for Mama. I eat slow and I look at her. She's looking outside at the sleet. She's looking real sad. I say to myself, I'm go'n make all this up one day. You see, one day, I'm go'n make all this up. I want say it now; I want tell her how I feel right now; but Mama don't like for us to talk like that.

"I can't eat all this," I say.

They ain't got but just three little old cakes there. I'm so hungry right now, the Lord knows I can eat a hundred times three, but I want my mama to have one.

Mama don't even look my way. She knows I'm hungry, she knows I want it. I let it stay there a little while, then I get it and eat it. I eat just on my front teeth, though, 'cause if cake touch that back tooth I know what'll happen. Thank God it ain't hurt me at all today.

After I finish eating I see the man go to the juke box. He drops a nickel in it, then he just stand there a little while looking at the record. Mama tells me keep my eyes in front where they belong. I turn my head like she say, but then I hear the man coming toward us.

"Dance, pretty?" he says.

Mama gets up to dance with him. But 'fore you know it, she done grabbed the little man in the collar and done heaved him 'side the wall. He hit the wall so hard he stop the juke box from playing.

"Some pimp," the lady back of the counter says. "Some pimp."

The little man jumps up off the floor and starts toward my mama. 'Fore you know it, Mama done sprung open her knife and she's waiting for him.

"Come on," she says. "Come on. I'll gut you from your neighbo to your throat. Come on."

I go up to the little man to hit him, but Mama makes me come and stand 'side her. The little man looks at me and Mama and goes on back to the counter.

"Some pimp," the lady back of the counter says. "Some pimp." She starts laughing and pointing at the little man. "Yes sir, you a pimp, all right. Yes sir-ree."

13

"Fasten that coat, let's go," Mama says.

"You don't have to leave," the lady says.

Mama don't answer the lady, and we right out in the cold again. I'm warm right now—my hands, my ears, my feet—but I know this ain't go'n last too long. It done sleet so much now you got ice everywhere you look.

We cross the railroad tracks, and soon's we do, I get cold. That wind goes through this little old coat like it ain't even there. I got on a shirt and a sweater under the coat, but that wind don't pay them no mind. I look up and I can see we got a long way to go. I wonder if we go'n make it 'fore I get too cold.

We cross over to walk on the sidewalk. They got just one sidewalk back here, and it's over there.

After we go just a little piece, I smell bread cooking. I look, then I see a baker shop. When we get closer, I can smell it more better. I shut my eyes and make 'tend I'm eating. But I keep them shut too long and I butt up 'gainst a telephone post. Mama grabs me and see if I'm hurt. I ain't bleeding or nothing and she turns me loose.

I can feel I'm getting colder and colder, and I look up to see how far we still got to go. Uptown is 'way up yonder. A half mile more, I reckon. I try to think of something. They say think and you won't get cold, I think of that poem, "Annabel Lee." I ain't been to school in so long—this bad weather—I reckon they done passed "Annabel Lee" by now. But passed it or not, I'm sure Miss Walker go'n make me recite it when I get there. That woman don't never forget nothing. I ain't never seen nobody like that in my life.

I'm still getting cold. "Annabel Lee" or no "Annabel Lee," I'm still getting cold. But I can see we getting closer. We getting there gradually.

Soon 's we turn the corner, I see a little old white lady up in front of us. She's the only lady on the street. She's all in black and she's got a long black rag over her head.

"Stop," she says.

Me and Mama stop and look at her. She must be crazy to be out in all this bad weather. Ain't got but a few other people out there, and all of them's men.

"Y'all done ate?" she says.

"Just finish," Mama says.

"Y'all must be cold then?" she says.

"We headed for the dentist," Mama says. "We'll warm up when we get there."

"What dentist?" the old lady says. "Mr. Bassett?"

"Yes, ma'am," Mama says.

"Come on in," the old lady says. "I'll telephone him and tell him y'all coming."

Me and Mama follow the old lady in the store. It's a little bitty store, and it don't have much in there. The old lady takes off her head rag and folds it up.

"Helena?" somebody calls from the back.

"Yes, Alnest?" the old lady says.

"Did you see them?"

"They're here. Standing beside me."

"Good. Now you can stay inside."

The old lady looks at Mama. Mama's waiting to hear what she brought us in here for. I'm waiting for that, too.

"I saw y'all each time you went by," she says. "I came out to catch you, but you were gone."

"We went back of town," Mama says.

"Did you eat?"

"Yes, Ma'am."

The old lady looks at Mama a long time, like she's thinking Mama might be just saying that. Mama looks right back at her. The old lady looks at me to see what I have to say. I don't say nothing. I sure ain't going 'gainst my mama.

"There's food in the kitchen," she says to Mama. "I've been keeping it warm."

Mama turns right around and starts for the door.

"Just a minute," the old lady says. Mama stops. "The boy'll have to work for it. It isn't free."

"We don't take no handout," Mama says.

"I'm not handing out anything," the old lady says. "I need by garbage moved to the front. Ernest has a bad cold an can't go out there."

"James'll move it for you," Mama says.

"Not unless you eat," the old lady says. "I'm old, but I have my pride, too, you know."

Mama can see she ain't go'n beat this old lady down, so she just shakes her head.

"All right," the old lady says. "Come into the kitchen."

She leads the way with that rag in her hand. The kitchen is a little bitty little old thing, too. The table and the stove just 'bout fill it up. They got a little room to the side. Somebody in there laying 'cross the bed—'cause I can see one of his feet. Must be the person she was talking to: Ernest or Alnest—something like that.

"Sit down," the old lady says to Mama. "Not you," she says to me. "You have to move the cans."

"Helena?" the man says in the other room.

"Yes, Alnest?" the old lady says.

"Are you going out there again?"

"I must show the boy where the garbage is, Alnest," the old lady says.

"Keep that shawl over your head," the old man says.

"You don't have to remind me, Alnest. Come, boy," the old lady says.

We go out in the yard. Little old back yard ain't no bigger than the store or the kitchen. But it can sleet here just like it can sleet in any big back yard. And 'fore you know it, I'm trembling.

"There," the old lady says, pointing to the cans. I pick up one of the cans and set it right back down. The can's so light, I'm go'n see what's inside of it.

"Here," the old lady says. "Leave that can alone."

I look back at her standing there in the door. She's got that black rag wrapped round her shoulders, and she's pointing one of her little old fingers at me.

"Pick it up and carry it to the front," she says. I go by her with the can, and she's looking at me all the time. I'm sure the can's empty. I'm sure she could've carried it herself—maybe both of them at the same time. "Set it on the sidewalk by the door and come back for the other one," she says.

I go and come back, and Mama looks at me when I pass her. I get the other can and take it to the front. It don't feel a bit heavier than that first one. I tell my-self I ain't go'n be nobody's fool, and I'm go'n look inside this can to see just what I been hauling. First, I look up the street, then down the street. Nobody coming.

Then I look over my shoulder toward the door. That little old lady done slipped up there quiet's mouse, watching me again. Look like she knowed what I was go'n do.

"Ehh, Lord," she says. "Children, children. Come in here, boy, and go wash your hands."

I follow her in the kitchen. She points toward the bathroom, and I go in there and wash up. Little bitty old bathroom, but it's clean, clean. I don't use any of her towels; I wipe my hands on my pants legs.

When I come back in the kitchen, the old lady done dished up the food. Rice, gravy, meat—and she even got some lettuce and tomato in a saucer. She even got a glass of milk and a piece of cake there, too. It looks so good, I almost start eating 'fore I say my blessing.

"Helena?" the old man says.

"Yes, Alnest?"

"Are they eating?"

"Yes," she says.

"Good," he says. "Now you'll stay inside."

The old lady goes in there where he is and I can hear them talking. I look at Mama. She's eating slow like she's thinking. I wonder what's the matter now. I reckon she's thinking 'bout home.

The old lady comes back in the kitchen.

"I talked to Dr. Bassett's nurse," she says. "Dr. Bassett will take you as soon as you get there."

"Thank you, ma'am," Mama says.

"Perfectly all right," the old lady says. "Which one is it?"

Mama nods toward me. The old lady looks at me real sad. I look sad, too.

"You're not afraid, are you?" she says.

"No, Ma'am," I say.

"That's a good boy," the old lady says. "Nothing to be afraid of. Dr. Bassett will not hurt you."

When me and Mama get through eating, we thank the old lady again.

"Helena, are they leaving?" the old man says.

"Yes, Alnest."

"Tell them I say good-bye."

"They can hear you, Alnest."

"Good-bye both mother and son," the old man says. "And may God be with you."

Me and Mama tell the old man good-bye, and we follow the old lady in the front room. Mama opens the door to go out, but she stops and comes back in the store.

"You sell salt meat?" she says.

"Yes."

"Give me two bits worth."

"That isn't very much salt meat," the old lady says.

"That's all I have," Mama says.

The old lady goes back of the counter and cuts a big piece off the chunk. Then she wraps it up and puts it in a paper bag.

"Two bits," she says.

"That looks like awful lot of meat for a quarter," Mama says.

"Two bits," the old lady says. "I've been selling salt meat behind this counter twenty-five years. I think I know what I'm doing."

"You got a scale there," Mama says.

"What?" the old lady says.

"Weigh it," Mama says.

"What?" the old lady says. "Are you telling me how to run my business?"

"Thanks very much for the food," Mama says.

"Just a minute," the old lady says.

"James," Mama says to me. I move toward the door.

"Just one minute, I said," the old lady says.

Me and Mama stop again and look at her. The old lady takes the meat out of the bag and unwraps it and cuts 'bout half of it off. Then she wraps it up again and juggs it back in the bag and gives the bag to Mama. Mama lays the quarter on the counter.

"Your kindness will never be forgotten," she says. "James," she says to me.

We go out, and the old lady comes to the door to look at us. After we go a little piece I look back, and she's still there watching us.

The sleet's coming down heavy, heavy now, and I turn up my coat collar to keep my neck warm. My mama tells me turn it right back down.

"You not a bum," she says. "You a man."

Nikki Giovanni (1943–)

Nikki Giovanni was a star of the Black Arts Movement and one of the first poets to advocate harsh militarism as a response to racism. Her militarism sparked her fame as a black poet and as a figure known nationally because of her high visibility, including appearances on talk shows. Though her national fame contradicted to some degree with the desire to destroy White America that her poetry voiced, Giovanni enjoyed the visibility and kept it in line with the political establishment of Black presence and pride.

Giovanni is perhaps most well known for the three collections of poetry she published between 1967 and 1970: Black Feeling/Black Talk *(1967),* Black Judgment *(1968), and* Re: Creation *(1970). She self-published and self-publicized her first title,* Black Feeling/Black Talk, *and the militancy and vital performance of poems such as "Nigger Can You Kill?" (or, "The True Import of the Present Dialogue, Black vs. Negro") with its critique of false Black consciousness that keeps Blacks from real revolution, rocketed her to public attention. With such poems, Giovanni issued a call to Black America to kill White oppressors and those Black people who were passive. An impatience for change became justification for open violence. Published by Broadside Press, the revolutionary themes, the accessibility of the language, and the incantatory rhythm of the poetry made* Black Judgment *and* Re: Creation *appealing to Black audiences and a wider national audience as well.*

And advocate of the Black Aesthetic, Giovanni believed a poet must use her craft toward social revolution and inspire her audience with her language. "For Saundra" clarifies the need for a poet to write about lived experience and social realities. "Nikki-Rosa," her 1968 signature poem, destroys the stereotype of the degenerate Black family with images of love and deep connection, arguing that the love is also the strength, the "wealth" of the Black community. "Ego Tripping" connects contemporary identity to African roots and ancestry, with the vernacular of the Black toast and the idea of a mythic Black woman who embodies and celebrates Black women across time.

Giovanni recorded her poetry with a gospel choir to create Truth Is on Its Way *(1971) and* The Way I Feel *(1974). She also made several more recordings to coincide with her philosophical belief held in common with other Black Arts poets that Black poetry cannot be separated from Black music, orality, and community. These attempts to reach a wider audience had exactly the effect desired, drawing Giovanni to the attention of multigenerational and international audiences.*

In 1972, Giovanni took her poetry in a new direction with the publication of My House, *a collection of love poems. The birth of her son in 1969 and* My House *signaled a general shift in her work. In* My House, *the personal and public come together in short poems and through simple language. Giovanni divides the collection into two sections— The Rooms Outside and The Rooms Inside—which has caused some to be critical of the di-*

chotomy she draws between public and private. Revolution still occurs, but as quieter transformation of reality.

The 1974 publication of Gemini: An Extended Autobiographical Statement on My First Twenty-five Years of Being a Black Poet is Giovanni's first journey into prose. The narrative chapters of this work are tall tales with clever titles and an upbeat "I" narrator. In the last chapter of the "autobiography," Giovanni voices the transition evident in the poetry of My House, a new future that is not fueled by militarism, for herself, and more importantly, for her son.

Not abandoning her earlier philosophy entirely, Giovanni's next book of poetry was The Woman and the Men (1975), a collection of new poems and selected poems from Re: Creation and Black Judgment. Yet, Cotton Candy on a Rainy Day (1978) personalized revolution even more with themes of isolation, loneliness, and a loss of the idealism that characterized her 1960s activism. Giovanni closes this collection with poems about friendship and love, hope on a personal level.

While continuing prolific publication of her own poetry, Giovanni extended this effort to capture the collectivity of artistic creation and the continuance of literary tradition by discussing issues of politics and identity with James Baldwin and Margaret Walker. A Dialogue: James Baldwin and Nikki Giovanni (1975) includes discussion between the two on the role and struggle of the Black intellectual in the 1960s and 70s in the way that bell hooks' and Cornel West's Breaking Bread (1991) discusses what it is to be an intellectual in the 1990s. A Poetic Equation: Conversations Between Nikki Giovanni and Margaret Walker (1974) documents the struggle toward Black female identity and intellectualism in the wake of rising feminism.

Sacred Cows and Other Edibles (1988) is a continuation of the autobiographical/political essay that energized Gemini. In Racism 101 (1994), a third collection of essays, Giovanni valorizes the tradition of storytelling in "Griots" and recognizes, in the tradition of Alice Walker's In Search of Our Mothers' Gardens (1984), the value of ever-present culture, of home as museum.

Giovanni also continues to create provocative and reflective poetry in her third decade of literary production. "All Eyez on U" is a tribute to 2pac Shakur, to whom she dedicates her most recent collection of poetry, Love Poems (1997). "Stardate Number 18628.190," the preface poem to The Selected Poems of Nikki Giovanni (1996), catalogs the functions of poetry, plays with ellipses to string and connect ideas, and moves from past to present and future to convey a vision of African American affirmation.

Despite the range of themes, political motivations, and genres over the course of her career, Giovanni has maintained a remarkably consistent and personal voice in her poetry and prose. She emphasizes in all of her work the search for love and acceptance alongside and within the general struggle for affirmation in African American communities. The voice of a strong and very human woman is the thread that ties all of her work together.

Born Yolande Cornelia Giovanni, Jr., in Knoxville, Tennessee on June 7, 1943, Nikki Giovanni grew up in Lincoln Heights, a predominantly Black neighborhood in Cincinnati, Ohio. Giovanni returned to Tennessee to study at Fisk University where she graduated with honors in 1967. She took her first creative writing classes at Fisk and continued at the University of Pennsylvania and Columbia University. During her college years, Giovanni was very active in SNCC, the Student Nonviolent Coordinating Committee.

Giovanni has taught at Rutgers University, Ohio State University, and the College of Mount St. Joseph. She has been a professor of English at Virginia Polytechnic Institute and State University since 1987 and, as poet, speaker, and essayist, shares her vision with audiences nationwide.

R. Joyce Lausch

Stardate Number 18628.190

This is not a poem . . . this is hot chocolate at the beginning of Spring . . . topped with hand whipped double cream . . . a splash of brandy to give it sass . . . and just a little cinnamon to give it class . . . This is not a poem

This is a summer quilt . . . log cabin pattern . . . see the corner piece . . . that was grandmother's wedding dress . . . that was grandpappa's favorite Sunday tie . . . that white strip there . . . is the baby who died . . . Mommy had pneumonia so that red flannel shows the healing . . . This does not hang from museum walls . . . nor will it sell for thousands . . . This is here to keep me warm

This is not a sonnet . . . though it will sing . . . Precious Lord . . . take my hand . . . Amazing Grace . . . how sweet the sound . . . Go down, Moses . . . Way down to the past . . . Way up to the future . . . It will swell with the voice of Marion Anderson . . . lilt on the arias of Leontyne . . . dance on the trilling of Battle . . . do the dirty dirty with Bessie . . . moan with Dinah Washington . . . rock and roll through the Sixties . . . rap its way into the Nineties . . . and go on out into Space with Etta James saying At Last . . . No, this is not a sonnet . . . but the truth of the beauty that the only authentic voice of Planet Earth comes from the black soil . . . tilled and mined . . . by the Daughters of the Diaspora

This is a rocking chair . . . rock me gently in the bosom of Abraham . . . This is a bus seat: No, I'm not going to move today . . . This is a porch . . . where they sat spitting at fireflies . . . telling young Alex the story of The African . . . This is a hook rug . . . to cover a dirt floor . . . This is an iron pot . . . with the left over vegetables . . . making a slow cooking soup . . . This is pork . . . simmering chitterlings . . . surprising everybody with our ability to make a way . . . out of no way . . . This is not rest when we are weary . . . nor comfort when we are sad . . . It is laughter . . . when we are in pain . . . It is "N'mind" when we are confused . . . It is "Keep climbing, chile" when the road takes the unfair turn . . . It is "Don't let nobody turn you round" . . . when our way is dark . . . It is the faith of our Mothers . . . who plaited our hair . . . put Vaseline on our faces . . . polished our run down shoes . . . patched our dresses . . . wore sweaters so that we could wear coats . . . who welcomed us and our children . . . when we were left alone to rear them . . . who said "Get your education . . . and nobody can put you back"

This is not a poem . . . No . . . It is a celebration of the road we have traveled . . . It is a prayer . . . for the roads yet to come . . . This is an explosion . . . The original Big Bang . . . that makes the world a hopeful . . . loving place

This is the Black woman . . . in all our trouble and glory . . . in all our past history and future forbearance . . . in all that ever made love a possibility . . . .
. . . . This is about us . . .
    bleached and natural . . . braided and straightened hair . . .
    made up . . . or . . . beaten up faces . . .
    tall . . . short . . . stately . . . bent . . .
    CC Riders . . . junkies . . . whores . . .
    wives . . . mothers . . . grandmothers . . . aunts
    working in the home or outside . . .
    working in the system or outside . . .
    working praying working to survive . . .
    giving pride . . . giving succor . . . giving voice . . . giving
    encouragement . . . giving whatever . . . we can give

This is a flag . . . that we placed over Peter Salem and Peter Poor . . . the 54th Regiment from Massachusetts . . . All the men and women lynched in the name of rape . . . Emmett Till . . . Medgar Evers . . . Malcolm X . . . Martin Luther King, Jr. . . . This a banner we fly for Respect . . . Dignity . . . the Assumption of Integrity . . . for a future generation to rally around

This is about us . . . Celebrating ourselves . . . And a well deserved honor it is . . . Light the candles, Essence . . . This is a rocket . . . Let's ride

Nikki-Rosa

    childhood remembrances are always a drag
    if you're Black
    you always remember things like living in Woodlawn
    with no inside toilet
    and if you become famous or something
    they never talk about how happy you were to have
    your mother
    all to yourself and
    how good the water felt when you got your bath
    from one of those
    big tubs that folk in chicago barbeque in
    and somehow when you talk about home
    it never gets across how much you
    understood their feelings
    as the whole family attended meetings about Hollydale
    and even though you remember
    your biographers never understand

your father's pain as he sells his stock
and another dream goes
And though you're poor it isn't poverty that
concerns you
and though they fought a lot
it isn't your father's drinking that makes any difference
but only that everybody is together and you
and your sister have happy birthdays and very good
Christmases
and I really hope no white person ever has cause
to write about me
because they never understand
Black love is Black wealth and they'll
probably talk about my hard childhood
and never understand that
all the while I was quite happy

For Saundra

i wanted to write
a poem
that rhymes
but revolution doesn't lend
itself to be-bopping

then my neighbor
who thinks i hate
asked—do you ever write
tree poems—i like trees
so i thought
i'll write a beautiful green tree poem
peeked from my window
to check the image
noticed the school yard was covered
with asphalt
no green—no trees grow
in manhattan

then, well, i thought the sky
i'll do a big blue sky poem
but all the clouds have winged
low since no-Dick was elected

so i thought again
and it occurred to me
maybe i shouldn't write
at all
but clean my gun
and check my kerosene supply

perhaps these are not poetic
times
at all

Revolutionary Dreams

i used to dream militant
dreams of taking
over america to show
these white folks how it should be
done
i used to dream radical dreams
of blowing everyone away with my perceptive powers
of correct analysis
i even used to think i'd be the one
to stop the riot and negotiate the peace
then i awoke and dug
that if i dreamed natural
dreams of being a natural
woman doing what a woman
does when she's natural
i would have a revolution

Ego Tripping

(THERE MAY BE A REASON WHY)

I was born in the congo
I walked to the fertile crescent and built
  the sphinx
I designed a pyramid so tough that a star
    that only glows every one hundred years falls
    into the center giving divine perfect light
I am bad

I sat on the throne
   drinking nectar with allah
I got hot and sent an ice age to europe
   to cool my thirst
My oldest daughter is nefertiti
   the tears from my birth pains
   created the nile
I am a beautiful woman

I gazed on the forest and burned
   out the sahara desert
   with a packet of goat's meat
and a change of clothes
I crossed it in two hours
I am a gazelle so swift
   so swift you can't catch me

   For a birthday present when he was three
I gave my son hannibal and elephant
He gave me rome for mother's day
My strength flows ever on
My son noah built new/ark and
I stood proudly at the helm
   as we sailed on a soft summer day
I turned myself into myself and was
   jesus
   men intone my loving name
   All praises All praises
I am the one who would save

I sowed diamonds in my back yard
My bowels deliver uranium
   the filings from my fingernails are
   semi-precious jewels
   On a trip north
I caught a cold and blew
My nose giving oil to the arab world
I am so hip even my errors are correct
I sailed west to reach east and had to round off
   the earth as I went
   The hair from my head thinned and gold was laid
   across three continents

I am so perfect so divine so ethereal so surreal
I cannot be comprehended
   except by my permission

I mean . . . I . . . can fly
   like a bird in the sky . . .

Cotton Candy On A Rainy Day

Don't look now
I'm fading away
Into the gray of my mornings
Or the blues of every night

Is it that my nails
   keep breaking
Or maybe the corn
   on my second little piggy
Things keep popping out
   on my face
     or
   of my life

It seems no matter how
I try I become more difficult
   to hold
I am not an easy woman
   to want

They have asked
   the psychiatrists   psychologists   politicians and
   social workers
What this decade will be
   known for
There is no doubt   it is
   loneliness

If loneliness were a grape
   the wine would be vintage
If it were a wood
   the furniture would be mahogany
But since it is life   it is

Cotton Candy
    on a rainy day
The sweet soft essence
    of possibility
Never quite maturing

I have prided myself
On being in that great tradition
    albeit circus
That the show must go on
Though in my community the vernacular is
    One Monkey Don't Stop the Show

We all line up
    at some midway point
To thread our way through
    the boredom and futility
Looking for the blue ribbon and gold medal

Mostly these are seen as food labels
We are consumed by people who sing
    the same old song   STAY:

                as sweet as you are
                in my corner
Or perhaps   *just a little bit longer*
But whatever you do   *don't change baby baby don't change*
Something needs to change
Everything   some say   will change
I need a change
    of pace   face   attitude and life
Though I long for my loneliness
I know I need something
Or someone
Or. . . . .

I strangle my words as easily as I do my tears
I stifle my screams as frequently as I flash my smile
    it means nothing
I am cotton candy on a rainy day
    the unrealized dream of an idea unborn

I share with the painters the desire
To put a three-dimensional picture
On a one-dimensional surface

All Eyez On U

(FOR 2PAC SHAKUR 1971–1996)

as I tossed and turned unable to achieve sleep unable to control anxiety unable
to comprehend why

2Pac is not with us

if those who lived by the sword died by the sword there would be no white men
on earth
if those who lived on hatred died on hatred there would be no KKK
if those who lived by lies died by lies there would be nobody on wall street in
executive suites in academic offices instructing the young
don't tell me he got what he deserved   he deserved a chariot and the accolades
of a grateful people

he deserved his life

it is as clear as a mountain stream as defining as a lightning strike as terrifying as
sun to vampires

2Pac told the truth

there were those who called it dirty   gansta rap inciting there were those who
never wanted to be   angry at the conditions but angry at the messenger who re-
ported: *your kitchen has roaches your toilet is overflowing your basement has so
much water the rats are in the living room
your house is in disorder*

and 2Pac told you about it

what a beautiful boy graceful carriage melodic voice sharp wit intellectual
breadth what a beautiful boy to lose

not me   never me   I do not believe east coast west coast   I saw them murder
Emmett Till I saw them murder Malcolm X   I saw them murder   Martin
Luther King   I witnessed them shooting Rap Brown I saw them beat LeRoi
James   I saw them fill their jails I see them burning churches   not me   never
me   I do not believe this is some sort of mouth action   this is some sort of political action and they picked well   they picked the brightest freshest fruit from
the tallest tree   what a beautiful boy

but he will not go away   as Malcolm did not go away   as Emmett Till did not
go away   your shooting him will not take him from us his spirit will fill our

hearts   his courage will strengthen us for the challenge   his truth will straighten our backbones

you know, Socrates had a mother   she too watched her son drink hemlock she too asked why   but Socrates stood firm and would not lie to save himself 2Pac has a mother   the lovely Afeni had to bury her son   it is not right

it is not right that this young warrior is cut down   it is not right for the old to bury the young   it is not right

this generation mourns 2Pac as my generation mourned Till as we all mourn Malcolm   this wonderful young warrior

Sonia Sanchez said when she learned of his passing she walked all day walking the beautiful warrior home to our ancestors I just cried as all mothers cry for the beautiful boy who said he and Mike Tyson would never be allowed to be free at the same time who told the truth abut them and who told the truth about us who is our beautiful warrior

there are those who wanted to make *him* the problem   who wanted to believe if they silenced 2Pac all would be quiet on the ghetto front there are those who testified that the problem wasn't the conditions but the people talking about them

they took away band   so the boys started scratching they took away gym   so the boys started break dancing the boys started rapping cause they gave them the guns and the drugs but not the schools and libraries

what a beautiful boy to lose

and we mourn 2Pac Shakur and we reach out to his mother and we hug our-selves in sadness and shame

and we are compelled to ask:
R U Happy, Mz Tucker? 2Pac is gone
R U Happy?

Griots

I must have heard my first stories in my mother's womb.
    Mother loved a good story and my father told good jokes, but it was her fa-ther, Grandpapa, who told the heroic tales of long ago. Grandpapa was a Fisk

University graduate (1905) who had majored in Latin. As he sometimes told the story, he had intended to be a diplomat until he met Grandmother, but that is probably another story altogether, he being Black and all in 1905 or thereabouts.

Grandpapa loved the stars. He knew the constellations and the gods who formed them, for whom they were named.

Grandpapa was twenty years the senior of Grandmother, so he was an old man when we were born. Grandmother's passion was flowers; his, constellations. One needn't have a great imagination to envision this courtship: the one with her feet firmly planted on earth, the other with his heart in the sky. It is only natural that I would love history and the gossip of which it is composed.

Fiction cannot take the place of stories. Aha, you caught me! Fiction is stories, you say. But no. Stories, at their best, pass along a history. It may be that there was no Ulysses with a faithful Penelope knitting and unraveling, but something representative of the people is conveyed. Something about courage, fortitude, loss, and recovery.

I, like most young ladies of color, used to get my hair done every Saturday. The beauty parlor is a marvelous thing. Every Saturday you got the saga of who was sleeping with whose husband; who was pregnant; who was abused by whose boyfriend or husband. Sometimes they would remember the children were there, but mostly the desire of the women to talk without the presence of the men overcame their desire to shield us from the real world.

My mother's family is from Albany, Georgia, but Grandmother and Grandpapa had moved to Knoxville, Tennessee. We four grandchildren spent our summers with Grandmother.

At night, when we were put to bed, my sister Gary and I would talk and sing and sometimes read under the covers using our Lone Ranger flashlight rings. Of course, we were caught. Grandmother would threaten us and take our rings. We would sneak out of our room, wiggling on our stomachs, to reach the window under which we sat and listened to Grandpapa and Grandmother talk.

Sitting under that window I learned that Eisenhower was not a good president; I learned that poll taxes are unfair. I heard Grandmother berate Grandpapa for voting Republican when "Lincoln didn't do all that much for colored people." I heard assessments of Black and white people of Knoxville and the world. No one is enhanced by this. I'm not trying to pretend they were; there were no stories of "the African" in my family, although I am glad there were in Alex Haley's.

We were just ordinary people trying to make sense of our lives, and for that I thank my grandparents. I'm lucky that I had the sense to listen and the heart to care; I'm glad they talked into the night, sitting in the glider on the front porch, Grandmother munching on fried fish and Grandpapa eating something sweet. I'm glad I understand that while language is a gift, listening is a responsibility. There must always be griots . . . else how will we know who we are?

Paper Dolls, Iron Skillets,
Libraries, and Museums

I used to cut out paper dolls, a thing I think no longer exists in the age of Barbie and Ken and those turtle things. My sister and I would sometimes draw our own clothes, color them, paste and glue wonderful accessories . . . but we never could get the tabs right . . . and the clothes fell off. Fortunately we were not easily discouraged, and Mommy always praised our efforts.

There are certain advantages to having an older sister. She took piano lessons first and played so well I know it was pointless for me to try. Well, I tried but it was the kind of effort one gives when one knows one is doomed to second place. She also took French first so I learned the alphabet, numbers, and a few dirty words before I enrolled in school. Our father was a math whiz. Give him a few numbers and he'd see the sequence; give him a problem and he would solve it. Gary, my sister, inherited that trait from him. It's all I can do to keep my checkbook straight. All this is leading up to a point. I had to find things that I could do well. Kickball is not actually a sport by which one can earn a living; I was good at dodgeball, but my temper is not suited to being graciously hit. That left tennis and poetry.

Had I not lived in a world that had so little regard for the wishes of Black girls, I may have tried the tennis circuit. Althea Gibson had, after all, shown that it could be done, if one subscribes to role-model theories, but, irony of all ironies, my parents didn't like the travel. And anyway, I started to smoke in college, so that killed that. My task? To find something I loved that did not require me to change my physical habits while allowing me to grow emotionally and intellectually. No problem.

I've always loved libraries. Spending most summers in Knoxville, Tennessee, where I was born, I established a wonderful daily routine. Breakfast in the morning, tennis, shower, lunch, library. To be quite honest, I'm not now and never was a breakfast fan, but it would just break Grandmother's heart if you didn't eat, not something, but a bit of everything. I ultimately moved to Knoxville and attended Austin High. When I went to college I was, well, chubby. Three weeks after registration I had dropped twelve pounds and could actually see my cheekbones and distinguish my eyes. But then, being human, I missed Grandmother's breakfasts. Moral of this story: People complain about what they have until they don't have it; then they miss it.

I never envisioned being a librarian because of the math. Dewey and the others still confuse me. I, in fact, which I say without bragging, will dial 411 all day long because I refuse to keep a phone book that I cannot use anyway. I've always made friends with librarians so that they didn't mind getting the books I needed or wanted. I simply am a firm believer that if you have incompetence in an area, you should turn to people who have expertise. Which brings me to museums.

As a Black woman I never visited a museum until I enrolled at Fisk in Nashville. Knoxville didn't have any that Black people seemed to visit; Cincinnati, our hometown, had them but we never seemed welcome. Both my sister and I are collectors. Though neither of us had articulated it until fairly recently, we now realize that we grew up in museums. Because the Black community had no public place to deposit our memories, the churches and Colored Schools, the Masonic and other lodges, but mostly the homes in which we and our playmates lived, were museums. The photographs of men and women in the armed services from the Civil War to the present; the framed letter saying great-great-grandfather was entitled to a pension for his service to the country; the books signed by Booker T. Washington, Langston Hughes, James Weldon Johnson, W.E.B. Du Bois; the piece of silver or crystal from "the plantation." The needlepoint chairs, pillows that were embroidered, handkerchiefs with delicate work, the quilts . . . oh, the beautiful quilts filled with gunnysacks, old army blankets, bags that once held one hundred pounds of flour or coffee beans, which weighted you down when you went to bed. The Black community is a living museum. This Christmas Gary fried chicken in Grandmother's iron skillets. Grandmother had inherited them from Grandpapa's family. Those things can't be purchased today. It takes a generation just to get them properly seasoned. And a lifetime of love to understand that they are.

Jewelle Gomez (1948–)

Much of Jewelle Gomez's work is motivated by her dedication to the place of lesbians in main-stream society. With a deep feminist commitment and an equal commitment to racial and cultural diversity, Gomez explores issues of lesbian identity, the complexities of same sex rela-tionships and communities, and relationships between gay populations and heterosexual mainstream society. Her portrayals of lesbian relationships are honest, sensitive, and very real. The characters in her fiction are fully alive and the images and moments she communicates through her poetry provide insight into the joy, pain, and endurance of lesbian living and lov-ing. She, like Audre Lorde, explores the position of "outsider," focusing on the complexity of female independence and community and blending political activism with poetic language.

Gomez was born September 11, 1948, in Boston, Massachusetts. When her parents sep-arated when she was two, Gomez lived with her paternal grandparents in Washington, DC, for six years before moving back to Boston where she lived with her maternal great-grand-mother, a retired textile laborer, until she was twenty-two. Though her family was not the tra-ditional nuclear family, Gomez was always surrounded by love and support. Her maternal grandmother and her father and stepmother lived nearby and she spent time with each of them. Spending most of her time with adults, Gomez was a precocious child and good student.

Gomez attended an all-girls public school in Boston in the wake of the Civil Rights movement. She received a full scholarship to Northeastern her first year. One of a small percentage of black students, Gomez joined students protesting the racial inequality on the campus. She graduated from Northeastern University in 1971 and continued her edu-cation at Columbia University School of Journalism as a Ford Foundation fellow, receiving a master's degree in 1973.

Gomez began her career in television while a student at Northeastern, working in production for station WGBH-TV, Boston, on "Say Brother" from 1968–1971. Working for WNET in New York City during the 1970s, Gomez contributed to the production of Chil-dren's Television Workshop.

Gomez began her literary career in the 1980s, publishing two collections of poetry, The Lipstick Papers (1980) and Flamingoes and Bears (1986). Inspired by Ntozake Shange's for colored girls ... (1977) and the Black Arts Movement, Gomez dedicated her-self to poetry, self-publishing The Lipstick Papers, a compilation of poems she wrote and revised throughout the 1970s. The voices in the poems are the voices that have been si-lenced or ignored in contemporary literature and history, like the voice of Assata Shakur, mother of a baby born in jail on Riker's Island. The personae of the poems in Flamingoes and Bears are more sexual and vibrant, and, certainly, a reflection of Gomez's growth and confidence as woman, lesbian, and writer. The allegorical marriages of flamingoes and bears signal resistance to society's judgment of lesbian couples.

While Gomez focused on poetry in the 1980s, she has broadened that focus to include both fiction and essay in the 1990s, publishing The Gilda Stories *(1991), her first novel; a collection of essays,* Forty-three Septembers *(1993); a third collection of poetry,* Oral Traditions *(1995); and, her most recent work, a collection of short fiction,* Don't Explain *(1998).*

Perhaps her most well-known work, The Gilda Stories *is experimental, a combination of history, romance, science fiction, and mystery. The title character, Gilda, is a vampire who, rather than Gothic, dark predator, is a healer and social activist. Taking blood for survival, Gilda and those like her search in the minds of their victims for a wound that needs healing, leaving an impression of peace and insight the victim will remember when he or she recovers. Still an outsider, Gilda is representative of those outside the mainstream in any community, too often vilified despite intention or true identity. Gilda and the vampires she interacts most meaningfully with are racially and ethnically diverse. Additionally, they are products of different historical contexts. The novel begins, for example, with Gilda's mortal life as a slave in 1850s Louisiana to her lives as immortal vampire in 1890s California, 1921 Missouri, 1955 Massachusetts, 1981 New York, and, finally, a futuristic 2002 New Hampshire.*

Gomez's most recent collection of fiction, Don't Explain, *also spans different historical contexts, including stories about lesbian survival from the homophobic and constraining 1950s forward. The title story "Don't Explain" features a lonely and isolated waitress, Letty, who finds community and acceptance in the home and lesbian community of a fellow waitress, bolder and younger Delia. The collection as a whole leans in the direction of the contemporary, but all of the stories center in the timeless complexities of human relationships. In this latest collection of fiction, Gomez also demonstrates her continued and daring willingness to openly communicate the lesbian erotic.*

A founding member of Gay and Lesbian Alliance against Defamation (GLAAD), a member of Feminist Anti-Censorship Taskforce (FACT), the board of advisors for the Cornell University Human Sexuality Archives, and the National Center for Lesbian Rights, Gomez's dedication to social involvement and action is obvious. She is a forceful public speaker, working her literary proficiency into the weave of her oratory.

As poet, novelist, short fiction writer, social activist, and teacher of creative writing, Gomez shines in each of her roles. She was the director of the Literature Program on the New York State Council on the Arts from 1989 to 1993, and a lecturer in Hunter College's departments of women's studies and English from 1989–90. Currently, she is serving as the Executive Director of San Francisco State's Poetry Center and Archives.

R. Joyce Lausch

Don't Explain

Boston 1959

Letty deposited the hot platters on the table effortlessly. She slid one deep-fried chicken, a club steak with boiled potatoes, and a fried porgy plate down her arm as if removing beaded bracelets. Each one landed with a solid clink on the shiny Formica in its appropriate place. The last barely settled before Letty turned back to the kitchen to get Savannah and Skip their lemonade and extra biscuits. Then to put her feet up. Out of the corner of her eye she saw Tip come in the lounge. His huge shoulders, draped in sharkskin, narrowly cleared the doorframe.

Damn! He's early tonight! she thought, but kept going. Tip was known for his extravagance; that's how he'd gotten his nickname. He always sat at Letty's station because they were both from Virginia, although neither had been back in years.

Letty had come up to Boston in 1946 and been waiting tables in the 411 Lounge since '52. She liked the casual community formed around it. The pimps were not big thinkers but good for a laugh; the musicians who played the small clubs around Boston often ate at the 411, providing some glamour—and now and then a jam session. The "business" girls were usually generous and always willing to embroider a wild story. After Letty's mother died there'd been no family to go back to down in Burkeville.

Letty took her newspaper from the locker behind the kitchen and filled a tall glass with the tart grape juice punch for which the cook, Henrietta, was famous.

"I'm going on break, Henrietta. Delia's takin' my station."

She sat in the back booth nearest the kitchen, beside the large blackboard which displayed the menu. When Delia came out of the bathroom, Letty hissed to get her attention. The reddish-brown of Delia's face was shiny with a country freshness that always made Letty feel a little shy.

"What's up, Miss Letty?" Her voice was soft and saucy.

"Take my tables for twenty minutes. Tip just came in."

The girl's already bright smile widened as she started to thank Letty.

"Go 'head, go 'head. He don't like to wait. You can thank me if he don't run you back and forth fifty times."

Delia hurried away as Letty sank into the coolness of the overstuffed booth and removed her shoes. After a few sips of her punch she rested her head on the back of the seat with her eyes closed. The sounds around her were as familiar as her own breathing: squeaking Red Cross shoes as Delia and Vinnie passed, the click of high heels around the bar, the clatter of dishes in the kitchen, and ice cascading into glasses. The din of conversation rose, leveled, and rose again over the jukebox. Letty had not played her record in days, but the words spun around in her head as if they were on a turntable:

> *Right or wrong don't matter*
> *When you're with me sweet*
> *Hush now, don't explain*
> *You're my joy and pain.*

Letty sipped her cool drink; sweat ran down her spine, soaking into the nylon uniform. July weather promised to give no breaks, and fans were working overtime like everybody else.

She saw Delia cross to Tip's table again. In spite of the dyed red hair, no matter how you looked at her, Delia was still a country girl. Long, self-conscious, shy—she was bold only because she didn't know any better. She'd moved up from Anniston with her cousin a year before and landed the job at the 411 immediately. She was full of fun, but that didn't get in the way of her working hard. Sometimes she and Letty shared a cab going uptown after work, when Delia's cousin didn't pick them up in her green Pontiac.

Letty caught Tip eyeing Delia as she strode on tight-muscled legs back to the kitchen. That lounge lizard! Letty thought to herself. Letty had trained Delia how to balance plates, how to make tips, and how to keep the customer's hands on the table. She was certain Delia would have no problem putting Tip in his place. In the year she'd been working at the 411, Delia hadn't gone out with any of the bar flies, though plenty had asked. Letty figured that Delia and her cousin must run with a different crowd. They talked to each other sporadically in the kitchen or during their break, but Letty never felt that wire across her chest like Delia was going to ask her something she couldn't answer.

She closed her eyes again for the few remaining minutes. The song was back in her head, and Letty had to squeeze her lips together to keep from humming aloud. She pushed her thoughts onto something else. But when she did she always stumbled upon Maxine. Letty opened her eyes. When she'd quit working at Salmagundi's and come to the 411 she'd promised herself never to think about any woman like that again. She didn't know why missing Billie so much brought it all back to her.

She heard the bartender, Duke, shout a greeting from behind the bar to the owner as he walked in. Aristotle's glance skimmed his dimly lit domain before he made his way to his stool, the only one at the bar with a back. That was Letty's signal. No matter that it was her break: she knew white people didn't like to see their employees sitting down, especially with their shoes off. By the time he was settled near the door, Letty was up, her glass in hand, and on her way through the kitchen's noisy swinging door.

"You finished your break already?" Delia asked.

"Ari just come in."

"Uh oh, let me git this steak out there. Boy, he sure is nosy!"

"Who, Tip?"

"Yeah. He ask me where I live, who I live with, where I come from, like he supposed to know me!"

"Well, just don't take nothing he say to heart and you'll be fine. And don't take no rides from him!"

"Yeah. He asked if he could take me home after I get off. I told him me and you had something to do." Letty was silent as she sliced the fresh bread and stacked it on plates for the next orders.

"My cousin's coming by, so it ain't a lie, really. She can ride us."

"Yeah," Letty said as Delia giggled and turned away with her platter.

Vinnie burst through the door like she always did, breathless and bossy. "Ari up there, girl! You better get back on station."

Letty drained her glass with deliberation, wiped her hands on her thickly starched white apron, and walked casually past Vinnie as if she'd never spoken. She heard Henrietta's soft chuckle float behind her. She went over to Tip, who was digging into the steak like his life depended on devouring it before the plate got dirty.

"Everything all right tonight?" Letty asked, her ample brown body towering over the table.

"Yeah, baby, it's all right. You ain't working this side no more?"

"I was on break. My feet can't wait for your stomach, you know."

Tip laughed. "*Break.* What you need a break for, big and healthy as you is!"

"We all get old, Tip. But the feet get old first, let me tell you that!"

"Not in my business, baby. Why you don't come on and work for me and you ain't got to worry 'bout your feet."

Letty sucked her teeth loudly, the exaggeration a part of the game they'd played over the years. "Man, I'm too old for that mess!"

"You ain't too old for me."

"Ain't nobody too old for *you*. Or too young, neither, looks like."

"Where you and that gal goin' tonight?"

"To a funeral," Letty responded dryly.

"Aw, woman, get on away from my food!" The gold cap on his front tooth gleamed from behind his greasy lips when he laughed. Letty was pleased. Besides giving away money, Tip liked to hurt people. It was better when he laughed.

The kitchen closed at 11:00. Delia and Letty slipped off their uniforms in the tiny bathroom and were on their way out the door by 11:15. Delia looked even younger in her knife-pleated skirt and white cotton blouse. Letty felt old in her slacks and long-sleeved shirt as she stood on Columbus Avenue in front of the neon 411 sign. The movement of car headlights played across her face, which was set in exhaustion. The dark green car pulled up and they got in quietly, both anticipating Sunday, the last night of their work week.

Delia's cousin was a stocky woman who looked about thirty-five, Letty's age. She never spoke much. Not that she wasn't friendly. She always greeted Letty with a smile and laughed at Delia's stories about the customers. Just close to the chest like me, that's all, Letty often thought. As they pulled up to the corner of Cunard Street, Letty opened the rear door. Delia turned to her and said, "I'm sorry you don't play your record on break no more, Miss Letty. I know you don't want to, but I'm sorry just the same."

Delia's cousin looked back at them with a puzzled expression but said nothing. Letty said goodnight, shut the car door, and turned to climb the short flight of stairs to her apartment. Cunard Street was quiet outside her window, and for once the guy upstairs wasn't blasting his record player. After her bath, Letty lay awake and restless in her bed. The electric fan was pointed at the ceiling, bouncing warm air over her, rustling her sheer nightgown.

Inevitably the strains of Billie Holiday's songs brushed against her, much like the breeze that moved around her. She felt silly when she thought about it, but the melody gripped her like a solid presence. It was more than the music. Billie was her hero. Letty saw Billie as big, like herself, with big hungers and a hard secret she couldn't tell anyone. Two weeks before, when Letty had heard that Lady was dead, sorrow had enveloped her. A door had closed that she could not consciously identify to herself or to anyone. It embarrassed her to think about. Like it did when she remembered how she'd felt about Maxine.

Letty had met Billie soon after she started working at the 411 when the singer had stopped in the club with several musicians on their way back from the Jazz Festival. There the audience, curious to see what a real, live junkie looked like, had sat back waiting for Billie to fall on her face. Instead she'd killed them dead with her liquid voice and rough urgency. Still, in the bar, the young, thin horn player had continued to reassure her: "Billie, you were the show, the whole show!"

Soon the cloud of insecurity receded from her face and it lit up with a center-stage smile. Once convinced, Billie became the show again, loud and commanding. She demanded her food be served up front, at the bar, and sent Henrietta, who insisted on waiting on her personally, back to the kitchen fifteen times. Billie laughed at jokes that Letty could barely hear as she bustled back and forth between the abandoned kitchen and her own tables. The sound of that laugh from the bar penetrated her bones. She'd watched and listened, certain she saw something no one else did. Vulnerability was held at bay, and behind that, a hunger even bigger than the one for food or heroin. Letty found reasons to walk up to the front—to use the telephone, to order a drink she paid for and left in the kitchen—just to catch the scent of her, the scent of sweat and silk emanating from her.

"Hey, baby," Billie said when Letty reached past her to pick up her drink from Duke.

"Henny sure can cook, can't she," Letty responded, hoping to see into Billie's eyes.

"Cook? She in these pots, sister!" the horn player shouted from down the bar, sitting behind his own heaping plateful of food.

Billie laughed, holding a big white napkin in front of her mouth, her eyes watering. Letty enjoyed the sound even though she still sensed something deeper, unreachable.

When Billie finished eating and gathered her entourage to get back on the road, she left a tip, not just for Henrietta but for each of the waitresses and the bartender. Generous just like the "business" girls, Letty was happy to note. She still had the two one-dollar bills in an envelope at the back of her lingerie drawer.

After that, Letty felt even closer to Billie. She played one of the few Lady Day records on the jukebox every night during her break. Everyone at the 411 had learned not to bother her when her song came on. Letty realized, as she lay waiting for sleep, that she'd always felt if she had been able to say or do something that night to make friends with Billie, it might all have been different. The faces of Billie, her former lover Maxine, and Delia blended in her mind in half-sleep. Letty slid her hand along the soft nylon of her gown to rest it between her full thighs. She pressed firmly, as if holding desire inside herself. Letty could have loved her enough to make it better.

Sunday nights at the 411 were generally quiet. Even the pimps and prostitutes used it as a day of rest. Letty came in early to have a drink at the bar and talk with Duke before going to the back to change into her uniform. She saw Delia through the window as the younger woman stepped out of the green Pontiac, looking as if she'd just come from Concord Baptist Church. "Satin Doll" played on the jukebox, wrapping the bar in mellow nostalgia for the Sunday dinners they'd serve.

Aristotle let Henrietta close the kitchen early on Sunday, and Letty looked forward to getting done by 9:30 or 10:00 and maybe enjoying some of the evening. When her break time came, she started for the jukebox automatically. She hadn't played anything by Billie in two weeks. Now, looking down at the inviting glare, she knew she still couldn't do it. She punched the buttons that would bring up Jackie Wilson's "Lonely Teardrops" and went to the back booth.

She'd almost dropped off to sleep when she heard Delia whisper her name. Letty opened her eyes and looked up into the girl's smiling face. Her head was haloed in tight, shiny curls.

"Miss Letty, won't you come home with me tonight?"

"What?"

"I'm sorry to bother you, but your break time almost up. I wanted to ask if you'd come over to the house tonight . . . after work. My cousin'll bring you back home after."

Letty didn't speak. Her puzzled look prompted Delia to start again.

"Sometime on Sunday my cousin's friends from work come over to play cards, listen to music, you know. Nothin' special, just some of the girls from the office building down on Winter Street where she work, cleaning. She, I mean we, thought you might want to come over tonight. Have a drink, play some cards—"

"I don't play cards much."

"Well, not everybody play cards . . . just talk . . . sitting around talking. My cousin said you might like to for a change."

Letty wasn't sure she liked the last part—*for a change*—as if they had to entertain an old aunt.

"I really want you to come, Letty. They always her friends, but none of them is my own friends. They all right, I don't mean nothin' against them, but it would be fun to have my own personal friend there, you know?"

Delia was a good girl. Perfect words to describe her, Letty thought, smiling. "Sure, honey. I'd just as soon spend my time with you as lose my money with some fools."

By ten o'clock the kitchen was clean. Once they'd changed out of their uniforms and were out on the street Delia apologized that they had to take a cab uptown. She explained that her cousin and her friends didn't work on Sunday so they were already at home. Letty almost declined, tempted to go home. But she didn't. She stepped into the street and waved down a Red and White cab with brisk, urban efficiency. All the way uptown Delia explained that the evening wasn't a big deal and cautioned Letty not to expect much. "Just a few friends, hanging around, drinking and talking." She was jumpy, and Letty tried to put her at ease. She had not expected her visit would make Delia so anxious.

The apartment was located halfway up Blue Hill Avenue in an area where a few blacks had recently been permitted to rent. They entered a long, carpeted hallway and heard the sounds of laughter and music ringing from the rooms at the far end.

Inside, with the door closed, Delia shed her nervousness. This was clearly her home turf, and Letty couldn't believe she ever really needed an ally to back her up. Delia stepped out of her shoes at the door and walked to the back with her same long-legged gait. They passed a closed door, which Letty assumed to be one of the bedrooms, then came to a kitchen ablaze with light. Food and bottles were strewn across the blue-flecked table top. A counter opened from the kitchen into the dining room, which was the center of activity. Around a large mahogany table sat five women in smoke-filled concentration, playing poker.

Delia's cousin looked up from her cards with the same slight smile she displayed when she picked them up at work. Here it seemed welcoming, not guarded as it did in those brief moments in her car. She wore brown slacks and a matching sweater. The pink, starched points of her shirt collar peeked out at the neck.

Delia crossed to her and kissed her cheek lightly. Letty looked around the table to see if she recognized anyone. The women all seemed familiar in the way that city neighbors can, but Letty was sure she hadn't met any of them before. Delia introduced them, and each acknowledged Letty without diverting her attention from her cards: Karen, a short, round woman with West Indian bangles almost up to her elbow; Betty, who stared intently at her cards through thick eyeglasses encased in blue cat's-eye frames; Irene, a big, dark woman with long black hair and a gold tooth in front. Beside her sat Myrtle, who was wearing army fatigues and a gold Masonic ring on her pinkie finger. She said hello in the softest voice Letty had ever heard. Hovering over her was Clara, a large redbone woman whose hair was bound tightly in a bun at the nape of her neck. She spoke with a delectable Southern accent that drawled her "How're you doin'" into a full paragraph draped around an inquisitive smile.

Letty felt Delia tense again. Then she pulled Letty by the arm toward the French doors behind the players. There was a small den with a desk, some books, and a television set. Through the second set of glass doors was a living room. At the record player was an extremely tall, brown-skinned woman. She bent over the wooden cabinet searching for the next selection, oblivious to the rest of the gathering. Two women sat on the divan in deep conversation punctuated with constrained laughter.

"Maryalice, Sheila, Dolores . . . this is Letty. She work with me at the 411."

They looked up at her quickly, smiled, then went back to their preoccupations. Two of them resumed their whispered conversation; the other returned to the record collection. Delia directed Letty back toward the foyer and the kitchen.

"Come on, let me get you a drink. You know, I don't even know what you drink!"

"Delia?" Her cousin's voice reached them over the counter, just as they stepped into the kitchen. "Bring a couple of beers back when you come, okay?"

"Sure, babe." Delia went to the refrigerator and pulled out two bottles. "Let me just take these in. I'll be right back."

"Go 'head, I can take care of myself in this department, girl." Letty surveyed the array of bottles on the table. Delia went to the dining room and Letty mixed a Scotch and soda. She poured slowly as the reality settled on her. These women were friends, perhaps lovers, like she and Maxine had been. The name she'd heard for women like these burst inside her head: *bulldagger*. Letty flinched, angry she had let it in, angry that it frightened her. "Ptuh!" She blew through her teeth as if spitting the word back at the air.

She did know these women, Letty thought, as she stood at the counter looking out at the poker game. They were oblivious to her, except for Terry. Letty finally remembered that that was Delia's cousin's name.

As Letty took her first sip, Terry called over to her, "We gonna be finished with this hand in a minute, Letty, then we can talk." This time her face was filled by a large grin.

"Take your time," Letty said. She went out through the foyer door and around to the living room. She walked slowly on the carpet and adjusted her eyes to the light, which was a bit softer. The tall woman, Maryalice, had just put a record on the turntable and sat down on a love seat across from the other two women. Letty stood in the doorway a moment before the tune began:

> *Hush now, don't explain*
> *Just say you'll return*
> *I'm glad you're back*
> *Don't explain . . .*

Letty was stunned. She realized the song sounded different among these women: Billie sang just to them. Letty watched Maryalice sitting with her long legs stretched out tensely in front of her. She was wrapped in her own thoughts, her eyes closed. She appeared curiously disconnected after what had clearly been a long search for this record. Letty watched her face as she swallowed several times. Then Letty sat beside her. They listened to the music while the other two women spoke in low voices.

Maryalice didn't move when the song was over.

"I met her once," Letty said.

"I beg your pardon?"

"Kinda met her. At the 411 Lounge where me and Delia work."

"Naw!" Maryalice said as she sat up.

"She was just coming back from a gig."

"Honestly?" Maryalice's voice caught with excitement.

"She just had dinner—smothered chicken, potato salad, green beans, side of stewed tomatoes, and an extra side of cornbread."

"Big eater."

"Child, everybody is when Henrietta's cooking. Billie was...," Letty searched for the words, "she was sort of stubborn."

Maryalice laughed. "You know, that's kinda how I pictured her."

"I figure she had to be stubborn to keep going," Letty said. "And not stingy, either!"

"Yeah," Maryalice said, enjoying the confirmation of her image of Billie.

Letty rose from the sofa and went to the record player. Delia stood tentatively watching from the doorway of the living room. Letty picked up the arm of the phonograph and replaced it at the beginning of the record. Letty noticed the drops of moisture on Maryalice's lashes, but she relaxed as Letty settled onto the seat beside her. They listened to Billie together, for the first time.

hattie gossett (1942–)

hattie gossett is a writer, playwright, performance poet, activist, and educator who lives in New York City. Her work has been published in numerous anthologies and in a prose-poetry collection Presenting . . . Sister No Blues in 1988. Currently she is a contributing writer for Essence magazine.

In "old woman," gossett captures the orality of voice that she is characteristic for. The old woman in this poem is a careful watcher and is keen on naming wrongdoing; the lines of her voice capture the disdain, which gossett as a writer achieves through her use of repetition and repeated line breaks, adding emphasis but also harshness. This orality is key in gossett's poetry, because, like Jayne Cortez or Sonia Sanchez, her work is intended not only to be read aloud, but also for performance, and the oral quality lends the necessary expressiveness.

In "a night at the fantasy factory," gossett uses orality over a longer poem, capturing the narrative of a young woman who has just gotten a job as a waitress. The poem begins with this woman's conversation with her girlfriend, which gossett only presents half of, yet her presentation is so well done that we can anticipate the responses on the other end and are literally eavesdropping on a conversation between two women. Again, line breaks and short lines add tone and emphasis here, but gossett also uses careful diction. Through the conversation, gossett paints a picture of urban desperation and violence, of poverty, but she also leaves the characters with some agency—one can hear the hope in the woman's voice that even as the job does not pay much, it will help her make (she hopes) ends meet without being too much trouble.

That gossett uses orality not just for its palpable quality but also to tell a narrative and paint a vivid picture of urban life is part of the achievement in this poem. Her subject touches on many aspects of the life in the city, even criticizing people like her who have "made it" and who have seemingly forgotten their connection to their home neighborhoods. The other skillful aspect of this poem is how precisely it chronicles the waitress' experience, moving from the telephone conversation to "setting up" for work. At this point, a narrator is introduced, who keeps a keen eye on the subject, and speaks almost as if subject and narrator are one. gossett again switches voices and perspective with the two short interchanges titled "butter #1" and "butter #2," which are dialogue sequences between the waitress and the cook. These two narrative moments further indicate the desperate and difficult quality of this urban life—the cook's conservation of butter for economic reasons, and the waitress' unenviable position of standing between two groups who dictate, on some level, her success in the job: the cook and the customer.

These poetic pieces use unconventional form but are insightful and well-designed portraits of an urban situation. gossett uses orality to not only represent vocal qualities, but also to enhance the images her poems foreground.

In "world view, world view, world view," gossett makes an explicit political comment on the position of poor women of color, arguably the women she has been writing about in the other poems, and their position in the world. Similar to claims by other Black women theorists, gossett argues that the Black woman's subjugated position is an important reference point for understanding the violence of the world, but also for gauging human potential. In spite of their marginalized positions, Black women hold up the whole world, she argues, harkening to the roles Black women have played in raising all children, providing labor, and building bridges between disparate communities. The political characteristic of her poetry resonates with Audre Lorde's suggestion (made in a poem) that "poetry is not a luxury." In fact, poetry is a necessary forum for those who are marginalized to speak about pain and oppression, and to engage their human agency. gossett's poems—in their edginess and grit, but also in the use of orality and performative techniques—are quintessential examples of the political voice of contemporary Black women's poetry.

Kevin Everod Quashie

old woman

you people look the other way too much
you act like you dont see
you know you see them slippin under that turnstile
lookin the other way
well god sees
yes he sees
and he keeps the record
and one day
yes one day
soon too
he will show you the record
and you will be sorry
actin like you dont see
well not me
i am a witness for my god
i see!
i see you!
i see!

a night at the fantasy factory
foxes! food! fun!
dining room 4p.m. till closing/thursday disco

YEAH I GOT THE JOB

yeah girl i got the waitress job
it dont pay much but it is off the books so i guess between this and
    unemployment i can make it
plus the bar is only 2blocks away which means i can walk back
    and forth
and i get to eat for free so i guess its okay
except
well the boss tried to get me to wear hot pants
yeah girl can you imagine
and when i went last night to work for the first time he told me
    he didn't like my headrag
you know i was hot
who the fuck does he think he is
but i need this job so i tried to be cool
i told the dude—no not the owner—i dont deal with him—the cook
    is my boss
hes the one giving orders about hot pants and headrags
anyway i smiled real big and made my voice real low and told him
    my stuff is strong enuff to shine through the most concealing
    outfit
yeah he went for it
but what i really wanted to tell him is that he aint paying me enuff
    money to have me work and take off my clothes too
no no i didnt say that
but i sure was thinking it
then when he cracked about the headrag i told him it is made out
    of expensive imported material (you know theyre always
    impressed when you talk about how much something costs)
    which matches my outfit and that i only wear it when my hair
    doesnt look right same way other women wear wigs
whatd he say?
well i dont think he dug it too tuff but he just mumbled and went
    on frying chicken and broiling steaks
whatd you say
he sounds like a drag?
hmmmmmmmmmmph!
girl you aint said nothing

well this too will eventually pass
what is it like being there
well its not too bad
red and white leather
red carpeting
scrupulously clean bathrooms
none of that ruff stuff in here honey
i guess you could call it a halfassed highclass sepiatone cops and
    robbers bar
middleage middlelevel detectives dopedealers numbers bankers
   civil servants doctors lawyers gambling den and after hours
    spot proprietors show biz types athletes plus some transit workers
    and other blue collar types who like the bigtime spenders
    atmosphere
few independent women here
mostly women looking for husbands/sugar daddies
willing to smile and be patted
in the dining room everyone is licking their chops over lobster steak
   shrimp
at the bar theyre drinking strictly topshelf
they strut and posture round the bar—their playground—like reject
   paper cutouts from *gentlemens quarterly* or *playboy*
sipping johnny walker red/chivas regal they can forget they came
   from backwater georgia or deadend street new york
they can believe that they have gone over to the other side
they can believe that when cops are lining us up against the wall
   the next time they will merely have to flash their gold
   american express cards and be waved on to safety
shame they dont read or i would recommend john williams *the man
   who cried i am* or fanon on the native elite
and on top of that theyre cheappppp!
they act like they dont know nothing about leaving 15% or 20%
   of the bill as a tip for me though when they downtown in white
   places they go outta their way to leave great big tips
but in harlem they can spend 30 or 40dollars and then they act
   like they doin you a big favor when they only leave a dollar or
   2 for a tip
when i am not busy which happens more often that i would like
   i sit in the corner and read or write
or just stare into space

world view
world view
world view

theres more poor than nonpoor
theres more colored than noncolored
theres more women than men

    all over the world the poor woman of color is the mainstay
        of the little daddy centered family which is the bottom-
        line of big daddys industrial civilization

    when she gets off her knees and stands up straight the whole
        thing can/will collapse

    have you noticed that even now she is flexing her shoulder
        muscles and strengthening her thigh and leg muscles?

    and her spine is learning to stretch out long her brain and
        heart are pumping new energy already you can see the
        load cracking at the center as she pushes it off her

she is holding up the whole world
what you gonna do?
you cant stop her
you gonna just stand there and watch her with your mouth open?
or are you gonna try to get down?
you cant stop her
she is holding up the whole world

setting up

while the late afternoon beersippers bet on the last figure of the
    daytrack singleaction the waitress turns on the lights shakes
    out the tablecloths and wipes the placemats
she lays down the tablecloths so last nights greasespots dont show
    and uses the placemats to cover the stubborn spots that wont
    be hidden
folded napkin and fork on the left
knife and spoon on the right
waterglass mouthdown at tip of knife
on each table ketchup hot sauce steak sauce salt&pepper (make

sure containers are full) ashtray and candle
pitchers of ice water menus blank checks pencils corkscrew winelist
    at the waitress station
by the time the figure comes out and the folks who work down-
    town start drifting in for their first drinks of the evening the
    waitress is cutting squares of butter making 2 big plastic bags
    of salad lining the breadbaskets with papernapkins filling up
    the saladdressing containers getting wineglasses from the bar
then in the bathroom applying makeup while smoking a joint
a party of 5 enters
right this way please gentlemen right this way

butter #1

only 1piece of butter a customer

okay what if someone asks for more

let me know   i will decide   dont give nobody no extra nothin
    lessen i tells you

butter #2

the customer wants sour cream *and* butter on his baked

whats he gittin

fried breast

shit! hes only spendin 3dollars and he wants a million dollars worth
    of extras—betcha he wants more salad dressing too

Michael S. Harper (1938–)

Michael S. Harper is most well known for writing about Blackness as part of American identity. Writing Black history into American history and contemporary life, speaking both to a majority and Black audience, and his refusal to separate his Black identity from his American identity have made him a somewhat controversial poet. Harper believes in documenting American experience with its history of injustices, and he explores the dual consciousness of being Black in the United States, mediating racist history and present realities. His distinctive voice bridges and links personal, racial, and historical past with complexity as he asserts that the African American and "American" traditions are not mutually exclusive. As a narrative poet, Harper includes and links Black idioms, literature, and traditions with American landscapes, institutions, and syntax.

Harper is also recognized for his incorporation of jazz themes and methods into his poetry. Jazz is the greatest influence on his style. He notes jazz greats like Charlie Parker and John Coltrane not only as worthy subjects within his poetry, but as artists who have most influenced his understanding of poetry and style. Harper writes with the ear in mind, focusing on sound and rhythm. His poems are meant to be read aloud or even sung. Blues refrains and the strategies of enjambment, idioms, irregular repetition, and varied line lengths make his poetry musical, while concrete images ground his complex philosophy of poetry's musicality and purpose. He believes that poetry, like jazz, requires a level of mastery before improvisation. Jazz modality as it works its way into his poetry is about unity, undoing the Cartesian binaries between African American and American, history and myth, past and present, individual and group.

Michael Harper celebrates artistic ancestry and creativity as healing forces not only in the jazz tradition, but also in the literary tradition, honoring writers like Ralph Ellison and Robert Hayden within his poetry and often reciting poems by these writers. He also venerates African American heroes from all walks of life, portraying them as vital mythic figures and integrating the power of myth and history with contemporary and historical African American figures whose stories have not been given such power.

Many of Harper's poems are personal poems of beauty and pain, especially those dealing with the deaths of his sons. His poetry is rich with both tradition and personal triumph. His poems sing with jazz undertone and rhythm as he expresses his views of Black American history and identity.

This complex and acclaimed poet, Michael S. Harper, was born in Brooklyn, New York, on March 18, 1938. Delivered by his grandfather who was a doctor to a father who was a postal worker and a mother who worked as a medical stenographer, Harper at one time thought about becoming a doctor to carry on the tradition of medicine in the family. He was discouraged from that goal, however, through the racism of educators both in secondary school and college who told him he should set his professional sights lower.

Harper's parents were economically stable enough to move the family to predominantly White West Los Angeles when Harper was thirteen. He stayed in the Los Angeles area to pursue his education, attending Los Angeles State College from 1956–1961 to earn both his B.A. and M.A. While a student, Harper worked in the postal system like his father and saw the racism that kept well-educated African American people in positions below their qualifications. He determined he would not be one of them.

In 1961, Harper started study at the prestigious Iowa Writers' Workshop at the University of Iowa. The only African American in his fiction and poetry classes, his sense of double consciousness, which would become a part of much of his published poetry, intensified. After earning his M.F.A. degree in 1963, Harper taught at various colleges along the West Coast as he continued to write and submit poems for publication.

Michael Harper's first collection of poetry, Dear John, Dear Coltrane, was published in 1970. A nomination for a National Book Award immediately distinguished him. This first collection was a compilation of ten years of work. While John Coltrane was the inspiration, he is not the central subject of the collection. The collection revolves around a theme of redemption. The isolation of the Black musician stands as metaphor for the African American experience. Establishing continuing themes of kinship, geography, and history, Harper centered his personal and family experience to engage the universal theme of self assertion and transcendence.

Harper published six more collections of poetry in the short timeframe of the next seven years. History Is Your Own Heartbeat (1971) links history and myth to personal experience, reclaiming the past in order to understand the relationships between self and history, past and present, and one person to all people. Photographs: Negatives: History as Apple Tree (1972) focuses on the multiple meanings of development and centers in part on his Chippewa great-grandmother's history and the way Native American history is part of American history. Song: I Want a Witness (1972) centers the Black religious tradition as metaphor for sermonlike and urgent exhortation for interdependent members of an American society to recognize abuses and change. Debridement (1973) is dedicated to two dead children and three living, with its military term title that means the cutting away of dead flesh to save the living. Nightmare Begins Responsibility (1975) boasts a wide variety and range of action, stark landscapes, and a commitment to writing as responsibility toward healing an American nightmare perpetuated by society's lack of commitment to interdependent relationships. Images of Kin (1977), which is primarily a collection of his earlier work in reverse chronological order, was Harper's second book nominated for a National Book Award.

Harper has published at a slower pace in the 1980s and 1990s, producing three more collections of poetry. Rhode Island: Eight Poems (1980) is not a major work but continues Harper's tradition of strong images. Healing Song for the Inner Ear (1984) focuses on Harper's personal history and heroes, but extends that focus to a more international scope. Honorable Amendments (1995), his most recent collection, provides a contemporary view of American culture and race.

In addition to his work and production as a poet, Michael Harper also edited an anthology of the poetry of one of his heroes, the Collected Poems of Sterling A. Brown, published in 1980. He also co-edited Every Shut Eye Ain't Asleep: An Anthology of Poetry by African Americans Since 1945 (1994) with Andrew Walton.

Harper has been a professor at Brown since 1970. He served as the director of the Creative Writing program from 1974 to 1983, seeing Gayl Jones, Sherley Anne Williams, and Melvin Dixon progress through the ranks to become successful writers.

R. Joyce Lausch

Eve (Rachel)

*'What has gone into that quality of voice, that distancing, that precise knowledge of
who she is, where she has come from, what costs have been to herself, but also to others,
the ones who did not survive.'*

*'the rib is but the unseen potential aspect of self, free of fleshly desire, waiting to be dis-
covered, to be named beyond definition, a conjugation of names in deeds.'*

I have been waiting to speak to you
for many years; one evening
I sat down to tell the story
of your mother's song of *Fante,*
"The Dance of the Elephants"
on the lips of her parents
escaping in disguise.
From the ribbed podium I have waited
for you to join my own daughter,
Rachel, in the arena of surrender,
where women bathe the wounds
in our dark human struggle to be human:
this must be earned in deeds.

There are blessings to remember:
your magical birth on the third
anniversary of your parents' wedding.
I was there among the family faces
strung on violin and cello,
your Irish grandmother's song of the bogs,
your hidden grandfather's raging at your loveliness,
at his own daughters swimming amidst swans.

I talk of you to your parents over these distancings,
our voices rising over gray Portland skies,
the lush green of your eyes
shuttered in springtime;
you can not be otherwise than your grandmothers'
healing songs sprouting through you,
a tree in essential bloom in standing water.

To be here in America?
Ask this of the word many times:
in your parents' books underlined in green,
in dark blotches of your life-giving womb,

in these riddles beckoning—
'old folk songs chanted underneath the stars,'
in the cadence of black speech:
'just like a tree; backwater, muddy water,'
in gentle eyes of these writers of kinship,
in the circle of light which is Little Crow,
skinned and diced folksaying his splintered story,
comforts in small utterances, remember,
Eve means rescue from bodily desire.

Our last welcome
is the love of liars
in tall tales to larger truths;
succor these voices in your blood
listening for doubletalk, stoicism, irony
where your heart-center funnels its loam,
where you will plant your own crafted shoes
in these bodies of soiled, broken, mending hands.

Healing Song

He stoops down eating sunflowers
snowballed at his prayer-rugged
table, 'message/solution/masses'
his ghetto-blues-plantation,
driven into inner/outer realities
as buffers drawn from his eyes.

Penned in that magnificent voice
where *victorola* mutters 'Koppin' songs,
his sedge burning night-trains,
this serape-man found wanting
only in that 'God Don't Like Ugly'
phrase; he draws his own lightning,
believing differently,
an angel surrendering angles of desire:
his masked heart-centered soul reveals.

Rused in dance steps of jubilo,
atavisms of worship shutting out sound,

his full essential flowering
balances in the 4 a.m. traduction,
his Emancipation Tree.

Hidden in ancient tetters
of autobiography,
he tropes of 1863 *moverings,*
his Osceolas already sacrificed
as Lincoln's mass production lines
funnel bodies to the Crater;
his Easter families agonize
at blue doors of transformation.

Self-accused in venial sins, his gorgeous
offerings lift blind pigs to Bessie's
witchdoctoring, her blue-black tongue
singing down Jesus,
'watch your goin' be like comin' back,'
he witnesses flesh pull down in anger,
killing calves of hunger to no higher law.

Ragboned Bob Hayden, shingled in slime,
reaches for his cereus ladder of midnight flight,
his seismographic heartbeats
sphinctered in rhiney polygraphs of light;
Dee-troit born and half-blind
in diction of arena and paradise,
his ambient nightmare-dreams streak his tongue;
mementos of his mother, of Erma, he image-makes
peopling the human family of God's mirror,
mingling realities, this creature of transcendence
a love-filled shadow, congealed and clarified.

Nightmare Begins Responsibility

I place these numbed wrists to the pane
watching white uniforms whisk over
him in the tube-kept
prison
fear what they will do in experiment

watch my gloved stickshifting gasolined hands
breathe *boxcar-information-please* infirmary tubes
distrusting white-pink mending paperthin
silkened end hairs, distrusting tubes
shrunk in his *trunk-skincapped*
shaven head, in thighs
distrusting-white-hands-picking-baboon-light
on this son who will not make his second night
of this wardstrewn intensive airpocket
where his father's asthmatic
hymns of *night-train,* train done gone
his mother can only know that he has flown
up into essential calm unseen corridor
going boxscarred home, *mamaborn, sweetsonchild*
gonedowntown into *researchtestingwarehousebatteryacid*
mama-son-done-gone/me telling her 'nother
train tonight, no music, no breathstroked
heartbeat in my infinite distrust of them:

and of my distrusting self
white-doctor-who-breathed-for-him-all-night
say it for two sons gone,
say nightmare, say it loud
panebreaking heartmadness:
nightmare begins responsibility.

The Meaning of Protest

> *Between the world and me*
> a black boy is a native
> son with a long dream
> if a white man will listen.
> Uncle Tom's children
> were eight men, all outsiders,
> fish bellies living
> underground.

> Pagan Spain taught us the church
> was woman as mystery, a penis
> the sword to butcher each other;

Black Power! we're not going
to the moon, and in Bandung
white man can't come,
he's on a savage holiday.

Blossoms in a peanut field
won't bring me home;
something in the hum
of cotton is a glue
that won't hold red soil still;
twelve million voices spliced
on an iron cross
between the world, and me, and you.

Song: *I Want a Witness*

Blacks in frame houses
call to the helicopters,
their antlered arms
spinning; jeeps pad
these glass-studded streets;
on this hill are tanks painted gold.

Our children sing
spirituals of *Motown,*
idioms these streets suckled
on a southern road.
This scene is about power,
terror, producing
love and pain and pathology;
in an army of white dust,
blacks here to *testify*
and *testify,* and *testify,*
and *redeem,* and *redeem,*
in black smoke coming,
as they wave their arms,
as they wave their tongues.

History as Apple Tree

Cocumscussoc is my village,
the western arm of Narragansett
Bay; Canonicus chief sachem;
black men escape into his tribe.

How does patent not breed heresy?
Williams came to my chief
for his tract of land,
hunted by mad Puritans,
founded Providence Plantation;
Seekonk where he lost
first harvest, building, plant,
then the bay from these natives:
he set up trade.
With Winthrop he bought
an island, *Prudence;*
two other, *Hope* and *Patience*
he named, though small.
His trading post at the cove;
Smith's at another close by.
We walk the Pequot trail
as artery or spring.

Wampanoags, Cowesets,
Nipmucks, Niantics,
came by canoe for the games;
matted bats, a goal line,
a deerskin filled with moss:
lacrosse. They danced;
we are told they gambled their souls.

In your apple orchard
legend conjures Williams' name;
he was an apple tree.
Buried on his own lot
off Benefit Street
a giant apple tree grew;
two hundred years later,
when the grave was opened,
dust and root grew
in his human skeleton:
bones became apple tree.

As black man I steal away
in the night to the apple tree,
place my arm in the rich grave,
black sachem on a family plot,
take up a chunk of apple root,
let it become my skeleton,
become my own myth:
my arm the historical branch,
my name the bruised fruit,
black human photograph: apple tree.

Here Where Coltrane Is

Soul and race
are private dominions,
memories and modal
songs, a tenor blossoming,
which would paint suffering
a clear color but is not in
this Victorian house
without oil in zero degree
weather and a forty-mile-an-hour wind;
it is all a well-knit family:
a love supreme.
Oak leaves pile up on walkway
and steps, catholic as apples
in a special mist of clear white
children who love my children.
I play "Alabama"
on a warped record player
skipping the scratches
on your faces over the fibrous
conical hairs of plastic
under the wooden floors.

Dreaming on a train from New York
to Philly, you hand out six
notes which become an anthem
to our memories of you:
oak, birch, maple,

apple, cocoa, rubber.
For this reason Martin is dead;
for this reason Malcolm is dead;
for this reason Coltrane is dead;
in the eyes of my first son are the browns
of these men and their music.

Brother John

Black man:
I'm a black man;
I'm black; I am—
A black man; black—
I'm a black man;
I'm a black man;
I'm a man; black—
I am—

Bird, buttermilk bird—
smack, booze and bitches
I am Bird
baddest nightdreamer
on sax in the ornithology-world
I can fly—higher, high, higher—
I'm a black man;
I am; I'm a black man—

Miles, blue haze,
Miles high, another bird,
more Miles, mute,
Mute Miles, clean,
bug-eyed, unspeakable,
Miles, sweet Mute,
sweat Miles, black Miles;
I'm a black man;
I'm black; I am;
I'm a black man—

Trane, Coltrane; John Coltrane;
it's tranetime; chase the Trane;

it's a slow dance;
it's the Trane
in Alabama; acknowledgment,
a love supreme,
it's black Trane; black;
I'm a black man; I'm black;
I am; I'm a black man—

Brother John, Brother John
plays no instrument;
he's a black man; black;
he's a black man; he is
Brother John; Brother John—

I'm a black man; I am;
black; I am; I'm a black
man; I am; I am;
I'm a black man;
I'm a black man;
I am; I'm a black man;
I am:

FOCUSED STUDY
Essex Hemphill (1957–1995)

Essex Hemphill was, at the time of his death, perhaps the most well-known Black gay male writer in the United States. His collection, Ceremonies, *had received widespread praise, and his years of gay and antiracism activist work had propelled him to incredible heights in the literary world. Hemphill was born in Chicago on April 16, 1957, and grew up mostly in Washington, DC. He studied English and journalism at the University of Maryland, before completing a degree in English at the University of the District of Columbia. Hemphill immediately became involved in various poetry and writing collectives on the East Coast, especially in Philadelphia with his friend and fellow writer, Joseph Beam.*

Hemphill published a chapbook of poetry, Earth Life, *in 1985, and then the collection* Conditions *in 1986. He contributed to the first contemporary collection of Black gay male writing,* In the Life, *which was edited by Beam. When Beam died, it was Hemphill who completed the vision for a second collection,* Brother to Brother, *which appeared in 1991 and won many literary awards. Hemphill received a fellowship grant from the National Endowment for the Humanities and later produced his first and only full collection of writing,* Ceremonies, *which appeared in 1992. But by then, he was already a star and a valued artist in various Black communities.*

What most characterizes Hemphill's work (and also contributes to the widespread regard in which his work and life are held) is his unrelenting interrogation of the politics of Blackness, especially as gender, class and poverty, and sexuality are considered in these politics. Hemphill's politics and his poetics, like those of other writers such as Audre Lorde and James Baldwin, projected a different kind of Black nationalism, where issues of sexuality and homophobia, sexism and misogyny were as relevant as the critique of racism and colonialism. Hemphill refused to have his sexuality—and his explicitness about sexuality—leave him out of conversations about the health of the Black nation. Furthermore, while he has explored sensuality between men explicitly in his work, unlike many contemporary gay writers, his focus on sex was not primarily for shock. Instead, Hemphill tells particular and sometimes painful stories in those representations, and reveals much about the way communal politics include and exclude.

In "American Hero," Hemphill is at his poetic best, weaving together two images—one of a Black man on a basketball court, and the other of a Black man at a club—to conflate the archetypes of the Black straight man and the Black gay man. The Black heterosexual man on the basketball court is the hero, a pillar of masculinity, the pride of Black people and the recipient of cheers from white fans; conversely, the Black gay man on the dance floor is the center of queer sexuality, the object of attention and desire. Hemphill's woven image not only indicts Black communities for their rejection of Black gay men as legitimate heroes, but also indicts white racism in both cases for objectifying Black men's bodies.

The clear and critical narrative voice that Hemphill creates in "American Hero" is followed by an equally marginalized and less subdued narrative voice in "Visiting Hours." Again, Hemphill uses a persona, that of a security guard, to make a political statement about the lack of opportunities that exist for Black people in urban spaces. His poetics are enhanced by his use of urban types—the basketball player, the club-goer, the security guard—which represent an intersection of race, class, gender, and sexuality, and reveal that the political bent of Hemphill's writing is not singular but multiple. His is a very layered critique of the U.S. society that he lives in.

Hemphill's poetry captures many of the major themes and movements of gay, lesbian, bisexual, and black liberation movements. In "Commitments," for example, he portrays a narrator who is noting his own invisibility in the Black family and community that he is a part of, even as his presence is evident in photographs, at weddings and funerals, and is indispensable to the functioning of the community. Here Hemphill is referencing two noticeable phenomena: one, the notion of invisibility as Ralph Ellison's landmark novel, *Invisible Man*, captured it; and two, the well-explored idea that Black gay and lesbian people are widely present yet highly invisible in Black culture (for example, the Black Church). Similarly, in "The Occupied Territories," Hemphill provides a commentary of the politics of sex which resurfaced under the fear of AIDS and other sexually-transmitted disease, but which also relates to the widespread homophobia of cultural traditions in the U.S. Many gay and lesbian writers and scholars had begun, at this point in literary and academic studies, to explore the notions of desire and pleasure, and to ask questions about the relationship between erotica, one's body, and apparatus of State control. Hemphill's poem contributes to these critiques.

"To Some Supposed Brothers" is Hemphill's pro-feminist anthem, and represents the alliance some Black gay men have made to Black feminist politics. Hemphill, who often spoke out in favor of women's rights and in particular, Black women's political activism, links the oppression of Black men—the dynamics he described in "American Hero"—to men's participation in violence against Black women. What is also effective about the poem is its use of rhythm and repetition, and its particular diction, which lends an oral quality to some stanzas. Finally, in "American Wedding" Hemphill takes on another cultural icon of tradition and oppression, the wedding ceremony. He rescripts the wedding to be a union and celebration of freedom and self-actualization, a celebration that is truly "American" because the stated but hardly realized goals of the country have been met. "In america," he writes, "I place my ring / on your cock / where it belongs." With these lines, and with an "america" that is not capitalized, Hemphill takes the marginalized image of a particular sexual practice of some gay men and makes it the image of strength and salvation for the country. "Every time we kiss," he continues, "we confirm the new world coming."

Hemphill's work is an insightful critique of masculinity. While "American Hero" reveals the tensions and collusions between Black male heterosexuality and homosexuality, and "To Some Supposed Brothers" challenges Black masculinity on its sexism. "Isn't It Funny," like so many of his prose pieces, exploits and celebrates maleness even as he problematizes it. Similarly, in the prose piece "In An Afternoon Light," Hemphill presents ways that narrow constructions of Black masculinity intervene with healthy relationships (sexual or nonsexual) between Black men. Hemphill seems here to be in accord with Joseph Beam's pronouncement that Black man loving Black man is a revolutionary act.

But Hemphill's exploration of masculinity is also a challenge to gay politics (across the racial spectrum) to come clean. His poem "Better Days" is juxtaposed with "Serious Moonlight" and "For My Own Protection," with all three poems making commentary on the risky and empty character of some gay men's lives. Hemphill poems argue that not only should health be a central concern for Black gay men, but the notion of health needs to be seriously redefined to better include all of the protections a Black gay male body needs in the world.

Finally, there is his epic poem "Heavy Breathing." The longest poetic sequence Hemphill wrote, "Heavy Breathing" is a virtual Black masterpiece, making reference to Langston Hughes, James Baldwin, Martin Luther King Jr., Aime Cesaire, and Malcolm X. He uses the language and rhetoric of the Black Church, the Civil Rights Movement, and Queer Nation to ask about the quality of life after heavy breathing. Like "American Hero," it is another moment of Hemphill conflating different social constructs—the heavy breathing of hot, hidden gay sex and the heavy breathing of public Civil Rights protest. Always committed to asking about the health of everyone in the Black nation, Hemphill posits the reality of gay sex as a necessary equivalent to Black liberation movements.

What Essex Hemphill understood so well, and what is evident in his work, is the idea that oppression is oppression, and that oppression is widespread. His poetry, while incredibly beautiful and lyrical, does not fail to give voice to pain, hurt, and disappointment, even as it articulates hope and promise. It is this sensibility—the undying hope and the big-hearted activism—that renders Hemphill's work memorable in various canons of American literature. He talks to and about gay Black men in America as if we in fact are what we are—human, complicated, and necessary. He is wry and clever, potent and prophetic, and loving. In his vision, he is comparable to only the best of our modern writers.

Kevin Everod Quashie

American Hero

I have nothing to lose tonight.
All my men surround me, panting,
as I spin the ball above our heads
on my middle finger.
It's a shimmering club light
and I'm dancing, slick in my sweat.
Squinting, I aim at the hole
fifty feet away. I let the tension go.
Shoot for the net. Choke it.
I never hear the ball
slap the backboard. I slam it
through the net. The crowd goes wild
for our win. I scored
thirty-two points this game
and they love me for it.
Everyone hollering
is a friend tonight.
But there are towns,

certain neighborhoods
where I'd be hard pressed
to hear them cheer
if I move on the block.

Heavy Breathing

. . . and the Negro every day lower, more cowardly, more sterile, less profound, more spent beyond himself, more separate from himself, more cunning with himself, less straight to himself,

I accept, I accept it all . . .

—*AIMÉ CÉSAIRE*
"Return to My Native Land"

At the end of heavy breathing,
very little of my focus intentional,
I cross against the light of Mecca.
I recall few instances of piety
and strict obedience.
Nationalism disillusioned me.
My reflections can be traced
to protest slogans
and enchanted graffiti.
My sentiments—whimsical—
the dreams of a young, yearning bride.
Yes, I possess a mouth such as hers:
red, petulant, brutally pouting;
or at times I'm insatiable—
the vampire in the garden, demented
by the blood of a succulent cock.
I prowl in scant sheaths of latex.
I harbor no shame.
I solicit no pity.
I celebrate my natural tendencies,
photosynthesis, erotic customs.
I allow myself to dream of roses
though I know
the bloody war continues.

I am only sure of this:
I continue to awaken

in a rumpled black suit.
Pockets bulging with tools
and ancestral fossils.
A crusty wool suit
with salt on its collar.
I continue to awaken
shell-shocked, wondering
where I come from
beyond mother's womb,
father's sperm.
My past may be lost
beyond the Carolinas
North and South.
I may not recognize
the authenticity
of my Negritude,
so slowly I awaken.

Science continues
dismantling chromosomes.
Tampering with genetic codes.
I am sure of this
as I witness Washington
change its eye color
from brown to blue;
what kind of mutants are we now?
Why is some destruction so beautiful?

Do you think I could walk pleasantly
and well-suited toward annihilation?
with a scrotal sack full
of primordial loneliness
swinging between my legs
like solid bells?

I am eager to burn
this threadbare masculinity,
this perpetual black suit
I have outgrown.

At the end of heavy breathing,
at the beginning of grief and terror,
on the X2, the bus I call a slave ship.
The majority of its riders Black.

Pressed to journey to Northeast,
into voodoo ghettos
festering on the knuckles
of the "Negro Dream."

The X2 is a risky ride.
A cargo of block boys, urban pirates,
the Colt 45 and gold-neck-chain-crew
are all part of this voyage,
like me, rooted to something here.

The women usually sit
at the front.
The unfortunate ones
who must ride in the back
with the fellas
often endure foul remarks;
the fellas are quick to call them
out of name, as if all females
between eight and eighty
are simply pussies with legs.

The timid men, scattered among
the boat crew and crack boys,
the frightened men
pretend invisibility
or fake fraternity
with a wink or nod.
Or they look the other way.
They have a sister on another bus,
a mother on some other train
enduring this same treatment.

There is never any protest.
No peer restraint. No control.
No one hollered STOP!
for Mrs. Fuller,
a Black mother murdered
in an alley near home.
Her rectum viciously raped
with a pipe. Repeatedly
sodomized repeatedly
sodomized before a crowd
that did not holler STOP!

Some of those watching knew her.
Knew her children.
Knew she was a member of the block.
Every participant was Black.
Every witness was Black.
Some were female
and Black.

There was no white man nearby shouting
"BLACK MAN, SHOVE IT IN HER ASS!
TAKE SOME CRACK! SHOVE IT IN HER ASS,
AND THE REST OF YOU WATCH!"

At the end of heavy breathing
the funerals of my brothers
force me to wear
this scratchy black suit.
I should be naked,
seeding their graves.
  I go to the place
  where the good feelin' awaits me
  self-destruction in my hand,
kneeling over a fucking toilet,
splattering my insides
in a stinking, shit-stained bowl.
I reduce loneliness to cheap green rum,
spicy chicken, glittering vomit.
  I go to the place
  where danger awaits me,
cake-walking
a precarious curb
on a corner
where the absence of doo wop
is frightening.
The evidence of war
and extinction surround me.
I wanted to stay warm
at the bar,
play to the mischief,
the danger beneath a mustache.
The drag queen's perfume
lingers in my sweater
long after she dances
out of the low-rent light,

the cheap shots and catcalls
that demean bravery.

And though the room
is a little cold and shabby,
the music grating,
the drinks a little weak,
we are here
witnessing the popular one
in every boy's town.
A diva by design.
Giving us silicone titties
and dramatic lip synch.
We're crotch to ass,
shoulder to shoulder,
buddy to buddy,
squeezed in sleaze.
We want her to work us.
We throw money
at her feet.
We want her
to work us,
let us see
the naked ass of truth.
We whistle for it,
applaud, shout vulgarities.
We dance like beasts
near the edge of light,
choking drinks.
Clutching money.
And here I am,
  flying high
    without ever leaving the ground
three rums firing me up.
The floor swirling.
Music thumping at my temple.
  In the morning
  I'll be all right.
  I know I'm hooked on the boy
  who makes slaves out of men.

I'm an oversexed
well-hung
Black Queen

influenced
by phrases like
"the repetition
of beauty."

   And you want me to sing
   "We Shall Overcome"?
   Do you daddy daddy
   do you want me to coo
   for your approval?
   Do you want me
   to squeeze my lips together
   and suck you in?
   Will I be a "brother" then?

I'm an oversexed
well-hung
Black Queen
influenced
by phrases like
"I am the love that dare not
speak its name."

   And you want me to sing
   "We Shall Overcome"?
   Do you daddy daddy
   do you want me to coo
   for your approval?
   Do you want me
   to open my hole
   and pull you in?
   Will I be "visible" then?

I'm an oversexed
well-hung
Black Queen
influenced
by phrases like
"Silence = death."

Dearly Beloved,
my flesh like all flesh
will be served
at the feast of worms.

I am looking
for signs of God
as I sodomize my prayers.
I move in and out of love
and pursuits of liberty,
spoon-fed on hypocrisy.
I throw up gasoline
and rubber bullets,
an environmental reflex.
Shackled to shimmy and sham,
I jam the freeway
with my vertigo. I return
to the beginning, to the opening of time
and wounds. I dance
in the searchlight
of a police cruiser.
I know I don't live *here* anymore
but I remain in this body
to witness.

I have been in the bathroom weeping
as silently as I could.
I don't want to alarm
the other young men.
It wasn't always this way.
I used to grin.
I used to dance.
The streets weren't always
slick with blood,
sick with drugs.
My life seems to be
marked down
for quick removal
from the shelf.
When I fuck
the salt tastes sweet.

At the end of heavy breathing
for the price of the ticket
we pay dearly, don't we darling?
Searching for evidence
of things not seen.
I am looking
for Giovanni's room

in this bathhouse.
I know he's here.

I cruise a black maze,
my white sail blowing full.
I wind my way through corridors
lined with identical doors
left ajar, slammed shut,
or thrown open to the dark.
some rooms are lit and empty,
their previous tenant
soon-to-be-wiped-away,
then another will arrive
with towels and sheets.

We buy time here
so we can fuck each other.
Everyone hasn't gone to the moon.
Some of us are still here,
breathing heavy,
navigating this deadly
sexual turbulence;
perhaps we are
the unlucky ones.

Occasionally I long
for a dead man
I never slept with.
I saw you one night
in a dark room
caught in the bounce of light
from the corridor.
You were intent
on throwing dick
into the depths
of a squirming man
bent to the floor,
blood rushing
to both your heads.

I wanted to give you
my sweet man pussy,
but you grunted me away
and all other Black men

who tried to be near you.
Our beautiful nigga lips and limbs
stirred no desire in you.
Instead you chose blonde,
milk-toned creatures to bed.
But you were still one of us,
dark like us, despised like us.

Occasionally I long
to fuck a dead man
I never slept with.
I pump up my temperature
imagining his touch
as I stroke my wishbone,
wanting to raise him up alive,
wanting my fallen seed
to produce him full-grown
and breathing heavy
when it shoots
across my chest;
wanting him upon me,
alive and aggressive,
intent on his sweet buggery
even if my eyes do
lack a trace of blue.

At the end of heavy breathing
the fire quickly diminishes.
Proof dries on my stomach.
I open my eyes, regret
I returned without my companion,
who moments ago held my nipple
bitten between his teeth,
as I thrashed about
on the mercy of his hand
whimpering in tongues.

At the end of heavy breathing
does it come to this?
Filtering language of necessity?
Stripping it of honesty?
Burning it with fissures
that have nothing to do with God?
The absolute evidence of place.

A common roof, discarded
rubbers, umbrellas,
the scratchy disc of memory.
The fatal glass slipper.
The sublimations
that make our erections falter.

At the end of heavy breathing
who will be responsible
for the destruction of human love?
Who are the heartless
sons of bitches
sucking blood from dreams
as they are born?
Who has the guts
to come forward
and testify?
Who will save
our sweet world?

We were promised
this would be a nigga fantasy
on the scale of Oz.
Instead we're humiliated,
disenchanted, suspicious.
I ask the scandal-infested leadership
"What is your malfunction? Tell us
how your automatic weapons
differ from the rest."

They respond with hand jive,
hoodoo hollering,
excuses to powder the nose,
or they simply disappear
like large sums of money.

And you want me to give you
a mandatory vote
because we are both Black
and descendants of oppression?
What will I get in return?
Hush money from the recreation fund?
A kilo of cocaine?
A boy for my bed

and a bimbo for my arm?
A tax break on my new home
west of the ghetto?

You promised
this would be a nigga fantasy
on the scale of Oz.
Instead, it's "Birth of a Nation"
and the only difference
is the white men
are played in Blackface

At the end of heavy breathing
as the pickaninny frenzy escalates,
the home crew is illin'
on freak drugs
and afflicted racial pride.
The toll beyond counting,
the shimmering carcasses
all smell the same.
No matter which way
the wind blows
I lose a god
or a friend.

My grieving is too common
to arouse the glance of angels.
My shame is too easy to pick up
like a freak from the park
and go.

Urged to honor paranoia,
trained to trust a dream,
a reverend, hocus-pocus
handshakes; I risk becoming schizoid
shuffling between Black English
and assimilation.
My dreamscape is littered
with effigies of my heroes.
I journey across
my field of vision
raiding the tundra
of my imagination.
Three African rooftops

are aflame in my hand.
Compelled by desperation,
I plunder every bit of love
in my possession.
I am looking for an answer
to drugs and corruption.
I enter the diminishing
circumstance of prayer.
Inside a homemade Baptist church
perched on the edge
of the voodoo ghetto,
the murmurs of believers
rise and fall, exhaled
from a single spotted lung.
The congregation sings
to an out-of-tune piano
while death is rioting,
splashing blood about
like gasoline,
offering pieces of rock
in exchange
for throw-away dreams.

The lines of takers are long.

Now is the time
to be an undertaker
in the ghetto,
a black dress seamstress.
Now is not the time
to be a Black mother
in the ghetto,
the father of sons,
the daughters of any of them.

At the end of heavy breathing
I engage in arguments
with my ancestral memories.
I'm not content
with nationalist propaganda.
I'm not content
loving my Black life
without question.
The answers of Negritude

are not absolute.
The dream of King
is incomplete.
I probe beneath skin surface.
I argue with my nappy hair,
my thick lips so difficult
to assimilate.
Up and down the block we battle,
cussing, kicking, screaming,
threatening to kill
with bare hands.

At the end of heavy breathing
the dream deferred
is in a museum
under glass and guard.
It costs five dollars
to see it on display.
We spend the day
viewing artifacts,
breathing heavy
on the glass
to see—
the skeletal remains
of black panthers,
pictures of bushes,
canisters of tears.

Visiting Hours

The government pays me
nine thousand dollars a year
to protect the East Wing.
So I haunt it.

Visiting hours are over.
The silent sentry is on duty.
An electric eye patrols the premises.
I'm just here
putting mouth on the place.

Modigliani whispers to Matisse.
Matisse whispers to Picasso.
I kiss the Rose in my pocket
and tip easy through this tomb of thieves.

I'm weighted down with keys,
flashlight, walkie-talkie, a gun.
I'm expected to die, if necessary,
protecting European artwork
that robbed color and movement
from my life.

I'm the ghost in the Capitol.
I did Vietnam.
My head is rigged with land mines,
but I keep cool,
waiting on every other Friday,
kissing the Rose,
catching some trim.

I'm not protecting any more Europeans
with my life.
I'll give this shit in here away
before I die for it.
Fuck a Remb-randt!

And if I ever go off,
you'd better look out, Mona Lisa.
I'll run through this gallery
with a can of red enamel paint
and spray everything in sight
like a cat in heat.

For My Own Protection

I want to start an organization
to save my life.
If whales, snails, dogs, cats
Chrysler and Nixon can be saved,
the lives of Black men are priceless

and can be saved.
We should be able to save each other.
I don't want to wait for the Heritage Foundation
to release a study saying
Black people are almost extinct.
I don't want to be the living dead
pacified with drugs, sex and rock-n-roll.
If a human chain can be formed
around nuclear missile sites,
then surely Black men can form
human chains around Anacostia, Harlem,
South Africa, Wall Street, Hollywood,
each other.

If we have to take tomorrow with blood
are we ready?
Do our s curls and dreadlocks and phillies
make us any more ready than a bush or conkaline?
I'm not concerned
about the attire of a soldier.
All I want to know
for my own protection
is are we capable
of whatever
whenever.

Commitments

I will always be there.
When the silence is exhumed.
When the photographs are examined
I will be pictured smiling
among siblings, parents,
nieces and nephews.

In the background of the photographs
the hazy smoke of barbecue,
a checkered red and white tablecloth
laden with blackened chicken,
glistening ribs, paper plates,
bottles of beer and pop.

In the photos
the smallest children
are held by their parents.
My arms are empty, or around
the shoulders of unsuspecting aunts
expecting to throw rice at me someday.

Or picture tinsel, candles,
ornamented, imitation trees,
or another table, this one
set for Thanksgiving,
a turkey steaming the lens.

My arms are empty
in those photos, too,
so empty they would break
around a lover.

I am always there
for critical emergencies,
graduations,
the middle of the night.

I am the invisible son.
In the family photos
nothing appears out of character.
I smile as I serve my duty.

The Occupied Territories

You are not to touch yourself
in any way
or be familiar with ecstasy.
You are not to touch
anyone of your own sex
or outside of your race
then talk about it,
photograph it, write it down

in explicit details, or paint it
red, orange, blue, or dance
in honor of its power, dance
for its beauty, dance
because it's yours.

You are not to touch other flesh
without a police permit.
You have no privacy—
the State wants to seize your bed
and sleep with you.
The State wants to control
your sexuality, your birth rate,
your passion.
The message is clear:
your penis, your vagina,
your testicles, your womb,
your anus, your orgasm,
these belong to the State.

You are not to touch yourself
or be familiar with ecstasy.
The erogenous zones
are not demilitarized.

In an Afternoon Light

On a recent afternoon in Philadelphia, I walked to the corner of 63rd and
Malvern Streets to catch a number 10 trolley, *my* imaginary streetcar named Desire. Waiting, when I arrived at the stop, was another Black man, sipping a bottle
of beer and smoking a cigarette. He wore sunshades and was built three sizes
larger than my compact frame. I guessed him to be in his thirties though his potbelly suggested an older age or the consumption of too much beer and soul food.
A blue hand towel was tossed over his right shoulder. A baseball jacket was
draped across his left thigh. He was sitting on the wall I sit on when I wait here.

Since there was no trolley in sight, I guarded walked over and sat at the far
end of the wall. He continued to drink his beer as I observed him from the corner
of my eye. I pretended to occupy myself with looking for an approaching trolley.
He abruptly ended our brief interlude of silence. For no apparent reason he

blurted out, "Man, the woman's movement is ruling the world. It's turning our sons into faggots and our men into punks."

"What do you mean?" I asked, raising my voice as loudly as he had raised his. Indignation and defensiveness tinged my vocal chords. I thought his remarks were directed specifically at me.

"You see all the cars going by?" he asked, gesturing at the minor traffic.

"Yeah, so what about it?"

"Well, can't you see that all the drivers in the cars are women—"

"Which only means more women are driving," I interjected.

"—because women have caused major changes in society, brother."

"So?"

"So women are ruling more things now. That's why I don't want my son to spend all his time with his mother, his grandmother, and those aunts of his. His mother and I don't live together, but I go visit him and take him downtown or to the movies or to the Boy's Club. I think that's important, so he'll know the difference."

"The difference in what?"

"The difference between a woman and a man. You know . . ."

"Which is supposed to be determined by what—how they use their sex organs? What I do know, brother, is that 13- and 14-year-old Black children are breeding babies they can't care for—crack babies, AIDS babies, accidental babies, babies that will grow up and inherit their parents' poverty and powerlessness. The truth is young people are fucking because they want to fuck. They're encouraged to fuck. Yet we don't talk to them frankly and honestly about sex, sexuality, or their responsibility."

"Okay brother, hold that thought. You're moving too fast. See, this is what I mean. Suppose you grow up in a home with your father being a minister and your mother is there all the time taking care of the house and kids. You grow up, go off to college and get a good education, then—"

"Yeah—"

"—then you decide you gonna be gay. You like men. I say you learned that. Education did that. Your folks didn't teach you that."

"That's bullshit, and you know it. It's stupid to suggest that women or education can make a man gay. What you fail to understand is that this is the natural diversity of human sexuality no matter what we call it. Also, my father is a minister, my mother was at home raising us before they divorced, and I went to college. And you know what?"

"What?"

"I'm a faggot."

"No you ain't!"

"Yes I am. In fact, I'm becoming a well-known faggot."

"I don't believe you."

"Why not?"

"Because you ain't switching and stuff."

"Yeah, all you think being gay is about is men switching—but you're wrong. I'm a faggot because I love *me* enough to be who I am. If your son becomes a faggot it won't be because of the way you or his mother raise him. It won't be because of television, movies, books, and education. It will be because he learns to trust the natural expression of his sexuality without fear or shame. If he learns anything about courage from you or his mother, then he'll grow up to be himself. You can't blame being straight or gay on a woman or education. The education that's needed should be for the purpose of bringing us all out of sexual ignorance. Our diverse sexuality is determined by the will of nature, and nature *is* the will of God."

He sat there for a moment staring at me, sipping his beer. He lit another cigarette. I realized then that he could beat me to a pulp if he chose to impose his bigger size on me, but I wasn't afraid for what I had said and revealed. On too many occasions I have sat silently as men like him mouthed off about gays and women and I said nothing because I was afraid. But not today. Not this afternoon. The longer I sit silently in my own community, my own home, and say nothing, I condone the ignorance and its by-products of violence and discrimination. I prolong my existence in a realm of invisibility and complicity. I prolong our mutual suffering by saying nothing.

In this tense interlude a bus and trolley approached. I was angry with having to encounter him on such a glorious spring day, but this is the kind of work social change requires. I consoled myself believing this.

When he rose I immediately rose too—a defensive strategy, a precaution.

"It's been good talking to you, brother. I'll think about what you've said." He extended his hand to me just as the bus and the trolley neared. I looked at his hand, known and unknown to me, offered tenuously, waiting to clasp my hand.

"Yeah, it was cool talking to you, too," I returned, as I hesitantly shook his hand. He swaggered to the bus and boarded with his beer hidden under the jacket he carried. I walked into the street to meet the trolley in an afternoon light devoid of shame.

To Some Supposed Brothers

You judge a woman
by the length of her skirt,
by the way she walks,
talks, looks, and acts;
by the color of her skin you judge
and will call her "Bitch!"
"Black bitch!"

if she doesn't answer your:
"Hey baby, watcha gonna say
to a man."

You judge a woman
by the job she holds,
by the number of children she's had,
by the number of digits on her check,
by the many men she may have lain with
and wonder what jive murphy
you'll run on her this time.

You tell a woman
every poetic love line
you can think of,
then like the desperate needle
of a strung out junkie
you plunge into her veins,
travel wildly through her blood,
confuse her mind, make her hate,
and be cold to the men to come,
destroying the thread of calm
she held.

You judge a woman
by what she can do for you alone
but there's no need
for slaves to have slaves.

You judge a woman
by impressions you think you've made.
Ask and she gives,
take without asking,
beat on her and she'll obey,
throw her name up and down the streets
like some loose whistle—
knowing her neighbors will talk.
Her friends will chew her name.
Her family's blood will run loose
like a broken creek.
And when you're gone,
a woman is left
healing her wounds alone.

But we so-called men,
we so-called brothers
wonder why it's so hard
to love *our* women
when we're about loving them
the way america
loves us.

Isn't It Funny

I don't want to hear you beg.
I'm sick of beggars.
If you a man
take what you want from me
or what you can.
Even if you have me
like some ol gal across town
you think you love.

Look at me!
standing here
with my dick as straight as yours.
What do you think this is?
The weather cock on a rooftop?

We sneak all over town
like two damn thieves
with whiskey on our breath,
no street lights on the backroads,
just the stars above us
as ordinary as they should be.

We always have to work it out,
walk it through, talk it over,
drink and smoke our way into sodomy.

I could take you in my room
but you're afraid the landlady
will recognize you.
I feel thankful I don't love you.
I won't have to suffer you later on.

But for now I say
Johnnie Walker,
have you had enough, Johnnie Walker?
Do-I-look-like-a-woman-now?
Against the fogged car glass
do I look like your cross town lover?
Do I look like Shirley?

When you reach for her
to kiss her lips, her lips
are thick like mine,
her hair is cut close too, like mine
isn't it . . .

American Wedding

In america,
I place my ring
on your cock
where it belongs.
No horsemen
bearing terror,
no soldiers of doom
will swoop in
and sweep us apart.
They're too busy
looting the land
to watch us.
They don't know
we need each other
critically.
They expect us to call in sick,
watch television all night,
die by our own hands.
They don't know
we are becoming powerful.
Every time we kiss
we confirm the new world coming.

What the rose whispers
before blooming

I vow to you.
I give you my heart,
a safe house.
I give you promises other than
milk, honey, liberty.
I assume you will always
be a free man with a dream.
In america,
place your ring
on my cock
where it belongs.
Long may we live
to free this dream.

Better Days

In daytime hours
guided by instincts that never sleep,
the faintest signals come to me
over vast spaces
of etiquette and restraint.
Sometimes I give in
to the pressing call of instinct,
knowing the code of my kind
better than I know
the National Anthem
or the Lord's Prayer.
I am so driven by my senses
to abandon restraint,
to seek pure pleasure
through every pore.
I want to smell the air around me
thickly scented
with a playboy's freedom.
I want impractical relationships.
I want buddies and partners,
names I will forget by sunrise.
I don't want to commit my heart.
I only want to feel good.

I only want to freak sometimes.
There are not other considerations.
A false safety
compels me to think
I will never need kindness,
so I don't recognize
that need in someone else.
But it concerns me,
going off to sleep and awakening
throbbing with wants—
that I am being consumed by want.
And I wonder where stamina comes from
to search all night until my footsteps
ring awake the sparrows,
and I go home, ghost walking,
driven indoors to rest
my hunters guise,
to love myself as fiercely
as I have in better days.

Serious Moonlight

In between love affairs
I stopped worrying about
my peculiar loneliness.
I don't search for reason or blame.
I don't worry that men come
and go through my life
wounded by my hand,
accomplices sometimes
to my own self-inflicted injuries.

I try not to worry too much
because Black men die too frequently
from strokes as fatal as hammer blows.
My hair is growing thin,
my stomach a little weak and nervous.
I have only tried once to kill myself,
but I was too young to understand

how to die.
So nothing happened
when I held my breath.
I'm still here hanging on
refusing to be intimidated.

I worry about this planet,
this human wilderness.
What is called "advanced civilization"
means we are all closer to death.
I worry about the tempers
between men who build bombs.
Men who seek different satisfactions
and collide.
Their collision could mean the end of life
as I come out of the morning subway
unaware their tempers flared
between Dupont Circle
and Judiciary Square.

I worry about melting down,
catching man-made diseases
in the bus stations,
being a suspect because I live in the South East,
because I'm the same color as the assailant,
the thief, the night,
because I think the street boat
will take me home
but it takes me out,
because I want everything to look lovely
I take a toke or two,
because PCP makes me do wild things,
makes me think I'm a white man
so I kill, steal and thrill myself,
but I'm too dark to escape the consequences,
I'm too proud to imitate a beast.

I don't worry about
where my next love is gonna come from.
It will sneak up on me
and rape me in the serious moonlight.

Where We Live: A Conversation with Essex Hemphill and Isaac Julien

Don Belton

At the twentieth century's close, independent filmmakers Marlon Riggs, Isaac Julien, and poet Essex Hemphill are likely the artists/activists whose work most richly articulates and extends the represented range of black gay men's identity. Their daring interventions advance the project of healing the whole of black masculinity by celebrating acts of dialogue, compassion, and love between black men across the spectrum of sexual orientation, as well as between black men and black women.

Riggs's landmark documentary *Tongues Untied,* along with Julien's *Looking for Langston,* a cinematic meditation on the life and legacy of the closeted Harlem Renaissance writer Langston Hughes, served stunning notice that black gay male silence and invisibility had ended. For two decades, Hemphill has crafted elegant poems that illuminate the life-giving geography of black men's love and grief.

Riggs died on April 5, 1994, of complications due to AIDS. In December of 1994, I brought Julien and Hemphill together for a conversation around the completion of Riggs's film *Black Is . . . Black Ain't,* which explores the nexus of black identity and masculinity. Hemphill appears in the film, along with cultural activists bell hooks, Michelle Wallace, Cornel West, and Angela Davis. I met with Julien and Hemphill at Hemphill's apartment in West Philadelphia. Hemphill showed an advance cassette copy of the film. The following is excerpted from conversation between Julien and Hemphill that afternoon.

HEMPHILL: I find myself resisting popular notions of black masculinity while at the same time being attracted to them. Early on, I learned ways to protect my masculinity or, I guess I should say, my homo-masculinity. I wasn't inclined to be athletic. In the black neighborhood I came from, there was an emphasis on being able to play basketball or football. I, instead, was attracted to gymnastics because of the way the body looked. But I knew instinctively that if I had said, "I want to be a gymnast," among the fellas I ran with I would have been labeled a sissy. As an adult, I've had to resist the idea that I'm not a man because I don't have children or a woman.

JULIEN: I think this is a good place to start. Initially, masculinity was about living up to the fiction of normative heterosexual masculinity. Growing up, I remember men in the community who were a part of my parents' circle commenting in Creole about how I was such a *petit macqot,* which is a small boy, *un petit garçon.* It was also a way of calling a young boy a sissy. A means of saying he's already displaying feminine traits. Maybe I wasn't interested in trying to conceal that part of my identity. So, in a way, it began a war early in my life, but not a bloody war. It was a war of positions in the sense I did not want to totally participate in being a straight black male in the conventional framework. My feelings for boys my age happened very early on—I must have been eight years old. In the playground, I saw the shorts fall off the goalkeeper's waist during a sports match. I remember feeling very erotically charged by the image. There was already in circulation the idea of black men having this hypermasculinity that was tough and resilient. It was tough growing up in London in the 1970s. You had to be tough to physically contest the everyday racist treatment by the police, by various authority figures and institutions. Therefore, you understood that this toughness was a mask and a defense. Questions around being black and male came to the forefront for me when I began to pursue my education and most of the other young men around me were being arrested.

HEMPHILL: We're faced with redefining what masculinity is. We're faced with constructing a masculinity for all of us, one that will be useful as opposed to disempowering. I think that, given issues like economic oppression, we feel safe holding onto the model constructed out of athletics, around street toughness and other conventional models of masculinity. You know, "My gun's bigger . . ." The gun is supposed to be an extension of you or your anger, and it's the bullet that strikes, not the fist. I can't think when I last saw two black men physically fighting. And not that I'm endorsing fighting, but I think the gun has become an apt metaphor for our isolation from our own rage and frustration. Our increasing isolation from one another's humanity. Then there's the masculinity that we're getting via television, film, and magazines. We need a masculinity that brings us more into contact with one another. A masculinity that is intimate and humane. A masculinity that allows if I feel like being soft my softness won't mean I'm a sissy or a punk.

JULIEN: In *Black Is . . . Black Ain't,* bell hooks and Michelle Wallace talk about the language of sexism and the presumptions around gender. That's really where everything begins to shut down. We both grew up experiencing scenes in which black men could not cry or express fear. Growing up, I very much identified with trying not to reproduce the dominant ideas of being a man. There's an overvaluation of strict gender codes in the black community. "Only sissies cry." When that was told to me, I said, "Fuck this. I'm not going to live like this." Those stories or fictions of "real" masculinity are learned early in life and then become ways of toughening young boys. That sort of information isn't useful to our community. I think there should be more of an investment in unlearning those codes, because they end breeding a certain inhumanity. Our redemption as a people is *not* a "dick thing," as bell hooks points out in the film.

HEMPHILL: I believe that many of the destructive lessons taught in our childhood homes is the result of the desperation of our parents. They were children at one point and were made to learn those same lessons. I don't know how we begin to unlearn that behavior.

JULIEN: Well, it's true that the codes we're meant to adhere to—masculine and feminine—are prescribed in childhood. As black boys and girls growing up in families attacked by racism from the outside, we are made to feel a kind of double restriction on the expression of ourselves in any way that might go against the grain of dominant ideas. We, as black men especially, are supposed to instill and police these codes within ourselves. But where are these codes coming from? I think that in America, but not only in America, there is this obsessive concentration on the family—the notion that everything can be resolved within the family. But this middle-class notion of "family" seems to me the space where we first learned how to fear one another and to fear the free expression of ourselves. As a result, the debate around black masculinity in the U.S. has become so topical with films like *Jungle Fever* and *Boyz in the Hood*. One of the problems with the *New York Times* article/symposium on black men [*Who Will Help the Black Man? New York Times*, 4 December 1994, v. 1, 74:1] is that it is exclusively a discussion by and about black middle-class, presumably heterosexual men. The question at the center of that discussion is really, How can we get black people, black men in particular, to get over in the American Dream? It should be obvious by now that's just a poor question. I also think the street tough machismo identity is bankrupt. It's just producing a competitive, nihilistic environment for black men to destroy themselves and each other. It's difficult to have a position on this without talking about the disappearance of real economic opportunity for the black working poor and the infiltration of drugs in our communities in both the U.S. and London. Marlon's film carries an important critique of black manhood along these lines.

HEMPHILL: Yes, and the critique bell hooks provides [in the film] of the black macho pose of the 60s and 70s is so powerful because if the sum of black political struggle is about empowering the black phallus at the expense of all other cultural issues, we cannot succeed. Or else that success will have no meaning. Our masculinity must encompass diversity and nuance. There should never be a question about whether Sally can drive a rig or whether Tommy can raise the children. There are also important class issues. The *Times* piece represented the black male middle class. I'd like to see that [discussion] take place with representatives from a broader range of possible black male identity. I'd have loved to have heard someone who flips hamburgers for minimum wage talk about how he views himself as a man. A construction worker. An emergency room doctor. I had problems with one of the participants in that article referring to working-class blacks as "black trash." Its a simple-minded analogy he was trying to draw—that you have white trash and you have black trash. Well, come on, baby [laughs], . . . who says any group of society is to be regarded as trash? So for me the *Times* piece was not a broad enough conversation. It was a safe conversation for the *New York Times*. Safe for the particular men who were included. And self-serving.

HEMPHILL: In a recent issue of the Nation of Islam's newspaper, *The Final Call,* Louis Farrakhan called for a "million-man march" on Washington, D.C. A march of one million black men on the nation's capital. The call itself is historic, though I've heard nothing about it in the mainstream press. But who's going to be on the stage when those one million black men assemble in Washington? You? Me? Would Marlon have been invited to speak? Hardly. It will be men who are considered safe. Safe for me equals ineffective—men who will not take risks in their intellect and who will not take risks in their compassion. I think of the ending of *Black Is . . . Black Ain't,* where bell hooks speaks about replacing the notion of black unity with the notion of communion. The root meaning of communion suggests that our union is based on a willingness to communicate with one another. It's a beautiful idea to pursue. [In the film] Michelle Wallace says, "I always get the feeling that when black people talk about unity and community that it's a turf war thing, you know—we're gonna get together and this is gonna be our block, and if you come on our block, you know, we're gonna kick your ass." Michelle says, "I always think I'm gonna be the one whose ass is gonna get kicked." I've always felt like that as well. I'm as black as anyone, but not by the criteria the nationalists construct.

I think we need to bear witness in the representation of black male identity. Those black men who will march will largely be lower- and working-class men— your grassroots level. The march may not be framed around their identities, but they have always been the essential part of the Nation of Islam's political base. Of any black political base. For that reason, I believe we ought to try to participate. So at least, for the record, there is the fact that we were there to claim our membership in our communities.

JULIEN: Why would we try to claim membership in black masculinity through the Nation of Islam?

HEMPHILL: Big spectacle-oriented groups like the Nation of Islam are winning minds and support among everyday black people. Either we are a part of black communities or we aren't. Our presence has always been crucial to our communities, yet within those communities and the larger society we're still rendered as nonexistent. We're still considered to be not interested in something like this. There is a danger in that. As black gay men we need a politic that touches the vast majority of our brothers where they're at. Otherwise as gay men we only represent a breakdown. . . .

For me, the way I live, my blackness is the priority. Period. Be it my identity as a gay person or as a person with AIDS or my identity as a writer . . . I'm still dealt with as black, first and foremost.

JULIEN: I think it's a product of segregationist thinking about sexuality and gender that we have to prioritize our identities.

HEMPHILL: I don't want you to misunderstand me. In 1991 or '92, when I was on tour in England, I had trouble with customs, and the trouble I had had everything to do with me being a black man in bomber jacket, in jeans and construction boots. All these other people are flowing by me in customs with no problem, but they stopped me every time, because I fit a certain profile. That's why my blackness has to be there first for me. It's a battle around that place where I am desperate and wanting to see some of the dying stop.

JULIEN: But a march won't stop that. Anyway, I think the image of one million black men marching on Washington is phallocentric and misogynist. I don't know. Maybe I'm just cynical.

HEMPHILL: I don't think it's cynicism. We share a similar concern and pessimism. I think we articulate it differently. I agree with you about the phallocentrism and misogyny. . . . I stopped three or four young brothers on my street last spring, and they were bigger than me. It was after school, after business hours. These young fellas had taken magic markers and written all over the storefront windows. And something in me just snapped. I'm sick of there being no intervention. I told them, "Don't do that. That's a black business. You're destroying property." I was scared to death, but I wasn't going to my apartment and locking my door. The truth is I might not be sitting here now because of that act. Even a simple intervention could cost our lives.

JULIEN: Generally, there's a breakdown of the civil society in America.

HEMPHILL: Various horrifying themes occur in all our communities. Why is there such tremendous disrespect among black men towards women, regardless of our sexual orientation? Even a statement like, "Miss Thing is gonna take me to a new level of sensuality." I was wondering why it's never "*Mr.* Thing." Why is it "*Thing*"?

JULIEN: I thought "Miss Thing" was about a parody of a sexist comment.

HEMPHILL: Think about the things you've heard among gay brothers about women. How much different are some of those statements from the ones by some heterosexual brothers? There hasn't been much discourse among black gay men about that. But I know sisters are anxious for that. Not just conversation, but deliberate work. I don't think current notions of masculinity work for any male. I don't think they work for anyone.

JULIEN: I think the social complexities around contemporary male identity are just deepened by issues of blackness and gayness.

HEMPHILL: This is why, for various reasons, including expediency. I've elected not to take a white lover when that option has been there. I feel like this is the worst country to try to love outside the race. I can't imagine what you deal with in your relationship [Mark Nash, Julien's life-partner of seven years, is white].

JULIEN: My experience being in America with Mark has not been one where I've been rejected. If blacks or whites want to reject me, they're not my friends and I don't feel I've lost anything.

HEMPHILL: It seems so incredibly important, the way that Marlon's use of the slogan "Black men loving black men is *the* revolutionary act" in *Tongues Untied* has been so fucked by so many people [because Marlon's partner, Jack Vincent, is white].

JULIEN: I just don't agree with a slogan like that. Who's to say what *the* revolutionary act is, anyway? Who can prescribe that? If I'd grown up in America, I don't know what I would be like. The positioning of a slogan like that—the way it is positioned in the film—is fine, I suppose, but when it's used as some kind of moral code to police interracial desire, then I think it's really about our shame about the range of our own desires.

HEMPHILL: The act of black men loving black men isn't only about our sexual expression. It means everything, including intervening downstairs when those young black men were defacing their neighborhood. That was about my love for them. If I didn't love us, I wouldn't care. You know—"Just go ahead. Get your magic markers and do the block. Do the block!"

JULIEN: I think it's very complicated, the discourse of love in relationship to yourself. Unlearning self-hatred and fear is hard work. I've had to be in America to really begin to understand that, being so marginalized here.

HEMPHILL: In some ways, I think we *have* failed.

JULIEN: We have to be willing not to reject that failure out of hand. That's essential to experiencing humanity.

FOCUSED STUDY
bell hooks (1952–)

*Born Gloria Watkins on September 25, 1952, in Hopkinsville, Kentucky, bell hooks re-
named herself, like Toni Cade Bambara, after a powerful woman in her heritage. Publishing her first small collection of poems,* And There We Went, *in 1978, hooks needed to
imagine a self who could speak out and be a strong woman. This image for her was her
maternal great grandmother.*

*hooks started attending Stanford at the age of nineteen and graduated in 1974, com-
pleting her education by earning a Ph.D. from the University of California at Santa Cruz in
1983. She has been a professor at Yale University and is currently Distinguished Professor
at City College in New York.*

hooks began working on her first book, Ain't I A Woman, *as an undergraduate, finished it during graduate school and published it in 1981, two years before receiving her
degree.* Feminist Theory: From Margin to Center *(1984) followed. These early works were
grounded in Black feminist theory, the philosophy that Black women need to articulate the
specificity of their realities and bring those realities to the forefront of a feminist theory, to
articulate and recognize a feminist theory that empowers Black women. In these works,
hooks identifies and condemns the ways in which Black women have been ignored or
marginalized by mainstream feminism. She also identifies the intersections of racism, sexism, and classism in the desire to dominate that fuels the hierarchical structure of American society. Authentic feminism, hooks argues, should seek to redefine power and
eradicate existing hierarchies, battling all -isms in combination rather than privileging
gender over race or class. This assertion is one that also dominates* Talking Back: Thinking
Feminist, Thinking Black *(1988), a collection of twenty-three essays dealing with issues
ranging from domestic violence, homophobia in black communities, and academic politics, all within a Black feminist context.*

Her next works, Yearning: Race, Gender, and Cultural Politics *(1990),* Black Looks:
Race and Representation *(1992), and* Outlaw Culture: Resisting Representations *(1994),
continue in feminist focus, but couple that focus with an emphasis on cultural criticism. As
part of her political agenda, hooks critiques representations of Blackness, especially Black
women, in popular media such as film. She also clarifies the directions Black cultural critics and artists should pursue in their work. In "Choosing the Margin as a Space of Radical
Openness," for example, hooks discusses the need for Black cultural critics and producers
of cultural texts to articulate memory, to center the specificities and variations of existence
in the margins in order to integrate counter-hegemonic, or resistant philosophy, into their
texts. In "Homeplace: A Site of Resistance," hooks explains the resistance evidenced in the
creation and maintaining of affirmative and liberating home space by women who battled the oppositions of time and service they were required to give to others rather than*

their own families. This celebration of Black cultural practice and tradition combines hooks' dedication to feminist practice and cultural criticism. Art on My Mind: Visual Politics *(1995) and* Reel to Real: Race, Sex, and Class at the Movies *(1996) extend the body of hooks's cultural criticism, making it not unreasonable to title bell hooks the nation's foremost Black woman cultural critic.*

In Breaking Bread: Insurgent Black Intellectual Life *(1991), hooks converses with Cornel West about what it means to be a Black intellectual committed to revolution on so many levels. The two structure their conversation as interview and dialogue; hooks interviews West and West interviews hooks, but the drive of the whole is interactive and open conversation. This conversation foregrounds the necessity of Black men and women to speak and cooperate with one another, clarifying the role of men in feminist objectives and highlighting the process of cooperation in social change. In West's interview of hooks, the two discuss issues ranging from art, literary tradition, and memory to sexuality and spirituality, creating a symbiotic world of ideas around their individual perspectives. hooks also discusses the process of establishing identity and the progression of political philosophy in her works.*

Her examination of all aspects of her identity in Breaking Bread *leads logically to her writing about teaching and healing in* Teaching to Transgress: Education as the Practice of Freedom *(1994) and* Sisters of the Yam: Black Women and Self-Recovery *(1993), respectively. In* Teaching to Transgress, *hooks discusses her own role as teacher, but also endows education with spiritual and liberating power, making the teacher responsible for engaging all students in real ways and discussing the necessity of both addressing and eliminating the realities of racism, sexism, and classism in the classroom. In* Sisters of the Yam, *hooks focuses on the inner lives of women, learning to love self through relationships, community, and assertiveness.*

*While much of her work contains autobiographical resonance, her latest pair of autobiographical works—*Bone Black *(1996) and* Wounds of Passion *(1997)—provide a unique look at bell hooks the Black woman and writer as they also expand the notion of autobiography. In* Bone Black, *hooks isolates moments in her childhood that highlight her development into womanhood and her understanding of the people and ideas surrounding her. An important figure in her early autobiography is her grandmother, Saru, a woman who taught her independence of space and assertion. Saru tells hooks stories that she collects and translates into the power she needs as a writer. The need for independence and love of space informs the sequel to* Bone Black, Wounds of Passion, *in which hooks communicates her growth and struggle as a writer and as a woman in the difficult central relationship she maintained throughout her undergraduate and graduate years. With the addition of* Remembered Rapture: The Writer at Work *(1999) and its celebration of literacy, hooks documents her writing life from its earliest forms to its current status.*

bell hooks is a public intellectual with a wide audience. She is writer, teacher, and lecturer and excels in each role. Her focus on crucial cultural issues—race, gender, self-definition, healing, and empowerment—enriches the tradition of Black feminist criticism and Black cultural criticism at once. hooks is a committed feminist, but she is also a very independent thinker, not afraid to speak her mind even at the risk of criticism from her communities. bell hooks is in every way a pursuer of truth and justice. A prolific writer, her contributions to Black autobiography adds to her already profound contribution to theoretical and intellectual traditions. Her astute perspective drives her investigation of arts, beliefs, and institutions by historical and social analysis and enriches understanding on all fronts.

With the 1999 hardcover of her second volume of poetry, A Woman's Mourning Song *(1993), and the forthcoming 2000 publication of* Speak to My Heart: A New Vision of Love, *a work dealing with issues of sexuality, the family, feminism, and the primacy of relationships, the role of bell hooks in continued thinking about African American culture and politics is resoundingly clear.*

R. Joyce Lausch

Choosing the Margin as a Space of Radical Openness

As a radical standpoint, perspective, position, "the politics of location" necessarily calls those of us who would participate in the formation of counter-hegemonic cultural practice to identify the spaces where we begin the process of re-vision. When asked, "What does it mean to enjoy reading *Beloved,* admire *Schooldaze,* and have a theoretical interest in post-structuralist theory?" (one of the "wild" questions posed by the Third World Cinema Focus Forum), I located my answer concretely in the realm of oppositional political struggle. Such diverse pleasures can be experienced, enjoyed even, because one transgresses, moves "out of one's place." For many of us, that movement requires pushing against oppressive boundaries set by race, sex, and class domination. Initially, then, it is a defiant political gesture. Moving, we confront the realities of choice and location. Within complex and ever shifting realms of power relations, do we position ourselves on the side of colonizing mentality? Or do we continue to stand in political resistance with the oppressed, ready to offer our ways of seeing and theorizing, of making culture, towards that revolutionary effort which seeks to create space where there is unlimited access to the pleasure and power of knowing, where transformation is possible? This choice is crucial. It shapes and determines our response to existing cultural practice and our capacity to envision new, alternative, oppositional aesthetic acts. It informs the way we speak about these issues, the language we choose. Language is also a place of struggle.

To me, the effort to speak about issues of "space and location" evoked pain. The questions raised compelled difficult explorations of "silences"—unaddressed places within my personal political and artistic evolution. Before I could consider answers, I had to face ways these issues were intimately connected to intense personal emotional upheaval regarding place, identity, desire. In an intense all-night-long conversation with Eddie George (member of Black Audio Film Collective) talking about the struggle of oppressed people to come to voice, he made the very "down" comment that "ours is a broken voice." My response was simply that when you hear the broken voice you also hear the pain contained within that brokenness—a speech of suffering; often it's that sound nobody wants to hear. Stuart Hall talks about the need for a "politics of articulation." He and Eddie have engaged in dialogue with me in a deeply soulful way, hearing my struggle for words. It is this dialogue between comrades that is a gesture of love; I am grateful.

I have been working to change the way I speak and write, to incorporate in the manner of telling a sense of place, of not just who I am in the present but where I am coming from, the multiple voices within me. I have confronted silence, inarticulateness. When I say, then, that these words emerge from suffering, I refer to that personal struggle to name that location from which I come to voice—that space of my theorizing.

Often when the radical voice speaks about domination we are speaking to those who dominate. Their presence changes the nature and direction of our words. Language is also a place of struggle. I was just a girl coming slowly into womanhood when I read Adrienne Rich's words, "This is the oppressor's language, yet I need it to talk to you." This language that enabled me to attend graduate school, to write a dissertation, to speak at job interviews, carries the scent of oppression. Language is also a place of struggle. The Australian aborigines say "that smell of the white man is killing us." I remember the smells of my childhood, hot water corn bread, turnip greens, fried pies. I remember the way we talked to one another, our words thickly accented black Southern speech. Language is also a place of struggle. We are wedded in language, have our being in words. Language is also a place of struggle. Dare I speak to oppressed and oppressor in the same voice? Dare I speak to you in a language that will move beyond the boundaries of domination—a language that will not bind you, fence you in, or hold you? Language is also a place of struggle. The oppressed struggle in language to recover ourselves, to reconcile, to reunite, to renew. Our words are not without meaning, they are an action, a resistance. Language is also a place of struggle.

It is no easy task to find ways to include our multiple voices within the various texts we create—in film, poetry, feminist theory. Those are sounds and images that mainstream consumers find difficult to understand. Sounds and scenes which cannot be appropriated are often that sign everyone questions, wants to erase, to "wipe out." I feel it even now, writing this piece when I gave it talking and reading, talking spontaneously, using familiar academic speech now and then, "talking the talk"—using black vernacular speech, the intimate sounds and gestures I normally save for family and loved ones. Private speech in public discourse, intimate intervention, making another text, a space that enables me to recover all that I am in language, I find so many gaps, absences in this written text. To cite them at least is to let the reader know something has been missed, or remains there hinted at by words—there in the deep structure.

Throughout *Freedom Charter,* a work which traces aspects of the movement against racial apartheid in South Africa, this statement is constantly repeated: *our struggle is also a struggle of memory against forgetting.* In much new, exciting cultural practice, cultural texts—in film, black literature, critical theory—there is an effort to remember that is expressive of the need to create spaces where one is able to redeem and reclaim the past, legacies of pain, suffering, and triumph in ways that transform present reality. Fragments of memory are not simply represented as flat documentary but constructed to give a "new take" on the old, constructed to move us into a different mode of articulation. We see this in films like *Dreaming Rivers* and *Illusions,* and in books like *Mama Day* by Gloria Naylor. Thinking again about space and location, I heard the statement "our struggle is also a struggle of memory against forgetting"; a politicization of memory that distinguishes nostalgia, that longing for something to be as once it was, a kind of useless act, from that remembering that serves to illuminate and transform the present.

I have needed to remember, as part of a self-critical process where one pauses to reconsider choices and location, tracing my journey from small town Southern black life, from folk traditions, and church experience to cities, to the university, to neighborhoods that are not racially segregated, to places where I see for the first time independent cinema, where I read critical theory, where I write theory. Along that trajectory, I vividly recall efforts to silence my coming to voice. In my public presentation I was able to tell stories, to share memories. Here again I only hint at them. The opening essay in my book, *Talking Back,* describes my effort to emerge as critical thinker, artist, and writer in a context of repression. I talk about punishment, about mama and daddy aggressively silencing me, about the censorship of black communities. I had no choice. I had to struggle and resist to emerge from that context and then from other locations with mind intact, with an open heart. I had to leave that space I called home to move beyond boundaries, yet I needed also to return there. We sing a song in the black church tradition that says, "I'm going up the rough side of the mountain on my way home." Indeed the very meaning of "home" changes with experience of decolonization, of radicalization. At times, home is nowhere. At times, one knows only extreme estrangement and alienation. Then home is no longer just one place. It is locations. Home is that place which enables and promotes varied and everchanging perspectives, a place where one discovers new ways of seeing reality, frontiers of difference. One confronts and accepts dispersal and fragmentation as part of the construction of a new world order that reveals more fully where we are, who we can become, an order that does not demand forgetting. "Our struggle is also a struggle of memory against forgetting."

This experience of space and location is not the same for black folks who have always been privileged, or for black folks who desire only to move from underclass status to points of privilege; not the same for those of us from poor backgrounds who have had to continually engage in actual political struggle both within and outside black communities to assert an aesthetic and critical presence. Black folks coming from poor, underclass communities, who enter universities or privileged cultural settings unwilling to surrender every vestige of who we were before we were there, all "sign" of our class and cultural "difference," who are unwilling to play the role of "exotic Other," must create spaces within that culture of domination if we are to survive whole, our souls intact.

Our very presence is a disruption. We are often as much an "Other," a threat to black people from privileged class backgrounds who do not understand or share our perspectives, as we are to uninformed white folks. Everywhere we go there is pressure to silence our voices, to co-opt and undermine them. Mostly, of course, we are not there. We never "arrive" or "can't stay." Back in those spaces where we come from, we kill ourselves in despair, drowning in nihilism, caught in poverty, in addiction, in every postmodern mode of dying that can be named. Yet when we few remain in that "other" space, we are often too isolated, too alone. We die there, too. Those of us who live, who "make it," passionately holding on to aspects of that "downhome" life we do not intend to lose while simultaneously seeking new knowledge and experience, invent spaces of radical openness. Without such spaces we would not survive. Our living depends on our ability to conceptualize alternatives, often improvised. Theorizing about this experience aesthetically, critically is an agenda for radical cultural practice.

For me this space of radical openness is a margin—a profound edge. Locating oneself there is difficult yet necessary. It is not a "safe" place. One is always at risk. One needs a community of resistance.

In the preface to *Feminist Theory: From Margin to Center,* I expressed these thoughts on marginality:

> To be in the margin is to be part of the whole but outside the main body. As black Americans living in a small Kentucky town, the railroad tracks were a daily reminder of our marginality. Across those tracks were paved streets, stores we could not enter, restaurants we could not eat in, and people we could not look directly in the face. Across those tracks was a world we could work in as maids, as janitors, as prostitutes, as long as it was in a service capacity. We could enter that world but we could not live there. We had always to return to the margin, to cross the tracks to shacks and abandoned houses on the edge of town.
>
> There were laws to ensure our return. Not to return was to risk being punished. Living as we did—on the edge—we developed a particular way of seeing reality. We looked both from the outside in and from the inside out. We focused our attention on the center as well as on the margin. We understood both. This mode of seeing reminded us of the existence of a whole universe, a main body made up of both margin and center. Our survival depended on an ongoing public awareness of the separation between margin and center and an ongoing private acknowledgement that we were a necessary, vital part of that whole.
>
> This sense of wholeness, impressed upon our consciousness by the structure of our daily lives, provided us with an oppositional world-view—a mode of seeing unknown to most of our oppressors, that sustained us, aided us in our struggle to transcend poverty and despair, strengthened our sense of self and our solidarity.

Though incomplete, these statements identify marginality as much more than a site of deprivation; in fact I was saying just the opposite, that it is also the site of radical possibility, a space of resistance. It was this marginality that I was naming as a central location for the production of a counter-hegemonic discourse that is not just found in words but in habits of being and the way one lives. As such, I was not speaking of a marginality one wishes to lose—to give up or surrender as part of moving into the center—but rather of a site one stays in, clings to even, because it nourishes one's capacity to resist. It offers to one the possibility of radical perspective from which to see and create, to imagine alternatives, new worlds.

This is not a mythic notion of marginality. It comes from lived experience. Yet I want to talk about what it means to struggle to maintain that marginality even as one works, produces, lives, if you will, at the center. I no longer live in that segregated world across the tracks. Central to life in that world was the ongoing awareness of the necessity of opposition. When Bob Marley sings, "We refuse to be what you want us to be, we are what we are, and that's the way it's going to be," that space of refusal, where one can say no to the colonizer, no to the downpressor, is located in the margins. And one can only say no, speak the voice of resistance, because there exists a counter-language. While it may resemble the colonizer's tongue, it has undergone a transformation, it has been irrevocably changed. When I left that concrete space in the margins, I kept alive in my heart ways of knowing reality which affirm continually not only the primacy of resistance but the necessity of a resistance that is sustained by remembrance of the past, which includes recollections of broken tongues giving us ways to speak that decolonize our minds, our very beings. Once mama said to me as I was about to go again to the predominantly white university, "You can take what the white people have to offer, but you do not have to love them." Now understanding her cultural codes, I know that she was not saying to me not to love people of other races. She was speaking about colonization and the reality of what it means to be taught in a culture of domination by those who dominate. She was insisting on my power to be able to separate useful knowledge that I might get from the dominating group from participation in ways of knowing that would lead to estrangement, alienation, and worse—assimilation and co-optation. She was saying that it is not necessary to give yourself over to them to learn. Not having been in those institutions, she knew that I might be faced again and again with situations where I would be "tried," made to feel as though a central requirement of my being accepted would mean participation in this system of exchange to ensure my success, my "making it." She was reminding me of the necessity of opposition and simultaneously encouraging me not to lose that radical perspective shaped and formed by marginality.

Understanding marginality as position and place of resistance is crucial for oppressed, exploited, colonized people. If we only view the margin as sign marking the despair, a deep nihilism penetrates in a destructive way the very ground of our being. It is there in that space of collective despair that one's creativity, one's imagination is at risk, there that one's mind is fully colonized, there that the freedom one longs for as lost. Truly the mind that resists colonization struggles for freedom one longs for as lost. Truly the mind that resists colonization struggles for freedom of expression. The struggle may not even begin with the colonizer; it may begin within one's segregated, colonized community and family. So I want to note that I am not trying to romantically re-inscribe the notion of that space of marginality where the oppressed live apart from their oppressors as "pure." I want to say that these margins have been both sites of repression and sites of resistance. And since we are well able to name the nature of that repression we know better the margin as site of deprivation. We are more silent when it comes to speaking of the margin as site of resistance. We are more often silenced when it comes to speaking of the margin as site of resistance.

Silenced. During my graduate years I heard myself speaking often in the voice of resistance. I cannot say that my speech was welcomed. I cannot say that my speech was heard in such a way that it altered relations between colonizer and colonized. Yet what I have noticed is that those scholars, most especially those who name themselves radical critical thinkers, feminist thinkers, now fully participate in the construction of a discourse about the "Other." I was made "Other" there in that space with them. In that space in the margins, that lived-in segregated world of my past and present. They did not meet me there in that space. They met me at the center. They greeted me a colonizers. I am waiting to learn from them the path of their resistance, of how it came to be that they were able to surrender the power to act as colonizers. I am waiting for them to bear witness, to give testimony. They say that the discourse on marginality, on difference has moved beyond a discussion of "us and them." They do not speak of how this movement has taken place. This is a response from the radical space of my marginality. It is a space of resistance. It is a space I choose.

I am waiting for them to stop talking about the "Other," to stop even describing how important it is to be able to speak about difference. It is not just important what we speak about, but how and why we speak. Often this speech about the "Other" is also a mask, an oppressive talk hiding gaps, absences, that space where our words would be if we were speaking, if there were silence, if we were there. This "we" is that "us" in the margins, that "we" who inhabit marginal space that is not a site of domination but a place of resistance. Enter that space. Often this speech about the "Other" annihilates, erases: "No need to hear your voice when I can talk about you better than you can speak about yourself. No need to hear your voice. Only tell me about your pain. I want to know your story. And then I will tell it back to you in a new way. Tell it back to you in such a way that it has become mine, my own. Re-writing you, I write myself anew. I am still author, authority. I am still the colonizer, the speaking subject, and you are now at the center of my talk." Stop. We greet you as liberators. This "we" is that "us" in the margins, that "we" who inhabit marginal space that is not a site of domination but a place of resistance. Enter that space. This is an intervention. I am writing to you. I am speaking from a place in the margins where I am different, where I see things differently. I am talking about what I see.

Speaking from margins. Speaking in resistance. I open a book. There are words on the back cover, *Never in the Shadows Again*. A book which suggests the possibility of speaking as liberators. Only who is speaking and who is silent. Only who stands in the shadows—the shadow in a doorway, the space where images of black women are represented voiceless, the space where our words are invoked to serve and support, the space of our absence. Only small echoes of protest. We are re-written. We are "Other." We are the margin. Who is speaking and to whom. Where do we locate ourselves and comrades.

Silenced. We fear those who speak about us, who do not speak to us and with us. We know what it is like to be silenced. We know that the forces that silence us, because they never want us to speak, differ from the forces that say speak, tell me your story. Only do not speak in a voice of resistance. Only speak from that space in the margin that is a sign of deprivation, a wound, an unfulfilled longing. Only speak your pain.

This is an intervention. A message from that space in the margin that is a site of creativity and power, that inclusive space where we recover ourselves, where we move in solidarity to erase the category colonized/colonizer. Marginality as site of resistance. Enter that space. Let us meet there. Enter that space. We greet you as liberators.

Spaces can be real and imagined. Spaces can tell stories and unfold histories. Spaces can be interrupted, appropriated, and transformed through artistic and literary practice.

As Pratibha Parma notes, "The appropriation and use of space are political acts."

To speak about that location from which work emerges, I choose familiar politicized language, old codes, words like "struggle, marginality, resistance." I choose these words knowing that they are no longer popular or "cool"—hold onto them and the political legacies they evoke and affirm, even as I work to change what they say, to give them renewed and different meaning.

I am located in the margin. I make a definite distinction between that marginality which is imposed by oppressive structures and that marginality one chooses as site of resistance—as location of radical openness and possibility. This site of resistance is continually formed in that segregated culture of opposition that is our critical response to domination. We come to this space through suffering and pain, through struggle. We know struggle to be that which pleasures, delights, and fulfills desire. We are transformed, individually, collectively, as we make radical creative space which affirms and sustains our subjectivity, which gives us a new location from which to articulate our sense of the world.

Homeplace

A SITE OF RESISTANCE

When I as a young girl the journey across town to my grandmother's house was one of the most intriguing experiences. Mama did not like to stay there long. She did not care for all that loud talk, the talk that was usually about the old days, the way life happened then—who married whom, how and when somebody died, but also how we lived and survived as black people, how the white folks treated us. I remember this journey not just because of the stories I would hear. It was a movement away from the segregated blackness of our community into a poor white neighborhood. I remember the fear, being scared to walk to Baba's (our grandmother's house) because we would have to pass that terrifying whiteness—those white faces on the porches staring us down with hate. Even when empty or vacant, those porches seemed to say "danger," "you do not belong here," "you are not safe."

Oh! that feeling of safety, of arrival, of homecoming when we finally reached the edges of her yard, when we could see the soot black face of our grandfather, Daddy Gus, sitting in his chair on the porch, smell his cigar, and rest on his lap. Such a contrast, that feeling of arrival, of homecoming, this sweetness and the bitterness of that journey, that constant reminder of white power and control.

I speak of this journey as leading to my grandmother's house, even though our grandfather lived there too. In our young minds houses belonged to women, were their special domain, not as property, but as places where all that truly mattered in life took place—the warmth and comfort of shelter, the feeding of our bodies, the nurturing of our souls. There we learned dignity, integrity of being; there we learned to have faith. The folks who made this life possible, who were our primary guides and teachers, were black women.

Their lives were not easy. Their lives were hard. They were black women who for the most part worked outside the home serving white folks, cleaning their houses, washing their clothes, tending their children—black women who worked in the fields or in the streets, whatever they could do to make ends meet, whatever was necessary. Then they returned to their homes to make life happen there. This tension between service outside one's home, family, and kin network, service provided to white folks which took time and energy, and the effort of black women to conserve enough of themselves to provide service (care and nurturance) within their own families and communities is one of the many factors that has historically distinguished the lot of black women in patriarchal white supremacist society from that of black men. Contemporary black struggle must honor this history of service just as it must critique the sexist definition of service as women's "natural" role.

Since sexism delegates to females the task of creating and sustaining a home environment, it has been primarily the responsibility of black women to construct domestic households as spaces of care and nurturance in the face of the brutal harsh reality of racist oppression, of sexist domination. Historically, African-American people believed that the construction of a homeplace, however fragile and tenuous (the slave hut, the wooden shack), had a radical political dimension. Despite the brutal reality of racial apartheid, of domination, one's homeplace was the one site where one could freely confront the issue of humanization, where one could resist. Black women resisted by making homes where all black people could strive to be subjects, not objects, where we could be affirmed in our minds and hearts despite poverty, hardship, and deprivation, where we could restore to ourselves the dignity denied us on the outside in the public world.

This task of making homeplace was not simply a matter of black women providing service; it was about the construction of a safe place where black people could affirm one another and by so doing heal many of the wounds inflicted by racist domination. We could not learn to love or respect ourselves in the culture of white supremacy, on the outside; it was there on the inside, in that "homeplace," most often created and kept by black women, that we had the opportunity to grow and develop, to nurture our spirits. This task of making a homeplace, of making home a community of resistance, has been shared by black women globally, especially black women in white supremacist societies.

Historically, black women have resisted white supremacist domination by working to establish homeplace. It does not matter that sexism assigned them this role. It is more important that they took this conventional role and expanded it to include caring for one another, for children, for black men, in ways that elevated our spirits; that kept us from despair, that taught some of us to be revolutionaries able to struggle for freedom. In his famous 1845 slave narrative, Frederick Douglass tells the story of his birth, of his enslaved black mother who was hired out a considerable distance from his place of residence. Describing their relationship, he writes:

> I never saw my mother, to know her as such more than four or five times in my life; and each of these times was very short in duration, and at night. She was hired by Mr. Stewart, who lived about twelve miles from my house. She made her journeys to see me in the night, traveling the whole distance on foot, after the performance of her day's work. She was a field hand, and a whipping is the penalty of not being in the field at sunrise . . . I do not recollect of ever seeing my mother by the light of day. She was with me in the night. She would lie down with me and get me to sleep, but long before I waked she was gone.

After sharing this information, Douglass later says that he never enjoyed a mother's "soothing presence, her tender and watchful care" so that he received the "tidings of her death with much the same emotions I should have probably felt at the death of a stranger." Douglass surely intended to impress upon the consciousness of white readers the cruelty of that system of racial domination which separated black families, black mothers from their children. Yet he does so by devaluing black womanhood, by not even registering the quality of care that made his black mother travel those twelve miles to hold him in her arms. In the midst of a brutal racist system, which did not value black life, she valued the life of her child enough to resist that system, to come to him in the night, just to hold him.

Now I cannot agree with Douglass that he never knew a mother's care. I want to suggest that this mother, who dared to hold him in the night, gave him at birth a sense of value that provided a groundwork, however fragile, for the person he later became. If anyone doubts the power and significance of this maternal gesture, they would do well to read psychoanalyst Alice Miller's book, *The Untouched Key: Tracing Childhood Trauma in Creativity and Destructiveness*. Holding him in her arms, Douglass' mother provided, if only for a short time, a space where this black child was not the subject of dehumanizing scorn and devaluation but was the recipient of a quality of care that should have enabled the adult

Douglass to look back and reflect on the political choices of this black mother who resisted slave codes, risking her life, to care for her son. I want to suggest that devaluation of the role his mother played in his life is a dangerous oversight. Though Douglass is only one example, we are currently in danger of forgetting the powerful role black women have played in constructing for us homeplaces that are the site for resistance. This forgetfulness undermines our solidarity and the future of black liberation struggle.

Douglass's work is important, for he is historically identified as sympathetic to the struggle for women's rights. All too often his critique of male domination, such as it was, did not include recognition of the particular circumstances of black women in relation to black men and families. To me one of the most important chapters in my first book, *Ain't I A Woman: Black Women and Feminism,* is one that calls attention to "Continued Devaluation of Black Womanhood." Overall devaluation of the role black women have played in constructing for us homeplaces that are the site for resistance undermines our efforts to resist racism and the colonizing mentality which promotes internalized self-hatred. Sexist thinking about the nature of domesticity has determined the way black women's experience in the home is perceived. In African-American culture there is a long tradition of "mother worship." Black autobiographies, fiction, and poetry praise the virtues of the self-sacrificing black mother. Unfortunately, though positively motivated, black mother worship extols the virtues of self-sacrifice while simultaneously implying that such a gesture is not reflective of choice and will, rather the perfect embodiment of a woman's "natural" role. The assumption then is that the black woman who works hard to be a responsible caretaker is only doing what she should be doing. Failure to recognize the realm of choice, and the remarkable re-visioning of both woman's role and the idea of "home" that black women consciously exercised in practice, obscures the political commitment to racial uplift, to eradicating racism, which was the philosophical core of dedication to community and home.

Though black women did not self-consciously articulate in written discourse the theoretical principles of decolonization, this does not detract from the importance of their actions. They understood intellectually and intuitively the meaning of homeplace in the midst of an oppressive and dominating social reality, of homeplace as site of resistance and liberation struggle. I know of what I speak. I would not be writing this essay if my mother, Rosa Bell, daughter to Sarah Oldham, granddaughter to Bell Hooks, had not created homeplace in just this liberatory way, despite the contradictions of poverty and sexism.

In our family, I remember the immense anxiety we felt as children when mama would leave our house, our segregated community, to work as a maid in the homes of white folks. I believe that she sensed our fear, our concern that she might not return to us safe, that we could not find her (even though she always left phone numbers, they did not ease our worry). When she returned home after working long hours, she did not complain. She made an effort to rejoice with us that her work was done, that she was home, making it seem as though there was nothing about the experience of working as a maid in a white household, in that space of Otherness, which stripped her of dignity and personal power.

Looking back as an adult woman, I think of the effort it must have taken for her to transcend her own tiredness (and who knows what assaults or wounds to her spirit had to be put aside so that she could give something to her own). Given the contemporary notions of "good parenting" this may seem like a small gesture, yet in many post-slavery black families, it was a gesture parents were often too weary, too beaten down to make. Those of us who were fortunate enough to receive such care understood its value. Politically, our young mother, Rosa Bell, did not allow the white supremacist culture of domination to completely shape and control her psyche and her familial relationships. Working to create a homeplace that affirmed our beings, our blackness, our love for one another was necessary resistance. We learned degrees of critical consciousness from her. Our lives were not without contradictions, so it is not my intent to create a romanticized portrait. Yet any attempts to critically assess the role of black women in liberation struggle must examine the way political concern about the impact of racism shaped black women's thinking, their sense of home, and their modes of parenting.

An effective means of white subjugation of black people globally has been the perpetual construction of economic and social structures that deprive many folks of the means to make homeplace. Remembering this should enable us to understand the political value of black women's resistance in the home. It should provide a framework where we can discuss the development of black female political consciousness, acknowledging the political importance of resistance effort that took place in homes. It is no accident that the South African apartheid regime systematically attacks and destroys black efforts to construct homeplace, however tenuous, that small private reality where black women and men can renew their spirits and recover themselves. It is no accident that this homeplace, as fragile and as transitional as it may be, a makeshift shed, a small bit of earth where one rests, is always subject to violation and destruction. For when a people no longer have the space to construct homeplace, we cannot build a meaningful community of resistance.

Throughout our history, African-Americans have recognized the subversive value of homeplace, of having access to private space where we do not directly encounter white racist aggression. Whatever the shape and direction of black liberation struggle (civil rights reform or black power movement), domestic space has been a crucial site for organizing, for forming political solidarity. Homeplace has been a site of resistance. Its structure was defined less by whether or not black women and men were conforming to sexist behavior norms and more by our struggle to uplift ourselves as a people, out struggle to resist racist domination and oppression.

That liberatory struggle has been seriously undermined by contemporary efforts to change that subversive homeplace into a site of patriarchal domination of black women by black men, where we abuse one another for not conforming to sexist norms. This shift in perspective, where homeplace is not viewed as a political site, has had negative impact on the construction of black female identity and political consciousness. Masses of black women, many of whom were not formally educated, had in the past been able to play a vital role in black liberation struggle. In the contemporary situation, as the paradigms for domesticity in black life mirrored white bourgeois norms (where home is conceptualized as politically neutral space), black people began to overlook and devalue the importance of black female labor in teaching critical consciousness in domestic space. Many black women, irrespective of class status, have responded to this crisis of meaning by imitating leisure-class sexist notions of women's role, focusing their lives on meaningless compulsive consumerism.

Identifying this syndrome as "the crisis of black womanhood" in her essay, "Considering Feminism as a Model for Social Change," Sheila Radford-Hill points to the mid-sixties as that historical moment when the primacy of black woman's role in liberation struggle began to be questioned as a threat to black manhood and was deemed unimportant. Radford-Hill asserts:

> Without the power to influence the purpose and the direction of our collective experience, without the power to influence our culture from within, we are increasingly immobilized, unable to integrate self and role identities, unable to resist the cultural imperialism of the dominant culture which assures our continued oppression by destroying us from within. Thus, the crisis manifests itself as social dysfunction in the black community—as genocide, fratricide, homicide, and suicide. It is also manifested by the abdication of personal responsibility by black women for themselves and for each other . . . The crisis of black womanhood is a form of cultural aggression: a form of exploitation so vicious, so insidious that it is currently destroying an entire generation of black women and their families.

This contemporary crisis of black womanhood might have been avoided had black women collectively sustained attempts to develop the latent feminism expressed by their willingness to work equally alongside black men in black liberation struggle. Contemporary equation of black liberation struggle with the subordination of black women has damaged collective black solidarity. It has served the interests of white supremacy to promote the assumption that the wounds of racist domination would be less severe were black women conforming to sexist role patterns.

We are daily witnessing the disintegration of African-American family life that is grounded in a recognition of the political value of constructing homeplace as a site of resistance; black people daily perpetuate sexist norms that threaten our survival as a people. We can no longer act as though sexism in black communities does not threaten our solidarity; any force which estranges and alienates us from one another serves the interests of racist domination.

Black women and men must create a revolutionary vision of black liberation that has a feminist dimension, one which is formed in consideration of our specific needs and concerns. Drawing on past legacies, contemporary black women can begin to reconceptualize ideas of homeplace, once again considering the primacy of domesticity as a site for subversion and resistance. When we renew our concern with homeplace, we can address political issues that most affect our daily lives.

Calling attention to the skills and resources of black women who may have begun to feel that they have no meaningful contribution to make, women who may or may not be formally educated but who have essential wisdom to share, who have practical experience that is the breeding ground for all useful theory, we may begin to bond with one another in ways that renew our solidarity.

When black women renew our political commitment to homeplace, we can address the needs and concerns of young black women who are groping for structures of meaning that will further their growth, young women who are struggling for self-definition. Together, black women can renew our commitment to black liberation struggle, sharing insights and awareness, sharing feminist thinking and feminist vision, building solidarity.

With this foundation, we can regain lost perspective, give life new meaning. We can make homeplace that space where we return for renewal and self-recovery, where we can heal our wounds and become whole.

bell hooks Interviewed by Cornel West

CW Begin by telling me what your motivation has been for becoming an intellectual. Talk about your work, and the politics of both your personal relationships and your politics of resistance.

bh A passion for ideas, for thinking critically, lay the groundwork for my commitment to intellectual life. That passion began in childhood. When I was young I had, and continue to have, an insatiable longing to read everything—know everything. To this day I remain the kind of reader for whom nothing is off limits, from children's books, Harlequin romances, car and fashion magazines, self-help books, all kinds of pulp, to economic, sociological, psychological, literary, and feminist theory. I love to read across disciplines. I am always astonished by academics who show no interest in work outside their discipline. For me, reading broadly has been absolutely essential to the kind of speculative critical thinking that informs my work. I have said in other writing that the difficulty many academics have when called to speak and write from an inclusive standpoint—one where ideas are looked at from a multidimensional perspective that begins with an analysis rooted in an understanding of race, gender, and class is due to the gap created by a lack of information. Since so many scholars and academics have been trained to think and study along narrow disciplinary lines, the knowledge they produce rarely addresses the complexity of our experience or our capacity to know. A pure passion to know was the yearning that seduced me into intellectual life. And that yearning has really been the impetus motivating me to synthesize and juxtapose in a complex way ideas, experiences that on the surface might not appear to have a point of convergence.

When I think about my intellectual development, where I am now, I am often amazed that the attitudes and commitments to intellectual work that were present in my childhood remain constant. In Terry Eagleton's essay "The Significance of Theory," he suggests that children make the best theorists because they often possess that unstoppable will to transgress the boundaries of accepted ideas, to explore and discover new ways of thinking and being.

My childhood engagement with ideas was intimately linked to struggle for self-recovery. Growing up in a family with strong elements of dysfunctionality, where I was psychologically wounded and at times physically hurt, the primary force which kept me going, which lifted my spirits was critical engagement with ideas. This engagement and concomitant development of critical consciousness enabled me to step back from the family situation and look at myself, my parents, my siblings from a critical, analytical perspective. This helped me to understand the personal history and experiences informing my parents' behavior. So, Cornel, what has made my relationship to theory unique is the way my life stands as testimony to the positive power of critical thinking.

Coupling a passion for ideas and a vivid imagination, I found in the world of creative writing a place of transcendence, a way to recover myself. Unlike many children in dysfunctional family settings who create imaginary playmates to sustain their spirits, I found early on that intense creative engagement with reading and writing poetry took me on an imaginative journey that uplifted and inspired me. I started writing poetry when I was ten, publishing my first poems in our Sunday school magazine. Receiving such affirmation at such an early age gave me an autonomous sense of self-esteem while instilling in me the understanding that my voice was important, that my vision could be articulated and shared.

I remember growing up in our house on First Street. We had a room for the sick and dying. We called it the middle room. In that room hung curtains with the Elizabeth Barrett Browning sonnet "How do I Love Thee Let Me Count the Ways." I would stand at the window reciting this sonnet over and over again. Reciting poetry was an important cultural practice in both Black schools and homes.

CW Was there a particular person exposing you to poetry at that time?

bh I grew up in the traditional Black church where you learned poems for Easter Sunday, Black History Month, and so on.

The last time I went home to my childhood church, Virginia Street Baptist Church . . .

CW In Kentucky?

bh Yes. Every Sunday there is a scheduled program when Sunday school ends, where we come up together as a congregation and somebody reports on the Sunday school lesson.

CW Yeah, we did that too.

bh And you might have a play, we used to have plays. And it made me think, who were these adult Black people acting out a play, made me remember that Black adults did these kinds of things as a group, that we had a context to memorize things, that I memorized things.

As an adolescent I went to Crispus Attucks High School, before it was integrated, and we used to have similar programs before pep rallies. In fact, my first memory of major public speaking is during pep rallies. We students would always have a talent show where folks would sing or perform whatever talent they had. My talent, naturally, was reciting poems.

CW Langston Hughes or who?

bh It started out ironically with James Whitecomb Rielly's "The Little Orphan Annie Poem." That was my favorite poem to recite.

CW Really, "Little Orphan Annie?"

bh Yes, because I could act out the parts. And it gave me a little taste of fame in my high school because people knew and liked my recitations.

CW That gave you a certain status.

bh Absolutely. A little notoriety is crucial for adolescent self-esteem. I also read the scripture during the morning offering from the time I was a little girl. I chose the passage from Matthew that goes, "If you haven't given to the least of these my brethren, you haven't given to me."

CW Powerful passage, powerful passage.

bh So here I'd be, a young girl reading scripture while folks would be shouting and the old ladies would be saying, "Oh how she reads!" and this solidified for me the relationship between artistic performance and artistic/intellectual production as forces which deeply move people spiritually and emotionally. This connection really had a tremendous impact on me.

CW Say something about your experience at Stanford and Wisconsin, because it is interesting that, despite this rich grounding in Black civil society, Black family, Black church, Black school, you chose to study at these highly prestigious, predominantly White institutions. How did it affect and alter you?

bh Well, it's very interesting, because I really did not understand class differences among Black people until I went to Stanford. Growing up in segregated Kentucky, it was irrelevant how much money any individual Black person did or did not have because we lived as a community in the same areas and, for the most part, under the same conditions. We all went to the same schools, we attended the same church. So, one could say, my "sense" of Blackness was monolithic, I thought all Black people existed in a kinship structure of larger community. Stanford was my first real departure from that way of life.

Stanford of the early 1970s had a lot of Black students from the African diaspora. St. Clair Drake was our major scholarly figure, and there were international Black students, as well as wealthy Black American students. It was a very, very difficult time in my life. College initiated my class awakening, shook up my agrarian, working-class notions of privilege, where privilege was defined as enough food, shelter, and care, yet here I was in an institution where "plenty" was defined through vacations in South America and Europe. It is as a result of these vantage points, these experiences, that I came to politically interrogate class differences among Black people. I realized for the first time that Black people, nationally and internationally, are not joined ideologically, politically, or culturally by virtue of skin color but that, in fact, the question of ideology, and political stance would very much determine the degree to which we could be joined together.

Also the years that I was at Stanford, the Black Muslims were a strong force on the campus.

CW Yeah, out in East Palo Alto . . .

bh Yes. Between Black power, SDS, SNCC, protest against the Vietnam war, and Stonewall, it was a very politicized time.

CW Now, was this class awakening preceded by a feminist awakening or did your feminist awakening develop through a class analysis?

bh My feminist awakening came as a result of growing up in a traditional, patriarchal household. With patriarchy meaning absolute rule by the father. Contrary to most of the studies that have been done by people like Moynihan, Frazier, or people that focus on urban cities, two-parent-headed households were the "norm" throughout my childhood. It is also important to keep in mind that, when we talk about Black people before 1900, at least ninety percent of those Black people were still in the agrarian South and that in Black southern familial tradition, the father was the understood head of the household, whether or not he was an earning provider in the home.

If a sociologist had come into the home of my grandmother or my mother they would have seen strong talking women and very silent men. And they might not have readily understood that any time my grandfather did decide to speak, his word was law. So it was very deceptive if you took that household in terms of how it appeared from an outsider's vantage point. Mother might be doing all the talking, she might also be doing all the apparent decision making. But no matter what my mother had approved of, if my father decided to open his mouth and say no, his word was law. There would be no ensuing discussion or argument about it. So it's really important to keep in mind when we talk about the place of Black males and Black father figures in the home, that many of us are coming from traditional households where the father was not only present but exerting a tremendous amount of authority and control.

CW Are you saying then that there were certain criticisms of Black patriarchy already implicit in your younger years?

bh Now remember, Cornel, I grew up in a household with five sisters and one brother, and we five older girls were seeing this younger brother get to do all kinds of things, get to have all kinds of privileges that we did not have.

We were also witnessing on a daily basis the fierceness of my father. If, for example, my father came home and something was not right about the house he would immediately and sometimes violently upbraid my mother. Instilling in all of us a fear of his moods, his brutal censure.

I can also remember walking up the stairs one day after having a conflict with my mother and saying, "I'm never going to get married, I'm never going to let any man tell me what to do." I attribute this early consciousness of male domination to my keen sense that inequity in my household was gender based.

Now I would like to add that my maternal grandfather, Daddy Gus, represented an alternative model of Black masculinity. He was always kind, gentle and non-dominating. He really represented for me a non-traditional masculine ideal. Seeing these differing styles of Black maleness has made me ever mindful of the need to resist constructing a negative monolithic paradigm of Black masculinity.

CW How old were you at this time?

bh Sixteen, fifteen, the time when one can begin to feel very acutely the sense of injustice brought about by sex role patterns.

CW With relation to your feminist development, can you share with me what went into your decision to write your dissertation on Toni Morrison?

bh I wrote my first book *Ain't I A Woman: Black Women and Feminism* as a nineteen-year-old undergraduate at Stanford. By then I was heavily engaged in women's studies classes and had begun, not only to think in a more sophisticated way about gender, but also more about the specific nature of Black female reality. This also began the "hot" time, when women of color were telling "women's studies" that they were only looking at White women's experience. Naturally, this brought about the mad search for the authentic Black female voice.

Many people don't think of Toni Morrison as an essayist, but she was really one of the first major Black female voices in social criticism, making specific commentary on gender in the early 1970s and late 1960s. I read her essays before reading her fiction. So, first and foremost, I saw Morrison as a mentor figure, a Black woman writing the kind of social critique I envisioned myself writing.

My favorite novel still is *The Bluest Eye*. Because it does in literature what Black feminists have just begun documenting in the realm of feminist theory, and that is to show graphically the intertwining of race, gender, and class. Early on in the novel there is that powerful moment when Claudia, speaking about her mother, says, "When I think of autumn, I think of someone with hands who does not want me to die." There is that immediate sense of winter, the cold, being poor, and the effect of poverty on the consciousness of young Black girls. I, and I believe many Black women, have an immediate identification with Morrison's novels because she grappled with what it means to be poor and Black, coming to consciousness of a political and sexual world around you.

Despite the clarity and magic in her later works, her first novel *The Bluest Eye* is for me the most powerful. It has a raw, subversive, political immediacy which is not as apparent in her later novels. Although *The Street,* written earlier by Ann Petry, comes close to invoking that immediacy—an opinion I've had the opportunity to share and elaborate on with Ann Petry herself.

CW I remember she came to your class at Yale.

bh It was an unforgettable moment when she stood there and told us that she knew before she had written a word that Lutie was going to kill Boots.

The Street also gives us that powerful intertwining of race, sex, and class. But, it doesn't give us girlhood in quite the same way as Morrison's *The Bluest Eye*. Morrison was trying to delineate, for a country which has historically discarded the experience of Black females, the processes and experiences which construct and shape Black women's identities. She shows fictively ways we make it despite the oppressive conditions of poverty and racial/sexual subordination but she also shows the wounds—the scars we carry into adulthood.

I also came to Morrison believing that White critics, and many of the Black people who were writing about Morrison, were not delving as deeply into the complexity of her work as her writing deserved.

CW But you haven't published any of this work.

bh I have never focused on publishing my literary criticism to the degree that I have feminist theory or cultural criticism, or even film criticism. In fact, I often explain to people that having written books that cut across class barriers makes it very difficult to focus on producing and publishing literary criticism, given its narrow and limited audience.

When *Ain't I a Woman* was first published I would get dozens of letters a week, where, say, a Black woman from a small town, out in the middle of nowhere, would tell me that she read my book at the public library and it transformed her life. Intellectual affirmation of this sort forces you to interrogate radical pedagogy as it relates to your individual notions of intellectual production. I sometimes feel an enormous sense of personal power in a positive way. I feel as though I have enabled some women and men to live more fully in the world. But this has also made it very difficult for me to put one hundred percent of my energy into literary criticism. I continue to write literary criticism but my efforts are directed much more towards that literature which is going to reach a wider audience and serve as a catalyst for personal and communal transformation.

CW With all this debate nowadays about public intellectuals, it is fascinating to see someone like yourself whose texts sell thirty, and forty thousand copies, whose texts sell across the academy and the community, who receives letters from Black prisoners—a brother talking about how your name is a household word in his prison. I can see your point about not wanting to be so narrowly "academicized" that it takes away this much broader audience. There must also be a good deal of tension and anxiety about having such a broad public on the one hand while still negotiating a viable career within the academy. You've written about some of your tensions within the academy, what some of its downfalls are. Can you say more about how you've handled these tensions?

bh I think that the major dilemma is the way professionalization within the academy limits those of us who want to speak to broader audiences.

I think back to the heated debate which centered around my choosing not to use footnotes in *Ain't I A Woman*. I actually spent a great deal of time deliberating on whether or not to use footnotes. I went into various communities and asked non-academic Black people if they read books with footnotes. The majority responded by saying that when they open a book with footnotes they immediately think that book isn't for them, that the book is for an academic person. And I've tried to explain, as well as justify, to, for the most part, academically-oriented individuals that my choice around footnotes was very much a choice informed by questions of class, access, and literacy levels rather than a simple devaluation of footnotes, or "shoddy, careless" scholarship. I am perpetually concerned with what kinds of codes, apart from interest, convey to a group of people the notion that a particular book isn't for them.

Which leads me back to the problem of professionalization in the academy, the editorial practice which would have all our articles sound alike. I was teasing an editor working on a piece of mine to appear in a literary journal about the edit he had done, and I said to him, "You know you've stripped this of my flavor, my essence." And we both laughed because he immediately invoked notions of "standard and rigor," when we both knew what he really meant to say was that my work was too personal, engaging, overtly political, too "Black" to conform to the journal's "style."

After finishing *Black Looks: Race and Representation* I said to myself, the world is going say I'm writing too much. A thought which raised all sorts of questions in my mind about Black women, success, and our sense of entitlement. I wonder if male academics—writers like Noam Chomsky, Fred Jameson, or Edward Said—sit around contemplating whether or not they're writing "too much."

I also live with the fear, like others in the academy, that a heavy-handed professionalism is going to come down on me and tell me that what I've written is of no value. I live with that fear because people who are evaluating you for tenure, for jobs, are not looking at something like the letter from the brother in prison. They're looking at me from the perspective of the journal editor, from the perspective of someone who's likely to say, bell hooks is not academic enough.

These tensions are ever present in a positive and negative way. Not just because I straddle academic and non-academic worlds, but because my voice is also evolving, and I think my new books, *Yearning* and *Black Looks,* are moving, in some ways, in a more "academic" direction. The bottom line is that bell hooks readers who always expect me to be straightforward, who expect me to be less abstract, sometimes have difficulty with these books . . .

CW How are these two books different from your last three?

bh I am engaging in a much more traditionally academic discourse to discuss issues of aesthetics. Ideally, what I'm trying to do is bridge these two things, as I say in my essay "Postmodern Blackness," it's not like I'm going to be talking about deconstruction in the academy and then go home to basic working-class Black life and not talk at all about the essay I'm writing on, say, postmodernism. And if folks ask me what postmodernism is, I'm certainly going to find a way to satisfy their curiosity. Yet it is this very transgression of intellectual boundaries that academics often resist most violently. It's not that we as academics are forbidden to transgress, but that the forces of social control within the academy, that would have it be primarily a location for the reinscription of the status quo, place a lot of pressure on people who are trying to speak to many audiences, trying to speak with the kind of poly-vocality and multi-vocality that allow us access to different audiences, to conform or be punished.

Take you, for instance. I tease you about giving up academe and becoming a prophet in the Black community, because I know you have the power to speak beyond Princeton, beyond a White, elitist location. I think that most Black people who enter academe end up being threatened by that access we can have to a world beyond the college or university setting alone.

CW Yes, it's true. Few intellectuals fuse intellectual power with deep moral concern and political engagement. Edward Said is somebody that comes to mind, but for every Edward Said there are one hundred and fifty academicians who, albeit interesting and competent, are narrow. So it follows that for every bell hooks there are one hundred and fifty academics threatened by your "poly-vocality."

This brings me to another point. You as a writer have already established a corpus. I won't mention your exact age but it is under forty. This is a very impressive amount of work for someone in their thirties to have achieved, and this corpus does not include your fiction, which remains as yet unpublished. But is the sense many of us share that you have not actually received the kind of critical and intellectual attention your work deserves shared by you as well? I realize I'm putting you on the spot here.

bh Naturally, this raises the questions about the meaning and importance attached to acclaim, recognition, and reward. I believe we are often rewarded in ways that are not visible to a larger audience, but certainly traditional rewards are often withheld from insurgent intellectuals.

Many people think that given the success of my work I must have colleges and universities all over the country anxious to offer me teaching positions, that I must get constant job offers, and exorbitant salary, yet this is not the case. And often it is on precisely this level that I feel I do not receive enough recognition or material reward for the work that I do. Another example would be the racist process I endured to receive tenure. White academics, some of whom had published very little, demanded proof of my continued intention of writing. Something like the anti-bellum slave auction, when the new master demanded proof of the slave women's fertility. Patricia Williams bears witness to this very process in her insightful and transgressive book *Alchemy of Race and Rights*.

CW Proof? What more "proof" did they need?

bh I think it is dangerous to downplay the significance of recognition and reward, because recognition and reward inspires one to keep going, to keep writing, it confirms that there is a listening audience. So, when one's work is downplayed, or unacknowledged, that has the potential to threaten the artist's sense of agency. As early as 1892, Anna Julia Cooper, in *In a Voice from the South,* was pointing out the fact that Black women are often silenced by the knowledge that there will be no receptive audience for their voices.

When I think about Black people who possess qualities one might define as genius or distinctive creativity, I wonder why many of them don't continue to produce at the rate which their initial promise might suggest. A great deal of it most assuredly has to do with the degree to which they are not recognized, supported (emotionally and materially) and/or encouraged. Understanding this makes me feel very fortunate, even blessed, because when the academy was not recognizing the value and legitimacy of my work, many non-academic folks— Black, White, Asian—were writing to me, telling me how much they valued and appreciated my work, which both surprised and sustained me. It was a tremendous honor because I was very much raised to believe that "a prophet is never received in his own home." I grew up with the idea that it is possible to not be received by the community from which you come. But, happily, my experience has been just the opposite.

There was a point after the publication of my first book, where I felt I couldn't go on anymore because I had been so brutally and harshly critiqued by established feminists. It was really those down-home people who were affirming me. This, more than anything else, brought home for me how important larger reward can be.

When Shahrazad Ali began to appear in *Newsweek* and *Time,* I was very resentful. I thought, here is a woman who's written a book which is completely disenabling to Black people and Black community, and yet she's getting all this play in the press while many Black folks don't even know there is a bell hooks, a Cornel West, a Michele Wallace, a Patricia Hill Collins, a Stuart Hall, a Toni Cade Bambara, an Audre Lorde, and all the Black scholars and thinkers who are working in the interest of renewed Black liberation struggle. It can be disheartening.

CW Precisely. Our influence could be so much greater if, in fact, Black intellectuals had broader visibility in the establishment journals, magazines, etc. Yet I feel it is significant that we do still have many ardent readers without the establishment heralding us in this regard.

And now a quick question about fiction. Very few people know that you write fiction extensively. Who is bell hooks the fiction writer?

bh My fiction is much more experimental and abstract than my social criticism and feminist writing and that has made me much more shy about it.

One of the ideas I speak extensively about wherever I go is the joy of our voices. The fact that we can speak in many different ways. Yet this very asset quickly becomes a liability within a market economy such as this one. Once a corporation or even an independent publishing house can market an author as a specific kind of voice, it becomes a label which is put on you. In fact, it's not very different from Hollywood, where actors constantly struggle to avoid being typecast. Let's face it, it is very hard in this culture for even greatly rewarded writers to write in different kinds of voices. Take someone as distinguished as Toni Morrison: people have come to expect a certain kind of lyrical prose and would be quite shocked and disheartened if Morrison were to alter dramatically the style of her fiction or write nonfiction. Or Alice Walker. The tremendous success of a novel like *The Color Purple* that is very sparse in its language was followed by a very verbose and wordy book like *Temple of My Familiar,* and many people couldn't get through it. So the public developed an expectation of who Alice Walker is, of what her voice is. The fact is, most of us Black folks who are coming from working-class and poor backgrounds speak in many voices; we have Black vernacular speech as well as a more standardized speech we can use. What we want is to have the capacity to use all those voices in much the same way as great jazz musicians like pianist Cecil Taylor do in their music.

I read an interview with him in *Downbeat* where he talks about playing White Western classical music as well as a whole range of other things. The joy of his life as a musician has been that capacity to exercise his range. Sadly enough, we haven't gotten to a place in U.S. society yet where we allow Black writers of any status and fame to write in the many voices which they may want to and/or are capable of writing in.

CW Will you publish your fiction under bell hooks? Why don't you publish under your real name, Gloria Watkins?

bh Right now I publish everything under bell hooks, but I would like to publish under even another name. I like play.

CW Tell me again why you chose the name bell hooks over the name given to you by your mother and father?

bh Growing up, I was a sharp-tongued kid. (Some people still think I'm a sharp-tongued woman.)

bell hooks, who I don't remember clearly, was my great grandmother. She was still alive when I was a tiny girl and I remember going to the corner store one day and as usual talking back to my mother, and the storekeeper immediately said, you must be bell hooks's granddaughter, he recognized that sharp tongue.

bell hooks really entered my mind as that figure in my childhood who had paved the way for me to speak. I am, in the African tradition, in the African American religious tradition, very conscious of ancestor acknowledgment as crucial to our well-being as a people. When I think back to the past, to my father's mother Sister Ray, Bell Hooks my great-grandmother, and Sarah Oldham my mother's mother, I think about women who have charted the way for me. Alice Walker, in her essay "In Search of Our Mother's Gardens," articulates that Black women come from a legacy of women who have made a path for us. Take the title of Beverly Guysheftall's early edited anthology, *Sturdy Black Bridges,* where she is saying our mothers have been bridges that we walked across. The world never heard of Bell Blair Hooks and yet it was this woman of fiery speech who transmitted to her daughter Sarah, and her daughter Rosa the capacity of strong speech. These women are the ancestors who make it possible for me to be who I am today.

As a girl we were required to enter my grandmother's house in the African way, so that if we had brought a little friend with us we had to first present them to my grandmother, who would inevitably ask, "Well who are her people?" And then our friend would have to go down the line of her relations. If you walked into the house and you did not acknowledge the elders first, you were punished. I would often think about this later when I went into feminist classrooms where we would do an exercise to test our knowledge of our mother's ancestral lines. Frequently, women didn't even know the name of their great grandmother. It is out of that spirit that I chose the name bell hooks.

The thing I like about the interviews with myself at the end of *Yearning* is that I try to convey my more playful side. I use Play here with a capital P. I think that there is an element of Play that is almost ritualistic in Black folk life. It serves to mediate the tensions, stress, and pain of constant exploitation and oppression. Play, in a sense, becomes a balm; in religious terms, we say there is a Balm in Gilead.

Black folks release the stress and tensions in their lives through constructive Play, and I've tried to keep that element alive in my life.

Yet, this also raises again the question of what does it mean for us as Black people to function in predominantly White institutions when one of the elements of Black consciousness that is very threatening to a White supremacist world is that spirit of Play? And it is threatening precisely because that spirit of Play is enabling, it enables you to lift yourself up when things seem down, to laugh, to perhaps joke about something which is very serious.

We have talked a great deal about nihilism as it is happening in Black communities, yet one of the forces that nihilism threatens to check is our capacity to Play. If we look at new books like Bernie Siegel's *Love Medicine* and new books on health, we see White psychologists and self-help gurus acknowledging the degree to which thinking positively enables one to survive, the degree to which positive approaches to illness and suffering enable one to transcend and heal. What is so threatening about the nihilism in Black life is that it intervenes on our capacity to think positively, create interludes of Play.

When I was young my brother would tell stories, or act out a play and lift our spirits up, lift us out of the doldrums. Now television and mass media have intervened, robbing us of the ability to share and interact to create enjoyment for ourselves.

I teach a seminar on Zora Neale Hurston, and my students always become annoyed because I try to show them how Arsenio Hall and Eddie Murphy's popularity is rooted in their use of these very kinds of traditional Black "signifying" and Play. Frequently, they take a serious subject and find an element in it that allows one to laugh, lifts one up. And I appreciate that about Arsenio, although his politics are often retrograde.

A scene in that righteously bad movie, *Harlem Nights,* really captures what I'm saying. Arsenio is in the cab weeping over the death of his male buddy, and his grief is rendered comic. The comedy lifts you up, breaks through an otherwise tedious film. It was a particularly Black form of dealing with the absurdity of our lives at times.

What has also handicapped us historically is that elements of Play have not been a part of the White supremacist Euro-centric mode of discourse within the academy. So, to some extent, social mobility required us to enter into a social contract where we suppress both the capacity and the desire to engage in cultural rituals of Play. Signifying is a skill, a method of disengagement which allows you to unwind. I think of it as breakdancing, an art where you see the body deconstructing itself, so to speak, showing you how you can move and control parts of a body one didn't realize existed within the realm of self-discipline or control.

CW Yes, you have a wonderful fusion of transgression, on the one hand, but also a way to hold the demons of meaninglessness at bay, on the other hand, which you are calling the absurd.

Looking at Spike Lee, it has always struck me that Spike's great talent, almost near genius, is his keen sense of Play and the comic. Unfortunately this is fused with retrograde sexual politics and a limiting, neo-nationalist orientation.

bh I would agree, Cornel, Spike is a genius when it comes to documenting that element of Play.

CW And that is one of the main reasons I still go to his movies. This issue of Play is crucial to discussions of Black cultural identity and survival. I'm very glad you brought it up.

Let's return to your work. The degree to which you infuse a kind of spirituality, through the integration of existential issues, issues of psychic survival, the absurd, political engagement, and a deep sense of history. Those levels are interwoven in so many ingenious ways in your work. Take for instance the devaluation of Black women which has been overlooked by White establishment but which has also been overlooked by male-dominated Black nationalist politics. How can we as a people talk seriously about spirituality and political engagement in order to project a future, while simultaneously coming to terms with the past?

bh It's interesting to me that you should combine discussion of Black spirituality with the devaluation of Black women because one of the things I've tried to say throughout my work, when I've talked about religion is that however we might fault the Black church, it has always been a place where Black women have had dignity and respect. Growing up with a sense of the value of Black womanhood came, in part, from the place I saw Black women hold in the church. I think it is very hard for many people to understand that, despite the sexism of the Black church, it was also a place where many Black women found they could drop the mask that was worn all day in Miss Anne's house; they could drop that need to serve others. Church was a place you could be and say, "Father I stretch my hands to thee," and you could let go. In a sense you could drop the layers of daily existence and get to the core of yourself.

The degradation Black women may have experienced in daily life would fall away in the church. It was noting this difference as a young woman that made me think about how the larger society devalues Black womanhood—a devaluation that is perpetuated in our own communities.

What gives me some measure of hope is seeing Shahrazad Ali on the Phil Donahue show with Haki Madhubuti and hearing him say that he did not sell *The Black Man's Guide to Understanding the Black Woman* in his bookstore because it advocated violence against Black women. A subversive and important moment which was undercut when Donahue rushed in and said, "That's censorship." It's telling that a White male "liberal" can make the issue of censorship more important than violence against Black women. We are still in a society were violence against Black womanhood is seen as unimportant, not worthy of concern. Pearl Cleage's short book of essays, *Mad at Miles,* addresses the way violence against Black women is often not taken seriously in our communities—particularly by men.

What I wanted so much to do in my first book was to say there is a history that has produced this circumstance of devaluation. It is not something inherent in Black women that we don't feel good about ourselves, that we are self-hating. Rather it is an experience which is socially circumscribed, brought into being by historical mechanisms. I have to acknowledge here, Cornel, that writing *Ain't I A Woman* was an expression of spiritual devotion to Black womanhood.

CW Would you say your political identity was nascent then?

bh Yes, I was reading Browning and Yeats, very much like Baraka when he was shaping his writerly sensibility. I was reading Wordsworth and Dickinson, I even had this sense that the writer could be removed, "objective." When I began confronting the reality of living as a Black woman in a White supremacist, capitalist patriarchy, the notion of "objectivity" vanished. I wrote *Ain't I A Woman* because I felt called to illuminate something that would change how people perceived Black women. The passage in the Bible that spoke to me during this period was Jacob wrestling with the angel. When the inner call to write that book came to me it was very much like an angel I had to wrestle with.

One of the most important books in my transformation as a young woman in college was *The Autobiography of Malcolm X*. Part of why I wrote the essay "Sitting at the Feet of the Messenger" is because people forget that as Malcolm was coming into his critical consciousness around the issues of capitalism and White supremacy, he was also grappling with himself as a spiritual human being and his sense of spiritual quest. So it makes sense that he was a powerful mentor for me because he grappled with history and his personal place in history.

The kind of organic intellectuality that you so often speak about we see personified in Malcolm's commitment to self-education while in prison. It was also an occasion for him to rethink his relationship to religiosity and spirituality. People don't talk about those passages where Malcolm tells us he could not get down on his knees and pray in the beginning, and the process of conversion and myatonia that came into his life, enabling him to participate in the experience of humility.

CW This is what strikes me as being unique about your work, that in your four volumes critiquing European imperialism, critiquing patriarchy, critiquing class exploitation, critiquing misogyny, critiquing homophobia, what I discern, as well, is a preoccupation with the dynamics of spiritual and personal change so that there is a politics of conversion shot through the political, economic, and social critiques.

When you talk about Malcolm in this way (hardly anybody talks about Malcolm in this way), it makes me think how so many of our dynamic young folk who have been politicized in the last few years by the Chuck Ds, Public Enemies, and others have missed that dimension of Malcolm, have disregarded or misunderstood his politics of conversion. As African Americans, we have yet to talk enough about how individuals actually change, the conversion of the soul that must occur before the role of love and care and intimacy can be meaningfully talked about.

bh I would start with the question of devotion and discipline because when I look at the evolution of my identity as a writer I see it intimately tied to my spiritual evolution. If we think of the slaves as bringing to new world Christianity a sense of personal relationship with God, evidenced most easily in Black spirituals like the one that says, "When I die tomorrow I will say to the Lord, Oh Lord you been my friend." This sense of immediate connection, we find again when we look at mystical religious experience globally—Sufism, Islamic mysticism. The idea that it is not our collective relationship to God that brings about enlightenment and transformation, rather our personal relationship to God. This is intimately linked to the discipline of being a writer. Which is also why it is important to understand the role of solitude and contemplation in Malcolm's life.

One of the things that is very different in my life from the life of my siblings is this ability to be alone, to be with my inner self. When we talk about becoming an intellectual, in the real life-enhancing sense of that word, we're really talking about what it is to sit with one's ideas, where one's mind becomes a workplace, where one really takes enormous amounts of time to contemplate and critically reflect on things. That experience of aloneness undergirds my intellectual practice and it is rooted in spiritual discipline where I have sought aloneness with God and listened to the inner voice of God as it speaks to me in the stillness of my life. I think a great deal about young Black folks engaged in intellectual/artistic production, and wonder if they understand the story of Christ going into the desert, if they know an inner place of absence in which they can be renewed and experience spiritual enlightenment.

CW How do you reconcile those crucial points about solitude with community and the emphasis Black people have on community?

bh I've certainly engaged fully with a number of religious traditions, but in all of them one holds up the notion that when you are truly able to be alone in that sense of Christ going into the garden of Gethsemane or going into the desert, or Buddha sitting under the Boti tree, it actually enables you to re-enter community more fully. This is something that I grapple with a great deal, the sense of collective communal experience. The great gift of enlightenment for whomever it comes to is the sense that only after we are able to experience ourselves within a context of autonomy, aloneness, independence, are we able to come into community with knowledge of our place, and feeling that what we have to give is for the good of the whole. Think, for example, of the question of what it means to save someone's life, which was raised in *Mo' Better Blues*. In order to intervene and save someone's life, one must know, first of all, how to take individual accountability for who we are, for life choices we make. I see how questions of accountability affect my own relationship to community precisely because as I develop intellectually and spiritually, I need greater periods of time alone. And it seems the greater my need to be alone, the greater my need to re-enter community as well.

CW Yes, this is the paradox of writing.

I wanted to say a word about your breaking the silence, as it were, around homophobia in the Black community. And by breaking the silence I don't mean to imply that homophobia hasn't been talked about because there are a number of published works by Black gays and lesbians. Rather, I mean breaking the silence as a heterosexual intellectual who takes the issues of sexual marginalization and devaluation seriously.

What went into your political decision to break this silence?

bh I'd like to give some background on this. Like so many Black folks from traditional communities, I grew up knowing that, say, the schoolteacher across the street was gay and being taught to respect him.

One of the things that hurt me most when *Ain't I A Woman* was first published without any specific commentary on lesbianism was that many Black lesbians such as Barbara Smith and Cheryl Clark actively decided to label me homophobic. That was particularly hurtful because I had lived my life in solidarity with gay and lesbian Black folks. Yet, I was not silenced by their critique; instead I was challenged to ask myself whether or not it is enough to engage in acts of solidarity with gay people in daily life if one does not speak publicly in such a manner that it mirrors those acts of solidarity. This led me to feel that it is important for me to speak openly and publicly about solidarity with gay people, and solidarity around the question of radical sexualities in general. Take for example brother Harlem Dalton's piece, *AIDS in Blackface,* which is one of the pieces in which we're seeing more of us speak openly, not just giving lip service to homophobia, in order to analyze what is making the Black community so homophobic. What is making popular, young Black culture so homophobic? Why are gays such a target for young rappers and Black comedy today? We've got to study these questions in a deeper manner so that we can come to grips with the question of homosexuality in Black community as something that has always been an aspect of our life. I actually feel that, as we have been more integrated into White society, we have actually adopted certain constructs of homophobia that were, in fact, inimical to early forms of Black cultural life. Toni Morrison, certainly, in editing the *Black Book* has spoken to this. Certain forms of persecution of the "other" in traditional Black life based on differences were held in question. There was a real sense of solidarity with anyone who was disenfranchised. I really see us altering that perspective as we enter a middle-class location and sensibility.

CW When you think, for example, of Black institutions, family, and church they are primarily patriarchal. This means there had to be a notion of the "other" and a subjugation of that "other" in order to maintain power.

bh But you never think about the fact that until racial integration every gay Black person in America lived within those families, those institutions, and what I'm saying is that while there was not public acceptance, there was integration into the life of the community. No one got up on Sunday mornings to beat up the Black gay piano player, or call him out.

CW That's true, but let's not glorify that past either, there were sermons preached against homosexuality, and the gay church organist or the lesbian singer could not live an "out" life. It was an understood contract: if you kept it to yourself and sat there quietly listening to the preacher haranguing homosexuality, you were allowed to participate fully in community life. There was integration and respect for gay and lesbian humanity, not lifestyle, and the price for that community acceptance was silence.

bh We have to distinguish between respect for an individual's humanity and respect for an individual's sexual preference. Yet, what I am trying to suggest is that now there is not even respect for gay humanity.

A very poignant essay in Spike's *Spin* issue focusing on gays and AIDS told the story of a Black man who was ostracized and shunned by Black community, and how painful and devastating that was. We need to call upon a traditional Black value system that did, in fact, maintain that no matter what is ailing you (and here we're talking about disease and traditional responses to diseases such as tuberculosis and leprosy), you were still a member of the community and therefore entitled to both care and dignity. There was a magnitude and a generosity within Christian love that could make one reach out and care for people around one. What we are seeing today is a complete breakdown of an ethics of care and responsibility. Today in Black communities we are seeing an ethic imbued with notions of "persecute the outsider," "persecute the different," some of which has to be the outcome of racial integration, where we have, in effect, come to condone and accept levels of persecution in our own daily life that at other historical moments would have been unthinkable.

CW I agree.

bh For instance, why is it that, when a Black person in a predominantly White institution sits at a cocktail party and hears derogatory statements made about Black people, they don't jump up and fight? And yet, forty years ago, it would have been unthinkable for a White person to say, in the presence of Black people, some of the same things which are said to us today. Take, for example, Madonna's *Truth or Dare*. This means, that, to some extent, we have, in consumer society, been made to feel that if we are being paid, we should be willing to submit to certain forms of degradation in exchange for that pay. This economic co-optation desensitizes us and diminishes our feelings of bondedness with all people who are oppressed and abused. It makes us more willing to persecute those that are oppressed and abused because we are ourselves submitting to certain forms of abuse on a daily basis.

CW Again, I agree, but I would like to come back to the issue of sexuality because talking about homophobia in the Black community actually raised the deeper issue of sexuality in general, and why it is that for Black Americans historically there has been the refusal, inability and/or fear to engage in shared public reflection on sexuality. Is this so because, in dealing with sexuality, there is a perceived threat to a certain kind of narrow conception of community that has traditionally held Black people together?

bh One of the things we are in great need of is a discourse that deals with the representation of Black bodies. It is no accident that one of the major themes in Shahrazad Ali's book is the body. By calling into question the way we confront our Black female bodies, Ali takes us back to those 19th century themes of White supremacy: the iconography of Black bodies as represented in the White supremacist imagination. We are doomed to silence and certain forms of sexual repression until we as a people can speak more openly about our own bodies and our notions of the body in general.

It has been painful for me to hear Black women say, for example, "Well there is some truth to what Shahrazad Ali says." In order to respond and intervene I find that I must enter into Ali's discourse directly and take on, say, the issue of Black women and body odor. I respond by saying that while we know fear and stress produce certain kinds of body odor it would be quite a different thing if Shahrazad Ali were problematizing the question of body odor in her critique. Perhaps saying instead that many Black women may have a distinctive body odor because we live in a society where we are continually and perpetually under a great deal of stress. Under a great deal of stress, in fact, about negative, White supremacist representations of our bodies.

What Black scholar has done any meaningful anthropological work around obsessive cleanliness in Black life?

I was visiting a Black woman friend of mine last weekend and we were laughing about how Black people always say, "Don't sit your butt on my bed." We can't fully understand why we find it difficult to publicly discuss sexuality if we don't look at some of our relations to the body and to disease. What do we think is going to happen if someone "sits their butt on your bed"?

CW Do you think this raises the question of sexual taboo?

bh The pervasiveness of AIDS in our community is really requiring that we have some open discussion of how we have sex, who we have sex with, and what sexuality means in our lives. What does it say about Black male sexuality when many Black men feel desexualized if called upon to use a condom? What kinds of sexuality are we speaking about when Black men feel intimidated sexually by any form of birth control? We can see these notions of sexuality as almost archaic in Western Culture today, as it is imperative for our health that we seek to understand the origin of these beliefs.

One of the major ironies of groups like 2 Live Crew is the representation of an openness about the body and of sexual graphicness which belies the reality of Black life. We know that even basic nudity is still seen by many Black people as an affront and assault on their sensibilities. In most Black homes, across class, there is tremendous unease in relation to the body, nakedness, and the representation of Blackness.

CW Part of this comes from White supremacist discourse associating Black being with Black bodies, as if we have no minds, no intelligence, are only the sum total of our visible physicality, and therefore the issue of whether Black people actually like and love their bodies becomes a crucial thing. I'm thinking specifically about the sermon that you invoked earlier in *Beloved*.

bh Oh, absolutely, which is all about the body.

CW Which is all about the body, and this is fascinating because Toni Morrison would say, "Look you've got to love yourself not only in the abstract; you've got to love your big lips; you've got to love your flat nose; you've got to love your skin, hands, all the way down." The issue of self-regard, self-esteem, and self-respect is reflected in bodily form.

bh This is interesting, because, when I teach *Passing*, Nella Larson's novella, in my introduction to African American literature class, I find that students are very resistant when I ask them to think about the fact that Clare, who has passed for a White ruling-class woman, but who comes back to Blackness, is the only character to really say, "I want to be Black so much I'm willing to sacrifice my husband, my child, my wealth, to live in Harlem." I ask them to think about whether or not she falls to her death because in a White supremacist county, the Black person who is most threatening is the one who loves Blackness, who loves the embodiment of

Blackness, the mark of Blackness on the skin, in the body. Cornel, my students could not deal with that. It was as though I were speaking taboo.

Do we fundamentally live in a culture where a Black person who deeply and profoundly loves Blackness is completely at odds with the culture on the whole? Is there no place for Black self-love in this culture? We are in a strange historical moment, in that Blackness is so openly commodified and simultaneously despised. Which should lead us to ask ourselves whether or not it is commodified in a manner that allows us to celebrate Black self-love, or does commodification once again reduce Blackness to spectacle and carnival? Which makes the commodificaton by White or Black culture not a gesture of love, but really a gesture of disdain.

I believe we are currently engaging a reinscription of the minstrel, particularly B-boy culture, where certain forms of bard suggest a celebration of Blackness. Yet once they are commodified and sold to us in certain forms, do they still carry a message of "Black is so fine, it's so wonderful to be Black"?—or do they carry that sense of spectacle where one might want to engage Blackness as a moment of transgressive pleasure without wanting to truly incorporate Blackness into one's life?

CW This is a crucial issue, which has to do with how we relate to a traditional Garvey, and Malcolm X, and Elijah Muhammad, other Black radicals who, despite their flaws and foibles, had a profound love for Black people and Blackness itself. Which is also why they are currently being appropriated in a gesture of fashion politic and flattened out into objects that no longer represent that uncompromised love of Blackness.

This also leads us to the issue of Black male/female relations. We've heard so much today about the crisis of the Black man and the Black woman, about the nihilism which is so much at the core of today's Black relationships. Could you tie together questions of Black self-regard and Black self-respect as they pertain to Black men and women forming and sustaining loving relationships?

bh In *Sisters of the Yam: Black Women and Self-Recovery* (a manuscript only recently completed), I talk extensively about how Black women's self-recovery informs to a large degree their ability to choose psychologically healthy partners and sustain relationships with them. I believe that it is impossible for two individuals not committed to their own and each other's well being to sustain a healthy and enduring relationship. I am also working on a book which I'm tentatively calling *Black Revolutionary Consciousness,* where I assert that mental health is a crucial frontier in new Black liberation struggle. The key to the sense of what it means to be critically affirming of Blackness; loving of Blackness lies in enhanced psychological health.

One of the things that really profoundly disturbed me was hearing a White woman scholar, Barbara Bowen, give a talk on 16th century misogynist pamphlets written as tracts to define women's place. She read one about tongues, how, if a woman talked too much, she was seen as less chaste and less worthy, and realizing just how historically linked this was to Shahrazad Ali's book, in that both represent misogynist tracts from different historical periods.

I was also fascinated by how Ali's book is represented to us as though it is opposed to a Euro-centric perspective when, in fact, it is completely rooted in a Euro-centric notion of the body. There is so little difference between these 16th century renaissance tracts about the female body and Ali's work. It allows you to realize that, without psychoanalytic exploration of the body, there can be no liberating discussion of gender relations in the Black community.

In *Black Looks,* I write an essay on Black men, and in it I say that what I found particularly moving in *Harlem Nights* was the way in which Quick, played by Eddie Murphy, only divulges his real name to the Black woman that he desires. And in that moment we see cinematically represented the dropping of the mask of masculinity and we see loving recognition. She goes on to repeat his name and he tells her it sounds wonderful when she says it. I chose to interpret that moment as saying to Black people that in the act of recognizing one another, we can also accept ourselves fully. Yet this liberatory message is undermined because her character goes on to betray him. Leaving us with a bleak vision of Black heterosexuality that tells us, when we drop the mask of our false selves in order to display our authentic selves, our authentic sense of being, we will be betrayed, we will be abandoned.

We really have got to begin to look at those psychoanalytic notions of how the self comes into being through a world of recognition and response, through being seen and loved as you really are. We are so obsessed as Black folks with appearances, with surfaces, so where then does that deep and profound inner recognition come from? We see this emotional dissonance in Black parenting, adults obsessively dressing Black children in fashion outfits. These are the ways in which we convey to kids early on that it is the surface representation of yourself that matters most, while the inner self is often left wanting, left without a sense of secure identity. Much of my new work is trying to look at this.

Mo' Better Blues is fundamentally a depressing film because the film ends with a sense that all we can reproduce is that which in the past has already wounded us. There is not a sense that we can revision the past.

Morrison has also pushed us to remember the past in ways and reinterpret it in ways that enable us to seek our own psychic healing.

One of my favorite albums is *Sexual Healing* by Marvin Gaye. For him also there seemed to be the sense that there is a sickness of the body, sickness within the body that affects the body politics. There is a way we can read "Sexual Healing" as not just being about literal desire, sex. Rather, Marvin Gaye was trying to communicate to Black people that there is a sickness in our body politics. The body politic of Blackness is in need of healing and he connects that to a notion of Christ as giving us the capacity to rejoice, similar to Baby Sugg's sermon in *Beloved,* saying we must be grateful for the bodies that we inhabit.

CW That's true, and yet I think the other side of Marvin's attempt to fuse spirituality and sexuality, the negative side, is that sexuality becomes an escape from a confrontation with the disease of the soul. The body then becomes a displacement from a grappling with that nihilism and hopelessness, making sexuality the only means by which one feels one can remain alive, given the living deadness of one's own being.

bh That is the critical tension; that's exactly what we are talking about. In my essay on Black men, I say it is no accident that young Black men have come to represent the outer limits of transgression, i.e., *Nasty As You Wanna Be, In Living Color,* etc. The young Black male body becomes the quintessential sign of moving beyond all limits. Perhaps this has been inscribed today because young Black men are threatened daily by violent death and disease.

In Elaine Scarry's book *The Body in Pain* she says that this culture doesn't have a language to articulate pain. An interesting point if you then apply it to the public representation of the young Black male body, through rapping, dancing, sports, a body that has a joy in living yet the daily circumstances of Black male life in the United States is not joy but the constant threat and seduction of death. And this is the tension we see in a figure like Marvin Gaye, who has a range of issues, including substance abuse, yet still identifies the crucial spiritual/sexual question for healing as coming to terms with the body. Which, of course, we know he failed to do within his lifetime.

CW Yes, another Black genius, robbed of his ability to live out, in your words, "the promise of that genius."

One question about your own life. I think continually, incessantly, and obsessively about the title of James Baldwin's book *The Price of the Ticket.* One of the fundamental things about Black intellectual life is the cost that one has to pay for prophetic vocation, and we know James Baldwin himself paid a very high cost for that. How would you begin to talk about the price of the ticket, the price one has to pay as a prophetic intellectual?

bh Well, I already answered that when I spoke earlier about discipline, solitude, and community. The Buddhist monk Thich Nhat Hanh says that when a person decides to truly be themselves, they are going to find themselves alone. I think often about Martin Luther King's decision to oppose the Vietnam War and how his speeches were tied to a certain sense of isolation. He says in his sermon that many preachers will not agree with him and he will find himself alone, at which point he quotes that famous passage from Romans, "Do not be conformed to this world but be ye transformed that you may know what the will of God is, that which is good and perfect . . ." I have grappled with an enormous sense of isolation. We've had many Black women academics but, to some extent, we are a new generation. We represent the first generation of Black women thinkers who don't have to have children, or manage a household, if we choose. Molly Haskell, a White woman film critic, says, "To claim one's strength as a woman is a fearful thing. Easier to idealize the man or denigrate him, worship at the feet of male authority then explore and exhibit one's own soul, luxuriate in one's own power and risk ending up alone. Once we take responsibility for our mental processes we take responsibility for our lives, that is what feminism has become for me, looking fiercely and accurately not passively and defensively at the pattern of our lives and acknowledging all the ways which we are not victims but are responsible for the way which we connect the past to the present." These words moved my deeply because I think one of the costs that we pay for uncompromised intellectual pursuit is certain forms of isolation, where, if one does not take care to find community, can be very disenabling and debilitating.

CW Which community does one re-enter with this kind of critical consciousness, this kind of prophetic vocation?

bh Part of the joy of having these kinds of conversations with you is that this is a form of re-entering community. One of the things I sometimes say teasingly to myself is, I take my community where I find it. I used to have a very utopian, idealized notion of community, long for the perfect relationship—me and another bohemian Black male intellectual, within the perfect Black community of like-minded souls. Now I'm learning to be nourished from wherever that sense of community comes from, and this way of thinking has enlarged my community. For too long we have conceptualized the Black community in narrow terms. We conceptualized it as a neighborhood that is all Black, something as superficial as that. When, in fact, it seems to me that it is by extending my sense of community that I am able to find nourishment, that I am able to think of this time spent with you in conversation as a kind of communion.

I think back to why we considered calling our dialogues together *Breaking Bread*—the sense of taking one's nourishment in that space where you find it.

Bone Black

CHAPTER 1

Mama has given me a quilt from her hope chest. It is one her mother's mother made. It is a quilt of stars—each piece taken from faded-cotton summer dresses—each piece stitched by hand. She has given me a beaded purse that belonged to my father's mother Sister Ray. They want to know why she has given it to me since I was not Sister Ray's favorite. They say she is probably turning over in her grave angry that I have something of hers.

Mama tells us—her daughters—that the girls in her family started gathering things for their hope chest when they were very young, gathering all the things that they would carry with them into marriage. The first time she opens hers for us I feel I am witnessing yet another opening of Pandora's box, that the secrets of her youth, the bittersweet memories, will come rushing out like a waterfall and push us back in time. Instead the scent of cedar fills the air. It reminds me of Christmas, of abandoned trees, standing naked in the snow after the celebrations are over. Usually we are not invited to share in the opening of the chest. Even though we stand near her watching, she acts as it we are not there. I see her remembering, clutching tightly in her hand some object, some bit of herself that she has had to part with in order to live in the present. I see her examining each hope to see if it has been fulfilled, it the promises have been kept. I pretend I do not see the tears in her eyes. I am glad she shares the opening of the chest this time with all of us. I am clutching the gifts she hands to me, the quilt, the beaded purse. She knows that I am often hopeless. She stores no treasures for my coming marriage. I do not want to be given away. I cannot contain my dreams until tomorrow. I cannot wait for someone else, a stranger, to take my hand.

That night in my sleep I dream of going away. I am taking the bus. Mama is standing waving good-bye. Later when I return from my journey I come home only to find there has been a fire, nothing remains of our house and I can see no one. There is only the dark and the thick smell of smoke. I stand alone weeping. The sound of my sobbing is like the cry of the peacock. Suddenly they appear with candles, mama and everyone. They say they have heard my sorrow pierce the air like the cry of the peacock, that they have come to comfort me. They give me a candle. Together we search the ashes for bits and pieces, any fragment of our lives that may have survived. We find that the hope chest has not burned through and through. We open it, taking out the charred remains. Someone finds a photo, one face has turned to ash, another is there. We pass around the fragments like bread and wine at communion. The chorus of weeping is our testimony that we are moved.

Louder than our weeping is a voice commanding us to stop our tears. We cannot see who is speaking but we are reminded of the stern sound of our mother's mother's voice. We listen. She tells us to sit close in the night, to make a circle of our bodies, to place the candles at the center of the circle. The candles burn like another fire only this time she says the fire burns to warm our hearts. She says Listen, let me tell you a story. She begins to put together in words all that has been destroyed in the fire. We are all rejoicing when the dream ends.

The next day I want to know what the dream means, who she is, this storyteller who comes in the night. Saru, mama's mother, is the interpreter of dreams. She tells me that I should know the storyteller, that I and she are one, that they are my sisters, family. She says that a part of me is making the story, making the words, making the new fire, that it is my heart burning in the center of the flames.

CHAPTER 17

Sitting at Saru's side as she smokes I hear about the reservations, about Indian women, the way in which the lighter-skinned black men wanted to marry them. She tells me that one of them, maybe her father, went there to find a bride, not a white-skinned bride, but a woman with skin the color of warm honey, with straight jet black hair, blacker than white folk's hair. Saru tells me that white folks and even some niggers like to make fun when a colored person says that they are part Indian but she says in those days there were many such unions, many such marriages. She talks sadly about this need in people to make other people deny parts of themselves. She tells me that a person cannot feel right in their heart if they have denied parts of their ancestral past, that this not feeling right in the heart is the cause of much pain. When she was a little girl black people remembered their homes in Africa, spoke languages different from English, and understood many things about life that white folks did not understand. She said they stopped talking about Africa because that was how the white folks wanted it. Saru thinks that black people could talk about their Indian kin because they knew them in the present, that this was a heritage other than slavery to lay claim to. She lays claim to it. She tells me the stories over and over so I will know them, so I will pass them on.

One story troubles my sleep. I do not tell her. I do not want her to know. I am afraid she will think I am not ready, not old enough to bear the stories. This story is about a magic woman who lives inside smoke. She hides in the smoke so no one can capture her. Smoke is to her what clay is to the red bird god. She can take the smoke and make it become many things. Using the smoke she turns herself into a male. She must be male to be a warrior. There are no women warriors. She fights fiercely against her enemies. They cannot understand when the arrows that pierce her body do not cause her to fall. When they try to capture her alive she takes the smoke wherever she can find it, in a dying fire, in the residue of a gunshot, from pipes, and turns the smoke into a snake that devours her enemies. Sometimes she turns the smoke into a bird of prey, a hawk or an owl, and sometimes a black wolf.

In my sleep I have seen the magic woman fighting battles, shooting her arrow into enemy after enemy. The part of the dream that troubles my sleep, the part I do not like to tell Saru is that the face of the young male warrior looks like my face. I stare into his eyes as if I am looking into a mirror. When Saru changes herself into a woman she no longer looks like me. To keep silent about this dream is to not understand its meaning. Saru has told me many times that dreams are messages sent to us by guardian spirits, that the wise one learns to listen to the message, to follow its wisdom.

When I tell Saru of my dream, of the young warrior who wears my face in battle, she says that this is the face of my destiny, that I am to be a warrior. I do not understand. I do not intend to fight in wars or battles. She says that there are many battlegrounds in life, that I will live the truth of the dream in time.

CHAPTER 29

His smells fill my nostrils with the scent of happiness. With him all the broken pieces of my heart get mended, put together again bit by bit. He can always tell when I am sad. He will ask me What have they been doing to you now. He knows that I am a wounded animal, that they pour salt on the open sores just to hear me moan. He tells me that in the end it will come out all right. He tells me Blessed are they that mourn for they shall be comforted. I am comforted by his presence. Soot-black-skinned man with lines etched deep in his face as if someone took a knife and carved them there. He is Daddy Gus, mama's father. From her I know that he has always been gentle, that he has never been a man of harsh words. I need his presence in my life to learn that all men are not terrible, are not to be feared. He, too, is one of the faithful, one of the right-hand men of god. When he speaks I listen very carefully to hear what is said. His voice comes from some secret place of knowing, a hidden cave where the healers go to hear messages from the beloved.

In my dream we run away together, hand in hand. We go to the cave. To enter we must first remove all our clothes, we must wash, we must rub our body with a red mud. We cover ourselves so completely that we are no longer recognizable as grandfather granddaughter. We enter without family ties or memory. The cave is covered with paintings that describe the way each animal has come to know that inside all of us is a place for healing, that we have only to discover it. Each animal searches and searches until they find the opening of the cave. As soon as they enter, the mind ceases, they feel at peace. They feel they are no longer blind, that they see for the first time. It is too much for the heart to bear. They stand together weeping, sobbing. When we enter the cave we also take time to weep, to lose ourselves in sorrow. We make a fire. In the fire are all the lost spirits that show us ways to live in the world. I do not yet have a language with which to speak with them. He knows. He speaks. I am the silent one, the one who bears witness. In the dream we leave the cave in quiet. Just as we reach the outside he begins talking to me without opening his mouth. He places his voice inside my head telling me that knowledge of the cave can be given to anyone, only they must be seeking, that until I can tell a seeker from someone who is just curious I must not speak about it.

We are again grandfather and granddaughter. My visits to him are frequent. He has a favorite chair by the stove in the living room. When I was much smaller I sat there cuddled in his lap like a cat, hardly moving, hardly alive so near to the stillness of death was the bliss I knew in his arms. His room is filled with treasures. Once the curtain has been drawn at the doorway so that the others cannot see, he tells me that everything has life, a tiny soul inside it—things like pocketknives, coins, bits of ribbon. He is always finding the treasures people have lost or abandoned. He hears their small souls crying in the wilderness. He gives them a place to rest. In his room treasures are everywhere. Every object has a story. He teaches me to listen to the stories things tell, to appreciate their history. He has many notebooks, little black notebooks filled with faded yellow paper. I understand from him that the notebooks are a place for the storage of memory. He writes with a secret pencil; the pages seem covered in ash, the ash left by the fire we have visited. This fire he says now burns inside us.

Angela Jackson (1951–)

Angela Jackson was born in Greenville, Mississippi, but mostly grew up in Chicago. She attended Northwestern University, where she developed a reputation as an undergraduate as a writer of great repute. It was during her undergraduate years that she also became a member of Chicago's Organization of Black American Culture Writers workshop, which was to be the greatest single influence upon her work. Jackson has published numerous collections of poetry and fiction, including Voodoo/Love Magic (1974), The Greenville Club (1977), Solo in Boxcar Third Floor E (1985), Dark Legs and Silk Kisses (1993), and her collected edition, And All These Roads Be Luminous (1998). She has received a fellowship from the National Endowment for the Arts and an American Book Award for Solo.

Jackson's gift as a poet is evident in her unmistakable ear and sense for language, which, as one critic suggests, might be a combination of her Southern heritage with its rich flavors and tonality, and her Midwestern urban sensibility. For sure, Jackson's involvement in the OBAC Writers Workshop, which was committed to Black Aesthetic as an ideology, is part the reason for her particular use of language: Her early style developed under the keen directive to find, use, and refine Black language—words that were signally and expressedly Black. But Jackson's use of language is not a narrow adherence to the tenets of Black Aestheticism; instead, she combines this interest in Black language, with melodious rhythms and narratives of urban life, to create beautiful poetry.

Jackson's "Foreword" is the opening piece and foreword for Carolyn Rodgers' prize-winning collection, how i got ovah. It is in this loving and celebratory piece that Jackson's interest in language and her melodic rhythms are most evident. She uses short lines, clipped sentences, and lower-cased letters, all of which are common Black Aesthetic poetic gestures. What achieves the rhythm of "testimony" in this poem is the orality of her language, the way the language in its directness jumps off the page like a sermon. Speaking directly to the reader, Jackson writes "her name is sister. she is yours. / everytime you look at her u see somebody u know. / she remind you of the church." These directed lines trigger and command memory and engage repetition to reinforce the song quality. Hers is a foreword that celebrates and also commands, ending with "she a witness. will glorify u. / will embarrass the ugly. / tell u bout yoself. / she a witness. humming her people / to the promise/d land." To the end Jackson's poetics are necessarily clever, as indicated by her use of "promise/d," which is both what is to come, and what has already been.

In her own work, Jackson uses her deft poetics and language skills to give life to urban situations, especially those that speak about women's experiences and memories of home. In "The Fitting Room," her narrator makes an immediate connection with the reader through the question, "you know what I mean," which is necessary, because the poem's success depends on its ability to speak to experiences the reader may have had.

Jackson uses clothing as a metaphor to point to the ways that the world does not fit one's body, and it is an apt metaphor because most people have had some experience of being in a fitting room and confronting items that do not fit. The triumph of this poem is its intimate narrator, who makes the difficult subject easier to bear and engage.

"Why I Must Make Language" is a stunning study in the use of words and line breaks. Jackson calls attention to her own political engagement of poetic language, and, in a poem that is somewhat her aesthetic manifesto, she isolates single words to highlight their power and to exploit their tone. In the opening of the poem, she delays the description of the star, "shining," to a one-word sentence that follows the mention of the star. The next sentence pays attention to the s and p sounds in the words "points," "pierce," "space," "simple," and "superb." Throughout the poem, Jackson captures wonderfully moments of alliteration and assonance, off- and slant-rhyme, which help to elucidate her point: that language is powerful, political, and only it can help us begin to express the wonder and beauty and terrible of the world. This language gives us access to our ancestors, to "the wild / and civilized / Sky." It is also important to note that Jackson's narrator claims not only to be using language, but to be making it, which offers a greater sense of agency.

The two short poems, "grits" and "greens," are companion pieces that reflect the aim of writing that Jackson describes in "Why I Must Make Language." Both poems evoke a sense of home, of things past and Southern, familial and motherly. Jackson uses the cultural construct of cooking to give life to these two images, both which serve to bring women from her past, and their grand actions, back to life.

Finally, in "Making the Name," she demands that the language name her right: It is in this poem, with its tensions about language's ability to misname, that highlights her careful and defiant title, "Why I Must Make Language." Similar to the motivation of the artists of the Black Aesthetic movement, but also those who embrace some post-modern and post-colonial critiques of language, Jackson recognizes that language's power is not neutral, and in fact can be damaging. One can be made drunk in and by language, and can be misnamed and unwritten in the space of words. Her echo of Aretha's powerful "call me" is a refusal to be invisible that calls upon a long cultural tradition of resistance to invisibility. Jackson is also speaking within a contemporary Black woman's tradition in her rich use of metaphors and alliterative rhyme.

Kevin Everod Quashie

The Fitting Room

FOR JACK LAZEBNIK AND "THE GHOST OF SENIOR HALL"

A person has to try on many lives
before she finds one that fits.
    You know what I mean?
People will tell her anything.
How the hat sits too big, and the slip
clings.
She has to be a child again
and see herself in the mirror
in her training bra, in order to dream
        of breasts.

Or like when you shop for shoes
you should do it in the evening
after your feet have swollen
from all your little steps.
The pair you choose then,
sensible and pleasing to foot and eye,
is the pair you will wear
until they wear
out.
I don't know what to make of this.
I don't know what this means,
even though I'm telling it to you.
Like love.
You can choose a man, then choose another,
and all he did was change pants.
But he's the same man in the same life
that didn't fit you, but you tried to squeeze in it
anyway and it was two sizes too small.

People look at you sometimes
and try to have you thinking you'll never find
anything with your measurements.
And you can change those if you want to wear
something bad enough.
Or somebody can cut you down to size.
And you can let them outdo you. Or
leave you in hot water until you draw up.
Then they'll call you country   talk about your trouble
shake their heads and admire how awful you look.
They'll say you a nice person but you got no style.
How does that suit you? Fine. Just fine.
Or

you have to keep taking off garments
and putting other ones on
until you see your self in the seeing glass
as this one has all the glamour and sense you mean
to say what is on your mind.
It looks like it was made with you in mind.
Tell me. You who've lived so long and so little,
     so many lives.
Do you
Do you like this one?

Why I Must Make Language

FOR ELEANOR HAMILTON

For
a Voice
like a star.
Shining.
With points to pierce
space,
and be
simple, superb
clarity.
Incandescent.
Some thing
a child might carry
down the black hall,
to make peace with Mystery.
Or woman
into a wooded place
where she may see
the shapes and
names of trees.
Anonymous awe be called
Glory.
Or man
might seek
in the cave
of a woman
and see the writing
on the wall,
and find some
luminosity.
Ancestors may descend
on streams of light.
Or
all look up
and listen
deep
into the night.
The wild
and civilized
Sky.

grits

all night
she watch the pot, cooked
her grits thick for hours
(not the quick kind) till grains disappear
into smooth with a slick

coat on top
hot enough
for a man to wear
(she said) on both
his faces.

greens

this is the kind of love you write home about
in sunlight the single aunt sits round
the harsh wood table and sighs. you know how

strong the smell of mustard greens is.
and bitter the turnip. spinach,
on the other hand, goes down easy.

all this cooking in her one pot when
you write home the kind of love
it is.

Making the Name

Call me, call me, call me, call me, baby.

—*Aretha Franklin*

name me a woman who can get so
drunk
    half a cup of syllables, first thing

in the morning, late at
night when the moon winks wicked
while I essay poetically past with my shoes in my hand
foolish on the curb of your voice

walking in my big feet and palm legs
all of me
fondled in the palm
wine
of your language, changed plain
water to wine, burnished
a brandy to slide
so
easy down
among all the jive and solemn verbs

call me she who
        is
        made word
inebriated, inebriant
    all done up and delicious

so I could stay out later than moonlight &
sneak in the backdoor of a wedding night with
    a giggle in my throat

    walking soft
in my bare feet and silk
    woven legs
in soot hair & eyes, a stream
of ssshes parting my lips, I would not
wake the war in you

beloved

        I am the name of peace,
        and drunken victory,
    the luscious part-
    ing of speech

Foreword

carolyn.
singer of sass and blues. has come again.
the skinny knock-kneed little mama of "paper soul"
the pain-struck girl of "songs of a black bird"
has been transformed.

she is all grown up now. boldly beautiful
"blues getting up" has got up and went. carolyn taken us
some where.
listen at her sanctified soul.
make u testify to truth.

her name is sister. she is yours.
everytime you look at her u see somebody u know.
she remind u of the church.
her eye is seeing holy. she remind u of the people on the corner
                    her words be leaning on the buildings there.
she you sister. she everywhere.
carolyn can do the happy in the aisles of yo mind.
she so country and street and proper too.
she africa and greenville, monroe and pinebluff. chicagonewyorkphilly
l.a. boston batonrouge neworleans atlanta macon and alligator too.
carolyn say "the blues got class." she the blues and something else
everything too.
carolyn is a poet. a downhome choir in herself.
she a witness. will glorify u.
              will embarrass the ugly.
tell u bout yoself.
she a witness. humming her people
              to the promise/d land.

Jesse Jackson (1941–)

Jesse Jackson was born in Greenville, South Carolina, on October 8, 1941. After high school, Jackson attended the University of Illinois, but transferred after only one year to North Carolina A&T in 1960. It was at North Carolina A&T that he earned a B.S. in Sociology and became a student activist and leader in the Civil Rights Movement. Later, Jackson attended Chicago Theological Seminary and was ordained as a Baptist minister in 1968.

Jackson's life has always been one of politics and social activism. He grew up in a Black America where the political center of Black life was in the church. Jackson worked with Dr. Martin Luther King, Jr. and other leaders of the Civil Rights Movement and was recognized early on for his leadership abilities and his skill of oratory. During the 1970s, after the movement had seen some of its leaders killed and others jailed, Jackson remained a political figure by building alliances with regional and national organizations, and eventually, by forming Operation PUSH and the Rainbow Coalition, a national political collective committed to peace and social justice, and an activist arm for the racially and economically disenfranchised. It is from the strength of the Coalition that Jackson made a run at the presidential nomination of the Democratic Party in 1984. He made a strong showing, finishing third of eight candidates. Still, it was his utterly mesmerizing primetime address to the Convention that cemented his place as a major figure in American politics. Since 1984, Jackson has served as a negotiator in international peace situations and has been involved in two presidential campaigns: In 1988, he made an even stronger showing that 1984, finishing second in the party; and in 1996, he gave another rousing address, which many consider to be even more elegantly crafted and delivered that the speech excerpted here.

Jackson's 1984 speech is a study in oratorical and rhetorical strategies. He begins the speech in the sermon tradition, offering a general comment on the occasion of the gathering. In fact, Jackson borrows the language of religious ceremony (for example, marriage and funeral) in his observation that "We are gathered here this week to nominate a candidate and write a platform which will expand, unify, direct, and inspire our party and the nation to fulfill this mission."

The sermon tradition that Jackson relies on for this speech engages signifying. As one of the central classical rhetorical strategies, signifying is, in one way, using repetition for emphasis and intensity. Noted African American literary scholar Henry Louis Gates, Jr. has argued that in Black speech and written traditions, signifying creates a multi-layered discourse. In Jackson's speech, as was the case with King, the Reverend C.L. Franklin, Sojourner Truth, and other great Black orators, the repetition of signifying merges with the use of typology (the use of Biblical narratives and personalities as tropes). Hence, Jackson makes several references to being on the mountaintop, or to the manger, which is intended to trig-

ger the appropriate Biblical stories, and links his argument to the struggle and triumph those examples represent. Jackson also uses non-Biblical figures and symbols in a similarly referential way. For example, he ends the speech with a reference to the famous lines engraved on the base of the Statue of Liberty, from poet Emma Lazarus: "Give me your tired, your poor, your huddled masses yearning to be free." Jackson also makes reference to Dr. King, with his constant evocation of the dream that the United States is and can be.

What Jackson achieves in the speech is not just a sense of rhythm, which repetition helps to create, but also an amazing tapestry of narratives that his audience is familiar with and that will move them to action. His arguments rely on pathos because they are aware of the audience, and they are effective because of such consideration. Jackson makes reference to ideals of democracy (the flag, for example), of pluralism in nature (the idea of the rainbow), and to Christian goodness. One great example of his achievement of an effective argument of pathos is the sentence "Our flag is red, white, and blue, but our nation is a rainbow—red, yellow, brown, black and white—and all are precious in God's sight." Jackson's text is the literal quilt he argues that America is, and in keeping with his message of multiculturalism, he later mentions Christian and Islamic traditions.

Jackson also uses arguments based on ethos, on his credibility as a speaker, to complement his appeal to the audience. This occurs largely near the end of the text, where he references his childhood, the modest beginnings, which further authorizes his ability to speak on issues of disenfranchisement. Jackson also cleverly but not arrogantly compares his situation to that of Jesus, and engages the Horatio Alger narrative by proclaiming success as a possibility for everyone under a just American state.

There are two other rhetorical strategies of note in Jackson's speech, one being his use of repetition and alliteration for emphasis. In the opening he proclaims "My constituency is the damned, the disinherited, the disrespected, and the despised," creating an emphatic reinforcement through the use of hard "d" sounds and synonyms. Jackson also utilizes reversals, where he inverts a paradigm or introduces a familiar idea that he then dismantles. For example, he argues "we must not measure greatness from the mansion down but from the manger up." Not only is there alliteration in the construction, but there is balance and reversal. Jackson tells us the negative half of the statement first, building anticipation for the affirmative half. These kinds of reversals are widely employed in Black sermon tradition.

Kevin Everod Quashie

The Candidate's Challenge: The Call of Conscience, the Courage of Conviction

Tonight we come together, bound by our faith in a mighty God, with genuine respect and love for our country, and inheriting the legacy of a great party—the Democratic party—which is the best hope for redirecting our nation on a more humane, just, and peaceful course. This is not a perfect party. We are not a perfect people. Yet we are called to a perfect mission: to feed the hungry, to clothe the naked, to house the homeless, to teach the illiterate, to provide jobs for the jobless, and to choose the human race over the nuclear race. We are gathered here this week to nominate a candidate and write a platform which will expand, unify, direct, and inspire our party and the nation to fulfill this mission.

My constituency is the damned, the disinherited, the disrespected, and the despised. They are restless and seek relief. They've voted in record numbers. They have invested faith, hope, and trust in us. The Democratic party must send them a signal that we care. I pledge my best not to let them down.

Leadership must heed the call of conscience—redemption, expansion, healing, and unity—for they are the keys to achieving our mission. Time is neutral and does not change things. With courage and initiative, leaders change things. No generation can choose the age or circumstances in which it is born, but through leadership it can choose to make the age in which it is born an age of enlightenment—an age of jobs, peace, and justice. Only leadership—that intangible combination of gifts, discipline, information, circumstance, courage, timing, will, and divine inspiration—can lead us out of the crisis in which we find ourselves. Leadership can mitigate the misery of our nation. Leadership can part the waters and lead our nation in the direction of the Promised Land. Leadership can lift the boats stuck at the bottom. . . .

Our flag is red, white, and blue, but our nation is a rainbow—red, yellow, brown, black, and white—and all are precious in God's sight. America is not like a blanket, one piece of unbroken cloth—the same color, the same texture, the same size. It is more like a quilt—many patches, many pieces, many colors, many sizes, all woven and held together by a common thread. The white, the Hispanic, the black, the Arab, the Jew, the woman, the Native American, the small farmer, the businessperson, the environmentalist, the peace activist, the young, the old, the lesbian, the gay, and the disabled make up the American quilt. Even in our fractured state, all of us count and fit in somewhere. We have proven that we can survive without each other. But we have not proven that we can *win* or *make progress* without each other. We must come together.

From Fannie Lou Hamer in Atlantic City in 1964 to the Rainbow Coalition in San Francisco today, from the Atlantic to the Pacific, we have experienced pain, but progress, as we obtained open housing; as young people got the right to vote; as we lost Malcolm, Martin, Medgar, Bobby, John, and Viola. The team that got us here must be expanded, not abandoned. Twenty years ago, tears welled up in our eyes as the bodies of Schwerner, Goodman, and Chaney were dredged from the depths of a river in Mississippi.* Twenty years later, our communities, black and Jewish, are in anguish, anger, and pain. Feelings have been hurt on

---

*Fannie Lou Hamer led the Mississippi Freedom Democratic party, which challenged the regular Mississippi Democratic party about their exclusion of blacks from the delegation at the Democratic National Convention in Atlantic City, N.J., in 1964. The others named all were civil rights advocates who were assassinated: Malcolm X; Martin Luther King, Jr.; Medgar Evers, chairman of the NAACP in Mississippi; Robert F. Kennedy; John F. Kennedy; and Viola Liuzzo, a white woman from Detroit killed while assisting in the Selma-to-Montgomery march for voting rights in 1965. Michael Schwerner, Andrew Goodman, and James Chaney were young civil rights workers murdered near Philadelphia, Mississippi, in the summer of 1964. Schwerner and Goodman were Jewish.

both sides. There is a crisis in communications. Confusion is in the air, but we cannot afford to lose our way. We may agree to agree, or agree to disagree on issues, but we must bring back civility to the tensions. We are copartners in a long and rich religious history—the Judeo-Christian traditions. Many blacks and Jews have a shared passion for social justice at home and peace abroad. We must seek a revival of the spirit, inspired by a new vision and new possibilities. We must return to higher ground. We are bound by Moses and Jesus, but also connected with Islam and Muhammed. We are bound by Dr. Martin Luther King, Jr., and Rabbi Abraham Heschel crying out from their graves for us to reach common ground. We are bound by shared blood and shared sacrifices. We are much too intelligent; much too bound by our Judeo-Christian heritage; much too victimized by racism, sexism, militarism, and anti-Semitism; much too threatened as historical scapegoats to go on divided one from another. We must turn from finger-pointing to clasped hands. We must share our burdens and our joys with each other once again. We must turn to each other and not on each other.

Twenty years later, we cannot be satisfied by just restoring the old coalition. Old wineskins must make room for new wine. We must heal and expand. The Rainbow Coalition is making room for Arab-Americans. They too know the pain and hurt of racial and religious rejection. They must not continue to be made pariahs. The Rainbow Coalition is making room for Hispanic-Americans who this very night are living under the threat of the Simpson-Mazzoli immigration bill and farm workers in Ohio who are fighting the Campbell Soup Company with a boycott to achieve legitimate worker rights.

The Rainbow is making room for the Native Americans, the most exploited people of all and a people with the greatest moral claim among us. We support them as they seek to preserve their ancestral homelands and the beauty of a land that once was all theirs. They can never receive a fair share for all that they have given, but they must finally have a fair chance to develop their great resources and to preserve their people and their culture.

The Rainbow includes Asian-Americans, now being killed in our streets—scapegoats for the failures of corporate, industrial, and economic policies. The Rainbow is making room for young Americans. Twenty years ago, our young people were dying in a war for which they could not even vote. Twenty years later, young America has the power to stop a war in Central America and the responsibility to vote in great numbers. Young America must be politically active in 1984. The choice is war or peace. We must make room for young America.

The Rainbow includes disabled Americans. The color "chrome" fits in the rainbow. The disabled have their handicap revealed and their genius concealed, while the able-bodied have their genius revealed and their disability concealed. But ultimately we must judge people by their values and their contribution. Don't leave anybody out. I would rather have Roosevelt in a wheelchair than Reagan on a horse.

The Rainbow is making room for small farmers. They have suffered tremendously under the Reagan regime. They will either receive 90 percent parity or 100 percent charity. We must address their concerns and make room for them.

The Rainbow includes lesbians and gays. No American citizen ought to be denied equal protection under the law.

We must be unusually committed and caring as we expand our family to include new members. All of us must be tolerant and understanding as the fears and anxieties of the rejected and of the party leadership express themselves in so many different ways. Too often what we call hate—as if it were deeply rooted in some philosophy or strategy—is simply ignorance, anxiety, paranoia, fear, and insecurity. We must be long-suffering as we seek to right the wrongs of our party and our nation. We must expand our party, heal our party, and unify our party. That is the means to our mission in 1984.

We are often reminded that we live in a great nation—and we do. But it can be greater still. The Rainbow is mandating a new definition of greatness. We must not measure greatness from the mansion down but from the manger up. Jesus said that we should not be judged by the bark we wear but by the fruit we bear. Jesus said that we must measure greatness by how we treat the least of these. . . .

Democracy guarantees opportunity; it does not guarantee success. Democracy guarantees the right to participate; it does not give a license to either a majority or a minority to dominate. The victory for the Rainbow Coalition in the platform debates today was not whether we won or lost the vote but that we raised the right issues. We could afford to lose the vote. Issues are negotiable. We could not afford to avoid raising the right questions. Our self-respect and our moral integrity were at stake. Our heads are perhaps bloody but unbowed. Our backs are straight, and our vision is clear. We can go home and face our people. And when we think, in this journey from slave ship to championship, that we have gone from the planks of the boardwalk in Atlantic City in 1964 to fighting to help to write the planks in the Democratic party platform in San Francisco in 1984, there is a deep and abiding sense of joy in our soul, in spite of the tears in our eyes. Although there are missing planks, there is a solid foundation upon which we can build.

The real challenge to our individual and collective Democratic leadership is to do three things: (1) provide hope, which will inspire people to struggle and achieve, (2) provide a plan that shows the people a way out of our dilemma, and (3) courageously lead the way out.

There is a way out. *Justice.* The requirement for rebuilding America is justice. The linchpin of progressive politics in America is not new programs in the North but new power in the South. That is why I argue over and over again, that from Lynchburg, Virginia, around to Texas, there is only one black congressperson out of 115. Nineteen years after passage of the Voting Rights Act, we're locked out of the House, the Senate, and the governor's mansion. The key to unlocking Southern power is getting the Voting Rights Act enforced and ending the new forms of political disenfranchisement.

The key to a Democratic victory in 1984 is enfranchisement of the progressive wing of the Democratic party. They are the ones who have been devastated by Reaganomics, and, therefore, it is in their self-interest to vote in record numbers to oust their oppressor. Those already poor and those who are being impoverished do not simply want a change in leaders, they want a change in direction. The poor are not looking to be embellished, they have a need to be empowered. The key to political enfranchisement is enforcement of the Voting Rights Act. Gerrymandering, annexations, at-large elections, inaccessible registrars, roll purges, dual registrations, and second primaries—these are the schemes that continue to disenfranchise the locked-out. Why do I fight these impediments? Because you cannot hold someone in the ditch without lingering there with them. If the Voting Rights Act is enforced, we'll get twelve to twenty black, Hispanic, female, and progressive congresspersons from the South. We can save the cotton, but we've got to fight the boll weevils. We've got to make a judgment.

It's not enough to hope ERA will pass. How can we pass ERA? If blacks vote in great numbers, progressive whites win. It's the only way progressive whites win. If blacks vote in great numbers, Hispanics win. If blacks, Hispanics, and progressive whites vote, women win. When women win, children win. When women and children win, workers win. We must all come up together. We must come up together. I tell you, with all of our joy and excitement, we must not save the world and lose our souls. We should never short-circuit enforcement of the Voting Rights Act at every level. If one of us rises, all of us must rise. Justice is the way out.

There is a way out. *Peace.* The only way we can have jobs at home is to have peace abroad. We should not act as if nuclear weaponry is negotiable and debatable. In 1984, other nations have nuclear weapons too. Now if we drop the bomb, six to eight minutes later, we, too, will be destroyed. The issue now is not about dropping the bomb on somebody; it's about dropping the bomb on everybody. We must choose developed minds over guided missiles and think our way out, not fight it out. We must develop a coherent strategic nuclear strategy. We used nuclear weapons once before on Japan. But we must declare that never again will we be the ones to engage in the "first use" of nuclear weapons. Our real security is in developed minds, not guided missiles. . . .

There is a way out. *Jobs.* If we enforce the Voting Rights Act as a way of achieving justice; and if we achieve peace through cutting the defense budget without cutting our defense, respect other nations of the world, and resolve conflicts through negotiations instead of confrontations; then we will have enough power and money to rebuild America. We can use the money we are currently squandering on the arms race to save the human race. We can use that money to build millions of new houses, to build hospitals, to train and pay our teachers and educate our young people, to provide health care and health-care training, to rebuild our cities and end rural poverty; use that money to rebuild 250,000 bridges, rebuild our railroads, and build mass-transit systems; use that money to put steelworkers back to work; use that money to rebuild the infrastructure of our country: repair our roads, our ports, our riverbeds, our sewer systems, and stop soil erosion; use that money to clean up our environment: our land, our water, and our air; use that money to make "America the Beautiful." We could put America back to work. . . .

What this campaign has shown above all else is that the key to our liberation is in our own hands and in our dream and vision of a better world. It is the vision that allows us to reach out to each other and to redeem each other. It is the dream that sustains us through the dark times and the dark realities. It is our hope that gives us a *why* for living when we do not see *how* to live. . . .

When I was a child in Greenville, South Carolina, the Rev. James Hall used to preach a sermon, every so often, about Jesus. He would quote Jesus as saying, "If I be lifted up, I'll draw all men unto me." When I was a child I didn't quite understand what he meant. But I understand it a little better now. If you raise up truth, it's magnetic. It has a way of drawing people. With all this confusion in the convention—bright lights, parties, and big fun—we must raise up a simple proposition: feed the hungry, and the poor will come running; study war no more, and our youth will come running. If we lift up a program to put America back to work as an alternative to welfare and despair, the unemployed will come running. If we cut the military budget without cutting our defense and use that money to rebuild bridges and put steelworkers back to work; use that money to provide jobs for our citizens; use that money to build schools and train teachers and educate our children; use that money to build hospitals and train doctors and nurses—the whole nation will come running to us.

As I lived in the ghettoes, in barrios, on reservations, and in the slums, I had a message for our youth. Young America, I know you face a cutback in jobs, large reductions in housing and food, inferior health care and education, and a general environment that tries to break your spirit. But don't put dope in your veins; put hope in your brains. Don't let them break your spirit. There is a way out. Our party must not only have the courage and the conscience to expose the slummy side. We must have the conviction and vision to show America the sunny side, the way out. When I see urban decay I see a sunny side and a slummy side. A broken window is the slummy side. Train that youth to be a carpenter. That's the sunny side. A missing brick? That's the slummy side. Train that youth to be a brick mason. That's the sunny side. The hieroglyphics of destitution on the walls? That's the slummy side. Train that youth to be a painter or an artist. That's the sunny side. Then unions must open up, embrace, and train our youth so they can help to rebuild America.

I am more convinced than ever that we can win. We'll vault up the rough side of the mountain—we can win. But I just want the youth of America to do me one favor. Exercise the right to dream. You must face reality—that which is. But then dream of the reality that ought to be, that must be. Live beyond the pain of reality with the dream of a bright tomorrow. Use hope and imagination as weapons of survival and progress. Use love to motivate you and obligate you to serve the human family.

Young people, dream of peace. Choose the human race over the nuclear race. We must bury the weapons and not burn the people. We are the first generation that will either freeze the weapons or burn the people and freeze the planet.

Young people, dream of a new value system. Dream of teachers, but teachers who will teach for life, not just for a living. Dream of doctors, but doctors who are more concerned with public health than personal wealth. Dream of lawyers, but lawyers who are more concerned with justice than a judgeship. Dream of artists, but artists who will convey music and message, rhythm, rhyme, and reason. Dream of priests and preachers, but priests and preachers who will prophesy and not profiteer. Dream of writers, but writers who will ascribe, describe, prescribe, not just scribble. Dream of authentic leaders who will mold public opinion against a headwind, not just ride the tailwinds of opinion polls. Dream of a world where we measure character by how much we share and care, not by how much we take and consume. Preach and dream. Our time has come.

We must measure character by how we treat the least of these, by who feeds the most hungry people, by who educates the most uneducated people, by who cares and loves the most, by who fights for the needy and seeks to save the greedy. We must dream and choose the laws of sacrifice, which lead to greatness, and not the laws of convenience, which lead to collapse.

In your dreaming you must know that unearned suffering is redemptive. Water cannot wash away the blood of martyrs. Blood is thicker than water. Water makes grass and flowers grow, but blood make sons and daughters of liberation grow. No matter how difficult the days and dark the nights, there is a brighter side somewhere. In Angola, Mozambique, Nicaragua, El Salvador, South Africa, Greenville, South Carolina, and Harlem, there is a brighter side.

Jesus was rejected from the inn and born in the slum. But just because you were born in the slum does not mean that the slum was born in you. With a made-up mind, which is the most powerful instrument in the world, you can rise above your circumstances. No mountain is too high, and no valley is too low; no forest is too dense, and no water is too deep—if your mind is made up. With eyesight, you may see misery. But with insight, you can see the brighter side.

Suffering breeds character, character breeds faith, and in the end faith will not disappoint. Faith, hope, and dreams will prevail. Weeping may endure for a night, but joy is coming in the morning. Troubles won't last always. Our time has come. No graves can hold our bodies down. Our time has come. No lie can live forever. Our time has come. We must leave our racial battlegrounds, come to economic common ground, and rise to moral higher ground. America, our time has come. Give me your tired, your poor, your huddled masses yearning to breathe free. And come November, there will be a change, because our time has come.

Kelvin Christopher James*

Kelvin Christopher James was born in Port of Spain, Trinidad, and graduated from the University of the West Indies with a science degree in 1967. James was a high school science teacher for a year in 1968, before emigrating to New York, where he earned his living as a clinical technologist at Harlem Hospital in New York City from 1973 to 1979. During these years, James completed his education at Columbia University, receiving one master's degree in 1975 (M.A.), one in 1976 (M.S.), and a doctorate in education in 1978.

A freelance writer since 1980, James has published a collection of short fiction, Jumping Ship and Other Stories (1992) and two novels, Secrets (1993) and Fling with a Demon Lover (1996). James's childhood days in Trinidad figure prominently in Jumping Ship. The stories in the collection connect, recreating the progression of home, emigration, and the issues surrounding assimilation to a new country and dominant culture. The collection is divided into three parts, the first centered in the Caribbean, the second focused on the "border" of emigration/immigration, and the final part grounded in the urban geography of the United States. The primary theme of the first section is the lure of seduction, the dangerous edge just under the surface of a seeming tropical paradise. Desire is frustrated in each of the stories in section one, resulting in rage or betrayal for each of the characters. Stories in section two structurally carry the reader from the islands to the United States. The idea of home is disrupted as the notions of migration and exile become central. In section three, all but one of the stories is set in New York City. The characters are, again, Black males, struggling against circumstances with dire consequences over which they have little control. While the protagonists of the stories in section three are predominantly "criminal," James undercuts stereotypes, emphasizing psychological and sociological complexity in identity and behavior. The voice of the whole is vitally male, exploring Black male identity and masculinity across environments and age.

In "Ties," a story from the third and longest section of the collection, Othello Jones narrates from prison the circumstances that landed him there, the witnessing of the death of his hero brother, Stone, and his plans for a future. Othello's first person perspective captures the complexities of his situation, including the disillusionment that has plagued his life, his idealizing of his older brother, and his resistance against a system that would confine him to stereotype.

In his first novel, Secrets, Kelvin Christopher James assumes the voice of a Caribbean girl, Uxann, who, overweight and shy, prefers her own company or, at most, the company of her strict father, Seyen, with whom she lives, or her best friend, Keah, a feisty opposite. Opposites attract and intrigue as Uxann's naivete and obedience meets Keah's headstrong

*Birth year not available.

480

will. When Keah is expelled from school for fornicating on school grounds, Seyen hires her to help Uxann with the chores. Passion and fury figure highly in the tragedy that this circumstance provokes. A novel about loss of innocence, Secrets proves James's poetic ability on a level of myth and intimacy.

Fling with a Demon Lover, James' second novel, has met less critical acclaim than his first two works. The novel features a New York school teacher, Sassela Jack, who leaves the security of her life, including a long-term relationship, for a Greek island where she becomes enmeshed in a relationship with a much younger lover, Ciam. The relationship dissipates into disturbing mystery, and the novel dissolves from dream to nightmare. James experiments with language, adopting unusual speech patterns and sentence structures, to create a mood that matches the spinning of his characters.

For his success in expressing the complexities of illusion and for his ability to ground geography within his fiction, we look forward to more word-work from Kelvin Christopher James.

R. Joyce Lausch

Ties

I met a man in the joint. He was from Trinidad and mentally fine-tuned to crazy. But he was also harmless, and we all took care of him. A gentleman philosopher, and honest as sunshine, Trinee had a saying for every situation. You listened to him, and you'd think he was a hundred years old. Yet he was as young as any of us.

Once I heard him say how, when Lion gets old, common Dog fucks him. I cracked up when he said this to make a point in a funny story. But there's serious sense in Trinee's nonsense. And I, for one, never want to grow old so feeble. Not unless things change around in this town.

I went to the joint because I wanted to live the American Dream. Not too much, or too fancy. Just the ordinary American Dream, featuring food, good appliances, some fine clothes, and a steady income. No fancy cars! They're not for me. I will always pay the taximan. I'd even take the trains rather than have sanitation trucks, dogs, and vandals make my ride ugly. Yes, all I wanted was an average portion of the apple pie, minus the car. Thing is, nobody ever showed me how to get it, except my brother, Stone. And he was a hard man.

Mama had named him Winston Shaka Jones. But his real name was Stone. He was six years older than I, and by the time I first could talk, he had the name already. He was a watchful guy, never spoke much about anything. That doesn't mean he was a thinker, now. Neither does it say that he was stupid. Stone was a one to do what someone told him. It had to be the right someone, of course. Mama used to tell Stone to make something of himself, because his father had made him a ravager. She always told him that: "Your father made you a ravager!" It was as though she fancied the sound of it. Stone never said anything back. You ever hear a rock talk?

Stone's father had raped Ma when she was sixteen. He was her father's good buddy, and could visit the house when Gramps was away. He raped her twice in one week. When she told her mother and Gramma told Gramps, he said some-body had to do her the favor sometime. But then Gramps was a no-good anyhow.

Once when Ma was upset, she told Stone what she thought of his father—mean, bitter things. Stone begged her then for permission to find the brute and end him. He was a fist-hearted fifteen-year-old man, but that night his tears were running full as he asked. Ma looked at him as if long lost, and then she said, "Don't bother, son." She hardly ever called us "son." Then she went over and held his face to her bosom. She was crying, too.

Stone was my man. From since I was in kindergarten, he was who I wanted to be. He was the nearest thing to Superman that I knew. He always got a job done, whatever the job. When I was about twelve, Stone took me under his wing. I was very careful to be cool about it. But I was happy as a soap bubble in sum-mer. He taught me to play ball, to fight dirty, to steal and rob and hustle and con people. Even though it was much harder than school stuff, I learned everything. Stone didn't like to teach the same thing twice. Soon I felt I could do some things better than he. But we had no hassles. For a while, it was all good life. Then Stone decided to make a soldier of himself. So he joined the army to see the world, and they showed him Vietnam.

Sometimes, in the joint, time gets long. It's best then to just sit and think. I call it "monking," because you can become so inspired, with revelations and under-standings. After a monking spell, you may get angry in a strange way. Every time you remember a wrong done you, a chill embraces you, forcing your belly mus-cles a little tighter, permanently. Make a check of all the brothers in jail. Those who look strong and lean, I bet they're either revenge-bent hating, or hugging madness close. If there's a difference.

Whenever I thought about Stone, I would read a book, any book. I read a good bit. I suppose I have a sort of angry prison education.

I admired Stone more than anyone else in creation. Yet he lived and died close to me, and I never knew him. Maybe I love him because I didn't know him. Maybe Stone was a mean guy. I don't know. I don't know if Stone had a sense of humor. I don't know what he liked in women. I never knew if he had a favorite beer. So now I get mad thinking of Stone. Somehow, someone stole my brother's personality from me. But then, I might've been careless with it. So I am cool.

Seven years in the joint taught me one or two tricks. A good one is how to be patient in anger. I learned patience from being bored working in the prison li-brary. In a few years, I had patiently read every book they stacked. That way I picked up a liberal education, too. Otherwise I could've been a reluctant book-keeper. That's what the authorities in the joint had decided to teach me to be. I guess they were trying to show me the pathway to upward social mobility. I didn't apply myself, though. I figured that if it was so hot, why weren't they all doing it? They wanted riches. And on the other side, I didn't expect many businessfolks would be eager to hire a bookkeeper with my record.

Watching the power of justice was another trick I learned. Up on the top edge of Central Park, like layers and layers of stubbornness, there is a great mass of black stone, a hard cap to the natural heart of the city. I always picture it when I think of the Justice System in this town. Being involved in that system is like being stuck in the middle of that unfeeling mass of hardness. That's if you don't have power: to slip, to slide, or explode out. And to folks like me, power comes in different guises. It's not easy to hold, or even recognize.

I have seen guys pray to the jailhouse lawyer as though he were God. Just because he, a prisoner like them, could comprehend that unnatural legal thinking, those traditional laws that changing times have made foolish. So, to them, the jailhouse lawyer is a great man. Guys would beg him to listen to their cases. They'd approach him as though it were Judgment Day and they have a fifty-fifty chance of getting in, and he's the one with the deciding vote. They're so reverent! You find out that these "common criminals" are men who could tell a good joke. Or movie buffs who want a good education for their kids. And it's the prison lawyer who has power to change them so. For too many a brother in jail, he is the best and last hope.

This lord of promise was no help to me, though. I had an open-and-shut case: accessory to murder of an officer and a civilian, attempted robbery, assault of all the officers who tried to kill me after they had handcuffed me, and a few misdemeanors they ganged up as the writing space ran out. The trial didn't take long. The prosecutor mentioned my address, and the judge became red in the face. Then his lips closed up tight like a disturbed oyster. My legal-aid defense counsel was like a little boy on a big seashore: You hardly noticed he was there.

What saved me some was my minority. I qualified as juvenile, unschooled, unable to understand the best ways to progress in regular society. So I got life, meaning three-to-ten. Not too bad. It kept me out of wars and other trouble.

When Stone came back from the government's war, we had begun some serious hustling. The difference from before was Stone. He moved with incredible smooths. This was from his Vietnam training. People who saw him armed knew he was dangerous. They did exactly what he said. Which was very nice, since we were able to stop mugging poor folks, and lived off the high-priced little stores, and such-like. It was quicker money, less time on the streets, and easier on everyone. We never hurt a soul.

Stone spent a lot of money on Mama, giving her a good time in the fancy life. I sort of let him. They had their special thing I stayed out of. Once he bought her a fine mink coat. Mrs. Saunders, who had a true eye for style, said Mama wore it like she was born to mink. And Mama seemed to believe that. For you wouldn't have believed her graciousness when Stone and I took her to those fancy-named restaurants. I'm sure Ma went to every Caribbean country boasting a hotel and an airport. Yes, she did make merry of her little self. She knew that Stone was trying to make up for his birthright. Just as she had to know we were robbing and stealing. But we never spoke about such things. What was there to say?

I got the idea for the numbers-joint takeoff by accident. It came on a cool fall day. Angel and I had been playing ball in the park, him in dungaree coveralls, me in jeans. He was going to show me the mightiest dunk shot ever by a six-foot-one, unknown high school player. He started fifteen feet right of the hoop, driving in powerfully from an angle, then he leapt for height and—only managed a mighty miss.

The ball took off, ricocheting over the fence and into the street. Then a telephone repairman ran out from behind a repair truck and tossed the ball back to us. The freaky thing was that the guy, even down to his coveralls, was Angel's double. We agreed that it was some kinda weird, then ended the game and started for the bodega to get something to cool down over. As we passed the telephone-repair van, Angel decided he'd play the van's license-plate number. And surprised me by going into a little doorway almost blocked by the repair van—a new but thriving numbers joint.

Half hour later, Stone was satisfied with my answers. I had told him that, yes, there was a fresh-dug, open trench between the curb and the truck. That the men were working on it. And that, yes, the numbers man with the gun sat his protection well inside the joint's door, as he didn't want to be conspicuous to the repairmen. Only then did Stone agree to go shopping with me. We bought apparatus that telephone repairmen carried: coveralls, two yellow hard hats, oversized plastic goggles, pliers, and some colored wire. And we were ready.

Next day, there were no newspaper stories about the stickup of a numbers joint. To street people, that meant no one had died, so the police were staying out of it. But the street also had it that the numbers people had lost about $100,000 worth of quite spendable money. They had no idea who'd taken them off. The two robbers had entered saying they were from the telephone company. Every man, woman, and child who heard the news wished they'd been the heroes.

About three hours after that nonstickup, two quietly dressed young men stepped into a small hardware store on the East Side. If anything was remarkable about them, it was that they were so circumspect in deportment. They virtually trod the pavement softly. The younger, more outgoing one asked the storekeeper for some rubber bands. He was courteous and spoke nicely. The other young man stood by silently. He remained just inside the door and carried in one hand a large, filled shopping bag. There was something magnetic about his silence. He seemed charged, alert, set like a rattleless viper. This quiet one was looking at the store's only other occupant: a brown-skinned, middle-aged woman. In that neighborhood, perhaps somebody's maid. She was in the store's phone booth occupied at frowning as she concentrated on her conversation.

While he was bagging the rubber bands, the shopkeeper glanced over to the watchful young man. The gesture was more of curiosity than caution, as if he didn't like the boy's quiet but wasn't threatened by it. The transaction completed, the young men turned to leave.

Then the door opened, and a new customer entered. Instantly, the quiet one fastened his gaze on the new man. And right then came a moment when time paused on the brink, before the events of its smooth flow jumbled on together.

Some things went so fast, they had to be recalled with effort to memory. And some things happened too slowly for ever forgetting.

The new man wrenched around to face the intense stare. Then he spread his legs and put his back to the door, defending it against the boys' exit. His reassuring voice announced, "All right, everybody, take it easy." The take-charge tone identified him. He was a well-trained plainclothes officer who knew trouble when he saw it.

The nice young man was quick in his response. "No trouble, Officer," he said, "no trouble at all. Ask the man." And the boy looked over to the shopkeeper.

The shopkeeper was smiling nervously. He didn't want trouble in his store. Meanwhile, the nice young man leaned privately on the hard one. He urged in a whisper, "Let's go, man. Chill out, chill out!" The defiant one responded reluctantly, like a rock shifted by a great effort. But he was moving. The nice one reached for the door handle. He was trying hard to be casual.

The new man now seemed embarrassed by his overreaction, and relinquished the door slowly. The nice boy moved aside for the other to leave ahead of him. But as this young man passed, the man reached over to poke suspiciously at the bag. He demanded, "What you got in there?" At that, the hard young man flowed into action.

Stone released the bag most gently. With no other motion, and before the bag had hit the floor, he was holding the poking hand. He twisted it somehow, and the officer's face was jerked down to collide with Stone's rapidly rising knee. At the same time, Stone's other hand reached for the man's hair. He grabbed it and twisted violently. And I heard the muffled, crunching sound with which life deserted the bewildered man. It was all done faster than I can say.

I was fascinated. I couldn't speak, and tears rushed to my eyes. I had never seen physical action so perfect. He had performed the brutal act of killing with a graceful finesse that was wonderful. He must've felt my emotion, for he glanced oddly at me, his face set proud. Then, as our eyes met, I saw him flinch and go dead. Same time, I heard the shot.

A big hole had splattered out the top of his chest. It went from a quick jagged white to a brown flowing red. I spun around to see the shopkeeper with the shotgun still in his hands. He was trembling badly, and spitting white froth from the side of his mouth. He looked older than he had just a moment before, and shook his head as though violently negating the scene, dislodging his glasses. He clutched the wavering shotgun with one hand, and snatched to right his glasses, but only succeeded in completely knocking them off.

My bullets must've hit him somewhere in the trunk region. I saw no wounds or bloody spots appear on his haggard face. He tried to brace unsuccessfully against some invisible, avenging whiplash. Then he crumpled down across the counter, and with a sobbing, gargling sound started to die.

I felt Stone pulling at my pants cuff. My eyes were rivers, and snot was running in between my open lips. I looked for something to blow my nose and wipe my face with. Stone kept tugging at my pants cuff. Impatient with the irritation, I blew out my nose onto the bloody floor. Then I dried my face with my jacket sleeves, and I looked to attend my main man.

Stone's left shoulder and arm were almost blown away. The thick blood was surging out of him and onto the floorboards. It seemed so much. Stone wanted something. He was trying to tell me what, but all I heard was a gurgle. His face showed a lot of damage, but mainly it looked sweat-dirty. Then he looked at my hand, and I understood. It was the gun he wanted. So I put it on his shoulder and let some blood run over it. Then I pulled up his good hand to hold it there, making him look like some macabre marksman at rest after firing. Then he did the one thing that could break my heart. Stone cried.

The tears were seeping through his half-closed eyes and running down the sides of his face into his ears. I thought it must feel uncomfortable. But I was at a loss for what to do, unable to move, or comfort him. All my life, he had taught me to take care of business. But I didn't know how to comfort someone when he was dying. So I just sat there in his sticky blood, crying and feeling protective.

He was trying to talk again, and couldn't because the blood was in his throat. After a while, he began to cough and cough and cough. I said, "Take it easy, man," concerned that his shoulder couldn't take such a jarring. Then he said something. It sounded like, "I ain't no rapist." But it was a wheezing rasp of a whisper. What was clear in it, though, was the righteousness of the innocent. Then Stone died.

I never told Mama about that part. I didn't want her to know what he was thinking last. For no one loved her more than Stone. I didn't.

I never found out what happened to Stone's body. I was in the hospital recovering from the arresting officers for a month after he died. Mama lasted about two years more. When I got to jail, she used to come see me once every month. But we didn't have much to talk the hour out. She really wanted to know more about Stone. She was asking me something I couldn't tell her.

After she passed, they took me once to see her grave. Her neighbors in the building had buried her. They had also petitioned for my pass to visit the cemetery. At the gravesite, no sadness came to me. Instead, I found myself wondering what had become of the mink coat, and all that jewelry Stone had bought her.

Jail was good to me. I was educated there. When I went in, I was like that officer Stone destroyed: just an average dummy with minimal education and a lot of good instincts. I learned to think in the joint. I came to understand that time is friendly if you keep yourself ready. And I had one joy there: a pleasure I fought with every day. You see, I didn't want to become dependent on it. For I had no control over it, "it" being the letter I got every two weeks.

Men in jail become pathetic in their dependencies. Without ever realizing, they make themselves into puppets. They are manipulated by everybody—by other prisoners, guards, officials, by chaplains, by entertainers, by their children and their women, and most of all, by their hopes.

This can cause some strange changes. I've seen lovermen go weird. From Romeos who broke and balled the ladies outside, lovesickness turns them into lisping, stubble-chinned, prison-yard queens. For salvation from prison, men have been born again, lost themselves in hobbies, developed occult philosophies, become militant or mental defectives. Sometimes they seek death with rash cunning, smiling all the while. Sometimes they just go mad. But they hardly ever recognize they're dancing for an uninterested puppeteer named Hope. For in prison, salvation is not your own to find. They have no saviors there.

Sometimes when I knew my letter was due, I would begin to avoid mail call. I learned to enjoy the pain of avoiding mail call. I'd do it gradually, a day at a time, holding myself in check when I felt the anticipation rise. After a while, I learned to like the thrill itself, minus the gratification. There were times when I suspended pleasure until I could pick up two letters at a time. Once I did three.

The letters always got to me looking old in their cream-colored six-by-three envelopes. Regardless of postmarked origin, which changed frequently, the return address was always one word: Harlem. I liked that. I read it as a defiant camaraderie. They were addressed in liquid black ink, used by an old-fashioned nib pen dipped in an inkpot. Fine lines were impressed on the envelope so that the writing was neat and straight. Yet the handwriting was nervous and unpracticed, a crochet of words formed letter by letter and linked by flourishes. It was mostly this time and concern in production that made these letters my constant comfort and solace.

They always began, *My dear son Othello* . . . They always ended with, *A Prayer for Those Awaiting Deliverance.* I never said the prayer, but I respected it. The letters themselves didn't give anything much in the form of news. I usually flushed them down the toilet just after reading. I kept the stamps, though. These I dated and put under my mattress in a prison envelope—my treasury. What these letters unspokenly said was that the old cleaning lady was keeping up her end.

After Old Man Death had walked away with his full bag, the shop knew a moment of relief. That was just a feeling, though. The fact was, I was sad and very frightened. There were blood and dead people all around. One of them was the law. There was also a shopping bag containing $126,000 wrapped in a bath towel. It was a bad spot to be in. I knew I should get out of there, but was too listless to move. Moreover, there was blood all over me. And I really didn't want to leave my man. But neither did I want to face those officers who were radioing their rapid approach.

As if from a distance, I heard Mama's voice saying softly, "You'd better soon get away from all this trouble, son." For a moment, terrifying thoughts of angels and the supernatural overwhelmed me. I actually gasped for breath. But immediately I realized she wouldn't have said that, or in just those tones. So then I was only surprised. I looked around. The old lady who'd been in the phone booth was walking toward the front door, carefully avoiding the spots of blood and disorder. She was obviously leaving, intent on minding her own business. In a confusion, I also knew there was nothing I was going to do about it.

Suddenly, without thought, I said, "Wait! Please, wait." She paused, one hand on the doorknob, and the words spilled out of me. "Here, take this," I said, grabbing the bag and holding it out to her. "Please, ma'am. . . . Use whatever you want. Please. Keep the rest safe for me. Anyhow you want. Here! These keys are to safe-deposit boxes. Take them. This is all my ID. Please, ma'am, hold it for me. I love my brother. I have to suffer with him. His name is Stone. Please!"

I was moving all the while: rushing things to her, handing the bag to her, explaining, pleading, and crying again. Sniffling like a baby. At last she said, "Okay, son, okay. I'll take care of your business for you, just as you ask. But now I need a change of air."

She had been peering at me head aslant, still half facing the door and looking uncertain. Then, when she said, "Okay," she smiled at me and winked. It was a spry wink, an okay-let's-do-it wink. And with that twinkle, she gained my absolute trust. Then she took the loot and walked out the door, still being careful to avoid the gore. The only things that I knew about her were her voice, that she'd worn a red scarf around her neck, and that her accent was Caribbean.

Leaving the joint is an emotional experience. Some men can hardly take it. They ask their people to come and meet them to help them go through the gates. You're glad to leave, of course. But if you've been in for a while, you're leaving old friends. Sometimes they're your only friends. And they're glad to see you go, but they also wish it was them leaving. So in the morning or the night before, when you tell them good-bye, you feel the coldness of their envy. Yet you ignore it. You're too glad to be getting away from that cage of anger and despair. And you know, too, that they're really glad for you. There's just no way they could show it.

But that's not the hardest part of regaining your freedom. The most difficult is stepping into that strange, spacious, glaring world again. You're like a country boy walking first time into a slick, big-city nightclub. Everyone is looking at you. And you know they all think you're a piece of shit. And you have to be cool, 'cause you're not sure about it yourself.

In addition to the usual "Harlem," there was a real address on the last two letters. It was near Marcus Garvey Park, and this was where I headed when I hit the city. That afternoon it was the only certain place in this world. Everywhere else was just a blurred understanding. I headed there express, no stops nowhere. Just having that place to go to made me forever owe the old lady. Lagniappe was that she let me come out on my own.

The house was a four-storied brownstone. It looked solid and secure—as Trinee would say, "as though it there since Hatchet was Hammer." I rang the super's bell as instructed in the letter.

After a minute, an older man opened the door, put his head out, and asked before I could speak, "You Othello Jones?" I didn't answer right away. After such a long time locked up, the sound of my name, public and free, was soul music. I savored its song, the cadences: la-la-la laaa.

"Yes, sir," I told him, "I'm Othello Jones."

The man smiled at me. "Well, sir boss, your room is on the top floor. It's nice, spacey, private. Can see the park up there. Lots of light. Mrs. Dean said I must see you have everything—even unto the fatted calf. . . ." He chuckled at his reference. I smiled away, too. Although not so much at what he said as for his manner. He went on, "She said you'd see her two weeks from tomorrow. She left some things with me for you. Looks like she's . . ." And he kept on talking, treating me like family and making me welcome.

Charles Johnson (1948–)

Winner of the 1998 MacArthur Fellowship, Charles Johnson has published five novels, including the widely celebrated Middle Passage *(1990), which won the National Book Award for fiction.* Middle Passage *is one of the only African American works to treat the brutal transition that slaves experienced upon being kidnapped from Africa and brought by ship to the Western Hemisphere. Unlike typical slave autobiographers, Johnson focuses on the ocean voyage itself.*

Johnson was born in Evanston, Illinois, in 1948. Because his first love was drawing, he worked as an editorial cartoonist while attending Southern Illinois University. In the early 1970s he published two collections of drawings. In 1974 he wrote Faith and the Good Thing, *a transgenre book heavily influenced by John Gardner, Ralph Ellison, and Buddhist thought.* Faith *uses philosophy and folktales to articulate Johnson's theories about African American traditions, fiction, and esthetics. After writing several screenplays, including* Booker *(1984), which appeared on PBS, Johnson became a teacher of creative writing at the University of Washington.*

The following three stories were excerpted from Africans in America: America's Journey through Slavery *(1998), a book companion to the PBS series of the same title. This extraordinary team publication was meticulously prepared and organized over a ten-year period by the WGBH Series Research Team, which included Patricia Smith, Steve Fayer, and scholars from around the world. The editors interweave Johnson's fictional stories with a historical account of slavery.*

In "The Soulcatcher," Frank is a slave who has escaped so long ago that he underestimates the power, love, and determination of the tiny Black Boston community of which he has become a part. Clement Walker, a soulless bounty hunter fueled by hatred and greed, overestimates his own immunity from the violent forces unleashed by slavery.

In "The Mayor's Tale," an unimaginative, egocentric, and exploitive White mayor awakens to discover that every Black man, woman, and child in the city has utterly disappeared. The mayor never sees Black laborers, or the "invisible" labor they produce, until they are gone and he is forced to do his own work. Because Johnson does not name the mayor, his wife, or their "northeastern city," they may all serve as synecdochic signifiers for every White, upper-middle class family in every "free" northern city.

"The Transmission," the first short story in Africans in America, *relates the haunting tale of Malawi, who has just been ripped from his people, the Allmuseri. Johnson gives us a window into Malawi's thoughts in order to provide an intimate and visceral experience of the first leg of slavery:*

> *They were dead, and this was the boat to the Underworld. In the darkness of its belly, the boy—his name was Malawi—lay pressed against its wet, wooden hull, naked and chained to a corpse that only before had been his older brother,*

Oboto. Down there, the air curdled, thick with the stench of feces and decaying flesh. Already the ship's rats were nibbling at Oboto's cold, stiff fingers. Malawi screamed them away whenever they came scurrying through a half a foot of salt water towards his brother's body.

Malawi's brother is an apprentice griot, "a living book who carried within himself, like a treasure, his people's entire history from time immemorial. Its recitation takes three full days." Before Oboto dies, he whispers all his knowledge into his brother's ear so that the Allmuseri, and he himself, will be immortal. The transmission also shelters Malawi from the insanity around him. Oboto tells him not to fear the White men:

> *They are barbarians. Malawi, I don't think the spirits respect them. How could they? They smell bad. They are unclean. They are dead here'—he touched his chest above his heart—'not us.'*

A "hook-nosed phantom" helps Malawi cast his brother into the sea, sympathizing with Malawi's deep grief. This brilliant scene elicits an awkward and almost guilty ambivalence from the reader. While the "hook-nosed phantom" is the first White to recognize Malawi's humanity, he still willingly participates in Malawi's enslavement.

Like Toni Morrison's fiction, "The Transmission" probes the themes of immortality, pain, spirituality, violation, resistance, global White supremacy, the role of art in healing, and the bottomless capacity of Black societies to empower individuals.

Dee Parmer Woodtor recently wrote, "Slavery is not dead and done, and it won't be until we find the words to talk about it." In "The Transmission," "The Soulcatcher," "The Mayor's Tale," and in numerous other stories, novels, and screenplays, Johnson courageously undertakes the awesome task of finding the words.

Nicole Lanson

The Soulcatcher

In that Boston market on a Thursday in 1853, there were two men, one black, one white, who were as intimately bound, in a way, as brothers, or perhaps it was better to say they were caught in a macabre dance, one that stretched from rural South Carolina to Massachusetts over a period of three long months of hiding, disguises, last-minute escapes, name changes, and tracking leads that led nowhere until it brought them both here to the bustling open-air market perched near the waterfront on a summer afternoon.

They were weary, these two. Hunter and Hunted.

The Hunter paused just at the periphery of the market, breathing in the salt-laced air, looking at the numerous stands filled with freshly baked bread, a variety of vegetables, fish caught earlier that day, and handicrafts—wood carvings, colorful quilts, and hand-sewn leather garments—sold by black and white Bostonians alike. The Negroes, he noticed, including the one he was looking for, had set up their stands toward the rear of the market, separating themselves from the others. A gnarled, little merchant with a Scottish brogue, and wearing a yeoman's cap and burnoose, suddenly pulled at the sleeve of the Hunter's jacket. He pointed with his other hand at boots on the table beside him. Irritated, the Hunter shook loose his arm from the merchant's grasp, then moved on a few paces through the crowded market, tilting down his hat brim a bit to hide his face, and positioned himself to one side of a hanging display of rugs. From there he could see the Negro he wanted but was not himself in plain view. He reached into a pocket sewn inside his ragged, gypsy cloak, felt around his pistol—a Colt .31—and his fingers closed on a folded piece of paper. The Hunter withdrew it. He opened it slowly, as he'd done nearly a hundred times in the last three months in dozens of towns in North Carolina, Virginia, Pennsylvania, and New York, in daylight and dark, when the trail he was following went cold and he sat before a campfire, wondering how long it would be before he would collect his bounty. The paper had been folded and creased so often a few of the words on it were feathery. In the upper right-hand corner he saw the long-dried stain of dark blood—his brother Jeremiah's—and below it this notice:

RUN away from <u>Charlotte</u> on *Sunday,* a Negro slave named FRANK, well known about the Country as a craftsman, has a scar on one of his Wrists, and has lost one or more of his fore Teeth; he is a very resourceful Fellow, skilled as a smithy and saddle-maker, loves Drink, and is very often in his Cups, but surly and dangerous when sober. Whither he has run to, I cannot say, but I will offer $200 to have him returned to me. He can read and write.

APRIL 2, 1853   JUBAL CATTON

From where he stood, the Hunter had a side view of a black craftsman seated before a table of wood carvings, talking to a nearby old Negress selling fish and a balding black man hawking produce. The Hunter was sure this was Frank. When last he'd seen him—just outside Norfolk—he was wearing Lowell pants and a jerkin. Today he was dressed better in a homespun suit. Under the table, he noticed, there was a flask, which the Negro occasionally lifted to his lips, then slid back out of sight. For a time, the Hunter was content simply to study him. He didn't want to rush. That's what Jeremiah always told him: *You move too quick, you'll startle the prey. When the moment's right to move, you'll know.* Now that he nearly had Frank trapped, the Hunter wished his brother could be there, at the market, for the catch. But Jeremiah was back in Charleston. Blind. When Frank bolted from Jubal Catton's farm, he'd stolen his master's Walker .44, and when they found him hiding in a barn, Frank fired at Jeremiah's face from five feet away, missing him—the nigger was a bad shot—but the blast seared his brother's eyes. Yes, thought the Hunter. He wished like hell Jeremiah was here now. They both still wanted that reward. But this runaway had made the hunt personal. During the first month he pursued Frank, his intent was to kill him. Then, as the weeks drew on, he realized slavery was worse than death. It was a little bit of death every day. It was even worse than being blind.

He would take him back, the Hunter decided. Jeremiah'd want it that way.

The Hunted reached under his table, grabbed the bottle by its neck, then drank just enough to take away the dryness in his throat. He never knew exactly why, but for some reason he'd always fought better drunk than sober. And it looked like he had a fight coming now, though he had thrown away his master's gun and had nothing to defend himself with but his bare hands. He thought, *All right, if that's the way it has to be*. He'd seen the white man—his name was Clement Walker—the moment he entered the market, or rather his nerves had responded, as they always did, when a soulcatcher was close by. He could smell them the way a rabbit did a hound. It was the way they looked at colored people, he supposed. Most whites didn't bother to look at you at all, like you were invisible. Or as unimportant as a fence post. Or if they were afraid of you, they'd look away altogether. But not soulcatchers. They wanted to see your face. Match it with a description on a wanted poster. Oh, yes, *they* looked. Real hard.

That was how he'd spotted the Hunter. But he didn't need that sixth sense anymore to recognize Walker. The Hunted rubbed his left shoulder, massaging the spot where the Hunter had months ago left a deep imprint of his incisors—this, during their tussle after he shot at Jeremiah Walker. No question he'd know Clement *any*where. The man was in his dreams or—more precisely—his nightmares since he left his master's farm. Not a day passed when Frank didn't look over his shoulder, expecting him to be there, holding a gun in one hand and manacles in the other. It was almost as if he was *inside* Frank now, the embodiment of all his fears.

His first instinct had been to flee when he saw him, but Lord, he felt tired of running. Of being alone. That he'd not counted on when he ran for freedom: the staggering loneliness. The suspicions. The constant living in fear that he might be taken back to the tortures of slavery at any time. For months, he'd been afraid to speak to anyone. Every white man was a potential enemy. No Negro could be fully trusted either. But along the way he'd been fortunate. More so than many fugitives. He met white ministers who were conductors for the Underground Railroad, men who fronted as his master long enough for him to traverse the states of North Carolina and Virginia; and here, in Boston, he'd found free blacks—the very portrait of Christian kindness and self-sacrifice—willing to risk their own lives to help him. They were deeply religious, these Negroes. Lambs of Jesus, he thought at first. They put him up in their homes, fed him, provided him with clothes and a fresh start. Even helped him pick a new name. Jackson Lee was the one he used now. And he deployed those many skills he'd learned as a slave, plus his own God-given talent, to rebuilding his life from scratch. At least, until now.

Out of the corner of his eye he could see the Hunter moving closer, circling round toward the front of the market, keeping the waterfront at Frank's back, to cut him off if he tried to run. This time the Hunted decided, no. He would stay, dying here among free black people. He'd been to their churches, heard their preachers say no man should fear death because the Son of God conquered that for all time. And no man could be enslaved, they said, if he was prepared to die.

The Hunter stopped in front of his table. He looked over the carvings, picked up one of a horse, and examined it, the faintest of smiles on his lips. "You do right fine work."

"Thank you."

"I once knew a fellah in Charleston was almost as good as you."

"That so?"

"Um-huh." The Hunter put the carving down. "Nigger named Frank. I don't suppose you know his work, do you?"

"No," he shook his head. "Never been to Charleston. Lived here my whole life. You kin ask anybody here 'bout that." He tilted his head toward the balding man, then at the old black woman selling fish. "Ain't that so?"

"Yes, sir." The balding man held out his hand at waist-level, his palm facing down. "I been knowin' Jackson since he was yea-high."

The old woman chimed in, "That's right. He belong to my church."

The Hunter's eyes narrowed, he looked at both of them irritably, said, "I think you two better mind your own damned business," then he swung his gaze back toward the Hunted. "I ain't here to play games with you, Frank."

"My name is Jackson Lee."

"Right, and I'm Andrew Jackson."

Slowly, the Hunter withdrew his pistol. His arm bent, close to his side, he pointed the barrel at the Hunted. "Get up."

Frank sat motionless, looking down the black, one-eyed barrel. "No."

"Then I'll shoot you, nigger. Right here."

"Guess you'll have to do that then."

The old woman said, "Mister! You don't have to do that!"

"Naw," the balding man pleaded. "He from round here!"

Frowning, the Hunter took a deep breath. "I *told* y'all to shut up and stay out of this! It ain't your affair!"

In the market there came first one shot, shattering the air. By the time the second exploded, merchants and patrons were screaming, scattering from the waterfront like windblown leaves, tipping over tables that sent potatoes, cabbages, and melons rolling into the street. When the thunderous pistol reports subsided, leaving only a silence, and the susurration of wind off the water, the only figures left in the debris of broken displays and stands were the Hunter—he was sprawled dead beneath a rug he'd pulled to the ground as he fell—and the Hunted. There were also his new friends: The black fish woman. The balding man. Both were members of Boston's chapter of the Liberty Association, devoted to killing bounty hunters on sight. The balding man was Frank's minister. The fish woman was the minister's mother. They were the ones who'd taken him in. Helped him set up his stall in the market. And they were much better shots than he was.

It was good, thought Frank, to have friends—hunters in their own right—like these.

The Transmission

They were dead, and this was the boat to the Underworld.

In the darkness of its belly, the boy—his name was Malawi—lay pressed against its wet, wooden hull, naked and chained to a corpse that only hours before had been his older brother, Oboto. Down there, the air was curdled, thick with the stench of feces and decaying flesh. Already the ship's rats were nibbling at Oboto's cold, stiff fingers. Malawi screamed them away whenever they came scurrying through a half a foot of salt water toward his brother's body. He held Oboto as the boat thrashed, throwing them from side to side, and the rusty chains bit deeper into his wrists. But by now, after seven weeks at sea, the rats were used to screams, moaning, and cries in the lightless entrails of the ghost ship. All night, after the longhaired, lipless phantoms drove them below—the men into the hold, the females into the longboats and cabins, the children under a tarpaulin on deck—Malawi heard the wailing of the other one hundred captives, some as they clawed at him for more room. (Perhaps, he thought, this was why the phantoms clipped their nails every few days.) He couldn't always understand the words of the others, but Malawi gleaned enough to gather from his yokefellows that they were in the hands of white demons taking them to hell where they would be eaten. Many of the others were from different tribes and they spoke different tongues. Some, he remembered, had been enemies of his people, the Allmuseri. Others traded with the merchants of his village, men like his father Mbwela, who was a proud man, one wealthy enough to afford two wives. But that was before he and Oboto were captured. They were no longer Hausa, Tefik, Fulani, Ibo, Kru, or Fanti. Now they were dead, one and all, and destined for the Underworld.

Every day since this journey began, Malawi had lost something; now he wondered if there was anything left to lose.

They had been herded after their long trek from the lush interior to the bustling trading fort overlooking the sea. They came in chains, shackled in twos at their necks, in a coffle that contained forty prisoners, a flock of sheep, and an ostrich. When they arrived at twilight, their feet were crusted with mud and their backs stung from the sticks their captors—warriors from the nearby Asante tribe—used to force them up whenever they fell during the exhausting month-long march. It was there, on that march, that the horrors began. Wearily, Malawi walked chained to Oboto. His father, Mbwela, and mother, Gwele (Mbwela's youngest wife), were shackled in front of him. His mother stumbled. One of the Asante struck her, and Gwele fought back, scratching at his eyes until he plunged a knife into her belly. In a rage such as Malawi had never seen, his father fell upon the Asante warrior, beating him to the ground, and would have killed him had not another of their captors swung his sword and unstrung Mbwela's head, but with a cut so poorly delivered his father did not die instantly but instead lay bleeding on the ground as the coffle moved on, with Mbwela cursing their captors, their incompetence, telling them how *he* would have done the beheading right.

How long it took to reach the fort, Malawi could not say. But he remembered their captors fired rifles to announce the coffle's arrival. Cannons at the fort thundered back a reply. Men fluent in several languages lifted their robes and ran to the fort's entrance to meet them. Their Asante captors chanted, *Hodi, hodi, hodi,* asking permission to trade. The dragomen replied, *Karibu,* meaning they could, and then Malawi and the other prisoners were driven toward the receiving house as people inside the fort pointed and stared. Like slices of walking earth, they must have seemed, so chalky from their long trek, a few stumbling, some bleeding from their feet, mothers long since mad, their eyes streaming and unseeing, carrying dead children, the rest staring round the fort in shock and bewilderment.

And Malawi was one of those. The bustling, slave market was like a dream—or, more exactly, like yet another nightmare from which he could not awaken, no matter how hard he rubbed his eyes. There were harem dancers in brightly colored costumes. Magnificent horses ridden by vast-bearded Arab traders who exchanged the cracking-fingers greeting of the coast. Bazaars. And musicians picking up the air and playing it on their *koras,* as if everyone had come from all over the earth to an unholy festival. In this place human life was currency, like a cowrie shell. Starving families brought their children to sell. Slaves, stripped naked, were held down by other black men as the strangely dressed phantoms branded their shoulders with red-hot pieces of bent wire. They'd been shaved clean, soaked in palm oil. And when the wire touched their skin, burning flesh blended with rich food smells in the market and made Malawi cough until his eyes watered. Then, when his vision cleared, he saw along the beach, just below the warehouses, phantoms bartering for black flesh. They traded firelocks, liquor, glittering beads, and textiles for people from the Angola, Fula, Sesi, and Yoruba tribes. If they resisted or fought back, they were whipped until blood cascaded from their wounds. The phantoms forced open their mouths to examine their teeth and gums as if they were livestock and, laughing, fingered their genitals. They paid one hundred bars apiece for each man; seventy-five bars for each woman. Malawi, whose father had been a merchant, saw that what they called a "bar" was worth a pound of black gunpowder or a fathom of cloth, and he saw that they accepted no children under the height of four feet four inches.

What, Malawi wondered, had he and the others done to deserve this? And, instantly, he knew: Those being sold were debtors. They were thieves. They were tribesmen who refused to convert to Islam. Were guilty of witchcraft. Or refused to honor the ruling tribe in their region. Or they'd been taken prisoner during tribal wars, just as he and Oboto had been captured.

He saw a bare-chested ghost, one with a goatish laugh and reddish whiskers, arguing with an Asante trader chewing on a khat leaf, yelling that the wrinkled old man he'd brought to sell, who was swearing and looked ill, had been drugged to conceal his sickness. No, *that* one the ghost didn't want. Not the elderly. Only the healthy men who could work, the young women who could bear, and the children. He and his brother would surely be picked—Malawi was sure of that—or at least they would choose Oboto, who was strong, with tightly strung muscles and sharp features like the tribes of the far north. Yes, they would want a man as strikingly beautiful, as brave and wise, as his brother.

Oboto touched Malawi's arm just before they were pushed into the warehouse, and Malawi saw—away in the distance beneath a day-old moon—a vessel a hundred times the size of the thatch-roofed homes in his village, with sails like white bird wings and great, skeletal trees springing from its deck and piercing the clouds. This he heard the phantoms call the *Providence*. Then it was dark as they were shoved into the warehouses. Families in his coffle were separated—husbands from wives; children from their parents—so those in their cells, then later on the ship, could not *talk* to each other. By some miracle, one he thanked his ancestors for, they'd blundered and not separated him from his brother, who had seen twenty harvests, five more than Malawi himself.

That night their jailers fed them a porridge made from roots and grainy honey beer. As they ate, Oboto told him, "Don't be afraid, little brother."

Malawi was indeed afraid but did not want to anger Oboto. "I'm not, as long as you are here—"

"No"—his brother cut him off—"*listen* to me. Even if I am *not* here, you must not be afraid. Malawi, I have been watching these people who raided our village, and the ones from the ship . . . They are not strong."

"But they have many guns," said Malawi, "and chains and great ships!"

"And they bleed when they are cut." Oboto moved closer to him as a guard passed their cell. He whispered, "I've seen them faint in the sun, and I watched one from that ship cry when he passed water, as if he was afflicted and doing so was painful. Did you see some of them up close? Their rotten teeth, I mean. A few are missing fingers. Or a hand. They touch others in places forbidden, and all the while they look afraid, fingering their rifles, looking over their shoulders. Their mothers have not yet finished with them. They are barbarians. Malawi, I *don't* think the spirits respect them. How could they? They smell bad. They are unclean. They are dead *here*"—he touched his chest above his heart—"not us. Some of the white men I saw, the ones with the whips, grovel before others in fear and have stripes on their backs as if *they* were slaves. The ones doing the hardest work, unloading crates from the ship for trade, don't understand as many tongues as you or I."

"Yes . . ." Malawi nodded slowly, for his brother spoke well, as always. "I saw that." As a merchant's son, he'd picked up enough Ibo and Bantu to converse passably well when he accompanied Mbwela on trips to buy and sell goods. And he'd seen one of the phantoms, a young man close to his brother's age, fall down in the heat when unloading a crate of goods from the *Providence*, and because he was slow in rising, one of the other ghosts beat him, bloodying his mouth. He'd seemed different from the other devils. His nose was hooked like that of a hornbill beneath blue eyes that could have been splinters from the sky. This was probably his first trip to Africa and it seemed no one had told him that it was a good idea to take fluids all day, even a little, because your body was constantly losing moisture, whether you were perspiring or not. "But," said Malawi, "I *am* afraid of them. I'm sorry. . . ."

"Don't be sorry." Oboto touched Malawi's arm gently. "I was afraid too when I saw them burning the village. When our parents died. And I prayed to our ancestors to let *me* die—yes, I did that during the journey here—but they helped me understand."

"What?" said Malawi. "Why they have taken so much from us?"

"No, they showed me what they cannot take. And I will show you."

Malawi knew—as their captors could not—that before the raid on their village Oboto was destined to be a *griot,* a living book who carried within himself, like a treasure, his people's entire history from time immemorial. Its recitation took three full days. When he was a child all the adults agreed that Oboto's gift of recall distinguished him for this duty, and from his fifth harvest he could be seen trailing behind gruff, old Ndembe, who was *griot* then but getting a bit forgetful in his sixties, repeating after his teacher every chapter of their tribe's history. He learned their songs for war and weddings, the words they sang when someone died or was born. He learned the chronicle of their kings and commoners, the exploits of their heroes, folklore, and words for every beast, plant, and bird as well as the rhymes their women sang when they made *fufu,* taking into himself one piece of their culture at a time, then stitching it into an ever-expanding tapestry that covered centuries of his people's hopes and dreams, tragedies and victories. Now Malawi realized their village had not been wiped from the face of the world; its remains were kept inside Oboto. And during that night in the warehouse, while the other prisoners wailed or wept, Oboto began to teach his younger brother, transmitting all he knew, beginning with the story of how their gods created the world, and then the first man and woman.

Oboto continued after he and Malawi were bathed, branded, and brought on board the *Providence.* During the night they were kept below, tightly packed together, and forced to lie on their right sides to lessen the pressure on their hearts. Those on the ship's right side faced forward; those on the left faced the stern. Hatches and bulkheads had been grated and apertures cut around the deck to improve the circulation of air, though in those depths Malawi wheezed when he whispered back the ancient words his brother chanted.

Come morning, they were forced topside. The phantoms covered their mouths with rags, went into the hold to drag from below those prisoners who'd died during the night, and then by 9 A.M. cleaned this unholy space with chloride lime so it could be inspected by the ship's captain. Up above, more phantoms washed and scrubbed the decks and splashed buckets of salt water on Malawi and the others, then from buckets fed them a pasty gruel the color of river mud in messes of ten. And all the while, Oboto quietly sang to his brother—in a language their captors could not understand—how their people long ago had navigated these very waters to what the phantoms called the New World, leaving their hieroglyphics and a calendar among the Olmecs, and a thousand years earlier ventured east, sprinkling their seed among the Dravidians before their cities were destroyed by Aryans who brought the Vedas and caste system to enslave them. On and on, like a tapestry, Oboto unfurled their past, rituals, and laws in songs and riddles as they ate or when the phantoms shaved their hair and clipped their nails every few days.

Slowly, after weeks of suffering, it dawned on Malawi that this transmission from his brother, upon which he fastened his mind night and day like a prayer, was holding madness at bay. It left him no time to dwell on his despair. Each day the prisoners were brought together for exercise. To dance and sing African melodies beneath mist-blurred masts and rigging that favored the webwork of a spider. Week after week, Oboto used that precious time to teach, at pains to pass along as much of their people's experiences as his younger brother could absorb, though after six weeks Malawi saw he was weakening. His voice grew fainter, so frail that at night when they lay crushed together, Malawi had to place his ear close to Oboto's lips, catching the whispered words as his brother's chest rose and fell, each of his weak exhalations a gift from a world they would never see again.

When Oboto's wind was gone, Malawi held him close and chanted his brother's spirit safely on its journey to join their ancestors and he kept the rats away. The hatch creaked open. Sunlight spilled into the hold, stinging his eyes. The phantoms came below cursing—they were always cursing—and drove the prisoners onto the deck. One of them, the hook-nosed phantom, began unchaining Malawi from Oboto. "I guess he was some kind of kin to you, wasn't he? That's too bad. I've lost family too, so I guess I know how you feel." He removed the last of the shackles from Oboto, then stood back, waiting for Malawi to release his brother. "Go on now, you can turn him loose. He's dead."

Malawi did not let go. He tried to lift his brother, slipping his arms under Oboto's shoulders, but found him too heavy. The phantom watched him struggle for a moment, then took Oboto by his feet, and together they carried the body onto the deck, with Malawi still singing his people's funeral songs. They stepped to the rail, Malawi blinking back tears by then, the edges of his eyes feeling blurred. Then he and the phantom swung his brother overboard, dropping him into wind-churned waters. Instantly, Oboto disappeared beneath the roily waves. For a few seconds Malawi's heart felt so still he wondered if he might be dead, too, then involuntarily the words he'd learned came flooding back into his thoughts, and he knew there was much in him—beyond the reach of the ghosts—that was alive forever.

The phantom, his yellow hair flattened to his forehead by spray, was watching Malawi closely, listening to the lay on his lips. He was very quiet. Malawi stopped. The boy said, "Naw, go on. I don't understand what you're singing, but I like it. It's beautiful. I want to hear more . . . C'mon."

Malawi looked at him for a moment, unable to understand all his strange words. He glanced back down at the waters, thinking that Oboto's songs had only taken him so far. Just to before the time his village was raided. His people's chronicle was unfinished. New songs were needed. And these *he* must do. Hesitantly at first, and then with a little more confidence, he began weaving the events since his and Oboto's capture onto the last threads his brother had given him.

Malawi sang and the phantom listened.

The Mayor's Tale

Once upon a time in a nation not very old the people of a large, northeastern city awoke one morning and discovered to their surprise (though they should have seen it coming) that something had changed in their lives.

The city's Mayor like many others went to sleep the night before, curled beneath the warm covers beside his Wife, feeling as he drifted off to sleep that all was well in the world. Their two children rested comfortably down the hallway in the great, three-story house; they were doing well at their studies, according to the tutor he'd hired for them, and it was likely both boys—then ages eight and twelve—would easily be accepted at the nation's oldest and most prestigious college when the time came for them to apply. His investments were performing better than expected, given the country's delicate political situation (but when, after all, was politics not a delicate matter?). Added to which, he'd worked hard all throughout 1850 to beat his competitors in neighboring cities along the eastern seaboard for a few lucrative contracts that would further industrialize his own city, which would assure his reelection, and he was meeting with representatives of those companies in the morning. Furthermore, his Wife of twenty years seemed pleased with her personal affairs, the charity work she and her friends did each weekend, and particularly with her abolitionist activities. He, being a progressive man, supported fully this cause of Negro manumission, both in his role as Mayor and, even more importantly, in his home, where he employed five free Negroes as servants. Indeed, he had cheered on and publicly supported the recent Compromise that abolished the slave trade in the District of Columbia. He treated his black help royally, or so the Mayor believed, and he overlooked what everyone in his social circle agreed were inherent and unfortunate deficiencies in colored people. These shortcomings, after all, were not *their* fault, but rather the unjust distribution of talent, beauty, and intelligence by Nature, so that those more generously endowed by Providence were duty bound to help them. Without white men, the Negro would be lost. They were like children in their dependency. The Mayor paid his servants handsomely and on time, was lavish with tips, inquired frequently into their health and well-being, told them repeatedly they were an important part of his family, and he proudly pointed them out when his friends, business associates, and political colleagues dined with his family or dropped by. And, as if that were not enough, the Mayor had a lovely, new mistress—a young singer of thirty (which was half his age), who gave him good reason to look forward to those weekends his Wife and her friends were away.

Yes, all was well—as well as a civilized man might expect—in the world on Wednesday, January 1, 1851.

Thursday, however, was quite another story. When he opened his eyes and stretched, having slept well—the sleep of the just, he'd say—the Mayor felt as rested as he did on Saturday, the day he normally slept in. But this wasn't the weekend. Or was it? For a moment he wasn't sure. He shook his Wife's shoulder, rousing her awake, and she said, "Why are you still here? Aren't you supposed to be at City Hall?" Like Immanuel Kant, the Mayor preferred his life "to be like the most regular of regular verbs." So he was at first bewildered, then upset, by this disruption of his schedule. He stumbled from bed, his bare feet landing on a floor so cold its chill went through him like a shock, squeezed a whoop from his lips, and sent him hopping around the room for his slippers. He found his wire-rim spectacles on a nightstand, then shivering so badly his teeth chattered, he bent over to better see the small, wooden clock. It was quarter past eleven. He'd slept all morning, missing at least five appointments.

And all the fireplaces were dark and cold.

The Mayor rang for his butler, Henry, who always awoke him and had each fireplace blazing by 5 A.M. No answer. He rang again, waiting and watching his breath steam the bedroom air as if he were standing outside on the ice-cold street. "Please get him to light the fireplaces now!" wailed his Wife. "I'm not leaving this bed until the house is warm! And tell the maid I'm *hungry!*" The Mayor sighed and said, "Yes, dear, I . . . I will. Henry must be sick this morning—he's never been remiss in his duties before, you know." He hurried to dress himself, and found to his great dismay that not only had his personal servant failed to wake him, but Henry had not prepared or set out his clothing for the day either. Because he was so late and had no idea where Henry put his freshly pressed linen, the Mayor grumbled and pulled on his wrinkled shirt from the day before (on the front was a red soup stain from a lunch he'd taken at his club, but he couldn't worry about that now), his uncreased trousers, his coat, then hurried downstairs and through the frigid hallways of his many-roomed house, calling for their servants. Again, there was no answer. In the kitchen, in the chambers set aside for their live-in help, and in the livery stable there was only silence. And not a black face to be found. Moreover, the horses had not been groomed. Or fed. His carriage was not ready. He would have to travel, he realized, the five miles to City Hall under his own locomotion!

Not being accustomed to walking, it took the Mayor two hours to traverse the distance between his home and office. He stopped to rest often, puffing, placing his hand against a wall, his heart racing and empty stomach growling. And what he saw—or rather didn't see—along the way to work startled him. There were no black people. It wasn't as if he looked for them every day. No, most of the time they blended into the background of his city, as unnoticeable as trees or weather vanes or lampposts—or maybe like the inner workings of a finely tuned watch. Obviously, no one paid attention to a timepiece's hidden mechanism until it ceased to work. But now, along the five-mile stretch between his home and City Hall, he saw chaos. Coal had not been delivered to homes, and this was the dead of winter! Barges had not been unloaded in the harbor. Fresh bread had not been delivered from bakeries. Roadwork lay unfinished, as if the fingers of God had plucked its dusky crews off the face of the earth. No windows were washed. No snow was shoveled. It was as if his city had run out of its primary source of power, coal. (A terrible pun, he knew, but on this awful day it seemed appropriate.) He wondered aloud as he galumphed down the nearly empty streets, "What in heaven's name is going on?" No carriages, driven by black coachmen, bore white passengers to and from the offices where they conducted the country's crucial business, domestic and international. Indeed, half the offices he saw were closed.

It was, therefore, a befuddled and disheveled Mayor who finally reached City Hall by 2 P.M. and slumped heavily behind his desk, wondering if his heart might fail him once and for all after his morning's exertions. Everything he'd accomplished this morning (which wasn't much) had taken two—perhaps three—times longer to do. His secretary, a young man named Daniel, looked very sad that Thursday. He told the Mayor the people with whom he'd missed appointments were furious. Two entrepreneurs of enormous wealth and influence who'd traveled a great distance to see him—one a railroad man, the other a maritime merchant—felt insulted by what they called Hizzoner's "malfeasance" and planned to cancel further discussions of their proposed contracts and in the future only do business with other cities.

"No!" whispered the Mayor.

His secretary said, "I'm afraid so, sir. Your political rivals will make great capital of this. Your reelection is only months away, and you promised in the last campaign to improve commerce, shipping, and transportation."

"I *know* what I promised, damn it!" The Mayor pounded his desk. "But it's not my fault! Nothing's been normal today!" He leaned back in his seat, red-faced, and began pulling at his fingers. "All the Negroes are gone. Have you noticed that? What on earth happened to them?"

"What *you* agreed to, I guess," said his secretary.

"*Me?* What are you babbling about, man? Talk sense! I never told the Negroes to go away! Have you been drinking?"

"No, sir. I'm quite sober, insofar as it appears we both will be out of a job by November. I'm referring to the Compromise in Congress, which you fully endorsed."

"What does *that* have to do with our Negroes being gone?"

Quietly, his secretary stepped from the Mayor's office to his own room, then returned after less than a minute with a copy of a newspaper from the day before. "Perhaps you should read this. Please read it *carefully,* sir. Meanwhile, if you don't mind, I'd like to repair to my office in order to finish sending our copies of my résumé to potential, future employers. And I have a dreadful headache today. . . ."

His secretary departed, leaving the Mayor more baffled than before. He opened the day-old newspaper, and there it was, the complex Compromise. In it, California became the thirty-first state. New Mexico and Utah were to be organized as territories and residents could decide for themselves whether to be free or slave. The slave trade was ended in D.C., and—*Wait!* He looked closer, bringing the paper closer to his eyes in order to read some changes in the Fugitive Slave Act of 1793. Vaguely, he recalled this item, but hadn't attended closely to its details. Under the amendment, federal commissioners were granted the power to issue warrants for runaway slaves. They could form posses to capture fugitive blacks. They could fine citizens if they refused to help in returning Negroes to their former masters, who had to do nothing more than submit an affidavit in court. The blacks were denied a jury trial. They could not testify to defend themselves. Slowly, he put the newspaper down. His man Henry . . . their cook . . . their three other servants and perhaps *all* the coloreds in his city were runaways. No doubt they'd changed their names. And once they learned of the amendment to the Fugitive Slave Act, they'd fled en masse during the night, probably to Canada. Who could blame them? And *he* had endorsed this disaster?

Gloomily, the Mayor left City Hall. Night was coming on . . . and streetlamps were unlit. He plodded on, realizing that until now he'd not seen how dependent the life of the city—and his own fortune—was on blacks. They were interwoven, albeit invisibly, into the fabric of everything; and, like the dangling string on a sweater which, if pulled, unraveled the entire garment, so too their removal caused everything—high and low, private and personal—to collapse. Without sealing the deal on those contracts, he would lose his office. He was certain of that now. His own businesses would suffer. My God, he might even lose his mistress and be left with only his Wife, who sometimes could be a shrew! Miserably, he tramped back home in the snow, which seeped into his shoes and dampened his feet so thoroughly he felt his toes had frozen in one solid block of flesh by the time he reached his front door, coughing, his nose burning and running badly, because—yes—he'd picked up a nasty cold.

The house was colder and darker than before. If anything, he only wanted a little sympathy now from his Wife. He did not see her downstairs. So, blowing his nose into his handkerchief, he climbed the steep stairs to their bedroom, dripping all the way. "Dear," he said, opening the door, "I have some bad news. . . ."

"Well," she crabbed, "you can save whatever it is until you find dinner for us. I haven't eaten all day. I'm *starving!* And so are the children!"

It dawned on him that she had not left their bed all day. "You couldn't find something for yourself in the kitchen?"

"Nothing's prepared! I haven't had to cook in years! You know that. I want you to go out right now and find us something to eat."

"Now?"

"Yes, *now*."

Slump-shouldered, feeling euchered, the Mayor went back outside, walking two miles in the darkness, with fresh snow beginning to fall, flaking on his shoulders. An hour later he arrived at the building that housed his club, thinking perhaps there they would wrap four plates of food, which he could carry home to his family. He tried the door. It was locked. Inside no lights were on whatsoever. Then he saw a sign in the ground-floor window. NO WAITERS OR COOKS TODAY. He stared blankly, helplessly, at the words. His mouth wobbled. *Of course,* he thought, *Of course. . . .*

And then Hizzoner broke down and wept in the snow.

Gayl Jones (1949-)

Gayl Jones was born in Lexington, Kentucky, and earned an MA and a DA in creative writing at Brown University.

Jones's first novels, Corregidora *(1975) and* Eva's Man *(1976), were edited by Toni Morrison at Random House.* Corregidora *treats three generations of Black women in Brazil.* Eva's Man *relates an account of a severely abused woman residing in a mental ward. Jones also published two plays and* White Rat *(1977), a collection of short stories. More recently she wrote* Liberating Voices *(1991), a scholarly treatment of African American literature and culture. She received a National Endowment for the Arts Fellowship and taught at the University of Michigan before, in 1980, choosing a sequestered private life.*

In White Rat *Jones relies on dialogue more than straightforward description and exposition. She concentrates on families and on hetero- and homosexual relationships, which, in her work, are often tangled and involve domination and disrespect. Solutions do not come easily. This focus is definitely evident in "Jevata," the selection included here.*

Keith D. Miller

Jevata

I didn't see Jevata when she ran Freddy away from her house, but Miss Johnny Cake said she had a hot poker after him, and would have killed him too, if he hadn't been faster than she was. Nobody didn't know what made her do it. I didn't know either then, and I'm over there more than anybody else is. Now I'm probably the onliest one who know what did happen—me and her boy David. Miss Johnny Cake don't even know, and it seem like she keep busier than anybody else on Green Street. People say what make Miss Johnny so busy is the Urban Renewal come and made her move out of that house she was living in for about forty years, and all she got to do now is sit out there on the porch and be busy. Once she told me she felt dislocated, and I told Jevata what she said, and Jevata said she act dislocated.

Miss Johnny Cake aint the onliest one talking about Jevata neither. All up and down Green Street they talking. They started talking when Jevata went up to

505

Lexington and brought Freddy back with her, and they aint quit. They used to talk when I'd come down from Davis town to visit her. Then I guess they got used to me. I called myself courting her then. We been friends every since we went over to Simmons Street School together, and we stayed friends. I guess all the courting was on my side though, cause she never would have me. I still come to see about her though. I was coming to see about her all during the time that Freddy was living with her.

"I don't see what in the world that good-lookin boy see in her," Miss Johnny Cake would say. "If I was him and eighteen, I wouldn't be courting the mama, I be courting the daughter. He aint right, is he, Mr. Floyd?"

I wouldn't say anything, just stand with my right foot up on the porch while she sat rocking. She was about seventy, with her gray hair in two plaits.

"I don't see what they got in common," Miss Johnny said.

"Same thing any man and woman got in common," I said.

"Aw, Mr. Floyd, you so nasty."

Before Freddy came, Jevata used to have something to say to people, but after he came she wouldn't say nothing to nobody. She used to say I was the only one that she could trust, because the others always talked about her too much. "Always got something to say about you. Caint even go pee without them having something to say about you." She would go on by and wouldn't say nothing to nobody. People said she got stuck up with that young boy living with her. "Woman sixty-five going with a boy eighteen," some of the women would say. "You seen her going up the street, didn't you? Head all up in the air, that boy trailin behind her. Don't even look right. I be ashamed for anybody to see me trying to go with a boy like that. Look like her tiddies fallen since he came, don't it? But you know she always have been like 'at though, always looking after boys. I stopped Maurice from going down there to play. But you know if he was like anybody else he least be trying to get some from the daughter too."

Now womens can get evil about something like that. Wasn't so much that Jevata was going with Freddy, as she wouldn't say nothing to them, while she was doing it. Now if she'd gone over there and said something to them, and let them all in her business and everything, they would felt all right then, and they wouldn't a got evil with her. "Rest of us got man trouble, Miss Jevata must got boy trouble," they'd laugh.

Now the boy's eighteen, but Jevata aint sixty-five though, she's fifty, cause I aint but two years older than her myself. I used to try to go with her way back when we was going to Simmons Street School together, but she wouldn't have me then, and she won't have me now. She married some nigger from Paris, Kentucky, one come out to Dixieland dance hall that time Dizzy Gillespie or Cab Calloway come out there. Name was Joe Guy. He stayed with her long enough to give her three children. Then he was gone. I was trying to go with her after he left, but she still wouldn't have me. She mighta eventually had me if he hadn't got to her, but after he got to her, seem like she wouldn't look at no mens. Onliest reason she'd look at me was because we'd been friends for so long. But first time I tried to get next to her right after he left, she said, "Shit, Floyd, me and you friends, always have been and always will be." I asked her to marry me, but she looked at me real evil. I thought she was going to tell me I could just quit coming to see her, but she didn't. After that she just wouldn't let me say nothing else about it, so I just come over there every chance I get. She got three childrens. Cynthy the oldest. She sixteen. Then she got a boy fourteen, name David, and a little boy five, name Pete. Sometime she call him Pete Junebug, sometime Little Pete.

Don't nobody know where in Lexington she went and got Freddy. Some people say she went down to the reform school they got down there and got him. It ain't that he's bad or nothing, it's just that they think something's wrong with him. I didn't know where she got him myself, because it was her business and I figured she tell me when she wanted to, and if she didn't wont to, she wouldn't.

Miss Johnny Cake lives over across the street from Jevata, and everytime I pass by there, she got to call me over. Sometimes I don't even like to pass by there, but I got to. She thinks I'm going to say something about Jevata and Freddy, but I don't. I just listen to what she's got to say. After she's said her piece, sometimes she'll look at me and say, "Clarify things to me, Mr. Floyd." I figure she picked that up from Reverend Jackson, cause he's always saying, "The Lord clarified this to me, the Lord clarified that to me." I ain't clarified nothing to her yet.

"He's kinda funny, ain't he?" she said one day. That was when Freddy and Jevata was still together. It seemed like Miss Johnny Cake just be sitting out there waiting for me to come up the street, because she would never fail to call me over. Sitting up there, old seventy-year-old woman, couldn't even keep her legs together. One a the men on the street told me she been in a accident, and something happened to that muscle in her thighs, that's supposed to help you keep your legs together. I believed him till he started laughing, and then I didn't know whether to believe him or not.

"That boy just don't act right, do he? He ain't right, is he, Mr. Floyd? Something wrong with him, aint it?" She waited, but not as if she expected an answer. I guess she'd got used to me not answering. "You reckon he's funny? Naw, cause he wouldn't be with her if he was funny, would he? I guess she do something for him. She must got something he wont. God knows I don't see it. Mr. Floyd, you just stand up there and don't say nothing. Cat got your tongue, and Freddy got hers." She looked at me grinning. I blew smoke between my teeth. "If you wonted to, I bet you could tell me everything that go on in that house."

I said I couldn't.

"Well, I know she sixty-five, cause she used to live down 'ere on Poke Street when I did. She might look like she forty-five, and tell everybody she forty-five, but she aint. Now, if that boy was *right,* he be trying to go with Cynthy anyway. That's what a *right* boy would do. But he aint right. He don't even *look* right, do he, Mr. Floyd?"

I told her he didn't look no different from anybody else to me.

Miss Johnny grinned at me. "You just don't wont to say nothin' against her, do you? Aint no reason for you to take up for him, though, cause he done cut you out, aint he?"

I said I was going across the street. She said she didn't see why I won't to take up for him, cut me out the way he did.

One day when I came down the street, Freddy was standing out in the yard, his shirt sleeves rolled up, standing up against the post, looking across the street at Miss Johnny, looking evil. I didn't think Miss Johnny would bother me this time. I waved to her and kept walking. She said, "Mr. Floyd, aint you go'n stop and have a few words with me? You got cute too?" I went over to her porch before I got a chance to say anything to Freddy. He was watching us, though. Green Street wasn't a wide street, and if she talked even a little bit as loud as she'd been talking, he would have heard.

"Nigger out there," she said, almost at a whisper. "Keep staring at me. Look at him."

She kept patting her knees. I didn't turn around to look at him. I was thinking, "He see those bloomers you got on."

"Look at him," she said, still low.

"Nice day, aint it?" I said, loud.

"Fine day," she said, loud, too, then whispered, "I wish he go in the house. I don't even like to look at him."

I said nothing. I lit a cigarette. She started rocking back and forth in her rocker, and closed her eyes, like she was in church. Or like I do when I'm in church.

"You have you a good walk?" she asked, her eyes still closed.

I said, "OK."

We were talking moderate, now.

"You a fool you know that? Walk all the way out here from Davis town, just to see that woman. She got what she need, over there."

I hoped he hadn't heard, but I knew he had. I wondered if I was in his place, if I would have come over and said something to her.

"You know you a fool, don't you?" she asked again, still looking like she was in church.

I didn't answer.

"You know you a fool, Mr. Floyd," she said. She rocked a while more then she opened her eyes.

"But I reckon you say you been a fool a long time, aint no use quit now."

I turned a little to the side so I could see out of the corner of my eye. He was still standing there. I couldn't tell if he was watching or not. I felt awkward about crossing the street now. I gave Miss Johnny a hard look before I crossed. She only smiled at me.

"Mr. Floyd," Freddy said. He always called me "Mr. Floyd." He was still looking across the street at Miss Johnny. I stood with my back to her. He asked me to walk back around the yard with him. I did. I stood with my back against the house, smoking a cigarette.

"I caint stand that old woman," he said. "You see how she was setting, didn't you? Legs all open. I never could stand womens sit up with their legs all open. 'Specially old women."

I said they told me she couldn't help it.

"I had a aunt use to do that," he said. "She can help it. She just onry. Aint nothing wrong with that muscle. She just think somebody wont to see her ass. Like my aunt. Used to think I wonted to see her ass, all the time."

I said nothing. Then I asked "How's Jevata . . . and the children?"

"They awright. Java and Junebug in the house. Other two at school."

I finished my cigarette and was starting in the house.

"Think somebody wont to see her ass," Freddy said. He stayed out in the yard.

Jevata was in the kitchen ironing. She took in ironing for some white woman lived out on Stanley Street.

"How you, Floyd?" she asked.

"Not complaining," I said. I sat down at the kitchen table. She looked past me out in the back yard where Freddy must have still been standing.

"What Miss Busy have to say about me today?" she asked, looking back at me.

"Nothin'."

"You can tell me," she said. "I won't get hurt."

"Miss Johnny wasn't doing nothing but out there talking bout the weather," I said.

"Weather over here?" she asked.

I smiled.

She looked back out in the yard. I thought Freddy was still standing out there, but when I turned around in my seat to look, he wasn't. He must have gone back around to the front of the house.

"How you been?" she asked me as if she hadn't asked before, or didn't remember asking.

She wasn't looking at me, but I nodded.

"I never did think I be doing this," she said. "You 'member that time I told you Joe and me went down to Yazoo, Mississippi and this ole, white woman come up to me and asked me did I iron, and I said 'Naw, I don't iron'. I wasn't gonna iron for *her,* anyway."

I said nothing. I had already offered to help Jevata out with money, but she wouldn't let me. I worked with horses, and had enough left over to help. Now, I was thinking, she had *four* kids to take care of.

"He found a job yet?" I asked.

She looked at me, irritated. She was sweating from the heat. "I told him he could take his time. He aint been here long. He need time to get adjusted."

I was wondering how much adjusting did he need. It was over half a year ago since she went and got him.

"You don't think Freddy's evil, do you?" she asked.

I looked at her. I didn't know why she asked that. I said, "Naw, I don't think he's evil." She went back to ironing. I just sat there in the kitchen, watching her. After a while Freddy came in through the back door. He didn't say anything. He passed by, and I saw him put his hand on her waist. She smiled but didn't turn around to look at him. He went on into the front of the house. I sat there about fifteen or twenty minutes longer, and then I got up and said I was going.

"Glad you stopped by," Jevata said.

I said I'd probably be back by sometime next week, then I went out the back way.

Miss Johnny not only caught me when I was coming to see Jevata, but she caught me when I was leaving.

"I never did think that bastard go in the house," she said. "Sometime I wish the Urban Renewal come and move me away from here. They dislocate me once, they might as well do it again."

I was thinking she probably heard Reverend Jackson say, "When the devil dislocate you, the Lord relocate you."

"How's Miss Jevata doing?" she asked.

"She's awright," I said.

"Awright as you can be with a nigger like that on your hands. If it was me, I be ashamed for anybody see me in the street with him. If he wont to go with somebody, he ought to go with Cynthy. I didn't tell you what I seen them doing last night?"

"What?" I asked frowning.

"I seen 'em standing in the door. Standing right up in the door kissing. Thought nobody couldn't see 'em with the light off. But you know how you can see in people's houses. Tha's the only time I seen 'em though. But still if they gonna do something like that, they ought to go back in there where caint nobody see 'em, and do it. Cause 'at aint right. Double sin as old as she is. And they sinned again, cause you spose to go in your closet and do stuff like that."

I said nothing.

"You know I'm right, Mr. Floyd."

I still said nothing.

"Naw, you prob'ly don't know if I'm right or not," she said.

I looked away from her, over across the street at Jevata's house.

"Tiddies all sinking in," she said. "I don't see what he see in her. Look like she aint got no tiddies no more. I don't see what he see in her. You think I'm crazy, don't you? I just don't like to see no old womens trying to go with young boys like that. I guess y'all ripe at that age, though, aint you?"

I said I couldn't remember back that far.

"Floyd, you just a nigger. You just mad cause you been trying to go with her yourself. I bet you thought yall *was* going together, didn't you? Everybody else thought so too, but not me. I didn't."

I turned around to look at her. She kept watching me.

"Aint no use you saying nothing neither, cause I know you wasn't. I can tell when a man getting it and when he aint."

I started to tell her I could tell when a woman wonts it and can't have it, but I just told her I'd be seeing her.

"You got a long walk back to Davis town, aint you, Mr. Floyd?"

The next time I was down to Jevata's only the girl was at home. I asked her where her mama was. She said she and Freddy took Junebug downtown to get him some shoes. She told me Jevata had been mad all morning.

"Mad about what?" I asked.

"Mad cause Miss Johnny told Freddy to go up to the store for her."

"To get what?"

"A bottle of Pepsi Cola."

"Did he go?"

"Naw, he sent Davey." Then she said, "I don't know what makes that woman so meddlesome, anyway."

We were in the living room. I hadn't set down when I heard Jevata wasn't there. She was still standing, her arms folded like she was cold. She was frowning.

"What is it?" I asked.

"I guess I do know why she so meddlesome, why they all so meddlesome," she said.

I waited for her to go on.

"They talking about them, aint they, Mr. Floyd? People all up and down the street talking, aint they?" She didn't ask the question as if she expected an answer. She was still looking at me, frowning. She was a big girl for sixteen. She could've passed for eighteen. And she acted older than she was. She acted about twenty.

"Sometimes I'm ashamed to go to school. Kids on this street been telling everybody up at school. But you know I wouldn't tell mama. I don't wont to hurt her. I wouldn't do anything to hurt her."

I was thinking Jevata probably already knew, or guessed that people who didn't even know her might be talking about her.

I didn't say anything.

"They saying nasty things," she said.

I still didn't say anything. She kept looking at me. I put my hand on her shoulder. She was the reason I understood how Jevata could feel about Freddy, those times I felt attracted to Cynthy, wanting to touch those big breasts. I took my hand away.

"Just keep trying not to hurt her," I said.

She was looking down at the floor. I kept watching her breasts. They were bigger than her mama's. I was thinking of Mose Mason, who they put out of church for messing with that little girl him and his wife adopted. The deacons came to the house and he said, "I aint doing nothing but feeling around on her tiddies. I aint doing nothin' y'all wouldn't do." They was mad, too. "They ack like they aint never wont to feel on nobody," Moses told me when we was sitting over in Tiger's Inn. "Shit, I bet they do more feeling Saturday night than it take me a whole damn week to do. And then they come sit up under the pulpit on Sunday morning and play like they hands aint never touched nothin' but the Holy Bible. Saying 'amen' louder than anybody. Shit, don't make me no difference, though, whether I'm with 'em or not cause the Baptist is sneaky, anyway. Sneak around and do they dirt."

"I can hear them," Cynthy said quietly. "I can hear her telling him to hold her. 'Hold me, Freddy,' she say. I can hear her telling him he's better to her than my daddy was."

I couldn't think of anything to tell her. I wanted to touch her again, but didn't dare.

When Jevata came in, she said, "Cynthy tell you what that bitch did?

I nodded.

"I know what she wonts, bitch," she said. "I know just what she wonts with him."

She asked me if I wanted something to eat. I said, Naw, I'd better be going. I'd been just waiting around to see her.

"Why did she try to kill 'im, Mr. Floyd?" Miss Johnny asked. It was a couple of weeks after Jevata had gone after Freddy with the poker.

"I don't know," I said. I had my right foot up on the porch and was leaning on my knee, smoking.

"Got after Cynthy, didn't he? I bet that's what he did."

"He didn't bother Cynthy," I said, angry. But I didn't know whether he did or not.

"I bet tha's what he did. I bet she went somewhere and come back and found them in that house." She started laughing.

"I don't know what happened," I said.

"Seem like she tell you, if she tell anybody," Miss Johnny said.

I threw my cigarette down on the ground, and mashed it out.

"I wish she let me come over there and get some dandelions like I used to, so I can make me some wine out of 'em," she said.

"If Freddy was over there, you could tell him to get you some," I said.

"I wouldn't tell 'at nigger to do nothing for me," she said. She was angry. I looked at her for a moment, and then I walked out of the yard.

When I got to Jevata's, she was sitting in the front room with her housecoat on, the same dirty yellow one Cynthy said she was wearing the day she threatened to kill Freddy. Cynthy said she hadn't been out of the house since she chased Freddy out. I asked her if she was all right.

"Aint complaining, am I?" she said. She said she had some Old Crow back there in the kitchen if I wanted some. I said, "Naw, thank you." She hadn't been drinking any herself, which surprised me. She didn't drink much anyway, but I thought maybe with Freddy gone, she might.

"Shit, Floyd, why you looking at me like that?" she asked.

"I didn't know I was looking at you any way," I said.

"Well, you was."

I said nothing.

"I seen Miss Bitch call you over there. What she wont this time?"

"She wonts to know why," I said.

"I aint told *you* why."

"And you won't, will you?"

She looked away from me, then she said, "You know it always have took me a long time, Floyd."

She didn't say anything else, and I tried not to look at her the way I had been looking. She sat on the edge of the couch with her hands together, like she was nervous, or praying. Her shoulders were pulled together in a way that made her look like she didn't have any breasts.

Cynthy came in the front room, and asked me how I was.

"Awright."

"Mama, supper's ready," she said.

"Stay for supper, won't you, Floyd?" Jevata asked me.

"Yeah."

"Cynthy, where's Freddy?" Jevata asked suddenly.

Cynthy looked at me quickly, then back at Jevata.

"He's not here, Mama," Cynthy said.

"Floyd, you aint seen Freddy, have you?" Jevata asked me.

I just looked at her. I couldn't even have replied as calmly as Cynthy had managed to. I just kept looking at her. Jevata laughed suddenly, a quick, nervous laugh, then said, "Naw, y'all, I don't mean Freddy, I mean where's Little Pete, y'all. I don't mean Freddy I feel like a fool now."

I said nothing.

"He's down the road playing with Ralph," Cynthy said.

"Well, tell him to come up here and get his supper."

"What about David, Mama?"

"You take his plate in there to him. I don't wont to see him."

"Yes, m'am."

I looked at Cynthy, puzzled, then I said I would take it. Jevata looked at me, but said nothing.

David was lying on the bed. I set his plate down on the chair by the bed. He didn't say anything.

"You know something about this, don't you?" I asked.

He still said nothing.

"I b'lieve you know what happened."

"Go way and leave me alone!" David said. "You aint my daddy."

I stood looking at him for a moment. He still lay on his belly. He had half turned around when he was hollering, but he hadn't looked at me. I finally left the room. When I came back in the kitchen, Little Pete was sitting at the table and Cynthy was putting the food on the table.

"Where's Jevata?" I asked.

Cynthy said nothing.

"I just ask her when Freddy was coming back and then she start acting all funny. I didn't do nothin', Mr. Floyd."

"I know you didn't," I said.

Cynthy looked at me and sat my plate down on the table. I sat down with them. Jevata didn't come back.

"Don't you think you better take your mama a plate," I said to Cynthy.

"She said she didn't wont nothin'," she said.

I stood up.

"She looked like she didn't wont nothin', Mr. Floyd," Cynthy said.

I sat back down.

I knew there was one place I could find out where Freddy was. I took the bus to Lexington, then went to the barber shop over in Charlotte Court, right off Georgetown Street.

"Any y'all know Freddy Coleman?" I asked.

They didn't answer. Then, one man sitting up in the chair, getting his hair trimmed around the sides, cause he didn't have any in the top, said, "What you got to do with him?"

"Nothin'," I said. "I just wont to know where he is."

"I used to know. He used to keep the yard down here at Kentucky Village."

Some of the other men started laughing. Kentucky Village was a school for delinquent boys. I asked what was funny.

"Close to them KV boys, wasn't he," one of the men said.

The man in the chair started laughing. "He never did do nothing. Just used to stand up there with the rake. Womens be passing by looking. Didn't do 'em no good." He asked me why I wanted him.

"I'm just looking for him," I said.

They looked at each other, like people who got a secret. They were trying not to laugh again.

"You can try that liquor store up the street. They tell me his baby hang out over there."

The rest of the men started laughing. I left them and went up to the liquor store. Somebody told me Freddy was living in an apartment up over some restaurant off Second Street.

I found the place and went upstairs and knocked on the door. He wasn't glad to see me.

"How you find me?" he asked.

I came in before he asked me to. I stayed standing.

"What do you wont?" he asked. "Finding out where I am for *her*?"

"Naw, for myself," I said.

I looked around. The living room was small. Only a couch and a couple of chairs, and a low coffee table. On the coffee table was a hat with feathers on it. It was a woman's hat. We were both standing. I didn't sit down without him asking me to. He wasn't saying anything and I wasn't. I was thinking he *was* a good-looking man, almost *too* good-looking. The onliest other man I knew was *that* good-looking was Mr. Pindar, a fake preacher that used to go around stealing people's money. He used to get drunks off the street and have them go before the congregation and play like he had changed their life. And people would believe it, too. He was so good-looking the women would believe it, and preached so good the men would believe it.

Freddy kept standing there looking at me. I kept looking at him.

"Where's my ostrich hat?" It was a man's voice, but somehow it didn't sound like a man.

Freddy looked embarrassed, he was frowning. He hollered he didn't know where it was.

"You seen my ostrich hat, honey?" the man asked again. He came in, like he was swaying, saw me and stopped cold. He said, "How do," snatched the hat from the table and went back in the other room.

Freddy wasn't looking at me. I said I'd better be going.

"He's crazy," Freddy said quickly. "He live down at Eastern State, and he's crazy."

Eastern State was the mental hospital.

"He got a room down at Eastern State," Freddy said. "They let him out everyday so he can get hisself drunk. That's all he do is get hisself drunk."

I said nothing. The man had come back in the room, and was standing near the door, pouting, his lower lip stuck out. Freddy hadn't turned to see him.

I started to go. Freddy reached out to put his hand on my arm, but didn't. He looked like he didn't want me to go.

"I was going to ask you to come back to her," I said, my eyes hard now. I ignored the man standing there, pouting. "I was going to tell you she needs you."

Freddy looked like he wanted to cry. "You know she kill me if I go back there," he said.

"Why?" I asked.

He said nothing.

I went toward the door again and he came with me. He still hadn't turned around to see the man. I asked him why again. Then I wanted another why. I asked him why did he go with her in the first place.

He said nothing for a long time, then he reached out to touch my arm again. I don't know if he would have stopped again this time, but I stood away from him.

"She was going to the carnaval. You know the one they have back behind Douglas Park every year, the one back there. She was passing through Douglas Park and seen me sitting up there all by myself. She ask me if I wont to go to the carnival. I don't know why she did. Maybe she thought I was lonesome, but I wasn't. I was sitting up there all by myself. She took me with her, you know. They had this man in this tent who was swallowing swords and knives, you know like they do. She wanted to take me there, so I went. We was standing up there watching this man, up close to him. We was standing up close to each other too, and then all a sudden Miss Jevata kind of turned her head to me, you know, and said kind of quiet like, 'You know, Miss Jevata could teach you how to swallow lightning,' she said. That was all she said. She didn't say nothing else and she didn't say that no more. I don't even know if anybody else heard her. But I think that's why I went back with her. That was the reason I went with her."

I said nothing. When I closed the door, I heard something hit the wall.

"Freddy did something to David, didn't he," I asked her.

"Naw, it wasn't David," Jevata said. She was sitting with her hands together.

I frowned, watching her.

"Petie come and told me Freddy tried to throw him down the toilet. I didn't believe him."

"If he tried he would've," I said. "What did him and David do?"

She kept looking at me. I was waiting.

"I seen him go in the toilet," she said finally. "Him and David went back in the toilet together. He didn't even have his pants zipped up when he come back to the house."

I was over by her when she burst out crying. When she stopped, she asked me if I could do something for her. I told her all she had to do was ask. When she told me she still loved Freddy, that she wanted me to get him back for her, I walked out the door.

I thought I wouldn't see her again. When the farm I worked for wanted me to go up to New Hampshire for a year to help train some horses, I went. I told myself when I did come back, I was through going out there, but I didn't keep my promise to myself.

When I got there, Miss Johnny wasn't sitting out on her porch, but Jevata was sitting out on hers—with a baby, sitting between her breasts. She was tickling the baby and laughing. When she looked up at me, she was still laughing.

"Floyd, Freddy back," she said. "Freddy come back."

I didn't know what to say to her. I asked if Cynthy was at home. She said yes. I went in the house. Cynthy was standing in the living room. She must have seen me coming.

"Freddy back?" I asked.

She put her hands to her mouth, and drew me toward the kitchen.

"Naw, she mean the baby," she said. "She named the baby Freddy."

"Is it his?" I asked.

She hesitated, frowning, then she said, "Yes." She got farther into the kitchen and I went with her.

"She didn't wont to have him at first. At first she tried to get rid of him."

I kept looking at her. She was a grown woman now. I remembered when I first started coming there, right after her daddy left. Everytime I'd come, she'd get the broom and start sweeping around my feet, like she was trying to sweep me out of the house. Now she looked at me, still frowning, but I could tell she was glad to see me. She said she knew I'd been sending them the money, but Jevata thought Freddy had.

I said nothing. I stood there for a moment, then I said I'd better be going.

"You will come back to see us?" she asked quickly, apprehensively. "We've missed you."

I looked at her. I started to move toward her, then I realized that she meant I might be able to help Jevata.

"Yes, I'll be back," I said.

She smiled. I went out the door.

"You little duck, you little duck, Freddy, you little duck," Jevata said, tickling the baby, who was laughing. A pretty child.

"You be back to see us, won't you, Floyd?" she asked when I started down the porch.

"Yes," I said, without turning around to look at her.

Barbara Jordan (1936–1996)

"Barbara Jordan was a patriot in the highest and best use of that word. She was a rare national treasure, an American original. Her extraordinary intellect and her equally extraordinary skills of expression enabled her to give brilliant utterance to what others felt but
could not say with such clarity." Such praise is not uncommon for Barbara Jordan. Born
February 21, 1936, into a poverty-stricken, all-Black ghetto of Houston, Texas, child of a
Baptist preacher, Jordan rose to the halls of the United States Congress where she was
elected to three terms as Congressional Representative from her home state. She was the
first Black person since the Reconstruction Era elected to that body. Educated at Texas
Southern University, Jordan graduated magna cum laude before moving on to receive her
law degree at Boston University in 1959. After practicing law for several years, Jordan decided to run for the Texas State Senate in 1966. Her stunning win—she received 80 percent
of the votes—catapulted her into the political arena where she worked for social reform,
cosponsoring a minimum-wage bill and a workers' compensation plan. In 1968, she was
the delegate to the Democratic National Convention in Chicago, working for Lyndon B.
Johnson. Elected to the United States Congress in 1972, Jordan came to national attention
as a member of the House Judiciary Committee charged with determining impeachment
proceedings against President Richard M. Nixon for his connection with the break-in of
the Democratic National Committee headquarters at Watergate. Jordan called for impeachment on July 25, 1974, a portion of which is excerpted here. In her speech, she displayed the passion and eloquence that solidified her position as a committed, powerful
figure of late twentieth century American politics. Jordan spoke for an entire nation in her
unqualified defense of the Constitution. "I am not going to sit here and be an idle spectator to the diminution, the subversion, the destruction of the Constitution."

She was determined that the Constitution take precedence over all else in the Watergate impeachment hearings of the House Judiciary Committee in 1974. Jordan begins her
speech by inserting herself into the narrative of the United States. She is unafraid to name
the racist past of the country, and she does so to further assert her right to be there, at this
critical juncture in U.S. political history. To confirm herself as one with every right to be a
part of these proceedings, Jordan uses three short, clipped statements, whose meaning is
unmistakably clear: "My faith in the Constitution is whole, it is complete, it is total." It is a
clever and powerful moment in Jordan's rhetoric, because juxtaposed against the opening
reminder of her own being left out by this Constitution, she is able to suggest—without actually saying so—that if she is able to revere the Constitution, then all men and women in
the country, including the President, must do the same. Further, Jordan relies on early
American government documents for support, which increases her credibility with the audience. Other features in Jordan's speech include her use of repetition for emphasis and

her invoking conclusion. Note that there are times, particularly at the beginning and end-ing of the speech, when Jordan pares down her language to its cleanest and clearest, which works to solidify her message.

Jordan was considered by many to be one of the most influential women in the United States. Her visibility and political breakthroughs put the focus on Black women's leadership abilities, along with her contemporaries Angela Davis, Shirley Chisholm, and Erika Huggins. But Jordan attempted to consciously identify with the needs of not only women and Blacks but also with other minorities: "I would say that being a woman, a black and member of Con-gress has enlarged my constituency beyond any dream I had of how large my constituency would become. I receive mail from all over the country. Not from just women and blacks, but from everybody, it seems, who wants to get something off their chest." Her unblinking, pas-sionate liberalism was based on making the American dream available to everybody.

Texas Senator Lloyd Bentsen was so enthralled with her powerful delivery during the Watergate hearings that he spoke of her in biblical terms. "I looked down to see if she was reading from stone tablets," said the Senator. "And we know that if God is a woman, she sounds like Barbara Jordan." Jordan died on January 17, 1996, and with her passing, American politics lost a giant and brilliant human.

Lenore Brady

Argument for Impeachment, 1974

Mr. Chairman, I join my colleague, Mr. Rangel, in thanking you for giving the junior members of this committee the glorious opportunity of sharing the pain of this inquiry. Mr. Chairman, you are a strong man and it has not been easy but we have tried as best we can to give you as much assistance as possible.

Earlier today we heard the beginning of the Preamble of the Constitution of the United States, "We, the people." It is a very eloquent beginning. But when that document was completed on the seventeenth of September in 1787 I was not included in that "We, the people." I felt somehow for many years that George Washington and Alexander Hamilton just left me out by mistake. But through the process of amendment, interpretation and court decision I have finally been included in "We, the people."

Today, I am an inquisitor. I believe hyperbole would not be fictional and would not overstate the solemness that I feel right now. My faith in the Constitu-tion is whole, it is complete, it is total. I am not going to sit here and be an idle spectator to the diminution, the subversion, the destruction of the Constitution.

"Who can so properly be the inquisitors for the nation as the representatives of the nation themselves?" (Federalist, number 65) The subject of its jurisdiction are those offenses which proceed from the misconduct of public men. That is what we are talking about. In other words, the jurisdiction comes from the abuse or violation of some public trust. It is wrong, I suggest, it is a misreading of the Constitution for any member here to assert that for a member to vote for an article of impeachment means that that member must be convinced that the president should be removed from office. The Constitution doesn't say that. The powers relating to impeachment are an essential check in the hands of this body, the legislature, against and upon the encroachment of the executive. In establishing the division between the two branches of the legislature, the House and the Senate, assigning to the one the right to accuse and to the other the right to judge, the framers of this Constitution were very astute. They did not make the accusers and the judges the same person. . . .

Common sense would be revolted if we engaged upon this process for petty reasons. Congress has a lot to do. Appropriations, tax reforms, health insurance, campaign finance reform, housing, environmental protection, energy sufficiency, mass transportation. Pettiness cannot be allowed to stand in the face of such overwhelming problems. So today we are not being petty. We are trying to be big because the task we have before us is a big one.

This morning in a discussion of the evidence we were told that the evidence which purports to support the allegations of misuse of the CIA by the president is thin. We are told that that evidence is insufficient. What that recital of the evidence this morning did not include is what the president did know on June 23, 1972. The president did know that it was Republican money, that it was money from the Committee for the Re-election of the President, which was found in the possession of one of the burglars arrested on June 17.

What the president did know on June 23 was the prior activities of E. Howard Hunt, which included his participation in the break-in of Daniel Ellsberg's psychiatrist, which included Howard Hunt's participation in the Dita Beard ITT affair, which included Howard Hunt's fabrication of cables designed to discredit the Kennedy administration.

We were further cautioned today that perhaps these proceedings ought to be delayed because certainly there would be new evidence forthcoming from the president of the United States. There has not even been an obfuscated indication that this committee would receive any additional materials from the president. The committee subpoena is outstanding and if the president wants to supply that material, the committee sits here.

The fact is that on yesterday, the American people waited with great anxiety for eight hours, not knowing whether their president would obey an order of the Supreme Court of the United States. . . .

Beginning shortly after the Watergate break-in and continuing to the present time the president has engaged in a series of public statements and actions designed to thwart the lawful investigation by government prosecutors. Moreover, the president has made public announcements and assertions bearing on the Watergate case which the evidence will show he knew to be false.

There assertions, false assertions, impeachable, those who misbehave. Those who "behave amiss or betray their public trust."

James Madison again at the constitutional convention: "A president is impeachable if he attempts to subvert the Constitution."

The Constitution charges the president with the task of taking care that the laws be faithfully executed, and yet the president has counseled his aides to commit perjury, willfully disregarded the secrecy of grand jury proceedings, concealed surreptitious entry, attempted to compromise a federal judge while publicly displaying his cooperation with the processes of criminal justice.

"A president is impeachable if he attempts to subvert the Constitution."

If the impeachment provision in the Constitution of the United States will not reach the offenses charged here, then perhaps that eighteenth century Constitution should be abandoned to a twentieth century paper shredder. Has the president committed offenses and planned and directed and acquiesced in a course of conduct which the Constitution will not tolerate? That is the question. We know that. We know the question. We should now forthwith proceed to answer the question. It is reason, and not passion, which must guide our deliberations, guide our debate, and guide our decision.

June Jordan (1938–)

June Jordan is a prolific contemporary writer who refuses to be categorized. As poet, children's author, dramatist, and essayist, Jordan has demonstrated her great flexibility as a writer as well as her dedication to her profession and the causes she believes in. With profound power and insight, Jordan connects the intricacies of her private life to the realm of the political.

Jordan was born in Harlem on July 19, 1938, the only child of working-class Jamaican parents. Jordan received most of her education in a predominantly White environment. Spending one year as the only Black student in a high school student body of 3,000 and then three years at a girls' preparatory school in Massachusetts, Jordan learned to love the literature she was exposed to, loving first the British Romantics. The appreciation for African American, women's, and global literatures that is so evident in her own literary production came later.

The deepest influences on her development as an intellectual and as a writer were her parents. Exposed from an early age to the classics of the Bible, Shakespeare, Edgar Allen Poe, and Paul Laurence Dunbar, she began writing poetry at age seven. While her early desire to be a poet was not always encouraged nor were her relationships with her parents ideal, Jordan was inspired by this early introduction to literature and her father's love for it. Her mother's dreams of becoming an artist and her suicide before realizing her dreams motivated Jordan's feminist writing and action. Her mother was the most significant example in the history of neglected lives and dreams of African American women that Jordan has dedicated herself to transforming.

For June Jordan, the personal and political cannot be separate. One of the most political and personal battles of her life was the inner and societal battle of her interracial marriage to Mike Meyer while she was an undergraduate at Barnard College in 1955. Her marriage and the birth of their son, Christopher David Meyer, coincided with her involvement in the first stirrings of the civil rights movement. When she met Malcolm X in 1964, she intensified her activism, joining the Freedom Riders to Baltimore. The seriousness of her involvement in the movement was partial reason for the dissolution of her marriage. In 1966, the year after her mother's suicide, she and Meyer divorced. The struggle to support her son and to write energized her efforts to incite change in the sexist, racist world around her.

Her first publication, a long poem, Who Look at Me (1968), is closely linked to a series of paintings that highlight the power dynamics of gaze in race relations. As the starting point of self-identification, eye contact is the central image of the poem; the subject becomes active in the course of the poem, looking back at the White people who define through looking at and, more importantly, looking at Black people to redefine and affirm.

In the few years before the 1971 publication of her first novel, Jordan worked with W. R. Buckminster-Fuller on an environmental redesign project for New York's East Side.

This project lead to the article, "Urban Redesign" for which she and Buckminster-Fuller won the 1971 Prix de Rome in environmental design. His Own Where, *a 1972 National Book Award nominee, draws upon Jordan's urban planning experience as Buddy, the protagonist of the novel, "remodels" space to create a place he can call his own. The novel also advocates the power, lyricism, and validity of Black English twelve years before its appearance in Alice Walker's* The Color Purple.

Jordan published three collections of poetry in the 1970s. Her first collection, Some Changes *(1971), centers on love relationships. The first two sections of the collection are dedicated to her parents, while the third is dedicated to a lover, an integration of sexuality, before the fourth section returns to the subject of family.* Some Changes *plays with the definition of family and engages with literary tradition, especially Eliot, Dickinson, and Shakespeare, transforming canonical style through assertion of Black identity.* New Days: Poems of Exile and Return *(1973) draws a parallel between the "exile" of Black life in the United States and Jordan's travel to Rome, which was relatively less like exile. One of the collection's most powerful poems, "Getting Down to Get Over," focuses on Jordan's recovery of her mother; an incantation of powerful personal force becomes a communal voice as the poem creates the face of the mother, bringing it back to center.* Things That I Do in the Dark *(1977) contains selected and new poems and shows the emergence of a Black feminist perspective, a reconsideration of violence as means for productive Black struggle, and an affirmation that violence is indeed still necessary especially in the context of global violence. Many of Jordan's poems, like "I Must Become a Menace to My Enemies," demonstrate her awareness of the need for revolution, even the militant revolution proposed by Nikki Giovanni and Amiri Baraka in their poetry. In form, structure, and language, Jordan's poetry demonstrates a recognition of Black Aesthetic; her language is accessible, her lyrics forceful and gentle at once, expressing the variation within resistance.*

Continuing the autobiographical bent of her poetry, her first collection of essays, Civil Wars *(1981), focuses on the challenges of being a Black woman, writer, and single mother. In the foreword to the collection, Jordan clarifies the connection between language and resistance. She asserts the purpose of her own language, both poetry and prose. A second collection of political essays,* On Call, *followed in 1985.* On Call *focuses on liberation struggles around the world, complex views of race and class, and the championing of Black English. Her early essays show her skill in translating the force of her poetry into prose.*

June Jordan's work in the 1990s has continued to be a balance of poetry and essay. She published a third collection of essays, Technical Difficulties, *in 1992, and her most recent,* Affirmative Acts, *in 1996. In each of these collections, the relationship between power and voice continues as Jordan addresses issues of race, global politics, capitalism, and sexuality. Jordan's prose celebrates the power of language to not only speak injustice but to create truth and freedom. In "I Am Seeking an Attitude," for example, Jordan powerfully asserts her identity as a woman, her alliance with women globally, and the necessity of continued feminist struggle.*

Jordan's most recent trilogy of poetry consists of Haruko: Love Poems *(1994),* June Jordan's Poetry for the People *(1995), and* Kissing God Goodbye *(1997). These collections focus more centrally than previous works on Jordan's relationships as a bisexual woman, her battle with cancer, and her interaction with the students she teaches.*

June Jordan's poetry and prose is marked by intensity of conviction and action. Her dedication to asserting, defending, and nurturing Black experience is the thread running through all of her work, prose and poetry. Grounded in the complex balancing of love and anger as it relates to her understanding of her parents and the hope and future represented in her son, the strong autobiographical dimension in her work elicits a powerful personal voice in transformation. Exercising wide breadth and diversity in both content and form, Jordan links this voice to individual and cultural survival.

Jordan has shared her skill and talent as a writer and teacher in many places rang-ing from Children's Workshop in Brooklyn to New York's City College, Sarah Lawrence, and Yale University. Since 1989, she has been a professor of African American studies and women's studies at the University of California at Berkeley where she runs the Poetry for the People program. She is also a columnist for The Progressive.

R. Joyce Lausch

Who Look At Me

DEDICATED TO MY SON, CHRISTOPHER

Who would paint a people
black or white?
       *

For my own I have held
where nothing showed me how
where finally I left alone
to trace another destination
       *

A white stare splits the air
by blindness on the subway
in department stores
The Elevator
            (that unswerving ride
where man ignores the brother
by his side)

A white stare splits obliterates
the nerve-wrung wrist from work
the breaking ankle or
the turning glory
of a spine
       *

Is that how we look to you
a partial nothing clearly real?

Who see a solid clarity
of feature
size and shape of some
one head
an unmistaken nose

the fact of afternoon
as darkening
his candle eyes

Older men with swollen neck
(when they finally sit down
who will stand up
for them?)

I cannot remember nor imagine pretty
people treat me
like a doublejointed stick
                    WHO LOOK AT ME
                    WHO SEE

the tempering sweetness
of a little girl who wears
her first pair of earrings
and a red dress

the grace of a boy removing
a white mask he makes beautiful

Iron grille across the glass
and frames of motion closed or
charred or closed

The axe lies on the ground
She listening to his coming sound

Him
just touching his feet
powerful and wary

anonymous and normal
parents and their offspring
posed in formal
                    *
I am
impossible to explain
remote from old and new interpretations
and yet
not exactly
                    *
look at the stranger as

he lies more gray then black
on that colorquilt
that
(everyone will say)
seems bright beside him

look
black sailors on the light
green sea the sky keeps blue
the wind blows high
and hard at night
for anyhow anywhere new
                    *
Who see starvation at the table
lines of men no work to do
my mother ironing a shirt?

Who see a frozen skin the midnight
of the winter and the hallway cold
to kill you like the dirt?

where kids buy soda pop
in shoeshine parlors
barber shops so they can hear
some laughing

Who look at me?

Who see the children
on their street the torn down door the wall
complete an early losing
                        games of ball
the search to find
a fatherhood a mothering of mind
a multimillion multicolored mirror
of an honest humankind?
                    *
look close
and see me black man mouth
for breathing (North and South)
A MAN

I am black alive and looking back at you.
                    *
see me brown girl throat
that throbs from servitude

see me hearing fragile
leap
and lead a black boy
reckless to succeed
to wrap my pride
around tomorrow and to go
there
without fearing

see me darkly covered ribs
around my heart across my skull
thin skin protects the part
that dulls from longing
                    *

Who see the block we face
the thousand miles of solid alabaster space
inscribed keep off keep out don't touch
and Wait Some More for Half as Much?
                    *

To begin is no more agony
than opening your hand
                    *

sometimes you have to dance
like spelling
the word joyless
                    *

Describe me broken mast
adrift but strong
regardless what may
come along
                    *

What do you suppose he hears
every evening?
                    *

I am stranded in a hungerland
of great prosperity
                    *

shelter happens seldomly and
like an accident
it stops
                    *

No doubt
the jail is white where I was born
but black will bail me out

*

We have lived as careful
as a church and prayer
in public

*

we reveal
a complicated past
of tinderbox and ruin
where we carried water
for the crops

we come from otherwere

victim to a rabid cruel cargo crime

to separate and rip apart
the trusting members of one heart

my family

I looked for you
I looked for you

*

(slavery:) the insolence

came to frontiers
of paralyze highways
freedom strictly underground

came here to hatred hope labor love
and lynchlength rope

came a family to a family

I found my father
silently despite the grieving
fury of his life
Afternoons he wore his hat
and held a walking stick

I found my mother
her geography
becomes our home

*

so little safety

almost nowhere like the place
that childhood plans
in a pounding happy space
between deliberate brown and clapping
hands
that preached a reaping to the wildly
    sleeping earth
brown hands that worked for rain a fire inside
    and food to eat
from birth brown hands
    to hold
                        *

New energies of darkness we
disturbed a continent
like seeds

and life grows slowly
so we grew

We became a burly womb
an evening harvest kept by prayers
a hallelujah little room

We grew despite the crazy killing scorn
that broke the brightness to be born

In part we grew
by looking back at you

that white terrain
impossible for black America to thrive
that hostile soil to mazelike toil
backbreaking people into pain
we grew by work by waiting
to be seen
black face black body and black mind
beyond obliterating
homicide of daily insult daily death
the pistol slur the throbbing redneck war
with breath

In part we grew
with heroes who could halt a slaveship
lead the crew

like Cinque (son
of a Mendi African Chief) he
led in 1839
the Amistad Revolt
from slavehood forced
a victory he
killed the captain killed the cook
took charge
a mutiny for manhood
people
called him killer but
some
the Abolitionists
looked back at robbery
of person
murdering of spirit
slavery requires
and one
John Quincy Adams (seventy-three)
defended Cinque who
by highest court decree
in 1841 stood free
and freely he returned
to Africa
victorious

In part we grew
grandmother husband son
together when the laborblinding day was done
In part we grew
as we were meant to grow
ourselves
with kings and queens no white man knew

we grew by sitting on a stolen chair
by windows and a dream
by setting up a separate sail
to carry life
to start the song

to stop the scream

*

These times begin the ending of all lies
the fantasies of seasons start and stop

the circle leads to no surprise
for death does not bewilder
only life can kill can mystify can start
and stop like flowers ripening a funeral
like (people) holding hands across the knife
that cuts the casket to an extraordinary size
                              *

Tell the whiplash helmets GO!
and take away
that cream and orange Chevrolet
stripped to inside steel and parked
forever on one wheel

Set the wild dogs chewing up
that pitiful capitulation
plastic flower plastic draperies
to dust the dirt

Break the clothesline
Topple down the clotheslinepole

O My Lives Among The Wounded Buildings
should be dressed in trees and grass
                              *
we will no longer wait for want for watch
for what we will

Getting Down to Get Over

DEDICATED TO MY MOTHER

MOMMA MOMMA MOMMA
momma momma
mammy
nanny
granny
woman
mistress
sista

luv

blackgirl
slavegirl

gal

honeychile
sweetstuff
sugar
sweetheart
baby
Baby Baby
MOMMA MOMMA
Black Momma
Black bitch
Black pussy
piecea tail
nice piecea ass

hey daddy! hey
bro!
we walk together (an')
talk together (an')
dance and *do*
(together)
dance and do/hey!
daddy!
bro!
hey!
nina nikki nonni nommo nommo
momma Black
Momma

Black Woman
Black
Female Head of Household
Black Matriarchal Matriarchy
Black Statistical
Lowlife Lowlevel Lowdown
Lowdown and *up*
to be Low-down
Black Statistical
Low Factor
Factotem
Factitious Fictitious

Figment Figuring in Lowdown Lyin
Annual Reports

Black Woman/Black
Hallelujah Saintly
patient
smilin
humble
givin thanks
for
Annual Reports and
Monthly Dole
and
Friday night
and
(*good* God!)
Monday mornin: Black and Female
martyr masochist
(A BIG WHITE LIE)
Momma Momma

What does Mothafuckin mean?
WHO'S THE MOTHAFUCKA
FUCKED MY MOMMA
messed yours over
and right now
be trippin on my starveblack
female soul
a macktruck
mothafuck
the first primordial
the paradig/digmatic
dogmatistic mothafucka who
is he?
hey!
momma momma

dry eyes on the
sky/dark/hidden/cryin Black
face
of the loneliness
the rape
the brokeup mailbox
an' no western union roses

come inside the kitchen
and no poem
take you through the whole night
and no big
Black
burly
hand
to holdin yours
to have to hold onto
no
big Black burly hand
no nommo
no Black prince
come riding from the darkness
on a beautiful black horse
no bro
no daddy

"I was sixteen when I met my father
In a bar.
In Baltimore.
He told me who he was
and what he does.
Paid for the drinks.
I looked.
I listened.
And I left him.
It was civil
perfectly
and absolute bull
shit.
The drinks was leakin waterweak
and never got down to my knees."

hey daddy
what they been and done to you
and what you been and done
to me
to momma
momma momma
hey
sugar daddy
big daddy
sweet daddy

Black Daddy
The Original Father Divine
the everlovin
deep
tall
bad
buck
jive
cold
strut
bop
split
tight
loose
close
hot
hot
hot
sweet SWEET DADDY
WHERE YOU BEEN AND
WHEN YOU COMIN BACK TO ME
HEY
WHEN YOU COMIN BACK
TO MOMMA
momma momma

And Suppose He Finally Say
"Look, Baby.
I Loves Me Some
Everything about You.
Let Me Be Your Man."
That reach around the hurtin
like a dream.
And I ain never wakin up
from that one.
momma momma
momma momma

II

Consider the Queen

hand on her hip
sweat restin from
the corn/bean/greens' field

steamy under the pale/sly
suffocatin sun

Consider the Queen

she fix the cufflinks
on his Sunday shirt
and fry some chicken
bake some cake
and tell the family
"Never mine about the bossman
don' know how a human
bein spozed to act. Jus'
never mind about him.
Wash your face.
Sit down. And let
the good Lord bless this table."

Consider the Queen

her babies pullin at the nipples
pullin at the momma milk

the infant fingers gingerly
approach caress the
soft/Black/swollen/momma breast

and there
inside the mommasoft
life-spillin treasure chest
the heart
breaks

rage by grief by sorrow
weary weary
breaks
breaks quiet
silently
the weary sorrow
quiet now the furious
the adamant the broken
busted beaten down and beaten up
the beaten beaten beaten
weary heart beats

tender-steady
and the babies suck/
the seed of blood
and love glows at the
soft/Black/swollen momma breast

Consider the Queen

she works when she works
in the laundry *in jail*
in the school house *in jail*
in the office *in jail*
on the soap box *in jail*
on the desk
on the floor
on the street
on the line
at the door
lookin fine
at the head of the line
steppin sharp from behind
in the light
with a song
wearing boots
or a belt
and a gun
drinkin wine when it's time

when the long week is done
but she works when she works
in the laundry in jail
she works when she works

Consider the Queen

she sleeps when she sleeps
with the king in the kingdom
she
sleeps when she sleeps
with the wall
with whatever it is who happens
to call
with me and with you
(to survive you make
do/you explore more and more)

so she sleeps when she sleeps
a really deep sleep

Consider the Queen

a full/Black/glorious/a purple rose
aroused by the tiger breathin
beside her
a shell with the moanin
of ages inside her
a hungry one feedin the folk
what they need

Consider the Queen.

III

Blackman
let that white girl go
She know what you ought to know.
(By now.)

IV

MOMMA MOMMA
momma momma
family face
face of the family alive
momma
mammy
momma
woman
sista
baby
luv

the house on fire/
poison waters/
earthquake/
and the air a nightmare/
turn
turn
turn around the
national gross product
growin

really gross/turn
turn
turn the pestilence away
the miserable killers
and Canarsie
Alabama
people beggin to be people
warfare on the welfare
of the folk/
hey
turn
turn away
the trickbag university/the
trickbag propaganda/
trickbag
tricklin of prosperity/ of
pseudo-"status"
lynchtree necklace
on the strong
round
neck of you
my momma
momma momma
turn away
the f.b.i./the state police/the cops/
the/everyone of the
infest/incestuous investigators
into you
and Daddy/into us
hey
turn
my mother
turn
the face of history
to your own
and please be smilin
if you can
be smilin
at the family

momma momma

let the funky forecast
be the last

one we will ever
want to listen to

And Daddy see
the stars fall down
and burn a light
into the singin
darkness of your eyes
my Daddy
my Blackman
you take my body in
your arms/you use
the oil of coconuts/of trees and
flowers/fish and new fruits
from the new world
to enflame me in this otherwise
cold place
please
meanwhile
momma
momma momma
teach me how to kiss
the king within the kingdom
teach me how to t.c.b./to make do
and be
like you
teach me to survive my
momma
teach me how to hold a new life
momma
help me
turn the face of history
to your face.

I Must Become a Menace to My Enemies

DEDICATED TO THE POET AGOSTINHO NETO,
PRESIDENT OF THE PEOPLE'S REPUBLIC OF ANGOLA: 1976

I

I will no longer lightly walk behind
a one of you who fear me:

Be afraid.
I plan to give you reasons for your jumpy fits
and facial tics
I will not walk politely on the pavements anymore
and this is dedicated in particular
to those who hear my footsteps
or the insubstantial rattling of my grocery
cart
then turn around
see me
and hurry on
away from this impressive terror I must be:
I plan to blossom bloody on an afternoon
surrounded by my comrades singing
terrible revenge in merciless
accelerating
rhythms
But
I have watched a blind man studying his face.
I have set the table in the evening and sat down
to eat the news.
Regularly
I have gone to sleep.
There is no one to forgive me.
The dead do not give a damn.
I live like a lover
who drops her dime into the phone
just as the subway shakes into the station
wasting her message
cancelling the question of her call:

fulminating or forgetful but late
and always after the fact that could save or
condemn me

I must become the action of my fate.

II

How many of my brothers and my sisters
will they kill
before I teach myself
retaliation?
Shall we pick a number?

South Africa for instance:
do we agree that more than ten thousand
in less than a year but that less than
five thousand slaughtered in more than six
months will
WHAT IS THE MATTER WITH ME?

I must become a menace to my enemies.

III

And if I
if I ever let you slide
who should be extirpated from my universe
who should be cauterized from earth
completely
(Iawandorder jerkoffs of the first the
    terrorist degree)
then let my body fail my soul
in its bedevilled lecheries

And if I
if I ever let love go
because the hatred and the whisperings
become a phantom dictate I o-
bey in lieu of impulse and realities
(the blossoming flamingos of my
    wild mimosa trees)
then let love freeze me
out.

I must become
I must become a menace to my enemies.

Roman Poem Number Nine

Return is not a way of going forward
after all
or back. In any case it seems
a matter of opinion how
you face although

the changing bed the different voice
around the different room

may testify to movement
entry exit it
is motion takes you in
and memory that lets you out again.
Or
as this love will let me say
the body travels faster than the keeping
heart will turn away.

Of Nightsong and Flight

There are things lovely and dangerous still

the rain
when the heat of an evening
sweetens the darkness with mist

and the eyes cannot see what the memory will
of new pain

when the headlights deceive
like the window wild birds believe to be air
and bash bodies and wings
on the glass

when the headlights show space
but the house and the room and the bed and your face
are still there

while I am mistaken
and try to drive by

the actual kiss
of the world everywhere

Foreword

All of this started with my uncle. He was a probation officer living with my aunt and her daughter on the third, the top, floor of our Brooklyn brownstone. Even when he washed and polished his car on weekends, my uncle sported a pistol, most of the time, and told amazing, terrific stories about how he did in this or that unfortunate other guy. I adored him and, I'm pretty sure, he liked me well enough; for example, after his tour in World War II, as a second lieutenant stationed mainly in Georgia, what he brought back for me, as a very special present, was a rather lusty, full-grown raccoon.

For a long while during childhood I was relatively small, short, and, in some other ways, a target for bully abuse. In fact, my father was the first regular bully in my life and there were many days when my uncle pounded down the two flights of stairs in our house to grab the chair, or the knife, or whatever, from my father's hands.

But outside intervention has its limits and, consequently, my uncle decided to teach me how to fight for myself. He showed me numerous ways to disarm/disable an assailant. But what he told me is what I best remember: "It's a bully. Probably you can't win. That's why he's picking the fight. But if you go in there, saying to yourself, 'I may not win this one but it's going to cost you; if you hit me you better hope to take me out. Because I'll be going for your life.'—If you go in there like that they'll leave you alone. And remember: it's a bully. It's not about fair. From the start: it's not about fair."

I quickly, and repeatedly, learned that jumping into a showdown breeds, and requires, a decent degree of optimism, or affirmation, if you prefer: The outcome matters less than the jumping into it; once you're on, there's an adrenalin plumping of self-respect that compensates for terror. I learned, in short, that fighting is a whole lot less disagreeable than turning tail or knuckling under. It feels better. Besides, he was right; I lost a lot of fights as a kid in Bedford-Stuyvesant. But nobody fought me twice. They said I was "crazy."

While my uncle was teaching me literal pugilistics, my parents were teaching me the Bible and sending me out for piano lessons, voice lessons, and the like. Early on, the scriptural concept that "in the beginning was the Word and the Word was with God and the Word was God"—the idea that the word could represent and then deliver into reality what the word symbolized—this possibility of language, of writing, seemed to me magical and basic and irresistible. I really do mean "early on": my mother carried me to the Universal Truth Center on 125th Street, every Sunday, before we moved from Manhattan. I must have been two years old, or three, when the distinctive belief of that congregation began to make sense to me: that "by declaring the truth, you create the truth." In other words, if you lost your wallet you declared, "There is no loss in Divine Mind"—and kept looking. Those words, per se, possessed the power to change the facts; the wallet would turn up again.

I loved words and I hated to fight. But if, as a Black girl-child in America, I could not evade the necessity to fight, then, maybe, I could choose my weaponry at least.

It was the week after the Harlem Riot of 1964, a week of lurching around downtown streets like a war-zone refugee (whenever I heard a police or fire engine siren I would literally hit the pavement to flatten myself before the putative level of the flying bullets) that I realized I now was filled with hatred for everything and everyone white. Almost simultaneously it came to me that this condition, if it lasted, would mean I had lost the point: not to resemble my enemies, not to dwarf my world, not to lose my willingness and ability to love.

This was self-interested, to be sure. As Mrs. Fannie Lou Hamer said, years later, as she stood on her porch in Mississippi, "Ain' no such a thing as I can hate anybody and hope to see God's face."

So, back in 1964, I resolved not to run on hatred but, instead, to use what I loved, words, for the sake of the people I loved. However, beyond my people, I did not know the content of my love: what was I *for?* Nevertheless, the agony of that moment propelled me into a reaching far and away to R. Buckminster Fuller, to whom I proposed a collaborative architectural redesign of Harlem, as my initial, deliberated movement away from the hateful, the divisive.

My first meeting with Bucky lasted several hours, just the two of us, alone. And when we separated, agreed on the collaboration for *Esquire* magazine, I felt safe in my love again. We would think and work together to design a three-dimensional, an enviable, exemplary life situation for Harlem residents who, otherwise, had to outmaneuver New York City's Tactical Police Force, rats, a destructive and compulsory system of education, and so forth, or die.

This was a way, a scale, of looking at things that escaped the sundering paralysis of conflict by concentrating on the point, the purpose of the fight: What kind of schools and what kind of streets and what kind of parks and what kind of privacy and what kind of beauty and what kind of music and what kind of options would make love a reasonable, easy response?

Forward from that evening in Fuller's room, at the St. Regis Hotel, my sometime optimism born of necessity hardened into a faithful confidence carried by dreams: detailed explorations of the alternatives to whatever stultifies and debases our lives.

My life seems to be an increasing revelation of the intimate face of universal struggle. You begin with your family and the kids on the block, and next you open your eyes to what you call your people and that leads you into land reform into Black English into Angola leads you back to your own bed where you lie by yourself, wondering if you deserve to be peaceful, or trusted or desired or left to the freedom of your own unfaltering heart. And the scale shrinks to the size of a skull: your own interior cage.

And then if you're lucky, and I have been lucky, everything comes back to you. And then you know why one of the freedom fighters in the sixties, a young Black woman interviewed shortly after she was beaten up for riding near the front of an interstate bus—you know why she said, "We are all so very happy."

It's because it's on. All of us and me by myself: we're on.

A New Politics of Sexuality

As a young worried mother, I remember turning to Dr. Benjamin Spock's *Common Sense Book of Baby and Child Care* just about as often as I'd pick up the telephone. He was God. I was ignorant but striving to be good: a good Mother. And so it was there, in that best-seller pocketbook of do's and don't's, that I came upon this doozie of a guideline: Do not wear miniskirts or other provocative clothing because that will upset your child, especially if your child happens to be a boy. If you give your offspring "cause" to think of you as a sexual being, he will, at the least, become disturbed; you will derail the equilibrium of his notions about your possible identity and meaning in the world.

It had never occurred to me that anyone, especially my son, might look upon me as an asexual being. I had never supposed that "asexual" was some kind of positive designation I should, so to speak, lust after. I was pretty surprised by Dr. Spock. However, I was also, by habit, a creature of obedience. For a couple of weeks I actually experimented with lusterless colors and dowdy tops and bottoms, self-consciously hoping thereby to prove myself as a lusterless and dowdy and, therefore, excellent female parent.

Years would have to pass before I could recognize the familiar, by then, absurdity of a man setting himself up as the expert on a subject that presupposed women as the primary objects for his patriarchal discourse—on motherhood, no less! Years passed before I came to perceive the perversity of dominant power assumed by men, and the perversity of self-determining power ceded to men by women.

A lot of years went by before I understood the dynamics of what anyone could summarize as the Politics of Sexuality.

I believe the Politics of Sexuality is the most ancient and probably the most profound arena for human conflict. Increasingly, it seems clear to me that deeper and more pervasive than any other oppression, than any other bitterly contested human domain, is the oppression of sexuality, the exploitation of the human domain of sexuality for power.

When I say sexuality, I mean gender: I mean male subjugation of human beings because they are female. When I say sexuality, I mean heterosexual institutionalization of rights and privileges denied to homosexual men and women. When I say sexuality I mean gay or lesbian contempt for bisexual modes of human relationship.

The Politics of Sexuality therefore subsumes all of the different ways in which some of us seek to dictate to others of us what we should do, what we should desire, what we should dream about, and how we should behave our-

This essay was adapted from the author's keynote address to the Bisexual, Gay, and Lesbian Student Association at Stanford University on April 29, 1991. It was published in *The Progressive*, July 1991.

selves, generally. From China to Iran, from Nigeria to Czechoslovakia, from Chile to California, the politics of sexuality—enforced by traditions of state-sanctioned violence plus religion and the law—reduces to male domination of women, heterosexist tyranny, and, among those of us who are in any case deemed despicable or deviant by the powerful, we find intolerance for those who choose a different, a more complicated—for example, an interracial or bisexual—mode of rebellion and freedom.

We must move out from the shadows of our collective subjugation—as people of color/as women/as gay/as lesbian/as bisexual human beings.

I can voice my ideas without hesitation or fear because I am speaking, finally, about myself. I am Black and I am female and I am a mother and I am bisexual and I am a nationalist and I am an antinationalist. And I mean to be fully and freely all that I am!

Conversely, I do not accept that any white or Black or Chinese man—I do not accept that, for instance, Dr. Spock—should presume to tell me, or any other woman, how to mother a child. He has no right. He is not a mother. My child is not his child. And, likewise, I do not accept that anyone—any woman or any man who is not inextricably part of the subject he or she dares to address—should attempt to tell any of us, the objects of her or his presumptuous discourse, what we should do or what we should not do.

Recently, I have come upon gratuitous and appalling pseudoliberal pronouncements on sexuality. Too often, these utterances fall out of the mouths of men and women who first disclaim any sentiment remotely related to homophobia, but who then proceed to issue outrageous opinions like the following:

- That it is blasphemous to compare the oppression of gay, lesbian, or bisexual people to the oppression, say, of black people, or of the Palestinians.

- That the bottom line about gay or lesbian or bisexual identity is that you can conceal it whenever necessary and, so, therefore, why don't you do just that? Why don't you keep your deviant sexuality in the closet and let the rest of us—we who suffer oppression for reasons of our ineradicable and always visible components of our personhood such as race or gender—get on with our more necessary, our more beleaguered struggle to survive?

Well, number one: I believe I have worked as hard as I could, and then harder than that, on behalf of equality and justice—for African-Americans, for the Palestinian people, and for people of color everywhere.

And no, I do not believe it is blasphemous to compare oppressions of sexuality to oppressions of race and ethnicity: Freedom is indivisible or it is nothing at all besides sloganeering and temporary, short-sighted, and short-lived advancement for a few. Freedom is indivisible, and either we are working for freedom or you are working for the sake of your self-interests and I am working for mine.

If you can finally go to the bathroom wherever you find one, if you can finally order a cup of coffee and drink it wherever coffee is available, but you cannot follow your heart—you cannot respect the response of your own honest body in the world—then how much of what kind of freedom does any one of us possess?

Or, conversely, if your heart and your honest body can be controlled by the state, or controlled by community taboo, are you not then, and in that case, no more than a slave ruled by outside force?

What tyranny could exceed a tyranny that dictates to the human heart, and that attempts to dictate the public career of an honest human body?

Freedom is indivisible; the Politics of Sexuality is not some optional "special-interest" concern for serious, progressive folk.

And, on another level, let me assure you: if every single gay or lesbian or bisexual man or woman active on the Left of American politics decided to stay home, there would be *no* Left left.

One of the things I want to propose is that we act on that reality: that we insistently demand reciprocal respect and concern from those who cheerfully depend upon our brains and our energies for their, and our, effective impact on the political landscape.

Last spring, at Berkeley, some students asked me to speak at a rally against racism. And I did. There were four or five hundred people massed on Sproul Plaza, standing together against that evil. And, on the next day, on that same plaza, there was a rally for bisexual and gay and lesbian rights, and students asked me to speak at that rally. And I did. There were fewer that seventy-five people stranded, pitiful, on that public space. And I said then what I say today: That was disgraceful! There should have been just one rally. One rally: freedom is indivisible.

As for the second, nefarious pronouncement on sexuality that now enjoys mass-media currency: the idiot notion of keeping yourself in the closet—that is very much the same thing as the suggestion that black folks and Asian-Americans and Mexican-Americans should assimilate and become as "white" as possible—in our walk/talk/music/food/values—or else. Or else? Or else we should, deservedly, perish.

Sure enough, we have plenty of exposure to white everything so why would we opt to remain our African/Asian/Mexican selves? The answer is that suicide is absolute, and if you think you will survive by hiding who you really are, you are sadly misled: there is no such thing as partial or intermittent suicide. You can only survive if you—who you really are—do survive.

Likewise, we who are not men and we who are not heterosexist—we, sure enough, have plenty of exposure to male-dominated/heterosexist this and that.

But a struggle to survive cannot lead to suicide: suicide is the opposite of survival. And so we must not conceal/assimilate/integrate into the would-be dominant culture and political system that despises us. Our survival requires that we alter our environment so that we can live and so that we can hold each other's hands and so that we can kiss each other on the streets, and in the daylight of our existence, without terror and without violent and sometimes fatal reactions from the busybodies of America.

Finally, I need to speak on bisexuality. I do believe that the analogy is interracial or multicultural identity. I do believe that the analogy for bisexuality is a multicultural, multi-ethnic, multiracial world view. Bisexuality follows from such a perspective and leads to it, as well.

Just as there are many men and women in the United States whose parents have given them more than one racial, more than one ethnic identity and cultural heritage to honor; and just as these men and women must deny no given part of themselves except at the risk of self-deception and the insanities that must issue from that; and just as these men and women embody the principle of equality among races and ethnic communities; and just as these men and women falter and anguish and choose and then falter again and then anguish and then choose yet again how they will honor the irreducible complexity of their God-given human being—even so, there are many men and women, especially young men and women, who seek to embrace the complexity of their total, always-changing social and political circumstance.

They seek to embrace our increasingly global complexity on the basis of the heart and on the basis of an honest human body. Not according to ideology. Not according to group pressure. Not according to anybody's concept of "correct."

This is a New Politics of Sexuality. And even as I despair of identity politics—because identity is given and principles of justice/equality/freedom cut across given gender and given racial definitions of being, and because I will call you my brother, I will call you my sister, on the basis of what you *do* for justice, what you *do* for equality, what you *do* for freedom and *not* on the basis of who you are, even so I look with admiration and respect upon the new, bisexual politics of sexuality.

This emerging movement politicizes the so-called middle ground: Bisexuality invalidates either/or formulation, either/or analysis. Bisexuality means I am free and I am as likely to want and to love a woman as I am likely to want and to love a man, and what about that? Isn't that what freedom implies?

If you are free, you are not predictable and you are not controllable. To my mind, that is the keenly positive, politicizing significance of bisexual affirmation:

To insist upon complexity, to insist upon the validity of all of the components of social/sexual complexity, to insist upon the equal validity of all of the components of social/sexual complexity.

This seems to me a unifying, 1990s mandate for revolutionary Americans planning to make it into the twenty-first century on the basis of the heart, on the basis of an honest human body, consecrated to every struggle for justice, every struggle for equality, every struggle for freedom.

FOCUSED STUDY
Randall Kenan (1963-)

Becoming a writer was plan B in Randall Kenan's life. For the first three years of his undergraduate stint at the University of North Carolina at Chapel Hill, Kenan majored in physics. Then, as he puts it, "writing just took hold of me." His writing career began in publishing and brought him back to his birthplace—New York. Born in Brooklyn on March 12, 1963 but raised in Chiquapin, North Carolina, Kenan returned north to take an entry-level position at Random House, a job he acknowledges he got with the help of Toni Morrison. He went on to become an editor at Knopf before beginning his teaching career at Sarah Lawrence, Vassar, and Colombia.

Critics have suggested that Kenan walks a fine line between parodying and honoring the Southern Grotesque tradition. While Kenan agrees, he also characterizes his writing as self-consciously postmodern, a narrative conception of the world in which intersections of time, place, and things result in new ways of writing, shifts of form that engage the reader in unexpected ways. Part of this complexity may originate in Kenan's rich and varied literary inheritance, which includes an eclectic mix of writers like Buchi Emecheta, Flannery O'Conner, Katherine Anne Porter, Joseph Mitchell, James Baldwin, Zora Neale Hurston, and Yukio Mishima, strong influences on his writing and literary philosophies. His work draws as well from Greek tragedy and the Bible.

More recently, Kenan, disturbed by the suggestion among some Black youth that ambition and achievement are antithetical to Black identity, set off on a seven-year journey throughout the United States in search of what it means to be Black and how Black cultural norms have developed and may evolve in the future. His effort produced his latest nonfiction work, Walking on Water: Black American Lives at the Turn of the Twenty-first Century *(1999). Kenan has also written a biography of James Baldwin (1992) as well as collaborated with photographer Norman Mauskopf on a pictorial,* A Time Not Here: The Mississippi Delta, *published in 1994.*

Most of Kenan's stories are set in Tims Creek, North Carolina, a fictional African American community touched by magic, inhabited by the living and the dead, whose lives are complicated by racial and sexual tensions. His first novel, A Visitation of Spirits, *published in 1989, introduced readers to this community. His collection of imaginative and unpredictable short stories,* Let the Dead Bury Their Dead and Other Stories *(1992), builds on this gallery of lovers, losers, dreamers, and misfits. Clarence Pickett develops clairvoyant abilities; Reverend Barden delivers a eulogy over the woman with whom he had been having a secret affair; his interior monologue is anything but holy. The title story, a parody of scholarship complete with footnotes and made-up documents, fuses folklore and the supernatural to trace the town's origins as a runaway slave community.*

The story, "Things of This World; or, Angels Unawares," weaves together themes of racial tension, White supremacy, youth (routine) violence, and death, as an angel of life and death, in the body of a prescient "Chinaman" named Chi, falls into the life of John Edgar Stokes, an aging African American living at the edge of town. Kenan sets up a classical narrative, one that is catholic in its elements: violence and prejudice, new friendship, spirituality and compassion. While his writing affirms the necessity for spiritual good and moral propriety, it also recognizes the untenable intersection of injustice and racism. Like an Old Testament prophet with a big heart and a right to embrace vengeance, Kenan challenges both legal and cultural structures as authority, seemingly acknowledging a higher and more personal authority to be held. Still, the aesthetic impulse of his work is a movement toward greater love.

Kenan is clearly in the tradition of Black writers who conjure complicated lived realities in their fiction and who are unafraid to deal with big ideas. Like Baldwin and Morrison, he is an artist of reckon, a writer of literary but also human consequence. In "The Foundations of the Earth," Kenan's magical deft is put on a loving and traditional 70-year-old Black grandmother, Maggie MacGowan Williams, who is coping not only with the death of her grandson, but also with the belated revelation that he was homosexual. Kenan nestles this story within the everydayness of life in this small rural town, and its people's real and performed concern for morality and godliness. But it is the grandmother's attempt to resurrect her dead grandbaby by inviting his White lover (Gabriel) to visit that, in fact, is the foundation of the earth. Here, these two people who are so socially different (like Chi and Stokes), are called to make a love for each other out of their humanness. Kenan's craft is subtle, and the tension is revealed and then eased with their mutual recognition that "life is hard," a simple comment that, in fact, holds all the moral imperative any person could need to live. This moment between Mrs. Williams and Gabriel gives lovely light to the depth and usefulness of the other conflicts presented in the story.

Randall Kenan is perhaps the next great African American writer, one who is poised to take his place in various national and international canons. His agility and his vision are stunning, leading Terry McMillan to proclaim him a "Black [Gabriel Garcia] Marquez." Places of honor are now being made for the loveliness Kenan has written and is dreaming of.

Lenore L. Brady

Things of This World
;OR, ANGELS UNAWARES

On the sixth of June of that year a man of decidedly Asian aspect appeared in Mr. John Edgar Stokes's front yard, near the crepe myrtle bush he had planted in the southwest corner back in 1967, which now had ornery drooping limbs that Mr. John Edgar had to prune each year. The man lay face down and motionless in the grass, his legs in the gully, feet pointing toward the road. He wore dusty jeans and a bright red-and-blue flannel shirt. His shoes, brogans.

Not until the dog, Shep, continued to make such a ruckus after he had yelled at him for a score of minutes to hush up, figuring it was just somebody passing in the road, did Mr. John Edgar come out of his kitchen where he had just lingered over his eggs, bacon, and coffee, and then washed the dishes, to investigate what the matter could be.

When he first saw the man Mr. John Edgar gave a barely audible *Huh,* almost a sigh as if he had been pushed in the chest by some invisible hand. He stood there staring, contemplating whether or not he did indeed see a Chinaman, or what looked to him to be a Chinaman, from the back, face down in the southwest corner of his yard. Glory be, he thought, might be one of them migrant workers. Mexican. Dead drunk.

As he approached the prone figure it occurred to him—and he was annoyed that it hadn't occurred to him on the first go-round—that the man might well be dead.

He called to the corpse: "Hey. Hey there. What you doing?"

But the figure did not move.

"I say, you there. Feller. Is you quick or dead?"

Mr. John Edgar looked around and scratched his head, wanting to have a witness before proceeding. Not particularly eager to flip the thing over and say "Morning" to the Grim Reaper. He felt a creepy sort of sensation in the back of his neck.

But as he neared the man he heard what amounted to a groan and, sure enough, saw a slight twitching in the shoulder region of the body, and a kind of spasm in the leg.

Mr. John Edgar crouched down and nudged the man. "Scuse me, boy. You ain't sleep, is you?"

The body roused a bit more, now moaning louder, the sound making a little more sense, seemed he was saying: "Fall" or "Fell" or "Falling."

"Son? You all right?" Mr. John Edgar poked him again, and as if in reward the man, with some effort and a great sigh, raised his head.

"Jesus, son." Though the man's eyes were closed, Mr. John Edgar could tell the man was not Mexican. A Chinaman. Just like he had seen on TV. Look at them eyes, he thought. Just as slanted as a cat's. The man had a gash on his forehead and the fresh blood trickled down his face, over some already dried. Blood oozed from his mouth. "Jesus."

Mr. John Edgar lifted the man before he even considered the act, reacting perhaps to the blood, his heart beating now a little faster. He didn't appear to have stumbled down drunk, Mr. John Edgar reasoned. Somebody must have beaten him. He felt a twinge of pity. Poor fool.

Mr. John Edgar lifted him and began toward the house. The man didn't seem to weigh more than a hundred pounds. If that. No more than two feed sacks. Still, carrying him wasn't too bad for an eighty-six-year-old man. Mr. John Edgar carried his groaning load into the kitchen and set him down on a cot he kept in the corner. He wet a rag and wiped the blood from the man's head and mouth. Didn't seem to be serious. But I ain't no doctor, he reminded himself. Might better call Doc Streeter.

At that very second the man's eyes blinked wide open with a start, but his voice was quite calm and soft: "No." His face held a look of such bewilderment and confusion and fear that Mr. John Edgar felt a tug in his belly.

"Boy, who messed you up like this?" Mr. John Edgar's voice came out firm and solid, tinged with a little anger, not at the Chinaman but at the fact that someone had perhaps taken advantage of him.

"Messed? . . . messed me? . . . mess? . . ."

"I say, did some of them white bastards jump you?"

"Jump? White? No. I . . . I fell . . ."

"You *fell?* What the hell you talking bout, boy? How you going to hurt yourself like that just falling down in my yard?"

The man looked around, taking in the kitchen, the oilcloth-covered table, the blue porcelain plates on the wall, the wrought-iron spider on the stove, the worn-through linoleum, the string of brilliant red peppers hanging over the door, Mr. John Edgar Stokes himself. He began to shiver.

"You all right, boy?"

Mr. John Edgar went to get him a blanket. As he put it over him, the man said "Thank you," seeming less frightened but still confused. "Thank you. You are kind."

"How did you get into this condition, son?"

"I'm fine, really. I'm fine. I just need to . . . to . . . a little. Yes. A little . . ."

Mr. John Edgar watched him, expecting him to say more, but the man had closed his eyes. Now Mr. John Edgar felt confident he was just sleeping.

He sat down on the other side of the room, ran his hand over his face. What the *hell?* Should he call Doc Streeter? He'd wait. Figure out what the problem was.

He put on some soup. By the time the kitchen was smelling of chicken and tomato and parsley and salt, the man had aroused himself. He seemed rested but still a bit weak.

Mr. John Edgar brought a cup of the soup to the man. "Bet you're hungry. It's going on eleven o'clock."

"Thank you. You're very kind."

He handed the man a cup of soup and a spoon, but the stranger began to tremble from the effort and the soup to slosh a bit.

"Here. Here." Mr. John Edgar took it and commenced to feed the man, spoonful by spoonful, carefully, grasping at this rare opportunity to nurture, and in some inexpressible way felt pleased each time the Chinaman swallowed and smiled. He finished the whole cup, burped, excused himself, and wiped his mouth with the back of his hand.

"That was good. I was hungry."

Mr. John Edgar walked to the sink. "So. You one of them migrant workers or something, is you? You don't look Mexican at all. How you come to be in Tims Creek? What's your . . . ?" Mr. John Edgar turned around to see the man had dozed off again into—if his face told no lies—what had to be a healing sleep.

"Well, go on and sleep then," Mr. John Edgar muttered under his breath, and went outside to finish propping up his tomato bushes in the garden, heavy laden with plump green tomatoes promising many platefuls of eating, stewed and raw-sliced, in just a few weeks.

Shep sat at the edge of the garden, watchfully, his tongue out, panting in the midmorning sun. Shep, Mr. John Edgar reasoned, was getting old, though he still gallivanted about like a wet-behind-the-ears puppy. His sire, Yoke, had lived to be eighteen. And Yoke's dame, Sam, had lived to the grand old age of twenty, not faltering one step till the day she died. Maybe the same would be true for Shep.

Already the temperature had reached the high eighties and the humidity was thick as moss. Sweat beaded on the tonsure of Mr. John Edgar's head as he stooped and poked and tied, inhaling the sharp odor of the plants.

He had almost forgotten about the man when he heard the toilet flush. Mr. John Edgar figured he had better go and look in on him.

The man sat on the cot, his head in his hands.

"You ain't crying there, is you, feller?"

The man looked up, a smidgen stronger, with a faint smile. "No. Not at all. I'm just still a bit tired." The man had no accent as Mr. John Edgar could place, which puzzled him a bit. But then he had seen Chinamen on TV who spoke English better than the whiteman.

"You from round here?"

"No. Just passing through."

"Where you headed?"

"To see a friend."

"Round here?"

"Yes."

"Would I know—?"

"Oh, how rude of me. My name is—" The man stood as if to shake Mr. John Edgar's hand but crumpled over.

"Now now, why don't you just lay back now? Mr. John Edgar helped him stretch out.

His head back on the pillow, cocked to one side, he said: "Chi. My name is Chi."

"Pleased to meet you, Mr. Chi. Now I should call Doc Streeter. He's the town doctor, you know. I spect you may need a look-see."

"No." The Chinaman said it with a firmness that took Mr. Edgar by surprise.

"No? What you mean, 'No'?"

"No. I'll be fine. It's not serious. I just fell. I know. I've done if before. No need for a doctor. I just need to rest. Trust me."

"Trust you? I don't know a damn thing about you."

"Please. I won't stay long."

Mr. John Edgar furrowed his brow and frowned. He narrowed his eyes like an owl about to say "Who." "Ain't nobody chasing you, is they?"

"No. Nobody's chasing me."

"You wouldn't lie to me, would you?"

"No, Mr. Stokes. I do not lie."

"Well." Mr. John Edgar scratched his head. "All right. For a little while. But if you get worser, I'm calling Doc Streeter. Okay?"

"I won't get worse. I promise."

He walked out of the room and then it struck him: *"Mr. Stokes"*? But when he went back into the kitchen the man was deep in slumber. How did he know my name? But the man might have seen it on the mailbox or on something in the house when he went to the bathroom, Mr. John Edgar reasoned while walking to the porch.

That night Mr. John Edgar made them liver and onions, and cabbage and carrots, with some cornbread and bitter lemonade to drink. Chi seemed to enjoy the food though he didn't say much. Mr. John Edgar, after a while of silence, went off telling tales: about laying tracks for the railroads in his youth, about the biggest snake he had killed, about the price of corn and how he now leased all his land to the biggest landowner in town, Percy Terrell, the son of old evil Malcolm Terrell, against his better judgment. He talked long after they had finished eating. Chi said very little, and by and by Mr. John Edgar came round to the idea of what Chi was going to do.

"Well, you can stay on here tonight if you want. Ain't nobody but me." He said it without a second thought, for he trusted this strange Chinese man for some reason, though he couldn't quite put a finger on why he did.

Chi accepted with a gracious thank-you and Mr. John Edgar showed him the second bathroom and told him he could take a bath if he wanted, and laid out clean towels and some fresh clothes he thought might fit him.

In bed, his false teeth out, rubbing his bare gums together pleasurably, enjoying the wet friction, Mr. John Edgar considered the foolishness of what he had done by inviting a complete stranger into his house: He could sassinate me this very night, cut my head clean off in the middle of the night. But I've lived my life. What would it matter?"

He turned on his side, oddly confident in his instinct, and glided off into sweet slumber.

The next morning he found Chi at the table looking somewhat better, a tad more dignified, upright, though he could tell the small Chinaman had not regained his full mettle. Mr. John Edgar scrambled up some eggs and fried up some bacon, and Chi munched with delight, saying Mr. John Edgar was a good cook.

Chi followed Mr. John Edgar around all that day: in the garden he helped him pick peas, chop collards and cabbage, and pull some of the last sweet corn; he rode with him into town in Mr. John Edgar's 1965 Ford pickup truck to buy some wire and nails and light bulbs; he helped him fix the roof of the pump house; all the while saying little, and Mr. John Edgar, perhaps induced by the Asian man's silence, talked on of his days of courting and sparking and of this gal Cindy and that gal Emma Jo and of that ole Callie Mae Harris's mama, Cleona, who was evil as a wet hen. Or he'd simply sit in silence enjoying the good company of his guest.

That night he roasted a hen, fried some mustard greens, and boiled some of the sweet corn they'd pulled that day and some rice. Again Chi complimented Mr. John Edgar's cooking, asking him where he'd learned to cook so well.

"A man living by himself'll pick up what he needs to, I reckon's all there is to it."

"You never married." Chi put it more as a statement than a question.

"No. Never got round to it."

They sat on the porch afterward, mostly in silence. Mr. John Edgar was now yarned out. After a spell of rocking he asked: "What it like in China?"

"I'm not from China."

"You ain't a Chinaman, then?"

"No."

"Oh." Mr. John Edgar wanted to ask where the hell he *was* from then, but felt somewhat embarrassed, figuring he should know. So they rocked, saying nothing, listening to the twilight noises leavened by the sound of trucks and cars on the highway in the far distance.

The next morning Mr. John Edgar rose at about five and decided to clean his gun. As he moved to put it back in the closet off the parlor, outside the window something caught his eye. Mr. John Edgar stood perplexed: There in the back-yard was Chi. Seemed at first to be doing some queer dance. No. No. Fighting some invisible somebody. No. Dancing. But no, the way he's a-moving . . .

As he watched Chi, with his arms moving like a puppet's, Mr. John Edgar wanted to think him crazy, but something about the look on his face, the reverence with which he moved, with grace, yes, that's what it was, the grace of his move-ments, like a cat, made him think better of it. Looked like a ritual of some kind. Was he casting a spell? Praying? Maybe this was how they prayed where this feller was from. Clutching the gun, Mr. John Edgar stood at the window watching, and presently Chi sat down in the dew-misted grass. Motionless, his legs folded up be-fore him, his head straight ahead toward the sun, his eyes closed.

Well, I'll be damned, Mr. John Edgar thought, half expecting the man to float; and at length, when he didn't, Mr. John Edgar Stokes took his gun back to the parlor.

By the time he got back to the kitchen, there sat Chi at the table, looking pert. He had regained all his dignity. The scar on his forehead was a mere red shadow, his black eyes glistened.

"Good morning, Mr. Stokes."

"Morning there, feller. Like some eggs and ham?"

"Thank you. Please."

Mr. John Edgar went about preparing the meal as he had done for scores of years, humming. He truly wanted to ask what the man had been doing in his backyard facing the morning sun, but felt by turns embarrassed and guilty and prying, as if he had witnessed something private between this foreigner and his Lord. Best not to be nosy. Mind your own business.

They lingered over coffee, Mr. John Edgar ticking off those things he had to do for the day, waiting patiently to hear the man say it was time to go, thinking his hospitality had reached its limit and the polite thing would be for the man to move on, seeing as he was hale and hearty. But at the same time he did enjoy the strange man's company. There was something comforting about it. So he got up to cut the grass, and as he stood at the shed door he heard a truck drive up.

Joe Allen Pearsall got out of his truck and Mr. John Edgar could tell he had bad news by the way he was slumped over in the shoulders, looking at the ground.

"Well, morning to you, Joe Allen. How you been?"

"All right, Mr. John Edgar. How you?"

Mr. John Edgar searched his own mind, trying to beat Joe Allen to the news. He hated surprises. Maybe something had happened to that crazy wife of his. Maybe somebody had died. Who? Zeke Cross? Carl Fletcher? Maggie Williams? Ada Mae . . .

"Mr. John Edgar. Something bad happened."

The old man wanted to say: "Well, I know that." But he said nothing, waiting for Joe Allen to complete his thought. Instead of letting more words drop out of his mouth—must be mighty bad or he woulda just said it—Joe Allen backed to the end of his truck, motioning for Mr. John Edgar to follow. He let the tailgate down.

They stood there for a good minute. Mr. John Edgar just stared, no saliva in his mouth. Not looking a Joe Allen, he asked: "Who done it?"

"Them Terrell boys. Say that he been shitting in their yard and that this morning he was in their cow pasture chasing a heifer. So . . . so . . . I was at the store when they done it."

By the time Chi had come around to the truck, Mr. John Edgar had the dog, Shep, already stiffening, up in his arms, the tongue hanging pendulously; drool, an admixture of blood and froth, leaving a gelatinous pool on the bed of the truck; the head a horrid confusion of tattered bone, flesh, white fluid, and what was left of a grey brain. Blood stained the tan coat.

As Mr. John Edgar carried Shep to the backyard, to where the yard met the garden, Joe Allen turned with questions in his eyes to the strange man at his side standing as perplexed and sad as he.

"Who . . . ?"

"I am Chi."

They stood, and it was obvious that Joe Allen wanted to ask Chi what he was doing there. But they were both distracted by the somber goings-on.

Mr. John Edgar laid Shep down and went into the shed to retrieve a shovel and an old quilt, faded yet still Joseph's coat-like in its patchwork colors.

"Let me do it, Mr. John Edgar." But he seemed neither to hear nor to see Joe Allen as he went about the task of digging a hole wide enough, long enough, deep enough. Chi and Joe Allen, useless pallbearers, watched Mr. John Edgar, who seemed neither to sweat a drop nor strain a muscle, as he went about the duty with a skill that would have made anybody who didn't know better think it his occupation.

Tenderly he swaddled the cooling pup in the quilt and lowered him to his forever bed. When the last shovelful of earth had been patted down, Mr. John Edgar picked up two large stones from a pile at the other end of the garden, stones swallowed by moss, and placed one at Shep's feet and one at his nose. He took a long pause, his breath miraculously even, a barely seen dew of sweat on his brown head, but he didn't seem to grieve or meditate or tremble in anger: he seemed only to wait, peering at the shallow grave, as if expecting the dog to claw out of the earth, brain intact, healed, panting, resurrected.

Presently he said under his breath: "Damn," turned and walked back to the shed, put the shovel down, and went into the house.

Chi and Joe Allen followed him with their eyes. Joe Allen shuffled awkwardly, clearly having no words or actions he felt would suffice. He regarded Chi with only slightly less suspicion than before.

"You from round here?"

"No."

"I didn't think so. Never seen you before. Helping Mr. John Edgar out, is you?"

"Yes. I've been staying with him for a few days."

"Have? Wh—?"

The door slammed with a loud crack and they both pivoted to see Mr. John Edgar, gun in hand, marching toward his truck.

"Oh, Jesus. We got to stop him." Joe Allen ran toward the truck. Chi close behind.

"Mr. John Edgar. Mr. John Edgar! Now you can't just . . . You can't . . ."

But the old man paid Joe Allen no heed, cranking up the truck and backing out, running over a few marigolds to avoid hitting Joe Allen's truck. He shot down the road, pushing the old truck as fast as she would go.

Come on, Joe Allen motioned to Chi. They took off after him. Joe Allen, in his haste, ran over more marigolds.

The Terrell General Store was no more than five miles from Mr. John Edgar Stokes's house, barely within the town limits. He pulled up, the truck lurching to a stop. All three Terrell boys congregated on the front porch of the large warehouse of a store. One called out: "Well, if it ain't John Edgar Stokes. To what do we owe the pleasure." They all laughed.

Their jocular tone changed when Mr. John Edgar got out of his automobile and they could see he was carrying a Smith & Wesson. One Terrell boy whispered to another: "Better get Daddy," and the boy zipped off like a housefly.

Mr. John Edgar, his head held high, barely gave the boys a glance, but it was clear that the half-look equated them in his mind with hog slop. Choking his gun by the neck, he stomped along the side of the store.

By the time the boys ran up to Mr. John Edgar, Joe Allen and Chi had arrived and were among the boys who hollered at him.

The Terrell boys jumped in front of Mr. John Edgar but he did not stop; merely leveled his gun, cocked it, and kept walking. The boys got out of the way. "Crazy old nigger. What's he doing?"

Percy Terrell came bursting out the back door: "John Edgar Stokes. What you doing back here? What you aiming to do with that gun? Deer season is over. Now, John Edgar—"

Mr. John Edgar stopped in front of a hutch of hound dogs. Five dogs in all. Percy's prize coon dogs. Yapping in the confusion.

Joe Allen ran up to him from behind and whispered: "You oughtn't to do this, Mr. John Edgar."

"Nigger, I will kill you," one of the Terrell boys said, fist clenched, trembling, face all red. He took a step forward and Mr. John Edgar raised the gun to the level of the boy's heart.

"John Edgar!" Percy Terrell howled. The boy's eyes twitched with fear, given two seconds to contemplate his mortality. Another Terrell stepped forward and Mr. John Edgar, implacable, pointed the gun toward him; after the boy froze, toward the third; and finally toward Percy Terrell himself. They stood stock-still, less from the reality of the gun than from the look in Mr. John Edgar Stokes's eyes, a curse of loathing and damnation as if from God's own Counsel on Earth.

In a motion approaching nonchalance, Mr. John Edgar reeled to the hound dogs and aimed at the one on the end, the one Percy called Billy.

"Hell, no!"

The bullet went through the chicken wire, pretty and neat, not breaking a strand. The dog didn't make sound the first. He just fell over on his side like a spent toy. Mr. John Edgar got him square in the head. The blood came dripping down.

The youngest Terrell lunged toward him, but Mr. John Edgar just cocked his gun again, shot the ground, cocked it again, and pointed it at the boy. Mr. John Edgar began backing away, shaking his head *no;* but now the look on his face said that any more killing he had to do would be incidental and painless. Another Terrell boy babbled loudly and incoherently, his rage making him the color of raw beef, his arms flailing, yammering a high-pitched patois of hate: "Paw we gotta kill him nigger sombitch killing cocksucker nigger Paw Paw do something."

Terrell shook his head gravely. "You done it now, you ole fart. John Edgar, you a dead man. You'll pay for this, you goddamn fool."

Mr. John Edgar got into his truck unaccosted and drove away, this time obeying the speed limit, followed by a shaken Joe Allen and Chi.

By the time Joe Allen and Chi got out of the truck, Mr. John Edgar had set himself down in his rocker on the front porch and was rocking.

"Now, Mr. John Edgar, you shouldn'ta done that, now. You reckon ole Terrell gone let you get away with that?"

Mr. John Edgar said not a word, answering Joe Allen with the creak of the chair on the floorboards, his gun in his lap.

Joe Allen tried to talk more but it became clear that Mr. John Edgar intended to keep silent. Flustered, Joe Allen went into the house and made a few phone calls. Chi sat with Mr. John Edgar in silence. Joe Allen came back, visibly worried, and just looked at the two of them. "Jesus H. Christ."

"The Builders" (also The Family) screenprint, 1974. Jacob Lawrence/Spike Mafford; Francine Seders Gallery, Ltd.

Elizabeth Catlett, Homage to My Young Black Sisters 1968, red cedar, 68 × 12 × 12 inches. Erwin Gaspin Photography; Neuberger Museum

Faith Ringgold, "Freedom of Speech," 1990. Acrylic on paper, 38 × 45 in. Faith Ringgold, Inc.

Gordon Parks "Bessie Fontenelle and son Richard," 1968, 17 5/8 × 24 3/4. Gordon Parks Photography

Dr. Streeter arrived first. The Reverend Barden came with Ed Phelps. Joe Allen recapped the entire incident, showing himself to be more than a little proud of what ole Mr. John Edgar had done, and smiled broadly at the end. The men all laughed and congratulated Mr. John Edgar in whoops and guffaws and slaps on the shoulder.

"Dog's dead, though." Mr. John Edgar continued to rock in the same rhythm, staring steelily into the front yard.

The men all became grave in countenance, heads bowed. It was Dr. Streeter who finally voiced everyone's unspoken curiosity. Turning to Chi, he scratched his white beard and fidgeted with his glasses in a lordly manner. "And who are you?"

Chi, who was standing now, looked as though he felt at home among this gathering. "My name is Chi. I am a friend."

"I see. You're not from around here, are you? Migrant worker or something?"

"No. Just passing through."

"We ought to hide him," Ed Phelps broke in. "Mr. John Edgar, you ought to hide. Ain't no telling what they'll do."

"Might not be a bad idea." Joe Allen looked worried.

Mr. John Edgar Stokes kept on rocking.

In the distance a siren came screaming. They could all see the sheriff's car zipping toward the house, followed by two other cars.

"Oh, Lord, my Lord." The Right Reverend Hezekiah Barden's face was wet with sweat. "What we gone do now? Terrell don't play, you know."

"You aren't afraid, are you, Reverend?" Dr. Streeter winked at Barden.

"Maybe we should pray?"

"Well,"—Dr. Streeter straightened his tie—"you better pray fast, Hez. Better pray fast."

Sheriff Roy Brinkley parked his car beside the road in front of the yard, the light still blinking on the top. Brinkley, a man of brood-sow girth and a small and jowly head, came rolling across the lawn with Percy Terrell at his right hand. The boys behind.

"Well, well, well." Dr. Streeter stood at the foot of the steps. "To what do we owe this visit from the county's finest?"

"Out of my way, Streeter. I ain't got time for your Yankee foolishness. You know why I'm here."

"Why?" Barden had composed himself, wiped away all the sweat with his Panama hankie. "Looks to me like the two things you're lacking is some white sheets and a cross."

"Now you know it ain't like that, Reverend." Brinkley himself was sweating now; the walk across the lawn had surely been an overexertion.

"Stop all this bullshit." Terrell pointed to Mr. John Edgar. "You all know good and well why we come here. To get him."

"To string him up?" Ed Phelps came down to ground level with Dr. Streeter.

"Yeah." Joe Allen stepped forward too. "Your boys killed his dog, you know. I don't see no sheriff coming for you."

"That was different and you know it." Brinkley wiped his red and sweating face with his bare hand.

"How come?" Ed Phelps shrugged.

"Cause John's dog was trespassing on Terrell's property. They was within their rights to shoot him. John was trespassing and maliciously destroyed property. He shoulda filed a complaint if he felt there was wrong-doing."

"Well, who do I file a complaint with now, you?"

"Shut up, Streeter." Terrell pointed. "This don't concern you."

"I'm not one of your employees, like the sheriff here. I can speak when and where I please."

"Well, talk all you want to. Roy, arrest that nigger and let's go so I don't have to listen to this fancy boy shoot off at the mouth. I got better things to do."

Rankled by what sounded like an order, Sheriff Brinkley advanced between Ed Phelps and Dr. Streeter and put his foot on the first step to the porch.

"Get the hell off my porch." Mr. John Edgar had stopped rocking.

"Now, John. You—" Brinkley took another step and Mr. John Edgar picked up his gun.

"I said get off my porch."

"You can't do this."

"I can and I am. I said get off my porch." He cocked the gun and took aim at Brinkley's belly.

Roy Brinkley trembled with anger, his belly quivering despite the tight brown uniform. "You broke the law, John Edgar Stokes. The law says you got to come with me."

"Well, the Bible say 'an eye for an eye,' don't it, Reverend? An Eye for an Eye and a Tooth for a Tooth. That's the onliest Law I'm studying about. Now get the hell off my porch or they'll have to scrape you off."

Sheriff Brinkley took one step back and almost fell into the Right Reverend Hezekiah Barden. He swung his great girth around and walked back to his squad car.

"Where the hell you going, Roy?" Terrell chased after him. "Arrest him. *Arrest* him, goddamn it. What do I pay . . . what were you elected to do? Goddamn it, arrest him, I say."

The men on the porch all laughed and slapped Mr. John Edgar's back. Mr. John Edgar again commenced to rocking, not smiling with the men.

Voices from the squad car carried to the porch.

"You fat fairy. You a goddamn coward is what you is. Scared of one old nigger with a buncha coons and a shotgun. He ain't gon—"

"Be quiet, Percy. Just hush."

"Scared is all you is. Scared. I gone take my boys and—"

"Hush, Percy." From the porch they heard static. "Luella? This is Sheriff Brinkley. I'm requesting assistance."

"Assistance, my left titty. You just scared. Afeared of a ole nigger."

"Hush, Percy, please! Yeah, at the residence of John Edgar Stokes in Tims Creek . . ."

On the porch the men became silent, looking to one another in puzzlement, looking to Chi in even greater puzzlement, each finding himself questioning the extent of his own courage on what had seemed earlier to have been a routine June day. The white men stood about the sheriff's car in the road; the black men on the porch, a strange Asian man in their midst. Chi said nothing, just looked from one group to another, seeming to drink it all into his Dead Sea-calm black eyes.

"Maybe." The Reverend Barden's face shone once again with sweat. "Maybe you ought to go on with them, John Edgar. Maybe . . ."

Two state patrol cars came down the road, one from each direction. Three tall troopers got out and conferred with Brinkley and Terrell. Two troopers were white, one black. They each had rifles in their hands. After a time they approached the house: the two white patrollers on either side, guns at the ready, the black one in the middle with Brinkley, Terrell, and his boys behind.

Before the steps Brinkley called out in a voice too loud: "In the name of the People of York County, the Governor of the Great State of North Carolina, and the Constitution of these United States of America, John Edgar Stokes, you are under arrest for willful and malicious destruction of property, resisting arrest, and threatening the life of an officer of the law. Now you come on down here and let me take you to the courthouse, why don't you?"

Mr. John Edgar just kept on rocking and rocking, as if the sights and sounds before him were no more than hoot owls and mist in the dark, unworthy of heed. All the men eyed one another tremulously, expecting everything, daring nothing.

"Go get him, son," Brinkley said to the black trooper.

As the black man, his eyes veiled behind smoky sunglasses, walked up the steps, Mr. John Edgar did nothing, outnumbered by two guns trained on his head and heart. The officer of the law took the gun from the old man without a struggle and pulled him forward, and Malcolm Streeter, M.D., was heard to say "Pernicious infamy. O foul and black traitor of fate." But the man placed handcuffs on Mr. John Edgar Stokes just the same, and Brinkley, rocking on his heels in his new-found self-confidence and delight, commenced to recite: "You have the right to remain silent . . ."

"What difference does it make in Terrell County?"

"Now you stay out of this, Streeter. This is the law talking."

"The law? Law? Jim Crow law if you ask me."

"Streeter, if you don't hush up I'll arrest you too."

"Go ahead, and you'll see more lawyers swarming over your precious courthouse than you're already going to see in about an hour. Come on, arrest me."

"Brinkley!" Terrell stepped forward. "Come on. We don't have to stand here and take this shit. Come on." They began to walk away.

"His master's voice," Streeter said through clenched teeth.

Brinkley looked back but Terrell beckoned *come on* from the squad car's open door.

"If you harm one hair on that saintly man's head, I'll have your badge, your career, and your life. You pusillanimous hippopotamus!"

Dr. Streeter's words rang out to no avail as they stuffed Mr. John Edgar Stokes into the back of the sheriff's car. Terrell gloated and waved at the men as he got into the front seat, and began laughing as they drove off.

Word got out in the community in a hurry, and scores of people from all around Tims Creek followed the car containing Mr. John Edgar to Crosstown, and watched, yelling and screaming, as he was processed and spirited away behind steel doors. Though Brinkley's people were besieged by black and white telling them they had committed a heinous sin by putting an eighty-six-year-old man behind bars, the clerks and officers remained tight-mouthed as ordered and would not speak of release. Dr. Streeter and the Right Reverend Barden thundered about human rights and the travesty of justice, and placed phone calls to the state capitol and beyond well into the early morning. Early the next day Mr. John Edgar was released on five hundred dollars' bail, which Dr. Streeter promptly posted. Reporters from the York County *Cryer* and the Raleigh *News and Observer* and the Wilmington *Star* asked him questions; photographers snapped his picture; women hugged his neck and men shook his hand. He said little. Getting into the backseat of Dr. Streeter's car, he looked up to see Chi. He asked him how he was doing.

"Fine, sir. I'm just fine. How are you holding up?"

"I do all right. For a old man."

Back home he sat in his parlor, contemplating the room, looking for pictures of family, knowing there were only a few: his mother, his father, both born slaves, dead for decades; his old sweetheart Lena Thompson, who he felt he would have married had he not waited so damn long; his nephew Joshua in Philadelphia; Joshua's two children. A daguerreotype, a large print, some snapshots, a few Polaroids, elementary-school pictures. Not much. Not enough to fill one of those good-size albums they sell at the department stores. All else was dull: mementos of affectless happenings he could barely remember; gifts bearing little significance. Mr. John Edgar Stokes sat in his parlor on the day after his release from the county jail, troubled yet transformed, studying not just the present but the eighty-six years that had led him there. Amazed to now be awaiting a hearing, a trial. It had come up all of a sudden like a summer storm, but unlike a thundercloud this wouldn't leave things pretty much the way it found them.

Folk came by to talk, but he had very little to say to them. They left feeling a vague unease, not able to articulate their disquiet. Thinking, in the end, that that fine old gentleman, who lived so long alone with his good dog, cooking, working in his garden, who had stopped farming some ten-odd years ago, had finally come upon the penultimate trouble of his life in the form of senility. Poor old gent.

He didn't have to cook, seeing as so many womenfolk in the community had brought over pies, collard greens, spareribs, fried chicken, potato salad. He and Chi ate in unperturbed quiet, and afterward they returned to the dimly lit parlor and sat in quietude.

By and by Mr. John Edgar looked up to Chi and said: "You know, I hated to kill that dog. I surely did. But I had to. Just had to." He paused, looking out into the June-warm blackness of evening. "Seems like up to now I been sitting right here in this chair waiting, waiting. But you know what?"

"No, sir."

"It sho was worth it. Worth it to see the look on that ole Terrell's face. I stood up to that cocksucker. Yes sir."

He smiled. Chi inclined his head thoughtfully and nodded with a strange look of understanding, complicity, and warmth.

"You know what else?"

"No. What, Mr. Stokes?"

"I wisht I could die. Die right now to spite his sorry ass. Yes sir. To show he ain't got no power over death. Yes sir. I could die right now—content."

"Could you?" Chi's black eyes seemed to shimmer in the lamp's faint light.

"Sho nuff could. With pleasure." He grinned.

When they found Mr. John Edgar Stokes he was sitting upright in a chair by his kitchen sink, his back straight as a swamp reed, not slouching one whit, clutching a large wooden spoon; his eyes stretched wide with astonishment, his mouth a gaping O—though his false teeth had held admirably to the gums—as if his last sight had been something more than truly remarkable, something wonderful and awesome to behold.

They found no sign of the man called Chi.

The Foundations of the Earth

I

Of course they didn't pay it any mind at first: just a tractor—one of the most natural things in the world to see in a field—kicking dust up into the afternoon sky and slowly toddling off the road into a soybean field. And fields surrounded Mrs. Maggie MacGowan Williams's house, giving the impression that her lawn stretched on and on until it dropped off into the woods far by the way. Sometimes she was certain she could actually see the earth's curve—not merely the bend of the small hill on which her house sat but the great slope of the sphere, the way scientists explained it in books, a monstrous globe floating in a cold nothingness. She would sometimes sit by herself on the patio late of an evening, in the same chair she was sitting in now, sip her Coca-Cola, and think about how big the earth must be to seem flat to the eye.

She wished she were alone now. It was Sunday.

"Now I wonder what that man is doing with a tractor out there today?"

They sat on Maggie's patio, reclined in that after-Sunday-dinner way—Maggie; the Right Reverend Hezekiah Barden, round and pompous as ever; Henrietta Fuchee, the prim and priggish music teacher and president of the First Baptist

Church Auxiliary Council; Emma Lewis, Maggie's sometimes housekeeper; and
Gabriel, Mrs. Maggie Williams's young, white, special guest—all looking out
lazily into the early summer, watching the sun begin its slow downward arc, feeling the baked ham and the candied sweet potatoes and the fried chicken with the
collard greens and green beans and beets settle in their bellies, talking shallow
and pleasant talk, and sipping their Coca-Colas and bitter lemonade.

"Don't they realize it's Sunday?" Reverend Barden leaned back in his chair
and tugged at his suspenders thoughtfully, eyeing the tractor as it turned into another row. He reached for a sweating glass of lemonade, his red bow tie afire in
the penultimate beams of the day.

"I . . . I don't understand. What's wrong?" Maggie could see her other guests
watching Gabriel intently, trying to discern why on earth he was present at Maggie MacGowan Williams's table.

"What you mean, what's wrong?" The Reverend Barden leaned forward and
narrowed his eyes at the young man. "What's wrong is: it's Sunday."

"So? I don't . . ." Gabriel himself now looked embarrassed, glancing to Maggie, who wanted to save him but could not.

"'So?' 'So?'" Leaning toward Gabriel and narrowing his eyes, Barden asked:
"You're not from a church-going family, are you?"

"Well, no. Today was my first time in . . . Oh, probably ten years."

"Uh-huh." Barden corrected his posture, as if to say he pitied Gabriel's being
an infidel but had the patience to instruct him. "Now you see, the Lord has declared Sunday as His day. It's holy. 'Six days shalt thou labor and do all thy work:
but the seventh day is the sabbath of the Lord thy God: in it thou shalt not do
any work, thou, nor thy son, nor thy daughter, thy manservant, nor thy maidser-
vant, nor thy cattle, nor thy stranger that is within thy gates: for in six days the
Lord made heaven and earth, the sea, and all that in them is, and rested the seventh day: wherefore, the Lord blessed the sabbath day, and hallowed it.' Exodus.
Chapter twenty, verses nine and ten."

"Amen." Henrietta closed her eyes and rocked.

"Hez." Maggie inclined her head a bit to entreat the good Reverend to desist.
He gave her an understanding smile, which made her cringe slightly, fearing her
gesture might have been mistaken for a sign of intimacy.

"But, Miss Henrietta—" Emma Lewis tapped the tabletop, like a judge in
court, changing the subject. "Like I was saying, I believe that Rick on *The Winds
of Hope* is going to marry that gal before she gets too big with child, don't you?"
Though Emma kept house for Maggie Williams, to Maggie she seemed more like
a sister who came three days a week, more to visit than to clean.

"Now go on away from here, Emma." Henrietta did not look up from her
empty cake plate, her glasses hanging on top of her sagging breasts from a silver
chain. "Talking about that worldly foolishness on TV. You know I don't pay that
mess any attention." She did not want the Reverend to know that she secretly
watched afternoon soap operas, just like Emma and all the other women in the congregation. Usually she gossiped to beat the band about this rich heifer and that

handsome hunk whenever she found a fellow TV-gazer. Buck-toothed hypocrite, Maggie thought. She knew the truth: Henrietta, herself a widow now on ten years, was sweet on the widower minister, who in turn, alas, had his eye on Maggie.

"Now, Miss Henrietta, we was talking about it t' other day. Don't you think he's apt to marry her soon?" Emma's tone was insistent.

"I *don't know*, Emma." Visibly agitated, Henrietta donned her glasses and looked into the fields. "I wonder who that is anyhow?"

Annoyed by Henrietta's rebuff, Emma stood and began to collect the few remaining dishes. Her purple-and-yellow floral print dress hugged her ample hips. "It's that ole Morton Henry that Miss Maggie leases that piece of land to." She walked toward the door, into the house. "He ain't no God-fearing man."

"Well, that's plain to see." The Reverend glanced over to Maggie. She shrugged.

They are ignoring Gabriel, Maggie thought. She had invited them to dinner after church services thinking it would be pleasant for Gabriel to meet other people in Tims Creek. But generally they chose not to see him, and when they did it was with ill-concealed scorn or petty curiosity or annoyance. At first the conversation seemed civil enough. But the ice was never truly broken, questions still buzzed around the talk like horseflies, Maggie could tell. "Where you from?" Henrietta had asked. "What's your line of work?" Barden had asked. While Gabriel sat there with a look on his face somewhere between peace and pain. But Maggie refused to believe she had made a mistake. At this stage of her life she depended on no one for anything, and she was certainly not dependent on the approval of these self-important fools.

She had been steeled by anxiety when she picked Gabriel up at the airport that Friday night. But as she caught sight of him stepping from the jet and greeted him, asking about the weather in Boston; and after she had ushered him to her car and watched him slide in, seeming quite at home; though it still felt awkward, she thought: I'm doing the right thing.

II

"Well, thank you for inviting me, Mrs. Williams. But I don't understand . . . . Is something wrong?"

"*Wrong?* No, nothing's wrong, Gabriel. I just thought it'd be good to see you. Sit and talk to you. We didn't have much time at the funeral."

"Gee . . . I—"

"You don't want to make an old woman sad, now do you?"

"Well, Mrs. Williams, if you put it like that, how can I refuse?"

"Weekend after next then?"

There was a pause in which she heard muted voices in the wire.

"Okay."

After she hung up the phone and sat down in her favorite chair in the den, she heaved a momentous sigh. Well, she had done it. At last. The weight of uncertainty would be lifted. She could confront him face to face. She wanted to know about her grandboy, and Gabriel was the only one who could tell her what she wanted to know. It was that simple. Surely, he realized what this invitation meant. She leaned back looking out the big picture window onto the tops of the brilliantly blooming crepe myrtle trees in the yard, listening to the grandfather clock mark the time.

III

Her Grandson's funeral had been six months ago, but it seemed much longer. Perhaps the fact that Edward had been gone away from home so long without seeing her, combined with the weeks and days and hours and minutes she had spent trying not to think about him and all the craziness that had surrounded his death, somehow lengthened the time.

At first she chose to ignore it, the strange and bitter sadness that seemed to have overtaken her every waking moment. She went about her daily life as she had done for thirty-odd years, overseeing her stores, her land, her money; buying groceries, paying bills, shopping, shopping; going to church and talking to her few good living friends and the few silly fools she was obliged to suffer. But all day, dusk to dawn, and especially at night, she had what the field-workers called "a monkey on your back," when the sun beats down so hot it makes you delirious; but her monkey chilled and angered her, born not of the sun but of a profound loneliness, an oppressive emptiness, a stabbing guilt. Sometimes she even wished she were a drinking woman.

The depression had come with the death of Edward, though its roots reached farther back, to the time he seemed to have vanished. There had been so many years of asking other members of the family: Have you heard from him? Have you seen him? So many years of only a Christmas card or birthday card a few days early, or a cryptic, taciturn phone call on Sunday mornings, and then no calls at all. At some point she realized she had no idea where he was or how to get in touch with him. Mysteriously, he would drop a line to his half-sister, Clarissa, or drop a card without a return address. He was gone. Inevitably, she had to ask: Had she done something evil to the boy to drive him away? Had she tried too hard to make sure he became nothing like his father and grandfather? I was as good a mother as a woman can claim to be, she thought: from the cradle on he had all the material things he needed, and he certainly didn't want for attention, for care; and I trained him proper, he was a well-mannered and upright young fellow when he left here for college. Oh, I was proud of that boy, winning a scholarship to Boston University. Tall, handsome like his granddad. He'd make somebody a good . . .

So she continued picking out culprits: school, the cold North, strange people, strange ideas. But now in her crystalline hindsight she could lay no blame on anyone but Edward. And the more she remembered battles with the mumps and the measles and long division and taunts from his schoolmates, the more she became aware of her true anger. He owes me respect, damn it. The least he can do is keep in touch. Is that so much to ask?

But before she could make up her mind to find him and confront him with her fury, before she could cuss him out good and call him an ungrateful, no-account bastard just like his father, a truck would have the heartless audacity to skid into her grandchild's car one rainy night in Springfield and end his life at twenty-seven, taking that opportunity away from her forever. When they told her of his death she cursed her weakness. Begging God for another chance. But instead He gave her something she had never imagined.

Clarissa was the one to finally tell her. "Grandma," she had said, "Edward's been living with another man all these years."

"So?"

"No, Grandma. Like man and wife."

Maggie had never before been so paralyzed by news. One question answered, only to be replaced by a multitude. Gabriel had come with the body, like an interpreter for the dead. They had been living together in Boston, where Edward worked in a bookstore. He came, head bowed, rheumy-eyed, exhausted. He gave her no explanation; nor had she asked him for any, for he displayed the truth in his vacant and humble glare and had nothing to offer but the penurious tribute of his trembling hands. Which was more than she wanted.

In her world she had been expected to be tearless, patient, comforting to other members of the family; folk were meant to sit back and say, "Lord, ain't she taking it well. I don't think I could be so calm if my grandboy had've died so young." Magisterially she had done her duty; she had taken it all in stride. But her world began to hopelessly unravel that summer night at the wake in the Raymond Brown Funeral Home, among the many somber-bright flower arrangements, the fluorescent lights, and the gleaming bronze casket, when Gabriel tried to tell her how sorry he was . . . How dare he? This pathetic, stumbling, poor trashy white boy, to throw his sinful lust for her grandbaby in her face, as if to bury a grandchild weren't bad enough. Now this abomination had to be flaunted.—Sorry, indeed! The nerve! Who the hell did he think he was to parade their shame about?

Her anger was burning so intensely that she knew if she didn't get out she would tear his heart from his chest, his eyes from their sockets, his testicles from their sac. With great haste she took her leave, brushing off the funeral director and her brother's wives and husband's brothers—they all probably thinking her overcome with grief rather than anger—and had Clarissa drive her home. When she got to the house she filled a tub with water as hot as she could stand it and a handful of bath oil beads, and slipped in, praying her hatred would mingle with the mist and evaporate, leaving her at least sane.

Next, sleep. Healing sleep, soothing sleep, sleep to make the world go away, sleep like death. Her mama had told her that sleep was the best medicine God ever made. When things get too rough—go to bed. Her family had been known as the family that retreated to bed. Ruined crop? No money? Get some shut-eye. Maybe it'll all be better in the morning. Can't be worse. Maggie didn't give a damn where Gabriel was to sleep that night; someone else would deal with it. She didn't care about all the people who would come to the house after the wake to the Sitting Up, talking, eating, drinking, watching over the still body till sunrise; they could take care of themselves.

The people came; but Maggie slept. From deeps under deeps of slumber she sensed her granddaughter stick her head in the door and whisper, asking Maggie if she wanted something to eat. Maggie didn't stir. She slept. And in her sleep she dreamed.

She dreamed she was Job sitting on his dung heap, dressed in sackcloth and ashes, her body covered with boils, scratching with a stick, sending away Eliphaz and Bildad and Zophar and Elihu, who came to counsel her, and above her the sky boiled and churned and the air roared, and she matched it, railing against God, against her life—*Why? Why? Why did you kill him, you heartless old fiend? Why make me live to see him die? What earthly purpose could you have in such a wicked deed? You are God, but you are not good. Speak to me, damn it. Why? Why? Why?* Hurricanes whipped and thunder ripped through a sky streaked by lightning, and she was lifted up, spinning, spinning, and Edward floated before her in the rushing air and quickly turned around into the comforting arms of Gabriel, winged, who clutched her grandboy to his bosom and soared away, out of the storm. Maggie screamed and the winds grew stronger, and a voice, gentle and sweet, not thunderous as she expected, spoke to her from the whirlwind: *Who is this that darkeneth counsel by words without knowledge? Gird up now thy loins like a man; for I will demand of thee, and answer thou me. Where wast thou when I laid the foundations of the earth? Declare if thou hast understanding . . . .* The voice spoke of the myriad creations of the universe, the stupendous glory of the Earth and its inhabitants. But Maggie was not deterred in the face of the maelstrom, saying: *Answer me, damn you: Why?,* and the winds began to taper off and finally halted, and Maggie was alone, standing on water. A fish, what appeared to be a mackerel, stuck its head through the surface and said: *Kind woman, be not aggrieved and put your anger away. Your arrogance has clouded your good mind. Who asked you to love? Who asked you to hate?* The fish dipped down with a plip and gradually Maggie too began to slip down into the water, down, down, down, sinking, below depths of reason and love, down into the dark unknown of her own mind, down, down, down.

Maggie MacGowan Williams woke the next morning to the harsh chatter of a bluejay chasing a mockingbird just outside her window, a racket that caused her to open her eyes quickly to blinding sunlight. Squinting, she looked about the room, seeing the chest of drawers that had once belonged to her mother and her mother's mother before that, the chairs, the photographs on the wall, the television, the rug thickly soft, the closet door slightly ajar, the bureau, the mirror atop the bureau, and herself in the mirror, all of it bright in the crisp morning light. She saw herself looking, if not refreshed, calmed, and within her the rage had gone, replaced by a numb humility and a plethora of questions. Questions. Questions. Questions.

Inwardly she had felt beatific that day of the funeral, ashamed at her anger of the day before. She greeted folk gently, softly, with a smile, her tones honey-flavored but solemn, and she reassumed the mantle of one-who-comforts-more-than-needing-comfort.

The immediate family had gathered at Maggie's house—Edward's father, Tom, Jr.; Tom, Jr.'s wife, Lucille; the grandbaby, Paul (Edward's brother); Clarissa. Raymond Brown's long black limousine took them from the front door of Maggie's house to the church, where the yard was crammed with people in their greys and navy blues, dark browns, and deep, deep burgundies. In her new humility she mused: When, oh when will we learn that death is not so somber, not something to mourn so much as celebrate? We should wear fire reds, sun oranges, hello greens, ocean-deep blues, and dazzling, welcome-home whites. She herself wore a bright dress of saffron and a blue scarf. She thought Edward would have liked it.

The family lined up and Gabriel approached her. As he stood before her—raven-haired, pink-skinned, abject, eyes bloodshot—she experienced a bevy of conflicting emotions: disgust, grief, anger, tenderness, fear, weariness, pity. Nevertheless she *had* to be civil, *had* to make a leap of faith and of understanding. Somehow she felt it had been asked of her. And though there were still so many questions, so much to sort out, for now she would mime patience, pretend to be accepting, feign peace. Time would unravel the rest.

She reached out, taking both his hands into her own, and said, the way she would to an old friend: "How have you been?"

IV

"But now, Miss Maggie . . ."

She sometimes imagined the good Reverend Barden as a toad-frog or an impotent bull. His rantings and ravings bored her, and his clumsy advances repelled her; and when he tried to impress her with his holiness and his goodness, well . . .

". . . that man should now better than to be plowing on a Sunday. Sunday! Why, the Lord said . . ."

"Reverend, I know what the Lord said. And I'm sure Morton Henry knows what the Lord said. But I am not the Lord, Reverend, and if Morton Henry wants to plow the west field on Sunday afternoon, well, it's his soul, not mine."

"But, Maggie. Miss Maggie. It's—"

"Well,"—Henrietta Fuchee sat perched to interject her five cents into the debate—"but, Maggie. It's your land! Now, Reverend, doesn't it say somewhere in Exodus that a man, or a woman in this case, a woman is responsible for the deeds of misdeeds of someone in his or her employ, especially on her property?"

"But he's not an emplo—"

"Well,"—Barden scratched his head—"I think I know what you're talking about, Henrietta. It may be in Deuteronomy . . . or Leviticus . . . part of the Mosaic Law, which . . ."

Maggie cast a quick glance at Gabriel. He seemed to be interested in and entertained by this contest of moral superiority. There was certainly something about his face . . . but she could not stare. He looked so *normal* . . .

"Well, I don't think you should stand for it, Maggie."

"Henrietta? What do you . . . ? Look, if you want him to stop, *you* go tell him what the Lord said. I—"

The Right Reverend Hezekiah Barden stood, hiking his pants up to his belly. "Well, *I* will. A man's soul is a valuable thing. And I can't risk your own soul being tainted by the actions of one of your sharecroppers."

"My soul? Sharecropper—he's not a sharecropper. He leases that land. I—wait! . . . Hezekiah! . . . This doesn't . . ."

But Barden had stepped off the patio onto the lawn and was headed toward the field, marching forth like old Nathan on his way to confront King David.

"Wait, Reverend." Henrietta hopped up, slinging her black pocketbook over her left shoulder. "Well, Maggie?" She peered at Maggie defiantly, as if to ask: *Where do you stand?*

"Now, Henrietta, I—"

Henrietta pivoted, her moral righteousness jagged and sharp as a shard of glass. "Somebody has to stand up for right!" She tromped off after Barden.

Giggling, Emma picked up the empty glasses. "I don't think ole Morton Henry gone be too happy to be preached at this afternoon."

Maggie looked from Emma to Gabriel in bewilderment, at once annoyed and amused. All three began to laugh out loud. As Emma got to the door she turned to Maggie. "Hon, you better go see that they don't get into no fistfight, don't you think? You know that Reverend don't know when to be quiet." She looked to Gabriel and nodded knowingly. "You better go with her, son," and was gone into the house; her molasses-thick laughter sweetening the air.

Reluctantly Maggie stood, looking at the two figures—Henrietta had caught up with Barden—a tiny cloud of dust rising from their feet. "Come on, Gabe. Looks like we have to go referee."

Gabriel walked beside her, a broad smile on his face. Maggie thought of her grandson being attracted to this tall white man. She tried to see them together and couldn't. At that moment she understood that she was being called on to re-align her thinking about men and women, and men and men, and even women and women. Together . . . the way Adam and Eve were meant to be together.

V

Initially she found it difficult to ask the questions she wanted to ask. Almost impossible.

They got along well on Saturday. She took him out to dinner; they went shopping. All the while she tried with all her might to convince herself that she felt comfortable with this white man, with this homosexual, with this man who had slept with her grandboy. Yet he managed to impress her with his easygoing manner and openness and humor.

"Mrs. W." He had given her a *nickname,* of all things. No one had given her a nickname since . . . "Mrs. W., you sure you don't want to try on some swimsuits?"

She laughed at his kind-hearted jokes, seeing, oddly enough, something about him very like Edward; but then that thought would make her sad and confused.

Finally that night over coffee at the kitchen table she began to ask what they had both gingerly avoided.

"Why didn't he just tell me?"

"He was afraid, Mrs. W. It's just that simple."

"Of what?"

"That you might disown him. That you might stop . . . well, you know, loving him, I guess."

"Does your family know?"

"Yes."

"How do they take it?"

"My mom's fine. She's great. Really. She and Edward got along swell. My dad. Well, he'll be okay for a while, but every now and again we'll have these talks, you know, about cures and stuff and sometimes it just gets heated. I guess it'll just take a little more time with him."

"But don't you *want* to be normal?"

"Mrs. W., I *am*. Normal."

"I see."

They went to bed at one-thirty that morning. As Maggie buttoned up her nightgown, Gabriel's answers whizzed about her brain; but they brought along more damnable questions and Maggie went to bed feeling betrayal and disbelief and revulsion and anger.

In church that next morning with Gabriel, she began to doubt the wisdom of having asked him to come. As he sat beside her in the pew, as the Reverend Barden sermonized on Jezebel and Ahab, as the congregation unsuccessfully tried to disguise their curiosity—("What is that white boy doing here with Maggie Williams? Who is he? Where he come from?")—she wanted Gabriel to go ahead and tell her what to think: *We're perverts* or *You're wrong-headed, your church has poisoned your mind against your own grandson; if he had come out to you, you would have rejected him. Wouldn't you?* Would she have?

Barden's sermon droned on and on that morning; the choir sang; after the service people politely and gently shook Gabriel and Maggie's hands and then stood off to the side, whispering, clearly perplexed.

On the drive back home, as if out of the blue, she asked him: "Is it hard?"

"Ma'am?"

"Being who you are? What you are?"

He looked over at her, and she could not meet his gaze with the same intensity that had gone into her question. "Being gay?"

"Yes."

"Well, I have no choice."

"So I understand. But is it hard?"

"Edward and I used to get into arguments about that, Mrs. W." His tone altered a bit. He spoke more softly, gently, the way a widow speaks of her dead husband. Or, indeed, the way a widower speaks of his dead husband. "He used to say it was harder being black in this country than gay. Gays can always pass for straight; but blacks can't always pass for white. And most can never pass."

"And what do you think now?"

"Mrs. W., I think *life* is hard, you know?"

"Yes. I know."

VI

Death had first introduced itself to Maggie when she was a child. Her grandfather and grandmother both died before she was five; her father died when she was nine; her mother when she was twenty-five; over the years all her brothers except one. Her husband ten years ago. Her first memories of death: watching the women wash a cold body: the look of brown skin darkening, hardening: the corpse laid out on a cooling board, wrapped in a winding-cloth, before interment: fear of ghosts, bodyless souls: troubled sleep. So much had changed in seventy years; now there were embalming, funeral homes, morticians, insurance policies, bronze caskets, a bureaucratic wall between deceased and bereaved. Among the many things she regretted about Edward's death was not being able to touch his body. It made his death less real. But so much about the world seemed unreal to her these dark, dismal, and gloomy days. Now the flat earth was said to be round and bumblebees were not supposed to fly.

What was supposed to be and what truly was. Maggie learned these things from magazines and television and books, she loved to read. From her first week in that small schoolhouse with Miss Clara Oxendine, she had wanted to be a teacher. School: the scratchy chalkboard, the dusty-smelling textbooks, labyrinthine grammar and spelling and arithmetic, geography, reading out loud, giving confidence to the boy who would never learn to read well, correcting addition and subtraction problems, the taste and the scent of the schoolroom, the heat of the potbellied stove in January. She liked that small world; for her it was large. Yet how could she pay for enough education to become a teacher? Her mother would smile, encouragingly, when young Maggie would ask her, not looking up from her sewing, and merely say: "We'll find a way."

However, when she was fourteen she met a man named Thomas Williams, he sixteen going on thirty-nine. Infatuation replaced her dreams and murmured to her in languages she had never heard before, whispered to her another tale: *You will be a merchant's wife.*

Thomas Williams would come a-courting on Sunday evenings for two years, come driving his father's red Ford truck, stepping out with his biscuit-shined shoes, his one good Sunday suit, his hat cocked at an impertinent angle, and a smile that would make cold butter drip. But his true power lay in his tongue. He would spin yarns and tell tales that would make the oldest storyteller slap his knee and declare: "Hot damn! Can't that boy lie!" He could talk a possum out of a tree. He spoke to Maggie about his dream of opening his own store, a dry-goods store, and then maybe two or three or four. An audacious dream for a seventeen-year-old black boy, son of a farmer in 1963—and he promised, oh, how he promised, to keep Maggie by his side through it all.

Thinking back, on the other side of time and dreams, where fantasies and wishing had been realized, where she sat rich and alone, Maggie wondered what Thomas Williams could possibly have seen in that plain brown girl. Himself the son of a farmer with his own land, ten sons and two daughters, all married and doing well. There she was, poorer than a skinned rabbit, and not that pretty. Was he looking for a woman who would not flinch at hard work?

Somehow, borrowing from his father, from his brothers, working two, three jobs at the shipyards, in the fields, with Maggie taking in sewing and laundry, cleaning houses, saving, saving, saving, they opened their store; and were married. Days, weeks, years of days, weeks of days, weeks of inventory and cleaning and waiting on people and watching over the dry-goods store, which became a hardware store in the sixties while the one store became two. They were prosperous; they were respected; they owned property. At seventy she now wanted for nothing. Long gone was the dream of a schoolhouse and little children who skinned their knees and the teaching of the ABCs. Some days she imagined she had two lives and she preferred the original dream to the flesh-and-blood reality.

Now, at least, she no longer had to fight bitterly with her pompous, self-satisfied, driven, blaspheming husband, who worked seven days a week, sixteen hours a day, money-grubbing and mean though—outwardly—flamboyantly generous; a man who lost interest in her bed after her first and only son, Thomas, Jr., arrived broken in heart, spirit, and brain upon delivery; a son whose only true achievement in life was to illegitimately produce Edward by some equally brainless waif of a girl, now long vanished; a son who practically thrust the few-week-old infant into Maggie's arms, then flew off to a life of waste, sloth, petty crime, and finally a menial job in one of her stores and an ignoble marriage to a woman who could not conceal her greedy wish for Maggie to die.

Her life now was life that no longer had bite or spit or fire. She no longer worked. She no longer had to worry about Thomas's philandering and what pretty young thing he was messing with now. She no longer had the little boy whom Providence seemed to have sent her to maintain her sanity, to moor her to the Earth, and to give her vast energies focus.

In a world not real, is there truly guilt in willing reality to cohere through the life of another? Is that such a great sin? Maggie had turned to the boy—young, brown, handsome—to hold on to the world itself. She now saw that clearly. How did it happen? The mental slipping and sliding that allowed her to meld and mess and confuse her life with his, his rights with her wants, his life with her wish? He would not be like his father or his grandfather; he would rise up, go to school, be strong, be honest, upright. He would be; she would be . . . a feat of legerdemain; a sorcery of vicariousness in which his victory was her victory. He was her champion. Her hope.

Now he was gone. And now she had to come to terms with this news of his being "gay," as the world called what she had been taught was an unholy abomination. Slowly it all came together in her mind's eye: Edward.

He should have known better. I should have known better. I must learn better.

VII

They stood there at the end of the row, all of them waiting for the tractor to arrive and for the Reverend Hezekiah Barden to save the soul of Morton Henry.

Morton say them standing there from his mount atop the green John Deere as it bounced across the broken soil. Maggie could make out the expression on his face: confusion. Three blacks and a white man out in the fields to see him. Did his house burn down? His wife die? The President declare war on Russia?

A big, red-haired, red-faced man, his face has so many freckles he appeared splotched. He had a big chew of tobacco in his left jaw and he spat out the brown juice as he came up the edge of the row and put the clutch in neutral.

"How you all today? Miss Maggie?"

"Hey, Morton."

Barden started right up, thumbs in his suspenders, and reared back on his heels. "Now I spect you're a God-fearing man?"

"Beg pardon?"

"I even spect you go to church from time to time?"

"Church? Miss Maggie, I—"

The Reverend held up his hand. "And I warrant you that your preacher—where *do* you go to church, son?"

"I go to—wait a minute. What's going on here? Miss Maggie—"

Henrietta piped up. "It's Sunday! You ain't supposed to be working and plowing fields on a Sunday!"

Morton Henry looked over to Maggie, who stood there in the bright sun, then to Gabriel, as if to beg him to speak, make some sense of this curious event. He scratched his head. "You mean to tell me you all come out here to tell me I ain't suppose to plow this here field."

"Not on Sunday you ain't. It's the Lord's Day."

"'The Lord's Day'?" Morton Henry was visibly amused. He tongued at the wad of tobacco in his jaw. "The Lord's Day." He chuckled out loud.

"Now it ain't no laughing matter, young man." The Reverend's voice took on a dark tone.

Morton seemed to be trying to figure out who Gabriel was. He spat. "Well, I tell you, Reverend. If the Lord wants to come plow these fields I'd be happy to let him."

"You . . ." Henrietta stomped her foot, causing dust to rise. "You can't talk about the Lord like that. You're using His name in vain."

"I'll talk about Him any way I please to." Morton Henry's face became redder by the minute. "I got two jobs, five head of children, and a sick wife, and the Lord don't seem too worried about that. I spect I ain't gone worry too much about plowing this here field on His day none either."

"Young man, you can't—"

Morton Henry looked to Maggie. "Now, Miss Maggie, this is your land, and if you don't want me to plow it, I'll give you back your lease and you can pay me my money and find somebody else to tend this here field!"

Everybody looked at Maggie. How does this look, she couldn't help thinking, a black woman defending a white man against a black minister? Why the *hell* am I here having to do this? she fumed. Childish, hypocritical idiots and fools. Time is just slipping, slipping away and all they have to do is fuss and bother about other folk's business while their own houses are burning down. God save their souls. She wanted to yell this, to cuss them out and stomp away and leave them to their ignorance. But in the end, what good would it do?

She took a deep breath. "Morton Henry. You do what you got to do. Just like the rest of us."

Morton Henry bowed his head to Maggie, "Ma'am," turned to the others with a gloating grin, "Scuse me," put his gear in first, and turned down the next row.

"Well—"

Barden began to speak but Maggie just turned, not listening, not wanting to hear, thinking: When, Lord, oh when will we learn? Will we ever? *Respect*, she thought. Oh how complicated.

They followed Maggie, heading back to the house, Gabriel beside her, tall and silent, the afternoon sunrays romping in this black hair. How curious the world had become that she would be asking a white man to exonerate her in the eyes of her own grandson; how strange that at seventy, when she had all the laws and rules down pat, she would have to begin again, to learn. But all this stuff and bother would have to come later, for now she felt so, so tired, what with the weekend's activities weighing on her three-score-and-ten-year-old bones and joints; and she wished it were sunset, and she alone on her patio, contemplating the roundness and flatness of the earth, and slipping softly and safely into sleep.

An Interview with Randall Kenan

Charles H. Rowell

This interview was conducted by telephone between Charlottesville, Virginia, and Oxford, Mississippi, on Wednesday, August 20, 1997.

ROWELL: What is a writing day like for you? What is the beginning of a work day for you as a writer? How does it proceed and end? What are your writing habits?

KENAN: My work days are never even. I think every project builds up its own momentum, and a lot of that inertia depends upon what you're working on at the time. If I'm working on a longer piece, I usually start out very slowly. I even dread getting started, and at first the process may be very painstaking. I might spend all day and just work on one paragraph, one page, and I might throw that out in the end. I might write ten pages and realize I can't use them. Generally, I find the longer I work on a project, the further, the deeper I get into it, the longer, within a given day, I spend with it. I might go from only working three hours a day at the beginning to working on it for eighteen hours near the end or even longer. I have gotten into projects, and gone without sleep for three days and just worked like a demon. But that focus is a matter of having built up momentum, learning about what I'm working on, fumbling about, groping, restructuring—trying to figure out what the heck it is I'm trying to do, what I'm working on is really about.

ROWELL: What are you referring to by "building up momentum"? What does that mean? Did that happen, for example, when you were working on *A Visitation of Spirits?*

KENAN: With *A Visitation of Spirits,* it took me a long time to figure out what the novel was really about. I had worked four years on a book that I thought was going to be that novel, and was stumped at one point, and put it down for a long time. There followed a period of months where I didn't physically work on it—unknown to me, I was actually working on it in my mind. I totally re-structured the story—consciously and unconsciously—in my brain, and, again, slowly, painstakingly, I tried to start things again. Over the course of months, I came to more clarity. To me that is what writing is about, coming to clarity on the page. I found that the narrative took over a large space in my mind and that homesteading led me to put my behind to the chair for longer and longer periods of time. The momentum I'm talking about is really about the willingness, the commitment you can give to a project, the amount of time you spend with it. When I speak of those days when I could do nothing but sit and write, I'm talking about a matter of me not really being aware of time. I can get up at seven o'clock in the morning, go to work, work through lunch, look up and the sun has gone down, and I was really not aware of the passage of time. Sometimes I even forget to eat. And it goes without saying, this anti-social behavior has been a big problem among me and my family and friends.

ROWELL: How do you explain to the beginning writer the seriousness of learn-ing your craft?

KENAN: I think that's one of the most difficult things in teaching writing, or work-ing with beginning writers—we take language for granted; we all use sentences. We've been speaking since we were a few years old. We read the newspaper. We look at TV. We listen to the radio. We chat with friends and strangers. We're im-mersed in language. That's part of what being a human being is about, to be bathed in words. When people start to write, of course they assume that they know all they need to know, and then wonder why it is that they can't produce stories like Chekhov or novels like Nabokov. They have the basic skills. So what's the problem? But that is only the beginning of learning to think like a writer, to see and recognize a narrative—or in some cases, the lack of a narrative.

Of course you must study grammar. Not knowing grammar for a writer is like a dancer not knowing foot positions or what certain positions are called. That knowledge is essential. Next a writer begins to understand elements of point-of-view, elements of how a character is made, understanding the differ-ent types of stories and how they all intersect and how they're inter-woven; a writer must come to some understanding of how to create and shape a dra-matic scene. These things might sound reductive, but I think we first start out as craftsmen and women and aspire to become artists. There is a big difference between being merely a builder, and being a builder of structures that will not fall, that tell somebody something about life, love and dying.

ROWELL: How did you come to the craft of fiction? I'm thinking of your rural North Carolina background. Were there writers in your family? Did you read a lot of novels when you were a youngster? Did some event or some professor, while you studied at the University of North Carolina, have anything to do with your electing writing as a career? Can you recall how and perhaps why you came to writing fiction?

KENAN: Well, the reasons are multi-fold. Writing was always something I certainly took for granted. It took me years, really, after I had left the environs of Chinquapin, to understand that I grew up in an oral tradition. I was lucky enough to come from a very rural community in which I was literally raised up by people who were in their seventies and eighties and they were very loquacious. That was the world in which I moved, in which people told stories, in which people understood the world they lived in through talking about it, through relating not only events that happened to them, but to their forefathers. Literally, in the 1960s and 1970s, I could touch my great-great-grand-Aunt and reach back into the middle of the 19th century. Think about it: When she was a girl, she had known people who were born at the turn of the century—the 18th century! My life was structured by these oral narratives, and I took this all for granted, just like everybody else. It just seemed the most natural thing in the world to me. My kinfolk were not writers, but that fundamental impetus to create a story, whether it's on the page, or through your mouth, was the milieu in which I spent my first seventeen years. I wasn't conscious of wanting to make writing a vocation. I was actually going to become a scientist. That was my dream. I was enamored of certain scientists who were science fiction writers. But you see, even then, writing was not something I started out following deliberately. I just did it. I didn't make a conscious decision that "Ah, ha! I'm going to become a science fiction writer!" I just did it. I wrote two very foul novels in high school and that was just the way I moved in the world. I really didn't think about it. Remember, I was growing up in rural, backwoods North Carolina, where nobody knew or even thought about writers, and though it may sound like a bucolic and rustic and wonderful place to city-dwellers, it was actually a very boring experience, on the whole. So I was escaping into my imagination a great deal.

By the time I got to college, I was heading for a major in physics. I started thinking about this writing thing more deliberately and took a writing course. That's where I encountered one of my mentors, Max Steele, whom I will always credit for turning me in a different direction. He was very impatient with my writing science fiction. He knew what I did not know; that I came from a background, specifically, rural, black southeastern North Carolina, that had not really been written about. North Carolina has many, many, many writers, and a long tradition of writers, but the absence of blackfolk writing in that tradition was conspicuous. I fought with Max for a long time, and he told me to read this book, read that book, write about home. And for the first time I really read black writers. I mean, I had read books by and about black people all my life, for class and such, but I had not really read them, thought about them. I read Toni Morrison. I read Gabriel García Márquez. I read Yukio Mishima. Those three writers, really, I credit more than others with getting me to begin to see the potential of the written word. I slowly came around to what Max was trying to tell me. Though I didn't change my view of what I wanted to do with science fiction, or think any less of it, I did begin to think more and more of contributing to this ongoing dialogue in fiction about our culture and about the landscape and about the people. It struck me that these people like my great-great-aunt Erie and the people I had grown up around, deserved to be explored on the page. Perhaps I was thinking that when they were gone, there would be some sort of record, that their stories would be guaranteed to be known to other people. Of course there are other joys and pleasures in writing that you take from the page and that aren't quite so grandiose. At the end of the day, that's really what keeps me going—the pleasure of the written word. And largely that's one of the many things I try to do when I sit down to write.

In a nutshell, in a very fat nutshell, that's how I came to start writing.

ROWELL: You've spoken of that small area in North Carolina, and you've mentioned three writers who directed you in learning your craft: Toni Morrison, Gabriel García Márquez, and Mishima. What did Mishima teach you that helps you to reinvent your North Carolina?

KENAN: I could speak for hours about Mishima. I came to Mishima not as most people do, as this man who committed suicide in this very gruesome, very political way. I first came to him through the short story, "Patriotism." It was the very first thing that I read by him. I was so struck by the style in which he approached physicality. "Patriotism" is the story of a man and wife who commit seppuku, ritual suicide as an act of contrition and honor. On its bare face the story is very horrific, yet it is also quite beautiful and full of grace. There were elements in that story which I said I wanted to attempt to emulate, in terms of bringing these visions I had in my head to the page. I then read his novel, *Confessions of a Mask,* and that blew me away on a number of levels. It was the most extraordinary account I had ever read theretofore of coming to consciousness about one's own sexuality, specifically, a male's attraction to other males. And it was at once sensitive and lyrical and it confirmed many of the things that I had felt while growing up, but had never articulated, never thought of articulating about myself as an erotic human being. And here was this message in a bottle sent all the way from post-War Japan! Reading this book challenged me to write from my perspective, from a perspective of southeastern North Carolina, from this perspective of being a black male, and attempt, again, to bring that sensitivity and lyricism, and above all that attention to unusual detail which is particularly Japanese, particular to Mishima, to my own work. Reading Mishima opened up the door to Japanese literature. Tanazaki. Abe. Kawabata. Those writers, just before and after World War II, have a particular cultural way of looking at characters, of looking at the world which is different, in many ways from a North American way of looking at the physical world. Their culture teaches them to look, to see certain things we Americans often ignore. I was attracted to their sense of the erotic, their definitions of beauty, how they construct their sense of honor and manners, their approach to filial piety, their over-all aesthetic. Of course there are similarities—we are all human beings in the end—but there are also fundamental, cultural differences. As I came to appreciate the differences, I came to look at African-American culture, in particular, with new eyes. It was as if I were approaching my own culture with the eyes of a foreigner. I found this exciting. Fresh. New. Some African writers—I think of Amos Tutulo or Bessie Head and to some degree Achebe—also have this sense about their work as well, but I came to them later.

ROWELL: Will you talk about the tradition of telling, storytelling and the love of language in the South? I think immediately of the black preacher's love of language. You spoke of storytellers earlier.

KENAN: Yeah, from before James Weldon Johnson's *God's Trombones* up through A.J. Verdelle's *The Good Negress*. I think it's become a cliché, in many ways, to speak too pointedly about the "Southerner's love of language and storytelling." But all clichés and stereotypes stem from some fundamental truth. I suspect that all human animals love language and stories best—after food, warmth and sex—how else can you account for the success of television? Probably what separates the South from the rest of the universe is their particular colorful use of their language—made out of African retentions and dim Elizabethanisms and Native American words, and that African vision of an animistic universe, and the basic sense of Calvinist doom, and a well-developed sense of the absurd. As Flannery O'Connor, again, said, you have your grotesques all over the world, but Southerners talk about them openly, and in that talking try to make some sense out of them and the world—the eccentric aunt, the uncle who shot the already dead mule—all those funny, existential, sad, human experiences. Southerners probably had to have language in order to express their sense of themselves. Of course, I'm not sure that's still the case as America has become more Southern, and the South more like the rest of America.

ROWELL: Will you say more about the representation of sexuality in Mishima and how it helped you to write about sexuality? I am suddenly thinking of what Alice Walker talked about years ago when she spoke of the need for models for writers—if I recall correctly she was talking about models for black women writers. Was/is Mishima a model for you?

KENAN: Well, as I have said, my relationship to Mishima is quite complex. We can't forget that he was an ardent Nationalist, which I actually find problematic. Of course there were some resonances with his political ideas vis-á-vis Japan's relationship to the United States government and African America's relationship to that same government—two groups effectively colonized, over-powered, and subjected to the same hegemony, militarily and economically, and the desire to see one's own culture survive and thrive; a certain cultural nationalism. Now some people even go so far as to call Mishima a Fascist. About all those things, I'm unclear and undecided. It all makes him a richer and more fascinating person. But as a writer, he made a career by destroying any pigeon-hole. He was a married man, who wrote some pivotal novels about gay men; he was Japanese, yet his most important literary influences were European, and he confounded folk on another of other notions. For me, to write about same sex love, about the South, about blackfolk, leads certain people to want to put me in this category or that category—which I find reductive and simple-minded. One of the first exciting elements of reading Mishima's work was how he made same-sex love at once unremarkable, and yet how he made the love—which had nothing to do with the sex of the participants—quite remarkable. That dichotomy is what I glommed onto. So perhaps, as a writer who didn't want to live in any one socio-political-regional-sexual house, I found a model in Mishima. Yet I wouldn't want to reduce what I found so fascinating about him to a single lesson, or that I actively tried to "do it like Mishima did it."

ROWELL: Some time ago, when I interviewed the lesbian writer Audre Lorde and asked her whether sexuality had anything to do with her writing, she responded that it did. What is your position on sexuality and the writer? Is the sexuality of the writer important to the text?

KENAN: That's always a tangled knot, and people have very strong feelings about that relationship. For me, I approach my sexuality in my writing in the same way I would approach my being black. I think it is a choice one makes in terms of how broad and deep one wants to make his or her work. Where do you write from? Do you write out of being a black person? Do you write out of being gay? Or do you write out of your experience as a human being? For instance, take Ralph Ellison. *Invisible Man*—and he wrote extensively about this—was written from Ellison's vision as a human being. The book was deeply informed and sensitized by the fact that he was black, and by the fact that he was from Oklahoma and that he went to Tuskeegee, and that he came to New York at a certain period in history. But those accumulative facts about his life did not stop him from writing a Bledsoe with great insight, nor did it stop him from writing about Reinhart with great sensitivity. I think that such ability comes from one's own ability to think of oneself as a human being, formed by this broader spectrum of other people. What writing can enable us to do, I believe, is to step into somebody else's shoes. If you are so bound up by those things that other people think define you, you'll never be able to get out of yourself. I look at a book that I am not completely enamored with and that is usually one of the things I would point toward as being a shortcoming: the writer was so constricted by what he was supposed to be—politically, socially, economically—that it ultimately short-circuited her ability to be somebody completely Other than themselves, and it therefore closed them off from understanding how this other person might view even the person writing or anything else in the world.

ROWELL: What did Toni Morrison offer you? You mentioned her among the three writers you found very important to you early on in your career as a writer. Gabriel García Márquez is the third writer.

KENAN: Perhaps incorrectly I twin García Márquez with Morrison, but not for what some might think of as the obvious reasons. The bedrock of what people think of a Southern literature is "realism." And as I said, my earliest influences, my earliest fascinations and passions, were for texts that were not bound by what would fit into most people's "realism." A critic once pointed out how much my stories reminded them of Poe. This was something I was completely unaware of. I thought back after reading that, and remembered, in fact, that my first attempts at stories, back in grade school, were dreadful imitations of Edgar Allen Poe stories. That was part and parcel of how I saw the world, a world in which religion was taken very seriously. My great-aunts and uncles would often sit around and talk about ghosts and the spirit world. Demons and the devils were very real things to me, so how could I see the world without them? When I encountered Morrison and when I encountered García Márquez, it was as if they had given me a license to go right on seeing the world the way I saw it. I was just dumbfounded when I read *A Hundred Years of Solitude,* because his view of the world in which these magical things happened as a matter of course, along with work and family arguments and worrying about bills, made perfect sense. Yet it was a worldview that was not consonant with this political, social realism that I was being instructed to follow. In truth I don't see social realism and so-called magic realism as being counter. I see them as being able to co-exist. That's what, in my own humble and stumbling way, I attempted to do—interject into the ongoing American dialogue, that social dialogue and that political dialogue, another dimension which was a world of mystery and the unknowable which, for me as a child and to the people around me, was very real and very present, and I wanted to be true to that way of looking at and living in the world. Morrison and García Márquez sent out powerful messages that my way of looking at things was okay. Don't worry, their books said, just write it the way you see it.

ROWELL: What in terms of craft did you learn from them?

KENAN: You know, in a review one time, someone once said something to the effect that if García Márquez and Morrison were to have a literary love-child, the result would be me. Now I was flattered to death by that statement; but it's also scared the shit out of me. What does that mean? Basically I feel the same way about both of them that I feel about Faulkner. I mean, I idolize them, but you have to worry about being yourself after a time. To this day I can recite the first page of *Sula.* I studied everything she did. I tried to write like Toni Morrison and, one fine morning, I realized that I was not a fortysomething year-old woman from Ohio with two children, and a Senior Editor at Random House and lecturer at Princeton and Yale. I was not Toni Morrison. Nor had I been born in Colombia, and been a reporter for a daily newspaper, not had I lived in Paris with a wife and children to support. I was not Gabo. I mean that in a very fundamental sense. I had to grow up in that sense, and get on with it. In order to do what I had to do, I had to define my own way of being, which is very painstaking, and, as James Baldwin said, is a daily process: You have to invent yourself every day. In my case that means a lot of reading, a lot of looking at my own background, and a lot of writing. Just as other writers I admire deeply, these two taught me supreme lessons about sentences, about character, about structure, but in the end, I believe a writer integrates a great many writers into their aesthetic vision. As I've said, I've learned from Mishima, I've learned from Issac Bashevis Singer, I've learned from Italo Calvino, I've learned a great deal from James Agee, and Katherine Anne Porter. In truth, it's Katherine Anne Porter who really got me to look at the short story the way I do.

Jamaica Kincaid (1949–)

Elaine Potter Richardson, known by most as Jamaica Kincaid, was born on May 25, 1949, in St. John's on the island of Antigua in the Caribbean. In 1965 she left Antigua and came to work as an au pair in New York City. This was an experience she had dreamed of since reading work by Charlotte Brontë, author of her favorite novel, Jane Eyre. *Brontë had spent a year in Belgium and Kincaid too dreamt of going there. But instead of Belgium, she ended up in New York City. Her experiences, which she has spoken of in interviews, reflect those of Lucy, the protagonist in her novel of the same name.*

She wanted the opportunity to experience the world, and the city provided her the freedom and anonymity she sought. Between 1969 and 1970, she studied photography at the New School for Social Research in New York City and also attended Franconia College in New Hampshire for a little while before returning to New York City. Upon completion of her studies, she began her career in publishing, working for several publications including Glamour *and* Mademoiselle *magazines.*

In 1973 she changed her name to Jamaica Kincaid. This was both an act of liberation and reinvention, reflecting her search for identity and anonymity. With a new name, she was able to recreate herself as an individual who felt no obligation to follow the norms of the society she had come from or the one she was now a part of. In this same year a friend introduced her to William Shawn, editor of the New Yorker *magazine. She was assigned to write the "Talk of the Town" pieces. This was the beginning of her career both as a journalist and author.* Girl *was the first in a long list of essays (85 in total) published by the magazine. She became a staff writer for the* New Yorker *in 1976, a position she held until 1995.*

In 1979, as she was settling into her position at the New Yorker, *Kincaid married Allen Shawn—a composer and professor at Bennington College and son of William Shawn. They have two children—Annie and Harold.*

Jamaica Kincaid gained wide acclaim for her first two complete works, At the Bottom of the River *(1978) and* Annie John *(1983), from which the selections included in this anthology are taken. In 1983 she was nominated for the PEN/Faulkner Award and won the Morton Dauwen Zabel Award of the American Academy and Institute of Arts and Letters for* At the Bottom of the River. *Her second major work,* Annie John, *was a finalist for the International Ritz Paris Hemingway Award in 1985. Both of these works are comprised of individual essays first published in the* New Yorker. At the Bottom of the River *has been critiqued for its complexity and inaccessibility. The essays are dark, written from a place we cannot touch, feel, or even know. They are part of a dream sequence or the unconscious. Most critics feel that they are deeply personal and that we (the readers) cannot translate them, nor are we meant to. Instead, we are to engage the sense of loss and mourning expressed in this work. Images of the child or infant swimming in the womb,* then in a world of limbo and finally in the dark, comprise the chronology of the ten pieces. Departure from the womb signifies a longing for the Mother and the desire to return to the safe waters of the womb. The inability to return results in a crisis of loss and the inability of the narrator to be seen, felt, or heard.

Annie John builds upon these same themes but expands the idea of Mother to include Antigua's relationship to Britain, its "Mother Country." Critics like Annie John because the language and style are deceptively simple. This book pays homage to Kincaid's ability to manipulate language. It is a book full of island images, childhood memories, and school rivalries. We (the readers) can identify with the narrator; we see ourselves in the characters and grasp whatever lies in Kincaid's beautiful language. But the sense of loss prevails, the mourning continues, and the narrator is once again bound to depart from the womb. Antigua is an island and the water that surrounds it is reminiscent of the amniotic fluid. Leaving this beautiful land and the imperialistic history that it epitomizes is as traumatic as departing from the Mother's womb.

While the United States has provided a large and appreciative audience, Kincaid continues to nurture strong links to her homeland and family through her writing. Themes of loss, domination, and the relationship between the powerful and the powerless dominate most of her work. These themes are linked to the subject of home—the island she had left and the ambivalent feelings she had towards it, and the relationship between mother and daughter that speaks both of love, loss of love, and a myriad of undeniable emotions.

Kincaid admits she sometimes writes out of her own experiences—it is easy to see this in Annie John, At the Bottom of the River, and Lucy. In one of the selected readings, "Columbus in Chains," for example, Kincaid writes of a punishment that involved copying the first and second books of Paradise Lost. John Milton's Paradise Lost had a great impact on Kincaid. She was able to identify with the themes and ideas inherent in this work and adopted them in her own writing. Lucy, the protagonist in the novel Lucy, says her mother named her after Lucifer—Satan in Paradise Lost. The character Lucy mimics Kincaid's journey from home—paradise (Satan's departure from the Garden of Eden)—and the crisis of identity this causes.

But it is not to Milton that we can attribute Kincaid's amazing style. In an interview with Diane Simmons, Kincaid says that two things changed her thinking about writing—the French film La Jetée made up of black-and-white still photographs, and the work of French experimental writer Alain Bobbe-Grillet. Simmons states that the works of these men freed both writer and reader of the need "to make conventionally coherent arrangements of experience and reality." As a result, Kincaid seemed to tap into her ability to write of her life and home "without recourse to a storytelling mode she had come to see as archaic and dishonest." She interweaves stories in what seems to be simple yet elegant, direct and indirect, complicated but precise language. She makes it sound natural and real, funny and sad, while at the same time addressing complex issues pertaining to colonialism, history, and personal identity.

In 1998 Kincaid edited and wrote the introduction for a book on gardening. While gardening is one of her hobbies, she does not exclude it from the kind of investigation that allows for critical thought. She reflects upon the fact that for the majority of the people in her homeland gardening is a means of livelihood, one that they do not engage in for relaxation but for survival. Kincaid never lets us off the hook, irrespective of the subject—she has a magic that draws us in and gets us to participate in her stories; nodding, laughing, crying, seething in anger, reacting, and interacting; allowing her to lead us down whatever road she takes.

In 1992 she was the recipient of the Lila Wallace Reader's Digest Fund Annual Writer's Award, and her novel The Autobiography of My Mother *was a finalist for the National Book Critics Circle Award for fiction and the PEN/Faulkner Award in 1997. Her work has been widely read, and she has been recognized and honored by schools like Williams College and Colgate University, which are among several that have awarded her honorary degrees. She has also been a visiting professor at Harvard University in Cambridge, Massachusetts.*

Caroline Irungu

In the Night

In the night, way into the middle of the night, when the night isn't divided like a sweet drink into little sips, when there is no just before midnight, midnight, or just after midnight, when the night is round in some places, flat in some places, and in some places like a deep hole, blue at the edge, black inside, the night-soil men come.

They come and go, walking on the damp ground in straw shoes. Their feet in the straw shoes make a scratchy sound. They say nothing.

The night-soil men can see a bird walking in trees. It isn't a bird. It is a woman who has removed her skin and is on her way to drink the blood of her secret enemies. It is a woman who has left her skin in a corner of a house made out of wood. It is a woman who is reasonable and admires honeybees in the hibiscus. It is a woman who, as a joke, brays like a donkey when he is thirsty.

There is the sound of a cricket, there is the sound of a church bell, there is the sound of this house creaking, that house creaking, and the other house creaking as they settle into the ground. There is the sound of a radio in the distance—a fisherman listening to merengue music. There is the sound of a man groaning in his sleep; there is the sound of a woman disgusted at the man groaning. There is the sound of the man stabbing the woman, the sound of her blood as it hits the floor, the sound of Mr. Straffee, the undertaker, taking her body away. There is the sound of her spirit back from the dead, looking at the man who used to groan; he is running a fever forever. There is the sound of a woman writing a letter; there is the sound of her pen nib on the white writing paper; there is the sound of the kerosene lamp dimming; there is the sound of her head aching.

The rain falls on the tin roofs, on the leaves in the trees, on the stones in the yard, on sand, on the ground. The night is wet in some places, warm in some places.

There is Mr. Gishard, standing under a cedar tree which is in full bloom, wearing that nice white suit, which is as fresh as the day he was buried in it. The white suit came from England in a brown package: "To: Mr. John Gishard," and so on and so on. Mr. Gishard is standing under the tree, wearing his nice suit and holding a glass full of rum in his hand—the same glass full of rum that he had in his hand shortly before he died—and looking at the house in which he used to live. The people who now live in the house walk through the door backward when they see Mr. Gishard standing under the tree, wearing his nice white suit. Mr. Gishard misses his accordion; you can tell by the way he keeps tapping his foot.

In my dream I can hear a baby being born. I can see its face, a pointy little face—so nice. I can see its hands—so nice, again. Its eyes are closed. It's breathing, the little baby. It's breathing. It's bleating, the little baby. It's bleating. The baby and I are now walking to pasture. The baby is eating green grass with its soft and pink lips. My mother is shaking me by the shoulders. My mother says, "Little Miss, Little Miss." I say to my mother, "But it's still night." My mother says, "Yes, but you have wet your bed again." And my mother, who is still young, and still beautiful, and still has pink lips, removes my wet nightgown, removes my wet sheets from my bed. My mother can change everything. In my dream I am in the night.

"What are the lights in the mountains?"

"The lights in the mountains? Oh, it's a jablesse."

"A jablesse! But why? What's a jablesse?"

"It's a person who can turn into anything. But you can tell they aren't real because of their eyes. Their eyes shine like lamps, so bright that you can't look. That's how you can tell it's a jablesse. They like to go up in the mountains and gallivant. Take good care when you see a beautiful woman. A jablesse always tries to look like a beautiful woman."

No one has ever said to me, "My father, a night-soil man, is very nice and very kind. When he passes a dog, he gives a pat and not a kick. He likes all the parts of a fish but especially the head. He goes to church quite regularly and is always glad when the minister calls out, 'A Mighty Fortress Is Our God,' his favorite hymn. He would like to wear pink shirts and pink pants but knows that this color isn't very becoming to a man, so instead he wears navy blue and brown, colors he does not like at all. He met my mother on what masquerades as a bus around here, a long time ago, and he still likes to whistle. Once, while running to catch a bus, he fell and broke his ankle and had to spend a week in hospital. This made him miserable, but he cheered up quite a bit when he saw my mother and me, standing over his white cot, holding bunches of yellow roses and smiling down at him. Then he said, 'Oh, my. Oh, my.' What he likes to do most, my father the night-soil man, is to sit on a big stone under a mahogany tree and watch small children playing play-cricket while he eats the intestines of animals stuffed with blood and rice and drinks ginger beer. He has told me this many times: 'My dear, what I like to do most,' and so on. He is always reading botany books and knows a lot about rubber plantations and rubber trees; but this is an interest I can't explain, since the only rubber tree he has ever seen is a specially raised one in the botanic gardens. He sees to it that my school shoes fit comfortably. I love my father the night-soil man. My mother loves my father the night-soil man. Everybody loves him and waves to him whenever they see him. He is very handsome, you know, and I have seen women look at him twice. On special days he wears a brown felt hat, which he orders from England, and brown leather shoes, which he also orders from England. On ordinary days he goes barehead. When he calls me, I say, 'Yes, sir.' On my mother's birthday he always buys her some nice cloth for a new dress as a present. He makes us happy, my father the night-soil man, and has promised that one day he will take us to see something he has read about called the circus."

In the night, the flowers close up and thicken. The hibiscus flowers, the flamboyant flowers, the bachelor's buttons, the irises, the marigolds, the white-headbush flowers, the lilies, the flowers on the daggerbush, the flowers on the turtleberry bush, the flowers on the soursop tree, the flowers on the sugar-apple tree, the flowers on the mango tree, the flowers on the guava tree, the flowers on the cedar tree, the flowers on the stinking-toe tree, the flowers on the dumps tree, the flowers on the papaw tree, the flowers everywhere close up and thicken. The flowers are vexed.

Someone is making a basket, someone is making a girl a dress or a boy a shirt, someone is making her husband a soup with cassava so that he can take it to the cane field tomorrow, someone is making his wife a beautiful mahogany chest, someone is sprinkling a colorless powder outside a closed door so that someone else's child will be stillborn, someone is praying that a bad child who is living prosperously abroad will be good and send a package filled with new clothes, someone is sleeping.

Now I am a girl, but one day I will marry a woman—a red-skin woman with black bramblebush hair and brown eyes, who wears skirts that are so big I can easily bury my head in them. I would like to marry this woman and live with her in a mud hut near the sea. In the mud hut will be two chairs and one table, a lamp that burns kerosene, a medicine chest, a pot, one bed, two pillows, two sheets, one looking glass, two cups, two saucers, two dinner plates, two forks, two drinking-water glasses, one china pot, two fishing strings, two straw hats to ward the hot sun off our heads, two trunks for things we have very little use for, one basket, one book of plain paper, one box filled with twelve crayons of different colors, one loaf of bread wrapped in a piece of brown paper, one coal pot, one picture of two women standing on a jetty, one picture of the same two women embracing, one picture of the same two women waving goodbye, one box of matches. Every day this red-skin woman and I will eat bread and milk for breakfast, hide in bushes and throw hardened cow dung at people we don't like, climb coconut trees, pick coconuts, eat and drink the food and water from the coconuts we have picked, throw stones in the sea, put on John Bull masks and frighten defenseless little children on their way home from school, go fishing and catch only our favorite fishes to roast and have for dinner, steal green figs to eat for dinner with the roast fish. Every day we would do this. Every night I would sing this woman a song; the words I don't know yet, but the tune is in my head. This woman I would like to marry knows many things, but to me she will only tell about things that would never dream of making me cry; and every night, over and over, she will tell me something that begins, "Before you were born." I will marry a woman like this, and every night, every night, I will be completely happy.

Columbus in Chains

Outside, as usual, the sun shone, the trade winds blew; on her way to put some starched clothes on the line, my mother shooed some hens out of her garden; Miss Dewberry baked the buns, some of which my mother would buy for my father and me to eat with our afternoon tea; Miss Henry brought the milk, a glass of which I would drink with my lunch, and another glass of which I would drink with the bun from Miss Dewberry; my mother prepared our lunch; my father noted some perfectly idiotic thing his partner in housebuilding, Mr. Oatie, had done, so that over lunch he and my mother could have a good laugh.

The Anglican church bell struck eleven o'clock—one hour to go before lunch. I was then sitting at my desk in my classroom. We were having a history lesson—the last lesson of the morning. For taking first place over all the other girls, I had been given a prize, a copy of a book called *Roman Britain,* and I was made prefect of my class. What a mistake the prefect part had been, for I was among the worst-behaved in my class and did not at all believe in setting myself up as a good example, the way a prefect was supposed to do. Now I had to sit in the prefect's seat—the first seat in the front row, the seat from which I could stand up and survey quite easily my classmates. From where I sat I could see out the window. Sometimes when I looked out, I could see the sexton going over to the minister's house. The sexton's daughter, Hilarene, a disgusting model of good behavior and keen attention to scholarship, sat next to me, since she took second place. The minister's daughter, Ruth, sat in the last row, the row reserved for all the dunce girls. Hilarene, of course, I could not stand. A girl that good would never do for me. I would probably not have cared so much for first place if I could be sure it would not go to her. Ruth I liked, because she was such a dunce and came from England and had yellow hair. When I first met her, I used to walk her home and sing bad songs to her just to see her turn pink, as if I had spilled hot water all over her.

Our books, *A History of the West Indies,* were open in front of us. Our day had begun with morning prayers, then a geometry lesson, then it was over to the science building for a lesson in "Introductory Physics" (not a subject we cared much for), taught by the most dingy-toothed Mr. Slacks, a teacher from Canada, then precious recess, and now this, our history lesson. Recess had the usual drama: this time, I coaxed Gwen out of her disappointment at not being allowed to join the junior choir. Her father—how many times had I wished he would become a leper and so be banished to a leper colony for the rest of my long and happy life with Gwen—had forbidden it, giving as his reason that she lived too far away from church, where choir rehearsals were conducted, and that it would be dangerous for her, a young girl, to walk home alone at night in the dark. Of course, all the streets had lamplight, but it was useless to point that out to him. Oh, how it would have pleased us to press and rub our knees together as we sat in our pew while pretending to pay close attention to Mr. Simmons, our choirmaster, as he waved his baton up and down and across, and how it would have pleased us even more to walk home together, alone in the "early dusk" (the way Gwen had phrased it, a ready phrase always on her tongue), stopping, if there was a full moon, to lie down in a pasture and expose our bosoms in the moonlight. We had heard that full moonlight would make our breasts grow to a size we would like. Poor Gwen! When I first heard from her that she was one of ten children, right on the spot I told her that I would love only her, since her mother already had so many other people to love.

Our teacher, Miss Edward, paced up and down in front of the class in her usual way. In front of her desk stood a small table, and on it stood the dunce cap. The dunce cap was in the shape of a coronet, with an adjustable opening in the back, so that it could fit any head. It was made of cardboard with a shiny gold paper covering and the word "DUNCE" in shiny red paper on the front. When the sun shone on it, the dunce cap was all aglitter, almost as if you were being tricked into thinking it a desirable thing to wear. As Miss Edward paced up and down, she would pass between us and the dunce cap like an eclipse. Each Friday morning, we were given a small test to see how well we had learned the things taught to us all week. The girl who scored lowest was made to wear the dunce cap all day the following Monday. On many Mondays, Ruth wore it—only, with her short yellow hair, when the dunce cap was sitting on her head she looked like a girl attending a birthday party in *The Schoolgirl's Own Annual.*

It was Miss Edward's way to ask one of us a question the answer to which she was sure the girl would not know and then put the same question to another girl who she was sure would know the answer. The girl who did not answer correctly would then have to repeat the correct answer in the exact words of the other girl. Many times, I had heard my exact words repeated over and over again, and I liked it especially when the girl doing the repeating was one I didn't care about very much. Pointing a finger at Ruth, Miss Edward asked a question the answer to which was "On the third of November 1493, a Sunday morning, Christopher Columbus discovered Dominica." Ruth, of course, did not know the answer, as she did not know the answer to many questions about the West Indies. I could hardly blame her. Ruth had come all the way from England. Perhaps she did not want to be in the West Indies at all. Perhaps she wanted to be in England, where no one would remind her constantly of the terrible things her ancestors had done; perhaps she had felt even worse when her father was a missionary in Africa. I could see how Ruth felt from looking at her face. Her ancestors had been the masters, while ours had been the slaves. She had such a lot to be ashamed of, and by being with us every day she was always being reminded. We could look everybody in the eye, for our ancestors had done nothing wrong except just sit somewhere, defenseless. Of course, sometimes, what with our teachers and our books, it was hard for us to tell on which side we really now belonged—with the masters or the slaves—for it was all history, it was all in the past, and everybody behaved differently now; all of us celebrated Queen Victoria's birthday, even though she had been dead a long time. But we, the descendants of the slaves, knew quite well what had really happened, and I was sure that if the tables had been turned we would have acted differently; I was sure that if our ancestors had gone from Africa to Europe and come upon the people living there, they would have taken a proper interest in the Europeans on first seeing them, and said, "How nice," and then gone home to tell their friends about it.

I was sitting at my desk, having these thoughts to myself. I don't know how long it had been since I lost track of what was going on around me. I had not noticed that the girl who was asked the question after Ruth failed—a girl named Hyacinth—had only got a part of the answer correct. I had not noticed that after these two attempts Miss Edward had launched into a harangue about what a worthless bunch we were compared to girls of the past. In fact, I was no longer on the same chapter we were studying. I was way ahead, at the end of the chapter about Columbus's third voyage. In this chapter, there was a picture of Columbus that took up a whole page, and it was in color—one of only five color pictures in the book. In this picture, Columbus was seated in the bottom of a ship. He was wearing the usual three-quarter trousers and a shirt with enormous sleeves, both the trousers and shirt made of maroon-colored velvet. His hat, which was cocked up on one side of his head, had a gold feather in it, and his black shoes had huge gold buckles. His hands and feet were bound in chains, and he was sitting there staring off into space, looking quite dejected and miserable. The picture had as a title "Columbus in Chains," printed at the bottom of the page. What had happened was that the usually quarrelsome Columbus had got into a disagreement with people who were even more quarrelsome, and a man named Bobadilla, representing King Ferdinand and Queen Isabella, had sent him back to Spain fettered in chains attached to the bottom of a ship. What just deserts, I thought, for I did not like Columbus. How I loved this picture—to see the usually triumphant Columbus, brought so low, seated at the bottom of a boat just watching things go by. Shortly after I first discovered it in my history book, I heard my mother read out loud to my father a letter she had received from her sister, who still lived with her mother and father in the very same Dominica, which is where my mother came from. Ma Chess was fine, wrote my aunt, but Pa

Chess was not well. Pa Chess was having a bit of trouble with his limbs; he was not able to go about as he pleased; often he had to depend on someone else to do one thing or another for him. My mother read the letter in quite a state, her voice rising to a higher pitch with each sentence. After she read the part about Pa Chess's stiff limbs, she turned to my father and laughed as she said, "So the great man can no longer just get up and go. How I would love to see his face now!" When I next saw the picture of Columbus sitting there all locked up in his chains, I wrote under it the words "The Great Man Can No Longer Just Get Up and Go." I had written this out with my fountain pen, and in Old English letter-ing—a script I had recently mastered. As I sat there looking at the picture, I traced the words with my pen over and over, so that the letters grew big and you could read what I had written from not very far away. I don't know how long it was before I heard that my name, Annie John, was being said by this bellowing dragon in the form of Miss Edward bearing down on me.

I had never been a favorite of hers. Her favorite was Hilarene. It must have pained Miss Edward that I so often beat out Hilarene. Not that I liked Miss Ed-ward and wanted her to like me back, but all my other teachers regarded me with much affection, would always tell my mother that I was the most charming stu-dent they had ever had, beamed at me when they saw me coming, and were very sorry when they had to write some version of this on my report card: "Annie is an unusually bright girl. She is well behaved in class, at least in the presence of her masters and mistresses, but behind their backs and outside the classroom quite the opposite is true." When my mother read this or something like it, she would burst into tears. She had hoped to display, with a great flourish, my report card to her friends, along with whatever prize I had won. Instead, the report card would have to take a place at the bottom of the old trunk in which she kept any important thing that had to do with me. I became not a favorite of Miss Edward's in the following way: Each Friday afternoon, the girls in the lower forms were given, instead of a last lesson period, an extra-long recess. We were to use this in ladylike recreation—walks, chats about the novels and poems we were reading, showing each other the new embroidery stitches we had learned to master in home class, or something just as seemly. Instead, some of the girls would play a game of cricket or rounders or stones, but most of us would go to the far end of the school grounds and play band. In this game, of which teachers and parents disapproved and which was sometimes absolutely forbidden, we would place our arms around each other's waist or shoulders, forming lines of ten or so girls, and then we would dance from one end of the school grounds to the other. As we danced, we would sometimes chant these words: "Tee la la la, come go. Tee la la la, come go." At other times we would sing a popular calypso song which usually had lots of unladylike words to it. Up and down the schoolyard, away from our teachers, we would dance and sing. At the end of recess—forty-five minutes—we were missing ribbons and other ornaments from our hair, the pleats of our linen tunics became unset, the collars of our blouses were pulled out, and we were soaking wet all the way down to our bloomers. When the school bell rang, we would make a whooping sound, as if in a great panic, and then we would throw ourselves on top of each other as we laughed and shrieked. We would then run back to our classes, where we prepared to file into the auditorium for evening prayers. After that, it was home for the weekend. But how could we go straight home after all that excitement? No sooner were we on the street than we would form little groups, depending on the direction we were headed in. I was never keen on joining them on the way home, because I was sure I would run into my mother. Instead, my friends and I would go to our usual place near the back of the churchyard and sit on the tombstones of people who had been buried there way before slavery was abolished, in 1833. We would sit and sing bad songs, use forbidden words, and, of course, show each other various parts of our bodies. While some of us watched, the others would walk up and down on the large tombstones showing off their legs. It was immediately a popular idea; everybody soon wanted to do it. It wasn't long before many girls—the ones whose mothers didn't pay strict attention to what they were doing—started to come to school on Fridays wearing not bloomers under their uniforms but underpants trimmed with lace and satin frills. It also wasn't long before an end came to all that. One Friday afternoon, Miss Edward, on her way home from school, took a shortcut through the churchyard. She must have heard the commotion we were making, because there she suddenly was, saying, "What is the meaning of this?"—just the very thing someone like her would say if she came unexpectedly on something like us. It was obvious that I was the ringleader. Oh, how I wished the ground would open up and take her in, but it did not. We all, shamefacedly, slunk home, I with Miss Edward at my side. Tears came to my mother's eyes when she heard what I had done. It was apparently such a bad thing that my mother couldn't bring herself to repeat my misdeed to my father in my presence. I got the usual punishment of dinner alone, outside under the breadfruit tree, but added on to that, I was not allowed to go to the library on Saturday, and on Sunday, after Sunday school and dinner, I was not allowed to take a stroll in the botanical gardens, where Gwen was waiting for me in the bamboo grove.

That happened when I was in the first form. Now here Miss Edward stood. Her whole face was on fire. Her eyes were bulging out of her head. I was sure that at any minute they would land at my feet and roll away. The small pimples on her face, already looking as if they were constantly irritated, now ballooned into huge, on-the-verge-of-exploding boils. Her head shook from side to side. Her strange bottom, which she carried high in the air, seemed to rise up so high that it almost touched the ceiling. Why did I not pay attention, she said. My impertinence was beyond endurance. She then found a hundred words for the different forms my impertinence took. On she went. I was just getting used to this amazing bellowing when suddenly she was speechless. In fact, everything stopped. Her eyes stopped, her bottom stopped, her pimples stopped. Yes, she had got close enough so that her eyes caught a glimpse of what I had done to my textbook. The glimpse soon led to closer inspection. It was bad enough that I had defaced my schoolbook by writing in it. That I should write under the picture of Columbus "The Great Man . . ." etc. was just too much. I had gone too far this time, defaming one of the great men in history, Christopher Columbus, discoverer of the island that was my home. And now look at me. I was not even hanging my head in remorse. Had my peers ever seen anyone so arrogant, so blasphemous?

I was sent to the headmistress, Miss Moore. As punishment, I was removed from my position as prefect, and my place was taken by the odious Hilarene. As an added punishment, I was ordered to copy Books I and II of *Paradise Lost,* by John Milton, and to have it done a week from that day. I then couldn't wait to get home to lunch and the comfort of my mother's kisses and arms. I had nothing to worry about there yet; it would be a while before my mother and father heard of my bad deeds. What a terrible morning! Seeing my mother would be such a tonic—something to pick me up.

When I got home, my mother kissed me absentmindedly. My father had got home ahead of me, and they were already deep in conversation, my father regaling her with some unusually outlandish thing the oaf Mr. Oatie had done. I washed my hands and took my place at table. My mother brought me my lunch. I took one smell of it, and I could tell that it was the much hated breadfruit. My mother said not at all, it was a new kind of rice imported from Belgium, and not breadfruit, mashed and forced through a ricer, as I thought. She went back to talking to my father. My father could hardly get a few words out of his mouth before she was a jellyfish of laughter. I sat there, putting my food in my mouth. I could not believe that she couldn't see how miserable I was and so reach out a hand to comfort me and caress my cheek, the way she usually did when she sensed that something was amiss with me. I could not believe how she laughed at everything he said, and how bitter it made me feel to see how much she liked him. I ate my meal. The more I ate of it, the more I was sure that it was breadfruit. When I finished, my mother got up to remove my plate. As she started out the door, I said, "Tell me, really, the name of the thing I just ate."

My mother said, "You just ate some breadfruit. I made it look like rice so that you would eat it. It's very good for you, filled with lots of vitamins." As she said this, she laughed. She was standing half inside the door, half outside. Her body was in the shade of our house, but her head was in the sun. When she laughed, her mouth opened to show off big, shiny, sharp white teeth. It was as if my mother had suddenly turned into a crocodile.

Etheridge Knight (1931–1991)

Known as a prison poet, Etheridge Knight writes not only of literal incarceration, but of the imposed imprisonment of racism and poverty and also of internal imprisonment, the chains of addiction and internalized racism. As imprisoned as he was both literally and figuratively, Knight sings, too, of freedom, of hope, of love, and of survival. His poems are witness to a strong and enduring spirit.

Born in Corinth, Mississippi, on April 19, 1931, into a poor family of seven children, Etheridge Knight completed only a ninth-grade education. He spent his adolescent years in menial jobs and in pool halls, bars, juke joints, and underground poker games. In these predominantly Black male environments, Knight honed his skills in verbal performance, mastering the art of "Black toasts" or "telling toasts," long narrative poems from the oral tradition that are performed from memory and with spirit. While his rough adolescent environment encouraged Knight's poetic experience, it also introduced him to addiction. Knight became addicted to drugs at an early age and would never fully free himself of addiction before his early death.

Etheridge Knight served in the United States Army from 1947–1951. As a soldier in the Korean War, he suffered a shrapnel wound, and his addiction to narcotics increased when he was treated with morphine. Arrested in 1960 for robbery of a purse in Indianapolis to support his drug habit, he served an eight-year prison sentence at Indiana State Prison in Michigan City. Convinced his prison sentence was unjustly long and racially motivated, Knight wrote poetry to curb his anger. He was encouraged by the prominent poet, Gwendolyn Brooks, and by Dudley Randall, whose new Broadside Press published his first collection, Poems from Prison, *in 1968.*

While in prison, he was introduced to fellow poet Sonia Sanchez and married her when he was released. The marriage was brief and unsuccessful due to his continuing drug addiction. He married second wife, Mary McNally, a few years later, adopted two children, and lived in Minneapolis until their separation in 1977. At this point, Knight moved to Memphis, Tennessee, for methadone treatment. Remarried to third wife, Charlene Blackburn, Knight had a third child, a son.

Etheridge Knight died March 10, 1991 of lung cancer, leaving a legacy of poetry and promise. Knight's poetry is not always as polemic as much of the poetry of the Black Arts movement was, but is full of his personal feelings of anguish, loneliness, frustration, and triumph in his struggle in prison and within the pull of addiction. Central to Knight's second collection of poetry, Belly Song and Other Poems *(1973), is the void and reality of the prison cell. Prison becomes not only literal space but also a symbol for the sociopolitical conditions of Black people. In "Belly Song," repetition creates a rhythm as Knight writes about surviving prison, reviving hope, memory, and healing.*

Two later collections, Born of a Woman: New and Selected Poems *(1980) and* Essential Etheridge Knight *(1986), compile prominent poems from* Poems from Prison *and* Belly Song *and continue the themes and style of these collections with poetry that values the dignity of every human life, including the lives of prison inmates, Knight's family members, and Knight himself. In* Born of Woman, *Knight highlights and celebrates the generative power of women. These later poems emphasize heritage, the continuity of tradition and family, and the collectivity of suffering and history. "Ilu, the Talking Drum," for example, moves from images of Africa to the South and back to Africa through pulse and rhythm, paralleling the movement of Blacks in the United States from slavery to cultural revolution and revival of heritage. Knight also continues to link resonant images to stark political messages. In "A Black Poet Leaps to His Death," Knight sings for a young Black man who has committed suicide, linking the tragedy to war in Lebanon, and filling the poem with mournful images of fall.*

Edheridge Knight is acknowledged as one of the most important and popular writers of the Black Arts Movement. Relying on the skills of his adolescence, Knight always recited poetry from memory. He felt, as part of the Black Arts philosophy, that art needed to be functional and for the benefit of the community. Through public recitation, Knight reinforced the orality of poetry as a way of celebrating the social and communal storytelling tradition of African American tradition. By writing forcefully and emotionally about the pain, rage, and sorrow of his experiences within the prison system, as a drug addict, and as a Black man and family member, Knight added a personal and emotional dimension to the militancy of the poetry of his time.

R. Joyce Lausch

Cell Song

Night Music Slanted
Light strike the cave
of sleep. I alone
tread the red circle
and twist the space
with speech.

Come now, etheridge, don't
be a savior; take
your words and scrape
the sky, shake rain

on the desert, sprinkle
salt on the tail
of a girl,

can there anything
good come out of
prison

The Idea of Ancestry

1

Taped to the wall of my cell are 47 pictures: 47 black
faces: my father, mother, grandmothers (1 dead), grandfathers (both dead), brothers, sisters, uncles, aunts,
cousins (1st & 2nd), nieces, and nephews. They stare
across the space at me sprawling on my bunk. I know
their dark eyes, they know mine. I know their style,
they know mine. I am all of them, they are all of me;
they are farmers, I am a thief, I am me, they are thee.

I have at one time or another been in love with my mother,
1 grandmother, 2 sisters, 2 aunts (1 went to the asylum),
and 5 cousins. I am now in love with a 7-yr-old niece
(she sends me letters written in large block print, and
her picture is the only one that smiles at me).

I have the same name as 1 grandfather, 3 cousins, 3 nephews,
and 1 uncle. The uncle disappeared when he was 15, just took
off and caught a freight (they say). He's discussed each year
when the family has a reunion, he causes uneasiness in
the clan, he is an empty space. My father's mother, who is 93
and who keeps the Family Bible with everybody's birth dates
(and death dates) in it, always mentions him. There is no
place in her Bible for "whereabouts unknown."

2

Each fall the graves of my grandfathers call me, the brown
hills and red gullies of mississippi send out their electric
messages, galvanizing my genes. Last yr / like a salmon quitting
the cold ocean-leaping and bucking up his birthstream /I
hitchhiked my way from LA with 16 caps in my pocket and a
monkey on my back. And I almost kicked it with the kinfolks.
I walked barefooted in my grandmother's backyard / I smelled the
    old
land and the woods / I sipped cornwhiskey from fruit jars with the
    men /
I flirted with the women / I had a ball till the caps ran out
and my habit came down. That night I looked at my grandmother
and split / my guts were screaming for junk / but I was almost

contented / I had almost caught up with me.
(The next day in Memphis I cracked a croaker's crib for a fix.)

This yr there is a gray stone wall damming my stream, and when
the falling leaves stir my genes, I pace my cell or flop on my bunk
and stare at 47 black faces across the space. I am all of them,
they are all of me, I am me, they are thee, and I have no children
to float in the space between.

Haiku

1

Eastern guard tower
glints in sunset; convicts rest
like lizards on rocks.

2

The piano man
is stingy at 3 A.M.
his songs drop like plum.

3

Morning sun slants cell.
Drunks stagger like cripple flies
On jailhouse floor.

4

To write a blues song
is to regiment riots
and pluck gems from graves.

5

A bare pecan tree
slips a pencil shadow down
a moonlit snow slope.

My Life, the Quality of Which

My life, the quality of which
From the moment
My Father grunted and comed
Until now
As the sounds of my words
Bruise your ears
IS
and can be felt
In the one word: DESPERATION

But you have to *feel* for it

Jefferson, Missouri
June 9, 1972

The Bones of My Father

1

There are no dry bones
here in this valley. The skull
of my father grins
at the Mississippi moon
from the bottom
of the Tallahatchie,
the bones of my father
are buried in the mud
of these creeks and brooks that twist
and flow their secrets to the sea.
but the wind sings to me
here the sun speaks to me
of the dry bones of my father.

2

There are no dry bones
in the northern valleys, in the Harlem alleys
young / black / men with knees bent
nod on the stoops of the tenements

and dream
of the dry bones of my father

And young white longhairs who flee
their homes, and bend their minds
and sing their songs of brotherhood
and no more wars are searching for
my father's bones.

3

There are no dry bones here.
We hide from the sun.
No more do we take the long straight strides.
Our steps have been shaped by the cages
that kept us. We glide sideways
like crabs across the sand.
We perch on green lilies, we search
beneath white rocks . . .
THERE ARE NO DRY BONES HERE

The skull of my father
grins at the Mississippi moon
from the bottom
of the Tallahatchie.

Connecticut
February 21, 1971

For Black Poets Who Think of Suicide

Black Poets should live—not leap
From steel bridges (like the white boys do).
Black Poets should live—not lay
Their necks on railroad tracks (like the white boys do).
Black Poets should seek—but not search too much
In sweet dark caves, nor hunt for snipe
Down psychic trails (like the white boys do).

For Black Poets belong to Black People. Are
The Flutes of Black Lovers. Are

The Organs of Black Sorrows. Are
The Trumpets of Black Warriors.
Let All Black Poets die as Trumpets,
And be buried in the dust of marching feet.

Ilu, The Talking Drum

The deadness was threatening us—15 Nigerians and 1 Mississippi
     nigger.
It hung heavily, like stones around our necks, pulling us down
to the ground, black arms and legs outflung
on the wide green lawn of the big white house
The deadness was threatening us, the day
was dying with the sun, the stillness—
unlike the sweet silence after love / making or
the pulsating quietness of a summer night—
the stillness was skinny and brittle and wrinkled
by the precise people sitting on the wide white porch
of the big white house . . .
The darkness was threatening us, menacing . . .
we twisted, turned, shifted positions, picked our noses,
stared at our bare toes, hissed air thru our teeth . . .
Then Tunji, green robes flowing as he rose,
strapped on Ilu, the talking drum,
and began:

kah doom / kah doom-doom / kah doom / kah doom-doom-doom
kah doom / kah doom-doom / kah doom / kah doom-doom-doom
kah doom / kah doom-doom / kah doom / kah doom-doom-doom
kah doom / kah doom-doom / kah doom / kah doom-doom-doom

the heart, the heart beats, the heart, the heart beats slow
the heart beats slowly, the heart beats
the blood flows slowly, the blood flows
the blood, the blood flows, the blood, the blood flows slow
kah doom / kah doom-doom / kah doom / kah doom-doom-doom
and the day opened to the sound
kah doom / kah doom-doom / kah doom / kah doom-doom-doom
and our feet moved to the sound of life
kah doom / kah doom-doom / kah doom / kah doom-doom-doom

and we rode the rhythms as one
from Nigeria to Mississippi
and back
kah doom / kah doom-doom / kah doom / kah doom-doom-doom

Belly Song

—FOR THE DAYTOP FAMILY

"You have made something
Out of the sea that blew
And rolled you on its salt bitter lips.
It nearly swallowed you.
But I hear
You are tough and harder to swallow than most . . ."

—S. Mansfield

    1

And I   and I / must admit
that the sea in you
    has sung / to the sea / in me
and I   and I / must admit
that the sea in me
    has fallen / in love
    with the sea in you
because you have made something
out of the sea
    that nearly swallowed you

And this poem
This poem
This poem / I give / to you.
This poem is a song / I sing / I sing / to you
from the bottom
    of the sea
       in my belly

This poem / is a song / about FEELINGS
about the Bone of feeling
about the Stone of feeling
    And the Feather of feeling

2

This poem
This poem
This poem / is /
a death / chant
and a grave / stone
and a prayer for the dead:
      for young Jackie Robinson.
a moving Blk / warrior who walked
among us
      with a wide / stride—and heavy heels
moving   moving   moving
thru the blood and mud and shit of Vietnam
moving   moving   moving
thru the blood and mud and dope of America
      for Jackie / who was /

a song
and a stone
and a Feather of feeling
    now dead
and / gone / in this month of love

This poem
This poem / is / a silver feather
and the sun-gold / glinting / green hills breathing
river flowing . . .

3

This poem
This poem
This poem / is / for ME—for me
and the days / that lay / in the back / of my mind
when the sea / rose up /
    to swallow me
and the streets I walked
    were lonely streets
    were stone / cold streets

This poem
This poem / is /
for me / and the nights
    when I
wrapped my feelings

in a sheet of ice
and stared
    at the stars
        thru iron bars
        and cried
in the middle of my eyes . . .

This poem
This poem
This poem / is / for me
    and my woman
    and the yesterdays
when she opened
    to me like a flower
    But I fell on her
    like a stone
I fell on her like a stone . . .

    4

And now—in my 40th year
    I have come here
to this House of Feelings
to this Singing Sea
and I   and I / must admit
that the sea in me
    has fallen / in love
with the sea in you
because the sea
that now sings / in you
    is the same sea
that nearly swallowed you—
    and me too.

Seymour, Connecticut
June 1971

A Black Poet Leaps to His Death

—FOR MBEMBE MILTON SMITH

was it a blast to the balls dear brother
with the wind ringing in the ear
that great rush against the air
that great push
                    into the universe

you are not now alone mbembe
of the innocent eyes   sadder
than a mondays rain   it is I
who hear your crush of bone
                your splatter of brain
                your tear of flesh
on the cold chicago stone

                and my october cry
when the yellow moon is ringed with blood
of children dead in the lebanese mud
        is as sharp as a kc switchblade
your pain is a slash across my throat
i feel a chill   can the poet belie
the poem
        old revolutionaries never die
it is said
        they just be born again
(check chuck colson and his panther from folsom)
but you are *dead*
mbembe   poetman in the home of the brave
the brown leaves whister across you grave
but it must have been a rush   a great gasp
        of breath
        the awesome leap to your death
o poet of the blood and bone
        of the short song
        and serious belief
i sing you release

                            October 1981

Ruth Ellen Kocher (1965–)

Born July 26, 1965, in Wilkes-Barre, Pennsylvania, Ruth Ellen Kocher spent most of her childhood and adolescence in one of the many housing projects constructed in the north-eastern United States in the early 1970s. She is the author of Desdemona's Fire, *a collection of poems published in 1999, which won the Naomi Long Madgett Poetry Award. Her poetry has also been published in a number of literary journals, including* African American Review, Antioch Review, Gettysburg Review, Ploughshares, Prairie Schooner, *and* Missouri Review, *which awarded her the Tom McAfee Discovery Feature.*

Kocher attended Pennsylvania State University, where she earned a B.A. in English. While there, she was encouraged and greatly influenced by the poet Bruce Weigl. She says of Weigl that his poetry on the Vietnam War made evident to her for the first time how lyric can wrench beauty from a tragic past. She was also a fellow at the Bucknell Seminar for Younger Poets. Later Kocher attended Arizona State University, where she earned an M.F.A. in creative writing, working on her development of narrative lyric with the poet Norman Dubie, who encouraged her to find not only what is beautiful in language, but what is unexpected. She went on to earn a Ph.D. in literature. Kocher is currently an assistant professor at Southern Illinois University, where she teaches creative writing and African American literature.

Kocher cites as poetic influences Louise Gluck, whose economy of language she admires, and Theodore Roethke for his experimentation with form. One of the themes Kocher repeatedly explores in her poetry is how one's relationships to parents and community influence the formation of self-perception and that ever-elusive thing called identity. Kocher's poems use a speaker who often explores issues of race and identity as tenuous circumstances dependent on familial, social, and self-perception. She often exploits the tensions between fiction and reality through retellings of classic tales in literature and mythology, using those images to complete her own incomplete history.

In "Poem to a Jazz Man," the speaker is a daughter who imagines her absent father's seduction of her mother and, in doing so, forges a connection with the father she never knew. The description of the man at the piano is as musical and seductive as the speaker imagines the man himself to be, an effect created by assonance, in this case the repetition of e sounds. Her mother, by contrast, is presented as two-dimensional, an Eve-like innocent whose naivete makes her an easy target for the man: "She didn't have a chance."

"Liturgy of the Light-Skinned" is a companion piece to "Jazz Man," the speaker again the daughter who, though a "myth" to her father and "not part of the story," writes the story of her origins. She compensates for details unknown to her by the inclusion of fantastic images that connote a fairytale-like tone (the lizards in the piano, the old widow) so that her history becomes its own myth. Repetition becomes a tool by which Kocher manip-

ulates paradox—making a story out of a not-story—and illustrates generational connections with her mother and grandmother.

In "Braiding," the speaker's interactions with three different hairdressers bring her to confront various aspects of her own identity. The poem braids three strands of description, using dialogue, interior monologue, and sensory images to evoke the three experiences with these women. The exchanges between the women and the speaker introduce culture and family that seem foreign to the speaker, something she seems able to experience only second hand through all of the women in this poem. In the first segment, the speaker sees herself mirrored in the hairdresser's biracial son, and in the sound of her spoken name she feels the woman's attempt to connect with her in "sisterly devotion." Part two uses humor and music to evoke the rhythm of easy banter among the salon workers and clients. In the final segment, the speaker remembers her adolescence, memories marked by realization of sexuality and of difference. Images of taste and smell give the recollection immediacy. The final internal monologue that concludes the poem suggest the speaker looks to these collected moments for an affirmation of the African ancestry from which she "always ran."

In the title poem to her collection, "Desdemona's Fire," Kocher evokes the fictional figures of Othello and Desdemona, a literary allusion by which she represents the interracial union of her speaker's parents and the biracial child's search for voice. Addressing the parents who refuse to accept her true self, the speaker shows each parent seeing only him- or herself reflected in the image of the child. The adult speaker insists on "writing myself into your story" by revisiting a childhood memory of self, during which she confronts the image each parent seems to hold of her. Picking up on the language and mirror imagery of "Liturgy," this poem also depicts a daughter's demand that each sees her not as the image of one or the other but as daughter to them both.

Vanessa Holford Diana

Poem to a Jazz Man

My mother doesn't seem to remember
any of this, but the music must have been sweet,
cool jazz taking her like snake charm,
pleasure and desire, a warm July night.
The tall black man at the piano must have teased
the keys into filling that hot air with speak-easy
sugared sounds. She didn't have a chance.
Some poor white girl from the edge of town,
singing Saturdays to pay her rent,
could never have known what the music could do,
how the man and the piano, his fingers, his soul,
could so easily enter her, grow there
into a small, dark-eyed song.

Child, she would say, you are just like him.

Liturgy of the Light-Skinned

On me you can smell a story,
iron and blue slag,
wooden floor boards
danced on all night.
There's a piano in this story
and a black man
whose fingers were not very long.
In the piano are the souls of lizards
who frantically
jump against the keys
seeing a light
they believe is the sun.
The man at the piano
is someone's father but
his daughter is a myth to him.
She is not part of the story.
The ending is not ending
when a woman
meets a child who is
not her own image.
The woman combs her own hair.
The mirror frames her face.
She thinks about the old woman
downstairs, the child at her feet, and wishes
that the lights in the house
would not go out
because the swollen limbs of her mother
have failed again,
but they do, every night
and so every night
the old woman and the young woman
are both mothers, share
the bitter blanket of arthritis
and aching. Darkness.
This is only the beginning.
I am the child and my mother
fights the rage of her mother,
the brimstone scowls at the wicked,
the hard light that passes through
her house. I am the daughter,
the lizard, the man who knows only myth
but thinks he's the sun. My mother looks at me
and I know I am not part of this story.

Braiding

I.

Each woman does it differently.
Brinette scolds her children
and weaves the holy ghost into my hair
knowing the difference in my skin
like her own son, large-boned
Creole boy with his daddy's
disposition. She says my name
determined to jog me, *Ruth,*
with emphasis on the fricative motion
of speaking, of women and sisterly
devotion to God and His signs:
that I have come to her
once again, on just the day
she needs cab fare to the AME.
God wants her there.

Long sliver of the right cold inside us,
take us over the fold, the good turn:
how we know everything wants us near,
back again to some comfort
without knowing. World?
Ours, never again.

II.

Kim owns a salon, does "hair design."
Her braiding marks a rhythm in my ear,
her three-inch nails clicking
the tripart criss-cross of Kan-eka-lon strands
while David explains to the next girl
how, the night before in drag,
he does a number at a family club,
loses the rice bags he used for breasts
during a pirouette to Donna Sommers
screeching ". . . hot stuff baby this evening,
hot stuff baby tonight."

This is back street,
Shake that, that mother, damn
all over everything you ever said
and want it back again

back where we belong,
take us there. Take us.

Kim says, Girl, you gotta big head,
and charges me more than she said,
takes a break and eats lunch
while the other girls' men
come in, one by one, for waves.

III.

All October. Orange mornings
and brown leaves and boyfriends calling
girl, calling you away from home
as if the woods would love you better.
Billy Joe. Billy Joe's hands.

My mother sent me to Brenda Brown's,
a neighborhood black lady, because
she'd know what to do with my hair,
would know the depth,
the hold of it. Brenda smoked cigarettes,
sat me down with her own kids
all munching Sugar Pops,
let the comb stew in the flame
so that, when she finally touched it
red hot to slicked down nap,
the heat would evaporate Afro sheen into breath,
hair into smoke that choked me all day.
She called my friend "Lily girl,"
colorless besides freckles that startled her face,
taught her how to do it,
how to move the comb
carefully away from you
like a brand turned over
and over until you're
ready to go.

When you're ready to know
why you always ran
go back again and listen,
voices, voices, all over you
taking the blanket of shadows,
all of their hands,

twisting the dark fold into a message:
hieroglyphic artifact of your own
wanting. Say it again,
you love me. You love my hair,
all coarseness and telling.

Desdemona's Fire

Birth, not death, is the hard loss.—Louise Glück

Trace the image
of yourselves,
dark arm, white thigh.
That the two of you
could have a child
is my story.
Imagine her,
child in a red nightgown
sleepwalking through the center
of her mother's kitchen
looking for the dog
she never had:
poor moor, poor she
as me, that other life
that came from you.

I am writing myself into your story,
not as a dream, not as the hierophant
whose silk robes drape over your feet
like white-water tide spilling. I am yours,

the alien hand.

Call me daughter
and you will be saved.
Call me wind that feeds your fire.
Call me water. Call me breath.
I am writing myself into your story
because you murder again
not knowing my birth.

If you spoke
as though you loved me,
strangers would forget
how we pass each other in the littered
morning,
fail among the milk cartons
and crushed cans rusted
into their cores.

Say it simply:
your eyes reflected in mine
as though our other lives
were not this one also.

What alien hand
keeps you splitting yourselves in two,
determined to create a life
that turns one morning toward the sink
and above the pitch of a radio,
sees her own reflection,
the dark circle of her own name:
girl in a red nightgown
who speaks
an ancient alphabet in her sleep.

Say it finally: the alien hand
that destroys your so many ways.

Yusef Komunyakaa (1947–)

Yusef Komunyakaa was born on April 29, 1947, in Bogalusa, Louisiana, seventy miles from New Orleans. Immediately after high school graduation in 1965, Komunyakaa entered the Army, serving in Vietnam both as a war correspondent and as editor of The Southern Cross, *a military newspaper. He was awarded a Bronze Star for his service.*

A poet with twenty years of publishing experience, Komunyakaa received minimal recognition before winning a 1994 Pulitzer Prize for Neon Vernacular *(1993), a collection of new poems and a wide range of selected poems from each of seven collections published in the 1970s and 1980s. Komunyakaa's Louisiana boyhood, his experiences in Vietnam, and his sense of African American history and artistic tradition figure largely in his poetry. Also, like poet Michael S. Harper, Komunyakaa commemorates the jazz tradition as subject and as stylistic method.*

Komunyakaa's publications previous to Neon Vernacular *illustrate the range of his poetic talent.* Dedications and Other Dark Horses *(1977), a chapbook, and* Lost in the Bonewheel Factory *(1979), Komunyakaa's first full-length book, focus on the hard realities of the human condition and the resilience of the human spirit. Several poems in* Bonewheel *and later collections follow the structure Komunyakaa employs in "Passions," in which he grounds a theme—passion—in still-life vivid images, creating a slideshow effect of sensory stimulation.* Copacetic *(1984) integrates blues and jazz style with lyrical poems of a narrative quality, focusing on his boyhood in the South and the beliefs, songs, and music of the folk. Tone and image bleak, "Blues Chant Hoodoo Survival" and "Back Then" foreground the continuum of resistance and endurance that characterizes African American history.* I Apologize for the Eyes in My Head *(1986) is characterized by experimentation with longer poems, contrasts of mood, ghosts symbolic of mortality, waiting death, and the losses of slavery, Jim Crow laws, love, and loved ones. The collection resonates with an overwhelming nostalgia for Louisiana boyhood and a central relationship in the city.* Toys in a Field *(1987) and* Dien Cai Dau *(1988) deal most centrally with Komunyakaa's experiences in Vietnam, especially the psychological and spiritual horrors of war for all involved. The poems of* Dien Cau Dau, *military slang for crazy, have a surreal quality and revolve around austere images to capture the liminal experience of war.* February in Sydney *(1989) exemplifies Komunyakaa's rhythmic, fluid, introspective voice. The title poem, for example, connects the jazz tradition to psychological survival as sounds become images.*

Komunyakaa's poetry of the 1990s continues to demonstrate variety in content, form, and style. In Magic City *(1992), generations and family relationships are central. Komunyakaa revisits his childhood, foregrounding the simultaneous simplicity and complexity of perspective and self-revelation in poems like "Nude Tango" and "Venus's-flytraps." The new poems in* Neon Vernacular *are about return, the "what ifs, "what's next," and "what has stayed the same" questions of a man reconstructing identity. His latest work,* Thieves of Paradise *(1988), sweeps time, returning to a mythic past in poems like "Memory Cave," and to his own Vietnam past in "Buried Light." In "Kosmos" and "Anodyne," Komunyakaa celebrates his own body as a timeless miracle and the embodiment of generations leading to his existence.*

Komunyakaa's art of image is profound. Communicating emotion and experience beyond the common capacity of language, the weaving of images in single poems and between poems creates a rich tapestry. What Komunyakaa's poetry accomplishes is a psychological portrait of an individual from childhood to adulthood with continual reminder that the individual is history and tradition, self and all else, at once. Narrative skill from Darkhorses *to* Thieves of Paradise *grounds philosophy and brings image to life.*

In addition to his own poetry, Komunyakaa has also co-edited, with Sascha Feinstein, The Jazz Poetry Anthology *(1991). His most recent work,* Blue Notes: Essays, Interview and Commentaries (Poets on Poetry) *(1999), was produced with co-editor Radiclani Clytus.*

Yusef Komunyakaa graduated with an M.F.A. degree from the University of California, Irvine, after earning a B.A. at the University of Colorado and an M.A. at Colorado State University. He first taught at the University of New Orleans and, for a short time, taught poetry to third through sixth graders in the city. Since 1985, Komunyakaa has been a professor of English at Indiana University. A traveler, Komunyakaa has spent time in Japan, St. Thomas, and Puerto Rico and spends part of each year in Australia.

R. Joyce Lausch

Passions

Coitus
Ah, pink tip of sixth sense,
oyster fat of lovepearl,
dew-seed & singing leaf-tongue,
lizard's head of pure thought.

Body Painting
To step into the golden lute
& paint one's soul
on the body. Bird
goddess & slow snake
in the flowered tree. Circle,
lineage, womb, mouth, leaf-footed
godanimal on a man's chest
who leaps into the moon
on a woman's belly.

Blue-green Iridescent Flies
Meat, excrement, a source

of life attracts this
message & definition
of the ultimate us.
They fly off
with the weight of the world.

Peepshow
A new moon rises
on an elevator over the mountain.

String Bass
The moon's at the window,
as she rocks in the arms
of this lonely player
like a tall Yoruba woman.

Pinball Machines
Encased in glass, a woman
opens her eyes. The room floods
with a century of bells.
Magnetic balls & sound of metal
seem enough to build a locomotive
moving through the room's wooden bones.

Butterflies
Incandescent anthologies
semi-zoological alphabets of fire,
these short lives transmigrate, topaz
memories cling to air, release wordflesh
from the cocoon of silk fear.

Psilocybe
One hundred purple rooms
in a mirror of black water.
I must enter each,
interrogated by a different demon.
In the distance I can hear
the sea coming. A woman at Laguna Beach.
Her eyes now seashells.
Her arms two far-off sails.
Like a tree drags the ground on a windy day
with yellow & red fruit too soft to eat,
she comes toward me. Stars cluster
her laughter like a nest of moth eyes—

her focus on the world.
The closer she comes, the deeper
I work myself away into music
that I hope can save us both.
A man steps from a junkyard of chrome
fenders & hubcaps,
pulling off masks.
At least a hundred scattered about.
The last one: I'm him.

Back Then

I've eaten handfuls of fire
back to the bright sea
of my first breath
riding the hipbone of memory
& saw a wheel of birds
a bridge into the morning
but that was when gold
didn't burn out a man's eyes
before auction blocks
groaned in courtyards
& nearly got the best of me
that was when the spine
of every ebony tree wasn't
a pale woman's easy chair
black earth-mother of us all
crack in the bones & sombre
eyes embedded like beetles
in stoic heartwood
seldom have I needed
to shake a hornet's nest
from the breastplate
fire over the ground
pain tears me to pieces
at the pottery wheel
of each dawn
an antelope leaps
in the heartbeat
of the talking drum

Blues Chant Hoodoo Revival

my story is
how deep the heart runs
to hide & laugh
with your hands
over your blank mouth
face behind the mask
talking in tongues
something tearing
feathers from a crow
that screams
from the furnace
the black candle
in a skull
sweet pain of meat

    let's pour the river's rainbow
    into our stone water jars
    bad luck isn't red flowers
    crushed under jackboots

your story is
a crippled animal
dragging a steel trap
across desert sand
a bee's sting inside your heart
& its song of honey
in my groin
a factory of blue jays
in honey locust leaves
wet pages of smoke
like a man
deserting his shadow
in dark woods
the dog that limps away
& rotten fruit on the trees
this story is
the speaking skull
on the mantelpiece
the wingspan of a hawk
at the edge of a coyote's cry
the seventh son's mojo hand

holding his life together
with a black cat bone
the six grandfathers
& spider woman
the dust wings
of ghost dance vision
deer that can't
stand for falling
wunmonije witch doctor
backwater blues
juju man
a silk gown on the floor
a black bowl
on a red lacquered table
x-rated
because it's true

       let's pour starlight
       from our stone water jars
       pain isn't just red flowers
       crushed under jackboots

my story is
inside a wino's bottle
the cup blood leaps into
eight-to-the-bar
a man on his knees
facing the golden calf
the silverfish of old lust
mama hoodoo
a gullah basket
woven from your hair
love note from the madhouse
thornbushes
naming the shape
of things to come
old murder weapons
strings of piano wire

       let's pour the night
       into our stone water jars
       this song isn't red flowers
       crushed under silence

our story is
a rifle butt
across our heads
arpeggio of bowed grass
among glass trees
where they kick down doors
& we swan-dive from
the brooklyn bridge
a post-hypnotic suggestion
a mosaic membrane
skin of words
mirrors shattered
in roadhouses
in the gun-barrel night
how a machine moves
deeper into piles
of bones
the way we
crowd at the foot
of the gallows

February in Sydney

Dexter Gordon's tenor sax
plays "April in Paris"
inside my head all the way back
on the bus from Double Bay.
Round Midnight, the '50s,
cool cobblestone streets
resound footsteps of Bebop
musicians with whiskey-laced voices
from a boundless dream in French.
Bud, Prez, Webster, & The Hawk,
their names run together riffs.
Painful gods jive talk through
bloodstained reeds & shiny brass
where music is an anesthetic.
Unreadable faces from the human void
float like torn pages across the bus
windows. An old anger drips into my throat,
& I try thinking something good,

letting the precious bad
settle to the salty bottom.
Another scene keeps repeating itself:
I emerge from the dark theatre,
passing a woman who grabs her red purse
& hugs it to her like a heart attack.
Tremolo. Dexter comes back to rest
behind my eyelids. A loneliness
lingers like a silver needle
under my black skin,
as I try to feel how it is
to scream for help through a horn.

Venus's-flytraps

I am five,
 Wading out into deep
  Sunny grass,
Unmindful of snakes
 & yellowjackets, out
  To the yellow flowers
Quivering in sluggish heat.
 Don't mess with me
  'Cause I have my Lone Ranger
Six-shooter. I can hurt
 You with questions
  Like silver bullets.
The tall flowers in my dreams are
 Bis as the First State Bank,
  & they eat all the people
Except the ones I love.
 They have women's names,
  With mouths like where
Babies come from. I am five.
 I'll dance for you
  If you close your eyes. No
Peeping through your fingers.
 I don't supposed to be
  This close to the tracks.
One afternoon I saw
 What a train did to a cow.
  Sometimes I stand so close

I can see the eyes
   Of men hiding in boxcars.
      Sometimes they wave
& holler for me to get back. I laugh
   When trains make the dogs
      Howl. Their ears hurt.
I also know bees
   Can't live without flowers.
      I wonder why Daddy
Calls Mama honey.
   All the bees in the world
      Live in little white houses
Except the ones in these flowers.
   All sticky & sweet inside.
      I wonder what death tastes like.
Sometimes I toss the butterflies
   Back into the air.
      I wish I knew why
The music in my head
   Makes me scared.
      But I know things
I don't supposed to know.
   I could start walking
      & never stop.
These yellow flowers
   Go on forever.
      Almost to Detroit.
Almost to the sea.
   My mama says I'm a mistake.
      That I made her a bad girl.
My playhouse is underneath
   Our house, & I hear people
      Telling each other secrets.

Nude Tango

While they were out buying Easter hats
With my brothers & sister,
I stole a third chocolate
Rabbit from the refrigerator
& tiptoed between two mirrors

Where the scent of my parents
Guarded the room. I swayed, bobbed,
Swayed, my shirt a white flag
When it landed on a bedpost.
Something I had to get past
In the pit of my belly.
What were my feet trying to do
When a shoe slid under the bed?
I tangoed one naked reflection
Toward another, creating a third,
As he sprung across the years
& pulled me into the woods:
If you say anything,
I'll kill your mama
A ripped shirt pocket
Flapped like a green tongue.
Thistled grass bloodied my knees.
God was in the sunlight
Toying with the knife.
Milkweed surrounded us,
Spraying puffs of seeds,
& I already knew the word *cock.*
I shoved out a hip,
Threw my arms around
My image, & fell to the floor
To let it pass over
Like an animal travelling
Through our lives
To leave a mythic smell.

Memory Cave

A tallow worked into a knot
of rawhide, with a ball of waxy light
tied to a stick, the boy
scooted through a secret mouth
of the cave, pulled by the flambeau
in his hand. He could see
the gaze of agate eyes
& wished for the forbidden

plains of bison & wolf, years
from the fermented honey
& musty air. In the dried
slag of bear & bat guano,
the initiate stood with sleeping
gods at his feet, lost
in the great cloud of their one
breath. Their muzzles craved
touch. How did they learn
to close eyes, to see into
the future? Before the Before:
mammon was unnamed & mist
hugged ravines & hillocks.
The elders would test him
beyond doubt & blood. Mica
lit the false skies where
stalactite dripped perfection
into granite. He fingered
icons sunlight & anatase
never touched. Ibex carved
on a throwing stick, reindeer
worried into an ivory amulet,
& a bear's head. Outside,
the men waited two days
for him, with condor & bovid,
& not in a thousand years
would he have dreamt a woman
standing here beside a man,
saying, "This is as good
as the stag at Salon Noir
& the polka-dotted horses."
The man scribbles *Leo Loves
Angela* below the boy's last bear
drawn with manganese dioxide
& animal fat. This is where
sunrise opened a door in stone
when he was summoned to drink
honey wine & embrace a woman
beneath a five-pointed star.
Lying there beside the gods
hefty & silent as boulders,
he could almost remember
before he was born, could see
the cliff from which he'd fall.

Kosmos

Walt, you shanghaied me to this
oak, as every blood-tipped leaf
soliloquized "Strange Fruit"
like the octoroon in New Orleans

who showed you how passion
ignited dogwood, how it rose
from inside the singing sap.
You heard primordial notes

murmur up from the Mississippi,
a clank of chains among the green
ithyphallic totems, betting your heart
could run vistas with Crazy Horse

& runaway slaves. Sunset dock
to whorehouse, temple to hovel,
your lines traversed America's
white space, driven by a train whistle.

*

Believing you could be three places
at once, you held the gatekeeper's daughter,
lured by the hard eyes of his son,
on a voyage in your head

to a face cut into Mount Rushmore.
You knew the curse in sperm
& egg, but had faith in the soil,
that it would work itself out

in generations, springs piercing bedrock.
Love pushed through jailhouses, into bedrooms
of presidents & horse thieves,
oil sucked into machines in sweatshops

& factories. I followed from my hometown
where bedding an oak is bread on the table;
where your books, as if flesh, were locked
in a glass case behind the check-out desk.

*

Wind-jostled foliage—a scherzo,
a bellydancer adorned in bells.
A mulatto moon halved into yesterday
& tomorrow, some balustrade

full-bloomed. But you taught home
was wherever my feet took me,
birdsong over stockyards or Orient,
fused by handshake & blood.

Seed & testament, naked
among fire-nudged thistle,
from the Rockies to below
sea level, to the steamy bayous,

I traipsed your footpath.
Falsehoods big as stumbling blocks
in the mind, lay across the road,
beside a watery swoon.

*

I'm back with the old folk
who speak your glossolalia of pure
sense unfolding one hundred years.
Unlocked chemistry, we're tied to sex,

spectral flower twisted out of
filigreed language & taboo
stubborn as crabgrass. You slept
nude under god-hewn eyes & ears.

Laughter in trees near a canebrake,
I know that song. Old hippie,
before Selma & People's Park,
your democratic nights a vortex

of waterlilies. The skin's cage
opened, but you were locked inside
your exotic Ethiopia. Everything
sprung back like birds after a shot.

Buried Light

A farmer sings about the Fourth Moon, as a girl and boy push rice shoots under slush, their hands jabbing like quick bills of long-legged birds. Their black silk clothes shine in watery light.

Afternoon crouches like three tigers, the sun a disc against a dream of something better. The water buffalo walks with bowed head, as if there's a child beneath his hide, no longer a mere creature willed to the plow.

Mud rises, arcing across the sun. Some monolithic god has fallen to his knees. Dead stars shower down. It was there waiting more than twenty years, some demonic egg speared by the plowshare. Mangled legs and arms dance in the muddy water till a silence rolls over the paddie like a mountain of white gauze.

Anodyne

I love how it swells
into a temple where it is
held prisoner, where the god
of blame resides. I love
slopes & peaks, the secret
paths that make me selfish.
I love my crooked feet
shaped by vanity & work
shoes made to outlast
belief. The hardness
coupling milk it can't
fashion. I love the lips,
salt & honeycomb on the tongue.
The hair holding off rain
& snow. The white moons
on my fingernails. I love
how everything begs
blood into song & prayer
inside an egg. A ghost
hums through my bones
like Pan's midnight flute
shaping internal laws

beside a troubled river.
I love this body
made to weather the storm
in the brain, raised
out of the deep smell
of fish & water hyacinth,
out of rapture & the first
regret. I love my big hands.
I love it clear down to the soft
quick motor of each breath,
the liver's ten kinds of desire
& the kidney's lust for sugar.
This skin, this sac of dung
& joy, this spleen floating
like a compass needle inside
nighttime, always divining
West Africa's dusty horizon.
I love the birthmark
posed like a fighting cock
on my right shoulder blade.
I love this body, this
solo & ragtime jubilee
behind the left nipple,
because I know I was born
to wear out at least
one hundred angels.

FOCUSED STUDY
Audre Lorde (1934–1992)

Renowned feminist lesbian poet, essayist and theorist, Audre Lorde was born Audrey Geraldine Lorde in Harlem New York on February 18, 1934. Lorde's childhood was deeply influenced by her Grenadian mother and by her position as the youngest of five sisters. Lorde had great difficulty learning to talk, communicating in full sentences only in adulthood. She spent most of her young school years as a student in Catholic schools where she learned early what it was to be an outsider.

Lorde worked her way through eight years (1951–1959) at Hunter College, where she would later be a distinguished professor, to get a bachelor's degree in library science. During her time at Hunter College, she spent one year at National University of Mexico in 1954. In 1961, Lorde earned a masters degree in library science from Columbia University.

In 1962, while working as a librarian in New York City, Audre Lorde married attorney Edwin Ashley Rollins. During the eight years of their marriage, she bore two children, Elizabeth and Jonathan. Lorde divorced Rollins in 1970 and moved her career to John Jay College of Criminal Justice, where she taught from 1970–1981. From that time until her death in 1992, she was a professor at Hunter College.

Audre Lorde's work, be it poetry, essay, or "biomythography," demonstrates her commitment to truth. She communicated with integrity the variety of her experiences and her place in the collective histories of Black women in the Caribbean, the United States, and Africa, continually promoting difference as opportunity for dialogue, rather than as threat. Especially in her well-known collection of essays, Sister Outsider (1984), Lorde affirms her multiple identities of lesbian, writer, Black woman, mother, and feminist.

Lorde's first collection of poetry, First Cities (1968), was written while she was a poet in residence at Tougaloo College in Mississippi. The collection is subtly nationalistic, falling gently in line with the work of fellow poets of the Black Arts Movement—Haki Madhubuti, Nikki Giovanni, and Mari Evans. Her second poetry collection, Cables to Rage (1970), focuses on themes of marriage, childrearing, love, and betrayal. The collection also contains Lorde's first open reference to her homosexuality.

During the 1970s, Lorde published five more volumes of poetry. From a Land Where Other People Live (1973) won a National Book Award and outspokenly advocates for third world peoples, addressing contemporary violence worldwide. In "The Winds of Orisha," Lorde articulates the watchfulness and suffering demanded of Black women who witness nightmarish violence everywhere there is injustice, oppression, and war. The New York Headshop and Museum (1974) is Lorde's most radical, angry, and complex anti-establishment collection, with poems expressing anguish beyond pain and anger. Between Our Selves (1976) is a chapbook of Lorde's long and most quoted poem. The publication of Coal (1976) was a telling indicator of Lorde's growing popularity and appeal to a wide audience. The title poem *demonstrates brilliant use of metaphor and control of language as Lorde links Blackness and voice to the metamorphosis of coal into diamond. In* The Black Unicorn *(1978), Lorde connects herself and other strong Black women to powerful women figures of African mythology, including the Amazon warriors and the goddess, Seboulisa. In "A Woman Speaks," "From the House of Yemanjá," and "A Litany for Survival," Lorde links timeless power, warring, and magic to the condition and survival of Black women throughout time.*

Audre Lorde's prose adds to the power of her poetry collections. With the publication of her first prose work, The Cancer Journals *(1980), Lorde became the first Black woman to write about her breast cancer experience. A later prose work,* Burst of Light *(1988), is also about Lorde's battle with cancer and awareness of mortality, and, like* The Cancer Journals, *is a combination of essay and Lorde's personal journal entries.*

For her prose work, Zami: A New Spelling of My Name *(1984), Lorde coined the genre title "biomythography" to encompass Zami's play with the genres of autobiography, poetry, fiction, and myth. Lorde's bold account of her first menstruation melds the Grenadian traditions of her mother with her own understanding of herself and timeless rite of passage. Zami also stands as the first account of a Black lesbian in the homophobic culture of the United States.*

In Sister Outsider: Essays and Speeches *(1984), Lorde links her own experiences to articulate women's strategies toward power. In the essay, "Uses of the Erotic: The Erotic as Power," Lorde argues for the energy of the erotic and feminism as a powerful politic and spiritual source. "Poetry Is Not a Luxury" expresses the necessity of articulating experience, of using language to transform reality. In every essay in the collection, difference, lived experience, and breaking silence establish power.*

Lorde's poetry and prose are mutually enriching. Each of her identities—Black woman, lesbian, theorist, poet, essayist—coalesces in her writing. Through her life of writing, Lorde fought against all forms of oppression both in the United States and globally. For Lorde, social protest is always inseparable from art and speech is a political act in and of itself.

In an interview with Claudia Tate, Lorde articulates the philosophies which guide her identification as a writer and impact the nature of her work, both poetry and prose. She speaks of her multiple identities—lesbian, feminist, Black woman, writer—and how each fits into who she is and what she writes. Primarily and with great impact, Lorde affirms her purpose and audience: "I write for those women who do not speak, for those who do not have a voice because they/we were so terrified, because we are taught to respect fear more than ourselves. We've been taught that silence would save us, but it won't. We must learn to respect ourselves and our needs more than the fear of our differences, and we must learn to share ourselves with each other." The vision Lorde shares with Tate is consistent with the vision evidenced in all of her work.

In the scholarly article, "'Coming Out Blackened and Whole': Fragmentation and Reintegration in Audre Lorde's Zami *and* The Cancer Journals," *Elizabeth Alexander foregrounds the physical body in Audre Lorde's prose. Alexander traces Lorde's use of language, showing the ways Lorde connects the physical body to liberation and self-definition.*

R. Joyce Lausch

Black Mother Woman

> *I cannot recall you gentle*
> *yet through your heavy love*
> *I have become*

an image of your once delicate flesh
split with deceitful longings.

When strangers come and compliment me
your aged spirit takes a bow
jingling with pride
but once you hid that secret
in the center of furies
hanging me
with deep breasts and wiry hair
with your own split flesh
and long suffering eyes
buried in myths of little worth.

But I have peeled away your anger
down to the core of love
and *look mother*
I Am
a dark temple where your true spirit rises
beautiful
and tough as chestnut
stanchion against your nightmare of weakness
and if my eyes conceal
a squadron of conflicting rebellions
I learned from you
to define myself
through your denials.

Conclusion

Passing men in the street who are dead
becomes a common occurrence
but loving one of them
is no solution.
I believe in love as I believe in our children
but I was born Black and without illusions
and my vision
which differs from yours
is clear
although sometimes restricted.

I have watched you at midnight
moving through casual sleep
wishing I could afford the non-desperate dreams
that stir you
to wither and fade into partial solutions.
Your nights are wintery long and very young
full of symbols of purity and forgiveness
and a meek jesus that rides through your cities
on a barren ass whose braying
does not include a future tense.
But I wear my nights as I wear my life
and my dying
absolute and unforgiven
nuggets of compromise and decision
fossilized by fierce midsummer sun
and when I dream
I move through a Black land
where the future
glows eternal and green
but where the symbols for now
are bloody and unrelenting
rooms
where confused children
with wooden stumps for fingers
play at war
who cannot pick up their marbles
and run away home
whenever nightmare threatens.

The Winds of Orisha

I.

This land will not always be foreign.
How many of its women ache to bear their stories
robust and screaming like the earth erupting grain
or thrash in padded chains mute as bottles
hands fluttering traces of resistance
on the backs of once lovers
half the truth

knocking in the brain like an angry steampipe
how many
long to work or split open
so bodies venting into silence
can plan the next move?

Tiresias took 500 years they say to progress into woman
growing smaller and darker and more powerful
until nut-like, she went to sleep in a bottle
Tiresias took 500 years to grow into woman
so do not despair of your sons.

II.

Impatient legends speak through my flesh
changing this earths formation
spreading
I will become myself
in incantation
dark raucous many-shaped characters
leaping back and forth across bland pages
and Mother Yemonja raises her breast to begin my
    labour
near water

the beautiful Oshun and I lie down together
in the heat of her body truth my voice comes stronger
Shango will be my brother roaring out of the sea
earth shakes our darkness swelling into each other
warning winds will announce us living
as Oya, Oya my sister my daughter
destroys the crust of the tidy beaches
and Eshu's black laughter turns up the neat sleeping sands.

III.

The heart of this country's tradition is its wheat men
dying for money
dying for water for markets for power
over all people's children
they sit in their chains on their dry earth
before nightfall
telling tales as they wait for their time
of completion
hoping the young ones can hear them

earth-shaking fears wreath their blank weary faces
most of them have spent their lives and their wives
in labour
most of them have never seen beaches
but as Oya my sister moves out of the mouths
of their sons and daughters against them
I will swell up from the pages of their daily heralds
leaping out of the almanacs
instead of an answer to their search for rain
      they will read me
the dark cloud
meaning something entire
and different.

When the winds of Orisha blow
even the roots of grass
quicken.

Coal

I
is the total black, being spoken
from the earth's inside.
There are many kinds of open
how a diamond comes into a knot of flame
how sound comes into a word, colored
by who pays what for speaking.

Some words are open like a diamond
on glass windows
singing out within the passing crash of sun
Then there are words like stapled wagers
in a perforated book—buy and sign and tear apart—
and come whatever wills all chances
the stub remains
an ill-pulled tooth with a ragged edge.
Some words live in my throat
breeding like adders. Others know sun
seeking like gypsies over my tongue
to explode through my lips
like young sparrows bursting from shell.
Some words
bedevil me.

Love is a word, another kind of open.
As the diamond comes into a knot of flame
I am Black because I come from the earth's inside
now take my word for jewel in the open light.

A Woman Speaks

Moon marked and touched by sun
my magic is unwritten
but when the sea turns back
it will leave my shape behind.
I seek no favor
untouched by blood
unrelenting as the curse of love
permanent as my errors
or my pride
I do not mix
love with pity
nor hate with scorn
and if you would know me
look into the entrails of Uranus
where the restless oceans pound.

I do not dwell
within my birth nor my divinities
who am *ageless* and *half-grown*
and still seeking
my sisters
witches in Dahomey
wear me inside their coiled cloths
as our *mother* did
mourning.
I have been *woman*
for a long time
beware my smile
I am treacherous with *old* magic
and the noon's *new* fury
with all your wide futures
promised
I am
woman
and not white.

From the House of Yemanjá

My mother had two faces and a frying pot
where she cooked up her daughters
into girls
before she fixed our dinner.
My mother had *two faces*
and a broken pot
where she hid out a perfect daughter
who was not me
I am the sun and moon and forever hungry
for her eyes.

I bear *two women* upon my back
one dark and rich and hidden
in the ivory hungers of the other
mother
pale as a witch
yet steady and familiar
brings me *bread* and *terror*
in my sleep
her breasts are huge exciting anchors
in the midnight storm.

All this has been
before
in my mother's bed
time has no sense
I have no brothers
and my sisters are cruel.

Mother I need
mother I need
mother I need your blackness now
as the august earth needs rain.
I am
the sun and moon and forever hungry
the sharpened edge
where day and night shall meet
and not be
one.

The Women of Dan Dance With Swords in Their Hands to Mark the Time When They Were Warriors

I did not fall from the sky
I
nor descend like a plague of locusts
to drink color and strength from the earth
and I do not come like rain
as a tribute or symbol for earth's becoming
I come *as a woman*
dark and open
some times I fall like night
softly
and terrible
only when I must die
in order to rise again.

I do not come like a secret warrior
with an unsheathed sword in my mouth
hidden behind my tongue
slicing my throat to ribbons
of service with a smile
while the blood runs
down and out
through holes in the two sacred mounds
on my chest.

I come like a woman
who I am
spreading out through nights
laughter and promise
and dark heat
warming whatever I touch
that is living
consuming
only
what is already dead.

A Litany for Survival

For those of us who live at the shoreline
standing upon the constant edges of decision
crucial and alone

for those of us who cannot indulge
the passing dreams of choice
who love in doorways coming and going
in the hours between dawns
looking inward and outward
at once before and after
seeking a now that can breed
futures
like bread in our children's mouths
so their dreams will not reflect
the death of ours;

For those of us
who were imprinted with fear
like a faint line in the center of our foreheads
learning to be afraid with our mother's milk
for by this weapon
this illusion of some safety to be found
the heavy-footed hoped to silence us
For all of us
this instant and this triumph
We were never meant to survive.

And when the sun rises we are afraid
it might not remain
when the sun sets we are afraid
it might not rise in the morning
when our stomachs are full we are afraid
of indigestion
when our stomachs are empty we are afraid
we may never eat again
when we are loved we are afraid
love will vanish
when we are alone we are afraid
love will never return
and when we speak we are afraid
our words will not be heard
nor welcomed
but when we are silent
we are still afraid.

So it is better to speak
remembering
we were never meant to survive.

Recreation

Coming together
it is easier to work
after our bodies
meet
paper and pen
neither care nor profit
whether we write or not
but as your body moves
under my hands
charged and waiting
we cut the leash
you create me against your thighs
hilly with images
moving through our word countries
my body
writes into your flesh
the poem
you make of me.

Touching you I catch midnight
as moon fires set in my throat
I love you flesh into blossom
I made you
and take you made
into me.

Power

The difference between poetry and rhetoric
is being
ready to kill
yourself
instead of your children.

I am trapped on a desert of raw gunshot wounds
and a dead child dragging his shattered black
face off the edge of my sleep
blood from his punctured cheeks and shoulders
is the only liquid for miles and my stomach

churns at the imagined taste while
my mouth splits into dry lips
without loyalty or reason
thirsting for the wetness of his blood
as it sinks into the whiteness
of the desert where I am lost
without imagery or magic
trying to make power out of hatred and destruction
trying to heal my dying son with kisses
only the sun will bleach his bones quicker.

The policeman who shot down a 10-year-old in Queens
stood over the boy with his cop shoes in childish blood
and a voice said "Die you little motherfucker" and
there are tapes to prove that. At his trial
this policeman said in his own defense
"I didn't notice the size or nothing else
only the color." and
there are tapes to prove that, too.

Today that 37-year-old white man with 13 years of police forcing
has been set free
by 11 white men who said they were satisfied
justice had been done
and one black woman who said
"They convinced me" meaning
they had dragged her 4'10" black woman's frame
over the hot coals of four centuries of white male approval
until she let go the first real power she ever had
and lined her own womb with cement
to make a graveyard for our children.

I have not been able to touch the destruction within me.
But unless I learn to use
the difference between poetry and rhetoric
my power too will run corrupt as poisonous mold
or lie limp and useless as an unconnected wire
and one day I will take my teenaged plug
and connect it to the nearest socket
raping an 85-year-old white woman
who is somebody's mother
and as I beat her senseless and set a torch to her bed
a greek chorus will be singing in 3/4 time
"Poor thing. She never hurt a soul. What beasts they are."

Love Poem

Speak earth and bless me
with what is richest
make sky flow honey out of my hips
rigid as mountains
spread over a valley
carved out by the mouth of rain.

And I knew when I entered her   I was
high wind in her forest's hollow
fingers whispering sound
honey flowed   from the split cup
impaled on a lance of tongues
on the tips of her breasts   on her navel
and my breath   howling into her entrances
through lungs of pain.

Greedy as herring-gulls
or a child
I swing out   over the earth
over and over   again.

(1971)

To the Poet Who Happens to Be Black
and the Black Poet Who Happens to Be a Woman

I
I was born in the gut of Blackness
from between my mother's particular thighs
her waters broke upon blue-flowered linoleum
and turn to slush in the Harlem cold
10 PM on a full moon's night
my head crested round as a clock
"You were so dark," my mother said
"I thought you were a boy."

II
The first time I touched my sister   alive
I was sure   the earth took note
but we were not new
false skin peeled off like gloves of fire

yoked flame   I was
stripped to the tips of my fingers
her song written into my palms my nostrils my belly
welcome home
in a language   I was pleased to relearn.

III
No cold spirit ever strolled through my bones
on the corner of Amsterdam Avenue
no dog mistook me for a bench
nor a tree   nor a bone
no lover envisioned my plump brown arms
as wings   nor misnamed me condor
but I can recall without counting
eyes
canceling me out
like an unpleasant appointment
postage due
stamped in yellow   red   purple
any color
except Black   and choice
and woman
alive.

IV
I cannot recall the words of my first poem
but I remember a promise
I made my pen
never to leave it
lying
in somebody else's blood.

(1985)

Chapter 11

When I was growing up in my mother's house, there were spices you grated and spices you pounded, and whenever you pounded spice and garlic or other herbs, you used a mortar. Every West Indian woman worth her salt had her own mortar. Now if you lost or broke your mortar, you could, of course, buy another one in the market over on Park Avenue, under the bridge, but those were usually

Puerto Rican mortars, and even though they were made out of wood and worked exactly the same way, somehow they were never really as good as West Indian mortars. Now where the best mortars came from I was never really sure, but I knew it must be in the vicinity of that amorphous and mystically perfect place called "home." And whatever came from "home" was bound to be special.

My mother's mortar was an elaborate affair, quite at variance with most of her other possessions, and certainly with her projected public view of herself. It stood, solid and elegant, on a shelf in the kitchen cabinet for as long as I can remember, and I loved it dearly.

The mortar was of a foreign fragrant wood, too dark for cherry and too red for walnut. To my child eyes, the outside was carved in an intricate and most enticing manner. There were rounded plums and oval indeterminate fruit, some long and fluted like a banana, others ovular and end-swollen like a ripe alligator pear. In between these were smaller rounded shapes like cherries, lying in batches against and around each other.

I loved to finger the hard roundness of the carved fruit, and the always surprising termination of the shapes as the carvings stopped at the rim and the bowl sloped abruptly downward, smoothly oval but suddenly businesslike. The heavy sturdiness of this useful wooden object always made me feel secure and somehow full; as if it conjured up from all the many different flavors pounded into the inside wall, visions of delicious feasts both once enjoyed and still to come.

The pestle was long and tapering, fashioned from the same mysterious rose-deep wood, and fitted into the hand almost casually, familiarly. The actual shape reminded me of a summer crook-necked squash uncurled and slightly twisted. It could also have been an avocado, with the neck of the alligator pear elongated and the whole made efficient for pounding, without ever losing the apparent soft firmness and the character of the fruit which the wood suggested. It was slightly bigger at the grinding end than most pestles, and the widened curved end fitted into the bowl of the mortar easily. Long use and years of impact and grinding within the bowl's worn hollow had softened the very surface of the wooden pestle, until a thin layer of split fibers coated the rounded end like a layer of velvet. A layer of the same velvety mashed wood lined the bottom inside the sloping bowl.

My mother did not particularly like to pound spice, and she looked upon the advent of powdered everything as a cook's boon. But there were some certain dishes that called for a particular savory blending of garlic, raw onion, and pepper, and souse was one of them.

For our mother's souse, it didn't matter what kind of meat was used. You could have hearts, or beefends, or even chicken backs and gizzards when we were really poor. It was the pounded-up saucy blend of herb and spice rubbed into the meat before it was left to stand so for a few hours before cooking that made that dish so special and unforgettable. But my mother had some very firm ideas about what she like best to cook and about which were her favorite dishes, and souse was definitely not one of either.

On the very infrequent occasions that my mother would allow one of us three girls to choose a meal—as opposed to helping to prepare it, which was a daily routine—on those occasions my sisters would usually choose one of those proscribed dishes so dear to our hearts remembered from our relatives' tables, contraband, and so very rare in our house. They might ask for hot dogs, perhaps, smothered in ketchup sauce, or with crusty Boston-baked beans; or american chicken, breaded first and fried crispy the way the southern people did it; or creamed something-or-other that one of my sister had tasted at school; what-have-you croquettes or anything fritters; or once even a daring outrageous request for slices of fresh watermelon, hawked from the back of a rickety wooden pickup truck with the southern road-dust still on her slatted sides, from which a young bony Black man with a turned-around baseball cap on his head would hang and half-yell, half-yodel—"Wahr—deeeeeee-mayyyyyyy-lawnnnnnnn."

There were many american dishes I longed for too, but on the one or two occasions a year that I got to choose a meal, I would always ask for souse. That way, I knew that I would get to use my mother's mortar, and this in itself was more treat for me than any of the forbidden foods. Besides, if I really wanted hot dogs or anything croquettes badly enough, I could steal some money from my father's pocket and buy them in the school lunch.

"Mother, let's have souse," I'd say, and never even stop to think about it. The anticipated taste of the soft spicy meat had become inseparable in my mind from the tactile pleasures of using my mother's mortar.

"But what makes you think anybody can find time to mash up all that stuff?" My mother would cut her hawk-grey eyes at me from beneath their heavy black brows. "Among-you children never stop to think," and she'd turn back to whatever it was she had been doing. If she had just come from the office with my father, she might be checking the day's receipts, or she might be washing the endless piles of dirty linen that always seemed to issue from rooming-houses.

"Oh, I'll pound the garlic, Mommy!" would be my next line in the script written by some ancient and secret hand, and off I'd go to the cabinet to get down the heavy wooden mortar and pestle.

I took a head of garlic out from the garlic bottle in the icebox, and breaking off ten or twelve cloves from the head, I carefully peeled away the tissue lavender skin, slicing each stripped peg in half lengthwise. I dropped them piece by piece into the capacious waiting bowl of the mortar. Taking a slice from a small onion, I put the rest aside to be used later over the meat, and cutting the slice into quarters, I tossed it into the mortar also. Next came the coarsely ground fresh black pepper, and then a lavish blanketing cover of salt over the whole. Last, if we had any, a few leaves from the top of a head of celery. My mother sometimes added a slice of green pepper, but I did not like the texture of the pepper-skin under the pestle, and preferred to add it along with the sliced onion later on, leaving it all to sit over the seasoned and resting meat.

After all the ingredients were in the bowl of the mortar, I fetched the pestle and placing it into the bowl, slowly rotated the shaft a few times, working it gently down through all the ingredients to mix them. Only then would I lift the pestle, and with one hand firmly pressed around the carved side of the mortar caressing the wooden fruit with my aromatic fingers, I thrust sharply downward, feeling the shifting salt and the hard little pellets of garlic right up through the shaft of the wooden pestle. Up again, down, around, and up—so the rhythm began.

The *thud push rub rotate up* repeated over and over. The muted thump of the pestle on the bed of grinding spice as the salt and pepper absorbed the slowly yielding juices of the garlic and celery leaves.

Thud push rub rotate up. The mingling fragrances rising from the bowl of the mortar.

Thud push rub rotate up. The feeling of the pestle held between my curving fingers, and the mortar's outside rounding like fruit into my palm as I steadied it against my body.

All these transported me into a world of scent and rhythm and movement and sound that grew more and more exciting as the ingredients liquefied.

Sometimes my mother would look over at me with that amused annoyance which passed for tenderness.

"What you think you making there, garlic soup? Enough, go get the meat now." And I would fetch the lamb hearts, for instance, from the icebox and begin to prepare them. Cutting away the hardened veins at the top of the smooth firm muscles, I divided each oval heart into four wedge-shaped pieces, and taking a bit of the spicy mash from the mortar with my fingertips, I rubbed each piece with the savory mix, the pungent smell of garlic and onion and celery enveloping the kitchen.

The last day I ever pounded seasoning for souse was in the summer of my fifteenth year. It had been a fairly unpleasant summer for me. I had just finished my first year of high school. Instead of being able to visit my newly found friends, all of whom lived in other parts of the city, I had had to accompany my mother on a round of doctors with whom she would have long whispered conversations. Only a matter of utmost importance could have kept her away from the office for so many mornings in a row. But my mother was concerned because I was fourteen and a half years old and had not yet menstruated. I had breasts but no period, and she was afraid there was something "wrong" with me. Yet, since she had never discussed this mysterious business of menstruation with me, I was certainly not supposed to know what all the whispering was about, even though it concerned my own body.

Of course, I knew as much as I could have possibly found out in those days from the hard-to-get books on the "closed shelf" behind the librarian's desk at the public library, where I had brought a forged note from home in order to be allowed to read them, sitting under the watchful eye of the librarian at a special desk reserved for that purpose.

Although not terribly informative, they were fascinating books, and used words like *menses* and *ovulation* and *vagina*.

But four years before, I had had to find out if I was going to become pregnant, because a boy from school much bigger than me had invited me up to the roof on my way home from the library and then threatened to break my glasses if I didn't let him stick his "thing" between my legs. And at that time I knew only that being pregnant had something to do with sex, and sex had something to do with that thin pencil-like "thing" and was in general nasty and not to be talked about by nice people, and I was afraid my mother might find out and what would she do to me then? I was not supposed to be looking at the mailboxes in the hallway of that house anyway, even though Doris was a girl in my class at St. Mark's who lived in that house and I was always so lonely in the summer, particularly that summer when I was ten.

So after I got home I washed myself up and lied about why I was late getting home from the library and got a whipping for being late. That must have been a hard summer for my parents at the office too, because that was the summer that I got a whipping for something or other almost every day between the Fourth of July and Labor Day.

When I wasn't getting whippings, I hid out at the library on 135th Street, and forged notes from my mother to get books from the "closed shelf," and read about sex and having babies, and waited to become pregnant. None of the books were very clear to me about the relationship between having your period and having a baby, but they were all very clear about the relationship between penises and getting pregnant. Or maybe the confusion was all in my own mind, because I had always been a very fast but not a very careful reader.

So four years later, in my fifteenth year, I was a very scared little girl, still half-afraid that one of that endless stream of doctors would look up into my body and discover my four-year-old shame and say to my mother, "Aha! So that's what's wrong! Your daughter is about to become pregnant!"

On the other hand, if I let Mother know that I knew what was happening and what these medical safaris were all about, I would have to answer her questions about how and wherefore I knew, since she hadn't told me, divulging in the process the whole horrible and self-incriminating story of forbidden books and forged library notes and rooftops and stairwell conversations.

It was a year after the rooftop incident, when we had moved farther uptown. The kids at St. Catherine's seemed to know a lot more about sex than at St. Mark's. In the eighth grade, I had stolen money and bought my classmate Adeline a pack of cigarettes and she had confirmed my bookish suspicions about how babies were made. My response to her graphic descriptions had been to think to myself, *there obviously must be another way that Adeline doesn't know about, because my parents have children and I know they never did anything like that!* But the basic principles were all there, and sure enough they were the same as I had gathered from *The Young People's Family Book.*

So in my fifteenth summer, on examining table after examining table, I kept my legs open and my mouth shut, and when I saw blood on my pants one hot July afternoon, I rinsed them out secretly in the bathroom and put them back on wet because I didn't know how to break the news to my mother that both her worries and mine were finally over. (All this time I had at least understood that having your period was a sign you were not pregnant.)

What then happened felt like a piece of an old and elaborate dance between my mother and me. She discovers finally, through a stain on the toilet seat left there on purpose by me as a mute announcement, what has taken place; she scolds, "Why didn't you tell me about all of this, now? It's nothing to get upset over, you are a woman, not a child anymore. Now you go over to the drugstore and ask the man for . . ."

I was just relieved the whole damn thing was over with. It's difficult to talk about double messages without having a twin tongue. Nightmarish evocations and restrictions were being verbalized by my mother:

"This means from now on you better watch your step and not be so friendly with every Tom, Dick, and Harry . . ." (which must have meant my staying late after school to talk with my girlfriends, because I did not even know any boys); and, "Now remember, too, after you wrap up your soiled napkins in newspaper, don't leave them hanging around on the bathroom floor where your father has to see them, not that it's anything shameful but all the same, remember . . ."

Along with all of these admonitions, there was something else coming from my mother that I could not define. It was the lurking of that amused/annoyed brow-furrowed half-smile of hers that made me feel—all her nagging words to the contrary—that something very good and satisfactory and pleasing to her had just happened, and that we were both pretending otherwise for some very wise and secret reasons. I would come to understand these reasons later, as a reward, if I handled myself properly. Then, at the end of it all, my mother thrust the box of Kotex at me (I had fetched it in its plain wrapper back from the drugstore, along with a sanitary belt), saying to me,

"But look now what time it is already, I wonder what we're going to eat for supper tonight?" She waited. At first I didn't understand, but I quickly picked up the cue. I had seen the beefends in the icebox that morning.

"Mommy, please let's have some souse—I'll pound the garlic." I dropped the box onto a kitchen chair and started to wash my hands in anticipation.

"Well, go put your business away first. What did I tell you about leaving that lying around?" She wiped her hands from the washtub where she had been working and handed the plain wrapped box of Kotex back to me.

"I have to go out, I forgot to pick up tea at the store. Now make sure you rub the meat good."

When I came back into the kitchen, my mother had left. I moved toward the kitchen cabinet to fetch down the mortar and pestle. My body felt new and special and unfamiliar and suspect all at the same time.

I could feel bands of tension sweeping across my body back and forth, like lunar winds across the moon's face. I felt the slight rubbing bulge of cotton pad between my legs, and I smelled the delicate breadfruit smell rising up from the front of my print blouse that was my own womansmell, warm, shameful, but secretly utterly delicious.

Years afterward when I was grown, whenever I thought about the way I smelled that day, I would have a fantasy of my mother, her hands wiped dry from the washing, and her apron untied and laid neatly away, looking down upon me lying on the couch, and then slowly, thoroughly, our touching and caressing each other's most secret places.

I took the mortar down, and smashed the cloves of garlic with the edge of its underside, to loosen the thin papery skins in a hurry. I sliced them and flung them into the mortar's bowl along with some black pepper and celery leaves. The white salt poured in, covering the garlic and black pepper and pale chartreuse celery fronds like a snowfall. I tossed in the onion and some bits of green pepper and reached for the pestle.

It slipped through my fingers and clattered to the floor, rolling around in a semicircle back and forth, until I bent to retrieve it. I grabbed the head of the wooden stick and straightened up, my ears ringing faintly. Without even wiping it, I plunged the pestle into the bowl, feeling the blanket of salt give way, and the broken cloves of garlic just beneath. The downward thrust of the wooden pestle slowed upon contact, rotated back and forth slowly, and then gently altered its rhythm to include an up and down beat. Back and forth, round, up and down, back, forth, round, round, up and down. . . . There was a heavy fullness at the root of me that was exciting and dangerous.

As I continued to pound the spice, a vital connection seemed to establish itself between the muscles of my fingers curved tightly around the smooth pestle in its insistent downward motion, and the molten core of my body whose source emanated from a new ripe fullness just beneath the pit of my stomach. That invisible thread, taut and sensitive as a clitoris exposed, stretched through my curled fingers up my round brown arm into the moist reality of my armpits, whose warm sharp odor with a strange new overlay mixed with the ripe garlic smells from the mortar and the general sweat-heavy aromas of high summer.

The thread ran over my ribs and along my spine, tingling and singing, into a basin that was poised between my hips, now pressed against the low kitchen counter before which I stood, pounding spice. And within that basin was a tiding ocean of blood beginning to be made real and available to me for strength and information.

The jarring shocks of the velvet-lined pestle, striking the bed of spice, traveled up an invisible pathway along the thread into the center of me, and the harshness of the repeated impacts became increasingly more unbearable. The tidal basin suspended between my hips shuddered at each repetition of the strokes which now felt like assaults. Without my volition my downward thrusts of the pestle grew gentler and gentler, until its velvety surface seemed almost to caress the liquefying mash at the bottom of the mortar.

The whole rhythm of my movements softened and elongated, until, dreamlike, I stood, one hand tightly curved around the carved mortar, steadying it against the middle of my body; while my other hand, around the pestle, rubbed and pressed the moistening spice into readiness with a sweeping circular movement.

I hummed tunelessly to myself as I worked in the warm kitchen, thinking with relief about how simple my life would be now that I had become a woman. The catalogue of dire menstruation-warnings from my mother passed out of my head. My body felt strong and full and open, yet captivated by the gentle motions of the pestle, and the rich smells filling the kitchen, and the fullness of the young summer heat.

I heard my mother's key in the lock.

She swept into the kitchen briskly, like a ship under full sail. There were tiny beads of sweat over her upper lip, and vertical creases between her brows.

"You mean to tell me no meat is ready?" My mother dropped her parcel of tea onto the table, and looking over my shoulder, sucked her teeth loudly in weary disgust. "What do you call yourself doing, now? You have all night to stand up there playing with the food? I go all the way to the store and back already and still you can't mash up a few pieces of garlic to season some meat? But you know how to do the thing better than this! Why you vex me so?"

She took the mortar and pestle out of my hands and started to grind vigorously. And there were still bits of garlic left at the bottom of the bowl.

"Now you do, so!" She brought the pestle down inside the bowl of the mortar with dispatch, crushing the last of the garlic. I heard the thump of wood brought down heavily upon wood, and I felt the harsh impact throughout my body, as if something had broken inside of me. Thump, thump, went the pestle, purposefully, up and down in the old familiar way.

"It was getting mashed, Mother," I dared to protest, turning away to the icebox. "I'll fetch the meat." I was surprised at my own brazenness in answering back.

But something in my voice interrupted my mother's efficient motions. She ignored my implied contradiction, itself an act of rebellion strictly forbidden in our house. The thumping stopped.

"What's wrong with you, now? Are you sick? You want to go to your bed?"

"No, I'm all right, Mother."

But I felt her strong fingers on my upper arm, turning me around, her other hand under my chin as she peered into my face. Her voice softened.

"Is it your period making you so slow-down today?" She gave my chin a little shake, as I looked up into her hooded grey eyes, now becoming almost gentle. The kitchen felt suddenly oppressively hot and still, and I felt myself beginning to shake all over.

Tears I did not understand started from my eyes, as I realized that my old enjoyment of the bone-jarring way I had been taught to pound spice would feel different to me from now on, and also that in my mother's kitchen there was only one right way to do anything. Perhaps my life had not become so simple, after all.

My mother stepped away from the counter and put her heavy arm around my shoulders. I could smell the warm herness rising from between her arm and her body, mixed with the smell of glycerine and rosewater, and the scent of her thick bun of hair.

"I'll finish up the food for supper." She smiled at me, and there was a tenderness in her voice and an absence of annoyance that was welcome, although unfamiliar.

"You come inside now and lie down on the couch and I'll make you a hot cup of tea."

Her arm across my shoulders was warm and slightly damp. I rested my head upon her shoulder, and realized with a shock of pleasure and surprise that I was almost as tall as my mother, as she led me into the cool darkened parlor.

Poetry Is Not a Luxury*

The quality of light by which we scrutinize our lives has direct bearing upon the product which we live, and upon the changes which we hope to bring about through those lives. It is within this light that we form those ideas by which we pursue our magic and make it realized. This is poetry as illumination, for it is through poetry that we give name to those ideas which are—until the poem—nameless and formless, about to be birthed, but already felt. That distillation of experience from which true poetry springs births thought as dream births concept, as feeling births idea, as knowledge births (precedes) understanding.

As we learn to bear the intimacy of scrutiny and to flourish within it, as we learn to use the products of that scrutiny for power within our living, those fears which rule our lives and form our silences begin to lose their control over us.

For each of us as women, there is a dark place within, where hidden and growing our true spirit rises, "beautiful/and tough as chestnut/stanchions against (y)our nightmare of weakness/"** and of impotence.

These places of possibility within ourselves are dark because they are ancient and hidden; they have survived and grown strong through that darkness. Within these deep places, each one of us holds an incredible reserve of creativity and power, of unexamined and unrecorded emotion and feeling. The woman's place of power within each of us is neither white nor surface; it is dark, it is ancient, and it is deep.

When we view living in the european mode only as a problem to be solved, we rely solely upon our ideas to make us free, for these were what the white fathers told us were precious.

---

*First published in *Chrysalis: A Magazine of Female Culture,* no. 3 (1977).

**From "Black Mother Woman," first published in *From A Land Where Other People Live* (Broadside Press, Detroit, 1973), and collected in *Chosen Poems: Old and New* (W.W. Norton and Company, New York, 1982), p. 53.

But as we come more into touch with our own ancient, noneuropean consciousness of living as a situation to be experienced and interacted with, we learn more and more to cherish our feelings, and to respect those hidden sources of our power from where true knowledge and, therefore, lasting action comes.

At this point in time, I believe that women carry within ourselves the possibility for fusion of these two approaches so necessary for survival, and we come closest to this combination in our poetry. I speak here of poetry as a revelatory distillation of experience, not the sterile word play that, too often, the white fathers distorted the word *poetry* to mean—in order to cover a desperate wish for imagination without insight.

For women, then, poetry is not a luxury. It is a vital necessity of our existence. It forms the quality of the light within which we predicate our hopes and dreams toward survival and change, first made into language, then into idea, then into more tangible action. Poetry is the way we help give name to the nameless so it can be thought. The farthest horizons of our hopes and fears are cobbled by our poems, carved from the rock experiences of our daily lives.

As they become known to and accepted by us, our feelings and the honest exploration of them become sanctuaries and spawning grounds for the most radical and daring of ideas. They become a safe-house for that difference so necessary to change and the conceptualization of any meaningful action. Right now, I could name at least ten ideas I would have found intolerable or incomprehensible and frightening, except as they came after dreams and poems. This is not idle fantasy, but a disciplined attention to the true meaning of "it feels right to me." We can train ourselves to respect our feelings and to transpose them into a language so they can be shared. And where that language does not yet exist, it is our poetry which helps to fashion it. Poetry is not only dream and vision; it is the skeleton architecture of our lives. It lays the foundations for a future of change, a bridge across our fears of what has never been before.

Possibility is neither forever not instant. It is not easy to sustain belief in its efficacy. We can sometimes work long and hard to establish one beachhead of real resistance to the deaths we are expected to live, only to have that beachhead assaulted or threatened by those canards we have been socialized to fear, or by the withdrawal of those approvals that we have been warned to seek for safety. Women see ourselves diminished or softened by the falsely benign accusations of childishness, of nonuniversality, of changeability, of sensuality. And who asks the question: Am I altering your aura, your ideas, your dreams, or am I merely moving you to temporary and reactive action? And even though the latter is no mean task, it is one that must be seen within the context of a need for true alteration of the very foundations of our lives.

The white fathers told us: I think, therefore I am. The Black mother within each of us—the poet—whispers in our dreams: I feel, therefore I can be free. Poetry coins the language to express and charter this revolutionary demand, the implementation of that freedom.

However, experience has taught us that action in the now is also necessary, always. Our children cannot dream unless they live, they cannot live unless they are nourished, and who else will feed them the real food without which their dreams will be no different from ours? "If you want us to change the world someday, we at least have to live long enough to grow up!" shouts the child.

Sometimes we drug ourselves with dreams of new ideas. The head will save us. The brain alone will set us free. But there are no new ideas still waiting in the wings to save us as women, as human. There are only old and forgotten ones, new combinations, extrapolations and recognitions from within ourselves—along with the renewed courage to try them out. And we must constantly encourage ourselves and each other to attempt the heretical actions that our dreams imply, and so many of our old ideas disparage. In the forefront of our move toward change, there is only poetry to hint at possibility made real. Our poems formulate the implications of ourselves, what we feel within and dare make real (or bring action into accordance with), our fears, our hopes, our most cherished terrors.

For within living structures defined by profit, by linear power, by institutional dehumanization, our feelings were not meant to survive. Kept around as unavoidable adjuncts or pleasant pastimes, feelings were expected to kneel to thought as women were expected to kneel to men. But women have survived. As poets. And there are no new pains. We have felt them all already. We have hidden that fact in the same place where we have hidden our power. They surface in our dreams, and it is our dreams that point the way to freedom. Those dreams are made realizable through our poems that give us the strength and courage to see, to feel, to speak, and to dare.

If what we need to dream, to move our spirits most deeply and directly toward and through promise, is discounted as a luxury, then we give up the core—the fountain—of our power, our womanness; we give up the future of our worlds.

For there are no new ideas. There are only new ways of making them felt—of examining what those ideas feel like being lived on Sunday morning at 7 A.M., after brunch, during wild love, making war, giving birth, mourning our dead—while we suffer the old longings, battle the old warnings and fears of being silent and impotent and alone, while we taste new possibilities and strengths.

Uses of the Erotic: The Erotic as Power*

There are many kinds of power, used and unused, acknowledged or otherwise. The erotic is a resource within each of us that lies in a *deeply female and spiritual plane,* firmly rooted in the power of our unexpressed or unrecognized feeling. In order to perpetuate itself, every oppression must corrupt or distort those various

---

*Paper delivered at the Fourth Berkshire Conference on the History of Women, Mount Holyoke College, August 25, 1978. Published as a pamphlet by Out & Out Books (available from The Crossing Press).

sources of power within the culture of the oppressed that can provide energy for change. For women, this has meant a suppression of the erotic as a considered source of power and information within our lives.

We have been taught to suspect this resource, vilified, abused, and devalued within western society. On the one hand, the superficially erotic has been encouraged as a sign of female inferiority; on the other hand, women have been made to suffer and to feel both contemptible and suspect by virtue of its existence.

It is a short step from there to the false belief that only by the suppression of the erotic within our lives and consciousness can women be truly strong. But that strength is illusory, for it is fashioned within the context of male models of power.

As women, we have come to distrust that power which rises from our deepest and nonrational knowledge. We have been warned against it all our lives by the male world, which values this depth of feeling enough to keep women around in order to exercise it in the service of men, but which fears this same depth too much to examine the possibilities of it within themselves. So women are maintained at a distant/inferior position to be *psychically milked,* much the same way ants maintain colonies of aphids to provide a life-giving substance for their masters.

But the erotic offers a well of replenishing and provocative force to the woman who does not fear its revelation, nor succumb to the belief that sensation is enough.

The erotic has often been misnamed by men and used against women. It has been made into the confused, the trivial, the psychotic, the plasticized sensation. For this reason, we have often turned away from the exploration and consideration of the *erotic as a source of power and information, confusing it with its opposite, the pornographic.* But pornography is a direct denial of the power of the erotic, for it represents the suppression of true feeling. Pornography emphasizes sensation without feeling.

The erotic is a measure between the beginnings of our sense of self and the chaos of our strongest feelings. It is an internal sense of satisfaction to which, once we have experienced it, we know we can aspire. For having experienced the fullness of this depth of feeling and recognizing its power, in honor and self-respect we can require no less of ourselves.

It is never easy to demand the most from ourselves, from our lives, from our work. To encourage excellence is to go beyond the encouraged mediocrity of our society is to encourage excellence. But giving in to the fear of feeling and working to capacity is a luxury only the unintentional can afford, and the unintentional are those who do not wish to guide their own destinies.

This internal requirement toward excellence which we learn from the erotic must not be misconstrued as demanding the impossible from ourselves nor from others. Such a demand incapacitates everyone in the process. For the erotic is not a question only of what we do; *it is a question of how acutely and fully we can feel in the doing.* Once we know the extent to which we are capable of feeling that sense of satisfaction and completion, we can then observe which of our various life endeavors bring us closest to that fullness.

The aim of each thing which we do is to make our lives and the lives of our children richer and more possible. Within the celebration of the erotic in all our endeavors, my work becomes a conscious decision—a longed-for bed which I enter gratefully and from which I rise up empowered.

Of course, women so empowered are dangerous. So we are taught to separate the erotic demand from most vital areas of our lives other than sex. And the lack of concern for the erotic root and satisfactions of our work is felt in our disaffection from so much of what we do. For instance, how often do we truly love our work even at its most difficult?

The principal horror of any system which defines the good in terms of profit rather than in terms of human need, or which defines human need to the exclusion of the psychic and emotional components of that need—the principal horror of such a system is that it robs our work of its erotic value, its erotic power and life appeal and fulfillment. Such a system reduces work to a travesty of necessities, a duty by which we earn bread or oblivion for ourselves and those we love. But this is tantamount to blinding a painter and then telling her to improve her work, and to enjoy the act of painting. It is not only next to impossible, it is also profoundly cruel.

As women, we need to examine the ways in which our world can be truly different. I am speaking here of the necessity for reassessing the quality of all the aspects of our lives and of our work, and of how we move toward and through them.

The very word *erotic* comes from the Greek word *eros,* the personification of love in all its aspects—born of Chaos, and *personifying creative power and harmony.* When I speak of the erotic, then, *I speak of it as an assertion of the life-force of women;* of that creative energy empowered, the knowledge and use of which we are now reclaiming in our language, our history, our dancing, our loving, our work, our lives.

There are frequent attempts to equate pornography and eroticism, two diametrically opposed uses of the sexual. Because of these attempts, it has become fashionable to separate the spiritual (psychic and emotional) from the political, to see them as contradictory and antithetical. "What do you mean, a poetic revolutionary, a meditating gunrunner?" In the same way, we have attempted to separate the spiritual and the erotic, thereby reducing the spiritual to a world of flattened affect, a world of the ascetic who aspires to feel nothing. But nothing is farther from the truth. For the ascetic position is one of the highest fear, the gravest immobility. The severe abstinence of the ascetic becomes the ruling obsession. And it is one not of self-discipline but of self-abnegation.

The dichotomy between the spiritual and the political is also false, resulting from an incomplete attention to our erotic knowledge. For the bridge which connects them is formed by the erotic—the sensual—those physical, emotional, and psychic expressions of what is deepest and strongest and richest within each of us, being shared: the passions of love, in its deepest meanings.

Beyond the superficial, the considered phrase, "It feels right to me," acknowledges the strength of the erotic into a true knowledge, for what that means is the first and most powerful guiding light toward any understanding. And understanding is a handmaiden which can only wait upon, or clarify, that knowledge, deeply born. The erotic is the nurturer or nursemaid of all our deepest knowledge.

The erotic functions for me in several ways, and the first is in providing the power which comes from sharing deeply any pursuit with another person. The sharing of joy, whether physical, emotional, psychic, or intellectual, forms a bridge between the sharers which can be the basis for understanding much of what is not shared between them, and lessens the threat of their difference.

Another important way in which the erotic connection functions is the open and fearless underlining of my capacity for joy. In the way my body stretches to music and opens into response, hearkening to its deepest rhythms, so every level upon which I sense also opens to the erotically satisfying experience, whether it is dancing, building a bookcase, writing a poem, examining an idea.

That self-connection shared is a measure of the joy which I know myself to be capable of feeling, a reminder of my capacity for feeling. And that deep and irreplaceable knowledge of my capacity for joy comes to demand from all of my life that it be lived within the knowledge that such satisfaction is possible, and does not have to be called *marriage*, nor *god*, nor *an afterlife*.

This is one reason why the erotic is so feared, and so often relegated to the bedroom alone, when it is recognized at all. For *once we begin to feel deeply all the aspects of our lives, we begin to demand from ourselves and from our life-pursuits that they feel in accordance with that joy which we know ourselves to be capable of.* Our erotic knowledge empowers us, becomes a lens through which we scrutinize all aspects of our existence, forcing us to evaluate those aspects honestly in terms of their relative meaning within our lives. And this is a grave responsibility, projected from within each of us, not to settle for the convenient, the shoddy, the conventionally expected, nor the merely safe.

During World War II, we bought sealed plastic packets of white, uncolored margarine, with a tiny, intense pellet of yellow coloring perched like a topaz just inside the clear skin of the bag. We would leave the margarine out for a while to soften, and then we would pinch the little pellet to break it inside the bag, releasing the rich yellowness into the soft pale mass of margarine. Then taking it carefully between our fingers, we would knead it gently back and forth, over and over, until the color had spread throughout the whole pound bag of margarine, thoroughly coloring it.

I find the erotic such a kernel within myself. When released from its intense and constrained pellet, it flows through and colors my life with a kind of energy that heightens and sensitizes and strengthens all my experience.

We have been raised to fear the *yes* within ourselves, our deepest cravings. But, once recognized, those which do not enhance our future lose their power and can be altered. The fear of our desires keeps them suspect and indiscriminately powerful, for to suppress any truth is to give it strength beyond endurance. The fear that we cannot grow beyond whatever distortions we may find within ourselves keeps us docile and loyal and obedient, externally defined, and leads us to accept many facets of our oppression as women.

When we live outside ourselves, and by that I mean on external directives only rather than from our internal knowledge and needs, when we live away from those erotic guides from within ourselves, then our lives are limited by external and alien forms, and we conform to the needs of a structure that is not based on human need, let alone an individual's. But when we begin to live from within outward, in touch with the power of the erotic within ourselves, and allowing that power to inform and illuminate our actions upon the world around us, then we begin to be responsible to ourselves in the deepest sense. For as we begin to recognize our deepest feelings, we begin to give up, of necessity, being satisfied with suffering and self-negation, and with the numbness which so often seems like their only alternative in our society. Our acts against oppression become integral with self, motivated and empowered from within.

In touch with the erotic, I become less willing to accept powerlessness, or those other supplied states of being which are not native to me, such as resignation, despair, self-effacement, depression, self-denial.

And yes, there is a hierarchy. There is a difference between painting a back fence and writing a poem, but only one of quantity. And there is, for me, no difference between writing a good poem and moving into sunlight against the body of a woman I love.

This brings me to the last consideration of the erotic. To share the power of each other's feelings is different from using another's feelings as we would use a kleenex. When we look the other way from our experience, erotic or otherwise, we use rather than share the feelings of those others who participate in the experience with us. And use without consent of the used is abuse.

In order to be utilized, our erotic feelings must be recognized. The need for sharing deep feeling is a human need. But within the european-american tradition, this need is satisfied by certain proscribed erotic comings-together. These occasions are almost always characterized by a simultaneous looking away, a pretense of calling them something else, whether a religion, a fit, mob violence, or even playing doctor. And this misnaming of the need and the deed give rise to that distortion which results in pornography and obscenity—the abuse of feeling.

When we look away from the importance of the erotic in the development and sustenance of our power, or when we look away from ourselves as we satisfy our erotic needs in concert with others, *we use each other as objects of satisfaction rather than share our joy in the satisfying*, rather than make connection with our similarities and our differences. To refuse to be conscious of what we are feeling at any time, however comfortable that might seem, is to deny a large part of the experience, and to allow ourselves to be reduced to the pornographic, the abused, and the absurd.

The erotic cannot be felt secondhand. As a Black lesbian feminist, I have a particular feeling, knowledge, and understanding for those sisters with whom I have danced hard, played, or even fought. This deep participation has often been the forerunner for joint concerted actions not possible before.

But this erotic charge is not easily shared by women who continue to operate under an exclusively european-american male tradition. I know it was not available to me when I was trying to adapt my consciousness to this mode of living and sensation.

Only now, I find more and more women-identified women brave enough to risk sharing the erotic's electrical charge without having to look away, and without distorting the enormously powerful and creative nature of that exchange. Recognizing the power of the erotic within our lives can give us the energy to pursue genuine change within our world, rather than merely settling for a shift of characters in the same weary drama.

For not only do we touch our most profoundly creative source, but we do that which is female and self-affirming in the face of a racist, patriarchal, and anti-erotic society.

Interview with Claudia Tate

CLAUDIA TATE: How does your openness about being a Black lesbian feminist direct your work and, more importantly, your life?

AUDRE LORDE: When you narrow your definition to what is convenient, or what is fashionable, or what is expected, what happens is dishonesty by silence. It is putting all of your eggs into one basket. That's not where all of your energy comes from.

Black writers, of whatever quality, who step outside the pale of what Black writers are supposed to write about, or who Black writers are supposed to be, are condemned to silences in Black literary circles that are as total and as destructive as any imposed by racism. This is particularly true for Black women writers who have refused to be delineated by male-establishment models of femininity, and who have dealt with their sexuality as an accepted part of their identity. For instance, where are the women writers of the Harlem Renaissance being taught? Why did it take so long for Zora Neale Hurston to be reprinted?

Now, when you have a literary community oppressed by silence from the outside, as Black writers are in America, and you have this kind of tacit insistence upon some unilateral definition of what "Blackness" is, then you are painfully and effectively silencing some of our most dynamic and creative talents, for all change and progress from within require the recognition of differences among ourselves.

ED. NOTE: Audre Lorde had preferred that the word "black" be capitalized throughout the interview.

When you are a member of an out-group, and you challenge others with whom you share this outsider position to examine some aspect of their lives that distorts differences between you, then there can be a great deal of pain. In other words, when people of a group share an oppression, there are certain strengths that they build together. But there are also certain vulnerabilities. For instance, talking about racism to the women's movement results in "Huh, don't bother us with that. Look, we're all sisters, please don't rock the boat." Talking to the Black community about sexism results in pretty much the same thing. You get a "Wait, wait . . . wait a minute: we're all Black together. Don't rock the boat." In our work and in our living, we must recognize that difference is a reason for celebration and growth, rather than a reason for destruction.

We should see difference as a dialogue, the same way we deal with symbol and image, in literary study. "Imaging" is the process of developing a dialectic, a tension between opposites that illuminates the differences and similarities between things in apparent opposition. It is the same way with people. We need to use these differences in constructive ways, creative ways, rather than in ways to justify our destroying each other.

With respect to myself specifically, I feel that not to be open about any of the different "people" within my identity, particularly the "mes" who are challenged by a status quo, is to invite myself and other women, by my example, to live a lie. In other words, I would be giving in to a myth of sameness which I think can destroy us.

I'm not into living lies, no matter how comfortable they may be. I really feel that I'm too old for both abstractions and games, and I will not shut off any of my essential sources of power, control, and knowledge. I learned to speak the truth by accepting many parts of myself and making them serve one another. This power fuels my life and my work.

C.T.: Has the social climate of the eighties suppressed the openness of the seventies?

LORDE: To begin with, all of these things are relative, and when we speak of the openness of the seventies, we are speaking more of an appearance than a reality. But as far as sexuality is concerned, it is true that in the seventies, Black lesbians and gay men saw a slowly increasing acknowledgment of their presence within the Black community. In large part this came about because of the number of us willing to speak out about our sexual identities. In the 1960s, many Black people who spoke from a complex Black identity suffered because of it, and were silenced in many ways. In the mistaken belief that unity must mean sameness, differences within the Black community of color, sex, sexuality, and vision were sometimes mislabeled, oversimplified, and repressed. We must not romanticize the sixties while we recognize its importance. Lesbians and gay men have always existed in Black communities, and in the sixties we played active and important roles on many fronts in that decade's struggle for Black liberation. And that has been so throughout the history of Black people in america, and continues to be so.

In the 1970s some of those differences which have always existed within the Black community began to be articulated and examined, as we came to learn that we, as a people, cannot afford to waste our resources, cannot afford to waste each other. The eighties present yet another challenge. On one hand, there is a certain move towards conservatism and greater repression within american society, and renewed attacks upon lesbians and gay men represent only the cutting edge of that greater repression which is so dangerous to us all as Black people. But because of this shift to the right, some voices once willing to examine the role of difference in our communities are falling silent, some once vocal people are heading for cover.

It's very distressing to hear someone say, "I can't really afford to say that or I can't afford to be seen with you." It's scary because we've been through that before. It was called the fifties. Yet more and more these days, "all of our asses are in the sling together," if you'll excuse the expression, and real alliances are beginning to be made. When we talk about "Dykes Against Racism Everywhere," and "Black and White Men Together," which are gay groups who have been doing active antiracial work in a number of communities, when we see the coalition of Black community organizations in the Boston area that got together to protest the wholesale murder of Black women in 1978 and '79, we are talking about real coalitions. We must recognize that we need each other. Both these trends are operating now. Of course, I'm dedicated to believing that it's through coalitions that we'll win out. There are no more single issues.

C.T.: Have your critics attempted to stereotype your work?

LORDE: Critics have always wanted to cast me in a particular role from the time my first poem was published when I was fifteen years old. My English teachers at Hunter High School said that a particular poem was much too romantic. It was a love poem about my first love affair with a boy, and they didn't want to print it in the school paper, which is why I sent it to *Seventeen* magazine.

It's easier to deal with a poet, certainly with a Black woman poet, when you categorize her, narrow her down so that she can fulfill your expectations, so she's socially acceptable and not too disturbing, not too discordant. I cannot be categorized. That has been both my weakness and my strength. It has been my weakness because my independence has cost me a lot of support. But you see, it has also been my strength because it has given me a vantage point and the power to go on. I don't know how I would have lived through the difficulties I have survived and continued to produce, if I had not felt that all of who I am is what fulfills me and fulfills the vision I have of the world, and of the future.

C.T.: For whom do you write? What is your responsibility to your audience?

LORDE: I write for myself and my children and for as many people as possible who can read me, who need to hear what I have to say—who need to use what I know. When I say myself, I mean not only the Audre who inhabits my body but all those feisty, incorrigible Black women who insist on standing up and saying "*I am* and you cannot wipe me out, no matter how irritating I am, how much you fear what I might represent." I write for these women for whom a voice has not yet existed, or whose voices have been silenced. I don't have the only voice or all of their voices, but they are a part of my voice, and I am a part of theirs.

My responsibility is to speak the truth as I feel it, and to attempt to speak it with as much precision and beauty as possible. I think of my responsibility in terms of women because there are many voices for men. There are very few voices for women and particularly very few voices for Black women, speaking from the center of consciousness, from the *I am* out to the *we are* and then out to the *we can*.

My mother used to say: "Island women make good wives; whatever happens they've seen worse." Well, I feel that as Black women we have been through all kinds of catastrophe. We've survived, and with style.

I feel I have a duty to speak the truth as I see it and to share not just my triumphs, not just the things that felt good, but the pain, the intense, often unmitigating pain. It is important to share how I know survival is survival and not just a walk through the rain. For example, I have a duty to share what it feels like at three o'clock in the morning when you know "they" could cut you down emotionally in the street and grin in your face. And "they" are your own people. To share what it means to look into another sister's eyes and have her look away and choose someone you know she hates because it's expedient. To know that I, at times, have been a coward, or less than myself, or oppressive to other women, and to know that I can change. All of that anxiety, pain, defeat must be shared. We tend to talk about what feels good. We talk about what we think is settled. We never seem to talk about the ongoing problems. We need to share our mistakes in the same way we share our victories because that's the only way learning occurs. In other words, we have survived the pain, the problems, the failures, so what we need to do is use this suffering and learn from it. We must remember and comfort ourselves with that fact that survival is, in itself, a victory.

I never thought I would live to be forty, and I feel, "Hey, I really did it!" I am stronger for confronting the hard issue of breast cancer, of mortality, dying. It is hard, extremely hard, but very strengthening to remember I could be silent my whole life long and then be dead, flat out, and never have said or done what I wanted to do, what I needed to do because of pain or fear. . . . If I wait to be assured I'm right before I speak, I would be sending little cryptic messages on the Ouiji board, complaints from the other side.

I really feel if what I have to say is wrong, then there will be some woman who will stand up and say Audre Lorde was in error. But my words will be there, something for her to bounce off of, something to incite thought, activity.

I write not only for my peers but for those who will come after me, to say I was there, and I passed on, and you will pass on, too. But you're here now, so do it. I believe very strongly in survival and teaching. I feel that is my work.

This is so important that it bears repeating. I write for those women who do not speak, for those who do not have a voice because they/we were so terrified, because we are taught to respect fear more than ourselves. We've been taught that silence would save us, but it won't. We *must* learn to respect ourselves and our needs more than the fear of our differences, and we must learn to share ourselves with each other.

C.T.: Is writing a way of growing, understanding?

LORDE: Yes. I think writing and teaching, child-rearing, digging rocks (which is one of my favorite pastimes), all of the things I do are very much a part of my work. They flow in and out of each other, help to nourish each other. That's what the whole question of survival and teaching means. That we keep our experience afloat long enough, that we share what we know, so that other people can build upon our experience. There are many ways of doing that in all aspects of our lives. So teaching for me is in many respects identical to writing. Both become ways of exploring what I need for survival. They are survival techniques. Because as I write, as I teach, I am answering those questions that are primary for my own survival, and I am exploring the response to these questions with other people; this is what teaching is. I think that this is the only way that real learning occurs. Learning does not happen in some detached way of dealing with a text alone, but from becoming so involved in the process that you can see how it might illuminate your life, and then how you can share that illumination.

C.T.: When did you start to write?

LORDE: I looked around when I was a young woman and there was no one saying what I wanted and needed to hear. I felt totally alienated, disoriented, crazy. I thought that there's got to be somebody else who feels as I do.

    I was very inarticulate as a youngster. I couldn't speak. I didn't speak until I was five, in fact, not really until I started reading and writing poetry. I used to speak in poetry. I would read poems, and I would memorize them. People would say, "Well, what do you think, Audre? What happened to you yesterday?" And I would recite a poem and somewhere in that poem there would be a line or a feeling I was sharing. In other words, I literally communicated through poetry. And when I couldn't find the poems to express the things I was feeling, that's when I started writing poetry. That was when I was twelve or thirteen.

C.T.: Do Black male and female writers dramatize characters and themes in distinctly different ways? Gayl Jones replied to this question by saying she thought one distinction has to do with the kinds of events men and women select to depict in literature. She thinks Black women writers tend to select particular and personal events rather than those which are generally considered to be representative.

LORDE: I think that's true. This reflects a difference between men and women in general. Black men have come to believe to their detriment that you have no validity unless you're "global," as opposed to personal. Yet, our *real power* comes from the personal; our real insights about living come from that deep knowledge within us that arises from our feelings. Our thoughts are shaped by our tutoring. As Black people, we have not been tutored for our benefit, but more often than not, for our detriment. We were tutored to function in a structure that already existed but that does not function for our good. Our feelings are our most genuine paths to knowledge. They are chaotic, sometimes painful, sometimes contradictory, but they come from deep within us. And we must key into those feelings and begin to extrapolate from them, examine them for new ways of understanding our experiences. This is how new visions begin, how we begin to posit a future nourished by the past. This is what I mean by matter following energy, and energy following feeling. Our visions begin with our desires.

Men have been taught to deal only with what they understand. This is what they respect. They know that somewhere feeling and knowledge are important, so they keep women around to do their feeling for them, like ants do aphids.

I don't think these differences between men and women are rigidly defined with respect to gender, though the Western input has been to divide these differences into male and female *characteristics*. We all have the ability to feel deeply and to move upon our feelings and see where they lead us. Men in general have suppressed that capacity, so they keep women around to do that for them. Until men begin to develop that capacity within themselves, they will always be at a loss and will always need to victimize women.

The message I have for Black men is that it is to their detriment to follow this pattern. Too many Black men do precisely that, which results in violence along sexual lines. This violence terrifies me. It is a painful truth which is almost unbearable. As I say in a new poem, it is "a pain almost beyond bearing" because it gives birth to the kind of hostility that will destroy us.

C.T.: To change the focus, though ever so slightly. Writing by Black Americans has traditionally dramatized Black people's humanity. Black male writers tend to cry out in rage in order to convince their readers that they too feel, whereas Black women writers tend to dramatize the pain, the love. They don't seem to need to intellectualize this capacity to feel, but focus on describing the feeling itself.

LORDE: It's one thing to talk about feeling. It's another to feel. Yes, love is often pain. But I think what is really necessary is to see how much of this pain I can use, how much of this truth I can see and still live unblinded. That is an essential question that we must all ask ourselves. There is some point at which pain becomes an end in itself, and we must let it go. On the other hand, we must not be afraid of pain, and we must not subject ourselves to pain as an end in itself. We must not celebrate victimization because there are other ways of being Black.

There is a very thin but a very definite line between these two responses to pain. And I would like to see this line more carefully drawn in some of the works by Black women writers. I am particularly aware of the two responses in my own work. And I find I must remember that the pain is not its own reason for being. It is a part of living. And the only kind of pain that is intolerable is pain that is wasteful, pain from which we do not learn. And I think that we must learn to distinguish between the two.

C.T.: How do you integrate social protest and art in your work?

LORDE: I see protest as a genuine means of encouraging someone to feel the inconsistencies, the horror of the lives we are living. Social protest is saying that we do not have to live this way. If we feel deeply, and we encourage ourselves and others to feel deeply, we will find the germ of our answers to bring about change. Because once we recognize what it is we are feeling, once we recognize we can feel deeply, love deeply, can feel joy, then we will demand that all parts of our lives produce that kind of joy. And when they do not, we will ask, "Why don't they?" And it is the asking that will lead us inevitably toward change.

So the question of social protest and art is inseparable for me. I can't say it is and either-or proposition. Art for art's sake doesn't really exist for me. What I saw was wrong, and I had to speak up. I loved poetry, and I loved words. But what was beautiful had to serve the purpose of changing my life, or I would have died. If I cannot air this pain and alter it, I will surely die of it. That's the beginning of social protest.

C.T.: How has your work evolved in terms of interest and craft? Let's look at the love poetry, for instance, which dominated your early work [*The First Cities* and *New York Head Shop*] and which appears in *The Black Unicorn*.

LORDE: Everyone has a first-love poem that comes out of that first love. Everybody has it, and it's so wonderful and new and great. But when you've been writing love poems after thirty years, the later poems are the ones that really hit the nitty gritty, that meet your boundaries. They witness what you've been through. Those are the real love poems. And I love them because they say, "Hey! We define ourselves as lovers, as people who love each other all over again; we become new again." These poems insist that you can't separate loving from fighting, from dying, from hurting, but love is triumphant. It is powerful and strong, and I feel I grow a great deal in all of my emotions, especially in the capacity to love.

C.T.: Your love poetry seems not only to celebrate the personal experience of love but also love as a human concept, a theme embracing all of life, a theme which appears more and more emphatically in your later work. Particularly interesting, for instance, are the lesbian love poems ["Letter for Jan" and "Walking Our Boundaries"]. It didn't seem to make much difference whether the poems depicted a relationship between two women, two men, or a man and a woman. . . . The poems do not celebrate the people but the love.

LORDE: When you love, you love. It only depends on how you do it, how committed you are, how many mistakes you make. . . . But I do believe that the love expressed between women is particular and powerful because we have had to love ourselves in order to live; love has been our means of survival. And having been in love with both men and women, I want to resist the temptation to gloss over the differences.

C.T.: I am frequently jarred by my sometimes unconscious attempt to identify the sex of the person addressed in the poem. Since I associate the speaker's voice with you, and since I'm not always conscious that you are a lesbian, the jarring occurs when I realize the object of affection is likewise a woman. I'm certain this disturbance originates in how society defines love in terms of heterosexuality. So if we are to see love as a "universal" concept, society pressures us to see it as heterosexual.

LORDE: Yes, we're supposed to see "universal" love as heterosexual. What I insist upon in my work is that there is no such thing as universal love in literature. There is *this* love in *this* poem. The poem happens when I, Audre Lorde, poet, deal with the particular instead of the "UNIVERSAL." My power as a person, as a poet, comes from who I am. I am a particular person. The relationships I have had, in which people kept me alive, helped sustain me, were sustained by me, were particular relationships. They help give me my particular identity, which is the source of my energy. Not to deal with my life in my art is to cut out the fount of my strength.

I love to write love poems. I love loving. And to put it into another framework, that is, other than poetry, I wrote a paper entitled "The Uses of the Erotic," where I examined the whole question of loving as a manifestation, love as a source of tremendous power. Women have been taught to suspect the erotic urge, the place that is uniquely female. So, just as we tend to reject our Blackness because it has been termed inferior, as women we tend to reject our capacity for feeling, our ability to love, to touch the erotic, because it has been devalued. But it is within this that lies so much of our power, our ability to posit, our vision. Because once we know how deeply we can feel, we begin to demand from all of our life pursuits that they be in accordance with these feelings. And when they don't we must raise the question why do I feel constantly suicidal, for instance? What's wrong? Is it me, or is it what I am doing? We begin to need to answer such questions. But we cannot when we have no image of joy, no vision of what we are capable of. After the killing is over. When you live without the sunlight, you don't know what it is to relish the bright light or even to have too much of it. Once you have light, then you can measure its intensity. So too with joy.

C.T.: Universities seem to be one major source of income for many writers, that is in terms of writer-in-residence positions. Have you had such appointments? What has been their effect?

LORDE: I've only had one writer-in-residence position, and that was at Tougaloo College in Mississippi fourteen years ago. It was pivotal for me. Pivotal. In 1968 my first book had just been published; it was my first trip into the Deep South; it was the first time I had been away from the children; the first time I worked with young Black students in a workshop situation. I came to realize that this was my work. That teaching and writing we're inextricably combined, and it was there that I knew what I wanted to do for the rest of my life.

I had been "the librarian who wrote." After my experience at Tougaloo, I realized that writing was central to my life and that the library, although I loved books, was not enough. Combined with the circumstances that followed my stay at Tougaloo: King's death, Kennedy's death, Martha's accident,* all of these things really made me see that life is very short, and what we have to do must be done now.

---

*Lorde's close personal friend.

I have never had another writer-in-residence position. The poem "Touring" from *The Black Unicorn* represents another aspect of being a travelling cultural worker. I go and read my poetry. I drop my little seeds and then I leave. I hope they spring into something. Sometimes I find out they do; sometimes I never find out. I just have to have faith, and fun along the way.

C.T.: Would you describe your writing process?

LORDE: I keep a journal and write in it fairly regularly. I get a lot of my poems out of it. It's like the raw material for my poems. Sometimes I'm blessed with a poem that comes in the form of a poem, but other times I've worked for two years on a poem.

For me, there are two very basic and different processes for revising my poetry. One is recognizing that a poem has not yet become itself. In other words, I mean that the feeling, the truth that the poem is anchored in is somehow not clearly clarified inside of me, and as a result it lacks something. Then it has to be re-felt. Then there's the other process which is easier. The poem is itself, but it has rough edges that need to be refined. That kind of revision involves picking the image that is more potent or tailoring it so that it carries the feeling. That's an easier kind of rewriting and re-feeling.

My journal entries focus on things I feel: feelings that sometimes have no place, no beginning, no end; phrases I hear in passing; something that looks good to me; sometimes just observations of the world.

I went through a period once when I felt like I was dying. I wasn't writing any poetry, and I felt that if I couldn't write I would split. I was recording in my journal, but no poems came. I know now that this period was a transition in my life.

The next year, I went back to my journal, and here were these incredible poems that I could almost lift out of it. Many of them are in *The Black Unicorn*. "Harriet" is one of them; "Sequelae" and "The Litany for Survival" are others. These poems came right out of the journal. But I didn't see them as poems then.

"Power" was in the journal too. It is a poem written about Clifford Glover, the ten-year-old Black boy shot by a cop who was acquitted by a jury on which a Black woman sat. In fact, the day I heard on the radio that O'Shea had been acquitted, I was going across town on 88th Street [New York City] and I had to pull over. A kind of fury rose up in me—the sky turned red. I felt so sick. I felt as if I would drive the car into a wall, into the next person I saw. So I pulled over. I took out my journal just to air some of my fury, to get it out of my fingertips. Those expressed feelings are that poem. That was just how "Power" was written.

C.T.: A transition has to occur before you can make poetry out of your journal entries.

LORDE: There is a gap between the journal and my poetry. I write this stuff in my journal, and sometimes I cannot even read my journals because there is so much pain and rage in them. I'll put it away in a drawer, and six months, a year or so later, I'll pick up the journal, and there will be the seeds of poems. The journal entries somehow have to be assimilated into my living; only then can I deal with what I have written down.

Art is not living. It is the use of living. The artist has the ability to take the living and use it in a certain way and produce art.

C.T.: Does Afro-American literature possess particular characteristics?

LORDE: Afro-American literature is certainly part of an African tradition. African tradition deals with life as an experience to be lived. In many respects, it is much like the Eastern philosophies in that we see ourselves as a part of a life force; we are joined, for instance, to the air, to the earth. We are part of the whole-life process. We live in accordance with, in a kind of correspondence with the rest of the world as a whole. And therefore living becomes an experience, rather than a problem, no matter how bad or how painful it may be. Change will rise endemically from the experience fully lived and responded to.

I feel this very much in African writing. And as a consequence, I have learned a great deal from Achebe, Tutuola, Ekwensi, from Flora Nwapa and Ama Ata Aido. Leslie Lacy, a Black American who lived temporarily in Ghana, writes about experiencing this transcendence in his book *The Rise and Fall of a Proper Negro.*

It's not a turning away from pain, error, but seeing these things as part of living, and learning from them. This characteristic is particularly African, and it is transposed into the best of Afro-American literature. In addition, we have the legends of our struggle and survival in the New World.

This transcendence appears in Ellison, a little bit in Baldwin. And it is present very much so in Toni Morrison's *Sula,* which is a most wonderful piece of fiction. And I don't care if she won a prize for *The Song of Solomon.* *Sula* is a totally incredible book. It made me light up inside like a Christmas tree. I particularly identified with the book because of the female-outsider idea. That book is one long poem. Sula is the ultimate Black female of our time, trapped in her power and her pain. Alice Walker uses that quality in *The Color Purple,* another wonderful novel of living as power.

C.T.: The recent writing by many Black women seems to explore human concerns somewhat differently than do the men. These women refuse to blame racism alone for every negative aspect of Black life. They are examining the nature of what passes between Black women and Black men—the power principles. Men tend to respond defensively to the writing of Black women by labeling them as the "darklings" of the literary establishment. Goodness knows, the critics, especially Black male critics, had a field day with Ntozake Shange's *For Colored Girls Who Have Considered Suicide When the Rainbow is Enuf.* And they are getting started on Alice Walker's *The Color Purple.* But there are cruel Black men, just as there are kind Black men. Can't we try to alter that cruelty by focusing on it?

LORDE: Let me read an excerpt from a piece in *The Black Scholar* for you, which I wrote a while back:

> As I have said elsewhere, it is not the destiny of Black America to repeat white America's mistakes. But we will, if we mistake the trappings of success in a sick society for the signs of a meaningful life. If Black men continue to do so, defining "femininity"

in its archaic European terms, this augurs ill for our survival as a people, let alone our survival as individuals. Freedom and future for Blacks do not mean absorbing the dominant white male disease. . . .

As Black people, we cannot begin our dialogue by denying the oppressive nature of male privilege. And if Black males choose to assume that privilege, for whatever reason, raping, brutalizing and killing women, then we cannot ignore Black male oppression. One oppression does not justify another.*

It's infuriating. Misguided Black men. And meanwhile they are killing us in the streets. Is that the nature of nationhood?

I find this divisiveness to be oppressive and very persistent. It's been going on for a long time. It didn't start with Ntozake. It's been coming more and more to the forefront now. If you ask any of the Black women writers over thirty whom you're interviewing, if she's honest, she will tell you. You know there's as much a Black literary mafia in this country as there is a white literary mafia. They control who gets exposure. If you don't toe the line, then you're not published; your works are not distributed. At the same time, as Black women, of course, we do not want to be used against Black men by a system that means both of us ill.

C.T.: Do you think that had it not been for the women's movement Black women would still be struggling to achieve their voice in the literary establishment?

LORDE: Without a doubt. Black women writers have been around a long time, and they have suffered consistent inattention. Despite this reality, you hear from various sources that Black women really have "it." We're getting jobs; we're getting this and that, supposedly. Yet we still constitute the lowest economic group in America. Meanwhile those of us who do not fit into the "establishment" have not been allowed a voice, and it was only with the advent of the women's movement—even though Black women are in disagreement with many aspects of the women's movement—that Black women began to demand a voice, as women and as Blacks. I think any of us who are honest have to say this. As Barabara Smith says, "All the women were white and all the Blacks were men, but some of us are still brave." Her book on Black women's studies [*Some of Us Are Brave*], which she edited along with Gloria Hull and Patricia Bell Scott, is the first one on the subject.

C.T.: Are you at a turning point in your career, your life?

LORDE: I think I have deepened and broadened my understanding of the true difficulty of my work. Twenty years ago when I said we needed to understand each other I had not really perfected a consciousness concerning how important differences are in our lives. But that is a theme which recurs in my life and in my work. I have become more powerful because I have refused to settle for

---

*"Feminism and Black Liberation: The Great American Disease" by Audre Lorde, *The Black Scholar*, X, 8–9 (April 1979), p. 19.

the myth of sorry sameness, that myth of easy sameness. My life's work continues to be survival and teaching. As I said before, teaching is also learning; teach what you need to learn. If we do this deeply, then it is most effective. I have, for example, deepened the questions that I follow, and so I have also deepened the ways I teach and learn.

The work I did on the erotic was very, very important. It opened up for me a whole area of connections in the absence of codified knowledge, or in the absence of some other clear choice. The erotic has been a real guide for me. And learning as a discipline is identical to learning how to reach through feeling the essence of how and where the erotic originates, to posit what it is based upon. This process of feeling and therefore knowing has been very, very constructive for me.

I believe in the erotic and I believe in it as an enlightening force within our lives as women. I have become clearer about the distinctions between the erotic and other apparently similar forces. We tend to think of the erotic as an easy, tantalizing sexual arousal. I speak of the erotic as the deepest life force, a force which moves us toward living in a fundamental way. And when I say living I mean it as that force which moves us toward what will accomplish real positive change.

When I speak of a future that I work for, I speak of a future in which all of us can learn, a future which we want for our children. I posit that future to be led by my visions, my dreams, and my knowledge of life. It is that knowledge which I call the erotic, and I think we must develop it within ourselves. I think so much of our living and our consciousness has been formed by death or by non-living. This is what allows us to tolerate so much of what is vile around us. When I speak of "the good," I speak of living; I speak of the erotic in all forms. They are all one. So in that sense I believe in the erotic as an illuminating principle in our lives.

C.T.: You've just finished a new work.

LORDE: Yes. *Zami: A New Spelling of My Name* was just published. It's a biomythography, which is really fiction. It has the elements of biography and history of myth. In other words, it's fiction built from many sources. This is one way of expanding our vision.

I'm very excited about this book. As you know, it's been a long time coming. Now that it's out, it'll do its work. Whatever its faults, whatever its glories, it's there.

You might call *Zami* a novel. I don't like to call it that. Writing *Zami* was a lifeline through the cancer experience. As I said in *The Cancer Journals,* I couldn't believe that what I was fighting I would fight alone and only for myself. I couldn't believe that there wasn't something there that somebody could use at some other point because I know that I could have used some other woman's words, whatever she had to say. Just to know that someone had been there before me would have been very important, but there was nothing. Writing *The Cancer Journals* gave me the strength and power to examine that experience, to put down into words what I was feeling. It was my belief that if this work were useful to just one woman, it was worth doing.

C.T.: What can you share with the younger generation of black women writers and writers in general?

LORDE: Not to be afraid of difference. To be real, tough, loving. And to recognize each other. I can tell them not to be afraid to feel and not to be afraid to write about it. Even if you are afraid, do it anyway because we learn to work when we are tired, so we can learn to work when we are afraid. Silence never brought us anything. Survive and teach; that's what we've got to do and to do it with joy.

"Coming Out Blackened and Whole": Fragmentation and Reintegration in Audre Lorde's *Zami* and *The Cancer Journals*

ELIZABETH ALEXANDER

1

"As a Black woman," said the late Audre Lorde, "I have to deal with identity or I don't exist at all. I can't depend on the world to name me kindly, because it never will. If the world defines you, it will define you to your disadvantage. So either I'm going to be defined by myself or not at all" ("Interview with Audre Lorde" with Karla Hammond 18). In essays from her *Sister Outsider* and *A Burst of Light* as well as in the more narratively autobiographical *Zami: A New Spelling of My Name* and *The Cancer Journals,* Lorde names differences among women. African Americans, lesbians, and other groups as empowering rather than divisive forces and as aspects of identity. The political ideal, as she sees it, should not be a melting pot where all difference is subsumed, usually bending to the descriptive and ideological might of the previously dominant group. Instead, Lorde argues, difference within the self is a strength to be called upon rather than a liability to be altered. She exhorts her readers to recognize how each of them is multifarious and need never choose one aspect of identity at the expense of the others. "There's always someone asking you to underline one piece of yourself," she said in a 1981 interview,

> whether it's *Black, woman, mother, dyke, teacher,* etc.—because that's the piece that they need to key in to. They want you to dismiss everything else. But once you do that, then you've lost because then you become acquired or bought by that particular es-

sence of yourself, and you've denied yourself all of the energy that it takes to keep all those others in jail. Only by learning to live in harmony with your contradictions can you keep it all afloat. . . . That's what our work comes down to. No matter where we key into it, it's the same work, just different pieces of ourselves doing it. ("Audre" 15)

Each of us, says Lorde, needs each of those myriad pieces to make us who we are and whole. Lorde works the science and logic of her own hybridity. "I had never been too good at keeping within straight lines, no matter what their width" (25), she writes in *Zami*. She must make a physical space for herself in a hybrid language, a composite, a creation of new language to make space for the "new" of the self-invented body.

The implications of this thinking for questions of identity are broad. For the self to remain simultaneously multiple and integrated, embracing the definitive boundaries of each category—race, gender, class, et cetera—while dissembling their static limitations, assumes a depth and complexity of identity construction that refutes a history of limitation. For the self to be fundamentally collaged—overlapping and discernibly dialogic—is to break free from diminishing concepts of identity. Lorde says, "When I say myself, I mean not only the Audre who inhabits my body but all those feisty, incorrigible black women who insist on standing up and saying '*I am* and you cannot wipe me out, no matter how irritating I am, how much you fear what I might represent'" (Interview 104). The self is comprised of multiple components within the self and evolved from multiple external sources, an African-American women's tradition or mythos.

The Cancer Journals is Lorde's memoir of her battle with the disease, but the scope of the meditation, as well as Lorde's formal freedom, makes it much more. For *Zami* she has invented a name for the book's new, collaged genre: *biomythography*. Neither autobiography, biography, nor mythology, biomythography is all of those things and none of them, a collaged space in which useful properties of genres are borrowed and reconfigured according to how well they help tell the story of a particular African-American woman's life. *Biomythography* both refers to each of its eponymous genres and defines itself in its present moment.

I will consider how in this biomythographic mode Lorde's vision of collaged self-construction is mirrored in her compositional choices. With *biomythography* Lorde names a new genre, creating a larger space for her myriad selves. "I feel that not to be open about any of the different 'people' within my identity," she said in an interview, "particularly the 'mes' who are challenged by a status quo, is to invite myself and other women, by my example, to live a lie. In other words, I would be giving in to a myth of sameness which I think can destroy us" (Interview 102).

Both *Zami* and *The Cancer Journals* favor nonlinear narration that plays with chronology as it needs to. Both are autobiographies of Lorde's body. Both books are also erotic autobiographies, with *Zami* in particular describing Lorde's sensual life in intricate detail. The African-American woman's body in Lorde's work—specifically, her own body—becomes a map of lived experience and a way of printing suffering as well as joy upon the flesh. Because the history of the black female sexual body is fraught with lies and distortion, the story of those bodies as told by their inhabitants must take place on new, self-charted terrain with the marks of a traumatic history like a palimpsest. Like Carriacou, the Caribbean home of Lorde's antecedents that she as a child could not find on any map at school, the body of flesh or land that does not accurately exist in white American eyes leaves the inhabitant open for self-invention and interpretation. The flesh, the text, remains scarred, marking the trail to self-creation.

Lorde is preoccupied with things bodily: that which is performed upon the body versus what the body performs and asserts. Cancer surgery and subsequent bodily struggles are the focus of *The Cancer Journals,* while the ingestion of X-ray crystals at a factory job and an illegal abortion are signal episodes in *Zami.* Sexual and spiritual woman-love are what the body performs and how it heals as well as the means by which Lorde finds voice and self-expression. She incorporates the intellectual and physical aspects of her life, reminding the reader that the metaphysical resides in a physical space, the body. Thus rage and oppression are metabolized to cancer, but she will also "write fire until it comes out my ears, my eyes, my noseholes—everywhere. Until it's every breath I breathe" ("Burst" 76–77). In Lorde's work, the body speaks its own history; she chooses corporeal language to articulate what she could not previously put into words.

In *The Cancer Journals,* for instance, Lorde dreams of a different vocabulary for considering this phenomenon. She recounts a dream in which "I had begun training to change my life" and follows a "shadowy teacher":

> Another young woman who was there told me she was taking a course in "language crazure," the opposite of discrazure (the cracking and wearing away of rock). I thought it would be very exciting to study the formation and crack and composure of words, so I told my teacher I wanted to take that course. My teacher said okay, but it wasn't going to help me any because I had to learn something else, and I wouldn't get anything new from that class. I replied maybe not, but even though I knew all about rocks, for instance, I still liked studying their composition, and giving a name to the different ingredients of which they were made. It's very exciting to think of me being all the people in this dream. (14–15)

"[T]he formation and crack and composure" of words mirrors the process of reconstituting the scarred self. Lorde thinks of herself as all of the people in the dream. She is at once the self who wants to learn about language, the self who explores new selves and ideas, the censorial teacher-self as well as the self who gives permission for new exploration, albeit grudgingly. The dream allows for the simultaneous existence of different selves coexisting as a single self, and the contemplation of form, crack, and composure mirrors how the self is continually brought back together from disassembled fragments. Perhaps she is playing also, in the way that dreams play tricks with language, with the words *crazure* and *discrazure,* with first being considered "crazy," as Lorde tells us she has been since elementary school, and then coming to see the roots of *craze* as, in fact, whole and sane. In crazure the lines and fissures are visible but the object—like Lorde herself—remains whole.

In *Zami* Lorde describes the process of constructing herself racially and sexually with race and gender both facts of biology and learned characteristics and social operatives. To be "blackened" reveals not only a process of becoming and being acted upon but also a state of being. Lorde restores the visual impact of "coming out" to suggest her assertion and arrival and also, of course, playing on lesbian "coming out." Hers is a process of becoming black and lesbian on her own terms as much as it is being named and seen as those things by a larger world. "Blackened" is a positive state to "come out" into, but it also implies being burnt and scarred. The statement's ending—"and whole"—suggests no contradiction between being scarred and being whole (*Zami* 5). In Lorde's work life experience ever marks and takes shape as visible body memory, as a collage whose assembled scraps always allude to their past and beyond to a collective race memory of the violence of rupture in the Middle Passage, as encoded by the African-American collage artist Romare Bearden. When Lorde refers to the *"journeywoman pieces of myself"* (*Zami* 5), she configures the self as simultaneously fragmented and reassembled.

Zami's first section is an unlabeled preprologue, a dedication of sorts in which Lorde asks questions in italics and then muses upon them in roman typeface. This introduces us to the dialogism of Lorde's work, in which process is always apparent and the self is presented as an unfinished work in transition and progress. Collage, too, is dialogic at its core, insofar as the cut and torn strips encode a dialogue between past and ever evolving present. That referentiality of using a scrap that on closer scrutiny can be identified both with its former life and as part of the present fiction recalls Bearden's earlier work, in which pieces were readily associated with their origins. Interestingly, Bearden later works continually with origami-like paper in ways less obviously allusive to a separate past than his earlier newspaper and magazine cutouts.[1] This gesture reflects the assurance of both self and voice in Bearden's mature work. By engaging visibly in the dialogic aspects of collage, *Zami* ruminates on how the self is put together and how the book is the body for Lorde's ideas about self-construction.

2

Images of black people's bodies in American culture have been either hypersexualized or desexualized to serve the imaginings and purposes of white American men and women. African-American men have been iconographically exploited as either black buck (in the nineteenth century, renegade slave; in the twentieth, athlete or criminal) or docile, smiling eunuch (in the nineteenth century, men seen as "Uncles"—Remus, or Jim on the river raft, without children on their own and with-

---

By engaging visibly in the dialogic aspects of collage, Zami ruminates on how the self is put together and how the book is the body for Lorde's ideas about self-construction.

out discernible sexuality—in the twentieth century, obsequious entertainers).
Black women, similarly, have been inconographically exploited as the hypersexualized Jezebel who entices the supposedly unrapacious master into her pallet or as
the desexualized Mammy who has no children or loves her white "babies" as her
own. Her body is very much a part of her image: as Mammy she is a comforting void
of avoirdupois, while the Jezebel's curvaceous body is prominently displayed like
an emblem of her social status or her essence. It is startling how, even today, there
is so little iconographic gray space with these images. Historian Gerda Lerner
writes that the postslavery mythology of blacks was created to maintain social control. She specifically addresses the mythicizing of black women's sexual freedom
and abandon so that they were seen as women who

> therefore, deserved none of the consideration and respect granted to white women.
> Every black woman was, by definition, a slut according to this racist mythology;
> therefore, to assault her and exploit her sexually was not reprehensible and carried
> with it none of the normal communal sanctions against such behavior. A wide range
> of practices reinforced this myth: the laws against intermarriage; the denial of the title
> "Miss" or "Mrs." to any black woman; the taboos against respectable social mixing of
> the races; the refusal to let black women customers try on clothing in stores before
> making a purchase; the assigning of single toilet facilities to both sexes of Blacks; the
> different legal sanctions against rape, abuse of minors and other sex crimes when
> committed against white or black women. Black women were very much aware of the
> interrelatedness of these practices and fought constantly—individually and through
> their organizations—both the practices and the underlying myth. (163–64)

This continual need to prove oneself sexually respectable—as if one ever could—
against such a backdrop of accusation and assumption made the frank discussion
of one's own sexuality dangerous. The need to name oneself, rather than leave it
to a hostile dominant culture, is shown in the way in *Zami* Lorde and her late-
teenaged friends call themselves "The Branded": "We became The Branded because we learned how to make a virtue out of it" (82).

Lorde's mapping of her body is all the more powerful against this history, as
is her reclaiming and redefining of the erotic in her groundbreaking essay, "Uses
of the Erotic: The Erotic as Power":

> The erotic has often been misnamed by men and used against women. It has been
> made into the confused, the trivial, the psychotic, the plasticized sensation. For this
> reason, we have often turned away from the exploration and consideration of the
> erotic as a source of power and information, confusing it with its opposite, the
> pornographic. But pornography is a direct denial of the power of the erotic, for it
> represents the suppression of true feeling. Pornography emphasizes sensation with-
> out feeling. (54)

Lorde carefully separates eroticism from abuse of sexuality, freeing herself and
those who would write after her from the idea that black women's sexuality is to

be whispered about and to be ashamed of. She reminds us that "[t]he very word *erotic* comes from the Greek word *eros,* the personification of love in all its aspects—born of Chaos, and personifying creative power and harmony. When I speak of the erotic, then, I speak of it as an assertion of the lifeforce of women; of that creative energy empowered, the knowledge and use of which we are now reclaiming in our language, our history, our dancing, our loving, our work, our lives" (55). Eroticism as she defines it has nothing at all to do with how African-American women are conventionally sexualized.

Lorde keeps readers aware of what the body feels, piece by piece, throughout the narratives. We are always aware of what her body is doing and feeling, from abortion cramps to sweat running between her breasts at 3 a.m. (*Zami* 117). This is in contrast to her mother's "euphemisms of body": "bamsy," "lower region," "between your [not 'my'] legs," all "whispered" (*Zami* 32). Further, Lorde talks about the body as a thing put together and taken apart. In both *The Cancer Journals* and *Zami* she isolates the breast and its symbolic meaning for motherhood and heterosexual beauty and then reconceives her own body by talking about what the breast means to her: yes, it gives her pleasure, but not apart from the rest of her body. The female breast can be prosthetically replaced, but Lorde needs to create and articulate her own grammar of physical significance.

Lorde continually refers to her physical self; phrases such as "when I was five years old and still legally blind" (*Zami* 21) give the reader a corporeal landmark in her life's chronology, calling attention again to the conflict black women frequently experience between public authority and self-authority. She is blind in the eyes of the law, yet she has already given us accounts of what she sees around her. We have before us, then, a legally blind narrative we have nonetheless come to trust. The emphasis on legality in "legally blind" calls up the ironies of legal and extralegal categories in African-American life: "chattel personal" defined full human beings, and so on. Lorde points to a distrust of the American common legal system and asks readers instead to trust her authority as she recounts the details she remembers seeing. Young Audre enters a "sight conservation class" but shows us a "blue wooden booth," "white women," "milk," "black mother," and "red and white tops" (*Zami* 21). It turns out that the seven or eight black children in her class all have "serious deficiencies of sight"; are all these children wrong and legally deficient? Lorde's authority supersedes legal status and public logic.

Lorde yokes the physical and conceptual when she recalls a doctor who "clip[ped] the little membrane under my tongue so I was no longer tongue-tied" (*Zami* 23). To be tongue-tied is to have an encumbered, surgically correctable tongue as well as to be at a loss for words or without language, and Lorde liberalizes this metaphorized tongue: she gives a physical home and tangible, corporeal image to the concept of self-expression. The tongue, the physical organ that enables speech, is clipped that she might speak, and Lorde mines that act of surgical violence, of bodily invasion, to talk about speaking, expression, recreation, and acting. Similarly, when struggling for money, Lorde sells her blood for plasma. Blood is a synecdoche for the surviving body and its sale a metaphor for the idea of "living off of her body," and Lorde refigures "selling one's body" as a tawdry sexual act (though most prostitutes do so to survive as well). That is, she sells a regenerative part so the whole can live.

Moreover, blood "belongs" inside of the body, but Lorde externalizes it, as she constantly turns her body inside out, showing us the hidden insides that amplify how the outside has been maligned and distorted; the metaphysical inside is never known unless she chooses to reveal it. Conversely, the X-ray crystals that Lorde counts in the factory are brought inside the body in another inversion of nature. She buries them deeper and deeper in her body, first secreting them in her thick socks, then taking them into her mouth, chewing them up and imbibing some part of them even as they are spit out in the bathroom.

Lorde's photograph makes up the full front cover of the first edition of *The Cancer Journals*. Here she makes herself, her body, empirical, the best evidence of her arguments and self-definitions. She illustrates that she is all she proclaims herself to be—fat and black and beautiful—but that cover is also a strange testament to her very physical existence: she is a survivor and alive. She shows us the inside of her body to gain a kind of documentary, empirical self-referencing, authority as an expert on her own life and as the maker of a life on paper. For neither that life, her own, nor that of any black woman, has ever existed in representation as its possessor experienced it. Consider the case of the Hottentot Venus, a southern African woman named Saartje Baartman (tribal name unknown) brought to Europe in the early nineteenth century under the impression that she was to earn money performing that she could take back to her family (see Gilman 232–35). Instead, she was exhibited nude in circuses and private balls in London and Paris; eager Europeans paid to see her steatopygia. A French scientist, Georges Cuvier, made a name for himself by performing experiments of an unspecified nature upon her body and by dissecting her buttocks and genitalia after her death at the age of 25. Baartman came to signify sexual and racial difference represented in extremis, as well as the attitude that black women's bodies were easily commodified and utterly dispensable. Baartman's case represents as well another side of the exploitation of black women: the burning desire to see further and further inside, to have access to every crack and crevice of a black woman's body and to that which she has tried to keep sacred. This underlines the power of Lorde showing us her insides, that sanctified, veiled territory that looks so different because she is showing it herself.

3

Zami's subtitle, "a new spelling of my name," hints that the alphabet—shapes that when put together make discernible meaning—will be rearranged. The "me" or "my" that name represents remains constant: Audre Lorde, as we her readers know her. But the moniker is what is new and what will unfold in the book; what the self is called and what it calls itself are not necessarily identical things. The theme of naming and renaming oneself is familiar within African-American culture, of course. Instead of the example of Malcolm X, whose *X* stands as a sign of empty space, negation and refutation of the white patriarch's legacy, Lorde re-spells her name altogether. She empties language, even letters, of previous signifiers as she plays with these received symbols. Lorde makes use of all that is available to her, just as African-American experience incorporates the joy of transported and reassembled culture as it remembers the ugly rupture of the Middle Passage. Lorde works with that same alphabet to make a newly named and new self altogether. *Spelling* works both as a noun (how the word is spelled) as well as an active verb form (the process of spelling). So Lorde engages in spelling and reinventing, a work in progress who has not necessarily settled at a fixed meaning or identity. "A" new spelling (as opposed to "the") means there is probably more to come.

The way Lorde sees before she gets glasses and the validity of that vision challenges conventional ways of seeing and knowing. The first story she writes as a child, Lorde tells us, is a collage as well as a rebus: "I like White Rose Salada tea" (*Zami* 29), with the rose represented by a picture clipped from the *New York Times Magazine* and by letters spelling her story. "How I Became a Poet" (*Zami* 31–34) challenges the concept of chapters. Unattributed quotations challenge the notion of authorship and attribution.

"Growing up Fat Black Female and almost blind in america requires so much surviving that you have to learn from it or die," Lorde writes in *The Cancer Journals* (40). She spells America with a lowercase *a,* again exercising her prerogative as maker of the body of the book and letting her spelled language bear her perspective on the world. She chooses not to capitalize the name of a country that she sees as "cold and raucous" (*Zami* 11). Carriacou is her ancestral home, but the body of the country, the physical spot, while not locatable in any official text (the map), is utterly integral to her sense of self and ancestry. "Once *home* was a far way off, a place I had never been to but knew well out of my mother's mouth" (*Zami* 13), she continues. If a body of land does not even appear on a paper map but incontrovertibly exists, emitting from her mother's actual body, she must trust her own authority and be utterly free to experience and know it according to an internal family barometer. Invisibility, rather than distorted visibility, ironically provides a higher degree of self-inventive freedom.

Harlem is capitalized while *america* is not; Lorde gives herself that authority of capitalization. For upper- and lower-case letters imply caste or class, both suggested and contained within *case*. Lorde plays with the spelling of her name from the beginning of the biomythography, describing her decision to drop the *y* on her birth name Audrey for love of the solidity and visual symmetry of Audre Lorde:

> I did not like the tail of the Y hanging down below the line in Audrey, and would always forget to put it on, which used to disturb my mother greatly. I used to love the evenness of AUDRELORDE at four years of age, but I remembered to put on the Y because it pleased my mother, and because, as she always insisted to me, that was

the way it had to be because that was the way it was. No deviation was allowed from her interpretations of correct. (*Zami* 24)

Lorde echoes this theme in *The Cancer Journals*. Discussing the politics of prostheses, she talks about carving one's physical self to someone else's idea of correctness rather than to one's own sense of symmetry. That dangling Y is in a way like a prosthetic limb or breast: once the new and natural shape of the body is to have one breast, just as the new and natural shape of the name is the indeed wonderfully even AUDRELORDE, addenda are prosthetic, unnecessary, and in their way de-forming.

Later, young Audre writes her name at school in what she thinks is her most glorious penmanship, moving slantwise down the page in another kind of symmetry. She works hard at this display, "half-showing off, half-eager to please" (*Zami* 25). She wants to write with pencil, which is how she has learned and the way she thinks is proper, but is given a crayon instead. Crayon, we are to think, is much coarser and less exact than the sharp pencil, for children and not for adults. Lorde makes do, but her teacher says, "I see we have a young lady who does not want to do as she is told" (26). This moment in which the narrator's "right" is presented in opposition to a public "right" is an important trope in black women's autobiography; without resistance, survival and growth are impossible in an unjust world. Since we have been set up to identify with the narrator, as readers we align ourselves against the tyrannical dominant culture and with the contested genius of the black girl-child. This is how we learn the lesson that to follow instructions, to play by what you think are the rules, does not always garner the expected perquisites.

In that instance of childhood we see Lorde asserting her own way of *writing*—not yet "spelling" explicitly, as the title would indicate, but spelling in the fundamental way that a child spells when every act of writing is a conscious act of putting together the pieces that make words that then hold meaning. To spell one's name is to create oneself in language, in Lorde's words, to put together "all the journeywoman pieces of myself" into one's most public signifier: the name.

Also present in *Zami* is the signal scene in African-American autobiography in which the slave learns to read and to transcend a received legal status, thus entering the domain in which literacy is experienced as freedom. Lorde learns to read and speak simultaneously "because of [her] nearsightedness," distilling from apparent deficiency a new way of learning. Describing this, Lorde establishes a firm link between literacy and self-expression:

I took the books from Mrs. Baker's hands after she was finished reading, and traced the large black letters with my fingers, while I peered again at the beautiful bright colors of the pictures. Right then I decided I was going to find out how to do that myself. I pointed to the black marks which I could now distinguish as separate letters, different from my sisters' more grown-up books, whose smaller print made the pages only one grey blur for me. I said, quite loudly, for whoever was listening to hear, "I want to read." (23)

This scene demonstrates Lorde's understanding that letters and words have physicality, that language has a body, and that the physical place in which communicated language resides is important. This leads the reader, herself engaged in an act of literacy as she reads the book, to reexperience that lost sense of the word's physicality. After this scene, Lorde's mother teaches her "to say the alphabet forwards and backwards as it was done in Grenada" (23). Lorde's logic, bodily and intellectual, finds sense in the so-called backwards as well as in the forwards.

Lorde describes her mother as follows: "My mother was a very powerful woman. This was so in a time when that word-combination of *woman* and *powerful* was almost unexpressable in the white american common tongue, except or unless it was accompanied by some aberrant explaining adjective like blind, or hunchback, or crazy, or Black" (*Zami* 15). For her mother to exist in language as she knows her, Lorde must trust her own knowledge and her own developing linguistic cosmos. She must also become attuned to what she knows outside of spoken language. She says that "my mother must have been *other* than woman" (16) because of her authority, because of the way she did not fit what "the white american common tongue" would represent as "Black and foreign and female in New York City in the twenties" (17). Lorde writes, "It was so often her [my mother's] approach to the world; to change reality. If you can't change reality, change your perceptions of it" (18). Lorde's mother in some regards provided a blueprint for Lorde's ability to change form to suit her needs, to change an outside perception of her body by inserting her own sense of form, both literary and physical. In an interview with Adrienne Rich, Lorde said she learned from her mother "[t]he important value of nonverbal communication, beneath language. My life depended on it. . . . eventually I learned how to acquire vital and protective information without words. My mother used to say to me, 'Don't just listen like a ninny to what people say in their mouth'" ("Interview with Audre Lorde" 715). Language makes space for self-articulation and allows the self-invented body to name itself and to exist. Like so many other African-American women writers, Lorde must make a physical space for herself in a hybrid and composite language wherein what she knows is frequently at odds with what the world tells her she should see.

4

On a family trip to Washington, DC, Lorde describes the agony of what her eyes actually see. The trip marks the hardest smack with direct racism and segregation that the family had experienced and takes place "on the edge of the summer when I was supposed to stop being a child" (*Zami* 68). Great preparation is made in the family for the trip; food is cooked and packed for the train along with suitcases. Lorde sees everything there "through an agonizing corolla of dazzling whiteness" (69) which at the same time dazzles and blinds. The color of Washington's buildings represent who runs them; it is beautiful, what the family members have come to see, but it is also what they are up against and what they are not, for when they stop on the hot summer day for vanilla ice cream (more blinding whiteness) they are not allowed to eat at the counter. Washington is "real" and "official" as a site of power, and Lorde, on the brink of a new maturity, sees what is painful in the white dazzle: "The waitress was white, and the counter was white, and the ice cream I never ate in Washington, D.C. that summer I left childhood was white, and the white heat and the white pavement and the white stone monuments of my first Washington summer made me sick to my stomach for the whole rest of that trip" (71). Here we see a direct example, as well, of how her body absorbs and metabolizes her life's experiences, including painful ones. Her body holds and manifests that which has happened to her psyche. She develops a long-lasting stomachache from the moment she is acted upon via the seeing power of her eyes, as though the white is a tincture of evil.

Lorde writes of the "secret fears which allow cancer to flourish" (*Cancer* 10). In both books taken together, cancer is inescapably a metaphor for the dangers of growing up poor, female, and black. She metabolizes the fears that others have of her, from teachers to exploitative employers. The episode where she describes her abortion and the episode when she works in Keystone Electronics most vividly illustrate this.

The abortion segment is graphic, necessarily. "Now all I had to do was hurt" (*Zami* 110), she writes, after she has had the catheter inserted into her uterus. This both isolates and delays bodily experience. The rubber eventually works its way out, as does the fetus. She keeps the reader ever aware of exactly how she is feeling: "[T]his action which was tearing my guts apart and from which I could die except I wasn't going to—this action was a kind of shift from safety towards self-preservation. It was a choice of pains. That's what living was all about" (*Zami* 111). The fetus is, of course, a part of her body as it grows inside of her, but it is a part that she wants to be rid of. To get rid of the life-burden of an unwanted child she must have this physical symbol of that invasion removed. Like a tumor, a fetus grows unwittingly.

Lorde has worked in two doctor's offices but cannot type and is young, poor, female, and black, so she ends up working in a factory that processes X-ray crystals used in radio and radar machinery. The place was "offensive to every sense, too cold and too hot, gritty, noisy, ugly, sticky, stinking, and dangerous" (*Zami* 126). She counts X-ray crystals with black and Puerto Rican women whose fingers are permanently darkened from exposure to the radiation: "Nobody mentioned that carbon tet destroys the liver and causes cancer of the kidneys. Nobody mentioned that the X-ray machines, when used unshielded, delivered doses of constant low radiation far in excess of what was considered safe even in those days" (*Zami* 126).

Workers could earn bonuses for "reading" crystals past a certain amount, but the factory bosses scrutinized them, making sure they did not discard crystals and claim credit for them. Lorde, in need of money, figures out a way to beat the system. She slips crystals into her socks every time she goes to the bathroom, and once inside the stall, "I chewed them up with my strong teeth and flushed the little shards of rock down the commode. I could take care of between fifty and a hundred crystals a day in that manner, taking a handful from each box I signed out" (*Zami* 146). She chews the crystals and spits them out; they are nonfood but nonetheless "metabolized"; as she tells us hatred, too, can be metabolized. The body, then, makes visible also what has been metaphorically imbibed. Lorde's cancer turns the body inside out, alluding to the internal lacerations of chewed X-ray crystals, which are themselves a manifestation of what a poor black female has to do to survive. Lorde earns unprecedented amounts of money—for the factory, of course—and is laid off shortly thereafter. The X-ray crystals have stained her fingertips, leaving her marked with the work of her class status and for the illness she will eventually develop. She says she has a sense of the fingers burning off (*Zami* 146). A reader of *The Cancer Journals* cannot escape the conclusion that this episode contributed largely to her subsequent illness.

By insistently reminding the reader of her bodily reality, Lorde works toward the body's integration through struggle, a synecdoche for the struggle of the self to remain whole. The women she admires are whole in their variegated bodies. One of the first images she presents of a woman outside of her family is of a woman named DeLois who walks on the street, her "big proud stomach" (*Zami* 4) attracting sunlight. She tells of one of her early, significant love affairs, in Mexico, with a woman, Eudora (*Zami* 161–76), who has had breast cancer—eerily presaging the future of Lorde's own healing, whole-ing process, just as it is " the love of women," though not explicitly erotic love, that heals her in *The Cancer Journals*. Making love, how the body acts, is a counterpart or antidote to what has been done to it. Making love (the erotic) as a creative act (as power) is a self-making self-defining act. Even autoerotic love, masturbation, is written about as a part of the process of healing the body and making it and the resident psyche whole again (*Cancer* 40).

5

Lorde survives despite "grow[ing] up fat, Black, nearly blind, and ambidextrous in a West Indian household" (*Zami* 24). "Ambidextrous" plays on the fact that she tells us about sleeping with both men and women, but it also deals more seriously with the notion of self-creation and incorporating power. To be ambidextrous, then, in another instance of bodily states, facts of nature, existing as metaphors for aspects of identity. She talks about her mother as being both, other, and says that she, too, wishes for ambidextrous self-culled sexual identity: "*I have always wanted to be both man and woman, to incorporate the strongest and richest parts of my mother and father within/into me. . . . I have felt the age-old triangle of mother father and child, with the "I" as its eternal core, elongate and flatten out into the elegantly strong triad of grandmother mother daughter, with the "I" moving back and forth flowing in either or both directions as needed*" (7). Identity is fluid, as is demonstrated by the elision of punctuation in "*mother father and child*" and "*grandmother mother daughter.*"

The essay "A Burst of Light" serves as a postscript to *The Cancer Journals*, synthesizing and further distilling many of its ideas. Lorde makes explicit con-

nections between becoming an authority on one's own body and cancer and politics, dying and struggling to live and work. Much of the essay is an exhausting
chronicle of the work she keeps up with around the globe as she is fighting the
disease; a refrain is "I" (or "we," with her lover, Frances) "did good work." She
fights experts and decides she does not want the borders of her body to be invaded. She rejects medical advice when it is her life at stake. When she says she
wants to have "[e]nough moxie to chew the whole world up and spit it out in
bite-sized pieces, useful and warm and wet and delectable because they came out
of my mouth" ("Burst" 62), the image recalls and inverts the chewed and spit out
X-ray crystals. *To metabolize* means to take in good and bad and then determine
what is useful in the shaping of the self. The act that probably poisoned her can
be reenacted to her advantage.

Lorde travels to a holistic healing center and finds a philosophy wherein
"the treatment of any disease, and cancer in particular, must be all of a piece,
body and mind, and I am ready to try anything so long as they don't come at me
with a knife" ("Burst" 83). Divisibility and invasion are worse even than cancer.

She rejects a prosthesis in part because the breast does not "perform," as a
leg or an arm does. She realizes it is not its own erotic world, not erotic unto itself, but rather part of a schema of eros she controls and that is integral within
her body. She explores what the body performs versus what is done to the body:
abortion, cancer surgery. Body language is a necessary part of naming herself in
her own tongue.

Lorde's work, as it focuses on her physical existence, emphasizes the literal
meaning of incorporation, of putting one's self into a body, or in this case, speaking of one's self in one's own body. The intellect lives and operates in the body.
The heart and soul express themselves through the body. The body manifests the
ills of an oppressive world that is especially punishing to women and poor people and people of color. The body is a very specific site in Lorde's work, the location where all this takes place. She is constantly reminding us that she is an
inhabitant of a body that has given birth to children, been nearly blind, and has
battled cancer and lost pieces of itself but remains whole, incorporated, integrated. It is "*[m]y body, a living representation of other life older longer wiser*"
(*Zami* 7). Bodies express what verbal language cannot.

6

I am a scar, a report from the frontlines, a talisman, a resurrection.

—Audre Lorde, "A Burst of Light: Living with Cancer"

In James Alan McPherson's "The Story of a Scar," the African-American male
protagonist sits in a plastic surgeon's waiting room and from the first page is
compelled to ask the African-American woman next to him, "As a concerned
person, and as your brother, I ask you, without meaning to offend, how did you
get that scar on the side of your face?" (97). She rebuffs his bold inquiry and his

presumption that she will "read" her own body for him. "'I ask *you*,' she said, 'as a nosy person with no connections in your family, how come your nose is all bandaged up?'" (97). His bandaged nose makes his nosiness legible. As the story proceeds from the man's narrative perspective, the woman tells her story, only to be continually interrupted by the man's presumptions about her narrative. He presumes to know her and to know what the mark on her face signifies. He presumes he has access to that signification because, after all, the mark is visible, and if a black woman's body is visible, it is therefore accessible, not only to white men, historically, but in this instance for black men as well.

But she will not let him get away with that and will not let her story be usurped. She "reads" him as well. "'You don't have to tell me a thing,' she said, 'I know mens goin' and comin'. There ain't a-one of you I'd trust to take my grand-mama to Sunday school'" (98). The male protagonist persists:

> The scar still fascinated me. . . . The scar was thick and black and crisscrossed with a network of old stitch patterns, as if some meticulous madman had first attempted to carve a perfect half-circle in her flesh, and then decided to embellish his handiwork. It was so grotesque a mark that one had the feeling it was the art of no human hand and could be peeled off like so much soiled putty. But this was a surgeon's office and the scar was real. It was as real as the honey-blond wig she wore, as real as her purple pantsuit. I studied her approvingly. Such women have a natural leaning toward the abstract expression of themselves. Their styles have private meanings, advertise secret distillations of their souls. Their figures, and their disfiguration, make meaningful statements. (98–99)

As it turns out, the woman has been marked by public violence by a man. Her scar is a history of sorts, a mark she is trying to change. The more she tells of her story the more she gives away of herself, leaving both of them on uncertain ground, but she will not simply cut to the chase and tell the *mere* "story of a scar"; she is telling a piece of her life, telling the story her way regardless of how the listener wants to receive it. The man characterizes her story as "tiresome ramblings," and she becomes angry: "This here's *my* story! . . . You dudes cain't stand to hear the whole of anything. You want everything broke down in little pieces. . . . That's how come you got your nose all busted up. There's some things you have to take your time about" (100).

When she finishes her story, her talk is not interrupted narratively for several pages; she takes over the narrative space of the story with her bodily truth. The male narrator then interrupts and gives a condescending and erroneous conclusion to her story (105). She then takes the space of a long pause and a dramatic drag on her cigarette. "'You know everything,' she said in a soft tone, much unlike her own. 'A black mama birthed you, let you suck her titty, cleaned your dirty drawers, and you still look at us through paper and movie plots'" (105–06).

After the story is finished, after he has had to listen to her truth, "[a] terrifying fog of silence and sickness crept into the small room, and there was no longer the smell of medicine" (111). There are no longer antidotes, only dis-ease, the fact of the scar and the story of a scar hanging in the air in the doctor's waiting room. That is when we learn of other doctors who have been unsuccessful in their attempts to modify her scar. In the very last line the man asks the woman's name, something that he thinks will provide information, when in fact is beside the point next to the story he has just been given. It is merely something for him to possess. When Audre Lorde says she gives us "a new spelling of my name," she insists that the names mean less than presumed, that you have to listen to a person tell his or her own story before assuming what the story holds. Lorde tells her own "story of a scar" in *Zami* and *The Cancer Journals* because she understands the imperative to both gather her multiple selves into one body and to name that body, rather than leave the (mis)naming to another.

Lorde continually states that she claims the different parts of herself—"I am lesbian, mother, warrior, . . ." speaking through difference. It is her credo, a way of living, that all people, but particularly those said to be marginalized, must refuse to be divisible and schizophrenic. It is in the way that she takes us through the history of her body, in both *Zami* and *The Cancer Journals,* that Lorde maps the new terrain of what over 100 years ago Linda Brent had to whisper and withhold from her readers: all that a corporeal history embodies. The link between Lorde and Brent is crucial: for both, the issue is control over one's own body and the power to see the voice as a literal functioning *member* of the corpus, an organ that works and must be self-tended.

Sexuality is broad and frequently forbidden discursive terrain for many black women in both writing and other sorts of public lives. When we do write, we write our sexualities into existence against a vast backdrop, a history, of misrepresentation and essentializing and perversion, appropriations of our bodies and stories about our bodies. This precedes our entry into the Euro-American written universe. Lorde claims that terrain for herself, defining what she thinks of as the erotic, inscribing in her books an actual, fleshly black woman's body. The effect is like that seen in African-American visual artist Howardena Pindell's 1988 painting, "Autobiography: AIR/CS560." After a near fatal car crash in 1979 and lengthy rehabilitation, Pindell suffered memory lapses and manifested her process of recovery and remembering in her work. She "used postcards from friends and collected them in her travels to help jar recollections or explain flashes of images. . . . Her automobile accident produced a need for memory" (Rouse 8). She also began lying on her canvases to leave an imprint of her body with which to work (Pindell). In the painting, then, Pindell left an impression of her fragmented and reassembled body as physical evidence both that the body exists and that she can imagistically create it. The narrative history of the body is a way of interpellating difference and claiming wholeness.

The link between Lorde and Brent is crucial: for both, the issue is control over one's own body and the power to see the voice as a literal functioning member *of the corpus, an organ that works and must be self-tended.*

In Lorde's work, as in Pindell's, it takes literal invasion for the self to be reconstituted. Why is the self not conceived as an a priori whole? These images literalize what is historically and metaphorically true in African-American women's writing: it is the fissure, the slash of the Middle Passage, the separation from the originary, that which the physical scar shows and alludes to—all that is an intractable part of African-American women's history—that makes possible the integrity of the scar, the integrity of the body's history, and a record of what the scar performs.

NOTES

1. For example, Bearden cuts paper in identifiable iconographic shapes such as the arc of a watermelon slice, the ruffle of a rooster comb, curls of steam engine smoke, or the shape of a guitar. Each of these has specific meaning in Bearden's African-American cosmology.

WORKS CITED

Gilman, Sander L. "Black Bodies, White Bodies: Toward an Iconography of Female Sexuality in Late Nineteenth-Century Art, Medicine, and Literature." *"Race," Writing, and Difference.* Ed. Henry Louis Gates, Jr. Chicago: U of Chicago P, 1986. 223–63.

Lerner, Gerda, ed. *Black Women in White America: A Documentary History.* 1972. New York: Vintage-Random, 1973.

Lorde, Audre. "Audre Lorde: An Interview." With Karla Hammond. *Denver Quarterly* 16 (1981): 10–27.

——."A Burst of Light: Living with Cancer." *A Burst of Light: Essays.* Ithaca: Firebrand, 1988. 49–134.

——. *The Cancer Journals.* San Francisco: Spinsters, 1980.

——. Interview. With Claudia Tate. *Black Women Writers at Work.* Ed. Tate. New York: Continuum, 1983. 100–116.

——."An Interview with Audre Lorde." With Karla Hammond. *American Poetry Review* Mar.–Apr. 1980: 18–21.

——. "An Interview with Audre Lorde." With Adrienne Rich. *Signs: Journal of Women in Culture and Society* 6 (1981): 713–36.

——. "Uses of the Erotic: The Erotic as Power." *Sister Outsider: Essays and Speeches.* Crossing Press Feminist Series. Freedom: Crossing, 1984. 53–59.

——. *Zami: A New Spelling of My Name.* Freedom: Crossing, 1982.

McPherson, James Alan. "The Story of a Scar." *Elbow Room: Stories.* Boston: Little, 1972. 97–112.

Pindell, Howardena. Lecture. Philadelphia Museum of Art. Philadelphia, 15 Apr. 1991.

Rouse, Terrie S. "Howardena Pindell: Odyssey." *Howardena Pindell: Odyssey.* New York: Studio Museum in Harlem, 1986. 5–12.

Haki Madhubuti (1942–)

When Don Lee was an infant, his mother, deserted by her husband, moved her family to Detroit. When Lee was sixteen, his mother died, and he left Michigan for Chicago.

Lee's early books of poetry were published by Dudley Randall's Broadside Press; in 1967 Lee co-founded Third World Press, which first operated from his basement.

A leader in the Black Arts Movement, Lee in 1973 changed his name to Haki Madhubuti. He has written prose and poetry prolifically, forging a close relationship with Gwendolyn Brooks, an esteemed, older poet.

At a time when major U.S. publishers displayed little interest in young African American writers—especially those of a political bent—Madhubuti used the Third World Press to promote a vibrant artistic tradition, especially in Detroit and Chicago.

Like other works of the Black Arts Movement, Madhubuti's poetry reflects the cadences of street talk and is often militantly anti-racist. Most of the poems here pay tribute to African American women and express appreciation for their resistance to sexism as well as to racism.

Keith D. Miller

The Secrets of the Victors

(the only fair fight is the one that is won
—Anglo-Saxon Proverb)

forever define the enemy as less than garbage,
his women as whores & gutter scum,
their children as thieves & beggars,
the men as rapists, child molestors & cannibals,
their civilization as savage and
beautifully primitive.

as you confiscate the pagan's land, riches & women
curse them to your god for not being productive,
for not inventing barbed wire and DDT,
perpetually portray the *natives*
as innocent & simple-minded while eagerly
preparing to convert them to *your way.*

dispatch your merchants with
tins & sweets, rot gut & cheap wines.
dispatch your priest armed with
words of fear, conditional love and
fairy tales about strangers dying for you.
dispatch your military
to protect your new labor pool.

if there is resistance
or any show of defiance
act swiftly & ugly & memoriable.
when you kill a man
leave debilitating fear in the hearts of his
father, brothers, uncles, friends & unborn sons.
if doubt exits as to your determination
wipe the earth with his
women, girl children & all that's sacred;
drunken them in bodacious horror.
upon quiet, summon the ministers to
bless the guilty as you publicly
break their necks.
after their memories fade intensify the teaching.

instruct your holy men
to curse violence   while
proclaiming the Land Safe
introducing
the thousand year Reign of the Victors
as your Scholars
re-write the history.

The Changing Seasons of Ife

she is quality and light
a face of carob and ivory
of broad smiles and eyes that work.
she dresses in purples
& touches of aquablue.
plants grow profusely in her earthpots.
she seeks standards,
will not accept questionable roses or tapped water.
her taste is antique and bountiful heritage,
her music often void of melody

is firetone and harsh truths.
it is known that
dark rhythms played in & out of her early years
leaving temporary scars that lined her future
as beauty has it
wine is shared with shadows on prolonged trips
her smile broad & brandy
makes small miracles
emerge.

Lady Day

hearing from you are smiles in winter
you   as you are
you warm and illuminating spaces
bring
blooming fruit in ice age times
with heated heated voices

believe me when i say
men will listen to you
most
will try to please you

there will be sun & thunder & mudslides
in your life
you will satisfy your days with work & laughter
and sunday songs.
your nights like most nights will
conjure up memories of easier seasons
happier suntimes and coming years

earthcolors and rainbows will enter your heart
when least expected
often
in small enduring ways   like this
lovesong.

Some of the Women are Brave

her strength may have come from
not having the good things early in life
like

her own bed, unused clothes,
"good looks," uncritical friends
or
from the knee of her great grandmother.
whatever path she took
she was learning to become small danger.

organizer of mothers,
overseer of broken contracts,
a doer of large deeds,
unafraid of sky scrapers & monotone
bureaucrats.
monotones labeled her demands crippling & unusual.
she urged drinkable water, working elevators,
clean playgrounds, heat, garbage collection
and the consolation of tenant's dreams.

many damned her,
others thought her professional agitator & provocateur
dismissing her as a
man hating bulldagger
that was communist inspired.

she was quick burn against the enemy
a stand up boxer unattached to niceties
and the place of women.
she was waterfalls in the brain
her potency as it comes
needs to be packaged & overnight expressed
to Black homes; to be
served with morning meals.

The Damage We Do

he loved his women
weak & small
so that he would not tire
of
beating them.
he sought the weakest & the smallest
so that they couldn't challenge

his rage of boxing
their heads up against refrigerators,
slamming their hands in doors,
stepping on them like roaches,
kicking them in their centers of life.
all of his women
were
weak and small and sick
& he an
embarrassment to the human form
was not an exception in america.

Sun and Storm

beyond weep and whisper,
beyond clown and show,
beyond why & where & not now
clear the voices

there is *storm* on the horizon.
beneath calm & cold & killer death
there is *vision* approaching.
beneath filth & fear & running asses
there is planning & hope & connecting trust.
beneath traffic stops and sex crazed negroes
there are new people arising
clothed in love & work & a will to advance.

newpeople
bold and sure   tested tough   fever wise
these are womenblack with brain and womb &
smiles that regenerate.
these are menblack with mind and seed &
strength of strength.
they are children-conscious and elder-wise
sweet lovers of life.
newpeople
known in afrika,
known in asia,
known in europe & the americas
with their rainbow smiles, willing minds,
and bridge-building backs as the
people of the sun.

Woman With Meaning

she is small and round,
round face and shoulders connected to half-sun breast,
on a round stomach that sits on rounded buttocks,
held up by short curved legs and circular feet,
her smile reveals bright teeth, and when it comes,
her eyes sing joy and her face issues in gladness,
she is brilliant beauty.

she likes colors,
her hair, which is worn in its natural form, is
often accented with vivid, cheerful scarfs. her make-up
is difficult to detect, it complements her oak-colored skin,
suggesting statuesque music. her scent is fresh mango
and moroccan musk. her clothes are like haitian paintings,
highly noticeable during her rhythmic walks,
as she steps like a dancer.

she is a serious woman,
her values,
her ideas,
her attitudes,
her actions are those of a reflective mind.
her child is her life,
her people their future,
she and her child live alone and the brothers
speak good words about them.

the brothers,
married and unmarried, want to help her.
it is difficult to be with her and not
lose one's sense of balance,
one's sense of place and wisdom.
that is what caring does.
her aloneness
hurts and tears at the inside of serious men.
some of the older men have tried
to tie her heart into theirs but
the commitment was never enough.
her sense of honor and history,
her knowing of sisterhood and rightness
force her to sleep alone each night.

the brothers
continue to speak good words about her,
many
when thinking of
her smile.
others light candles and pray.
some send her notes, gifts and poems,
all
hoping for the unexpected.

Clarence Major (1936–)

Clarence Major's artistic career spans not only half of the twentieth century but also many genres and most of the globe. A noted painter, photographer, poet, novelist, editor, essayist, and scriptwriter, Major is the author of eight novels and nine books of poetry. His work has been recognized throughout America and Europe with such awards as the Pushcart Prize in 1976 for his poem "Funeral" and in 1989 for the story "My Mother and Mitch." Among numerous other honors, Major received the Western States Book Award for fiction in 1986 for My Amputations; *he was also awarded the Franco American Commission for Education Exchange 1981–1983 as well as a Le Prix Maurice Edgar Coindreau nomination in 1982 for the French translation of* Reflex and Bone Structure. *Major teaches African American literature and creative writing and writes and paints during his free time.*

A native of Atlanta, Georgia, Major was born on December 31, 1936 to Clarence and Inez Huff Major. He received a Bachelor of Science degree from State University of New York at Albany and a PhD in 1978 from the Union for Experimenting Colleges and Universities in Ohio. This experimental program let him take classes and teach at a variety of colleges and universities from Howard to Sarah Lawrence. He spent twelve years at University of Colorado, Boulder, and moved to UC Davis in 1989. He also served in the United States Air Force as a record specialist from 1955–1957.

As broad as Major's production has been, his influences are equally as wideranging. "I grew up reading Hemingway, Faulkner, Richard Wright, Dos Passos, the usual American writers, but before I discovered American writers I was reading French poets—Verlaine and Baudelaire." As a writer, Major has been linked with Ezra Pound, Denise Levertov, and Robert Creely, but also with June Jordan, Michael Harper, Al Young, Ishmael Reed, and William Melvin Kelley.

Clarence Major is considered at the forefront of experimental poetry and prose. Critics claim him as an avant-gardiste (like Kelley and Reed), but Major's works defy easy categorization. He has consistently been praised for his unique use of language with its thematic and technical complexities. Each novel seems to have a different voice, each poem its own struggle and ease with the language. As Major comments, "I like to try new things and the most challenging thing about writing fiction is selecting the right voice and point of view and developing the work, understanding the voice. I like to play with different voices, I think that's the most interesting part of creating fiction." These multivoiced renderings reflect Major's African and Native American heritage.

More innovative works like My Amputations *mix the rhythms of American slang with the languages of history, science, mythology, and the occult, an alchemy that expresses the violence that he believes is an integral part of life for Southern Blacks and that shapes their lives and attitudes. This alchemy of language is at once deception and self-*

revelation. Much of his fiction reminds us that reality is not simply something out there: Ours is a "man-made world, influenced by our ability to reflect, re-imagine, reinterpret and reform it."

Major's affinity for language also emerges in his work on The Dictionary of Afro-American Slang *(1970) and its updated and expanded version* Juba to Jive: A Dictionary of African-American Slang *(1994). Both editions are important for their explorations of the living languages spoken daily by many Americans yet omitted from many standard English dictionaries.*

His story collection, Fun and Games *(1990), from which "Letters" is excerpted, was nominated for a Los Angeles Times Book Critics Award. "Letters" relies on a mock-epistolary tradition to communicate the changing, unstable relationship between Julie Ingram and Allen Morris, former lovers who seek a temporary connection. From the expansive verbal gestures of the first letter in the story to the truncated, impersonal memo-like last, the story is written across shrinking surfaces of language that oppose the enormity of the loss of connection between them. Through their gossip—sharing intimacies of their past—their struggle unfolds, a struggle that resides in their different and differing racial and sexual politics. The personal nature of the letter mixes with its function in the narrative as a public writing. The letters themselves become tools of self-expression rather than tools of mutual intimacies. Major cleverly uses the letter as part meditation, part performance, and he writes a story where two people are trying to negotiate these two (sometimes) conflicting functions.*

In his poems, Major uses synesthesia (the mixing of senses) and repetition to create a musical rhythm and structure. As in "Letters," Major's craft is precise and complicated in his poetry—and nothing occurs because of chance. The following poems are taken from his 1998 collection, Configurations, *and reflect Major's poetics of gesture and movement that articulate integration of body, mind, and spirit, a connection that depends on the coupling of the material world with the spiritual.*

Lenore L. Brady

Letters

Dear Julie: I guess the thing about your letter that surprised me the most was the way you ended it. I mean with the word love. Somehow I didn't expect it and to see it was a surprise. But I know you meant it in a new sense, not the old sense we once thought we shared. But maybe even more a surprise than the word love was the letter itself. I guess I never expected to hear from you. Especially since you refused to talk to me when I called you in Jericho. And now you propose we become pen pals. Well I can say right now I'm not much for writing letters and never have been. Never had a pen pal. But I'm willing to try. I mean I will try to answer any letter you write and to let you know what I'm doing from time to time. But I'm not sure if it's worth it. If you know what I mean. In any case I am sure I can't tell you all my thoughts. I doubt if anybody can tell anybody all his thoughts. But I can tell you what has happened since we last met. Coming back here to New York was rough. At first. Especially having to stay in the same apartment me and Gail Smith shared. So I was determined to move. You will notice on the envelope my new address. I have a larger apartment and the neighborhood is nicer. I'm a bachelor again and beginning to like it. I have a new job I like very much. I'm Assistant Circulation Director of the new Black magazine for women, *Stance*. I'm sure you've seen it because it's everywhere in the nation on all newsstands. If you haven't seen it let me know and I'll send you a copy. It's a good magazine and we're proud of it and see a big future for it. I was in on the beginning of it. Along with the president and chief executive and the vice president I helped put together the proposal that got us our initial investors. And though there has been only one issue so far we have three in dummy on the drawing boards. We have problems of course but we have hope. Most of our problems at the moment have to do with personnel. So far most of the people we have employed have been good and willing to work for less than they could earn elsewhere. A few have caused serious trouble however. We had to let our editor-in-chief go last week and she was an absolute bitch about it. The following day we got a phone call from an unknown party telling us our building was about to go up in a blast. Naturally we called the police and they had us all clear out while they searched the place but they found no bomb. In my own department things are going well. We have good circulation. One the biggest distributors in the country is handling *Stance*. Though in order to keep their service we have to maintain a certain standard. I suppose you're wondering how I, without a college education, managed to get into this line of work. Aside from luck it is the result of planning. A very good friend of mine, Jake Johnson, brought me into the initial group, knowing my talent for business affairs. Anyway this will give you a little idea of where my head is at lately. As for my personal life I have been trying to stay away from any serious involvement with anybody right now. I give all my energy to the magazine. I did see Gail two of three times about six weeks ago. It was a mistake. I think she hates me now. I ran into her one day just as she was coming out of the telephone building where she works. I wanted her to sit down with me in a nearby restaurant and have coffee and talk. But she refused. So we stood there in front of the building and I felt like crying she was so mean. She called me every filthy name she could think of. I guess I really hurt her leaving like I did. I don't suppose there is any way to change that now. You can't undo the past. Then I didn't see her anymore until she called one night and asked if she could see me. I agreed. And you can imagine how it turned out. Sex should never be like that. Then I didn't see her again for about a week. I needed to talk with someone that night and called her. She was alone and lonely too. So we ended up making the same mistake again. It got to be very sick. Afterward we both felt bad. And I made up my mind not to see her again. Even if she called in desperation. But it has been many weeks now and she hasn't called. So I hope and trust she has found her way. She's really a good person and deserves happiness. I think she'll do all right too. And as I said I'm doing all right giving myself fully to my work. I enjoy working with the people in my department and my hours are pretty flexible.

And already we are close to a circulation of a hundred thousand copies per month. It's a monthly magazine. So much for myself and my world. It was really great to hear that you are getting into things you find interesting. But the Black Panther Party newspaper isn't the only Black publication around. Read *Stance*. Make sure you read it and let me know what you think. After all it is for Black women. By the way I read an article in the *Amsterdam News* about your Uncle Elmer Blake. Doctor Blake. It said that he just won some sort of impressive award for a book he wrote on the Harlem scene in the 1920s. Should be an interesting book. I have always felt that the 1920s would be a great time to have been alive and grown. Anyway this letter is getting a bit long and I have work to do. Again I must say it was good to hear from you. Keep in touch.
Yours, Al.

Dear Al: I have looked everywhere for *Stance* but apparently it is not for sale in Boston. No one seems to have heard of it here yet. Perhaps because it is a new publication. From what you say it sounds very interesting and I am anxious to see it. Please send me a copy. Guess what. In addition to all my other activities I have now taken up the guitar. I am studying with this really great guy from Berkeley who studied under world famous Andrés Segovia. And I really love the instrument. And it is good for my head to be making my own music. I love music so much. Did I tell you in my previous letter that I see my old friend Sara. Two weeks ago she had to give up her home and now lives in an apartment not far from here. She has gone through a lot but I think now she's growing stronger and opening to new areas of interest. She takes clay modeling on Wednesday nights with me. Her little girl Cynthia is growing so fast and she calls me Aunt Julie. Not that I encourage it. In fact it gives me a very strange feeling. One I can live without. One of these days when I meet Mister Right I want to have children. But I'm in no hurry. Did you ever read the autobiography of Malcom X. It's a great great book if you haven't read it you should stop whatever you're doing right now and go out and buy a copy. By the way thanks for telling me about the article in the *Amsterdam News*. Mom bought a copy of Uncle Blake's book and I saw it last time I was at her place. You'd think he'd have sent us a copy but then I think he's always considered us stupid or something. The trouble with him is all his life he's been a stiff stuckup puritan. And my family tends to be free and open. Open to new ideas. Mom still asks about you. In fact I showed her your letter and she was happy about your success. She may write to you sometime. May even stop in to see you when she's in N.Y. I guess I told you about Dad losing his job. Now it appears he is planning to go to work for the NAACP. I have no direct contract with him. But he is in touch with Barbara. Mom and I hear about him through Barbara. He and Barbara were always close. He called Oscar once and talked with him for an hour. Oscar of course is with Mom. It just happened that Mom answered the phone when he called. And would you believe all Dad said to her was, May I speak to Oscar. Wouldn't even acknowledge her presence. Not even as much as a hello. Wow. He must be changing a lot because at least he was always respectful toward Mom. But I'm not trying to understand it anymore. It is beyond me. Barbara is in Paris now and she hears from Dad a lot. She says the French are cold people. Won't tolerate anyone who can't speak French. Barbara of course speaks a little French. But I know what she means because Paris turned me off too. White countries in general turn me off. I love Africa. As you well know. I also enjoyed teaching the history of Africa to black kids that time in Brooklyn. May one day get back into this sort of work. It gives me a very good feeling, working with children. You remember my cousin, Gloria. In a letter from her I learn many things. Are you ready for this. You remember The Corked Pussy Cat. Well a Hollywood company has made a movie in which it is one of the main scenes; but they're calling the place by another name. Gloria says Rose Marie was recently pregnant. She may have gotten pregnant last August up at Duck Pond. She really screws around a lot. She's 16 years old now. Anyway they sent her to New York for an abortion. But Rose Marie's relation to the family has been altered by this whole experience. And my uncle being the type of man he is compounds the situation. My cousin Patrick was drafted last month but ran away to Canada and nobody has heard from him since. I don't blame him. But it is sad that he may not be able to come back home for many years. He was very close to his mother, Aunt Alla. By the way Gloria says she's seeing a new doctor who may really help her. I hope so. I recently ran into her African friend. The one who was there at Duck Pond remember. His name is Bill Gwala. He's a friend of a friend of mine, Clark Nkosi. Who is also a friend of Odum. Remember Odum. Anyway I have been dating Bill Gwala but not seriously. I think Africans are mentally too far from me. There's always something there in a relationship with an African that is not quite right for me. Anyway he and I went out together several times. He asked about you. Well I have to get ready for my modern dance class. And tonight I'm going out dancing with Bill. Don't forget to send me a copy of your magazine.

Peace, Julie.

Dear Julie: By now you should have the copy of *Stance* I sent. What do you think? This has been a hell of a week for me. I haven't stopped one minute. I must be going on nervous energy. I certainly have had little or no sleep. But I'm wrapped up in what I'm doing. The work is more and more exciting every day. I found your letter waiting yesterday when I returned from Fisk University in Tennessee where I spoke to the students there about *Stance*. I gave out a lot of free copies and I think we'll be getting many subscribers from that area as a result of my trip. It is in the area of paid circulation that I am trying to build *Stance*. Subscriptions mean more in my department than newsstand sales. Tomorrow I am to speak at New York University about *Stance*. I have been invited there by the Black students. They seem to have a great thing going, their own thing, and it's a good source to tap. I have always wanted to put my energy into something like this, something that takes me into contact with people. I am discovering that my life is turning out beautiful after all. Got to go now. Let me hear your reaction to *Stance*.

Yours, Al.

Dear Al: Here is my official response to *Stance:* I don't like it. What I dislike about it is its glossy smugness, its supercommercial jive hangups. The girl on the cover looks like she's squatting to take a youknowwhat. I mean the expression on her face is constipated. And the wig she's wearing looks like dimestore quality. And what happened to the color? She looks orange. And I've never seen any orange black people in my life. And why are there so many cigarette ads? I counted at least seven. Cigarette ads and makeup. The makeup I guess is all right, but I couldn't understand so many cigarette ads. Is it some sort of secret conspiracy to inflict all black women with cancer? You know genocide. I noticed your name is in 15th place on the list of staff personnel. I don't know why but somehow I expected you to be closer to the top. Another thing I found confusing was the fact that the table of contents did not always agree with the pages on which the various features and articles appeared. For example on page 26 there are these words: "The Plight of The Black Woman Novelist In Modern American Literature" by Ruth Smith, but according to the table of contents page 26 should contain: "Thirty-Five Views of Black Women on Black Men" by Nancy Giacchi. I looked through the entire publication at least seven times after reading everything in it and I couldn't find even a trace of the article by Nancy Giacchi. Was this a printer's error? Anyway, I did find the sections on beauty and food and home decoration interesting. The pictures of the grapes with the water drops on them was great. You should do more of this kind of stuff. I also liked the fantastic purple and green rug in the picture of a livingroom on page 61. I'd like to own one like that. The caption doesn't say where it can be bought. I was wondering if you could give me this information? No hurry because I don't have the bread at the moment. My allowance from Dad ended when he married Roslyn Carter. Anyway these are my responses to *Stance*. And I am sincerely sorry they were not more positive. And I hope you do not think badly of me for giving you my honest impression.
Until next time, Julie.

Dear Al: Having heard nothing from you in all these weeks I thought I'd write again, though I think you owe me a letter, since I was the one who wrote last, way back in November. Maybe it was the beginning of December. Anyway, here it is a new year. Barbara flew back from France to spend Christmas with us. It was great. We were all together at Mom's place. Dad didn't even call. Still, it was wonderful. I hope you had a pleasant holiday season. By the way, I saw another issue of *Stance* on a newsstand in Harvard Square. I looked through it and it certainly looked better than the first one. I thought you'd be pleased to hear this. The cover was great. Keep up the good work. I've been vaguely playing with the notion of going down to Mexico for awhile. You may remember I mentioned Clark Nkosi. We were friends for a long time and never thought of each other in romantic terms. That is until recently. Now he's been invited to teach in Mexico City and will be leaving here shortly. He wants me to go with him down there. I haven't made up my mind yet, but I will have to very soon. This is the first time I've started having an affair with a person who was at first a friend. It has always been the other way around. After an affair ends, the man and I become friends. Usually. As in our case. I often think of you, Al. But for a long time I couldn't bear to remember what happened between us. I was so hurt. I had expected us to be together for the rest of our lives. I think I resented you, too. As though our failure to make it was all your fault. I tend to be childish in this way, but I'm working on myself trying to do better. Anyway, with Clark things are different. We simply let things happen. I haven't made any elaborate plans to give the rest of my life to him. And I am sure the thought has never entered his mind. We both value our freedom. He's a brilliant man and he's writing a book. A novel about modern day Africa in which he's trying to show the interplay, exchange and conflict between the natives and the colonialists. I've read sections of it and it's great, sure to be a bestseller. Obviously, I have tremendous respect for him. But I won't go on about my affairs. It has been so long since I heard from you, I hardly know what to say. I hope your work is still going well. Write when you can. Sincerely, Julie.

Dear Julie: I received your letters but was not able to answer before now because I have been both very busy and was in the hospital for a week. I spent a week in Harlem Hospital with two broken ribs and a broken jaw. I'm much better now. Back at work. It was kind of freakish the way it happened. I was in a bar near Times Square and got into a fight with a white guy. I don't remember what we were arguing about. They say we were arguing about something. But it turned out the place was filled with his friends and they all jumped me. I guess I'm lucky to be alive. I must have been very drunk because all I can remember is the bartender refusing to serve me a drink. But this must have been long before the fight started. Anyway, I'm still alive. My momma was my nurse. So I could not have had better care. For a week I stayed up there with Momma and Pop in their apartment after I was released from the hospital. It was good in a way because I got to know my pop a little better. He and I talked a lot while I was there. And he told me things about his childhood I never knew. The hard times he's had. And I think it gave me a greater respect for him as a person. Momma of course is Momma and she was simply great, both in the hospital and later. I can walk around now but not too fast. And I can talk, too, but not too fast. Sounds funny now but when it happened it wasn't so funny. And the crazy part is I've never gone out to pick a fight with anybody. But I've never let anybody fuck with me either. Ever since I was a little kid I've always drawn the line. Anyway, that's the big event in my recent history. I'm back at work now here and things have really piled up. I have a helper, too. A young guy fresh out of college. I'm training him. Teaching him the business. So he'll know everything about circulation I know. Anyway, take care and if you go to Mexico watch out, you might get a suntan. Sincerely yours, Allen Morris.

Dear Allen Morris: I've been busy writing letters, letters, letters. And receiving them. It seems all at once everybody I've ever known has written to me. Anki

and Christer are back in Stockholm. They say it is very dark and cold there. As usual. But they spend part of the year there every year. My friend Nicholas Zieff has just surprised us all by getting married. He has married a lovely woman. I think she's simply delightful. She is also a teacher and they have a lot more in common. The wedding was small since this was the second time for them both. A few days ago I ran into José Cruz and he asked if he could stop by sometime. Tonight we're having supper together in an Indian restaurant. He's just been promoted on his job and is in good spirits. He's a wonderful person and I've always admired him. My old friend Johnny Hawkins was recently in town for an engagement at a nightclub. Saw the notice in a local paper but didn't go to see him. Though I was tempted to. Despite the hassles, Johnny and I had good times together. And looking back on the relationship I realize I loved him deeply and probably still do. And always will. Sorry I must end this letter so quickly, but I have tons of letters to write.
Sincere regards, Julie Ingram.

   Dear Julie My Friend: Thank you for your recent letter. This is just a note to acknowledge having received it. I am head over heels in work. Still training my helper who is turning out to be a very good worker. Take care.
Sincerely yours, Al.

   Al: Please forgive my haste. Am seriously thinking of moving to Mexico City. Making plans. But haven't been feeling well lately. A friend of mine, an African named Hourari, was shot two days ago at an airport in Ghana. I don't know details. Trying to find out exactly what happened. Though it may not be possible. This leaves me deeply distressed. What kind of world are we living in? Best regards, your friend, Julie.

   My Dearest Julie: Do you remember the blind colored man I helped across the street that time in Boston? Well, I've been thinking about him a lot. How he took me to be a white person. This self-hatred in our race. How we kill each other. It is a painful situation. We here at *Stance* are having a famous Negro psychologist write an article on the subject for one of our spring issues. Hope you are well.
Your friend, Al.

   Dear Al: Clark Nkosi left for Mexico three days ago. I finally decided not to go with him. Mom needs me and besides all my best friends are here. I am planning to step up my activity. I am a very active physical person. In addition to modern dance and clay modeling, I am planning now to start classes in filmmaking, pottery and poetry, acrobatics and puppetry, drama and jewelry making. I had also thought about figure drawing but I probably won't have time for so much. I am also looking for a job, one that will allow me time to do other things.

Dear Julie Ingram: I received your recent letter and am happy to know that you are still happy and well. Am working hard and am also very happy. Keep in touch.
Sincerely yours, Allen Morris.

My Seasonal Body

For that whole year I was in the weight of myself.
I was a hundred and fifty pounds of sadness

in a warm locality with sky and boats and sea.

I was solitary and lonely.

I was sixteen with holes in my head for eyes.
I was so so serious.

The weight of my young self was so heavy.
So heavy.

The Way the Roundness Feels

A secret world turns in us.
Your fingers cruise the rotunda.
You handle your own canoe in water.
I hear your loud heart thumping under my hand.
Listen to my face. Stay with me.
I move around in the recurring circle
        that is my absence.
Feel the shape.
Feel how it must be in here
        where I sway.
Your neck and breasts are round.
So are our teacups.
They are necessarily shaped this way.
White, silver, and gold—the dark and light colors
        of our wholeness
are here in the shadows around us.
Your mouth, I know your lips.
Your hands, I know your fingers.

I feel you moving all through these words.
From inside of me you are speaking,
giving shape to my thoughts.

First

A woman is sitting in a doorway
of a thatched-roof house.
Paul is painting her as part
of the background
for The Great Tree.
Up close, I realize the woman
is my mother and she's in a trance.
In the single eye in her head
she sees the wall
that separates her life
from her death.
Her first memory is red
and cold, wet and cold.
Her last is like the first.

The String

My mother tied
a string around her finger
and just as she was
trying to tie it to mine
my sister ran off with it,
trying it first around a tree
then a bush, then
around the house
and up through
the moon and back.
By the time
she returned my mother
was old. She yanked at the string
as though it were a plant
in dry earth.
I picked up the string
and took it from there.

1990

Paule Marshall (1929–)

Paule Marshall was born Valenza Pauline Burke on April 9, 1929, in Stuyvesant Heights, Brooklyn, New York. While her parents had immigrated from the West Indies ten years before her birth, Marshall grew up in an immigrant community, surrounded by people still trying to maintain "home" traditions. These traditions separated Caribbean immigrants psychologically and socially from African American communities, often creating conflict. Marshall was greatly influenced by this conflict and also by her observation of Caribbean immigrants, including her own parents, working to make the most of their situation in the United States and losing themselves in pursuit of the American Dream. Marshall integrates the confluence of her experiences in her work, writing about the effects of colonialism on West Indian peoples, the experience of immigration, the pursuit of American materialism, the place of women in families of Caribbean immigrants, and the conflict and contradiction of the meaning of blackness in the context of Caribbean and African American communities.

Brown Girl, Brownstones, first published in 1959 and reissued by The Feminist Press in 1981, is regarded by many to be the beginning of contemporary African American women's writing. Ahead of its time, the novel was well received when it was published, but experienced dramatically increased recognition when African American women writers like Alice Walker and Ntozake Shange claimed Marshall as literary predecessor. Focusing on a Black woman's reality in a Black context, Brown Girl, Brownstones in many ways meshes perfectly with the aims and content of much contemporary African American women's writing. Marshall challenged stereotypes of race and gender, highlighting the complexities of intersecting aspects of identity.

Brown Girl, Brownstones is about an immigrant family, struggling to maintain traditional values in a new environment. Silla, the headstrong mother committed to making things work, and Deighton, the father who lives in the unrealistic but more pleasant world of his dreams, leave Selina caught in the middle, trying to formulate her own identity somewhere between the two extremes. Selina, a first-generation American-born daughter, struggles to define herself within and against her family's values and the demeaning control of the men with whom she becomes romantically involved. Because of its expression of the Caribbean and African American intersection and the coming of age of a young Black girl, Brown Girl, Brownstones is often studied for both its feminist and postcolonial emphasis.

Following the success of Brown Girl, Brownstones, Marshall has produced three more novels in the span of her career, each written in a different decade: The Chosen Place, the Timeless People (1969), Praisesong for the Widow (1983), and Daughters (1991). She also published a collection of four novellas in Clap Hands and Sing (1961). And, finally, her most quoted essay, "From the Poets in the Kitchen," is published as pref-

ace to Reena and Other Stories *(1983), a collection of a small number of woman-centered short stories and a novella issued in collection by The Feminist Press. In "From the Poets in the Kitchen," Marshall focuses on the influence of women's space and conversation, celebrating the inspiration of these women who gently inspired her words. In honoring the "ordinary" women in her own life, Marshall also celebrates the oral tradition and the value of women's communities.*

In 1950, Paule Marshall married Kenneth E. Marshall and bore a son. While her husband was supportive to some degree, he resented her leaving the house to write, arguing that she was neglecting her duties as mother. Not willing to give up her love of language, Marshall learned the challenge of being both mother and writer. She and her husband divorced in 1963.

Graduating from Brooklyn College in 1953 with a degree in English, Marshall had only read two African American writers, Paul Laurence Dunbar and James Wright. While Marshall was influenced by these writers and most crucially influenced by the culture and tradition of the women who surrounded her when she was young, she was also influenced by the literary talent of those she came to admire most in her study of literature—Joseph Conrad, Thomas Mann, and Charles Dickens. Marshall did eventually encounter James Baldwin and Ralph Ellison after college graduation and praised their works highly, especially Ellison's Shadow and Act *(1964). And, in the late 1960s, she finally found her way to Zora Neale Hurston, Dorothy West, and Gwendolyn Brooks, whose novel* Maud Martha*(1953) especially impressed her with its depiction of a realistic Black woman character like the characters she aims to create in her own work.*

Partially because her themes were not common in the literature of her time, Marshall struggled for most of her life to make a living as a writer. Post-college graduation, Marshall pursued work first as a librarian and then as a journalist, an unusual aspiration for a Black woman in the 1950s. While contracted to do rather unfulfilling writing for a small Black magazine Our World, *Marshall began work on* Brown Girl, Brownstones. *The greatest benefits of her career in journalism were the travel assignments, including trips to the Caribbean and South America, which inspired the settings for the novellas in* Clap Hands and Sing *(1961). The common thematic thread in each of the novellas is the psychological cost of materialism, a cost seen in the breakdown of relationships for each of the main characters. This collection also evinces Marshall's commitment to the importance of comparative Black cultures, an idea that the Black Arts movement would advocate later in the 1960s.*

The Chosen Place, the Timeless People, *like* Clap Hands and Sing, *is also primarily set outside the United States, highlighting the problematic intersections of developed and underdeveloped nations. In a time when Black cultural nationalism was just beginning to dominate social and political fronts, this novel was, like* Brown Girl, Brownstones, *ahead of its time. A long and episodic novel,* The Chosen Place *focuses on displaced Africans returning to the Caribbean to embrace the notion of community, the idea of a unified Black people. The dark history of slavery and the cultural conflict between tourism and native Caribbean people resonates and troubles the novel. Having visited Barbados only once, this novel is filled with images of what she heard of the place and of the vestiges of the traditions and culture that surrounded her in the United States.*

Marshall was one of the first to pronounce the reality of Black experience as being other than monolithically urban, male, and African American. Not only does she highlight the experiences of Caribbean immigrants, but she does so with provocative attention to intersections of gender, culture, sexuality, and class. Focusing on Black people in Black cultures and the variety in Black experiences, Marshall's concentration would be further developed by women writing in the 1970s who would also receive greater recognition for their work than Marshall, until recently, received for hers. Though she received a Guggenheim Award and a National Endowment of the Arts award and taught at both Yale and Columbia, her work has not been for the majority of her life as well known as that of her male contemporaries.

In line with the support she received from Black feminists in the 1970s, Marshall developed a more feminist focus in her own work in the 1980s. Praisesong for the Widow's Avey Johnson is a middle-class, middle-aged woman living a life smooth on the surface, but undercut by internal dissatisfaction. On a luxury cruise to Carriacou, Avey abandons the posh and meaningless vacation and experiences the ways of the native people. In chapter four of Praisesong's final section, Avey begins the journey that will transform her. In the course of the novel, Avey regains health through African ritual. She gains strength through recognizing her place in an African communal past.

Supplementing her writing with teaching in the 1980s and 1990s, Marshall was a professor of English and Creative Writing at Virginia Commonwealth University from 1987 until the mid-1990s. Daughters, her most recent novel, continues her focus on Caribbean and U.S. identity and has been well received. Her most recent tribute was receipt of the prestigious MacArthur Award in 1992.

R. Joyce Lausch

From the Poets in the Kitchen
1983

Some years ago, when I was teaching a graduate seminar in fiction at Columbia University, a well known male novelist visited my class to speak on his development as a writer. In discussing his formative years, he didn't realize it but he seriously endangered his life by remarking that women writers are luckier than those of his sex because they usually spend so much time as children around their mothers and their mothers' friends in the kitchen.

What did he say that for? The women students immediately forgot about being in awe of him and began readying their attack for the question and answer period later on. Even I bristled. There again was that awful image of women locked away from the world in the kitchen with only each other to talk to, and their daughters locked in with them.

But my guest wasn't really being sexist or trying to be provocative or even spoiling for a fight. What he meant—when he got around to explaining himself more fully—was that, given the way children are (or were) raised in our society, with little girls kept closer to home and their mothers, the woman writer stands a better chance of being exposed, while growing up, to the kind of talk that goes on among women, more often than not in the kitchen; and that this experience gives her an edge over her male counterpart by instilling in her an appreciation for ordinary speech.

It was clear that my guest lecturer attached great importance to this, which is understandable. Common speech and the plain, workaday words that make it up are, after all, the stock in trade of some of the best fiction writers. They are the principal means by which characters in a novel or story reveal themselves and give voice sometimes to profound feelings and complex ideas about themselves and the world. Perhaps the proper measure of a writer's talent is skill in rendering everyday speech—when it is appropriate to the story—as well as the ability to tap, to exploit, the beauty, poetry and wisdom it often contains.

"If you say what's on your mind in the language that comes to you from your parents and your street and friends you'll probably say something beautiful." Grace Paley tells this, she says, to her students at the beginning of every writing course.

It's all a matter of exposure and a training of the ear for the would-be writer in those early years of apprenticeship. And, according to my guest lecturer, this training, the best of it, often takes place in as unglamorous a setting as the kitchen.

He didn't know it, but he was essentially describing my experience as a little girl. I grew up among poets. Now they didn't look like poets—whatever that breed is supposed to look like. Nothing about them suggested that poetry was their calling. They were just a group of ordinary housewives and mothers, my mother included, who dressed in a way (shapeless house-dresses, dowdy felt hats and long, dark, solemn coats) that made it impossible for me to imagine they had ever been young.

Nor did they do what poets were supposed to do—spend their days in an attic room writing verses. They never put pen to paper except to write occasionally to their relatives in Barbados. "I take my pen in hand hoping these few lines will find you in health as they leave me fair for the time being," was the way their letters invariably began. Rather, their day was spent "scrubbing floor," as they described the work they did.

Several mornings a week these unknown bards would put an apron and a pair of old house shoes in a shopping bag and take the train or streetcar from our section of Brooklyn out to Flatbush. There, those who didn't have steady jobs would wait on certain designated corners for the white housewives in the neighborhood to come along and bargain with them over pay for a day's work cleaning their houses. This was the ritual even in the winter.

Later, armed with the few dollars they had earned, which in their vocabulary became "a few raw-mouth pennies," they made their way back to our neighborhood, where they would sometimes stop off to have a cup of tea or cocoa together before going home to cook dinner for their husbands and children.

The basement kitchen of the brownstone house where my family lived was the usual gathering place. Once inside the warm safety of its walls the women threw off the drab coats and hats, seated themselves at the large center table, drank their cups of tea or cocoa, and talked. While my sister and I sat at a smaller table over in a corner doing our homework, they talked—endlessly, passionately, poetically, and with impressive range. No subject was beyond them. True, they would indulge in the usual gossip: whose husband was running with whom, whose daughter looked slightly "in the way" (pregnant) under her bridal gown as she walked down the aisle. That sort of thing. But they also tackled the great issues of the time. They were always, for example, discussing the state of the economy. It was the mid and late 30's then, and the aftershock of the Depression, with its soup lines and suicides on Wall Street, was still being felt.

Some people, they declared, didn't know how to deal with adversity. They didn't know that you had to "tie up your belly" (hold in the pain, that is) when things got rough and go on with life. They took their image from the bellyband that is tied around the stomach of a newborn baby to keep the navel pressed in.

They talked politics. Roosevelt was their hero. He had come along and rescued the country with relief and jobs, and in gratitude they christened their sons Franklin and Delano and hoped they would live up to the names.

If F.D.R. was their hero, Marcus Garvey was their God. The name of the fiery, Jamaican-born black nationalist of the 20's was constantly invoked around the table. For he had been their leader when they first came to the United States from the West Indies shortly after World War I. They had contributed to his organization, the United Negro Improvement Association (UNIA), out of their meager salaries, bought shares in his ill-fated Black Star Shipping Line, and at the height of the movement they had marched as members of his "nurses' brigade" in their white uniforms up Seventh Avenue in Harlem during the great Garvey Day parades. Garvey: He lived on through the power of their memories.

And their talk was of war and rumors of wars. They raged against World War II when it broke out in Europe, blaming it on the politicians. "It's these politicians. They're the ones always starting up all this lot of war. But what they care? It's the poor people got to suffer and mothers with their sons." If it was *their* sons, they swore they would keep them out of the Army by giving them soap to eat each day to make their hearts sound defective. Hitler? He was for them "the devil incarnate."

Then there was home. They reminisced often and at length about home. The old country. Barbados—or Bimshire, as they affectionately called it. The little Caribbean island in the sun they loved but had to leave. "Poor—poor but sweet" was the way they remembered it.

And naturally they discussed their adopted home. America came in for both good and bad marks. They lashed out at it for the racism they encountered. They took to task some of the people they worked for, especially those who gave them only a hard-boiled egg and a few spoonfuls of cottage cheese for lunch. "As if anybody can scrub floor on an egg and some cheese that don't have no taste to it!"

Yet although they caught H in "this man country," as they called America, it was nonetheless a place where "you could at least see your way to make a dollar." That much they acknowledged. They might even one day accumulate enough dollars, with both them and their husbands working, to buy the brownstone houses which, like my family, they were only leasing at that period. This was their consuming ambition: to "buy house" and to see the children through.

There was no way for me to understand it at the time, but the talk that filled the kitchen those afternoons was highly functional. It served as therapy, the cheapest kind available to my mother and her friends. Not only did it help them recover from the long wait on the corner that morning and the bargaining over their labor, it restored them to a sense of themselves and reaffirmed their self-worth. Through language they were able to overcome the humiliations of the work-day.

But more than therapy, that freewheeling, wide-ranging, exuberant talk functioned as an outlet for the tremendous creative energy they possessed. They were women in whom the need for self-expression was strong, and since language was the only vehicle readily available to them they made of it an art form that—in keeping with the African tradition in which art and life are one—was an integral part of their lives.

And their talk was a refuge. They never really ceased being baffled and overwhelmed by America—its vastness, complexity and power. Its strange customs and laws. At a level beyond words they remained fearful and in awe. Their uneasiness and fear were even reflected in their attitude toward the children they had given birth to in this country. They referred to those like myself, the little Brooklyn-born Bajans (Barbadians), as "these New York children" and complained that they couldn't discipline us properly because of the laws here. "You can't beat these children as you would like, you know, because the authorities in this place will dash you in jail for them. After all, these is New York children." Not only were we different, American, we had, as they saw it, escaped their ultimate authority.

Confronted therefore by a world they could not encompass, which even limited their rights as parents, and at the same time finding themselves permanently separated from the world they had known, they took refuge in language. "Language is the only homeland," Czeslaw Milosz, the emigré Polish writer and Nobel Laureate, has said. This is what it became for the women at the kitchen table.

It served another purpose also, I suspect. My mother and her friends were after all the female counterpart of Ralph Ellison's invisible man. Indeed, you might say they suffered a triple invisibility, being black, female and foreigners. They really didn't count in American society except as a source of cheap labor. But given the kind of women they were, they couldn't tolerate the fact of their invisibility, their powerlessness., And they fought back, using the only weapon at their command: the spoken word.

Those late afternoon conversations on a wide range of topics were a way for them to feel they exercised some measure of control over their lives and the events that shaped them. "Soully-gal, talk yuh talk!" they were always exhorting each other. "In this man world you got to take yuh mouth and make a gun!" They were in control, if only verbally and if only for the two hours or so that they remained in our house.

For me, sitting over in the corner, being seen but not heard, which was the rule for children in those days, it wasn't only what the women talked about—the content—but the way they put things—their style. The insight, irony, wit and humor they brought to their stories and discussions and their poet's inventiveness and daring with language—which of course I could only sense but not define back then.

They had taken the standard English taught them in the primary schools of Barbados and transformed it into an idiom, an instrument that more adequately described them—changing around the syntax and imposing their own rhythm and accent so that the sentences were more pleasing to their ears. They added the few African sounds and words that had survived, such as the derisive suck-teeth sound and the word "yam," meaning to eat. And to make it more vivid, more in keeping with their expressive quality, they brought to bear a raft of metaphors, parables, Biblical quotations, sayings and the like:

"The sea ain' got no back door," they would say, meaning that it wasn't like a house where if there was a fire you could run out the back. Meaning that it was not to be trifled with. And meaning perhaps in a larger sense that man should treat all of nature with caution and respect.

"I has read hell by heart and called every generation blessed!" They sometimes went in for hyperbole.

A woman expecting a baby was never said to be pregnant. They never used that word. Rather, she was "in the way" or, better yet, "tumbling big." "Guess who I butt up on in the market the other day tumbling big again!"

And a woman with a reputation of being too free with her sexual favors was known in their book as a "thoroughfare"—the sense of men like a steady stream of cars moving up and down the road of her life. Or she might be dubbed "a free-bee," which was my favorite of the two. I liked the image it conjured up of a woman scandalous perhaps but independent, who flitted from one flower to another in a garden of male beauties, sampling their nectar, taking her pleasure at will, the roles reversed.

And nothing, no matter how beautiful, was ever described as simply beautiful. It was always "beautiful-ugly": the beautiful-ugly dress, the beautiful-ugly house, the beautiful-ugly car. Why the word "ugly," I used to wonder, when the thing they were referring to was beautiful, and they knew it. Why the antonym, the contradiction, the linking of opposites? It used to puzzle me greatly as a child.

There is the theory in linguistics which states that the idiom of a people, the way they use language, reflects not only the most fundamental views they hold of themselves and the world but their very conception of reality. Perhaps in using the term "beautiful-ugly" to describe nearly everything, my mother and her friends were expressing what they believed to be a fundamental dualism in life: the idea that a thing is at the same time its opposite, and that these opposites, these contradictions make up the whole. But theirs was not a Manichaean brand of dualism that sees matter, flesh, the body, as inherently evil, because they constantly addressed each other as "soully-gal"—soul: spirit; gal: the body, flesh, the visible self. And it was clear from their tone that they gave one as much weight and importance as the other. They had never heard of the mind/body split.

As for God, they summed up His essential attitude in a phrase. "God," they would say, "don' love ugly and He ain' stuck on pretty."

Using everyday speech, the simple commonplace words—but always with imagination and skill—they gave voice to the most complex ideas. Flannery O'Connor would have approved of how they made ordinary language work, as she put it, "double-time," stretching, shading, deepening its meaning. Like Joseph Conrad they were always trying to infuse new life in the "old old words worn thin . . . by . . . careless usage." And the goals of their oral art were the same as his: "to make you hear, to make you feel . . . to make you *see.*" This was their guiding esthetic.

By the time I was 8 or 9, I graduated from the corner of the kitchen to the neighborhood library, and thus from the spoken to the written word. The Macon Street Branch of the Brooklyn Public Library was an imposing half block long edifice of heavy gray masonry, with glass-paneled doors at the front and two tall metal torches symbolizing the light that comes of learning flanking the wide steps outside.

The inside was just as impressive. More steps—of pale marble with gleaming brass railings at the center and sides—led up to the circulation desk, and a great pendulum clock gazed down from the balcony stacks that faced the entrance. Usually stationed at the top of the steps like the guards outside Buckingham Palace was the custodian, a stern-faced West Indian type who for years, until I was old enough to obtain an adult card, would immediately shoo me with one hand into the Children's Room and with the other threaten me into silence, a finger to his lips. You would have thought he was the chief librarian and not just someone whose job it was to keep the brass polished and the clock wound. I put him in a story called "Barbados" years later and had terrible things happen to him at the end.

I sheltered from the storm of adolescence in the Macon Street library, reading voraciously, indiscriminately, everything from Jane Austen to Zane Grey, but with a special passion for the long, full-blown, richly detailed 18th- and 19th-century picaresque tales: "Tom Jones," "Great Expectations," "Vanity Fair."

But although I loved nearly everything I read and would enter fully into the lives of the characters—indeed, would cease being myself and become them—I sensed a lack after a time. Something I couldn't quite define was missing. And then one day, browsing in the poetry section, I came across a book by someone called Paul Laurence Dunbar, and opening it I found the photograph of a wistful, sad-eyed poet who to my surprise was black. I turned to a poem at random. "Little brown-baby wif spa'klin' / eyes / Come to yo' pappy an' set on his knee." Although I had a little difficulty at first with the words in dialect, the poem spoke to me as nothing I had read before of the closeness, the special relationship I had had with my father, who by then had become an ardent believer in Father Divine and gone to live in Father's "kingdom" in Harlem. Reading it helped to ease somewhat the tight knot of sorrow and longing I carried around in my chest that refused to go away. I read another poem. "'Lias! 'Lias! Bless de Lawd! / Don' you know de day's / erbroad? / Ef you don' get up, you scamp / Dey'll be trouble in dis camp." I laughed. It reminded me of the way my mother sometimes yelled at my sister and me to get out of bed in the mornings.

And another: "Seen my lady home las' night / Jump back, honey, jump back. / Hel' huh han' an' sque'z it tight . . ." About love between a black man and a black woman. I had never seen that written about before and it roused in me all kinds of delicious feelings and hopes.

And I began to search then for books and stories and poems about "The Race" (as it was put back then), about my people. While not abandoning Thackeray, Fielding, Dickens and the others, I started asking the reference librarian, who was white, for books by Negro writers, although I must admit I did so at first with a feeling of shame—the shame I and many others used to experience in those days whenever the word "Negro" or "colored" came up.

No grade school literature teacher of mine had ever mentioned Dunbar or James Weldon Johnson or Langston Hughes. I didn't know that Zora Neale Hurston existed and was busy writing and being published during those years. Nor was I made aware of people like Frederick Douglass and Harriet Tubman—their spirit and example—or the great 19th-century abolitionist and feminist Sojourner Truth. There wasn't even Negro History Week when I attended P.S. 35 on Decatur Street!

What I needed, what all the kids—West Indian and native black American alike—with whom I grew up needed, was an equivalent of the Jewish shul, someplace where we could go after school—the schools that were shortchanging us—and read works by those like ourselves and learn about our history.

It was around that time also that I began harboring the dangerous thought of someday trying to write myself. Perhaps a poem about an apple tree, although I had never seen one. Or the story of a girl who could magically transplant herself to wherever she wanted to be in the world—such as Father Divine's kingdom in Harlem. Dunbar—his dark, eloquent face, his large volume of poems—permitted me to dream that I might someday write, and with something of the power with words my mother and her friends possessed.

When people at readings and writers' conferences ask me who my major influences were, they are sometimes a little disappointed when I don't immediately name the usual literary giants. True, I am indebted to those writers, white and black, whom I read during my formative years and still read for instruction and pleasure. But they were preceded in my life by another set of giants whom I always acknowledge before all others: the group of women around the table long ago. They taught me my first lessons in the narrative art. They trained my ear. They set a standard of excellence. This is why the best of my work must be attributed to them; it stands as testimony to the rich legacy of language and culture they so freely passed on to me in the wordshop of the kitchen.

CHAPTER 4

At two o'clock that afternoon, the hour Avey Johnson had been scheduled to leave for the airport, she found herself back down on the wharf instead. In front of her stretched the harbor filled with the shabby boats. Behind her, on the slopes of the hill, rose the crowded pastel town.

She wasn't altogether sure how she had gotten there, everything had moved so swiftly once she had given in. After quickly finishing dressing and closing up the rum shop, the man had led her up a winding network of steep sandy paths to the bluff and the main road overlooking the beach. There, a car that also served as a taxi had materialized outside a shop belonging to a friend his age. In minutes, with the granddaughter of the shopowner, a young woman in her twenties, at the wheel (she announced she had also once gone on the excursion), they were on their way to her hotel. When they arrived the man sent their driver with her to collect the few things she needed. With the young woman's help this was quickly done. Before Avey Johnson knew it, her luggage was being carted away to the storage room, the reservation for her flight home had been changed (to the further mystification of the desk clerk) and she was back in the car beside the old man, headed for the wharf.

Just as they were leaving the rum shop he had formally introduced himself. Dressed by then in the rusty jacket to the pants, and wearing a tie and what looked like a clergyman's discarded black hat, he had stopped her at the door and with an Old World courtliness held out his hand. "Lebert Joseph's the name. I din' introduce myself proper before. And you is Mistress who . . . ?"

She had to laugh. "That's right. Here we are about to go off on a trip together and we don't even know each other's names." And taking his hand, she had told him hers—but only after having to pause for a long moment to think of it. When it did come to her and she said it aloud, it sounded strange, almost like someone else's name.

He had left her for the moment to go in search of the boat he traveled on each year. Before bounding away on the uneven legs, he had deposited her in the arcade to one of the warehouses lining the harbor road. "Stay right here, oui, out the sun and this mob of people. You's not to leave. I gon' be back just now."

She stood there, wondering at herself, filled with misgivings, yet waiting as obedient as a child for him to return. On the ground beside her stood the smallest of her suitcases, containing her night things and a change of clothes, and next to it a battered valise belonging to the man. Her pocketbook was on her arm. She had remembered to put on her watch. And she had thought to wear a hat this time. It was the same one she had flung into the corner last night.

She had wanted during the brief stop-off at the hotel to change out of the pink shirtdress. It had become stained with perspiration from her long walk up the beach and even more wrinkled than when she had put it on from the two hours spent sitting in the rum shop. But there had not been enough time.

Little had changed on the wharf since yesterday. As large a crowd of out-islanders was to be seen thronging the area between the roadway and the sea, and those up front, nearest the water, were eagerly boarding the long line of schooners and sloops tied up at the edge. The air rang with the Patois they insisted on speaking these two or three special days of the year. *"They can speak the King's English good as me and you but the minute they set foot on the wharf for the excursion is only Patois you hearing."* The bright polished surface of the sky appeared to reflect the myriad colors and patterns of their clothes and the umbrellas the women were carrying. Underscoring the festive din was the solemn note she had detected yesterday and wondered about: a sound like the summoning of a church bell only they could hear distinctly.

She was feeling more dazed and confused than ever, yet there now seemed to be a small clear space in her mind; looking out from it she found the scene on the wharf less overwhelming today, less strange. The milling, moving tide of bodies, the colors and sounds, the pageantry of the umbrellas were like frames from a home movie she remembered Marion had made her last trip to Ghana. She had filmed something she had called a durban or was it durbar? There had been a showing of the movie for the parents and children at her school, and Marion had insisted that she come. In the talk Marion had given along with the film she had spoken of something called a New Yam, of a golden stool that descended from the sky, and of ancestors who were to be fed.

Moreover, the scene in front of her also vaguely called to mind something from her own life. Just what, she couldn't say. But the surging crowd, the rapidly filling boats, the sheen of sunlight on the water were reminiscent of something. And slowly it came to her, drifting up out of the void she sensed in her: the annual boat ride up the Hudson River to Bear Mountain!

Each summer before her father, on orders from her great-aunt, took her to spend August in Tatem, she would go with the family up the river to Bear Mountain Park on the excursion sponsored by the neighborhood social club.

As early as six in the morning would find them among the small but growing crowd already gathered on the pier at 125th Street. Behind them, hidden by the tall buildings along Riverside Drive lay Harlem and Seventh Avenue where they lived. Across the Hudson, New Jersey rose like the landfall of another country. But the green unbroken palisade over there scarcely claimed their attention.

Every eye those mornings would be trained south, toward the Battery, where the S.S. *Robert Fulton* was scheduled to make its appearance at eight o'clock out of the rising mist downriver.

The *Robert Fulton* was invariably late.

"You would think that old boat could get here on time at least once, just to surprise us": her mother, wearing the bright floral print dress she had made for the occasion. With the new dress on, her hair freshly marcelled and her face powdered, she didn't look as if she had been up half the night frying chicken, making potato salad and preparing the inevitable rice for her father. Lord, deliver me from these Gullahs and their rice rice rice! she was always saying.

"What's it got to be on time for? Ain't nobody here but us darkies": her father, looking the dandy. He had exchanged the gray work clothes he wore every day as one of a crew of janitors in a large apartment building downtown for a lemon-yellow sport shirt and a pair of tan slacks with razor-sharp creases down the front. As an extra touch he had tied one of her mother's colorful head scarves like an ascot at the open collar of the shirt. (She had long since vowed never to marry a man who didn't know how to tie a scarf just that way.) The scarf was special for the boat ride. Later he would use it to cover his face as he napped stretched out on the grass at Bear Mountain during the afternoon heat.

"I said what's it got to be on time for? Ain't nobody here but us . . ."

"Negroes, you! Or Coloreds. Don't you see the children standing here? Always bringing down the race."

But behind the cut-eye she dealt him she had been subtly smiling. A smile Avey knew that was part of their private language. That night, on the run home over the black river, under the stars, they had danced to the live band inside the main cabin, her father clasping her mother in the floral dress close to him, his face which was dark like her own pressed against her mother's with its light coppery mix of red and brown—the color of her three brothers.

That night, standing watching them along with her brothers and the other children crowded near the bandstand, she had felt her body flush hot and cold in turns, and she had understood something for the first time, the knowledge coming to her like one of the stars above the boat bursting in a shower of splintered light inside her: simply, that it was out of this holding and clasping, out of the cut-eyes and the private smiles that she and her brothers had come.

Boat rides up the Hudson! Sometimes, standing with her family amid the growing crowd on the pier, waiting for the *Robert Fulton* to heave into sight, she would have the same strange sensation as when she stood beside her great-aunt outside the church in Tatem, watching the elderly folk inside perform the Ring Shout. As more people arrived to throng the area beside the river and the cool morning air warmed to the greetings and talk, she would feel what seemed to be hundreds of slender threads streaming out from her navel and from the place where her heart was to enter those around her. And the threads went out not only to people she recognized from the neighborhood but to those she didn't know as well, such as the roomers just up from the South and the small group of

West Indians whose odd accent called to mind Gullah talk and who it was said were as passionate about their rice as her father.

The threads streaming out from her even entered the few disreputable types who occasionally appeared in their midst from the poolrooms and bars where the posters advertising the boat ride were displayed. They were the ones who could be counted on to act the fool or worse once they had in a few drinks. Some years, on the return run down the river, there would be a sudden eruption among the dancers inside the cabin or out on one of the decks and two figures, locked together in what looked like a violent bunnyhug of a dance, would come grappling and spinning and cursing out of the scattering crowd. There might be the flash of a blade in the starlight, followed by the sight and smell of blood, and her father saying in love and disgust as he quickly herded them away, "My people, my people. They don't feel they had a good time lessen somebody gets cut."

She would even feel the threads entering them.

Then it would seem to her that she had it all wrong and the threads didn't come from her, but from them, from everyone on the pier, including the rowdies, issuing out of their navels and hearts to stream into her as she stood there holding the bag containing the paper plates and cups, napkins and tablecloth which she was in charge of. She visualized the threads as being silken, like those used in the embroidery on a summer dress, and of a hundred different colors. And although they were thin to the point of invisibility, they felt as strong entering her as the lifelines of woven hemp that trailed out into the water at Coney Island. If she cared to she could dog-paddle (she couldn't swim) out to where the Hudson was deepest and not worry. The moment she began to founder those on shore would simply pull on the silken threads and haul her in.

While the impression lasted she would cease being herself, a mere girl in a playsuit made out of the same material as her mother's dress, someone small, insignificant, outnumbered, the object of her youngest brother's endless teasing; instead, for those moments, she became part of, indeed the center of, a huge wide confraternity.

By the time the *Robert Fulton* finally made its appearance, the crowd on the pier would have grown so large it would look as if all of Harlem was there. And the numbers lent a certain importance to the occasion. They raised it above the ordinary. It didn't seem that they were just going on a day's outing up a river to a state park a few miles away, but on a voyage—a full-scale voyage—to someplace far more impressive. No one there could have said where this place was. None present could have called its name. Yet the eagerness with which they swarmed up the gangplank the moment it was laid, the high drama in their voices and laughter and gestures, in the bright, brash, here-I-come, see-me-here colors they had on said they were confident of reaching there. And they weren't just going to this place, wherever it was, whatever its name, just to loll on the grass and eat fried chicken and potato salad and to nap or play bid whist during the afternoon heat. But to lay claim: *"We gon' put on our robes and shout all over God's heaven!"*

Boat rides up the Hudson were always about something that momentous and global.

For a moment, caught up in the memory, she failed to notice Lebert Joseph as he came rushing up.

He had found the schooner, he announced out of breath, after having searched up and down the wharf. It was all the way at the southern end, a good distance from where they were. And it was about to sail. "We gon' have to make haste, oui." He was already snatching up the two bags and moving off.

They were to cover almost the entire length of the wharf, the man charging ahead at an almost comical near-run, Avey Johnson struggling despite her long legs to keep up behind. For most of the way he stayed close to the line of buildings, out of the heart of the crowd. But as they neared the end of the dock area, he abruptly turned and plunged into its midst, clearing a swift path for them with his shouts, the startling black suit and hat he wore and the fact that everyone there knew him. "M'sieur Joseph!" they hailed him.

The two of them finally reached the edge of the wharf and he brought her to a halt before a two-master lying among the last boats there. And immediately her doubts and misgivings flared up again. Because although the schooner she found herself facing was larger than most of the others, it was as much of a relic, with the same scarred and battered look and exhausted air. Why had she expected anything different! Up front it boasted the crudely carved figurehead of a saint on the bow. And this was also the worse for wear, the salt spray having eaten away most of the face and the sandaled feet and the long girdled robe it had on. Only the crucifix in its hand had by some miracle remained intact. This it held out over the water as though it were a divining rod that had once led the way to a rich lode of gold.

"The *Emanuel C*," he announced as he rushed her on board up a makeshift gangplank. He was holding her firmly by the elbow.

The main deck was scarcely larger than her living room at home. And it was packed. A small multitude of out-islanders—men, women and children—had already claimed every inch of space on the worn planking. Those who had boarded early had made seats for themselves on the covered hatch, the cleats for the ropes and the piles of cargo lying about from the schooner's regular run. A lively group of young men had encamped on top of the small deckhouse midship. The only seating as such was a long bench built into the starboard flank of the boat, where a number of old women and mothers with babies sat crowded together. To shield them from the sun an awning made from a discarded sail had been strung between the deckhouse and the rigging over their heads.

Everyone else was standing.

Lebert Joseph led her across to the oldest among the women on the bench. And the moment she saw them sitting there in their long somber dresses, their black hands folded in their laps and their filmy eyes overseeing everything on deck, she experienced a shock of recognition that for a moment made her forget her desire to bolt. They were—she could have sworn it!—the presiding mothers

of Mount Olivet Baptist (her own mother's church long ago)—the Mother Cald-
wells and Mother Powes and Mother Greens, all those whose great age and long
service to the church had earned them a title even more distinguished than "sister" and a place of honor in the pews up front. From there their powerful
"Amens" propelled the sermon forward each Sunday. Their arms reached out to
steady those taken too violently with the spirit. And toward the end of the service when the call went out: *"Come/Will you come . . . ?"* and the sinners and
backsliders made their shamefaced calvary up to the pulpit, it was their exhorta-
tions which helped to bring them through.

The only thing those before her on the bench lacked were the fans from the
local mortician with a picture of Jesus feeding the lambs on one side and the address of the funeral parlor on the other. These they should have been holding on
their laps or panning slowly back and forth across their faces.

Space was quickly made for her between a stout woman in her eighties with
large capable hands and a gold-rimmed smile, and her thinner neighbor of the
same age or older, who wore her white hair in a crown of braids above her
dimmed eyes and a shawl around her shoulders. The face she turned to Avey
Johnson was simply bone and a lined yellowish sheeting of skin. Old people who
have the essentials to go on forever.

Waving Lebert Joseph aside, they took charge. They relieved him of her suit-
case and placed it out of the way under the bench. Her pocketbook was gently
taken from her arm and laid flat on her lap. Reaching up, they removed her
hat—doing it with such delicacy she scarcely felt it leave her head—and placed it
on top of the pocketbook: there was no need for it with the thick canvas awning
overhead. Then they indicated the railing just behind her: she was to rest her
head there whenever she felt like it.

By the time the *Emanuel C* edged away from the wharf and under power of a
fitful motor began threading its way through the other boats in the harbor, Avey
Johnson found herself comfortably settled and the worst of her fears put to rest.
She felt so reassured that when they reached the outer harbor minutes later and
the first of the sails went up, she greeted it with something of the excitement she
had felt as a child when the *Robert Fulton,* with a blast of its horn, would swing
out into the Hudson, the boat ride finally under way.

The lesser foresail was up; and shortly afterwards with much shouting and
hauling of the ropes on the part of the small crew, the large mainsail went aloft.
The sight of it made the housewife in her recoil. Both sails could stand a good
bleaching, a good, old-fashioned bluing. But even as she sat there feeling embarrassed on their account, a wind swept up of the sea, unfurled them and then,
with a sound like a giant bellows, filled them; and from just so many yards of
patched and dingy canvas, they were transformed into sails that called to mind
those huge ecclesiastical banners the Catholics parade through the streets on the
feast days of their saints. And for no reason, not understanding why, she caught
herself thinking: it had been done in the name of the Father and of the Son.

And the sea? Glancing over her shoulder at the waves no more than six feet below, she saw that it was as Lebert Joseph had described it earlier: "a sea smooth as silk."

As unworried suddenly as Thomasina Moore setting off on the listing sloop, she watched the island with its coastal hills and distant mountains and steep little town slowly recede and drop to the level of a sandbar over the widening plain of the sea. At the same time, her gaze shifting leisurely between the two, she was observing the out-islanders as they stood chatting amid the confusion of their belongings and the many children on board. No one appeared bothered in the least by the crowding or the searing sun on their heads or their sometimes unsteady footing.

Once as the schooner gave a sudden roll and pitch a young woman in a brightly patterned sundress with a wide skirt grabbed the arm of the man beside her. Thrown off balance himself he was no help, so that for a moment they staggered about in their little patch of deck space, laughing and clinging to each other, until the boat righted itself.

Was she perhaps the taxi driver's old girlfriend? The one he said had thrown him over for a man who would accompany her on the excursion? What was her name again . . . ? Sylvie. He had spoken of her with bittersweet regret.

She leaned her head back on the railing and smiled reassuredly at Lebert Joseph, who was keeping a watchful eye on her from the crowded hatch nearby where space had been made for him to sit. She closed her own eyes. Breathed deep the salt air which, it was said, could cure anything. Allowed her mind to drift on the sound of the wind in the transformed sails and the singing voices around her. Martinique. That was where she had first heard it—the Patois. And its odd cadence, its vivid music had reached into a close-off corner of her mind to evoke the sound of voices in Tatem. She hadn't even realized what had happened, that a connection had been made, until two nights later when her great-aunt had appeared. She had stood there large as life in the middle of her dream, and as a result there was a hole the size of a crater where her life of the past three decades had been.

Avey Johnson stirred fitfully as the bewildering events of the last few days laid siege to her again, and immediately—her eyes still closed—she felt her elderly neighbors on the bench turn toward her. A quieting hand came to rest on her arm and they both began speaking to her in Patois—soothing, lilting words full of maternal solicitude. And just as they had relieved her of the heavy pocketbook and her hat earlier, their murmurous voices now set about divesting her of the troubling thoughts, quietly and deftly stripping her of them as if they were so many layers of winter clothing she had mistakenly put on for the excursion.

And as her mind came unburdened she began to float down through the gaping hole, floating, looking, searching for whatever memories were to be found there. While her body remained anchored between the old women who were one and the same with the presiding mothers of Mount Olivet in their pews up front, her other self floated down. And the deeper it went, the smaller everything became. The large, somewhat matronly handbag on her lap shrank to a little girl's pocketbook of white patent leather containing a penny for the collection plate and a handkerchief scented with her mother's cologne. There were suddenly new hightop shoes that buttoned along the sides on her feet, and a pair of little sheer marquisette gloves on her hands. A bow of pale blue satin that felt bigger than her head matched the Easter outfit she had on. And above the racing of the silken sea just below the railing she soon began to hear—the sound reaching her clearly over the years—the inflammatory voice from the pulpit.

Colleen McElroy (1935–)

As a poet and writer of short fiction and memoir, Colleen McElroy travels through memory and geography, linking past with present and self with communities. Her verse and prose feature a sense of freshness and renewal even as they also foreground contradiction and isolation. McElroy is very conscious of gender and heritage, adding to the richness of her creation in all genres.

Colleen McElroy was born October 19, 1935, in St. Louis. When her parents divorced in 1938, she and her mother moved in with her grandmother. Five years later, her mother married an army sergeant and the family moved around the country in line with his military responsibilities. Spending significant amounts of time before adulthood in St. Louis, Wyoming, Kansas City, and Munich, Germany, McElroy developed a strong sense of place. She continues to travel, visiting such locations as Japan, Europe, South America, Africa, Southeast Asia, Majorca, and including those experiences in her poetry.

McElroy attended college in Germany before transferring to Kansas City where she received her bachelor's degree. She continued her education by studying speech and hearing sciences at the University of Pittsburgh and returned to Kansas City to do graduate work in neurological and language learning patterns. During this time, McElroy married, had two children, and divorced.

With her children, McElroy moved to Washington state and became director of Speech and Hearing Sciences at Western Washington University. She also studied at the University of Washington to receive a Ph.D. in ethnolinguistic patterns of dialect differences and oral traditions. She later became a professor there, and, in 1983, became the first African American woman to be granted tenure.

In her mid-thirties, McElroy married poet David McElroy and began writing seriously herself. Her love for the landscape of Pacific Northwest and her home in Bellingham, Washington, intersected with encouragement from poets Denise Levertov and Richard Hugo as well as her discovery of Black poets Langston Hughes, Gwendolyn Brooks, and Margaret Walker.

Colleen McElroy published her first collection of poetry in 1973, a chapbook, The Mules Done Long Since Gone, *a work that resonates with the Northwest landscape and newfound poetic influence.* Music From Home *(1976), a second collection, centers self, her roles as mother and woman.* Winters Without Snow *(1979) documents the pain of a second divorce, showing a range of emotion and maintaining a high level of intimacy. Because her impetus to write centers in the personal, McElroy's early poetry is self-conscious. Images that connect past to present abound as McElroy explores herself and creates meaning.*

In 1983, her collection Queen of the Ebony Isles *was selected and published by the Wesleyan University Press Poetry Series. The collection received an American Book Award in 1985. The poems of this collection are also self-conscious, tracing the generations of mother and child. McElroy revisits the summers of her childhood in "Monologue for St. Louis," expressing the alienation she feels as a lover of words through the images of garden and grapes. She links her past to her daughter's present in "In My Mother's Room," connecting her sprawled sleeping mother to her position between that well-earned exhaustion and the anxious innocence of her daughter. In "Queen of the Ebony Isles," McElroy personifies the passionate, energy-zapping intensity of sexuality and womanhood, creating an image both grotesque and beautiful. Queen of the Ebony Isles is a collection that links many aspects of identity—mother, lover, woman.*

McElroy's later poetry including Bone Flames *(1987)* and What Madness Brought Me Here: Collected Poems 1968–88 *(1990), is characterized by focus on travel, communities of women, and self-reflexive address of the power of poetic language.* What Madness Brought Me Here: Collected Poems 1968–88 *(1990) provides a forum for the range of McElroy's development as a poet, allowing her poems to speak to one another across the years of original publication dates. In "Pike Street Bus," McElroy foregrounds the process and function of poetry, personifying the poem as storyteller and narrating in simple language the beauty and bleakness of the people around her. In "Tapestries," McElroy values the knowledge and ways of being of the women closest to her—her family—and also emphasizes her difference, her travel and separation, as what she has to bring back to that community. McElroy's most recent collection of verse,* Travelling Music *(1998), more philosophical and outside of self than previous work, hints at the direction future poetry may take. With humor that tends toward illuminating the ironies of existence, the collection maintains the personal voice established in other volumes.*

McElroy has also published two collections of short stories, Jesus and Fat Tuesday *(1987)* and Under the Cardboard Pines *(1990). In the stories of* Jesus and Fat Tuesday, *McElroy plumbs her characters' spirits and minds to reveal their truths and challenges.* Under the Cardboard Pines *(1990) revolves around history and memory, as stories intertwine and draw the reader in. "Imogene" from McElroy's first collection of fiction,* Jesus and Fat Tuesday *(1987), exemplifies the honesty with which McElroy conveys the experiences and perceptions of her characters, bleak as they may be. Imogene is driven by a need to feel beautiful and worthwhile. She lives in desperation and illusion, her seemingly greatest concerns of being out of cigarettes and gaining weight hiding the realities of self-abuse and unhappiness. Balancing third-person distance and description with Imogene's first-person thoughts, she captures the contradiction between Imogene's reality and her illusion. She communicates Imogene's tenuous psychological survival with sensitivity and the same hope Imogene herself has.*

Expanding her work with poetry and fiction to the realm of nonfiction prose, McElroy has also published a poetic memoir, A Long Way from St. Louie *(1997), and an ethnographic memoir,* Over the Lip of the World: Among the Storytellers of Madagascar *(1998).* A Long Way from St. Louie *is an extended meditation on life's journey. Part travel narrative and part poem, the memoir settles in neither and is enriched by both. In short vignettes and lyric poems, McElroy documents her travels with a keen sense of her own difference as a Black woman and a poetic eye for the vividness of places and peoples.*

Her most recent work, Over the Lip of the World *(1988), combines memoir and ethnography, featuring McElroy's Fulbright-funded research in Madagascar. She shares with readers the oral traditions and myths of the island through personal narrative and through collection of selected stories and song-poems that communicate Madagascan ideas about origin and the rules governing individual and social behaviors and relationships. This ethnographic study is yet another form of McElroy's fascination with the ways language governs life, a fascination that drives the spectrum of her work.*

R. Joyce Lausch

Colleen McElroy

Monologue for Saint Louis

home again and the heart barely there
when choked by clusters of words
thick as the clumps of blue-black
grapes we snitched every summer
from the neighbor's arbor
succulent pockets of flesh laced
with green staining our lips and fingers

it is summer again and I am home
vowing penance for all my disappearances
since that first summer
when the arbor was clotted
with pockets of grapes latticed on each
interlocking vine

now earthworms have trellised the arbor
and that crumbling heap of rotting black
sticks cannot shield us from wind or words
we are the women we whispered about each summer
familiar houses and schoolyards have disappeared
childhood streets are blocked with singular black

one-way signs aligned like a lacework
of warnings or accusing fingers
I am home again
and my cousins sit in their cloaks of black
skin dragging me through twisted vines
of genetic maps thick with childhood vows

they remember each summer
how each year I vowed to return home
forever but I am lost in a riddle of words
home is a vacant lot its back yard clotted
with a stainless-steel arch and clusters
of tiny parks sprouting like trelliswork

enclosing some strange summer
resort my cousins have disappeared
into like the shadows of beasts and bad air
that infect this flat country and I am home
a stranger in love with words
with tart sweet clusters of poems

In My Mother's Room

(for Vanessa)

my mother lies spread-eagle upon the bed
I am in the next room with my daughter
slowly passing away the evening
in a late summer's drone of hours
muffled sounds of children's games
drift through the window
along with the odor of thick honeysuckle
and the flicker of yellow fireflies
the warp and weft of their flight
draws me to the edge of a time when I was
a child, this house my prison
and my mother sprawled naked on the bed
signaled hours to be spent alone
hiding in a book
or in my room under the clapboard eaves
now my father sits by himself in the garden

my mother snores
her mouth open in a sagging *oh*
her flowered bathrobe
slipping from the edge of the bed
in a cascade of roses
I am slumped in the overstuffed chair
watching the TV grind past endless hours
my daughter frowns
but will not look directly at us
fully clothed, I am as vulnerable
as my mother, whose childbearing scars
are slightly visible as she lies under
the humid blanket of another midwestern summer
cankered by antagonisms
we are shadows of black into black
one of the other
I can draw my own body into the damp outline she will leave when she awakens
one day, I will walk into this house
lift her flowered robe from my shoulders
then stumble and sink onto that bed
in perfect mimicry
my legs will flow into the age-old patterns

my pubic hairs will curl tightly
into the early evening heat
and I will breathe the labors
of a hundred midwestern summers

but tonight, I am fully clothed
and I smile at my daughter's frowns
she has wrapped herself in innocence
against this scene
I motion her to the door
toward the scent of flowers and children playing
knowing all too soon
she will finally
finger her breasts
and disappear into crowds
of us naked women

Queen of the Ebony Isles

this old woman follows me from room to room
screams like my mother   angers like my child
teases me   rolling her tattooed hips forward
and out   steals my food   my name   my smile
when you call her I come running

when we were young and perfect
we danced together and oh we loved well
all the husbands and lovers   children and books
the sunshine and long walks on lonely nights
now she sucks me thin with her affairs

weaves romantic shadows over the windows
and curses my sober moods   kisses everyone
and insists on wearing red shoes
she hums the same songs over and over
something about love and centuries turning upon us

each time she changes the verse
shifting the words like cards in a game
of solitaire   the hot patent-leather colors
her mercurial moods as she flies about
her red heels glittering and clicking out of tune

she has seen too many comic strips
believes she's as deadly lovely
as Dragon Lady and Leopard Girl   I resist
but her limbs are daring   oiled for movement

without me who are you she asks   I am heavy
with silence   my hands are maps of broken lines
without her all sounds are hollow   I am numbed
cold and cannot read the cycles of the moon
even the sun   the sun cannot warm me

aloneness is a bad fiddle I play against my own
burning   bet your kinky muff she cackles knowing
the symptoms   then draped in feather boas
she drags me toward yet another lover   beckoning
with her brash reds pulsing like haunting violins

on midnight-blue nights she screams
into the eyes of the moon   twirling her war machine
like some Kamikaze pilot   her heat bakes my skin
even blacker   she's never happy unless we're falling
in love or hate   she grows younger while I

age and age   bandage wounds and tire too easily
she says   play the game   play the game she says
when I complain she says I'm hearing voices
she's hacked my rocking chair into firewood
I am the clown in all her dreams

when she looks into the mirror from my eyes
I want to float away unscathed
drift like patches of early morning fog
she thinks I stay because I love her
one day soon I'll move while she's sleeping

Pike Street Bus

Poem, we're going this way,
With that bus,
Its driver fat and full
Of unspent words like you.
Tell them about it, poem.

It starts this way,
A slow lumbering thing
Turning the corner.
Then the lead line drops.
The bus is stuck like
The driver's face
In the rearview mirror
As he watches sparks dance
In front of Pike Market,
Watches the line throw fire.
The broccoli's put away,
Apples gone, fish face sideways
In neat rows under a layer
Of white paper.
There's heavy breathing
On the bus.

The driver's face is swollen,
The grey evening settles
In lines around his mouth.
His belly peeks out, dull white
Where a missing button
Lets his shirt stand open.
He leaves the bus, catching sight
Of the lead line hanging
Toward the broken pavement.
A few faces turn to watch;
Others look sideways.
She stares straight on,
Her black face tired,
Her arms remembering forty offices,
Mop handle imprints still cling
To her palms. Her eyes are old
Before her time.

Say it for her, poem.
Tell her dreams of places
Where she's always young,
Smiling and sitting straight
Like the picture that stares out
From her dresser. She's crisp;
Caught by the camera alive,
In love, not knowing this night,
This bus.
Ignore the drunk that staggers on,

Lurching toward the coin box.
He hangs at an angle
Against Seattle's fading sun.
He leans back, falling
Into his past, using his coins
For balance before diving
For the slot; a handful
Of attention on his face
As the change drops.

Plunging toward a seat
Smashing against her feet
And dreams, his mind leaves
Him once again. She rubs
Her cleaning woman knees,
Stroking toward the pain on the floor.
Extra fat on her chin bobbing
As she remembers how she last saw
Her man; sitting barefoot
Atop a kettledrum, pounding
At an eight-hour day.

Tapestries

when I was eight I listened to stories of love
and etiquette while my mother's sisters
sat on Grandma's horsehair sofa
naked under their starched dresses
words flew from their fingers
in a dance as old as the moon
but I dreamed of other places
of dark bodies bending
to a language too dreamlike
and concise to decode

above them a tapestry desert stretched
into distant corners where I imagined
ancient rituals grotesque and graceful
conjuring up the moon-flecked
seasons of the earth
but my mother's sisters wove tales
that collapsed the world
into sarcastic snips of language

their black thighs opened
billows of powdery musk
rising from their legs like dust
from some raw and haunting land

I had a choice
two scenes their dark secrets
spread for my viewing
the usual desert palm trees camels
a cautious rug merchant one hand
on the tent, face turned towards the horizon
turning back like Thomas Jefferson
towards his black *anima,* like Lot's wife
or the thousands of black women
who fled slavery preferring instead
the monastic beds of the River Niger

it is said those waters flowed
red for years
shades of ochre fuchsia and russet
as layers of blood sifted
through the silt of the river
the velvet sands on that tapestry
were red and flowed into all corners
my aunts sat in a line beneath this scene
refusing to turn back
wagging their heads against the world's sins

I have seen more than my aunts dared to see
how each Sunday they sat bare-assed and defiant
their dark female caverns linking thighs
into matching hills of lemon ebony and mocha flesh
how the wooden humps reflected off my grandmother's
whalebone hairpins when she leaned into the light
the crumbling walls of the city of Benin
Kamehameha's feathered cape in the Bishop museum

I have seen Buenos Aires
where ladies dine inside their mirrors
Berlin where my blackness
was examined in six languages
Bogotá where there are no traffic signals
and even pregnant women are targets
fat clumsy figures playing toreador
with foreign made limousines

in the Middle East fairy chimneys
of volcanic tuffs spiral into the sunlight
their colors glowing like stained glass
in the half-light of the desert
shades of ochre russet and ebony
thrust into tidal waves of magma
and firestorm of ash
like beads on a rosary linking
village to village

when I was eight my prudish aunts
sat like squat pigeons on the horsehair sofa
brazen under their stiff-collared dresses
and I gathered dreams of love
from a tapestry woven in velvet
a blood-colored crescent moon, three palm trees
two burgundy camels, all arched around
a shadowy figure entering a tent
the world behind him barren and flat

some days pressed by the low ceiling
or a troubled sky I drift back to that room
the scene spreads before me
the delicate red tracery
of some ancient artisan
clinging to threadbare spots
the nomad who is forever coming home
the tent with its doorway of secrets
the dark face turned towards the corner
staring at some fixed point
on the amber horizon of that velvet desert
as if to say how vast
and naked the world seems to be

Imogene

She was out of cigarettes and someone was making love down the hall. Low moans, abrupt intakes of breath, then fading sounds. She slammed her feet into her worn sandals, leaning against the dresser for balance.

She had scrambled around the room, turning things over, searching nervously for a cigarette or part of one to calm her. It was happening all over again.

Feeling on top of it one minute, and doom the next. She had been anxious about him last night, unsure of him. So tonight, she'd waited, waited until she had to go out, until the noise and her dry throat forced her to the door.

When she looked up from the dresser, the image in the mirror refused to be familiar at first, then was all too familiar—her face bloated, her skin faded under lemony shadows.

Jesus, I've gained weight, she thought.

The moaning erupted again and she clutched her stomach, but by the time she'd reached the stairs, she could hear the couple grinding into each other once more. The audible breathing, and inevitable currents, lowing and building.

It was cool on the street. The night air brushed against her face, rolled over her and she fell into the comfort of darkness. Despite its grittiness, it was a California summer's night. The few palm trees dotting this side of Oakland looked as out of place as she felt, something left over from some other town and dragged to this place to be ignored by everything but dirt. Her forehead was damp with sweat and old makeup. She hadn't felt the wetness back in her room, but now it was heavy, pulling at her, adding extra weight. She wiped her face with the sleeve of her sweater.

Shouldn't let him see me sweating. Won't!

But she couldn't just shake off knowing he hadn't come looking for her. It was late and he hadn't come up to the room to find her.

She glanced back at the triplex. A wooden box. Someone had painted each section in different pastel colors, once upon a time. Now, like all the other houses on the block, it was faded, the paint chipped and windows missing. How many houses like this had she seen? How many one room traps of many rooms? She decided she must be as tired as the building looked. Even the uneven tiles in the doorway reminded her of the rumpled bed she was deserting.

She walked quickly, ducking her head at the slightest movement: a floating scrap of paper, shadows of trees, a flash of light reflected off long, low, chrome-plated cars. She thought she heard someone call her name from the doorway of an all-night convenience store, but she didn't look up. She hurried past it all, toeing in, her body curved, no hips, no bust, not seeing anyone but knowing someone recognized her. They would talk. Say how she'd cut them cold. She'd make it up though. Tomorrow, she'd ask questions, smile. Ask about brothers or cousins. Ask about cars. Questions with answers she'd learned to ignore.

Learn. Humph! What do I learn? All these years and no reason for me to believe he's different.

He wasn't the most handsome man she'd known and it wasn't that she couldn't look for someone else. No, not the most handsome, but style! *I can still pick them. Six feet tall and light on his feet. Moves like a hunter. Like one of those mountain cats. Knows every hidden place. Some college too. And a good dresser. Ohh-hh, he can look good. Fine suits and clean fingernails.*

But it wasn't the way he looked. She could see that in the movies any day. It was the touching, the reaching out and finding him there when she needed him.

How many others had she felt, but never touched? He was her man, the one she could love and feel. That sweet-awful feeling of knowing how someone else felt. Not guessing. Not faking. So little to ask.

She walked faster, shuffling a little to keep her sandals on her feet as the uneven cracks of the sidewalk jutted out in front of her. She pulled her elbows into her sides, cutting off the breeze and closing in the dampness.

It was he way he tilted his head. *Yes, that must be it,* she thought suddenly. A kind of unconscious lift just before he smiled. And his hands. *Yeah, his hands. Not the way he held his head. That was it.* Those broad fingers and their sure, swift movements.

Two dogs raced each other across the street. The little one skitterish, running first in front, then behind the bigger one. The big one striding, breaking his stride once to turn and half-heartedly growl at her. She hesitated, narrowed her eyes to a squint and eased out her breath. They moved into the bushes and she stumbled to the next corner. The shadows elongated her legs across the half arc of light from the street lamp. She was pleased to think this added a few extra inches to her short figure.

She wished she'd stayed in her room. She should try to forget him. Not make any excuses to go out, despite the welcome relief of the night air. She should forget all about him, his hands and thighs.

Thighs, that was it. I've always been a fool for thighs.

Her mind clicked on the image of smoothness under pants that gripped muscles. She imagined him under her, over her. Her hands on the long inclines of his thighs, pulling them against her, almost into her. She wrapped her arms tightly around her waist.

Suddenly, the sharp blast of a car horn shattered the rhythms of the street: 5 rapid stabs and 2 steady beats. Shave-and-a-haircut. Always insulting, no matter how many times she heard it. She lowered her head as the driver's wide-brimmed hat turned in her direction.

No need to wave. No reason to speak. Just cruising. A good night for cruising. A clear sky. Maybe he's out here somewhere. Maybe he's gone across the Bay, into the city. Maybe he's looking for someone else.

A man passed her just as she stepped off the curb. *Too easy. A dead mark,* she thought. She could hear him pause, but she didn't turn when he said hello.

By the time she reached the BART bridge, she'd talked herself in and out of seeing him again at least half-a-dozen times. A train whizzed by overhead. The lighted cars let her see the heads of people. *I'll bet he's across the Bay,* she thought. *Gone over before dark cause he knows I won't follow him there.*

She stopped for a second and watched the train disappear around the curve. She thought vaguely about the city, but as usual, she couldn't connect herself to anything she knew, to what she imagined might happen on the other side of the Bay. Even on those nights when someone had taken her for a drive close enough to the water so she could see the city lights and skyline, none of that world connected for her. Oakland. That was enough.

The intersection on the other side of the BART overpass was free of cars. She was the only figure visible in the streetlight. Her skirt tightened as she stepped back onto the sidewalk. The material clutched her hips and the waistband bit her flesh. She pulled at her sweater.

Got to lose weight. Damn skirt's too old. Old skirt. Old me.

She dismissed the thought and pulled her sweater tighter against the swirling wind and its debris. She could sense the man she'd passed still standing on the corner at the other side of the BART bridge. He was watching her walk out of his line of vision.

Goddamn men. Where was he? Dumb. I'm dumb. Why worry? He'll wait. Why shouldn't he? Shit! She knew he could find someone else, particularly if she kept him waiting too long.

She had believed in him, had told him so. She'd believed in all of them, even the one she'd married. *God, he was good. Almost for a month.* That had been a good sign. But he'd left, like all the others. *The good looking ones run faster,* she thought.

And she had known they would, but she'd wanted to hang on, feel secure with them. She had searched their faces each time, hoping for the right one, looking for the final, the honest, one. *Every time.*

She groped in her pocket for a cigarette and then remembered why she'd left her room. Then she remembered her purse, left on the bed. Or under it. She rarely forgot it, but all that moaning down the hall and the dry feeling without cigarettes in that funky little room.

Damn! Need a drink. Get a drink somewhere. If I could just get him to care. We could move. Try another city.

She'd told him that once. She'd told him she was willing to move, to find a good job and work with the sun up, to make friends. And then she'd have the nights with only his lips flush against hers, his shoulders pushing as he turned her over and over.

God, he's good, she thought again. And she thought about how easily he made the whole world turn smooth and silky. How he made her body feel innocent.

The Tambourine was near by, its pulsing neon sign already in sight. She had credit there. He liked the place. He'd be there. Plots, tricks, plans. She really needed that drink. Across the street from the Tambourine, she stopped and watched the door of the bar for a second. If he was not there, then one drink. fifteen minutes at most.

The heavy odor of liquor billowed against her as she opened the door. The stale beer and smoke reminded her of armpits and she closed her elbows in and headed blindly for a barstool. Her legs brushed the polished wood as she swung herself onto the seat. She'd seen him immediately and felt the rush of blood behind her eyelids. She forced herself to turn towards the bottles lining the back of the bar. *Double bourbon. Yeah, that's it.* She nodded and ordered.

He was alone, not looking her way, but he'd seen her. When she walked in, she saw him check his watch, then reach for a cigarette. She licked her lips, immediately wiped them dry again with the bar napkin, her fingers brushing the slight mustache covering her upper lip, and in the reflection in the mirror back of the bar, her eyes checked the oily space across the broad plane of her nose.

Bastard! Once, if I could wait for him to come to me just once!

She signaled the bartender and walked to the table, drinking as she crossed the room. Someone reached out, touching her thigh. She caught only the coarse color of denim as the hand withdrew. The bourbon was good and the glass cold. She held the icy surface against her forehead. The glass was half empty by the time she'd crossed the floor.

He had a fresh cigarette already in his hand when he turned to face her. When she'd lowered herself into the chair, he placed the cigarette between her lips and lit a match with one stroke of his thumbnail. She inhaled, trying not to look directly at him, then chased the smoke with a sip of bourbon. His hand brushed her cheek and he pouted a fake kiss at her. She looked down at her drink, trying to wish away the hot feeling left by his hand.

He turned to speak, his voice bone-deep and caressing her weakness like a suede glove.

"Let's take a walk, baby."

She didn't move. He began a smile, then pulled at his shirt cuffs and shifted his body towards her. He took her hand, rubbing her fingers, stroking her palm. Then he pulled her fingers to his lips, kissed the tips, then her palms. She forced herself to smile.

"You're a good woman," he cooed, his voice lower this time, almost a murmur, a whisper heavy with the secret they shared.

Despite herself, she looked up, searching for his eyes but he'd turned to pick up his cigarettes. She dropped her eyes again, the pain of wanting him ballooning like hot steam in her chest, just below her collarbone. She removed her hand from his. Then he got up, taking her hand again and leaning over to kiss her lightly on the cheek.

"Com'on," he said. "Let's go."

She rose halfway out of the chair, finished her drink in one swallow, then let him lead her from the table. He held her hand clear to the doorway. A few people looked at them and she felt protected. When he felt her hesitate, he turned and winked at her. She let herself relax. *He waited,* she thought. *He was here, waiting, all the time.*

He took long steps, his short city boots hitting the floor in a cowboy's cadence. He stopped to maneuver her around a table, his shoulders blocking the glare of the neon sign above the bar. Everything about him suggested even lines: his legs, his arms, the angle of his jaw, his shoulders, even the razor-edge crease of his trousers cupping the bulge that sweetly curved into the nest of his crotch. His body was a little too thin, but he was wearing blue, the outfit she'd bought last week. A powdery blue jacket, the material soft, full of shadows and clouds of color, the nap rippling with each movement of his body. A diagonally cut zipper was partly opened, and his dark silk shirt contrasted with the softness of the jacket. Above the silk collar, his skin was velvety black.

Even in the doorway of the dimly lit bar, the sight of his smooth skin made her feel flushed. He led her to the sidewalk and as the door to the bar swung shut, he turned and waved to the bartender, and she noticed how the faint creases around his eyes and razor stubble on his chin added handsomeness to his face the way a pipe did for some men.

"The car," he gestured, "over there."

Quick. Too quick, she thought. He saw her frown.

"It's cool. Don't sweat it. I'm here, right? Can't stay in that room all night. Easy, baby, easy."

He led her across the street. She lowered her shoulders from their tensed hunch, trying to walk in long strides, trying to look as if she were about to enjoy the evening. Anyone could see she was with him. She was his. That was all. Nothing else. He walked close to her side, and she tried matching his pace, her hips swaying gently under the tightness of her skirt, her sandals flopping rhythmically, breaking the other noises of the street. When she looked down the length of the block, another BART train whipped past on its way to the city.

They reached the car. He put his hand on the handle, the gun metal grey of the door glinting slickly against the knobby weave of his jacket.

"You ok?" he asked.

She nodded. He gave her arm a reassuring squeeze and opened the car door. It opened soundlessly, the black leather seats sleek and smooth, almost breathing into the light that fell upon them. He blocked her view, the back of his neck catching the light as he leaned forward, leaned over the front seat toward the rear of the car.

"Mr. Preston? It's ok. She's here. You been real patient."

He stepped back, standing between her and the open car. His smile was smooth now, and he patted her cheek again before pushing a stray hair into place, and pulling her sweater squarely onto her shoulders.

"Fifty bucks, baby," he said. "I'll be in the Tambourine."

Then he kissed her forehead and moved aside, helping her into the back seat. She didn't turn to look at him as the door shut. She closed her eyes and pushed her body across the seat. The slickness of the leather licked her skirt, gripping and holding it above her knees. As she squirmed over the seat, she wet her lips again, smoothing the dryness out of the flesh.

She kept her eyes closed, holding onto his image, holding her squint and letting her face relax so that her lashes touched her cheeks. The man in the back seat breathed with a sharp intake. *A scotch drinker,* she thought. The man's rough hands moved swiftly past her knees to her wet crotch and she shuddered. But her thoughts were clear: she remembered her man, how he had smiled and the warm feeling when his hands brushed her face just before she'd slid into the car and the door had closed. She hoped he would be in a good mood when she got back to the Tambourine. Her sweater fell open and she let her body go soft, leaning into the seat, stroking the smooth leather with her free hand.

Reginald McKnight (1956–)

With attention to the intersections of race, gender, and social class, Reginald McKnight expands interpretation of African and African American history. Foregrounding connection between people of African descent through the fulcrum of the Middle Passage, like his predecessor Ralph Ellison and contemporary Toni Morrison, McKnight focuses on spiritual health. In McKnight's fiction, characters survive and achieve through creativity and acknowledgment of racial difference and heritage.

Reginald McKnight was born February 26, 1956, in Fürstenfeldbruck, Germany. He started his education at Pikes Peak Community College in Colorado Springs, Colorado, where he earned an associate's degree before continuing his education at Colorado College, where he earned a bachelor's degree in African literature. He earned a master's degree at Denver University in 1987.

McKnight's first collection of short stories, Moustapha's Eclipse (1988), was the end result of his Denver University master's thesis and won the Dur Heinz Literature Prize as well as an O Henry Award. The Kind of Light That Shines on Texas (1992), a second collection of short stories, was preceded by his first novel, I Get on the Bus (1990). In I Get on the Bus, McKnight draws on his own experience of teaching English as a second language in Senegal. In the novel, a Peach Corps volunteer, Evan, contracts malaria while in Senegal. As he recovers, a Senegalese woman tells him stories in a language he cannot understand. His sickness is not only literal, but symbolic of the way he is implicated, a part of a communal soul, in the destructive grip of history and colonialism. The line between illness and health is blurred and Evan cannot be cured by Western reason, but must have the spirit of African imagination to be restored to true health. Belief in spirit, magic, and imagination are the only means to Evan's healing, health, and continuance.

The stories in The Kind of Light That Shines on Texas center in the lives of post–Civil Rights, middle-class African Americans. In the title story, Clinton Oates is one of three Black children in a sixth-grade classroom in the heart of 1960s Texas. Each of the children survive in different ways, Ah-so, the girl, through silent attention, Marvin, big and ominous, through the silence of sleep, and Clint through "Uncle Tom" endurance of his teacher's racist jokes and persistent privileging of White children. Clint doesn't understand the politics of racism, knows that he has no more in common with Marvin or Ah-so than with many of the other children, but also knows that he is somehow bound to them despite the contradiction. Through the insight of a child, McKnight reveals the pain and pride of racial identity. In each of the stories in the collection, the protagonist, in search of self, is wary, uncertain of his circumstances and effect. With humor and insight, McKnight details the uncertainty of self-perception and environment, the conditions of rootlessness, and the persistence of cultural difference.

McKnight's third and most recent collection of short fiction, White Boys *(1998), also features characters from the Black middle class who are displaced and misunderstood. The protagonist of the title story is a young boy in Texas whose family is deeply affected by the tensions surrounding racist perceptions and fear. The young African American boy tries to trust a new White friend, neighbor, and classmate and tries to believe that their friendship is evidence of the disappearance of racism in contemporary American life, but he is cautious. His White friend is tortured by his family's racist hate, kept just beneath the surface of their relationship with their neighbors. Both come to understand that despite subtleties of appearance, racism still seethes. In settings ranging from Texas to Senegal, McKnight's characters realize the cultural difference does indeed matter despite their desire to reduce its impact in their own lives. His first-person narratives highlight the conflict between the self-perceptions of characters and their lived realities.*

In addition to his fiction, McKnight has published African American Wisdom *(1994), a collection of folk sayings and reflections on African American culture.*

R. Joyce Lausch

The Kind of Light That Shines on Texas

I never liked Marvin Pruitt. Never liked him, never knew him, even though there were only three of us in the class. Three black kids. In our school there were fourteen classrooms of thirty-odd white kids (in '66, they considered Chicanos provisionally white) and three or four black kids. Primary school in primary colors. Neat division. Alphabetized. They didn't stick us in the back, or arrange us by degrees of hue, apartheidlike. This was real integration, a ten-to-one ratio as tidy as upperclass landscaping. If it all worked, you could have ten white kids all to yourself. They could talk to you, get the feel of you, scrutinize you bone deep it they wanted to. They seldom wanted to, and that was fine with me for two reasons. The first was that their scrutiny was irritating. How do you comb your hair—why do you comb your hair—may I please touch your hair—were the kinds of questions they asked. This is no way to feel at home. The second reason was Marvin. He embarrassed me. He smelled bad, was at least two grades behind, was hostile, dark skinned, homely, close-mouthed. I feared him for his size, pitied him for his dress, watched him all the time. Marveled at him, mystified, astonished, uneasy.

He had the habit of spitting on his right arm, juicing it down till it would glisten. He would start in immediately after taking his seat when we'd finished with the Pledge of Allegiance, "The Yellow Rose of Texas," "The Eyes of Texas Are upon You," and "Mistress Shady." Marvin would rub his spit-flecked arm with his left hand, rub and roll as if polishing an ebony pool cue. Then he would rest his head in the crook of his arm, sniffing, huffing deep like black-jacket boys huff bagsful of acrylics. After ten minutes or so, his eyes would close, heavy. He would sleep till recess. Mrs. Wickham would let him.

There was one other black kid in our class. A girl they called Ah-so. I never learned what she did to earn this name. There was nothing Asian about this big-shouldered girl. She was the tallest, heaviest kid in school. She was quiet, but I don't think any one of us was subtle or sophisticated enough to nickname our classmates according to any but physical attributes. Fat kids were called Porky or Butterball, skinny ones were called Stick or Ichabod. Ah-so was big, thick, and African. She would impassively sit, sullen, silent as Marvin. She wore the same dark blue pleated skirt every day, the same ruffled white blouse every day. Her skin always shone as if worked by Marvin's palms and fingers. I never spoke one word to her, nor she to me.

Of the three of us, Mrs. Wickham called only on Ah-so and me. Ah-so never answered one question, correctly or incorrectly, so far as I can recall. She wasn't stupid. When asked to read aloud she read well, seldom stumbling over long word, reading with humor and expression. But when Wickham asked her about Farmer Brown and how many cows, or the capital of Vermont, or the date of this war or that, Ah-so never spoke. Not one word. But you always felt she could have answered those questions if she'd wanted to. I sensed no tension, embarrassment, or anger in Ah-so's reticence. She simply refused to speak. There was something unshakable about her, some core so impenetrably solid, you got the feeling that if you stood too close to her she could eat your thoughts like a black star eats light. I didn't despise Ah-so as I despised Marvin. There was nothing malevolent about her. She sat like a great icon in the back of the classroom, tranquil, guarded, sealed up, watchful. She was close to sixteen, and it was my guess she'd given up on school. Perhaps she was just obliging the wishes of her family, sticking it out till the law could no longer reach her.

There were at least half a dozen older kids in our class. Besides Marvin and Ah-so there was Oakley, who sat behind me, whispering threats into my ear; Varna Willard with the large breasts; Eddie Limon, who played bass for a high school rock band; and Lawrence Ridderbeck, who everyone said had a kid and a wife. You couldn't expect me to know anything about Texan educational practices of the 1960s, so I never knew why there were so many older kids in my sixth-grade class. After all, I was just a boy and had transferred into the school around midyear. My father, an air force sergeant, had been sent to Viet Nam. The air force sent my mother, my sister, Claire, and me to Connolly Air Force Base, which during the war housed "unaccompanied wives." I'd been to so many different schools in my short life that I ceased wondering about their differences. All I knew about the Texas schools is that they weren't afraid to flunk you.

Yet though I was only twelve then, I had a good idea why Wickham never once called on Marvin, why she let him snooze in the crook of his polished arm. I knew why she would press her lips together, and narrow her eyes at me whenever I correctly answered a question, rare as that was. I know why she badgered Ah-so with questions everyone knew Ah-so would never even consider answering. Wickham didn't like us. She wasn't gross about it, but it was clear she didn't want us around. She would prove her dislike day after day with little stories and jokes. "I just want to share with you all," she would say, "a little riddle my daughter told me at the supper table th'other day. Now, where do you go when you injure your knee?" Then one, two, or all three of her pets would say for the rest of us, "We don't know, Miz Wickham," in that skin-chilling way suck-asses speak, "where?" "Why, to Africa," Wickham would say, "where the knee grows."

The thirty-odd white kids would laugh, and I would look across the room at Marvin. He'd be asleep. I would glance back at Ah-so. She'd be sitting still as a projected image, staring down at her desk. I, myself, would smile at Wickham's stupid jokes, sometimes fake a laugh. I tried to show her that at least one of us was alive and alert, even though her jokes hurt. I sucked ass, too, I suppose. But I wanted her to understand more than anything that I was not like her other nigra children, that I was worthy of more than the non-attention and the negative attention she paid Marvin and Ah-so. I hated her, but never showed it. No one could safely contradict that woman. She knew all kinds of tricks to demean, control, and punish you. And she could swing her two-foot paddle as fluidly as a big-league slugger swings a bat. You didn't speak in Wickham's class unless she spoke to you first. You didn't chew gum, or wear "hood" hair. You didn't drag your feet, curse, pass notes, hold hands with the opposite sex. Most especially, you didn't say anything bad about the Aggies, Governor Connelly, LBJ, Sam Houston, or Waco. You did the forbidden and she would get you. It was that simple.

She never got me, though. Never gave her reason to. But she could have invented reasons. She did a lot of that. I can't be sure, but I used to think she pitied me because my father was in Viet Nam and my uncle A.J. had recently died there. Whenever she would tell one of her racist jokes, she would always glance at me, preface the joke with, "Now don't you nigra children take offense. This is all in fun, you know. I just want to share with you all something Coach Gilchrest told me th'other day." She would tell her joke, and glance at me again. I'd giggle, feeling a little queasy. "I'm half Irish," she would chuckle, "and you should hear some of those Irish jokes." She never told any, and I never really expected her to. I just did my Tom-thing. I kept my shoes shined, my desk neat, answered her questions as best I could, never brought gum to school, never cursed, never slept in class. I wanted to show her we were not all the same.

I tried to show them all, all thirty-odd, that I was different. It worked to some degree, but not very well. When some article was stolen from someone's locker or desk, Marvin, not I, was the first accused. I'd be second. Neither Marvin, nor Ah-so nor I were ever chosen for certain classroom honors—"Pledge leader," "flag holder," "noise monitor," "paper passer outer," but Mrs. Wickham once let me be "eraser duster." I was proud. I didn't even care about the cracks my fellow students made about my finally having turned the right color. I had done something that Marvin, in the deeps of his never-ending sleep, couldn't even dream of doing. Jack Preston, a kid who sat in front of me, asked me one day at recess whether I was embarrassed about Marvin. "Can you believe that guy?" I said. "He's like a pig or something. Makes me sick."

"Does it make you ashamed to be colored?"

"No," I said, but I meant yes. Yes, if you insist on thinking us all the same. Yes, if his faults are mine, his weaknesses inherent in me.

"I'd be," said Jack.

I made no reply. I was ashamed. Ashamed for not defending Marvin and ashamed that Marvin even existed. But if it had occurred to me, I would have asked Jack whether he was ashamed of being white because of Oakley. Oakley, "Oak Tree," Kelvin "Oak Tree" Oakley. He was sixteen and proud of it. He made it clear to everyone, including Wickham, that his life's ambition was to stay in school one more year, till he'd be old enough to enlist in the army. "Them slopes got my brother," he would say. "I'mna sign up and git me a few slopes. Gonna kill them bastards deader'n shit." Oakley, so far as anyone knew, was and always had been the oldest kid in his family. But no one contradicted him. He would, as anyone would tell you, "snap yer neck jest as soon as look at you." Not a boy in class, excepting Marvin and myself, had been able to avoid Oakley's pink bellies, Texas titty twisters, moon pie punches, or worse. He didn't bother Marvin, I suppose, because Marvin was closer to his size and age, and because Marvin spent five sixths of the school day asleep. Marvin probably never crossed Oakley's mind. And to say that Oakley hadn't bothered me is not to say he had no intention of ever doing so. In fact, this haphazard sketch of hairy fingers, slash of eyebrow, explosion of acne, elbows, and crooked teeth, swore almost daily that he'd like to kill me.

Naturally, I feared him. Though we were about the same height, he outweighed me by no less than forty pounds. He talked, stood, smoked, and swore like a man. No one, except for Mrs. Wickham, the principal, and the coach, ever laid a finger on him. And even Wickham knew that the hot lines she laid on him merely amused him. He would smile out at the classroom, goofy and bashful, as she laid down the two, five, or maximum ten strokes on him. Often he would wink, or surreptitiously flash us the thumb as Wickham worked on him. When she was finished, Oakley would walk so cool back to his seat you'd think he was on wheels. He'd slide into his chair, sniff the air, and say, "Somethin's burnin. Do y'all smell smoke? I swanee, I smell smoke and fahr back here." If he had made these cracks and never threatened me, I might have grown to admire Oakley, even liked him a little. But he hated me, and took every opportunity during the six-hour school day to make me aware of this. "Some Sambo's gittin his ass broke open one of these days," he'd mumble. "I wanna fight somebody. Need to keep in shape till I git to Nam."

I never said anything to him for the longest time. I pretended not to hear him, pretended not to notice his sour breath on my neck and ear. "Yep," he'd whisper. "Coonies keep y' in good shape for slope killin." Day in, day out, that's the kind of thing I'd pretend not to hear. But one day when the rain dropped down like lead balls, and the cold air made your skin look plucked, Oakley whispered to me, "My brother tells me it rains like this in Nam. Maybe I oughta go out at recess and break your ass open today. Nice and cool so you don't sweat. Nice and wet to clean up the blood." I said nothing for at least half a minute, then I turned half right and said, "Thought you said your brother was dead." Oakley, silent himself, for a time, poked me in the back with his pencil and hissed, *"Yer* dead." Wickham cut her eyes our way, and it was over.

It was hardest avoiding him in gym class. Especially when we played murderball. Oakley always aimed his throws at me. He threw with unblinking intensity, his teeth gritting, his neck veining, his face flushing, his black hair sweeping over one eye. He could throw hard, but the balls were squishy and harmless. In fact, I found his misses more intimidating than his hits. The balls would whizz by, thunder against the folded bleachers. They rattled as though a locomotive were passing through them. I would duck, dodge, leap as if he were throwing grenades. But he always hit me, sooner or later. And after a while I noticed that the other boys would avoid throwing at me, as if I belonged to Oakley.

One day, however, I was surprised to see that Oakley was throwing at everyone else but me. He was uncommonly accurate, too; kids were falling like tin cans. Since no one was throwing at me, I spent most of the game watching Oakley cut this one and that one down. Finally, he and I were the only ones left on the court. Try as he would, he couldn't hit me, nor I him. Coach Gilchrest blew his whistle and told Oakley and me to bring the red rubber balls to the equipment locker. I was relieved I'd escaped Oakley's stinging throws for once. I was feeling triumphant, full of myself. As Oakley and I approached Gilchrest, I thought about saying something friendly to Oakley: Good game, Oak Tree, I would say. Before I could speak, though, Gilchrest said, "All right boys, there's five minutes left in the period. Y'all are so good, looks like, you're gonna have to play like men. No boundaries, no catch outs, and you gotta hit your opponent three times in order to win. Got me?"

We nodded.

"And you're gonna use these," said Gilchrest, pointing to three volleyballs at his feet. "And you better believe they're pumped full. Oates, you start at that end of the court. Oak Tree, you're at th'other end. Just like usual, I'll set the balls at mid-court, and when I blow my whistle I want y'all to haul your cheeks to the middle and th'ow for all you're worth. Got me?" Gilchrest nodded at our nods, then added, "Remember, no boundaries, right?"

I at my end, Oakley at his, Gilchrest blew his whistle. I was faster than Oakley and scooped up a ball before he'd covered three quarters of his side. I aimed, threw, and popped him right on the knee. "One–zip!" I heard Gilchrest shout. The ball bounced off his knee and shot right back into my hands. I hurried my throw and missed. Oakley bent down, clutched the two remaining balls. I remember being amazed that he could palm each ball, run full out, and throw left-handed or right-handed without a shade of awkwardness. I spun, ran, but one of Oakley's throws glanced off the back of my head. "One–one!" hollered Gilchrest. I fell and spun on my ass as the other ball came sailing at me. I caught it. "He's out!" I yelled. Gilchrest's voice boomed, "No catch outs. Three hits. Three hits." I leapt to my feet as Oakley scrambled across the floor for another ball. I chased him down, leapt, and heaved the ball hard as he drew himself erect. The ball hit him dead in the face, and he went down flat. He rolled around, cupping his hands over his nose. Gilchrest sped to his side, helped him to his feet, asked him whether he was OK. Blood flowed from Oakley's nose, dripped in startlingly bright spots on the floor, his shoes, Gilchrest's shirt. The coach removed Oakley's T-shirt and pressed it against the big kid's nose to stanch the bleeding. As they walked past me toward the office I mumbled an apology to Oakley, but couldn't catch his reply. "You watch your filthy mouth, boy," said Gilchrest to Oakley.

The locker room was unnaturally quiet as I stepped into its steamy atmosphere. Eyes clicked in my direction, looked away. After I was out of my shorts, had my towel wrapped around me, my shower kit in hand, Jack Preston and Brian Nailor approached me. Preston's hair was combed slick and plastic looking. Nailor's stood up like frozen flames. Nailor smiled at me with his big teeth and pale eyes. He poked my arm with a finger. "You fucked up," he said.

"I tried to apologize."

"Won't do you no good," said Preston.

"I swanee," said Nailor.

"It's part of the game," I said. "It was an accident. Wasn't my idea to use volleyballs."

"Don't matter," Preston said. "He's jest lookin for an excuse to fight you."

"I never done nothing to him."

"Don't matter," said Nailor. "He don't like you."

"Brian's right, Clint. He'd jest as soon kill you as look at you."

"I never done nothing to him."

"Look," said Preston, "I know him pretty good. And jest between you and me, it's 'cause you're a city boy—"

"Whadda you mean? I've never—"

"He don't like your clothes—"

"And he don't like the fancy way you talk in class."

"What fancy—"

"I'm tellin him, if you don't mind, Brian."

"Tell him then."

"He don't like the way you say 'tennis shoes' instead of sneakers. He don't like coloreds. A whole bunch a things, really."

"I never done nothing to him. He's got no reason—"

"*And,*" said Nailor, grinning, "*and,* he says you're a stuck-up rich kid." Nailor's eyes had crow's-feet, bags beneath them. They were a man's eyes.

"My dad's a sergeant," I said.

"You chicken to fight him?" said Nailor.

"Yeah, Clint, don't be chicken. Jest go on and git it over with. He's whupped pert near ever'body else in the class. It ain't so bad."

"Might as well, Oates."

"Yeah, yer pretty skinny, but yer jest about his height. Jest git 'im in a headlock and don't let go."

"Goddamn," I said, "he's got no reason to—"

Their eyes shot right and I looked over my shoulder. Oakley stood at his locker, turning its tumblers. From where I stood I could see that a piece of cotton was wedged up one of his nostrils, and he already had the makings of a good shiner. His acne burned red like a fresh abrasion. He snapped the locker open and kicked his shoes off without sitting. Then he pulled off his shorts, revealing two paddle stripes on his ass. They were fresh red bars speckled with white, the white speckles being the reverse impression of the paddle's suction holes. He must not have watched his filthy mouth while in Gilchrest's presence. Behind me, I heard Preston and Nailor pad to their lockers.

Oakley spoke without turning around. "Somebody's gonna git his skinny black ass kicked, right today, right after school." He said it softly. He slipped his jock off, turned around. I looked away. Out the corner of my eye I saw him stride off, his hairy nakedness a weapon clearing the younger boys from his path. Just before he rounded the corner of the shower stalls, I threw my toilet kit to the floor and stammered, "I—I never did nothing to you, Oakley." He stopped, turned, stepped closer to me, wrapping his towel around himself. Sweat streamed down my rib cage. It felt like ice water. "You wanna go at it right now, boy?"

"I never did nothing to you." I felt tears in my eyes. I couldn't stop them even though I was blinking like mad. "Never."

He laughed. "You busted my nose, asshole."

"What about before? What'd I ever do to you?"

"See you after school, Coonie." Then he turned away, flashing his acne-spotted back like a semaphore. "Why?" I shouted. "Why you wanna fight me?" Oakley stopped and turned, folded his arms, leaned against a toilet stall. "Why you wanna fight *me*, Oakley?" I stepped over the bench. "What'd I do? Why me?" And then unconsciously, as if scratching, as if breathing, I walked toward Marvin, who stood a few feet from Oakley, combing his hair at the mirror. "Why not him?" I said. "How come you're after *me* and not *him*?" The room froze. Froze for a moment that was both evanescent and eternal, somewhere between an eye blink and a week in hell. No one moved, nothing happened; there was no sound at all. And then it was as if all of us at the same moment looked at Marvin. He just stood there, combing away, the only body in motion, I think. He combed his hair and combed it, as if seeing only his image, hearing only his comb scraping his scalp. I knew he'd heard me. There's no way he could not have heard me. But all he did was slide the comb into his pocket and walk out the door.

"I got no quarrel with Marvin," I heard Oakley say. I turned toward his voice, but he was already in the shower.

I was able to avoid Oakley at the end of the school day. I made my escape by asking Mrs. Wickham if I could go to the rest room.

"'Rest room,'" Oakley mumbled. "It's a damn toilet, sissy."

"Clinton," said Mrs. Wickham. "Can you *not* wait till the bell rings? It's almost three o'clock."

"No ma'am," I said, "I won't make it."

"Well I should make you wait just to teach you to be more mindful about . . . hygiene . . . uh things." She sucked in her cheeks, squinted. "But I'm feeling charitable today. You may go." I immediately left the building, and got on the bus. "Ain't you a little early?" said the bus driver, swinging the door shut. "Just left the office," I said. The driver nodded, apparently not giving me a second thought. I had no idea why I'd told her I'd come from the office, or why she found it a satisfactory answer. Two minutes later the bus filled, rolled, and shook its way to Connolly Air Base. When I got home, my mother was sitting in the living room, smoking her Slims, watching her soap opera. She absently asked me how my day had gone and I told her fine. "Hear from Dad?" I said.

"No, but I'm sure he's fine." She always said that when we hadn't heard from him in a while. I suppose she thought I was worried about him, or that I felt vulnerable without him. It was neither. I just wanted to discuss something with my mother that we both cared about. If I spoke with her about things that happened at school, or on my weekends, she'd listen with half an ear, say something like, "Is that so?" or "You don't say?" I couldn't stand that sort of thing. But when I mentioned my father, she treated me a bit more like an adult, or at least someone who was worth listening to. I didn't want to feel like a boy that afternoon. As I turned from my mother and walked down the hall I thought about the day my father left for Viet Nam. Sharp in his uniform, sure behind his aviator specs, he slipped a cigar from his pocket and stuck it in mine. "Not till I get back," he said. "We'll have us one when we go fishing. Just you and me, out on the lake all day, smoking and casting and sitting. Don't let Mama see it. Put it in y'back pocket." He hugged me, shook my hand, and told me I was the man of the house now. He told me he was depending on me to take good care of my mother and sister. "Don't you let me down, now, hear?" And he tapped his thick finger on my chest. "You almost as big as me. Boy, you something else." I believed him when he told me those things. My heart swelled big enough to swallow my father, my mother, Claire. I loved, feared, and respected myself, my manhood. That day I could have put all of Waco, Texas, in my heart. And it wasn't till about three months later that I discovered I really wasn't the man of the house, that my mother and sister, as they always had, were taking care of me.

For a brief moment I considered telling my mother about what had happened at school that day, but for one thing, she was deep down in the halls of *General Hospital,* and never paid you much mind till it was over. For another thing, I just wasn't the kind of person—I'm still not, really—to discuss my problems with anyone. Like my father I kept things to myself, talked about my problems only in retrospect. Since my father wasn't around I consciously wanted to be like him, doubly like him, I could say. I wanted to be the man of the house in some respect, even if it had to be in an inward way. I went to my room, changed my clothes, and laid out my homework. I couldn't focus on it. I thought about Marvin, what I'd said about him or done to him—I couldn't tell which. I'd done something to him, said something about him; said something about and done something to myself. *How come you're after me and not him?* I kept trying to tell myself I hadn't meant it that way. *That* way. I thought about approaching Marvin, telling him what I really meant was that he was more Oakley's age and weight than I. I would tell him I meant I was no match for Oakley. *See, Marvin,* what I meant was that he wants to fight a colored guy, but is afraid to fight you 'cause you could beat him. But try as I did, I couldn't for a moment convince myself that Marvin would believe me. I meant it *that* way and no other. Everybody heard. Everybody knew. That afternoon I forced myself to confront the notion that tomorrow I would probably have to fight both Oakley and Marvin. I'd have to be two men.

I rose from my desk and walked to the window. The light made my skin look orange, and I started thinking about what Wickham had told us once about light. She said that oranges and apples, leaves and flowers, the whole muticolored world, was not what it appeared to be. The colors we see, she said, look like they do only because of the light or ray that shines on them. "The color of the thing isn't what you see, but the light that's reflected off it." Then she shut out the lights and shone a white light lamp on a prism. We watched the pale splay of colors on the projector screen; some people oohed and aahed. Suddenly, she switched on a black light and the color of everything changed. The prism colors vanished, Wickham's arms were purple, the buttons of her dress were as orange as hot coals, rather than the blue they had been only seconds before. We were all very quiet. "Nothing," she said, after a while, "is really what it appears to be." I didn't really understand then. But as I stood at the window, gazing at my orange skin, I wondered what kind of light I could shine on Marvin, Oakley, and me that would reveal us as the same.

I sat down and stared at my arms. They were dark brown again. I worked up a bit of saliva under my tongue and spat on my left arm. I spat again, then rubbed the spittle into it, polishing, working till my arm grew warm. As I spat, and rubbed, I wondered why Marvin did this weird, nasty thing to himself, day after day. Was he trying to rub away the black, or deepen it, doll it up? And if he did this weird nasty thing for a hundred years, would he spit-shine himself invisible, rolling away the eggplant skin, revealing the scarlet muscle, blue vein, pink and yellow tendon, white bone? Then disappear? Seen through, all colors, no colors. Spitting and rubbing. Is this the way you do it? I leaned forward, sniffed the arm. It smelled vaguely of mayonnaise. After an hour or so, I fell asleep.

I saw Oakley the second I stepped off the bus the next morning. He stood outside the gym in his usual black penny loafers, white socks, high-water jeans, T-shirt, and black jacket. Nailor stood with him, his big teeth spread across his bottom lip like playing cards. If there was anyone I felt like fighting, that day, it was Nailor. But I wanted to put off fighting for as long as I could. I stepped toward the gymnasium, thinking that I shouldn't run, but if I hurried I could beat Oakley to the door and secure myself near Gilchrest's office. But the moment I stepped into the gym, I felt Oakley's broad palm clap down on my shoulder. "Might as well stay out here, Connie," he said. "I need me a little target practice." I turned to face him and he slapped me, one-two, with the back, then the palm of his hand, as I'd seen Bogart do to Peter Lorre in *The Maltese Falcon*. My heart went wild. I could scarcely breathe. I couldn't swallow.

"Call me a nigger," I said. I have no idea what made me say this. All I know is it kept me from crying. "Call me a nigger, Oakley."

"Fuck you, ya black-ass slope." He slapped me again, scratching my eye. "I don't do what coonies tell me."

"Call me a nigger."

"Outside, Coonie."

"Call me one. Go ahead!"

He lifted his hand to slap me again, but before his arm could swing my way, Marvin Pruitt came from behind me and calmly pushed me aside. "Git out my way, boy," he said. And he slugged Oakley on the side of his head. Oakley stumbled back, stiff-legged. His eyes were big. Marvin hit him twice more, once again to the side of the head, once to the nose. Oakley went down and stayed down. Though blood was drawn, whistles blowing, fingers pointing, kids hollering, Marvin just stood there, staring at me with cool eyes. He spat on the ground, licked his lips, and just stared at me, till Coach Gilchrest and Mr. Calderon tackled him and violently carried him away. He never struggled, never took his eyes off me.

Nailor and Mrs. Wickham helped Oakley to his feet. His already fattened nose bled and swelled so that I had to look away. He looked around, bemused, wall-eyed, maybe scared. It was apparent he had no idea how bad he was hurt. He didn't blink. He didn't even touch his nose. He didn't look like he knew much of anything. He looked at me, looked me dead in the eye, in fact, but didn't seem to recognize me.

That morning, like all other mornings, we said the Pledge of Allegiance, sang "The Yellow Rose of Texas," "The Eyes of Texas Are upon You," and "Mistress Shady." The room stood strangely empty without Oakley, and without Marvin, but at the same time you could feel their presence more intensely somehow. I felt like I did when I'd walk into my mother's room and could smell my father's cigars or cologne. He was more palpable, in certain respects, than when there in actual flesh. For some reason, I turned to look at Ah-so, and just this once I let my eyes linger on her face. She had a very gentle-looking face, really. That surprised me. She must have felt my eyes on her because she glanced up at me for a second and smiled, white teeth, downcast eyes. Such a pretty smile. That surprised me too. She held it for a few seconds, then let it fade. She looked down at her desk, and sat still as a photograph.

James Alan McPherson (1943–)

In advertising his first collection of short fiction, Hue and Cry *(1969), McPherson wrote: "It is my hope that this collection of stories can be read as a book about people, all kinds of people: old, young, lonely, homosexual, confused, used, discarded, wronged. As a matter of fact, certain of these people happen to be black, and certain of them happen to be white; but I have tried to keep the color part of most of them far in the background, where these things should rightly be kept." This statement communicates McPherson's valuing of craft and the universality of human experience. Sometimes criticized and sometimes praised for his stance, especially in context of his literary beginnings in simultaneity with the Black Arts movement that advocated recognition and affirmation of cultural difference, McPherson's work adds to the spectrum of literary production of the late 1960s and the 1970s.*

James Alan McPherson was born September 16, 1943, in Savannah, Georgia. With a mother who was a domestic worker and an electrician father, McPherson grew up in a working class Black community and was aided by the patronage of his parents' White friends. The importance of his parents' White friends and their contributions to his life taught McPherson the politics and arbitrariness of the color line; he credits his development as an individual and as a writer to both communities.

Though he attended segregated schools, McPherson learned that education was the way he could surmount Jim Crow politics. He determined to get a good education beyond high school through whatever means were offered. He attended Morgan State University in Maryland for a short time as an exchange student, before transferring to and earning a bachelor's degree from Morris Brown College in Atlanta in 1965. The same year he graduated from Morris Brown, he began studies at Harvard Law School.

Balancing his study and his love of writing, McPherson wrote and submitted stories for publication. His second short story, "Gold Coast," won a fiction contest sponsored by the At-lantic Monthly. McPherson completed his law degree in 1968, however, before moving on to teach writing at the law school and work on his M.F.A. degree at the University of Iowa.

The politics of McPherson's short stories are conservative, more in line with Civil Rights movement than with the Black Power movement of the 1960s. While McPherson worked as janitor his first year at Harvard and two school years at Morris Brown, he also benefited from minority student recruitment and a union dispute that allowed him otherwise unavailable summer work as a waiter. In fact, most of McPherson's college work was as a waiter on the Northern Railroad, a job that translated into the content of many of his short stories. In his first collection of stories, Hue and Cry, *for example, "Solo Song for Doc" and "On Trains" are both set in the context of the railroad industry.*

McPherson's short stories of the 1960s and 1970s bring African American issues of identity to the center, while addressing issues of age, race, class, and gender discrimination in intersection. Against all forms of discrimination, McPherson creates characters who embody diverse cultures, people moving beyond stereotype. Centering the human condition and relationships, the ironies and paradoxes of American life, especially concerning race, drive the responses of his characters and inform the difficulties they have connecting to each other. His characters embody resiliency and value systems and habits that are dying out under the pressure of paradox. McPherson's background as young, gifted, enterprising, and Southern creeps into his characters as he reconciles American and Southern aspects of Black identity.

Ralph Ellison, himself a believer in privileging craft, was a major influence and big supporter of Hue and Cry. The collection was very well-received, earning McPherson a National Institute of Arts and Letters grant and a Rockefeller grant in 1970 and a Guggenheim fellowship in 1972. The collection emphasized integration and cultural pluralism and craft over politics in a time when alternative philosophies of the Black Arts movement were dominant.

His second collection, Elbow Room (1977), was honored with a Pulitzer Prize and also aided McPherson in becoming one of the first Black writers to receive the MacArthur Foundation grant, an award he was given in 1981. The stories in Elbow Room are multivoiced and contemporary. In "The Story of a Scar," the narrator and a woman in the waiting room of a doctor's office share the spotlight. The woman tells the narrator the "story" of a dark purple and jagged scar running down the left side of her face, a story filled with rough jealousy and the complexities of gender identity, concepts of masculinity, and racial unity. The conversation of the narrator and the woman serves as frame for the story she tells, disrupting the flow of the past with reminder of the present. She claims authority, yet also remains anonymous, a subtle and powerful move that lingers in the final question of the story. The story highlights the fact that too often conflicts of identity and misunderstanding result in violence to others.

McPherson's most recent work, Crabcakes (1998), is a collection of short, interrelated prose pieces, on the border of memoir. The pieces that carry the heft of the project focus on a house McPherson purchased in Baltimore, the two elderly Black people who lived there for the small amount McPherson asked as rent, and the way his purchase and obligation to them filters into his life. A second emphasis in the work is McPherson's discussion and relation of Eastern philosophies to events in his life.

McPherson has held short professorships at University of Iowa (1968–1969), the University of Santa Cruz (1969), Morgan State University (1969–1970), and the University of Virginia (1976–1981).

R. Joyce Lausch

The Story of a Scar

Since Dr. Wayland was late and there were no recent newsmagazines in the waiting room, I turned to the other patient and said: "As a concerned person, and as your brother, I ask you, without meaning to offend, how did you get that scar on the side of your face?'

The woman seemed insulted. Her brown eyes, which before had been wandering vacuously about the room, narrowed suddenly and sparked humbling reprimands at me. She took a draw on her cigarette, puckered her lips, and blew

a healthy stream of smoke toward my face. It was a mean action, deliberately ir-
reverent and cold. The long curving scar on the left side of her face darkened. "I
ask *you*," she said, "as a nosy person with no connections in your family, how
come your nose is all bandaged up?"

It was a fair question, considering the possible returns on its answer. Dr. Wayland would remove the bandages as soon as he came in. I would not be asked again.
A man lacking permanence must advertise. "An accident of passion," I told her. "I
smashed it against the headboard of my bed while engaged in the act of love."

Here she laughed, but not without intimating, through heavy, broken
chuckles, some respect for my candor and the delicate cause of my affliction.
This I could tell from the way the hardness mellowed in her voice. Her appetites
were whetted. She looked me up and down, almost approvingly, and laughed
some more. This was a robust woman, with firm round legs and considerable
chest. I am small. She laughed her appreciation. Finally, she lifted a brown palm
to her face, wiping away tears. "You *cain't* be no married man," she observed. "A
wife ain't worth *that* much."

I nodded.

"I knowed it," she said. "The best mens don't git married. They do they
fishin' in goldfish bowls."

"I am no adulterer," I cautioned her. "I find companionship wherever I can."

She quieted me by throwing out her arm in a suggestion of offended modesty. She scraped the cigarette on the white tile beneath her foot. "You don't have
to tell me a thing," she said. "I know mens goin' and comin'. There ain't a-one of
you I'd trust to take my grandmama to Sunday school." Here she paused, seemingly lost in some morbid reflection, her eyes wandering across the room to Dr.
Wayland's frosted glass door. The solemnity of the waiting room reclaimed us.
We inhaled the antiseptic fumes that wafted from the inner office. We breathed
deeply together, watching the door, waiting. "Not a-one," my companion said
softly, her dark eyes wet.

The scar still fascinated me. It was a wicked black mark that ran from her
brow down over her left eyelid, skirting her nose but curving over and through
both lips before ending almost exactly in the center of her chin. The scar was
thick and black and crisscrossed with a network of old stitch patterns, as if some
meticulous madman had first attempted to carve a perfect half-circle in her flesh,
and then decided to embellish his handiwork. It was so grotesque a mark that
one had the feeling it was the art of no human hand and could be peeled off like
so much soiled putty. But this was a surgeon's office and the scar was real. It was
as real as the honey-blond wig she wore, as real as her purple pantsuit. I studied
her approvingly. Such women have a natural leaning toward the abstract expression of themselves. Their styles have private meanings, advertise secret distilla-
tions of their souls. Their figures, and their disfigurations, make meaningful
statements. Subjectively, this woman was the true sister of the man who knows
how to look while driving a purple Cadillac. Such craftsmen must be approached
with subtlety if they are to be deciphered. "I've never seen a scar quite like that
one," I began, glancing at my watch. Any minute Dr. Wayland would arrive and

take off my bandages, removing me permanently from access to her sympathies. "Do you mind talking about what happened?"

"I *knowed* you'd git back around to that," she answered, her brown eyes cruel and level with mine. "Black guys like you with them funny eyeglasses are a real trip. You got to know everything. You sit in corners and watch people." She brushed her face, then wiped her palm on the leg of her pantsuit. "I read you the minute you walk in here."

"As your brother . . ." I began.

"How can you be my brother when your mama's a man?" she said.

We both laughed.

"I was pretty once," she began, sniffing heavily. "When I was sixteen my mama's preacher was set to leave his wife and his pulpit and run off with me to *Deetroit* City. Even with this scar and all the weight I done put on, you can still see what I had." She paused. "*Cain't* you?" she asked significantly.

I nodded quickly, looking into her big body for the miniature of what she was.

From this gesture she took assurance. "I was twenty when it happen," she went on. "I had me a good job in the post office, down to the Tenth Street branch. I was a sharp dresser, too, and I had me my choice of mens; big ones, puny ones, old mens, married mens, even D. B. Ferris, my shift supervisor, was after me on the sly—don't let these white mens fool you. He offered to take me off the primaries and turn me on to a desk job in hand-stampin' or damaged mail. But I had my pride. I told him I rather work the facin' table, *every shift,* than put myself in his debt. I shook my finger in his face and said, 'You ain't foolin' me, with your *sly self!* I know where the *wild goose went;* and if you don't start havin' some *respect* for black women, he go'n come *back!*' So then he turn red in the face and put me on the facin' table. Every shift. What could I do? You ain't got no rights in the post office, no matter what lies the government tries to tell you. But I was makin' good money, dressin' bad, and I didn't want to start no trouble for myself. Besides, in them days there was a bunch of good people workin' my shift: Leroy Boggs, Red Bone, 'Big Boy' Tyson, Freddy May . . ."

"What about that scar?" I interrupted her tiresome ramblings. "Which one of them cut you?"

Her face flashed a wall of brown fire. "This here's *my* story!" she muttered, eyeing me up and down with suspicion. "You dudes cain't stand to hear the whole of anything. You want everything broke down in little pieces." And she waved a knowing brown finger. "That's how come you got your nose all busted up. There's some things you have to take your time about."

Again I glanced at my watch, but was careful to nod silent agreement with her wisdom. "It was my boyfriend that caused it," she continued in a slower, more cautious tone. "And the more I look at you the more I can see you just like him. He had that same way of sittin' with his legs crossed, squeezin' his sex juices up to his brains. His name was Billy Crawford, and he worked the parcel-post window down to the Tenth Street branch. He was nine years older than me and was goin' to school nights on the GI Bill. I was twenty when I met him durin' lunch break down in the swing room. He was sittin' at a table against the wall, by hisself, eatin' a cheese sandwich with his nose in a goddamn book. I didn't know any better then. I sat down by him. He looked up at me and say, 'Water seeks its own level, and people do, too. You are not one of the riffraff or else you would of sit with them good-timers and bullshitters 'cross the room. Welcome to my table.' By riffraff he meant all them other dudes and girls from the back room, who believed in havin' a little fun playin' cards and such durin' lunch hour. I thought what he said was kind of funny, and so I laughed. But I should of knowed better. He give me a cheese sandwich and started right off preachin' at me about the lowlife in the back room. Billy couldn't stand none of 'em. He hated the way they dressed, the way they talked, and the way they carried on durin' work hours. He said if all them tried to be like him and advanced themselfs, the Negro wouldn't have no problems. He'd point out Eugene Wells or Red Bone or Crazy Sammy Michaels and tell me, 'People like them think they can homestead in the post office. They think these primaries will need human hands for another twenty years. But you just watch the Jews and Puerto Ricans that pass through here. *They* know what's goin' on. I bet you don't see none of them settin' up their beds under these tables. They tryin' to improve themselfs and get out of here, just like me.' Then he smile and held out his hand. 'And since I see you're a smart girl that keeps a cold eye and some distance on these bums, welcome to the club. My name's Billy Crawford.'

"To tell you the truth, I liked him. He was different from all the jive-talkers and finger-poppers I knew. I liked him because he wasn't ashamed to wear a white shirt and a black tie. I liked the way he always knew just what he was gonna do next. I liked him because none of the other dudes could stand him, and he didn't seem to care. On our first date he took me out to a place where the white waiters didn't git mad when they saw us comin'. That's the kind of style he had. He knew how to order wine with funny names, the kind you don't never see on billboards. He held open doors for me, told me not to order rice with gravy over it or soda water with my meal. I didn't mind him helpin' me. He was a funny dude in a lot of ways: his left leg was shot up in the war and he limped sometimes, but it looked like he was struttin'. He would stare down anybody that watched him walkin'. He told me he had cut his wife loose after he got out of the army, and he told me about some of the games she had run on him. Billy didn't trust women. He said they all was after a workin' man's money, but he said that I was different. He said he could tell I was a God-fearin' woman and my mama had raised me right, and he was gonna improve my mind. In those days I didn't have no objections. Billy was fond of sayin', 'You met me at the right time in your life.'

"But Red Bone, my co-worker, saw what was goin' down and began to take a strong interest in the affair. Red was the kind of strong-minded sister that mens just like to give in to. She was one of them big yellow gals, with red hair and a loud rap that could put a man in his place by just soundin' on him. She like to wade through the mail-room, elbowin' dudes aside and sayin', 'You don't wanna mess with *me,* fool! I'll *destroy* you! Anyway, you ain't nothin' but a dirty thought I had when I was three years old!' But if she liked you she could be warm and soft, like a mama. 'Listen,' she kept tellin' me, 'that Billy Crawford is a potential punk. The more I watch him, the less man I see. Every time we downstairs havin' fun I catch his eyeballs rollin' over us from behind them goddamn books! There ain't a rhythm in his body, and the only muscles he exercises is in his eyes.'

"That kind of talk hurt me some, especially comin' from her. But I know it's the way of some women to bad-mouth a man they want for themselfs. And what woman don't want a steady man and a good provider?—which is what Billy was. Usually, when they start downgradin' a steady man, you can be sure they up to somethin' else besides lookin' out after you. So I told her, 'Billy don't have no bad habits.' I told her, 'He's a hard worker, he don't drink, smoke, nor run around, and he's gonna git a *college* degree.' But that didn't impress Red. I was never able to fig-ure it out, but she had something in for Billy. Maybe it was his attitude; maybe it was the little ways he let everybody know that he was just passin' through; maybe it was because Red had broke every man she ever had and had never seen a man with no handholes on him. Because that Billy Crawford was a strong man. He worked the day shift, and could of been a supervisor in three or four years if he wanted to crawl a little and grease a few palms; but he did his work, quiet-like, pulled what overtime he could, and went to class three nights a week. On his day off he'd study and maybe take me out for a drink after I got off. Once or twice a week he might let me stay over at his place, but most of the time he'd take me home to my Aunt Alvene's, where I was roomin' in those days, before twelve o'clock.

"To tell the truth, I didn't really miss the partyin' and the dancin' and the good-timin' until Red and some of the others started avoidin' me. Down in the swing room durin' lunch hour, for example, they wouldn't wave for me to come over and join a card game. Or when Leroy Boggs went around to the folks on the floor of the mail room, collectin' money for a party, he wouldn't even ask me to put a few dollars in the pot. He'd just smile at me in a cold way and say to some-body loud enough for me to hear, 'No, sir; ain't no way you can git quality folk to come out to a Saturday night fish fry.'

"Red squared with me when I asked her what was goin' down. She told me, 'People sayin' you been wearin' a high hat since you started goin' with the profes-sor. The talk is you been throwin' around big words and developin' a strut just like his. Now I don't believe these reports, being your friend and sister, but I do think you oughta watch your step. I remember what my grandmama used to tell me: "It don't make no difference how well you fox-trot if everybody else is dancin' the two-step." Besides, that Billy Crawford is a potential punk, and you gonna be one lonely girl when somebody finally turns him out. Use your mind, girl, and stop bein' silly. Everybody is watchin' you!'

"I didn't say nothin', but what Red said started me to thinkin' harder than I had ever thought before. Billy had been droppin' strong hints that we might git married after he got his degree, in two or three years. He was plannin' on being a high school teacher. But outside of being married to a teacher, what was I go'n git out of it? Even if we did git married, I was likely to be stuck right there in the post office with no friends. And if he didn't marry me, or if he was a punk like Red believed, then I was a real dummy for givin' up my good times and my best days for a dude that wasn't go'n do nothin' for me. I didn't make up my mind right then, but I begin to watch Billy Crawford with a different kind of eye. I'd just turn around at certain times and catch him in his routines: readin', workin', eatin', runnin' his mouth about the same things all the time. Pretty soon I didn't have to watch him to know what he was doin'. He was more regular than Monday mornings. That's when a woman begins to tip. It ain't never a decision, but somethin' in you starts to lean over and practice what you gonna say whenever another man bumps into you at the right time. Some women, especially married ones, like to tell lies to their new boyfriends; if the husband is a hard worker and a good provider, they'll tell the boyfriend that he's mean to them and ain't no good when it comes to sex; and if he's good with sex, they'll say he's a cold dude that's not concerned with the problems of the world like she is, or that they got married too young. Me, I believe in tellin' the truth: that Billy Crawford was too good for most of the women in this world, me included. He deserved better, so I started lookin' round for somebody on my own level.

"About this time a sweet-talkin' young dude was transferred to our branch from the 39th Street substation. The grapevine said it was because he was makin' woman-trouble over there and caused too many fights. I could see why. He dressed like he was settin' fashions every day; wore special-made bell-bottoms with so much flare they looked like they was starched. He wore two diamond rings on the little finger of his left hand that flashed while he was throwin' mail, and a gold tooth that sparkled all the time. His name was Teddy Johnson, but they called him 'Eldorado' because that was the kind of hog he drove. He was involved in numbers and other hustles and used the post office job for a front. He was a strong talker, a easy walker, that dude was a *woman* stalker! I have to give him credit. He was the last *true* son of the Great McDaddy—"

"Sister," I said quickly, overwhelmed suddenly by the burden of insight. "I *know* the man of whom you speak. There is no time for this gutter-patter and indirection. Please, for my sake and for your own, avoid stuffing the shoes of the small with mythic homilies. This man was a bum, a hustler and a small-time punk. He broke up your romance with Billy, then he lived off you, cheated on you, and cut you when you confronted him." So pathetic and gross seemed her elevation of the fellow that I abandoned all sense of caution. "Is your mind so *dead,*" I continued, "did his switchblade slice so *deep,* do you have so little *respect* for yourself, or at least for the idea of *proportion* in this sad world, that you'd sit here and *praise* this brute!?"

She lit a second cigarette. Then, dropping the match to the floor, she seemed to shudder, to struggle in contention with herself. I sat straight on the blue plastic couch, waiting. Across the room the frosted glass door creaked, as if about to open; but when I looked, I saw no telling shadow behind it. My companion crossed her legs and held back her head, blowing two thoughtful streams of smoke from her broad nose. I watched her nervously, recognizing the evidence of past destructiveness, yet fearing the imminent occurrence of more. But it was not her temper or the potential strength of her fleshy arms that I feared. Finally she sighed, her face relaxed, and she wet her lips with the tip of her tongue. "You know everything," she said in a soft tone, much unlike her own. "A black mama birthed you, let you suck her titty, cleaned your dirty drawers, and you still look at us through paper and movie plots." She paused, then continued in an even softer and more controlled voice. "Would you believe me if I said that Teddy Johnson loved me, that this scar is to him what a weddin' ring is to another man? Would you believe that he was a better man than Billy?"

I shook my head in firm disbelief.

She seemed to smile to herself, although the scar, when she grimaced, made the expression more like a painful frown. "Then would you believe that I was the cause of Billy Crawford goin' crazy and not gettin' his college degree?"

I nodded affirmation.

"Why?" she asked.

"Because," I answered, "from all I know already, that would seem to be the most likely consequence. I would expect the man to have been destroyed by the pressures placed on him. And, although you are my sister and a woman who has already suffered greatly, I must condemn you and your roughneck friends for this destruction of a man's ambitions."

Her hardened eyes measured my face. She breathed heavily, seeming to grow larger and rounder on the red chair. "My brother," she began in an icy tone, "is as far from what you are as I am from being patient." Now her voice became deep and full, as if aided suddenly by some intricately controlled wellspring of pain. Something aristocratic and old and frighteningly wise seemed to have awakened in her face. "Now this is the way it happened," she fired at me, her eyes wide and rolling. I want you to *write* it on whatever part of your brain that ain't already covered with page print. I want you to *remember* it every time you stare at a scarred-up sister on the street, and *choke* on it before you can work up spit to condemn her. I was *faithful* to that Billy Crawford. As faithful as a woman could be to a man that don't ever let up or lean back and stop worryin' about where he's gonna be ten years from last week. Life is to be *lived,* not traded on like *dollars!* . . . All that time I was goin' with him, my feets itched to dance, my ears hollered to hear somethin' besides that whine in his voice, my body wanted to press up against somethin's besides that facin' table. I was young and pretty; and what woman don't want to enjoy what she got while she got it? Look around sometime: there ain't *no mens,* young nor old, chasin' *no older womens,* no matter how pretty they *used to be!* But Billy Crawford couldn't see nothin' besides them *goddamn books* in front of his face. And what the Jews and Puerto Ricans was doin'. Whatever else Teddy Johnson was, he was a dude that knowed how to live. He wasn't out to *destroy* life, you can believe *that!* Sure I listened to his rap. Sure I give him the come-on. With Billy workin' right up front and watchin' everything, Teddy was the only dude on the floor that would talk to me. Teddy would say, 'A girl that's got what you got needs a man that have what I have.' And that ain't all he said, either!

"Red Bone tried to push me closer to him, but I am not a sneaky person and didn't pay her no mind. She'd say, 'Girl, I think you and Eldorado ought to git it on. There ain't a better lookin' dude workin' in the post office. Besides, you ain't goin' *nowheres* with that professor Billy Crawford. And if *you* scared to tell him to lean up off you, I'll do it *myself,* bein' as I am your sister and the one with your interest in mind.' But I said to her, 'Don't do me no favors. No matter what you think of Billy, I am no sneaky woman. I'll handle my own affairs.' Red just grin and look me straight in the eye and grin some more. I already told you she was the kind of strong-minded sister that could look right down into you. Nobody but a woman would understand what she was lookin' at.

"Now Billy wasn't no dummy durin' all this time. Though he worked the parcel-post window up front, from time to time durin' the day he'd walk back in the mail room and check out what was goin' down. Or else he'd sit back and listen to the gossip durin' lunch hour, down in the swing room. He must of seen Teddy Johnson hangin' round me, and I know he seen Teddy give me the glad-eye a few times. Billy didn't say nothin' for a long time, but one day he pointed to Teddy and told me, 'See that fellow over there? He's a bloodletter. There's some people with a talent for stoppin' bleedin' by just being around, and there's others that start it the same way. When you see that greasy smile of his you can bet it's soon gonna be a bad day for somebody, if they ain't careful. That kind of fellow's been walkin' free for too long.' He looked at me with that tight mouth and them cold brown eyes of his. He said, 'You know what I mean?' I said I didn't. He said, 'I hope you don't ever have to find out.'

"It was D. B. Ferris, my shift supervisor, that set up things. He's the same dude I told you about, the one that was gonna give me the happy hand. We never saw much of him in the mail room, although he was kinda friendly with Red Bone. D. B. Ferris was always up on the ramps behind one of the wall slits, checkin' out everything that went down on the floor and tryin' to catch somebody snitchin' a letter. There ain't no tellin' how much he knew about private things goin' on. About this time he up and transferred three or four of us, the ones with no seniority, to the night shift. There was me, Red, and Leroy Boggs. When Billy found out he tried to talk D. B. Ferris into keepin' me on the same shift as his, but Ferris come to me and I told him I didn't mind. And I didn't. I told him I was tired of bein' watched by him and everybody else. D. B. Ferris looked up toward the front where Billy was workin' and smiled that old smile of his. Later, when Billy asked me what I said, I told him there wasn't no use tryin' to fight the government. 'That's true,' he told me—and I thought I saw some meanness in his eyes—'but there are some other things you can fight,' he said. At that time my head was kinda light, and I didn't catch what he meant.

"About my second day on the night shift, Teddy Johnson began workin' overtime. He didn't need the money and didn't like to work nohow, but some nights around ten or eleven, when we clocked out for lunch and sat around in the swing room, in would strut Teddy. Billy would be in school or at home. Usually, I'd be sittin' with Red and she'd tell me things while Teddy was walkin' over. "Girl, it *must* be love to make a dude like Eldorado work overtime. *He* needs to work like *I* need to be a Catholic.' Then Teddy would sit down and she'd commence to play over us like her life depended on gittin' us together. She'd say, 'Let's go over to my place this mornin' when we clock out. I got some bacon and eggs and a bottle of Scotch.' Teddy would laugh and look in my eyes and say, 'Red, we don't wanna cause no trouble for this here fine young thing, who I hear is engaged to a college man.' Then I'd laugh with them and look at Teddy and wouldn't say nothin' much to nobody.

"Word must of gotten back to Billy soon after that. He didn't say nothin' at first, but I could see a change in his attitude. All this time I was tryin' to git up the guts to tell Billy I was thinkin' about breaking off, but I just couldn't. It wasn't that I thought he needed me; I just knew he was the kind of dude that doesn't let a girl decide when somethin' is over. Bein' as much like Billy as you are, you must understand what I'm tryin' to say. On one of my nights off, when we went out to a movie, he asked, 'What time did you get in this mornin'?' I said, 'Five-thirty, same as always.' But I was lyin'. Red and me had stopped for breakfast on the way home. Billy said, 'I called you at six-thirty this morning, and your Aunt Alvene said you was still out.' I told him, 'She must have been too sleepy to look in my room.' He didn't say more on the subject, but later that evenin', after the movie, he said, 'I was in the war for two years. It made me a disciplined man, and I hope I don't ever have to lose my temper.' I didn't say nothin', but the cold way he said it was like a window shade flappin' up from in front of his true nature, and I was scared.

"It was three years ago this September twenty-second that the thing happened. It was five-thirty in the mornin'. We had clocked out at four-forty-five, but Red had brought a bottle of Scotch to work, and we was down in the swing room drinkin' a little with our coffee, just to relax. I'll tell you the truth: Teddy Johnson was there, too. He had come down just to give us a ride home. I'll never forget that day as long as I live. Teddy was dressed in a pink silk shirt with black ruffles on the sleeves, the kind that was so popular a few years ago. He was wearin' shiny black bell-bottoms that hugged his little hips like a second coat of skin, and looked like pure silk when he walked. He sat across from me, flashin' those diamond rings every time he poured more Scotch in our cups. Red was sittin' back with a smile on her face, watchin' us like a cat that had just ate.

"I was sittin' with my back to the door and didn't know anything, until I saw something change in Red's face. I still see it in my sleep at night. Her face seemed to light up and git scared and happy at the same time. She was lookin' behind me, over my shoulder, with all the smartness in the world burnin' in her eyes. I turned around. Billy Crawford was standin' right behind me with his hands close to his sides. He wore a white shirt and a thin black tie, and his mouth was tight like a little slit. He said, 'It's time for you to go home,' with that voice of his that was too cold to be called just mean. I sat there lookin' up at him. Red's voice was even colder. She said to me, 'You gonna let him order you around like that?' I didn't say nothin'. Red said to Teddy, 'Aint *you* got something to say about this?' Teddy stood up slow and swelled out his chest. He said, 'Yeah. I got somethin' to say,' looking hard at Billy. But Billy just kept lookin' down at me. 'Let's go,' he said. 'What you got to say?' Red Bone said to Teddy. Teddy said to me, 'Why don't *you* tell the dude, baby?' But I didn't say nothin'. Billy shifted his eyes to Teddy and said, 'I got nothing against you. You ain't real, so you don't matter. You been strutting the streets too long, but that ain't my business. So keep out of this.' Then he looked down at me again. 'Let's go,' he said. I looked up at the way his lips curled and wanted to cry and hit him at the same time. I felt like a trigger bein' pulled. Then I heard Red sayin', 'Why don't you go back to bed with them *goddamn books, punk!* And leave decent folks *alone!'* For the first time Billy glanced over at her. His mouth twitched. But then he looked down at me again. 'This here's the *last time* I'm asking,' he said. That's when I exploded and started to jump up. 'I ain't goin' *nowhere!'* I screamed. The last plain thing I remember was tryin' to git to his face, but it seemed to turn all bright and silvery and hot, and then I couldn't see nothin' no more.

"They told me later that he sliced me so fast there wasn't time for nobody to act. By the time Teddy jumped across the table I was down, and Billy had stabbed me again in the side. Then him and Teddy tussled over the knife, while me and Red screamed and screamed. Then Teddy went down holdin' his belly, and Billy was comin' after me again, when some of the dudes from the freight dock ran in and grabbed him. They say it took three of them to drag him off me, and all the time they was pullin' him away he kept slashin' out at me with that knife. It seemed like all the walls was screamin' and I was floatin' in water, and I thought I was dead and in hell, because I felt hot and prickly all over, and I could hear some woman's voice that might have been mine screamin' over and over, 'You devil! . . . You *devil!'*"

She lit a third cigarette. She blew a relieving cloud of smoke downward. The thin white haze billowed about her purple legs, dissipated, and vanished. A terrifying fog of silence and sickness crept into the small room, and there was no longer the smell of medicine. I dared not steal a glance at my watch, although by this time Dr. Wayland was agonizingly late. I had heard it all, and now I waited. Finally her eyes fixed on the frosted glass door. She wet her lips again and, in a much slower and pained voice, said, "This here's the third doctor I been to see. The first one stitched me up like a turkey and left this scar. The second one refused to touch me." She paused and wet her lips again. "This man fixed your nose for you," she said softly. "Do you think he could do somethin' about this scar?"

I searched the end table next to my couch for a newsmagazine, carefully avoiding her face. "Dr. Wayland is a skilled man," I told her. "Whenever he's not late. I think he may be able to do something for you."

She sighed heavily and seemed to tremble. "I don't expect no miracle or nothin'," she said. "If he could just fix the part around my eye I wouldn't expect nothin' else. People say the rest don't look too bad."

I clutched a random magazine and did not answer. Nor did I look at her. The flesh around my nose began to itch, and I looked toward the inner office door with the most extreme irritation building in me. At that moment it seemed a shadow began to form behind the frosted glass, signaling perhaps the approach of someone. I resolved to put aside all notions of civility and go into the office before her, as was my right. The shadow behind the door darkened, but vanished just as suddenly. And then I remembered the most important question, without which the entire exchange would have been wasted. I turned to the woman, now drawn together in the red plastic chair, as if struggling to sleep in a cold bed. "Sister," I said, careful to maintain a casual air. "Sister . . . what is your name?"

E. Ethelbert Miller (1950–)

E. Ethelbert Miller is something of a legend in Washington, DC art circles: He has worked for the African American Resource Center of Howard University since 1974 and has been director for 25 years; he founded and directs the Ascension Poetry Reading Series; and has had September 28,1979, proclaimed by the Mayor of DC "E. Ethelbert Miller Day." He has also received three regional awards: the Mayor's Art Award for Literature (1982), the Public Humanities Award (1988), and the Columbia Merit Award (1993). His presence in the DC art scene, which includes being a mentor to many young writers, is an amazing force and includes other northeast localities outside of DC.

Born November 20,1950, in New York City, Miller attended Howard University starting in 1968. Influenced by the Black Arts and civil rights movements, Miller changed his major from history to Afro-American Studies. He graduated in 1972 and worked as the assistant director of the Resource Center; two years later, he became director. It is in this capacity that Miller established himself as an "aesthetic entrepeneur," for both his encouragement of younger artists and his wide knowledge of African American arts, but also for his contributions to the literature as a critic and especially a poet, editor, and reader. Miller has edited numerous volumes, including In Search of Color Everywhere (1994) and Women Surviving Massacres and Men (1977), and has authored five collections of poetry to date, including Season of Hunger/Cry of Rain (1982), Where Are the Love Poems for Dictators (1986), First Light: New and Selected Poems (1994), and Whispers, Secrets and Promises (1998). His memoir, titled Fathering Words, is due to be published later this year.

What is most evident about Miller's poetry is his incredible command of the brief prosaic poem. He weaves words like a painter with the sparsest of tools—two colors and three strokes—giving lovely life to images that tell a narrative, reveal a tension or a fear, capture a neighborhood. Miller's poetic landscapes are not bound by particular themes, and in fact his travels to Africa, Cuba, and Nicaragua all offer him subjects for poetic consideration. He speaks of things Southern and urban, international and local, and explores the relationships that exist between people. His work is also largely but not explicitly autobiographical—he uses his experience as backdrop to help him develop the rich textures of his poems. His poems are intimate, and sometimes bluesy, and his work is similar to some of Lucille Clifton's poems but also to the works of Langston Hughes and Gwendolyn Brooks.

In "Panama," Miller is at his finest, using the line and stanza break to offset the word "seen" and enhance the intensity of the poem. The separation of "seen" also coincides with the notion of a forgotten language, of memories and home countries lost. The intimacy of the poem, both in its short length but also its diction and familiarity, is a nice contrast to the commentary on emigration and cultural assimilation. This is characteristic of Miller's work—that his poems are particular and precise, but are also political. Similarly, in "Urban Zen" and *"black boys," Miller captures images of urban life and presents them in compact melodies with a subtle, grace commentary. As a writer, Miller is not, as James Baldwin would say, an observer, uninvolved and detached; instead, he is a witness, one who is committed to the environment he lives in and writes about and whose alliances are clear and strong.*

Miller is also skilled at capturing the beauty of an interaction between two people. What is amazing about his poems, which deal with relationships, is that they speak with the voices of both parties, even as Miller only writes from the perspective of one of the people involved. In "Fire," he writes of his brother's desire to be a priest, yet it is his fear that we learn the most about. The juxtapositioning in this poem is key, opening with his age, and then two lines later, his brother's. These bits of information are structurally unconnected, but they are linked in what they communicate to the reader about one boy's new manhood dreams and another's thriving youthful awe. The poignancy of this relationship between older brother and young is highlighted again in "Aaron," the lovely poem where Miller fuses Biblical allusion and popular culture (Charleston Heston in "The Ten Commandments"). The breath-taking beauty of the poem is in the knowledge one has of the Moses–Aaron relationship, but especially in the positioning of these the last two stanzas—the first, which communicates the fear that Miller had of his brother as the older sibling; and the second, which reveals the humanity and love that Miller, the younger, performs. Miller gives new textuality to Black men's relationships with each other, but also to Aaron's relationship with Moses, in these last few lines.

Miller's aesthetic might be best described as one that is "a metaphor / for things left / unsaid," especially in his use of seamless but unarticulated transition. In fact, because Miller's pieces are for the most part incredibly short, they demand that the reader participate in making meaning between the lines, words, stanzas; the reader not only fills in the gaps, but also interprets the gaps as Miller might have intended them. These poems are, to echo the title of one his collections, whispers and secrets that hold great promise because they are so open, so intimate and inviting. In "Conjure," Miller deploys the modifier "this," which he (mis)uses as a noun to give a sense of precision even as the referent is unspecified. The repetition of "this" is like an invocation, performing the conjuring of the poem's title. Even when he seems to identity the "this" as a movement, it is still left open with the concluding stanza, which is the singular word, "this." In this poem, as with others, Miller achieves pauses and emphases through repetition, not with punctuation marks, which is another example of how deft a poet and artist he is.

E. Ethelbert Miller has incredible skills as a poet, one whose words are like pictures and images that, when placed next to each other, tell narratives and reflect politics that are whispers and secrets, but also promises and prayers. His poems are intimate, accessible, and musical, and in the tradition of a muse, he makes significant commentary on the condition of human life. He is unafraid to think and write of big things, but does so in very personal, bluesy ways.

Kevin Everod Quashie

Panama

in the early twenties
a boat brought
my father to America

his first impressions
were spoken in Spanish

years later when he
had forgotten the
language he could not
remember what he had

seen

Fire

i am ten years old
and share a room with my brother.
at seventeen he dreams of becoming
a priest or monk. i am too young
to know the difference. in our room
the small bureau is an altar covered
with white cloth. two large candles
stand on each end. my fear of fire
begins in this room.

October 31

(FOR JUNE)

tonight i have flashes
of being the streaks of silver
in your hair

Whispers, Secrets and Promises

afternoon
and your eyes walk
across the table into
my hands

this is the beginning
of confessions and faith

or how you braid your
hair

a metaphor
for things left
unsaid

Conjure

this is how
I remember you
undressing in moonlight

this is
the kiss
that opened hands

this movement
so gentle

this

Aaron

after watching
heston part the
red sea for the
first time
my brother ran
to his room
and pulled the
blanket from
his bed

he stood in the
doorway proudly
proclaiming
himself moses

he was the
oldest so what
he said was law

for my sister
and I

later that night
while my brother
slept I crawled
into his bed and
picked the lint
from his hair

in small town usa

in small town usa
it doesn't matter if you can count
all the black people on one hand
and have a finger for yourself
it's 7 am and you look out the window
of your hotel and there's an old black
woman coming to work to scrub and clean
and this woman reminds you of your mother
tired but getting to work early and on time
never late as you close the curtain
and climb back into bed knowing you are
not alone and this woman is nearby
getting things ready for you and when you
leave your room you make your bed
and fold your towels hoping in this
small way to make it easier for this
woman you now pass in the hall
and you both wonder who will speak first
during this moment when being black is
all there is

Urban Zen

I.

my blood
in the street
on our block

II.

beer
bottles
covering
the
cement
grass

III.

car
alarm
ringing
who
hears?

IV.

two
quarters
in my pocket
spare change
for he who
asks

V.

on the bus
no room
still we
stop
for
more

VI.

card
board
instead
of glass
for a window

VII.

my
neighbor

          moved
          to
          where?

black boys

          young black boys
          sitting with their
          backs against a wall
          sneakers sparkling
          while others stand
          with hands pushed
          deep into jeans
          pants resting on
          their hips as casual
          as gunfire

untitled

     when there are no more poems to be written
     go & wake the dead
     tell them that the war is over
     that victory is ours
     tell them that the living too
     have found peace

another love affair/another poem

        it was afterwards
        when we were in the shower
        that she said

        "you're gonna write a poem about this"

        "about what?" i asked

                    8/5/78

E. Ethelbert Miller

untitled

when
you're
small

white
folks
always

want
to touch
your head

for
good
luck

Toni Morrison (1931–)

One could compile a lovely litany of accolades on Toni Morrison, but I will simply say that she is America's finest living writer. It is not only her possession of a Nobel Prize or just about every major national and international literary award that makes such a pronouncement possible; instead, it is the ease and deft and spirit and breadth of her writing, the way she captures human life in its most pained and powerful moments, and how she renders the reader breathless and hopeful, awakened and soothed. Morrison's impact on American literature is widespread, and one could almost call a cadre of writers, including well-established ones like Randall Kenan and Gloria Naylor, Morrisonian. This is not mere conjecture or hyperbole; Morrison is a wonder, a genius, and a miracle; her work is beauty, sorrow, and redemption.

Born Chloe Anthony Wofford in Lorain, Ohio, Morrison attended Howard University and, in 1955, earned a Master's Degree from Cornell University in English. For two years, Morrison worked at Texas Southern University and then later taught at Howard. In 1964, she became a senior editor at Random House, a position that perhaps changed the course of contemporary Black literature. In this position, Morrison nurtured to publication works by Angela Davis, Toni Cade Bambara, June Jordan, and Gayl Jones, as well as the encyclopedic The Black Book (1970). It was also in that year that a small short story that she had written while in a writing group, appeared as the elegant and poetic and complicated narrative of a little Black girl and the desire not necessarily for new eyes, but for something deeper—love and the opportunity to be seen. The Bluest Eye was widely regarded as a well-crafted novel, and along with works by Alice Walker, Maya Angelou, Nikki Giovanni, Bambara, and Paule Marshall, signaled a new renaissance in Black women's cultural production.

After The Bluest Eye, Morrison produced Sula (1974), a slim, powerful tale of the lives of two Black girls who grow up to be Black women in a world that has little to no regard for those not male and White. This work confirmed what many already knew—that Morrison was gifted and well-versed in narrative techniques, and even more skilled at representation of human life. Critics noted her keen sense of language, at once poetic and accessible, language so beautiful that it made dimensioned pictures out of the stories her novels told. Sula was nominated for a National Book Award and placed Morrison squarely in the pantheon of writers of distinction.

What perhaps was so lovely, so urgent and appealing, about Morrison's work was that she represented Black characters with a textured interior that had only rarely before been articulated in writing. Morrison's works struggled to touch the edges, and then the center, of Black interior life, and the scorch, horror, and thrill was not only hers, but that of her readers. Already, White America was itching to claim Morrison as its own, with reviewers implicitly and explicitly suggesting, even demanding, that she put her amazing skill to use on subjects more universal than Black communities. This racist suggestion is one that Morrison still hears today, even as it is packaged more carefully as if to mask its unmistakable odor.

Song of Solomon, *which appeared in 1977, is considered Morrison's finest moment of storytelling. It also brought her national recognition beyond the scope of the literary and academic elite: Her book was the first by an African American since Richard Wright to be made a Book-of-the-Month Club main selection.* Solomon *received the National Critics Circle Award, as well as the American Academy and Institute of Arts and Letters Award, and sold incredibly well.*

Morrison's first best-seller, Tar Baby, *appeared in 1981, followed quickly by her appearance on the cover of* Newsweek *magazine. In many ways,* Tar Baby *was a diversion for Morrison, especially in landscape and in the presence of White characters as major figures. Nonetheless, Morrison's craft and commitment did not wane, nor did her critical nor mass popularity: The book spent four months atop the best-seller list, and Morrison was elected to the American Academy and Institute of Arts and Letters.*

It was a few years before another novel came, but when it did, many readers wondered how they would ever read it, and how they had ever lived without it: Beloved *arrived in 1987 to Morrison's claim that it was the first of a trilogy on love.* Beloved *quickly garnered praise as a notable book of the century and won a Pulitzer Prize, among other honors, after being incomprehensibly ignored for the National Book Award. It is not an overstatement to say that this book has a significant and unmovable place in the canons of American literature, especially for the way that it articulates horrors and history through the loving act of a mother headstrong and desperate. Her second of the love trilogy was* Jazz, *published in 1991, which explores the love of a man for a woman. The narrative is a virtual venture into jazz mechanics and again exhibited Morrison's virtuosity. That same year, Morrison published a series of essays called* Playing in the Dark: Whiteness and the Literary Imagination. *This small scholarly monograph argued profoundly for the construction of Whiteness in early American literature as a tool to legitimize Black inferiority. Morrison wisely suggests that the central preoccupation of all early American literature is the boding Black presence. As if there needed to be further evidence of her intellectual rigor and her national reputation, both works were featured on the front cover of the* New York Times Book Review.

Then, in 1993, came the Nobel Prize, the first time that an African American was so honored. Her lecture and speech of acceptance, which is printed in its entirety here, is itself a literary masterpiece and has been widely read and studied. Since then, Morrison has completed her trilogy with Paradise *(1998) and edited collections of essays on contemporary issues that affect Black America:* Race-ing Justice, EnGendering Power: Essays on Anita Hill, Clarence Thomas and the Construction of Social Reality *(1992) and* Birth of a Nation Hood *(1998) on the O.J. Simpson debacle. She has also written and produced a play,* Dreaming Emmett *(1986), and continues to write for* The New Yorker *as well as other publications. She is the Robert F. Gooheen Professor of Humanities at Princeton University.*

In The Nobel Lecture, *a key Morrison aesthetic is evident: Her interest in the lives of Black people who live in rural areas, like the Ohio she grew up in and that she understands historically and emotionally to be a key part of Black America's consciousness. In this text, which is an insightful and moving commentary on language and power, Morrison uses repetition for emphasis, but also exploits it to achieve orality and poetic ease in her language. Her words glide and sway, but are not without sting and stick. In fact, Morrison cleverly turns the occasion of her meditation into a narrative about meditations between an old woman and some children, which makes it also a meditation for the reader. She also evokes folk sen-*

sibilities with her use of the classically colloquial *"once upon a time."* Morrison is arguing here, among other things, that narrative is, especially because of its exchange and commitment of energy, a potentially liberating force that needs to be put to better use.

Also included for focused study on Morrison is the essay "Rootedness: The Ancestor as Foundation," in which Morrison explores the role of ancestors in her work, but also in Black tradition. Her comments here are insightful, especially in relation to the old woman in her Nobel Lecture, and "Rootedness" exists still as one of the clearest pieces of Black literary criticism. Her conversation with Gloria Naylor (from 1985) is lovely not only because it illuminates how these two women fit into a tradition of Black women's writing, but also because of the way both writers complicate this tradition. It is a moment of listening in on two great minds as they riff off each other, creating their own lovely narrative through their combined spoken words. Finally, there is Morrison's essay "Home," which she gave at a conference in celebration and engagement of Cornel West's Race Matters and which not only traces Morrison's own writing process through her first six novels, but which dares to ask hard questions about the legacy and utility of race.

For almost thirty years now, Morrison has been Black America's comet—ancient and sweeping, but also always on the outer edges of things. Her work and her presence continue to mean that there are no easy answers allowed and that the language and, more importantly, the lives we live, must be accountable, and must be made to do the work of freedom. She is, quite simply, a living wonder and a prophet.

Kevin Everod Quashie

The Nobel Lecture

MEMBERS OF THE
SWEDISH ACADEMY,
LADIES AND GENTLEMEN:

Narrative has never been merely entertainment for me. It is, I believe, one of the principal ways in which we absorb knowledge. I hope you will understand, then, why I begin these remarks with the opening phrase of what must be the oldest sentence in the world, and the earliest one we remember from childhood: "Once upon a time . . ."

"Once upon a time there was an old woman. Blind but wise." Or was it an old man? A guru, perhaps. Or a *griot* soothing restless children. I have heard this story, or one exactly like it, in the lore of several cultures.

"Once upon a time there was an old woman. Blind. Wise."

In the version I know the woman is the daughter of slaves, black, American, and lives alone in a small house outside of town. Her reputation for wisdom is without peer and without question.

Among her people she is both the law and its transgression. The honor she is paid and the awe in which she is held reach beyond her neighborhood to places far away; to the city where the intelligence of rural prophets is the source of much amusement.

One day the woman is visited by some young people who seem to be bent on disproving her clairvoyance and showing her up for the fraud they believe she is. Their plan is simple: they enter her house and ask the one question the answer to which rides solely on her difference from them, a difference they regard as a profound disability: her blindness. They stand before her, and one of them says,

"Old woman, I hold in my hand a bird. Tell me whether it is living or dead."

She does not answer, and the question is repeated. "Is the bird I am holding living or dead?"

Still she does not answer. She is blind and cannot see her visitors, let alone what is in their hands. She does not know their color, gender or homeland. She only knows their motive.

The old woman's silence is so long, the young people have trouble holding their laughter.

Finally she speaks, and her voice is soft but stern. "I don't know," she says. "I don't know whether the bird you are holding is dead or alive, but what I do know is that it is in your hands. It is in your hands."

Her answer can be taken to mean: if it is dead, you have either found it that way or you have killed it. If it is alive, you can still kill it. Whether it is to stay alive is your decision. Whatever the case, it is your responsibility.

For parading their power and her helplessness, the young visitors are reprimanded, told they are responsible not only for the act of mockery but also for the small bundle of life sacrificed to achieve its aims. The blind woman shifts attention away from assertions of power to the instrument through which that power is exercised.

Speculation on what (other than its own frail body) that bird in the hand might signify has always been attractive to me, but especially so now, thinking as I have been about the work I do that has brought me to this company. So I choose to read the bird as language and the woman as a practiced writer. She is worried about how the language she dreams in, given to her at birth, is handled, put into service, even withheld from her for certain nefarious purposes. Being a writer, she thinks of language partly as a system, partly as a living thing over which one has control, but mostly as agency—as an act with consequences. So the question the children put to her, "Is it living or dead?," is not unreal, because she thinks of language as susceptible to death, erasure; certainly imperiled and salvageable only by an effort of the will. She believes that if the bird in the hands of her visitors is dead, the custodians are responsible for the corpse. For her a dead language is not only one no longer spoken or written, it is unyielding language content to admire its own paralysis. Like statist language, censored and censoring. Ruthless in its policing duties, it has no desire or purpose other than to maintain the free range of its own narcotic narcissism, its own exclusivity and dominance. However, moribund, it is not without effect, for it actively thwarts the intellect, stalls conscience, suppresses human potential. Unreceptive to interrogation, it cannot form or tolerate new ideas, shape other thoughts, tell another story, fill baffling silences. Official language smitheried to sanction ignorance and preserve privilege is a suit of armor, polished to shocking glitter, a husk from which the knight departed long ago. Yet there it is; dumb, predatory, sentimental. Exciting reverence in schoolchildren, providing shelter for despots, summoning false memories of stability, harmony among the public.

She is convinced that when language dies, out of carelessness, disuse, indifference, and absence of esteem, or killed by fiat, not only she herself but all users and makers are accountable for its demise. In her country children have bitten their tongues off and use bullets instead to iterate the void of speechlessness, of disabled and disabling language, of language adults have abandoned altogether as a device for grappling with meaning, providing guidance, or expressing love. But she knows tongue-suicide is not only the choice of children. It is common among the infantile heads of state and power merchants whose evacuated language leaves them with no access to what is left of their human instincts, for they speak only to those who obey, or in order to force obedience.

The systematic looting of language can be recognized by the tendency of its users to forgo its nuanced, complex, mid-wifery properties, replacing them with menace and subjugation. Oppressive language does more than represent violence; it is violence; does more than represent the limits of knowledge; it limits knowledge. Whether it is obscuring state language or the faux language of mindless media; whether it is the proud but calcified language of the academy or the commodity-driven language of science; whether it is the malign language of law-without-ethics, or language designed for the estrangement of minorities, hiding its racist plunder in its literary cheek—it must be rejected, altered and exposed. It is the language that drinks blood, laps vulnerabilities, tucks its fascist boots under crinolines of respectability and patriotism as it moves relentlessly toward the bottom line and the bottomed-out mind. Sexist language, racist language, theistic language—all are typical of the policing languages of mastery, and cannot, do not, permit new knowledge or encourage the mutual exchange of ideas.

The old woman is keenly aware that no intellectual mercenary or insatiable dictator, no paid-for politician or demagogue, no counterfeit journalist would be persuaded by her thoughts. There is and will be rousing language to keep citizens armed and arming; slaughtered and slaughtering in the malls, courthouses, post offices, playgrounds, bedrooms and boulevards; stirring, memorializing language to mask the pity and waste of needless death. There will be more diplomatic language to countenance rape, torture, assassination. There is and will be more seductive, mutant language designed to throttle women, to pack their throats like pâté-producing geese with their own unsayable, transgressive words; there will be more of the language of surveillance disguised as research; of politics and history calculated to render the suffering of millions mute; language glamorized to thrill the dissatisfied and bereft into assaulting their neighbors; arrogant pseudo-empirical language crafted to lock creative people into cages of inferiority and hopelessness.

Underneath the eloquence, the glamour, the scholarly associations, however stirring or seductive, the heart of such language is languishing, or perhaps not beating at all—if the bird is already dead.

She has thought about what could have been the intellectual history of any discipline if it had not insisted upon, or been forced into, the waste of time and life that rationalizations for and representations of dominance required—lethal discourses of exclusion blocking access to cognition for both the excluder and the excluded.

The conventional wisdom of the Tower of Babel story is that the collapse was a misfortune. That it was the distraction or the weight of many languages that precipitated the tower's failed architecture. That one monolithic language would have expedited the building, and heaven would have been reached. Whose heaven, she wonders? And what kind? Perhaps the achievement of Paradise was premature, a little hasty if no one could take the time to understand other languages, other views, other narratives. Had they, the heaven they imagined might have been found at their feet. Complicated, demanding, yes, but a view of heaven as life; not heaven as post-life.

She would not want to leave her young visitors with the impression that language should be forced to stay alive merely to be. The vitality of language lies in its ability to limn the actual, imagined and possible lives of its speakers, readers, writers. Although its poise is sometimes in displacing experience, it is not a substitute for it. It arcs toward the place where meaning may lie. When a President of the United States thought about the graveyard his country had become, and said, "The world will little note nor long remember what we say here. But it will never forget what they did here," his simple words were exhilarating in their life-sustaining properties because they refused to encapsulate the reality of 600,000 dead men in a cataclysmic race war. Refusing to monumentalize, disdaining the "final word," the precise "summing up," acknowledging their "poor power to add or detract," his words signal deference to the uncapturability of the life it mourns. It is the deference that moves her, that recognition that language can never live up to life once and for all. Nor should it.

Language can never "pin down" slavery, genocide, war. Nor should it yearn for the arrogance to be able to do so. Its force, its felicity, is in its reach toward the ineffable.

Be it grand or slender, burrowing, blasting or refusing to sanctify; whether it laughs out loud or is a cry without an alphabet, the choice word or the chosen silence, unmolested language surges toward knowledge, not its destruction. But who does not know of literature banned because it is interrogative; discredited because it is critical; erased because alternate? And how many are outraged by the thought of a self-ravaged tongue?

Word-work is sublime, she thinks, because it is generative; it makes meaning that secures our difference, our human difference—the way in which we are like no other life.

We die. That may be the meaning of life. But we *do* language. That may be the measure of our lives.

"Once upon a time . . ." Visitors ask an old woman a question. Who are they, these children? What did they make of that encounter? What did they hear in those final words: "The bird is in your hands"? A sentence that gestures toward possibility, or one that drops a latch? Perhaps what the children heard was, "It is not my problem. I am old, female, black, blind. What wisdom I have now is in knowing I cannot help you. The future of language is yours."

They stand there. Suppose nothing was in their hands. Suppose the visit was only a ruse, a trick to get to be spoken to, taken seriously as they have not been before. A chance to interrupt, to violate the adult world, its miasma of discourse about them. Urgent questions are at stake, including the one they have asked: "Is the bird we hold living or dead?" Perhaps the question meant: "Could someone tell us what is life? What is death?" No trick at all; no silliness. A straightforward question worthy of the attention of a wise one. An old one. And if the old and wise who have lived life and faced death cannot describe either, who can?

But she does not; she keeps her secret, her good opinion of herself, her gnomic pronouncements, her art without commitment. She keeps her distance, enforces it and retreats into the singularity of isolation, in sophisticated, privileged space.

Nothing, no word follows her declaration of transfer. That silence is deep, deeper than the meaning available in the words she has spoken. It shivers, this silence, and the children, annoyed, fill it with language invented on the spot.

"Is there no speech," they ask her, "no words you can give us that help us break through your dossier of failures? through the education you have just given us that is no education at all because we are paying close attention to what you have done as well as to what you have said? to the barrier you have erected between generosity and wisdom?

"We have no bird in our hands, living or dead. We have only you and our important question. Is the nothing in our hands something you could not bear to contemplate, to even guess? Don't you remember being young, when language was magic without meaning? When what you could say, could not mean? When the invisible was what imagination strove to see? When questions and demands for answers burned so brightly you trembled with fury at not knowing?

"Do we have to begin consciousness with a battle heroes and heroines like you have already fought and lost, leaving us with nothing in our hands except what you have imagined is there? Your answer is artful, but its artfulness embarrasses us and ought to embarrass you. Your answer is indecent in its self-congratulation. A made-for-television script that makes no sense if there is nothing in our hands.

"Why didn't you reach out, touch us with your soft fingers, delay the sound bite, the lesson, until you knew who we were? Did you so despise our trick, our modus operandi, that you could not see that we were baffled about how to get your attention? We are young. Unripe. We have heard all our short lives that we have to be responsible. What could that possibly mean in the catastrophe this world has become; where, as a poet said, "nothing needs to be exposed since it is already barefaced"? Our inheritance is an affront. You want us to have your old, blank eyes and see only cruelty and mediocrity. Do you think we are stupid enough to perjure ourselves again and again with the fiction of nationhood? How dare you talk to us of duty when we stand waist deep in the toxin of your past?

"You trivialize us and trivialize the bird that is not in our hands. Is there no context for our lives? No song, no literature, no poem full of vitamins, no history connected to experience that you can pass along to help us start strong? You are an adult. The old one, the wise one. Stop thinking about saving your face. Think of our lives and tell us your particularized world. Make up a story. Narrative is radical, creating us at the very moment it is being created. We will not blame you if your reach exceeds your grasp; if love so ignites your words that they go down in flames and nothing is left but their scald. Or if, with the reticence of a surgeon's hands, your words suture only the places where blood might flow. We know you can never do it properly—once and for all. Passion is never enough; neither is skill. But try. For our sake and yours forget your name in the street; tell us what the world has been to you in the dark places and in the light. Don't tell us what to believe, what to fear. Show us belief's wide skirt and the stitch that unravels fear's caul. You, old woman, blessed with blindness, can speak the language that tells us what only language can: how to see without pictures. Language alone protects us from the scariness of things with no names. Language alone is meditation.

"Tell us what it is to be a woman so that we may know what it is to be a man. What moves at the margin. What it is to have no home in this place. To be set adrift from the one you knew. What it is to live at the edge of towns that cannot bear your company.

"Tell us about ships turned away from shorelines at Easter, placenta in a field. Tell us about a wagonload of slaves, how they sang so softly their breath was indistinguishable from the falling snow. How they knew from the hunch of the nearest shoulder that the next stop would be their last. How, with hands prayered in their sex, they thought of heat, then sun. Lifting their faces as though it was there for the taking. Turning as though there for the taking. They stop at an inn. The driver and his mate go in with the lamp, leaving them humming in the dark. The horse's void steams into the snow beneath its hooves and the hiss and melt are the envy of the freezing slaves.

"The inn door opens; a girl and a boy step away from its light. They climb into the wagon bed. The boy will have a gun in three years, but now he carries a lamp and a jug of warm cider. They pass it from mouth to mouth. The girl offers bread, pieces of meat and something more: a glance into the eyes of the one she serves. One helping for each man, two for each woman. And a look. They look back. The next stop will be their last. But not this one. This one is warmed."

It's quiet again when the children finish speaking, until the woman breaks into the silence.

"Finally," she says. "I trust you now. I trust you with the bird that is not in your hands because you have truly caught it. Look. How lovely it is, this thing we have done—together."

YOUR MAJESTIES,
YOUR HIGHNESSES,
LADIES AND GENTLEMEN;

I entered this hall pleasantly haunted by those who have entered it before me. That company of laureates is both daunting and welcoming, for among its lists are names of persons whose work has made whole worlds available to me. The sweep and specificity of their art have sometimes broken my heart with the courage and clarity of its vision. The astonishing brilliance with which they practiced their craft has challenged and nurtured my own. My debt to them rivals the profound one I owe to the Swedish Academy for having selected me to join that distinguished alumni.

Early in October an artist friend left a message which I kept on the answering service for weeks and played back every once in a while just to hear the trembling pleasure in her voice and the faith in her words. "My dear sister," she said, "the prize that is yours is also ours and could not have been placed in better hands." The spirit of her message with its earned optimism and sublime trust marks this day for me.

I will leave this hall, however, with a new and much more delightful haunting than the one I felt upon entering: that is the company of the laureates yet to come. Those who, even as I speak, are mining, sifting and polishing languages for illuminations none of us has dreamed of. But whether or not any one of them secures a place in this pantheon, the gathering of these writers is unmistakable and mounting. Their voices bespeak civilizations gone and yet to be; the precipice from which their imaginations gaze will rivet us; they do not blink or turn away.

It is, therefore, mindful of the gifts of my predecessors, the blessing of my sisters, in joyful anticipation of writers to come that I accept the honor the Swedish Academy has done me, and ask you to share what is for me a moment of grace.

December, 1993

Rootedness: The Ancestor as Foundation

" . . . *If anything I do, in the way of writing novels or whatever I write, isn't about the village or the community or about you, then it isn't about anything. I am not interested in indulging myself in some private exercise of my imagination . . . which is to say yes, the work must be political. . . .*"

There is a conflict between public and private life, and it's a conflict that I think ought to remain a conflict. Not a problem, just a conflict. Because they are two modes of life that exist to exclude and annihilate each other. It's a conflict that should be maintained now more than ever because the social machinery of this country at this time doesn't permit harmony in a life that has both aspects. I am impressed with the story of—probably Jefferson, perhaps not, who walked home alone after the presidential inauguration. There must have been a time when an artist could be genuinely representative *of* the tribe and *in* it; when an artist could have a tribal or racial sensibility and an individual expression of it. There were spaces and places in which a single person could enter and behave as an individual within the context of the community. A small remnant of that you can see sometimes in Black churches where people shout. It is a very personal grief and a personal statement done among people you trust. Done within the context of the community, therefore safe. And while the shouter is performing some rite that is extremely subjective, the other people are performing as a community in protecting that person. So you have a public and a private expression going on at the same time. To transfer that is not possible. So I just do the obvious, which is to keep my life as private as possible; not because it is all that interesting, it's just important that it be private. And then, whatever I do that is public can be done seriously.

The autobiographical form is classic in Black American or Afro-American literature because it provided an instance in which a writer could be representative, could say, "My single solitary and individual life is like the lives of the tribe; it differs in these specific ways, but it is a balanced life because it is both solitary and representative." The contemporary autobiography tends to be 'how I got over—look at me—alone—let me show you how I did it.' It is inimical, I think, to some of the characteristics of Black artistic expression and influence.

The label "novel" is useful in technical terms because I write prose that is longer than a short story. My sense of the novel is that it has always functioned for the class or the group that wrote it. The history of the novel as a form began when there was a new class, a middle class, to read it; it was an art form that they needed. The lower classes didn't need novels at that time because they had an art form already: they had songs, and dances, and ceremony, and gossip, and celebrations. The aristocracy didn't need it because they had the art that they had patronized, they had their own pictures painted, their own houses built, and they made sure their art separated them from the rest of the world. But when the industrial revolution began, there emerged a new class of people who were neither peasants nor aristocrats. In large measure they had no art form to tell them how to behave in this new situation. So they produced an art form: we call it the novel of manners, an art form designed to tell people something they didn't know. That is, how to behave in this new world, how to distinguish between the good guys and the bad guys. How to get married. What a good living was. What would happen if you strayed from the fold. So that early works such as *Pamela,* by Samuel Richardson, and the Jane Austen material provided social rules and explained behavior, identified outlaws, identified the people, habits, and customs that one should approve of. They were didactic in that sense. That, I think, is probably why the novel was not missed among the so-called peasant cultures. They didn't need it, because they were clear about what their responsibilities were and who and where was evil, and where was good.

But when the peasant class, or lower class, or what have you, confronts the middle class, the city, or the upper classes, they are thrown a little bit into disarray. For a long time, the art form that was healing for Black people was music. That music is no longer *exclusively* ours; we don't have exclusive rights to it.

Other people sing it and play it; it is the mode of contemporary music every-where. So another form has to take that place, and it seems to me that the novel is needed by African-Americans now in a way that it was not needed before—and it is following along the lines of the function of novels everywhere. We don't live in places where we can hear those stories anymore; parents don't sit around and tell their children those classical, mythological archetypal stories that we heard years ago. But new information has got to get out, and there are several ways to do it. One is in the novel. I regard it as a way to accomplish certain very strong functions—one being the one I just described.

It should be beautiful, and powerful, but it should also *work*. It should have something in it that enlightens; something in it that opens the door and points the way. Something in it that suggests what the conflicts are, what the problems are. But it need not solve those problems because it is not a case study, it is not a recipe. There are things that I try to incorporate into my fiction that are directly and delib-erately related to what I regard as the major characteristics of Black art, wherever it is. One of which is the ability to be both print and oral literature: to combine those two aspects so that the stories can be read in silence, of course, but one should be able to hear them as well. It should try deliberately to make you stand up and make you feel something profoundly in the same way that a Black preacher requires his congregation to speak, to join him in the sermon, to behave in a certain way, to stand up and to weep and to cry and to accede or to change and to modify—to ex-pand on the sermon that is being delivered. In the same way that a musician's music is enhanced when there is a response from the audience. Now in a book, which closes, after all—it's of some importance to me to try to make that connection—to try to make that happen also. And, having at my disposal only the letters of the al-phabet and some punctuation, I have to provide the places and spaces so that the reader can participate. Because it is the affective and participatory relationship be-tween the artist or the speaker and the audience that is of primary importance, as it is in these other art forms that I have described.

To make the story appear oral, meandering, effortless, spoken—to have the reader *feel* the narrator without *identifying* that narrator, or hearing him or her knock about, and to have the reader work *with* the author in the construction of the book—is what's important. What is left out is as important as what is there. To describe sexual scenes in such a way that they are not clinical, not even ex-plicit—so that the reader brings his own sexuality to the scene and thereby par-ticipates in it in a very personal way. And owns it. To construct the dialogue so that it is heard. So that there are no adverbs attached to them: "loudly," "softly," "he said menacingly." The menace should be in the sentence. To use, even for-mally, a chorus. The real presence of a chorus. Meaning the community or the reader at large, commenting on the action as it goes ahead.

In the books that I have written, the chorus has changed but there has al-ways been a choral note, whether it is the "I" narrator of *Bluest Eye,* or the town functioning as a character in *Sula,* or the neighborhood and the community that responds in the two parts of town in *Solomon.* Or, as extreme as I've gotten, all of nature thinking and feeling and watching and responding to the action going on in *Tar Baby,* so that they are in the story: the trees hurt, fish are afraid, clouds report, and the bees are alarmed. Those are the ways in which I try to incorporate, into that traditional genre the novel, unorthodox novelistic characteristics—so that it is, in my view, Black, because it uses the characteristics of Black art. I am not suggesting that some of these devices have not been used before and elsewhere—only the reason why I do. I employ them as well as I can. And those are just some; I wish there were ways in which such things could be talked about in the criticism. My general disappointment in some of the criticism that my work has received has nothing to do with approval. It has something to do with the vocabulary used in order to describe these things. I don't like to find my books condemned as bad or praised as good, when that condemnation or that praise is based on criteria from other paradigms. I would much prefer that they were dismissed or embraced based on the success of their accomplishment within the culture out of which I write.

I don't regard Black literature as simply books written *by* Black people, or simply as literature written *about* Black people, or simply as literature that uses a certain mode of language in which you just sort of drop g's. There is something very special and very identifiable about it and it is my struggle to *find* that elusive but identifiable style in the books. My joy is when I think that I have approached it; my misery is when I think I can't get there.

[There were times when I did.] I got there in several separate places when I knew it was exactly right. Most of the time in *Song of Solomon,* because of the construction of the book and the tone in which I could blend the acceptance of the supernatural and a profound rootedness in the real world at the same time with neither taking precedence over the other. It is indicative of the cosmology, the way in which Black people looked at the world. We are very practical people, very down-to-earth, even shrewd people. But within that practicality we also accepted what I suppose could be called superstition and magic, which is another way of knowing things. But to blend those two worlds together at the same time was enhancing, not limiting. And some of those things were "discredited knowledge" that Black people had; discredited only because Black people were discredited therefore what they *knew* was "discredited." And also because the press toward upward social mobility would mean to get as far away from that kind of knowledge as possible. That kind of knowledge has a very strong place in my work.

I have talked about function in that other question, and I touched a little bit on some of the other characteristics [or distinctive elements of African-American writing], one of which was oral quality, and the participation of the reader and the chorus. The only thing that I would add for this question is the presence of an ancestor; it seems to me interesting to evaluate Black literature on what the writer does with the presence of an ancestor. Which is to say a grandfather as in Ralph Ellison, or a grandmother as in Toni Cade Bambara, or a healer as in Bambara or Henry Dumas.

There is always an elder there. And these ancestors are not just parents, they are sort of timeless people whose relationships to the characters are benevolent, instructive, and protective, and they provide a certain kind of wisdom.

How the Black writer responds to that presence interests me. Some of them, such as Richard Wright, had great difficulty with that ancestor. Some of them, like James Baldwin, were confounded and disturbed by the presence or absence of an ancestor. What struck me in looking at some contemporary fiction was that whether the novel took place in the city or in the country, the presence or absence of that figure determined the success or the happiness of the character. It was the absence of an ancestor that was frightening, that was threatening, and it caused huge destruction and disarray in the work itself. That the solace comes, not from the contemplation of serene nature as in a lot of mainstream white literature, nor from the regard in which the city was held as a kind of corrupt place to be. Whether the character was in Harlem or Arkansas, the point was there, this timelessness was there, this person who represented this ancestor. And it seemed to be one of those interesting aspects of the continuum in Black or African-American art, as well as some of the things I mentioned before: the deliberate effort, on the part of the artist, to get a visceral, emotional response as well as an intellectual response as he or she communicates with the audience.

The treatment of artists by the people for whom they speak is also of some interest. That is to say, when the writer is one of them, when the voice is not the separate, isolated ivory tower voice of a very different kind of person but an implied "we" in a narration. This is disturbing to people and critics who view the artist as the supreme individual. It is disturbing because there is a notion that that's what the artist is—always in confrontation with his own society, and you can see the differences in the way in which literature is interpreted. Whether or not Sula is nourished by that village depends on your view of it. I know people who believe that she was destroyed by it. My own special view is that there was no other place where she could live. She would have been destroyed by any other place; she was permitted to "be" only in that context, and no one stoned her or killed her or threw her out. Also it's difficult to see who the winners are if you are not looking at it from that point of view. When the hero returns to the fold—returns to the tribe—it is seen by certain white critics as a defeat, by others as a triumph, and that is a difference in what the *aims* of the art are.

In *Song of Solomon* Pilate is the ancestor. The difficulty that Hagar [youngest of the trio of women in that household] has is how far removed she is from the experience of her ancestor. Pilate had a dozen years of close, nurturing relationships with two males—her father and her brother. And that intimacy and support was in her and made her fierce and loving because she had that experience. Her daughter Reba had less of that and related to men in a very shallow way. Her daughter had even less of an association with men as a child, so that the progression is really a diminishing of their abilities because of the absence of men in a nourishing way in their lives. Pilate is the apogee of all that: of the best of that which is female and the best of that which is male, and that balance is disturbed if it is not nurtured, and if it is not counted on and if it is not reproduced. That is the disability we must be on guard against for the future—the female who reproduces the female who reproduces the female. You know there are a lot of people who talk about the position that men hold as of primary importance, but actually it is if we don't keep in touch with the ancestor that we are, in fact, lost.

The point of the books is that it is *our* job. When you kill the ancestor you kill yourself. I want to point out the dangers, to show that nice things don't always happen to the totally self-reliant if there is no conscious historical connection. To say, see—this is what will happen.

I don't have much to say about that [the necessity to develop a specific Black feminist model of critical inquiry] except that I think there is more danger in it than fruit, because any model of criticism or evaluation that excludes males from it is as hampered as any model of criticism of Black literature that excludes women from it. For critics, models have some function. They like to talk in terms of models and developments and so on, so maybe it's of some use to them, but I suggest that even for them there is some danger in it.

If anything I do, in the way of writing novels (or whatever I write) isn't about the village or the community or about you, then it is not about anything. I am not interested in indulging myself in some private, closed exercise of my imagination that fulfills only the obligation of my personal dreams—which is to say yes, the work must be political. It must have that as its thrust. That's a perjorative term in critical circles now: if a work of art has any political influences in it, somehow it's tainted. My feeling is just the opposite: if it has none, it is tainted.

The problem comes when you find harangue passing off as art. It seems to me that the best art is political and you ought to be able to make it unquestionably political and irrevocably beautiful at the same time.

A Conversation:
Gloria Naylor and Toni Morrison

Gloria Naylor/1985

Hudson, river c. 315 mi. long, rising in NE New York in L. Tear of the Clouds near Mt. Marcy in the Adirondacks and flowing generally S., forming N.Y.-N.J. line for c. 17 mi. near its mouth in Upper New York Bay. . . . At New York City Holland and Lincoln tunnels, railroad tunnel, subways, ferries, and George Washington Bridge link N.Y. and

N.J. Above New York City river widens at Tappan Zee. On W bank PALISADES stretch N from N.J. Catskill Mts. descend to Husdon Valley. First explored by Henry Hudson in 1609. Major highway for Indians and early settlers. Has many historic, literary, and artistic associations.

(The Columbia Viking Desk Encyclopedia)

There is a blue house that sits on this river between two bridges. One is the George Washington that my bus has just crossed from the Manhattan side, and the other is the Tappan Zee that it's heading toward. My destination is that blue house, my objective is to tape a dialogue between myself and another black American writer, and I stepped on this bus seven years ago when I opened a slim volume entitled *The Bluest Eye*. Where does the first line of any novel—like any journey—actually begin? . . . *Quiet as it's kept, there were no marigolds in the fall of 1941* . . . I encountered those words, crystallized from the stream of a lifetime where they had been flowing through experiences seen and unseen, felt and un-felt, heard and unheard. That sentence was the product of a thousand tributaries before it would ultimately swell with an existence of its own, flowing off to become yet another source to uncountable possibilities.

From grade school I had been told that I had potential, while I only knew that I felt most complete when expressing myself through the written word. So I scribbled on bits of looseleaf and in diaries—to hide it all away. I wrote because I had no choice, but that was a long road from gathering the authority within myself to believe that I could actually *be* a writer. The writers I had been taught to love were either male or white. And who was I to argue that Ellison, Austen, Dickens, the Brontës, Baldwin and Faulkner weren't masters? They were and are. But inside there was still the faintest whisper: Was there no one telling my story? And since it appeared there was not, how could I presume to? Those were frustrating years until I enrolled in a creative writing seminar at Brooklyn College. My instructor's philosophy was that in order for us to even attempt to write good literature, we must read good literature. And so her reading list included Tillie Olsen, Henry James—and Toni Morrison. I have tried hard but I can't remember if we read *The Bluest Eye* at the beginning, middle, or end of the semester. Time has been swallowed except for the moment I opened that novel because for my memory that semester is now *The Bluest Eye,* and *The Bluest Eye* is the beginning. The presence of the work served two vital purposes at that moment in my life. It said to a young poet, struggling to break into prose, that the barriers were flexible; at the core of it all is language, and if you're skilled enough with that, you can create your own genre. And it said to a young black woman, struggling to find a mirror of her worth in this society, not only is your story worth telling but it can be told in words so painstakingly eloquent that it becomes a song.

Now that I saw it could be done, the questions was, who had done it? Intellectually, I accepted that the author of *The Bluest Eye* was a black woman, and it gave me a measure of pride that *we* had been here all along, creating American literature. Yet, I stared at the name, Toni Morrison, on the book's cover and it seemed as far removed from me as the separate universe I assumed all artists moved in—they were "different" people. Then a newspaper clipping, announcing that Toni Morrison would be reading from her latest novel, *Song Of Solomon,* gave me my first opportunity to see this ethereal creature. When I walked into that room the striking resemblance between this writer and my second cousin jolted me. *She looked like Jessie.* The caramel skin, wide full mouth, the liquid eyes capable of lightning jumps from an almost childlike vulnerability to a piercing assessment of the surrounding climate. The round head that would tip sharply to the side just before a burst of laughter. I didn't approach her after that first reading, but then and several times afterwards, I would simply sit and watch intently—every movement, every gesture. I knew all of her novels practically by heart then, but I was waiting—perhaps a bit fearfully—for some evidence that would shatter the growing revelation that she was a real person. It never came. And that refrain kept playing itself over and over in my mind until it shrieked itself along with her into reality—*She looked like Jessie.* I knew without a doubt that Jessie and I shared the same blood. And so that meant, somehow, the writer who could create a *Bluest Eye* was just like me. I went home one night after one of her readings, stared into my bathroom mirror, and I began to cry . . . *After the funeral the well-meaning came to console and offer their dog-eared faith in the form of coconut cakes, potato pies, fried chicken, and tears . . .* Where does the first line of a novel actually begin and end? Through these experiences, so many before and after them, my own sentence was crystallized.

That had been my encounter with the work and the writer. But now two books later as my bus pulls up in back of her home, I am finally going to meet the woman. How can I possibly begin? What do you say to someone who has played this type of role in your life?

Well, first, you say, "Hello" . . .

It is now many hours later. Across the Hudson, the New York shore is becoming a hazy blue-gray as evening approaches. The river moves against her grounds with a hypnotic rhythm that seems to suspend you a touch above time and place. I settle back into a deep, wide lounge that accepts my body as the view from her windows receives my spirit and gently expands it over the waves. It is a peaceful moment. While I am in the midst of the contentment most guests experience with attentive hosts, there is an added facet to my comfort: I have come to the realization that I like this woman. I had no guarantee of that before today, knowing that the artist and her art, while inextricably tied, are still two separate entities. And I had prepared myself so there would have been no harm done had I left there acknowledging her genius, but now aware that she was someone I would not voluntarily spend another afternoon with. So I considered it a gift that I would leave with more than an absence of harm—a newly possessed acquaintance with a good human being.

Through the day I have seen that there is so much that is different about us: I'm at the beginning of my career, she's at the height of hers; I am reticent and cautious, she is open and dramatic. We are from two generations, city and small town. I am childless and she is a devoted parent. But we are, after all, women; and so as I turn the tape recorder on, we continue talking as any two women might who happen to be fiercely proud of their identities and dedicated to their work.—GN

TM: The book that I'm writing now is called *Beloved*. I had an idea that I didn't know was a book idea, but I do remember being obsessed by two or three little fragments of stories that I heard from different places. One was a newspaper clipping about a woman named Margaret Garner in 1851. It said that the Abolitionists made a great deal out of her case because she had escaped from Kentucky, I think, with her four children. She lived in a little neighborhood just outside of Cincinnati and she had killed her children. She succeeded in killing one; she tried to kill two others. She hit them in the head with a shovel and they were wounded but they didn't die. And there was a smaller one that she had at her breast. The interesting thing, in addition to that, was the interviews that she gave. She was a young woman. In the inked pictures of her she seemed a very quiet, very serene-looking woman and everyone who interviewed her remarked about her serenity and tranquility. She said, "I will not let those children live how I have lived." She had run off into a little woodshed right outside her house to kill them because she had been caught as a fugitive. And she had made up her mind that they would not suffer the way that she had and it was better for them to die. And her mother-in-law was in the house at the same time and she said, "I watched her and I neither encouraged her nor discouraged her." They put her in jail for a little while and I'm not even sure what the denouement is of her story. But that moment, that decision was a piece, a tail of something that was always around, and it didn't get clear for me until I was thinking of another story that I had read in a book that Camille Billops published, a collection of pictures by Van der Zee, called *The Harlem Book of the Dead*. Van der Zee was very lucid. He remembered everybody he had photographed. There was this fashion of photographing beloved, departed people in full dress in coffins or in your arms. You know, many parents were holding their children beautifully dressed in their arms and they were affectionate photographs taken for affectionate reasons. In one picture, there was a young girl lying in a coffin and he says that she was eighteen years old and she had gone to a party and that she was dancing and suddenly she slumped and they noticed there was blood on her and they said, "What happened to you?" And she said, "I'll tell you tomorrow. I'll tell you tomorrow." That's all she would say. And apparently her ex-boyfriend or somebody who was jealous had come into the party with a gun and a silencer and shot her. And she kept saying, "I'll tell you tomorrow" because she wanted him to get away. And he did, I guess; anyway, she died. Now what made those stories connect, I can't explain, but I do know that, in both instances, something seemed clear to me. A woman loved something other than herself so much. She had placed all of the value of her life in something outside herself. That the woman who killed her children loved her children so much; they were the best part of her and she would not see them sullied. She would not see them hurt. She would rather kill them, have them die. You know what that means?

GN: I do, yes.

TM: And that this woman had loved a man or had such affection for a man that she would postpone her own medical care or go ahead and die to give him time to get away so that, more valuable than her life, was not just his life but something else connected with his life. Now both of those incidents seem to me, at least on the surface, very noble, you know, in that old-fashioned sense, noble things, generous, wide-spirited, love beyond the call of . . .

GN: . . . of a very traditional kind of female . . .

TM: That's right. Always. It's peculiar to women. And I thought, it's interesting because the best thing that is in us is also the thing that makes us sabotage ourselves, sabotage in the sense that our life is not as worthy, or our perception of the best part of ourselves. I had about fifteen or twenty questions that occurred to me with those two stories in terms of what it is that really compels a good woman to displace the self, her self. So what I started doing and thinking about for a year was to project the self not into the way we say "yourself," but to put a space between those words, as though the self were really a *twin* or a thirst or a friend or something that sits right next to you and watches you, which is what I was talking about when I said "the dead girl." So I had just projected her out into the earth. So how to do that? How to do that without being absolutely lunatic and talking about some medical students that nobody wants to hear about. So I just imagined the life of a dead girl which was the girl that Margaret Garner killed, the baby girl that she killed.

GN: How old was the child?

TM: Less than two. I just imagined her remembering what happened to her, being someplace else and returning, knowing what happened to her. And I call her Beloved so that I can filter all these confrontations and questions that she has in that situation, which is 1851, and then to extend her life, you know, her search, her quest, all the way through as long as I care to go, into the twenties where it switches to this other girl. Therefore, I have a New York uptown-Harlem milieu in which to put this love story, but Beloved will be there also.

GN: Always Beloved being the twin self to whatever woman shows up throughout the work.

TM: She will be the mirror, so to speak. I don't know, I'm just gonna write and see what happens to it. I have about 250 pages and it's overwhelming me. There's a lot of danger for me in writing it, which is what I am very excited about. The effort, the responsibility as well as the effort, the effort of being worth it, that's not quite it. The responsibility that I feel for the woman I'm calling Sethe, and for all of these people; these unburied, or at least unceremoniously buried, people made literate in art. But the inner tension, the artistic inner tension those people create in me; the fear of not properly, artistically, burying them, is extraordinary. I feel this enormous responsibility in exactly the way you describe the ferocity you felt when somebody was tampering with a situation that was gonna hurt . . .

GN: My people . . .

TM: Your people. Exactly. I have to have now very overt conversations with these people. Before I could sort of let it disguise itself as the artist's monologue with herself but there's no time for that foolishness now. Now I have to call them by their names and ask them to reappear and tell me something or leave me alone even. But it does mean that I feel exactly the way you do about this. They are such special company that it is very difficult to focus on other people. There is a temptation to draw away from living people, people who are extremely important to you and who are real. They're in competition a great deal with this collection of imagined characters. But these are demands that I can meet, and I know I can because they would not have spoken to me had I not been the one.

GN: Had you not been somehow worthy. I consider it being worthy to be used as that medium.

TM: They won't talk to you otherwise.

GN: No, I understand. Just before the women who lived on Brewster Place had faded back to from wherever they came, I had gotten a bound copy of the book—which I really call a tombstone because that's what it represents, at least for my part of the experience—and those women wrote me a little epigraph which I recorded in the front of the book. They told me that I must always remember them, remember how they came to be, because they were the ones who were real to me and they were the ones I had to worry about. They wanted me to know that they cared about me and that they understood that I had cared deeply about them. And having said that, they just sort of faded on off. . . . A lot of people don't think that our characters become that tangible to us.

TM: Some people are embarrassed about it; they both fear and distrust it also; they don't solidify and recreate the means by which one enters into that place where those people are. I think the more black women write, the more easily one will be able to talk about those thing. Because I have almost never found anyone whose work I respected or who took their work that seriously, who did not talk in the vocabulary that you and I are using; it's not the vocabulary of literary criticism.

GN: No, it's not.

TM: And it's not taught. People speak, of course, of the muse and there are other words for this. But to make it as graphic a presence or a collection of presence as I find it absolutely to be, it's not even a question of trying to make it that way—that's the way that it appears. There are not a lot of people to whom one speaks that way. But I know that that's what it is. It isn't a question of searching it out. It's a question of my perceptions and in that area, I know.

GN: They become so tangible that not only do you deal with them affectionately, but sometimes you deal with them very irately. Listening to you talking about the self, I can remember with *Linden Hills* the woman who was imprisoned in that basement. I actually invented a mirror, if you will, for her after she had gone through all her experiences. After she had dug up the remnants of the other Nedeed women, I created a way for her to see her own reflection in a pan of water because she had no self up until that moment. And when she realized that she had a face, then maybe she had other things going for her as well, and she could take her destiny in her own hands. But the point of all that was what was going to happen step by step once she discovered herself—she was going to barge up out of that basement, etc.—and I had *my* ending all set. But when this character who had lived with me now for two years finally discovered her face in that pan of water, she decided that she liked being what she was. She liked being a wife and a mother and she was going upstairs and claim that identity. And I said, "Oh, Lord, woman, don't you know what the end of this book has got to be? You've gotta tear that whole house down to the ground, or my book won't make any sense." Obviously, she didn't care. And I was angry with her for a good week—I just stopped writing and ran around the house cursing her. But then again that was *her* life and her decision. So the ball was thrown back into my lap—my job was to figure out a way for this woman to live her life and for me to end that book the way I wanted to.

TM: Break her arm and make her . . .

GN: Exactly. But it's marvelous, Toni. There's something so wonderful about being and even grappling with those things and being in the midst of just watching them coming to fruition.

TM: Oh, yes.

GN: You know, when I finished *Linden Hills,* I said to myself, of course, the first day or two days after, "Never again! I must have been crazy!"

TM: "This had been too hard!"

GN: And just last week, I was thinking, "God, you know, that was fun!" Truly! And I can see it reflected in your eyes—the fun of it, now the challenge of it.

TM: It's truly amazing. And the wonderful thing is when I go and sit down and try to write—maybe I need a color, I need the smell, I need something, and I don't have it. And as soon as I get concave, a small thing comes and when I pick up that yellow lined tablet, Gloria, it is always there; not necessarily when you call it, not even when you want it, but always when you need it. And, as they say, "right on time."

GN: But do you ever wonder, since we have no control over when it comes, if we have no control over when it will leave—forever?

TM: Well, I thought after *Tar Baby* I would just quit. I had written four books. You know, I would just stop and do nothing and then I got involved in filming them which I had always stayed away from. I don't want to see it in another form; besides, I can't think that way. But then little by little, some people whom I respect bought *Tar Baby* and I got involved in producing *Song of Solomon,* and in both instances there were people who wanted fidelity, wanted faithfulness in the film to the book. As I got more involved in that, I had some conflict with the novel I've just described. But what happened was that—you see, the mercy of these people is incredible because when you get in their lives, other things happen also so you don't have to decide *whether* you'll do the novel—all of it surfaced at the same time. One idea shot up another and another and another. So I didn't find these projects in competition with each other. But I think, at the moment, that I won't write anything after *Beloved*.

GN: I know you said that before.

TM: That's exactly what I said. But I thought that about each book so no one pays any attention to me on that score. This is the one. This is it. Maybe I'll write a play or maybe I'll write a short story. Maybe I won't. At any rate, what's gratifying is that—see, this is going to sound very arrogant, but when I wrote *The Bluest Eye,* I was under the distinct impression, which was erroneous, that it was on me, you know, that nobody else was writing like that, nobody, and nobody was going to.

GN: Well, you were right about that. Yes, you were!

TM: And I thought, "No one is ever going to read this until I'm dead. No one's going to do this." I really felt that—you know, I kept it sort of tight, but I thought, "Nobody's going to write about these people that way."

GN: That's not arrogant. That's the truth.

TM: They're going to make them into some little comic relief or they're going to sap it up. No one is going to see what I saw which was this complex poetic life. And it was as grand and as intricate and as profound as anybody had walked this earth. That's what I thought. And no one is going to write from the inside with that kind of gentleness, not romanticizing them, but knowing that whatever happened to them, there was that heartbeat, that love, that understanding. That's what I thought.

GN: Also, because your unique signature would have to be on that since the story was filtered through you. Whatever may have happened in the past and future . . .

TM: Well, I don't feel that way anymore.

GN: You don't feel that . . . no, I don't think—it could have, yes, the subject matter; I don't want to argue with you. I think the subject matter could have been tackled and, if we go back, we can look at it having been tackled in various ways. Wallace Thurman, *The Blacker the Berry*. Same subject matter, two different texts. The sensibilities were different. No, you're saying that no one could have done it that way, quite true. Arrogance would be to say no one could have done it that well and that's up to us to say that, that's not up to you to say that. Not well, but that way.

TM: But now I feel that, thank God, some things are done now. I used to think it was like a plateau; now there are these valleys, if you will, full of people who are entering this terrain, and they're doing extraordinary things with novels and short stories about black women and that's not going to stop; that's not going to ever stop.

GN: No, no, because one is built on another.

TM: And there won't be these huge gaps, either, between them. It's possible to look at the world now and find oneself properly spoken of in it.

GN: Because oneself spoke up for oneself.

TM: That's the point. It wasn't anybody else's job. I'm sitting around wondering why A, B, or C didn't tell my story. That's ridiculous, you know. This is *our* work and I know that it is ours because I have done it and you know it is because you've done it. And you will do it again and again and again. I don't know. It's a marvelous beginning. It's a real renaissance. You know, we have spoken of renaissances before. But this one is ours, not somebody else's.

GN: But being the pioneer of that renaissance within the contemporary time period, how do you feel about that, about watching the black women writers who have now come up after you. In a sense, Toni, you were the first widely accepted black woman writer.

TM: No. Paule Marshall, whom I had not read at that time, had written that incredible book before me.

GN: *Brown Girl, Brown Stones.*

TM: Yes, stunning, in the fifties. And, of course, there was Zora Neale Hurston and, you know, there were women before, so that's what I meant when I said—I was just ill-read, that's all, because I had gone to those schools where . . .

GN: Ill-taught.

TM: Ill-taught. And they didn't have those books in my libraries so it was a long time before I had a thrill of being introduced to such women. It was a double thrill for me because I was introduced to them after I had written, you see. And many people who are trying to show certain kinds of connections between myself and Zora Neale Hurston are always dismayed and disappointed in me because I hadn't read Zora Neale Hurston except for one little short story before I began to write. I hadn't read her until after I had written. In their efforts to establish a tradition, that bothers them a little bit. And I said, "No, no, you should be happy about that." Because the fact that I had never read Zora Neale Hurston and wrote *The Bluest Eye* and *Sula* anyway means that the tradition really exists. You know, if I had read her, then you could say that I consciously was following in the footsteps of her, but the fact that I never read her and still there may be whatever they're finding, similarities and dissimilarities, whatever such critics do, makes the cheese more binding, not less, because it means that the world as perceived by black women at certain times does exist, however they treat it and whatever they select out of it to record, there is that. I hadn't read Jean Toomer either. I didn't read him until I came into publishing and was . . . well, that was the time when there was the sort of flurry of reprints so people could get things. I was reading African novels and things like that, but, you know, all sorts of things that were just unavailable to me. They weren't at Cornell and they certainly weren't at Howard University in the days that I was there.

But your question about how I felt—it's like, there's nothing quite like seeing, for me there's nothing like reading a really, really fine book; I don't care who wrote it. You work with one facet of a prism, you know, just one side, or maybe this side, and it has millions of sides, and then you read a book and there is somebody who is a black woman who has this sensibility and this power and this talent and she's over here writing about that side of this huge sort of diamond thing that I see, and then you read another book and somebody has written about another side. And you know that eventually that whole thing will be lit—all of these planes and all of the facets. But it's all one diamond, it's all one diamond. I claim this little part, you did this one, but there's so much room, oh, my God. You haven't even begun and there's so much room and each one is another facet, another face of this incredible stone, this fantastic jewel that throws back light constantly and is constantly changing because even the face that I may have cleaned or cleared or dealt with will change. It looked like it was saffron light to me, but maybe twenty years later it looks blue. That's the way I feel about it. Geometrically all those things touch in a way, but each person has his own space, his own side of the diamond to work on. That's so gratifying, so exciting. That eliminates the feeling I had at the beginning—that of solitude. That my work doesn't have anything to do with life as it goes on, but as though there were something secret in my head when I was writing the book.

Is that so? Is that the way it was? I read the conversation between Gloria Naylor and me again; remember it again; listen to tapes of it. It's all there—not so orderly or so exact, but right nevertheless. Still, is that so? What am I missing and why do I care? It's okay to print whatever in any newspaper, magazine, or journal from the college weekly to *Vogue,* from *Il Tempo* to the Cleveland *Plain Dealer.* I never comment on the interview; never write letters correcting errors or impressions. I am content to read proof and content not to see proof at all. So what's missing from this one that made me want to add to it and made Gloria want to preface it? Neither of us wanted an interview and we hope this is not one. An interview is my trying to get to the end of it; an interview is my trying to help the reporter or student fill in the blank spaces under the questions so she or he will believe he or she has some information; it is my saying eight or ten things eight or ten times into a tape recorder in precisely the same way I've said them before. And my mind drifts so when I am being interviewed that I hardly remember it. For while I am talking (about my work, the state of one thing, the future of another), the alert part of my mind is "interviewing" the interviewer: Who are you? Why are you doing this? This is not the way to find out anything; an hour? Why do you want to be good at it?

I see them select or make up details to add to the fixed idea of me they came in the door with—the thing or person they want me to be. I sense it and, if I am feeling lazy, I play to it—if not I disappear—shift into automatic and let them have any shadow to play with, hoping my smoke will distract them into believing I am still there.

Because an interview is not an important thing.

But a conversation—well now—that's something. Rare and getting more so. And this meeting between Gloria Naylor and me was going to be that. Not one but *two* people present on the scene, talking the kind of talk in which something of consequence is willing to be revealed; some step forward is taken; some moment or phrase flares like a lightning bug and both of us see it at the same time and will remember it the same way. We didn't care how we "came off" or if we said something useful or memorable to anybody else—or whether what we said was good copy. In fact, we would use the good offices of the *Southern Review* assignment to meet and see if we liked each other or not. No observers.

She brought a tape recorder which we treated like a nuisance—which it was—so much so we forgot to turn it on all morning. Until the afternoon it lay on the table like an envelope addressed to "Occupant" that we were going to get around to opening in a minute, in a minute—when we had time. She had no list of questions; took no notes. Whatever would be missing from the "piece"; that what-was-so, we would provide. I would say what I was thinking when I said ————. What I thought when she said ————. When we laughed. Or were interrupted by telephone or one of my children or something on the stove. But are these the things that make up a conversation: What happens between and around what is said? the silence after one word? the frown after another?

I meant to be ready, of course. She followed my directions and arrived when she said she would. I have never found a reliable way to be on time. Either I sit in airports two hours before flight time or stand perspiring at gates whose little signs have been taken down. But I meant to be dressed at least. I'd been up since five o'clock getting all sorts of things done, none of which included putting on shoes or street clothes. That tickled her and she laughed about it off and on the whole day. That was good because her smile really is one, and it's hard not to join in with one of your own.

She says my work was critical to her decision to write prose. She believes that, but I know my work may have figured in *when* she would write a novel but not *whether*.

She is troubled about political and/or vs. aesthetic responsibility; about whether having children would hurt or derail her work; about the limits of her obligations to the community.

She is amazed by the joy it gives her—writing. Fiercely attentive to the respect it demands of her.

She is angry and hurt by deceptions in publishing—its absence of honor. She is amused by her self; pleased by her triumphs. In short, worried about all the right things. Pleased about all the real things.

I look at her and think for the thousandth time how fine it is now. So many like her and more coming. Eyes scrubbed clean with a Fuller brush, young black women walking around the world who can (and do) say "I write is what I do. I do this and that too—but write is what I *do*, hear?" Women who don't have to block what they know; keep secret what they feel; who welcome their own rage and love because it has voice, place, point and art—and the art is *hers,* not somebody else's. She wears on her head the "hat" she made—not one she bought made by somebody else.

She likes my chair. The river. The warm bread. "Do you ever leave this place? What for?"

I remind her of someone and she likes that. A link. I am not alien.

It was a conversation. I can tell, because I said something I didn't know I knew. About the "dead girl." That bit by bit I had been rescuing her from the grave of time and inattention. Her fingernails maybe in the first book; face and legs, perhaps, the second time. Little by little bringing her back into living life.

So that now she comes running when called—walks freely around the house, sits down in a chair; looks at me, listens to Gloria Naylor and anybody else she wants to. She cannot lie. Doesn't know greed or vengeance. Will not fawn or pontificate. There is no room for pupils in her eyes. She is here now, alive. I have seen, named and claimed her—and oh what company she keeps.—**TM**

Home

From the beginning I was looking for a sovereignty—an authority—that I believed was available to me only in fiction writing. In that activity alone did I feel coherent, unfettered. There, in the process of writing, was the willed illusion, the control, the pleasure of nestling up ever closer to meaning. There alone the delight of redemption, the seduction of origination. But I have known for a good portion of the past twenty-nine years that those delights, those seductions, are deliberate inventions necessary to both do the work and legislate its mystery. It became increasingly clear how language both liberated and imprisoned me. Whatever the forays of my imagination, the keeper, whose keys tinkled always within earshot, was race.

I have never lived, nor has any of us, in a world in which race did not matter. Such a world, one free of racial hierarchy, is usually imagined or described as dreamscape—Edenesque, utopian, so remote are the possibilities of its achievement. From Martin Luther King's hopeful language, to Doris Lessing's four-gated city, to Jean Toomer's "American," the race-free world has been posited as ideal, millennial, a condition possible only if accompanied by the Messiah or situated in a protected preserve—a wilderness park.

But, for the purposes of this talk and because of certain projects I am engaged in, I prefer to think of a-world-in-which-race-does-*not*-matter as something other than a theme park, or a failed and always-failing dream, or as the father's house of many rooms. I am thinking of it as home. "Home" seems a suitable term because, first, it lets me make a radical distinction between the metaphor of house and the metaphor of home and helps me clarify my thoughts on racial construction. Second, the term domesticates the racial project, moves the job of unmattering race away from pathetic yearning and futile desire; away from an impossible future or an irretrievable and probably nonexistent Eden to a manageable, doable, modern human activity. Third, because eliminating the potency of racist constructs in language is the work I can do. I can't wait for the ultimate liberation theory to imagine its practice and do its work. Also, matters of race and matters of home are priorities in my work and both have in one way or another initiated my search for that elusive sovereignty as well as my abandonment of the search once I recognized its disguise.

As an already- and always-raced writer, I knew from the very beginning that I could not, would not, reproduce the master's voice and its assumptions of the all-knowing law of the white father. Nor would I substitute his voice with that of his fawning mistress or his worthy opponent, for both of these positions (mistress or opponent) seemed to confine me to his terrain, in his arena, accepting the house rules in the dominance game. If I had to live in a racial house, it was important, at the least, to rebuild it so that it was not a windowless prison into which I was forced, a thick-walled, impenetrable container from which no cry could be heard, but rather an open house, grounded, yet generous in its supply of windows and doors. Or, at the most, it became imperative for me to transform this house completely. Counterracism was never an option.

I was tempted to convert it into a palace where racism didn't hurt so much; to crouch in one of its many rooms where coexistence offered the delusion of agency. At some point I tried to use the race house as a scaffolding from which to launch a movable feast that could operate, be celebrated, on any number of chosen sites. That was the authority, the glossy comfort, the redemptive quality, the freedom writing seemed at first to promise.

Yet in that freedom, as in all freedoms (especially stolen ones), lies danger. Could I redecorate, redesign, even reconceive the racial house without forfeiting a home of my own? Would life in this renovated house mean eternal homelessness? Would it condemn me to intense bouts of nostalgia for the race-free home I have never had and would never know? Or would it require intolerable circumspection, a self-censoring bond to the locus of racial architecture? In short, wasn't I (wouldn't I always be) tethered to a death-dealing ideology even (and especially) when I honed all my intelligence toward subverting it?

These questions, which have engaged so many, have troubled all of my work. How to be both free and situated; how to convert a racist house into a race-specific yet nonracist home. How to enunciate race while depriving it of its lethal cling? They are questions of concept, of language, of trajectory, of habitation, of occupation, and, although my engagement with them has been fierce, fitful, and constantly (I think) evolving, they remain in my thoughts as aesthetically and politically unresolved.

Frankly, I look to the contributors of this conference for literary and extraliterary analyses and for much of what can be better understood about matters of race. I believe, however, that my own writerly excursions and my use of a house/home antagonism are related to the topics addressed at this conference because so much of what seems to lie about in discourses on race concerns legitimacy, authenticity, community, belonging. In no small way, these discourses are about home: an intellectual home; a spiritual home; family and community as home; forced and displaced labor in the destruction of home; dislocation of and alienation within the ancestral home; creative responses to exile, the devastations, pleasures, and imperatives of homelessness as it is manifested in discussions on feminism, globalism, the diaspora, migrations, hybridity, contingency, interventions, assimilations, exclusions. The estranged body, the legislated body, the violated, rejected, deprived body—the body as consummate home. In virtually all of these formations, whatever the terrain, race magnifies the matter that matters.

Let me try to be explicit in the ways the racial house has troubled my work.

There was a moment of some significance to me that followed the publication of *Beloved*. It concerns the complex struggle and frustration inherent in creating figuratively logical narrative language that insists on race-specificity without race prerogative.

Someone saw the last sentence of *Beloved* as it was originally written. In fact, it was the penultimate sentence if one thinks of the last word in the book (the resurrection of the title, the character, and the epigraph) as the very last sentence. In any case the phrase "Certainly no clamor for a kiss," which appears in the printed book, is not the one with which I had originally closed the book. My friend was startled by the change. I told him that my editor had suggested an alteration in the language of the sentence without, of course, offering a sample of what the change might be.

The friend railed at my editor for his audacity and at me, too, for considering, let alone agreeing to, the change. I then went to some pains to explain to him why I did it, but became entangled in what the original phrase had meant, or rather what the original last word of the phrase had meant to me. How long it took to arrive at it, how I thought it was the perfect final word; that it connected everything together from the epigraph and the difficult plot to the struggles of the characters through the process of re-membering the body and its parts, re-membering the family, the neighborhood, and our national history. How it reflected this remembering, revealed its necessity, clarified its complexity, and provided the bridge I wanted from the beginning of the book to its end, as well as the beginning of the book that was to follow.

As I went on belaboring the importance of the word, my friend became angrier and angrier. It seemed clear to him from my sustained defense of the word I had abandoned that I was still convinced of it rightness. Nevertheless, I said, I thought there was something to be considered in the editor's objection (which was simply that—not a command). The editor wondered if a better word could be found to end the book because the one I had chosen was too dramatic, too theatrical. At first I disagreed with him: it was a simple, common word. But I was open to his opinion that, in the context of the previous passages, it stood out like a sore thumb. That may even have been his phrase.

Still I resisted the revision for some time (a long time, considering that we were in the galley or late manuscript stage—I am not sure which). I went away and thought about how completely reliable the editor's instincts and recommendations had always been. I decided, finally, to let the decision rest on whether I could indeed find a better word. One that produced the same meaning and had the same effect.

I was eager to find a satisfactory replacement, because the point that gripped me was that even if the word I had chosen was the absolute right one, something

was wrong with it if it called attention to itself—awkwardly, inappropriately—
and did not complete the meaning of the text, but dislodged it. It wasn't a question of simply substituting one word for another that meant the same thing: I
might have to rewrite a good deal in order to assure myself that a certain syn-
onym was preferable. Eventually, I did discover a word that seemed to accomplish what the original one did with less mystification: "kiss."

The discussion with my friend made me realize that I am still unhappy about it
because "kiss" works at a level a bit too shallow. It searches for and locates a quality
or element of the novel that was not, and is not, its primary feature. The driving force
of the narrative is not love, or the fulfillment of physical desire. The action is driven
by necessity, something that precedes love, follows love, informs love, shapes it, and
to which love is subservient. In this case the necessity was for connection, acknowledgment, a paying-out of homage still due. "Kiss" clouds that point.

I was inclined to believe that there were poorly lit passages leading up to
that original word if indeed it was so very misunderstood and so strongly and
wrongly unsettling. I have been reading recently some analyses of revisions of
texts out of copyright and thinking about the ways in which books get not only
reread but also rewritten—both in one's own language (with the ambivalence of
the writer and the back-and-forth between editor and writer), and in translation.
The liberties translators take that enhance; the ones taken that diminish. And for
me, the alarm. There is always the threat of not being taken seriously, of having
the work reduced to social anthropology, of having the politics of one's own language, the politics of another language bury, rather than expose, the reader's
own politics.

My effort to manipulate American English was not to take standard English
and use vernacular to decorate it, or to add "color" to dialogue. My efforts were
to carve away the accretions of deceit, blindness, ignorance, paralysis, and sheer
malevolence embedded in raced language so that other kinds of perception were
not only available but were inevitable. That is the work I thought my original last
word accomplished; then I became convinced that it did not, and now am sorry I
made the change. The trouble it takes to find just one word and know that it is
that note and no other that would do is an extraordinary battle. To have found it
and lost it is, in retrospect, infuriating. Well, what does it matter? Can a book really fall apart because of one word, even if it's in a critical position? Probably not.

But maybe it can, if the writing is emphasizing racial specificity minus racist
hierarchy in its figurative choices. In this instance I settled for the latter. I gave
up a word that was racially charged and figuratively coherent for one that was
only the latter, because my original last word was so clearly disjunctive, a sore
thumb, a jarring note combining as it did two linguistically incompatible functions—except when signaling racial exoticism. It is difficult to sign race while
designing racelessness.

Actually, I think my editor was right. The original word was the "wrong"
word. But I also know that my friend was right: the "wrong" word, in this case,
was also the only word. Since language *is* community, if the cognitive ecology of

a language is altered, so is the community. As you can see, my assertion of agency outside the raced house turned into genuflection in its familiar yard.

That experience of regret highlights for me the need to rethink the subtle yet persuasive attachments we may have to the architecture of race. We need to think about what it means and what it takes to live in a redesigned racial house and—evasively and erroneously—call it diversity or multiculturalism as a way of calling it home. We need to think about how invested some of the best theoretical work may be in clinging to the house's redesign as simulacrum. We need to think about what new dangers present themselves when escape or self-exile from the house of racial construction is announced or achieved.

I risk here, perhaps, charges of encouraging futile attempts to transcend race or pernicious efforts to trivialize it. It would worry me a great deal if my remarks—or my narratives—were to be so completely misunderstood. What I am determined to do is to take what is articulated as an elusive race-free paradise and domesticate it. I am determined to concretize a literary discourse that (outside of science fiction) resonates exclusively in the register of permanently unrealizable dream. It is a discourse that (unwittingly) allows racism an intellectual weight to which it has absolutely no claim. My confrontation is piecemeal and very slow. Unlike the successful advancement of an argument, narration requires the active complicity of a reader willing to step outside established boundaries of the racial imaginary. And, unlike visual media, narrative has no pictures to ease the difficulty of that step.

In writing novels the adventure for me has been explorations of seemingly impenetrable, race-inflected, race-clotted topics. In the first book I was interested in racism as a cause, consequence, and manifestation of individual and social psychosis. In the second I was preoccupied with the culture of gender and the invention of identity, both of which acquired astonishing meaning when placed in a racial context. In *Song of Solomon* and *Tar Baby* I was interested in the impact of race on the romance of community and individuality. In *Beloved* I wanted to explore the revelatory possibilities of historical narration when the body-mind, subject-object, past-present oppositions, viewed through the lens of race, collapse. In *Jazz* I tried to locate American modernity as a response to the race house. It was an attempt to blow up its all-encompassing shelter, its all-knowingness, and its assumptions of control. In the novel I am now writing, I am trying first to enunciate and then eclipse the racial gaze altogether.

In *Jazz* the dynamite fuse to be lit was under the narrative voice—the voice that could begin with claims of knowledge, inside knowledge, and indisputable authority ("I know that woman. . . .") and end with the blissful epiphany of its vulnerable humanity and its own needs. In my current project I want to see whether or not race-specific, race-free language is both possible and meaningful in narration. And I want to inhabit, walk around, a site clear of racist detritus; a place where race both matters and is rendered impotent; a place "already made for me, both snug and wide open. With a doorway never needing to be closed, a view slanted for light and bright autumn leaves but not rain. Where moonlight can be counted on if the sky is clear and stars no matter what. And below, just yonder, a river called Treason to rely on." I want to imagine not the threat of freedom, or its tentative panting fragility, but the concrete thrill of borderlessness—a kind of out of doors safety where "a sleepless woman could always rise from her bed, wrap a shawl around her shoulders and sit on the steps in the moonlight. And if she felt like it she could walk out the yard and on down the road. No lamp and no fear. A hiss-crackle from the side of the road would never scare her because what ever it was that made that sound, it wasn't something creeping up on her. Nothing for miles around thought she was prey. She could stroll as slowly as she liked, thinking of food preparations, of family things, or lift her eyes to stars and think of war or nothing at all. Lampless and without fear she could make her way. And if a light shone from a window up a ways and the cry of a colicky baby caught her attention, she might step over to the house and call out softly to the woman inside trying to soothe the baby. The two of them might take turns massaging the infant stomach, rocking, or trying to get a little soda water down. When the baby quieted they could sit together for a spell, gossiping, chuckling low so as not to wake anybody else. The woman could decide to go back to her bed then, refreshed and ready to sleep, or she might stay her direction and walk further down the road—on out, beyond, because nothing around or beyond considered her prey."

■

That description is meant to evoke not only the safety and freedom outside the race house, but to suggest contemporary searches and yearnings for social space that is psychically and physically safe.

■

The overweening, defining event of the modern world is the mass movement of raced populations, beginning with the largest forced transfer of people in the history of the world: slavery. The consequences of which transfer have determined all the wars following it as well as the current ones being waged on every continent. The contemporary world's work has become policing, halting, forming policy regarding, and trying to administer the movement of people. Nationhood—the very definition of citizenship—is constantly being demarcated and redemarcated in response to exiles, refugees, *Gastarbeiter,* immigrants, migrations, the displaced, the fleeing, and the besieged. The anxiety of belonging is entombed within the central metaphors in the discourse on globalism, transnationalism, nationalism, the break-up of federations, the rescheduling of alliances, and the fictions of sovereignty. Yet these figurations of nationhood and identity are frequently as raced themselves as the originating racial house that defined them. When they are not raced, they are, as I mentioned earlier, imaginary landscape, never inscape; Utopia, never home.

I applaud and am indebted to scholars here and elsewhere who are clearing intellectual and moral space where racial constructs are being forced to reveal their struts and bolts, their technology and their carapace, so that political action, legal and social thought, and cultural production can be generated sans racist cant, explicit or in disguise.

The defenders of Western hegemony sense the encroachment and have already defined the possibility of imagining race without dominance—without hierarchy—as "barbarism." We are already being asked to understand such a world as the destruction of the four-gated city, as the end of history. We are already being asked to know such a world as aftermath—as rubbish, as an already damaged experience, as a valueless future. Once again, the political consequences of new and threatening theoretical work is the ascription of an already-named catastrophe. It is therefore more urgent than ever to develop nonmessianic language to refigure the raced community, to decipher the deracing of the world. It is more urgent than ever to develop an epistemology that is neither intellectual slumming nor self-serving reification. Participants in this conference are marking out space for critical work that neither bleeds the raced house for the gains it provides in authenticity and insiderdom, nor abandons it to its own signifying gestures. To the extent the world-as-home that we are working for is already described in the raced house as waste, the work this conference draws our attention to is not just interesting—it may save our lives.

The campuses where we mostly work and frequently assemble will not, under the close scrutiny of conferences such as this one, remain alien terrain. Our campuses will not retain their fixed borders while tolerating travel from one kind of race-inflected community to another as interpreters, native guides. They will not remain a collection of segregated castles from whose balustrades we view—even invite—the homeless. They will not remain markets where we permit ourselves to be auctioned, bought, silenced, downsized, and vastly compromised depending on the whim of the master and the going rate. Nor will they remain oblivious to the work of conferences such as this one because they cannot enforce or afford the pariah status of race theory without forfeiting the mission of the university itself.

Hostility to race studies, however, is not limited to political and academic critics. There is much wariness in off-campus communities, especially minority communities where resentment against being described and spoken for can be intense, regardless of the researcher's agenda. The distrust that race studies often receive from the authenticating off-campus community is legitimate only when the scholars themselves have not recognized their own participation in the maintenance of the race house. The wariness is justified only when scholars have not unapologetically recognized that the valuable work they do can be done best in this environment; when they have not envisioned academic life as straddling opposing worlds or as escapist flight. W.E.B. Du Bois's observation about double consciousness is a strategy, not a prophecy or a cure. Beyond the dichotomous double consciousness, the new space this conference explores is formed by the inwardness of the outside, the interiority of the "othered," the personal that is always embedded in the public. In this new space one can imagine safety without walls, can iterate difference that is prized but unprivileged, and can conceive of a third, if you will pardon the expression, world "already made for me, both snug and wide open, with a doorway never needing to be closed."

Home.

Thylias Moss (1954–)

Thylias Moss is known for her lively poetry performances, for being able to inhabit character and voice and to give to poetry what the form in fact represents: a spoken life. In 1991, she won the Dewar's Profiles Performance Artist Award for her deft skill as a reader. Her poetry on the page is also well received and awarded, including the prestigious Witter Bynner Prize from the American Academy and Institute of Arts and Letters in 1981. She has been a Guggenheim Fellow and a MacArthur Fellow, and has been shortlisted to the National Critics Circle Award.

Moss was born and grew up in Cleveland, Ohio, which gave her experiences of the urban Midwest and a flavor of the Southern ruralness for which Ohio is known. She began her college studies at Syracuse University, earning her Bachelor's degree from Oberlin in 1981. After completing a Master of Fine Arts degree from the University of New Hampshire under the guidance of Charles Simic, she taught at Phillips Academy in Andover, and at Brandeis University, before accepting a position at the University of Michigan where she currently teaches Creative Writing. Though she is best known for her poetry and her performances, she has also authored a children's book, I Want to Be (1998), and has written a memoir that is as yet unpublished. Her works of poetry include At Redbones (1990), Rainbow Remnants on Rock Bottom Ghetto Sky (1991), Small Congregations (1993), Last Chance for the Tarzan Holler (1998), and most recently, Tale of a Sky-Blues Dress (1999).

Moss's poetry exhibits a keen sense of language, especially the language of places where Black people live, work, and socialize. For example, the selected and new poems in Small Congregations deftly capture the language of Black life that is reminiscent of church: The language is sacred and profane, mythic and earthy. Like Rita Dove, Moss gives poetic representation to the ritual and holiness that is human life and has an understanding of dreams and invented desires. Her poems represented here explore the intersection of labor and work in a context that is sometimes southern and rural, sometime urban, but always gendered and racialized, though not necessarily in debilitating ways. In "Washing Bread," Moss exhibits the ritual of washing clothes in a river, a day practice from days long gone. She uses images such as white, cleansing, laying, sickness, and crosses to reinforce the sacred of the moment, which is still also a material moment of labor.

Moss is skilled at various poetic forms, but she is particularly good at the prose poem, especially because she is a great storyteller. In "The Warmth of Hot Chocolate," she discusses angels in common day life, which nicely references the images from "Washing Bread." These angels, those who "ride and tame the air," are also people who try to commit suicide, like the poem's narrator, who is willful and self-aware and comments on the potency of everyday life. This narrator is a version of the woman washer in the earlier poem.

"Renegade Angels," which is one of her better known prose poems, begins with the encompassing opening: "Every night women in love gather outside the window and it is nothing special." This is the catholicity, the humanizing broadness, that Moss's poetic observations give to a reader. She is unafraid of big topics and of writing about the observations of human sociology that she has noted in her living. She writes about these observations in the language of prayer: "My eyes do not close without seeing what darkness holds, the letdown hair of women and welcome." Like all her prose, the language is tight; her using "letdown" as a adjective helps to achieve that tightness, and the alliteration of "women" and "welcome" provides the necessary rhythm. In "Remembering Kitchens" and "Sunrise Comes to Second Avenue," Moss continues in the merger and revelation of the sacred and/or the profane. Her poetic subjects seem to resonate with ideas that Paule Marshall expresses about the power of women's spaces and especially of the daily and the working routine.

Moss is a major American poetic voice, continuing the tradition of poets like Lucille Clifton, Audre Lorde, and Yusef Komunyakaa.

Kevin Everod Quashie

Washing Bread

In the river a woman washes
big white slices of bread
like shirts.

When she wrings them
milky water runs from wrists to elbows
and she remembers the loaf bloating
with starvation.

When she lays the bread on nearby rocks
she is a nurse swabbing fever.
It dries and gets dirty again.
Her children eat
pieces of their crosses.

The Warmth of Hot Chocolate

Somebody told me I didn't exist even though he was looking dead at me. He said that since I defied logic, I wasn't real for reality is one of logic's definitions. He said I was a contradiction in terms, that one side of me cancelled out the other side leaving nothing. His shaking knees were like polite maracas in the small clicking they made. His moustache seemed a misplaced smile. My compliments did not deter him from insisting he conversed with an empty space since there was no such thing as an angel who doesn't believe in God. I showed him where my wings had been recently trimmed. Everybody thinks they grow out of the back, some people even assume shoulder blades are all that man has left of past glory, but my wings actually grow from my scalp, a heavy hair that stiffens for flight by the release of chemical secretions activated whenever I jump off a bridge. Many angels are discovered when people trying to commit suicide ride and tame the air. I was just such an accident. We're simply a different species, not intrinsically holy, just intrinsically airborne. Demons have practical reasons for not flying; it's too hot in their home base to endure all the hair; besides, the heat makes the chemicals boil away so demons plummet when they jump and keep falling. Their home base isn't solid. Demons fall perpetually, deeper and deeper into evil until they reach a level where even to ascend is to fall.

I think God covets my wings. He forgot to create some for himself when he was forging himself out of pure thoughts rambling through the universe on the backs of neutrons. Pure thoughts were the original cowboys. I suggested to God that he jump off a bridge to activate the wings he was sure to have, you never forget yourself when you divvy up the booty, but he didn't have enough faith that his fall wouldn't be endless. I suggested that he did in fact create wings for himself but had forgotten; his first godly act had been performed a long time ago, after all.

I don't believe in him; he's just a comfortable acquaintance, a close associate with whom I can be myself. To believe in him would place him in the center of the universe when he's more secure in the fringes, the farthest corner so that he doesn't have to look over his shoulder to nab the backstabbers who want promotions but are tired of waiting for him to die and set in motion the natural evolution. God doesn't want to evolve. Has been against evolution from its creation. He doesn't figure many possibilities are open to him. I think he's wise to bide his time although he pales in the moonlight to just a glow, just the warmth of hot chocolate spreading through the body like a subcutaneous halo. But to trust him implicitly would be a mistake for he then would not have to maintain his worthiness to be God. Even the thinnest, flyweight modicum of doubt gives God the necessity to prove he's worthy of the implicit trust I can never give because I protect him from corruption, from the complacence that rises within him sometimes, a shadowy ever-descending brother.

Renegade Angels

Every night women in love gather outside the window and it is nothing special; coming out is what stars do, clouds, the sun when it builds up the nerve and then has to just blurt out. Their thoughts collect there, outside, the window of no value to them unless they marvel at coincidence; the window is just how I know it happens. I am not part of the circle although every game I played as a girl was round. By morning there is fruit on branches not meant to bear witness anymore, that birds avoid and that embarrasses me so I don't taste it; I don't find out if they're edible berries, and even if they were, I'd let them shrink and drop dried; I can't see myself snatching berries, especially not from a shrub so brambled, the branches look as if the feet of little birds tangled and broke off to appease beaks that had to get into those berries no matter what. This is the wrong thing to say because someone will start thinking that women in love set traps, bait bushes, trick birds, act out fables in which birds are made to always fly, to exhaust their wings, to be up soaring to death because they can't resort to landing. This is how the great hoverers are made. But women in love can do more than this, making is too traditionally and industrially valued to be a special accomplishment, a reason to gather when light isn't that good and there are no decent shadows, and the lit square and rectangular windows are irregular stars so big in their closeness they can't be wished on and personalized; stars are better the more distant they are so that to wish on them is to empower pinpricks. My eyes do not close without seeing what darkness holds, the letdown hair of women and welcome. And I remember where I was when I was fertilized, where as a zygote I was stamped with most destinies but Eagle Scout, where I was when I divided and doubled without taking up additional space for a long time, before testing the limits of the skin that did not fail and being delivered; with a woman, deep inside a woman, expanding a woman's body from the inside, depending on a woman, filling a woman. This is what I remember while I'm saying that other prayer and singing the song I took, as a girl, as jingle: all day, all night, the angels watching over me. Outside my window. In honor of them for forty years I bleed libation.

Remembering Kitchens

In the kitchen we compensate for missiles
in the world by fluting edges of crust
to bake rugged, primping rosettes and peaks
on cakes that are round tables with white
butter cloths swirled on, portable
Communion altars.

On the Sundays, ham toasted itself
with lipid melts, the honey veneer
waxed pork conceit to unnameable luster
and humps of rump poked
through the center of pineapple slices
so as to form tonsured clerical heads,
the Sundays being exceptional.

The waiting for the bread
helped us learn, when it arrived steaming
like kicked-up chariot dust then died down
quickly to the staid attitude of its brown dress,
the lovely practical.
In the center of the table
we let it loaf. When that was through
we sliced it into a file to rival the keeping
of the Judgment notes. So we kept our own,
a second set, and judged the judges, toasting
with cranberry water in Libbey glasses
that came from deep in the Duz. All this
in moon's skim light.

Somehow the heat of the stove,
flames shooting up tall and blue, good looking
in the uniform, had me pulling down the door,
the seat of the Tappan's pants, having the heat push
against me, melting off my pancake makeup, nearly
a chrysalis moment, my face registering then
at least four hundred degrees, and rising
in knowledge, the heat rising too, touching
off the sensors for the absolute mantra
of the ringing, the heat sizzling through cornices
and shingles, until the house is a warm alternative
to heavenly and hellish extremes,
and I remove Mama's sweet potato pie, one made
—as are her best—in her sleep when she can't
interfere, when she's dreaming at the countertop
that turns silk beside her elegant leaning, I slice it
and put the whipped cream on quick, while the pie
is hot so the peaks of cream will froth; these
are the Sundays my family suckles grace.

Sunrise Comes to Second Avenue

Daylight announces
the start of a day six hours old.

We all have thankless
jobs to do. Consider

the devotion of fishes singing
hymns without voices.

The clock's hands searching
for the lost face, a place

for the Eucharist. The man
bedded down on the roadway,

the asphalt pope out of bread,
breath and blessings.

The streetcleaner
sweeping up confessions.

Harryette Mullen*

Harryette Mullen is a poet whose language dances, sways and dazzles, making multiple references to Black texts and experience and using word play to expand and explode poetic and cultural conventions. She is entirely modern and post-modern, at once using the repetition and variation that characterized modernist writers like Gertrude Stein and Jean Toomer and the merger of disparate parts that is prevalent in post-modernity's emphasis of collagism. Her most recent collection of poetry, Muse and Drudge *(1995), is a blues- and jazz-influenced masterpiece, a study in signifying and rhythm.*

Mullen was born in Florence, Alabama, but grew up in Fort Worth, Texas. She earned a BA in English from the University of Texas at Austin and a PhD from the University of California, Santa Cruz. Since earning her doctorate, Mullen has taught at Cornell and UCLA (her current appointment) and has produced four volumes of poetry, including Tree Tall Woman *(1981),* Trimmings *(1991), and* S*PerM**K*T *(1992), and a scholarly study titled* Freeing the Soul: Race, Subjectivity, and Difference in Slave Narratives *(1999). Mullen is unusual in that she has been able to gain wide praise for her scholarly work, as well as for her creative work; she has received a Rockefeller Foundation Fellowship and the Gertrude Stein Award in Innovative American Poetry.*

In commentary on her work, especially Muse *and* Drudge, *Mullen once asserted that "writing poetry ... is more a matter of texture than form." This aesthetic commitment is evident in much of her poetry, especially in its untraditional use of the quatrain (four-line), a form mostly used in ballads and other folk literature. Mullen's use of the quatrain does not rely on rhyme, however, and when there is rhyme, it is often slanted and imprecise: In the second stanza below, the end words all have similar vowel and consonant sounds, creating a rhythm and beat that is not entirely the smooth sing-song of, for example, a limerick. Further, Mullen's line-length and meter varies, which further pushes the convention of the quatrain.*

Having self-identified with foundational Black poets such as Langston Hughes, Paul Lawrence Dunbar, Sterling Brown, and Margaret Walker, and with more contemporary writers like Etheridge Knight, Al Young, Gwendolyn Brooks, and Lucille Clifton, Mullen evidences an interest in folkcraft, in poetic voices that capture pieces of Black life. Her text is multivoiced, what one critic has called a hybrid text that merges seemingly disparate voices. In the opening stanza, Mullen makes reference to common folk phrases in the first and third lines, juxtaposing these lines with voices that counter the hope of the saying. "I dream a world" has to contend with "and then what," and vice versa. What Mullen achieves is a poem that reads like a dictionary of Black cultural folklore and texts, a poem that is like a quilt in its use and revision of social and cultural linguistic codes.

---

*Birth year not available.

Reading Mullen requires both a relaxed appreciation of the musicality and texture and careful attention paid to the deftness of her artistry and its juxtaposition of word next to word. For example, in the twelfth stanza, Mullen uses the word "distressed," which also sounds like "dress(ed)," which fleshes out her reference to clothes, skin color, and politics in these short four lines. Or, in the fifteenth stanza, Mullen plays with long vowel and consonant sounds, in the line "loose booty muddy bosom," while engaging the language of Black urban popular culture. In these moments, Mullen is most clearly a musician, riffing and scatting like John Coltrane or Sarah Vaughn. This is the texture she referred to in her comment cited earlier. And in the tradition of jazz, Mullen both "pay[s] dues, respects, and 'props' to tradition while still claiming the freedom to wander to the other side of far." She is one of Black America's most innovative and lovely poets.

Kevin Everod Quashie

Muse and Drudge (pages 3–7)

I dream a world
and then what
my soul is resting
but my feet are tired

half the night gone
I'm holding my own
some half forgotten tune
casual funk from a darker back room

handful of gimme
myself when I am real
how would you know
if you've never tasted

a ramble in brambles
the blacker more sweeter juicier
pores sweat into blackberry tangles
going back native natural country wild briers

country clothes hung on her all and sundry
bolt of blue have mercy ink perfume
that snapping turtle pussy
won't let go until thunder comes

call me pessimistic
but I fall for sour pickles
sweets for the heat
awrr reet peteet patootie

shadows crossed her face
distanced by the medium
riffing through it
too poor to pay attention

sepia bronze mahogany
say froggy jump salty
jelly in a vise
buttered up broke ice

sun goes on shining
while the debbil beats his wife
blues played lefthanded
topsy-turvy inside out

under the weather
down by the sea
a broke johnny walker
mister meaner

bigger than a big man
cirrus as a heart attracts
more power than a loco motive
think your shit don't stink

edge against a wall
wearing your colors
soulfully worn out
stylishly distressed

battered like her face
embrazened with ravage
the oxidizing of these
agonizingly worked surfaces

that other scene offstage
where by and for her he descends
a path through tangled sounds
he wants to make a song

blue gum pine barrens
loose booty muddy bosom
my all day contemplation
my midnight dream

something must need fixing
raise your window high
the carpenter's here
with hammer and nail

what you do to me
got to tell it
sing it shout out
all about it

ketchup with reality
built for meat wheels
the diva road kills
comfort shaking on the bones

trouble in mind
naps in the back
if you can't stand
sit in your soul kitsch

pot said kettle's mama must've
burnt them turnip greens
kettle deadpanned not missing a beat
least mine ain't no skillet blonde

Gloria Naylor (1950–)

Gloria Naylor is often mentioned in the company of Toni Morrison and Alice Walker as an influential fiction writer of the Black feminist literary movement, a fitting grouping because Naylor credits her exposure to Morrison's The Bluest Eye while in college as the turning point in her writing career. Before that time, Naylor had not been exposed to literature representing the Black female experience, and reading Morrison's work inspired her to begin writing fiction herself. Like Morrison, Zora Neale Hurston and Alice Walker have been important influences in Naylor's work.

Naylor was born January 25, 1950, in New York City and was educated at Brooklyn College of the City University of New York, where she earned her B.A., and Yale University, where she earned her M.A. She has written five novels: The Women of Brewster Place: A Novel in Seven Stories (1982), which won the National Book Award for best first novel; Linden Hills (1985); Mama Day (1988); Bailey's Café (1992); and The Men of Brewster Place (1998). Naylor also wrote a play based on Bailey's Café (1994) and edited Children of the Night: The Best Short Stories by Black Writers, 1967 to the Present (1995). In addition, she founded an independent film company called One Way Productions, Inc., which is reportedly going to produce a film of Mama Day, the screenplay for which Naylor is writing. Besides the National Book Award, Naylor's additional awards include a Guggenheim Fellowship; Distinguished Writer Award, Mid-Atlantic Writers Association; National Endowment for the Arts fellowship; Candace Award, National Coalition of 100 Black Women; and the Lillian Smith Award.

As its title suggests, The Women of Brewster Place: A Novel in Seven Stories collects multiple stories of Black women to explore a variety of experiences across class, age, and sexuality, a move that challenges monolithic stereotypes while dramatizing several very different tales of struggle and resilience. The collective effect of grouping these stories is a community characterization, a multiple narrative structure Naylor utilizes in her other fiction as well. In "The Two," a chapter from Brewster, Naylor dramatizes the struggles of a young lesbian woman to find acceptance in a community that refuses to tolerate what they consider her "difference." Lorraine yearns for a place where she can find "some peace," where she doesn't feel different. But the "ancient pattern" of prejudice, which the other residents of Brewster Place have faced throughout their lives, has taught them to reject what is not "like them." Such prejudice is widespread—Lorraine has also lost a teaching job, been rejected by her father, and been forced to move from two previous communities because of her homosexuality.

Naylor uses dialogue during the tenants' meeting to illustrate a number of perspectives among the community members; some even reason that Lorraine and her partner Theresa aren't so different from them after all. But nevertheless the community as a group *ultimately fails to recognize Lorraine's viewpoint that "Black people were all in the same boat . . . and if they didn't row together, they would sink together." Much of the tragedy in this chapter depicts various forms of such "sinking": the arguments between Lorraine and Theresa, Ben's retreat into drunkenness, and especially the terrible violence committed by C.C. and his peers. All of these actions stem from desperate attempts to escape the pain that social ostracism, economic struggle, and racism create. The acts of sexual violation committed by Mr. Clyde and the boys in Brewster Place show the connections between economics, racism, and rape as an exercise of power. In the shocking conclusion of the chapter, Naylor depicts the consequences of a fractured community's failure to embrace all of its members and provide them with a safe space of nurturing and acceptance.*

That Naylor continues to utilize the communal characterization of Brewster *in her third novel,* Mama Day, *and also in her fourth novel,* Bailey's Café, *shows her ongoing concern with depicting diversity and interrelatedness in the communities she creates.*

Vanessa Holford Diana

The Two

At first they seemed like such nice girls. No one could remember exactly when they had moved into Brewster. It was earlier in the year before Ben was killed— of course, it had to be before Ben's death. But no one remembered if it was in the winter or spring of that year that the two had come. People often came and went on Brewster Place like a restless night's dream, moving in and out in the dark to avoid eviction notices or neighborhood bulletins about the dilapidated condition of their furnishings. So it wasn't until the two were clocked leaving in the mornings and returning in the evenings at regular intervals that it was quietly absorbed that they now claimed Brewster as home. And Brewster waited, cautiously prepared to claim them, because you never knew about young women, and obviously single at that. But when no wild music or drunken friends careened out of the corner building on weekends, and especially, when no slightly eager husbands were encouraged to linger around that first-floor apartment and run errands for them, a suspended sigh of relief floated around the two when they dumped their garbage, did their shopping, and headed for the morning bus.

The women of Brewster had readily accepted the lighter, skinny one. There wasn't much threat in her timid mincing walk and the slightly protruding teeth she seemed so eager to show everyone in her bell-like good mornings and evenings. Breaths were held a little longer in the direction of the short dark one—too pretty, and too much behind. And she insisted on wearing those thin Qiana dresses that the summer breeze molded against the maddening rhythm of the twenty pounds of rounded flesh that she swung steadily down the street. Through slitted eyes, the women watched their men watching her pass, knowing the bastards were praying for a wind. But since she seemed oblivious to whether these supplications went answered, their sighs settled around her shoulders too. Nice girls.

And so no one even cared to remember exactly when they had moved into Brewster Place, until the rumor started. It had first spread through the block like a sour odor that's only faintly perceptible and easily ignored until it starts growing in strength from the dozen mouths it had been lying in, among clammy gums and scum-coated teeth. And then it was everywhere—lining the mouths and whitening the lips of everyone as they wrinkled up their noses at its pervading smell, unable to pinpoint the source or time of its initial arrival. Sophie could— she had been there.

It wasn't that the rumor had actually begun with Sophie. A rumor needs no true parent. It only needs a willing carrier, and it found one in Sophie. She had been there—on one of those August evenings when the sun's absence is a mockery because the heat leaves the air so heavy it presses the naked skin down on your body, to the point that a sheet becomes unbearable and sleep impossible. So most of Brewster was outside that night when the two had come in together, probably from one of those air-conditioned movies downtown, and had greeted the ones who were loitering around their building. And they had started up the steps when the skinny one tripped over a child's ball and the darker one had grabbed her by the arm and around the waist to break her fall. "Careful, don't wanna lose you now." And the two of them had laughed into each other's eyes and went into the building.

The smell had begun there. It outlined the image of the stumbling woman and the one who had broken her fall. Sophie and a few other women sniffed at the spot and then, perplexed, silently looked at each other. Where had they seen that before? They had often laughed and touched each other—held each other in joy or its dark twin—but where had they seen *that* before? It came to them as the scent drifted down the steps and entered their nostrils on the way to their inner mouths. They had seen that—done that—with their men. That shared moment of invisible communion reserved for two and hidden from the rest of the world behind laughter or tears or a touch. In the days before babies, miscarriages, and other broken dreams, after stolen caresses in barn stalls and cotton houses, after intimate walks from church and secret kisses with boys who were now long forgotten or permanently fixed in their lives—that was where. They could almost feel the odor moving about in their mouths, and they slowly knitted themselves together and let it out into the air like a yellow mist that began to cling to the bricks on Brewster.

So it got around that the two in 312 were *that* way. And they had seemed like such nice girls. Their regular exits and entrances to the block were viewed with a jaundiced eye. The quiet that rested around their door on the weekends hinted of all sorts of secret rituals, and their friendly indifference to the men on the street was an insult to the women as a brazen flaunting of unnatural ways.

Since Sophie's apartment windows faced theirs from across the air shaft, she became the official watchman for the block, and her opinions were deferred to whenever the two came up in conversation. Sophie took her position seriously and was constantly alert for any telltale signs that might creep out around their drawn shades, across from which she kept a religious vigil. An entire week of drawn shades was evidence enough to send her flying around with reports that as soon as it got dark they pulled their shades down and put on the lights. Heads nodded in knowing unison—a definite sign. If doubt was voiced with a "But I pull my shades down at night too," a whispered "Yeah, but you're not *that* way" was argument enough to win them over.

Sophie watched the lighter one dumping their garbage, and she went outside and opened the lid. Her eyes darted over the crushed tin cans, vegetable peelings, and empty chocolate chip cookie boxes. What do they do with all them chocolate chip cookies? It was surely a sign, but it would take some time to figure that one out. She saw Ben go into their apartment, and she waited and blocked his path as he came out, carrying his toolbox.

"What ya see?" She grabbed his arm and whispered wetly in his face.

Ben stared at her squinted eyes and drooping lips and shook his head slowly. "Uh, uh, uh, it was terrible."

"Yeah?" She moved in a little closer.

"Worst busted faucet I seen in my whole life." He shook her hand off his arm and left her standing in the middle of the block.

"You old sop bucket," she muttered, as she went back up on her stoop. A broken faucet, huh? Why did they need to use so much water?

Sophie had plenty to report that day. Ben had said it was terrible in there. No, she didn't know exactly what he had seen, but you can imagine—and they did. Confronted with the difference that had been thrust into their predictable world, they reached into their imaginations and, using an ancient pattern, weaved themselves a reason for its existence. Out of necessity they stitched all of their secret fears and lingering childhood nightmares into this existence, because even though it was deceptive enough to try and look as they looked, talk as they talked, and do as they did, it had to have some hidden stain to invalidate it—it was impossible for them both to be right. So they leaned back, supported by the sheer weight of their numbers and comforted by the woven barrier that kept them protected from the yellow mist that enshrouded the two as they came and went on Brewster Place.

Lorraine was the first to notice the change in the people on Brewster Place. She was a shy but naturally friendly woman who got up early, and had read the morning paper and done fifty sit-ups before it was time to leave for work. She came out of her apartment eager to start her day by greeting any of her neighbors who were outside. But she noticed that some of the people who had spoken to her before made a point of having something else to do with their eyes when she passed, although she could almost feel them staring at her back as she moved on. The ones who still spoke only did so after an uncomfortable pause, in which they seemed to be peering through her before they begrudged her a good morning or evening. She wondered if it was all in her mind and she thought about mentioning it to Theresa, but she didn't want to be accused of being too sensitive again. And how would Tee even notice anything like that anyway? She had a lousy attitude and hardly ever spoke to people. She stayed in that bed until the last moment and rushed out of the house fogged-up and grumpy, and she was used to being stared at—by men at least—because of her body.

Lorraine thought about these things as she came up the block from work, carrying a large paper bag. The group of women on her stoop parted silently and let her pass.

"Good evening," she said, as she climbed the steps.

Sophie was standing on the top step and tried to peek into the bag. "You been shopping, huh? What ya buy?" It was almost an accusation.

"Groceries." Lorraine shielded the top of the bag from view and squeezed past her with a confused frown. She saw Sophie throw a knowing glance to the others at the bottom of the stoop. What was wrong with this old woman? Was she crazy or something?

Lorraine went into her apartment. Theresa was sitting by the window, reading a copy of *Mademoiselle*. She glanced up from her magazine. "Did you get my chocolate chip cookies?"

"Why good evening to you, too, Tee. And how was my day? Just wonderful." She sat the bag down on the couch. "The little Baxter boy brought in a puppy for show-and-tell, and the damn thing pissed all over the floor and then proceeded to chew the heel off my shoe, but, yes, I managed to hobble to the store and bring you your chocolate chip cookies."

Oh, Jesus, Theresa thought, she's got a bug up her ass tonight.

"Well, you should speak to Mrs. Baxter. She ought to train her kid better than that." She didn't wait for Lorraine to stop laughing before she tried to stretch her good mood. "Here, I'll put those things away. Want me to make dinner so you can rest? I only worked half a day, and the most tragic thing that went down was a broken fingernail and that got caught in my typewriter."

Lorraine followed Theresa into the kitchen. "No, I'm not really tired, and fair's fair, you cooked last night. I didn't mean to tick off like that; it's just that . . . well, Tee, have you noticed that people aren't as nice as they used to be?"

Theresa stiffened. Oh, God, here she goes again. "What people, Lorraine? Nice in what way?"

"Well, the people in this building and on the street. No one hardly speaks anymore. I mean, I'll come in and say good evening—and just silence. It wasn't like that when we first moved in. I don't know, it just makes you wonder; that's all. What are they thinking?"

"I personally don't give a shit what they're thinking. And their good evenings don't put any bread on my table."

"Yeah, but you didn't see the way that woman looked at me out there. They must feel something or know something. They probably—"

"They, they, they!" Theresa exploded. "You know, I'm not starting up with this again, Lorraine. Who in the hell are they? And where in the hell are we? Living in some dump of a building in this God-forsaken part of town around a bunch of ignorant niggers with the cotton still under their fingernails because of you and your theys. They knew something in Linden Hills, so I gave up an apartment for you that I'd been in for the last four years. And then they knew in Park Heights, and you made me so miserable there we had to leave. Now these mysterious theys are on Brewster Place. Well, look out that window, kid. There's a big wall down that block, and this is the end of the line for me. I'm not moving anymore, so if that's what you're working yourself up to—save it!"

When Theresa became angry she was like a lump of smoldering coal, and her fierce bursts of temper always unsettled Lorraine.

"You see, that's why I didn't want to mention it." Lorraine began to pull at her fingers nervously. "You're always flying up and jumping to conclusions—no one said anything about moving. And I didn't know your life has been so miserable since you met me. I'm sorry about that," she finished tearfully.

Theresa looked at Lorraine, standing in the kitchen door like a wilted leaf, and she wanted to throw something at her. Why didn't she ever fight back? The very softness that had first attracted her to Lorraine was now a frequent cause for irritation. Smoked honey. That's what Lorraine had reminded her of, sitting in her office clutching that application. Dry autumn days in Georgia woods, thick bloated smoke under a beehive, and the first glimpse of amber honey just faintly darkened about the edges by the burning twigs. She had flowed just that heavily into Theresa's mind and had stuck there with a persistent sweetness.

But Theresa hadn't known then that this softness filled Lorraine up to the very middle and that she would bend at the slightest pressure, would be constantly seeking to surround herself with the comfort of everyone's goodwill, and would shrivel up at the least touch of disapproval. It was becoming a drain to be continually called upon for this nurturing and support that she just didn't understand. She had supplied it at first out of love for Lorraine, hoping that she would harden eventually, even as honey does when exposed to the cold. Theresa was growing tired of being clung to—of being the one who was leaned on. She didn't want a child—she wanted someone who could stand toe to toe with her and be willing to slug it out at times. If they practiced that way with each other, then they could turn back to back and beat the hell out of the world for trying to invade their territory. But she had found no such sparring partner in Lorraine, and the strain of fighting alone was beginning to show on her.

"Well, if it was that miserable, I would have been gone a long time ago," she said, watching her words refresh Lorraine like a gentle shower.

"I guess you think I'm some sort of a sick paranoid, but I can't afford to have people calling my job or writing letters to my principal. You know I've already lost a position like that in Detroit. And teaching is my whole life, Tee."

"I know," she sighed, not really knowing at all. There was no danger of that ever happening on Brewster Place. Lorraine taught too far from this neighborhood for anyone here to recognize her in that school. No, it wasn't her job she feared losing this time, but their approval. She wanted to stand out there and chat and trade makeup secrets and cake recipes. She wanted to be secretary of their block association and be asked to mind their kids while they ran to the store. And none of that was going to happen if they couldn't even bring themselves to accept her good evenings.

Theresa silently finished unpacking the groceries. "Why did you buy cottage cheese? Who eats that stuff?"

"Well, I thought we should go on a diet."

"If *we* go on a diet, then you'll disappear. You've got nothing to lose but your hair."

"Oh, I don't know. I thought that we might want to try and reduce our hips or something." Lorraine shrugged playfully.

"No, thank you. We are very happy with our hips the way they are," Theresa said, as she shoved the cottage cheese to the back of the refrigerator. "And even when I lose weight, it never comes off there. My chest and arms just get smaller, and I start looking like a bottle of salad dressing."

The two women laughed, and Theresa sat down to watch Lorraine fix dinner. "You know, this behind has always been my downfall. When I was coming up in Georgia with my grandmother, the boys used to promise me penny candy if I would let them pat my behind. And I used to love those jawbreakers—you know, the kind that lasted all day and kept changing colors in your mouth. So I was glad to oblige them, because in one afternoon I could collect a whole week's worth of jawbreakers."

"Really. That's funny to you? Having some boy feeling all over you."

Theresa sucked her teeth. "We were only kids, Lorraine. You know, you remind me of my grandmother. That was one straight-laced old lady. She had a fit when my brother told her what I was doing. She called me into the smokehouse and told me in this real scary whisper that I could get pregnant from letting little boys pat my butt and that I'd end up like my cousin Willa. But Willa and I had been thick as fleas, and she had already given me a step-by-step summary of how she'd gotten into her predicament. But I sneaked around to her house that night just to double-check her story, since that old lady had seemed so earnest. 'Willa, are you sure?' I whispered through her bedroom window. 'I'm tellin' ya, Tee,' she said. 'Just keep both feet on the ground and you home free.' Much later I learned that advice wasn't too biologically sound, but it worked in Georgia because those country boys didn't have much imagination."

Theresa's laughter bounced off of Lorraine's silent, rigid back and died in her throat. She angrily tore open a pack of the chocolate chip cookies. "Yeah," she said, staring at Lorraine's back and biting down hard into the cookie, "it wasn't until I came up north to college that I found out there's a whole lot of things that a dude with a little imagination can do to you even with both feet on the ground. You see, Willa forgot to tell me not to bend over or squat or—"

"Must you!" Lorraine turned around from the stove with her teeth clenched tightly together.

"Must I what, Lorraine? Must I talk about things that are as much a part of life as eating or breathing or growing old? Why are you always so uptight about sex or men?"

"I'm not uptight about anything. I just think it's disgusting when you go on and on about—"

"There's nothing disgusting about it, Lorraine. You've never been with a man, but I've been with quite a few—some better than others. There were a couple who I still hope to this day will die a slow, painful death, but then there were some who were good to me—in and out of bed."

"If they were so great, then why are you with me?" Lorraine's lips were trembling.

"Because—" Theresa looked steadily into her eyes and then down at the cookie she was twirling on the table. "Because," she continued slowly, "you can take a chocolate chip cookie and put holes in it and attach it to your ears and call it an earring, or hang it around your neck on a silver chain and pretend it's a necklace—but it's still a cookie. See—you can toss it in the air and call it a Frisbee or even a flying saucer, if the mood hits you, and it's still just a cookie. Send it spinning on a table—like this—until it's a wonderful blur of amber and brown light that you can imagine to be a topaz or rusted gold or old crystal, but the law of gravity has got to come into play, sometime, and it's got to come to rest—sometime. Then all the spinning and pretending and hoopla is over with. And you know what you got?"

"A chocolate chip cookie," Lorraine said.

"Uh-uh." Theresa put the cookie in her mouth and winked. "A lesbian." She got up from the table. "Call me when dinner's ready, I'm going back to read." She stopped at the kitchen door. "Now, why are you putting gravy on that chicken, Lorraine? You know it's fattening."

The Brewster Place Block Association was meeting in Kiswana's apartment. People were squeezed on the sofa and coffee table and sitting on the floor. Kiswana had hung a red banner across the wall, "Today Brewster—Tomorrow America!" but few understood what that meant and even fewer cared. They were there because this girl had said that something could be done about the holes in their walls and the lack of heat that kept their children with congested lungs in the winter. Kiswana had given up trying to be heard above the voices that were competing with each other in volume and length of complaints against the landlord. This was the first time in their lives that they felt someone was taking them seriously, so all of the would-be-if-they-could-be lawyers, politicians, and Broadway actors were taking advantage of this rare opportunity to display their talents. It didn't matter if they often repeated what had been said or if their monologues held no relevance to the issues; each one fought for the space to outshine the other.

"Ben ain't got no reason to be here. He works for the landlord."

A few scattered yeahs came from around the room.

"I lives in this here block just like y'all," Ben said slowly. "And when you ain't got no heat, I ain't either. It's not my fault 'cause the man won't deliver no oil."

"But you stay so zooted all the time, you never cold no way."

"Ya know, a lot of things ain't the landlord's fault. The landlord don't throw garbage in the air shaft or break the glass in them doors."

"Yeah, and what about all them kids that be runnin' up and down the halls."

"Don't be talking 'bout my kids!" Cora Lee jumped up. "Lot of y'all got kids, too, and they no saints."

"Why you so touchy—who mentioned you?"

"But if the shoe fits, steal it from Thom McAn's."

"Wait, please." Kiswana held up her hands. "This is getting us nowhere. What we should be discussing today is staging a rent strike and taking the landlord to court."

"What we should be discussin'," Sophie leaned over and said to Mattie and Etta, "is that bad element that done moved in this block amongst decent people."

"Well, I done called the police at least a dozen times about C. C. Baker and them boys hanging in that alley, smoking them reefers, and robbing folks," Mattie said.

"I ain't talkin' 'bout them kids—I'm talkin' 'bout those two livin' 'cross from me in 312."

"What about 'em?"

"Oh, you know, Mattie," Etta said, staring straight at Sophie. "Those two girls who mind their business and never have a harsh word to say 'bout nobody—them the two you mean, right, Sophie?"

"What they doin'—livin' there like that—is wrong, and you know it." She turned to appeal to Mattie. "Now, you a Christian woman. The Good Book say that them things is an abomination against the Lord. We shouldn't be havin' that here on Brewster and the association should do something about it."

"My Bible also says in First Peter not to be a busybody in other people's matters, Sophie. And the way I see it, if they ain't botherin' with what goes on in my place, why should I bother 'bout what goes on in theirs?"

"They sinning against the Lord!" Sophie's eyes were bright and wet.

"Then let the Lord take care of it," Etta snapped. "Who appointed you?"

"That don't surprise me comin' from *you*. No, not one bit!" Sophie glared at Etta and got up to move around the room to more receptive ears.

Etta started to go after her, but Mattie held her arm. "Let that woman be. We're not here to cause no row over some of her stupidness."

"The old prune pit," Etta spit out. "She oughta be glad them two girls are that way. That's one less bed she gotta worry 'bout pullin' Jess out of this year. I didn't see her thumpin' no Bible when she beat up that woman from Mobile she caught him with last spring."

"Etta, I'd never mention it in front of Sophie 'cause I hate the way she loves to drag other people's business in the street, but I can't help feelin' that what they're doing ain't quite right. How do you get that way? Is it from birth?"

"I couldn't tell you, Mattie. But I seen a lot of it in my time and the places I've been. They say they just love each other—who knows?"

Mattie was thinking deeply. "Well, I've loved women, too. There was Miss Eva and Ciel, and even as ornery as you can get, I've loved you practically all my life."

"Yeah, but it's different with them."

"Different how?"

"Well . . ." Etta was beginning to feel uncomfortable. "They love each other like you'd love a man or a man would love you—I guess."

"But I've loved some women deeper than I ever loved any man," Mattie was pondering. "And there been some women who loved me more and did more for me than any man ever did."

"Yeah." Etta thought for a moment. "I can second that, but it's still different, Mattie. I can't exactly put my finger on it, but . . ."

"Maybe it's not so different," Mattie said, almost to herself. "Maybe that's why some women get so riled up about it, 'cause they know deep down it's not so different after all." She looked at Etta. "It kinda gives you a funny feeling when you think about it that way, though."

"Yeah, it does," Etta said, unable to meet Mattie's eyes.

Lorraine was climbing the dark narrow stairway up to Kiswana's apartment. She had tried to get Theresa to come, but she had wanted no part of it. "A tenants' meeting for what? The damn street needs to be condemned." She knew Tee blamed her for having to live in a place like Brewster, but she could at least try to make the best of things and get involved with the community. That was the problem with so many black people—they just sat back and complained while the whole world tumbled down around their heads. And grabbing an attitude and thinking you were better than these people just because a lot of them were poor and uneducated wouldn't help, either. It just made you seem standoffish, and Lorraine wanted to be liked by the people around her. She couldn't live the way Tee did, with her head stuck in a book all the time. Tee didn't seem to need anyone. Lorraine often wondered if she even needed her.

But if you kept to yourself all the time, people started to wonder, and then they talked. She couldn't afford to have people talking about her, Tee should understand that—she knew from the way they had met. Understand. It was funny because that was the first thing she had felt about her when she handed Tee her application. She had said to herself, I feel that I can talk to this woman, I can tell her why I lost my job in Detroit, and she will understand. And she had understood, but then slowly all that had stopped. Now Lorraine was made to feel awkward and stupid about her fears and thoughts. Maybe Tee was right and she was too sensitive, but there was a big difference between being personnel director for the Board of Education and a first-grade teacher. Tee didn't threaten their files and payroll accounts but, somehow, she, Lorraine, threatened their children. Her heart tightened when she thought about that. The worst thing she had ever wanted to do to a child was to slap the spit out of the little Baxter boy for pouring glue in her hair, and even that had only been for a fleeting moment. Didn't Tee understand that if she lost this job, she wouldn't be so lucky the next time? No, she didn't understand that or anything else about her. She never wanted to bother with anyone except those weirdos at that club she went to, and Lorraine hated them. They were coarse and bitter, and made fun of people who weren't like them. Well, she wasn't like them either. Why should she feel different from the people she lived around? Black people were all in the same boat—she'd come to realize this even more since they had moved to Brewster—and if they didn't row together, they would sink together.

Lorraine finally reached the top floor; the door to Kiswana's apartment was open but she knocked before she went in. Kiswana was trying to break up an argument between a short light-skinned man and some woman who had picked up a potted plant and was threatening to hit him in the mouth. Most of the other tenants were so busy rooting for one or the other that hardly anyone noticed Lorraine when she entered. She went over and stood by Ben.

"I see there's been a slight difference of opinion here," she smiled.

"Just nigger mess, miss. Roscoe there claim that Betina ain't got no right being secretary 'cause she owe three months' rent, and she say he owe more than that and it's none of his never mind. Don't know how we got into all this. Ain't what we was talkin' 'bout, no way. Was talkin' 'bout havin' a block party to raise money for a housing lawyer."

Kiswana had rescued her Boston Fern from the woman and the two people were being pulled to opposite sides of the room. Betina pushed her way out of the door, leaving behind very loud advice about where they could put their secretary's job along with the block association, if they could find the space in that small an opening in their bodies.

Kiswana sat back down, flushed and out of breath. "Now we need someone else to take the minutes."

"Do they come with the rest of the watch?" Laughter and another series of monologues about Betina's bad-natured exit followed for the next five minutes.

Lorraine saw that Kiswana looked as if she wanted to cry. The one-step-forward-two-steps-backwards progression of the meeting was beginning to show on her face. Lorraine swallowed her shyness and raised her hand. "I'll take the minutes for you."

"Oh, thank you." Kiswana hurriedly gathered the scattered and crumpled papers and handed them to her. "Now we can get back down to business."

The room was now aware of Lorraine's presence, and there were soft murmurs from the corners, accompanied by furtive glances while a few like Sophie stared at her openly. She attempted to smile into the eyes of the people watching her, but they would look away the moment she glanced in their direction. After a couple of vain attempts her smile died, and she buried it uneasily in the papers in her hand. Lorraine tried to cover her trembling fingers by pretending to decipher Betina's smudged and misspelled notes.

"All right," Kiswana said, "now who had promised to get a stereo hooked up for the party?"

"Ain't we supposed to vote on who we wants for secretary?" Sophie's voice rose heavily in the room, and its weight smothered the other noise. All of the faces turned silently toward hers with either mild surprise or coveted satisfaction over what they knew was coming. "I mean, can anybody just waltz in here and get shoved down our throats and we don't have a say about it?"

"Look, I can just go," Lorraine said. "I just wanted to help, I—"

"No, wait." Kiswana was confused. "What vote? Nobody else wanted to do it. Did you want to take the notes?"

"She can't do it," Etta cut in, "unless we was sitting here reciting the ABC's, and we better not do that too fast. So let's just get on with the meeting."

Scattered approval came from sections of the room.

"Listen here!" Sophie jumped up to regain lost ground. "Why should a decent woman get insulted and y'll take sides with the likes of them?" Her finger shot out like a pistol, which she swung between Etta and Lorraine.

Etta rose from her seat. "Who do you think you're talkin' to, you old hen's ass? I'm as decent as you are, and I'll come over there and lam you in the mouth to prove it!"

Etta tried to step across the coffee table, but Mattie caught her by the back of the dress; Etta turned, tried to shake her off, and tripped over the people in front of her. Sophie picked up a statue and backed up into the wall with it slung over her shoulder like a baseball bat. Kiswana put her head in her hands and groaned. Etta had taken off her high-heeled shoe and was waving the spiked end at Sophie over the shoulders of the people who were holding her back.

"That's right! That's right!" Sophie screamed. "Pick on me! Sure, I'm the one who goes around doin' them filthy, unnatural things right under your noses. Every one of you knows it; everybody done talked about it, not just me!" Her head moved around the room like a trapped animal's. "And any woman—any woman who defends that kind of thing just better be watched. That's all I gotta say—where there's smoke, there's fire, Etta Johnson!"

Etta stopped struggling against the arms that were holding her, and her chest was heaving in rapid spasms as she threw Sophie a look of wilting hate, but she remained silent. And no other woman in the room dared to speak as they moved an extra breath away from each other. Sophie turned toward Lorraine, who had twisted the meeting's notes into a mass of shredded paper. Lorraine kept her back straight, but her hands and mouth were moving with a will of their own. She stood like a fading spirit before the ebony statue that Sophie pointed at her like a crucifix.

"Movin' into our block causin' a disturbance with your nasty ways. You ain't wanted here!"

"What have any of you ever seen me do except leave my house and go to work like the rest of you? Is it disgusting for me to speak to each one of you that I meet in the street, even when you don't answer me back? Is that my crime?" Lorraine's voice sank like a silver dagger into their consciences, and there was an uneasy stirring in the room.

"Don't stand there like you a Miss Innocent," Sophie whispered hoarsely. "I'll tell ya what I seen!"

Her eyes leered around the room as they waited with a courtroom hush for her next words.

"I wasn't gonna mention something so filthy, but you forcin' me." She ran her tongue over her parched lips and narrowed her eyes at Lorraine. "You forgot to close your shades last night, and I saw the two of you!"

The silence in the room tightened into a half-gasp.

"There you was, standin' in the bathroom door, drippin' wet and as naked and shameless as you please . . ."

It had become so quiet it was now painful.

"Calling to the other one to put down her book and get you a clean towel. Standin' in that bathroom door with your naked behind. I saw it—I did!"

Their chests were beginning to burn from a lack of air as they waited for Lorraine's answer, but before the girl could open her mouth, Ben's voice snaked from behind her like a lazy breeze.

"Guess *you* get out the tub with your clothes on, Sophie. Must make it mighty easy on Jess's eyes."

The laughter that burst out of their lungs was such a relief that eyes were watery. The room laid its head back and howled in gratitude to Ben for allowing it to breathe again. Sophie's rantings could not be heard above the wheezing, coughing, and backslapping that now went on.

Lorraine left the apartment and grasped the stairway railing, trying to keep the bile from rising into her throat. Ben followed her outside and gently touched her shoulder.

"Miss, you all right?"

She pressed her lips tightly together and nodded her head. The lightness of his touch brought tears to her eyes, and she squeezed them shut.

"You sure? You look 'bout ready to keel over."

Lorraine shook her head jerkily and sank her nails deeply into her palm as she brought her hand to her mouth. I mustn't speak, she thought. If I open my mouth, I'll scream. Oh, God, I'll scream or I'll throw up, right here, in front of this nice old man. The thought of the churned up bits of her breakfast and lunch pouring out of her mouth and splattering on Ben's trousers legs suddenly struck her as funny, and she fought an overwhelming desire to laugh. She trembled violently as the creeping laughter tried to deceive her into parting her lips.

Ben's face clouded over as he watched the frail body that was so bravely struggling for control. "Come on now, I'll take you home." And he tried to lead her down the steps.

She took her head in a panic. She couldn't let Tee see her like this. If she says anything smart to me now, I'll kill her, Lorraine thought. I'll pick up a butcher knife and plunge it into her face, and then I'll kill myself and let them find us there. The thought of all those people in Kiswana's apartment standing over their bleeding bodies was strangely comforting, and she began to breathe more easily.

"Come on now," Ben urged quietly, and edged her toward the steps.

"I can't go home." She barely whispered.

"It's all right, you ain't gotta—come on."

And she let him guide her down the stairs and out into the late September evening. He took her to the building that was nearest to the wall on Brewster Place and then down the outside steps to a door with a broken dirty screen. Ben unlocked the door and led her into his damp underground rooms.

He turned on the single light bulb that was hanging from the ceiling by a thick black cord and pulled out a chair for her at the kitchen table, which was propped up against the wall. Lorraine sat down, grateful to be able to take the weight off of her shaky knees. She didn't acknowledge his apologies as he took the half-empty wine bottle and cracked cup from the table. He brushed off the crumbs while two fat brown roaches raced away from the wet cloth.

"I'm makin' tea," he said, without asking her if she wanted any. He placed a blackened pot of water on the hot plate at the edge of the counter, then found two cups in the cabinet that still had their handles intact. Ben put the strong black tea he had brewed in front of her and brought her a spoon and a crumpled pound bag of sugar. Lorraine took three heaping teaspoons of sugar and stirred the tea, holding her face over the steam. Ben waited for her face to register the effects of the hot sweet liquid.

"I liked you from first off," he said shyly, and seeing her smile, he continued. "You remind me lots of my little girl." Ben reached into his hip pocket and took out a frayed billfold and handed her a tiny snapshot.

Lorraine tilted the picture toward the light. The face stamped on the celluloid paper bore absolutely no resemblance to her at all. His daughter's face was oval and dark, and she had a large flat nose and a tiny rounded mouth. She handed the picture back to Ben and tried to cover her confusion.

"I know what you thinkin'," Ben said, looking at the face in his hands. "But she had a limp—my little girl. Was a breech baby, and the midwife broke her foot when she was birthed and it never came back right. Always kinda cripped along—but a sweet child." He frowned deeply into the picture and paused, then looked up at Lorraine. "When I seen you—the way you'd walk up the street all timid-like and tryin' to be nice to these-here folks and the look on your face when some of 'em was just downright rude—you kinda broke up in here." He motioned toward his chest. "And you just sorta limped along inside. That's when I thought of my baby."

Lorraine gripped the teacup with both hands, but the tears still squeezed through the compressed muscles in her eyes. They slowly rolled down her face but she wouldn't release the cup to wipe them away.

"My father," she said, staring into the brown liquid, "kicked me out of the house when I was seventeen years old. He found a letter one of my girlfriends had written me, and when I wouldn't lie about what it meant, he told me to get out and leave behind everything that he had ever bought me. He said he wanted to burn them." She looked up to see the expression on Ben's face, but it kept swimming under the tears in her eyes. "So I walked out of his home with only the clothes on my back. I moved in with one of my cousins, and I worked at night in a bakery to put myself through college. I would send him a birthday card each year, and he always returned them unopened. After a while I stopped putting my return address on the envelopes so he couldn't send them back. I guess he burned those too." She sniffed the mucus up into her nose. "I still send those cards like that—without a return address. That way I can believe that, maybe, one year before he dies, he'll open them."

Ben got up and gave her a piece of toilet paper to blow her nose in.

"Where's your daughter now, Mr. Ben?"

"For me?" Ben sighed deeply. "Just like you—livin' in a world with no address."

They finished their tea in silence and Lorraine got up to go.

"There's no way to thank you, so I won't try."

"I'd be right hurt if you did." Ben patted her arm. "Now come back anytime you got a mind to: I got nothing, but you welcome to all of that. Now how many folks is that generous?"

Lorraine smiled, leaned over, and kissed him on the cheek. Ben's face lit up the walls of the dingy basement. He closed the door behind her, and at first her "Good night, Mr. Ben" tinkled like crystal bells in his mind. Crystal bells that grew larger and louder, until their sound was distorted in his ears and he almost believed that she had said "Good night, Daddy Ben"—no—"Mornin' Daddy Ben, mornin' Daddy Ben, mornin' . . ." Ben's saliva began to taste like sweating tin, and he ran a trembling hand over his stubbled face and rushed to the corner where he had shoved the wine bottle. The bells had begun almost to deafen him and he shook his head to relieve the drumming pain inside of his ears. He knew what was coming next, and he didn't dare waste time by pouring the wine into a cup. He lifted the bottle up to his mouth and sucked at it greedily, but it was too late. *Swing low, sweet chariot.* The song had started—the whistling had begun.

It started low, from the end of his gut, and shrilled its way up into his ears and shattered the bells, sending glass shards flying into a heart that should have been so scarred from old piercings that there was no flesh left to bleed. But the glass splinters found some minute, untouched place—as they always did—and tore the heart and let the whistling in. And now Ben would have to drink faster and longer, because the melody would now ride on his body's blood like a cancer and poison everywhere it touched. *Swing low, sweet chariot.* It mustn't get to his brain. He had a few seconds before it got to his brain and killed him. He had to be drunk before the poison crept up his neck muscles, past his mouth, on the way to his brain. If he was drunk, then he could let it out—sing it out into the air before it touched his brain, caused him to remember. *Swing low, sweet chariot.* He couldn't die there under the ground like some animal. Oh, God, please make him drunk. And he promised—he'd never go that long without a drink again. It was just the meeting and then that girl that had kept him from it this long, but he swore it would never happen again—just please, God, make him drunk.

The alcohol began to warm Ben's body, and he felt his head begin to get numb and heavy. He almost sobbed out his thanks for this redeeming answer to his prayers, because the whistling had just reached his throat and he was able to open his mouth and slobber the words out into the room. The saliva was dripping from the corners of his mouth because he had to take huge gulps of wine between breaths, but he sang on—drooling and humming—because to sing was salvation, to sing was to empty the tune from his blood, to sing was to unremember Elvira, and his daughter's "Mornin', Daddy Ben" as she dragged her twisted foot up his front porch with that song hitting her in the back.

Swing low

"Mornin', Ben. Mornin', Elvira."

Sweet chariot

The red pick-up truck stopped in front of Ben's yard.

Comin' for to carry me home

His daughter got out of the passenger side and began to limp toward the house.

Swing low

Elvira grinned into the creviced face of the white man sitting in the truck with tobacco stains in the corner of his mouth. "Mornin', Mr. Clyde. Right nice day, ain't it, sir?"

Sweet chariot

Ben watched his daughter come through the gate with her eyes on the ground, and she slowly climbed up on the porch. She took each step at a time, and her shoes grated against the rough boards. She finally turned her beaten eyes into his face, and what was left of his soul to crush was taken care of by the bell-like voice that greeted them. "Mornin', Daddy Ben. Mornin', Mama."

"Mornin', baby," Ben mumbled with his jaws tight.

Swing low

"How's things up at the house?" Elvira asked. "My little girl do a good job for you yesterday?"

Sweet chariot

"Right fine, Elvira. Got that place clean as a skinned rat. How's y'all's crops comin'?"

"Just fine, Mr. Clyde, sir. Just fine. We sure appreciate that extra land you done rented us. We bringin' in more than enough to break even. Yes, sir, just fine."

The man laughed, showing the huge gaps between his tobacco-rotted teeth. "Glad to do it. Y'all some of my best tenants. I likes keepin' my people happy. If you needs somethin', let me know."

"Sure will, Mr. Clyde, sir."

"Aw right, see y'all next week. Be by the regular time to pick up the gal."

"She be ready, sir."

The man started up the motor on the truck, and the tune that he whistled as he drove off remained in the air long after the dust had returned to the ground. Elvira grinned and waved until the red of the truck had disappeared over the horizon. Then she simultaneously dropped her arm and smile and turned toward her daughter. "Don't just stand there gawkin'. Get in the house—your breakfast been ready."

"Yes, Mama."

When the screen door had slammed shut, Elvira snapped her head around to Ben. "Nigger, what is wrong with you? Ain't you heared Mr. Clyde talkin' to you, and you standin' there like a hunk of stone. You better get some sense in you head 'fore I knock some in you!"

Ben stood with his hands in his pockets, staring at the tracks in the dirt where the truck had been. He kept balling his fists up in his overalls until his nails dug into his palms.

"It ain't right, Elvira. It just ain't right and you know it."

"What ain't right?" The woman stuck her face into his and he backed up a few steps. "That that gal work and earn her keep like the rest of us? She can't go to the fields, but she can clean house, and she'll do it! I see it's better you keep your mouth shut 'cause when it's open, ain't nothin' but stupidness comin' out." She turned her head and brushed him off as she would a fly, then headed toward the door of the house.

"She came to us, Elvira." There was a leaden sadness in Ben's voice. "She came to us a long time ago."

The thin woman spun around with her face twisted into an airless knot. "She came to us with a bunch of lies 'bout Mr. Clyde 'cause she's too damn lazy to work. Why would a decent widow man want to mess with a little black nothin' like her? No, anything to get out of work—just like you."

"Why she gotta spend the night then?" Ben turned his head slowly toward her. "Why he always make her spend the night up there alone with him?"

"Why should he make an extra trip just to bring her tail home when he pass this way every Saturday mornin' on the way to town? If she wasn't lame, she could walk it herself after she finish work. But the man nice enough to drop her home, and you want to bad-mouth him along with that lyin' hussy."

"After she came to us, you remember I borrowed Tommy Boy's wagon and went to get her that Friday night. I told ya what Mr. Clyde told me. 'She ain't finished yet, Ben.' Just like that—'She ain't finished yet.' And then standin' there whistlin' while I went out the back gate." Ben's nails dug deeper into his palms.

"So!" Elvira's voice was shrill. "So it's a big house. It ain't like this shit you got us livin' in. It take her longer to do things than most folks. You know that, so why stand there carryin' on like it mean more than that?"

"She ain't finished yet, Ben." Ben shook his head slowly. "If I was half a man I woulda—"

Elvira came across the porch and sneered into his face. "If you was half a man, you coulda given me more babies and we woulda had some help workin' this land instead of a half-grown woman we gotta carry the load for. And if you was even quarter a man, we wouldn't be a bunch of miserable sharecroppers on someone else's land—but we is, Ben. And I'll be damned if I see the little bit we got taken away 'cause you believe that gal's lowdown lies! So when Mr. Clyde come by here, you speak—hear me? And you act as grateful as your pitiful ass should be for the favors he done us."

Ben felt a slight dampness in his hands because his fingernails had broken through the skin of his palms and the blood was seeping around his cuticles. He looked at Elvira's dark braided head and wondered why he didn't take his hands out of his pockets and stop the bleeding by pressing them around it. Just lock his elbows on her shoulders and place one hand on each side of her temples and then in toward each other until the blood stopped. His big callused hands on the bones of her skull pressing in and in, like you would with a piece of dark cloth to cover the wounds on your body and clot the blood. Or he could simply go into the house and take his shotgun and press his palms around the trigger and handle, emptying the bullets into her sagging breasts just long enough—just pressing hard enough—to stop his palms from bleeding.

But the gram of truth in her words was heavy enough to weigh his hands down in his pockets and keep his feet nailed to the wooden planks in the porch, and the wounds healed over by themselves. Ben discovered that if he sat up drinking all night Friday, he could stand on the porch Saturday morning and smile at the man who whistled as he dropped his lame daughter home. And he could look into her beaten eyes and believe that she had lied.

The girl disappeared one day, leaving behind a note saying that she loved them very much, but she knew that she had been a burden and she understood why they had made her keep working at Mr. Clyde's house. But she felt that if she had to earn her keep that way, she might as well go to Memphis where the money was better.

Elvira ran and bragged to the neighbors that their daughter was now working in a rich house in Memphis. And she was making out awful well because she always sent plenty of money home. Ben would stare at the envelopes with no return address, and he found that if he drank enough every time a letter came, he could silence the bell-like voice that came chiming out of the open envelope— "Mornin' Daddy Ben, mornin' Daddy Ben, mornin' . . ." And then if he drank enough every day he could bear the touch of Elvira's body in the bed beside him at night and not have his sleep stolen by the image of her lying there with her head caved in or her chest ripped apart by shotgun shells.

But even after they lost the sharecropping contract and Elvira left him for a man who farmed near the levee and Ben went north and took a job on Brewster, he still drank—long after he could remember why. He just knew that whenever he saw a mailman, the crystal bells would start, and then that strange whistling that could shatter them, sending them on that deadly journey toward his heart.

He never dreamed it would happen on a Sunday. The mailman didn't run on Sundays, so he had felt safe. He hadn't counted on that girl sounding so much like the bells when she left his place tonight. But it was okay, he had gotten drunk in time, and he would never take such a big chance again. No, Lord, you pulled me through this time, and I ain't pressin' your mercy no more. Ben stumbled around his shadowy damp rooms, singing now at the top of his voice. The low, trembling melody of "Swing Low, Sweet Chariot" passed through his greasy windows and up into the late summer air.

Lorraine had walked home slowly, thinking about the old man and the daughter who limped. When she came to her stoop, she brushed past her neighbors with her head up and didn't bother to speak.

Theresa got off the uptown bus and turned the corner into Brewster Place. She was always irritable on Friday evenings because they had to do payroll inventories at the office. Her neck ached from bending over endless lists of computer printouts. What did that damn Board of Education think—someone in accounting was going to sneak one of their relatives on the payroll? The biggies had been doing that for years, but they lay awake at night, thinking of ways to keep the little guys from cashing in on it too. There was something else that had been turning uncomfortably in her mind for the last few weeks, and just today it had lain still long enough for her to pinpoint it—Lorraine was changing. It wasn't exactly anything that she had said or done, but Theresa sensed a firmness in her spirit that hadn't been there before. She was speaking up more—yes, that was it—whether the subject was the evening news or bus schedules or the proper way to hem a dress. Lorraine wasn't deferring to her anymore. And she wasn't apologizing for seeing things differently from Theresa.

Why did that bother her? Didn't she want Lorraine to start standing up for herself? To stop all that sniveling and handwringing every time Theresa raised her voice? Weren't things the way she had wanted them to be for the last five years? What nagged at Theresa more than the change was the fact that she was worrying about it. She had actually thought about picking a fight just to see how far she could push her—push her into what? Oh, God, I must be sick, she thought. No, it was that old man—that's what it was. Why was Lorraine spending so much time with that drunk? They didn't have a damn thing in common. What could he be telling her, doing for her, that was causing this? She had tried—she truly had—to get Lorraine to show some backbone. And now some ignorant country winehead was doing in a few weeks what she couldn't do for the last five years.

Theresa was mulling this over when a little girl sped past her on skates, hit a crack in the sidewalk, and fell. She went to walk around the child, who looked up with tears in her eyes and stated simply, "Miss, I hurt myself." She said it with such a tone of wonder and disappointment that Theresa smiled. Kids lived in such an insulated world, where the smallest disturbance was met with cries of protest. Oh, sweetheart, she thought, just live on and you'll wish many a day that the biggest problem in your life would be a scraped knee. But she was still just a little girl, and right now she wanted an audience for her struggle with this uninvited disaster.

Theresa bent down beside her and clucked her teeth loudly. "Oh, you did? Let's see." She helped her off the ground and made an exaggerated fuss over the scraped knee.

"It's bleeding!" The child's voice rose in horror.

Theresa looked at the tiny specks of blood that were beading up on the grimy knee. "Why, it sure is." She tried to match the note of seriousness in the child's tone. "But I think we have a little time before you have to worry about a transfusion." She opened her pocketbook and took out a clean tissue. "Let's see if we can fix it up. Now, I want you to spit on this for me and I'll wipe your knee."

The girl spit on the tissue. "Is it gonna hurt?"

"No, it won't hurt. You know what my grandma used to call spit? God's iodine. Said it was the best thing for patching anything up—except maybe a broken leg."

She steadied the girl's leg and gently dabbed at the dirty knee. "See, it's all coming off. I guess you're gonna live." She smiled.

The child looked at her knee with a solemn face. "I think it needs a Band-Aid."

Theresa laughed. "Well, you're out of luck with me. But you go on home and see if your mama has one for you—if you can remember which knee it was by then."

"What are you doing to her?" The voice pierced the air between the child and Theresa. She looked up and saw a woman rushing toward them. The woman grabbed the child to her side. "What's going on here?" Her voice was just half an octave too high.

Theresa stood up and held out the dirty and bloody tissue. "She scraped her knee." The words fell like dead weights. "What in the hell did you think I was doing?" She refused to let the woman avoid her eyes, enjoying every minute of her cringing embarrassment.

"Mama, I need a Band-Aid, you got a Band-Aid?" The child tugged on her arm.

"Yes, yes, honey, right away." The woman was glad to have an excuse to look down. "Thank you very much," she said, as she hurried the child away. "She's always so clumsy. I've told her a million times to be careful on those skates, but you know . . ."

"Yeah, right," Theresa said, watching them go. "I know." She balled the tissue in her hand and quickly walked into the building. She slammed the apartment door open and heard Lorraine running water in the bathroom.

"Is that you, Tee?"

"Yeah," she called out, and then thought, No, it's not me. It's not me at all. Theresa paced between the kitchen and living room and then realized that she still had the tissue. She threw it into the kitchen garbage and turned on the faucet to its fullest pressure and started washing her hands. She kept lathering and rinsing them, but they still felt unclean. Son-of-a-bitch, she thought, son-of-a-fucking-bitch! She roughly dried her hands with some paper towels and fought the impulse to wash them again by starting dinner early. She kept her hands moving quickly, chopping more onions, celery, and green peppers than she really needed. She vigorously seasoned the ground beef, jabbing the wooden spoon repeatedly into the red meat.

When she stopped to catch her breath and glanced toward the kitchen window, a pair of squinty black eyes were peering at her from the corner of a shade across the air shaft. "What the hell . . . ?" She threw down her spoon and ran over to the window.

"You wanna see what I'm doing?" The shade was pulled up with such force it went spinning on its rollers at the top of the window. The eyes disappeared from the corner of the shade across the air shaft.

"Here!" Theresa slammed the window up into its casing. "I'll even raise this so you can hear better. I'm making meat loaf, you old bat! Meat loaf!" She stuck her head out of the window. "The same way other people make it! Here, I'll show you!"

She ran back to the table and took up a handful of chopped onions and threw them at Sophie's window. "See, that's the onions. And here, here's the chopped peppers!" The diced vegetables hit against the windowpane. "Oh, yeah, I use eggs!" Two eggs flew out of the window and splattered against Sophie's panes.

Lorraine came out of the bathroom, toweling her hair. "What's all the shouting for? Who are you talking to?" She saw Theresa running back and forth across the kitchen, throwing their dinner out of the window. "Have you lost your mind?"

Theresa picked up a jar of olives. "Now, here's something *freaky* for you— olives! I put olives in my meat loaf! So run up and down the street and tell that!" The jar of olives crashed against the opposite building, barely missing Sophie's window.

"Tee, stop it!"

Theresa put her head back out the window. "Now olives are definitely weird, but you gotta take that one up with my grandmother because it's her recipe! Wait! I forgot the meat—can't have you think I would try to make meat loaf without meat." She ran back to the table and grabbed up the bowl.

"Theresa!!" Lorraine rushed into the kitchen.

"No, can't have you thinking that!" Theresa yelled as she swung back her arm to throw the bowl through Sophie's window. "You might feel I'm a *pervert* or something—someone you can't trust your damn children around!"

Lorraine caught her arm just as she went to hurl the bowl out of the window. She grabbed the bowl and shoved Theresa against the wall.

"Look," Lorraine said, pressing against the struggling woman, "I know you're pissed off, but ground sirloin is almost three dollars a pound!"

The look of sincere horror on Lorraine's face as she cradled the bowl of meat in her arm made Theresa giggle, and then slowly she started laughing and Lorraine nodded her head and laughed with her. Theresa laid her head back against the wall, and her plump throat vibrated from the full sounds passing through it. Lorraine let her go and put the bowl on the table. Theresa's sides were starting to ache from laughing, and she sat down in one of the kitchen chairs. Lorraine pushed the bowl a little further down the table from her, and this set them off again. Theresa laughed and rocked in the chair until tears were rolling down her cheeks. Then she crossed that fine line between laughter and tears and started to sob. Lorraine went over to her, cradled her head in her chest, and stroked her shoulders. She had no idea what had brought on all of this, but it didn't matter. It felt good to be the one who could now comfort.

The shade across the air shaft moved a fraction of an inch, and Sophie pressed one eye against her smeared and dripping windowpane. She looked at the two women holding each other and shook her head. "Um, um, um."

The next day Lorraine was on her way back from the supermarket, and she ran into Kiswana, who was coming out of their building, carrying an armful of books.

"Hi," she greeted Lorraine, "you sure have a full load there."

"Well, we ran out of vegetables last night." Lorraine smiled. "So I picked up a little extra today."

"You know, we haven't seen you at the meetings lately. Things are really picking up. There's going to be a block party next weekend, and we can use all the help we can get."

Lorraine stopped smiling. "Did you really think I'd come back after what happened?"

The blood rushed to Kiswana's face and she stared uncomfortably at the top of her books. "You know, I'm really sorry about that. I should have said something—after all, it was my house—but things just sort of got out of hand so quickly, I'm sorry, I . . ."

"Hey, look, I'm not blaming you or even that woman who made such a fuss. She's just a very sick lady, that's all. Her life must be very unhappy if she has to run around and try to hurt people who haven't done anything to her. But I just didn't want any more trouble, so I felt I ought to stay away."

"But the association is for all of us," Kiswana insisted, "and everyone doesn't feel the way she did. What you do is your own business, not that you're doing anything, anyway. I mean, well, two women or two guys can't live together without people talking. She could be your cousin or sister or something."

"We're not related," Lorraine said quietly.

"Well, good friends then," Kiswana stammered. "Why can't good friends just live together and people mind their own business. And even if you're not friends, even . . . well, whatever." She went on miserably, "It was my house and I'm sorry, I . . ."

Lorraine was kind enough to change the subject for her. "I see you have an armful yourself. You're heading toward the library?"

"No." Kiswana gave her a grateful smile. "I'm taking a few classes on the weekends. My old lady is always on my back about going back to school, so I enrolled at the community college." She was almost apologetic. "But I'm only studying black history and the science of revolution, and I let her know that. But it's enough to keep her quiet."

"I think that's great. You know, I took quite a few courses in black history when I went to school in Detroit."

"Yeah, which ones?"

While they were talking, C. C. Baker and his friends loped up the block. These young men always moved in a pack, or never without two or three. They needed the others continually near to verify their existence. When they stood with their black skin, ninth-grade diplomas, and fifty-word vocabularies in front of the mirror that the world had erected and saw nothing, those other pairs of tight jeans, suede sneakers, and tinged sunglasses imaged nearby proved that they were alive. And if there was life, there could be dreams of that miracle that would one day propel them into the heaven populated by their gods—Shaft and Superfly. While they grew old awaiting that transformation they moved through the streets, insuring that they could at least be heard, if not seen, by blasting their portable cassette players and talking loudly. They continually surnamed each other Man and clutched at their crotches, readying the equipment they deemed necessary to be summoned at any moment into Superfly heaven.

The boys recognized Kiswana because her boyfriend, Abshu, was director of the community center, and Lorraine had been pointed out to them by parents or some other adult who had helped to spread the yellow mist. They spotted the two women talking to each other, and on a cue from C. C., they all slowed as they passed the stoop. C. C. Baker was greatly disturbed by the thought of a Lorraine. He knew of only one way to deal with women other than his mother. Before he had learned exactly how women gave birth, he knew how to please or punish or extract favors from them by the execution of what lay curled behind his fly. It was his life-line to that part of his being that sheltered his self-respect. And the thought of any woman who lay beyond the length of its power was a threat.

"Hey, Swana, better watch it talkin' to that dyke—she might try to grab a tit!" C. C. called out.

"Yeah, Butch, why don't ya join the WACS and really have a field day."

Lorraine's arms tightened around her packages, and she tried to push past Kiswana and go into the building. "I'll see you later."

"No, wait." Kiswana blocked her path. "Don't let them talk to you like that. They're nothing but a bunch of punks." She called out to the leader, "C. C., why don't you just take your little dusty behind and get out of here. No one was talking to you."

The muscular tan boy spit out his cigarette and squared his shoulders. "I ain't got to do nothin'! And I'm gonna tell Abshu you need a good spankin' for taking up with a lesbo." He looked around at his reflections and preened himself in their approval. "Why don't ya come over here and I'll show ya what a real man can do." He cupped his crotch.

Kiswana's face reddened with anger. "From what I heard about you, C. C., I wouldn't even feel it."

His friends broke up with laughter, and when he turned around to them, all he could see mirrored was respect for the girl who had beat him at the dozens. Lorraine smiled at the absolutely lost look on his face. He curled his lips back into a snarl and tried to regain lost ground by attacking what instinct told him was the weaker of the two.

"Ya laughing at me, huh, freak? I oughta come over there and stick my fist in your cunt-eatin' mouth!"

"You'll have to come through me first, so just try it." Kiswana put her books on the stoop.

"Aw, Man, come on. Don't waste your time." His friends pulled at his arm. "She ain't nothing but a woman."

"I oughta go over there and slap that bitch in her face and teach her a lesson."

"Hey, Man, lay light, lay light," one whispered in his ear. "That's Abshu's woman, and that big dude don't mind kickin' ass."

C. C. did an excellent job of allowing himself to be reluctantly pulled away from Kiswana, but she wasn't fooled and had already turned to pick up her books. He made several jerky motions with his fist and forefinger at Lorraine.

"I'm gonna remember this, Butch!"

Theresa had watched the entire scene out of the window and had been ready to run out and help Kiswana if the boy had come up on the stoop. That was just like Lorraine to stand there and let someone else take up for her. Well, maybe she'd finally learned her lesson about these ignorant nothings on Brewster Place. They weren't ever going to be accepted by these people, and there was no point in trying.

Theresa left the window and sat on the couch, pretending to be solving a crossword puzzle when Lorraine came in.

"You look a little pale. Were the prices that bad at the store today?"

"No, this heat just drains me. It's hard to believe that we're in the beginning of October." She headed straight for the kitchen.

"Yeah," Theresa said, watching her back intently. "Indian Summer and all that."

"Mmm." Lorraine dumped the bags on the table. "I'm too tired to put these away now. There's nothing perishable in there. I think I'll take some aspirin and lay down."

"Do that," Theresa said, and followed her into the bedroom. "Then you'll be rested for later. Saddle called—he and Byron are throwing a birthday party at the club, and they want us to come over."

Lorraine was looking through the top dresser drawer for her aspirin. "I'm not going over there tonight. I hate those parties."

"You never hated them before." Theresa crossed her arms in the door and stared at Lorraine. "What's so different now?"

"I've always hated them." Lorraine closed the drawer and started searching in the other one. "I just went because you wanted to. They make me sick with all their prancing and phoniness. They're nothing but a couple of fags."

"And we're just a couple of dykes." She spit the words into the air.

Lorraine started as if she'd been slapped. "That's a filthy thing to say, Tee. You can call yourself that if you want to, but I'm not like that. Do you hear me? I'm not!" She slammed the drawer shut.

So she can turn on me but she wouldn't say a word to that scum in the streets, Theresa thought. She narrowed her eyes slowly at Lorraine. "Well, since my friends aren't good enough for the Duchess from Detroit," she said aloud, "I guess you'll go spend another evening with your boyfriend. But I can tell you right now I saw him pass the window just before you came up the block, and he's already stewed to the gills and just singing away. What do you two do down there in that basement—harmonize? It must get kinda boring for you, he only knows one song."

"Well, at least he's not a sarcastic bitch like some people."

Theresa looked at Lorraine as if she were a stranger.

"And I'll tell you what we do down there. We talk, Theresa—we really, really talk."

"So you and I don't talk?" Theresa's astonishment was turning into hurt. "After five years, you're going to stand there and say that you can talk to some dried-up wino better than you can to me?"

"You and I don't talk, Tee. You talk—Lorraine listens. You lecture—Lorraine takes notes about how to dress and act and have fun. If I don't see things your way, then you shout—Lorraine cries. You seem to get a kick out of making me feel like a clumsy fool."

"That's unfair, Lorraine, and you know it. I can't count the times I've told you to stop running behind people, sniveling to be their friends while they just hurt you. I've always wanted you to show some guts and be independent."

"That's just it, Tee! You wanted me to be independent of other people and look to you for the way I should feel about myself, cut myself off from the world, and join you in some crazy idea about being different. When I'm with Ben, I don't feel any different from anybody else in the world."

"Then he's doing you an injustice," Theresa snapped, "because we are different. And the sooner you learn that, the better off you'll be."

"See, there you go again. Tee the teacher and Lorraine the student, who just can't get the lesson right. Lorraine, who just wants to be a human being—a lousy human being who's somebody's daughter or somebody's friend or even somebody's enemy. But they make me feel like a freak out there, and you try to make me feel like one in here. That only place I've found some peace, Tee, is in that damp ugly basement, where I'm not different."

"Lorraine." Theresa shook her head slowly. "You're a lesbian—do you understand that word?—a butch, a dyke, a lesbo, all those things that kid was shouting. Yes, I heard him! And you can run in all the basements in the world, and it won't change that, so why don't you accept it?"

"I have accepted it!" Lorraine shouted. "I've accepted it all my life, and it's nothing I'm ashamed of. I lost a father because I refused to be ashamed of it—but it doesn't make me any *different* from anyone else in the world."

"It makes you damned different!"

"No!" She jerked open the bottom drawer of her dresser and took out a handful of her underwear. "Do you see this? There are two things that have been a constant in my life since I was sixteen years old—beige bras and oatmeal. The day before I first fell in love with a woman, I got up, had oatmeal for breakfast, put on a beige bra, and went to school. The day after I fell in love with that woman, I got up, had oatmeal for breakfast, and put on a beige bra. I was no different the day before or after that happened, Tee."

"And what did you do when you went to school that next day, Lorraine? Did you stand around the gym locker and swap stories with the other girls about this new love in your life, huh? While they were bragging about their boyfriends and the fifty dozen ways they had lost their virginity, did you jump in and say, 'Oh, but you should have seen the one I gave it up to last night?' Huh? Did you? Did you?"

Theresa was standing in front of her and shouting. She saw Lorraine's face crumple, but she still kept pushing her.

"You with your beige bras and oatmeal!" She grabbed the clothes from Lorraine's hand and shook them at her. "Why didn't you stand in that locker room and pass around a picture of this great love in your life? Why didn't you take her to the senior prom? Huh? Why? Answer me!"

"Because they wouldn't have understood," Lorraine whispered, and her shoulders hunched over.

"That's right! There go your precious 'theys' again. They wouldn't understand—not in Detroit, not on Brewster Place, not anywhere! And as long as they own the whole damn world, it's them and us, Sister—them and us. And that spells different!"

Lorraine sat down on the bed with her head in her hands, and heavy spasms shook her shoulders and slender back. Theresa stood over her and clenched her hands to keep herself from reaching out and comforting her. Let her cry. She had to smarten up. She couldn't spend the rest of her life in basements, talking to winos and building cardboard worlds that were just going to come crashing down around her ears.

Theresa left the bedroom and sat in the chair by the living room window. She watched the autumn sky darken and evening crystallize over the tops of the buildings while she sat there with the smugness of those who could amply justify their methods by the proof of their victorious ends. But even after seven cigarettes, she couldn't expel the sour taste in her mouth. She heard Lorraine move around in the bedroom and then go into the shower. She finally joined her in the living room, freshly clothed. She had been almost successful in covering the puffiness around her eyes with makeup.

"I'm ready to go to the party. Shouldn't you start getting dressed?"

Theresa looked at the black pumps and the green dress with black print. Something about the way it hung off of Lorraine's body made her feel guilty.

"I've changed my mind. I don't feel up to it tonight." She turned her head back toward the evening sky, as if the answer to their tangled lives lay in its dark face.

"Then I'm going without you." The tone of Lorraine's voice pulled her face unwillingly from the window.

"You won't last ten minutes there alone, so why don't you just sit down and stop it."

"I have to go, Tee." The urgency in her words startled Theresa, and she made a poor attempt of hiding it.

"If I can't walk out of this house without you tonight, there'll be nothing left in me to love you. And I'm trying, Theresa; I'm trying so hard to hold on to that."

Theresa would live to be a very old woman and would replay those words in her mind a thousand times and then invent a thousand different things she could have said or done to keep the tall yellow woman in the green and black dress from walking out of that door for the last time in her life. But tonight she was a young woman and still in search of answers, and she made the fatal mistake that many young women do of believing that what never existed was just cleverly hidden beyond her reach. So Theresa said nothing to Lorraine that night, because she had already sadly turned her face back to the evening sky in a mute appeal for guidance.

Lorraine left the smoky and noisy club and decided to walk home to stretch the time. She had been ready to leave from the moment she had arrived, especially after she saw the disappointment on everyone's face when she came in without Theresa. Theresa was the one who loved to dance and joke and banter with them and could keep a party going. Lorraine sat in a corner, holding one drink all night and looking so intimidated by the people who approached her that she killed even the most persistent attempts at conversation. She sensed a mood of quiet hysteria and self-mockery in that club, and she fled from it, refusing to see any possible connection with her own existence.

She had stuck it out for an hour, but that wasn't long enough. Tee would still be up, probably waiting at that window, so certain that she would be returning soon. She thought about taking a bus downtown to a movie, but she really didn't want to be alone. If she only had some friends in this city. It was then that she thought about Ben. She could come up the street in back of Brewster Place and cut through the alley to his apartment. Even if Tee was still in that window, she couldn't see that far down the block. She would just tap lightly on his door, and if he wasn't too drunk to hear her, then he wouldn't be too far gone to listen tonight. And she had such a need to talk to someone, it ached within her.

Lorraine smelled the claw-edged sweetness of the marijuana in the shadowy alley before she had gone more than fifty feet in. She stopped and peered through the leaden darkness toward the end and saw no one. She took a few more cautious steps and stopped to look again. There was still no one. She knew she would never reach Brewster like this; each time she stopped her senseless fears would multiply, until it would be impossible to get through them to the other side. There was no one there, and she would just have to walk through quickly to prove this to her pounding heart.

When she heard the first pair of soft thuds behind her, she willed herself not to stop and look back because there was no one there. Another thud and she started walking a little faster to reassure herself of this. The fourth thud started her to running, and then a dark body that had been pressed against the shadowy building swung into her path so suddenly she couldn't stop in time, and she bumped into it and bounced back a few inches.

"Can't you say excuse me, dyke?" C. C. Baker snarled into her face.

Lorraine saw a pair of suede sneakers flying down behind the face in front of hers and they hit the cement with a dead thump. Her bladder began to loosen, and bile worked its way up into her tightening throat as she realized what she must have heard before. They had been hiding up on the wall, watching her come up that back street, and they had waited. The face pushed itself so close to hers that she could look into the flared nostrils and smell the decomposing food caught in its teeth.

"Ain't you got no manners? Stepping on my foot and not saying you sorry?"

She slowly backed away from the advancing face, her throat working convulsively. She turned to run in the direction of the formless thuds behind her. She hadn't really seen them so they weren't there. The four bodies that now linked themselves across the alley hit her conscious mind like a fist, and she cried out, startled. A hand shot itself around her mouth, and her neck was jerked back while a hoarse voice whispered in her ear.

"You ain't got nothing to say now, huh? Thought you was real funny laughing at me in the streets today? Let's see if you gonna laugh now, dyke!" C. C. forced her down on her knees while the other five boys began to close in silently.

She had stepped into the thin strip of earth that they claimed as their own. Bound by the last building on Brewster and a brick wall, they reigned in that unlit alley like dwarfed warrior-kings. Born with the appendages of power, circumcised by a guillotine, and baptized with the steam from a million nonreflective mirrors, these young men wouldn't be called upon to thrust a bayonet into an Asian farmer, target a torpedo, scatter their iron seed from a B-52 into the wound of the earth, point a finger to move a nation, or stick a pole into the moon—and they knew it. They only had that three-hundred-foot alley to serve them as stateroom, armored tank, and executioner's chamber. So Lorraine found herself, on her knees, surrounded by the most dangerous species in existence—human males with an erection to validate in a world that was only six feet wide.

"I'm gonna show you somethin' I bet you never seen before." C. C. took the back of her head, pressed it into the crotch of his jeans, and jerkily rubbed it back and forth while his friends laughed. "Yeah, now don't that feel good? See, that's what you need. Bet after we get through with you, you ain't never gonna wanna kiss no more pussy."

He slammed his kneecap into her spine and her body arched up, causing his nails to cut into the side of her mouth to stifle her cry. He pushed her arched body down onto the cement. Two of the boys pinned her arms, two wrenched open her legs, while C. C. knelt between them and pushed up her dress and tore at the top of her pantyhose. Lorraine's body was twisting in convulsions of fear that they mistook for resistance, and C. C. brought his fist down into her stomach.

"Better lay the fuck still, cunt, or I'll rip open your guts."

The impact of his fist forced air into her constricted throat, and she worked her sore mouth, trying to form the one word that had been clawing inside of her—"Please." It squeezed through her paralyzed vocal cords and fell lifelessly at their feet. Lorraine clamped her eyes shut and, using all of the strength left within her, willed it to rise again.

"Please."

The sixth boy took a dirty paper bag lying on the ground and stuffed it into her mouth. She felt a weight drop on her spread body. Then she opened her eyes and they screamed and screamed into the face above hers—the face that was pushing this tearing pain inside of her body. The screams tried to break through her corneas out into the air, but the tough rubbery flesh sent them vibrating back into her brain, first shaking lifeless the cells that nurtured her memory. Then the cells went that contained her powers of taste and smell. The last that were screamed to death were those that supplied her with the ability to love—or hate.

Lorraine was no longer conscious of the pain in her spine or stomach. She couldn't feel the skin that was rubbing off of her arms from being pressed against the rough cement. What was left of her mind was centered around the pounding motion that was ripping her insides apart. She couldn't tell when they changed places and the second weight, then the third and fourth, dropped on her—it was all one continuous hacksawing of torment that kept her eyes screaming the only word she was fated to utter again and again for the rest of her life. Please.

Her thighs and stomach had become so slimy from her blood and their semen that the last two boys didn't want to touch her, so they turned her over, propped her head and shoulders against the wall, and took her from behind. When they had finished and stopped holding her up, her body fell over like an unstrung puppet. She didn't feel her split rectum or the patches in her skull where her hair had been torn off by grating against the bricks. Lorraine lay in that alley only screaming at the moving pain inside of her that refused to come to rest.

"Hey, C. C., what if she remembers that it was us?"

"Man, how she gonna prove it? Your dick ain't got no fingerprints." They laughed and stepped over her and ran out of the alley.

Lorraine lay pushed up against the wall on the cold ground with her eyes staring straight up into the sky. When the sun began to warm the air and the horizon brightened, she still lay there, her mouth crammed with paper bag, her dress pushed up under her breasts, her bloody pantyhose hanging from her thighs. She would have stayed there forever and have simply died from starvation or exposure if nothing around her had moved. There was no wind that morning, so the tin cans, soda bottles, and loose papers were still. There wasn't even a stray cat or dog rummaging in the garbage cans for scraps. There was nothing moving that early October morning—except Ben.

Ben had come out of the basement and was sitting in his usual place on an old garbage can he had pushed up against the wall. And he was singing and swaying while taking small sips from the pint bottle he kept in his back pocket. Lorraine looked up the alley and saw the movement by the wall. Side to side. Side to side. Almost in perfect unison with the sawing pain that kept moving inside of her. She crept up on her knees, making small grunting sounds like a wounded animal. As she crawled along the alley, her hand brushed a loose brick, and she clawed her fingers around it and dragged it along the ground toward the movement on Brewster Place. Side to side. Side to side.

Mattie left her bed, went to the bathroom, and then put on her tea kettle. She always got up early, for no reason other than habit. The timing mechanism that had been embedded in her on the farm wasn't aware that she now lived in a city. While her coffee water .was heating up, she filled a pitcher to water her plants. When she leaned over the plants at the side of the apartment, she saw the body crawling up the alley. She raised the window and leaned out just to be sure the morning light wasn't playing tricks with her eyes. "Merciful Jesus!" She threw a coat over her nightgown, slipped on a pair of shoes, and tried to make her arthritic legs hurry down the steps.

Lorraine was getting closer to the movement. She raised herself up on her bruised and stiffened knees, and the paper bag fell out of her mouth. She supported herself by sliding against the wall, limping up the alley toward the movement while clawing her brick and mouthing her silent word. Side to side. Side to side. Lorraine finally reached the motion on top of the garbage can. Ben slowly started to focus her through his burgundy fog, and just as he opened his lips to voice the words that had formed in his brain—"My God, child, what happened to you?"—the brick smashed down into his mouth. His teeth crumbled into his throat and his body swung back against the wall. Lorraine brought the brick down again to stop the moving head, and blood shot out of his ears, splattering against the can and bottom of the wall. Mattie's screams went ricocheting in Lorraine's head, and she joined them with her own as she brought the brick down again, splitting his forehead and crushing his temple, rendering his brains just a bit more useless than hers were now.

Arms grabbed her around the waist, and the brick was knocked from her hand. The movement was everywhere. Lorraine screamed and clawed at the motions that were running and shouting from every direction in the universe. A tall yellow woman in a bloody green and black dress, scraping at the air, crying, "Please. Please."

Pat Parker (1944–1989)

Pat Parker's legacy as a poet, activist, and sister is evidenced largely by the spirit of many contemporary Black women writers who have survived her. Parker's incredible ability to write searing and honest criticisms that also captured the tender and the human is evidenced in the poetic aesthetics of Cheryl Clarke, Audre Lorde, Jayne Cortez, Sapphire, among others. When Parker died of breast cancer in 1989, the loss was one that various communities of Black people noted and mourned, especially communities of Black women and Black lesbians specifically; her death also served to reignite the commitment to conversations about health in Black feminist discourses. This impact is noted most centrally in The Black Women's Health Book, *edited by Evelyn C. White, which pays a special tribute to Parker's life and poetry.*

Parker was born on January 20, 1944, and grew up in Houston, Texas. As a young adult, Parker moved to Oakland, California in the early 1970s, after having been involved in various facets of the civil rights movement. She became medical coordinator of the Oakland Feminist Women's Health Center, a position she held from 1978 to 1987. It is her activity through this center that propelled her to the heights of Black feminist activism, and she is partly responsible for the contemporary attention that is paid to Black women's health. She has written three collections of poetry that have generally lapsed out of print, but are recollected in Movement in Black *(1978; recently republished and expanded, 1999),* Pit Stop, *and* Womanslaughter. *She also published* Jonestown and Other Madness *(1985).*

Parker's gift is her ability to capture and further the poetic voice of resistance that originates in various civil rights and Black power movements in the 1960s, and the organization of Black feminist consciousness-raising groups in the 1970s. The aesthetics of the work these Black women produced included a merger of issues of global and international politics with issues of love and other "domestic" matters. In "love isn't," Parker juxtaposes the familiar love narrative, which posits an economically secure heterosexual couple enjoying their paradise, with the day-to-day shock and ugly of urban realities for people on the social margin; each stanza serves as a reversal and critique of the previous. Yet, Parker does not only suggest that urban life is harsh and unrelenting, but in fact reveals the commitment to love and betterment that exists in her politics. The ethic of care that she employs in the final stanza is not only prophetic and cautioning, but it softens the hard edges that she had earlier presented. Parker's images, especially the final poetic turn, serves as a reminder of the capacity and desire for love that motivates her liberation politics.

Similarly, in "legacy," Parker begins with refutation, except she names the social opinions that the poem is intended to counter, but does not offer a refutation until the final stanza. This delay builds expectation for a potent ending, and yet Parker delivers yet another turn: She again uses softness and a gesture of human kindness as the force with which she will reject social violence and hatred. This technique, Parker's deployment of delay, is an excellent example of irony, for her tone is partly wry, and it undercuts the expectation that those in opposition to her (and perhaps some of her readers) might have. In this poem especially, Parker is able to create an oral poem, through her use of repetition and her use of subjects in the poem; that is, one can almost hear the voice of a mother speaking to her child, which further affirms the ironic and loving impulse of Parker's revolutionary politics.

The untitled poem also uses irony and sarcasm to deliver a difficult message—a critique of Black male sexism and patriarchal violence against Black women. Parker begins with an epigraph from the slave freedom fighter and underground railroad leader Harriet Tubman that is defiant and self-regarding. Yet, Parker begins that poem with the loving and political greeting "brother," which not only creates a narrative voice, but is also conversational and familiar. Again, the end of the poem is where the strength is, and the sweet relevance of Parker's words are revealed line by line, ending with an uncompromised punctuation.

Perhaps the piece that best reflects Parker's skill at wit and sarcasm is "For the white person who wants to know how to be my friend," where the title introduces Parker's humor with its instructive tone. Parker's poem is a listing of all too familiar insults made by White people in their clumsy attempts to befriend a Black person. Yet she also reveals how complicated race and its corresponding social narratives are, especially in her opening lines, which suggest the realness and importance and still, the irrelevance of race. Parker's humor is not to be mistaken for levity, and in fact the poem argues that race and its social practice is a conundrum that in fact requires constant critical interrogation.

What Parker gives us in these poems are glimpses of the incredible spirit and voice of resistance that made her such an indispensable member of Black artistic and activist communities.

Kevin Everod Quashie

love isn't

I wish I could be
the lover you want
come joyful
bear brightness
like summer sun

Instead
I come cloudy
bring pregnant women
with no money
bring angry comrades
with no shelter

I wish I could take you
run over beaches

lay you in sand
and make love to you

Instead
I come rage
bring city streets
with wine and blood
bring cops and guns
with dead bodies and prison

I wish I could take you
travel to new lives
kiss ninos on tourist buses
sip tequila at sunrise

Instead
I come sad
bring lesbians
without lovers
bring sick folk
without doctors
bring children
without families

I wish I could be
your warmth
your blanket

All I can give
is my love.

I care for you
I care for our world
if I stop
caring about one
it would be only
a matter of time
before I stop
loving
the other.

legacy

FOR ANASTASIA JEAN

*'Anything handed down
from, or as from an
ancestor to a descendant.'*

Prologue

There are those who think
or perhaps don't think
that children and lesbians
together can't make a family
that we create an extension
of perversion.

They think
or perhaps don't think
that we have different relationships
with our children
that instead of getting up
in the middle of the night
for a 2 AM and 6 AM feeding
we rise up and chant
'you're gonna be a dyke
you're gonna be a dyke.'

That we feed our children
lavender Similac
and by breathing our air
the children's genitals distort
and they become hermaphrodites.

They ask
'What will you say to them
what will you teach them?'

Child
that would be mine
I bring you my world
and bid it be yours.

[untitled]

*"There are two things I've got a right to, and these
are death or liberty. One or the other i mean to have."*
Harriet Tubman

Brother
  I don't want to hear
  about
  how *my* real enemy
  is the system.
i'm no genius,
  but i do know
  that system
you hit me with
  is called
  a fist.

For the white person who wants to know how to be my friend.

The first thing you do is to forget that i'm Black.
Second, you must never forget that i'm Black.

You should be able to dig Aretha,
but don't play her every time i come over.
And if you decide to play Beethoven—don't tell me
his life story. They made us take music appreciation too.

Eat soul food if you like it, but don't expect me
to locate your restaurants
or cook it for you.

And if some Black person insults you,
mugs you, rapes your sister, rapes you,
rips your house or is just being an ass—
please, do not apologize to me
for wanting to do them bodily harm.
It makes me wonder if you're foolish.

And even if you really believe Blacks are better lovers than
whites—don't tell me. I start thinking of charging stud fees.

In other words—if you really want to be my friend—*don't*
make a labor of it. I'm lazy. Remember.

Richard Perry (1944-)

Richard Perry was born January 13, 1944, in New York City. He attended City College of New York, earning a Bachelor's degree in 1970, and completed an M.F.A. from Columbia two years later. Since then, Perry has taught at the Pratt Institute in Brooklyn and is currently an associate professor of English. In his career, Perry has published three novels, Changes (1974), Montgomery's Children (1984), and No Other Tale to Tell (1994). He has received numerous awards for his work, including two from the New Jersey State Council of the Arts and a National Endowment for the Arts fellowship.

"Blues for My Father, My Mother, and Me" is a lovely story that uses the blues aesthetic to reveal the unarticulated pain of a family who has endured violence and loss, and now is left, as its narrator does at the end, to pick up the broken pieces. Perry sets up the narrator, Jason Strong, as the blues artist, for it is his reflections and thoughts that guide the reader's vision of his family. Jason's narration is a complicated, moving consciousness that mixes past and present in a swaying melody, juxtaposing pain and sweetness, and forcing himself, his parents, and the reader to reconcile life's ugly with its possibility. Perry achieves this in the story by using a gradual unfolding of the narrative, bolstered by scenes that leave great images in the reader's mind. This exploitation of the power of a photographic scene is what makes the scene where Jason's father stands futilely with his pants at a puddle beneath his feet and with a thundering voice so memorable. In that moment, the reader, like Jason, is challenged to merge the power and the impotence, which also resonates with Jason's own inability to have children as the result of racial violence, and his father's invocation of him as the last "Strong man." These images also connect with Jason's embrace of his father.

According to novelist Ralph Ellison, in the tradition of the blues, the jagged edge of pain is fingered, embraced, acknowledged. Perry gives us a story that intersects the private and seething pain of each of the characters—the mother's loss of her only girl child and her resentment of her husband's militant race politics; the father's loss of the only son he liked and respected, and his resentment of his wife's betrayal of him; the living son's anger at being abused and disregarded; the dead son's attempt to be his father's son, in spite of his own misgivings. Perry's narrative, like James Baldwin's in "Sonny's Blues" or Toni Morrison's in Jazz, presents a conflict between Black northern and southern life, suggesting that there is no unearned rest in either place. That the peace that Jason is seeking and that he has a renewed faith in at the story's end is one that is long worked for and always at the risk of a society's hateful intentions toward Black people.

But there is also the blues in Perry's language, the way he captures the language and wit of Black folk culture. When the mother says, "Old is what you get when you don't die," it is a moment of Perry infusing his narrative with the wisdom of the blues, for the blues offer reflections on the lessons for living. Another manifestation of blues aesthetic in the narrative is the textured, thick language—a language that is so well crafted that one can almost feel it—that Perry uses, especially in Jason's description of his visit to his father's bedside: "I sit here, sinking beneath menthol and despair," Jason says, which recreates for the reader the palpability of the air in the room.

The way Perry closes the story, with the father playing "something intricate on the guitar, [something that] makes it sound like laughing and crying at the same time," and the son picking up the pieces, the mother, cautious, at the threshold of the door, makes a commentary on the notion of strength and masculinity. The "blues" in the title is not only this song, but also the narrative Jason has just narrated, and he too now is a blues singer, with the capacity to speak sweetness and pain, and with an unrelenting commitment to hope, which, in the end, is where strength really is.

Kevin Everod Quashie

Blues for My Father, My Mother, and Me

On Saturday, my mother calls. Dudley Strong is ill. No, nothing serious, a little pleurisy in his side. But he is moodier than usual. He sleeps fitfully and has bad dreams. Twice in the last week he woke screaming for Marcus. Perhaps if I came, not long, she knows I'm busy.

I try to stay away from my parents. I saw them last nine months ago at my brother's funeral. My mother didn't talk to me when I was a kid. My father always preferred my brother. I used to believe it was because Marcus was the older, but whatever the reason, it hurts. Still, it hasn't stopped me from making a life for myself. I've got a job, an apartment, and a couple of friends. A woman or two seem to enjoy my company. Sometimes I get a little lonely, but show me some people who don't.

I'll leave to see my parents in the morning. I have not been out today. I stayed in the darkroom, processing film I shot a week ago in Soho. Only two of the photographs developed revealed a smiling face. The smell of chemicals lines my throat. I swallow hard and something opens up inside, and I'm missing my brother.

"It's been tough," Marcus said. "I'm not crying, but it seems like for a long spell now, I've just been marking time. I'm ready to devote myself to what I have to do. I see that lasting change takes lasting struggle."

We were having a drink in the West End Bar on Broadway. It was one of the few times he allowed me a glimpse of what his life was like then, in the summer of 1971. He said he was dreaming all the time of Bobby Johnson, of Schwerner, Chaney and Goodman. Mississippi had ripped something out of Marcus. He'd been so confident, so brash. Mississippi had found his soft spot, taught him the meaning of fear, self-doubt, and failure. For a long time after he came North he

was disconnected, floated from Harlem to Newark to Greenwich Village searching for the "radical" solution. His eyes were empty and his shoulders slumped. I
worried, but there was nothing I could do. Then he got a regular job and found a
shrink, and I thought he'd turned the corner.

The last time I saw him was six months before he died. He'd joined a group
that planned to blow up the Statue of Liberty and the Stock Exchange. I thought
he'd given up on all of that; I said he was crazy. He said I was part of the problem. That there could be no revolution without risk. That it was men like him
who offered a way out, and that if I insisted on standing in the middle, then the
middle was where I'd fall.

At the end he was sounding just like my father, and we were shouting. It's
not good to imagine that your brother died angry at you. For a while I blamed
myself.

My parents are another story. All the way up on the bus from New York to
Kingston, I turn it over in my head. Sure they make me guilty, like anybody's
parents can, but my reasons for staying away are better than most. The air in my
parents' house is laced with their mutual hate, and I can't breathe it. I can't even
figure out if something happened to make them the way they are, or if each just
grew into despising the other. Sometimes I go through my childhood week by
month, trying to recall some word, some gesture or expression that would tell
me. But I never find anything. The way they are just is, that's all.

But it's such a waste. What's more important then family? I look at young
couples in the street and I talk under my breath to them, telling them not to
blow it. Don't fuck up the children, I say. Love one another. I'll never have my
own kids, so I get very touchy about the subject. Maybe that's why I miss Marcus
so, because now I can't have him. And it eats me up that we parted the way we
did. I hate guilt. I'm guilty because I've mostly stayed away from my parents the
last eight years. They're seventy-seven and seventy-four. They'll die soon. I don't
know how I'll handle it. I feel like there's something awful in me that their
deaths will activate, some unprotected place that, once bruised, will never heal.
But I don't want to think about that now. I settle back in my seat and try to let
the bus wheels hum me to sleep. After a while I sit up, stare out the window at
the bright December sky.

I stand in front of the house I grew up in. It's small, two storied, has a porch
my father screened himself. I am remembering waiting here for him to come
home from work, wondering if he'd be drunk or sober. The foods he wore on his
waiter's uniform, his music. My mother holding silence to her shoulders like a
shawl. My brother, sure of himself from the time he understood the meaning of
self. And me, a stranger in this house, lost, really, until I discovered cameras and
the magic of darkrooms.

But I don't live here anymore. I'm twenty-seven and I've got my own place. I
go up the porch steps, through the living room. I'm met by the smell of baking,
the figure of my mother at the kitchen sink.

"Mama?"

She turns: the broad nose, the impossibly angled cheekbones. "Jason?"

"How you doing?"

"Didn't expect you so soon."

I cross the room, take her in my arms. "You gain a few pounds, lady?"

"You know I ain't never been no size. Too old to get some now."

"Old? Come on. What's old?"

She pulls back from me, begins, as if I have violated her, to adjust her clothing needlessly. "Old," she says, "is what you get when you don't die."

There's a silence, building with a rush, that and the dull ache she triggers in my chest with distance. She has fully rearranged herself. "Dad upstairs?"

"Last I looked."

"Guess I'll go see him."

She doesn't look at me. It's as if I've come and gone already. I go back through the living room, climb the stairs.

At the top I pause in the door of the room I shared with my brother. Both beds are tightly made as if we would sleep in them again, as if we would lie again in darkness and share our dreams. I miss my brother. I turn down the hall toward my parents' door, open it enough to stick my head into the darkened room.

"Dad?"

"Marcus?"

"Jason." I step into the smell of menthol.

"I must have been dreaming," he says. "I keep dreaming about him."

"How you feeling?"

"Not too good." His head flops toward me, features forming in the dimness as my eyes grow accustomed to the dark. His face is withered and grizzled; he needs a haircut and a shave. "Got this cold in my side. . . ."

"Want me to open a window?"

"The light," he grunts, "hurts my eyes. Sit. Rest yourself."

His guitar lies across the only chair. I lean the instrument against the wall, drag the chair to the bed. "Been playing?"

"Playing?"

"Guitar."

"Naw."

". . . Beautiful day outside."

"I guess so. When you seen your brother?"

Daylight leaks past the drawn shades, weak and tentative, the way light must enter the mausoleums of dead men. "Marcus is dead."

"I won't see another spring," he says. "I won't last the winter."

"Don't talk like that. Mama says it's only pleurisy."

"Your *mama*." He spits the word out and struggles to lift his head from the pillow. There's a charge in the room, electric; I recognize the hate. "Your mama," he says, eyes small and ugly in the dimness, "she the reason for me going to prison. She the one told." He is looking not at me, but at the window where the light creeps through. "She hated Garvey. Hated Black. All she care about is that lily white Jesus of her'n. He had the way. He had the plan. That's why they got him. He died for us," my father says fiercely, and for a moment I don't know if he's talking about the black Garvey or the white Christ.

"Dad, I don't believe Mama did that."

"Never did believe she could do nothing, did you? Ask her."

"Did you?"

"Didn't need to."

"Then how . . . ?"

"Because," my father says, "she told me."

I sit here, sinking beneath menthol and despair. A long time ago, my father worked for Marcus Garvey, had been his driver and personal gofer, and then my father left for a job in a meat-packing plant. When Garvey was sent to prison on charges of mail fraud, my father became part of a group that plotted to break him out. Someone had betrayed them, and my father spent three years in jail.

Now he is telling me that his wife had been the traitor. Was this the reason for the way they were? If so, why hadn't he left; was his punishment of her in the staying? Why hadn't he considered *his* life, his misery? My father was fifty when I was born, my mother forty-seven. Marcus was fourteen months my senior. Why had they had us then?

Why had my mother betrayed him?

Why is he telling *me?*

Had Marcus known?

I sit, disgusted, feeling sorry for myself, waiting for my father to continue. But it's as if I'm no longer here, as if he's slipped back into the half-demented world I've disturbed with my presence. I try not to be bitter, but I can't help it. He's probably, in the bright place of his memory, sitting on the porch, playing checkers with his oldest son, while I stand in the dark outside the circle they make, watching. I listen to the labored snarl of his breathing, and I am thinking that I should get up and leave this house, leave him, forever.

"And you know what?" my father says.

"What?"

"Marcus ain't dead."

"Dad. . . ."

"Move out the way. Let me up."

"Dad. . . ."

"Move out the way, boy."

I move. It's the voice of his prime, full of power and authority, and I respond reflexively as I did when a child. He throws the blanket from his body, and then he looms above me, reeking of menthol. "Now where is my clothes?" he says, and, after a moment's indecision, makes his way like a drunken man to the closet. He is struggling to pull a pair of pants on over his pajamas. He is trying to put both feet into the same leg.

"Dad. Where you going?"

"Get my son."

"Where?"

"Want to come, come. Don't, don't."

I'm shaking. I cross to him, reach and grab his arm. "Come back to bed."

"Told you I'm going to get my son. Best let go of me." His voice is menacing, in his eyes a disbelief that I dare dictate to him, that I dare touch his body with impunity. I'm shaking. He is my father, no matter what he did to me, no matter how he felt about me, or feels now; he is my father. But I know what I have to do.

"Come back to bed. Marcus is dead."

"Ain't."

"He's dead," I shout. "I identified the body. They emptied shotguns in his face. Now come on back to bed."

"Going to see my son," he thunders. "Get out my way."

So it has come to this again. I watch him, towering above me, pants in a puddle at his feet. I think back nearly eight years to June, 1964, to the night before the morning Marcus and I left for Mississippi, when my father found out and waited up for Marcus and vowed to block Marcus' passage with his body, vowed to break his son's bones if need be, if that's what it took to keep him from going South. And Marcus coming into the room, frenzied, shaking my bed, and me awakening, thinking he was my father finally come to seek revenge. *I didn't tell,* I said. The lamp turned over, the bulb exploded like a pistol shot and Marcus was astride me in the dark, screaming *traitor,* both fists flailing at my face. My father stood in the doorway, didn't move. So this is his revenge, I thought. . . .

And all because, months before, when I saw them about to fight, I threw my body between my parents, and when my father, crazed with drink and rage, kept coming, I hit him. Not out of loyalty to my mother, but out of fear and a longing for peace. But I could never explain that to him; he wouldn't let me, only grunted when I tried. And now he was pushing me all the way out into the darkness by disconnecting me from my brother's love, his precious elder son who was going to Mississippi to risk his life for a thing as frail as freedom. My father's revenge was beautifully conceived and structured, the perfect poetry of a madman's shattered heart.

I was nineteen, but I understood this. I understood it in the way that young men suddenly realize that the earth does not exist to do their bidding, and that they are not immune to death. The understanding allowed me to accept when the policemen the neighbors called said that one of us, me or Marcus, had to cool off for the night in jail, and my father picked me. It also drove me from this house, all the way to Mississippi, with Marcus, who finally believed me. I hadn't planned to go. I thought my father was right, those folks would kill you. It didn't make any sense to me to risk my life like that. But I went because there was no place else to go and I learned to believe in nonviolence and I hoped and turned the other cheek until three men with axe handles beat between my thighs until my flesh was purple, until their daughters were safe, until what they'd done meant that I would have no children. I hate those men. But that I was there in the first place is still my father's fault.

He has accomplished the putting on of his pants, is struggling into a shirt, lurching for the door, the shirt unbuttoned, his feet bare. I grab his arm and spin him and slap him across the face.

The last time I hit my father he touched his face and stared at his fingers in disbelief. Now, with a growl, he cocks his fist and swings at my head. But my father is an old, sick man this morning, and I step inside the punch and embrace him. He is grunting, hammering at my back with both hands, but the blows don't hurt. I hold him tighter, his chin on my shoulder, and I feel the madness spending its strength. His hands fall to his sides; his knees buckle. I half carry, half drag him to the bed and lay him across it. I bump against the end table, setting in motion the empty vase which totters and falls, smashes against the floor. I leave it, peel the pants off, get him under the blanket. Then I just stand looking down at him, and I am frightened at what I feel: vengeance, pain, shame, love.

"You didn't," he says, "have to hit me." His face is turned, his eyes hidden.

"I'm sorry."

"Marcus. . . ."

"I'm *Jason*. Not Marcus."

"He's dead," my father says. "And I won't last the winter."

Something wells in me. I would never have thought my father could make me cry. I reach and touch his shoulder. "Sure you will. You'll outlive all of us."

"I ain't got no quarrel. . . . I done lived a long time." He faces me, eyes alive with hurt. "You all I got left now. You the last Strong man. The name is yours. You got to carry on."

I don't trust myself to speak. My father doesn't know; I never told him. Marcus was the last Strong man.

"Mouth's dry. Could you get me some water?"

I'm shaking, spent, everything moving two ways inside me. I go downstairs. My mother sits at the table, eyes like a threatened bird's, shoulders hunched. "What was all that fuss?"

"Oh . . . Dad got upset. He'll be all right. He wants some water."

She stares at me, as if trying to discover what water has to do with it, and then her gaze veers toward the counter and the cooling bread. "Ain't him I'm worried about."

I sigh, abused by their mutual hate, their private drama. "What's wrong, Mama? What is it?"

"What's he saying about me?"

I wave away the question. "He's sick. You can't listen to everything he says."

"He told what I did?"

I nod.

"I didn't *mean* for him to go to prison," she wails. "I was scared, that's why I told. The man said nothing would happen if it got stopped in time."

"Mama. . . ."

"I didn't *mean* it."

I close my eyes. "I know."

"And let me tell you something. My baby would've lived wasn't for him not being home. He the cause of my child dying."

The room begins to turn. I reach behind me for a wall; it's not there. I make it to the safety of the counter, hold to it with both hands. "What child?"

"It don't make no difference now."

"*Mama*. What child?" The room is turning, my mother's face the only still point. "Mama!"

She is rocking, holding herself, eyes fixed upon the floor. "We had a girl, your daddy and me. That's right. Was why he quit Garvey in the first place, we needed money. When Garvey went to jail for stealing, your daddy blamed himself as if his quittin' was the cause. Your daddy in prison and I'm left alone with a three-month baby, see? My milk went bad. From worrying. My baby died." She looks at me and blinks. "You had a sister. Been forty-seven had she lived. In August."

"Jesus, Mama. Did you tell him?"

"Tell him what?"

"How you *feel*," I whisper.

"Tell him? He knew."

She is curious, vaguely annoyed, and I hear the click as she dismisses my foolishness. "And then," she says, "to have him think I meant it. He had to have something on me, cause he know he the cause that baby dying. The way he know he the cause of Marcus ending up the way he did. It was what your daddy taught him. *Black* that, *black* this. He had to have something on me, to make us even."

It's more than she's spoken to me at one time in all my life. Winter sits on her face, gray and deadly, and when she speaks again her voice has lost its energy, gone flat. "This morning I went to take him his breakfast. He said he didn't like the way I looked at him. That I looked at him like he was a piece of dirt. And I told him . . . if the shoe fits, wear it."

"Maybe," I start, then say it anyway. "Maybe you shouldn't have said that."

Her eyes meet mine, then slide past to the window where the sun comes through. But I catch in the instant of our meeting her accusation, this and the knowledge that as she's suspected, nothing has changed. And as I begin to speak, to say that the path to peace did not lie in confrontation, I stop, thinking, who knew? Perhaps the *only* path to peace was confrontation, and my mother nods and says, almost triumphantly, "Sticking up for your father. Wasn't you, it was Marcus."

"I'm not taking sides. I just know he's suffering."

"Oh? *He's* suffering." And she looks at me and her face says I'm a grown man, yet stupid, have sight, but still can't see. "I birthed Marcus," she says, and blinks.

"I know. Listen. It'll be all right. He'll get over it."

"Maybe so. . . . But will I?"

I don't say anything. I move to the sink, fill a glass, then remember there is always a bottle of water in the refrigerator. Her voice arches behind me.

"Boy, let me tell you. You don't know the half. The *years*. But I won't cry no more. I won't."

I turn. Tears stream down her face. "Mama . . ." I step toward her; she holds her hands up.

"Go tend your father. He the one sick."

"What can I do? *Tell* me."

"Take your father his water."

I don't know where it comes from, but the thought explodes that someplace people are happy, someplace someone laughs. And all of it swells and bears down on me. The years of silence, of pain, and lost connections. I've had enough, not because I'm strong, but because I need and I'm grieving. I'm grieving for my parents, and for my brother, and I grieve for me. "There's nobody left but us now, Mama. Can't we make it better? Can't we try?"

She stares at me. If there's a feeling in her eyes, I can't read it. I look at her, all wrapped up in stubbornness and revenge, and I feel a sharp and searing rage. Then it drains, leaving me hollow, nothing to hold to. I wish my brother were here. I take a deep breath, try to get things to flow one way inside me. I go back upstairs, help my father to sit up, prop pillows behind his back.

"Did you dig a well?" he asks.

I consider strangling him. He drinks the water and smacks his lips. "Thankee, thankee. Now get me that guitar if you please."

I get the guitar. He picks a chord, tunes the instrument. "He really dead?"

"Dad," I say wearily.

"All right." He smiles a mocking, privileged smile. "What you want to hear?"

I want to say it doesn't matter. I want to say play a funeral dirge. Play the National Anthem. "Anything, Dad. Anything."

"You know 'Blues For The Boogie Man'?"

"No."

"How about 'I Have Had My Fun If I Don't Get Well No More'?"

"Yeah."

"Well, let's do it."

He begins to sing. I sit for a while, throat lined with menthol, feeling lost and tired and unconnected. I want to shout, to scream. I want to go to sleep in a sunlit room; I want to be held by someone who loves me. My father does something intricate on the guitar, makes it sound like laughing and crying at the same time, and I realize that though I've remembered the music, I've forgotten how good he is. Now I begin to focus on his song. It's an old song, one I recall from childhood; it is connected also to summer nights in Mississippi when I was afraid and wanted to leave there. Those voices in the South were deep and powerful, or high and sweet, and no matter how bad you felt they helped you make it through until the morning. My father's voice is thin, but not without strength, not without a stubborn desire to have the record show that although he was out there in the wilderness, half-mad, battered and barely alive, he was hanging tough. I'm feeling blue and washed out, but now at least I know. Everybody has a story;

there's always a reason why. My parents had told their stories to me. I had seen the tales as burdens, dusty, unclaimed baggage whose weight they now insisted I should bear. But perhaps I am wrong. Perhaps each telling is a gift, a way of connecting to the only flesh they share.

I don't know, but as I listen to my father sing, I sense a developing of hope. And I realize that I will make it, that some of my parents' toughness is in me, that if they have never bestowed upon me a perfect love, they have bequeathed to me my spirit. My parents' lives were hard, but they were not wasted; they'd lived them the best way they knew. Neither was a life that I wanted to live, but I didn't have to. And I didn't have to let their lives color mine.

Even as I think this I feel something slip inside, go out of me, deepen the darkness of my father's room. None of what I want can be achieved without struggle. I'm tired, and more than a little afraid, and besides, there's all that history. I will always be my parents' child; some things I'll never forget. And I don't know if I'm strong enough to remember without yielding to bitterness and the urge to revenge, even when I know each prevents me from connecting.

My father sings. I hear steps on the staircase and my mother comes along the hall, stands in the doorway. She doesn't say anything, but she is here. As I am. My father sings. I go to my knees where the vase lies shattered, and I begin to pick up the pieces.

Ishmael Reed (1938–)

Ishmael Reed grew up in Buffalo, New York; as a young man he lived New York City and came in contact with the Black Arts Movement. He thought highly of Larry Neal, a leading figure in Black Arts.

In 1967 he moved near San Francisco. For many years he has taught at the University of California at Berkeley, sometimes leaving for academic appointments at Yale, Harvard, SUNY Buffalo, and elsewhere.

Reed has written and edited many books, including novels, poems, and polemical essays. His most familiar works include two novels–Yellow Black Radio Broke-Down (1969) and Mumbo Jumbo (1972)–and his New and Collected Poems (1988).

Decidedly a maverick, Reed enjoys provoking controversy. Advocating "Neohoodooism," he offers trickster characters and madcap, take-no-prisoners rhetoric that satirizes not only suburban White culture, but also African American literature. Yet he pays a certain homage to blues and jazz traditions, which he knows well. Because he shatters literary forms and subverts intellectual conventions, he has been termed a postmodernist.

In "I am a Cowboy in the Boat of Ra" and the wildly satiric "Flight to Canada," Reed telescopes time and space. He patterns "Middle Class Blues" after blues songs and offers an imaginative protest in "Untitled."

Keith D. Miller

I am a Cowboy in the Boat of Ra

'The devil must be forced to reveal any such physical evil (potions, charms, fetishes, etc.) still outside the body and these must be burned.' (Rituale Romanum, published 1947, endorsed by the coat-of-arms and introductory letter from Francis Cardinal Spellman)

I am a cowboy in the boat of Ra,
sidewinders in the saloons of fools
bit my forehead   like   O
the untrustworthiness of Egyptologists
who do not know their trips. Who was that
dog-faced man? they asked, the day I rode
from town.

School marms with halitosis cannot see
the Nefertiti fake chipped on the run by slick
germans, the hawk behind Sonny Rollins' head or
the ritual beard of his axe; a longhorn winding
its bells thru the Field of Reeds.

I am a cowboy in the boat of Ra. I bedded
down with Isis, Lady of the Boogaloo, dove
down deep in her horny, stuck up her Wells-Far-ago
in daring midday getaway. 'Start grabbing the
blue,' I said from top of my double crown.

I am a cowboy in the boat of Ra. Ezzard Charles
of the Chisholm Trail. Took up the bass but they
blew off my thumb. Alchemist in ringmanship but a
sucker for the right cross.

I am a cowboy in the boat of Ra. Vamoosed from
the temple i bide my time. The price on the wanted
poster was a-going down, outlaw alias copped my stance
and moody greenhorns were making me dance;
    while my mouth's
shooting iron got its chambers jammed.

I am a cowboy in the boat of Ra. Boning-up in
the ol West i bide my time. You should see
me pick off these tin cans whippersnappers. I
write the motown long plays for the comeback of
Osiris. Make them up when stars stare at sleeping
steer out here near the campfire. Women arrive
on the backs of goats and throw themselves on
my Bowie.

I am a cowboy in the boat of Ra. Lord of the lash,
the Loup Garou Kid. Half breed son of Pisces and
Aquarius. I hold the souls of men in my pot. I do
the dirty boogie with scorpions. I make the bulls
keep still and was the first swinger to grape the taste.

I am a cowboy in his boat. Pope Joan of the
Ptah Ra. C/mere a minute willya doll?
Be a good girl and
bring me my Buffalo horn of black powder
bring me my headdress of black feathers

bring me my bones of Ju-Ju snake
go get my eyelids of red paint.
Hand me my shadow

I'm going into town after Set

I am a cowboy in the boat of Ra

look out Set	here i come Set
to get Set	to sunset Set
to unseat Set	to Set down Set

usurper of the Royal couch
—imposter RAdio of Moses' bush
party pooper O hater of dance
vampire outlaw of the milky way

The Middle Class Blues

Monologue

I can't believe it's 1994. Back in 84 it meant something, but nowadays being middle class and a nickel won't buy you a cup of coffee. During the rest of the 80s the frig was still full and you could always mambo in Guadalajara during the discount off seasons. But by the beginning of the 90s, the only difference between us and the poor was that everything they owned was on their backs while everything we owned was being lent to us by the banks. The banks were on our backs. I was over my head in billy dues. Me and the Mrs. argued so about money that one day she just upped and left. And these were supposed to be our golden years. Some golden years. I can't seem to save over a couple of hundred dollars and I'm spending a third more than I'm making. It's only a matter of time before I have to visit one of those bankruptcy consultants. Talking about the new poor. Never thought it would happen to me. What happened to the old poor? I dunno. They were kicked out of the bus stations, the parks and the welfare hotels a long time ago. Some say they went South. Others say that the society people had them shipped to Central America because down there they know how to handle the poor. Wherever they are, they must have been desperate. They left behind their blues. I'm lucky I guess. I can still afford a martini.

I
I got the middle class blues
I play by middle class rules
O, this middle class life
Is a life full of strife
The bourgeois state can be

A sweet and sour pill
When the first rolls around
You gotta deal with the bills

So hey, Mr. Bartender,
Bring me a dry vermouth and gin
Fix me a black olive and a big martini
Before I hit the wind

II
I constantly get headaches
And my back is often sore
Being the first one on the freeway
Is becoming such a chore
At work they got a robot
That soon will have my job
I'm too old to start all over
Too old to learn to rob

So hey, Mr. Bartender
Bring me a dry vermouth and gin
Fix me a black olive and a big martini
Before I hit the wind

III
The roof is always leaking
The plumbing needs some screws
Everybody on the block, it seems
Knows how to bar-b-cue
My next door neighbors are ticked at me
My lawn is turning brown
There's always something that must be fixed
Everytime you turn around

Hey, hey, Mr. Bartender
Bring me a dry vermouth and gin
Fix me a black olive and a big martini
Before I hit the wind

IV
My son is getting married
To a woman older than me
He just turned twenty the other
week
She's going on sixty-three

My daughter's on narcotics
Her eyes are always red
The car wouldn't start this morning
And I toss and turn in bed

So hey, Mr. Bartender
Bring me a dry vermouth and gin
Fix me a black olive and a big martini
Before I hit the wind

V
The communists say I'm an ingrate
The capitalists took my house
The old people say I neglect them
The young call me a louse
The tax man sent me a letter
He's coming here tonight
Sometimes it gets so heavy
At home, I'm never right

So hey, Mr. Bartender
Bring me a dry vermouth and gin
Fix me a black olive and a big martini
Before I hit the wind

VI
The Doctor says it's no good
To have this stress and mess
The ulcers that will get you
A classy middle class nest
A cat that won't eat store food
Must have its abalone
And don't forget the deadline
To pay the alimony

So hey, Mr. Bartender
Bring me a dry vermouth and gin
Fix me a black olive and a big martini
Before I hit the wind

VII
Well, I'm tired of paying the dentist
And going under the knife
And doing all the things you do

To stay the bourgeois life
The rich they live in heaven
The poor they live in hell
And I live somewhere in between
A sign outside says for sale

So hey, Mr. Bartender
Bring me a dry vermouth and gin
Fix me a black olive and a big martini
Let me go on get this wind

Untitled

Alaska's rape
dismemberment
disassembled piece by piece
and shipped to the lower
forty-eight so that people
in Dallas may own whale-
sized cadillacs and lear
jets which cost Alaska an
arm and a leg just like
ravished Jamaica whose
stolen sugar built Mansfield
Park where idle gang rapers
discuss flower beds and
old furniture
Jamaica, Alaska, sisters
dragged into an alley
used and abandoned

Flight to Canada

Dear Massa Swille:
What it was?
I have done my Liza Leap
& am safe in the arms
of Canada, so

Ain't no use your Slave
Catchers waitin on me
At Trailways
I won't be there

I flew in non-stop
Jumbo jet this A.M. Had
Champagne
Compliments of the Cap'n
Who announced that a
Runaway Negro was on the
Plane. Passengers came up
And shook my hand
& within 10 min. I had
Signed up for 3 anti-slavery
Lectures. Remind me to get an
Agent

   Traveling in style
Beats craning your neck after
The North Star and hiding in
Bushes anytime, Massa
Besides, your Negro dogs
Of Hays & Allen stock can't
Fly

   By now I s'pose that
Yellow Judas Cato done tole
You that I have snuck back to
The plantation 3 maybe 4 times
Since I left the first time

   Last visit I slept in
Your bed and sampled your
Cellar. Had your prime
Quadroon give me
She-Bear, Yes, yes

   You was away at a
Slave auction at Ryan's Mart
In Charleston & so I knowed
You wouldn't mind
Did you have a nice trip, Massa?

I borrowed your cotton money
to pay for my ticket & to get
Me started in this place called
Saskatchewan Brrrrrrr!
It's cold up here but least
Nobody is collaring hobbling gagging
Handcuffing yoking chaining & thumbscrewing
You like you is they hobby horse

    The Mistress Ms. Lady
Gived me the combination
To your safe, don't blame
The feeble old soul, Cap'n
I told her you needed some
More money to shop with &
You sent me from Charleston
To get it. Don't worry
Your employees won't miss
It & I accept it as a
Down payment on my back
Wages

    I must close now
Massa, by the time you gets
This letter old Sam will have
Probably took you to the
Deep Six
That was rat poison I left
In your Old Crow

        Your boy
        Quickskill

        1976

Carolyn Rodgers (1945–)

Carolyn Rodgers's legacy is as one of the writers who represented the Black Arts movement and, still, whose poetry captures the themes and ideas of Black feminist movements that came in the late 1960s and early 1970s. Like Pat Parker, Audre Lorde, and Jayne Cortez, but also Ethelbert Miller and Lucille Clifton, Rodgers has an interest in refiguring poetic language and capturing the vernacular speech patterns but also everyday experience. Yet, she is committed, as evidenced in her 1975 collection how i got ovah, to paradigms of love and healing, of being able to recognize and affirm the tender and human in Black urban reality.

A native of Chicago, Rodgers earned a B.A. degree from Roosevelt University and became heavily involved in the Chicago Black artistic scene. Like Angela Jackson, Rodgers attended the Organization of Black American Culture's writing workshops, and it was there that she seriously developed her talents. She founded the Third World Press, which published her first two volumes of poetry, Paper Soul (1968) and Song of a Black Bird (1969). A few years later, Rodgers would seemingly shift her attention to religious and spiritual themes, yet it was not really a shift, because her work had always been interested in how people under derisive social conditions respond, in how their souls survived and triumphed, or broke.

The title poem "how i got ovah" resonates with Langston Hughes' "Negro Speaks of Rivers" and with Nikki Giovanni's "Ego Trippin" in its assertion of a power and ancient Black subjectivity, its use of African images and geography as a way to claim heritage. This allusion to Hughes and to one of his most well-known poems is not coincidental, for Rodgers identifies Hughes as one of her mentors. What is wonderful about this poem is its positive self-appraisal, which is characteristic of the Black Arts poetics, and also how oral the language is: The words and their rhythms literally jump off the page, especially with the inclusion of the exclamation "yea," which sounds like a jazz artist acknowledging the sweetness of the scat movement that just finished. In creation of a strong "I" persona with an unfettered sense of self-regard, Rodgers captures the Black revolutionary's capacity to enact change.

"Some Body Call (for help)" is a Black Arts masterpiece in its use of line breaks, spacing, word variation, and repetition to recreate a sense of spoken language on the page. In the title itself, Rodgers separates the three words by capitalization, which makes "somebody" also mean "some body," and mutes the "for help" by placing it on a separate line, in parenthesis, and off to the side. She uses short lines, phonetic spelling, and capitalization to add rhythm and intensity, to capture the language of the street as closely as possible on page. What Rodgers' techniques here reveals is the Black Arts Movement's interest in reforming language to make it appropriate and relevant to Black life, a re-form that recognizes language's elasticity and its rigidity; that language is, at best, representational.

Interestingly, this revision in Black Aesthetics parallels a similar interrogation of language in post-structuralist and deconstructionist literary schools.

In "Blue," Rodgers again uses a strong poetic voice to bring the piece to life. Like Richard Perry's deft use of revelation in his bluesy short story "Blues for My Father, My Mother, and Me," Rodgers' speaker paints a picture of patched-up love through her reflection on the present moment: that her lover is leaving. The heartbreak of the speaker comes real in the poem with the repetition of "what you say" and the final pang that shatters the reflection and throws the speaker and reader back to the harsh present: "what you say / when he gone." Interestingly, this poem is a nice companion to "A Round," in that it suggests a theme that Rodgers muses on in many of her poems—the path to one's self, or how to get over. In "A Round" we have Rodgers at her most bluesy, with her use of wit and repetition, and her philosophical commentary residing in a short, common statement that feels more everyday than it does like a poem. Again, Rodgers is linguistically playful, with her doubletake on the word "around," which is highly relevant to the commentary her poem is making.

Kevin Everod Quashie

Blue

what you say
when somebody tell you
he gon leave
and take the threadbare love he brung to your seasons
raggedy love you took & stitched into
the weavings of your reasonings,
feelings you mended & pieced together
and knitted for yourself a life to slip into.
what you say when you find out he gon
make you switch places with his beginning
when he decides to end it all
and the reason ain't clear
cause you really can't hear him
when he don't be saying "i love you."
what you say,
when he gone.

A Round

the long way
is often the
short way
for me.
to get where i am going
i sometimes have to end up
in circles

Carolyn Rodgers

how i got ovah

i can tell you
about them
i have shaken rivers
out of my eyes
i have waded eyelash deep
have crossed rivers
have shaken the water weed out
of my lungs
have swam for strength
pulled by strength
through waterfalls with electric beats
i have bore the shocks
of water deep deep
waterlogs are my bones
i have shaken the water free of my hair
have kneeled on the banks
and kissed my ancestors of the dirt
whose rich dark root fingers rose up reached out
grabbed and pulled me rocked me cupped me
gentle strong and firm
carried me
made me swim for strength
cross rivers
though i shivered
was wet was cold
and wanted to sink down
and float as water, yea—
i can tell you.
i have shaken rivers
out of my eyes.

Some Body Call

(for help)

i remember the night
he beat
her
we all heard her scream
him break some glass
her beg
dont do it

the hit
imagined the cut
heard the door open
her running running running
in the hall   way
screaming blood blood
saw bloods
(in my head
would not open my door
the po-lees came   (some   body   called)
say who cut de lady
in de mouth who put her out
wid no coat no shoes
                            (some body called
                              some body called
                                                for help)
heard the pigs take her take him a way
beat him, he beat her, beat him down the stairs
heard him call
                (for help)

no body opened no door.
next morning
there was
this blood
on the walls
see
little smudges here there
from hand from mouth (no doubt)
running running along the walls in splatters in sblobs
running running
                        i could wipe the stains away
                        i could do that i could
                        but i thought   (surely)
                                                4 weeks past)
someone (else) would have
why, the janitor
empties the garbage
mops the hall   way floors every
day but he dont touch the blood
                            must be because he dont
                            hear her screeeeeeaaammmming
                            do he dont he NEED to
                            e-rase that blood runningstill   still
                    on the walls the second floors the first floors all   over

Bloods

running running running
  against the walls

                         BLOODS
             running running running
                 in hall ways
running running running
                        through they world
                            CUT-TING into each other
             Some   Body   PLEASE call
                                  for help

Sonia Sanchez (1934–)

Sonia Sanchez, writer of poetry, plays, screenplays, and children's fiction, was born Wilsonia Benita Driver in 1934 in Birmingham, Alabama, and moved to New York's Harlem with her father, stepmother, and sister when she was nine years old. Sanchez attended Hunter College in New York, earning a Bachelor of Arts degree in political science, then did postgraduate work in poetry at New York University. While there, Sanchez developed an instrumental relationship with poet Louis Bogan, who influenced Sanchez particularly in her use of form. She went on to teach at various institutions, Becoming the first college professor to offer a course specifically on African American women authors. Sanchez has held teaching positions at the Downtown Community School in San Francisco, the University of Pittsburgh, Rutgers University, the City College of the City University of New York, Amherst College, Spelman College, and Newcomb College of Tulane University. She is currently the Laura H. Carnell Professor of English at Temple University where she teaches Black American literature and creative writing.

Often criticized for her disruptive use of traditional poetic form, Sanchez in fact has a very significant understanding of form as both limitation and generating tool. Defying the restrictive and Eurocentric boundaries set by Western canonical uses of meter, tone, and language, Sanchez also depends upon an engagement with form that is particularly evident in her use of the praise poem, haiku and tanka. She infuses the poetic with the personal and the political, working toward a form that articulates all three.

The haiku found in this volume evidences the way in which Sanchez utilizes, and radically alters, traditional poetic form. While adhering to the severe limitations set forth by the haiku structure, Sanchez transforms the readers' understandings of the traditional haiku with her personal and political images and rhetoric.

The poem "Homecoming" represents a political and aesthetic "re-birth." First published in 1969 in a book of the same name, "Homecoming" recounts and reenacts the process through which Sanchez literally and figuratively came home. Comparing the "tourist/style" gaze to the Black "woman" gaze Sanchez has discovered/matured into, the poet looks at the ways in which her vision and her process of seeing needed reclamation and reidentification. "Small Comment," another poem from Homecoming included in this anthology, exemplifies the shifting politics that Sanchez found within her own work and within her community. The poem explores the ways politics go from words to action. She places the defining ability in the reader's own hands, an act that attempts to mobilize her readership towards political and personal growth.

The poem "Personal Letter No. 3" was first published in We a BaddDDD People (1970). This poem stands out as one of Sanchez' most poignant treatments of the ways in which Black women are made to simultaneously enact superhuman strength and endurance and are expected to fail at this enactment.

In 1978, a collection of Sonia Sanchez' work titled I've Been a Woman *was published. This collection charts one woman's progression toward a political, aesthetic, and spiritual understanding of Blackness and womanhood. "Poem No. 3" offers a glimpse into a very personal and highly resonant moment. The poem "Philadelphia: Spring, 1985," is a movement toward a reconstruction both of a devastating event and of a communal acknowledgment of loss. The poem in two parts addresses the destruction of the MOVE headquarters and of the deaths of eleven men, women, and children. Here the event is delicately handled with a language and tone that reverberates in stillness and fragility.*

Sonia Sanchez' more recent work continues to press the issue of private and public, doing so in ways that connect to her histories, both as an individual and as a member of a tradition and heritage. In her book of poems, Does Your House Have Lions? *(1995), Sonia Sanchez invokes a variety of voices from her past and present. Taking her brother's death from AIDS as content and motivation, Sanchez engages in a multilayered song in which her brother's life, his alienation from his family, his and his family's reactions to his struggles with HIV, and his subsequent death are played out and replayed toward a climax where his voice moves from one state of existence to another. The excerpt in this anthology, titled "Sister's Voice," is found at the beginning of Sanchez' book and introduces a body in motion. Focusing on the body of the speaker's brother moving away from familial pain and abandonment, "dancing" toward possibility and choice, "embracing" new "geographies," the sister introduces the body's eventual decomposition and movement away not only from its familial and ancestral foundations, but from those foundations that literally hold the body intact.*

In addition to the texts already mentioned, Sonia Sanchez has published a number of other significant poetry collections, as well as plays and children's books. Her continuing legacy in poetry and in her promotion of African American cultural expression has been honored by many institutions and universities. Among her many awards, Sanchez has received a PEN Writing Award, a grant from the National Institute of the Arts and Letters, a National Endowment for the Arts Award, the Lucretia Mott Award, an honorary Ph.D. from Wilberforce University, and an American Book Award from the Before Columbus Foundation.

Sonia Sanchez has said that her work serves apparently contradictory, but nonetheless simultaneous, purposes: to foster and advocate change on personal, regional, and global levels, and to promote a sense of tradition and historical rootedness to Black American individuals and communities. The paradox of a body of work that necessitates both change and stability is not irreconcilable, or even particularly unique, Sanchez maintains. It is through an understanding that the self that wishes to be as strong as bone, and the self that wishes to be as brittle as stone, is realizable in a body that dances to, as it creates, sounds and words centuries old.

Claudia Barbosa Nogueira

Small Comment

the nature of the beast is the
man or to be more specific
the nature of the man is his
bestial nature or to
bring it to its elemental terms
the nature of nature is
the bestial survival of the

fittest the strongest the richest
or to really examine
the scene we cd say that
the nature of any beast is
bestial unnatural and natural
in its struggle for superiority
and survival but to really
be with it we will say that the man
is a natural beast bestial in
his lusts natural in his
bestiality and expanding
and growing on the national
scene to be the most
bestial and natural of
any beast. you dig?

Personal Letter No. 3

nothing will keep
us young you know
not young men or
women who spin
their youth on
cool playing sounds.
we are what we
are what we never
think we are.
no more wild geo
graphies of the
flesh. echoes. that
we move in tune
to slower smells.
it is a hard thing
to admit that
sometimes after midnight
i am tired
of it all.

Haiku

Was it yesterday
love we shifted the air and
made it blossom Black?

sister's voice

this was a migration unlike
the 1900s of black men and women
coming north for jobs. freedom. life.
this was a migration to begin
to bend a father's heart again
to birth seduction from the past
to repay desertion at last.

imagine him short and black
thin mustache draping thin lips
imagine him country and exact
thin body, underfed hips
watching at this corral of battleships
and bastards. watching for forget
and remember. dancing his pirouette.

and he came my brother at seventeen
recruited by birthright and smell
grabbing the city by the root with clean
metallic teeth. commandant and infidel
pirating his family in their cell
and we waited for the anger to retreat
and we watched him embrace the city and the street.

first he auctioned off his legs. eyes.
heart. in rooms of specific pain.
he specialized in generalize
learned newyorkese and all profane.
enslaved his body to cocaine
denied his father's signature
damned his sister's overture.

and a new geography greeted him.
the atlantic drifted from offshore
to lick his wounds to give him slim
transfusion as he turned changed wore
a new waistcoat of solicitor
antidote to his southern skin
ammunition for a young paladin.

and the bars. the glitter. the light
discharging pain from his bygone anguish

of young black boy scared of the night.
sequestered on this new bank, he surveyed the fish
sweet cargoes crowded with scales feverish
with quick sales full sails of flesh
searing the coastline of his acquiesce.

and the days rummaging his eyes
and the nights flickering through a slit
of narrow bars. hips. thighs.
and his thoughts labeling him misfit
as he prowled, pranced in the starlit
city, coloring his days and nights
with gluttony and praise and unreconciled rites.

Homecoming

i have been a
way so long
once after college
i returned tourist
style to watch all
the niggers killing
themselves with
three-for-oners
with
needles
that cd
not support
their stutters.
                now woman
i have returned
leaving behind me
all those hide and
seek faces peeling
with freudian dreams.
this is for real.
            black
        niggers
            my beauty.
baby.
i have learned it
ain't like they say
in the newspapers.

Philadelphia: Spring, 1985

1.

/a phila. fireman reflects after
seeing a decapitated body in the MOVE ruins/

to see those eyes
orange like butterflies
over the walls.

i must move away
from this little-ease
where the pulse
shrinks into itself
and carve myself in white.

O to press the seasons
and taste the quiet juice
of their veins.

2. */memory/*

a.

Thus in the varicose town
where eyes splintered the night with glass
the children touched at random
sat in places where legions rode.

And O we watched the young birds
stretch the sky
until it streamed white ashes
and O we saw mountains lean on seas
to drink the blood of whales
then wander dumb with their wet bowels.

b.

Everywhere young
faces breathing in crusts.
breakfast of dreams.
The city, lit by a single fire,
followed the air into disorder.
And the sabbath stones singed our eyes
with each morning's coin.

c.

Praise of a cureless death they heard
without confessor;
Praise of cathedrals
pressing their genesis from priests;
Praise of wild gulls who came and drank
their summer's milk,
then led them toward the parish snow.

How still the spiderless city.
The earth is immemorial in death.

Sapphire (1950–)

" ... nobody said that what was cannot be changed," Sapphire writes in "Are You Ready to Rock?" In the first line of the first poem of her book, American Dreams (1994), Sapphire sets the tenor and the promise of her work. Beginning with an ellipsis, a lower case letter, and the word "nobody," Sapphire embarks on a mission to embody her language with the urgency of history and the power of revelation and transformation. Starting in mid-sentence, Sapphire rewrites the past, and so, re-visions and re-creates the future. Sapphire's beginning her sentence, poem, and book with a lower case letter problematizes Western grammatical standards and language use. Her work challenges her first word, "nobody," by supplying the voice that speaks just what that "nobody" was said to say. And this voice does not emerge from a no-body, Sapphire apparently contests, but a specifically Black female one.

Sapphire—poet, dancer, novelist, teacher, and performance artist—writes stories of bodies, the histories of abuse, wounds, rapes, addictions, mutilations, murders, hungers, scars, desires, and healings. She writes of what she reads, hears, sees, and experiences. Using current events, the work of other artists and scholars, testimonies and histories, popular Black urban culture, and her own life as inspiration and context, her work is charged with a political and spiritual sensibility.

Born Ramona Lofton in Fort Ord, California, in 1950, Sapphire attended San Francisco City College and New York City College, where she earned a Bachelor's degree in dance. She also attended graduate school at Brooklyn College. She has worked as an exotic dancer, a performance artist, a caseworker for children and their parents, and a teacher of reading and writing. To date, Sapphire has three book-length publications: Meditations on the Rainbow: Poetry, which was published in 1987; American Dreams, a work incorporating poetry and prose from which the excerpts in this anthology are taken (1994); and the novel Push, published in 1996. This last work met with a great deal of criticism, as well as praise, for its relentlessly frank portrayal of a young Black woman struggling as a survivor of incest and a lifetime of abuse and degradation.

The poem "Strange Juice (or the murder of Latasha Harlins)" recounts an incident wherein a 15-year-old African American girl was shot by a Korean shopkeeper in New York. The shopkeeper, Soon Ja Du, was convicted of voluntary manslaughter, but was given a sentence of probation and community service. The poem, told in the first person, records the thoughts of the already dead narrator, Latasha Harlins. Utilizing the framework of a life flashing before the eyes of one about to die, Sapphire explodes notions of time and space. The murdered young Black female body becomes a nexus where present actions and details are noted and interpreted, while the history of the struggles of African Americans spills into the stories of riots soon to follow. Latasha Harlins' dead body becomes more than a symbol for the complicated and violent effects of poverty, racism, and sexism, however, because it is a body in a process, a body that has been affected by and affects that around her. It is not only a sentient and omniscient (yet dead) body, but a specific body with a specific voice that evolves and becomes inflamed with known purpose.

Sapphire's work does not shy away from very difficult issues, nor does it attempt to hide its subjectivity. In the above poem, the narrator's anti-Asian and anti-women comments are not couched or explained away. These spaces of discomfort, where hatred and bigotry become entangled with a rhetoric of survival and success, seem to be terrain that Sapphire repeatedly explores. What Sapphire does so masterfully with these areas is extend them under the readers' feet; specifically, she demands that the reader go beyond mere association with characters or ideas, go beyond judgments made from the safe and powerful position we, as readers, occupy.

In the poem mentioned at the beginning of this essay, "Are You Ready to Rock?" Sapphire describes and outlines a process by which readers/citizens/consumers are constructed. Likewise, she demonstrates a way to problematize this construction. The question posed in the title, for example, is addressing popular cultural phenomenon, rock n' roll, that has gone from its roots in African American musical traditions to become highly commercialized and, in a sense, de- or misracialized. The question also, however, reflects Sapphire's intent on infusing her poem with pain and asks the reader if he or she is ready to feel and see and hear the hurting body and to rock that body toward healing. The desire to find oneself represented in and through a frequently racist, misogynistic, and homophobic popular culture as a means of validation is complicated by Sapphire's offering a reading that sees the pain that the songs and icons depicted in "Are You Ready to Rock?" can, and cannot, express and sees the necessity for the text, and the bodies therein, to be touched, rocked, and reclaimed.

Sapphire says that she finds inspiration and strength in the works of other contemporary Black poets, particularly Sonia Sanchez and Jayne Cortez. The emphasized oral quality of these poets' writings, the rhythms that accentuate movement and struggle, the histories told in language beautiful and accessible, the insistence on voicing pain, sorrow, joy, desire, and above all, strength, are all evident in the poems of the three. Sapphire, who has also been compared to Langston Hughes and Audre Lorde, is particularly strong in her ability to evoke, in detail, the moments when a body, devastated by a history of abuse and oppression, begins to resemble a person, looking at herself, and recognizing a self in motion.

Claudia Barbosa Nogueira

Are You Ready to Rock?

. . . nobody said that what was cannot be changed. This is an adventure in light waves & new days tiptoeing across a poisoned land selling flowers to soul survivors. We smile for Tina Turner & those fabulous legs that finally carried her to freedom. We hear you, honey, walking to freedom with thirty-six cents & a gas credit card. *What's Love Got to Do With It* when it leaves you brain damaged, bleeding in the snow, blind, limbless, discarded & deserted. Jerry Hall says you can never be sure your man is not gonna run off & leave you. That's terrible. I'm not being sarcastic. I feel like someone poured acid on my face & is banging in my dreams with telephone poles.

oh oh OH
please don't leave me
please don't leave me
please please please
don't go
baby
please don't go.
thank god for that
black boy from Augusta, GA
who grew up to be a man
running down his yellow wife
beating her bloody with a lead pipe.
yet still, when I hurt
I put that record on—
when I'm in the black hurt
it goes all thru my soul
& I scream:
baby please don't go.
All over women douse themselves with perfume, put on push-up bras & slide
into tight red dresses flashing the hold card of youth & desirability. With no pity
on paraplegics, heartbroken sharecroppers or stock market executives, they
creep out back doors into different colored arms sending knives thru the hearts
of men who owned them. & when you're young & pretty & you can feel he
wants you, you tear his eyes out with blue syphilis from the back door man cause
you know you a woman who got to bleed every month & finally turn to sour
milk & fat & die alone or too young or someone will put a gun to your head in a
moment of justifiable passion that the judge understands (after all how would *he*
feel if *his* wife fucked the gardener) & your brains mingle with the oil stains on
the driveway & your memory is a mantra lesbians & nuns with shaved heads
chant at battered women's shelters.

om nama kali ma
om nama kali ma
wear your love like heaven
but don't leave the woods
Little Red Riding Hood
& if I was you I'd be careful
of grandma too.
oh blue moon
black guitar fingers
string around
your clitoris
scream like broken glass
coca cola bottles
wipe out your vagina

detonating your eyes
into hills Red Cloud
rode across like fire,
after the infantry
burning the cornfields
of a mother's love
who slept while
your father smeared
his dick with ice cream
& entreated you
to suck it.
The world sleeps
under orange dioxin rains
eating tuna fish sandwiches
made of dead dolphins.
no one sees the bruises
not even after I swallow
everything in sight—pills, poison.
no one asks me what's wrong
they tell me I'm crazy
crazy
crazy
Crazy Horse
riding free against the cavalry
Harriet Harriet
Tubman
mumbling
falling out
in the swamp
comin'
comin'
comin' fo'
to carry me
home,
not my mother
not my sister
not my brother
it's me
he did it
to *me*
oh lord

standin' in the
need of prayer,
where were you

oh lord
when I was bleeding
from the asshole
at three years old.
sometimes I feel
like a motherless child
a long
long
long
way
from home.
if dogs run free then why can't we
which way mister
which way to 42nd Street
not my mother
not my father
it's me
it's me
it's me oh lord
standin' on the cement rock
where Mary stood.

oh Mary
don't you weep,
try some crack
against the memory
of your mother
sleeping
while your father was
creeping.
oh Martha
don't you moan,
let me get a snapshot
of you going down
on the dog
& let me tell you
if you don't be a good little girl
I'll show it to everybody.

oh baby please
oh baby please

wear your love like heaven
wear your love like heaven

maybe white men won't be so mean
she thinks as she smears lipstick
on her thick black lips

sliding the comb thru her blonde hair
patting powder on her white cheeks
she thinks, black guys are different
not like my father
at least I can feel 'em
when we fuck,
I couldn't *feel* daddy
even though he ate
up my life
& spit it in my face.

20 years
30 years
38 years
38 years
then you remember
you remember in a dream
or in a classroom full of kids
teaching the difference between
a noun & a pronoun,
you remember over a hamburger
at McDonald's or
someone touches your breast
in a way that seems ancient,
you remember sitting on
the toilet watching your
blood drip red on top of toilet paper & shit,
you remember
reading a poem,
you remember
masturbating.

& your life
is never the same.
Finally
you know.
You know
why you felt
so different
so long,

why you felt
so low
like you shoulda
been flushed
down the toilet
before you were born,
now you know
why you went willingly,
to the back door,
whore house
& white bitch's kitchen
now you know
why you didn't feel
like shit,
couldn't say no,
couldn't ask for what you needed,
couldn't get close
couldn't love anybody
couldn't get your shit together
couldn't market yourself
couldn't believe you could do it
couldn't read
couldn't drive
couldn't stop having babies
or eating
or smoking
or fucking,
now you know
why you are you.
now you know why while dogs ran free
you stayed home,
alone,
looking out the window
of a war zone,
always smiling
or crying
over this man
or that woman.
now you know why
the sky is crying
& maybelline
just couldn't
be true
& Corina
Corina

never
stops
eating
& Little Eva
is a crack head.
now you know why
with a job on Wall Street,
nice white boy husband
& a house in the country
she tore her
wrists apart
& bled into
the nite
dying
alone
on the
bathroom floor
you had scrubbed
earlier that day.
now you know
now you know
& now that you know,
you can begin
to heal.

Strange Juice (or the murder of Latasha Harlins)

I remember my boyfriend, the dark behind the brown of his eyes and how he look in his leather. I was walking with that good feeling thinking about him, the next day of school—maybe I go, maybe I don't. You know, who gives a fuck. And nothing special, you know, nothing is so special except now I'm dead. It's the day I died. And the sky was red-brown gauze. You could see patches of blue if you look up but I don't hardly ever look up. My eyes on the ground checking out my feet in orange Reeboks. What else I remember? Now that I look back it seems like the collard greens piled up on plywood boards at the door was huge green tears that tried to warn me. The day was the same but different. I didn't do nothin'. I slid open the glass door of the refrigerator that keeps all the beverages cool, it's so hot here. My eyes glance up at the camera pointed like a gun from the corner of the wall. Fuck it. I slip the cold bottle of orange juice in my back-pack, go to the counter. I'll get some gum, if she say something I'll say, aw bitch I was gonna buy this juice, you think I'm stupid. Wonder what we gonna do in school tomorrow. I be so glad to get out the ninth grade, go to high school. If I'm late for homeroom one more time—

"Oh bitch please! I was gonna pay for—OOG FU WOO SHIT SUE! Speak English hoe! Take your damn juice. I wasn't stealing nothin' from you chink ass hoe!"

She grabbed me. Bitch! I hit that hoe upside her jaw. Who the fuck she think she is putting her hands on somebody. Fuck this hoe, I ain't gon' argue with this bitch. I turn my back. And I walk away. I see the collard greens again only now they're growing like big trees then I see a red dirt road in the middle of the salad bar, no lie, like I'm high or something. Then everything is normal Koreatown fruit stand again. Del Monte corn out of a can poured in a stainless steel tub, iceberg, romaine, bran muffins and brownies wrapped in clear plastic. Fuck it I'm not thirsty no way.

1.

I don't hear the blast till I'm dead
I don't feel nothin' either
as I split in half
a dog yelps
and every sound I ever heard
flies out my mouth on green wings.
Crimson waterfalls open in my skull
and my bones come aloose,
the dog is screaming
like a siren now
and in the distance a bucket of water
spills over on a dusty red dirt road
and my heart quits
falls face first in
shattered glass on a
concrete floor.
The camera keeps
rolling.
My left leg twitches.
I don't cry.
Fifteen.
Green as greens
passing from sight
under broken bottles of light.

2.

I don't remember what I did wrong.
Somebody hit you, you hit 'em back.
She didn't' have to shoot me.
I was born here

and someone can shoot me and go home
and eat turkey on Thanksgiving—
what kinda shit is that?
Videotape the bitch killing me,
the hoe's own videotape
recording
the end of my days
reeling obscenely
for tv cameras—
my blood
sweet Jesus!
Rolling 20s
Bounty Hunters
PJs
Imperial Courts
NWA
LAPD
South Central
Hollywood
18th Street Diamond Riders
Easy Riders
it's a brown thing
it's a black thing
Crips
Bloods, Mexicans together forever tonight.
I don't remember . . .
I jus' wanted some juice
and now I'm dead.
Killed by a model minority
success story.
Listen, is anybody gonna
say anything?
I was gonna get a new orange leather jacket
to match my Reeboks.
I was passing math *and*
doing good in English.
Fuck history, I'm tired of hearing
'bout George Washington
and Columbus.
I told that cracker, "Shit, mutherfucker
what about us?"
No, I *wasn't* pregnant,
but I was gonna have a baby,
definitely, one day.

I like Luther Vandross, Tone-Lōc
and Queen Latifah.
Listen, is anybody gonna
say anything?
Community service!
A white bitch
with a pink slit
between her legs
like mine,
drips red.
A white girl that probably got
into law school on the
affirmative action birthed
by black people's struggle,
sitting on a seat
that was opened up
for her by Rosa Parks and
Fannie Lou Hamer,
nig—no, black people, African
Americans, like me, marching
under fire, hoses, broken glass
gasolined bodies
testicles sliced off,
strange fruit, tossed to dogs.
Swinging from trees.

This white judge woman
hooded in mahogany-walled
chambers decides my life
is not worth nothing.
A fifteen-year-old black girl
equals zero in this white bitch's book.
She sentences this yellow gunslinger
to community service and probation.
What are the terms of her probation,
that she don't kill nobody white?
Does anybody hear me?
Without my tongue.
Fifteen and out of time.
Listen to the gasoline on the wind.
Listen to my blood rhyme—
drip drop on the sidewalk.
Hear me children—
and BURN.

Ntozake Shange (1948–)

Out of the literary and cultural productions of the 1960s came one of Black America's great traveling griots, Ntozake Shange. Shange was born Paulette Williams on October 18, 1948. She developed her interests for the arts and literature through the encouragement and nurturing of her parents. Being in the company of her parents' group of talented friends, including W.E.B. DuBois, Dizzy Gillespie, and Miles Davis, surely nurtured a young Shange for a place in cultural leadership. Coupled with this youthful exposure to the arts and letters, Shange endured and survived many personal and emotional challenges during her undergraduate years at Barnard College, including a divorce. During her graduate studies at UCLA, she expressed her sense of self-determination by taking on an African name: "Ntozake," she who comes with her own things, and "Shange," she who walks like a lion. This moment of self-naming was a literal rejuvenation.

After her graduate degree, Shange taught at various colleges in California and performed poetry and dance with various groups, including her own company. Shange moved to New York, and her choreopoem (a series of poems choreographed like a dance sequence) eventually made its way to Broadway. At that time in 1975, it was only the second work by an African American woman to make it that far (following Lorraine Hansberry). The play, for colored girls who have considered suicide/when the rainbow is enuf, went on to win an Obie and an Outer Critics Circle award.

Walking proud and fierce with her own ideas, Shange creates her own revolution, her own drama that continues to flourish at the end of the millennium. Her creation, for colored girls, is a work full of Black women's experiences. This dance- and music-filled play of prose was revolutionary, especially in its presentation of contemporary Black women's voicing of their struggles with life in urban America. Never before had these women's voices graced the stage in this way: It spoke frustrations, exposed covered wounds about Black love relationships, evoked and questioned and reaffirmed sisterhood—all told as a tale of survival through old and new evils. Shange gave us these women from all over the country, and in their experiences, only two things are for sure and true—that they are in pain and that they are interested in being their own agents and having a sense of self-regard.

The whole of this play is summed up in the opening monologue with the lady in brown. In the "dark phrases of womanhood of never havin been a girl / half-notes scattered / without rhythm," one hears the voice of a girlhood suppressed and violated, a sanity balanced on "beer cans & shingles." Shange reveals the complicated relationship between Black women and some Black men who do violence to Black women, under the coercion of silence that is encouraged as part of the necessary alliance to a unified Black political struggle. Of course, at the center of this struggle is usually Black men's experi-

ences and needs, while Black women's are subjugated. It is the plight of Black woman-hood: "don't tell nobody don't tell a soul." Shange's lady asks "are we animals? have we gone crazy?", which reflects the levels of self- and community-destructive complicity that Black women are being asked to bear. What many people missed in critiquing Shange's characters and situations is that she also writes this for Black men, or at least, the message is necessary for Black men to hear and engage as part of their survival practice.

What Shange's colored girls *proved is not only that she was unafraid, but that a Black woman's voice could be heard in the theater, and be successful. Since the success of that work, Shange has produced various novels, including* Sassafrass, Cypress, and Indigo *(1982),* Betsey Brown *(1985),* Lilliane *(1997), and volumes of poetry, including the evocative* Nappy Edges *(1978) and* A Daughter's Geography *(1983). What is most noticeable about Shange's poetry is how much it uses variant spelling and contractions to create a musical rhythm that operates in a way different than language convention. It is one of the gifts of the Black Arts movement that infuses itself into Shange's writing, allowing her to represent the real-lifeness of her characters' worlds. Shange creates with her poems, similar to her work in* for colored girls, *a museum of people, whose lives are dynamic and colorful, and who characterize Black America. But, in the tradition of those Black women (and some men) writers, who take a decided interest in matters of the heart and soul as vital to the health of Black politics (some of whom include Audre Lorde, Angela Davis, James Baldwin, Toni Morrison, Alice Walker), Shange's poems are remarkably spiritual, picking up where the end of* colored girls *left off—"i found god in myself / and i loved her / loved her fiercely."*

Shange's work here captures heritage and history, pain and triumph, and the sweet and complicated contours of Black living. She is an amazing poet not only because she writes well, but also because she is committed to the political and marginalized lives of those who are her sisters.

Ja'Milla C. K. Lomas

FROM *for colored girls who have considered suicide/when the rainbow is enuf*

The stage is in darkness. Harsh music is heard as dim blue lights come up. One after another, seven women run onto the stage from each of the exits. They all freeze in postures of distress. The follow spot picks up the lady in brown. She comes to life and looks around at the other ladies. All of the others are still. She walks over to the lady in red and calls to her. The lady in red makes no response.

      lady in brown
dark phrases of womanhood
of never havin been a girl
half-notes scattered
without rhythm / no tune
distraught laughter fallin
over a black girl's shoulder
it's funny / it's hysterical
the melody-less-ness of her dance
don't tell nobody don't tell a soul
she's dancin on beer cans & shingles

this must be the spook house
another song with no singers
lyrics / no voices
& interrupted solos
unseen performances

are we ghouls?
children of horror?
the joke?

don't tell nobody don't tell a soul
are we animals? have we gone crazy?

i can't hear anythin
but maddening screams
& the soft strains of death
& you promised me
you promised me . . .
somebody / anybody
sing a black girl's song
bring her out
to know herself
to know you
but sing her rhythms
carin / struggle/ hard times
sing her song of life
she's been dead so long
closed in silence so long
she doesn't know the sound
of her own voice
her infinite beauty

she's half-notes scattered
without rhythm / no tune
sing her sighs
sing the song of her possibilities
sing a righteous gospel
let her be born
let her be born
& handled warmly.

  lady in brown
i'm outside chicago

  lady in yellow
i'm outside detroit

  lady in purple
i'm outside houston

  lady in red
i'm outside baltimore

  lady in green
i'm outside san francisco

  lady in blue
i'm outside manhattan

  lady in orange
i'm outside st. louis

  lady in brown
& this is for colored girls who have considered suicide
but moved to the ends of their own rainbows.

hands & holding

  1)

  hands & holding
  tongues & clits
  go well together

the way
the sun kisses the ocean at dawn
you have fallen
from the inside
of laughin congas
i hear you smilin
in the tunnel
women glissade
from tree limbs
their hips are so glad
to see you

2)

in the night / ochun's candles
make ether-glow waves
thru the hairs on yr stomach
i have spoken to stars
confined to black holes
from the milky way
they want to fall round you
i am envied by ladies
brighter even than the sun

3)

you were curled
under the window
like kittens at mykko's tits
some visitors
took you towards the true rainbow
you slept
eyes wide water soft
i sat at the end of the rainbow
makin gumbo in a pot of gold

4)

a trinidadian woman
tells me a hot-blooded man
dances like slow winds
in haitian hills/
yr touch is firm
like roots to soil

5)

i cannot speak
yr eyes have
stolen my tongue
only knows
to move from yr lips
to yr thigh

senses of heritage

my grandpa waz a doughboy from carolina
the other a garveyite from lakewood
i got talked to abt the race & achievement
bout color & propriety/
nobody spoke to me about the moon

daddy talked abt music & mama bout christians
my sisters/ we
always talked & talked
there waz never quiet
trees were status symbols

i've taken to fog/
the moon still surprisin me

the old men

the old men meet
round 2:00 maybe ten to
share nudges & loneliness

#1 opens his door always in dressin gown
& stockin cap/ he invites #2 in
they sit on the porch/ brown stiff
beer cans sit awkward in their fingers
thick knuckles like small ax-handles

#3 leans on the picket fence
there is no grass here/
small wine bottles/ #4 walks round the corner

his top left pocket frayin/ the old men
walk with
old pictures   secrets   wishes

the old men
sit on either side of the stoop
hands dangle between their legs
1 tips the brim of his straw hat/ #3
stretches a lame leg
#4 chews his beer cud-like
sadness like the regularity of young women passin
#2 nods his head same as the bleached willow
#4 pulls his moustache into the corners
of his mouth/ they're from round here/
they meet everyday with old pictures   secrets   wishes

an ol fashion lady

she's got whiskers
bout quarter inch long 'n
a tattered grey sweater
hangin round mismatched
shoulders one reachin
toward the a&p sign
the other barely holdin on
her hat they's a pieced
together daisy 'n some
witherin blue velvet
like the evenin jacket
under the sweater wit
gold lamé appliqué
set off by these teensy
butterflies with pink 'n
lavender wings flyin
over two/ three missin
buttons at her bosom
reachin a good 6 inches
towards this rope round her waist
she waz steppin lively now
on 8th avenue movin
awkward round comely
females feelin mangoes
sortin beans & lookin at

brassieres 'n girdles
she waz movin
her shrivelin head from side
to side   askin who

which one of us wd
go in wit her to the
beauty shop testifyin
that our old friend wdnt
say nothin that
she wd be still she wd pay
like anybody else
to get her hair fixed
somethin like lena
in stormy weather

i live in music

i live in music
is this where you live
i live here in music
i live on c# street
my friend lives on b♭ avenue
do you live here in music
sound
falls round me like rain on other folks
saxophones wet my face
cold as winter in st. louis
hot like peppers i rub on my lips
thinkin they waz lilies
i got 15 trumpets where other women got hips
& a upright bass for both sides of my heart
i walk round in a piano like somebody
else/ be walkin on the earth
i live in music
          live in it
               wash in it
i cd even smell it
wear sound on my fingers
sound falls   so fulla music
ya cd make a river where yr arm is &
hold yrself
               hold yrself in a music

Reginald Shepherd (1963–)

Reginald Shepherd was born in New York and received a B.A. from Bennington College in 1988. He then completed M.F.A. degrees from Brown University (1991) and the University of Iowa (1993). His first collection of poems, Some Are Drowning, appeared in 1994 and was widely praised. He has received numerous awards, including "Discovery"/The Nation (1993), Paumanok (for Poetry, 1994) and a National Endowment for the Arts fellowship (1995). He currently teaches at Northern Illinois University and has two forthcoming publications, Wrong and The History of His Body.

In the three poems from his collection Some Are Drowning, Shepherd uses language and images that are lush and thick, which recreates the feel of being submerged, as if under water. In "Wide Sargasso Sea," he uses the region of the North Atlantic between the Caribbean and the Azores as a poetic symbol through which he can explore loss and death and peril. The reference to the Sargasso Sea is one that is often used in Caribbean and African American literature to remember the perils of slavery and how slave ships and cargo moved over the earth's water. Like Shepherd's poem, which is a travel through memory and an attempt to reconcile what is worth remembering, the Sargasso Sea is also thick and calm, known for its abundance of seaweeds. Shepherd uses prose-like sentences, lines that are complexly constructed, to achieve this density.

In "Slaves," he begins with a grand opening "These are the years of the empty hands," which echoes a popular folk saying. "Slaves" poses the question of what one is to make of these many years past, ones with "slaves / thrown overboard to save the ship" and for whom "no words / remain." The poetic voice in this poem is self-conscious, making direct reference to the audience and the need to reclaim the losses that are being washed clean by waves of revised history. The narrator is defiant, but also pained, and willing to embrace all this suffering over all these years. Shepherd's poem moves easily between concrete images of modern America ("Outside our lives, my mythical / American, dingy rollers fringed with soot deposit / cracked syringes and used condoms on beaches tinted gray / by previous waves"), and ethereal musings on memory and one's "unhealed history."

One of Shepherd's skills is his ability to use classical poetic conceits in his work. Often, Shepherd will make reference to Greek and Roman mythic figures as a way to refigure the narratives of the Golden Era. This is evidence of Shepherd's training as a poet, and "A Muse" is a lovely example. Shepherd plays on the phrase "a muse" and its homonym, "amuse," and partially reverses the muse as a classical poetic construct—instead of the poetic voice being inspired by the muse, the poem can be read as a muse narrating the life of its subject. Reading it this way, the muse becomes less detached and instead is engaged in the common of everyday living. In fact, the final stanza seems to merge the muse and its subject's environment, so that the "it's hard to breathe" is also the experience of the muse. Some critics have determined *that Shepherd's language and classical references undercut the power of his voice as a Black writer, yet it is clear here that Shepherd is well aware of his engagement of the classical.*

In "Soul Music," which comes from his collection Angel, Interrupted, *Shepherd writes a sweeping text of urban gay soulness—the music, the clothing, the desire, the solo, the movement, the youthful energy. Shepherd lightens his characteristically heavy and thick lines, recapturing the orality using less complex sentence structures.*

Nonetheless, it is the panorama of images that makes this piece, like so much of Shepherd's work, muscular and rich. Shepherd's voice makes a necessary contribution to images and conversations of Black gay experience.

Kevin Everod Quashie

Wide Sargasso Sea

The bodies of the black men smolder
and then are still; tendrils of Jamestown
nicotine redeem the burned to burn again,
cured on white sheets. There's a stain indelible
as indigo. Or tired of all that, watch instead
his lashes sweep downwards on their arc,
which gives neither breeze nor shade:
pendant palm fronds sweep the glittering sands
of yet another El Dorado, the island paradise
of smallpox and sugarcane, and blue-eyed
planters' sons at play. But better to make bitter the kiss,
char the face into the stuccoed wall,
than taste the honeyed ash of foreign lips,
the cool and soothing poisoned rum:
the fatal aloe heals all wounds. If such are
the broken skin, I'll be
the scar, the boiling tar beneath the cobblestones
of Spanish Town. And parched the bedrooms, the corpus only
of what the light had eaten away: torn photographs
bear the print of bloodied lips
into sepia and annatto, marooned refusals
on black and burning archipelagoes. Shall I
address such heroes of the here
and now as have survived my memory?
Or let them lie where they have fallen?

Slaves

These are the years of the empty hands. And what
were those just past, swift with the flash of alloyed hulls
but carrying no cargo? Outside our lives, my mythical

America, dingy rollers fringed with soot deposit
cracked syringes and used condoms on beaches tinted gray
by previous waves, but when an hour waits just for a moment,
everyting begins again. All of it is yours, the longed-for
mundane: men falling from a cloud-filled sky like flakes of snow
onto the ocean, your mother immersed in ordinary misery
and burning breakfast, still alive in the small tenement
kitchen. You understand I use the second person
only as a marker: beyond these sheltered bays are monsters,
and tarnished treasures of lost galleons
it's death to bring to light. The ships put out
and they sink; before the final mast descends, the shadow
of a single sailor is burned across the sun, then wrapped
in strands of cirrus, his European skin a gift
to the black and unknown ocean floor. Of the slaves
thrown overboard to save the ship, no words
remain. What memorials the public beach becomes
in late October, scattered with Puerto Rican families
on muddied sand still lighter than a black man's
pound of flesh: it abrades my skin. I can't touch
that perfected picture of myself, no white wave
will wash either hand clean. There is a wind
riding in on the tainted waves, and what it cannot
make whole it destroys. You would say that all along
I chose wrong, antonyms of my own face
lined up like buoys, but there is another shore
on the far side of that wind. Everything is there,
outside my unhealed history, outside my fears. I
can see it now, and every third or fourth wave is clear.

A Muse

He winds through the party like wind, one of the just
who live alone in black and white, bewildered

by the eden of his body. (*You, you talk like winter
rain.*) He's the meaning of almost-morning walking home

at five A.M., the difference a night makes
turning over into day, simple birds staking claims

on no sleep. Whatever they call those particular birds.
He's the age of sensibility at seventeen, he isn't worth

the time of afternoon it takes to write this down.
He's the friend that lightning makes, raking

the naked tree, thunder that waits for weeks to arrive;
he's the certainty of torrents in September, harvest time

and powerlines down for miles. He doesn't even know
his name. In his body he's one with air, white as a sky

rinsed with rain. It's cold there, it's hard to breathe,
and drowning is somewhere to be after a month of drought.

Soul Music

*It is never the thing but the version
of the thing.* It's never the picture of excellence
and clear skin (the passions trained and cultivated,
tropical flowers opening under artificial light
to decorate the fashionably bare interior
of the borrowed soul) walking into the periphery
of sight, a Puerto Rican boy
in a green suede jacket with PERVERT
stitched on the chest. *What I feel, here in this room,
desiring you, is music.* (And if
he goes to bed with me, then I'll feel
other things.) So this is camp, living out
lines in a poem I read long ago, living lyrics
this season's diva sings on the headphones
of my roommate's Walkman (the authenticity
of recorded sound, with the hiss of reproduction
underneath). I'm lip-synching inconspicuously
enough, I hope, that no one overhears
and laughs. *My heart, my heart beats like
a drum* (I ran halfway here, afraid
the post office would close before I mailed this
to you), stuttered remix echoing hesitations
of the spangled moment I make mine (*remembering*

the very first time I heard this song, saw the man
it means), prompting them, while fluorescent light pours down
like clear water on a summer afternoon
(*like the cool waters of an oasis,* click, rewind
that summer, play), while late December snow
speckles dirty windows (spangles them, even)
with the beginning of a long Chicago winter.
(Nothing but music to see me through, and seeing
you alone or in a crowd, a glimpse out of the corner
of my eye.) Every song has a story, if I have to write
one, and here goes. PLEASURE, it says in turquoise letters
on your black baseball cap, like this song
I'm rewinding to hear again: beauty
standing in line at the post office
to change his address (another native
of the given body, always
on the move). I mail my package (a tape I copied
for someone) and move on (*remembering the very first*
time my heart beat like a drum). Pleasure
walks into a crowded room again
to wait his turn.

Anna Deavere Smith (1950–)

Born September 18, 1950, in Baltimore, Maryland, Smith is named after both parents, Anna Young Smith, her mother, and Deavere Smith, her father. The oldest of five children, she was raised Black middle class with a father in the tea and coffee business and a mother as elementary school principal. Despite middle-class status, Smith spent her childhood in a very segregated neighborhood, and it wasn't until high school that she interacted with people of other races and cultures.

Fascinated by the impact of language in everyday life, Smith completed a bachelor's degree in linguistics at Beaver College in 1971. She then pursued an M.F.A. degree at the American Conservatory Theatre, graduating in 1976.

Opting out of the academic route, Smith combined her two interests and began carrying a tape recorder around, recording the voices she encountered in order to perform their words and the experiences they conveyed on the stage. Her first play, On the Road (1983), was the product of research begun in 1979. As part of her exploration of her surroundings and the stories people had to tell, Smith entered communities filled with the tension of racism and resulting destructive actions and attitudes. She wanted to understand all of the perspectives contributing to tension and conflict.

In her Pulitzer Prize–nominated Fires in the Mirror: Crown Heights, Brooklyn, and Other Identities, Smith includes the results of interviewing fifty different people to illuminate the tensions between the Black and Hassidic populations of Brooklyn. Performing all parts in the one-woman play, Smith recreates the neighborhood. Including the perspectives from the spectrum of community members, she highlights the pain on all sides, the reasons behind the conflict.

Continuing this style and tradition in Twilight: Los Angeles, 1992 (1992), Smith was rewarded with two Tony Award nominations, an Obie award, a Drama Desk Award, and an Outer Critics Circle Special Achievement Award. Based on the Rodney King incident and the riots that followed, Smith's play takes on the feel of journalism, becomes both documentary and drama in performance. The excerpt from "The Territory," one section of Twilight, relays the perspectives of a former L.A. Police Commission president, an anti-police abuse activist, an actor, a former gang member, and a gang truce advocate's mother. This section, with the addition of the perspectives not included here of an L.A.-based writer, Mike Davis, and Cornel West, a Black intellectual, sets the stage for the intersection and clash of perspective that follows. Again, Smith performs the words and perspective of each of over two dozen people she interviewed about the effects of the incident and the anger and violence surrounding it.

Smith's works are unique in part because she is both writer and performer. Her other productions include Aye, Aye, Aye, I'm Integrated (1984), Piano (1991), and the ballet Hymn (1993), co-authored with choreographer Judith Jamison. Smith's performance ex-

tends from plays not her own such as Mother Courage and Tartuffe to the popular soap opera All My Children (1993) and the film Philadelphia (1993).

Received well by the public for her realistic depictions of cultural identities and attitudes about racial issues, Smith is sometimes criticized by critics for relying too heavily on stereotypes. She, however, has the approval of those she performs and reaches her goal of helping Black and White people understand each other more fully. In writing, producing and performing her work, Smith shows her dedication to not only the works themselves, but to the illumination of divisive racial conflicts. She strives to show the tension, to make it clear in order to foreground the possibilities of resolution, healing, and peace.

R. Joyce Lausch

The Territory

These Curious People
Stanley K. Sheinbaum, Former president,
Los Angeles Police Commission

(A beautiful house in Brentwood. There is art on all the walls. The art has a real spirit to it. These are the paintings by his wife, Betty Sheinbaum. There is a large living room, an office off the living room which you can see. It is mostly made of wood, lots of papers and books. The office of a writer. There are glass windows that look out on a pool, a garden, a view. Behind us is a kitchen where his wife, Betty was, but eventually she leaves. Stanley is sitting at a round wooden table with a cup of coffee. He is in a striped shirt and khaki pants and loafers. He has a beard. He is tall, and about seventy-three years old. He seems gruff, but when he smiles or laughs, his face lights up the room. It's very unusual. He has the smile and laugh of a highly spiritual, joyous, old woman, like a grandmother who has really been around. There is a bird inside the house which occasionally chirps.)

Very
interesting thing happened.
Like a week and a half (*very thoughtfully trying to
        remember*),
Maxine Waters calls me up—
You know who she is?
We're very good friends—
she calls me up and she says,
"Ya gotta come with me.
I been going down to Nickerson Gardens
and
the cops come in and break up these gang meetings
and these are gang meetings
for the purpose of truces."
(*I was momentarily distracted*)

Pay attention.
The next Saturday afternoon,
the next day even,
I go down with her,
uh,
to,
uh,
Nickerson Gardens
(*an abrupt stop, and*
second pause, as if he's forgotten something for a moment)
and I see a whole bunch of, uh,
police car
sirens and the lights
and I say, "What the hell's going on here?"
So sure enough, I pull in there
(*three-second pause*).
We pull in there
and, uh,
I ask a cop what's going on
and he says,
"Well, we got a call for help."
There's a gang meeting over there.
There's a community park there and there's a gym
and I go down to the . . .
we go down to the gang meeting
and half of 'em
outside of the
gym
and half of 'em
inside
and here's about a hundred cops lined up over here
and about another hundred
over here
and, uh,
I go
into the, uh,
into the group of gang members who were outside.
Even Maxine got scared by this.
I gotta tell you I was brought up in Harlem.
I just have a feel for what I can do and what I can't do
and I did that.
And I spent about
two, two
hours talkin' to these guys.

Some of these guys were ready to kill me.
(*A bird chirps loudly; maybe this is a parakeet or an inside
bird*)
I'm the police commissioner
and therefore a cop
and therefore all the things that went along with being a
    cop.
It was a very interesting experience, God knows.
One guy who was really disheveled and disjointed
and disfigured
opens up his whole body
and it's clear he's been shot across . . .
not in that . . . not in that day,
months or years before,
and, you know,
these guys have been through the wars down there
and,
you know, I hung around long enough that I could talk to
    them,
get some insights.
But the cops were mad,
they were really mad
that I would go talk to them
and not talk to them
and I knew that if I went and talked to them
I'd have bigger problems here
But I also knew as I was doing this,
I knew they were gonna be pissed.
Two days I got a letter
and I was . . .
the letter really pleased me in some way.
It was very respectful.
"You went in and talked to our enemy."
Gangs are their enemy.
And so
I marched down to Seventy-seventh
and, uh,
I said, "Fuck you,
I can come in here
anytime I want and talk to you."
Yeah, at roll call.
I said, uh,
"This is a shot I had at talking to these
curious people

about whom I know nothing
and I wanna learn.
Don't you want me to learn about 'em?"
You know, that kind of thing.
At the same time, I had been on this kick,
as I told you before, of . . .
of fighting for what's right for the cops,
because they haven't gotten what they should.
I mean, this city has abused both sides.
The city has abused the cops.
Don't ever forget that.
If you want me to give you an hour on that, I'll give you an
    hour on
that.
Uh,
and at the end,
uh,
I knew I hadn't won when they said,
"So which side are you on?"
When I said, I said, it's . . .
my answer was
"Why do I have to be on a side?"
Yu, yuh, yeh know.
Why do I have to be on a side?
There's a problem here.

WHEN I FINALLY GOT MY VISION/NIGHTCLOTHES
MICHAEL ZINZUN, REPRESENTATIVE, COALITION AGAINST POLICE ABUSE

(In his office at Coalition Against Police Abuse. There are very bloody and disturbing photographs of victims of police abuse. The most disturbing one was a man with part of his skull blown off and part of his body in the chest area blown off, so that you can see the organs. There is a large white banner with a black circle and a panther. The black panther is the image from the Black Panther Party. Above the circle is "All Power to the People." At the bottom is "Support Our Youth, Support the Truce.")

I witnessed police abuse.
It was
about one o'clock in the morning
and, um,
I was asleep,
like
so many of the other neighbors,
and I hear this guy calling out for help.

So my self and other people came out in socks
and gowns
and, you know,
nightclothes
and we came out so quickly we saw the police had this
    brother
handcuffed
and they was beatin' the shit out of him!
You see,
Eugene Rivers was his name
and, uh,
we had our community center here
and they was doin' it right across the street from it.
So I went out there, 'long with other people and we
    demanded they stop.
They tried to hide him by draggin' him away and we
    followed him
and told him they gonna stop.
They singled me out.
They began Macing the crowd, sayin' it was hostile.
They began
shootin' the Mace to get everybody back.
They singled me out.
I was handcuffed.
Um,
when I got Maced I moved back
but as I was goin' back I didn't go back to the center,
I ended up goin' around this . . .
it was a darkened
unlit area.
And when I finally got my vision
I said I ain't goin' this way with them police behind me,
so I turned back around, and when I did,
they Maced me again
and I went down on one knee
and all I could do was feel all these police stompin' on my
    back.
(*He is smiling*)
And I was thinkin' . . . I said
why, sure am glad they got them soft walkin' shoes on,
because when the patrolmen, you know, they have them
cushions,
so every stomp,
it wasn't a direct hard old . . .

yeah
type thing.
So
then they handcuffed me.
I said they . . .
well,
I can take this,
we'll deal with this tamarr [sic],
and they handcuffed me.
And then one of them lifted my
head up—
I was on my stomach—
he lifted me from behind
and hit me with a billy club
and struck me in the
side of the head,
which give me about forty stitches—
the straight billy club,
it wasn't a
P-28, the one with the side handle.
Now, I thought in my mind, said hunh,
they couldn't even knock me out,
they in trouble now.
You see what I'm sayin'?
'Cause I knew what we were gonna do,
'cause I dealt with police abuse
and I knew how to organize.
I say they couldn't even knock me out,
and so as I was layin' there
they was all standin' around me.
They still was Macing, the crowd was gettin' larger and larger and
larger
and more police was comin'.
One these pigs stepped outta the crowd with his flashlight,
caught me right in my eye,
and you can still see the stitches (*He lowers his lid and shows it*)
and
exploded the optic nerve to the brain,
ya see,
and boom (*He snaps his fingers*)
that was it.
I couldn't see no more since then.
I mean, they . . .
they took me to the hospital

and the doctor said, "Well, we can sew this eyelid up and these
stitches here
but
I don't think we can do nothin' for that eye."
So when I got out I got a CAT scan,
you know,
and
they said,
"It's gone."
So I still didn't understand it but I said
well,
I'm just gonna keep strugglin'.
We mobilized
to the point where we were able
to get two officers fired,
two officers had to go to trial,
and
the city on an eye
had to cough up one point two million dollars
and so
that's why
I am able to be here every day,
because that money's bein' used to further the struggle.
I ain't got no big Cadillac,
I ain't got no gold . . .
I ain't got no
expensive shoes or clothes.
What we do have
is an opportunity to keep struggling and to do research and to
organize.

THEY
JASON SANFORD, ACTOR

*(A rainstorm in February 1993. Saturday afternoon. We are in an office at the Mark
Taper Forum. Lamplight. A handsome white man in his late twenties wearing blue
jeans and a plaid shirt and Timberland boots. He played tennis in competition for years
and looks like a tennis player.)*

Who's they?
That's interesting,
'cause the they is
a combination of a lot of things.
Being brought up in Santa Barbara,

it's a little bit different saying "they" than being brought up in,
um,
LA,
I think,
'cause
being brought up in Santa Barbara
you don't see a lot of blacks.
You see Mexicans,
you see some Chinese,
but you don't see blacks.
There was maybe two black people in my school.
I don't know, you don't say
black
or you don't say
Negro
or,
no,
yeah,
you really don't.
I work with one.
Um,
because
of what I look like
I don't know if I'd been beaten.
I sure the hell would have been arrested
and pushed down on the ground.
I don't think it would have gone as far.
It wouldn't have.
Even the times that I have been arrested
they always make comments
about God, you look like Mr.,
uh,
all-American white boy.
That has actually been said to me
by a . . . by a
cop.
Ya know,
"Why do you have so many warrants?"
Ya know . . .
"Shouldn't you be takin' care of this?"
Ya know . . .
"You look like an all-American white boy.
You look responsible."
And

I remember being arrested in Santa Barbara one time
and
driving back
in the cop car
and having a conversation about tennis
with the cops.
So,
ah,
I'm sure I'm seen by the police totally different
than a black man.

BROAD DAYLIGHT
ANONYMOUS YOUNG MAN
FORMER GANG MEMBER

(Saturday, fall, sunny. He is wearing black pants and an oversized tee shirt. He is living with his mother after having recently gotten out of jail. His mother lives in a fancy apartment building, with pool, recreation room, etc. We are in one of the lounges. He has a goatee and wears his hair pulled back in a ponytail. He is black but looks Latino.)

They kind of respected their elders,
as far as,
not robbing them,
but then a lot of . . .
as I got older I noticed,
like the younger ones,
the lot of the
respect,
it
just like
disappeared,
'cause I . . . when I was younger it was like
if the police had
me and a couple other guys in the middle of the street
on our knees,
the older people would
come out and question.
They like . . .
"Take 'em to jail,"
because of that loss of respect,
you know,
of the elders
by the younger ones,
losing the respect of the elders.

When I went to the Valley
I felt more respect,
because when
I was in the
Valley
I was right there with rivals.
It's like I could walk right over
and it was rivals
and the way I felt was like
strong,
'cause when I moved out there
I didn't bring
all my homeboys
with me
and it's like I used to tell them,
my rivals,
I used to tell 'em, "Man,
I'm a one-man army."
I would joke about it.
I say,
"I don't need my homeboys
and everything."
Me and my brother,
we used to call ourselves the Blues Brothers,
because it was two of us
and we
would go and we either have our blue rags hanging and go
    right up
there in their neighborhood where there are
Bloods
and go right up in the apartments
and there could be a crowd of 'em
and we would pass by—
"What's up, cuz?"—
and keep goin'
and every now and then
they might say
something
but the majority of 'em
knew that I keep a gun on me
and every now and then
there would be broad daylight like this.
Some of 'em
would try and test me and say,

"well, he ain't fixin' ta shoot me in this broad daylight,"
you know,
and then
when they do
then you know
I either end up chasin' 'em,
shootin' at 'em or shootin'
whatever.
'Cause they thought ain't nobody that stupid
to shoot people in broad daylight.
And I was the opposite.
My theory was when you shoot somebody in broad daylight
people gonna be mostly scared,
they not gonna just sit there and look at you,
you know, to identify you.
I figure there's gonna be like
"I gotta run"
and I figure they just gonna be too scared to see who you
    are to
identify you.
That's where the reputation
came,
'cause they didn't know when I was comin',
broad daylight
or at night.
My favorite song?
I like oldies.
My favorite song is by Atlantic Star.
It's called
"Am I Dreamin'?"

LIGHTNING BUT NO RAIN
THERESA ALLISON, FOUNDER OF MOTHERS RECLAIMING OUR CHILDREN (MOTHERS ROC), MOTHER OF GANG TRUCE ARCHITECT DEWAYNE HOLMES

(Amazing black hat and bracelets on both arms. Beautiful rings.)

Mothers ROC came about right after my nephew was
    killed,
November the 29th of '91.
After the death of my nephew, my son
Dewayne
thought about a peace among,
you know, the, the guys in the project—

I don't want to say gangs—
the young men.
The truce, they started meeting every Sunday,
so I thought about
a group of mothers gettin' together,
so I thought about
the words
Reclaiming Our Children.
I knew that there was
a lot of kids going to prison,
a lot of kids going to the cemetery
by the hands of our enemy,
the unjust system.
Then my son Dewayne was sentenced for a crime he did
     not do.
When they killed Tiny—
when I say "they," I mean the police.
They shot forty-three times.
Five bullets went into Tiny.
No bullets went in nobody's else's body.
I think what they do, they want to make it look like a
     drive-by
shooting.
See, when the gangs
shoot at each other,
it's a lot of 'em
fire
(*She shows the shooting with her hand*)
bullets.
When they killed Tiny, they were in unmarked cars.
When they shot my nephew, they were dressed like gang
     members,
duck-walkin',
with hard beanies, jackets, no badges or anything,
all over the project,
like
birds!
This was going to be listed as a drive-by shooting,
and then they were gonna put
it on another project.
This is what they do all the time.
And for some reason the lights was out in the project,
'cause Tiny was goin' around
gatherin' up the children,

'cause when the lights go out in the projects,
there's a lot of shooting.
So when I left the Fox Hill Mall
I felt something was wrong,
but I didn't think it was my family,
'cause that day look like the crucifixion of Jesus.
I told people, "Doesn't this look like
the crucifixion of Jesus?" and they say,
"You right."
It was the weirdest time of my life,
it was the weirdest feeling.
It was lightning,
no rain!
And when I got back home my daughter was runnin' down
    La Brea
wid her two little girls and she was cryin'.
My daughter told me then
that Tiny,
that Tiny had been killed.
The day we had Tiny's funeral
it was so many people,
and me
being a strong Catholic,
it reminded me of the time
that Jesus took that one loaf of bread and made a whole,
it was just like that.
All of Tiny's death told me
that
a change must come,
really
a change got to come.
My son changed.
(*She's crying*)
Other guys in Watts changed.
Our life totally changed
from happy people
to hurting people.
I mean hurting people,
I mean *hurting*,
pain.
When we came back from the funeral,
we had a demonstration,
so I had a
great coalition.

I mean, I,
I mean it was . . .
I'm tellin' ya,
I'm tellin' you eight hundred fifty people,
nothin' but Spanish people,
that caravan,
I had white folks!
That in itself . . .
They don't want,
they don't want the peace,
they don't want us comin' together.
So after that they wanted my son more.
They wanted Dewayne more.
So when they attack my son,
again the lights was out in the project for some reason.
He was walkin' slow.
They told him
to give him his driver's license,
but they kept insisting he was another person,
Damian Holmes,
or some other Holmes they use,
other than Dewayne Holmes.
So they had him in a car.
So some people ran and got me.
We surrounded the police car,
we gonna turn it over,
we gonna turn it over.
Some laid on the ground.
I laid at the front part of the bumper, and one little girl—
 she was
about eighteen but she looked like twelve—
she was underneath the back wheel, so they couldn't
 roll.
If they rolled, they would have hit somebody,
people were all over the ground.
I told him, I said, "My son don't have a
warrant."
He said, "Oh yes he does."
I said, "Okay, run his name through this computer."
"Oh, we can't do that."
I said, "You a lie.
You do it anytime you want to arrest them."
So they kept saying they couldn't use it, they had to take
 him to the

station,
to run his name.
"But maybe he doesn't have anything."
"We just have to take him to the station."
Now, you
know and I know too,
before the police stop you for a traffic ticket
they done ran your license plate.
I mean, they know who you are,
you know.
They knew he was,
they knew he was Dewayne Holmes,
they knew he was Sniper!
I said, "Look, I'm not gonna move.
You not gonna kill my son like you killed my nephew."
So the police happened to pull the car up a little bit and hit
　　my leg.
Dewayne said, "Don't you hit my mother!"
But we, I already told him, "We gonna turn the car over,
　　Dewayne,
we gonna turn it over."
They were not gonna kill my son.
And that was their intention, to kill my son,
they still wanna kill my son,
they do! (*She cries*)
So then
the sergeant came
and he told the man,
he said, "It's not your son.
I made a mistake."
Somebody yell outta the car,
"Make 'em tell him they're sorry."
So the cop had to say,
"I'm sorry,"
that they didn't want to have . . .
After that Dewayne couldn't walk,
go from one side of the project to another.
They was trying to get my son,
to stop us, to stop
the demonstration,
to stop
us from protestin' against them,
to stop the world from knowing
that they corrupt.

LA supposed to be the best police officers in the world,
and if everybody all over the world knows
they the corrupt one,
then
that's the problem,
they been doin' it.
They used to take our kids
from one project
and drop 'em into another gang
zone and leave 'em in there
and let those guys kill 'em
and then say it's a gang-related thing,
hear me?
They picked my son up several times
and dropped him in another project
when he was just a little boy.
They've done it to my kid,
they'll do it to your kid.
It's the color, because we're Black.
The woman that killed Tiny,
she had a big
plaque—woman of the year!
Yeah, she shot him in the face,
her and her partner, we call 'em Cagney and Lacey,
and she is . . .
a little—
I can't give you the name—
how she use to go in an' pull these kids,
I mean from twelve years old,
and kick 'em and hit their heads against trees
and stomp on the ground.
Why you got to do Black kids like that?
Why couldn't you handcuff 'em and take 'em to jail?
Why couldn't they handcuff my nephew Tiny
and just take him to jail?
After they done shot him down,
he couldn't move! *(she cries)*
Why they have to shoot him in the face?
Doesn't seem like they killin' him
to keep from him sayin' what they said to him.
(Crying and an abrupt change)
They coverin' up!
'Cause they know they killed him wrong!
I'm not sayin' they were just gunnin' for Tiny,

but they not men enough,
they not men or women enough to say, "Hey, I killed the
   wrong person."
These police officers are just like you and I.
Take that damn uniform off of 'em,
they the same as you and I.
Why do they have so much power?
Why does the system work for them?
Where can we go
to get the justice that they have?
Ts tuh!
Where? *(crying)*
Then they took my child!
I was tired.
I have heart problems.
I went away
and they took him while I was gone.

Quincy Troupe (1943–)

Born July 24, 1943, in New York City, Quincy Troupe's father, Quincy Troupe, Sr., was the second-greatest catcher in the Negro baseball leagues. Troupe grew up in St. Louis before attending Grambling College in Louisiana where he earned a bachelor's degree in history and political science in 1963. Troupe spent two years in Paris before moving to Los Angeles where he earned an additional associate's degree in journalism in 1967. While in Los Angeles, Troupe joined the Watts Writers Workshop, a group headed by Budd Schulberg and created as a way to respond to the Watts riots without violence. As a result of his involvement, Troupe published Watts Poets: A Book of New Poetry and Essays *in 1968. A second anthology* Giant Talk: An Anthology of Third World Writings, *which Troupe co-edited with Rainer Schulte, followed in 1975 and evidences Troupe's continued dedication to publishing marginalized voices.*

Troupe has published five collections of his own verse: Embryo: Poems 1967-1971 *(1972);* Snake-Back Solos: Selected Poems 1969-1977 *(1979), which won the American Book Award in 1980;* Skulls Along the River *(1984);* Weather Reports: New and Selected Poetry *(1991); and his most recent,* Avalanche *(1996).*

Troupe's early poetry of Embryo *and* Snake-Back Solos *is characterized by self-reflexivity as he focuses on the power and function of poetry. A complementary focus is history, the connection of Black peoples to each other through common ancestry. "In Texas Grass," a poem from* Embryo, *foregrounds those "forgotten" by systems promising equality. The central image of rusting train cars is metaphor for Black men still waiting for promises of opportunity to be kept. "Blood-Rivers" pulses and flows with the rhythm of the heart and breath as it communicates the span of history to the present through the thread of spirit and liberation. Troupe emphasizes the orality of the poem through spacing, pauses within the line, and repetition. Origin and continuation drive Troupe's early poetry.*

In his later work, Troupe balances narrative with long strings of images and sounds. He returns to his personal past with more emphasis while still communicating the omnipresence of history. In "St. Louis Teenage Days," the lines are long and full, driven by the narrative of teenage ego and understanding. While American culture plays centrally into many of his later poems, it is not at the expense of history and legacy, as evidenced by "Impressions 2."

The poems of his most recent collection, Avalanche, *are rich with the rhythms of urban language and urban images. In "Eye Change Dreams" and "Old Black Ladies Standing on Bus Stop Corners #2," a revision of an earlier poem, Troupe captures the beauty, danger, and hard reality of the city, its activity, and its people. Exercising the repetition and rhythm for which he is most known, Troupe's latest collection is a cohesive part of his literary legacy.*

In all of his poetry, *Quincy Troupe celebrates Black life and art. Honoring the heroes of Black music, literature, and athletics, his verse is heavily influenced by the rhythms of Black music and speech. Focusing strongly on the nuances and rhythms of language, he strives to meld the forms of poetry and music. He is also dedicated to constant revision of his craft, revisiting and restructuring poems from previous collections in his later works. His focus in later works has also become more interior, exploring connections between the self, other people, and the environment. Enduring influences on his verse are poets Pablo Neruda, Aimé Césaire, Jean Toomer, and Sterling Brown.*

While Troupe has focused most on his own verse, he has continued important editorial work. He edited the anthology James Baldwin: The Legacy *(1989) and co-authored* Miles: The Autobiography *(1989).*

Troupe has worked both as the editor for Shrewd *and* Confrontation: A Journal of Third World Literature *and* American Rag *and as a teacher of creative writing and African American and Third World literatures at UCLA, University of Southern California, Ohio University, Berkeley, City University of New York, and the University of Ghana at Legion. He currently teaches at University of California San Diego and is the senior editor of the journal* River Styx.

R. Joyce Lausch

In Texas Grass

all along the rail
road tracks of texas
old train cars lay
rusted & overturned
like new african governments
long forgotten by the people
who built & rode them
till they couldnt run no more,
they remind me of old race horses
who've been put out to pasture
amongst the weeds
rain sleet & snow
till they die, rot away,
like photos fading
in grandma's picture book,
of old black men in mississippi/texas
who sit on dilapidated porches,
that fall away
like dead man's skin,
like white people's eyes,
& on the peeling photos,
old men sit sad-eyed
waiting, waiting for
worm dust, thinking of

the master & his long forgotten
promise of 40 acres & a mule,
& even now, if you pass across
this bleeding flesh
changing landscape,
you will see the fruited
countryside, stretching, stretching,
old black men, & young black men,
sittin on porches
waiting, waiting for rusted
trains in texas grass

Blood-Rivers

FOR K. CURTIS LYLE

as the ancient black rhythm
as the goat-skin drum
seeking lifes' pure music
hears the deep feeling,
touches the heart-beat source,
probes earth pulsations,
records the rivers endless spirit
as by God's elliptical magic
as the clock turns centuries
through the bones falling to dust

as the life keeps whispering
                              through ashes,

where summers are reborn
                     blood-rivers always evoking
the heart-bred flames of creation,
as the poem plunges into itself
the goat-skin drum sings
history of freedom,

freedom   freedom drums the goat-
                       skin voice of the drum
as the winds embracing Mt. Kilimanjaro
the sound of Ohnedaruth's horn
drums the goatskin voice of the drum

as action is the thought
as love keys the keeper
poetic expression is liberation,

& we are sounds of wind-music,
pumping blood into the heart, transforming,
as new rituals
                    paint flames against the night
the changing music liberates itself,
as in blood-felt rhythm
as in heart-felt rhythm
the genius of the singing
as breath falls drum-deep into another
as into clay embrace of the mother
we weld our joys   linking
the intergalactic barrier
the rhythm liberating   fire

St. Louis Teenage Days

FOR DONALD TROUPE & JAMES BRYANT

during those jettisoned days of smooth skin
& bright eyes turning new imagination
looping days spent dunking dreams of becoming
great & famous basketball players popping in
twenty-foot, rainbowing jump-shots
banking in clotheslining two-pointers
leanin into ears of brickhouse stallions
shooting, we fired tongues hot as lava
fished for love, words steaming
water coughed up poo-pooing
those skint-back days
locked in emerging blues

roy rogers & tom mix riding static skies of t.v.
screens then kookla fran & ollie, howdy
doody cracked our faces into cheese, split our sides
with hysterical laughter sewn into eyes bright as diamonds
moonlighting on iced, pimp fingers, as new keys
we sought to understand needs
we thought were real, but never quite understood
the meaning of cadillacs creased into our lives

then as symbols of pimps
we imitate even now & who we thought then
we really were fantasies
dominating dreams

so we turned our spirits inside out, like pockets wagging
or tongues of dogs lolling under sun stricken august, heat
wagging tails of language
groping for syllables, ancestral
half remembered vowels rolling over forgotten consonants, gliding
into confused speech, brokered pig-latin communicated through masks
veiling all meaning, even from ourselves, we grew into characters
sliding from words no one knew the meaning of
weaving new blues beneath american skies
eyes locked to that fifty dollar gold piece some call the sun
our lives on the run, like outlaws, speeding towards something
hidden beneath those blues, what the old black men sung of
our lives spending time with rumors of freedom
we thought we already had
so hung around corners, wooing players of cooing
feather touch glide, lean & tonguing players
of the slippery, side glances, slide
slip & fly off into scoobie-doo, doowopping language
rhythm taking us away until we really moved away from
ourselves, fading & dying within ghoulish tragedies
integrating toilet stools, roaches, their legs
stiff with death, falling into our lives
from everywhere we turned, perfumed with disinfectant
light, growing riots of furniture inside halloween
trickster tenements that remind of tombstones
we weaved our imaginations through
wheezing sunsets anchored to blues
rivers swallowing skies, we threw our eyes
into fishing for new dreams, we listened
for the death of innocence coming
& falling like light down the night

& so those jettisoned days of snapping shut rat traps
have run away from us now, like stale breath
wine memories of dying friends sucking up air like beached fish
dropped into twilight intervals, river stroked skies, dreams
fishing for what we knew was there, hip
beyond our knowing then
under rat trapping skies, jettisoned smooth skin glowing
then, bright penny eyes turning elliptical

new tongues rapping hot as lava rivers, dreams, turning then
imagination burning fast touchdowns, running for daylight—
like slaves—on real grass, love words whispered
in ears of brickhouse stallions
kookla fran & ollie, wagging lolling tongues of language, hip
beyond our knowing then, those days gone like those old blues
those old black men sang of

gone now, falling down the night like shooting light
gone now, surer than shit flushed down toilets
those days & nights, necessary flights
that innocence flashing

like memory light across deepening darkness

Impressions 2

FOR JEAN TOOMER & AMOS RYCE

iridescent skin of sunsetting rivers
flowing through red memory soil
of georgia carrying a legacy along inside
karintha dusk, orange discs on these rivers
of sundown eyes, sun faces of skulls
grinning red karintha dusk
swims through these licking finger flames
karintha dusks, carrying black songs along
coursing veins of mystery
smoke song curling over pine needle-cones
high above speech dark wind breaking through
cloud forms, songs breaking in the thickening
drumming blood, carrying dusk beauty along
inside mud, carrying crucified faces
along karintha songs, coursing through
rivers carrying skulls at dusk like nails
laced into burnt dusk skin, revealing veins
rhythms tonguing waves, karintha dusks
sun face blues of skulls & rain
sunface blues holding skulls & rain
carries the song into heroin-lynched veins
carries bright bones through blues & floods
carries this history to grow from mud
river blues carrying this legacy along
river blues carrying this rage to flames

Old Black Ladies Standing on Bus Stop Corners #2

FOR MY GRANDMOTHER, LEONA SMITH

blue black & bow bent under, beautiful
blue black & bow bent under, beautiful
blue black & bow bent under, beautiful

& it never did matter
whether the weather
was flame-tongue-licked
or as cold as a welldigger's asshole
in late december when santa claus
was working his cold money bullshit
that made financiers grin ear to ear
all the way to secret bank vaults
overflowing with marble eyes
of dirt-poor children

blue black & bow bent under, beautiful
blue black & bow bent under, beautiful
blue black & bow bent under, beautiful

never did matter
whether the days were storm raked
unzipped by lightning streaking clouds
dropping tornadoes that skipped crazy
to their own exploding beat
shooting hailstone death—
that popped like old bones—
crashing into the skulled
sunken eyes of tired old ladies
tired old black ladies
standing on bus stop corners
pain wrapped as shawls around their necks

blue black & bow bent under, beautiful

& "mama" it didn't matter
that your pained scarred feet overworked
numb legs grew down out of old worn dresses
seemingly fragile, gaunt & skeletal frail
as two old mop sticks—scarecrow legs—
didn't matter because you stood there anyway
defying nature's chameleon weather—

cold as a welldigger's asshole, then oven-hot—
defying all reason, you stood
there, testifying over 300 years
stretching back, of madness & treason

blue black & bow bent under, beautiful

no, it didn't matter
because the beauty of your heroic life
grown lovely in twisted swamps
grown lovely in a loveless land
grown pure & full from wombs
of concrete blood & bones
of concrete blood & bones & death
of death & sweat chained to breath
didn't matter dark proud flower
who stood tall scrubbed by cold
& rain & heat & age carrying
the foreign name given your grandfather—
who swayed body high
twisting & turning in the breeze
like billie's "strange fruit"—

because you stood there anyway
unforgettably silent in your standing
beautiful work-scarred black lady
numb legs & bow bent under beautiful
stood there on pain-scarred feet overworked
numb legs
& bow bent under beautiful
under the memory of your grandfather swaying high
up there in a burning southern breeze

now sweet music love sings soft tender beauty
                              deep in your washed aging windows—
& you give me strength
                                    during the mad, bizarre days—

& we have learned to love your life
& we will vindicate the pain & silence of your life
the memory of your grandfather with the foreign name
& who sways high up there in history over your legs
                              blue black & bow bent under beautiful
the weight of over 300 years carried

of blood & bones & death in mud
of breath & sweat chained to death
                              numb legs & bow bent under beautiful
under the memory of your grandfather
swaying high up there in the burning breeze

                  didn't matter whether the weather was flame-tongue-licked
or as cold as a welldigger's asshole in late december
because you stood there anyway
in full bloom of your strength & rare beauty
& made us strong

blue black & bow bent under, beautiful
blue black & bow bent under, beautiful
blue black & bow bent under, beautiful

Eye Change Dreams

FOR JOE OVERSTREET, CORRINE JENNINGS & GEORGE LEWIS

eye change dreams at 42nd street, times square
as swirling people wearing technicolor attitudes speed
through packed days, carrying speech that machine-guns out
in rhythms equaling movement of averted stares
squares even sashay by quick in flip
mimicking motions, as slick street hustlers roll their eyes around
like marbles searching for hits, lick their chops after clicking onto
some slow-witted hicks dribbling spit down their lips
eating hot dogs paid with fifty-dollar bills
in broad daylight—
                              yeah, tell me about it, trick—

escalator sidewalks moving everything along
so swiftly everyone thinks it's their own feet carrying
          their bodies, grooving to a different song
                              than say, in gloster, mississippi

where time is a turtle moving after a flood has crawled back
into the space it came out of in the first place
hear no beepers here
in gloster, no portable telephones panicking anywhere
only the constant slow humming glide of bloated mosquitoes

as they slide through air & bank in for fresh blood-kills
                         wind-tongue guiding them into the target
                                        wobbling on their zigzag ride above bearded

irises waving sword-shaped leaves in the breeze
as if preparing to do righteous battle with anyone or something
like people living in the big apple (their game faces constantly in place—
& they even wear them into bathrooms, so scared to death they are
of running into some cold-blooded rat there
staking out their own notion of territorial space)
try keeping their fluctuating dreams up to speed
switching up each & every moment, in midtown manhattan,
                 manic chameleons
everywhere, here, changing faces at high noon, say,
on 42nd street & 8th avenue, claustrophobic
heat-drenching crowds packed in, in august, locks in on flesh cold
as a triple life sentence served out at comstock—
people here switching up gears, trying to sidestep panic
                         in the middle of slapstick dreams
                                        & in the center of it all

a con man who looks like swifty lazar, the late hollywood agent,
tools around inside a white rolls royce, peddling gimmicks for old
          false-tooth legends,
who look so bizarre in public devoid of heavy makeup—
comic, even—outside of their dream machines, illusions—
tattered memorabilia the con man peddles at some tacky bazaar
inside a rundown building, in a cobwebbed room, where he hawks
          fading photographs of
zsa zsa gabor in her prime, before she started breaking down
in front of our eyes, wearing all that weird graphic white
pancake makeup over her everchanging face-lifts, masking the dreams
we wear ourselves, inside our switching, ballistic imaginations
bewitching us here as we move through times square
popping with the charge of electrical currents

energy eye imagined this poem having when eye first started writing it
than having to deal with how it slowed down midway through,
when eye hit that part about gloster, a third of the way down,
& tried to avoid all those zigzagging mosquitoes
divebombing in for fresh blood-kills—
my direction moving all over the place after that, changing up the focus,
the rhythm, the way my dipstick lines started composing themselves—
at that point in time, they began making it all up

as they went along, as if they were different musicians improvising
this poem—like the swifty lazar look-alike peddling old hollywood
wonders before the fall, before they became toothless legends,
before they became zsa zsa gabor

this sputnik verbal drumstick—a thing to be eaten
after all—promises way more than it could ever deliver
traveling at the speed of complete bullshit, as if were—

a technicolored times-square attitude, without rhyme,
riding in on a broomstick, heartsick & caustic

homesick for that good old big-apple charge

Alice Walker (1944-)

One of the most popular and prolific African American women writers, Walker began her career with a dedication to southern life and women. Since then, and not at the expense of her commitment to her southern heritage, Walker's topic range has broadened to include genital mutilation in Africa, which she discusses in her fifth novel Possessing the Secret of Joy (1992), and environmentalism, a topic that is pronounced in her essay collection, Living by the Word (1988). Throughout all of her work, Walker has remained true to the advocacy of Black women and Black female identity that earned her controversial novel The Color Purple (1982) a Pulitzer Prize. In addition to The Color Purple, Walker is the author of four other novels, three essay collections, two children's books, two short story collections, and five volumes of poetry.

Alice Walker was born in 1944, the eighth child of southern sharecroppers in Eatonville, Georgia. Her observation and participation in the grueling labor and injustice of sharecropping served as the impetus of her first novel, The Third Life of Grange Copeland (1970), which documents the journey of a sharecropper from Georgia to degrading racism in New York and back again with more respect for the women central to his life.

At age eight, Walker lost an eye when her brother accidentally shot her in the eye, a loss that made her acutely aware of being different and motivated her to start recording her thoughts and feelings in a notebook. This early sense of loss and difference undoubtedly contributes to the sensitivity of her writing. The disability also allowed her to leave Eatonville in 1961 to attend Spelman College in Atlanta on a disability scholarship.

During her two years at Spelman, Walker was exposed to the rise of the civil rights movement, a topic that permeates many of the stories in You Can't Keep a Good Woman Down (1981) and several of the essays in In Search of Our Mothers' Gardens (1983). Walker's second novel, Meridian (1976), focuses most centrally on the civil rights movement, providing an insightful portrayal of the politics of sex and race in the movement. Her initial exposure to civil rights philosophy and action while at Spelman spurred her to an active role. From 1965 to 1968, Walker participated in voter registration drives and campaigned for welfare and children's rights in the South.

After two years at Spelman, Walker transferred to Sarah Lawrence. During her time at Sarah Lawrence and at the age of twenty-three, Walker produced her first collection of poetry, Once (1968). The poems were dually motivated by a summer trip to Africa and by the suicidal powerlessness, despair, and shame she felt in dealing with an unwanted pregnancy that ended in an illegal abortion.

In 1967, Alice Walker married Melvyn Leventhal, a white Jewish civil rights lawyer. Their daughter, Rebecca, was born while they were living in Mississippi during a time when interracial marriage was illegal. They worked to desegregate Mississippi schools be-

fore Walker's move to New York City and their divorce in 1977. Walker moved to northern California, where she still resides, to finish The Color Purple.

Walker's publications in the 1970s, with a focus on southern women and their experiences, helped provide a locus for the explosion of Black women's literature that coincided with and would follow her earliest publications. In her work, the 1960s valorization of Black manhood gave way to more complex analyses of the societal forces of racism, sexism, and economic stress. In Revolutionary Petunias *(1972), her second collection of poetry, and in her first collection of short stories,* In Love and Trouble: Stories of Black Women *(1973), Walker expresses convincingly the oppression of Black women and the ways they resist and overcome despite often being at the mercy of the men they are involved with and/or forces of society and nature. Through figures like Mrs. Johnson, the preservationist of Black heritage in "Everyday Use," Walker captured the strength, resilience, and wisdom of "ordinary" southern women.*

In the title essay of In Search of Our Mothers' Gardens *and in other essays in the collection, Walker documents the legacy of creativity linked to spirituality and nature. She honors her own mother and other Black women through celebration of the creative traditions of sewing, quilting, cooking, and gardening. By clarifying the value of domestic art, Walker countered traditional definitions of art that valued textual and visual arts while ignoring or discounting other forms and established a place for Black women in history as producers of unique and priceless art.*

Another work of "recovery" for which Walker is acknowledged with gratitude and which is central to In Search of Our Mothers' Gardens *is her adamant search and valuing of unappreciated literary predecessor, Zora Neale Hurston. Writing about her search for information about Hurston's life in the essay collection and again in the poems in* Good Night Willie Lee *(1979), Walker helped establish Hurston's place within the Black female literary tradition. She solidified that place through her own editorial work on Hurston's* I Love Myself When I Am Laughing and Then Again When I Am Looking Mean and Impressive *(1979).*

The work for which Walker is most well know is The Color Purple, *awarded not only a Pulitzer Prize, but also the National Book Award and the American Book Award.* The Color Purple *is the first novel written by an African American woman to receive a Pulitzer Prize and the third and completion of a series of three novels Walker announced in the 1970s. Criticized for its depiction of incest, domestic abuse, positive articulation of lesbianism, and harsh depiction of Mister, the central Black male character,* The Color Purple *was also praised for its courage in showing the complexities of Black life. Walker says that the story was based on the experiences of her great-grandmother, who was raped at age twelve. Through Celie's work toward self-love and her triumph over the abusiveness of her circumstances, Walker was able to reimagine her great-grandmother's story. The Steven Spielberg film production was also both criticized and praised for many of the same reasons the book was, but was criticized most for its "Hollywood" hollowing of the intensity of the issues and of its even more one-sided depiction of Mister. Walker responds to the process and aftermath of* The Color Purple *in her recent book,* The Same River Twice *(1996).*

Her scope widening from the South outward, Walker's works of the 1980s and 1990s explore and express the realities of women's lives in broader contexts. Dually committed to her African American community and to her community of women, Walker's contributions to a broadening of feminist philosophy is profound. In In Search of Our Mothers' Gardens, *Walker coined the term "womanism" to distinguish a feminism grounded in spirituality, true sisterhood, and revolutionary action.*

In You Can't Keep a Good Woman Down *(1981), she treats the difficult topics of abortion, interracial rape, pornography, and welfare, the political realms that affect women directly and that women have had little power within. In "Advancing Luna—And Ida B. Wells," for example, the incident of an interracial rape figures centrally, and the impossibility of truly resolving all that surrounds the issue manifests itself in the addendums and postscripts that follow, each adding to the basic structure of the story.*

First making her work global with Nettie's journey to Africa in The Color Purple, *Walker has continued to explore a more global focus in the African center of* Possessing the Secret of Joy *and in* The Temple of My Familiar *(1989), which is set in Europe, Africa, and Central America as well as the United States.* The Temple of My Familiar *retains a couple of the characters from* The Color Purple *and explores in greater depth the African connection, the need for many people of African origin to revisit and regain spiritual heritage. Tashi, Celie's daughter's friend in Africa, reappears in* Possessing the Secret of Joy *as a woman who has experienced the trauma of female circumcision.*

The relationships of human beings to the natural world has also become a prevalent recent focus. In Horses Make the Landscape Look More Beautiful *(1984) and in* Living By the Word, *Walker links the oppressions of racism and sexism to the kinds of violations humans commit in their relationship with the living natural environment. Through such works, she has demonstrated a consistent willingness to address the most difficult topics for the benefit of women, the growth and healing of African American families and communities, and the well being of human beings globally.*

The publication of her collected poems, Her Blue Body Everything We Know *(1991), and the founding of her own press, Wild Trees Press, which has published among others, J. California Cooper, has confirmed Walker's lasting importance as womanist, writer, and loving thinker. The volume of her publication and her international popularity with the general public and academic audiences alike make her arguably the most significant woman writer of the latter half of the twentieth century. From her first works to her most contemporary, Walker has valorized strong and resourceful Black women, expanding the literary attention to and the role of the Black women writers.*

R. Joyce Lausch

Everyday Use

FOR YOUR GRANDMAMA

I will wait for her in the yard that Maggie and I made so clean and wavy yesterday afternoon. A yard like this is more comfortable than most people know. It is not just a yard. It is like an extended living room. When the hard clay is swept clean as a floor and the fine sand around the edges lined with tiny, irregular grooves, anyone can come and sit and look up into the elm tree and wait for the breezes that never come inside the house.

Maggie will be nervous until after her sister goes; she will stand hopelessly in corners, homely and ashamed of the burn scars down her arms and legs, eyeing her sister with a mixture of envy and awe. She thinks her sister has held life always in the palm of one hand, that "no" is a word the world never learned to say to her.

You've no doubt seen those TV shows where the child who has "made it" is confronted, as a surprise, by her own mother and father, tottering in weakly from backstage. (A pleasant surprise, of course: What would they do if parent and child came on the show only to curse out and insult each other?) On TV mother and child embrace and smile into each other's faces. Sometimes the mother and father weep, the child wraps them in her arms and leans across the table to tell how she would not have made it without their help. I have seen these programs.

Sometimes I dream a dream in which Dee and I are suddenly brought together on a TV program of this sort. Out of a dark and soft-seated limousine I am ushered into a bright room filled with many people. There I meet a smiling, gray, sporty man like Jonny Carson who shakes my hand and tells me what a fine girl I have. Then we are on the stage and Dee is embracing me with tears in her eyes. She pins on my dress a large orchid, even though she has told me once that she thinks orchids are tacky flowers.

In real life I am a large, big-boned woman with rough, man-working hands. In the winter I wear flannel nightgowns to bed and overalls during the day. I can kill and clean a hog as mercilessly as a man. My fat keeps me hot in zero weather. I can work outside all day, breaking ice to get water for washing; I can eat pork liver cooked over the open fire minutes after it comes steaming from the hog. One winter I knocked a bull calf straight in the brain between the eyes with a sledge hammer and had the meat hung up to chill before nightfall. But of course all this does not show on television. I am the way my daughter would want me to be: a hundred pounds lighter, my skin like an uncooked barley pancake. My hair glistens in the hot bright lights. Johnny Carson has much to do to keep up with my quick and witty tongue.

But that is a mistake. I know even before I wake up. Who ever knew a Johnson with a quick tongue? Who can even imagine me looking a strange white man in the eye? It seems to me I have talked to them always with one foot raised in flight, with my head turned in whichever way is farthest from them. Dee, though. She would always look anyone in the eye. Hesitation was no part of her nature.

"How do I look, Mama?" Maggie says, showing just enough of her thin body enveloped in pink skirt and red blouse for me to know she's there, almost hidden by the door.

"Come out into the yard," I say.

Have you ever seen a lame animal, perhaps a dog run over by some careless person rich enough to own a car, sidle up to someone who is ignorant enough to be kind to him? That is the way my Maggie walks. She has been like this, chin on chest, eyes on ground, feet in shuffle, ever since the fire that burned the other house to the ground.

Dee is lighter than Maggie, with nicer hair and a fuller figure. She's a woman now, though sometimes I forget. How long ago was it that the other house burned? Ten, twelve years? Sometimes I can still hear the flames and feel Maggie's arms sticking to me, her hair smoking and her dress falling off her in little black papery flakes. Her eyes seemed stretched open, blazed open by the flames reflected in them. And Dee. I see her standing off under the sweet gum tree she used to dig gum out of; a look of concentration on her face as she watched the last dingy gray board of the house fall in toward the red-hot brick chimney. Why don't you do a dance around the ashes? I'd wanted to ask her. She had hated the house that much.

I used to think she hated Maggie, too. But that was before we raised the money, the church and me, to send her to Augusta to school. She used to read to us without pity; forcing words, lies, other folks' habits, whole lives upon us two, sitting trapped and ignorant underneath her voice. She washed us in a river of make-believe, burned us with a lot of knowledge we didn't necessarily need to know. Pressed us to her with the serious way she read, to shove us away at just the moment, like dimwits, we seemed about to understand.

Dee wanted nice things. A yellow organdy dress to wear to her graduation from high school; black pumps to match a green suit she'd made from an old suit somebody gave me. She was determined to stare down any disaster in her efforts. Her eyelids would not flicker for minutes at a time. Often I fought off the temptation to shake her. At sixteen she had a style of her own: and knew what style was.

I never had an education myself. After second grade the school was closed down. Don't ask me why: in 1927 colored asked fewer questions than they do now. Sometimes Maggie reads to me. She stumbles along good-naturedly but can't see well. She knows she is not bright. Like good looks and money, quickness passed her by. She will marry John Thomas (who has mossy teeth in an earnest face) and then I'll be free to sit here and I guess just sing church songs to myself. Although I never was a good singer. Never could carry a tune. I was always better at a man's job. I used to love to milk till I was hooked in the side in '49. Cows are soothing and slow and don't bother you, unless you try to milk them the wrong way.

I have deliberately turned my back on the house. It is three rooms, just like the one that burned, except the roof is tin; they don't make shingle roofs any more. There are no real windows, just some holes cut in the sides, like the portholes in a ship, but not round and not square, with rawhide holding the shutters up on the outside. This house is in a pasture, too, like the other one. No doubt when Dee sees it she will want to tear it down. She wrote me once that no matter where we "choose" to live, she will manage to come see us. But she will never bring her friends. Maggie and I thought about this and Maggie asked me, "Mama, when did Dee ever *have* any friends?"

She had a few. Furtive boys in pink shirts hanging about on washday after school. Nervous girls who never laughed. Impressed with her they worshiped the well-turned phrase, the cute shape, the scalding humor that erupted like bubbles in lye. She read to them.

When she was courting Jimmy T she didn't have much time to pay to us, but turned all her faultfinding power on him. He *flew* to marry a cheap city girl from a family of ignorant flashy people. She hardly had time to recompose herself.

When she comes I will meet—but there they are!

Maggie attempts to make a dash for the house, in her shuffling way, but I stay her with my hand. "Come back here," I say. And she stops and tries to dig a well in the sand with her toe.

It is hard to see them clearly through the strong sun. But even the first glimpse of leg out of the car tells me it is Dee. Her feet were always neat-looking, as if God himself had shaped them with a certain style. From the other side of the car comes a short, stocky man. Hair is all over his head a foot long and hanging from his chin like a kinky mule tail. I hear Maggie suck in her breath. "Uhnnnh," is what it sounds like. Like when you see the wriggling end of a snake just in front of your foot on the road. "Uhnnnh."

Dee next. A dress down to the ground, in this hot weather. A dress so loud it hurts my eyes. There are yellows and oranges enough to throw back the light of the sun. I feel my whole face warming from the heat waves it throws out. Earrings gold, too, and hanging down to her shoulders. Bracelets dangling and making noises when she moves her arm up to shake the folds of the dress out of her armpits. The dress is loose and flows, and as she walks closer, I like it. I hear Maggie go "Uhnnnh" again. It is her sister's hair. It stands straight up like the wool on a sheep. It is black as night and around the edges are two long pigtails that rope about like small lizards disappearing behind her ears.

"Wa-su-zo-Tean-o!" she says, coming on in that gliding way the dress makes her move. The short stocky fellow with the hair to his navel is all grinning and he follows up with "Asalamalakim, my mother and sister!" He moves to hug Maggie but she falls back, right up against the back of my chair. I feel her trembling there and when I look up I see the perspiration falling off her chin.

"Don't get up," says Dee. Since I am stout it takes something of a push. You can see me trying to move a second or two before I make it. She turns, showing white heels through her sandals, and goes back to the car. Out she peeks next with a Polaroid. She stoops down quickly and lines up picture after picture of me sitting there in front of the house with Maggie cowering behind me. She never takes a shot without making sure the house is included. When a cow comes nibbling around the edge of the yard she snaps it and me and Maggie *and* the house. Then she puts the Polaroid in the back seat of the car, and comes up and kisses me on the forehead.

Meanwhile Asalamalakim is going through motions with Maggie's hand. Maggie's hand is as limp as a fish, and probably as cold, despite the sweat, and she keeps trying to pull it back. It looks like Asalamalakim wants to shake hands but wants to do it fancy. Or maybe he don't know how people shake hands. Anyhow, he soon gives up on Maggie.

"Well," I say. "Dee."

"No, Mama," she says. "Not 'Dee,' Wangero Leewanika Kemanjo!"

"What happened to 'Dee'?" I wanted to know.

"She's dead," Wangero said. "I couldn't bear it any longer, being named after the people who oppress me."

"You know as well as me you was named after your aunt Dicie," I said. Dicie is my sister. She named Dee. We called her "Big Dee" after Dee was born.

"But who was *she* named after?" asked Wangero.

"I guess after Grandma Dee," I said.

"And who was she named after?" asked Wangero.

"Her mother," I said, and saw Wangero was getting tired. "That's about as far back as I can trace it," I said. Though, in fact, I probably could have carried it back beyond the Civil War through the branches.

"Well," said Asalamalakim, "there you are."

"Uhnnnh," I heard Maggie say.

"There I was not," I said, "before 'Dicie' cropped up in our family, so why should I try to trace it that far back?"

He just stood there grinning, looking down on me like somebody inspecting a Model A car. Every once in a while he and Wangero sent eye signals over my head.

"How do you pronounce this name?" I asked.

"You don't have to call me by it if you don't want to," said Wangero.

"Why shouldn't I?" I asked. "If that's what you want us to call you, we'll call you."

"I know it might sound awkward at first," said Wangero.

"I'll get used to it," I said. "Ream it out again."

Well, soon we got the name out of the way. Asalamlakim had a name twice as long and three times as hard. After I tripped over it two or three times he told me to just call him Hakim-a-barber. I wanted to ask him was he a barber, but I didn't really think he was, so I didn't ask.

"You must belong to those beef-cattle peoples down the road," I said. They said "Asalamalakim" when they met you, too, but they didn't shake hands. Always too busy: feeding the cattle, fixing the fences, putting up salt-lick shelters, throwing down hay. When the white folks poisoned some of the herd the men stayed up all night with rifles in their hands. I walked a mile and a half just to see the sight.

Hakim-a-barber said, "I accept some of their doctrines, but farming and raising cattle is not my style." (They didn't tell me, and I didn't ask, whether Wangero (Dee) had really gone and married him.)

We sat down to eat and right away he said he didn't eat collards and pork was unclean. Wangero, though, went on through the chitlins and corn bread, the greens and everything else. She talked a blue streak over the sweet potatoes. Everything delighted her. Even the fact that we still used the benches her daddy made for the table when we couldn't afford to buy chairs.

"Oh, Mama!" she cried. Then turned to Hakim-a-barber. "I never knew how lovely these benches are. You can feel the rump prints." she said, running her hands underneath her and along the bench. Then she gave a sigh and her hand closed over Grandma Dee's butter dish. "That's it!" she said. "I knew there was something I wanted to ask you if I could have." She jumped up from the table and went over in the corner where the churn stood, the milk in it clabber by now. She looked at the churn and looked at it.

"This churn top is what I need," she said. "Didn't Uncle Buddy whittle it out of a tree you all used to have?"

"Yes," I said.

"Uh huh," she said happily. "And I want the dasher, too."

"Uncle Buddy whittle that, too?" asked the barber.

Dee (Wangero) looked up at me.

"Aunt Dee's first husband whittled the dash," said Maggie so low you almost couldn't hear her. "His name was Henry, but they call him Stash."

"Maggie's brain is like an elephant's," Wangero said, laughing. "I can use the churn top as a centerpiece for the alcove table," she said, sliding a plate over the churn, "and I'll think of something artistic to do with the dasher."

When she finished wrapping the dasher the handle stuck out. I took it for a moment in my hands. You didn't even have to look close to see where hands pushing the dasher up and down to make butter had left a kind of sink in the wood. In fact, there were a lot of small sinks; you could see where thumbs and fingers had sunk into the wood. It was beautiful light yellow wood, from a tree that grew in the yard where Big Dee and Stash had lived.

After dinner Dee (Wangero) went to the trunk at the foot of my bed and started rifling through it. Maggie hung back in the kitchen over the dishpan. Out came Wangero with two quilts. They had been pieced by Grandma Dee and then Big Dee and me had hung them on the quilt frames on the front porch and quilted them. One was in the Lone Star pattern. The other was Walk Around the Mountain. In both of them were scraps of dresses Grandma Dee had worn fifty and more years ago. Bits and pieces of Grandpa Jarrell's Paisley shirts. And one teeny faded blue piece, about the size of a penny matchbox, that was from Great Grandpa Ezra's uniform that he wore in the Civil War.

"Mama," Wangero said sweet as a bird. "Can I have these old quilts?"

I heard something fall in the kitchen, and a minute later the kitchen door slammed.

"Why don't you take one or two of the others?" I asked. "These old things was just done by me and Big Dee from some tops your grandma pieced before she died."

"No," said Wangero. "I don't want those. They are stitched around the borders by machine."

"That'll make them last better," I said.

"That's not the point," said Wangero. "These are all pieces of dresses Grandma used to wear. She did all this stitching by hand. Imagine!" She held the quilts securely in her arms, stroking them.

"Some of the pieces, like those lavender ones, come from old clothes her mother handed down to her," I said, moving up to touch the quilts. Dee (Wangero) moved back just enough so that I couldn't reach the quilts. They already belonged to her.

"Imagine!" she breathed again, clutching them closely to her bosom.

"The truth is," I said, "I promised to give them quilts to Maggie, for when she marries John Thomas."

She gasped like a bee had stung her.

"Maggie can't appreciate these quilts!" she said. "She'd probably be backward enough to put them to everyday use."

"I reckon she would," I said. "God knows I been saving 'em for long enough with nobody using 'em. I hope she will!" I didn't want to bring up how I had offered Dee (Wangero) a quilt when she went away to college. Then she had told me they were old-fashioned, out of style.

"But they're *priceless!*" she was saying now, furiously; for she has a temper. "Maggie would put them on the bed and in five years they'd be in rags. Less than that!"

"She can always make some more," I said. "Maggie knows how to quilt."

Dee (Wangero) looked at me with hatred. "You just will not understand. The point is these quilts, *these* quilts!"

"Well," I said, stumped. "What would *you* do with them?"

"Hang them," she said. As if that was the only thing you *could* do with quilts.

Maggie by now was standing in the door. I could almost hear the sound her feet made as they scraped over each other.

"She can have them, Mama," she said, like somebody used to never winning anything, or having anything reserved for her. "I can 'member Grandma Dee without the quilts."

I looked at her hard. She had filled her bottom lip with checkerberry snuff and it gave her face a kind of dopey, hangdog look. It was Grandma Dee and Big Dee who taught her how to quilt herself. She stood there with her scarred hands hidden in the folds of her skirt. She looked at her sister with something like fear but she wasn't mad at her. This was Maggie's portion. This was the way she knew God to work.

When I looked at her like that something hit me in the top of my head and ran down to the soles of my feet. Just like when I'm in church and the spirit of God touches me and I get happy and shout. I did something I never had done before: hugged Maggie to me, then dragged her on into the room, snatched the quilts out of Miss Wangero's hands and dumped them into Maggie's lap. Maggie just sat there on my bed with her mouth open.

"Take one or two of the others," I said to Dee.

But she turned without a word and went out to Hakim-a-barber.

"You just don't understand," she said, as Maggie and I came out to the car.

"What don't I understand?" I wanted to know.

"Your heritage," she said. And then she turned to Maggie, kissed her, and said, "You ought to try to make something of yourself, too, Maggie. It's really a new day for us. But from the way you and Mama still live you'd never know it."

She put on some sunglasses that hid everything above the tip of her nose and her chin.

Maggie smiled; maybe at the sunglasses. But a real smile, not scared. After we watched the car dust settle I asked Maggie to bring me a dip of snuff. And then the two of us sat there just enjoying, until it was time to go in the house and go to bed.

Advancing Luna—and Ida B. Wells

I met Luna the summer of 1965 in Atlanta where we both attended a political conference and rally. It was designed to give us the courage, as temporary civil rights workers, to penetrate the small hamlets farther south. I had taken a bus from Sarah Lawrence in New York and gone back to Georgia, my home state, to try my hand at registering voters. It had become obvious from the high spirits and sense of almost divine purpose exhibited by black people that a revolution was going on, and I did not intend to miss it. Especially not this summery, student-studded version of it. And I thought it would be fun to spend some time on my own in the South.

Luna was sitting on the back of a pickup truck, waiting for someone to take her from Faith Baptist, where the rally was held, to whatever gracious black Negro home awaited her. I remember because someone who assumed I would also be traveling by pickup introduced us. I remember her face when I said, "No, no more back of pickup trucks for me. I know Atlanta well enough, I'll walk." She assumed of course (I guess) that I did not wish to ride beside her because she was white, and I was not curious enough about what she might have thought to explain it to her. And yet I was struck by her passivity, her *patience* as she sat on the truck alone and ignored, because someone had told her to wait there quietly until it was time to go.

This look of passively waiting for something changed very little over the years I knew her. It was only four or five years in all that I did. It seems longer, perhaps because we met at such an optimistic time in our lives. John Kennedy and Malcolm X had already been assassinated, but King had not been and Bobby Kennedy had not been. Then too, the lethal, bizarre elimination by death of this militant or that, exiles, flights to Cuba, shoot-outs between former Movement friends sundered forever by lies planted by the FBI, the gunning down of Mrs. Martin Luther King, Sr., as she played the Lord's Prayer on the piano in her church (was her name Alberta?), were still in the happily unfathomable future.

We believed we could change America because we were young and bright and held ourselves *responsible* for changing it. We did not believe we would fail. That is what lent fervor (revivalist fervor, in fact; we would *revive* America!) to our songs, and lent sweetness to our friendships (in the beginning almost all interracial), and gave a wonderful fillip to our sex (which, too, in the beginning, was almost always interracial).

What first struck me about Luna when we later lived together was that she did not own a bra. This was curious to me, I suppose, because she also did not need one. Her chest was practically flat, her breasts like those of a child. Her face was round, and she suffered from acne. She carried with her always a tube of that "skin-colored" (if one's skin is pink or eggshell) medication designed to dry up pimples. At the oddest times—waiting for a light to change, listening to voter registration instructions, talking about her father's new girlfriend, she would apply the stuff, holding in her other hand a small brass mirror the size of her thumb, which she also carried for just this purpose.

We were assigned to work together in a small, rigidly segregated South Georgia town that the city fathers, incongruously and years ago, had named Freehold. Luna was slightly asthmatic and when overheated or nervous she breathed through her mouth. She wore her shoulder-length black hair with bangs to her eyebrows and the rest brushed behind her ears. Her eyes were brown and rather small. She was attractive, but just barely and with effort. Had she been the slightest bit overweight, for instance, she would have gone completely unnoticed, and would have faded into the background where, even in a revolution, fat people seem destined to go. I have a photograph of her sitting on the steps of a house in South Georgia. She is wearing tiny pearl earrings, a dark sleeveless shirt with Peter Pan collar, Bermuda shorts, and a pair of those East Indian sandals that seem to adhere to nothing but a big toe.

The summer of '65 was as hot as any other in that part of the South. There was an abundance of flies and mosquitoes. Everyone complained about the heat and the flies and the hard work, but Luna complained less than the rest of us. She walked ten miles a day with me up and down those straight Georgia highways, stopping at every house that looked black (one could always tell in 1965) and asking whether anyone needed help with learning how to vote. The simple mechanics: writing one's name, or making one's "X" in the proper column. And then, though we were required to walk, everywhere, we were empowered to offer prospective registrants a car in which they might safely ride down to the county courthouse. And later to the polling places. Luna, almost overcome by the heat, breathing through her mouth like a dog, her hair plastered with sweat to her head, kept looking straight ahead, and walking as if the walking itself was her reward.

I don't know if we accomplished much that summer. In retrospect, it seems not only minor, but irrelevant. A bunch of us, black and white, lived together. The black people who took us in were unfailingly hospitable and kind. I took them for granted in a way that now amazes me. I realize that at each and every house we visited I *assumed* hospitality, I *assumed* kindness. Luna was often startled by my "boldness." If we walked up to a secluded farmhouse and half a dozen dogs ran up barking around our heels and a large black man with a shotgun could be seen whistling to himself under a tree, she would become nervous. I, on the other hand, felt free to yell at this stranger's dogs, slap a couple of them on the nose, and call over to him about his hunting.

That month with Luna of approaching new black people every day taught me something about myself I had always suspected: I thought black people superior people. Not simply superior to white people, because even without thinking about it much, I assumed almost everyone was superior to them; but to everyone. Only white people, after all, would blow up a Sunday-school class and grin for television over their "victory," *i.e.,* the death of four small black girls. Any atrocity, at any time, was expected from them. On the other hand, it never occurred to me that black people *could* treat Luna and me with anything but warmth and concern. Even their curiosity about the sudden influx into their midst of rather ignorant white and black Northerners was restrained and courteous. I was treated as a relative, Luna as a much welcomed guest.

Luna and I were taken in by a middle-aged couple and their young school-aged daughter. The mother worked outside the house in a local canning factory, the father worked in the paper plant in nearby Augusta. Never did they speak of the danger they were in of losing their jobs over keeping us, and never did their small daughter show any fear that her house might be attacked by racists because we were there. Again, I did not expect this family to complain, no matter what happened to them because of us. Having understood the danger, they had assumed the risk. I did not think them particularly brave, merely typical.

I think Luna liked the smallness—only four rooms—of the house. It was in this house that she ridiculed her mother's lack of taste. Her yellow-and-mauve house in Cleveland, the eleven rooms, the heated garage, the new car every year, her father's inability to remain faithful to her mother, their divorce, the fight over the property, even more bitter than over the children. Her mother kept the house and the children. Her father kept the car and his new girlfriend, whom he wanted Luna to meet and "approve." I could hardly imagine anyone disliking her mother so much. Everything Luna hated in her she summed up in three words: "*yellow and mauve.*"

I have a second photograph of Luna and a group of us being bullied by a Georgia state trooper. This member of Georgia's finest had followed us out into the deserted countryside to lecture us on how misplaced—in the South—was our energy, when "the Lord knew" the North (where he thought all of us lived, expressing disbelief that most of us were Georgians) was just as bad. (He had a point that I recognized even then, but it did not seem the point where we were.)

Luna is looking up at him, her mouth slightly open as always, a somewhat dazed look on her face. I cannot detect fear on any of our faces, though we were all afraid. After all, 1965 was only a year after 1964 when three civil rights workers had been taken deep into a Mississippi forest by local officials and sadistically tortured and murdered. Luna almost always carried a flat black shoulder bag. She is standing with it against her side, her thumb in the strap.

At night we slept in the same bed. We talked about our schools, lovers, girl-friends we didn't understand or missed. She dreamed, she said, of going to Goa. I dreamed of going to Africa. My dream came true earlier than hers: an offer of a grant from an unsuspected source reached me one day as I was writing poems under a tree. I left Freehold, Georgia, in the middle of summer, without regrets, and flew from New York to London, to Cairo, to Kenya, and, finally, to Uganda, where I settled among black people with the same assumptions of welcome and kindness I had taken for granted in Georgia. I was taken on rides down the Nile as a matter of course, and accepted all invitations to dinner, where the best local dishes were superbly prepared in my honor. I became, in fact, a lost relative of the people, whose ancestors had foolishly strayed, long ago, to America.

I wrote to Luna at once.

But I did not see her again for almost a year. I had graduated from college, moved into a borrowed apartment in Brooklyn Heights, and was being evicted after a month. Luna, living then in a tenement on East 9th Street, invited me to share her two-bedroom apartment. If I had seen the apartment before the day I moved in I might never have agreed to do so. Her building was between Avenues B and C and did not have a front door. Junkies, winos, and others often wandered in during the night (and occasionally during the day) to sleep underneath the stairs or to relieve themselves at the back of the first-floor hall.

Luna's apartment was on the third floor. Everything in it was painted white. The contrast between her three rooms and kitchen (with its red bathtub) and the grungy stairway was stunning. Her furniture consisted of two large brass beds in-herited from a previous tenant and stripped of paint by Luna, and a long, high-backed church pew which she had managed somehow to bring up from the South. There was a simplicity about the small apartment that I liked. I also liked the notion of extreme contrast, and I do to this day. Outside our front window was the decaying neighborhood, as ugly and ill-lit as a battleground. (And al-legedly as hostile, though somehow we were never threatened with bodily harm by the Hispanics who were our neighbors, and who seemed, more than anything, *bewildered* by the darkness and filth of their surroundings.) Inside was the church pew, as straight and spare as Abe Lincoln lying down, the white walls as spotless as a monastery's, and a small, unutterably pure patch of blue sky through the window of the back bedroom. (Luna did not believe in curtains, or couldn't afford them, and so we always undressed and bathed with the lights off and the rooms lit with candles, causing rather nun-shaped shadows to be cast on the walls by the long-sleeved high-necked nightgowns we both wore to bed.)

Over a period of weeks, our relationship, always marked by mutual respect, evolved into a warm and comfortable friendship which provided a stability and comfort we both needed at that time. I had taken a job at the Welfare Department during the day, and set up my typewriter permanently in the tiny living room for work after I got home. Luna worked in a kindergarten, and in the evenings taught herself Portuguese.

It was while we lived on East 9th Street that she told me she had been raped during her summer in the South. It is hard for me, even now, to relate my feeling of horror and incredulity. This was some time before Eldridge Cleaver wrote of being a rapist / revolutionary; of "practicing" on black women before moving on to white. It was also, unless I'm mistaken, before LeRoi Jones (as he was then known; now of course Imamu Baraka, which has an even more presumptuous meaning than "the King") wrote his advice to young black male insurrectionaries (women were not told what to do with *their* rebelliousness): "Rape the white girls. Rape their fathers." It was clear that he meant this literally and also as: to rape a white girl *is* to rape her father. It was the misogynous cruelty of this latter meaning that was habitually lost on black men (on men in general, actually), but nearly always perceived and rejected by women of whatever color.

"Details?" I asked.

She shrugged. Gave his name. A name recently in the news, though in very small print.

He was not a Movement star or anyone you would know. We had met once, briefly. I had not liked him because he was coarse and spoke of black women as "our" women. (In the early Movement, it was pleasant to think of black men wanting to own us as a group; later it became clear that owning us meant exactly *that* to them.) He was physically unattractive, I had thought, with something of the hoodlum about him: a swaggering, unnecessarily mobile walk, small eyes, rough skin, a mouthful of wandering or absent teeth. He was, ironically, among the first persons to shout the slogan everyone later attributed solely to Stokeley Carmichael—Black Power! Stokeley was chosen as the originator of this idea by the media, because he was physically beautiful and photogenic and articulate. Even the name—Freddie Pye—was diminutive, I thought, in an age of giants.

"What did you do?"

"Nothing that required making a noise."

"Why didn't you scream?" I felt I would have screamed my head off.

"You know why."

I did. I had seen a photograph of Emmett Till's body just after it was pulled from the river. I had seen photographs of white folks standing in a circle roasting something that had talked to them in their own language before they tore out its tongue. I knew why, all right.

"What was he trying to prove?"

"I don't know. Do you?"

"Maybe you filled him with unendurable lust," I said.

"I don't think so," she said.

Suddenly I was embarrassed. Then angry. Very, very angry. *How dare she tell me this!* I thought.

Who knows what the black woman thinks of rape? Who has asked her? Who cares? Who has even properly acknowledged that *she* and not the white woman in this story is the most likely victim of rape? Whenever interracial rape is mentioned, a black woman's first thought is to protect the lives of her brothers, her father, her sons, her lover. A history of lynching has bred this reflex in her. I feel it as strongly as anyone. While writing a fictional account of such a rape in a novel, I read Ida B. Wells's autobiography three times, as a means of praying to her spirit to forgive me.

My prayer, as I turned the pages, went like this: *"Please forgive me. I am a writer."* (This self-revealing statement alone often seems to me sufficient reason to require perpetual forgiveness; since the writer is guilty not only of always wanting to know—like Eve—but also of trying—again like Eve—to find out.) *"I cannot write contrary to what life reveals to me. I wish to malign no one. But I must struggle to understand at least my own tangled emotions about interracial rape. I know, Ida B. Wells, you spent your whole life protecting, and trying to protect, black men accused of raping white women, who were lynched by white mobs, or threatened with it. You know, better than I ever will, what it means for a whole people to live under the terror of lynching. Under the slander that their men, where white women are concerned, are creatures of uncontrollable sexual lust. You made it so clear that the black men accused of rape in the past were innocent victims of white criminals that I grew up believing black men literally did not rape white women. At all. Ever. Now it would appear that some of them, the very twisted, the terribly ill, do. What would you have me write about them?"*

Her answer was: *"Write nothing. Nothing at all. It will be used against black men and therefore against all of us. Eldridge Cleaver and LeRoi Jones don't know who they're dealing with. But you remember. You are dealing with people who brought their children to witness the murder of black human beings, falsely accused of rape. People who handed out, as trophies, black fingers and toes. Deny! Deny! Deny!"*

And yet, I have pursued it: *"Some black men themselves do not seem to know what the meaning of raping someone is. Some have admitted rape in order to denounce it, but others have accepted rape as a part of rebellion, of 'paying whitey back.' They have gloried in it."*

"They know nothing of America," she says. *"And neither, apparently, do you. No matter what you think you know, no matter what you feel about it, say nothing. And to your dying breath!"*

Which, to my mind, is virtually useless advice to give to a writer.

Freddie Pye was the kind of man I would not have looked at then, not even once. (Throughout that year I was more or less into exotica: white ethnics who knew languages were a peculiar weakness; a half-white hippie singer; also a large Chinese mathematician who was a marvelous dancer and who taught me to waltz.) There was no question of belief.

But, in retrospect, there was a momentary *suspension* of belief, a kind of *hope* that perhaps it had not really happened; that Luna had made up the rape, "as white women have been wont to do." I soon realized this was unlikely. I was the only person she had told.

She looked at me as if to say: "I'm glad *that* part of my life is over." We continued our usual routine. We saw every interminable, foreign, depressing, and poorly illuminated film ever made. We learned to eat brown rice and yogurt and to tolerate kasha and odd-tasting teas. My half-black hippie singer friend (now a well-known reggae singer who says he is from "de I-lands" and not Sheepshead Bay) was "into" tea and kasha and Chinese vegetables.

And yet the rape, the knowledge of the rape, out in the open, admitted, pondered over, was now between us. (And I began to think that perhaps—whether Luna had been raped or not—it had always been so; that her power over my life was exactly the power *her word on rape* had over the lives of black men, over *all* black men, whether they were guilty or not, and therefore over my whole people.)

Before she told me about the rape, I think we had assumed a lifelong friendship. The kind of friendship one dreams of having with a person one had known in adversity; under heat and mosquitoes and immaturity and the threat of death. We would each travel, we would write to each other from the three edges of the world.

We would continue to have an "international list" of lovers whose amorous talents or lack of talents we would continue (giggling into our dotage) to compare. Our friendship would survive everything, be truer than everything, endure even our respective marriages, children, husbands—assuming we *did,* out of desperation and boredom someday, marry, which did not seem a probability, exactly, but more in the area of an amusing idea.

But now there was a cooling off of our affection for each other. Luna was becoming mildly interested in drugs, because everyone we knew was. I was envious of the openendedness of her life. The financial backing to it. When she left her job at the kindergarten because she was tired of working, her errant father immediately materialized. He took her to dine on scampi at an expensive restaurant, scolded her for living on East 9th Street, and looked at me as if to say: "Living in a slum of this magnitude must surely have been your idea." As a cullud, of course.

For me there was the welfare department every day, attempting to get the necessary food and shelter to people who would always live amid the dirty streets I knew I must soon leave. I was, after all, a Sarah Lawrence girl "with talent." It would be absurd to rot away in a building that had no front door.

I slept late one Sunday morning with a painter I had met at the Welfare Department. A man who looked for all the world like Gene Autry, the singing cowboy, but who painted wonderful surrealist pictures of birds and ghouls and fruit with *teeth*. The night before, three of us—me, the painter, and "an old Navy buddy" who looked like his twin and who had just arrived in town—had got high on wine and grass.

That morning the Navy buddy snored outside the bedrooms like a puppy waiting for its master. Luna got up early, made an immense racket getting breakfast, scowled at me as I emerged from my room, and left the apartment, slamming the door so hard she damaged the lock. (Luna had made it a rule to date black men almost exclusively. My insistence on dating, as she termed it, "anyone" was incomprehensible to her, since in a politically diseased society to "sleep with the enemy" was to become "infected" with the enemy's "political germs." There is more than a grain of truth in this, of course, but I having too much fun to stare at it for long. Still, coming from Luna it was amusing, since she never took into account the risk her own black lovers ran by sleeping with "the white woman," and she had apparently been convinced that a summer of relatively innocuous political work in the South had cured her of any racial, economic, or sexual political disease.)

Luna never told me what irked her so that Sunday morning, yet I remember it as the end or our relationship. It was not, as I at first feared, that she thought my bringing the two men to the apartment was inconsiderate. The way we lived allowed us to *be* inconsiderate from time to time. Our friends were varied, vital, and often strange. Her friends especially were deeper than they should have been into drugs.

The distance between us continued to grow. She talked more of going to Goa. My guilt over my dissolute if pleasurable existence coupled with my mounting hatred of welfare work, propelled me in two directions: south and to West Africa. When the time came to choose, I discovered that *my* summer in the South had infected me with the need to return, to try to understand, and write about, the people I'd merely lived with before.

We never discussed the rape again. We never discussed, really, Freddie Pye or Luna's remaining feelings about what had happened. One night, the last month we lived together, I noticed a man's blue denim jacket thrown across the church pew. The next morning, out of Luna's bedroom walked Freddie Pye. He barely spoke to me—possibly because as a black woman I was expected to be hostile toward his presence in a white woman's bedroom. I was too surprised to exhibit hostility, however, which was only a part of what I felt, after all. He left.

Luna and I did not discuss this. It is odd, I think now, that we didn't. It was as if he was never there, as if he and Luna had not shared the bedroom that night. A month later, Luna went alone to Goa, in her solitary way. She lived on an island and slept, she wrote, on the beach. She mentioned she'd found a lover there who protected her from the local beachcombers and pests.

Several years later, she came to visit me in the South and brought a lovely piece of pottery which my daughter much later dropped and broke, but which I glued back together in such a way that the flaw improves the beauty and fragility of the design.

Afterwords, Afterwards
Second Thoughts

That is the "story." It has an "unresolved" ending. That is because Freddie Pye and Luna are still alive, as am I. However, one evening while talking to a friend, I heard myself say that I had, in fact, written *two* endings. One, which follows, I considered appropriate for such a story published in a country truly committed to justice, and the one above, which is the best I can afford to offer a society in which lynching is still reserved, at least subconsciously, as a means of racial control.

I said that if we in fact lived in a society committed to the establishment of justice for everyone ("justice" in this case encompassing equal housing, education, access to work, adequate dental care, et cetera), thereby placing Luna and Freddie Pye in their correct relationship to each other, *i.e.*, that of brother and sister, *compañeros*, then the two of them would be required to struggle together over what his rape of her had meant.

Since my friend is a black man whom I love and who loves me, we spent a considerable amount of time discussing what this particular rape meant to us. Morally wrong, we said, and not to be excused. Shameful; politically corrupt. Yet, as we thought of what might have happened to an indiscriminate number of innocent young black men in Freehold, Georgia, had Luna screamed, it became clear that more than a little of Ida B. Wells's fear of probing the rape issue was running through us, too. The implications of this fear would not let me rest, so that months and years went by with most of the story written but with me incapable, or at least unwilling, to finish or to publish it.

In thinking about it over a period of years, there occurred a number of small changes, refinements; puzzles, in angle. Would these shed a wider light on the continuing subject? I do not know. In any case, I returned to my notes, hereto appended for the use of the reader.

Luna: Ida B. Wells—Discarded Notes

Additional characteristics of Luna: At a time when many in and out of the movement considered "nigger" and "black" synonymous, and indulged in a sincere attempt to fake Southern "hip" speech, Luna resisted. She was the kind of WASP who could not easily imitate another's ethnic style, nor could she even exaggerate her own. She was what she was. A very straight, clear-eyed, coolly observant young woman with no talent for existing outside her own skin.

Imaginary Knowledge

Luna explained the visit from Freddie Pye in this way:
  "*He called that evening, said he was in town, and did I know the Movement was coming North? I replied that I did know that.*"
  When could he see her? he wanted to know.
  "*Never,*" *she replied.*

He had burst into tears, or something that sounded like tears, over the phone. He was stranded at wherever the evening's fund-raising event had been held. Not in the place itself, but outside, in the street. The "stars" had left, everyone had left. He was alone. He knew no one else in the city. Had found her number in the phone book. And had no money, no place to stay.

Could he, he asked, crash? He was tired, hungry, broke—and even in the South had had no job, other than the Movement, for months. Et cetera.

When he arrived, she had placed our only steak knife in the waistband of her jeans.

He had asked for a drink of water. She gave him orange juice, some cheese, and a couple of slices of bread. She had told him he might sleep on the church pew and he had lain down with his head on his rolled-up denim jacket. She had retired to her room, locked the door, and tried to sleep. She was amazed to discover herself worrying that the church pew was both too narrow and too hard.

At first he muttered, groaned, and cursed in his sleep. Then he fell off the narrow church pew. He kept rolling off. At two in the morning she unlocked her door, showed him her knife, and invited him to share her bed.

Nothing whatever happened except they talked. At first, only he talked. Not about the rape, but about his life.

"He was a small person physically, remember?" Luna asked me. (She was right. Over the years he had grown big and, yes, burly, in my imagination, and I'm sure in hers.) "That night he seemed tiny. A child. He was still fully dressed, except for the jacket and he, literally, hugged his side of the bed. I hugged mine. The whole bed, in fact, was between us. We were merely hanging to its edges."

At the fund-raiser—on Fifth Avenue and 71st Street, as it turned out—his leaders had introduced him as the unskilled, barely literate, former Southern fieldworker that he was. They had pushed him at the rich people gathered there as an example of what "the system" did to "the little people" in the South. They asked him to tell about the thirty-seven times he had been jailed. The thirty-five times he had been beaten. The one time he had lost consciousness in the "hot" box. They told him not to worry about his grammar. "Which, as you may recall," said Luna, "was horrible." Even so, he had tried to censor his "aint's" and his "us'es." He had been painfully aware that he was on exhibit, like Frederick Douglass had been for the Abolitionists. But unlike Douglass he had no oratorical gift, no passionate language, no silver tongue. He knew the rich people and his own leaders perceived he was nothing: a broken man, unschooled, unskilled at anything. . . .

Yet he had spoken, trembling before so large a crowd of rich, white Northerners—who clearly thought their section of the country would never have the South's racial problems—begging, with the painful stories of his wretched life, for their money.

At the end, all of them—the black leaders, too—had gone. They left him watching the taillights of their cars, recalling the faces of the friends come to pick them up: the women dressed in African print that shone, with elaborately arranged hair, their jewelry sparkling, their perfume exotic. They were so beautiful, yet so strange. He could not imagine that one of them could comprehend his life. He did not ask for a

ride, because of that, but also because he had no place to go. Then he had remem-
bered Luna.

Soon Luna would be required to talk. She would mention her confusion over
whether, in a black community surrounded by whites with a history of lynching
blacks, she had a right to scream as Freddie Pye was raping her. For her, this was the
crux of the matter.

And so they would continue talking through the night.

This is another ending, created from whole cloth. If I believed Luna's story about
the rape, and I did (had she told anyone else I might have dismissed it), then this
reconstruction of what might have happened is as probable an accounting as any
is liable to be. Two people have now become "characters."

I have forced them to talk until they reached the stumbling block of the
rape, *which they must remove themselves,* before proceeding to a place from which
it will be possible to insist on a society in which Luna's word alone on rape can
never be used to intimidate an entire people, and in which an innocent black
man's protestation of innocence of rape is unprejudicially heard. Until such a society is created, relationships of affection between black men and white women
will always be poisoned—from within as from without—by historical fear and
the threat of violence, and solidarity among black and white women is only
rarely likely to exist.

Postscript: Havana, Cuba, November 1976

I am in Havana with a group of other black American artists. We have spent the
morning apart from our Cuban host bringing each other up to date on the kind
of work (there are no apolitical artists among us) we are doing in the United
States. I have read "Luna."

High above the beautiful city of Havana I sit in the Havana Libre pavilion
with the muralist/photographer in our group. He is in his mid-thirties, a handsome, brown, erect individual whom I have know casually for a number of years.
During the sixties he designed and painted street murals for both SNCC and the
Black Panthers, and in an earlier discussion with Cuban artists he showed impatience with their explanation of why we had seen no murals covering some of the
city's rather dingy walls: Cuba, they had said, unlike Mexico, has no mural tradition. "But the point of a revolution," insisted Our Muralist, " is to make new traditions!" And he had pressed his argument with such passion for the *usefulness,*
for revolutionary communication, of his craft, that the Cubans were both exas-
perated and impressed. They drove us around the city for a tour of their huge
billboards, all advancing socialist thought and the heroism of men like Lenin,
Camilo, and Che Guevara, and said, "These, *these* are our 'murals'!"

While we ate lunch, I asked Our Muralist what he'd thought of "Luna." Especially the appended section.

"Not much," was his reply. "Your view of human weakness is too biblical," he said. "You are unable to conceive of the man without conscience. The man who cares nothing about the state of his soul because he's long since sold it. In short," he said, "you do not understand that some people are simply evil, a disease on the lives of other people, and that to remove the disease altogether is preferable to trying to interpret, contain, or forgive it. Your 'Freddie Pye,'" and he laughed, "was probably raping white women on the instructions of his government."

Oh ho, I thought. Because, of course, for a second, during which I stalled my verbal reply, this comment made both very little and very much sense.

"I *am* sometimes naive and sentimental," I offered. I am sometimes both, though frequently by design. Admission in this way is tactical, a stimulant to conversation.

"And shocked at what I've said," he said, and laughed again. "Even though," he continued, "you know by now that blacks would be hired to blow up other blacks, and could be hired *by someone* to shoot down Brother Malcolm, and hired *by someone* to provide a diagram of Fred Hampton's bedroom so the pigs could shoot him easily while he slept, you find it hard to believe a black man could be hired *by someone* to rape white women. But think a minute, and you will see why it is the perfect disruptive act. Enough blacks raping or accused of raping enough white women and any political movement that cuts across racial lines is doomed.

"Larger forces are at work than your story would indicate," he continued. "You're still thinking of lust and rage, moving slowly into aggression and purely racial hatred. But you should be considering money—which the rapist would get, probably from your very own tax dollars, in fact—and a maintaining of the status quo; which those hiring the rapist would achieve. I know all this," he said, "because when I was broke and hungry and selling my blood to buy the food and the paint that allowed me to work, I was offered such 'other work.'"

"But you did not take it."

He frowned. "There you go again. How do you know I didn't take it? It paid, and I was starving."

"You didn't take it," I repeated.

"No," he said. "A black and white 'team' made the offer. I had enough energy left to threaten to throw them out of the room."

"But even if Freddie Pye *had been* hired *by someone* to rape Luna, that still would not explain his second visit."

"Probably nothing will explain that," said Our Muralist. "But assuming Freddie Pye *was* paid to disrupt—by raping a white woman—the black struggle in the South, he may have wised up enough later to comprehend the significance of Luna's decision not to scream."

"So you are saying he *did have* a conscience?" I asked.

"Maybe," he said, but his look clearly implied I would never understand anything about evil, power, or corrupted human beings in the modern world.

But of course he is wrong.

Womanist Definition

Womanist 1. From *womanish*. (Opp. of "girlish," i.e., frivolous, irresponsible, not serious.) A black feminist or feminist of *color*. From the black folk expression of mothers to female children, "You acting womanish," i.e., like a woman. Usually referring to *outrageous, audacious, courageous* or *willful* behavior. Wanting to know more and in greater depth than is considered "good" for one. Interested in grownup doings. Acting grown up. Being grown up. Interchangeable with another black folk expression: "You trying to be grown." Responsible. In charge. *Serious*.

*   *   *

2. *Also:* A *woman who loves other women*, sexually and/or nonsexually. Appreciates and prefers women's culture, women's emotional flexibility (values tears as natural counter-balance of laughter), and women's strength. Sometimes loves individual men, sexually and/or nonsexually. Committed to survival and wholeness of entire people, male *and* female. *Not a separatist,* except periodically, for health. Traditionally universalist, as in: "Mama, why are we brown, pink, and yellow, and our cousins are white, beige, and black?" Ans.: "Well, you know the colored race is just like a flower garden, with every color flower represented." Traditionally capable, as in: "Mama, I'm walking to Canada and I'm taking you and a bunch of other slaves with me." Reply: "It wouldn't be the first time."

*   *   *

3. Loves music. Loves dance. Loves the moon. *Loves* the Spirit. Loves love and food and roundness. Loves struggle. *Loves* the Folk. Loves herself. *Regardless*.

*   *   *

4. Womanist is to feminist as purple to lavender.

Motheroot

Creation often
needs two hearts
one to root
and one to flower
One to sustain
in time of drouth
and hold fast
against winds of pain
the fragile bloom

> *that in the glory*
> *of its hour*
> *affirms a heart*
> *unsung, unseen.*
>
> —*MARILOU AWIAKTA,*
>   *Abiding Appalachia*

In Search of Our Mothers' Gardens

> I described her own nature and temperament. Told how they needed a larger life for their expression. . . . I pointed out that in lieu of proper channels, her emotions had overflowed into paths that dissipated them. I talked, beautifully I thought, about an art that would be born, an art that would open the way for women the likes of her. I asked her to hope, and build up an inner life against the coming of that day. . . . I sang, with a strange quiver in my voice, a promise song.
>
> —*Jean Toomer, "Avey,"*
>   CANE

The poet speaking to a prostitute who falls asleep while he's talking—

When the poet Jean Toomer walked through the South in the early twenties, he discovered a curious thing: black women whose spirituality was so intense, so deep, so *unconscious,* that they were themselves unaware of the richness they held. They stumbled blindly through their lives: creatures so abused and mutilated in body, so dimmed and confused by pain, that they considered themselves unworthy even of hope. In the selfless abstractions their bodies became to the men who used them, they became more than "sexual objects," more even than mere women: they became "Saints." Instead of being perceived as whole persons, their bodies became shrines: what was thought to be their minds became temples suitable for worship. These crazy Saints stared out at the world, wildly, like lunatics—or quietly, like suicides; and the "God" that was in their gaze was as mute as a great stone.

Who were these Saints? These crazy, loony, pitiful women?

Some of them, without a doubt, were our mothers and grandmothers.

In the still heat of the post-Reconstruction South, this is how they seemed to Jean Toomer: exquisite butterflies trapped in an evil honey, toiling away their lives in an era, a century, that did not acknowledge them, except as "the *mule* of the world." They dreamed dreams that no one knew—not even themselves, in any coherent fashion—and saw visions no one could understand. They wandered or sat about the countryside crooning lullabies to ghosts, and drawing the mother of Christ in charcoal on courthouse walls.

They forced their minds to desert their bodies and their striving spirits sought to rise, like frail whirlwinds from the hard red clay. And when those frail whirlwinds fell, in scattered particles, upon the ground, no one mourned. Instead, men lit candles to celebrate the emptiness that remained, as people do who enter a beautiful but vacant space to resurrect a God.

Our mothers and grandmothers, some of them: moving to music not yet written. And they waited.

They waited for a day when the unknown thing that was in them would be made known; but guessed, somehow in their darkness, that on the day of their revelation they would be long dead. Therefore to Toomer they walked, and even ran, in slow motion. For they were going nowhere immediate, and the future was not yet within their grasp. And men took out mothers and grandmothers, "but got no pleasure from it." So complex was their passion and their calm.

To Toomer, they lay vacant and fallow as autumn fields, with harvest time never in sight: and he saw them enter loveless marriages, without joy; and become prostitutes, without resistance; and become mothers of children, without fulfillment.

For these grandmothers and mothers of ours were not Saints, but Artists; driven to a numb and bleeding madness by the springs of creativity in them for which there was no release. They were Creators, who lived lives of spiritual waste, because they were so rich in spirituality—which is the basis of Art—that the strain of enduring their unused and unwanted talent drove them insane. Throwing away this spirituality was their pathetic attempt to lighten the soul to a weight their work-worn, sexually abused bodies could bear.

What did it mean for a black woman to be an artist in our grandmothers' time? In our great-grandmothers' day? It is a question with an answer cruel enough to stop the blood.

Did you have a genius of a great-great-grandmother who died under some ignorant and depraved white overseer's lash? Or was she required to bake biscuits for a lazy backwater tramp, when she cried out in her soul to paint watercolors of sunsets, or the rain falling on the green and peaceful pasturelands? Or was her body broken and forced to bear children (who were more often than not sold away from her)—eight, ten, fifteen, twenty children—when her one joy was the thought of modeling heroic figures of rebellion, in stone or clay?

How was the creativity of the black woman kept alive, year after year and century after century, when for most of the years black people have been in America, it was a punishable crime for a black person to read or write? And the freedom to paint, to sculpt, to expand the mind with action did not exist. Consider, if you can bear to imagine it, what might have been the result if singing, too, had been forbidden by law. Listen to the voices of Bessie Smith, Billie Holiday, Nina Simone, Roberta Flack, and Aretha Franklin, among others, and imagine those voices muzzled for life. Then you may begin to comprehend the lives of our "crazy," "Sainted" mothers and grandmothers. The agony of the lives of women who might have been Poets, Novelists, Essayists, and Short-Story Writers (over a period of centuries), who died with their real gifts stifled within them.

And, if this were the end of the story, we would have cause to cry out in my paraphrase of Okot p'Bitek's great poem:

> O, my clanswomen
> Let us all cry together!
> Come,
> Let us mourn the death of our mother,
> The death of a Queen
> The ash that was produced
> By a great fire!
> O, this homestead is utterly dead
> Close the gates
> With *lacari* thorns,
> For our mother
> The creator of the Stool is lost!
> And all the young women
> Have perished in the wilderness!

But this is not the end of the story, for all the young women—our mothers and grandmothers, *ourselves*—have not perished in the wilderness. And if we ask ourselves why, and search for and find the answer, we will know beyond all efforts to erase it from our minds, just exactly who, and of what, we black American women are.

One example, perhaps the most pathetic, most misunderstood one, can provide a backdrop for our mother's work: Phillis Wheatley, a slave in the 1700s.

Virginia Woolf, in her book *A Room of One's Own,* wrote that in order for a woman to write fiction she must have two things, certainly: a room of her own (with key and lock) and enough money to support herself.

What then are we to make of Phillis Wheatley, a slave, who owned not even herself? This sickly, frail black girl who required a servant of her own at times—her health was so precarious—and who, had she been white, would have been easily considered the intellectual superior of all the women and most of the men in the society of her day.

Virginia Woolf wrote further, speaking of course not of our Phillis, that "any woman born with a great gift in the sixteenth century [insert "eighteenth century," insert "black woman," insert "born or made a slave"] would certainly have gone crazed, shot herself, or ended her days in some lonely cottage outside the village, half witch, half wizard [insert "Saint"], feared and mocked at. For it needs little skill and psychology to be sure that a highly gifted girl who had tried to use her gift for poetry would have been so thwarted and hindered by contrary instincts [add "chains, guns, the lash, the ownership of one's body by someone else, submission to an alien religion"], that she must have lost her health and sanity to a certainty."

The key words, as they relate to Phillis, are "contrary instincts." For when we read the poetry of Phillis Wheatley—as when we read the novels of Nella Larsen or the oddly false-sounding autobiography of that freest of all black women writers, Zora Hurston—evidence of "contrary instincts" is everywhere. Her loyalties were completely divided, as was, without question, her mind.

But how could this be otherwise? Captured at seven, a slave of wealthy, doting whites who instilled in her the "savagery" of the Africa they "rescued" her from . . . one wonders if she was even able to remember her homeland as she had known it, or as it really was.

Yet, because she did try to use her gift for poetry in a world that made her a slave, she was "so thwarted and hindered by . . . contrary instincts, that she . . . lost her health. . . ." In the last years of her brief life, burdened not only with the need to express her gift but also with a penniless, friendless "freedom" and several small children for whom she was forced to do strenuous work to feed, she lost her health, certainly. Suffering from malnutrition and neglect and who knows what mental agonies, Phillis Wheatley died.

So torn by "contrary instincts" was black, kidnapped, enslaved Phillis that her description of "the Goddess"—as she poetically called the Liberty she did not have—is ironically, cruelly humorous. And, in fact, has held Phillis up to ridicule for more than a century. It is usually read prior to hanging Phillis's memory as that of a fool. She wrote:

> The Goddess comes, she moves divinely fair,
> Olive and laurel binds her *golden* hair.
> Wherever shines this native of the skies,
> Unnumber'd charms and recent graces rise. [My italics]

It is obvious that Phillis, the slave, combed the "Goddess's" hair every morning; prior, perhaps, to bringing in the milk, or fixing her mistress's lunch. She took her imagery from the one thing she saw elevated above all others.

With the benefit of hindsight we ask, "How could she?"

But at last, Phillis, we understand. No more snickering when your stiff, struggling, ambivalent lines are forced on us. We know now that you were not an idiot or a traitor; only a sickly little black girl, snatched from your home and country and made slave; a woman who still struggled to sing the song that was your gift, although in a land of barbarians who praised you for your bewildered tongue. It is not so much what you sang, as that you kept alive, in so many of our ancestors, *the notion of song.*

Black women are called, in the folklore that so aptly identifies one's status in society, "the *mule* of the world," because we have been handed the burdens that everyone else—*everyone* else—refused to carry. We have also been called "Matriarchs," "Superwomen," and "Mean and Evil Bitches." Not to mention "Castraters" and "Sapphire's Mama." When we have pleaded for understanding, our character has been distorted; when we have asked for simple caring, we have been handed empty inspirational appellations, then stuck in the farthest corner. When we have asked for love, we have been given children. In short, even our plainer gifts, our labors of fidelity and love, have been knocked down our throats. To be an artist and a black woman, even today, lowers our status in many respects, rather than raises it: and yet, artists we will be.

Therefore we must fearlessly pull out of ourselves and look at and identify with our lives the living creativity some of our great-grandmothers were not allowed to know. I stress *some* of them because it is well known that the majority of our great-grandmothers knew, even without "knowing" it, the reality of their spirituality, even if they don't recognize it beyond what happened in the singing at church—and they never had any intention of giving it up.

How they did it—those millions of black women who were not Phillis Wheatley, or Lucy Terry or Frances Harper or Zora Hurston or Nella Larsen or Bessie Smith; or Elizabeth Catlett, or Katherine Dunham, either—brings me to the title of this essay, "In Search of Our Mothers' Gardens," which is a personal account that is yet shared, in its theme and its meaning, by all of us. I found, while thinking about the far-reaching world of the creative black woman, that often the truest answer to a question that really matters can be found very close.

In the late 1920s my mother ran away from home to marry my father. Marriage, if not running away, was expected of seventeen-year-old girls. By the time she was twenty, she had two children and was pregnant with a third. Five children later, I was born. And this is how I came to know my mother: she seemed a large, soft, loving-eyed woman who was rarely impatient in our home. Her quick, violent temper was on view only a few times a year, when she battled with the white landlord who had the misfortune to suggest to her that her children did not need to go to school.

She made all the clothes we wore, even my brothers' overalls. She made all the towels and sheets we used. She spent the summers canning vegetables and fruits. She spent the winter evenings making quilts enough to cover all our beds.

During the "working" day, she labored beside—not behind—my father in the fields. Her day began before sunup, and did not end until late at night. There was never a moment for her to sit down, undisturbed, to unravel her own private thoughts; never a time free from interruption—by work or the noisy inquiries of her many children. And yet, it is to my mother—and all our mothers who were not famous—that I went in search of the secret of what has fed that muzzled and often mutilated, but vibrant, creative spirit that the black woman has inherited, and that pops out in wild and unlikely places to this day.

But when, you will ask, did my overworked mother have time to know or care about feeding the creative spirit?

The answer is so simple that many of us have spent years discovering it. We have constantly looked high, when we should have looked high—and low.

For example: in the Smithsonian Institution in Washington, D.C., there hangs a quilt unlike any other in the world. In fanciful, inspired, and yet simple and identifiable figures, it portrays the story of the Crucifixion. It is considered rare, beyond price. Though it follows no known pattern of quilt-making, and though it is made of bits and pieces of worthless rags, it is obviously the work of a person of powerful imagination and deep spiritual feeling. Below this quilt I saw a note that says it was made by "an anonymous Black woman in Alabama, a hundred years ago."

If we could locate this "anonymous" black woman from Alabama, she would turn out to be one of our grandmothers—an artist who left her mark in the only materials she could afford, and in the only medium her position in society allowed her to use.

As Virginia Woolf wrote further, in *A Room of One's Own:*

Yet genius of a sort must have existed among women as it must have existed among the working class. [Change this to "slaves" and "the wives and daughters of sharecroppers."] Now and again an Emily Brontë or a Robert Burns [change this to "a Zora Hurston or a Richard Wright"] blazes out and proves its presence. But certainly it never got itself on to paper. When, however, one reads of a witch being ducked, of a woman possessed by devils [or "Sainthood"], of a wise woman selling herbs [our root workers], or even a very remarkable man who had a mother, then I think we are on the track of a lost novelist, a suppressed poet, of some mute and inglorious Jane Austen. . . . Indeed, I would venture to guess that Anon, who wrote so many poems without signing them, was often a woman. . . .

And so our mothers and grandmothers have, more often than not anonymously, handed on the creative spark, the seed of the flower they themselves never hoped to see: or like a sealed letter they could not plainly read.

And so it is, certainly, with my own mother. Unlike "Ma" Rainey's songs, which retained their creator's name even while blasting forth from Bessie Smith's mouth, no song or poem will bear my mother's name. Yet so many of the stories that I write, that we all write, are my mother's stories. Only recently did I fully realize this: that through years of listening to my mother's stories of her life, I have absorbed not only the stories themselves, but something of the manner in which she spoke, something of the urgency that involves the knowledge that her stories—like her life—must be recorded. It is probably for this reason that so much of what I have written is about characters whose counterparts in real life are so much older than I am.

But the telling of these stories, which came from my mother's lips as naturally as breathing, was not the only way my mother showed herself as an artist. For stories, too, were subject to being distracted, to dying without conclusion. Dinners must be started, and cotton must be gathered before the big rains. The artist that was and is my mother showed itself to me only after many years. This is what I finally noticed:

Like Mem, a character in *The Third Life of Grange Copeland,* my mother adorned with flowers whatever shabby house we were forced to live in. And not just your typical straggly country stand of zinnias, either. She planted ambitious gardens—and still does—with over fifty different varieties of plants that bloom profusely from early March until late November. Before she left home for the fields, she watered her flowers, chopped up the grass, and laid out new beds. When she returned from the fields she might divide clumps of bulbs, dig a cold pit, uproot and replant roses, or prune branches from her taller bushes or trees—until night came and it was too dark to see.

Whatever she planted grew as if by magic, and her fame as a grower of flowers spread over three counties. Because of her creativity with her flowers, even my memories of poverty are seen through a screen of blooms—sunflowers, petunias, roses, dahlias, forsythia, spirea, delphiniums, verbena . . . and on and on.

And I remember people coming to my mother's yard to be given cuttings from her flowers; I hear again the praise showered on her because whatever rocky soil she landed on, she turned into a garden. A garden so brilliant with colors, so original in its design, so magnificent with life and creativity, that to this day people drive by our house in Georgia—perfect strangers and imperfect strangers—and ask to stand or walk among my mother's art.

I notice that it is only when my mother is working in her flowers that she is radiant, almost to the point of being invisible—except as Creator: hand and eye. She is involved in work her soul must have. Ordering the universe in the image of her personal conception of Beauty.

Her face, as she prepares the Art that is her gift, is a legacy of respect she leaves to me, for all that illuminates and cherishes life. She has handed down respect for the possibilities—and the will to grasp them.

For her, so hindered and intruded upon in so many ways, being an artist has still been a daily part of her life. This ability to hold on, even in very simple ways, is work black women have done for a very long time.

This poem is not enough, but it is something, for the woman who literally covered the holes in our walls with sunflowers:

> They were women then
> My mama's generation
> Husky of voice—Stout of
> Step
> With fists as well as
> Hands
> How they battered down
> Doors
> And ironed
> Starched white
> Shirts
> How they led
> Armies
> Headragged Generals
> Across mined

> Fields
> Booby-trapped
> Kitchens
> To discover books
> Desks
> A place for us
> How they knew what we
> *Must* know
> Without knowing a page
> Of it
> Themselves.

Guided by my heritage of a love of beauty and a respect for strength—in search of my mother's garden, I found my own.

And perhaps in Africa over two hundred years ago, there was just a mother; perhaps she painted vivid and daring decorations in oranges and yellows and greens on the walls of her hut; perhaps she sang—in a voice like Roberta Flack's—*sweetly* over the compounds of her village; perhaps she wove the most stunning mats or told the most ingenious stories of all the village storytellers. Perhaps she was herself a poet—though only her daughter's name is signed to the poems that we know.

Perhaps Phillis Wheatley's mother was also an artist.

Perhaps in more than Phillis Wheatley's biological life is her mother's signature made clear.

Michele Faith Wallace (1952–)

Michele Wallace was at the forefront of Black feminist cultural discourse in the late 1970s and 1980s, beginning with her infamous book, Black Macho and the Myth of the Super-woman, *published in 1978. In that work, Wallace's candid analysis of Black male-female relationships ignited and fueled a conversation and critique that directly and indirectly re-sulted in the production of other central works of Black feminist studies. Wallace's writing, which merges cultural and literary studies with popular culture, is similar to work by bell hooks, June Jordan, Audre Lorde, and Cornel West.*

Born in 1952 to musician Robert Earl and artist Faith Jones, Wallace grew up in New York surrounded by art and was fortunate to have traveled to major European countries while still young. She attended City College of the City University of New York, earning a B.A. in 1974, and an M.A. in 1984. In between those two degrees, Wallace wrote for Newsweek *and became an instructor then assistant professor at her alma mater. She was a founding member of the National Black Feminist Organization and once president of Art Without Walls. Currently, Wallace is associate professor of English, Women's Studies, and Cinema Studies at City College. She has published two other works since* Black Macho, Invisibility Blues *and* Black Popular Culture *(a project she organized) and continues to write regularly for the* Village Voice *and* The New York Times, *among other publications.*

Wallace endured harsh criticism and strong praise for Black Macho, *which, in spite of its sometimes incomplete thesis, was an attempt to be honest and did stimulate conver-sations in Black and non-Black America about race and gender. Wallace was daring and relied heavily on her own personal experience (which was one of the criticisms leveled against her, considering she was 26 when the book was published); these two characteris-tics continue to be a part of the insightful criticism she has produced since 1978. In "Enter-tainment Tomorrow," Wallace does an effective job of explicating the term "popular culture," both by providing a definition, but also by giving and critiquing examples of pop-ular culture. Wallace asserts that at the heart of popular culture is the recognition of the power of art, that all art is in fact political, but also of its potential for surface, of the ways that art's existence is not an inherent radical politic. She provides various angles of view-ing popular culture but settles on the idea that such cultural production must not only have a mass quality, but it must generate from the masses. As an example, Wallace pro-vides a critique of Jesse Jackson's 1988 speech at the Democratic National Convention, raising questions that are somewhat similar to those political scientist Adolph Reed, Jr. raises. In Wallace's comments on Jackson's campaign are a number of pop cultural stud-ies elements, including the interdisciplinary approach of her questions and insights and the unresolved tension between positive and negative potency of the subject. Wallace does not end with a nice summary declaring Jackson's speech either failure or success, but in-*

stead suggests that there is a mixed quality, and the only basis for appraisal is its impact upon people's lives.

In the second part of the essay, Wallace relies upon personal narrative as a text for cultural critique, revealing the power and surface that is evident in her own residential community, which reflects an incredible ethnic and racial diversity. This diversity is a condition that may appear to be politically radical but is also largely due to chance and circumstance. How one reads the situation, then, depends on what about the situation one finds interesting and powerful. This realization of the multiple ways that cultural texts can be read is one of the central tenets of popular cultural studies. In the clear presentation of an aesthetic of cultural studies, Wallace's essay is similar to the aesthetic articulation made in Trey Ellis' "New Black Aesthetic."

Kevin Everod Quashie

Entertainment Tomorrow

What follows will be both a defense of and a critique of what is usually called 'entertainment.' My main concern is not the production of mass culture because I cannot defend its production, given its roots in a heartless capitalist economy of global exploitation. Besides, critiques of this institution are plentiful enough. But from the point of view of the pleasure we get from participating in mass culture, a great deal more remains to be said. As the least altruistic and most self-indulgent aspect of culture, our tastes in entertainment may be the truest indication of our collective potential for tolerance and our political limits, our likelihood of doing better the next time. Particularly when entertainment utilizes multicultural strategies, it expands our cultural and political horizons, and stretches our intellectual and creative muscles.

More important than whether it teaches us something or not is that it can show us new ways to feel. Having fun is one way to begin to subvert the deadly authority that runs our country and plagues our lives because it's a way to remember what the body really feels and what we want freedom to be when we finally get there. I learned this first from my artist mother and my musician father. There was always music and black was always beautiful in our house. Moreover, growing up in a Harlem where 'entertainment' was the chief export confirmed this lesson. In the 60s, the white New Left cut its teeth not only on the serious doings of the Civil Rights Movement but also on Afro-American country and urban blues, and its rhythm & blues/rock 'n' roll offspring. And unlike the political leadership, the music always told the truth.

At its worst, however, mass culture can cajole us into buying what we've already got too much of: racism, sexism, American chauvinism, loving the rich and hating the poor. Just think of a television show like *Dallas,* which trivializes white supremacist greed. Other low points include *The Morton Downey Show.*

Fairly serious political issues become goofy cartoon characters, as in a recent show on *Who Speaks for Black America?* at Harlem's Apollo Theatre during which Roy Innis called the black audience 'ignorant' and knocked to the floor scandal-plagued Reverend Al Sharpton. How that must have played in Peoria. Or a movie like *Betrayed,* where racism becomes this mysterious and rare disease unrelated to historical agency, class conflict or cultural difference. As the plot unfolds, we discover that racism is not only genetic in Midwestern farmers but also macho and irresistible to women. Deborah Winger, an FBI agent who is fighting racism (not my sense of that organization's historical record), falls hopelessly in love with Tom Beringer, whose agrarian roots and working-class background seem to make inevitable his little spare-time hobby of murdering blacks and Jews. Or there's Geraldo Rivera and Oprah Winfrey and the whole morning and afternoon TV line-up. They offer a flood of misinformation, nationalistic propaganda, melodramatic distortion and hyperbolic hogwash. Worst of all, once I tune them in, I can't seem to bring myself to tune them out.

But the best of what I mean by mass entertainment involves the spontaneous and usually unchoreographed conjunction of one or more forms of 'popular culture' and the technological apparatus of the mass cultural. By 'popular culture' I mean that culture which still comes from 'the people,' from the bottom up, although it can no longer claim to be uncontaminated by the poison of consumerism and the self-loathing it is ostensibly designed to ameliorate. In fact, popular culture is now deeply influenced by mass cultural appropriations of its formal qualities, which it may then reappropriate and revise in increasingly innovative gestures of autonomy. While the intricacy of this process makes popular culture virtually indistinguishable from mass culture, we can, nevertheless, identify the occurrence of the popular cultural by the ruptures it creates: not only its various ways of breaking with capitalist production—which becomes more and more difficult to do—but also by its ability to superimpose, upon the commercialism of one of the mass cultural forms, another agenda concerning 'the people.'

The prime recent example is Jesse Jackson's speech at the 1988 Democratic National Convention in Atlanta, during which the televisual intersected with Afro-American popular cultural traditions of the black church and black political speechmaking. As the time for the speech approached, I wondered how Jackson would handle the failure of the Rainbow Coalition to capture or dominate the ticket. The lifeless frame provided by the convention and the network coverage seemed impossible to salvage. The hollowness of the pseudo-event was palpable. In his speech, would Jackson manufacture an advantage, as every other pronouncement at this convention seemed manufactured (Randolph's folksy 'That old dog won't hunt' to describe Republican policies; Teddy Kennedy's 'Where was George?'; Barbara Jordan's defense of Bensten), or would Jackson level? And how would he handle the potential for widespread disillusionment among his supporters?

Although the media persistently claimed the opposite, Jackson's support had never been a cult of personality. That's why it called itself a coalition. Diverse groups who have had little understanding of each other's priorities in the past were banding together to advance the collective interests of the marginalized. I don't feel especially confident about my ability to evaluate mainstream political events, mostly because it seems impossible to know what is really going on. But when it comes to mass art, like everybody else, I'm a bit of a connoisseur, and Jackson's speech was mass art with a vengeance.

A consummate act of entertainment, it transcended all previous standards in my television viewing history for staged, nonviolent, televisual excitement. It was off the scale in terms of the energy it generated and, interestingly enough, in defense of the electronic forms, television and radio really scooped the story because the newspapers were virtually powerless to do it justice. It was representation, not substantive political change, that scored the victory here—by no means a trivial matter when it comes to dealing with why most Americans find it impossible to imagine a black president. Could this failure of imagination (in which commercial television and radio are usually only too happy to assist) have anything to do with the general aversion among registered voters to necessary economic reforms like feeding and housing the poor, or more humane foreign policies like dumping US political loyalties to the white supremacist regime of South Africa? I think so.

Jackson's was ostensibly a concession speech, a throw-in-the-towel-in-the-race-for-the-White House speech, and yet it seemed, alternatively, a radical Baptist sermon on despair and the dignity of 'unwed' mothers, a history lesson on the Civil Rights Movement and the integration of the Democratic Party, a confession, a sharp denunciation of the global politics of drugs, a strong defense of AIDS victims and the rights of the gay community, and much more. The concrete visions of the various trajectories of the speech, the branches of the various constituencies of the Rainbow Coalition, would (and did), no doubt, conflict—especially when it came to that part when he briefly, and dutifully, proposed tolerance for the Democratic Party right.

Yet the sheer daring and dazzling style in revitalizing once again the form of the political sermon—à la Martin Luther King, Jr, Adam Clayton Powell, Jr, Malcolm X, Reverend Daughtry (and there have been women, as well, such as Fannie Lou Hamer)—in the direction of the improvisational blues statement, told the Afro-American audience, at least, a lot about what could *not* be said. Remember, the form, as King, Malcolm X and Hamer employed it, was always about telling people things they didn't want to hear. It was about the necessarily innovative exercise of subverting boundaries and limitations still believed to be insurmountable. In other words, it was about the long haul.

Jackson did the key thing that a public speaker can do in order to subvert his own authority and engage the issue of 'the people' while himself in the untenable position of speaking to an audience of millions through the unfriendly medium of a network television camera. He identified himself with the silenced and powerless black woman who was his mother. He invoked his mother's teenage, 'unwed' difficulty in raising him. He proposed his mother's patchwork quilting as a standard by which to measure his political effectiveness. This use of the female figure was a critical aspect of his performance. It began when he went out into the audience to fetch Rosa Parks—the woman who was arrested for violating bus segregation in Montgomery, Alabama in the 1950s—as the 'mother' of the Civil Rights Movement. On the one hand, he was presenting himself as a conventional symbol of Democratic power politics. Even the introductions of his children, who were uniformly clean cut, articulate and well dressed, followed that format. On the other hand, Jackson's speech also seemed to be saying, 'Their grandma, and my mother, was a powerless black woman and so am I. Her powerlessness then is still my powerlessness now at this convention.'

Yet by this defense of Jackson's speech, I do not mean that it is the same as 'the real thing,' the victory of concrete political transformation and growth. Still, Jackson's speech was designed to do the very important work of helping us to imagine change, on the theory that what we can imagine, we can make happen. In the process, there was strong insinuation of battles far from won, the Civil Rights Movement chief among them. The difficulty we have as a culture in acknowledging such levels of accomplishment, particularly on the part of blacks, is a major part of what's wrong with how we do things. If Ted Kennedy or Lloyd Bentsen or anybody white had made such an extraordinary speech, it would have been lauded immediately and repeatedly, as an absolutely unforgettable event, to be endlessly interpreted and analyzed by left and liberal commentators.

On the other hand, I wouldn't try to offer any defense whatsoever for why Jackson would want to make peace with the despicable Mayor Koch of New York. Not only was Koch racist and unhelpful when Jackson was campaigning in the New York primaries, Koch seems, generally, to be advancing a program of urban fascism, the paramount aim of which is to disappear people of color, the homeless, street people, and anybody with a punk haircut.

Koch's long-term strategy became evident in the recent police riots in Tompkins Square Park on the Lower Eastside. Community demonstrators were protesting the city's attempt to close the park at midnight, thereby denying the homeless a place to sleep, and the restless a place to congregate and party. The police responded with surprising force and violence very late at night. Afraid to venture into the area (the rumor was that blacks were particular targets), I got most of my information from WBAI (which supplied the best coverage), as well as newspapers and television (which lagged several days behind). This was early August. While Lower Eastsiders, a fairly upwardly mobile and politically astute group, seem to have won the media battle (the closing of the park has been temporarily suspended), cool weather promises a re-escalation of Koch's cleanup efforts.

As for the Jackson strategy in all of this, it worked differently in practice than in theory. Jackson appeared none too pleased with Koch in the flesh, as a photo in *The New York Times* showing the concerned faces of Manhattan Borough President David Dinkins, Rep. Charles Rangel, Stanley Hill, the executive director of the Municipal Workers' Union, and Jackson himself, would indicate. To dissociate himself from Koch's policies even further, Jackson addressed an ongoing homelessness protest and demonstration at City Hall Park.

John Jiler recaps the group's history in the September 13 issue of *The Village Voice:* 'In June he [Koch] told the Parks people to get rid of them, but the move backfired. As a sanitation team began to devour the little village of cardboard and plastic, the press got wind of it and covered the event like a blanket. "Kochville," they began calling the settlement. As the homeless dug in, the mayor sizzled.'

That the Rainbow Coalition must lie down with Dukakis and Bensten is not my idea of fun either. Such are the all-too-familiar limitations of form: a dance is still just a dance no matter how 'black' it is. Form is not enough. Mass culture has made its millions by offering a substitute for substance—in automobiles and televisions, political parties and constitutional amendments—as everybody knows but keeps forgetting. So runs the critique.

What's Cookin' in Hell's Kitchen

Of course, the issue on the Lower Eastside and all over New York, except on Park Avenue, is labeled 'gentrification' by the press, which seems to pose the question of whether or not starving, homeless people can live side by side in peace with Wall Street lawyers (everybody's favorite image of the Yuppie). But the real issues are cultural tolerance—the kind of thing the city of Yonkers is willing to blow its entire municipal budget in order to avoid—and the potential for wholesale reform in housing the poor, and not-so-poor, the welfare system, the Board of Education, the prisons, drug programs, the police department, hospitals and health care, not to mention the management of public spaces. Most of us are not Wall Street lawyers. Most of us are not sleeping in the park, either. Yet. So why don't the media talk more about the Rainbow?

Last summer, my first in New York in three years, I lived in a small one-room apartment (about the size of many kitchens in 'middle America') with my spouse equivalent Gene in an area known as Hell's Kitchen. The uproar of dissonant musical tastes, the bellow and clamor of domestic violence at all hours, the crack vials in the hallway, the large numbers of homeless people sleeping in the streets, and the aggressiveness of the drug trade just down the block made it seem like 'hell' after the last three and a half years of comparative bliss in an under-populated Norman, Oklahoma and a beach-ridden San Diego, California. And yet, like everything else having to do with culture, I was of two minds about it. On the one hand, the poverty, the violence, the corruption, and the rampant economic exploitation were scary and awful, and it was as clear in New York City as it must be in many of the cities of the Third World that existing notions of 'government,' 'law and order,' 'profit' and the economic needed immediate revision. People were sleeping on the hard, nasty sidewalk. Children could barely get out of the schoolyard for the drug pushers. And sooner or later, the white man (a drug dealer) and the black woman (paying the rent, or so she claimed in their loud arguments) in the first floor front were going to succeed in killing one another and the police would finally have to come.

On the other hand, there was wisdom in those streets about culture-in-the-making and culture-on-the-run—the choices people make, and don't make, about how they will live despite too little space, not enough money, and the nearly insurmountable difficulties of communication and intimacy under the circumstances. I was moved and fascinated by the extraordinary struggles for survival and pleasure that were constantly going on around me, the mutual flow of black school children, Latino shopkeepers, white building supers, Chinese restaurateurs, Korean fruitstand owners, African vendors, addicts, winos, the regularly or sporadically unemployed and under-employed, the elderly, the disabled, the gay, the married, the lonely.

I don't mean we were all in the streets singing 'We Shall Overcome' with linked arms. Like kept to like and ignored everything and everybody else in a fairly heartless way. You could probably walk around with that fried egg on your head that Bette Midler used to sing about and nobody would say anything. But my suspicion was that beneath the veneer of imperturbability everybody wore for self-protection, there was a different kind of paying attention: the first stage of tolerance, the last stage of apathy, or both.

In my leisure time, I didn't go to the movies much. Instead I jogged around and around in circles in De Witt Clinton Park on Eleventh Avenue, a place that Curtis Slewa of the Guardian Angels now says, one year later, is too drug-infested for the homeless, much less a jogging writer. But when I then ran in the mornings—besides the hotdog vendor, the short woman with eight dogs and the classful of young retarded adults playing ball—I often found homeless people still asleep on the benches or on the grass, people I came to recognize as individuals. There was a guy who used to build a cage over himself out of cardboard boxes, as he lay on a park bench under the trees. There was a young white male, who did not look homeless, who used to pace up and down chain-smoking and arguing with himself. There was a white female/black male couple that I used to see regularly enough to wonder about their domestic arrangements. How long had they been together? Had they met while homeless? Did they have sex on the grass? What did they talk about? I always wondered about the couples especially.

About midsummer I began to fantasize about making a movie about a character I would call C. Wright. She was a homeless black woman, twenty years old, addicted to crack, an 'unwed' mother whose child was being raised in a foster home, and who occasionally slept in De Witt Clinton park during the summer of 1988. She had become homeless not too long ago while still living at home when her father was laid off. In my imaginary movie, this information would be provided in a flashback in which an alcoholic mother and an abusive father first demand that she give up her baby, then drive her into the streets because of their own poverty.

One morning C. Wright wakes up in the park and sees a handsome young black man jogging in her direction. A former high school track star herself, she manages to pull herself together enough to start running again. To make a long story short, she subsequently marries the handsome young man, reclaims her child from the foster home, and goes on to win the New York Marathon. I used to see an American Express ad in the black magazines in which a young black family is shown having a day in the park. The young attractive 'mother' is jogging in the front. Behind her follows the young attractive 'husband' and 'father' on a bicycle with a small child strapped into a safety seat on the back. The black father has that bemused look, as though he isn't sure he will be able to keep up with the mother, who is commodification's version of a black feminist. This was the sort of future I tried to construct for C. Wright, and yet the plot presented certain large gaps in plausibility.

How would she obtain her running shoes? Where would she shower? How would she get enough clean water to drink? Enough fresh fruit and vegetables and fish to eat? How would she ever manage to 'just say no' to crack, cheap wine, and chicken McNuggets? Where would the money come from for an apartment so that she could get a decent night's sleep? Finally, the logistics overwhelmed, and I gave up thinking about C. Wright's movie.

Marilyn Nelson Waniek (1946–)

Marilyn Nelson Waniek was born in Cleveland, Ohio, on April 26, 1946. She studied at the University of California, Davis, earning a B.A. in 1968; she earned graduate degrees from the Universities of Pennsylvania and of Minnesota (1970 and 1979 respectively). Waniek has taught at many institutions, including St. Olaf College, University of Connecticut, Reed College, and, currently, Louisiana State University. As a child, Waniek lived on various army bases and, as a result, developed an interest in various American ethnic heritages, especially the intergenerationality of identity, which she explores in The Homeplace (1990), a work that resonates with Rita Dove's Thomas and Beulah (1986) and for which Waniek received a National Book Award Nomination. She was also awarded a National Endowment for the Arts fellowship in 1982.

Waniek writes children's books as well as adult books of poetry, although it is for the latter that she is most well known. In these works, Waniek's style is at once lyric and elegant and classical, but also loose and rural, resonant with the subjects that she writes about. In "The House on Moscow Street," Waniek brings to life the house that is "the ragged source of memory" and motivates her investigation of love over the years, from the time of slavery up to her present life. Waniek unearths a narrative of her family, and it is this house that serves as a locating place: "In the middle bedroom's hard, / high antique double bed / the ghost of Aunt Jane, ... does not appear. / Nor does Pomp's ghost," she writes, linking the characters' lives to spaces in the homeplace. Her poetry here remains entirely narrative without losing any of the lyricism, particularly because Waniek uses complete sentences to express her thoughts here.

The poems from her collection, For the Body, are more prayerful and thick with spirituality, as evidenced by "Dedication," which repeatedly uses fragments to create the effect of a chant. Waniek's interest here is less to create a narrative and more to invoke a particular poetic and spiritual sense: "For the heart / in its stone boat / that falls always / through this clear, / this black water." In "My Grandfather Walks in the Woods," Waniek's prayerful tone is turned on her grandfather's image, a sweet meditation that admires him, but also the landscape around him. Again, Waniek uses fragments and short simple sentences for poetic effect. But Waniek's voice is not only celebratory, but also critical, as in "The American Dream," which uses the anaphora "I want" to present and critique consumerism but also racism and American nationalism. Similarly, in "The Leaves Are Losing the War," she enters a comment against a culture of violence and war, but her use of nature as a motif foreshadows and supports the hope and agency in the final stanza: "We make our small surrenders, / accept defeat. / Onto our shoulders the sky / drops gray stars." What contributes to the loveliness of this closing is Waniek's incredible balance between the four lines of the stanza—not perfect metric harmony, but each first line balanced *by a shorter one with about half the metrical length. Waniek's skill as a poet is precise and accurate without being cluttered and inaccessible.*

In "Compline," Waniek makes direct reference to prayer, titling the poem after the time of day in canonical religious practice that is reserved for rest, prayer, and reflection. Again, she uses simple language to create a narrative voice that is identifiable, resonant: a parent, maybe even a mother, asleep and tired, whose mind wanders to and wonders on travel, on the possibility of escape. But escape to where? which is the question that fuels that realization of thanks, of admiration for the blessings of the present world. What Waniek's poetry challenges the reader to do is something that the poetry allows her own self to do—to name and claim the triumphant and sweet and bitter that is our lives. Her work is always prayerful, never superficial, and invitingly well-crafted.

Kevin Everod Quashie

The House on Moscow Street

It's the ragged source of memory,
a tarpaper-shingled bungalow
whose floors tilt toward the porch,
whose back yard ends abruptly
in a weedy ravine. Nothing special:
a chain of three bedrooms
and a long side porch turned parlor
where my great-grandfather, Pomp, smoked
every evening over the news,
a long sunny kitchen
where Annie, his wife,
measured cornmeal
dreaming through the window
across the ravine and up to Shelby Hill
where she had borne their spirited,
high-yellow brood.

In the middle bedroom's hard,
high antique double bed
the ghost of Aunt Jane,
the laundress
who bought the house in 1872,
though I call with all my voices,
does not appear.
Nor does Pomp's ghost,
with whom one of my cousins believes
she once had a long and intimate
unspoken midnight talk.
He told her, though they'd never met,

that he loved her; promised
her raw widowhood would heal
without leaving a scar.

The conveniences in an enclosed corner
of the slant-floored back side porch
were the first indoor plumbing in town.
Aunt Jane put them in,
incurring the wrath of the woman
who lived in the big house next door.
Aunt Jane left the house
to Annie, whose mother she had known
as a slave on the plantation,
so Annie and Pomp could move their children
into town, down off Shelby Hill.
My grandmother, her brother, and five sisters
watched their faces change slowly
in the oval mirror on the wall outside the door
into teachers' faces, golden with respect.
Here Geneva, the randy sister,
damned their colleges,
daubing her quicksilver breasts
with gifts of perfume.

As much as love,
as much as a visit
to the grave of a known ancestor,
the homeplace moves me not to silence
but to righteous, praise Jesus song:

Oh, catfish and turnip greens,
hot-water cornbread and grits.
Oh, musty, much-underlined Bibles;
generations lost to be found,
to be found.

Dedication

    For the heart
    in its stone boat
    that falls always
    through this clear,

this black water.
For the heart,
the most desperate organ.
The heart, bailing us out.

For the brain,
the center of miracles,
with its dreams of flying
over the woods and meadows,
the body hanging by its beard.
For the brain, the maker,
its tiny star light.

And for the hands,
for all the working class
of the body: feet, belly, legs.
For all the other unsung
we have no nice names for.
For our proletariat,
our common man.

For all the body
whose messages we do not heed.
For the body,
riding its pain and pleasure.
For the body,
living like a beacon
out into death.

My Grandfather Walks in the Woods

Somewhere
in the light above the womb,
black trees
and white trees
populate a world.

It is a March landscape,
the only birds around are small
and black.
What do they eat,
sitting in the birches
like warnings?

The branches of the trees
are black and white.
Their race is winter.
They thrive in cold.

There is my grandfather
walking among the trees.
He does not notice
his fingers are cold.
His black felt hat
covers his eyes.

He is knocking on each tree,
listening to their voices
as they answer slowly
deep, deep from their roots.
I am John, he says,
are you my father?

They answer
with voices like wind
blowing away from him.

The American Dream

I want to go shopping
and buy myself.
I want to suddenly turn
american, sold at the counter
by some sleight-of-mind
salesman who'll trap my dreams
and put me in an automatic cage.

I want my face to stop looking
like an african housewife,
my feet to stop dancing to
lost music.

I want to get out of
my VW some saturday afternoon
and walk through silent glass doors.
I want to pick myself up
in Safeway.

The Leaves Are Losing the War

The leaves are losing the war.
They dive headfirst into the grass,
their broken wings all flaming.
The birds have mostly taken
their brief songs
and hoarded them away
but there are sparrows
still gay in their courage
and a platoon of strange geese
is waiting by the lake.
They are waiting for a signal:
for the sun to run out.

Everything is khaki:
the trees brown, the grass,
even the people are quiet now,
muffled in wool to the ears.
Under their coats
young girls' breasts are private
and the hands of the boys have forgotten
their summer yearnings.
Every morning the bus is full
of people looking away.

We make our small surrenders,
accept defeat.
Onto our shoulders the sky
drops gray stars.

Compline

The evening is as quiet
as a monk at prayer.
The children asleep,
the TV steel-green;
the Christmas tree cradles
fifty electric candles.
Stretched out on the couch
I at last close my eyes.

And immediately
fall asleep.
Despite miles of highways
paved with good intentions.
The car feels safe,
there's a whole tank of gas,
only one or two headlights grow
in my windshield and mirror.

Where am I going?
Can you tell me,
my dear

friend?
Because damned if I know.
The miles-per-hour landscape
offers a million illegible exits.
Was the one I sped past
twenty years ago
the right way?
The one I passed
today?

I wake with a start:
no answers.
I turn off the tree,
nudge the toys into a corner,
and tiptoe from
bedroom to bedroom
to bedroom. It is good
to give thanks.

Michael S. Weaver (1951–)
(Afaa M. Weaver)

Often when one thinks of language one thinks of the written or spoken manifestation. But in the wonderful tradition of the African "talking drum," Michael Weaver understands that music and visual art are two overlooked mediums that hold special significance in African American culture. Weaver combines various media to create powerful poetry that continually interrogates the past as a pathway to understanding and negotiating African American life today.

Born November 26, 1951, in Baltimore, Maryland, Weaver's early "love of paper and pencils" perpetuated his later love of language and the power it holds for transforming our world. He attended the University of Maryland at College Park from 1968–1970 and later earned his B.A. from Regents College in 1986. In 1987 he received his M.A. from Brown University. Weaver currently teaches at Rutgers University and resides with his wife and their daughter Kala in Philadelphia, Pennsylvania. Weaver has published four books of poetry: Water Song *(1985),* My Father's Geography *(1992),* Stations in a Dream *(1993), and* Timber and Prayer *(1995). In addition to this he has written two plays—*Rosa *(1993) and* Elvira and the Lost Prince *(1993)—and a collection of short stories,* The Day Sugar Daddy Died *(1997).*

The two best known of his works are My Father's Geography, *a collection of poems that look carefully at the journey of what Toni Morrison calls "re-memory," and* Timber and Prayer, *which pays homage to the musical tradition that has shaped African American culture. Weaver's "ardent feelings about what the word can do, how it can enliven and sustain the consciousness of the reader . . . and the influences of the Great Migration, the blues, jazz, classical music and the modernist painters" illuminate his discourse. The voice of God in "Ego" "caught in the crackling commotion of thought" exemplifies the power and redemption of spirituality that is at the same time all around us and fragile, if one stops and listens, respecting the sacredness of the moment.*

Weaver describes a journey of self framed by migration and movement often under the worst of circumstances. In his elegy "Christmas, 1941" written for his father and mother, Weaver brings us along on their journey from southern familiarity to the jazz rising from every steaming corner of the city and the possibilities. The wooden house on the farm of his father, "that stood . . . that was . . . that heard" shows the strength of foundation forged through oppression. The hope and possibility of "what the city was like, what groaning blues it kept," all conjure a poem that paints a picture of apprehension and yet tremendous hope. The final poem, "Salvation," is another elegy that interrogates the grief and celebration of a comrade no longer physically present but whose spirit mingles in the physical remains. The "high tenor, the sound of wood . . . crack[ling] . . . a chip of bone . . . rattles" helps the reader to experience the great dichotomy of "the definite . . . the imprecise." This dichotomy forms the basis of African American life, forms the blues, and the mixture of joyous sadness, and being "born under a bad sign" is a theme that runs not only within the confines of this poem but through all of Weaver's beautiful work.

Weaver's fascination with visual imagery brings each line to life vividly. The language that he loves so is developed into riffs that we play again and again, interrogating and searching for a "philosophy or creed," only to realize they were there in ourselves all along

Michael Pfister

Ego

God's voice
is caught in
the crackling commotion
of thought,
like dried leaves—
breaking.

Christmas, 1941

FOR MARK JOSEPH WEAVER

My father and his mother
came north on a train
powered by black smoke
billowing back from
an old, huffing engine
that drove its wheels
with relentless metal arms.
He was nineteen,
a big, strapping boy
sprouted from the ways
of a small farm,
raised in the wooden house
that stood twenty-seven years
after this trip to Baltimore,
the wooden house that was
a large box of planks

sitting up on columns
of stones piled and held together
with mortar, the wooden house
that heard the hoorays
when he was born.

His mother's guard and charge,
he sat entranced at the window,
wondering what the city was like,
what groaning blues it kept
in its cheeks like snuff,
what shifting love it held
where people were as thick
as wasps pouring from a nest.

At home the city
was Lawrenceville, a hamlet
he could stand on the edge of
and holler and be heard
on the other side of town,
a sleepy face of a place
with a five-and-dime
and old men in overalls
who blurred the distinction
between country and city,
between unbound and bound.

He reached into the paper box
for another piece of chicken
and met his mother's glance,
taunting and half-stern,
reminding him they had a ways to go
and he looked around to study
the other passengers who
looked back half-friendly
with eyes that sang out,
Go on way from here boy,
Ain't nobody studyin bout you,
or they sang out lovingly
like new grandparents with eyes
that promised to dream along
with him until they were north,
north of the guiding grimace
of Richmond, north of the capital of the North,

Washington, which surprised him
when the train rumbled through it.

In Baltimore his mother eyed him
like a nurse with a blind man,
as the buildings and the traffic
struck him dumb and dazzled,
and his mouth fell open
to suck in the city's liquid magic
that boiled on the notes
of a music of heart upon heart,
conscience upon conscience,
trudging soul upon trudging soul
where people amass to live
and to die together. He forgot
the night bird's song,
the whippoorwill's aria,
and the ripping cut of hot fields
as he walked in a new Jerusalem.

Salvation

FOR DONALD FAULCON AT LAKE MONTEBELLO

In symbol,
I blow your ashes
over the lake's ripples
that roll in under
the western end
of the world.
Your high tenor,
the sound of wood
that is cut to burn,
crackles. Your ashes
draw a body that
dissipates, lives
only for an instant.
The ashes spread
from tip to tip.
You claim
an eternal deed
on the place we believed

we would always
return to, until
the last second.
I pray that
you can hear
my wish where
you have command
of the light
that illumines my grief.
I pray that you can
see me where
all human futility
is spun like funny silk
on a wisdom's loom.
I pray that you can
laugh and mimic my laugh
in a private corner
like the space where
our lives intersected.
I am now alone
in the mind's
recounting of itself.
Life flips backward.
From the ashes,
a chip of bone
remains, rattles
in the urn. It is
the valley's single
icon of rebirth.
I take the bone
in my hand
to feel the definite,
to feel the imprecise.
I remember this is a day
like any other day
when we understood
a philosophy or a creed,
and the lake drank
our laughter as comic
or as congenial and wise
as where we begin
or where we end
this collecting
we call a life.

Cornel West (1953–)

A native of Tulsa, Oklahoma, Cornel West attended high school in Sacramento, California, before graduating from Harvard University. He earned a Ph.D. in philosophy from Princeton University and returned to teach there for six years. Since 1994 he has been a professor of African American Studies at Harvard.

West's first book, Prophesy Deliverance! *(1982), advocates a socially concerned African American Christianity that draws from Marxism. His* American Evasion of Philosophy *(1989) engages the work of Ralph Waldo Emerson and the tradition of American pragmatism, especially the career of John Dewey. West next wrote and co-edited several other rigorous, philosophical works. In the 1990s, he authored and co-authored thoughtful books for a more general audience, including* Breaking Bread *(1991, with bell hooks);* Race Matters *(1993);* Jews and Blacks *(1995, with Michael Lerner); and* The Future of the Race *(1996, with Henry Louis Gates, Jr.). In his collaboration with Michael Lerner and elsewhere, West focuses on the sometimes supportive, sometimes problematic relations between African Americans and Jewish Americans.*

An extremely popular and inspiring speaker, West lectures widely across the United States, mainly on African American topics. His oratorical persona is part passionate Baptist preacher, part streetcorner "brother," and part Harvard intellectual. He consistently advocates Christian socialism and the end of every form of racism, sexism, classism, and homophobia.

West's first essay here is a thoughtful reflection on the civil rights and Black-Is-Beautiful movements of the 1950s and 1960s. His second essay carefully weighs Malcolm X's unparalleled gift to articulate African American anger and frustration. West also evaluates the contributions and the inverted racial supremacy of Elijah Muhammad and the Nation of Islam. And he considers the degree that Malcolm X succeeded, at the end of his life, in expressing an egalitarian vision.

Keith D. Miller

The Paradox of the African American Rebellion

The distinctive feature of African American life in the sixties was the rise on the historical stage of a small yet determined petite bourgeoisie promoting liberal reforms, and the revolt of the masses, whose aspirations exceeded those of liberalism but whose containment was secured by political appeasement, cultural control and state repression. African America encountered the modern American capitalist order (in its expansionist phase)—as urban dwellers, industrial workers and franchised citizens—on a broad scale for the first time. This essay will highlight the emergence of the black parvenu petite bourgeoisie—the new, relatively privileged, middle class—and its complex relations to the black working poor and underclass. I will try to show how the political strategies, ideological struggles and cultural anxieties of this predominantly white-collar stratum both propelled the freedom movement in an unprecedented manner and circumscribed its vision, analysis and praxis within liberal capitalist perimeters.

For interpretive purposes, the sixties is not a chronological category which encompasses a decade, but rather a historical construct or heuristic rubric which renders noteworthy historical processes and events intelligible. The major historical processes that set the context for the first stage of the black freedom movement in the sixties were the modernization of Southern agriculture, the judicial repudiation of certain forms of southern racism and the violent white backlash against perceived black progress. The modernization of Southern agriculture made obsolete much of the traditional tenant labor force, thereby forcing large numbers of black rural folk into southern and northern urban centers in search of employment. The judicial repudiation of certain forms of Southern racism, prompted by the gallant struggles of the National Association for the Advancement of Colored People (NAACP) and exemplified in the *Brown v. Board of Education* decision of 1954, was not only a legal blow against tax-supported school segregation; it also added historical momentum and political legitimacy to black struggles against racism. Yet there quickly surfaced an often violent white reaction to this momentum and legitimacy. For example, Rev. George W. Lee was fatally shot in May 1955 for refusing to take his name off the voter registration list. Sixty-three-year-old Lamar Smith was killed in broad daylight in August 1955 for trying to get out the black vote in an upcoming primary election. And most notably, Emmett L. Till, a fourteen-year-old lad from Chicago visiting his relatives, was murdered in late August 1955. These wanton acts of violence against black people in Mississippi, though part of the American Southern way of life, reflected the conservative white reaction to perceived black progress. In 1955, this white reaction was met with widespread black resistance.

The greatness of Rev. Dr. Martin Luther King, Jr.—the major American prophet of this century and black leader in the sixties—was his ability to mobilize and organize this Southern resistance, such that the delicate balance between the emerging "new" black petite bourgeoisie, black working poor and black underclass was maintained for a few years. The arrest of Rosa Parks on December 1, 1955 in Montgomery, Alabama—as a result of one of a series of black acts of civil disobedience against Montgomery's bus line that year—led to the creation of the Montgomery Improvement Association (MIA), the adoption of a citywide black boycott and the placement of King at the head of the movement. After nearly a year of the boycott, the US Supreme Court declared Alabama's state and local bus segregation laws unconstitutional. Judicial repudiation of Southern racism again gave the black struggle for freedom momentum and legitimacy.

King is the exemplary figure of the first stage of the black freedom movement in the sixties not only because he was its gifted and courageous leader or simply because of his organizational achievements, but, more important, because he consolidated the most progressive potential available in the black Southern community at that time: the cultural potency of prophetic black churches, the skills of engaged black preachers, trade-unionists and professionals, and the spirit of rebellion and resistance of the black working poor and underclass. In this sense, King was an organic intellectual of the first order—a highly educated and informed thinker with organic links to ordinary folk. Despite his petit bourgeois origins, his deep roots in the black church gave him direct access to the life-worlds of the majority of black southerners. In addition, his education at Morehouse College, Crozier Theological Seminary and Boston University provided him with opportunities to reflect upon various anticolonial struggles around the world, especially those in India and Ghana, and also entitled him to respect and admiration in the eyes of black people, including the "old," black, middle class (composed primarily of teachers and preachers). Last, his Christian outlook and personal temperament facilitated relations with progressive non-black people, thereby insuring openness to potential allies.

King institutionalized his sense of the social engagement of black churches, his Christian-informed techniques of nonviolence and his early liberal vision of America, with the founding in February, 1957 in New Orleans of the Southern Christian Leadership Conference (SCLC). This courageous group of prophetic black preachers from ten Southern states served as the models for young black Southern activists. I stress the adjective "Southern" not simply because most black people in the USA at this time lived in the South, but also because the core of the first stage of the black freedom movement was a church-led movement in the belly of the violence-prone, underindustrialized, colonylike southern USA. Of course, the North was quite active—especially Harlem's Rev. Adam Clayton Powell, Jr. in Congress and the Nation of Islam's Malcolm X in the streets—but activity in the North was not the major thrust of this first stage.

Like David against Goliath, black activists openly challenged the entrenched, racist, white status quo in the South. Widespread white economic sanctions and physical attacks on black people, fueled by the so-called "Southern Manifesto" promoted in 1956 by Senator J. Strom Thurmond of South Carolina along with over a hundred congressmen, rendered both the Democratic and Republican parties relatively silent regarding the civil rights issues affecting black people. Two diluted civil rights bills (in 1957 and 1960) limped through Congress, and the Supreme Court, owing to congressional pressure, took much of the bite out of its earlier Brown decision. Black resistance intensified.

Inspired by the praxis of King, MIA and SCLC—as well as the sit-in techniques employed by the Congress of Racial Equality (CORE) in the North—four black freshmen students at North Carolina Agricultural and Technical College in

Greensboro staged a sit-in at the local Woolworth's on February 1, 1960. Within a week, their day-to-day sit-in had been joined by black and white students from the Women's College of the University of North Carolina, North Carolina College and Duke University. Within two weeks, the sit-in movement had spread to fifteen other cities in Virginia, Tennessee and South Carolina. Within two months, there were sit-ins in seventy-eight cities. By the end of 1960, over fifty thousand people throughout the South had participated in sit-in demonstrations, with over twenty-five percent of the black students in predominantly black colleges participating. In short, young black people (and some progressive white people) had taken seriously King's techniques of nonviolence and the spirit of resistance.

This spontaneous rebellion of young black people against the Southern taboo of black and white people eating together in public places exemplified a major component in the first stage of the black freedom movement: the emergence of politicized, black, parvenu, petit bourgeois students. These students, especially young preachers and Christian activists, prefigured the disposition and orientation of the vastly increasing number of black college students in the sixties: they would give first priority to social activism and justify their newly acquired privileges by personal risk and sacrifice. So the young black student movement was not simply a rejection of segregation in restaurants. It was also a revolt against the perceived complacency of the "old" black petite bourgeoisie. It is no accident that at the first general conference on student sit-in activity, which began Good Friday (April 15) 1960, the two keynote speakers—Rev. James Lawson and Rev. Martin Luther King, Jr.—launched devastating critiques of the NAACP and other "old" black middle class groups. King articulated this viewpoint when he characterized the sit-in movement as "a revolt against those Negroes in the middle class who have indulged themselves in big cars and ranch-style homes rather than in joining a movement for freedom." The organization which emerged later in the year from this gathering—the Student Nonviolent Coordinating Committee—(SNCC)—epitomized this revolt against the political reticence of the "old" black middle class.

The major achievement of SNCC was, in many ways, its very existence. SNCC initiated a new style and outlook among black students in particular and the "new" black petite bourgeoisie in general. Its activist, countercultural orientation even influenced disenchanted white students on elite university campuses. Yet SNCC's central shortcoming was discernible at its inception: if pushed far enough, the revolt against middle-class status and outlook would not only include their models but also themselves, given their privileged student status and probable upward social mobility.

The influence of SNCC's new style was seen when James Farmer departed from the program directorship of the NAACP to become National Director of CORE. Within six weeks, he announced that CORE would conduct "Freedom Rides"—modeled on the 1947 Journey of Reconciliation led by CORE—to challenge segregation in interstate bus depots and terminals. On May 4, 1961, seven black people and six white people left Washington, D.C. Within ten days, one of the buses had been burned to the ground and many riders had been viciously attacked in Birmingham and Montgomery. This "Freedom Ride" was disbanded in Montgomery on May 17. A second "Freedom Ride" was initiated by SNCC, led by Diane Nash, composed of white and black people from CORE and SNCC. Violence ensued again, with twenty-seven people arrested and given suspended two-month sentences and fines of two hundred dollars. They refused to pay and were taken to Parchman Prison.

These two "Freedom Rides"—though responsible for the desegregation of bus and train stations on September 22, 1961, by the Interstate Commerce Commission—served as a portent of the two basic realities which would help bring the initial stage of the black freedom movement to a close: first, the slow but sure rift between SNCC and King, and second, the ambiguous attitude of Democratic Party liberals to the movement. Both aspects came to the fore at the crucial August 1961 staff meeting at SNCC at the Highlander Folk School in Tennessee. It was well known that the Kennedy administration had called for a "cooling off" period, motivated primarily by its fear of alienating powerful Southern Democratic comrades in Congress. At the meeting, Tim Jenkins, a fellow traveller of the Democratic Party, proposed that SNCC drop its emphasis on direct action and focus on voter education and registration. The majority of the SNCC staff opposed Jenkins's project, owing to its connections with the Kennedy administration and the open approval of it by King's SCLC. In the eyes of many SNCC members, the "Establishment" against which they were struggling began to encompass both the Democratic Party's liberals and the SCLC's black activist liberals. This slow rupture would result in some glaring defeats in the civil rights movement, most notably the Albany (Georgia) Movement in December 1961, and also led to the gradual breakaway of SNCC from the techniques of nonviolence.

Yet in 1963, the first stage of the black freedom movement would culminate in its most successful endeavors: Birmingham and the March on Washington. The televised confrontation between the civil rights marchers and the Commissioner of Public Safety, Eugene "Bull" Connor, as well as the dramatic arrest of King, gave the movement much sympathy and support throughout the country. And the use of hundreds of black children in the struggle reinforced this effective histrionic strategy. Despite the bombing of the black Gaston Hotel, of King's brother's home, and black spontaneous rebellions in Birmingham, the massive nonviolent direct action—including over three thousand people imprisoned—proved successful. The city of Birmingham, often referred to as the "American Johannesburg," accepted the black demands for desegregation and black employment opportunities. Furthermore, President Kennedy responded to the Birmingham campaign with a televised address to the nation in which he pledged his support for a comprehensive civil rights bill. However, the assassination of Medgar Evers, state executive secretary of the Mississippi NAACP, only hours after Kennedy's speech cast an ominous shadow over the Birmingham victory.

The famous March on Washington in August 1963—the occasion for King's powerful and poignant "I have a dream" speech—was not the zenith of the civil rights movement. The movement had peaked in Birmingham. Rather the March on Washington was the historic gathering of that coalition of liberal forces—white trade unionists, Christians, Jews and civil rights activists—whose potency was declining, whose fragile cohesion was falling apart. The central dilemma of the first stage of the black freedom movement emerged: the existence and sustenance of the civil rights movement neither needed nor required white aid or allies, yet its *success* required white liberal support in the Democratic Party, Congress and the White House.

The March on Washington exemplified this debilitating limitations of the civil rights movement. With white liberal support, the movement would achieve limited success, but slowly lose its legitimacy in the eyes of the now more politicized black petit bourgeois students, working poor and underclass. Without white liberal support, the movement could raise more fundamental issues of concern to the black working poor and underclass, yet thereby render the movement marginal to mainstream American politics and hence risk severe repression. It comes as no surprise that the March on Washington witnessed both the most powerful rhetoric and the most salient reality of the civil rights movement: King's great speech and the Kennedy administration's supervision of the March.

In summary, the first stage of the black freedom movement in the sixties—the civil rights struggle—began as a black response to white violent attacks and took the form of a critique of everyday life in the American South. This critique primarily consisted of attacking everyday cultural folkways which insulted black dignity. It was generated, in part, from the multifarious effects of the economic transformation of dispossessed Southern rural peasants into downtrodden industrial workers, maids and unemployed city dwellers within the racist American South. In this regard, the civil rights movement prefigured the fundamental concerns of the American New Left: linking private troubles to public issues, accenting the relation of cultural hegemony to political control and economic exploitation.

The major achievements of the civil rights movement were noteworthy: the transformation of everyday life (especially the elimination of terror as a primary mode of social control) of central regions in the American South; the federal commitment to the civil and voting rights of African Americans; and the sense of confidence among black people that effective mobilization and organization were not only possible but imperative if the struggle for freedom was to continue. The pressing challenges were immense: transforming the power relations in the American South and North, obtaining federal support for employment and economic rights of the underprivileged, sustaining black organizational potency in the face of increasing class differentiation within the black community, and taking seriously the long-overlooked specific needs and interests of black women. The first stage came to a close principally because the civil rights struggle achieved its liberal aims, namely, absorption into mainstream American politics, reputable interest-group status in the (soon to falter) liberal coalition of the Democratic Party.

The second stage centered primarily on the issue of the legitimacy and accountability of the black political leadership. Like the first stage, this historical movement was engendered by a sense of black resistance and rebellion, and led by black petit bourgeois figures. Yet these "new," black, middle-class figures had been highly politicized and radicalized by the strengths and weaknesses of King's movement, by the rise of the New Left movement among white privileged students and by the revolutionary anticolonial struggles in the Caribbean (Cuba), Africa (Ghana and Guinea), Latin America (Chile and Bolivia) and Southeast Asia (Vietnam). The transitional events were the Mississippi Freedom Summer in 1964, the Democratic National Convention in Atlantic City, late August 1964, and the Selma campaign of 1965. The Freedom Summer brought to the surface the deep cultural and personal problems of interracial political struggle in America: white attitudes of paternalism, guilt and sexual jealousy, and black sensibilities of one-upsmanship, manipulation and sexual adventure. The Atlantic City convention illustrated the self-serving machinery of the Democratic Party, whose support even King at this point solicited at the risk of white-controlled compromise. Finally, King's Selma campaign, initiated by SNCC years earlier, was sustained primarily by federal support, escort and legitimacy. In short, the bubble was about to burst: the vision, analysis and praxis of significant elements of the black freedom movement were to move beyond the perimeters of prevailing American bourgeois politics.

The Watts explosion in August 1965 revealed the depths of the problem of legitimacy and accountability of black political leadership. The rebellion and resistance (especially in northern urban centers) could no longer find an organizational form of expression. In the cities, it had become sheer anarchic energy and existential assertion without political direction and social vision. The Watts rebellion was a watershed event in the black freedom movement, in that it drew the line of demarcation between those who would cling to liberal rhetoric, ties to the Democratic Party and middle-class concerns, and those who would attempt to go beyond liberalism, expose the absorptive role and function of the Democratic Party and focus more on black proletarian and lumpenproletarian interests.

The pressing challenges of the second stage were taken up by Martin Luther King, Jr. His Chicago campaign in 1966—though rejected by most of his liberal black and white comrades in SCLC—pushed for the radical unionization of slum-dwellers against exploitative landlords. His aborted poor people's campaign of 1967 to 68, initiated after his break with President Johnson and the Democratic Party, which had been precipitated by his fierce opposition to the Vietnam War, was even more attuned to black, Latino and white working poor and underclass concerns. Yet, despite his immense talent, energy and courage, it became clear that King lacked the organization and support to address these concerns. Notwithstanding his 1968 murder—preceded by intense FBI harassments and threats—the widespread ideological fragmentation and increased class and strata differentiation in African America precluded King from effectively meeting the pressing challenges. His new focus on the urban poor led to black middle-class abandonment of his movement; his nonviolent approach perturbed black committed leftists who welcomed his new focus; his Christianity disturbed black secularists and Muslims already working in urban ghettoes; and his integrationist perspective met with staunch opposition from black nationalists who were quickly seizing hegemony over the black freedom movement. In other words, King was near death politically and organizationally before he was murdered, though he will never die in the hearts and minds of progressive people in the USA and abroad.

Ironically, King's later path was blazed by his early vociferous critic, Malcolm X. Even as a narrow black nationalist under the late Honorable Elijah Muhammad, Malcolm X rejected outright white liberal support and ties to the Democratic Party, and he highlighted the plight of urban black working poor and unemployed people. More than any other black figure during the first stage, Malcolm X articulated the underlying, almost visceral, feelings and sensibilities of black urban America—North and South, Christian and non-Christian, young and old. His early rhetoric was simply prescient: too honest, too candid, precisely the things black folk often felt but never said publicly due to fear of white retaliation, even in the early sixties. In fact, his piercing rhetoric had primarily a cathartic function for black people; it purged them of their deferential and defensive attitudes toward white people.

Although Malcolm X moved toward a more Marxist-informed humanist position just prior to his assassination by rival Black Muslims in February 1965, he became the major symbol for (and of) the second stage of the black freedom movement in the sixties. What were accented were neither his political successes nor his organizational achievements, but rather his rhetorical eloquence and homespun honesty. Malcolm X did not hesitate to tell black and white America "like it is," even if it resulted in little political and practical payoff. This eloquence and honesty was admired at a distance by the black working poor and underclass: it expressed their gut feelings and addressed their situation but provided little means or hope as to how to change their predicament. The "old," black, middle class was horrified; they publicly and secretly tried to discredit him. The "new" black petite bourgeoisie, especially black students, welcomed Malcolm X's rhetoric and honesty with open arms. It resonated with their own new newly acquired sense of political engagement and black pride; it also spoke to a more fundamental problem they faced—the problem of becoming black leaders and elites with organic, existential and rhetorical ties to the black community.

In a complex way, Malcolm X's candid talk both fueled more protracted black rebellion and provided a means to contain it. In short, his rhetoric was double-edged and functioned in contradictory ways. On the one hand, it served as an ideological pillar for revolutionary black nationalism. On the other hand, his rhetoric was employed by manipulative black petit bourgeois politicians, professionals, administrators and students to promote their own upward social mobility. The adulation of Malcolm X in the black community is profound. Yet an often overlooked component of this adulation among the "new" black middle class was (and is) their subtle use of his truth-telling for their narrow, self-serving aims. The relative silence regarding his black sexist values and attitudes also reveals the deep patriarchal sensibilities in the black community.

The revolt of the black masses, with hundreds of rebellions throughout the country, set the framework for the second stage. The repressive state apparatus in American capitalist society jumped at this opportunity to express its contempt for black people. And the basic mechanism of pacifying the erupting black ghettoes—the drug industry—fundamentally changed the content and character of the black community. The drug industry, aided and abetted by underground capitalists, invaded black communities with intense force, police indifference and political silence. It accelerated black white-collar and solid blue-collar working-class suburban flight, and transformed black poor neighborhoods into terrains of human bondage to the commodity form, enslavement to the buying and selling of drugs. For the first time in African American history, fear and trepidation among black folk toward one another became pervasive. As crime moved toward civil terrorism, black distrust of and distance from the black poor and underclass deepened. And, of course, black presence in jails and prisons rapidly increased.

The revolt of the black masses precipitated a deep crisis—with political, intellectual and existential forms—among the "new" black petite bourgeoisie. What should the appropriate black middle-class response be to such black working poor and underclass rebellions? This complex response is best seen in the internal dynamics of the Black Power movement. This movement, more than any other at the time, projected the aspirations and anxieties of the recently politicized and radicalized black petite bourgeoisie. From Adam Clayton Powell, Jr.'s Howard University baccalaureate address of 1966, through the Meredith March, to the Newark Black Power Conference, the message was clear: beneath the rhetoric of Black Power, black control and black self-determination was a budding, "new," black, middle class hungry for power and starving for status. Needless to say, most young black intellectuals were duped by this petit bourgeois rhetoric, primarily owing to their own identity crisis and self-interest. In contrast, the "new" black business, professional and political elites heard the bourgeois melody behind the radical rhetoric and manipulated the movement for their own benefit. The rebellious black working poor and underclass often either became dependent on growing welfare support or seduced by the drug culture.

The second stage was primarily a black nationalist affair. The veneration of "black" symbols, rituals, styles, hairdos, values, sensibilities and flag escalated. The "Black Is Beautiful" slogan was heard throughout the black community and James Brown's "Say It Loud, I'm Black and I'm Proud" became an exemplary—and healthy—expression of the cultural reversal of alienating Anglo-American ideals of beauty and behavior. Yet this cantankerous reversal (like the black rediscovery of jazz) was principally a "new" black middle-class phenomenon.

The working poor and underclass watched as the "new" black middle class visibly grappled with its new identity, social position and radical political rhetoric. For the most part, the black underclass continued to hustle, rebel when appropriate, get high and listen to romantic proletarian love songs produced by Detroit's Motown; they remained perplexed at their idolization by the "new" black, middle class, which they sometimes envied. The black working poor persisted in their weekly church attendance, struggled to make ends meet and waited to see what the beneficial results would be after all the bourgeois "hoopla" was over. In short, the black nationalist moment, despite its powerful and progressive critique of American cultural imperialism, was principally the activity of black petit bourgeois self-congratulation and self-justification upon reaching an anxiety-ridden, middle-class status in racist American society.

To no surprise, the leading black, petit bourgeois, nationalist groups such as SNCC (after 1966), CORE, Ron Karenga's US and Imamu Amiri Baraka's Congress of African People were viewed by black proletarian and lumpenproletarian organizations as "porkchop nationalists" who confused superficial nation-talk with authentic cultural distinctiveness, middle-class guilt with working-class aspirations, and identity crises with revolutionary situations. The late Honorable Elijah Muhammad's Nation of Islam, though petit bourgeois in intent, was staunchly working poor and underclass (and especially strong in American prisons) in composition. Devoid of leading black intellectuals yet full of eloquent spokesmen, the nation of Islam put to shame the "porkchop nationalists," not only by being "blacker than thou" in both mythology and ideology, but also by producing discernible results in the personal, organizational and financial life of its members and the black community.

The Black Panther Party (founded in Oakland, California, 1966) was the leading black lumpenproletarian revolutionary party in the sixties. It thoroughly rejected and consistently struggled against petit bourgeois nationalism from a viewpoint of strong black leftist internationalism. Yet it was overwhelmed by the undisciplined character of black underclass life, seduced by the histrionic enticements of mass media and crushed by state repression. The only other major national response of black progressives against black petit bourgeois nationalism was George Wiley's Fannie Lou Hamer's National Welfare Rights Organization (founded in August 1967). But it was unable to sustain broad membership, and thereby control encroaching bureaucratic leadership. The League of Revolutionary Black Workers (founded in Detroit, Michigan, 1969), though regional in scope, was the most important revolutionary group among black industrial workers in the country. It eventually split over the issue of the role of black nationalism in a Marxist organization.

The rift between black petit bourgeois nationalists and black revolutionary leftists was best illustrated in the American response to James Forman's historic Black Manifesto. Forman, a former executive director of SNCC, ex-minister of Foreign Affairs of the Black Panther Party, and leader of the short-lived Black Workers' Congress, proposed at the National Black Economic Development Conference in Detroit and later, more dramatically, at New York City's Riverside Church's 11:00 p.m. service, reparation funds of five hundred million dollars from white Christian churches and Jewish synagogues in order to finance the black revolutionary overthrow of the US government. The "revolution" would turn into an "armed, well-disciplined, black-controlled government."

The symbolic gesture represented the peak of the black nationalist moment in the sixties, though it was enacted by a black Marxist. It also signified liberal white America's absorption and domestication of black nationalism. Despite the Manifesto's Marxist critique and demand of American capitalist society—such as the call for a black revolutionary vanguard party and even the call for white progressive people to accept this black leadership—the most salient issue became that of reparations to existing black middle-class groups.

The white American response to these demands on the ecclesiastical, educational and corporate levels was widespread. Of course, the major funds were not given to Forman's group (though it received about three hundred thousand dollars), but rather to church agencies, denominational caucuses, minority-oriented programs and, above all, black businesses and banks. Regardless of Forman's naive revolutionary intent, the black petit bourgeois nationalists triumphed. Soon the federal government and even the Nixon administration would openly support such moves in the name of "black self-determination" and "black capitalism."

The hegemonic role of black petit bourgeois nationalism had four deleterious consequences for African America. First, it isolated progressive black leftists such that orthodox Marxism became the primary refuge for those concerned with class struggle and Internationalism. And even in these new Marxist formations the Black Nation Thesis—the claim that black people constitute a nation with the USA—once again became the widely accepted understanding of African American oppression. Second, the machismo lifestyles of black nationalists (of the petit bourgeois and revolutionary varieties) so marginalized black women that the black feminist movement of the seventies and eighties was often forced to sever ties with black male-dominated groups, thereby encouraging an understandable but innocuous black feminist separatism. Third, black nationalism disarmed and delimited a large number of young black intellectuals by confining them to parochial black rhetoric, pockets of "internal dialogues," which resulted in posing almost insurmountable walls of separation between progressive white, brown, red, yellow and black intellectuals. Last, black nationalist rhetoric contributed greatly to the black freedom movement's loss of meaningful anchorage and organic ties to the black community, especially the churches. In short, besides the severe state repression and the pervasive drug invasion, the black petit bourgeois nationalist perspectives and practices were primarily responsible for the radically decentered state of the black freedom movement in the seventies and eighties. This was so principally because they undergirded the needs and interests of the "new" black middle class.

The sixties in African American history witnessed an unforgettable appearance of the black masses on the historical stage, but they are quickly dragged off—killed, maimed, strung out, imprisoned or paid off. Yet history continues and the growing black petite bourgeoisie still gropes for identity, direction and vision. This black middle class is "new" not simply because significant numbers of black people recently arrived in the world of higher education, comfortable living and professional occupations, but also because they achieved such status against the backdrop of undeniable political struggle, a struggle in which many of them participated. And the relation of their unprecedented opportunities and privileges to the revolt of the black masses is quite obvious to them. This is why the "new" black middle class will more than likely refuse to opt for political complacency. Its own position hangs on some form of political participation, on resisting subtle racist practices, housing policies and educational opportunities. Only persistent pressure can ensure a managerial job at IBM, partnership in a Wall Street firm, a home in Westchester or a slot at Harvard College, whereas in the past little resistance by the "old" black middle class was required to service the black community, live in the Gold Coast of Washington, D.C. or send the kid to Howard, Fisk or Morehouse. The roots of the "new" black middle class are in political struggle, in SCLC, SNCC, CORE, in the values and sensibilities these groups generated.

The major challenge of the "new," black, petite bourgeoisie is no longer whether it will take politics seriously (as posed in E. Franklin Frazier's classic *Black Bourgeoisie* in 1957). Rather it is what kind of politics the "new" black middle class will promote in the present national context of austere economic policies, declining state support of black rights and escalating racist violence and the prevailing international context of the crisis of capitalism, the nuclear arms race and anti-imperialist struggles. Like any other petite bourgeoisie, the "new" black middle class will most likely pursue power-seeking life styles, promote black entrepreneurial growth, and perpetuate professional advancement. Yet the rampant racism in American society truncates such life-styles, growth and advancement. The "new" black middle class can become only a "truncated" petite bourgeoisie in American society, far removed from real ownership and control over the crucial sectors of the economy and with intractable ceilings imposed upon their upward social mobility.

Presently, there are three major political options for this "truncated" black middle class: electoral politics in the bosom of the centrist Democratic Party or conservative Republican Party; social democratic and democratic socialist politics on the margin of the liberal wing of the Democratic Party (for instance, the Democratic Socialists of America) and inside grass-roots, black leftist, nationalist, preparty formations (for instance, the National Black United Front); or orthodox revolutionary politics far removed from both bourgeois American politics and black grass-roots groupings. The effects of the second stage of the black freedom movement in the sixties—beneath and between the endless ideological debates about violence versus nonviolence, the viability of black-white coalitions, reform versus revolution—primarily consisted of an oscillation between the first and third options, between vulgar realpolitik and antiquated orthodoxy, bourgeois politics and utopian rhetoric, with no mediating moment, hence little acknowledgment of the historical complexity of the prevailing African American predicament.

The prospects of galvanizing and organizing renewed black resistance are open-ended. The major tasks are repoliticizing the black working poor and underclass, revitalizing progressive black proletarian and petit bourgeois organizations, retooling black organic and traditional intellectuals, and forging meaningful alliances and beneficial fusions with progressive Latino, Asian, Native American and white groups.

Despite the historical limitations of the "new" black petite bourgeoisie, the African American predicament dictates that this group play a crucial role in carrying out these tasks. This is principally because the black middle class—preachers, teachers, lawyers, doctors and politicians—possess the requisite skills and legitimacy in the eyes of the majority of African Americans for the articulation of the needs and interests of African America. This unfortunate but inescapable situation requires that the politicized progressive wing of the black petite bourgeoisie and stable working class incessantly push beyond the self-serving liberalism of major black leaders and raise issues of fundamental concern to the black working poor and underclass. In short, the "new" black middle class must not be prematurely abandoned or denigrated. Rather, black progressives must keep persistent pressure on, and radical fire under, their liberal reformism until more effective political mobilization and organization emerge among the black working poor and underclass.

The repoliticizing of the black working poor and underclass should focus primarily on the black cultural apparatus, especially the ideological form and content of black popular music. African American life is permeated by black popular music. Since black musicians play such an important role in African American life, they have a special mission and responsibility: to present beautiful music which both sustains and motivates black people and provides visions of what black people should aspire to. Despite the richness of the black musical tradition and the vitality of black contemporary music, most black musicians fall far short of this crucial mission and responsibility. There are exceptions—Gil Scott-Heron, Brian Jackson, Stevie Wonder, Kenneth Gamble and Leon Huff—but more political black popular music is needed. Jamaican reggae music and Nigeria's Fela Anikulapo Kuti can serve as inspiring models in this regard. The radical politicization of black popular music, as best seen in Grandmaster Flash and the Furious Five's "The Message" and "New York, New York" (despite their virulent sexism) in the early years of rap is a necessary, though not sufficient, condition for the repoliticization of the black working poor and underclass. Black activists must make black musicians accountable in some way to the urgent needs and interests of the black community.

The major prerequisite for renewed organizational black resistance is the political revitalization of existing black groups—fraternities, sororities, lodges, trade unions and, especially, black churches. Without black religious participation, there can be no widespread black resistance. The prophetic wing of the black church has always been at the center of the black freedom movement. Without a strong organizational base with deep organic connections in the black community, there can be no effective renewed black resistance. Only the political revitalization of black prophetic churches can provide this broad organizational base—as Rev. Herbert Daughtry's African Peoples' Christian Organization and other such groups are attempting to do.

The role of black intellectuals—organic ones closely affiliated with the everyday operations of black organizations or traditional ones nesting in comfortable places geared toward theoretical and historical analyses, social visions and practical conclusions—is crucial for renewed black resistance. Without vision, the black freedom movement is devoid of hope. Without analysis, it lacks direction. Without protracted struggle, it ossifies. Yet the vision must be guided by profound, not provincial, conceptions of what it is to be a human being, an African human being in predominantly white, postindustrial, capitalist America, and of how human potential can be best realized in an overcoming of existing economic exploitation, racial and sexual oppression. Likewise, the analysis must be informed by the most sophisticated and cultivated, not self-serving and cathartic, tools available in order to grasp the complexity and specificity of the prevailing African American predicament on the local, regional, national and international levels. Last, the political praxis, though motivated by social vision and guided by keen analysis, must be grounded in moral convictions. Personal integrity is as important as correct analysis or desirable vision. It should be noted that while black intellectuals deserve no special privilege and treatment in the black freedom movement, the services they provide should be respected and encouraged.

It should be obvious that African Americans cannot fundamentally transform capitalist, patriarchal, racist America by themselves. If renewed black resistance is to achieve its aim, alliances and coalitions with other progressive peoples are inescapable. Without such alliances and coalitions, African Americans are doomed to unfreedom. Yet, the more consolidated the black resistance, the better the chance for meaningful and effective alliances and coalitions with others. Of course, each alliance and coalition must be made in light of the specific circumstances and the particular contexts. The important point here is that any serious form of black resistance must be open to such alliances and coalitions with progressive Latino, Asian, Native American and white peoples.

In conclusion, the legacy of the black freedom movement in the sixties still haunts us. In its positive form, it flows through our veins as blood to be spilt if necessary for the cause of human freedom, and in the visions, analyses and practices that build on, yet go beyond, those in the sixties. In its negative form, it reminds us of the tenuous status of the "new" black petite bourgeoisie—its progressive potential and its self-serving interests, its capacity to transcend its parochial past and its present white subordination. The challenge of the black freedom movement in the late twentieth century is neither a discovery of another Rev. Martin Luther King, Jr.—though it would not hurt—nor a leap of faith in a messianic black working class or underclass—though the role of both is crucial. Rather the challenge is a fusing and transforming of indigenous forms of American radicalism—of which black resistance is a central expression—into a major movement which promotes workers' self-management, cultural heterogeneity (including nonracist and nonsexist ways of life) and individual liberties.

Malcolm X and Black Rage

You don't stick a knife in a man's back nine inches and then pull it out six inches and say you're making progress.

—*Malcolm X*

No matter how much respect, no matter how much recognition, whites show towards me, as far as I'm concerned, as long as it is not shown to every one of our people in this country, it doesn't exist for me.

—*Malcolm X*

Malcolm X articulated Black rage in a manner unprecedented in American history. His style of communicating this rage bespoke a boiling urgency and an audacious sincerity; the substance of what he said highlighted the chronic refusal of most Americans to acknowledge the sheer absurdity that confronts human beings of African descent in this country—the incessant assaults on Black intelligence, beauty, character, and possibility. His profound commitment to affirm Black humanity at any cost and his tremendous courage to accent the hypocrisy of American society made Malcolm X the prophet of Black rage—then and now.

Malcolm X was the prophet of Black rage primarily because of his great love for Black people. His love was neither abstract nor ephemeral. Rather, it represented a concrete connection with a degraded and devalued people in need of *psychic conversion*. This connection is why Malcolm X's articulation of Black rage was not directed first and foremost at white America. Malcolm spoke love to Black people; he believed the love that motivated Black rage had to be felt by Black people in order for the rage to take on institutional forms. This love would produce a psychic conversion in Black people in that they would affirm themselves as human beings, no longer viewing their bodies, minds, and souls through white lenses, but believing themselves capable of taking control of their own destinies.

In American society—especially during Malcolm X's life in the 1950s and early '60s—such a psychic conversion could easily result in death. A proud, self-affirming

Black person who truly believed in the capacity of Black people to throw off the yoke of white racist oppression and control their own destiny usually ended up as one of those strange fruit that Southern trees bore, about which the great Billie Holiday poignantly sang. So when Malcolm X articulated Black rage, he knew he also had to exemplify in his own life the courage and sacrifice that any truly self-loving Black person needs in order to confront the frightening consequences of being self-loving in American society. In other words, Malcolm X crystallized sharply the relation of Black affirmation of self, Black desire for freedom, Black rage against American society, and the likelihood of early Black death. Black psychic conversion—the decolonization of the mind, body, and soul that strips white supremacist lies of their authority, legitimacy, and efficacy—begins with a bold and defiant rejection of Black degradation and is sustained by urgent efforts to expand those spaces wherein Black humanity is affirmed; it often ends with early death owing to both white contempt for such a subversive sensibility and, among those captive to Black self-contempt and self-doubt, a Black disbelief.

Malcolm X's notion of psychic conversion holds that Black people must no longer view themselves through white lenses. His claim is that Black people will never value themselves as long as they subscribe to a standard of valuation that devalues them. For example, Michael Jackson may rightly wish to be viewed as a person, not a color (neither black nor white), but his facial revisions reveal a self-measurement based on a white yardstick. Despite the fact that Jackson is one of the greatest entertainers who has ever lived, he still views himself, at least in part, through white aesthetic lenses that devalue some of his African characteristics. Needless to say, Michael Jackson's example is but the more honest and visible instance of a rather pervasive self-loathing among many wealthy and professional-class Black people. Malcolm X's call for psychic conversion often strikes horror into this privileged group because so much of who they are and what they do is evaluated in terms of their wealth, status, and prestige in American society. On the other hand, this group often understands Malcolm X's claim more than others precisely because they have lived so intimately in a white world in which the devaluation of Black people is so often taken for granted or unconsciously assumed. It is no accident that the Black middle class has always had an ambivalent relation to Malcolm X—an open rejection of his militant strategy of wholesale defiance of American society and a secret embrace of his bold truth-telling about the depths of racism in American society. One rarely encounters a picture of Malcolm X (as one does Martin Luther King, Jr.) in the office of a Black professional, but there is no doubt that he dangles as the skeleton in the closet lodged in the racial memory of most Black professionals.

In short, Malcolm X's notion of psychic conversion is an implicit critique of W. E. B. Du Bois's idea of "double-consciousness." From Malcolm X's viewpoint, double-consciousness pertains more to those Black people who live "betwixt and between" the Black and white worlds—traversing and crisscrossing these worlds yet never settled in either. Hence, they crave peer acceptance in both, receive genuine approval from neither, yet persist in viewing themselves through the lenses of the dominant white society. For Malcolm X, this "double-consciousness" is less a description of the Black mode of being in America than a particular kind of colonized mind-set of a special group in Black America. Psychic conversion calls for not simply a rejection of the white lenses through which one sees oneself but, more specifically, a refusal to measure one's humanity by appealing to any white supremacist standard. Du Bois's double-consciousness seems to lock Black people into the quest for white approval and disappointment due mainly to white racist assessment, whereas Malcolm X suggests that this tragic syndrome can be broken. But how?

Malcolm X does not put forward a direct answer to this question. First, his well-known distinction between "house negroes" (who love and protect the white master) and "field negroes" (who hate and resist the white master) suggests that the masses of Black people are more likely to acquire decolonized sensibilities and hence less likely to be "co-opted" by the white status quo. Yet this rhetorical device, though insightful in highlighting different perspectives among Black people, fails as a persuasive description of the behavior of "well-to-do" Black folk and "poor" Black folk. In other words, there are numerous instances of "field negroes" with "house negro" mentalities and "house negroes" with "field negro" mentalities. Malcolm X's often-quoted distinction rightly highlights the propensity among highly assimilated black professionals to put "whiteness" (in all its various forms) on a pedestal, but it also tends to depict "poor" Black people's notions and enactments of "blackness" in an uncritical manner. Hence his implicit critique of Du Bois's idea of double-consciousness contains some truth yet offers an inadequate alternative.

Second, Malcolm X's Black nationalist viewpoint claims that the only legitimate response to white supremacist ideology and practice is Black self-love and Black self-determination free of the tension generated by double-consciousness. This claim is both subtle and problematic. It is subtle in that every Black Freedom Movement is predicated on an affirmation of African humanity and a quest for Black control over the destinies of Black people. Yet not every form of Black self-love affirms African humanity. Furthermore, not every project of Black self-determination consists of a serious quest for Black control over the destinies of Black people. Malcolm's claim tends to assume that Black nationalisms have a monopoly on Black self-love and Black self-determination. This fallacious assumption confuses the issues highlighted by Black nationalisms with the various ways in which Black nationalists and others understand these issues.

For example, the grand legacy of Marcus Garvey forces us never to forget that Black self-love and Black self-respect sit at the center of any possible Black Freedom Movement. Yet this does not mean that we must talk about Black self-love and Black self-respect in the way in which Garvey did, that is, on an imperial model in which Black armies and navies signify Black power. Similarly, the tradition of Elijah Muhammad compels us to acknowledge the centrality of Black self-regard and Black self-esteem, yet that does not entail an acceptance of how Elijah Muhammad talked about achieving this aim—by playing a game of Black supremacy that awakens us from our captivity to white supremacy. My point here is that a focus on the issues rightly targeted by Black nationalists and an openness to the insights of Black nationalists does not necessarily result in an acceptance of Black nationalist ideology. Malcolm X tended to make such an unwarranted move.

Malcolm X's notion of psychic conversion is based on the idea of Black spaces in American society in which Black community, humanity, love, care, concern, and support flourish. He sees this Black coming-together as the offspring of the recognition of a boiling Black rage. Facilitating this coming-together is where Malcolm X's project really falters. The fundamental challenge is: How can the boiling Black rage be contained and channeled in the Black spaces such that destructive and self-destructive consequences are abated? The greatness of Malcolm X is, in part, that he raises this question with a sharpness and urgency never before posed in Black America. Unfortunately, in his short life he never had a chance to grapple with it or solve it in idea and deed. Instead, until 1964, he adopted Elijah Muhammad's response to this challenge and castigated Martin Luther King, Jr.'s response to it.

In contrast to Malcolm X, Elijah Muhammad and Martin Luther King, Jr., understood one fundamental truth about Black rage: It must neither be ignored nor ignited. Both leaders, in their own ways, knew how to work with Black rage in a constructive manner, shape it through moral discipline, channel it into political organization, and guide it by charismatic leadership. Malcolm X could articulate Black rage much better than Elijah Muhammad or Martin Luther King, Jr.—but for most of his public life he tended to ignite Black rage and harness it for the Nation of Islam. Hence Malcolm's grappling with how to understand Black rage and what to do with it was subordinate to Elijah Muhammad's project of Black separate spaces for Black community, humanity, love, care, concern, and support. Malcolm X, however, did have two psychic conversions—the first was to the Nation of Islam, but the second, in 1964, was to orthodox Islam that rejected any form of racial supremacy.

The project of Black separatism—to which Malcolm X was beholden for most of his life after his first psychic conversion—suffered from deep intellectual and organizational problems. Unlike Malcolm X's notion of psychic conversion, Elijah Muhammad's idea of religious conversion was predicated on an obsession with white supremacy. The basic aim of Black Muslim theology—with its distinct Black supremacist account of the origins of white people—was to counter white supremacy. Yet this preoccupation with white supremacy still allowed white people to serve as the principal point of reference. That which fundamentally motivates one still dictates the terms of what one thinks and does—so the motivation of a Black supremacist doctrine reveals how obsessed one is with white supremacy. This is understandable in a white racist society—but it is crippling for a despised people struggling for freedom, in that one's eyes should be on the prize, not the perpetuator of one's oppression. In short, Elijah Muhammad's project remained captive to the supremacy game—a game mastered by the white racists he opposed and imitated with his *Black* supremacy doctrine.

Malcolm X's notion of psychic conversion can be understood and used such that it does not necessarily *entail* Black supremacy; it simply rejects Black captivity to white supremacist ideology and practice. Hence, as the major Black Muslim spokesperson, he had many sympathizers, though few of them actually became Muslim members. Why did Malcolm X permit his notion of psychic conversion to serve the Black supremacist claims of the Nation of Islam—claims that undermine much of the best of his call for psychic conversion? Malcolm X remained a devoted follower of Elijah Muhammad until 1964 partly because he believed the other major constructive channels of Black rage in America—the Black church and Black music—were less effective in producing and sustaining psychic conversion than the Nation of Islam. He knew that the electoral political system could never address the existential dimension of Black rage—hence he, like Elijah, shunned it. Malcolm X also recognized, as do too few Black leaders today, that the Black encounter with the absurd in racist American society yields a profound spiritual need for human affirmation and recognition. Hence the centrality of religion and music—those most spiritual of human activities—in Black life.

Yet, for Malcolm, much of Black religion and Black music had directed Black rage away from white racism and toward another world of heaven and sentimental romance. Needless to say, Malcolm's conception of Black Christianity as a white man's religion of pie-in-the-sky and Black music as soupy "I Love You B-a-b-y" romance is wrong. While it's true that most—but not all—of the Black music of Malcolm's day shunned Black rage, the case of the church-based Civil Rights movement would seem to counter his charge that Black Christianity serves as a sedative to put people to sleep rather than to ignite them to action. Like Elijah Muhammad (and unlike Malcolm X), Martin Luther King, Jr., concluded that Black rage was so destructive and self-destructive that without a moral theology and political organization, it would wreak havoc on Black America. His project of nonviolent resistance to white racism was an attempt to channel Black rage in political directions that preserved Black dignity and changed American society. But his despair at the sight of Watts in 1965 or Detroit and Newark in 1967 left him more and more pessimistic about the moral channeling of Black rage in America. To King, it looked as if cycles of chaos and destruction loomed on the horizon if these moral channels were ineffective or unappealing to the coming generation. For Malcolm, however, the Civil Rights movement was not militant enough. It failed to speak clearly and directly to and about Black rage.

Malcolm X also seems to have had almost no intellectual interest in dealing with what is distinctive about the Black church and Black music: *their cultural hybrid character in which the complex mixture of African, European, and Amerindian elements are constitutive of something that is new and Black in the modern world.* Like most Black nationalists, Malcolm X feared the culturally hybrid character of Black life. This fear resulted in the dependence on Manichean (black-and-white or male/female) channels for the direction of Black rage—

forms characterized by charismatic leaders, patriarchal structures, and dogmatic pronouncements. The Manichean theology kept the white world at bay even as it heralded dominant white notions such as racial supremacy per se or the nation-state per se. The authoritarian arrangements imposed a top-down disciplined corps of devoted followers who contained their rage in an atmosphere of cultural repression (regulation of clothing worn, books and records consumed, sexual desire, etc.) and paternalistic protection of women.

The complex relation of cultural hybridity and critical sensibility (or jazz and democracy) evident here raises interesting questions. If Malcolm X feared cultural hybridity, to what degree or in what sense was he a serious democrat? Did he believe that the cure to the egregious ills of a racist American "democracy" was more democracy that included Black people? Did his relative silence regarding the monarchies he visited in the Middle East bespeak a downplaying of the role of democratic practices in empowering oppressed peoples? Was his fear of cultural hybridity partly rooted in his own reluctance to come to terms with his own personal hybridity, for example, his "redness," light skin, close white friends, and so on?

Malcolm X's fear of cultural hybridity rested on two political claims: that cultural hybridity downplayed the vicious character of white supremacy and that it so intimately linked the destinies of Black and white people that the possibility of Black freedom was unimaginable. Malcolm's fundamental focus on the varieties, subtleties, and cruelties of white racism made him suspicious of any discourse about cultural hybridity. Those figures who were most eloquent and illuminating about Black cultural hybridity in the 1950s and early '60s, such as Ralph Ellison and Albert Murray, were, in fact, political integrationists. Their position seemed to pass over too quickly the physical terror and psychic horror of being Black in America. To put it bluntly, Malcolm X identified much more with the mind-set of Richard Wright's Bigger Thomas in *Native Son* than with that of Ralph Ellison's protagonist in *Invisible Man*.

Malcolm X's deep pessimism about the capacity and possibility of white Americans to shed their racism led him, ironically, to downplay the past and present bonds between Blacks and whites. For if the two groups were, as Martin Luther King, Jr., put it, locked into "one garment of destiny," then the very chances for Black freedom were nil. Malcolm X's pessimism also kept him ambivalent about American democracy—for if the majority were racist, how could the Black minority ever be free? His definition of a "nigger" was "a victim of American democracy"—had not the *Herrenvolk* democracy of the United States made Black people noncitizens or anticitizens of the republic? Of course, the aim of a constitutional democracy is to safeguard the rights of the minority and avoid the tyranny of the majority. Yet the concrete practice of the U.S. legal system from 1883 to 1964 promoted a tyranny of the white majority much more than a safeguarding of the rights of Black Americans. In fact, these tragic facts drove Malcolm X to look elsewhere for the promotion and protection of Black people's rights—to institutions such as the United Nations and the Organization of

African Unity. One impulse behind his internalization of the Black Freedom struggle in the United States was a deep pessimism about America's will to racial justice, no matter how democratic the nation was or is.

Malcolm X's fear of cultural hybridity also rested on a third concern: his own personal hybridity as the grandson of a white man, which blurred the very boundaries so rigidly policed by white supremacist authorities. For Malcolm X, the distinctive feature of American culture was not its cross-cultural syncretism but rather its enforcement of a racial caste system that defined any product of this syncretism as abnormal, alien, and other to both Black and white communities. Like Garvey, Malcolm X saw such hybridity—for example, mulattoes—as symbols of weakness and confusion. The very idea of not "fitting in" the U.S. discourse of whiteness and blackness meant one was subject to exclusion and marginalization by both whites and Blacks. For Malcolm X, in a racist society, this was a form of social death.

One would think that Malcolm X's second conversion, in 1964, might have allayed his fear of cultural hybridity. Yet there seems to be little evidence that he revised his understanding of the radically culturally hybrid character of Black life. Furthermore, his deep pessimism toward American democracy continued after his second conversion—though no longer on mythological grounds but solely on the historical experiences of Africans in the modern world. It is no accident that the non-Black persons Malcolm X encountered who helped change his mind about the capacity of white people to be human were outside of America and Europe—Muslims in the Middle East. Needless to say, Malcolm found the most striking feature of the Islamic regimes not to be their undemocratic practices but their acceptance of his Black humanity. This great prophet of Black rage—with all his brilliance, courage, and conviction—remained blind to basic structures of domination based on class, gender, and sexual orientation in the Middle East.

The contemporary focus on Malcolm X, especially among Black youth, can be understood as both the open articulation of Black rage (as in film videos and on tapes targeted at whites, Jews, Koreans, Black women, Black men, and others), and desperate attempts to channel this rage into something more than a marketable commodity for the culture industry. The young Black generation is up against forces of death, destruction, and disease unprecedented in the everyday life of Black urban people. This raw reality of drugs and guns, despair and decrepitude generates a raw rage that, among past Black spokespersons, only Malcolm X was able to approximate. The issues of psychic conversion, cultural hybridity, Black supremacy, authoritarian organization, borders and boundaries in sexuality, and other matters all loom large at present—the same issues Malcolm X left dangling at the end of the short life in which he articulated Black rage and affirmed Black humanity.

If we are to build on the best of Malcolm X, we must preserve and expand his notion of psychic conversion (best seen in the works of bell hooks) that cements networks and groups in which Black community, humanity, love, care, and concern can take root and grow. These spaces—beyond Black music and Black religion—reject Manichean ideologies and authoritarian arrangements in the name of moral visions, subtle analyses of wealth and power, and concrete strategies of principled coalitions and democratic alliances. These visions, analyses, and strategies never lose sight of Black rage, yet they focus this rage where it belongs: on any form of racism, patriarchy, homophobia, or economic injustice that impedes the opportunities of people to live lives of dignity and decency. Poverty is as much a target of rage as degraded identity.

Furthermore, the cultural hybrid character of Black life leads us to highlight a metaphor alien to Malcolm X's theology—yet consonant with his performances to audiences—namely, the metaphor of jazz. I use the term "jazz" here not so much as a term for a musical art-form as for a mode of being in the world, an improvisational mode of protean, fluid, and flexible dispositions toward reality suspicious of either/or viewpoints, dogmatic pronouncements, and supremacist ideologies. To be a jazz freedom fighter is to attempt to galvanize and energize world-weary people into forms of organization with accountable leadership that promotes critical exchange and broad reflection. The interplay of individuality and unity is not one of uniformity and unanimity imposed from above but rather of conflict among diverse groupings that reach a dynamic consensus subject to questioning and criticism. As with a soloist in a jazz quartet, quintet, or band, individuality is promoted in order to sustain and increase the *creative* tension with the group—a tension that yields higher levels of performance to achieve the aim of the collective project. This kind of critical and democratic sensibility flies in the face of any policing of borders and boundaries of "blackness," "maleness," "femaleness," or "whiteness." Black people's rage ought to target white supremacy but also realize that maleness can encompass feminists such as Frederick Douglass or W. E. B. Du Bois. Black people's rage should not overlook homophobia; it also should acknowledge that heterosexuality can be associated with so-called straight antihomophobes—just as the struggle against Black poverty can be supported by progressive elements of the well-to-do regardless of race, gender, or sexual orientation.

Malcolm X was the first great Black spokesperson who looked ferocious white racism in the eye, didn't blink, and lived long enough to tell America the truth about this glaring hypocrisy in a bold and defiant manner. Unlike Elijah Muhammad and Martin Luther King, Jr., he did not live long enough to forge his own distinctive ideas and ways of channeling Black rage in constructive channels to change American society. Only if we are as willing as Malcolm X to grow and confront the new challenges posed by the Black rage of our day will we take the Black freedom struggle to a new and higher level.

John Edgar Wideman (1941–)

John Edgar Wideman began his academic career as a basketball star. Recruited by the University of Pennsylvania, he earned a place in the Philadelphia Big Five Basketball Hall of Fame. In 1963, when it became clear that his basketball talents would not take him to the NBA, he accepted a Rhodes Scholarship to attend Oxford University, where he earned a degree in eighteenth-century literature. He later accepted a Kent Fellowship at the prestigious University of Iowa Writers' Workshop. He left Iowa to become the first tenured Black professor at the University of Pennsylvania. An interesting beginning for one of America's most prominent writers.

Wideman was born in Washington, DC, but spent most of his early years in Homewood, a Black section of Pittsburgh and a place where he locates much of his fiction.

Wideman's early novels, A Glance Away (1967) and Hurry Home (1970), echo the esthetic practices of such White writers as T.S. Eliot, James Joyce, and William Faulkner; yet they display Wideman's mastery and originality with the language. He uses the conventions of realistic, modernist narrative only to push them, explode their forms with wordplay, multiple points of view, and stream of consciousness. In his third novel, The Lynchers (1973), Wideman began to incorporate Black vernacular dialect, Black historical tradition, and Black racial sentiment to create a more powerful narrative. He later recognized The Lynchers as problematic because it speaks a myth of the Black community that mainly recognizes pain, degradation, and hopelessness.

Wideman's fiction began to turn with Hiding Place (1981), the first volume of his Homewood Trilogy, which also includes Damballah (1981) and Sent for You Yesterday (1983). Still utilizing modernist techniques, Wideman incorporates myths and traditions of his own family and the Homewood community. Throughout the Homewood Trilogy, the reliance on place and community has been compared with Faulkner's Yoknapatawpha County. Wideman states: "The narrative method is less Faulknerian montage—the abutting or juxtaposing of varying, even contradictory perspectives—than it is mosaic, the gradual revelation of a design through the accretion of discrete fragments."

By the time Wideman finished Sent, he rejected notions of closure and frame as he reflected an African oral tradition that rejects closure and uniformity as various people refocus stories through myriad lenses. One of his most powerful stories is Brothers and Keepers (1984), a memoir that explores his struggles with his past and his painful, yet rewarding relationship with his imprisoned brother, Robby. Reuben (1987) continues to expand narrative structure through sliding points of view; shifting tenses; complicated syntax; and the selective elimination of grammatical protocols, such as quotation marks. It is meditation within and without the temporal and spatial panorama. In Philadelphia Fire (1990) Wideman mines this stylistic vein for his innovative novelistic interrogation of the 1985 bombing of the cult MOVE.

Wideman's writing offers a complex experience of words, images, and time, a clash and merger of formal and street language. It is an intense, lyrical chronicling of the Black experience in urban America and its roots in the rural past. One of his most persistent themes is the status and condition of African American men. He explores their relationships with women, with each other, with the Black community, and with the dominant White society. This exploration identifies African American males' sources of frustration, violence, and self-destruction, as well as possibilities for survival and success.

Throughout his short stories, Wideman suggests that, while earlier generations of African Americans grappled with economic and racial oppression, they at least had a strong sense of family and community—elements of support that now seem severely strained. "all stories are true" spins a personal, familial, and ancestral spiderweb of voices within three conversations in the narrative: The one occurring in the narrator's mind; the one imagined and spoken with the narrator's mother; and the one occurring with his incarcerated brother. These conversations continue Wideman's investigation of the violence, suffering, and daily struggle in the contemporary inner city. The sheltering, generative, powerful, living enormity of Black culture is symbolized by the lush Green Triangle, where a "massive tree centuries old holds out against the odds" and where a leaf becomes hope, freedom. There is strength beyond the appearance of weakness and vulnerability under the guise of strength, the paradoxes of maternity and history. Wideman plays with such paradoxes in order to reveal the hope for internal order and peace, the healing in which political structures and external limitations hold no sway.

"casa grande," narrative within narrative, past within present, combines a prison visit with a story written by Wideman's son when he was ten years old. The child's lost story becomes an analogy for his adult son's life of imprisonment. Thoughts of the Hohokam, an ancient people in Arizona whose name means "those who are gone, who are used up," percolate through the narrative, suggesting that what has vanished from sight is saved by memory.

"fever" uses Philadelphia's late eighteenth-century yellow fever epidemic as a point of transport. The story unexpectedly shifts to the 1985 present in the aftermath of the MOVE massacre. Memories of the Middle Passage float against earth-bound images: bodies that rock in the watery womb of the Atlantic juxtapose bodies that rot in a city destined to be the birthplace of American politics. Wideman seems to ask: What does it take to become an American? The main character of "Fever" is Richard Allen, who founded the African Methodist Episcopal Church, a man torn between religion and science, duty to family and freedom. As in many of Wideman's stories, a single narrative voice and time are inadequate to express the complexities of American history. He weaves the languages of science, religion, and racism together with words of love and healing, pointing toward the power of language to destroy and to heal.

Lenore Brady

all stories are true

And for fear of him the guards trembled and became like dead men.

MATTHEW 28:4.

My mother is standing on her porch. May 10, 1991. Early morning and the street is quiet now, as peaceful as it gets here, as peaceful as it always stays in other neighborhoods, invisible, not a half mile away behind the tree-topped ridge that separates Tokay, Susquehanna, Dunfermline, Seagirt from their neighbors to the west. The litany of streets always sweet on my tongue. I think I murmur their names, a silence unless you are inside my skull, sing them as a kind of background music that doesn't break the quiet of morning. If I'm not reciting them to myself, I hear the names anyway coming from somewhere else, a place that also knows what lies within the sound of these streets said to oneself again and again. Footsteps, voices, a skein of life dragged bead by bead through a soft needle's eye. And knows the names of streets can open like the gates of a great city, everyone who's ever inhabited the city, walked its streets, suddenly, like a shimmer, like the first notes of a Monk solo, breathing, moving, a world quickens as the gates swing apart. And knows my mother is not alone on her porch this May morning. Knows she hears beneath the stillness enveloping her the sound of street names, what is animated when they are recalled. The presence of other souls as palpable as light playing in the edges of her robe. Her mother and father and children. Her brother and sisters. Grands and great-grands. The man I have become and those whom I've lost becoming him. The song of street names a medium in which we all float, suspended, as if each of us is someone's precious, precious child who must never be allowed to slip from the arms cradling, rocking. And knows my mother is listening to time, time voiced in no manmade measurements of days or minutes or years, time playing as it always must, background or foreground or taking up all the space we have, a tape of the street names chanted that releases every Homewood footstep she's ever heard or dreamed.

I'm afraid for her. Experience one of those moments of missing her intensely, her gone, final good-byes said, though she is here, just ten feet away, through the front door screen, framed by two of the rusty wrought iron columns supporting the roof. A moment where fear of losing her overwhelms me to such an extent that I am bereft, helpless, unconsoled even by her presence, one price I pay for other moments when she's thousands of miles away and I've needed her and she is there, *there* beside me. After nine months of chemo her hair has grown in again, softer, curlier. Many shades of bushy gray and a crown of lighter hair, nearly white, nearly spun to invisibility by morning. I'm aware as I seldom am of her dimensions, how tall, how wide, how much this woman on the porch with her newborn's hair weighs. I need what is tangible, no matter how small she turns out to be, to offset words like frail and vulnerable I can't help saying to myself, words popping up though I try not to think them. I hate words with the power to take her away. *Frail. Old.* The effort of denying them makes her disappear anyway. My eyes cross Tokay, counting cobblestones as they go, remarking the incredible steepness of the street slanting out of my field of vision, the broken curbs and littered gutters, settling on the gigantic tree islanded in the delta where Seagirt and Tokay converge and Bricelyn begins. If the downtown wedge of skyscrapers where three rivers meet is the city's Golden Triangle, this could be its Green Triangle. A massive tree centuries old holds out against the odds here across from my mother's house, one of the biggest trees in Pittsburgh, anchored in a green tangle of weeds and bushes, trunk thick as a Buick, black as night after rain soaks its striated hide. Huge spread of its branches canopies the foot of the hill where the streets come together. Certain times of day in summer it shades my mother's front porch. If it ever tore loose from its moorings, it would crush her house like a sledgehammer. As big as it is, its roots must run under her cellar. The sound of it drinking, lapping nourishment deep underground is part of the quiet when her house is empty. How the tree survived a city growing around it is a mystery. For years no more than a twig, a sapling, a switch someone could have snapped off to beat a balky animal, swat a child's behind. I see a dark fist exploding through the asphalt, thrusting to the sky, the fingers opening, multiplying, fanning outward to form a vast umbrella of foliage. The arm behind it petrifies, other thick limbs burst from knots of hardened flesh, each one duplicating the fan of leaves, the delicate network of branches, thinning, twisting as they climb higher and farther from the source. Full-blown in a matter of seconds, ready to stand here across from my mother's house forever, till its time to be undone in the twinkling of an eye, just the way it arrived.

I didn't say any of this to my mother as I pushed through the screen door with my cup of coffee to join her on the porch. Then it was just one quiet thing after the other, a matter of seconds, the sight of her standing still, her back to me, me thinking thoughts that flashed at warp speed but would take forever to unpack, the door creaking, her turning slowly towards the noise, *You up, Baby,* a quick welcoming smile before she turns back to whatever it was, wherever she was gazing when I saw her first, small, bathed in the soft, remorseless light of morning, when I heard the sound of Homewood street names playing, transforming a commonplace scene into something else, restoring the invisible omnipresence of time, the enabling medium, what brought you to this moment and will carry you away, how things begin and end, always, you about to step out onto your mother's porch, catching her staring off at something, somewhere, home again, morning again, steamy coffee mug in one hand, sure of what you will do next, your fingers press the doorframe, pushing, absolutely unsure, fearing what will happen next, wondering what's in her eyes, behind them this morning in May, and which ghosts crowd the porch, regretting her privacy you are invading with yours. Who will the two of you together summon if you steal her attention, if you are ready and willing to offer yours, if you can break away from the tune playing over and over in your head and maybe in hers of the street names, sorrow and loss in every syllable when you say them to yourself the way you must to locate yourself here, back home in Pittsburgh this morning, Tioga Susquehanna Seagirt Cassina, praying your mother won't move, won't be gone before you reach her.

You hug each other. Not hard, not soft. Briefly. Long enough to remember everything.

I love my flowers.

A guy was selling them in the gas station. At Braddock and Penn. You know. The two big stations across from one another. A white guy in Mickey Mouse bermudas. He said these hadn't been out in the sun. Too much direct sun's not good for them, he said. These were shoved under a folding table he had set up. Pansies or some other kind, I forget. They just looked pretty to me and I thought you'd like something pretty and growing.

Impatiens. They're beautiful.

And you already have a hook by the door to hang them.

I used to keep a few little plants out here. Then one night just before Easter the flowers grew feet. Woke up one morning and everybody's flowers were gone. I only had a couple nice little plants. Nothing special. But they were gone just like everybody else's up and down both blocks. Flowers grew feet that night and walked away.

You mean somebody ripped off people's flowers.

Should have heard Eva. See the house with the green and white aluminum awning. That's Eva's. You know who I mean, don't you. Small brown-skinned woman always dressed nice. Used to ride the bus to town with me to work. Eva had big-time flowers on her porch. Gone that morning like everybody else's and Eva's fit to be tied. She said she was marching down to the corner and beat the black off him with her own two hands if she caught him with one of her flowers. Said she'd know her flowers if she saw them, pot or no pot or new pot she'd know her own flowers and strangle him with her bare hands if she caught him with her flowers.

Somebody selling flowers on the corner.

Right there on Bennett. Day after the night the flowers walked.

No. You got to be kidding.

Huh uh. Some guy down there big as life selling flowers. Had his stand right on Bennett and Bricelyn. No pots. Dog probably sold people's pots somewhere else. He wasn't completely crazy. A flower sale day after everybody's flowers disappeared off their porches.

He's lucky he didn't get shot.

Eva said she was going down there and look for her flowers. Tear him up if she found any. But how could you know for sure. I kinda looked for mine when I passed by that way, but he had everything tied up in plastic bags of dirt so how you supposed to tell. Flowers are flowers. Eva swore she'd know hers, but I didn't notice any commotion down there. Did his business all day. Gone next morning. Walked away like the flowers walked. Never saw the guy before. Don't care if I ever see him again.

A brazen brother.

That's how they do us. Steal anything and everything. Stained-glass windows out the church. I worry about one of them getting into the house.

Sorry-assed junkies.

Dope turns them crazy. Knock you down as soon as look at you. Kids you've watched grow up around here. I don't believe they intend to hurt anybody, but when that sickness is down on them, my, my, my, they'll do anything. I shudder when I think of your brother crazy that way. Him hurting someone or someone hurting him. Those so-called friends of his he'd bring home. Yes ma'am and no ma'am me and all the time I know their dope eyes counting up what they could come back and steal. Tommy knew it, too. God have mercy on me for saying this about my own son, but I believe now that's why he brought some of them around. To steal from me.

Coffee's not hot. Not cold. I try the porch railing with my hand. It feels solid enough. I remember helping Wade from next door mix concrete for the porch. The good feel of doing hard work with my brothers, the three of us, Dave, Ote and me, Wade's crew sweating into the wet cement, the moment during one cold Iron City break we all felt the presence of the brother missing who should be with us building this porch for our mother. I sit on the rail anchored in our concrete. Ask about Wade.

Poor man had a tough year. Dog died, wife died, he hit that paperboy. Old Wade was way down. Said he wouldn't have made it if it hadn't been for the boy's parents. They didn't blame him. People who witnessed the accident said Wade never had a chance. Going normal speed. The boy rode his bike straight into Wade's car. And thank goodness Wade was on his way to work. So he hadn't been drinking. Wade said if the parents had blamed him for the boy's death, he wouldn't have pulled through.

Dog died. Wife died. That's a rather strange order to put things in, Mother Dear.

You know what I mean. Didn't mean one thing worse than the other or first things first. You know I didn't mean anything like that.

I'm just teasing.

Teasing your fuddle-brained old mother. I know. I know most the time nobody understands what I'm talking about. Half the time don't know my own self. Pay me no mind. I didn't intend any disrespect. Wade Loved Nadine dearly and misses her terribly. Loved that raggedy, stump-tailed dog, too. It was just one terrible thing after another falling on the poor man. I don't know how he survived. Thought for awhile he was going to drink himself to death. But he'd clean up every morning and drive off to work. Wade's a strong man. A good man, too, in his way.

Sounds like he was Job last year.

I prayed for him. All alone in his house. I know how that feels, rattling around in a house all by yourself.

The porch is holding up fine, isn't it. A little crack by the glider and one where the steps come up but this porch will be here awhile.

Youall did quite a job.

Wade the only one who knew what he was doing. Me and Dave and Ote supplied the muscle.

It was one hot day. I was worried about youall. None of you used to working out in the broiling sun that way.

Little sweat mixed in the cement makes it stronger, last longer. Why you think the Pyramids been standing all these centuries. Good African blood gluing the stones.

What do you think about this idea going around that Egyptians were black.

Better late than never, Mom. I guess. Most of them a mixture of black Africans and brown Asiatics. Look at what part of the world we're talking about. Look at them today. Not exactly a matter of color, though. More about culture. People migrating and invading and mixing since the dawn of time. Everybody's a mongrel. The wonder is it's taken this long for the obvious to be said out loud. Wonder is it's 1991 and the obvious still resisted in some quarters.

I try to change the faces of the people in the Bible. I can't do it. They still look like the faces I saw in Sunday school, in the little picture books we had to study from. No black faces, except for that one dark wise man with Jesus in the manger. When I close my eyes, I still can't put black faces on the Bible people.

Well, we must have had the same books when I was in Sunday school. Maybe that's one of the reasons you had to drag me. Child abuse every Sunday morning.

Bit more child abuse might not have been a bad idea. I felt terrible knowing I was raising a bunch of little heathens.

Anyway, what I started to say is we used those same jive comic books, but the Bible people never were white to me. They never had a color, really. The funny-looking robes and beards and turbans stuck in my mind. But as far as color, well it's Reverend Felder I think of when I think of Bible days and Bible stories. Him up on the pulpit of A.M.E. Zion shouting and strutting and banging his big fists. Old Frank Felder black as coal and that's the color of everything he preached. Like his voice tar-brushed the Bible. If the faces in the books weren't black it didn't matter cause black was in charge, telling the story.

I did think of Job more than once when I prayed for Wade. And I guess Job surely did have Wade's face and Wade's face, God bless him, surely isn't white. Poor man bent down under all his burdens. I needed the story of Job to understand how Wade could handle it. Strength to bear up to the worst, no matter what, has to come from somewhere. I needed God and Job. Needed them both to understand how Wade survived what he did.

You know, Mom, people look at you and what you've had to deal with and you're just as much a miracle to them as you say Wade is to you.

God doesn't give you more than you can handle.

Not everybody has that kind of god.

I worry about your brother. Where will he turn now. He's still a Muslim, isn't he. He still goes by his Muslim name.

Told me not long ago he's not as active in the group as he once was. But he does pray. Not as regular as he once did, he says, but he keeps the faith.

I hope he has something. Because this last blow. The pardons board turning him down again without a hearing. He believed they'd almost have to let him go. Didn't see how they could say no.

They say whatever they want to say.

Other times he held something back. In his heart he hoped they'd give him a chance, believed he'd earned a chance, but like you say. He knows they don't have to answer to anybody. Do what they want to do. Every time but this he'd held something back to fight the no.

He's in danger now. Like when he was first locked up and wild and determined to tear the prison apart with his bare hands. Worse now because he's on his own. No crew of young wild ones like him fighting back. All he has is us. And we're out here. All he has really is the chance anybody has. To keep pushing on and try to make something of a life, whatever.

Don't think I can go with you today. I'm too shaky today to face that evil prison. Tell him I'll come next week with Denise and Chance.

Don't want to leave you if you're feeling badly.

I'll be all right here. You go talk to your brother. It's just one of those days. I'll take my pills and sit myself down awhile. I'll get it together, Babe.

Is something specific hurting.

Just one of those not so good days. I'm shaky. I have bad days every now and then. Hug him for me. Tell him I love him. I'll be fine here.

I rise with her. The porch one of those quiet, extrawide, featureless elevators in the hospital where she goes Tuesdays for treatments. Below us the map of streets, veins, arteries. We wait on this floor, at this height. The porch rocks like a Ferris wheel car stopped at the apex of the ride. Perhaps the huge motor's broken. Cable snapped. Gears stripped. We wait and listen for music to drift up from the streets.

My brother's arms are prison arms. The kind you see in the street that clue you where a young brother's been spending his time. Bulging biceps, the rippled look of ropy sinews and cords of muscle snaking around the bones. Skinned. Excess flesh boiled away in this cauldron. Must be noisy as a construction site where the weightlifters hang out in the prison yard. Metal clanking. Grunts and groans. Iron pumped till shoulders and chests swell to the bursting point. Men fashioning arms thick enough to wrestle fate, hold off the pressure of walls and bars always bearing down. Large. Big. Nothing else to do all day. Size one measure of time served. Serious time. Bodies honed to stop-time perfection, beyond vulnerability and pain. I see them in their sun-scoured playground sprawled like dazed children.

Hot today in the visiting area, fiery heat like the day we paddled round in Wade's cement. Row row row your concrete boat. It ain't heavy, it's your brother.

Hey, bro, I'd be the last one to deny I'm fucked up. We both know good and well I've had problems all my life doing what I been supposed to do. Here I sit in this godforsaken hole if anybody needs proof I couldn't handle. Something's wrong wit me, man, but the people who runs this joint, something's real wrong wit them, too.

Pressure in my face muscles from the permanent squint I'm wearing to keep sun out of my eyes. A mask of age. Forehead furrowed, cheeks tensed and hollow, eyes narrow, tiny creases incised at their corners, vision dimmed by the hazy porch of lashes and brow pouting to shade the eyes. Sun cooks my right side. I look past my brother to avoid the direct glare, beyond him to the bricks of the visiting room wall, the glass doors opening to the roofless enclosure where we sit. I listen closely but he's a blur in the center of the space across the round table where my eyes would naturally focus if I wasn't hiding from the sun. I don't need to see him. He will be wearing the same face I am. Pinched and sweaty. Older than it should be. Glazed eyes seeking something other than me to fix on, so what I say is a voice-over, as his is to me, listening while I tour the stones stacked forty feet high that surround us, the glass doors black as water, reflecting scraps of the yard.

Motherfuckers don't say shit for three months. Know I'm on pins and needles every minute of every day since I filed my commutation papers, but don't nobody say one god-blessed single solitary word good or bad for three months. I'm going crazy wit the waiting. And too scared to ask anybody what's happening cause you know how that works. Ask a question and they say *no* just to spite you, just to get you out their face. Limbo, man, for three months. Then last week I'm by the desk in the visiting room waiting for Denise and Chance and the guard at the desk hands me the phone, call for you. Lieutenant's on the line and he says to me Board turned you down. Tells me I can cancel my visit and speak to him now or check by his office later. That's it. Boom. Turned down.

Like getting hit in the chest wit a hammer. Couldn't breathe, man. Couldn't catch my breath for three days. Still can't breathe right. Felt like somebody had taken a hammer and whammed me in the heart.

No warning. No explanation. I'm standing in the visiting room trying to catch my breath and Denise and the baby be in here in a minute. Dying, man, and ready to die. My life was over soon's the lieutenant said Board turned you down.

Weird thing is the night before I had a dream. Woke me up. Couldn't go back to sleep. Dreamed I was in one the offices around here and my papers was on the desk. My papers. What I'd been waiting for all these months and finally there they sat. On top the desk and nobody else around. All I had to do was peep at the last sheet, right. There it'd be in black and white. Yes or no. Couldn't believe it be this easy. So much waiting and praying and begging and cursing boneheads out cause they wouldn't give me a clue. Wouldn't tell me nothing, nothing, and now alls I had to do was turn to the last page and I'd know.

Awful thing was I already knew the answer. Couldn't peep at the bottom sheet cause I already knew. Knew in my heart so I kept standing, staring, too scared to read what I knew I'd find.

Right when the dream ended I did look. Couldn't hold out. Looked and saw *denied* stamped on the last page. Whole dream came back to me soon as I put down that phone in the visiting room. Been *denied* all along. And all along I guess I knowed.

Nothing for three months then I'm waiting for a visit from my old lady and son and I get a phone call. Turned you down. Bam. Take that.

Like a hammer in my chest. Tell me that ain't evil, man. Saying no is bad enough. They don't have to treat people like dirt saying it.

My own fault I'm in here. I know I done some bad things. I'm in here, man, doing my time. Oh huh. Hard time. Lots of time for doing wrong. But they treat us like dog shit in here and that's wrong too. Guys get killed in here. Go crazy. But nobody cares. Long as they keep us locked up they can do us anyway they want. Figure we in here, so they don't owe us nothing. But wrong is wrong, ain't it. Just cause we down, is it right to keep on kicking us. Guys get meaner and crazier in here. Every day you see the ones can't take it slipping further and further off. Distance in their eyes, bro. Ain't nobody home in them eyes. They shuffle around here like ghosts. Stop speaking to people. Stop keeping theyselves clean. Gone, man. If you been around here any length of time you seen it happen to a lot of guys. You understand how easy it is to tune out and drop off the edge into your own little world. Another planet. You see why guys go off. Why they so cold and mean if they ever hit the street again.

Now our eyes are meeting. The sun's part of the meeting. A sting, a rawness you try to blink away but only make worse as sweat drips and irritates. Only one other table occupied when you sat down at yours. Now no free ones. The visiting room wall forms one end of the outdoor enclosure. Its other three walls rise forty feet at least, smooth blocks of stone topped by razor wire, a walkway, a guard tower in the far corner. At the base of the sheer stone walls fresh plantings, shrubbery dense and spiky bordering the concrete pavement. A few trees, also recently planted, have been spaced along the inside of the walls, each in a square collar of earth the size of a missing section of paving. You register these details for later. You think it will be crucial at some point to remember this yard exactly. You are uncertain why. Then, still listening to what he's saying, you realize how little of your brother's life you can share. This yard, detail by detail, is part of what you do share. You would be compromised if you come away with only a vague recollection. To fight this place, to force it to disappear, you must not miss anything. The map of it in your head makes its horror real, but also is what you must depend upon to plan an escape.

I think I'm finally beginning to understand why they so evil to us. They're scared of the black man. Really scared. More scared than I ever knew. More scared than they know themselves. When I first come in the joint. I knew something about the fear. Knew we had something on them. Wild as we was we didn't give them no chance to run game on us. We had learned the hard way coming up running the streets what they thought of us. Crazy killers. Animals. Dope fiends. Niggers you got to lock up or kill before they kill you. That was the deal. So we played the hand dealed us. We was stone outlaws. Fuck wit us you better be prepared to take us down cause if you don't we coming down on you. I was young and hot-blooded and that cowboy and indian gangster shit okay wit me. Bring it on. Let's git down and dirty. Rock and roll. We saw fear in their eyes. We fucked with them to keep it there. But they didn't kill me and, all praises to Allah, I didn't kill a guard. I changed. Wasn't really me in the first place. I was just playing the outlaw role I thought I needed to play to survive the joint. I changed but they stayed scared of me. And they hate me for keeping them scared. My buddy Rick. You remember Ricky from up the hill on Tokay. Took him dying to make me really understand what I'm telling you now. You know he got sick in here. Come in when I did, one of our wild bunch. Take no shit from nobody, none of us. But Rick changed, too. Wised up. Then he got sick, real sick, like I said. They wouldn't treat him. Wouldn't try to find out what was wrong. Why should they. If you scared of somebody, why you gon try and help them, fix them up, make them well so they can jump in your chest again. Huh uh. Ricky just rotted. Chased him away from the clinic. Or handed him a aspirin. You know the story. He shrunk down to nothing. Ninety-three goddamn pounds. Finally they had to stick him in the clinic. Let him rot in the clinic till his mother got to somebody and they transferred Ricky out of here and chained him to a bed in a locked ward in a real hospital and diagnosed stomach cancer. By that time Ricky too far gone to help. Drugged him up so he just nodded away. Didn't know people when they came to see him his mother said. Said he was so weak they unchained him. A cop in the room when she visited, but Ricky just laying there. A pitiful sight, plugged up to machines, not even recognizing his own mama. She was in a chair beside his bed on a Sunday she said it must have been Sunday cause she'd been there a couple hours that afternoon and she works six days a week so it must have been Sunday and Rick been sleeping like he always did the whole time so she was just sitting half sleep herself when Ricky's hand reached over and patted hers where she'd laid it on the blanket. She couldn't believe it she said. Tears started rolling down her cheeks she told me because what his touching her meant she thought was that he was ready to die. Too far gone to get better so she just knew Rick using his last strength to say good-bye.

The cop in the room had a different idea. See, he was still scared of Ricky so Ricky moving that hand meant Ricky was dangerous again. Cop jumped up and started refastening the chains.

None of it makes any goddamn sense. Who they keep. Who they let go. Never give you any reasons. They don't have to give reasons for what they do. They just do it. Denied. They stamp your papers *denied* and that's all the reason they got to give. Denied.

One the dudes they didn't deny, a white boy, he busted out of here not too long ago. Busted out and stayed out till he got tired of running and turned hisself in. Escaped the joint, man, and now they granted him a hearing with the full parole board. What kind of sense do it make.

Maybe you ought to arrange a little vacation for yourself before you apply next time.

Don't think I ain't thought about it. Been keeping my eye on that tree over there. Shimmy up, leap over on the wall. Gone.

Not much of a tree yet.

Yeah, well, it's still pretty scraggly. But I been watching it.

Long time before those branches grow as high as the wall. And you'd still have a pretty good leap.

Guys in here would try. Plenty of them. Scoot up that tree in a minute. Do a super monkey jump.

Branches awful skinny at the top. Even for a monkey.

Right. Right. Skinny enough so you get up there it'll bend to the wall. Ride it like a surfboard.

You got it all figured out, bro.

Told you I've been keeping my eye on that little tree.

This is where you and Denise were when the leaf got out.

At the table closest to the wall. In the shade. Uh huh. We was sitting there but by the time that leaf blew up near the top of the wall both of us on our feet cheering. Other people had got into it, too. Saw what we was watching and that leaf had a whole lot of fans when it sailed over the wall. Would have thought people cheering for the Steelers or somebody's lottery number hit. Wasn't nothing but a leaf me and Denise noticed that had started blowing higher and higher. Each time the wind would grab it, it would circle up higher. Over in that corner like it was riding a draft or a whirlwind or some damn something keeping it up. You know how something dumb catch your attention and you can't let it go. Leaf kept spinning round and round and rising each time it spinned. Like on a yo-yo. After watching it a while you know that leaf has flying out of here on its mind. Every little whip and twist and bounce starts to matter. Before you know it you're blowing with your breath to help it over the wall and you know something inside you will be hurt if that silly leaf can't finish what it started. Whole visiting yard whooping and hollering when it finally blew over the wall.

Denise cried. And damn. It was everything I could do to keep the tears out of my eyes. Everybody in here needed that leaf to go free.

Kind of magic, man, if you was here in the yard and seen it. Know I sound dumb trying to tell you how it was. But that's how it was. Specially for Denise and me cause earlier in the visit she told me she was carrying my baby. We'd already picked names: Jazz Melody for a girl, Chance Mandela if it was a boy. Couldn't help taking the leaf as a sign.

Chance because the odds were stacked against him ever being conceived, let alone born.

Million to one, bro. And Mandela cause Mandela's my man. You know. In the joint like me but still taking care of business.

Chance Mandela. When Mom called and told me he was born the day after Mandela walked out of prison, I couldn't believe it.

Little day late rascal. But my little guy was close. Real close. Bust out right behind Nelson.

The leaf, the day, the name. Pretty amazing, little brother. Has to be a sign. Gives you something special to fight for. A son, a family. You've come too far to let this denial turn you around.

I think a lot about it. Everything I mean. When I'm alone at night in my cell. Ain't never really alone no more since they double-bunking everybody, but you know what I mean. When I think about giving up, truth is, nothing but me can pull me back from the edge. I got to do it for me. No matter how much I love Chance and Denise and Mom and youall, nothing, not all the love in the world can fill the hole that opens up when I get down, really down. Only way to save myself is to do it for me. I got to be the reason. I got to be worth saving. Can't live a life for nobody else. Nobody can live one for me. You understand what I'm saying.

I'm trying.

The leaf. I told you how it finally blowed free overtop the wall. Couldn't see it no more. Denise grabbed my hand. She was crying and we was bouncing up and down. People shouting. Some even clapped. But you know something. I'm gonna tell you something I don't tell nobody when I tell about the leaf. The dumb thing blew back in here again.

casa grande

About a month ago I discovered a long-lost story written by my son:

A Trip to Jupiter

One morning I woke up floating in space because the gravity pull decreased. I was sailing nice and smoothly right towards Jupiter. I sailed for 0:100 hours and then landed. The atmosphere was very cool and I heard a sound: "Mee, Meep. Earthling intruder."

"Where are you earthling name caller." I asked.

"Right before your eyes. I am green with black spots but no thing can see me. I cannot see you. Where are you?"

"Who, me? Oh. Well I guess I might be near the end of the universe because it is very cool here. I also think I might be on Saturn because of the rings."

"Well, earthling you are dumb because you are on the biggest planet in the Universe, Jupiter. The rings you see are our moons. They make a circle around our planet. Earthling, are you well educated?"

"I am. I am. Mr. Unknown."

"Well you don't sound that way. Our schools are green and our only force is a cannon that shoots out Juperballs. Juperballs are balls from the sky and they kill whatever they touch. We have great leaders named: Nansi, Rasher, Lack, Spirital and Malcomba. Spirital is our only man from another planet, Earth. You live in Earth too, right?"

"I do. But how do you know?"

"We Jupers have 3 different powers. Each Juper has different powers. Mine happen to be: disappearing power, able to speak English, and E.S.P. My E.S.P. allows me to look into your body and know everything about you. For instance: You're 10 years old, you go to Washington school, and you're from a family of 5. Well I have to now go back to tending the Juperlies. Goodbye." And he went away. When I got back I told everyone what I had learned and where I had been and the writers named me student of the year. But when I told my parents they didn't believe one bit of it. They just laughed. "Ha, ha, ha," they said.

My son wrote his story, as he says, when he was ten years old. Eleven years later, just after he'd turned twenty-one and I had celebrated his birthday with him in the Arizona prison where he's serving a life sentence, I was attempting to write in my journal about the way it feels when the terrible reality of his situation comes down on me, when I exchange for a fraction of a second my life for his. Longer than that I can't bear. Even that fraction of a second, brief and illusory as it is, has the effect of a pebble dropped at dawn in a still, clear lake. Everything changes and keeps on changing, but not with the simple elegance of ripple within ripple expanding rhythmically outward. What I feel when I cannot help myself and our shadows collide, are superimposed for a millisecond, is the instability of the earth's core, the tremor of aging that's already started in my left thumb, convulsing my entire body, the planes and frames of being rattling and shattering, a voice too familiar to name crying out in pain and I can't do a damn thing about any of it. I couldn't write either so I straightened up my study instead. That's when I found "Trip to Jupiter" in a manila folder in a box of our kids' things and read it again for the first time in eleven years, thinking as I read, My god, here's something I've totally forgotten, totally lost.

That's what I thought anyway until later that same day, browsing my journal, I came across an entry from the previous year, written after another visit with my son:

He sits on a planet ten million light years away, waiting for time to change the place he is to another. Darkness shrouds him. He would be invisible from ten feet if there were someone else on the planet looking at the space where he sits. He peoples the darkness with many such *someones,* teaches them the language of this planet to which he is exiled, instructs them how not to be blind to his presence. They help him pass this time till it becomes another. To himself he is far too visible, a presence screaming light, insistent, tedious as neon. Dim warmth beneath his skin defines him, fills the void he must occupy until time drifts as far as it must drift to open again for him.

He dreams a forest of green creatures, some tall as trees, many man-size, others a foot or two high. They repeat themselves, could be the same prickly, stumped-armed form over and over until you dream differently, stare at the cacti clustered around you, scattered on rolling hills, in stark ranks on the desert floor.

They say the Hohokam dwelt here. Those who are gone, who are used up is what the word *hohokam,* borrowed from the Pima Indian language, means. Hohokam cremated their dead in shallow pits. Only ash and bits and pieces of ornament and bone remain. Named Hohokam by archeologists because the ones who dwelt here are gone, gone, gone and cannot speak their own names, sing their songs, claim this land they peopled nine centuries ago when the Gila River was young and filled with fish and waterfowl nested on its green banks and game roamed the marshes, when this dry land supported fruits and vegetables and flowers no one has seen growing here in a thousand years. Because they left so little behind, not even skulls for anthropologists to measure, the Hohokam culture remains mysterious. No one knows where they originated nor why they disappeared completely after flourishing here for hundreds of years, building towns, canals, their Casa Grande I decide to visit since I've some this far anyway, this close, and my heart is bursting so I'll come up for air here, near Coolidge, Arizona, off Route 289, just fifteen miles from the prison at Florence, blend in with the old white people hoping to find in these ruins something they didn't bring with them, hoping to leave something burdensome behind in the dust they do not need or will not miss when the vacation's over and its home again, home again.

On his distant planet he invents the word *hohokam*. It slips into his unconscious as a way of understanding where he once was. The sound of it almost like laughter, a joke on himself he can tell over and over without becoming bitter. Where he stays it doesn't snow but something is always falling from the sky, gritty, grainy, like shredded husks of insects—wings, legs, antennae, dried blood sucked from long-dead hosts, the desert floor lifted and reversed so it is a ceiling, then shaken ever so gently, sifted through the finest sieve down on his head *hohokam hohokam*. It could be a word of welcome, a whispered promise, That which is, soon goes away.

I can't help thinking the cacti are deformed. Truncated men missing limbs, heads, fingers, feet. Clearly each cactus is incomplete. Not what it should, could be. Or once was. Asymmetry reigns. Ladders with rungs missing. Functionless protuberances. Each cripple a warped facsimile of the perfect form yet to be achieved by a builder who keeps trying in spite of countless disasters jammed upright, headfirst into the desert sand.

Among these legions of failures some believe they are better than others. They laugh at the lost ones, the outcast, the *hohokam*. Their laughter rises and becomes dry rain on the planet where he sits in darkness, where time runs backwards, *Zamani* to *Sasa,* Great-time to Little-time, and oceans disappear down a drain no bigger than the pinhead upon which he dances his angels, counts them as they exhaust themselves and one by one plummet back to earth.

fever

To Mathew Carey, Esq., who fled Philadelphia in its hour of need and upon his return published a libelous account of the behavior of black nurses and undertakers, thereby injuring all people of my race and especially those without whose unselfish, courageous labours the city could not have survived the late calamity.

> *Consider Philadelphia from its centrical situation, the extent of its commerce, the number of its artificers, manufacturers and other circumstances, to be to the United States what the heart is to the human body in circulating the blood.*
>
> ROBERT MORRIS, 1777.

He stood staring through a tall window at the last days of November. The trees were barren women starved for love and they'd stripped off all their clothes, but nobody cared. And not one of them gave a fuck about him, sifting among them, weightless and naked, knowing just as well as they did, no hands would come to touch them, warm them, pick leaves off the frozen ground and stick them back in place. Before he'd gone to bed a flutter of insects had stirred in the dark outside his study. Motion worrying the corner of his eye till he turned and focused where light pooled on the deck, a cone in which he could trap slants of snow so they materialized into wet, gray feathers that blotted against the glass, the planks of the deck. If he stood seven hours, dark would come again. At some point his reflection would hang in the glass, a ship from the other side of the world, docked in the ether. Days were shorter now. A whole one spent wondering what goes wrong would fly away, fly in the blink of an eye.

Perhaps, perhaps it may be acceptable to the reader to know how we found the sick affected by the sickness; our opportunities of hearing and seeing them have been very great. They were taken with a chill, a headache, a sick stomach, with pains in their limbs and back, this was the way the sickness in general began, but all were not affected alike, some appeared but slightly affected with some of these symptoms, what confirmed us in the opinion of a person being smitten was the colour of their eyes.

Victims in this low-lying city perished every year, and some years were worse than others, but the worst by far was the long hot dry summer of '93, when the dead and dying wrested control of the city from the living. Most who were able, fled. The rich to their rural retreats, others to relatives and friends in the countryside or neighboring towns. Some simply left, with no fixed destination, the prospect of privation or starvation on the road preferable to cowering in their homes awaiting the fever's fatal scratching at their door. Busy streets deserted, commerce halted, members of families shunning one another, the sick abandoned to suffer and die alone. Fear ruled. From August when the first cases of fever appeared below Water Street, to November when merciful frosts ended the infestation, the city slowly deteriorated, as if it, too, could suffer the terrible progress of the disease: fever, enfeeblement, violent vomiting and diarrhea, helplessness, delirium, settled dejection when patients *concluded they must go (so the phrase for dying was), and therefore in a kind of fixed determined state of mind went off.*

In some it raged more furiously than in others—some have languished for seven and ten days, and appeared to get better the day, or some hours before they died, while others were cut off in one, two or three days, but their complaints were similar. Some lost their reason and raged with all the fury madness could produce, and died in strong convulsions. Others retained their reason to the last, and seemed rather to fall asleep then die.

Yellow fever: an acute infectious disease of subtropical and tropical New World areas, caused by a filterable virus transmitted by a mosquito of the genus *Aëdes* and characterized by jaundice and dark colored vomit resulting from hemorrhages. Also called *yellow jack.*

Dengue: an infectious, virulent tropical and subtropical disease transmitted by mosquitos and characterized by fever, rash and severe pains in the joints. Also called *breakbone fever, dandy.* [Spanish, of African origin, akin to Swahili *kindinga.*]

Curled in the black hold of the ship he wonders why his life on solid green earth had to end, why the gods had chosen this new habitation for him, floating, chained to other captives, no air, no light, the wooden walls shuddering, battered, as if some madman is determined to destroy even this last pitiful refuge where he skids in foul puddles of waste, bumping other bodies, skinning himself on splintery beams and planks, always moving, shaken and spilled like palm nuts in the diviner's fist, and Esu casts his fate, constant motion, tethered to an iron ring.

In the darkness he can't see her, barely feels her light touch on his fevered skin. Sweat thick as oil but she doesn't mind, straddles him, settles down to do her work. She enters him and draws his blood up into her belly. When she's full, she pauses, dreamy, heavy. He could kill her then; she wouldn't care. But he doesn't. Listens to the whine of her wings lifting till the whimper is lost in the roar and crash of waves, creaking wood, prisoners groaning. If she returns tomorrow and carries away another drop of him, and the next day and the next, a drop each day, enough days, he'll be gone. Shrink to nothing, slip out of this iron noose and disappear.

Aëdes aegypti; a mosquito of the family *Culicidae,* genus *Aëdes* in which the female is distinguished by a long proboscis for sucking blood. This winged insect is a vector (an organism that carries pathogens from one host to another) of yellow fever and dengue. [New Latin *Aëdes,* from Greek *aedes,* unpleasant:*a* −, not + *edos,* pleasant . . .]

All things arrive in the waters and waters carry all things away. So there is no beginning or end, only the waters' flow, ebb, flood, trickle, tides emptying and returning, salt seas and rivers and rain and mist and blood, the sun drowning in an ocean of night, wet sheen of dawn washing darkness from our eyes. This city is held in the water's palm. A captive as surely as I am captive. Long fingers of river, Schuylkill, Delaware, the rest of the hand invisible; underground streams and channels feed the soggy flesh of marsh, clay pit, sink, gutter, stagnant pool. What's not seen is heard in the suck of footsteps through spring mud of unpaved streets. Noxious vapors that sting your eyes, cause you to gag, spit and wince are evidence of a presence, the dead hand cupping this city, the poisons that circulate through it, the sweat on its rotting flesh.

No one has asked my opinion. No one will. Yet I have seen this fever before, and though I can prescribe no cure, I could tell stories of other visitations, how it came and stayed and left us, the progress of disaster; its several stages, its horrors and mitigations. My words would not save one life, but those mortally affrighted by the fever, by the prospect of universal doom, might find solace in knowing there are limits to the power of this scourge that has befallen us, that some, yea, most will survive, that this condition is temporary, a season, that the fever must disappear with the first deep frosts and its disappearance is as certain as the fact it will come again.

They say the rat's-nest ships from Santo Domingo brought the fever. Frenchmen and their black slaves fleeing black insurrection. Those who've seen Barbados's distemper say our fever is its twin born in the tropical climate of the hellish Indies. I know better. I hear the drum, the forest's heartbeat, pulse of the sea that chains the moon's wandering, the spirit's journey. Its throb is source and promise of all things being connected, a mirror storing everything, forgetting nothing. To explain the fever we need no boatloads of refugees, ragged and wracked with killing fevers, bringing death to our shores. We have bred the affliction within our breasts. Each solitary heart contains all the world's tribes, and its precarious dance echoes the drum's thunder. We are our ancestors and our children, neighbors and strangers to ourselves. Fever descends when the waters that connect us are clogged with filth. When our seas are garbage. The waters cannot come and go when we are shut off one from the other, each in his frock coat, wig, bonnet, apron, shop, shoes, skin, behind locks, doors, sealed faces, our blood grows thick and sluggish. Our bodies void infected fluids. Then we are dry and cracked as a desert country, vital parts wither, all dust and dry bones inside. Fever is a drought consuming us from within. Discolored skin caves in upon itself, we burn, expire.

I regret there is so little comfort in this explanation. It takes into account neither climatists nor contagionists, flies in the face of logic and reason, the good doctors of the College of Physicians who would bleed us, purge us, quarantine, plunge us in icy baths, starve us, feed us elixirs of bark and wine, sprinkle us with gunpowder, drown us in vinegar according to the dictates of their various healing sciences. Who, then, is this foolish, old man who receives his wisdom from pagan drums in pagan forests? Are these the delusions of one whose brain the fever has already begun to gnaw? Not quite. True, I have survived other visitations of the fever, but while it prowls this city, I'm in jeopardy again as you are, because I claim no immunity, no magic. The messenger who bears the news of my death will reach me precisely at the stroke determined when it was determined I should tumble from the void and taste air the first time. Nothing is an accident. Fever grows in the secret places of our hearts, planted there when one of us decided to sell one of us to another. The drum must pound ten thousand years to drive that evil away.

Fires burn on street corners. Gunshots explode inside wooden houses. Behind him a carter's breath expelled in low, labored pants warns him to edge closer to housefronts forming one wall of a dark, narrow, twisting lane. Thick wheels furrow the unpaved street. In the fire glow the cart stirs a shimmer of dust, faint as a halo, a breath smear on a mirror. Had the man locked in the traces of the cart cursed him or was it just a wheeze of exertion, a complaint addressed to the unforgiving weight of his burden? Creaking wheels, groaning wood, plodding footsteps, the cough of dust, bulky silhouette blackened as it lurches into brightness at the block's end. All gone in a moment. Sounds, motion, sight extinguished. What remained, as if trapped by a lid clamped over the lane, was the stench of dead bodies. A stench cutting through the ubiquitous pall of vinegar and gunpowder. Two, three, four corpses being hauled to Potter's Field, trailed by the unmistakable wake of decaying flesh. He'd heard they raced their carts to the burial ground. Two or three entering Potter's Field from different directions would acknowledge one another with challenges, raised fists, gather their strength for a last dash to the open trenches where they tip their cargoes. Their brethren would wager, cheer, toast the victor with tots of rum. He could hear the rumble of coffins crashing into a common grave, see the comical chariots bouncing, the men's legs pumping, faces contorted by fires that blazed all night at the burial ground. Shouting and curses would hang in the torpid night air, one more nightmare troubling the city's sleep.

He knew this warren of streets as well as anyone. Night or day he could negotiate the twists and turnings, avoid cul-de-sacs, find the river even if his vision was obscured in tunnel-like alleys. He anticipated when to duck a jutting signpost, knew how to find doorways where he was welcome, wooden steps down to a cobbled terrace overlooking the water where his shod foot must never trespass. Once beyond the grand houses lining one end of Water Street, in this quarter of hovels, beneath these wooden sheds leaning shoulder to shoulder were cellars and caves dug into the earth, poorer men's dwellings under these houses of the poor, an invisible region where his people burrow, pull earth like blanket and quilt round themselves to shut out cold and dampness, sleeping multitudes to a room, stacked and crosshatched and spoon fashion, themselves the only fuel, heat of one body passed to others and passed back from all to one. Can he blame the lucky ones who are strong enough to pull the death carts, who celebrate and leap and roar all night around the bonfires? Why should they return here? Where living and dead, sick and well must lie face to face, shivering or sweltering on the same dank floor.

Below Water Street the alleys proliferate. Named and nameless. He knows where he's going but fever has transformed even the familiar. He'd been waiting in Dr. Rush's entrance hall. An English mirror, oval framed in scalloped brass, drew him. He watched himself glide closer, a shadow, a blur, then the shape of his face materialized from silken depths. A mask he did not recognize. He took the thing he saw and murmured to it. Had he once been in control? Could he tame it again? Like a garden ruined overnight, pillaged, overgrown, trampled by marauding beasts. He stares at the chaos until he can recall familiar contours of earth, seasons of planting, harvesting, green shoots, nodding blossoms, scraping, digging, watering. Once upon a time he'd cultivated this thing, this plot of flesh and blood and bone, but what had it become? Who owned it now? He'd stepped away. His eyes constructed another face and set it there, between him and the wizened old man in the glass. He'd aged twenty years in a glance and the fever possessed the same power to alter suddenly what it touched. This city had grown ancient and fallen into ruin in two months since early August, when the first cases of fever appeared. Something in the bricks, mortar, beams and stones had gone soft, had lost its permanence. When he entered sickrooms, walls fluttered, floors buckled. He could feel roofs pressing down. Putrid heat expanding. In the bodies of victims. In rooms, buildings, streets, neighborhoods. Membranes that preserved the integrity of substances and shapes, kept each in its proper place, were worn thin. He could poke his finger through yellowed skin. A stone wall. The eggshell of his skull. What should be separated was running together. Threatened to burst. Nothing contained the way it was supposed to be. No clear lines of demarcation. A mongrel city. Traffic where there shouldn't be traffic. An awful void opening around him, preparing itself to hold explosions of bile, vomit, gushing bowels, ooze, sludge, seepage.

Earlier in the summer, on a July afternoon, he'd tried to escape the heat by walking along the Delaware. The water was unnaturally calm, isolated into stagnant pools by outcroppings of wharf and jetty. A shelf of rotting matter paralleled the river edge. As if someone had attempted to sweep what was unclean and dead from the water. Bones, skins, entrails, torn carcasses, unrecognizable tatters and remnants broomed into a neat ridge. No sigh of the breeze he'd sought, yet fumes from the rim of garbage battered him in nauseating waves, a palpable medium intimate as wind. Beyond the tidal line of refuge, a pale margin lapped clean by receding waters. Then the iron river itself, flat, dark, speckled by sores of foam that puckered and swirled, worrying the stillness with a life of their own.

Spilled. Spoiled. Those words repeated themselves endlessly as he made his rounds. Dr. Rush had written out his portion, his day's share from the list of dead and dying. He'd purged, bled, comforted and buried victims of the fever. In and out of homes that had become tombs, prisons, charnel houses. Dazed children wandering the streets, searching for their parents. How can he explain to a girl, barely more than an infant, that the father and mother she sobs for are gone from this earth? Departed. Expired. They are resting, child. Asleep forever. In a far, far better place, my sweet, dear suffering one. In God's bosom. Wrapped in His incorruptible arms. A dead mother with a dead baby at her breast. Piteous cries of the helpless offering all they own for a drink of water. How does he console the delirious boy who pummels him, fastens himself on his leg because he's put the boy's mother in a box and now must nail shut the lid?

Though light-headed from exhaustion, he's determined to spend a few hours here, among his own people. But were these lost ones really his people? The doors of his church were open to them, yet these were the ones who stayed away, wasting their lives in vicious pastimes of the idle, the unsaved, the ignorant. His benighted brethen who'd struggled to reach this city of refuge and then, once inside the gates, had fallen, prisoners again, trapped by chains of dissolute living as they'd formerly been snared in the bonds of slavery. He'd come here and preached to them. Thieves, beggars, loose women, debtors, fugitives, drunkards, gamblers, the weak, crippled and outcast with nowhere else to go. They spurned his church so he'd brought church to them, preaching in gin mills, whoring dens, on street corners. He'd been jeered and hooted, spat upon, clods of unnameable filth had spattered his coat. But a love for them, as deep and unfathomable as his sorrow, his pity, brought him back again and again, exhorting them, setting the gospel before them so they might partake of its bounty, the infinite goodness, blessed sustenance therein. Jesus had toiled among the wretched, the outcast, that flotsam and jetsam deposited like a ledge of filth on the banks of the city. He understood what had brought the dark faces of his brethren north, to the Quaker promise of this town, this cradle and capital of a New World, knew the misery they were fleeing, the bright star in the Gourd's handle that guided them, the joy leaping in their hearts when at last, at last the opportunity to be viewed as men instead of things was theirs. He'd dreamed such dreams himself, oh yes, and prayed that the light of hope would never be extinguished. He'd been praying for deliverance, for peace and understanding when God had granted him a vision, hordes of sable bondsmen throwing off their chains, marching, singing, a path opening in the sea, the sea shaking its shaggy shoulders, resplendent with light and power. A radiance sparkling in this walkway through the water, pearls, diamonds, spears of light. This was the glistening way home. Waters parting, glory blinking and winking. Too intense to stare at, a promise shimmering, a rainbow arching over the end of the path. A hand tapped him. He'd waited for it to blend into the vision, for its meaning to shine forth in the language neither word nor thought, God was speaking in His visitation. Tapping became a grip. Someone was shoving him. He was being pushed off his knees, hauled to his feet. Someone was snatching him from the honeyed dream of salvation. When his eyes popped open he knew the name of each church elder manhandling him. Pale faces above a wall of black cloth belonged to his fellow communicants. He knew without looking the names of the men whose hands touched him gently, steering, coaxing, and those whose hands dug into his flesh, the impatient, imperious, rough hands that shunned any contact with him except as overseer or master.

Allen, Allen. Do you hear me? You and your people must not kneel at the front of the gallery. On your feet. Come. Come. Now. On your feet.

Behind the last row of pews. There ye may fall down on your knees and give praise.

And so we built our African house of worship. But its walls could not imprison the Lord's word. Go forth. Go forth. And he did so. To this sinful quarter. Tunnels, cellars and caves. Where no sunlight penetrates. Where wind off the river cuts like a knife. Chill of icy spray channeled here from the ocean's wintry depths. Where each summer the brackish sea that is mouth and maw and bowel deposits its waste in puddles stinking to high heaven.

Water Street becomes what it's named, rises round his ankles, soaks his boots, threatens to drag him down. Patrolling these murky depths he's predator, scavenger, the prey of some dagger-toothed creature whose shadow closes over him like a net.

When the first settlers arrived here they'd scratched caves into the soft earth of the riverbank. Like ants. Rats. Gradually they'd pushed inland, laying out a geometrical grid of streets, perpendicular, true angled and straight edged, the mirror of their rectitude. Black Quaker coats and dour visages were remembrances of mud, darkness, the place of their lying in, cocooned like worms, propagating dreams of a holy city. The latest comers must always start here, on this dotted line, in this riot of alleys, lanes, tunnels. Wave after wave of immigrants unloaded here, winnowed here, dying in these shanties, grieving in strange languages. But white faces move on, bury their dead, bear their children, negotiate the invisible reef between this broken place and the foursquare town. Learn enough of their new tongue to say to the blacks they've left behind, *thou shalt not pass.*

I watched him bring the scalding liquid to his lips and thought to myself that's where his color comes from. The black brew he drinks every morning. Coloring him, changing him. And hue I had not considered until that instant as other than absence, something nonwhite and therefore its opposite, what light would be if extinguished, sky or sea drained of the color blue when the sun disappears, the blackness of cinders. As he sips, steam rises. I peer into the cup that's become mine, at the moon in its center, waxing, waning. A light burning in another part of the room caught there, as my face would be if I leaned over the cup's hot mouth. But I have no wish to see my face. His is what I study as I stare into my cup and see not absence, but the presence of wood darkly stained, wet plowed earth, a boulder rising from a lake, blackly glistening as it sheds crowns and beards and necklaces of water. His color neither neglect nor abstention, nor mystery, but a swelling tide in his skin of this bitter morning beverage it is my habit to imbibe.

We were losing, clearly losing the fight. One day in mid-September fifty-seven were buried before noon.

He'd begun with no preamble. Our conversation taken up again directly as if the months since our last meeting were no more than a cobweb his first words lightly brush away. I say conversation but a better word would be soliloquy because I was only a listener, a witness learning his story, a story buried so deeply he couldn't recall it, but dreamed pieces, a conversation with himself, a reverie with the power to sink us both into its unreality. So his first words did not begin the story where I remembered him ending it in our last session, but picked up midstream the ceaseless play of voices only he heard, always, summoning him, possessing him, enabling him to speak, to be.

Despair was in my heart. The fiction of our immunity had been exposed for the vicious lie it was, a not so subtle device for wresting us from our homes, our loved ones, the afflicted among us, and sending us to aid strangers. First they blamed us, called the sickness Barbados fever, a contagion from those blood-soaked islands, brought to these shores by refugees from the fighting in Santo Domingo. We were not welcome anywhere. A dark skin was seen not only as a badge of shame for its wearer. Now we were evil incarnate, the mask of long agony and violent death. Black servants were discharged. The draymen, carters, barbers, caterers, oyster sellers, street vendors could find no custom. It mattered not that some of us were born here and spoke no language but the English language, second-, even third-generation African Americans who knew no other country, who laughed at the antics of newly landed immigrants, Dutchmen, Welshmen, Scots, Irish, Frenchmen who had turned our marketplaces into Babel, stomping along in their clodhopper shoes, strange costumes, haughty airs, Lowlander gibberish that sounded like men coughing or dogs barking. My fellow countrymen searching everywhere but in their own hearts, the foulness upon which this city is erected, to lay blame on others for the killing fever, pointed their fingers at foreigners and called it Palatine fever, a pestilence imported from those low countries in Europe where, I have been told, war for control of the sea-lanes, the human cargoes transported thereupon, has raged for a hundred years.

But I am losing the thread, the ironical knot I wished to untangle for you. How the knife was plunged in our hearts, then cruelly twisted. We were proclaimed carriers of the fever and treated as pariahs, but when it became expedient to command our services to nurse the sick and bury the dead, the previous allegations were no longer mentioned. Urged on by desperate counselors, the mayor granted us a blessed immunity. We were ordered to save the city.

I swear to you, and the bills of morality, published by the otherwise unreliable Mr. Carey, support my contention, that the fever dealt with us severely. Among the city's poor and destitute the fever's ravages were most deadly and we are always the poorest of the poor. If an ordinance forbidding ringing of bells to mourn the dead had not been passed, that awful tolling would have marked our days, the watches of the night in our African American community, as it did in those environs of the city we were forbidden to inhabit. Every morning before I commenced my labors for the sick and dying, I would hear moaning, screams of pain, fearful cries and supplications, a chorus of lamentations scarring daybreak, my people awakening to a nightmare that was devouring their will to live.

The small strength I was able to muster each morning was sorely tried the moment my eyes and ears opened upon the sufferings of my people, the reality that gave the lie to the fiction of our immunity. When my duties among the whites were concluded, how many nights did I return and struggle till dawn with victims here, my friends, parishioners, wandering sons of Africa whose faces I could not look upon without seeing my own. I was commandeered to rise and go forth to the general task of saving the city, forced to leave this neighborhood where my skills were sorely needed. I nursed those who hated me, deserted the ones I loved, who loved me.

I recite the story many, many times to myself, let many voices speak to me till one begins to sound like the sea or rain or my feet those mornings shuffling through thick dust.

We arrived at Bush Hill early. To spare ourselves a long trek in the oppressive heat of day. Yellow haze hung over the city. Plumes of smoke from blazes in Potter's Field, from fires on street corners curled above the rooftops, lending the dismal aspect of a town sacked and burned. I've listened to the Santo Domingans tell of the burning of Cap François. How the capital city was engulfed by fires set in cane fields by the rebelling slaves. Horizon in flames all night as they huddled offshore in ships, terrified, wondering where next they'd go, if any port would permit them to land, empty-handed slaves, masters whose only wealth now was naked black bodies locked in the hold, wide-eyed witnesses of an empire's downfall, chanting, moaning, uncertain as the sea rocked them, whether or not anything on earth could survive the fearful conflagration consuming the great city of Cap François.

Dawn breaking on a smoldering landscape, writhing columns of smoke, a general cloud of haze the color of a fever victim's eyes. I turn and stare at it a moment, then fall in again with my brother's footsteps trudging through untended fields girding Bush Hill.

From a prisoner-of-war ship in New York harbor where the British had interned him he'd seen that city shed its graveclothes of fog. Morning after morning it would paint itself damp and gray, a flat sketch on the canvas of sky, a tentative, shivering screen of housefronts, sheds, sprawling warehouses floating above the river. Then shadows and hollows darkened. A jumble of masts, spars, sails began to sway, little boats plied lanes between ships, tiny figures inched along wharves and docks, doors opened, windows slid up or down, lending an illusion of depth and animation to the portrait. This city infinitely beyond his reach, this charade other men staged to mock him, to mark the distance he could not travel, the shore he'd never reach, the city, so to speak, came to life and with its birth each morning dropped the palpable weight of his despair. His loneliness and exile. Moored in pewter water, on an island that never stopped moving but never arrived anywhere. The city a mirage of light and air, chimera of paint, brush and paper, mattered naught except that it was denied him. It shimmered. Tolled. Unsettled the watery place where he was sentenced to dwell. Conveyed to him each morning the same doleful tidings: *The dead are legion, the living a froth on dark, layered depths. But you are neither, and less than both.* Each night he dreamed it burning, razed the city till nothing remained but a dry, black crust, crackling, crunching under his boots as he strides, king of the nothing he surveys.

We passed holes dug into the earth where the sick are interred. Some died in these shallow pits, awash in their own vomited and voided filth, before a bed in the hospital could be made ready for them. Others believed they were being buried alive, and unable to crawl out, howled till reason or strength deserted them. A few, past caring, slept soundly in these ditches, resisted the attendants sent to rouse them and transport them inside, once they realized they were being resurrected to do battle again with the fever. I'd watched the red-bearded French doctor from Santo Domingo with his charts and assistants inspecting this zone, his *salle d'attente* he called it, greeting and reassuring new arrivals, interrogating them, nodding and bowing, hurrying from pit to pit, peering down at his invisible patients like a gardener tending seeds.

An introduction to the grave, a way into the hospital that prefigured the way most would leave it. That's what this bizarre rite of admission had seemed at first. But through this and other peculiar stratagems, Deveze, with his French practice, had transformed Bush Hill from lazarium to a clinic where victims of the fever, if not too weak upon arrival, stood a chance of surviving.

The cartman employed by Bush Hill had suddenly fallen sick. Faithful Wilcox had never missed a day, ferrying back and forth from town to hospital, hospital to Potter's Field. Bush Hill had its own cemetery now. Daily rations of dead could be disposed of less conspicuously in a plot on the grounds of the estate, screened from the horror-struck eyes of the city. No one had trusted the hospital. Tales of bloody chaos reigning there had filtered back to the city. Citizens believed it was a place where the doomed were stored until they died. Fever victims would have to be dragged from their beds into Bush Hill's cart. They'd struggle and scream, pitch themselves from the rolling cart, beg for help when the cart passed a rare pedestrian daring or foolish enough to be abroad in the deadly streets.

I wondered for the thousandth time why some were stricken, some not. Dr. Rush and this Deveze dipped their hands into the entrails of corpses, stirred the black, corrupted blood, breathed infected vapors exhaled from mortified remains. I'd observed both men steeped in noxious fluids expelled by their patients, yet neither had fallen prey to the fever. Stolid, dim Wilcox maintained daily concourse with the sick and buried the dead for two months before he was infected. They say a woman, undiscovered until boiling stench drove her neighbors into the street crying for aid, was the cause of Wilcox's downfall. A large woman, bloated into an even more cumbersome package by gases and liquids seething inside her body, had slipped from his grasp as he and another had hoisted her up into the cart. Catching against a rail, her body had slammed down and burst, spraying Wilcox like a fountain. Wilcox did not pride himself on being the tidiest of men, nor did his job demand one who was overfastidious, but the reeking stench from that accident was too much even for him and he departed in a huff to change his polluted garments. He never returned. So there I was at Bush Hill, where Rush had assigned me with my brother, to bury the flow of dead that did not ebb just because the Charon who was their familiar could no longer attend them.

The doctors believe they can find the secret of the fever in the victims' dead bodies. They cut, saw, extract, weigh, measure. The dead are carved into smaller and smaller bits and the butchered parts studied but they do not speak. What I know of the fever I've learned from the words of those I've treated, from stories of the living that are ignored by the good doctors. When lancet and fleam bleed the victims, they offer up stories like prayers.

It was a jaunty day. We served out white guests and after they'd eaten, they served us at the long, linen-draped tables. A sumptuous feast in the oak grove prepared by many and willing hands. All the world's eyes seemed to be watching us. The city's leading men, black and white, were in attendance to celebrate laying the cornerstone of St. Thomas Episcopal African Church. In spite of the heat and clouds of mettlesome insects, spirits were high. A gathering of whites and blacks in good Christian fellowship to commemorate the fruit of shared labor. Perhaps a new day was dawning. The picnic occurred in July. In less than a month the fever burst upon us.

When you open the dead, black or white, you find: the dura mater covering the brain is white and fibrous in appearance. The leptomeninges covering the brain are clear and without opacifications. The brain weighs 1,450 grams and is formed symmetrically. Cut sections of the cerebral hemispheres reveal normal-appearing gray matter throughout. The white matter of the corpus callosum is intact and bears no lesions. The basal ganglia are in their normal locations and grossly appear to be without lesions. The ventricles are symmetrical and filled with crystal-clear cerebrospinal fluid.

The cerebellum is formed symmetrically. The nuclei of the cerebellum are unremarkable. Multiple sections through the pons, medulla oblongata and upper brain stem reveal normal gross anatomy. The cranial nerves are in their normal locations and unremarkable.

The muscles of the neck are in their normal locations. The cartilages of the larynx and the hyoid bone are intact. The thyroid and parathyroid glands are normal on their external surface. The mucosa of the larynx is shiny, smooth and without lesions. The vocal cords are unremarkable. A small amount of bloody material is present in the upper trachea.

The heart weighs 380 grams. The epicardial surface is smooth, glistening and without lesions. The myocardium of the left ventricle and septum are of a uniform meaty-red, firm appearance. The endocardial surfaces are smooth, glistening and without lesions. The auricular appendages are free from thrombi. The valve leaflets are thin and delicate, and show no evidence of vegetation.

The right lung weighs 400 grams. The left lung 510 grams. The pleural surfaces of the lungs are smooth and glistening.

The esophageal mucosa is glistening, white and folded. The stomach contains a large amount of black, noxious bile. A veriform appendix is present. The ascending, transverse and descending colon reveal hemorrhaging, striations, disturbance of normal mucosa patterns throughout. A small amount bloody, liquid feces is present in the ano-rectal canal.

The liver weighs 1,720 grams. The spleen weighs 150 grams. The right kidney weighs 190 grams. The left kidney weighs 180 grams. The testes show a glistening white tunica albuginea. Sections are unremarkable.

Dr. Rush and his assistants examined as many corpses as possible in spite of the hurry and tumult of never-ending attendance on the sick. Rush hoped to prove his remedy, his analysis of the cause and course of the fever correct. Attacked on all sides by his medical brethren for purging and bleeding patients already in a drastically weakened state, Rush lashed back at his detractors, wrote pamphlets, broadsides, brandished the stinking evidence of his postmortems to demonstrate conclusively how the sick drowned in their own poisoned fluids. The putrefaction, the black excess, he proclaimed, must be drained away, else the victim inevitably succumbs.

Dearest:

I shall not return home again until this business of the fever is terminated. I fear bringing the dread contagion into our home. My life is in the hands of God and as long as He sees fit to spare me I will persist in my labors on behalf of the sick, dying and dead. We are losing the battle. Eighty-eight were buried this past Thursday. I tremble for your safety. Wish the lie of immunity were true. Please let me know by way of a note sent to the residence of Dr. Rush that you and our dear Martha are well. I pray every hour that God will preserve you both. As difficult as it is to rise each morning and go with Thomas to perform our duties, the task would be unbearable if I did not hold in my heart a vision of these horrors ending, a blessed shining day when I return to you and drop this weary head upon your sweet bosom.

Allen, Allen, he called to me. Observe how even after death, the body rejects this bloody matter from nose and bowel and mouth. Verily, the patient who had expired at least an hour before, continued to stain the cloth I'd wrapped round him. We'd searched the rooms of a regal mansion, discovering six members of a family, patriarch, son, son's wife and three children, either dead or in the last frightful stages of the disease. Upon the advice of one of Dr. Rush's most outspoken critics, they had refused mercury purges and bleeding until now, when it was too late for any earthly remedy to preserve them. In the rich furnishings of this opulent mansion, attended by one remaining servant whom fear had not driven away, three generations had withered simultaneously, this proud family's link to past and future cut off absolutely, the great circle broken. In the first bedroom we'd entered we'd found William Spurgeon, merchant, son and father, present manager of the family fortune, so weak he could not speak, except with pained blinks of his terrible golden eyes. Did he welcome us? Was he apologizing to good Dr. Rush for doubting his cure? Did he fear the dark faces of my brother and myself? Quick, too quickly, he was gone. Answering no questions. Revealing nothing of his state of mind. A savaged face frozen above the blanket. Ancient beyond years. Jaundiced eyes not fooled by our busy ministrations, but staring through us, fixed on the eternal stillness soon to come. And I believe I learned in that yellow cast of his eyes, the exact hue of the sky, if sky it should be called, hanging over the next world where we abide.

Allen, Allen. He lasted only moments and then I wrapped him in a sheet from the chest at the foot of his canopied bed. We lifted him into a humbler litter, crudely nailed together, the lumber still green. Allen, look. Stench from the coffin cut through the oppressive odors permeating this doomed household. See. Like an infant the master of the house had soiled his swaddling clothes. Seepage formed a dark river and dripped between roughly jointed boards. We found his wife where she'd fallen, naked, yellow above the waist, black below. As always the smell presaged what we'd discover behind a closed door. This woman had possessed closets of finery, slaves who dressed, fed, bathed and painted her, and yet here she lay, no one to cover her modesty, to lift her from the floor. Dr. Rush guessed from the discoloration she'd been dead two days, a guess confirmed by the loyal black maid, sick herself, who'd elected to stay when all others had deserted her masters. The demands of the living too much for her. She'd simply shut the door on her dead mistress. No breath, no heartbeat, Sir. I could not rouse her, Sir. I intended to return, Sir, but I was too weak to move her, too exhausted by my labors, Sir. Tears rolled down her creased black face and I wondered in my heart how this abused and despised old creature in her filthy apron and turban, this frail, worn woman, had survived the general calamity while the strong and pampered toppled round her.

I wanted to demand of her why she did not fly out the door now, finally freed of her burden, her lifelong enslavement to the whims of white people. Yet I asked her nothing. Considered instead myself, a man who'd worked years to purchase his wife's freedom, then his own, a so-called freeman, and here I was following in the train of Rush and his assistants, a functionary, a lackey, insulted daily by those I risked my life to heal.

Why did I not fly? Why was I not dancing in the streets, celebrating God's judgment on this wicked city? Fever made me freer than I'd ever been. Municipal government had collapsed. Anarchy ruled. As long as fever did not strike me I could come and go anywhere I pleased. Fortunes could be amassed in the streets. I could sell myself to the highest bidder, as nurse or undertaker, as surgeon trained by the famous Dr. Rush to apply his lifesaving cure. Anyone who would enter houses where fever was abroad could demand outrageous sums for negligible services. To be spared the fever was a chance for anyone, black or white, to be a king.

So why do you follow him like a loyal puppy, you confounded black fool? He wagged his finger. *You* . . . His finger a gaunt, swollen-jointed, cracked-bone, chewed thing. Like the nose on his face. The nose I'd thought looked more like finger than nose. *Fool. Fool.* Finger wagging, then the cackle. The barnyard braying. Berserk chickens cackling in his skinny, goiter-knobbed throat. You are a fool, you black son of Ham. You slack-witted, Nubian ape. You progeny of Peeping Toms and orangutans. Who forces you to accompany that madman Rush on his murderous tours? He kills a hundred for every one he helps with his lame-brain, nonsensical, unnatural, Sangrado cures. Why do you tuck your monkey tail between your legs and skip after that butcher? Are you his shadow, a mind-less, spineless black puddle of slime with no will of its own?

You are a good man, Allen. You worry about the souls of your people in this soulless wilderness. You love your family and your God. You are a beacon and steadfast. Your fatal flaw is narrowness of vision. You cannot see beyond these shores. The river, that stinking gutter into which the city shovels its shit and ex-tracts its drinking water, that long-suffering string of spittle winds to an ocean. A hundred miles downstream the foamy mouth of the land sucks on the Atlantic's teat, trade winds saunter and a whole wide world awaits the voyager. I know, Allen. I've been everywhere. Buying and selling everywhere.

If you would dare be Moses to your people and lead them out of this land, you'd find fair fields for your talent. Not lapdogging or doggy-trotting behind or fetch doggy or lie doggy or doggy open your legs or doggy stay still while I beat you. Follow the wound that is a river back to the sea. Be gone, be gone. While there's still time. If there is time, *mon frère.* If the pestilence has not settled in you already, breathed from my foul guts into yours, even as we speak.

Here's a master for you. A real master, Allen. The fever that's supping on my in-nards. I am more slave than you've ever been. I do its bidding absolutely. Cough up my lungs. Shit hunks of my bowel. When I die, they say my skin will turn as black as yours, Allen.

Return to your family. Do not leave them again. Whatever the Rushes promise, whatever they threaten.

Once, ten thousand years ago I had a wife and children. I was like you, Allen, proud, innocent, forward looking, well-spoken, well-mannered, a beacon and steadfast. I began to believe the whispered promise that I could have more. More of what, I didn't ask. Didn't know, but I took my eyes off what I loved in order to obtain this more. Left my wife and children and when I returned they were gone. Forever lost to me. The details are not significant. Suffice to say the circum-stances of my leaving were much like yours. Very much like yours, Allen. And I lost everything. Became a wanderer among men. Bad news people see coming from miles away. A pariah. A joke. I'm not black like you, Allen. But I will be soon. Sooner than you'll be white. And if you're ever white, you'll be as dead as I'll be when I'm black.

Why do you desert your loved ones? What impels you to do what you find so painful, so unjust? Are you not a man? And free?

Her sleepy eyes, your lips on her warm cheek, each time may be the last meeting on this earth. The circumstances are similar, my brother. My shadow. My dirty face.

The dead are legion, the living a froth on dark, layered depths.

Master Abraham. There's a gentleman to see you, Sir. The golden-haired lad bound to me for seven years was carted across the seas, like you, Allen, in the bowels of a leaky tub. A son to replace my son his fathers had clubbed to death when they razed the ghetto of Antwerp. But I could not tame the inveterate hate, his aversion and contempt for me. From my aerie, at my desk secluded among barrels, bolts, crates and trunks of the shop's attic, I watched him steal, drink, fornicate. I overheard him denounce me to a delegate sent round to collect a tithe during the emergency. 'Tis well known in the old country that Jews bring the fever. Palatine fever that slays whole cities. They carry it under dirty fingernails, in the wimples of lizardy private parts. Pass it on with the evil eye. That's why we hound them from our towns, exterminate them. Beware of Master Abraham's glare. And the black-coated vulture listened intently. I could see him toting up the account in his small brain. Kill the Jew. Gain a shop and sturdy prentice, too. But I survived till fever laid me low and the cart brought me here to Bush Hill. For years he robbed and betrayed me and all my revenge was to treat him better. Allow him to pilfer, lie, embezzle. Let him grow fat and careless as I knew he would. With a father's boundless kindness I destroyed him. The last sorry laugh coming when I learned he died in agony, fever shriven, following by a day his Water Street French whore my indulgence allowed him to keep.

In Amsterdam I sold diamonds, Allen. In Barcelona they plucked hairs from my beard to fashion charms that brought ill fortune to their enemies. There were nights in dungeons when the mantle of my suffering was all I possessed to wrap round me and keep off mortal cold. I cursed God for choosing me, choosing my people to cuckold and slaughter. Have you heard of the Lamed-Vov, the Thirty-six Just Men set apart to suffer the reality humankind cannot bear? Saviors. But not Gods like your Christ. Not magicians, or sorcerers with bags of tricks, Allen. No divine immunities. Flesh and blood saviors. Men like we are, Allen. If man you are beneath your sable hide. Men who cough and scratch their sores and bleed and stink. Whose teeth rot. Whose wives and children are torn from them. Who wander the earth unable to die, but men always, men till God plucks them up and returns them to His side where they must thaw ten centuries to melt the crust of earthly grief and misery they've taken upon themselves. Ice men. Snow-men. I thought for many years I might be one of them. In my vanity. My self-pity. My foolishness. But no. One lifetime of sorrows enough for me. I'm just another customer. One more in the crowd lined up at his stall to purchase his wares.

You do know, don't you, Allen, that God is a bookseller? He publishes one book—the text of suffering—over and over again. He disguises it between new boards, in different shapes and sizes, prints on varying papers, in many fonts, adds prefaces and postscripts to deceive the buyer, but it's always the same book.

You say you do not return to your family because you don't want to infect them. Perhaps your fear is well-founded. But perhaps it also masks a greater fear. Can you imagine yourself, Allen, as other than you are? A free man with no charlatan Rush to blame. The weight of your life in your hands.

You've told me tales of citizens paralyzed by fear, of slaves on shipboard who turn to stone in their chains, their eyes boiled in the sun. Is it not possible that you suffer the converse of this immobility? You, sir, unable to stop an endless round of duty and obligation. Turning pages as if the next one or the next will let you finish the story and return to your life.

Your life, man. Tell me what sacred destiny, what nigger errand keeps you standing here at my filthy pallet? Fly, fly, fly away home. Your house is on fire, your children burning.

I have lived to see the slaves free. My people frolic in the streets. Black and white. The ones who believe they are either or both or neither. I am too old for dancing. Too old for foolishness. But this full moon makes me wish for two good legs. For three. Straddled a broomstick when I was a boy. Giddy-up, Giddy-up. Galloping m'lord, m'lady, around the yard I should be sweeping. Dust in my wake. Chickens squawking. My eyes everywhere at once so I would not be caught out by mistress or master in the sin of idleness. Of dreaming. Of following a child's inclination. My broom steed snatched away. Become a rod across my back. Ever cautious. Dreaming with one eye open. The eye I am now, old and gimpy limbed, watching while my people celebrate the rumor of Old Pharaoh's capitulation.

I've shed this city like a skin, wiggling out of it tenscore and more years, by miles and els, fretting, twisting. Many days I did not know whether I'd wrenched freer or crawled deeper into the sinuous pit. Somewhere a child stood, someplace green, keeping track, waiting for me. Hoping I'd meet him again, hoping my struggle was not in vain. I search that child's face for clues to my blurred features. Flesh drifted and banked, eroded by wind and water, the landscape of this city fitting me like a skin. Pray for me, child. For my unborn parents I carry in this orphan's potbelly. For this ancient face that slips like water through my fingers.

Night now. Bitter cold night. Fires in the hearths of lucky ones. Many of us till abide in dark cellars, caves dug into the earth below poor men's houses. For we are poorer still, burrow there, pull earth like blanket and quilt round us to shut out cold, sleep multitudes to a room, stacked and crosshatched and spoon fashion, ourselves the fuel, hear of one body passed to others and passed back from all to one. No wonder then the celebration does not end as a blazing chill sweeps off the Delaware. Those who leap and roar round the bonfires are better off where they are. They have no place else to go.

Given the derivation of the words, you could call the deadly, winged visitors an *unpleasantness from Egypt*.

Putrid stink rattles in his nostrils. He must stoop to enter the cellar. No answer as he shouts his name, his mission of mercy. Earthen floor, ceiling and walls buttressed by occasional beams, slabs of wood. Faint bobbing glow from his lantern. He sees himself looming and shivering on the walls, a shadowy presence with more substance than he feels he possesses at this late hour. After a long day of visits, this hovel his last stop before returning to his brother's house for a few hours of rest. He has learned that exhaustion is a swamp he can wade through and on the far side another region where a thin trembling version of himself toils while he observes, bemused, slipping in and out of sleep, amazed at the likeness, the skill with which that other mounts and sustains him. Mimicry. Puppetry. Whatever controls this other, he allows the impostor to continue, depends upon it to work when he no longer can. After days in the city proper with Rush, he returns to these twisting streets beside the river that are infected veins and arteries he must bleed.

At the rear of the cave, so deep in shadow he stumbles against it before he sees it, is a mound of rags. When he leans over it, speaking down into the darkness, he knows instantly this is the source of the terrible smell, that something once alive is rotting under the rags. He thinks of autumn leaves blown into mountainous, crisp heaps, the north wind cleansing itself and the city of summer. He thinks of anything, any image that will rescue him momentarily from the nauseating stench, postpone what he must do next. He screams no, no to himself as he blinks away his wife's face, the face of his daughter. His neighbors had promised to check on them, he hears news almost daily. There is no rhyme or reason in whom the fever takes, whom it spares, but he's in the city every day, exposed to its victims, breathing fetid air, touching corrupted flesh. Surely if someone in his family must die, it will be him. His clothes are drenched in vinegar, he sniffs the nostrum of gunpowder, bark and asafetida in a bag pinned to his coat. He's prepared to purge and bleed himself, he's also ready and quite willing to forgo these precautions and cures if he thought surrendering his life might save theirs. He thinks and unthinks a picture of her hair, soft against his cheek, the wet warmth of his daughter's backside in the crook of his arm as he carries her to her mother's side where she'll be changed and fed. No. Like a choking mist, the smell of decaying flesh stifles him, forces him to turn away, once, twice, before he watches himself bend down into the brunt of it and uncover the sleepers.

Two Santo Domingan refugees, slave or free, no one knew for sure, inhabited this cellar. They had moved in less than a week before, the mother huge with child, man and woman both wracked by fever. No one knows how long the couple's been unattended. There was shame in the eyes and voices of the few from whom he'd gleaned bits and pieces of the Santo Domigans' history. Since no one really knew them and few nearby spoke their language, no one was willing to risk, et cetera. Except for screams one night, no one had seen or heard signs of life. If he'd been told nothing about them, his nose would have led him here.

He winces when he sees the dead man and woman, husband and wife, not entwined as in some ballad of love eternal, but turned back to back, distance between them, as if the horror were too visible, too great to bear, doubled in the other's eyes. What had they seen before they flung away from each other? If he could, he would rearrange them, spare the undertakers this vision.

Rat feet and rat squeak in the shadows. He'd stomped his feet, shooed them before he entered, hollered as he threw back the covers, but already they were accustomed to his presence, back at work. They'd bite indiscriminately, dead flesh, his flesh. He curses and flails his staff against the rags, strikes the earthen floor to keep the scavengers at bay. Those sounds are what precipitate the high-pitched cries that first frighten him, then shame him, then propel him to a tall packing crate turned on its end, atop which another crate is balanced. Inside the second wicker container, which had imported some item from some distant place into this land, twin brown babies hoot and wail.

We are passing over the Dismal Swamp. On the right is the Appalachian range, some of the oldest mountains on earth. Once there were steep ridges and valleys all through here but erosion off the mountains created landfill several miles deep in places. This accounts for the rich loamy soil of the region. Over the centuries several southern states were formed from this gradual erosion. The cash crops of cotton and tobacco so vital to southern prosperity were ideally suited to the fertile soil.

Yeah, I nurse these old funky motherfuckers, all right. White people, specially old white people, lemme tell you, boy, them peckerwoods stink. Stone dead fishy wet stink. Talking all the time bout niggers got BO. Well, white folks got the stink and gone, man. Don't be putting my hands on them, neither. Never. Huh uh. If I touch them, be wit gloves. They some nasty people, boy. And they don't be paying me enough to take no chances wit my health. Matter of fact they ain't paying me enough to really be expecting me to work. Yeah. Starvation wages. So I ain't hardly touching them. Or doing much else either. Got to smoke a cigarette to get close to some of them. Piss and shit theyselves like babies. They don't need much taking care anyway. Most of them three-quarters dead already. Ones that ain't is crazy. Nobody don't want them round, that's why they here. Talking to theyselves. Acting like they speaking to a roomful of people and not one soul in the ward paying attention. There's one old black dude, must be a hundred, he be muttering away to hisself nonstop everyday. Pitiful, man. Hope I don't never get that old. Shoot me, bro, if I start to getting old and fucked up in body and mind like them. Don't want no fools like me hanging over me when I can't do nothing no more for my ownself. Shit. They ain't paying me nothing so that's what I do. Nothing. Least I don't punch em or tease em or steal they shit like some the staff. And I don't pretend I'm God like these so-called professionals and doctors flittin round here drawing down that long bread. Naw. I just mind my own business, do my time. Cop a little TV, sneak me a joint when nobody's around. It ain't all that bad, really. Long as I ain't got no ole lady and crumb crushers. Don't know how the married cats make it on the little bit of chump change they pay us. But me, I'm free. It ain't that bad, really.

By the time his brother brought him the news of their deaths . . .

Almost an afterthought. The worst, he believed, had been overcome. Only a handful of deaths the last week of November. The city was recovering. Commerce thriving. Philadelphia must be revictualed, refueled, rebuilt, reconnected to the countryside, to markets foreign and domestic, to products, pleasures and appetites denied during the quarantine months of the fever. A new century would soon be dawning. We must forget the horrors. The Mayor proclaims a new day. Says let's put the past behind us. Of the eleven who died in the fire he said extreme measures were necessary as we cleansed ourselves of disruptive influences. The cost could have been much greater, he said I regret the loss of life, especially the half dozen kids, but I commend all city officials, all volunteers who helped return the city to the arc of glory that is its proper destiny.

When they cut him open, the one who decided to stay, to be a beacon and steadfast, they will find: liver (1,720 grams), spleen (150 grams), right kidney (190 grams), left kidney (180 grams), brain (1,450 grams), heart (380 grams) and right next to his heart, the miniature hand of a child, frozen in a grasping gesture, fingers like hard tongues of flame, still reaching for the marvel of the beating heart, fascinated still, though the heart is cold, beats not, the hand as curious about this infinite stillness as it was about thump and heat and quickness.

NOTES

"Fever"—Absalom Jones and Richard Allen's "Narrative" (1794): Gary B. Nash's *Forging Freedom* (1988), Harvard University Press; and especially J.H. Powell's *Bring Out Your Dead* (1949), University of Pennsylvania Press, were useful sources for this meditation on history.

An Interview with John Edgar Wideman

BY CHARLES H. ROWELL

This interview was conducted by telephone between Charlottesville, Virginia, and Amherst, Massachusetts, during the morning of Tuesday, October 17, 1989.

ROWELL: John, what brought you to writing and publishing creative texts? When you were a student at the University of Pennsylvania, you were captain of the basketball team. Then later you became a Rhodes Scholar at Oxford University. How did you resist becoming a professional basketball player? In other words, what made you take the risk of becoming a creative writer?

WIDEMAN: Well, for me, I guess, it wasn't really a risk. Writing was something I had done as long as I could remember—and I simply wanted to try it seriously, full-time. I was very obviously young and ignorant, and I thought if you wanted to do things and if they were important to you that you could do them. And so I had that kind of optimism and, I guess, in a way arrogance. But storytelling and writing have been a part of my life forever, and I have enjoyed them for a long time.

This goes back, Charles, to when I was in grade school in Homewood in Pittsburgh. There was no auditorium in the grade school that I went to, which, by the way, was the same one that my mother attended in the 1920s—the same building, same location, obviously, and probably the same pencils and paper, I think. But this school had no auditorium, and so any time there was an assembly people simply sat on the steps in the center hallway, and I found myself, on more than one occasion, being called out by teachers to talk to the entire school when we had an assembly, when we had a program. Also, during homeroom I would get a chance to get up and tell stories, and that was my thing. I guess I was pretty good at it, because I could hold people's attention. I was fascinated by that. Even as a kid I recognized this as power and attention—the attention that I could get, the sense of control that I could have for a few moments, and just the whole fun of spinning out a story and making something up and, as I was making it up, engaging other people. So storytelling was a very satisfactory, personal kind of experience for me, going way back.

And then there were great storytellers in my family, and family gatherings—picnics and weddings, church socials, funerals, wakes—were occasions for other people to exercise their storytelling abilities and talents. So I had around me a kind of world, a creative world, an imaginative world, which I could draw from and which I very much wanted to participate in.

Let me bring it a little closer to the time we're talking about. By the time I had graduated from college and had gone to graduate school, I was thoroughly interested in the romantic notion of being a writer. What power the writer could have—and now I'm talking about the literate tradition—the sense of the writer as adventurer, the writer as explorer. That part of it was something that appealed to me greatly.

ROWELL: You entered the literary scene in 1967 with the publication of *A Glance Away,* your first novel. That was during the height of the Black Arts Movement. One critic (I think it was Addison Gayle) has described the Movement as "a Northern urban phenomenon." You are Northern and urban. In fact, you spent a great deal of your life in Pittsburgh, but you were born in Washington, D.C. Why were you never part of the Black Arts Movement? *Hurry Home, The Lynchers,* and your first novel suggest that you did not at all subscribe to the tenets of the Black Arts Movement. Without provoking any people out there in our age group who were the architects and the advocates of the Movement, will you comment on why you and many Southern writers like Albert Murray, or the younger Ernest Gaines, or the even younger Alice

Walker, were not really part of the Black Arts Movement? Then, too, there were also the non-Southern Black writers like Michael Harper and Jay Wright who were never part of the Black Arts Movement.

WIDEMAN: Well, this is an enormously complex issue and also, at some level, pretty simple. For one thing, I was out of the country. I was away in another country, England. That was between 1963 and 1967, and so at a time when I might have become intimately, physically, literally involved with the Movement I couldn't. I read about it in the newspaper; I was a distant sort of witness. That's part of it. The second part of it might be that I've always been sort of a loner, and very suspicious of groups and organizations and movements, and suspicious and not really at ease in that kind of situation. Maybe because of an ego that's too large or maybe because of some healthy skepticism or whatever. I won't try to figure that out. But, personally, my sense was that I didn't—I still don't have—an affinity for groups. If something is important to me, maybe I'll talk about it to one person, or maybe I'll talk about it to no one. I try to resolve things on a personal level, and I realize that there's some problems there, but I'm just trying to get at, maybe, why I was not attracted to the Black Arts Movement.

But there are many more general issues also that need to be touched on when someone asks why a person is part of the Black Arts Movement and why they're not. First of all, Alice Walker and myself . . . Albert Murray is really a generation ahead of us . . . if you look back now and ask what was produced, what came out of the sixties that remains of some significance to Afro-American literature, then I would hope that people would say that we were part of it, the Black Arts Movement. (As long as you don't put capital letters on "black arts movement.") In other words, there were many, many things happening. It was a multifaceted cultural event, this growth, this consciousness that was arising in the sixties, and the artwork that was being produced in the sixties. During the sixties, some of the activity was recognized and anointed—that is, got the publicity, got the attention, and a lot was missed. Just as the writers who are "significant" at this present moment are significant for a lot of reasons, but not necessarily because they're the best writers. So when we look back at the sixties, with the advantage of hindsight, we see a different configuration than we did then. When we're in the middle of something we always see as through a glass darkly. We mistook, during the sixties, a lot of attitudinizing and posturing for the real thing, for the leading edge. We confused dogma with innovation, adopted ideas that really weren't all that significant or that were only of secondary significance. And so, as we've tried with the Harlem Renaissance, we're reevaluating the sixties. That period is 20 years away from us now. We have a different picture of what went on, because we've seen what has lasted. Black Arts theorists—and we must remember there were many points of view—should not be dismissed. They deserve study and reconsideration. What was actually happening was complex, irreducible as life always is. It comes down to the individual, the individual artist, who for one reason or another has that strange combination of gifts and luck and perserverance that has made his/her work endure. The current events, ideological and aesthetic preoccupations of a given time, of the sixties for instance, are always the surface below which the significant activity occurs. Very few people understand at the time where the real action is.

It's not a simple question of repudiating certain figures and certain attitudes of the sixties. For instance, the notion that black people had to tell their own stories, that black people needed to investigate the language, that black people are on the edge of a kind of precipice and that, as a people, we might very well disappear if we didn't start to, number one, demand equality in the political sense, if we didn't begin to investigate our past, if we didn't begin to see ourselves as part of a world, a Third World—all these ideological and philosophical breakthroughs were crucial to reorienting us, and they still provide a basis for much of the thinking and the writing that is significant today. But it's one thing to make lists and programs and then write stories or paint pictures that very baldly reproduce ideas. It's another thing to struggle and refine a medium to embody ideas in an artistic way that will last. And so those of us who are still writing now, I hope, really are beneficiaries of what was going on at all levels in the sixties. I hope we've carried forward the ideas that are most significant, profound, important. I see continuities, rather than simply a break with or repudiation of the Black Arts Movement of the sixties.

ROWELL: My next question relates, in part, to the previous one on the Black Arts Movement, but its focus is what I continue to witness as the audience's demand of or prescription for black writers in the United States. How do you respond—or do you respond at all—to readers, especially black readers in the United States, frequently demanding "critical realism" from black writers? That is to say, readers so frequently desire to have the black writer engage, socially and politically, his or her own fiction. How do you respond to such a demand?

WIDEMAN: I don't respond well to anybody who tells me what to do. Whether it's in sports or dress, and certainly not in something as personal and intimate as literature. I listen and I try to make sense of criticism, but I listen much better when I'm not commanded to do something, when I don't feel pushed and shoved. So the bullyish tone and one-dimensional demands that characterized certain critics during the sixties, if anything, made me more sure that as a write I was responsible to something other than somebody else's ideas of what I should write and how I should write. Especially since I was working very hard to escape the strictures, to break out of the mould imposed by my "classic," Europeanized education. I didn't want to be J. Alfred Prufrock, I didn't want to be Hemingway anymore, I wanted to strike out on my own. And so I wasn't looking for anybody to give me another set of parameters or another path that I had to follow or another load or burden or harness on my back. It was important that I exercise independence and find my own voice, my own prerogative, at this time.

ROWELL: I'm fascinated by your expression "intimate as literature." Will you talk about that? How is literature "intimate"? I love that phrase, "intimate as literature."

WIDEMAN: Writing for me is an expressive activity, so it's as intimate as my handwriting, or the way I dance, or the way I play basketball. And when I do those things they're not simply instrumental; that is, when I write I'm not only writing to give a message; when I play basketball I'm not doing it simply to score points or to win. But in all those activities—and I think this is true of Afro-American art in general—there are ways of being who I am, and so I need to find the space to express what I am, who I am. Writing for me is a way of opening up, a way of sharing, a way of making sense of the world, and writing's very appeal is that it gives me a kind of hands-on way of coping with the very difficult business of living a life. What could be more intimate than that, what has more significance than that? Writing is like breathing, it's like singing, it takes the whole body and mind and experience. It's also anarchistic. I like to write because it allows me to do things my way, to say them my way. So what if everybody else's way is different.

ROWELL: I want to go back to a question I asked earlier about critics' and general readers' demands on black writers. The case of Irving Howe on Richard Wright is one we all know about. Ralph Ellison and James Baldwin responded—each in his own way—to Howe. Some years later Albert Murray responded to James Baldwin in *The Omni-Americans*. Do you think this dialogue, or this discourse, is unfinished? Is the black writer now free to proceed to write? I admit, of course, the way I raise the question loads the case. You can tell where I come from aesthetically.

WIDEMAN: Number one, Charles, I'm having a hard time hearing you, but for me one of the most important functions for writing—Afro-American writing, Eskimo writing, whatever—is identical with one of the most important functions of any art, and that is to be a medium of expression, a free medium of expression, a way that people can say what they want to say, do what they want to do, play in a way that they want to play. Art should be something that in many senses goes against the grain of the culture. That's one of is values, disruptive as well as integrative. It's the place where there's craziness, where there's unpredictability, where there is freedom of expression. Art should always be something that to some degree shocks and changes people and worries people and contradicts what the king says. Achebe makes the point that the writer or the artist is always the enemy of the king. Writing, art, is subversion, it turns the world on its head, it makes up things. That's its power, that's its joy. Play, illusion. Any constraints on that, any kind of rules or any allegiances that are externally imposed, have to be looked at by the artist with a lot of suspicion, a lot of skepticism. And that's the point of view where I come from. Which is not to say that an artist cannot be socially responsible, but I think the issue here is that the notion of social responsibility is really quite a wide one. The policing of that responsibility will be done or should be done by the audience. If you are on an ego trip, if you are too deeply involved in some kind of idiosyncratic masturbatory activity, well, people will eventually peek your whole card and not care about what you do. Or critics will come down on your case, etc., etc., but we can't police the activity before things are done, we can't direct art, we can't tell people what to write about, we can't ask people to follow rules. Rules are the anathema as well as the bones of art.

ROWELL: Am I correct in assuming that what you have just said is part of what one might describe as your theory of art? And I don't mean to make it so tight as to say that you have given a manifesto for art. That is, are these some of the aesthetic imperatives you have set for yourself as a fiction writer?

WIDEMAN: Right, in a casual way, I guess I have come to a very distinct set of ideas about writing at this point. But I think I have different ideas at different times in my life, and if you look at one of my books it probably contains an implicit theory of art, a theory of composition. As I grow older and look at the world, I see art as a gift to people, certainly a gift to the artist, though sometimes it's also a curse. Art is an area where the human personality gets to fulfill itself in a way that it doesn't in most other activities. This is not to make the artist a cult hero, or a priest, or anything like that, but simply to say that all human beings have the capacity for wonder, for play, for imagination, and that's the capacity, the faculty that modern civilization, mass civilization, is eroding, crushing, and so the artist has a crucial role. I like to think of everybody, of anybody with a healthy life, as an artist to some extent. What my grandmother did, what my aunts do, what my brothers do when they tell stories, is a form of artistic expression, a form of salvation. Life is tough, and we need the ability to dream, to make things, and that ability is epitomized by the artist. It doesn't mean the artist is sanctified, but the artist is someone with whom we can identify, who causes us to remember that there are sides to the human personality—creative, imaginative sides—that allow us to escape, transcend, remake, transform a life that is too often pretty brutal, nasty and short.

ROWELL: You mention that there might be a shift if you looked back on your texts, specifically *Hurry Home* and *The Lynchers*. Do you see a shift between those texts and *Damballah* and *Sent for You Yesterday,* for example?

WIDEMAN: Oh, I hope there are many shifts and changes, because as a writer I want to grow. But I see both continuities and shifts. All my books are about family, family relationships, and reordering and transformation of family. Also I think in all of them, one of the major subjects is writing and imagination. As I grew as a writer, I very consciously decided to change some of what I was trying to do stylistically in the earlier books. What I mean by *stylistically* is how I connected my books to what I assumed was the Great Tradition, the writers who came before. In my first three books, the ways I tried to assert continuity with tradition and my sense of tradition were quite different than my understanding of these matters in *Damballah, Hiding Place, Sent For You Yesterday.* It became clearer and clearer to me as I wrote that the tradition in which I wanted to place myself was much richer than I had first imagined. That is, for my first books, the tradition was mainly European, mainly literate. Because I was a black man and had grown up in a black community I sort of divided my books. Blackness provided the local habitation and names; the scenes, people, conversations, were largely drawn from my early experience, because that's what I knew best. But I was trying to hook that world into what I thought was something that would give those situations and people a kind of literary resonance, legitimize that world by infusing echoes of T.S. Eliot, Henry James, Faulkner, English and Continental masters. I was attempting through the use of metaphors, images and allusion, through structural parallels, to connect with what I thought of as the Great Tradition. For me, at the time, that strategy was valid, and I think some of what works in my early books validates that approach. But as I grew and learned more about writing, I found, or rediscovered I guess, that what Bessie Smith did when she sang, what Clyde McFater did, what John Coltrane did, what Ralph Ellison did, what Richard Wright did, what the anonymous slave composer and the people who spoke in the slave narratives did, what they were doing was drawing from a realm of experience, a common human inheritance, that T.S. Eliot, Faulkner, Tolstoi, and Austen were also drawing from. As a writer I didn't need to go by way of European tradition to get to what really counted, the common, shared universal core. I could take a direct route and get back to that essential mother lode of pain, love, grief, wonder, the basic human emotions that are the stuff of literature. I could get back to that mother lode through my very own mother's voice. Some people might argue, and I'd partly agree, that understanding and reading *The Wasteland,* being totally blown away by that poem as a kid, taught me how to get back to my own mother's voice. Nothing's easy, you can't skip stages. My writing is what it is because it did follow a particular circuitous path. I blundered into dead ends, made mistakes, had infatuations at one point or another, models that I imitated without really understanding what I was imitating. But that kind of trial and error and back and forth is what learning to write is all about, and that's how I visualize progress in art, not linear but circular, mysteriously wrapped up in time's mysterious unfolding. Circles. Layers. What seemed complex becomes simple, and what seems simple becomes complex.

ROWELL: You've commented on your use of private history in the writing of *Fever* (1989), a collection of stories. In the title story of that collection and in your forthcoming novel (1990) on the Philadelphia Fire, you introduce us to "public history" as one of your sources. What does this mean for you as a writer? Is this another shift or stage in your writing career?

WIDEMAN: It's not exactly new because I took a lynching and made a story about that. And it wasn't based on a specific lynching, but at the beginning of the book there is a litany of actual lynchings and atrocities committed against black people. But there is a difference. I think that certain public events occur and they have lots of significance, they are very important, they define powerful currents, they are events we shouldn't ignore, that we shouldn't forget, that we should try to make sense of. But at the same time because of the speed of the media and because of the activity that goes around us all the time, the accelerated push of contemporary life, we miss these events. Then there is also the very conscious censorship and infantilization and lying and distortion the media perpetrates. And there's the political reality of the social environment that we live in, where in individual life counts for less and less. We are being pushed into a communal, anthill, living willy-nilly whether we like it or not. Blackness is being attacked not simply in the old ways because of difference, difference vis-à-vis whiteness, but just because it's different. There's no time for somebody who asks too many questions. No time for people who want to bring up the past, and reconsider the past. There's no time for people whose lives present a different agenda than the agenda that is central—the majority agenda. And so I'm looking at this kind of situation and I see things happening and I see them getting buried. *Fever* was based on an actual occurrence of yellow fever in Philadelphia, Pennsylvania in the 1790s. Like Antonin Artaud, I think that societies, in some metaphysical sense, create the diseases they need and that those diseases are metaphors for the basic problems of those societies. It's no coincidence that the yellow fever epidemic, described by many at the time as the end of the world, was allegedly brought to the Americas by slaves from the West Indies. We need to stop the wheel and look at things again, try to understand what they mean.

The events in Philadelphia in 1985, the MOVE massacre, really began in 1978 when a bunch of MOVE people were arrested and put in jail forever for allegedly killing a policeman. The concerted, ruthless campaign of a city government—ironically, a city government under the control of a black mayor—to destroy difference is one of the most important public events that I've observed. It was particularly important because it was buried. A whole city is afflicted by amnesia. In the press it got a little play for awhile, but then it was forgotten. And I think that, maybe in the same sense that you can see the universe in a blade of grass, if we look at certain events long enough and hard enough through the lens of fiction, maybe we can learn more of what we need to know. If we don't try, if we don't fight for the little light there is, then we're going to suffer. In "Fever" and the stories that go with it, and in *Philadelphia Fire,* I'm trying to make myself stop, look, listen, and think about what's happening to us.

ROWELL: You have referred to *Damballah* as a novel. I've always thought of it as a coherent collection of interrelated short stories. *Fever,* of course, is a collection of short stories in the traditional sense of a collection. Is that correct?

WIDEMAN: I sort of thought that too, Charles, but I'm not so sure now. Because a lot of the stories were reworked and reorganized for the volume, and over half were new. And it doesn't have the kind of organic unity that *Damballah* had. But I'd like to think that the stories have unity in this sense. There's something really rotten in the state of Denmark. Something's really screwed. And the stories are ways of coping with the malaise which is in the air. "Fever," which is the final story in the book, attempts to render that essence, that unnameable uneasiness, that quality of decay or threat or collective anguish that permeates many of the other stories. Many of the other stories are about trouble, either people who are in trouble or who've fallen, and people who are working very hard to keep themselves from falling. And so the idea of the book, of the collection, is that this fever is amongst us still. This fever is something that we are subject to. Its ravages are still among us. So watch out folks. The final story in the book attempts to bridge, to synthesize past, present, and future sources of this fever, which to me clearly is the unresolved question of slavery, the unresolved question of racism, the unresolved question of majority rule that leads to majority domination and oppression.

ROWELL: You are not only a fiction writer and an essayist. You are also an excellent literary critic. Do you see the literary critic or literary theorists as having specific functions or roles? If so, is that reflected in your own writing of criticism?

WIDEMAN: I still think in the old-fashioned sense that the best criticism is a kind of handmaiden to the arts. Good critics through precept and example remind people that writing is fun, that writing is enjoyable, that writing has a serious side, a constructive side, that if you put work into it, it rewards that work. I think of critics also as a sort of conscience, as well as tour guides. Criticism can be a creative activity in which the critic dreams, the critic plays, the critic experiences a work of art and comes back changed or thoughtful or angry. Those emotions are a kind of evidence or witness to the power of fiction. And I think the best criticism makes us remember what it's like to have a powerful experience with this made-up stuff, this imaginary stuff. And so there's an organic relationship between good writing and good criticism. Too often that meeting doesn't occur. So we keep trying. We should keep trying.

ROWELL: I shall never forget seeing a photograph of you in an issue of *Sports Illustrated,* where you were standing before a chalkboard. On that board, you had written statements about Albert Murray. You've also written literary criticism about his work. You've also written about Zora Neale Hurston, about Charles Chestnutt, and about Gayle Jones. These writers are Southerners. Do you find something in them, artistically, in a positive way, that you don't find in other African-American writers? I'm thinking now about your interest in voice, in an article you wrote for the *American Poetry Review.* Voice, of course, is of primary importance in the elegant writing in *Damballah,* and in the texts which follow it.

WIDEMAN: I think there is such a thing as a core to Afro-American culture. There is a core culture. And part of it can be identified. And you can have fun talking about what you think the core is, but there is definitely one there. We'll never be able to define it once and for all, because then we'll probably start slipping into ideology rather than description. But there is a core and it has to do with the South. It has to do with the locus of that "letter from home" phrase you mentioned before. There was an understanding in me of Southern culture although I never ventured further south than Ohio until I was about 20 years old. As a kid I didn't know I was a carrier of Southern culture in Pittsburgh. My parents were not born in the South. You would have to go all the way back to my grandfathers, both of whom were born in the South. But indirect exposure to that core culture generated by the African background is enough to stamp us. It's what we all share. Knowing the deep structures of African-American culture can tell you more about people than knowing the part of the country that they come from.

ROWELL: Your work obviously indicates that you have studied different literary traditions. In fact, you talked about those traditions earlier in this interview. In terms of what you have set for yourself as a writer, as an artist, how do you view yourself in relation to other American writers, specifically African-American and European-American writers?

WIDEMAN: I like the idea of a writing community. And I'd like to feel myself a part of one. I'd like to feel that we are all in the same ballgame. I like that sense of respect, mutual respect, that you get when you go to the playground. When you go to the playground to play basketball there are no referees. And the game can't be played unless there is a certain degree of mutual respect and understanding about the rules. And I think it would be wonderful if we had that kind of community and that kind of mutual respect and understanding in this country, rather than cutthroat, commercialized competition and competitiveness. If the rewards were more evenly distributed, if we weren't all fighting the blockbuster syndrome, in which a piece of writing either goes to the top or gets no attention at all. If we had more good bookstores. If the literary establishment had a wider sense of what's valuable. If there weren't so many goddamned unexamined assumptions about what's good. If we taught writing and language more rationally, more humanely in schools, maybe this ideal sense of a literary heritage and a literary community would be a reality. Of course it isn't, and I guess I'm simply describing what it might be at its best and what I'd like to relate to and feel myself part of.

ROWELL: Obviously European-American musicians have learned a whole lot from African-American music. You can say that they've been to school in African-American music. Do you find anything in African-American literary tradition that European-American writers can benefit from? Have you seen evidence of their using the tradition? If I wanted to load the case, I would say that, obviously, Mark Twain learned something from the slave narrative. It is obvious too the Tennessee Williams and William Faulkner were aware of the poetic beauty of African-American speech. Faulkner apparently knew the African-American folk-sermon.

WIDEMAN: I think your examples are well-chosen. You can't really separate the strands out very easily. And what's incumbent upon critics and writers and all of us is to understand the interpenetration that's always existed from the very beginning. The tension that existed between the literate and oral traditions is epitomized always in the black tradition. And all writers learned from that. It is no coincidence that some of the earliest appearances of Afro-American dialect or vernacular occurred in eighteenth-century American drama, that from the very beginning our fellow Americans, European-Americans, were listening to what we said and how we said it, and it entered into their artistic creations at the very moment those artistic creations began. And that's just a kind of a simplified identifiable influence. You begin there and it just proliferates. You can't scratch very deeply below the surface before you discover evidence of cross-cultural borrowing, revision, etc. All American art has these kinds of multicultural strands, these layered influences that you can identify and point to, and then if you want to go further then that, the unconscious life of the arts which of course is very important, the unconscious life any American has as part of its armature, as part of its furniture, the sense of a captive population, of oppression, of invisible people and people who were forced into a certain caste. The American imagination, in its subconscious and unconscious, is permeated by the facts of our history, the facts of our lives. So you can't talk about Americans and not talk about Afro-Americans.

ROWELL: We—the *Callaloo* staff and I—are about to sponsor a symposium (November 8–11, 1989) which I'm calling "Economic Censorship and Canon Formation." In that title I'm referring to poverty and, hence, black Americans' lack of autonomy. Will you talk about the implications of this problem for black writers in the United States, and about how economic censorship has played a major role in canon formation in and outside African-American literature?

WIDEMAN: You will have a lot to talk about in your seminar. And the problem breaks down into many, many different aspects. For instance, in my experience, as a kid, the people around me, the black people, were of crucial importance to my life. These were my folks, these were the people from whom I'd learned to walk, talk, dance, and love, and that was my world. So of course these people weren't marginal in any sense of the word. Nor were they a minority, because they were mostly the majority of people I saw. But from somebody else's point of view they were marginal, and we were a minority. And as I grew up that message was passed along to me: that my people were marginal and that I was a minority, and that we really didn't count for much. Part of the reason why that message penetrated my consciousness was because of economic conditions. It was clear that we didn't have power, we didn't have big houses, we didn't have fancy cars, and those that did were sort of criminal people, sort of outlaws, so this economic marginality reinforced my sense of the fact that we were outside the mainstream, and for the longest time to me that meant that maybe my life was not that important. And that maybe if you wanted to write about something important, surely you wouldn't pick these people off here in this little quadrant, in this little camp over here. You want to write about the big life, Europe, Sartre and all that shit. So at the very beginning there's an invidious effect, a drastic loss of selfworth caused by economic marginalization and class consciousness and all that. That's one answer.

And maybe at the other end is the materialism of this particular American experiment in civilization. It's a society in which, black or white, what you possess, what you can show, what you can pile up, is an index to how important you are and how successful you are, and that materialism pervades every institution and every value, and it's a hell of a rock to get past, it's a hell of a hard nut to crack. It's almost impossible for a writer, and getting more and more difficult for any artist, to have a decent career in this country. And by decent career I mean not making a mint, but being able to support yourself with writing of quality. Once that impossibility happens—and it has happened, it's true today—then art begins to occupy less and less of a significant place in the society. And for the minority writer, the effects of that kind of economic exclusion are exacerbated because if only a few are going to be chosen, you know damn well we are going to be a very few of those few, if any. And if the literary society or the literary culture is going to be made up of people who are featured in *Time* magazine and featured in *USA Today* and who are profiled in *People* and stuff like that, then the chances for us to penetrate these upper levels are very, very small indeed. You get the sense among younger writers that if they don't get up to that level then they've failed, that their ticket to the lottery didn't come up. What's lost is the notion that art has something to do with honesty. It has something to do with self-expression, self-respect and inner satisfaction, it has something to do with fighting for a voice and achieving that voice and sharing it with a group of readers who care about what you do. Those values get lost in the shuffle.

Sherley Anne Williams (1944–)

Sherley Anne Williams was born August 25, 1944, in Bakersfield, California. The third of four daughters, Williams was born to parents who were agricultural laborers, working the cotton and fruit fields of California. Fesse Winson, her father, died of tuberculosis when Williams was eight. Eight years later with the death of her mother, Williams became the charge of her older sister, Ruise. With encouragement from her sister and high school teachers, Williams attended Fresno State, earning a bachelor's degree in history in 1966.

Not beginning to write for publication until after her graduation and continuing her education at Howard University, Williams' first published story "Tell Martha Not to Moan" appeared in the Massachusetts Review *in 1967 and was included in Toni Cade Bambara's anthology,* The Black Woman *(1970). The narrator of "Tell Martha Not to Moan" is a welfare recipient, unlucky in love, who speaks the Black English she is most comfortable with.*

Staying only a year at Howard, Williams worked as a community educator in Washington, D.C., from 1970 to 1972, before finishing her master's degree at Brown University where she also taught in the Black studies department for a year. The manuscript Give Birth to Brightness: A Thematic Study in Neo–Black Literature, *a comparative study of Baraka's* The Dutchman and the Slave, *James Baldwin's* Blues for Mister Charlie, *and Ernest Gaines'* Of Love and Dust, *was a product of the tutelage of Sterling Brown and her years at Howard and Brown and was published in 1972.*

Nineteen seventy-two also saw Williams' return to her California State University at Fresno as an associate professor of English. Continuing to research African American literature and history and to write, Williams taught at California State University at Fresno and then at the University of California at San Diego.

Williams was a professor at University of California at San Diego when The Peacock Poems *(1975), her first volume of poetry, was nominated for an American Book Award. Within the blues motif, Williams draws on childhood and her son, John Malcolm. The collection is grounded in the pain of the blues singer and the metaphor of the female peacock who is plain and silent, unlike her male counterpart. The Black woman, in the course of the collection, comes to "sing" her experiences as nurturer, sexual being, and whole woman. In "Drivin' Wheel," for example, Williams communicates with raw honesty the difficulty of meaningful communication between a man and the woman narrator. Gaps within and between lines capture the gaps between the totality of their thoughts and emotions and what they actually communicate as well as the barriers, both psychological and political, which keep them from connection. The intersection of gender roles and political belief are expressed both through fable and through the narrator's sad resignation. In "1 Poem   2 Voices   A Song," Williams* captures the power of music in language. She brings the blues to life through images and style, leaving the real power, however, in the observer's mind and reaction to the song.

Some One Sweet Angel Chile *(1982)*, Williams' second poetry collection, is both personal and historical, sharing the perspectives of women across history, including Bessie Smith, blues singer, and Hannah, a nineteenth-century northern Black woman who goes south to teach school. Williams' own childhood self is the focus of the third section. In "The Empress Brand Trim," a woman seizes and flaunts without shame the strength of her own sexuality. "I Want Aretha to Set This to Music" is a blues lyric, a woman's lonely lament with a repeated cry, "hear it?," demanding response. "you were never miss brown to me" highlights the community of strong women in Williams' own background. Strength is the theme that ties the three sections together.

Dessa Rose *(1986)*, Williams' first novel, established her reputation. An expansion of a short story, "Meditations on History," Dessa Rose foregrounds history and oral tradition. Two historically authentic situations from the center of the novel—an 1829 Kentucky slave uprising led by a pregnant Black woman and the history of a White woman who sheltered runaway slaves on her North Carolina farm. Angela Davis's essay "Reflection on the Black Woman's Role in the Community of Slaves" was Williams' first motivation and primary source for this historical perspective. Williams also researched Herbert Aptheker's American Negro Slave Revolts *(1943)*. The friendship that develops between Dessa, the woman leader of the slave revolt, and Miss Rufel, the North Carolina White woman, challenges stereotypes of Black women and southern White domesticity. The multiple perspectives in the story, including Dessa's personal narrative voice, her recounting of story for a White man, and the White man's interpretation of it, foreground the common process of slave narrative and emphasize the possibility that much of the "authentic" perspective was lost in the process. Dessa Rose is a real depiction of slavery from several angles with the perspective of a strong Black woman at its center.

Sherley Anne Williams is a talented multi-genre writer, excelling as a writer of short story, drama, literary criticism, poetry, and the novel. Combining Black oral tradition and Western literary forms and balancing the concerns of social class alongside race, Williams communicates the variety of Black women's experiences, including her own. She explores Black life in the context of Black communities and relationships, not primarily Black in relation to White.

Williams is currently a professor of African American literature at the University of California at San Diego.

R. Joyce Lausch

Drivin Wheel
myth story and life

> I want you to come on, baby,
> here's where you get
> yo steak, potatoes and tea.

first story

The darkened bedroom, the double bed,
the whispers of the city night,
against it her voice, husky, speaking
past the one soft light.

        I am   through you   wholly woman. You
        say I am cold   am hard   am vain. And
        I know I am fool and bitch. And black.
        Like my mother before me and my
        sisters around me. We share the same
        legacy   are women to the same
        degree.

And I ain't even touched what's between us.
A sullen, half tearful thought.
Others lay below the surface of her mind,
rushing, gone, finally caught.

             Not circumstance; history
        keeps us apart. I'm black. You black. And
        how have niggas proved they men? Fightin
        and fuckin as many women as
        they can. And even when you can do
        all the things a white man do you may
        leave fightin behind but fuckin stay
        the same.

             For us it's havin babies and how
        well we treats a man and how long we
        keep him. And how long don't really have
        that much to do with how well. I just
        can't be woman to yo kinda man.

second song

   my man is a fine fine man
   the superman of his time
       the black time   big time
   in a mild mannered disguise
   revealed only as needed:
       the heart steel   heart stone   heart
   and its erratic beating.
             Inner and outer
   rine and heart and running.

Running.   Hanging.   Caught by that powerful joint.
But my man can pull his ownself's coat
come at last to see that dick is just that same old rope.

Yeah.

A mild mannered.

disguise: laughing country boy astride
          a laughing goat.

first fable

We do not tell ourselves all the things we
know or admit, except perhaps in dreams,
oblique reminiscence, in sly yearnings, all
the people we feel ourselves to be.
Except
perhaps in dreams   the people we
feel . . .

Three. A prideful panther who
stalks a white wolf, a goatish rooster who was lured on
by a grey fox and a head, a body
and, lying to one side, a heart.
The head, the heart, the body had always
been apart. The rooster called
them Humpty Dumpty things and urged
the panther to attack. The rooster was accustomed
to command, ruling the panther through
words he had taught the panther to
talk; the words only said what he wanted
the panther to know. He would crow
or blow upon his horn
and the panther would forget
all the questions he had ever known.
And once in a while, just for show,
the rooster would allow the panther
to have his way.
Now, the panther thought it too good
a body to waste, too good a brain to be
forever cut from its source.
Let's put them together, man,
he called. You begin with the heart.
But the rooster
knew that rebuilt Humpty Dumpty men have a
way of taking worlds apart, have new ways of

putting them together again. He lived in the world
of already was and it was all he ever wanted
to know.
                    Not so fast, the rooster cried.
But the panther had already touched the heart
and for the first time he realized
that Not So Fast meant Don't Go. He
could feel something new, something
indefinable pumping through him. The rooster's
words failed to sway him. The rooster, angered,
sank his talons into the panther's shoulder.
The panther turned and, instinctively,
went upside the rooster's head.
The rooster absorbed the first blow;
he was smart enough to know it was coming.
But the second was a surprise, beyond
his comprehension. He died with the question
Why   still unspoken.

                         . . . in glancing asides
we are seen, or in oblique reference. And still
left to answer is how we can pull it all together.

fourth life

They lie up in the darkened bedroom
and listen to the whispers of the city night;
each waits upon the other
to make the final move to the light
or toward the door. They have met
history; it is them. Definitions from the past
—she bitch and fool; he
nigga and therefore jive—seem the last

reality. And, once admitted, mark
the past as them. They are defeated.
She moves to strap on her shoes.

          You said,

                              and he speaks.
voice and hand holding her seated,
his head moving into the circle of light.

               You said we are more than the
          sum jiveness, the total foolishness.

You are wholly woman, right? Isn't that
more than bitch?

What do it matter, huh?

His hand holds her, holds the wary
wearied question. He speaks, slow:

Matter a helluva lot. We can't
get together less we stay together.

His lips brush her cheek; she buries

her fingers in his bush. The question will always
be present, so too the doubt it leaves in its wake.
To question and to answer is to confront. To deal.
History is them; it is also theirs to make.

1 Poem   2 Voices   A Song

FOR SHERMAN MCKINNEY

his body be arched when he play—like Miles—
only leaner   legs stiff
hips forward   and the top
of him   seem like it drift
his shoulders be hunched   protectin his gift

He put horn to lip and blew
that he had been through the world
blew against rock beats in clear
soprano tones.

he said it be like a battle—
him and that horn—be pain.
I know it like an hour with the blues
blowin help him call his name.

Now,
fragmented by the
tripping lights, the band
is a fusilade
a kaleidoscope

of sound. And then. Then
he moves, arrogant,
slouching across the
stage and his raucous
voice reverberates
in the hand-held mike
rapping, calling out
a litany of
heroes: Lummumba.
Mao.   Martin.   Malcolm.
Jackson. . . . yeahyeah. Yeah!

he speak when he see a brother
wave   say   what it is, dude?
they nod   say   you got it   man.
he smile cause he know it be true.

this sherman song   the one he blew:
        I been through the world
        (hear it.   hear it.   hear it   feeeeel
        it.   Blow!)
                    but only
        the best has touched me.

The Empress Brand Trim

ruby reminisces:

                    He was still Uncle
                    Jack to me the first
                    time they come to New
                    York and I knew she
                    was special cause he
                    didn't run his women
                    in front of us kids.
                    She rehearsed that first
                    record right there in
                    our parlor and I
                    stayed out of school to
                    watch her. I didn't know
                    it then but my whole
                    life changed. She didn't look
                    no older than me—

bigger and darker,
sure, but no older,
and I was a teen-
ager—a pretty
girl; I sang; I danced.

She carried herself
like she didn't know she
was ugly, almost
like she didn't know she
was black—buying dark
glasses in Chicago
cause fans recognized
her in the streets or
that night in Concord—
she chased the *Klan* out
from behind our tent;
said she hadn't never
heard of such shit.

She loved womens and
mens. The womens was
on the Q.T., of
course, cause Jack wouldn't play
that. But wasn't nothing
he could do about
the mens. She'd go to
a party and pick out the
finest brown. "I'mo
give *you* some Empress
Brand trim. Tonight you
pay homage to the
Pussy Blues made."
And they always did.

I Want Aretha to Set
This to Music:

I surprise girlhood
in your face; I know
my own, have been a
prisoner of my own

dark skin and fleshy
lips, walked that same high
butty strut despite
all this; rejected
the mask my mother
wore so stolidly
through womanhood and
wear it now myself.

I see the mask, sense
the girl and the woman
you became, wonder
if mask and woman
are one, if pain is
the sum of all your
knowing, victim the
only game you learned.

Old and in pain and
bearing up bearing up
and hurt and age These
are the signs of our
womanhood but I'll
make book Bessie did
more than just endure.

hear it?

                              hear it?

Oh I'm lonesome now
        but I won't be lonesome long
Say I'm lonely now
        but I don't need to be lonesome long
You know it take a man wid some style and passion
        to make a single woman sing these lonely songs

                one-sided bed Blues

Never had a man talk to me
        to say the things he say
Never had a man talk like this, honey,
        say the things you say.

Man talk so strong
     till I can't tell Night from Day.

His voice be low words come slow
     and he be movin all the while
His voice be low words come slow
     and he be movin, Lawd! all the while.
I'm his radio and he sho
     know how to tune my dial.

My bed one-sided from me
     sleepin alone all the time
My bed *wop*-sided from me
     sleepin alone so much of the time
And the fact that it empty
     show how this man is messin wid my mind.

what's out there knockin
   Is what the world
   don't get enough of

you were never miss brown to me

I

We were not raised to look in
a grown person's mouth when they
spoke or to say ma'am or sir—
only the last was sometimes
thought fast even rude but daddy
dismissed this: it was yea and
nay in the Bible and this
was a New Day.   He liked even
less honorary forms—Uncle,
Aunt, Big Mamma—mamma to
who? he would ask.   Grown
people were Mr. and Miss
admitting one child in many
to the privilege of their
given names.   We were raised to
make "Miss Daisy" an emblem

of kinship and of love; you
were never Miss Brown to me.

II

I call you Miss in tribute
to the women of that time,
the mothers of friends, the friends
of my mother, mamma
herself, women of mystery
and wonder who traveled some
to get to that Project.   In the
places of their childhoods, the
troubles they had getting grown,
the tales of men they told among
themselves as we sat unnoted
at their feet we saw some image
of a past and future self.
The world had loved them even
less than their men but this did
not keep them from scheming on
its favor. It was this that
made them grown and drew from our
unmannerly mouths "Miss"
before their first names.

I call
you Daisy and acknowledge
my place in this line: I am
the women of my childhood
just as I was the women of
my youth, one with these women
of silence who lived on the
cusp of their time and knew it;
who taught what it is to be grown.

August Wilson (1945–)

The son of a White father and an African American mother, August Wilson grew up in Pittsburgh, quit high school, and began to write. Early in his career, he saw his plays produced in St. Paul and Minneapolis; then, in 1984, his drama Ma Rainey's Black Bottom (1984) opened on Broadway. The director was Lloyd Richards, who continued to collaborate with Wilson. Productions of subsequent plays earned Wilson many fellowships and awards. Joe Turner's Come and Gone (1986), Two Trains Running (1990), and Seven Guitars (1996) earned critical acclaim. Fences (1986) and The Piano Lesson (1987) each garnered a Pulitzer Prize.

Wilson's plays typically focus on the plight of poor African Americans trapped in northern cities (especially Pittsburgh) during earlier decades of this century. He repeatedly stresses a debt to blues singers and musicians (notably Bessie Smith)—an influence especially evident in Ma Rainey's Black Bottom and Joe Turner's Come and Gone. The central character in Joe Turner's lands in Pittsburgh after spending years on a chain gang. Fashioned by a Black ancestor, the piano in The Piano Lesson is an emblem of the struggle for African American memory, identity, and success. Set during the 1960s, Two Trains Running features African American habitues of a diner who experience tension and solidarity in their efforts to cope. In Seven Guitars Wilson again spotlights the urban poor.

Wilson's language is invariably intense and poetic. His characters' lines often seem fresh, yet inevitable, like the notes in Charlie Parker solo. As his characters wrestle with racism, poverty, gender division, and despair, their struggle seems metaphysical as well.

"The Ground on Which I Stand" (1998) is a recent, provocative, and controversial speech by Wilson.

The protagonist of Fences is Troy Maxson (played on Broadway by James Earl Jones), an eloquent and sometimes charming figure proud of his years playing baseball in the Negro Leagues. Now, retired from the sport, he is impoverished and troubled. His relationships to his son and wife are severely strained; and, for all his bravado and apparent grandeur, he seems pathetic and his life a failure.

Partly because, in Maxson, Wilson created a character as arresting as virtually any figure in twentieth-century American drama, Wilson is the most important American playwright of his generation.

Keith D. Miller

Fences

Fences opened on April 30, 1985, at the Yale Repertory Theatre in New Haven, Connecticut, with the following cast:

Troy Maxson	*James Earl Jones*
Jim Bono	*Ray Aranha*
Rose	*Mary Alice*
Lyons	*Charles Brown*
Gabriel	*Russell Costen*
Cory	*Courtney B. Vance*
Raynell	*Cristal Coleman* and *LaJara Henderson* at alternate performances

Director: Lloyd Richards
Set Design: James D. Sandefur
Costume Design: Candice Donnelly
Light Design: Danianne Mizzy
Music Director: Dwight Andrews
Production Stage Manager: Joel Grynheim
Stage Manager: Terrence J. Witter
Castings: Meg Simon/ Fran Kumin

Fences was initially presented as a staged reading at the Eugene O'Neill Theater Center's 1983 National Playwrights Conference.

Characters

Troy Maxson	
Jim Bono	Troy's *friend*
Rose	Troy's *wife*
Lyons	Troy's *oldest son by previous marriage*
Gabriel	Troy's *brother*
Cory	Troy and Rose's *son*
Raynell	Troy's *daughter*

Setting

The setting is the yard that fronts the only entrance to the Maxson household, an ancient two-story brick house set back off a small alley in a big-city neighborhood. The entrance to the house is gained by two or three steps leading to a wooden porch badly in need of paint.

A relatively recent addition to the house and running its full width, the porch lacks congruence. It is a sturdy porch with a flat roof. One or two chairs of dubious value sit at one end where the kitchen window opens onto the porch. An old-fashioned icebox stands silent guard at the opposite end.

The yard is a small dirt yard, partially fenced, except for the last scene, with a wooden sawhorse, a pile of lumber, and other fence-building equipment set off to the side. Opposite is a tree from which hangs a ball made of rags. A baseball bat leans against the tree. Two oil drums serve as garbage receptacles and sit near the house at right.

The Play

Near the turn of the century, the destitute of Europe sprang on the city with tenacious claws and an honest and solid dream. The city devoured them. They swelled its belly until it burst into a thousand furnaces and sewing machines, a thousand butcher shops and bakers' ovens, a thousand churches and banks and hospitals and funeral parlors. The city grew. It nourished itself and offered each man a partnership limited only by his talent, his guile, and his willingness and capacity for hard work. For the immigrants of Europe, a dream dared and won true.

The descendants of African slaves were offered no such welcome or participation. They came from places called the Carolinas and the Virginias, Georgia, Alabama, Mississippi, and Tennessee. They came strong, eager, searching. The city rejected them and they fled and settled along the riverbanks and under bridges in shallow, ramshackle houses made of sticks and tar paper. They collected rags and wood. They sold the use of their muscles and their bodies. They cleaned houses and washed clothes, they shined shoes, and in quiet desperation and vengeful pride, they stole, and lived in pursuit of their own dream: that they could breathe free, finally, and stand to meet life with the force of dignity and whatever eloquence the heart could call upon.

Act One

SCENE ONE

It is 1957. TROY and BONO enter the yard engaged in conversation. TROY is fifty-three years old, a large man with thick heavy hands; it is this largeness that he strives to fill out and make an accommodation with. Together with his blackness, his largeness informs his sensibilities and the choices he has made in his life. Of the two men, BONO is obviously the follower. His commitment to their friendship of thirty-odd years is rooted in his admiration of TROY's honesty, capacity for hard work, and his strength, which BONO seeks to emulate.

It is Friday night, payday, and the one night of the week the two men engage in a ritual of talk and drink. TROY is usually the most talkative and at times he can be crude and almost vulgar, though he is capable of rising to profound heights of expression. The men carry lunch buckets and wear or carry burlap aprons and are dressed in clothes suitable to their jobs as garbage collectors.

BONO: Troy, you ought to stop that lying!

TROY: I ain't lying! The nigger had a watermelon this big. (*TROY indicates with his hands.*)

Talking about . . . "What watermelon, Mr. Rand?" I liked to fell out! "What watermelon, Mr. Rand?" . . . And it sitting there big as life.

BONO: What did Mr. Rand say?

TROY: Ain't said nothing. Figure if the nigger too dumb to know he carrying a watermelon, he wasn't gonna get much sense out of him. Trying to hide that great big old watermelon under his coat. Afraid to let the white man see him carry it home.

BONO: I'm like you . . . I ain't got no time for them kind of people.

TROY: Now what he look like getting mad 'cause he see the man from the union talking to Mr. Rand?

BONO: Well, as long as you got your complaint filed, they can't fire you. That's what one of them white fellows tell me.

TROY: I ain't worried about them firing me. They gonna fire me 'cause I asked a question? That's all I did. I went to Mr. Rand and asked him why. "Why you got the white mens driving and the colored lifting?" Told him, "What's the matter, don't I count? You think only white fellows got sense enough to drive a truck. That ain't no paper job! Hell, anybody can drive a truck. How come you got all whites driving and the colored lifting?" He told me take it to the union. Well, hell, that's what I done! Now they wanna come up with this pack of lies.

BONO: I told Brownie if the man come and ask him any questions . . . just tell the truth! It ain't nothing but something they done trumped up on you 'cause you filed a complaint on them.

TROY: Brownie don't understand nothing. All I want them to do is change the job description. Give everybody a chance to drive the truck. Brownie can't see that. He ain't got that much sense.

BONO: How you figure he making out with that gal be up at Taylor's all the time . . . that Alberta gal?

TROY: Same as you and me. Getting just as much as we is. Which is to say nothing.

BONO: It is, huh? I figure you doing a little better than me . . . and I ain't saying what I'm doing.

TROY: Aw, nigger, look here . . . I know you. If you had got anywhere near that gal, twenty minutes later you gonna be looking to tell somebody. And the first one you gonna tell . . . that you gonna want to brag to . . . is gonna be me.

BONO: I ain't saying that. I see where you be eyeing her.

TROY: I eye all the women. I don't miss nothing. Don't never let nobody tell you Troy Maxson don't eye the women.

BONO: You been doing more than eyeing her. You done bought her a drink or two.

TROY: Hell yeah, I bought her a drink! What that mean? I bought you one, too. What that mean 'cause I buy her a drink? I'm just being polite.

BONO: It's all right to buy her one drink. That's what you call being polite. But when you wanna be buying two or three . . . that's what you call eyeing her.

TROY: Look here, as long as you known me . . . you ever known me to chase after women?

BONO: Hell yeah! Long as I done known you. You forgetting I knew you when.

TROY: Naw, I'm talking about since I been married to Rose?

BONO: Not since you been married to Rose. That's the truth. I can say that.

TROY: All right then! Case closed.

BONO: I see you be walking up around Alberta's house.

TROY: What you watching where I'm walking for? I ain't watching after you.

BONO: I seen you walking around there more than once.

TROY: Hell, you liable to see me walking anywhere! That don't mean nothing 'cause you see me walking around there.

BONO: Where she come from anyway? She just kinda showed up one day.

TROY: Tallahassee. You can look at her and tell she one of them Florida gals. They got some big healthy women down there. Grow them right up out the ground. Got a little bit of Indian in her. Most of them niggers down in Florida got some Indian in them.

BONO: I don't know about that Indian part. But she damn sure big and healthy. Woman wear some big stockings. Got them great big old legs and hips as wide as the Mississippi River.

TROY: Legs don't mean nothing. You don't do nothing but push them out of the way. But them hips cushion the ride.

BONO: Troy, you ain't got no sense.

TROY: It's the truth! Like you riding on Goodyears!

(ROSE *enters from the house. She is ten years younger than* TROY, *and her devotion to him stems from her recognition of the possibilities of her life without him: a succession of abusive men and their babies, a life of partying and running the streets, the church, or aloneness with its attendant pain and frustration. She recognizes* TROY'*s spirit as a fine and illuminating one and she either ignores or forgives his faults, only some of which she recognizes. Though she doesn't drink, her presence is an integral part of the Friday-night rituals. She alternates between the porch and the kitchen, where supper preparations are under way.*)

ROSE: What you all out here getting into?

TROY: What you worried about what we getting into for? This is men talk, woman.

ROSE: What I care what you are talking about? Bono, you gonna stay for supper?

BONO: I thank you, Rose. But Lucille say she cooking up a pot of pig feet.

TROY: Pig feet! Hell, I'm going home with you! Might even stay the night if you got some pig feet. You got something in there to top them pig feet, Rose?

ROSE: I'm cooking up some chicken. I got some chicken and collard greens.

TROY: Well, go on back in the house and let me and Bono finish what we was talking about. This is men talk. I got some talk for you later. You know what kind of talk I mean. You go on and powder it up.

ROSE: Troy Maxson, don't you start that now!

TROY: (*Puts his arm around* ROSE.) Aw, woman . . . come here. Look here, Bono . . . when I met this woman . . . I got out that place, say, "Hitch up my pony, saddle up my mare . . . there's a woman out there for me somewhere." I looked here. Looked there. Saw Rose and latched on to her. I latched on to her and told her—I'm gonna tell you the truth—I told her, "Baby, I don't wanna marry, I just wanna be your man." Rose told me . . . Tell him what you told me, Rose.

ROSE: I told him if he wasn't the marrying kind, then move out the way so the marrying kind could find me.

TROY: That's what she told me. "Nigger, you in my way. You blocking the view! Move out the way so I can find me a husband." I thought it over two or three days. Come back—

ROSE: (*Interrupting.*) Ain't no two or three days nothing. You was back the same night.

TROY: Come back, told her, "Okay, baby . . . but I'm gonna buy me a banty rooster and put him out there in the backyard, and when he see a stranger come, he'll flap his wings and crow . . ." Look here, Bono, I could watch the front door by myself; it was that backdoor I was worried about.

ROSE: Troy, you ought not talk like that. Troy ain't doing nothing but telling a lie.

TROY: Only thing is, when we first got married—forget the rooster—we ain't had no yard!

BONO: I hear you tell it. Me and Lucille was staying down there on Logan Street. Had two rooms with the outhouse in the back. I ain't mind the outhouse none. But when that goddamn wind blow through there in the winter, that's what I'm talking about! To this day I wonder why in the hell I ever stayed down there for six long years. But see, I didn't know I could do better. I thought only white folks had inside toilets and things.

ROSE: There's a lot of people don't know they can do better than they doing now. That's just something you got to learn. A lot of folks still shop at Bella's.

TROY: Ain't nothing wrong with shopping at Bella's. She got fresh food.

ROSE: I ain't said nothing about if she got fresh food. I'm talking about what she charge. She charge ten cents more than the A&P.

TROY: The A&P ain't never done nothing for me. I spends my money where I'm treated right. I go down to Bella, say, "I need a loaf of bread, I'll pay you on Friday," she give it to me. What sense that make when I got money to go and spend it somewhere else and ignore the person who done right by me? That ain't in the Bible.

ROSE: We ain't talking about what's in the Bible. What sense it make to shop there when she overcharge?

TROY: You shop where you want to. I'll do my shopping where the people been good to me.

ROSE: Well, I don't think it's right for her to overcharge. That's all I was saying.

BONO: Look here . . . I got to get on. Lucille going be raising all kind of hell.

TROY: Where you going, nigger? We ain't finished this pint. Come on, finish this pint.

BONO: Well, hell, I am . . . if you ever turn the bottle loose.

TROY: (*Hands him the bottle.*) The only thing I say about the A&P is I'm glad Cory got that job down there. Help him take care of his school clothes and things. Gabe done moved out and things getting tight around here. He got that job. He can start to look out for himself.

ROSE: Cory done went and got recruited by a college football team.

TROY: I told that boy about that football stuff. The white man ain't gonna let him get nowhere with that football. I told him when he first come to me with it. Now you come telling me he done went and got more tied up in it. He need to go and get recruited in how to fix cars or something where he can make a living.

ROSE: He ain't talking about making no living playing football. It's just something the boys in school do. They gonna send a recruiter by to talk to you. He'll tell you he ain't talking about making no living playing football. It's a honor to be recruited.

TROY: It ain't gonna get him nowhere. Bono'll tell you that.

BONO: If he be like you in the sports, he's gonna be all right. Ain't but two men ever played baseball as good as you. That's Babe Ruth and Josh Gibson. Thems the only two men hit a baseball farther than you.

TROY: What it ever get me? Ain't got a pot to piss in or a window to throw it out of.

ROSE: Times have changed since you was playing baseball, Troy. That was before the war. Times have changed a lot since then.

TROY: It's the same now as it was then. The white man ain't gonna let him get nowhere with that football.

ROSE: They got lots of colored boys playing ball now. Baseball and football.

BONO: You right about that, Rose. Times have changed. Troy just come along too early.

TROY: There ought not never have been no time called too early! Now, you take that fellow . . . What's that fellow they had playing left field for the Yankees back then? You know who I'm talking about, Bono. Used to play left field for the Yankees?

ROSE: Selkirk?

TROY: Selkirk! That's it! Man batting .269, understand? .269. What kind of sense that make? I was hitting .432 with thirty-seven home runs! Man batting .269 and playing left field for the Yankees! I saw Josh Gibson's daughter yesterday. She walking around with raggedy shoes on her feet. Now I bet you Selkirk's daughter ain't walking around with raggedy shoes. I bet you that!

ROSE: They got a lot of colored baseball players now. Jackie Robinson was the first. Folks had to wait for Jackie Robinson.

TROY: I done seen a hundred niggers play baseball better than Jackie Robinson. Hell, I know some teams Jackie Robinson couldn't even make! What you talking about Jackie Robinson. Jackie Robinson wasn't nobody. I'm talking about if you could play ball, then they ought to have let you play. Don't care what color you were. Come telling me I come along too early. If you could play, then they ought to have let you play. (TROY *takes a long drink from the bottle.*)

ROSE: You gonna drink yourself to death. You don't need to be drinking like that.

TROY: Death ain't nothing. I done seen him, done wrestled with him. You can't tell me nothing about Death. Death ain't nothing but a fastball on the outside corner. And you know what I'll do to that! Look here, Bono . . . am I lying? You get one of them fastballs about waist high over the outside corner of the plate where you can get the meat of the bat on it . . . and good God! You can kiss it good-bye. Now, am I lying?

BONO: Naw, you telling the truth there. I seen you do it.

TROY: If I'm lying, that's 450 feet worth of lying!

(*Pause.*)

That's all death is to me. A fastball on the outside corner.

ROSE: I don't know why you want to get on talking about Death.

TROY: Ain't nothing wrong with talking about Death. That's part of life. Everybody gonna die. You gonna die, I'm gonna die, Bono's gonna die. Hell, we all gonna die.

ROSE: But you ain't got to talk about it. I don't like to talk about it.

TROY: You the one brought it up. Me and Bono was talking about baseball . . . you tell me I'm gonna drink myself to Death. Ain't that right, Bono? You know I don't drink this but one night out of the week. That's Friday night. I'm gonna drink just enough to where I can handle it. Then I cuts it loose. I leave it alone. So don't you worry about me drinking myself to death. 'Cause I ain't worried about Death. I done seen him. I done wrestled with him. Look here, Bono . . . I looked up one day and Death was marching straight at me. Like Soldiers on Parade! The Army of Death marching straight at me. The middle of July, 1941. It got real cold just like to be winter. It seem like Death himself reached out and touched me on the shoulder. He touch me just like I touch you. I got cold as ice and Death standing there grinning at me.

ROSE: Troy, why don't you hush that talk.

TROY: I say, "What you want, Mr. Death? You be wanting me? You done brought your army to be getting me?" I looked him dead in the eye. I wasn't fearing nothing. I was ready to tangle. Just like I'm ready to tangle now. The Bible say be ever vigilant. That's why I don't get but so drunk. I got to keep watch.

ROSE: Troy was right down there in Mercy Hospital. You remember he had pneumonia? Laying there with a fever talking plumb out of his head.

TROY: Death, he ain't said nothing. He just stared at me. He had a thousand men to do his bidding and he wasn't going to get a thousand and one. Not then! Hell, I wasn't but thirty-seven years old.

(*Pause.*)

Death standing there staring at me . . . carrying that sickle in his hand. Finally he say, "You want bound over for another year?" See, just like that . . . "You want bound over for another year?" I told him, "Bound over hell! Let's settle this now!" It seem like he kinda fell back when I said that, and all the cold went out of me. I reached out and grabbed that sickle and threw it just as far as I could throw it . . . and me and him commenced to wrestling. We wrestled for three days and three nights. I can't say where I found the strength from. Every time it seemed like he was gonna get the best of me, I'd reach way down deep inside myself and find the strength to do him one better.

ROSE: Every time Troy tell that story he find different ways to tell it. Different things to make up about it.

TROY: I ain't making up nothing. I'm telling you the facts of what happened. I wrestled with Death for three days and three nights and I'm standing here to tell you about it.

(Pause.)

All right. At the end of the third night we done weakened each other to where both of us could hardly move. Death stood up, throwed on his robe . . . had him a white robe with a hood on it. He threwed on that robe and went off to look for his sickle. Say, "I'll be back." Just like that. "I'll be back." I told him, say, "You gonna have to find me!" I wasn't no fool. I wasn't going looking for him. Death ain't nothing to play with. And I know he's gonna get me. I know I got to join his army . . . his camp followers. But as long as I keep my strength and see him coming, as long as I keep up my vigilance, he's gonna have to fight to get me. I ain't going easy.

BONO: Well, look here, since you got to keep up your vigilance . . . let me have the bottle.

TROY: Aw hell, I shouldn't have told you that part. I should have left out that part. That vigilance part.

ROSE: Troy be talking that stuff and half the time don't even know what he be talking about.

TROY: Bono know me better than that. He know I don't talk nothing lessen I got a good handle on it as the truth. Ain't that right, Bono?

BONO: That's right. I know you. I know you got some Uncle Remus in your blood. You got more stories than the devil got sinners.

TROY: Aw hell, I done seen him too! Done talked with the devil.

ROSE: Troy, don't nobody wanna be hearing all that stuff. (LYONS *enters the yard from the street. Thirty-four years old,* TROY's *son by a previous marriage, he sports a neatly trimmed goatee, sport coat, white shirt, tieless and buttoned at the collar. Though he fancies himself a musician, he is more caught up in the rituals and "idea" of being a musician than in the actual practice of the music. The music offers him a "life-style and stance from which he can ignore the sociological context of his existence and celebrate the music's ability to provide a maintenance of equilibrium despite the precarious circumstances of day-to-day living." He has come to borrow money from* TROY, *and while he knows he will be successful, he is uncertain as to what extent his life-style will be held up to scrutiny and ridicule.*)

LYONS: Hey, Pop.

TROY: What you come Hey, Popping me for?

LYONS: How you doing, Rose?

(He kisses her.)

Mr. Bono, how you doing?

BONO: Hey, Lyons, how you been?

TROY: He must have been doing all right. I ain't seen him around here last week.

ROSE: Troy, leave the boy alone. He come by to see you and you wanna start all that nonsense.

TROY: I ain't bothering Lyons.

(*Offers him the bottle.*)

Here . . . get you a drink. We got an understanding. I know why he come by to see me and he know I know.

LYONS: Come on, Pop . . . I just stopped by to say hi, see how you was doing.

TROY: You ain't stopped by yesterday.

ROSE: You gonna stay for supper, Lyons? I got some chicken cooking in the oven.

LYONS: No, Rose . . . thanks. I was just in the neighborhood and thought I'd stop by for a minute.

TROY: You was in the neighborhood all right, nigger. You telling the truth there. You was in the neighborhood 'cause it's my payday.

LYONS: Well, hell, since you mentioned it, let me have ten dollars.

TROY: I'll be damned! I'll die and go to hell and play blackjack with the devil before I give you ten dollars.

BONO: That's what I wanna know about . . . this devil you done seen.

LYONS: What? Pop done seen the devil? You too much, Pops.

TROY: Yeah, I done seen him. Talked to him too!

ROSE: You ain't seen no devil. I done told you that man ain't had nothing to do with the devil. Anything you can't understand, you want to call it the devil.

TROY: Look here, Bono . . . I went down to see Hertzberger about some furniture. Got three rooms for two-ninety-eight. That what it say on the radio. Three rooms . . . two-ninety-eight. Even made up a little song about it. Go down there . . . man tell me I can't get no credit. I'm working everyday and can't get no credit. What to do? I got an empty house with some raggedy furniture in it. Cory ain't got no bed. He's sleeping on a pile of rags on the floor. Working every day and can't get no credit. Come back home—Rose'll tell you—madder than hell. Sit down, try to figure what I'm gonna do. Come a knock on the door. Ain't been living here but three days. Who know I'm here? Open the door . . . devil standing there bigger than life. White fellow . . . got on good clothes and everything. Standing there with a clipboard in his hand. I ain't had to say nothing. First words come out of his mouth was "I understand you need some furniture and can't get no credit." I liked to fell over. He say I'll give you all the credit you want, but you got to pay the interest on it. I told him give me three rooms worth and charge whatever you want. Next day a truck pulled up here and two men unloaded them three rooms. Man what drove the truck give me a book. Say send ten dollars a month to the address in the book and everything will be all right. Say if I miss a payment the devil was coming back and it'll be hell to pay. That was fifteen years ago. To this day, the first of the month I send my ten dollars, Rose'll tell you.

ROSE: Troy lying.

TROY: I ain't never seen that man since. Now, you tell me who else that could have been but the devil? I ain't sold my soul or nothing, you understand. I wouldn't have truck with the devil about nothing like that. He ain't mentioned nothing like that. I just got my furniture and pays my ten dollars the first of the month just like clockwork.

BONO: How long you say you been paying this ten dollars a month?

TROY: Fifteen years!

BONO: Hell, ain't you finished paying for it yet? How much the man done charged you.

TROY: Aw hell, I done paid for it. I done paid for it ten times over! The fact is I'm scared to stop paying it.

ROSE: Troy lying. We got that furniture from Mr. Glickman. He ain't paying no ten dollars a month to nobody.

TROY: Aw hell, woman. Bono know I ain't that big a fool.

LYONS: I was just getting ready to say . . . I know where there's a bridge for sale.

TROY: Look here, I'll tell you this . . . it don't matter to me if he was the devil. It don't matter if the devil give credit. Somebody has got to give it.

ROSE: It ought to matter. You going around talking about having truck with the devil . . . God's the one you gonna have to answer to. He's the one gonna be at the judgment.

LYONS: Yeah, well, look here, Pop . . . let me have that ten dollars. I'll give it back to you. Bonnie got a job working at the hospital.

TROY: What I tell you, Bono? The only time I see this nigger is when he wants something. That's the only time I see him.

LYONS: Come on, Pop, Mr. Bono don't want to hear all that. Let me have the ten dollars. I told you Bonnie working.

TROY: What that mean to me? "Bonnie working." I don't care if she working. Go ask her for the ten dollars if she working. Talking about Bonnie working . . . why ain't you working?

LYONS: Aw, Pop, you know I can't find no decent job. Where am I gonna get a job at? You know I can't get no job.

TROY: I told you I know some people down there. I can get you on the rubbish if you want to work. I told you that the last time you came by here asking me for something.

LYONS: Naw, Pop . . . thanks. That ain't for me. I don't wanna be carrying no-body's rubbish. I don't wanna be punching nobody's time clock.

TROY: What's the matter? You too good to carry rubbish? Where you think that ten dollars you talking about come from? I'm just supposed to haul people's rubbish and give my money to you 'cause you too lazy to work. You too lazy to work and wanna know why you ain't got what I got.

ROSE: What hospital Bonnie working at? Mercy?

LYONS: She's down at Passavant working in the laundry.

TROY: Ain't got nothing as it is. I give you that ten dollars and I got to eat beans the rest of the week. Naw, you ain't getting no ten dollars here.

LYONS: You ain't got to be eating no beans. I don't know why you wanna say that.

TROY: I ain't got no extra money. Gabe done moved over to Miss Pearl's paying her the rent and things done got tight around here. I can't afford to be giving you every payday.

LYONS: I ain't asked you to give me nothing. I asked you to loan me ten dollars. I know you got ten dollars.

TROY: Yeah, I got it. Why you think I got it? 'Cause I don't throw my money away out there in the streets. You living the fast life, wanna be a musician, running around in them clubs and things . . . then you learn to take care of yourself. You ain't gonna find me going and asking nobody for nothing. I done spent too many years without.

LYONS: You and me is two different people, Pop.

TROY: I done learned my mistake and learned to do what's right by it. You still trying to get something for nothing. Life don't owe you nothing. You owe it to yourself. Ask Bono. He'll tell you I'm right.

LYONS: You got your way of dealing with the world . . . I got mine. The only thing that matters to me is the music.

TROY: Hell, I can see that! It don't matter how you gonna eat, where your next dollar is coming from. You telling the truth there.

LYONS: I know I got to eat. But I got to live too. I need something that gonna help me to get out of the bed in the morning. Make me feel like I belong in the world. I don't bother nobody. I just stay with my music 'cause that's the only way I can find to live in the world. Otherwise there ain't no telling what I might do. Now I don't come by here criticizing you and the way you live. I just come by to ask you for ten dollars. I don't wanna hear all that about how I live.

TROY: Boy, your mama did a hell of a job raising you.

LYONS: You can't change me, Pop. I'm thirty-four years old.

ROSE: Let the boy have ten dollars, Troy.

TROY: (*To* LYONS.) What the hell you looking at me for? I ain't got no ten dollars. You know what I do with my money.

    (*To* ROSE.)

    Give him ten dollars if you want him to have it.

ROSE: I will. Just as soon as you turn it loose.

TROY: (*Handing* ROSE *the money.*) There it is. Seventy-six dollars and forty-two cents. You see this, Bono? Now, I ain't gonna get but six of that back.

ROSE: You ought to stop telling that lie. Here, Lyons. (*She hands him the money.*)

LYONS: Thanks, Rose. Look . . . I got to run. I'll see you later.

TROY: Wait a minute. You gonna say, "Thanks, Rose," and ain't gonna look to see where she got that ten dollars from?

LYONS: I know she got it from you, Pop. Thanks. I'll give it back to you.

TROY: There he go telling another lie. Time I see that ten dollars he'll be owed me thirty more.

LYONS: See you, Mr. Bono. Thanks, Pop. I'll see you again.

    (LYONS *exits the yard.*)

TROY: I don't know why he don't go and get him a decent job and take care of that women he got.

BONO: He'll be all right, Troy. The boy's still young.

TROY: The boy is thirty-four years old.

ROSE: Let's not get off into all that.

BONO: Look here . . . I got to be going. I got to be getting on. Lucille gonna be waiting.

TROY: (*Puts his arm around* ROSE.) See this woman, Bono? I love this woman. I love this woman so much it hurts. I love her so much . . . I done run out of ways to love her. So I got to go back to basics. Don't you come by my house Monday morning talking about time to go to work . . . 'cause I'm still gonna be stroking!

ROSE: Troy! Stop it now!

BONO: I ain't paying him no mind, Rose. That ain't nothing but gin-talk. Go on, Troy. I'll see you Monday.

TROY: Don't you come by my house, nigger! I done told you what I'm gonna be doing.

(*The lights go down to black.*)

Act One

SCENE TWO

The lights came up on ROSE *hanging up clothes. She hums and sings softly to herself.* TROY *enters from the house. It is the following morning.*

ROSE: 'Morning. You ready for breakfast? I can fix it soon as I finish hanging up these clothes?

TROY: I got the coffee on. That'll be all right. I'll just drink some of that this morning.

ROSE: That 642 hit yesterday. That's the second time this month. Miss Pearl hit for a dollar . . . seem like those that need the least always get lucky. Poor folks can't get nothing.

TROY: Them numbers don't know nobody. I don't know why you fool with them. You and Lyons both.

ROSE: It's something to do.

TROY: You ain't doing nothing but throwing your money away.

ROSE: Troy, you know I don't play foolishly. I just play a nickel here and a nickel there.

TROY: That's two nickels you done thrown away.

ROSE: Now I hit sometimes . . . that makes up for it. It always comes in handy when I do hit. I don't hear you complaining then.

TROY: I ain't complaining. I just say it's foolish. Trying to guess out of six hundred ways which way the number gonna come. If I had all the money niggers throw away on numbers for one week—just one week—I'd be a rich man.

ROSE: Well, you wishing and calling it foolish ain't gonna stop folks from playing numbers. That's one thing for sure. Besides, some good things come from playing numbers. Look where Pope done bought him that restaurant off of numbers.

TROY: I can't stand niggers like that. Man ain't had two dimes to rub together. He walking around with his shoes all run over bumming money for cigarettes. All right. Got lucky there and hit the numbers—

ROSE: Troy, I know all about it.

TROY: Had good sense, I'll say that for him. He ain't throwed his money away. I seen niggers hit the numbers and go through two thousand dollars in four days. Man brought him that restaurant down there, fixed it up real nice, and then didn't want nobody to come in it! A Negro go in there and can't get no kind of service. I seen a white fellow come in there and order a bowl of stew. Pope picked all the meat out the pot for him. Man ain't had nothing but a bowl of meat! Negro come behind him and ain't got nothing but the potatoes and carrots. Talking about what numbers do for people you picked a wrong example. Ain't done nothing but make him a worse fool than he was before.

(Pause.)

Where's Cory? Cory in the house? *(Calls.)* Cory?

ROSE: He gone out.

TROY: Out, huh? He gone out 'cause he know I want him to help me with this fence. I know how he is. That boy afraid of work. He ain't done a lick of work in his life.

ROSE: He had to go to football practice. Coach wanted them to get in a little extra practice before the season start.

TROY: I got his practice . . . running out of here before he get his chores done.

ROSE: Troy, what is wrong with you this morning? Don't nothing set right with you. Go on back in there and go to bed . . . get up on the other side.

TROY: Why something got to be wrong with me? I ain't said nothing wrong with me.

ROSE: You got something to say about everything. First it's the numbers, then it's the way the man runs his restaurant, then you done got on Cory. What's it gonna be next? Take a look up there and see if the weather suits you . . . or is it gonna be how you gonna put up the fence with the clothes hanging in the yard.

TROY: You hit the nail on the head there! Damn if that wasn't what I was thinking.

ROSE: I know you like I know the back of my hand. Go on in there and get you some coffee . . . see if that straighten you up. 'Cause you ain't right this morning.

(GABRIEL is heard singing off stage. TROY's brother, he is seven years younger than TROY. Injured in World War II, he has a metal plate in his head. He carries an old trumpet tied around his waist and believes with every fiber of his being that he is the Archangel Gabriel. He carries a chip basket with an assortment of discarded fruits and vegetables he has picked up in the strip district and which he attempts to sell.)

GABRIEL: (*Singing.*)
>   Yes mam I got plums
>   You ask me how I sell them

TROY: (*Hearing* GABRIEL.) Just what I need this morning.

GABRIEL: (*Singing.*)
>   Oh ten cents apiece
>   Three for a quarter
>   Come and buy now
>   'Cause I'm here today
>   And tomorrow I'll be gone
>   (GABRIEL *enters.*)

GABRIEL: Hey, Rose!

ROSE: How you doing, Gabe?

GABRIEL: There's Troy. Hey, Troy!

TROY: Hey, Gabe

ROSE: (*To* GABRIEL.) What you got there?

GABRIEL: You know what I got, Rose. I got fruits and vegetables.

ROSE: (*Looking in basket.*) Where's all these plums you talking about?

GABRIEL: I ain't got no plums today, Rose. I was just singing that. Have some to-morrow. Put me in a big order for plums. Have enough plums tomorrow for St. Peter and everybody.

>   (*To* ROSE.)
>   Troy's mad at me.

TROY: I ain't mad at you. What I got to be mad at you about? You ain't done nothing to me.

GABRIEL: I just moved over to Miss Pearl's to keep out from in your way. I ain't mean no harm by it.

TROY: Who said anything about that? I ain't said nothing about that.

GABRIEL: You ain't mad at me, is you?

TROY: Naw, I ain't mad at you Gabe. If I was mad at you I'd tell you about it.

GABRIEL: Got me two rooms. In the basement. Got my own door too. Wanna see my key?

>   (*He holds up a key.*)
>   That's my own key! Ain't nobody else got a key like that.
>   That's my key! My two rooms!

TROY: Well, that's good, Gabe. You got your own key . . . that's good.

ROSE: You hungry, Gabe? I was just fixing to cook Troy his breakfast.

GABRIEL: You got some biscuits? I'll take some biscuits. Did you know when I was in heaven, every morning me and St. Peter would sit down by the gate and eat some big fat biscuits. Oh, yeah! We had us a good time. We'd eat us them biscuits and then St. Peter would go off to sleep and tell me to wake him up when it's time to open the gates for the judgment.

ROSE: Well, come on . . . I'll make up a batch of biscuits.

(ROSE *exits into the house.*)

GABRIEL: Troy, St. Peter got your name in the book. I seen it. It say, "Troy Maxson." I say, "I know him! He got the same name like what I got. That's my brother!"

TROY: How many times you gonna tell me that, Gabe? He got your name in there too?

GABRIEL: Ain't got my name in the book. Don't have to have my name. I done died and went to heaven. He got your name, though. One morning St. Peter was looking at his book, marking it up for the judgment, and he let me see your name. Got it in there under M. Got Rose's name too. I ain't seen it like I seen yours, but I know it's in there. Great big book. Got everybody's name what was ever been born. That's what he told me. But I seen your name. Seen it with my own eyes.

TROY: Go on in the house there. Rose going to fix you something to eat.

GABRIEL: Oh, I ain't hungry. I done had breakfast with Aunt Jemina. She come by and cooked me up a whole mess of flapjacks. Remember how we used to eat them flapjacks?

TROY: Yeah, I remember. Go on in the house and get you something to eat now.

GABRIEL: I got to go sell my plums. I done sold some tomatoes. Got me two quarters. Wanna see?

(He shows TROY *his quarters.*)

I'm gonna save them and buy me a new horn so St. Peter can hear me when it's time to open the gates.

(GABRIEL *stops suddenly.* Listens.)

Hear that? That's the hellhounds. I got to chase them out of here. Go on get out of here! Get out!

(GABRIEL *exits singing.*)

Better get ready for the judgment
Better get ready for the judgment
My lord is coming down
Better get ready for the judgment
Better get ready for the judgment morning
Better get ready for the judgment
My god is coming down

(ROSE *enters from the house.*)

TROY: He gone off somewhere.

ROSE: He ain't eating right. Miss Pearl say she can't get him to eat nothing.

TROY: What you want me to do about it, Rose? I done did everything I can for the man. I can't make him get well. Man got half his head blown away . . . what you expect?

ROSE: Seem like something ought to be done to help him.

TROY: Man don't bother nobody. He just mixed up from that metal plate he got in his head. Ain't no sense for him to go back into the hospital.

ROSE: Least he be eating right. They can help him take care of himself.

TROY: Don't nobody wanna be locked up, Rose. What you wanna lock him up for? Man go over there and fight the war, get half his head blown off, and they give him a lousy three thousand dollars. And I had to swoop down on that.

ROSE: Is you fixing to go into that again?

TROY: That's the only way I got a roof over my head . . . 'cause of that metal plate.

ROSE: Ain't no sense you blaming yourself for nothing. You done what was right by him. Can't nobody say you ain't done what was right by him. Look how long you took care of him . . . till he wanted to have his own place and moved over there with Miss Pearl.

TROY: That ain't what I'm saying, woman! I'm just stating the facts. If my brother didn't have that metal plate in his head, I wouldn't have a pot to piss in or a window to throw it out of. And I'm fifty-three years old. Now you try and understand that!

(*TROY gets up from the porch and starts to exit the yard.*)

ROSE: Where you going off to? You been running out of here every Saturday for weeks. I thought you was gonna work on this fence?

TROY: I'm gonna walk down to Taylor's. Listen to the ballgame. I'll be back in a bit. I'll work on it when I get back.

(*TROY exits the yard. The lights go to black.*)

Act One

SCENE THREE

The lights come up on the yard. It is four hours later. ROSE is taking down the clothes from the line. CORY enters carrying his football equipment.

ROSE: Your daddy liked to had a fit with you running out of here this morning without doing your chores.

CORY: I told you I had to go to practice.

ROSE: He say you were supposed to help him with this fence.

CORY: He always say that every Saturday and then he don't never do nothing. Did you tell him about the recruiter?

ROSE: Yeah, I told him.

CORY: What he say?

ROSE: He ain't said nothing too much. You go in there and get started on your chores before he gets back. Go on and scrub down them steps before he gets back here hollering and carrying on.

CORY: I'm hungry. What you got to eat, Mama?

ROSE: Go on and get started on your chores. I got some meat loaf in there. Go on and make you a sandwich . . . and don't leave no mess in there.

(*CORY exits into the house. ROSE continues to take down the clothes. TROY enters the yard and sneaks up and grabs her from behind.*)

Troy! Go on, now. You liked to scared me to death. What was the score of the game? Lucille had me on the phone and I couldn't keep up with it.

TROY: What I care about the game? Come here, woman. (*He tries to kiss her.*)

ROSE: I thought you went down Taylor's to listen to the game. Go on, Troy! You supposed to be putting up this fence.

TROY: (*Attempting to kiss her again.*) I'll put it up when I finish with what is at hand.

ROSE: Go on, Troy. I ain't studying you.

TROY: (*Chasing after her.*) I'm studying you . . . fixing to do my homework!

ROSE: Troy, you better leave me alone.

TROY: Where's Cory? That boy brought his butt home yet?

ROSE: He's in the house doing his chores.

TROY: (*Calling.*) Cory! Get your butt out here, boy!

(ROSE *exits into the house with the laundry.* TROY *goes over to the pile of wood, picks up a board, and starts sawing.* CORY *enters from the house.*)

TROY: You just now coming in here from leaving this morning?

CORY: Yeah, I had to go to football practice.

TROY: Yeah, what? What kind of talk is that?

CORY: Yessir.

TROY: I ain't but two seconds off you noway. The garbage sitting in there overflowing . . . you ain't done none of your chores . . . and you come in here talking about, "Yeah."

CORY: I was just getting ready to do my chores now.

TROY: Your first chore is to help me with this fence on Saturday. Everything else come after that. Now get that saw and cut them boards.

(CORY *takes the saw and begins cutting the boards.* TROY *continues working. There is a long pause.*)

CORY: The Pirates done won five in a row.

TROY: I ain't thinking about the Pirates. Got an all-white team. Got that boy . . . that Puerto Rican boy . . . Clemente. Don't even half-play him. That boy could be something if they give him a chance. Play him one day and sit him on the bench the next.

CORY: He gets a lot of chances to play.

TROY: I'm talking about playing regular. Playing every day so you can get your timing. That's what I'm talking about.

CORY: They got some white guys on the team that don't play every day. You can't play everybody at the same time.

TROY: If they got a white fellow sitting on the bench, you can bet your last dollar he can't play! The colored guy got to be twice as good before he get on the team. That's why I don't want you to get all tied up in them sports. Man on the team and what it get him? They got colored on the team and don't play them. Same as not having them. All them teams the same.

CORY: The Braves got Hank Aaron and Wes Covington. Hank Aaron hit two home runs today. That makes forty-three.

TROY: Hank Aaron ain't nobody. That's the way you supposed to do. That's how you supposed to play the game. Ain't nothing to it. It's just a matter of timing . . . getting the right follow-through. Hell, I can hit forty-three home runs right now!

CORY: Not off no major-league pitching you couldn't.

TROY: We had better pitching in the Negro League. I hit seven home runs off of Satchel Paige. You can't get no better than that!

CORY: Sandy Koufax. He's leading the league in strikeouts.

TROY: I ain't thinking of no Sandy Koufax nothing.

CORY: You got Warren Spahn and Lew Burdette. I bet you couldn't hit no home runs off of Warren Spahn.

TROY: I'm through with it now. You go on and get them boards cut.

> (*Pause.*)
>
> Your mama tells me you got recruited by a college football team? Is that right?

CORY: Yeah. Coach Zellman say the recruiter gonna be coming by to talk to you. Get you to sign the permission papers.

TROY: I thought you supposed to be working down there at the A&P. Ain't you supposed to be working down there after school?

CORY: Mr. Stawicki say he gonna hold my job for me until after the football season. Say starting next week I can work weekends.

TROY: I thought we had an understanding about this football stuff? You suppose to keep up with your chores and hold that job down at the A&P. Ain't been around here all day on a Saturday. Ain't none of your chores done . . . and now you telling me you done quit your job.

CORY: I'm gonna be working weekends.

TROY: You damn right you are! And ain't no need for nobody coming around here to talk to me about signing nothing.

CORY: Hey, Pop, you can't do that. He's coming all the way from North Carolina.

TROY: I don't care where he coming from. The white man ain't gonna let you get nowhere with that football no way. You go and get your book-learning where you can learn to do something besides carrying people's garbage.

CORY: I get good grades, Pop. That's why the recruiter wants to talk with you. You got to keep up your grades to get recruited. This way I'll be going to college. I'll get a chance—

TROY: You gonna get your butt down there to the A&P and get your job back.

CORY: Mr. Stawicki done already hired somebody else 'cause I told him I was playing football.

TROY: You a bigger fool than I thought . . . to let somebody take away your job so you can play some football. That's downright foolishness. Where you gonna get your money to take out your girlfriend and whatnot? What kind of foolishness is that to let somebody take away your job?

CORY: I'm still gonna be working weekends.

TROY: Naw . . . naw. You getting your butt out of here and finding you another job.

CORY: Come on, Pop! I got to practice. I can't work after school and play football too. Coach Zellman say the team needs me—say—

TROY: I don't care what nobody else say. I'm the boss . . . you understand? I'm the boss around here. I do the only saying what counts.

CORY: Come on, Pop!

TROY: I asked you. Did you understand?

CORY: Yeah . . . Yessir.

TROY: You go down there to that A&P and see if you can get your job back. If you can't do both, then you quit the football team. You've got to take the crooked with the straights.

CORY: Yessir.

> (*Pause.*)
>
> Can I ask you a question?

TROY: What the hell you wanna ask me? Mr. Stawicki the one you got the questions for.

CORY: How come you ain't never liked me?

TROY: Liked you? Who the hell say I got to like you? What law is there say I got to like you? Wanna stand up in my face and ask a damn fool-ass question like that. Talking about liking somebody. Come here, boy, when I talk to you.

> (*CORY comes over to where TROY is working. He stands slouched over and TROY shoves him on his shoulder.*) Straighten up, goddammit! I asked you a question. What law is there say I got to like you?

CORY: None.

TROY: Well, all right then! Don't you eat every day?

> (Pause.)
>
> Answer me when I talk to you! Don't you eat every day?

CORY: Yeah.

TROY: Nigger, as long as you in my house you put that sir on the end of it when you talk to me!

CORY: Yes . . . sir.

TROY: You eat every day. Got a roof over your head. Got clothes on your back.

CORY: Yessir.

TROY: Why you think that is?

CORY: 'Cause of you.

TROY: Aw, hell I know it's 'cause of me . . . but why do you think that is?

CORY: (*Hesitant.*) 'Cause you like me.

TROY: Like you? I go out of here every morning, bust my butt, putting up with them crackers' every day . . . 'cause I like you? You about the biggest fool I ever saw.

> (Pause.)

It's my job. It's my responsibility! You understand that? A man got to take care of his family. You live in my house, sleep you behind on my bedclothes, fill you belly up with my food . . . 'cause you my son. You my flesh and blood. Not 'cause I like you! 'Cause I owe a responsibility to you! 'Cause it's my duty to take care of you. Let's get this straight right here—before it go along any further—I ain't got to like you. Mr. Rand don't give me my money come payday 'cause he likes me. He gives me 'cause he owe me. I done give you everything I had to give you. I gave you your life! Me and your mama worked that out between us. And liking your black ass wasn't part of the bargain. Don't you try and go through life worrying about if somebody like you or not. You best be making sure they doing right by you. You understand what I'm saying, boy?

CORY: Yessir.

TROY: Then get the hell out of my face, and get on down to that A&P.

(ROSE *has been standing behind the screen door for much of the scene. She enters as* CORY *exits.*)

ROSE: Why don't you let the boy go ahead and play football, Troy? Ain't no harm in that. He's just trying to be like you with the sports.

TROY: I don't want him to be like me! I want him to move as far away from my life as he can get. You the only decent thing that ever happened to me. I wish him that. But I don't wish him a thing else from my life. I decided seventeen years ago that boy wasn't getting involved in no sports. Not after what they did to me in the sports.

ROSE: Troy, why don't you admit you was too old to play in the major leagues? For once . . . why don't you admit that?

TROY: What do you mean too old? Don't come telling me I was too old. I just wasn't the right color. Hell, I'm fifty-three years old and I can do better than Selkirk's .269 right now!

ROSE: How was you gonna play ball when you was over forty? Sometimes I can't get no sense out of you.

TROY: I got good sense, woman. I got sense enough not to let my boy get hurt over playing no sports. You been mothering that boy too much. Worried about if people like him.

ROSE: Everything that boy do he do for you. He wants you to say "Good job, son." That's all.

TROY: Rose, I ain't got time for that. He's alive. He's healthy. He's got to make his own way. I made mine. Ain't nobody gonna hold his hand when he get out there in that world.

ROSE: Times have changed from when you was young, Troy. People change. The world's changing around you and you can't even see it.

TROY: (*Slow, methodical.*) Woman . . . I do the best I can do. I come in here every Friday. I carry a sack of potatoes and a bucket of lard. You all line up at the door with your hands out. I give you the lint from my pockets. I give you my sweat and my blood. I ain't got no tears. I done spent them. We go upstairs in that room at night and I fall down on you and try to blast a hole into forever. I get up Monday morning . . . find my lunch on the table. I go out. Make my way. Find my strength to carry me through to the next Friday.

(*Pause.*)

That's all I got, Rose. That's all I got to give. I can't give nothing else.

(TROY *exits into the house. The lights go down to black.*)

Act One

SCENE FOUR

It is Friday, two weeks later. CORY *enters from the house carrying his football equipment. The phone rings.*

CORY: (*Calling.*) I got it!

(*He answers the phone and stands in the screendoor talking.*)

Hello? Hey, Jesse. Naw . . . I was just leaving now.

ROSE: (*Calling from inside the house.*) Cory!

CORY: I told you man, them spikes is all tore up. You can use them if you want but they ain't no good. Earl got some spikes.

ROSE: (*Calling.*) Cory!

CORY: Size nine, I think.

(*Calling to* ROSE.)

Mam? I'm talking to Jesse.

(*Into phone.*)

When she say that? Aw, you lying, man. I'm gonna tell her you said that.

ROSE: (*Calling.*) Cory, don't you go nowhere!

CORY: I got to go to the game, Ma!

(*Into the phone.*)

Yeah, hey look, I'll talk to you later. Yeah, I'll meet you over Earl's house.

(*He hangs up the phone and calls to* ROSE.)

Bye, Ma!

(ROSE *enters from the house.*)

ROSE: Cory, where you going off too? You got all that stuff pulled out and thrown all over your room.

CORY: I was looking for my spikes. Jesse wanted to borrow my spikes.

ROSE: Get up there and get that cleaned up before your daddy gets back in here.

CORY: I got to go. I'll clean it up when I get back.

(CORY *exits.*)

ROSE: That's all he need to do is see that room all messed up.

(ROSE *exits into the house as* TROY *and* BONO *enter the yard.* TROY *is dressed in clothes other than his work clothes.*)

BONO: He told him the same thing he told you. Take it to the union.

TROY: Brownie ain't got that much sense. Man wasn't thinking about nothing. He wait until I confront them on it, then he wanna come crying seniority.
(*Calls.*)
Hey, Rose!

BONO: I wish I could have seen Mr. Rand's face when he told you.

TROY: He couldn't get it out of his mouth! Liked to bit his tongue! When they called me down there to the commissioner's office, he thought they was gonna fire me . . . like everybody else.

BONO: I didn't think they was gonna fire you . . . I thought they was gonna put you on the warning paper.

TROY: Hey, Rose!
(*To* BONO.)
Yeah . . . Mr. Rand like to bit his tongue.
(TROY *breaks the seal on the bottle, takes a drink, and hands it to* BONO.)
Hey, Rose!

ROSE: (*Entering from the house.*) Hush all that hollering man! I know you out here. What they say down there at the commissioner's office?

TROY: You supposed to come when I call you, woman. Bono'll tell you that.
(*To* BONO.)
Don't Lucille come when you call her?

ROSE: Man, hush your mouth. I ain't no dog . . . talk about come when you call me.

TROY: (*Puts his arm around* ROSE.) You hear this, Bono? I had me an old dog used to get uppity like that. You say, comere, Blue . . . and he just lay there and look at you. End up getting a stick and chasing him away trying to make him come.

ROSE: I ain't studying you and your dog. I remember you used to sing that old song.

TROY: (*He sings.*)
I had a dog his name was Blue
You know Blue was mighty true
You know Blue was a good old dog
Blue treed a possum in a hollow log.

ROSE: Don't nobody wanna hear you sing that old song. Used to have Cory running around here singing that song.

BONO: Hell, I remember that myself.

TROY: That was my daddy's song. My daddy made up that song.

ROSE: I don't care who made it up. Don't nobody wanna hear you sing it.

TROY: (*Makes a song like calling a dog.*) Come here, woman.

ROSE: You come in here carrying on, I reckon they ain't fired you. What they say down there at the commissioner's office?

TROY: Look here, Rose . . . Mr. Rand called me into his office today when I got back from talking to them people down there. It come from up top . . . he called me in and told me they was making me a driver.

ROSE: Troy, you kidding!

TROY: No I ain't. Ask Bono.

ROSE: Well, that's great, Troy. Now you don't have to hassle them people no more.

TROY: Brownie got mad when he heard about . . . run to Mr. Rand talking about he got seniority. Tell her what Mr. Rand told him, Bono.

BONO: Told him take it to the union . . . same as he told Troy.

(LYONS *enters from the street.*)

TROY: Aw hell, I wasn't looking to see you today. I thought you was in jail. Got it all over the front page of the *Courier* about them raiding Sefus' place . . . where you be hanging out with all them thugs.

LYONS: Hey, Pop . . . that ain't got nothing to do with me. I don't go down there gambling. I go down there to sit in with the band. I ain't got nothing to do with the gambling part. They got some good music down there.

TROY: They got some rogues . . . is what they got.

LYONS: How you been, Mr. Bono? Hi, Rose.

BONO: I see where you playing down at the Crawford Grill tonight.

ROSE: How come you ain't brought Bonnie like I told you. You should have brought Bonnie with you, she ain't been over in a month of Sundays.

LYONS: I was just in the neighborhood . . . thought I'd stop by.

TROY: Here he come with that I-was-in-the-neighborhood stuff.

BONO: Your daddy got a promotion on the rubbish. He's gonna be the first colored driver. Ain't got to do nothing but sit up there and read the paper like them white fellows.

LYONS: Hey, Pop . . . if you knew how to read you'd be all right.

TROY: What you care if I can read or not? I read about all them thugs you be hanging out with. I read about them going to jail. I read that.

BONO: Naw . . . naw . . . you mean if the nigger knew how to *drive* he'd be all right. Been fighting with them people about driving and ain't even got a license. Mr. Rand know you ain't got no driver's license?

TROY: Driving ain't nothing. All you do is point the truck where you want it to go and keep from hitting the rest of them cars and things out there. Driving ain't nothing.

BONO: Do Mr. Rand know you ain't got no driver's license? That's what I'm talking about. I ain't asked if driving was easy. I asked if Mr. Rand know you ain't got no driver's license.

TROY: He ain't got to know. The man ain't got to know my business.

LYONS: (*Going into his pocket.*) Say, look here, Pop . . .

TROY: I knew it was coming. Didn't I tell you, Bono? I know what kind of "Look here, Pop" that was. The nigger fixing to ask me for some money. It's Friday night. It's my payday. All them rogues down there on the avenue—the ones that ain't in jail—and Lyons is hopping in his shoes to get down there with them.

LYONS: See, Pop . . . if you give somebody else a chance to talk sometime, you'd see that I was fixing to pay you back your ten dollars like I told you. Here . . . told you I'd pay you when Bonnie got paid.

TROY: Naw . . . you go ahead and keep that ten dollars. Put it in the bank. The next time you feel like you wanna come by here and ask me for something, you go on down there and get that.

LYONS: Here's your ten dollars, Pop. I told you I don't want you to give me nothing. I just wanted to borrow ten dollars.

TROY: Naw . . . you go on and keep that for the next time you want to ask me.

LYONS: Come on, Pop . . . here go your ten dollars.

ROSE: Why don't you go on and let the boy pay you back, Troy?

LYONS: Here you go, Rose. If you don't take it I'm gonna have to hear about it for the next six months.

(*He hands her the money.*)

ROSE: You can hand yours over here too, Troy.

TROY: You see this, Bono. You see how they do me.

BONO: Yeah, Lucille do me the same way.

(GABRIEL *is heard singing off stage. He enters.*)

GABRIEL: Hey! Hey! There's Troy's boy!

LYONS: How you doing, Uncle Gabe?

GABRIEL: Lyons . . . the King of the Jungle! Rose . . . hey, Rose. Got a flower for you.
(*He takes a rose from his pocket.*)
Picked it myself. That's the same rose like what you is!

ROSE: That's right nice of you, Gabe.

LYONS: What you been doing, Uncle Gabe?

GABRIEL: Oh, I been chasing hellhounds and waiting on the time to tell St. Peter to open the gates.

LYONS: You been chasing hellhounds, huh? Well, you doing the right thing, Uncle Gabe. Somebody got to chase them.

GABRIEL: Oh, yeah . . . I know it. The devil's strong. The devil ain't no pushover. Hellhounds snipping at everybody's heels. But I got my trumpet waiting on the judgment time.

LYONS: Waiting on the battle of Armageddon, huh?

GABRIEL: Ain't gonna be too much of a battle when God get to waving that judgment sword. But the peoples gonna have a hell of a time trying to get into heaven if them gates ain't open.

LYONS: (*Putting his arm around* GABRIEL.) You hear this, Pop. Uncle Gabe, you all right!

GABRIEL: (*Laughing with* LYONS.) Lyons! King of the Jungle.

ROSE: You gonna stay for supper, Gabe. Want me to fix you a plate?

GABRIEL: I'll take a sandwich, Rose. Don't want no plate. Just wanna eat with my hands. I'll take a sandwich.

ROSE: How about you, Lyons? You staying? Got some short ribs cooking.

LYONS: Naw, I won't eat nothing till after we finished playing.

> (*Pause.*)

> You ought to come down and listen to me play, Pop.

TROY: I don't like that Chinese music. All that noise.

ROSE: Go on in the house and wash up, Gabe . . . I'll fix you a sandwich.

GABRIEL: (*To* LYONS *as he exits.*) Troy's mad at me.

LYONS: What you mad at Uncle Gabe for, Pop.

ROSE: He thinks Troy's mad at him 'cause he moved over to Miss Pearl's.

TROY: I ain't mad at the man. He can live where he want to live at.

LYONS: What he move over there for? Miss Pearl don't like nobody.

ROSE: She don't mind him none. She treats him real nice. She just don't allow all that singing.

TROY: She don't mind that rent he be paying . . . that's what she don't mind.

ROSE: Troy, I ain't going through that with you no more. He's over there 'cause he want to have his own place. He can come and go as he please.

TROY: Hell, he could come and go as he please here. I wasn't stopping him. I ain't put no rules on him.

ROSE: It ain't the same thing, Troy. And you know it.

(GABRIEL *comes to the door.*)

> Now, that's the last I wanna hear about that. I don't wanna hear nothing else about Gabe and Miss Pearl. And next week . . .

GABRIEL: I'm ready for my sandwich, Rose.

ROSE: . . . when that recruiter come from that school, I want you to sign that paper and go on and let Cory play football. Then that'll be the last I have to hear about that.

TROY: (*To* ROSE *as she exits into the house.*) I ain't thinking about Cory nothing.

LYONS: What? Cory got recruited? What school he going to?

TROY: That boy walking around here smelling his piss, thinking he's grown. Thinking he's gonna do what he want irrespective of what I say. Look here, Bono . . . I left the commissioner's office and went down to the A&P—that boy ain't working down there. He lying to me all the time. Telling me he got his job back, telling me he working weekends, telling me he working after school. Mr. Stawicki tell me he ain't working down there at all!

LYONS: Cory just growing up. He's just busting at the seams trying to fill out your shoes.

TROY: I don't care what he's doing. When he get to the point where he wanna disobey me . . . then it's time for him to move on. Bono'll tell you that. I bet he ain't never disobeyed his daddy without paying the consequences.

BONO: I ain't never had a chance. My daddy came on through, but I ain't never knew him to see him . . . or what he had on his mind or where he went. Just moving on through. Searching for the New Land. That's what the old folks used to call it. See a fellow moving around from place to place, woman to woman, called it searching for the New Land. I can't say if he ever found it. I come along, didn't want no kids. Didn't know if I was gonna be in one place long enough to fix on them right as their daddy. I figured I was going searching too. As it turned out, I been hooked up with Lucille near about as long as your daddy been with Rose. Going on sixteen years.

TROY: Sometimes I wish I hadn't known my daddy. My daddy ain't cared nothing about no kids. A kid to him wasn't nothing. All he wanted was for you to learn how to walk so he could start you to working. When it come time for eating, he ate first. If there was anything left over, that's what you got. Man would sit down and eat two chickens and give you the wing.

LYONS: You ought to stop that, Pop. Everybody feed their kids. No matter how hard times is, everybody care about their kids. Make sure they have something to eat.

TROY: The only thing my daddy cared about was getting them bales of cotton in to Mr. Lubin. That's the only thing that mattered to him. Sometimes I used to wonder why he was living. Wonder why the devil hadn't come and got him. Get them bales in to Mr. Lubin and find out he owe him money . . . and don't do nothing but walk around cussing for the next two months. That was the worse time to cross his path. Seem like he was mad at the world and would strike out at anything underfoot.

LYONS: He should have just went on and left when he saw he couldn't get nowhere. That's what I would have done.

TROY: How he gonna leave with eleven kids? And where he gonna go? He ain't knew how to do nothing but farm. No, he was trapped, and I think he knew it. But I'll say this for him: he felt a responsibility toward us. Maybe he ain't treated us the way I felt he should have, but without that responsibility he could have walked off and left us, made his own way.

BONO: A lot of them did. Back in those days what you talking about, niggers used to travel all over. They get up one day and see where the day ain't sitting right with them and they walk out their front door and just take on down one road or another and keep on walking.

LYONS: There you go! That's what I'm talking about.

BONO: Ain't owned nothing but what was on their back, so you didn't have to worry about leaving nothing behind or carrying nothing with you for that matter. Just walk on till you come to something else. Ain't you never heard of nobody having the walking blues? Well, that's what you call it when you just take off like that.

TROY: My daddy ain't had them walking blues what you talking about. He stayed right there with his family. But he was just as evil as he could be. My mama couldn't stand him . . . couldn't stand that evilness. She run off when I was about eight. She sneaked off one night after he had gone to sleep. Told me she was coming back for me. I ain't never seen her no more. All his women run off and left him. He wasn't good for nobody. When my turn come to head out, I was fourteen and got to sniffing around Joe Canewell's daughter. Had us an old mule we called Greyboy. My daddy sent me out to do some plowing and I tied up Greyboy and went to fooling around with Joe Canewell's daughter. We done found us a nice little spot, got real cozy with each other. She about thirteen and we done figured we was grown anyway, so we down there enjoying ourselves . . . ain't thinking about nothing. We didn't know Greyboy had got loose and wandered back to the house and my daddy was looking for me. We down there by the creek enjoying ourselves when my daddy come up on us, surprised us. He had them leather straps off the mule and commenced to whupping me like there was no tomorrow. I jumped up, mad and embarrassed. I was scared of my daddy. When he commenced to whupping on me, quite naturally I run to get out of the way.

(*Pause.*)

Now I thought he was mad 'cause I ain't done my work. But I see where he was chasing me off so he could have the gal for himself. When I see what the matter of it was, I lost all fear of my daddy. Right there is where I become a man . . . at fourteen years of age.

(*Pause.*)

Now it was my turn to run him off. I picked up the same reins that he had used on me. I picked up them reins and commenced to whupping on him. The gal jumped up and run off, and when my daddy turned to face me, I could see why the devil had never come to get him: 'cause he was the devil himself. I don't know what happened. When I woke up I was laying right there by the creek and Blue—this old dog we had—was licking my face. I thought I was blind. I couldn't see nothing. Both my eyes were swollen shut. I layed there and cried. I didn't know what I was gonna do. The only thing I knew was the time had come for me to leave my daddy's house. And right there the world suddenly got big. And it was a long time before I could cut it down to where I could handle it. Part of that cutting down was when I got to the place where I could feel him kicking in my blood and knew that the only thing that separated us was the matter of a few years.

(GABRIEL *enters from the house with a sandwich.*)

LYONS: What you got there, Uncle Gabe?
GABRIEL: Got me a ham sandwich. Rose gave me a ham sandwich.
TROY: I don't know what happened to him. I done lost touch with everybody except Gabriel. But I hope he's dead. I hope he found some peace.
LYONS: That's a heavy story, Pop. I didn't know you left home when you was fourteen?

(*The telephone rings.*)

TROY: And didn't know nothing. The only part of the world I knew was the forty-two acres of Mr. Lubin's land. That's all I knew about life.

LYONS: Fourteen's kinda young to be out on your own. I don't even think I was ready to be out on my own at fourteen. I don't know what I would have done.

TROY: I got up from the creek and walked on down to Mobile. I was through with farming. Figured I could do better in the city. So I walked the two hundred miles to Mobile.

LYONS: Wait a minute . . . you ain't walked no two hundred miles, Pop. Ain't nobody gonna walk no two hundred miles. You talking about some walking there.

BONO: That's the only way you got anywhere back in them days.

LYONS: Shhh. Damn if I wouldn't have hitched a ride with somebody.

TROY: Who you gonna hitch it with? They ain't had no cars and things like they got now. We talking about 1918.

ROSE: (*Entering.*) What you all out here getting into?

TROY: (*To* ROSE.) I'm telling Lyons how good he got it. He don't know nothing about this I'm talking.

ROSE: Lyons that was Bonnie on the phone. She say you supposed to pick her up.

LYONS: Yeah, okay, Rose.

TROY: I walked on down to Mobile and hitched up with some of them fellows that was heading this way. Got up here and found out not only couldn't you get a job, you couldn't find no place to live. I thought I was in freedom. Shhh. Colored folks living down there on the riverbanks in whatever kind of shelter they could make for themselves. Right down there under the Brady Street Bridge. Living in shacks made of sticks an' tar paper. Messed around there and went from bad to worse. Started stealing. First it was food. Then I figured, hell, if I steal money I can buy me some food. Buy me some shoes, too. One thing led to another. Met your mama—I was young and anxious to be a man—met your mama and had you. What I do that for? Now I got to worry about feeding you and her. Got to steal three times as much. Went out one day looking for somebody to rob . . . That's what I was, a robber. I'll tell you the truth. I'm ashamed of it today. But it's the truth. Went to rob this fellow—pulled out my knife, and he pulled out a gun. Shot me in the chest. It felt just like somebody had taken a hot branding iron and laid it on me. When he shot me, I jumped at him with my knife. They tell me I killed him. They put me in the penitentiary and locked me up for fifteen years. That's where I met Bono. That's where I learned how to play baseball. Got out that place and your mama had taken you and went on to make life without me. Fifteen years was a long time for her to wait. But that fifteen years cured me of that robbing stuff. Rose'll tell you. She asked me when I met her if I had gotten all that foolishness out of my system. And I told her, "Baby, it's you and baseball all what count with me." You hear me, Bono? I meant it too. She say, "Which one comes first?" I told her, "Baby, there ain't no doubt it's baseball, but you stick and get old with me and we'll both outlive this baseball." Am I right, Rose? And it's true.

ROSE: Man, hush your mouth. You ain't said no such thing. Talking about, "Baby, you know you'll always be number one with me." That's what you was talking.

TROY: You hear that, Bono? That's why I love her.

BONO: Rose'll keep you straight. You get off the track, she'll straighten you up.

ROSE: Lyons, you better get on home and get Bonnie. She waiting on you.

LYONS: (*Getting up to go.*) Hey, Pop, why don't you come down to the Grill and hear me play?

TROY: I ain't going down there. I got to get up in the morning. I'm too old to be sitting around in them clubs.

LYONS: You ain't got to stay long.

TROY: Naw, I'm gonna get my supper and go on to bed.

LYONS: Well, I got to go. I'll see you again.

TROY: Don't you come around here on my payday!

ROSE: Pick up the phone and let somebody know you coming. And bring Bonnie with you. You know I'm always glad to see her.

LYONS: Yeah, I'll do that, Rose. You take care now. See you, Pop. See you, Mr. Bono. See you, Uncle Gabe.

GABRIEL: Lyons! King of the Jungle!

(*LYONS exits.*)

TROY: Is supper ready, woman? Me and you got some business to take care of. I'm gonna tear it up too!

ROSE: Troy, I done told you now!

TROY: (*Puts his arm around BONO.*) Aw hell, woman . . . this is Bono. Bono like family. I done known this nigger since . . . How long I done know you?

BONO: It's been a long time.

TROY: I done known this nigger since Skippy was a pup. Me and him done been through some times.

BONO: You sure right about that.

TROY: Hell, I done know him longer than I known you. And we still standing shoulder to shoulder. Hey, look here, Bono . . . a man can't ask for no more than that.
(*Drinks to him.*)
I love you, nigger.

BONO: Hell, I love you too, but I got to get home to see my woman. You got yours. I got to go get mine.
(*BONO starts to exit as CORY enters the yard dressed in his football uniform. He gives TROY a hard, uncompromising look.*)

CORY: What you do that for, Pop?
(*He throws his helmet down in the direction of TROY.*)

ROSE: What's the matter? Cory, what's the matter?

CORY: Papa done went up to the school and told Coach Zellman I can't play football no more. Wouldn't even let me play the game. Told him to tell the recruiter not to come.

ROSE: Troy—

TROY: What you Troying me for. Yeah, I did it. And the boy know why I did it.

CORY: Why you wanna do that to me? This the one chance I had.

ROSE: Ain't nothing wrong with Cory playing football, Troy.

TROY: The boy lied to me, Rose. I told the nigger if he wanna play football to keep up his chores and hold down that job at the A&P. That was the conditions. Stopped down there to see Mr. Stawicki—

CORY: I can't work after school during football season, Pop! I tried to tell you that Mr. Stawicki's holding my job for me. You don't ever want to listen to nobody. And then you wanna go and do this to me!

TROY: I ain't done nothing to you. You done it to yourself.

CORY: Just 'cause you didn't have a chance! You just scared I'm gonna be better than you, that's all.

TROY: Come here.

ROSE: Troy—

(CORY reluctantly crosses over to TROY.)

TROY: All right! See. You done made a mistake.

CORY: I didn't even do nothing!

TROY: I'm gonna tell you what your mistake was. See . . . you swung at the ball and didn't hit it. That's strike one. See, you in the batter's box now. You swung and you missed. That's strike one. Don't you strike out!

(Lights fade to black.)

Act Two

SCENE ONE

The following morning. CORY is at the tree hitting the ball with the bat. He tries to mimic TROY, but his swing is awkward, less sure. ROSE enters from the house.

ROSE: Cory, I want you to help me with this cupboard.

CORY: I ain't quitting the team. I don't care what Poppa say.

ROSE: I'll talk to him when he gets back. He had to go see about your Uncle Gabe. The police done arrested him. Say he was disturbing the peace. He'll be back directly. Come on in here and help me clean out the top of this cupboard.
  (CORY exits into the house. ROSE sees TROY and BONO coming down the alley.)
  Troy, what they say down there?

TROY: Ain't said nothing. I give them fifty dollars and they let him go. I'll talk to you about it. Where's Cory?

ROSE: He's in there helping me clean out these cupboards.

TROY: Tell him to get his butt out here.

(ROSE exits into the house. TROY and BONO go over to the pile of wood. BONO picks up the saw and begins sawing.)

TROY: All they want is the money. That makes six or seven times I done went down there and got him out. See me coming they stick out their hands.

BONO: Yeah, I know what you mean. That's all they care about is that money. They don't care about what's right.

(Pause.)

Nigger, why you got to go and get some hard wood? You ain't doing nothing but building a little old fence. Get you some soft pine wood. That's all you need.

TROY: I know what I'm doing. This is outside wood. You put pine wood inside the house. Pine wood is inside wood. This here is outside wood. Now you tell me where the fence is gonna be?

BONO: You don't need this wood. You can put it up with pine wood and it'll stand as long as you gonna be here looking at it.

TROY: How you know how long I'm gonna be here, nigger? Hell, I might just live forever. Live longer than old man Horsely.

BONO: That's what Magee used to say.

TROY: Magee was a damn fool. Now you tell me who you ever heard of gonna pull their own teeth with a pair of rusty pliers?

BONO: The old folks . . . my granddaddy used to pull his teeth with pliers. They ain't had no dentists for the colored folks back then.

TROY: Get clean pliers! You understand? Clean pliers! Sterilize them! Besides we ain't living back then. All Magee had to do was walk over to Doc Goldblums.

BONO: I see you and that Tallahassee gal—that Alberta—I see you all done got tight.

TROY: What you mean "got tight"?

BONO: I see where you be laughing and joking with her all the time.

TROY: I laughs and jokes with all of them, Bono. You know me.

BONO: That ain't the kind of laughing and joking I'm talking about.

(CORY enters from the house.)

CORY: How you doing, Mr. Bono?

BONO: How you doing, Cory?

TROY: Get that saw from Bono and cut some wood. He talking about the wood's too hard to cut. Stand back there, Jim, and let that young boy show you how it's done.

BONO: He's sure welcome to it.

(CORY takes the saw and begins to cut the wood.)

Look at that. Big old strong boy. Look like Joe Louis. Hell, I must be getting old the way I'm watching that boy whip through that wood.

CORY: I don't see why Mama want a fence around the yard noways.

TROY: Damn if I know either. What the hell she keeping out with it? She ain't got nothing nobody want.

BONO: Some people build fences to keep people out . . . and some people build fences to keep people in. Rose wants to hold on to you all. She loves you.

TROY: Hell, nigger, I don't need nobody to tell me my wife loves me. Cory, go on in the house and see if you can find that other saw.

CORY: Where's it at?

TROY: I said find it! Look for it till you find it.

(CORY *exits into the house.*)

What's that supposed to mean? Wanna keep us in?

BONO: Troy, I done known you seem like damn near all my life. You and Rose both. I done known both of you all for a long time. I remember when you met Rose. When you was hitting them baseballs out the park. A lot of them old gals was after you then. You had the pick of the litter. When you picked Rose, I was happy for you. That was the first time I knew you had any sense. I said, "My man Troy knows what he's doing; I'm gonna follow this nigger, he might take me somewhere." I been following you too. I done learned a whole heap of things about life watching you. I done learned how to tell where the shit lies, how to tell it from the alfalfa. You done learned me a lot of things. You showed me how to not make the same mistakes, to take life as it comes along and keep putting one foot in front of the other.

(*Pause.*)

Rose a good woman, Troy.

TROY: Hell, nigger, I know she a good woman. I been married to her for eighteen years. What you got on your mind, Bono?

BONO: I just say she a good woman. Just like I say anything. I ain't got to have nothing on my mind.

TROY: You just gonna say she a good woman and leave it hanging out there like that? Why you telling me she a good woman?

BONO: She loves you, Troy. Rose loves you.

TROY: You saying I don't measure up. That's what you trying to say. I don't measure up 'cause I'm seeing this other gal. I know what you trying to say.

BONO: I know what Rose means to you, Troy. I'm just trying to say I don't want to see you mess up.

TROY: Yeah, I appreciate that, Bono. If you was messing around on Lucille, I'd be telling you the same thing.

BONO: Well, that's all I got to say. I just say that because I love you both.

TROY: Hell, you know me . . . I wasn't out there looking for nothing. You can't find a better woman than Rose. I know that. But seems like this woman just stuck on to me where I can't shake her loose. I done wrestled with it, tried to throw her off me, but she just stuck tighter. Now she's stuck on for good.

BONO: You's in control . . . that's what you tell me all the time. You responsible for what you do.

TROY: I ain't ducking the responsibility of it. As long as it sets right in my heart, then I'm okay. 'Cause that's all I listen to. It'll tell me right from wrong every time. And I ain't talking about doing Rose no bad turn. I love Rose. She done carried me a long ways and I love and respect her for that.

BONO: I know you do. That's why I don't want to see you hurt her. But what you gonna do when she find out? What you got then? If you try and juggle both of them, sooner or later you gonna drop one of them. That's common sense.

TROY: Yeah, I hear what you saying, Bono. I been trying to figure a way to work it out.

BONO: Work it out right, Troy. I don't want to be getting all up between you and Rose's business, but work it so it come out right.

TROY: Aw hell, I get all up between you and Lucille's business. When you gonna get that woman that refrigerator she been wanting? Don't tell me you ain't got no money now. I know who your banker is. Mellon don't need that money bad as Lucille want that refrigerator. I'll tell you that.

BONO: Tell you what I'll do. When you finish building this fence for Rose, I'll buy Lucille that refrigerator.

TROY: You done stuck your foot in your mouth now!

(TROY grabs up a board and begins to saw. BONO starts to walk out the yard.)

Hey, nigger . . . where you going?

BONO: I'm going home. I know you don't expect me to help you now. I'm protecting my money. I wanna see you put that fence up by yourself. That's what I want to see. You'll be here another six months without me.

TROY: Nigger, you ain't right.

BONO: When it comes to my money, I'm right as fireworks on the Fourth of July.

TROY: All right, we gonna see now. You better get out your bank book.

(BONO exits, and TROY continues to work. ROSE enters from the house.)

ROSE: What they say down there? What's happening with Gabe?

TROY: I went down there and got him out. Cost me fifty dollars. Say he was disturbing the peace. Judge set up a hearing for him in three weeks. Say to show cause why he shouldn't be recommitted.

ROSE: What was he doing that cause them to arrest him?

TROY: Some kids was teasing him and he run them off home. Say he was howling and carrying on. Some folks seen him and called the police. That's all it was.

ROSE: Well, what'd you say? What'd you tell the judge?

TROY: Told him I'd look after him. It didn't make no sense to recommit the man. He stuck out his big greasy palm and told me to give him fifty dollars and take him on home.

ROSE: Where's he at now? Where'd he go off to?

TROY: I ain't the man's keeper. He's gone on about his business. He don't need nobody to hold his hand.

ROSE: Well, I don't know. Seem like that would be the best place for him if they did put him into the hospital. I know what you're gonna say. But that's what I think would be best.

TROY: I'm gonna go down there and show cause all right. The man done had his life ruined fighting for what? And they wanna take and lock him up. Let him be free. He don't bother nobody.

ROSE: Well, everybody got their own way of looking at it, I guess. Come on and get your lunch. I got a bowl of lima beans and some cornbread in the oven. Come on get something to eat. Ain't no sense you fretting over Gabe.

(ROSE turns to go into the house.)

TROY: Rose, I got something to tell you.

ROSE: Well, come on, wait till I get this food on the table.

TROY: Rose!

> *(She stops and turns around.)*
>
> I don't know how to say this.
>
> *(Pause.)*
>
> I can't explain it none. It just sort of grows on you till it gets out of hand. It starts out like a little bush . . . and the next think you know it's a whole forest.

ROSE: Troy . . . what are you talking about?

TROY: I'm talking, woman, let me talk. I'm trying to find a way to tell you . . . I'm gonna be a daddy. I'm gonna be somebody's daddy.

ROSE: Troy . . . you're not telling me this? You're gonna be . . . what?

TROY: Rose . . . now . . . see . . .

ROSE: You telling me you gonna be somebody's daddy? You telling your *wife* this?

(GABRIEL enters from the street. He carries a rose in his hand.)

GABRIEL: Hey, Troy! Hey, Rose!

ROSE: I have to wait eighteen years to hear something like this.

GABRIEL: Hey, Rose . . . got a flower for you.

> *(He hands it to her.)*
>
> That's a rose. Same rose like what you is.

ROSE: Thanks, Gabe.

GABRIEL: Troy, you ain't mad at me, is you? Them bad mens come and put me away. You ain't mad at me, is you?

TROY: Naw, Gabe, I ain't mad at you.

ROSE: Eighteen years and you wanna come with this.

GABRIEL: *(Takes a quarter out of his pocket.)* See what I got? Got a brand-new quarter.

TROY: Rose, it's just—

ROSE: Ain't nothing you can say, Troy. Ain't no way of explaining that.

GABRIEL: Fellow that give me this quarter had a whole mess of them. I'm gonna keep this quarter till it stops shining.

ROSE: Gabe, go on in the house there. I got some watermelon in the frigidaire. Go on and get you a piece.

GABRIEL: Say, Rose . . . you know I was chasing hellhounds and them bad mens come and get me and take me away. Troy helped me. He come down there and told them they better let me go before he beat them up. Yeah, he did!

ROSE: You go on and get you a piece of watermelon, Gabe. Them bad mens is gone now.

GABRIEL: Okay, Rose . . . gonna get me some watermelon. The kind with the stripes on it.

(GABRIEL *exits into the house.*)

ROSE: Why, Troy? Why? After all these years to come dragging this in to me now. It don't make no sense at your age. I could have expected this ten or fifteen years ago, but not now.

TROY: Age ain't got nothing to do with it, Rose.

ROSE: I done tried to be everything a wife should be. Everything a wife could be. Been married eighteen years and I got to live to see the day you tell me you been seeing another woman and done fathered a child by her. And you know I ain't never wanted no half-nothing in my family. My whole family is half. Everybody got different fathers and mothers . . . my two sisters and my brother. Can't hardly tell who's who. Can't never sit down and talk about Papa and Mama. It's your papa and your mama and my papa and my mama—

TROY: Rose, stop it now.

ROSE: I ain't never wanted that for none of my children. And now you wanna drag your behind in here and tell me something like this.

TROY: You ought to know. It's time for you to know.

ROSE: Well, I don't want to know, goddamn it!

TROY: I can't just make it go away. It's done now. I can't wish the circumstances of the thing away.

ROSE: And you don't want to either. Maybe you want to wish me and my boy away. Maybe that's what you want? Well, you can't wish us away. I've got eighteen years of my life invested in you. You ought to have stayed upstairs in my bed, where you belong.

TROY: Rose, now listen to me, we can get a handle on this thing. We can talk this out, come to an understanding.

ROSE: All of a sudden it's "we." Where was "we" at when you was down there rolling around with some God-forsaken woman? "We" should have come to an understanding before you started making a damn fool of yourself. You're a day late and a dollar short when it comes to an understanding with me.

TROY: It's just . . . She gives me a different idea, a different understanding about myself. I can step out of this house and get away from the pressures and problems . . . be a different man. I ain't got to wonder how I'm gonna pay the bills or get the roof fixed. I can just be a part of myself that I ain't never been.

ROSE: What I want to know is, do you plan to continue seeing her? That's all you can say to me.

TROY: I can sit up in her house and laugh. Do you understand what I'm saying. I can laugh out loud . . . and it feels good. It reaches all the way down to the bottom of my shoes.

(*Pause.*)

Rose, I can't give that up.

ROSE: Maybe you ought to go on and stay down there with her . . . if she a better woman than me.

TROY: It ain't about nobody being a better woman or nothing. You ain't the blame, Rose. A man couldn't ask for no woman to be a better wife than you've been. I'm responsible for it. I done locked myself into a pattern trying to take care of you all that I forgot about myself.

ROSE: What the hell was I there for? That was my job, not somebody else's.

TROY: Rose, I done tried all my life to live decent . . . to live a clean, hard, useful life. I tried to be a good husband to you. In every way I knew. Maybe I come into the world backwards, I don't know. But you born with two strikes on you before you come to the plate. You got to guard it closely . . . looking for the curveball on the inside corner. You can't afford to let none get past you. You can't afford a call strike. If you going down, you going down swinging. Everything lined up against you. What you gonna do? I fooled them, Rose. I bunted. When I found you and Cory and a halfway decent job, I was safe. Couldn't nothing touch me. I wasn't gonna strike out no more. I wasn't going back to the penitentiary. I wasn't gonna lay in the streets with a bottle of wine. I was safe. I had me a family. A job. I wasn't gonna get that last strike. I was on first looking for one of them boys to knock me in. To get me home.

ROSE: You should have stayed in my bed, Troy.

TROY: Then, when I saw that gal, she firmed up my backbone. And I got to thinking that if I tried, I just might be able to steal second. Do you understand . . . after eighteen years I wanted to steal second.

ROSE: You should have held me tight. You should have grabbed me and held on.

TROY: I stood on first base for eighteen years and I thought . . . Well, goddamn it, go on for it!

ROSE: We're not talking about baseball! We're talking about you going off to lay in bed with another woman . . . and then bring it home to me. That's what we're talking about. We ain't talking about baseball.

TROY: Rose, you're not listening to me. I'm trying the best I can to explain it to you. It's not easy for me to admit that I been standing in the same place for eighteen years.

ROSE: I been standing with you! I been right here with you, Troy. I got a life too. I gave eighteen years of my life to stand in the same spot with you. Don't you think I ever wanted other things? Don't you think I had dreams and hopes? What about my life? What about me? Don't you think it ever crossed my mind to want to know other men? That I wanted to lay up somewhere and forget about my responsibilities? That I wanted someone to make me laugh so I could feel good? You not the only one who's got wants and needs. But I held on to you, Troy. I took all my feelings, my wants and needs, my dreams, and I buried them inside you. I planted a seed and watched and prayed over it. I planted myself inside you and waited to bloom. And it didn't take me no eighteen years to find out the soil was hard and rocky and it wasn't never gonna bloom. But I held on to you, Troy. I held you tighter. You was my husband. I owed you everything I had. Every part of me I could find to give you. And upstairs in that room, with the darkness falling in on me, I gave everything I had to try and erase the doubt that you wasn't the finest man in the world. And wherever you was going I wanted to be there with you. 'Cause you was my husband, 'cause that's the only way I was gonna survive as your wife. You always talking about what you give and what you don't have to give. But you take too. You take and don't even know nobody's giving!

> (ROSE *turns to exit into the house;* TROY *grabs her arm.*)

TROY: You're gonna listen to me. It ain't like what you saying!

ROSE: Troy, let go of my arm. You're hurting me.

TROY: You say I take and don't give.

ROSE: Troy, you're hurting my arm. Let go.

TROY: I done give you everything I got. Don't you tell me about not taking and giving. Don't you tell that lie on me.

ROSE: Troy!

TROY: Don't you tell that lie on me!

> (CORY *enters from the house.*)

CORY: Mama!

ROSE: Troy, you're hurting me.

TROY: Don't you tell me about no taking and giving.

> (CORY *comes up behind* TROY *and grabs him.* TROY, *surprised, is thrown off balance just as* CORY *throws a glancing blow that catches him on the chest and knocks him down.* TROY *is stunned, as is* CORY.)

ROSE: Troy. Troy. NO!
> (TROY *gets to his feet and starts at* CORY.)
Troy . . . no. Please! Troy!
> (ROSE *pulls on* TROY *to hold him back.* TROY *stops himself.*)

TROY: (*To* CORY.) All right. That's strike two. You stay away from around me, boy. Don't you strike out. You living with a full count. Don't you strike out.
> (TROY *exits out the yard as the lights go down.*)

Act Two

SCENE TWO

It is six months later, early afternoon. TROY *enters from the house and starts to exit the yard.* ROSE *enters from the house.*

ROSE: Troy, I want to talk to you.

TROY: All of a sudden, after all this time, you want to talk to me, huh? You ain't wanted to talk to me for months. You ain't wanted to talk to me last night. You ain't wanted no part of me then. What you wanna talk to me about now?

ROSE: Tomorrow's Friday.

TROY: I know what day tomorrow is. You think I don't know tomorrow's Friday? My whole life I ain't done nothing but look to see Friday coming, and you got to tell me it's Friday.

ROSE: I want to know if you're coming home.

TROY: I always come home, Rose. You know that. There ain't never been a night I ain't come home.

ROSE: That ain't what I mean, Troy, and you know it. I want to know if you're coming straight home after work.

TROY: I figure I'd cash my check, hang out at Taylor's with the fellows . . . maybe play a game of checkers.

ROSE: Troy, I can't live like this. I won't live like this. It's been going on six months now you ain't been coming home.

TROY: I be here every night. Every night of the year. That's 365 days.

ROSE: I want you to come home tomorrow after work.

TROY: Rose, I don't mess up my pay. You know that now. I take my pay and I give it to you. I don't have no money but what you give me back. I just want to have a little time to myself . . . a little time to enjoy life.

ROSE: What about me? When's my time to enjoy life?

TROY: I don't know what to tell you, Rose. I'm doing the best I can do.

ROSE: You ain't been home from work but time enough to change your clothes and run out . . . and you wanna call that the best you can do?

TROY: I'm going over to the hospital to see Alberta. She went into the hospital this afternoon. Look like she might have the baby early. I won't be gone long.

ROSE: Well, you ought to know. . . . They went over to Miss Pearl's and got Gabe today. She said you told them to go ahead and lock him up.

TROY: I ain't said no such thing. Whoever told you that is a liar. Miss Pearl ain't doing nothing but telling a big fat lie.

ROSE: She ain't had to tell me. I read it on the papers.

TROY: I ain't told them nothing of the kind.

ROSE: I saw it right there on the papers.

TROY: What it say, huh? What it say?

ROSE: It said you told them to take him.

TROY: They got that all screwed up. The way they screw up everything. I ain't worried about what they got on the paper.

ROSE: Say the government send part of his check to the hospital and the other part to you.

TROY: I ain't got nothing to do with that if that's the way it works. I ain't made up the rules about how it work.

ROSE: You did Gabe just like you did Cory. You wouldn't sign the paper for Cory, but you signed for Gabe. You signed that paper.

(*The telephone is heard ringing inside the house.*)

TROY: I told you I ain't signed nothing, woman. The only thing I signed was the release form. I ain't signed nothing about sending Gabe away.

ROSE: I said send him to the hospital—you said let him be free—now you done went down there and signed him to the hospital for half his money. You went back on yourself, Troy. You gonna have to answer for that.

(ROSE *exits into the house to answer the phone.*)

TROY: (*Calling after her.*) See now . . . you been over there talking to Miss Pearl. She done got mad 'cause she ain't getting Gabe's rent money. That's all it is. She's liable to say anything.

ROSE: (*From inside the house.*) Troy, I seen where you signed the paper.

TROY: What she doing got papers on my brother anyway? Miss Pearl telling a big fat lie. And I'm gonna tell her about it too!

(TROY *paces about the yard. Presently* ROSE *enters*).

You ain't seen nothing I signed.

ROSE: Troy, that was the hospital. Alberta had the baby.

TROY: What she have? What is it?

ROSE: It's a girl.

TROY: I better get on down to the hospital to see her.

ROSE: Troy . . .

TROY: Rose, I got to go see her now. That's only right. What's the matter? The baby's all right, ain't it?

ROSE: Alberta died having the baby.

TROY: Died? You say she's dead? Alberta's dead?

ROSE: They said they done all they could. They couldn't do nothing for her.

TROY: The baby? How's the baby?

ROSE: They say it's healthy.

TROY: (*More to himself than* ROSE.) I had that sickle in my hand. I just didn't throw it far enough.

ROSE: I wonder who's gonna bury her?

TROY: She had family, Rose. She wasn't living in the world by herself.

ROSE: I know she wasn't living in the world by herself.

TROY: Next thing you gonna want to know if she had any insurance.

ROSE: Troy, you ain't got to talk like that.

TROY: That's the first thing that jumped out your mouth. "Who's gonna bury her?" Like I'm fixing to take on that task for myself.

ROSE: I am your wife. Don't push me away.

TROY: I ain't pushing nobody away. Just give me some space. That's all. Just give me some room to breathe.

(ROSE *exits into the house.* TROY *walks about the yard.*)

TROY: (*With a quiet rage that threatens to consume him.*) All right, Mr. Death. See now . . . I'm gonna tell you what I'm gonna do. I'm gonna take and build me a fence around this yard. See? I'm gonna build me a fence around what belongs to me. And then I want you to stay on the other side. See? You stay over there until you're ready for me. Then you come on. Bring your army. Bring your sickle. Bring your wrestling clothes. I ain't gonna fall down on my vigilance this time. You ain't gonna sneak up on me no more. When you ready for me, when the top of your list say Troy Maxson, that's when you come around here. You come up and knock on the front door and ask for me. Then we gonna find out what manner of man you are. Ain't nobody else got nothing to do with this. This is between you and me. Man to man. You stay on the other side of that fence until you ready for me. Then you come up and knock on the front door. Anytime you want. I'll be ready for you.

(*The lights go down to black.*)

Act Two

SCENE THREE

The lights come up on the porch. It is late evening three days later. ROSE *sits listening to the ball game waiting for* TROY. *The final out of the game is made and* ROSE *switches off the radio and enters the house. Presently* TROY *enters the yard carrying an infant wrapped in blankets. He stands back from the house and calls.*

TROY: Rose . . . Rose!

(ROSE *enters and stands on the porch. There is a long, awkward silence, the weight of which grows heavier with each passing second.*)

Rose . . . I'm standing here with my daughter in my arms. She ain't but a wee bitty little old thing. She don't know nothing about grown-ups' business. She innocent . . . and she ain't got no mama.

ROSE: What you telling me for, Troy?

(*She turns and exits into the house.*)

TROY: Well . . . I guess we'll just sit out here on the porch.

(*He sits down on the porch. There is an awkward indelicateness about the way he handles the baby. His largeness engulfs and seems to swallow it. He speaks loud enough for* ROSE *to hear.*)

A man's got to do what's right for him. I ain't sorry for nothing I done. It felt right in my heart, and if it set right there, a man can't be blamed.

(To the baby.)

Ain't that right? What you smiling at? You smiling 'cause your daddy's telling the truth? Your daddy's a big man. Got these great big old hands. But sometimes he's scared. And right now your daddy's scared 'cause we sitting out here and ain't got no home. Oh, I been homeless before. I ain't had no little baby with me. But I been homeless. You just be out on the road by your lonesome and you see one of them trains coming and you just kinda go like this.

(He sings as a lullaby.)

Please, Mr. Engineer, let a man ride the line

Please, Mr. Engineer, let a man ride the line

I ain't got no ticket, please let me ride the blinds

(ROSE enters from the house. TROY hearing her steps behind him, stands and faces her.)

She's my daughter, Rose. My own flesh and blood. I can't deny her no more than I can deny them boys. We's the same. They my children.

(Pause.)

You and them boys is my family. You and them and this child is all I got in the world. World get so big sometimes a man can't hardly wrestle with it none. He need some help. This here little bitty thing is my daughter. I don't know too much about babies. So I guess what I'm saying is, I'd appreciate it if you'd help me take care of her.

ROSE: Okay, Troy. You're right. I'll take care of your baby for you 'cause, like you say, she's innocent and you can't visit the sins of the father upon the child. A motherless child has got a hard time.

(She takes the baby from him.)

From right now . . . this child got a mother. But you a womanless man.

(ROSE turns and exits into the house with the baby. Lights go down to black.)

Act Two

SCENE FOUR

It is two months later. LYONS enters from the street. He knocks on the door and calls.

LYONS: Hey, Rose! *(Pause.)* Rose!

ROSE: *(From inside the house.)* Stop all that hollering. You gonna wake up Raynell. I just got her to sleep.

LYONS: I just stopped by to pay Papa this twenty dollars I owe him. Where's everybody at?

ROSE: He should be here in a minute. I'm getting ready to go down to the church. Sit down and wait on him.

LYONS: I got to go pick up Bonnie over her mother's house.

ROSE: Well, sit it down there on the table. He'll get it.

LYONS: *(Enters the house and sets the money on the table.)* Tell Papa I said thanks. I'll see you again.

ROSE: Alright, Lyons. We'll see you.

(LYONS starts to exit as CORY enters.)

CORY: Hey, Lyons.

LYONS: What's happening, Cory. Say man, I'm sorry I missed your graduation. You know I had a gig and couldn't get away. Otherwise you know I would have been there. So what you doing?

CORY: I'm trying to find a job.

LYONS: I know how that go. It's rough out here. Jobs are scarce.

CORY: Yeah, I know. I been looking all over.

LYONS: Look here, I got to run. Talk to Papa . . . he know some people. He'll be able to help get you a job. Talk to him . . . see what he say.

CORY: Yeah, okay, Lyons.

LYONS: You take care. I'll talk to you soon. We'll find some time to talk.

(LYONS exits the yard. CORY wanders over to the tree, picks up the bat and assumes a batting stance. He studies an imaginary pitcher and swings. Dissatisfied with the result, he tries again. TROY enters. They eye each other for a beat. CORY puts the bat down and exits the yard. TROY starts into the house as ROSE exits with RAYNELL. She is carrying a cake.)

TROY: I'm coming in and everybody's going out.

ROSE: I'm taking this cake down to the church for the bake sale. Lyons was by to see you. He stopped by to pay you your twenty dollars. It's laying in there on the table.

TROY: *(Going into his pocket.)* Well, here go this money.

ROSE: Put it in there on the table, Troy. I'll get it.

TROY: What time you coming back?

ROSE: Ain't no use in you studying me. It don't matter what time I come back.

TROY: I just asked you a question, woman. What's the matter . . . can't I ask you a question?

ROSE: Troy, I don't want to go into it. Your dinner's in there on the stove. All you got to do is heat it up. And don't you be eating the rest of them cakes in there. I'm coming back for them. We have a bake sale at the church tomorrow.

(ROSE exits the yard. TROY sits down on the steps, takes a pint bottle from his pocket, opens it, and drinks. He begins to sing.)

TROY:

Had an old dog his name was Blue
You know Blue as a good old dog

Blue trees a possum in a hollow log
You know from that he was a good old dog.

(BONO *enters the yard.*)

BONO: Hey, Troy.

TROY: Hey, what's happening, Bono?

BONO: I just thought I'd stop by to see you.

TROY: What you stop by and see me for? You ain't stopped by in a month of Sundays. Hell, I must owe you money or something.

BONO: Since you got your promotion I can't keep up with you. Used to see you every day. Now I don't even know what route you working.

TROY: They keep switching me around. Got me out in Greentree now . . . hauling white folks' garbage.

BONO: Greentree, huh? Well, at least you ain't got to be lifting them barrels. Damn if they ain't getting heavier. I'm gonna put in my two years and call it quits.

TROY: I'm thinking about retiring myself. How's Lucille?

BONO: She all right. Her arthritis get to acting up on her sometime. Saw Rose on my way in. She going down to the church, huh?

TROY: Yeah, she took up going down there. All them preachers looking for somebody to fatten their pockets.

(*Pause.*)

Got some gin here.

BONO: Naw, thanks. I just stopped by to say hello.

TROY: Hell, nigger, you can take a drink. I ain't never known you to say no to a drink. You ain't got to work tomorrow.

BONO: I just stopped by. I'm fixing to go over to Skinner's. We got us a domino game going over his house every Friday.

TROY: Nigger, you can't play no dominoes. I used to whup you four games out of five.

BONO: Well, that learned me. I'm getting better.

TROY: Yeah? Well, that's all right. You sure had a good teacher.

BONO: Look here . . . I got to be getting on. Stop by sometime, huh?

TROY: Yeah, I'll do that, Bono. Lucille told Rose you bought her a new refrigerator.

BONO: Yeah, I finally broke down on that score.

TROY: I knew you would. I knew she's get you.

BONO: Yeah . . . okay. I'll be talking to you.

TROY: Yeah, take care, Bono. Good to see you. I'm gonna stop over.

BONO: Yeah, Okay, Troy.

(BONO *exits.*)

TROY: (*Drinks from the bottle and sings.*)

Old Blue's feets was big and round

Never 'llowed a possum to touch the ground
Old Blue died and I dig his grave
Let him down with a golden chain
Every night when I hear old Blue bark
I know Blue treed a possum in Noah's Ark.

(CORY *enters the yard. They eye each other for a beat.* TROY *is sitting in the middle of the steps.* CORY *walks over.*)

CORY: I got to get by.

TROY: Say what? What's you say?

CORY: You in my way. I got to get by.

TROY: You got to get by where? This is my house. Bought and paid for. In full. Took me fifteen years. And if you wanna go in my house and I'm sitting on the steps you say excuse me. Like your mama taught you.

CORY: Come on, Pop . . . I got to get by.

(CORY *starts to maneuver his way past* TROY. TROY *grabs his leg and shoves him back.*)

TROY: You just gonna walk over top of me?

CORY: I live here too!

TROY: (*Advancing toward him.*) You just gonna walk over top of me in my own house?

CORY: I ain't scared of you.

TROY: I ain't asked if you was scared of me. I asked you if you was fixing to walk over top of me in my own house? That's the question. You ain't gonna say excuse me? You just gonna walk over top of me?

CORY: If you wanna put it like that.

TROY: How else am I gonna put it?

CORY: I was walking by you to go into the house 'cause you sitting on the steps drunk, singing to yourself. You can put it like that.

TROY: Without saying excuse me?

(CORY *doesn't respond.*)

I asked you a question. Without saying excuse me?

CORY: I ain't got to say excuse me to you. You don't count around here no more.

TROY: Oh, I see . . . I don't count around here no more. You ain't got to say excuse me to your daddy. All of a sudden you done got so grown that your daddy don't count around here no more. Around here in his own house and yard that he done paid for with the sweat of his brow. You done got so grown to where you gonna take over. You gonna take over my house. Is that right? You gonna wear my pants. You gonna go in there and stretch out on my bed. You ain't got to say excuse me 'cause I don't count around here no more. Is that right?

CORY: That's right. You always talking this dumb stuff. Now, why don't you just get out my way.

TROY: I guess you got someplace to sleep and something to put in your belly. You got that, huh? You got that? That's what you need. You got that, huh?

CORY: You don't know what I got. You ain't got to worry about what I got.

TROY: You right! You one hundred percent right! I done spent the last seventeen years worrying about what you got. Now it's your turn, see? I'll tell you what you do. You grown . . . we done established that. You a man. Now, let's see you act like one. Turn your behind around and walk out this yard. And when you get out there in the alley, you can forget about this house. See? 'Cause this is my house. You go on and be a man and get your own house. You can forget about this. 'Cause this is mine. You go on and get yours 'cause I'm through with doing for you.

CORY: You talking about what you did for me . . . What'd you ever give me?

TROY: Them feet and bones! That pumping heart! I give you more than anybody else is ever gonna give you.

CORY: You ain't never gave me nothing. You ain't never done nothing but hold me back. Afraid I was gonna be, better than you. All you ever did was try and make me scared of you. I used to tremble every time you called my name. Every time I heard your footsteps in the house. Wondering all the time, What's Papa gonna say if I do this? What's he gonna say if I do that? What's Papa gonna say if I turn on the radio? And Mama, too—she tries, but she's scared of you.

TROY: You leave your mama out of this. She ain't got nothing to do with this.

CORY: I don't know how she stand you . . . after what you did to her.

TROY: I told you to leave your mama out of this!
    (*He advances toward* CORY.)

CORY: What you gonna do . . . give me a whupping? You can't whup me no more. You're too old. You just an old man.

TROY: (*Shoves him on his shoulder.*) Nigger! That's what you are. You just another nigger on the street to me!

CORY: You crazy! You know that?

TROY: Go on now! You got the devil in you. Get on away from me!

CORY: You just a crazy old man . . . talking about I got the devil in me.

TROY: Yeah, I'm crazy! If you don't get on the other side of that yard, I'm gonna show you how crazy I am! Go on . . . get out my yard.

CORY: It ain't your yard. You took Uncle Gabe's money he got from the army to buy the house . . . and then you put him out.

TROY: (*Advances to him.*) You get your black ass out my yard!
    (TROY's *advance backs* CORY *up against the tree.* CORY *grabs up the bat.*)

CORY: I ain't going nowhere! Come on . . . put me out! I ain't scared of you.

TROY: That's my bat! Put my bat down!

CORY: Come on! Put me out.

    (TROY *stops his advance.*)

CORY: What's the matter? You so bad . . . put me out!

TROY: That's strike three. You done struck out now. All right! Let's see what you gonna do now!

CORY: (*Backing up.*) Come on! Come on!

TROY: You gonna have to use it. You want to draw back that bat on me . . . you gonna have to use it.

(CORY *has retreated to the alley as* ROSE *enters carrying the baby.*)

ROSE: Cory! What you doing with that bat?

TROY: (*To* CORY.) Go on . . . don't you come around here no more.

ROSE: Troy, what's going on?

TROY: Rose, this boy don't live here no more. If he want to come back in here, he's gonna have to use that bat.
(*To* CORY.)
Go on! Get on away from around my house.

CORY: (*Throws the bat down in* TROY'S *direction.*)
I'll be back for my things, Mama.

TROY: They better be out there on the other side of that yard.

(CORY *exits down the alley.* TROY *watches after him.*)

ROSE: Cory! Troy, you just can't put the boy out like that.

TROY: I don't want to hear it, Rose, I promised myself when the day come that boy want to get up in my face and challenge me, he going on away from here. So I don't want to hear nothing you got to say.
(ROSE *turns and exits into the house.*)
'Cause it don't matter no more. I can't taste nothing.
Hallelujah! I can't taste nothing no more!

(*The lights fade to black.*)

Act Two

SCENE FIVE

The time is 1965. An unpainted, weather-beaten fence surrounds the house. RAYNELL, *a rather tall, gangly girl of seven, barefoot and wearing a flannel nightgown, enters the yard and crosses over to a small plot of ground off to the side. The screen door bangs shut.* ROSE *calls from the house.*

ROSE: Raynell!

RAYNELL: Mam?

ROSE: What you doing out there?

RAYNELL: Nothing.

ROSE: *(Coming to the door.)* Girl, get in here and get your shoes on. What you doing?

RAYNELL: Seeing if my garden growed.

ROSE: I told you it ain't gonna grow overnight. You got to wait.

RAYNELL: It don't look like it never gonna grow, dag!

ROSE: I told you a watched pot never boils. Get in here and get your shoes on.

RAYNELL: This ain't even no pot, Mama!

ROSE: You got have to give it a chance. It'll grow. Now you come on and do what I told you. We got to be getting ready. This ain't no morning to be playing around. Hear me?

RAYNELL: Yes, mam.

>   *(ROSE turns and goes into the house. RAYNELL pokes at her garden with a stick. CORY enters. He is dressed in a Marine sergeant's uniform and carries a duffel bag. His posture is that of a military man and his speech has a clipped sternness.)*

CORY: Hi.
>   *(Pause.)*
>   I bet your name is Raynell.

RAYNELL: Uh huh.

CORY: Is your mama home?

>   *(RAYNELL runs up on the porch to the screen door.)*

RAYNELL: Mama . . . there's some man out here. Mama?
>   *(ROSE comes to the door.)*

ROSE: Cory? Lord have mercy!
>   *(ROSE and CORY embrace in a tearful reunion.)*
>   Look at you. My goodness . . . just look at you.

CORY: How have you been, Mama? It's good to see you.

ROSE: If you ain't a sight for sore eyes! Done got all grown up.

CORY: Don't cry, Mama. What you crying about?

ROSE: I'm just so glad to see you. I didn't know if you was gonna make it or not. What took you so long?

CORY: You know how the Marines are, Mama. They have to have all their paperwork straight before they let you do anything.

ROSE: You seen Raynell? Isn't she grown? Raynell?

RAYNELL: Mam?

ROSE: Come here and say hello to your brother. Come on . . . this is your brother, Cory. You remember Cory?

RAYNELL: No, mam.

CORY: She don't remember me, Mama.

ROSE: Well, we talk about you. She heard us talk about you.

(*To* RAYNELL.)

This is your brother, Cory. Come on and say hello.

RAYNELL: Hi.

CORY: Hi. So you're Raynell. Mama told me a lot about you.

ROSE: Now, you go on in there and put your shoes on and lay out that dress like I told you.

RAYNELL: Mama, it's too big. Can't I wear the other one with the bow?

ROSE: Don't you give me no sass now. You go on and do what I told you.

RAYNELL: (*As she exits.*) Yes, mam.

ROSE: She's a good girl. She give me a little back talk every now and then. But she's a good child.

(*Pause.*)

I was hoping you'd bring your girlfriend so I could get a chance to meet her.

CORY: She had to work. She told me to tell you hello and she'd meet you some other time.

ROSE: Well, I'm sure glad you made it. I done called up there about Lyons. They say they gonna let him come. Gabriel's still in the hospital. I don't know if they gonna let him come or not. If it wasn't for Jim Bono and Miss Pearl I don't know how I would have made it these past few days. Ain't had nobody but me. And Raynell . . . she too young to understand. I try to get down to see Lyons every chance I get. But with working and taking care of Raynell and going to church and whatnot . . . there just ain't that many hours in the day.

CORY: I didn't know you was working, Mama.

ROSE: Ain't been but about a year or so. Your daddy retired and I got tired of sitting in the house doing nothing. The ward chairman got me on down there cleaning up at the courthouse. I could have got Miss Pearl to write and tell you, but her arthritis got so bad I hate to ask her anymore.

CORY: I see you got your fence built.

ROSE: Oh, that's been up there ever since Raynell wasn't but a wee little bitty old thing. Your daddy finally got around to putting that up to keep her in the yard. The thing's near about fallen down now. Ain't too much else changed. He still got that old piece of rag tied to that tree. He was out here swinging that bat. I was just ready to go back in the house. He swung that bat and then he just fell over. Seem like he swung it and stood there with this grin on his face . . . and then he just fell over. They carried him on down to the hospital, but I knew there wasn't no need.

CORY: Mama . . . I don't know how to tell you this, but I've got to tell you. I'm not going to Papa's funeral.

ROSE: Boy, hush your mouth. That's your daddy you're talking about. I don't wanna hear that kind of talk this morning. I done raised you to come to this? You standing there all healthy and grown talking about you ain't going to your daddy's funeral?

CORY: Mama, listen . . .

ROSE: I don't want to hear it, Cory. You just get that thought out your head.

CORY: I can't drag Papa with me everywhere I go. I've got to say no to him. One time in my life I've got to say no.

ROSE: Don't nobody have to listen to nothing like that. I know you and your daddy ain't seen eye to eye, but I ain't got to listen to that kind of talk this morning. Whatever was between you and your daddy . . . the time has come to put it aside. Just take it and set it over there on the shelf and forget about it. Disrespecting your daddy ain't gonna make you a man, Cory. You got to find a way to come to that on your own. Not going to your daddy's funeral ain't gonna make you a man.

CORY: The whole time I was growing up, living in his house, Papa was like a shadow that followed you everywhere. It weighed on you and sunk in your flesh. It would wrap around you and lay there until you couldn't tell which one was you anymore. That shadow digging in your flesh. Trying to crawl in. Trying to live through you. Everywhere I looked Troy Maxson was staring back at me: hiding under the bed, in the closet. I'm just saying I've got to find a way to get rid of that shadow, Mama.

ROSE: You just like him. You got him in you good.

CORY: Don't tell me that, Mama.

ROSE: You Troy Maxson all over again.

CORY: I don't want to be Troy Maxson. I want to be me.

ROSE: You can't be nobody but who you are, Cory. That shadow wasn't nothing but you growing into yourself. You either got to grow into it or cut it down to fit you. But that's all you got to make life with. That's all you got to measure yourself against that world out there. Your daddy wanted you to be everything he wasn't . . . and at the same time he tried to make you into everything he was. I don't know if he was right or wrong, but I know he meant to do more good than he meant to do harm. He wasn't always right. Sometimes when he touched, he bruised. And sometimes when he took me in his arms, he cut. When I first met your daddy I thought, Here is a man I can lay down with and make a baby. That's the first thing I thought when I seen him. I was thirty years old and had done seen my share of men. But when he walked up to me and said, "I can dance a waltz that'll make you dizzy," I thought, Rose Lee, here is a man that you can open yourself up to and be filled to bursting. Here is a man that can fill all them empty spaces you been tipping around the edges of. One of them empty spaces was being somebody's mother. I married your daddy and settled down to cooking his supper and keeping clean sheets on the bed. When your daddy walked through the house, he was so big he filled it up. That was my first mistake. Not to make him leave some room for me, for my part in the matter. But at that time I wanted that. I wanted a house that I could sing in. And that's what your daddy gave me. I didn't know to keep up his strength I had to give up little pieces of mine. I did that. I took on his life as mine and mixed up the pieces so that you couldn't hardly tell which was which anymore. It was my choice. It was my life and I didn't have to live it like that. But that's what life offered me in the way of being a woman, and I took it. I grabbed hold of it with both hands. After a while he didn't seem so big no more. Sometimes I'd catch him just sitting and staring at his hands, just sitting there staring like he was watching the silence eat away at them. By the time Raynell came into the house, me and your daddy had done lost touch with each other. I didn't want to make my blessing off of nobody's misfortune, but I took on to Raynell like she was all them babies I had wanted and never had. Like I'd been blessed to relive a part of my life. And if the Lord see fit to keep up my strength, I'm gonna do her just like your daddy did you . . . I'm gonna give her the best of what's in me.

(RAYNELL *enters from the house.*)

RAYNELL: Mama, can I wear my white shoes? This here hurt my feet.

ROSE: Well, they just gonna have to hurt your feet for a while. You ain't said they hurt your feet when you went down there to the store and got them.

RAYNELL: They ain't hurt then. My feet done got bigger.

ROSE: You leave them shoes on your feet and go back in there and get that black belt like I told you.

RAYNELL: I can't find it. These here look all right to me.

ROSE: Girl, go on back in that house and get that belt like I told you!

RAYNELL: (*As she exits.*) Dag! I told you I don't know where to find it.

ROSE: Don't you give me no back talk. You look around and find that belt. Look in that drawer upstairs.

(LYONS *enters from the street.*)

LYONS: Hey . . . hey, look here . . . is that Cory?

CORY: Hey, Lyons.

ROSE: (*Embracing* LYONS.) Lord have mercy.

LYONS: It'll be all right, Rose. Everything's gonna be all right. Looking at Cory standing there. He done come home. Standing there all big and grown. It's gonna be all right now.

(LYONS *and* CORY *embrace awkwardly.*)

　　Look at you, man. Look at you. A sergeant in the United States Marines! How you been, man?

CORY: I been all right.

LYONS: You look good. Don't he look good, Rose?

ROSE: Yeah . . . He come in a little while ago. A sight for sore eyes.

LYONS: Where's Uncle Gabe? He in the house?

ROSE: They don't know if they gonna let him come or not. I just talked to them a little while ago.

LYONS: Where's Raynell? Cory, you seen Raynell?

CORY: Yeah, she was in the yard when I came in.

LYONS: Ain't she precious? She gonna break a whole lot of hearts.

ROSE: You all come on in the house and let me fix you some breakfast . . . keep your strength up.

CORY: I ain't hungry, Mama.

LYONS: You can fix me something, Rose. I'll be in there in a minute. I'm gonna stay out here and talk to Cory a minute.

ROSE: Cory, you sure you don't want nothing? I know they ain't feeding you right.

CORY: No, Mama . . . thanks. I don't feel like eating. I'll get something later.

(ROSE *exits into the house.*)

LYONS: So how you been?

CORY: I been doing okay.

LYONS: Yeah. So when you get in?

CORY: A little while ago. This morning.

LYONS: Look at you . . . Got them sergeant stripes!

(*Pause.*)

I heard you thinking about getting married?

CORY: Yeah, I am. I figure it's about time.

LYONS: Me and Bonnie been split up about four years now. I guess she just got tired of all the changes I was putting her through.

(*Pause.*)

The Marines, huh? Sergeant. I knew you was gonna make something of yourself. Your head always was in the right direction. You gonna stay in. You gonna make it a career? Put in your twenty years?

CORY: I don't know. I got six in already. I think that's enough.

LYONS: Stick with Uncle Sam and retire early. There ain't nothing out here. I guess Rose told you what happened to me. They got me down the workhouse.

CORY: Yeah, she told me.

LYONS: You got to take the crooked with the straight. That's what Papa used to say. I thought I was being slick cashing other people's checks.

CORY: How much time you doing?

LYONS: They gave me three years. I got that beat now. I ain't got but nine months. It ain't so bad. You just learn to deal with it like anything else.

CORY: You still playing?

LYONS: Hey, you know I'm gonna do that. There's some fellows down there . . . we got us a band. We gonna stay together when we get out and see if we can make something out of it. But, yeah, I'm still playing. It still help me to get out of the bed in the morning. As long as it do that, I'm gonna be right there playing to make some sense out of it.

ROSE: (*At the screen door.*) Lyons, I got these eggs in the pan.

LYONS: Let me go get these eggs, man. Go eat and get ready to bury Papa.

(LYONS *starts toward the house. He stops at the door and salutes.*)

Sergeant!

(*To* RAYNELL.) Hey, precious!

(LYONS *exits into the house.* CORY *walks about the yard. He goes over to the tree and picks up* TROY'S *bat.* RAYNELL *enters from the house.*)

RAYNELL: You in the Army or the Marines?

CORY: The Marines.

RAYNELL: Papa said it was the Army.

>(*Pause.*)

>Did you know Blue?

CORY: Blue? Who's Blue?

RAYNELL: Papa's dog what he sing about all the time.

>(*After a long pause,* CORY *begins singing.*)

CORY: I had a dog his name was Blue

>You know how Blue was mighty true

>You know Blue was a good old dog

>Blue treed a possum in a hollow log

>You know from that he was a good old dog.

(RAYNELL *joining the singing.*)

CORY and RAYNELL: Blue trees a possum out on a limb

>Blue looked at me and I looked at him

>Grabbed that possum and put him in a sack

>Blue stayed there till I came back

>Old Blue's feets was big and round

>Never allowed a possum to touch the ground.

>Old Blue died and I dug his grave

>I dug his grave with a silver spade

>Let him down with a golden chain

>And every night I call his name

>Go on, Blue, you good dog, you!

>Go on, Blue, you good dog, you!

>Old Blue laid down and died like a man

>Now he's treeing possums in the Promised Land.

>I'm gonna tell you this to let you know:

>Blue's gone where the good dogs go.

>When I hear old Blue bark

>When I hear old Blue bark

>Blue treed a possum in Noah's Ark

>Blue treed a possum in Noah's Ark.

ROSE: (*Comes to the door and calls.*) Raynell. Get in here and get them other shoes like I told you.

RAYNELL: I'll be back.

(RAYNELL *exits into the house.* ROSE *comes out into the yard.*)

ROSE: Cory, we gonna be ready to go in a few minutes.

(GABRIEL *enters waving his trumpet. He is dressed in a crumpled suit, shirt and tie, and a battered hat.*)

GABRIEL: Hey, Rose! I'm here, Rose. Hey, Rose. I'm here!
ROSE: Gabe? Lord . . . look here Lyons!

(LYOS *enters from the house, followed by* RAYNELL.)

GABRIEL: Hey, Rose. It's time. It's time to tell St. Peter to open the gates. Troy, you ready? You ready, Troy? I'm gonna tell St. Peter to open the gates. You get ready now.

(*With great fanfare, he braces himself to blow. The trumpet is without a mouthpiece. He puts the end of it into his mouth and blows with great force, like a man who has been waiting some twenty-odd years for this single moment. No sound comes out of the trumpet. He braces himself and blows again with the same result. A third time he blows. There is a weight of impossible description that falls away and leaves him bare and exposed to a frightful realization. It is a trauma that a sane and normal mind would be unable to withstand. He begins to dance. A slow, strange, dance, eerie and life-giving. A dance of atavistic signature and ritual. He begins to howl in what is an attempt at song, or perhaps a song turning back into itself in an attempt at speech. He finishes his dance and the gates of heaven stand open as wide as God's closet.*)
That's the way that go!

The Ground on Which I Stand

Thank you. Some time ago I had an occasion to speak to a group of international playwrights. They had come from all over the world. From Colombia and Chile, Papua New Guinea, Poland, China, Nigeria, Italy, France, Great Britain. I began my remarks by welcoming them to my country. I didn't always think of it as my country; but since my ancestors have been here since the early 17th century, I thought it an appropriate beginning as any. So if there are any foreigners here in the audience, "Welcome to my country."

I wish to make it clear from the outset that I do not have a mandate to speak for anyone. There are many intelligent blacks working in the American theater who speak in loud and articulate voices. It would be the greatest of presumptions to say I speak for them. I speak only for myself and those who may think as I do.

I have come here today to make a testimony, to talk about the ground on which I stand and all the many grounds on which I and my ancestors have toiled, and the ground of theater on which my fellow artists and I have labored to bring forth its fruits, its daring and its sometimes lacerating, and often healing, truths.

The first and most obvious ground I am standing on is this platform I have so graciously been given at the 11th biennial conference of the Theater Communications Group. It is the Theater Communications Group to which we owe much of our organization and communication. I am grateful to them for entrusting me with the grave responsibility of sounding this keynote, and it is my hope to discharge my duties faithfully. I first attended the Conference in 1984, and I recall John Hirsh's eloquent address on "The Other" and mark it as a moment of enlightenment and import. I am proud and thankful to stand here tonight in my embrace of that moment and to find myself here on this platform. It is a moment I count well and mark with privilege.

In one guise the ground I stand on has been pioneered by the Greek dramatists, by Euripides, Aeschylus and Sophocles, by William Shakespeare, by Shaw and Ibsen, and by the American dramatists Eugene O'Neill, Arthur Miller and Tennessee Williams. In another guise the ground that I stand on has been pioneered by my grandfather, by Nat Turner, Denmark Vesey, by Martin Delaney, Marcus Garvey and the Honorable Elijah Muhammad. That is the ground of the affirmation of the value of one being, an affirmation of his worth in the face of the society's urgent and sometimes profound denial. It was this ground as a young man coming into manhood, searching for something to which to dedicate my life, that I discovered in the Black Power movement of the 1960s. I felt it a duty and an honor to participate in that historic moment, as the people who had arrived in America chained and malnourished in the hold of a 350-foot Portuguese, Dutch, or English sailing ship were now seeking ways to alter their relationship to the society in which they lived, and perhaps more important, searching for ways to alter the shared expectations of themselves as a community of people. The Black Power movement of the 1960s. I find it curious but no small accident that I seldom hear those words Black Power spoken, and when mention is made of that part of our history, that part of black history in America, whether in the press or in conversation, reference is made to the civil rights movement as though the Black Power movement, an important social movement by America's ex-slaves, had in fact never happened. But the Black Power movement of the 1960s was in fact a reality . . . that is the kiln in which I was fired and has much to do with the person I am today and the ideas and attitudes that I carry as part of my consciousness.

I mention this because it is difficult to disassociate my concerns with theater from the concerns of my life as a black man, and it is difficult to disassociate one part of my life from another. I have strived to live it all seamless . . . art and life together, inseparable and indistinguishable. The ideas I discovered and embraced in my youth when my idealism was full blown I have not abandoned in middle age when idealism is something less than blooming but wisdom is starting to bud. The ideas of self-determination, self-respect, and self-defense that governed my life in the 1960s I find just as valid and self-urging in 1996. The need to alter our relationship to the society and to alter the shared expectations of ourselves as a racial group I find of greater urgency now than it was then.

I am what is known, at least among the followers and supporters of the ideas of Marcus Garvey, as a race man. That is simply that I believe that race matters. That is the largest, most identifiable, and most important part of our personality. It is the largest category of identification because it is the one that most influences your perception of yourself, and it is the one to which others in the world of men most respond. Race is also an important part of the American landscape, as America is made up of an amalgamation of races from all parts of the globe. Race is also the product of a shared gene pool that allows for group identification, and it is an organizing principle around which cultures are formed. When I say culture, I am speaking about the behavior patterns, arts, beliefs, institutions, and all other products of human work and thought as expressed in a particular community of people.

There are some people who will say that black Americans do not have a culture. That cultures are reserved for other people, most notably Europeans of various ethnic groupings, and that black Americans make up a sub-group of American culture that is derived from the European origins of its majority population. But black Americans are Africans, and there are many histories and many cultures on the African continent.

Those who would deny black Americans their culture would also deny them their history and the inherent values that are a part of all human life.

Growing up in my mother's house at 1727 Bedford Avenue in Pittsburgh, Pennsylvania, I learned the language, the eating habits, the religious beliefs, the gestures, the notions of common sense, attitudes towards sex, concepts of beauty and justice, and the responses to pleasure and pain that my mother had learned from her mother and which you could trace back to the first African who set foot on the continent. It is this culture that stands solidly on these shores today as a testament to the resiliency of the African-American spirit.

The term black or African American not only denotes race; it denotes condition and carries with it the vestige of slavery and the social segregation and abuse of opportunity so vivid in our memory. That this abuse of opportunity and truncation of possibility is continuing and is so pervasive in our society in 1996 says much about who we are and much about the work that is necessary to alter our perceptions of each other and to effect meaningful prosperity for all.

The problematic nature of the relationship between white and black for too long led us astray from the fulfillment of our possibilities as a society. We stare at each other across a divide of economics and privilege that has become an encumbrance on black Americans' ability to prosper and on the collective will and spirit of our national purpose.

I speak about economics and privilege, and if you will look at one significant fact that affects us all in the American Theater . . . it is that of the 66 LORT theaters there is only one that can be considered black. From this it could be falsely assumed that there aren't sufficient numbers of blacks working in the American theater to sustain and support more theaters.

If you do not know, I will tell you that Black Theater in America is alive . . . it is vibrant . . . it is vital . . . it just isn't funded. Black Theater doesn't share in the economics that would allow it to support its artists and supply them with meaningful avenues to develop their talent and broadcast and disseminate ideas crucial to its growth. The economics are reserved as privilege to the overwhelming abundance of institutions that preserve, promote, and perpetuate white culture.

This is not a complaint. That is an advertisement. Since the funding sources, both public and private, do not publicly carry avowed missions of exclusion and segregated support, this is obviously either a glaring case of oversight . . . or we the proponents of Black Theater have not made our presence or our needs known. I hope here tonight to correct that.

I do not have the time in this short talk to reiterate the long and distinguished history of Black Theater—often accomplished amid adverse and hostile conditions—but I would like to take the time to mark a few high points.

There are and have always been two distinct and parallel traditions in black art. That is art that is conceived and designed to entertain white society and art that feeds the spirit and celebrates the life of Black America by designing its strategies for survival and prosperity.

An important part of Black Theater that is often ignored but is seminal to its tradition is its origins on the slave plantations of the South. Summoned to the big house to entertain the slaveowner and his guests, the slave began a tradition of theater as entertainment for whites that reached its pinnacle in the heyday of the Harlem Renaissance. This entertainment for whites consisted of whatever the slave imagined or knew that his master wanted to see and hear. This tradition has its present life counterpart in the crossover artists that slant their material for white consumption.

The second tradition occurred when the African in the confines of the slave quarters sought to invest his spirit with the strength of his ancestors by conceiving in his art, in his song and dance, a world in which he was the spiritual center and his existence was a manifest act of the creator from whom life flowed. He then could create art that was functional and furnished him with a spiritual temperament necessary for his survival as property and the dehumanizing status that was attendant to that.

I stand myself and my art squarely on the self-defining ground of the slave quarters and find the ground to be hallowed and made fertile by the blood and bones of the men and women who can be described as warriors on the cultural battlefield that affirmed their self-worth. As there is no idea that cannot be contained by black life, these men and women found themselves to be sufficient and secure in their art and their instructions.

It was this high ground of self-definition that the black playwrights of the 1960s marked out for themselves. Ron Milner, Ed Bullins, Philip Hayes Dean, Richard Wesley, Lonne Elder III, Sonia Sanchez, Barbara Ann Teer and Amiri Baraka were among those playwrights who were particularly vocal and whose talent confirmed their presence in the society and altered the American Theater, its meaning, its craft, and its history. The brilliant explosion of black arts and letters of the 1960s remains, for me, the hallmark and the signpost that points the way to our contemporary work on the same ground. Black playwrights everywhere remain indebted to them for their brave and courageous forays into an area that is marked with land mines and the shadows of snipers who would reserve the territory of arts and letters and the American Theater as their own special province and point blacks toward the ball fields and the bandstands.

That Black Theater today comes under such assaults should surprise no one as we are on the verge of reclaiming and reexamining the purpose and pillars of our art and laying out new directions for its expansion. As such we make a target for cultural imperialists who seek to empower and propagate their ideas about the world as the only valid ideas, and see blacks as woefully deficient, not only in arts and letters but in the abundant gifts of humanity.

In the 19th century, the lack of education, the lack of contact with different cultures, the expensive and slow methods of travel and communication fostered such ideas, and the breeding ground of ignorance and racial intolerance promoted them.

The King's English and the lexicon of a people given to such ignorance and intolerance did not do much to dispel such obvious misconceptions but provided them with a home: in *Webster's Third New International Dictionary,*

> BLACK . . . outrageously wicked, dishonorable, connected with the devil, menacing, sullen, hostile, unqualified, illicit, illegal violators of public regulations, affected by some undesirable condition, etc.
> WHITE . . . free from blemish, moral stain or impurity; outstandingly righteous, innocent, not marked by malignant influence, notably auspicious, fortunate, decent, a sterling man.

Such is the linguistic environment that informs the distance that separates blacks and whites in America and which the cultural imperialists, who cannot imagine a life existing and even flourishing outside their benevolent control, embrace.

Robert Brustein, writing in an article/review titled "Unity from Diversity," is apparently disturbed that "there is a tremendous outpouring of work by minority artists" which he attributes to cultural diversity. He writes that the practice of extending invitations to a national banquet from which a lot of hungry people have long been excluded is a practice that can lead to confused standards. He goes on to establish a presumption of inferiority of the work of minority artists, and I quote,

"Funding agencies have started substituting sociological criteria for aesthetic criteria in their grant procedures, indicating that 'elitist' notions like quality and excellence are no longer functional." He goes on to say, "It's disarming in all senses of the word to say that we don't share common experiences that are measurable by common standards. But the growing number of truly talented artists with more universal interests suggests that we may soon be in a position to return to a single value system."

Brustein's surprisingly sophomoric assumption that this tremendous outpouring of work by minority artists leads to confusing standards and that funding agencies have started substituting sociological for aesthetic criteria, leaving aside notions like quality and excellence, shows him to be a victim of 19th-century thinking and the linguistic environment that posits blacks as unqualified. Quite possibly this tremendous outpouring of works by minority artists may lead to a raising of standards and a raising of the levels of excellence, but Mr. Brustein cannot allow that possibility.

To suggest that funding agencies are rewarding inferior work by pursuing sociological criteria only serves to call into question the tremendous outpouring of plays by white playwrights who benefit from funding given to the 66 LORT theaters.

Are those theaters funded on sociological or aesthetic criteria? Do we have 66 excellent theaters? Or do those theaters benefit from the sociological advantage that they are run by whites and cater to largely white audiences?

The truth is that often, where there are aesthetic criteria of excellence, it is sociological criteria that have traditionally excluded blacks. I say raise the standards and remove the sociological consideration of race as privilege . . . and we will meet you at the crossroads . . . in equal numbers . . . prepared to do the work of extending and developing the common ground of American Theater.

We are capable of work of the highest order . . . we can answer to the high standards of world-class art. Anyone who doubts our capabilities at this last stage is being intellectually dishonest.

We can meet on the common ground of theater as a field of work and endeavor. But we cannot meet on the common ground of experience.

Where is the common ground in the horrifics of lynching? Where is the common ground in the maim of a policeman's bullet? Where is the common ground in the hull of a slave ship and the deck of a slave ship with its refreshments of air and expanse?

We will not be denied our history.

We have voice, and we have temper. We are too long along this road from the loss of our political will, we are too far along the road of reassembling ourselves, too far along the road to regaining spiritual health than to allow such transgression of our history to go unchallenged.

The commonalities we share are the commonalities of culture. We decorate our houses. That is something we do in common. We do it differently because we value different things. We have different manners and different values of social intercourse. We have different ideas of what a party is. There are some commonalities to our different ideas. We both offer food and drink, but because we have different culinary values, different culinary histories . . . we offer different food and drink to our guests.

In our culinary history we have learned to make do with the feet and ears and tails and intestines of the pig rather than the loin and the ham and the bacon. Because of our different histories with the same animal, we have different culinary ideas. But we share a common experience with the pig as opposed to say Muslims and Jews who do not share that experience.

We can meet on the common ground of the American Theater.

We cannot share a single value system if that value system is the values of white Americans based on their European ancestors. We reject that as Cultural Imperialism. We need a value system that includes our contributions as Africans in America. Our agendas are as valid as yours. We may disagree, we may forever be on opposites sides of aesthetics, but we can only share a value system that is inclusive of all Americans and recognizes their unique and valuable contributions. The ground together. We must develop the ground together. We reject the idea of equality among equals, but rather we say the equality of all men.

The common values of the American Theater that we can share are plot . . . dialogue . . . characterization . . . design. How we both make use of them will be determined by who we are . . . what ground we are standing on and what our cultural values are.

Theater is part of the art history in terms of its craft and dramaturgy but is part of the social history in terms of how it is financed and governed. By making money available to theaters willing to support colorblind casting, the financiers and governors have signaled not only their unwillingness to support Black Theater but their willingness to fund dangerous and divisive assaults against it. Colorblind casting is an aberrant idea that has never had any validity other than as a tool of the Cultural Imperialist who views their American Culture, rooted in the icons of European Culture, as beyond reproach in its perfection. It is inconceivable to them that life could be lived and even enriched without knowing Shakespeare or Mozart. Their gods, their manners, their being is the only true and correct representation of humankind. They refuse to recognize black conduct and manners as part of a system that is fueled by its own philosophy, mythology, history, creative motif, social organization and ethos. The idea that blacks have their own way of responding to the world, their own values, style, linguistics, their own religion, and aesthetics is unacceptable to them.

For a black actor to stand on the stage as part of a social milieu that has denied him his gods, his culture, his humanity, his mores, his ideas of himself and the world he lives in is to be in league with a thousand nay-sayers who wish to corrupt the vigor and spirit of his heart.

To cast us in the role of mimics is to deny us our own competence.

Our manners, our style, our approach to language, our gestures, and our bodies are not for rent. The history of our bodies, the maimings . . . the lashings . . . the lynchings . . . the body that is capable of inspiring profound rage and pungent cruelty . . . is not for rent. Nor is the meaning of the history of our bodies for rent.

To mount an all black production of *Death of A Salesman* or any other play conceived for white actors as an investigation of the human condition through the specific of white culture is to deny us our own humanity, our own history, and the need to make our own investigations from the cultural ground on which we stand as black Americans. It is an assault on our presence, our difficult but honorable history in America, and an insult to our intelligence, our playwrights, and our many and varied contributions to the society and the world at large. The idea of colorblind casting is the same idea of assimilation that black Americans have been rejecting for the past 380 years. For the record we reject it again. We reject any attempt to blot us out, to reinvent history and ignore our presence or to maim our spiritual product. We must not continue to meet on this path. We will not deny our history, and we will not allow it to be made to be of little consequence, to be ignored or misinterpreted.

In an effort to spare us the burden of being "affected by an undesirable condition" and as a gesture of benevolence, many whites, like the proponents of colorblind casting, say "Oh, I don't see color." We want you to see us. We are black and beautiful. We are not patrons of the linguist environment that has us as "unqualified, and violators of public regulations." We are not a menace to society. We are not ashamed. We have an honorable history in the world of men. We come from a long line of honorable people with complex codes of ethics and social discourse who devised myths and systems of cosmology and systems of economics, who were themselves part of a long social and political history. We are not ashamed and do not need you to be ashamed for us. Nor do we need the recognition of our blackness to be couched in abstract phrases like "artist of color." Who are you talking about? A Japanese artist? An Eskimo? A Filipino? A Mexican? A Cambodian? A Nigerian? An African American? Are we to suppose [to think] that if you put all of them on one side of the scale and one white person on the other side . . . that it would balance out? That whites carry that much spiritual weight? That one white person balances out the rest of humanity lumped together as nondescript "People of Color"? We reject that. We are unique, and we are specific.

We do not need colorblind casting. We need some theaters to develop our playwrights. We need those misguided financial resources to be put to a better use. We cannot develop our playwrights with the meager resources at our disposal. Why is it difficult to imagine 9 black theaters but not 66 white ones? Without theaters we cannot develop our talents. If we cannot develop our talents, then everyone suffers. Our writers. The theater. The audience. Actors are deprived of material, our communities are deprived of the jobs in support of the art: the company manager, the press co-ordinator, the electricians, the carpenters, the concessionaires, the people that work in the wardrobe, the box office staff, the ushers and the janitors. We need some theaters. We cannot continue like this. We have only one life to develop our talent, to fulfill our potential as artists. One life and it is short, and the lack of the means to develop our talent is an encumbrance on that life.

We did not sit on the sidelines while the immigrants of Europe through hard work, skill, cunning, guile, and opportunity built America into an industrial giant of the 20th century. It was our labor that provided the capital. It was our labor in the shipyards and the stockyards and the coal mines and the steel mills. Our labor built the roads and the railroads. And when America was challenged, we strode on the battlefield, our boots strapped on and our blood left to soak into the soil of places whose names we could not pronounce, against an enemy whose only crime was ideology. We left our blood in France and Korea and the Philippines and Vietnam and our only reward has been the deprivation of possibility and the denial of our moral personality.

It cannot continue. The ground together. The American ground on which I stand and which my ancestors purchased with their perseverance, with their survival, with their manners, and with their faith.

It cannot continue . . . as well other assaults upon our presence and our history cannot continue. When the *New York Times* published an article on Michael Bolton and lists as his influence the names of four white singers and then as an afterthought tosses in the phrase . . . "and the great black rhythm and blues singer," it cannot be anything but purposeful with intent to maim. These great black rhythm and blues singers reduced to an afterthought are on the edge of oblivion. One stroke of the editor's pen and the history of American music is revised, and Otis Redding, Jerry Butler, and Rufus Thomas are consigned to the dust-bin of history while Joe Cocker, Mick Jagger, and Rod Stewart are elevated to the status of the originators and creators of a vital art that is a product of our spiritual travails, and the history of music becomes a fabrication, a blatant forgery which, under the hallowed auspices of the *New York Times,* is presented as the genuine article.

We cannot accept these assaults. We must defend and protect our spiritual fruits. To ignore these assaults would be to be derelict in our duties. We cannot accept them. Our political capital will not permit them.

So much of what makes this country rich in art and all manner of spiritual life is the contributions that we as African Americans have made. We cannot allow others to have authority over our cultural and spiritual products. We reject, without reservations, any attempts by anyone to rewrite our history so as to deny us the rewards of our spiritual labors and to become the cultural custodians of our art, our literature, and own lives. To give expression to the spirit that has been shaped and fashioned by our history is of necessity to give voice and vent to the history itself.

It must remain for us a history of triumph.

The time has come for black playwrights to confer with one another . . . to come together to meet each other face to face, to address questions of aesthetics and ways to defend ourselves from the naysayers who would trumpet our talents as insufficient to warrant the same manners of investigation and exploration as the majority. We need to develop guidelines for the protection of our cultural property, our contribution, and the influence they accrue. It is time we took the responsibility for our talents in our own hands. We cannot depend on others. We cannot depend on the directors, the managers, or the actors to do the work we should be doing for ourselves. It is our lives and the pursuit of our fulfillment that are being encumbered by false ideas and perceptions of ourselves.

It is time to embrace the political dictates of our history and answer the challenge to our duties. I further think we should confer in a city in our ancestral homeland in the Southern part of the United States in 1998, so that we may enter the millennium united and prepared for a long future of prosperity.

From the hull of a ship to self-determining, self-respecting people. That is the journey we are making.

We are robust in spirit, we are bright with laughter, and we are bold in imagination. Our blood is soaked into the soil, and our bones lie scattered the whole way across the Atlantic ocean, as Hansel crumbs, to mark the way back home.

We are no longer in the House of Bondage, and soon we will no longer be victims of the counting houses who hold from us ways to develop and support our talents and our expressions of life and its varied meanings. Assaults upon that body politic that demean and ridicule and depress the value and worth of our existence, that seek to render it immobile and to extinguish the flame of freedom lit eons ago by our ancestors upon another continent—these assaults must be met with a fierce and uncompromising defense.

If you are willing to accept it . . . it is your duty to affirm and urge that defense, that respect, and that determination.

I must mention here with all due respect to W.E.B. DuBois that the concept of a Talented Tenth creates an artificial superiority. It is a fallacy and a dangerous idea that only serves to divide us further. I am not willing to throw away as untalented 90% of my blood; I am not willing to dismiss the sons and daughters of those people who gave more than lip service to the will to live and made it a duty to prosper in spirit if not in provision. I am not willing to dismiss them as untalented cannon fodder and unwitting sheep to the Talented Tenth's shepherd. All God's children got talent. It is a dangerous idea to set one part of the populace above and aside from the other. We do a grave disservice to ourselves not to seek out and embrace and enable all of our human resources as a people. All blacks in America—with very few exceptions—all blacks, no matter what our status, no matter the size of our bank accounts, no matter how many and what kind of academic degrees we can place beside our names, no matter the furnishings and square footage of our homes, the length of our closets and the quality of the wool and cotton that hangs there—we all in America originated from the same place— the slave plantations of the South. We all share a common past and despite how some of us might think and how it might look—we all share a common present and will share a common future.

We can make a difference. Artists, playwrights, actors—we can be the spearhead of a movement to reignite and reunite our people's positive energy for a political and social change that is reflective of our spiritual truths rather than economic fallacies. Our talents, our truth, our belief in ourselves is all in our hands. What we make of it will emerge from the self a baptismal spray that names and defines. What we do now becomes history by which our grandchildren will judge us.

We are not off on a tangent. The foundation of the American Theater is the foundation of European Theater that begins with the great Greek dramatist. It is based on the proscenium stage and the poetics of Aristotle. This is the theater that we have chosen to work in. We embrace the values of that theater but reserve the right to amend, to explore, to add our African consciousness and our African aesthetic to the art we produce.

To pursue our cultural expression does not separate us. We are not separatists as Mr. Brustein asserts. We are Americans trying to fulfill our talents. We are not the servants at the party. We are not apprentices to the kitchens. We are not the stableboys to the King's huntsmen. We are Africans. We are Americans. The irreversible sweep of history has decreed that. We are artists who seek to develop our talents and give expression to our personalities. We bring advantage to the common ground that is the American Theater.

All theaters depend on an audience for its dialogue. To the American Theater, subscription audiences are its life blood. But the subscription audience holds the seats of our theaters hostage to the mediocrity of its tastes and serves to impede the further development of an audience for the work that we do. While intentional or not, it serves to keep blacks out of the theater where they suffer no illusion of welcome anyway. A subscription thus becomes not a support system but makes the patrons members of a club to which the theater serves as a clubhouse. It is an irony that the people who can most afford a full price ticket get discounts for subscribing while the single ticket buyer who cannot afford a subscription is charged the additional burden of support to offset the subscription buyer's discount. It is a system that is in need of overhaul to provide not only a more equitable access to tickets but access to influence as well.

I look for and challenge students of art's management to be bold in their exploration of new systems of funding theaters, including profit-making institutions and ventures, and I challenge black artists and audiences to scale the walls erected by theater subscriptions to gain access to this vital area of spiritual enlightenment and enrichment that is the theater.

All theater goers have opinions about the work they witness. Critics have an informed opinion. Sometimes it may be necessary for them to gather more information to become more informed. As playwrights grow and develop as the theater changes, the critic has an important responsibility to guide and encourage that growth. However, in the discharge of their duties, it may be necessary for them to also grow and develop. A stagnant body of critics, operating from the critical criteria of forty years ago, makes for a stagnant theater without the fresh and abiding influence of contemporary ideas. It is the critics who should be in the forefront of developing new tools for analysis necessary to understand new influences.

The critic who can recognize a German neo-romanticism influence should also be able to recognize an American influence from blues or black church rituals, or any other contemporary American influence.

The true critic does not sit in judgment. Rather he seeks to inform his reader instead of adopting a posture of self-conscious importance in which he sees himself a judge and final arbiter of a work's importance or value.

We stand on the verge of an explosion of playwriting talent that will challenge our critics. As American playwrights absorb the influence of television and use new avenues of approach to the practice of their craft, they will prove to be wildly inventive and imaginative in creating dramas that will guide and influence contemporary life for years to come.

Theater can do that. It can disseminate ideas, it can educate even the miseducated . . . because it is art, and all art reaches across that divide that makes order out of chaos and embraces the truth that overwhelms with its presence and that connects man to something larger than himself and his imagination.

Theater asserts that all of human life is universal. Love, Honor, Duty, Betrayal belong and pertain to every culture of race. The way they are acted out on the playing field may be different, but betrayal is betrayal whether you are a South Sea Islander, Mississippi farmer, or an English Baron. All of human life is universal, and it is theater that illuminates and confers upon the universal the ability to speak for all men.

The ground together. We have to do it together. We cannot permit our lives to waste away, our talents unchallenged. We cannot permit a failure to our duty. We are brave and we are boisterous, our mettle is proven, and we are dedicated.

The ground together. The ground of the American theater on which I am proud to stand . . . the ground which our artistic ancestors purchased with their endeavors . . . with their pursuit of the American spirit and its ideals.

I believe in the American Theater. I believe in its power to inform about the human condition. I believe in its power to heal. To hold the mirror as it were up to nature. To the truths we uncover to the truths we wrestle from uncertain and sometimes unyielding realities. All of art is a search for ways of being, of living life more fully. We who are capable of those noble pursuits should challenge the melancholy and barbaric, to bring the light of angelic grace, peace, prosperity, and the unencumbered pursuit of happiness to the ground on which we stand.

MORE CONTEMPORARY AFRICAN AMERICAN WRITERS

The following is a list of other contemporary African American writers, and though not exhaustive, this list can serve as a guide for further exploration.

Opal Palmer Adisa
Elizabeth Alexander
Raymond Andrews
Doris Jean Austin
Calvin Baker
Houston A. Baker, Jr.
James Baldwin
Amiri Baraka
George Barlow
Gerald Barrax
Hal Bennett
Connie Briscoe
Wesley Brown
Xam Wilson Cartiir
Veronica Chambers
Cheryl Clarke
George Elliott Clarke
Pearl Cleage
Michelle T. Clinton
Cyrus Colter
J. California Cooper
Steven Corbin
Doris Davenport
Thulani Davis
Samuel R. Delaney
William Demby
Eric Jerome Dickey
Michael Eric Dyson
Grace Edwards-
   Yearwood
Thomas Sayers Ellis
Lolita Files
Arthur Flowers

Bill Freeman
Henry Louis Gates, Jr.
Christopher Gilbert
Marita Golden
James Earl Hardy
E. Lynn Harris
Peter Harris
Safiya Henderson-
   Holmes
Carolivia Herron
John Holman
Darryl Holmes
Eugene Howard
Gloria T. Hull
Kristin Hunter
Sheneska Jackson
Richard P. Jones
Alison Joseph
Joyce Anne Joyce
William Melvin Kelly
John Keene
Dolores Kendrick
Adrienne Kennedy
Kimberla Lawson-Roby
Helen Elaine Lee
Sarah Lawrence
   Lightfoot
Rikki Lights
Benilde Little
Nathaniel Mackey
Naomi Long Madgett
Nathan McCall
John McCluskey, Jr.

Diane McKinney-
   Whetstone
Mark McMorris
Sharon Mitchell
Opal Moore
Bruce Morrow
Elizabeth Nunez
Carl Phillips
Darryl Pinckney
Connie Porter
Patricia Powell
Jewell Parker Rhodes
Lucinda Roy
Kate Rushin
Carl Hanson Rux
Darieck Scott
Fatima Shaik
April Sinclair
Barbara Smith
Sharan Strange
Askia Muhammad Touri
Lorenzo Thomas
Natasha Trethewey
Omar Tyree
AJ Verdelle
Michael Warr
Van Whitfield
John A. Williams
Patricia J. Williams
George C. Wolfe
Cheryl Woodruff
Jay Wright
Al Young

CREDITS

INDEX